FIELDING'S
CARIBBEAN

Other Fielding Titles

Fielding's Alaska Cruises and the Inside Passage
Fielding's America West
Fielding's Asia's Top Dive Sites
Fielding's Australia
Fielding's Bahamas
Fielding's Baja California
Fielding's Bermuda
Fielding's Best and Worst — The surprising results of the Plog Survey
Fielding's Birding Indonesia
Fielding's Borneo
Fielding's Budget Europe
Fielding's Caribbean
Fielding's Caribbean Cruises
Fielding's Caribbean on a Budget
Fielding's Diving Australia
Fielding's Diving Indonesia
Fielding's Eastern Caribbean
Fielding's England including Ireland, Scotland & Wales
Fielding's Europe
Fielding's Europe 50th Anniversary
Fielding's European Cruises
Fielding's Far East
Fielding's France
Fielding's France: Loire Valley, Burgundy & the Best of French Culture
Fielding's France: Normandy & Brittany
Fielding's France: Provence and the Mediterranean
Fielding's Freewheelin' USA
Fielding's Hawaii
Fielding's Hot Spots: Travel in Harm's Way
Fielding's Indiana Jones Adventure and Survival Guide™
Fielding's Italy
Fielding's Kenya
Fielding's Las Vegas Agenda
Fielding's London Agenda
Fielding's Los Angeles Agenda
Fielding's Mexico
Fielding's New Orleans Agenda
Fielding's New York Agenda
Fielding's New Zealand
Fielding's Paradors, Pousadas and Charming Villages of Spain and Portugal
Fielding's Paris Agenda
Fielding's Portugal
Fielding's Rome Agenda
Fielding's San Diego Agenda
Fielding's Southeast Asia
Fielding's Southern California Theme Parks
Fielding's Southern Vietnam on Two Wheels
Fielding's Spain
Fielding's Surfing Australia
Fielding's Surfing Indonesia
Fielding's Sydney Agenda
Fielding's Thailand, Cambodia, Laos and Myanmar
Fielding's Travel Tool™
Fielding's Vietnam, including Cambodia and Laos
Fielding's Walt Disney World and Orlando Area Theme Parks
Fielding's Western Caribbean
Fielding's The World's Most Dangerous Places™
Fielding's Worldwide Cruises

FIELDING'S
CARIBBEAN

By
David Swanson
and
Kevin Garrett

Fielding Worldwide, Inc.
308 South Catalina Avenue
Redondo Beach, California 90277 U.S.A.

Fielding's Caribbean

Published by Fielding Worldwide, Inc.

Text Copyright ©1998 Fielding Worldwide, Inc.

Maps, Icons & Illustrations Copyright ©1998 Fielding Worldwide, Inc.

Photo Copyrights ©1998 to Individual Photographers

Some maps ©MAGELLAN Geographix, Santa Barbara, California,
☎ *(800) 929-4MAP*, www.magellangeo.com

FIELDING WORLDWIDE INC.

PUBLISHER AND CEO	**Robert Young Pelton**
GENERAL MANAGER	**John Guillebeaux**
OPERATIONS DIRECTOR	**George Posanke**
ELECTRONIC PUBLISHING DIRECTOR	**Larry E. Hart**
PUBLIC RELATIONS DIRECTOR	**Beverly Riess**
ACCOUNT SERVICES MANAGER	**Christy Harp**
PROJECT MANAGER	**Chris Snyder**
MANAGING EDITOR	**Amanda K. Knoles**
COVER DESIGNED BY	**Digital Artists, Inc.**
COVER PHOTOGRAPHERS — Front Cover	**Larry Ulrich/Tony Stone Images**
Back Cover	**Julie Houck/Westlight**
INSIDE PHOTOS	**Kevin Garrett, Joe Petrocik, Carol Lee, Benford Associates, Grenada Tourist Office, Karen Weiner, Escalera Associates, Robinson, Yesavich & Pepperdine, Inc., Saba Tourist Office, Trombone Associates, Corel Professional Photos**

Inquiries should be addressed to: Fielding Worldwide, Inc., 308 South Catalina Avenue, Redondo Beach, California 90277 U.S.A., ☎ *(310) 372-4474*, Facsimile *(310) 376-8064*, 8:30 a.m.–5:30 p.m. Pacific Standard Time.
Website: http://www.fieldingtravel.com
e-mail: fielding@fieldingtravel.com

ISBN 1-56952-137-9

Printed in the United States of America

Letter from the Publisher

The Caribbean can be a daunting place when it comes to choosing the perfect island getaway. Our focus is making sure you get the best experience for your time and money. To assist you we have created handy comparison tables for accommodations and restaurants complete with best buy and highest rated listings so you can get the most for your money. You'll also find the introductions tighter and with a definite accent on the romantic and adventurous.

Authors David Swanson and Kevin Garrett, faced with covering and reviewing hundreds of "tropical getaways on white sandy beaches," bring a youthful enthusiasm along with a true love of the Caribbean to this book. They have tackled the formidable task of giving the reader a balanced overview of the region as well as highlighting the unique personality of each island. In the year leading up to publication, every island has been visited at least once. In these pages you will find the famous, the hidden and the overlooked all rated and reviewed in our new easy-to-use format. Supporting their efforts have been the staff and researchers at Fielding Worldwide who have done an impressive job of gathering, checking, sorting and compiling more than 1500 attractions, hotels and restaurants. Special thanks to our staff for making it all come together. If it helps you find that one perfect place for your once-a-year getaway, then we have done our job.

Today, the concept of independent travel has never been bigger. Our policy of *brutal honesty* and a highly personal point of view has never changed; it just seems the travel world has caught up with us.

Enjoy your Caribbean adventure.

RYP

Robert Young Pelton
Publisher and CEO
Fielding Worldwide, Inc.

ABOUT THE AUTHORS

David Swanson

Although David Swanson's first travels were in the back of a Volkswagen bus through the American Southwest, the Rockies and western Canada as part of annual summer trips with his family, he has been enthusiastically hoofing the globe on a regular basis since his first trip to Europe in 1982. The journals from that trip also represented his first forays into travel writing, a career that blossomed into a full-time profession after he abandoned his nine-to-five job in 1993. Since then, his writing has appeared in the *Los Angeles Times*, *San Francisco Examiner*, *Chicago Sun-Times*, *Dallas Morning News*, *Cleveland Plain Dealer*, *Denver Post*, *American Way*, *Caribbean Travel and Life*, *Latitudes* and a number of other newspapers and publications. Swanson is also the author of *Fielding's Walt Disney World and Orlando*. A Southern California native, he currently lives in Boston and has gained a whole new appreciation for winter trips to sunnier climes since his move away from the West Coast. When Swanson isn't writing, he's bicycling, hiking, and enjoying obscure movies, and occasionally he ponders his former career in film marketing and publicity.

For this book, Swanson wrote all of the chapters dealing with islands in the Eastern Caribbean—everything from the Virgin Islands south to Trinidad.

Kevin Garrett

After learning to scuba dive on Grand Cayman while on assignment for *Islands* magazine, Kevin Garrett's passion for the Caribbean grew even stronger. He and his wife Echo, also a writer, moved to Atlanta from New York City four years ago, with the intention of making the Caribbean their backyard. A contributing writer to *Elegant Bride* and a regular columnist for *Investor's Business Daily,* Garrett's stories have also appeared in *Biztravel.com, Bridal Guide, Executive Getaways, Fantastic Flyer, The Self-Employed Professional* and *The Atlanta Journal-Constitution.* He co-wrote chapters on Tennessee and his native Georgia for three different guidebooks. Garrett also specializes in commercial travel and lifestyle photography, and his photos have appeared in *The Atlanta Journal-Constitution, Elegant Bride, Los Angeles,* and several other publications. When not looking at the world through a lens, he enjoys reading great travel writing and wrestling with his two young sons.

For this book, Garrett handled the eight Western Caribbean chapters, including the ABC Islands, Puerto Rico and the Turks and Caicos.

Fielding Rating Icons

The Fielding Rating Icons are highly personal and awarded to help the besieged traveler choose fr[o]m among the dizzying array of activities, attractions, hotels, restaurants and sights. The awarding of an ico[n] denotes unusual or exceptional qualities in the relevant category.

RATINGS
Fielding Award · Author Selection · Money Saver · Expensive · Quality · Warning · Danger · Inexpensive
Spacious · Cramped · Mild Disapproval · Timesaving

CULTURAL
Museum/Art · Interesting Architecture · History · Book Reference · Artistically Important · Musically Interesting · Cultural Archeology · Crafts
Theatre · Festivals

SIGHTS
Picturesque · Great Scenery · Market · Beaches · Cultural · Fortress · Castles · Church

WHERE TO STAY
Simple · Luxurious · Cottage · Bed & Breakfast · Scenic · Business · Honeymoon · Chateau

TRAVEL TIPS
Arrival/Departure · By Air · By Water · By Train · By Car · Bus/Local Transit · Barge · River Boat
Calendar · Itinerary · Compass · Kids

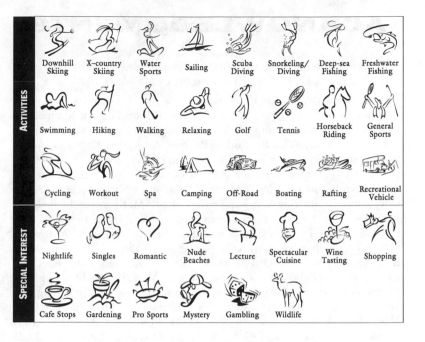

ACTIVITIES

Downhill Skiing	X–country Skiing	Water Sports	Sailing	Scuba Diving	Snorkeling/ Diving	Deep-sea Fishing	Freshwater Fishing
Swimming	Hiking	Walking	Relaxing	Golf	Tennis	Horseback Riding	General Sports
Cycling	Workout	Spa	Camping	Off-Road	Boating	Rafting	Recreational Vehicle

SPECIAL INTEREST

Nightlife	Singles	Romantic	Nude Beaches	Lecture	Spectacular Cuisine	Wine Tasting	Shopping
Cafe Stops	Gardening	Pro Sports	Mystery	Gambling	Wildlife		

What's in the Stars

Fielding's Five Star Rating System for the Caribbean

★★★★★ Exceptional hotels, restaurants and attractions—the finest in the region.

★★★★ Excellent in most respects

★★★ Very good quality

★★ Meritorious and worth considering

★ Modest or simple establishment

Restaurants are star-rated and classified by dollar signs as:

$	Inexpensive	up to $14 for entrées
$$	Moderate	$14–$18
$$$	Expensive	$18 and up

ACKNOWLEDGMENTS

The first group of people we'd like to praise are the vacationers we spoke with on various islands who told us their likes and dislikes.

An army of P.R. representatives assisted us with travel coordination, information and fact-checking. These individuals include Candice Kimmel and Lisa Blau at Adams Unlimited; Edwina Arnold; Kim Thorpe of the Barbados Tourism Authority; Tim Benford of Benford Associates; Keith Dawson of the British Virgin Islands Tourist Board; the staff of Cheryl Andrews Marketing; Myron Clement and Joe Petrocik of the Clement-Petrocik Company; Steve Johnson and Kim Hurtault of Dominica's National Development Corporation; Catherine Van Kampen and Kelly McKeone of FCB/Leber Katz Partners; Gerald Hill of French Caribbean International; Debra Gawron; Edwin Frank of the Grenada Board of Tourism; Paul Murphy at Hill and Knowlton; Philip Rose at the Jamaica Tourist Board; the staff at Kahn Communications; Gail Knopfler; Mia K. Casey and Lyla Naseem at Laura Davidson Public Relations; Ralph Locke; Marcella Martinez and Mary Brennan of Marcella Martinez Associates; Amy Adkinson, Chad Thompson, Luana Wheatley and their associates at Martin Public Relations; Marilyn Marx; Joan Medhurst and the staff of Medhurst and Associates; Kurt Genden at Middleton and Gendron; Kathy Owens at Patrice Tanaka & Company; Alison Ross at Peter Martin Associates; Jenny Craven, Kathy Strempel and Laura Avedisian at Progressive Public Relations; Norbert Beatty of Ruder-Finn; Glenn C. Holme of the Saba Tourist Bureau; Belinda Scott of the St. Vincent and the Grenadines Tourist Office; Roland Lopes of the St. Eustatius Tourist Bureau; Ronnie Pieters, Rolando Marin and associates at Tourism Corporation Bonaire; Regina Henry and Jay Kash of Trombone Associates; and Mary Jane Kolassa of Yesawich, Pepperdine and Brown.

The staff at Fielding Worldwide, particularly John Guillebeaux and Kathy Knoles, has been supportive and tolerant of us, as always. Finally, we'd like to thank our respective families and mates, Chris Principio and Echo Garrett, for their loving support and feedback. That they put up with us with smiles when we wing back from yet another round of research as well as when we're buried in notes, hotel brochures and restaurant menus, is above and beyond the call of duty.

—**David Swanson and Kevin Garrett**

TABLE OF CONTENTS

LIST OF MAPS

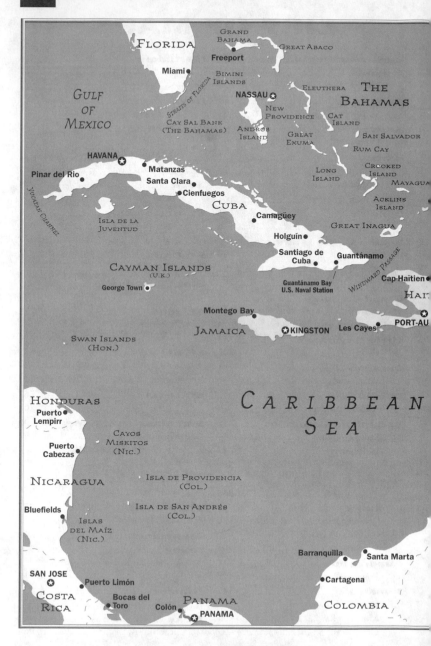

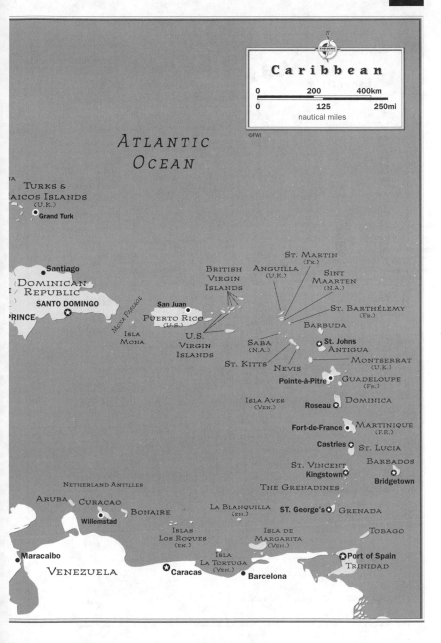

Caribbean

| 0 | 200 | 400km |
| 0 | 125 | 250mi |

nautical miles

©FWI

ATLANTIC
OCEAN

TURKS &
AICOS ISLANDS
(U.K.)
● Grand Turk

● Santiago

DOMINICAN
REPUBLIC
SANTO DOMINGO ✪
PRINCE

MONA PASSAGE

ISLA
MONA

San Juan
PUERTO RICO
(U.S.)

BRITISH
VIRGIN
ISLANDS

U.S.
VIRGIN
ISLANDS

ST. MARTIN
(Fr.)
ANGUILLA
(U.K.)
SINT
MAARTEN
(N.A.)
ST. BARTHÉLEMY
(Fr.)
BARBUDA

SABA
(N.A.)
ST. KITTS
NEVIS
ST. Johns ✪
ANTIGUA
MONTSERRAT
(U.K.)

Pointe-à-Pitre ● GUADELOUPE
(Fr.)

ISLA AVES
(Ven.)
Roseau ✪ DOMINICA

Fort-de-France ● MARTINIQUE
(F.R.)

Castries ✪ ST. LUCIA

ST. VINCENT
Kingstown✪
THE GRENADINES
BARBADOS
✪
Bridgetown

NETHERLAND ANTILLES

ARUBA CURACAO
BONAIRE
● Willemstad
LA BLANQUILLA
(En.)
ST. George's✪ GRENADA

ISLAS
LOS ROQUES
(En.)
ISLA DE
MARGARITA
(Ven.)
TOBAGO

● Maracaibo
ISLA
LA TORTUGA
(Ven.)
VENEZUELA Caracas ✪
● Barcelona
✪Port of Spain
TRINIDAD

Map Legend

Essentials

Hotel	Military Airbase	Cruise Port
Youth Hostel	Army Base	View
Restaurant	Naval base	Stadium
Bank	Fort	Building
Telephone	University	Zoo
Tourist Info.	School	Garden
Hospital		

Activities

Pub/Bar	Beach
Music Club	Campground
Post Office	Picnic Area
Parking	Golf Course
Taxi	Boat Launch
Subway	Diving
Metro	Fishing
Market	Water Skiing
Shopping	Snow Skiing
Cinema	Bird Sanctuary
Theater	Wildlife Sanctuary
Int'l Airport	Park
Regional Airport	Park Headquarters
Police Station	Mine
Courthouse	Lighthouse
Gov't. Building	Windmill
Attraction	

Historical

Archeological Site
Battleground
Castle
Monument
Museum
Ruin
Shipwreck

Religious

Church
Buddhist Temple
Hindu Temple
Mosque
Pagoda
Synagogue
Cemetery
Hebrew Cemetery
Muslim Cemetery

Physical

International Boundary
County/Regional Boundary
PARIS ○ National Capital
Montego Bay • State/Parish Capital
Los Angeles ● Major City
Quy Nhon ○ Town/Village
5 Motorway/Freeway
163 Highway
1AB Freeway Exit
Primary Road
Secondary Road
Subway
Trolley/Street Car

Biking Routed
Hiking Trail
Dirt Road
Railroad
RR Railroad Station
Ferry Route
▲ Mountain Peak
Lake
River
Cave
Coral Reef
Waterfall
Hot Spring

©FWI

TO OUR READERS

So you're off to the Caribbean—lucky you! Will you spend your days trekking through rainforests and inspecting colonial ruins? Exploring coral reefs teeming with sea creatures? Grooving away the night to the reggae and calypso beats? Or simply in a semi-comatose state of bliss on the beach, striving for the perfect tan?

Whatever your idea of paradise in the Caribbean—this book delivers. We know that just as no two beaches are exactly the same, neither are two people's ideas of the perfect vacation. Power to the adventurers among us who wouldn't dream of wasting time just lolling in the sun, and kudos to those who seek nothing more from their Caribbean getaway than the perfect tan. Most folks, we've found, fall somewhere in the middle, and we've provided plenty of information on shopping, attractions and sporting activities to give a clear picture of what each destination offers.

For most of us, monetary restrictions will be the primary consideration when planning a vacation. You'll find this book covers virtually every property on each island, from the poshest of the posh to the least expensive on the lower end. Happily, most islands offer a healthy assortment of mid-range choices, and with our brutally honest ratings system, you'll know just what to expect.

As Paul Simon says, one man's ceiling is another man's floor. For each person thrilled to ecstasy by the idea of giant, free-form pools, structured activities and theme parties, there's another who considers such a resort his or her personal version of hell. You may not go for cold-water showers and large insects as roommates, but the true bohemians among us could just as soon spend cash on other pleasures. And that's the beauty of the Caribbean: it's all there, from snooty country clubs to dependable Holiday Inns to seedy no-tell motels. You'll find it all in these pages.

To use this book in the most efficient way, start by reading the introductions for each island, which give you thumbnail sketches of what to expect at each destination. From there, read "Bird's-Eye View," "History," and "People." "Where to Stay" and Where to Eat" provide details on exactly what to expect—and how much it will cost you. And before you leave, be sure to read the "Island Directory" following each chapter for helpful nuts and bolts information, as well as the section upfront called "Caribbean Planner."

Leave room in your suitcase for this guide, of course, but remember, the best vacation pleasures are often the surprises. While we've obviously written this book to help guide your perfect holiday, we also caution against over-planning. Leave enough time—and an open mind—to let some of the true allure of the Caribbean find you. We promise, it will.

CARIBBEAN PLANNER

What is it about the idea of a tropical island that sets our pulses racing and hearts swooning? It's the lure of palm-dotted beaches, no doubt, and a sea so incredibly clear you can inspect your pedicure in five feet of water. It's balmy evenings when trade winds caress your hair, soothe your spirit and make everyone look and feel sensuous. It's the sheer romance of escaping the bills and the boss, not worrying about wind-chill factors and having only to decide if it's time to turn over and tan your back or if you're up to a night dive.

While the many islands of the Eastern Caribbean are strewn closely together as if a giant tossed a handful of land into the sea, those of the West are generally much more spread out, with miles of deep blue sea between landfalls. While the East is generally known for its smashing resorts and excellent shopping, the isles of the West are famed for their superior diving and untamed natural beauty. But that in itself is a huge generalization, as each island has its own treasures and pleasures. With the notable exception of hot, humid weather and that alluring crystalline sea, Aruba has less in common with St. John than Arkansas has with California.

While a rose may still be a rose no matter what it's called, lumping the Caribbean islands together under one category is, categorically, unfair. Each island has its own history, its own culture, its own personality. Seen one, seen them all is not the reality of the Caribbean. And *vive la différence!*

By Air

A number of airlines serve the Caribbean from North America, but service today is dominated by one carrier in particular: American Airlines and its commuter affiliate, American Eagle. Combined, it is estimated they transport approximately 70 percent of the region's travelers, most of them connecting through the airline's hubs in San Juan, Puerto Rico en route to islands in the Eastern Caribbean, and Miami, Florida for most destinations in the Western Caribbean.

The good news heralded by the dominance of one carrier is genuinely comprehensive and reliable air service. There are still the occasional lost luggage and delayed flight glitches, but they are by far the exception, not the rule, and American has instilled a level of Caribbean professionalism that sets a new standard for other regional carriers to live up to. The bad news is the expected: high airfares. American's influence in the Caribbean is such that most other carriers are happy to allow the airline to dictate the region's exorbitant fares. Believe it or not, from North America, low season airfare to the Caribbean is usually more expensive than a low season ticket to major European cities, despite the latter being more than twice the distance.

Relief may be on the horizon. In 1997, Air Jamaica stole a page from American's game plan and set up Montego Bay, Jamaica as a hub to serve other Caribbean islands from North America. At press time, Air Jamaica flies to Montego Bay from ten U.S. cities (including the only Caribbean service from the west coast, out of Los Angeles), and flies to seven islands from Montego Bay, including Cuba. The airline has also signed a letter of intent for a cooperative agreement with Delta. An added bonus with Air Jamaica is a stopover plan that allows you to book a ticket to a non-Jamaican destination, but also spend time on Jamaica, at no additional charge (some of American's fares allow a similar stopover in San Juan).

Other airlines with service from North America to the Caribbean are Air Canada, Air France, ALM, BWIA, Cayman Airways, Continental, Delta, Dominicana, Northwest, TWA, United and USAirways. There are numerous carriers within the region that hop between islands, with the dominant inter-island carrier being LIAT (see "Island Hopping," below). For additional information about air transportation to the individual islands, see the "Arrival and Departure" section in the "Directory" for each chapter.

To save money, it generally helps to purchase your ticket as far in advance as possible, and to keep your eyes open for special promotions, many of which are announced in your local newspaper's Sunday travel section. Don't expect great deals from the northeast when a blizzard is wending through your neighborhood—in general, fares are at their highest between Christmas and Easter, but they also increase during summer when island residents go on vacation. Monday through Thursday travel is usually less expensive than weekend flights. A travel agent can pull up a variety of fares and should provide you the lowest option, but it doesn't hurt to check around on your own, as well. Since San Juan is served by the largest variety of airlines (thus keeping prices lower) ask your travel agent to try "breaking" the itinerary through San Juan; the price of one round-trip ticket from home to San Juan and another from San Juan to your final destination—even on two separate airlines—may be lower than a single ticket.

Charter flights are also worth investigating and can sometimes save big bucks in high season, but are only offered to a few islands from select U.S. cities. Charter companies lease aircraft for exactly when they feel they can fill it, target specific markets and destinations with limited advertising budgets, and don't award frequent flyer miles—all factors which allow them to keep fares lower. Most charter service is usually limited to a weekly schedule and last-minute cancellations are not uncommon—use a credit card (and a travel agent) to make your purchase and minimize any potential refund hassles.

Package Tour Operators

No, we're not talking about a guided tour with a strict itinerary, but a vacation wholesaler—a middleman who buys hotel and airline space in bulk and passes a portion of the savings off to you. Packages are also appealing because they offer "one stop shopping" for your vacation: purchase your airfare, hotel and, perhaps, car rental in one transaction. Additionally, a reputable tour operator should offer an added degree of protection in the event of flight cancellations or other obstacles.

The downside? Occasionally, a package may not be to your advantage since a tour operator's room rates and airfare are negotiated well in advance of your booking. If a fare war pops into the picture, the wholesaler may be undercut by an airline's sale. Similarly, if a particular hotel is having trouble keeping rooms full, they may offer better rates directly to the general public. It pays to familiarize yourself with the price of the various elements in any package you are considering.

Additionally, smaller, boutique inns have traditionally been passed over by tour operators in favor of the bigger and more expensive hotels. Some of our favorite Caribbean hotels do not work with wholesalers, which can make their room prices unattractive compared to their competition (it's not uncommon for the base price of an air/hotel package to be lower than the least expensive round-trip airfare). One possible solution is to book a package with the minimum stay (usually three or four nights) at, say, Joe's Mega-Resort, and then switch to the lodging you prefer—most package operators will allow you to postpone your return date, even if you're not staying at the hotel linked to the package. This also opens up the option of island-hopping.

But most importantly, with few exceptions, tour operators are not regulated by state or federal agencies, allowing some of these businesses to fold, leaving their customers holding worthless airline tickets and hotel bookings.

The United States Tour Operators Association requires its 55 members to post a $1 million bond against consumer losses, though most tour operators—many of them quite legitimate—are not big enough to meet such standards. Your best protection is to go through a travel agent that is a member of the American Society of Travel Agents and to make your purchase with a credit card; the travel agent should know whether a tour operator is in good shape, and a credit card will help to protect you in the event of default.

The **United States Tour Operators Association** can provide a list of their members ☎ *(212) 599-6599*. The **Caribbean Tourism Organization** provides names of their recommended wholesalers for the region ☎ *(212) 635-9530*. For travel agent referrals in your community, contact the **American Society of Travel Agents** ☎ *(703) 739-2782*.

Island Hopping

Island hopping expeditions in the Caribbean—whether by ramshackle mailboat or via chartered puddle jumper—are one of the most appealing ways to discover the region and, in particular, some of the out-of-the-way outposts that aren't served by jets.

The easiest way to create an island hopping itinerary is via LIAT, the regional carrier that serves 23 Eastern Caribbean islands, plus Georgetown, Guyana and Caracas, Venezuela (though LIAT does fly to San Juan and the Virgin Islands, they do not serve the continental U.S.). Individual one-way fares can be as little as $30 or as much as $200, but LIAT has a pair of excellent island-hopping deals that access most of the destinations in the Eastern Caribbean.

LIAT's Mini Explorer allows you to visit three islands within 21 days for $249 (you can end your trip on the third island, or return to your original starting point for a total of four segments). The two hitches are that the itinerary must be reserved in advance and cannot be changed once ticketed, and the ticket must be purchased within the continental United States (you cannot buy it in the Caribbean). For the truly ambitious, the Super Explorer allows you to visit all 25 destinations in the LIAT network within 30 days for $449. Again, the itinerary must be locked in place before you start, but the Super Explorer may be booked and ticketed within the Caribbean as well as the U.S. Among the destinations LIAT does not serve are Virgin Gorda, St. Barthelemy, Saba, St. Eustatius and Bequia. LIAT's San Juan office can be reached at ☎ *(800) 468-0482* (have patience—the understaffed office can let it ring a long time before answering) or in Antigua ☎ *(268) 462-0700*.

When flying on LIAT, always travel lightly, observe check-in times to avoid losing your seat on overbooked flights, reconfirm your reservation at least once in the days prior to your trip, and note also that these planes leave early as often as late. Not for nothing is the airline's oft-muttered acronym, "Leave Island Any Time."

Trinidad-based BWIA has a similar island hopping fare, but a smaller route network. At press time, within the Caribbean, BWIA flies to Antigua, Barbados, Grenada, Kingston (Jamaica), Georgetown (Guyana), St. Lucia, St. Maarten and Trinidad. The airline's 30-day Caribbean Air Pass allows unlimited travel to those eight destinations for $449. The one advantage over LIAT's deal is that BWIA is a jet-only airline. The main disadvantage is that BWIA's service between these destinations is not daily.

There is also service between most of the islands in the Eastern Caribbean by sea. Some of the islands (particularly the U.S. and British Virgin Islands, Anguilla, and the Grenadines) have reliable if bumpkin ferries plying the link several times daily—these tend to be pretty inexpensive.

The stretch between Guadeloupe and St. Lucia is connected via sleek French ferry systems with prices that are only somewhat less than flying. See "Getting Around" in the "Directory" for each chapter for information on these inter-island links. Note that crossing the channels between islands can be very rough and is not suited for anyone remotely prone to seasickness.

If you are planning an island-hopping itinerary for your Caribbean sojourn, it pays to consult a travel agent who is an expert on the region, someone who can build on the wealth of information you already hold in your hands, with their own knowledge. One outfit that is well-versed in the vagaries of island travel is Connecticut-based **Caribbean Connection** ☎ *(800) 893-1100* or *(203) 261-8603*. They work hard to match their clients with the right islands, seek out special hotels at most price levels, and assemble creative island-hopping packages that cater to a variety of whims.

By Sea

There's nothing like a cruise for relaxing and getting away from it all. These floating hotels pamper guests and provide lots of onboard activities for those who get restless just lying on deck soaking up the rays. Cruise ships stop at most of the islands, and several even have their own private islands where passengers spend the day enjoying watersports and a beach barbecue.

Life at sea is so pleasant it can be hard to drag yourself off the ship at the ports of call. Obviously you're not going to soak up much island flavor in five or six hours, but there's still plenty to do and see—besides the requisite shopping—at each island. And take note that if you sign up for one of the official cruise line excursions, you'll pay much more than if you venture off alone. The disadvantage is that if you don't get back on time, you're in trouble—ships sail exactly when they say they will, and don't take a head count first. Bring your passport ashore just in case you—literally—miss the boat.

A cruise can be as short as three days and as long as several weeks; seven-day trips are most popular in the Caribbean. What you pay varies widely according to the type of cabin you select. The most expensive are the suites with balconies—a true treat if you can afford it—while the cheapest fares go to those who have a tiny inside cabin (no window) on a lower deck. Generally, the higher up you are, the higher the price. Watch the newspapers for deals on last-minute cruises—cruise lines will slash fares a few weeks out rather than sail empty.

Once you cruise with a line, it will try hard to get you back. The major lines reward frequent cruisers with deep discounts and two-for-one fares. While it's fun to try out different cruise lines, these promotions go a long way to assure brand loyalty. Also note the loyalty of your travel agent (cruises are virtually always booked through an agent rather than directly through the line). A good travel agent will send flowers and/or a bottle of wine to your cabin. If you've used the same agent a few times and have not received these perks, it's time to try an agency that will let you know your business is appreciated.

For information on cruising, contact the **Cruise Lines Association** *500 Fifth Avenue, New York, NY 10110;* ☎ *(212) 921-0066.* Also see *Fielding's Worldwide Cruises* for comprehensive reviews of each ship and line, and *Fielding's Caribbean Cruises* for more information about sailing the Caribbean.

Lodging

Some of the world's most romantic resorts are found in the Caribbean. So, alas are some sleazy and roach-ridden dumps. Most fall in between. And although we aim to be comprehensive, we've jettisoned the "no-star" hovels from this book in favor of seeking out unique and charismatic options in the budget range.

Once you decide on an island for your trip—no easy choice in itself—your next task is to select your accommodations. The choices are immense: luxury resorts that cater to almost every whim; all-inclusive properties where everything from soup to nuts and a variety of activities is included in the rates; glamorous villas with a pool and your own staff; atmospheric inns with rich history and perhaps colorful owners; apartments and condominiums where service is of the do-it-yourself variety; to budget properties where management may be indifferent, room decor from another (not-yet-quaint) era, and amenities sparse.

For most of us, the first way to narrow lodging options is to decide on a budget. The region has two basic seasons: high season generally extends from mid December through mid-April, and low season is the remaining eight months of the year. A number of hotels have a third set of rates—usually called shoulder season—that lasts for a month or so after Easter, and pops up again prior to Christmas. The prices listed in *Fielding's Caribbean* are a range, from the least expensive room in low season to the most expensive in high season (all figures were carefully researched and updated in the two months prior to publication)—a standard room in high season will be priced somewhere between these two points.

The figure we print is the rack rate—that is, the prices quoted in the hotel's rate card. If you are booking a room well in advance of your trip, you should be able to obtain a better price from all but the budget options.

Sometimes this will come in the form of a package. It can be as simple as an off-season special ("stay five nights and the sixth is free" is common), or it can be a honeymoon- or sports-oriented package which may contain a number of your meals and activities, and assorted extras for only slightly more than the nightly rate (the free welcome drink is a skimpy perk, but tax and service charge included is a true boon). Most hotels sell a single or double for the same price, though a surcharge for a third or fourth occupant is not uncommon. Typically children under a certain age (as young as 12 or as old as 17—it varies by property), are free. Be sure you understand the hotel's tax and service charge policy (see "Those Damn Surcharges," below).

Beyond a bed, it's important to know what you're paying for at a hotel—services and amenities vary widely in the region. The most common denominator is the meal plan. In the Caribbean, most properties offer a European Plan (or EP), which does not include any meals as part of your stay.

Other meal arrangements you'll see scattered through the various chapters are: Continental Plan (CP, which includes continental breakfast daily—usually juice, coffee and rolls), Breakfast Plan (BP, a full American-style breakfast), Modified American Plan (MAP, two full meals daily), or Full American Plan (FAP, three meals daily). Unless otherwise specified, we've used EP rates for establishing hotel prices throughout the book. Alcoholic drinks are not usually included in any of these plans, but it pays to check up front. Some hotels offer a meal plan in addition to the EP rate, ranging anywhere from $30 to $100 per person, per day, but its value depends on the quality of the food you're tied to. If you're staying at an isolated property you may have little option; at a big hotel with a slew of restaurants, the meal plan may provide enough diversity and quality to be worth investigating. Similarly, if the hotel you will be staying at offers a meal plan with a "dine around" option (common on Barbados), you won't be stuck perusing the same menu and setting night after night. However, if good food is important to you, consider the overall quality of dining on the island you will be visiting. Islands like Anguilla, Barbados, Puerto Rico, St. Thomas, Sint Maarten/Saint Martin and St. Barthelemy offer a variety of superlative restaurants you'll be sorry to miss if you're chained to one dining spot for the length of your stay.

Activities and sports are another area that should be considered when comparing hotels. Some hotels will tell you that watersports are included in the rates. Great, but what watersports do they offer? At one property the term watersports might embrace snorkeling equipment and a few tired rafts; at another it might include diving, water skiing, para sailing, etc. With each hotel description, we've noted the general array of watersports available, as well as other sports and activities provided by the property.

Once you have established a budget for your lodgings, you're ready to narrow the field a little further by deciding what type of accommodations you want to stay in. We have grouped the various properties into five basic categories. The **Hotels and Resorts** category encompasses a far-flung field, ranging from posh pleasure domes with a beach, a plethora of sports and activities, and perhaps a spa, room service and svelte courtesy, to simple local business hotels where the only perk is an underused pool. **Inns** are a Caribbean specialty, usually a couple dozen rooms or less, with owner-managers available to help you discover their island, and the history their buildings may shelter. Inns are usually right for romantics who want an added level of seclusion, for independent or solo travelers, and sometimes for families who don't want the impersonality of a big hotel (not all inns accept children year-round). Physically challenged visitors should always inquire about accessibility issues—elevators are unheard of and stairs can present problems. **Apartments and condominiums** are found on virtually every island, sometimes in great abundance. Though they lack the character of an inn and (usually) the activities and services of a resort, their kitchens offer a path to savings. If you are truly planning to use your accommodations for cooking, check before you book to see exactly how well you can rely on it: is it a kitchen that you can really craft meals in, or a kitchenette with little more than a hot plate perched on a mini-fridge and few utensils or cookware?

Because the Caribbean is no backpacker's paradise, **Low Cost Lodging** is usually in the eye of the beholder. If you're thinking of the type of carefree travel available in southeast Asia or even southern Europe, think again. In high season, "low cost" is $75-100 a night on some islands—and these places are typically no-frills abodes. Plan your vacation for the off-season, and steer to the islands that offer the greatest variety of less expensive accommodations: Dominica, the Dominican Republic, Grenada, Saba, St. Eustatius, St. Vincent, Tobago and Trinidad are good starting points. If the lodging options listed herein do not fit your wallet, pick up a copy of *Fielding's Caribbean on a Budget.*

All-Inclusives

A fast-growing trend in the Caribbean has been the development of all-inclusive properties. The phenomenon seems to have somewhat plateaued recently, but we suspect this is just a breather as the industry reassesses the market before its next spurt of growth. The concept, for those not familiar with the term, is that your lodging, meals, drinks, activities and entertainment are calculated into one set price. The all-inclusive package may also include excursions, a diverse roster of sports like golf and diving, and even your tax and gratuities. The concept is enormously appealing to many travelers because the cost of a vacation is pretty well set in stone before you depart— and because everything one needs is right on site, guests never have to leave the resort. Travel agents love to sell them because not only are all-inclusives relatively easy to book, requiring little research on their part, but agents receive—in effect—a commission on not only airfare and a hotel room, but on your meals and activities as well.

All-inclusives are sprinkled throughout the region, but have established a notable presence in the Dominican Republic, on Jamaica, Antigua, St. Lucia and, recently, Barbados. Some, such as the Sandals chain, Couples and Rendezvous, accept only heterosexual couples. Honeymooners and lovers staring dreamily into each other's eyes and making out at the pool is the norm. There are properties that cater to singles—notably Jamaica's Hedonism— that are tropical meat markets where attracting a partner is top priority. Club Med, which fostered the whole craze three decades ago, used to be known as a premiere singles spot, but the French-run company is increasingly courting the family market with lots of special activities for kids. Indeed, the family audience appears to be the next frontier for the industry. The Sandals organization—the unqualified leader in Caribbean all-inclusives—recently sprouted a Beaches brand; here, families, singles and couples are all welcomed to the polished Sandals environment. A relative newcomer to the field is St. James Hotels, which in 1997 turned three of its four appealing Barbados properties into family-friendly all-inclusives and has expansion plans that include a new resort on Grenada.

The category offers all levels of luxury. Most tend to be fairly cookie-cutter berths, but what they lack in room amenities or decor is made up for with enough goings-on outside the rooms to keep the busiest vacationers happy morning, noon and night. A few, like LeSport and LaSource, even throw in spa treatments. When perusing the brochures, you need to be eagle-eyed to spot the differences between properties and exactly what amenities and extras are provided, but perusing the fine print will help you better understand what to expect.

Despite the numerous advantages offered, not all of us are fans of the all-inclusive concept, at least in the mainstream. Perhaps the biggest drawback is that, because most activities and all dining and imbibing off property are not included, these hotels tend to be the destination in and of themselves, rather than the island. This is fine if you're simply looking to escape the world for a few days, but if you're a traveler interested in getting to know an island and its inhabitants, all-inclusives tend to mount rose-colored glasses on their guests—reality is filtered. Usually these properties invest heavily in fences and guards to keep locals and freeloaders out—the tactic might be good for security, but it does more to instill an "us and them" atmosphere than anything else, and puts a real damper on cultural exchange. An island like Jamaica is dynamic and colorful enough that if you stay at an all-inclusive, you really haven't seen the island.

Meals are another red flag. Food at all-inclusives tends to be mediocre, at best. At the so-called "Fine Dining Restaurant" of Barbados' Almond Beach Village—where the number of tables is not adequate to accommodate the number of guests clamoring for a candlelight dinner—the Italian food proffered would not pass muster at an amusement park (the sprig of basil atop a green-goo-drizzled creme brulee was the crowning glory). And drinks? At the average all-inclusive, your orange "juice" at breakfast is made from powder out of a can, the rum punch at lunch is loaded with a wallop of artificial fruit punch, at sundown you'll order a Jack Daniels but receive Jim Beam without explanation and at dinner, when you request wine, you will usually have just two choices: the red flavor or the white. What is more distressing still is that even those of us who choose not to go the all-inclusive route suffer on the food front. When accommodations on an island like St. Lucia make a dramatic shift toward all-inclusive arrangements, as they have during the last decade, independent restaurants have fewer customers to draw from and either lower their food standards or close entirely (currently, more than half of St. Lucia's hotel rooms are part of all-inclusive properties).

In the end, the decision to stay at an all-inclusive resort is a personal one, and many vacationers are perfectly happy with them. Though often fairly expensive, the concept does work for people who want to firmly lock down the price of their vacation up front, and they can be a pretty good deal for those inclined to participate in a lot of sports (most all-inclusives are not a good deal if you plan to spend your vacation by the pool with a book in hand). If, for you, the style of accommodations or quality of dining at a resort takes a back seat to the quantity of activities and food, an all-inclusive may be just the ticket for your ideal vacation.

And, a final note. There are a number of fine properties that are, for all practical purposes, all-inclusive—even if they prefer not to be called one.

They range from elegant Curtain Bluff in Antigua to private island resort Petit St. Vincent in the Grenadines. As you browse through our descriptions, you'll find a number of hotels with wonderful accommodations, an MAP or FAP meal plan, and a panoply of activities and sports included in the rates. A spring break atmosphere is not tolerated at most of these places, but a truly Caribbean vacation is served.

FIELDING'S AUTHOR'S SELECTIONS

Rating	Accommodation	Rates	Chapter
★★★	Anguilla Great House Beach Resort	$120–$230	Anguilla
★★★★	Covecastles	$425–$995	Anguilla
★	Lloyd's Guest House	$60–$80	Anguilla
★★★	Copper and Lumber Store Hotel	$85–$325	Antigua
★★★	Hawksbill Beach Resort	$155–$385	Antigua
★★★	Siboney Beach Club	$130–$290	Antigua
★★★	Divi Aruba Beach Resort	$175–$600	Aruba
★★★	Coconut Creek Hotel	$226–$496	Barbados
★	Pink Coral Inn	$35–$60	Barbados
★★	Guavaberry Spring Bay	$95–$142	British Virgin Islands
★★★	Long Bay Beach Hotel	$85–$360	British Virgin Islands
★★	Sandcastle	$85–$175	British Virgin Islands
★★★	Sugar Mill Hotel	$135–$265	British Virgin Islands
★★★	Pirate's Point Resort	$135–$200	Cayman Islands
★★★★	Avila Beach Hotel	$90–$430	Curaçao
★★★	Habitat Curaçao	$165–$220	Curaçao
★★	Castaways Beach Hotel	$82–$130	Dominica
★★	Papillotte Wilderness Retreat	$70–$100	Dominica
★★★	Petit Coulibri Guest Cottages	$115–$225	Dominica
★★★	Punta Cana Beach Resort	$75–$280	Dominican Republic
★★★★	Calabash	$205–$545	Grenada
★★★	Caribbee Inn	$90–$250	Grenada
★★	La Sagesse Nature Center	$50–$95	Grenada
★★★	Secret Harbour Resort	$130–$230	Grenada
★★	Siesta Hotel	$60–$135	Grenada
★★★★	Auberge de la Vieille Tour	$136–$390	Guadeloupe
★★★	Auberge les Petit Saints	$65–$127	Guadeloupe
★★★	La Toubana	$109–$237	Guadeloupe
★★★	Le Jardin Malanga	$176–$320	Guadeloupe
★★★	The Caves	$295–$600	Jamaica
★★	Jake's	$75–$250	Jamaica

FIELDING'S AUTHOR'S SELECTIONS

Rating	Accommodation	Rates	Chapter
★★★	Rockhouse	$80–$165	Jamaica
★★★★	Strawberry Hill	$195–$525	Jamaica
★★★	Leyritz Plantation	$68–$148	Martinique
★★	Huricane Cove Bungalows	$95–$265	Nevis
★★	Oualie Beach Hotel	$100–$255	Nevis
★★★	Gran Hotel El Convento	$190–$1200	Puerto Rico
★★★	Captain's Quarters	$70–$135	Saba
★★★	Eden Rock	$220–$680	St. Barthélémy
★★	Sea Horse Hotel	$80–$295	St. Barthélémy
★★★★	Buccaneer Hotel	$150–$280	St. Croix
★★	Hilty House Inn	$70–$110	St. Croix
★★	King's Alley Hotel	$79–$158	St. Croix
★★	King's Well	$55–$100	Sint Eustatius
★★★	Estate Concordia Studios	$95–$190	St. John
★★★★	Ottley's Plantation Inn	$190–$255	St. Kitts
★★★★	Anse Chastanet	$120–$530	St. Lucia
★★	Hummingbird Beach Resort	$30–$130	St. Lucia
★★★	Grand Case Beach Club	$105–$335	Saint Martin
★★★	L'Esplanade Caraibe Hotel	$100–$320	Saint Martin
★★★	Cupecoy Beach Club	$100–$350	Sint Maarten
★★	Pasanggrahan Royal Inn	$78–$148	Sint Maarten
★★★	Island Beachcomber	$95–$145	St. Thomas
★★	L'Hotel Boynes	$85–$175	St. Thomas
★★	Frangipani Hotel	$30–$150	St. Vincent
★★	Old Fort Country Inn	$90–$160	St. Vincent
★★	Spring on Bequia	$50–$205	St. Vincent
★★★★	Young Island Resort	$210–$640	St. Vincent
★★★	Asa Wright Nature Center	$106–$210	Trinidad
★★	Mt. Plaisir Estate	$48–$81	Trinidad
★★★	Ocean Club	$165–$860	Turks and Caicos
★★★	Windmills Plantation	$475–$695	Turks and Caicos

A NOTE ON OUR STAR RATINGS

Fielding's five-star rating system for hotels is designed not just to tally a list of bests and worsts, but to separate the ordinary from the extraordinary. It's a subjective rating system, based on our personal inspection of more than 1000 Caribbean properties over the years. We favor the unique and memorable over the stuffy and pretentious, service that is attentive and gracious above servitude and glowering, and a setting and ambiance that is truly West Indian and tropical rather than one with manufactured beaches and architecture that could be anywhere. In the process, we knock a few favorites, but we also highlight treasures the other guidebooks miss. Awarding the star ratings is the bane of our existence—even a scale of 1 to 100 would not be sufficient to assail the many unique traits that make a resort or inn special, or anathema. In practice, the difference that separates one four star resort from another can be substantial, and similarly, the difference between a three-star and a four-star property on the same island can be niggling.

Use the stars as your guide, but always read the description of individual properties to ascertain whether it's right for you. Finally, our favorites are noted with an "Author's Selection" icon. Culled from all price levels, and excluding only the five-star hotels from consideration, these properties are the places we remember most fondly when we return home. The best of the best—hotels that offer the region's highest level of accommodation, service, food and pampering—are awarded the "Fielding Award" icon.

Getting Around

Some islands are so tiny you'll easily get around on foot. Others use the mini moke as the preferred mode of transportation. Several have excellent bus systems and good taxi fleets—it varies widely by island. For details, see "Getting Around" in the directory in the back of each island chapter.

The biggest decision will be whether or not to rent a car. Chain and locally owned rental companies are available on virtually every island, and summer rates are often cheaper than during the prime winter season.

If you're staying at an all-inclusive resort and plan to rarely leave the property, there's no need to rent a car. If, however, you plan to explore and try different restaurants each evening, you're often better off renting a car than paying lots of taxi fares. You'll also be more independent.

Road conditions vary from island to island. Some have modern paved roads, but too often, the roadways are narrow, rutted and filled with hairpin turns. Driving is often on the left side of the road, which can be dangerous if you're not used to it. On the plus side, most islands have few major roads, so getting lost is rarely a problem. Consider renting a convertible so you can soak up every possible ray of sunshine, or a four-wheel-drive to easily navigate the often torturous roads on some islands.

A few tips on car rentals: Always reserve as far in advance as possible during the winter, as the cars get snatched up during prime tourist seasons. Check to see if they'll deliver the car to your hotel—many do at no extra charge (a number of hotels have car rental firms based in their lobbies). Before leaving home, check your car insurance policy to see if rental cars are covered. They often are, and this allows you to refuse the rental company's outrageously priced insurance, which saves big bucks. If you're not covered, seriously consider buying the rental insurance, as island drivers can be wackier than even those in Boston and, as stated, the roads are often awful.

Taxi service also varies. Some islands have metered cabs, but many more use standardized fares. In those cases, always ask what the trip will cost before you get in. If you're hiring a cabbie for a day's sight-seeing, you'll usually be able to negotiate a fare. On some islands fares increase dramatically at night and on Sundays. In others, cabs disappear by midnight. If you're relying on taxis, be sure you'll be able to catch one if you plan to stay out late. Always treat your cabdriver with courtesy and respect. It can pay off when you hit it off and the cabbie—virtually always a native—turns you on to interesting facts and places you'd never otherwise find.

Packing the Suitcase

First and foremost, try to pack lightly enough so you can carry your luggage on the plane, as opposed to checking it. The biggest advantage is that you'll avoid the all-too-common problem of lost luggage. While suitcases are usually located over time, if you've landed on a smaller island like St. Vincent (which is served only once a day by a small American Eagle plane), you'll be without your luggage for 24 hours or more. But also, by carrying your belongings on board, you'll whisk through customs (where applicable) well ahead of your fellow travelers waiting forlornly at the luggage carousel. Everything goes slower in the Caribbean—and luggage retrieval is no exception. Most airlines will only let you carry on two bags that measure no more than 62 inches (width plus length plus height). In all cases, carry-ons must fit under your seat or in the overhead compartment. This is much harder on the tiny planes that hop from island to island, but if you hand your bag to them on the runway, rather than check it, you'll still get it back more quickly.

As humidity is quite high throughout the Caribbean, bring natural fabrics; lightweight cotton is the best. Casual clothes are fine just about anywhere both day and night (when it's not, it's noted in the hotel or restaurant description) An exception are some historic churches, which may have a no-shorts rule. Respect this custom; it's especially easy for women, who can wear a light sundress.

The nights are generally warm and sultry, but some clubs and restaurants will invariably overdo the air conditioning, so tuck in a light jacket or sweater. If you're going to be trekking through the jungle or rainforest, obviously you want sturdy shoes and raingear. The nicer hotels equip their rooms with umbrellas; you may want to pack a small portable one just in case. Don't forget to bring a beach bag to hold your sunscreen lotion, hat or visor and a few dollars for lunch (your carry-on bag can serve this purpose).

Bring sandals or flip-flops for the beach (black sand gets particularly hot!) and good sneakers or walking shoes for touring. Lots of villages have cobblestone streets, and the old forts usually have dubious pathways, so you'll appreciate sturdy shoes. Unless you're into tottering around on high heels, you can leave them at home; flat dressy sandals will do even at the finer resorts.

Consider buying a sarong once you arrive. These large, colorful pieces of rectangular cloth can be tied in a variety of ways, from halter dress to shirt, fold up into practically nothing, are easy to handwash and make great souvenirs to boot. You'll find them in many shops and marketplaces. You'll also find lots of hats—mainly straw—and it's a good idea to pick one up. The sun is very strong throughout the region, and just because you are dutifully sight-seeing rather than lazing on the beach doesn't mean you won't get burned.

The sunbathers on a few (mostly French) islands go topless; whether or not you do too is a personal choice. However, it's considered rude to go to a nude beach and keep your clothes on. In any event, wearing swimsuits anywhere but the pool or beach is generally a no-no. Other essentials include mosquito repellant, a portable water bottle and film. You'll generally save a lot of money by buying these items stateside rather than on the island.

Finer hotels outfit their bathrooms with hair dryers, shampoo, conditioner and body lotion, but these products are usually of a cheap quality, so if you're particular, bring your own. It's well worth checking out the "introductory" or travel sizes of personal care items at the drug store or supermarket, or buying small plastic containers to fill. There's no need to lug your whole bottle of shampoo—just bring what you'll need for your stay.

Women should pack a few tampons or sanitary pads; on a few islands, they may be hard to find. Also bring a small sewing kit, extra eyeglasses and motion-travel wristbands or medication if you're prone to seasickness and will be boating. There's nothing like the fit of your own snorkel mask, so bring that along, too. Men who use electric shavers may need an electric converter—see the "directory" at the end of each island chapter for electrical currents. Prescription medications and eyeglasses should always be carried on your person when traveling, not checked with your luggage.

What not to bring: a travel iron (virtually all hotels supply one on request—and besides, this is the Caribbean and wrinkles are acceptable), expensive jewelry (why add to the myth that Americans are all rich, and the possibility of getting ripped off?), cowboy boots (too hot) and beach towels (unless you're staying in guest houses, they are usually supplied). Rather than dragging your whole address book along—which you'd hate to lose anyway—copy the addresses of friends to whom you plan to send postcards onto self-adhesive labels that you can stick on the cards.

Fanny packs are excellent for carrying your money and a small camera, and cooler than backpacks. Always lock your passport, extra money, plane ticket and other valuables in the in-room safe or check them at the front desk.

Remember, unless you're extremely fashion conscious, it's inevitable you'll wear the same comfortable clothes again and again, so pack lightly. And be sure to leave room in your suitcase for souvenirs!

Money Managing

Unless you plan to bring huge sums of money with you or are staying a very long time, it's much more convenient to not bring traveler's checks to the Caribbean. There are two reasons for this advice: many establishments tack on at least a five percent surcharge when cashing them; and worse, few places don't take them at all. On the other hand, you always run a risk when carrying cash. If you do opt for traveler's checks, be sure to carry the numbered receipts separately from your money—you'll need them for a refund in the event of loss or theft. Members of the Automobile Club of America (AAA) can get free traveler's checks, as can American Express cardholders.

A credit card is essential, even if you don't plan to use it. Most hotels won't give you a room without a credit card imprint, even if you're paying in cash. The same is true for car rental companies. This may be annoying, but perfectly understandable as hotels get ripped off constantly and with a credit card, at least have a chance of recouping their losses. Also, you never know what emergencies may arise, so always carry a credit card. Visa and Master-Card are the most widely accepted and American Express is often honored, while the Discover card is now accepted at an increasingly diverse array of hotels and shops.

U.S. dollars are accepted virtually everywhere and are the "official" currency of Puerto Rico, the U.S. *and* British Virgin Islands. In most cases, you won't even need to change money—though it can work to your advantage, particularly in the French islands. If you do want to convert to local currency, you're best off doing so at a bank, where the rate of exchange is invariably better than at hotels. In all instances, avoid the black market. In poorer nations such as the Dominican Republic, you're setting yourself up for scams or outright robbery.

Unless you're a whiz at division and multiplication, shoppers may want to carry a small calculator to figure out how prices translate into U.S. dollars. The calculator can also be used to communicate and negotiate when you're dealing with someone who doesn't speak English.

Automatic teller machines (ATMs) are becoming more common throughout most islands, but are not prevalent enough that you can really rely on them—except on San Juan and the U.S. Virgins. It's a good idea to tuck a few blank checks into your wallet—if you really get into trouble cash-wise, some major hotels will cash one for you (after a lot of begging). If you're really stuck, you can always get a cash advance on your credit card at a casino—but be warned that the service charges are exorbitant (about $17 for each $100).

When traveling about the island, always carry small bills. They are much more convenient for paying taxi and restaurant fares. Plus, it's rude to dicker over a price at the marketplace, get the seller down from $18 to $9, then present a $20 bill. Keep a supply of singles for tipping doormen and other personnel at your hotel, as necessary.

Above all, use your in-room safe (they are becoming increasingly standard) or check your valuables with the front desk. Nothing will ruin a vacation faster than getting ripped off—it's worth the few minutes of hassle to play it safe.

Documents

Each island requires some sort of identification to enter; details are given in the directory at the back of each chapter. Generally, you're best off with a passport, though some nations accept a photo I.D. such as a driver's license. (Often, expired passports are also acceptable.) Visas are generally not required for citizens of the United States, Canada and the European Economic Community, but again, rules vary by island.

You'll need to show proof that you're just a visitor and are not planning to make the island your new home (a return plane ticket will suffice). If you arrive at immigrations looking particularly bedragled, you may be required to prove you have enough funds for the length of your stay.

When you purchase your plane ticket, the agent will inform you of any special documents needed. If he or she fails to volunteer this information, ask. Cruise ship passengers need to bring a passport along, but usually don't need to show it at ports of call. Still, it's a good idea to take it along with you when debarking the ship, just in case.

Customs and Duties

As if coming home from a glorious Caribbean holiday isn't depressing enough, you have to go through customs, unless Puerto Rico is your vacation spot (in that case, you'll skip customs and can bring back as much stuff as you want). Otherwise, you'll fill out a simple form stating how much you spent on goods you're bringing back—if it's more than $400, you'll have to list each item. When shopping in duty-free stores, be sure to save the receipts to show proof of purchase.

Rules vary by region, but here's the general scoop on duty-free shopping:

You can bring $1200 worth of goods back from the Virgin Islands.

Six hundred dollars for Antigua, Barbuda, Barbados, British Virgin Islands, Dominica, Grenada, Montserrat, Saba, St. Eustatius, St. Kitts, Nevis, St. Lucia, Sint Maarten (the Dutch side), St. Vincent, the Grenadines, Trinidad and Tobago.

Four hundred dollars for Anguilla, Guadeloupe, Martinique, St. Martin (the French side) and St. Barthelemy.

If you stay on an island less than 48 hours or have been outside the United States within 30 days of your current trip, you can only bring back $25 worth of duty-free goods, except, again, for Puerto Rico.

If you've gone over the limit, you'll be taxed at a flat rate of 10 percent (5 percent for the U.S. Virgins) on the first $1000 of merchandise. Except for gifts under $50 sent directly to the recipient, all items shipped home are considered dutiable.

Some people try to beat customs by wearing their new Rolex or emerald earrings and acting as if they've always owned them. This is not especially recommended—you may need to show proof you did indeed leave the U.S. with these expensive items. Conversely, if you're traveling with a Rolex or suspiciously large rock on your finger, it's a good idea to bring the receipt along to prove you already owned it.

A NOTE ON DRUGS:

Don't even think of trying to get illegal drugs into an island or back home. It's just not worth the risk, and while few people busted in the Caribbean have Midnight Express-style horror stories to tell, remember you are in a foreign country and you're under its rules. Carry prescription drugs in their original containers to avoid hassles.

For more information on duty-free allowances, contact the U.S. Customs Service *P.O. Box 7404, Washington, DC 20044; for taped information, call* ☎ *(202) 927-2095.*

Insurance and Refunds

You can insure against everything from your valuables being stolen to your rental car crashing to bad weather ruining your trip—it's up to you and how much of a gambler you are. A must: car rental collision insurance, unless your car owner's policy covers rental cars (many do, and it's well worth checking before you leave home, as this is a big savings).

Always check the small print when booking a hotel and airline ticket. These days most airlines charge $50 (and more) if you change your flights; if you decide to scrap the whole trip, airline tickets are often nonrefundable. Most hotels require two to four weeks notice (in advance of your arrival date) to refund your deposit without penalty. In most, the hotel rate card will outline the policy. If you are unsure, or are working through a travel agent, ask to have the policy clarified to avoid any last minute surprises. When cruising, consider the optional insurance policy that lets you cancel at the last minute, for any reason, and still get a refund.

When to Go

Islanders know how to throw a party, and festivals full of song and dance occur year-round in the Caribbean. On some islands, there are even more festivals during the off-season, which serves to attract visitors who are keen for off-season bargains. Although Carnival is generally celebrated as the advent of Lent, it can happen anytime in the Caribbean, even during the summer. Throughout the year individual islands celebrate their own arts and crafts traditions, as well as various other religious and folklore celebrations. Sports competitions happen according to the high season for that sport, attracting athletes and fishermen from all over the world. (Singles should note these events as prime times to visit and the chance for meeting someone "tall and tan and young and handsome" soars sky-high.) For more information, check under "When to Go" in the directory of each individual island.

Cultural Festivals	
February	Barbados' Holetown Festival
March	Barbados' Holder's Season
June	Dominica's Festival of Creative Arts
June	Trinidad's Muslim Hosay

July	Tobago Heritage Festival
July–August	Barbados' Crop-Over Festival
Late July	Nevis' Culturama
Late July, early August	British Virgin Islands' Emancipation Festival
August	Guadeloupe's Fete des Cuisinieres
Late October	Cayman Islands' Pirate Week Festival

Music

January	Barbados' Jazz Festival
January	St. Barthélémy Music Festival
January	St. Croix's Blues Heritage Festival
February	Jamaica's Reggae Sunsplash Music Festival
May	St. Lucia Jazz Fest
June	Puerto Rico's Festival Pablo Casals
Late June	St. Kitts Music Festival
July	Dominican Republic's Merengue Festival
August	Jamaica's Sun Fest
October	Curaçao Jazz Festival
November	Trinidad's Pan Jazz Festival
December	Puerto Rico's Hatillo Festival of the Masks

Sports

January	Antigua's Tennis Week
January	Grenada's New Year's Fiesta Yacht Race
January	Jamaica's Classic Golf Tournament
March	Curaçao International Sailing Regatta
March	Sint Maarten's Heineken Regatta
April	Antigua Sailing Week
April	Antigua's Windsurfing Week
April	British Virgin Islands Spring Regatta
April	U.S. Virgin Islands International Rolex Spring Regatta
May	Guadeloupe's Intercontinental Kite Challenge
May 30	Anguilla's Boat Racing Day
June	Aruba's Hi-Winds Amateur World Challenge

June and July	U.S. and British Virgin Islands' Hook In and Hold On Boardsailing Regatta
August	Guadeloupe's Tour de la Guadeloupe
Early August	Martinique's Tour des Yoles Rondes (yawl race)
August	Grenada's Carriacou Regatta
August	Virgin Islands Open Atlantic Blue Marlin Tournament
October	Bonaire's Sailing Regatta
December	St. Lucia's Atlantic Rally for Cruisers

Secret Tips for Caribbean Survival

Duty Free Does Not Necessarily Mean Cheaper

The term "duty free" means that retailers are not required to pay import taxes on certain items, so can pass these savings directly along to the consumer. Often that translates to prices 30 to 40 percent less than in the United States. Even islands not officially duty free still often have duty-free shops at the airport or around the island, such as St. Lucia's Pointe Seraphine. Furthermore, on your way to an island, you can shop duty free in major U.S. airports by showing your boarding pass.

While most duty-free items are truly a bargain, it ain't always necessarily so. Cigarettes, for example, often cost close to $17 per carton at airport-duty free shops, and you can often do better on the island itself (and even in some U.S. supermarkets). If you're planning to buy expensive French perfume or a good piece of jewelry, do some comparison shopping before leaving the United States to see how prices stack up. And remember, if the product is defective, you'll have a much easier time getting satisfaction from your local store than a little shop in the Caribbean. Use common sense in your bargain hunting. Electronic equipment and cameras can be heavily discounted, but do you really want to haul your purchases back to the islands to have a warranty honored if something goes wrong?

Good duty-free bargains can generally be found on French perfumes, Dutch porcelain, Swiss crystal, fine bone china and woolens from England, linens and gemstones, especially emeralds. Prices are especially good on European-owned territories such as St. Martin, St. Barts, Martinique and Guadeloupe. Antigua, Barbados, St. Kitts, Grenada, St. Lucia and the British Virgins are good spots for imports from England.

Those Damn Surcharges

Most folks are genuinely amazed when checking out of a hotel and seeing their final hotel tab. Where did all these service charges come from? What's this government tax? What on earth is an energy surcharge? While it's always a good idea to go over your bill with a fine-tooth comb, most of these charges, alas, are legitimate—at least in the sense that they're posted in a lobby and/or noted on the hotel rate card.

All hotels charge a government tax of anywhere from 5–15 percent of your nightly room rate. The service charge, which averages 10–15 percent, is supposedly for maids and other staff—whether they actually ever see it or not is another matter. Still, don't feel obligated to tip extra if the service charge is included. Many hotels automatically tack on a service charge whenever you charge a meal or drink to your room; and room service checks virtually always include a service charge. In these cases, it's not necessary to tip the bartender or waiter. If you're not sure, ask. Energy surcharges are sometimes added to the bill to help defray the costs of electricity when local prices are quite high. Note that all these charges are not always mentioned in the brochure or when you inquire about rates. Some all-inclusive properties include the tax and service charge in their rates, but clarify exactly what is included (and what is not).

The biggest killers are the telephone surcharges. Ironically, it seems the more expensive the hotel, the higher the telephone rates. Many charge up to $1 per local phone call. If you dial direct to the United States, be prepared for exorbitant fees. If you must call the States direct, have your party call you back—you'll save a lot of money that way. Also consider buying a phone card, which are springing up all over the United States and on the islands, wherein you pay a flat fee (say, $20) for a prescribed amount of time. These cards, which do not require a credit card to obtain, are often much cheaper per minute than dialing direct from your hotel or a payphone. When you can use your stateside carrier's card (such as AT&T, Sprint and MCI) you'll invariably save, but note that their 800 access numbers are often not reachable from the Caribbean, even with operator assistance (sometimes U.S. phone cards can be used only from specifically noted phone booths—which may number as few as one or two on some islands).

Beware of the mini-bar—that tempting bottle of Red Stripe probably costs double or triple the usual price. If you don't trust your will power regarding raiding the fridge and gobbling down all those $5 candy bars (which cost 50 cents in the store) leave the mini-bar key at the front desk.

Health Precautions

There are very few health risks throughout the Caribbean. In most cases, the water is safe to drink (even if it doesn't taste so great); always inquire at your hotel if you're not sure. They'll give you an honest answer—the last thing these people want is a bunch of sick guests on their hands.

The biggest health threat in the Caribbean—as, alas, the world over these days—is from AIDS and other sexually transmitted diseases. It's best to bring condoms from home because they are not always as readily available on smaller islands (latex condoms offer much more protection than those made of lambskin).

It's always a good idea to carry along a small bottle of stomach medicine such as Mylanta, diarrhea remedies such as Pepto Bismol or Imodium, and pain relievers like aspirin or Tylenol. Don't assume you'll be able to find such items on the island (no problem in Jamaica, but lots of luck on Sint Eustatius or Cuba). If you require injections, bring your own sterile syringes and consider buying disposable ones from a U.S. pharmacy before you leave.

Malaria is generally no longer a threat (except in the Dominican Republic and Haiti), which is good news, since you can usually count on providing free meals for mosquitoes and no-see-ums. For the latest news on Caribbean health conditions, call the **Centers for Disease Control's International Travelers' Hotline** ☎ *(404) 332-4559*.

Watch out for the sun—it's going to be a lot stronger than you think, especially on overcast days when you may forget to apply sunscreen. Though getting a killer tan is high on many tourists' list of things to do, start slowly with a strong sunscreen, then once you work up a good base tan, gradually switch to a lower number (of course dermatologists recommend no tan at all, but try convincing vacationers of that).

The high humidity will probably make you perspire more than usual. Drink lots of fluids to avoid dehydration (water is best) to replace the ones you're oozing through your pores. Guests at all-inclusive properties invariably go wild the first night with all those free drinks—then pay dearly for it the next day. Keep that in mind as you order your fourth piña colada.

Buying prepared food from street vendors is generally safe, but do check out the operation. Is the meat kept refrigerated? Are the utensils clean? When buying bottled water, especially on the street, check that the tamper-proof band is intact. Some unscrupulous vendors will refill bottles with tap water.

Weather—or Not

The Caribbean Basin is one of the most temperate in the Western Hemisphere, a key reason it has been a vacation destination for many years. Daytime coastal temperatures within the region fluctuate minimally throughout the year, but average from the mid-70s to mid-80s. December and January are usually the coolest months, May through September the warmest. If you are headed to elevations higher than 1000 feet above sea level, you may experience nights chilly enough to warrant a sweater, but otherwise, shorts and a T-shirt are our preferred dress code. Humidity is a constant, though with daytime highs limited to the 80s, it's not usually overbearing. The driest month for most islands is March, with average humidity in the 60-65 percent range. October and November are the most uncomfortable, averaging 70-80 percent humidity. Rainfall occurs year-round, but the true rainy season in the Caribbean is June through December—the islands average anywhere from five to 10 inches of rain per month during this period. The dry season, February through April, brings only two or three inches of rain each month to most islands. Fortunately, showers are usually brief, even in the wet season, though occasionally a weather system moves in that brings regular downpours for up to several days. If a cloud-free vacation during the rainy season is paramount, consider visiting one of the less mountainous islands that receive more modest amounts of rain.

Californians cope with earthquakes, East Coasters deal with blizzards and Midwesterners have floods. In the Caribbean, the enemy is the hurricane— devastating storms that creep across the Atlantic from West Africa, bringing winds of at least 75 miles per hour, torrential rains, and waves that vacuum away postcard perfect beaches. An even bigger obstacle for the islands is the impression that the region is disaster-prone from the start of hurricane season in June until the season's finish in November.

Admittedly, chances are you've saved up for your vacation and you don't want anything like a storm to play havoc with your plans. But the lasting damage from Hurricanes Luis and Marilyn in September 1995 is also one of perception that extends well beyond the five islands that bore the brunt of their winds and rain. Hoteliers from St. Lucia tell us that September bookings have gone into a black hole since 1995—travelers now assume hurricanes are a virtual certainty during that month. In reality, a September visit will save you loads of money compared to a high- or even shoulder-season trip, and you'll experience the islands with a smaller contingent of tourists. When traveling to the Caribbean during the late summer/early fall, it's wise to keep an alternate plan (island) in your back pocket, just in case. Tune your TV to the Weather Channel in the days leading up to your trip and stay abreast of what might be brewing. For what it's worth, your intrepid authors have traveled to the Caribbean many times during hurricane season for research, and we look forward to enjoying the fewer people and lower room rates and airfares for years to come.

If you're open to a late-summer or early fall Caribbean vacation but still don't want to deal with even the notion of a hurricane, know that several islands lie outside the Atlantic/Caribbean hurricane belt and haven't been so much as grazed by a major storm in many decades. Four in particular—Aruba, Bonaire, Curacao and Trinidad—are a safe bet. A few others—Barbados, Grenada, the Grenadines and Tobago—lie at the edge of the hurricane belt and are rarely touched by major storms.

Travel for Seniors

Senior citizens are often entitled to great discounts, and should always look into such deals before traveling. The **National Council of Senior Citizens** *1331 F Street, NW, Washington, D.C. 20004;* ☎ *(202) 347-8800* is a nonprofit organization that publishes a monthly newsletter that includes travel tips and bargains; it's well worth the $12 per year membership/subscription. Also contact **Grand Circle Travel** *(347 Congress Street, Boston, MA 02210;* ☎ *(617) 350-7500* or *(800) 248-3737* for a free copy of "101 Tips for the Mature Traveler." The agency also offers escorted tours and cruises for older folks. Also catering to people over 50 is **SAGA International Holidays** *222 Berkeley Street, Boston, MA 02116;* ☎ *(800) 343-0273.*

Island Etiquette

While some of your best vacation photos will be candid shots of locals, keep in mind that many folks—older ones especially—often don't appreciate being part of your tourist experience. Always ask before snapping someone's photo and take a refusal with grace. If you promise to send a copy of a photo to an islander, do not fail to follow through when you return home. Kids, on the other hand, usually love to get the attention and will often ask you to take their picture. Indulge them, even if you're down to your last shot.

Carry small bills when dealing with street vendors and in marketplaces where you'll be negotiating prices.

In museums and restaurants, keep your negative feelings to yourself (or at least whisper them to your companion) about lousy decor or greasy food. You may find you just hate conch, but remember that it's a staple in many island diets, so try not to be judgmental. On the other hand, if the food is truly inedible, you have every right to send it back.

No one should have to endure lousy service, but extra patience will be required in the Caribbean. Everything is on a slower pace, and that certainly includes the cooks and waitstaff.

Respect local rules and customs regarding the formality of dress. In most cases shorts and T-shirts are just fine, but most churches ban them, even if you're just ducking in for a quick peek. Bathing suits are nearly always improper anywhere but on the beach or at the pool. If you want to go topless, make sure it's considered acceptable on the island (only on the French islands is it *de rigeur*).

Make a genuine effort to speak the language on islands such as Guadeloupe, Martinique and the Dominican Republic, where English speakers are rare. No matter how terrible your syntax or pronunciation, such efforts are greatly appreciated, and people will be much more apt to help you out than if you just walk up expecting them to speak your language.

Above all, do your fellow countrymen a big favor, and don't act like the Ugly American. It's no wonder everyone thinks we're all rich the way some U.S. travelers flash around large bills and expensive jewelry (and actually, if we can afford a Caribbean vacation—even on the cheap—we are pretty rich compared with most locals). Be sensitive to the fact that on most of these islands, life is much simpler and less materialistic. Remember, too, that you are a guest in this foreign land. Sure, you're paying for it, but that doesn't mean you've bought the right to impose your values on people of different cultures. However, it's amazing how far a smile will go.

ANGUILLA

Cove Castles Resort in Anguilla is famous for its ultramodern villas.

When Anguilla's striking paucity of attractions and activities is called to the attention of the island's U.S. tourism representative, her reply is short, sweet and to the point: "Life's a beach, and then you dine." To be sure, if you're in search of lush forests, heroic views, vigorous culture, trendy shopping or rich historical sights, proceed to another chapter. These attributes are virtually nonexistent on this sleepy isle, one of the last outposts of the British Empire and home to about 9000 easygoing, permanent residents. So what does Anguilla (pronounced "An-*gwee*-la") offer?

In a word, beaches. This is an island blessed with one of the most breathtaking collections of shimmering white-sand beauties that graces the globe. One unofficial spokesperson is Ron Hall, the dedicated "island finder" for *Conde Nast Traveler*, who put Anguilla on a headstrong list of his Ten Favorite Islands—the only Caribbean isle to make his final cut. "When it comes to beaches," he wrote, Anguilla "leaves the others way behind." It doesn't hurt that the island also boasts dining fine enough to write home about, and a handful of some of the region's most visually arresting resorts that share a bold architectural theme—blindingly chic, sexy Mediterranean motifs—that makes the most of the torpid surroundings.

But the real secret to Anguilla's success is languid tranquility—a peaceful essence that will bore one traveler to tears, while the next will extol these qualities as exactly what a Caribbean vacation is all about. Loll in Shoal Bay's warm, undulating sea as it licks and caresses loamy flats of powdery white sand, then wash ashore and swig on a rum punch at one of the island's colorful beach bars. Finish off the night with a sumptuous meal at an intimate nest like Koal Keel and, well, that pretty much sums up life on Anguilla. If these virtues push your buttons, the island may be just your cup of tea. Alas, most good things come with a price, and the final bill on Anguilla can be quite high, ranking right up with St. Barts as one of the region's most expensive destinations. But, if you're comfortable clinging to the notion that you can't take it with you, then come to relax in Anguilla, where the most strenuous item on the daily menu of activities is debating which perfect beach is the most perfect of all.

A spindly shape—long and relatively flat—earned Anguilla its name, French for "eel" (or Spanish or Italian, depending on whom you talk to). The 35-square-mile island is a coral formation nudged above sea level by centuries of geologic uplift, pockmarked by an unknown quantity of limestone caves, and ringed by a succession of bays, coves and salt ponds. With a highest point of just 213 feet above sea level, the island seduces only enough clouds to produce an average of 35 inches of rain per year, allowing little cultivation. Anguilla's dry, scrubby appearance inspired Lidia Shave to form the **Anguilla Beautification Club**, which has made admirable attempts to add greenery to the island's dusty topography. The club plants trees and flowers, and tourists are encouraged to donate funds and "adopt" their own tree

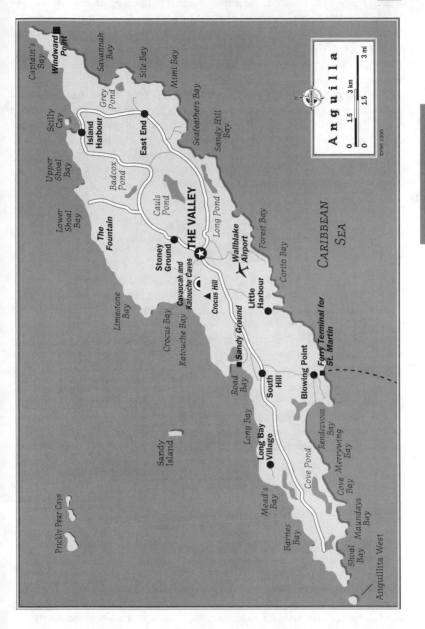

(ABC Trees, P.O. Box 274, Anguilla, BWI). Plentiful goats are the major "wild" life, but other creatures you're likely to encounter include lizards, pelicans, frigate birds and bananaquits; the area around Cauls Pond is quite good for birdwatching.

Anguilla has no city or town, just a series of communities and informal housing developments scattered along its 16-mile length. The major ones are **The Valley** (population: 500), which is in the center of the island near the Wallblake airport and serves as the center of government; **Sandy Ground**, where the island's deep water harbor is located; and **Blowing Point**, the ferry dock for St. Martin, just five miles south of Anguilla. There are only four traffic lights on the island, but plenty of speed bumps to keep the autos subdued. Anguilla took a beating from Hurricane Luis in 1995, but lasting damage is hard to spot today.

People

Anguilla is home to about 10,100 people who, while technically citizens of Great Britain, have a culture and style all their own. You won't find a strong British influence as on other colonies such as Bermuda; the ambience here is pure Caribbean. In fact, the number-one sport is the decidedly non-British pastime of boat racing. Because its limestone land makes for poor agriculture, slavery never really took hold here and there is scant evidence of tension between the races.

Anguillans are a proud, friendly and polite people; it's considered rude to jump in with a question or statement without first uttering the requisite "good morning" or "good afternoon." The island has a British education system in which elementary students graduate to one comprehensive school located in the Valley. For North American grade 12 and 13 equivalencies, students take Caribbean and British exams. There is no college or university on the island, so those interested in higher education attend schools in England, the United States, Jamaica or other Caribbean countries.

History

Long before the Europeans arrived in the Caribbean, Arawak Indians inhabited Anguilla's hot and dusty scrubland. Over the past 10 years, some 40,000 Amerindian artifacts have been uncovered by the Anguilla Archaeological and Historical Society from some 50 sites, indicating Anguilla may have been an important ceremonial site, even a pilgrimage, for this native American tribe. By the time the English settled in the 1650s, the Arawaks had vanished—probably decimated by European conquistadors and marauding pirates. When the dry climate foiled all British attempts at farming, their former slaves divided up the land, cultivated pigeon peas and corn, and then finally turned to the sea, building and trading sloops and schooners and fishing in rich waters. In 1967, the British forced Anguilla into an uncomfortable tri-island alliance when the Associated State of St. Kitts-Nevis-Anguilla was signed into law. The single act stimulated a determined, if not exactly violent, rebellion, which found Anguillans marching a coffin around the island, burning the Government House and sending its 12 policemen packing. World headlines roared with news of "The Eel that Squeeled" (sic) as the Brits sent in paratroopers, only to be met on the shore by cheering Anguillians singing the British national anthem and waving Union Jacks. Finally the Brits succumbed and gave Anguilla what it really wanted—a benevolent overlord who took the pains to build a badly needed phone system, a new pier and roads.

Tourism sprouted on Anguilla later than on most other Caribbean islands. The first major resort opened in the mid-1980s. Others followed, spurring a population boom, and now tourism is the island's only major economy. In 1996, the island flirted with cruise ship landings as a sort of post-hurricane financial aid, but residents wisely determined the intrusion might be disastrous to their more-important accommodations and dining industry; today, only ships smaller than 200 passengers are allowed to call.

An amusing recounting of the Anguillan revolution is offered in *Under an English Heaven*, by Donald E. Westlake, available at local bookstores and boutiques.

Easily one of the best destinations for beach-lovers in the Caribbean, Anguilla boasts some 12 miles of glistening white strands divided and stashed into 30-odd spots around the island. Some of the best are concentrated west of Sandy Ground and Blowing Point, and include famous **Rendezvous Bay**, the island's longest sweep of sand—nearly two miles of dunes facing the rolling hills of St. Martin. Good for long, lonely walks at any hour, Rendezvous is studded with seashells and elegant hunks of driftwood, as well as coconuts that wash ashore. Anguillan glamour shines at **Maundays Bay**, graced by the

Fielding **ANGUILLA**

LINGERING IN ANGUILLA

ANGUILLA

A British-dependent territory, Anguilla is the northernmost of the leeward islands. The shape of the island may have spawned its name, which in Spanish means "eel." Today, Anguilla is a beach-lover's treasure—the main island is rimmed with long, white sand beaches dotted with stands of picture-postcard palm trees that face bright blue waters. Offshore, the diving on wrecks put down as artifical reefs is appealing.

Fountain Cave

Located near Shoal Bay East, the Fountain is a dome-shaped cavern that shelters several freshwater pools. Discovered in 1979, the cavern contains petroglyphs on the walls. A 16-foot stalagmite has been carved with the image of Jocahu, a Taino Indian god. The government hopes to develop the cave as a site for visitors.

Cove Bay

Near Maundays Bay, you can relax in your own private paradise—provided you bring along your own picnic and towels. This soft-sand beach edged with coconut trees has no facilities.

Shoal Bay West

Once one of the Caribbean's best-kept secrets, this beach is still worth a visit, if only to sit on the powder white sands and watch the waves lap the water. Beach chairs and umbrellas are available.

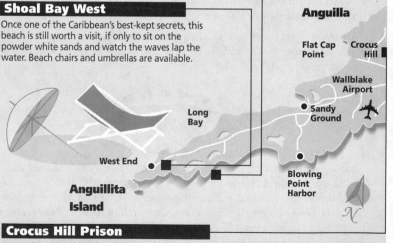

Anguilla

Flat Cap Point   Crocus Hill

Wallblake Airport

Sandy Ground

Long Bay

West End

Anguillita Island

Blowing Point Harbor

Crocus Hill Prison

At an elevation of 213 feet, the ruins of the prison occupy the island's highest point.

Island Harbor

This fishing village is set near a long, slender beach that fronts a safe harbor. Local fishermen put out to sea in handmade boats.

Scilly Cay

From the water, this spit of land looks like a castaway's hideout—thatched huts and a few palm trees rise from the sandy beach. The waters here are neon-blue, perfect for swimming or snorkeling, but most visitors come for the lobster and potent rum punch.

Captain's Bay

Rent a four-wheel-drive and head to this remote beach on the northeastern end, where limestone cliffs edge the sand. The surf pounds the shore, making the water too rough for swimming, but you'll savor the isolation.

Scrub Island

Sailboat Racing

The island's national sport, and the islanders and visiting boaters alike participate in sailboat races held during Carnival and on other holidays.

Shoal Bay East

Island Harbor

The Valley

The Quarter

Forest Bay

The Museum at Arawak

Situated in the Arawak Beach Resort, this small, privately operated museum has displays of Arawak artifacts, as well as replicas of everyday utensils once used by the natives.

The Valley

This small town is where you'll find the Roman Catholic church and Wallblake House. Built around 1796 by Will Blake, this plantation great house is the subject of legends. Now owned by the Catholic Church, the structure can be toured by appointment. Built in 1966, the nearby St. Gerard's Catholic Church has rock walls and stained glass windows.

cupolas of Cap Juluca along most of its seagrape-lined sweep, while just beyond is quieter **Shoal Bay West**, where the striking villas of Covecastles add futuristic élan to the setting. **Sandy Ground** (Road Bay) is a hub for watersports and boating activities, as well as home to the island's only deep-water port and a small crop of restaurants; quite picturesque from the bluffs at either end.

Continuing east along the north coast, lovely **Katouche** is tucked below the bluffs of Crocus Hill with fine snorkeling for those who can locate the trail from Old Ta, while **Little Bay** is a stunner. Less than a hundred feet wide, this tiny cove is backed by steep cliffs and its dollop of velvety sand descends gently into a miragelike hue of turquoise; it's typically approached by boat, but a precipitate trail can be pointed out to you by locals. **Shoal Bay East**—locally referred as two beaches, upper and lower—is one of the island's most popular hangouts, in part because of the live music and inexpensive restaurants, but saunter off from its central hub and you'll find a piece to call your own. At Anguilla's east end are several, less-visited outposts with their own special attributes: **Captain's Bay** (awesome waves and the unofficial nude beach), **Junks Hole Bay** (great beach bar with johnny cakes and red snapper), **Savannah Bay** (palms and privacy); each is best reached on foot or by four-wheel drive.

Underwater

Swimming through the carcasses of downed ships provides a delightful scuba conundrum: the wrecks are dead, yet teeming with life as the sea consumes their skeletal remains. Anguilla is a decidedly low-key dive destination, happily content to sink abandoned ships off its northern coast for the delight of visitors and fish alike. Seven of these artificial reefs have been put down over the past decade—four in 1990 alone during the island's offshore cleanup campaign—allowing Anguilla to proclaim itself the "wreck dive capital of the Caribbean." The most exciting wreck activity is somewhat less deliberate: a pair of Spanish galleons were recently discovered off **Junks Hole Bay** for which excavation is just starting for bronze religious medallions (the site is unlikely to be open to the public until 1998). Because the remaining wrecks are more recent, they are a number of years away from true encrustation but, combined with an assortment of attractive nearby reefs, Anguilla is a pleasurable dive destination. The island's waters have not suffered from overuse, and the government recently created a Marine Parks system and instituted a mooring permit policy to minimize damage to reefs. An added attraction in March are the humpback whales that navigate the strait between Windward

Point and Scrub Island. Snorkeling is excellent at a number of north coast locations and on the nearby reefs; check out Frenchman's Reef and the east side of Shoal Bay, both accessible from shore.

Dive Shops

The Dive Shop

Sandy Ground; ☎ *(264) 497-2020.*

The island's oldest dive shop (since 1985), a PADI Five Star facility working with all levels of divers. Formerly known as Tamariain Watersports. Resort courses, $100. Two-tank dive, $80.

Anguillan Divers

Island Harbor; ☎ *(264) 497-4750.*

Smaller PADI facility, with courses to Divemaster; open since 1991. Dives the adventurous reefs off Windward Point and the eastern channel. Two-tank dive, $70. Resort course, $75.

Being slender in shape, and only modestly endowed with gentle limestone hills, coraline Anguilla would hardly seem to boast a wealth of hiking options. Scrubby **Crocus Hill** represents the island's high point, a mere hiccup in the Eastern Caribbean at just 213 feet above sea level, which helps keep the island's focus firmly glued on its stunning beaches. However, a topographical map from the Land and Survey Department will display some of the tracks that cross Anguilla's interior, while several offshore islands can be reached by charter boats and provide additional exploration possibilities. Although there are no companies that specialize in touring the island on foot, the **Anguilla Archeological and Historical Society** sometimes conducts walks. Keep in mind that the island's beaches and brushy interior are scrubby and exposed; bring ample water and sunscreen for any excursions.

Man-made attractions are delightfully few and far between on Anguilla, but there are a few sights to fill in the spare hours between beaches. On the outskirts of The Valley is **Crocus Hill**, the island's highest point and the location of an old prison—a view of the entire island is possible. On the slopes of Crocus Hill are some of the island's oldest homes, some of them brightly painted and photogenic. Several caves wind through the island's limestone interior: the National Trust hopes to open the most important, **Fountain Cavern**, as a National Park soon (check with the Tourist Board). It was an important Amerindian ceremonial site 1600 years ago and contains petroglyphs, artifacts and a fresh water source. Replicas from another Amerindian site, **Big Spring Cave**, near Island Harbour, are on display at the mini-museum at Arawak Beach Resort. For more information about the Amerindian culture and sites, contact the **Anguilla Archeological and Historical Society** ☎ *(264) 497-4164.* Birdwatching has developed a following over the last several years and in 1994 the **Anguilla Beautification Club** planted 5000 mangroves to recreate habitats for marine birds and fish. **Cauls Pond**, **Long Salt Pond** and **Grey Pond** are among the best areas to see some of Anguilla's permanent winged residents, including the snowy egret, yellow-crowned night heron and white-cheeked pintails, as well as some of the winter visitors.

Several small offshore islands are idyllic landings for swimming, snorkeling and sunning. **Gorgeous Scilly Cay** is privately owned and home to a memorable, if expensive, restaurant open for lunch (see "Where to Eat"); you may be able to swing over for an afternoon of sunbathing if you buy a round of drinks. **Sandy Island**, little more than a miragelike dune deposited two miles off Road Bay, was scalped of its palm trees by Hurricane Luis, but the beach bar is back, and snorkeling through the aquamarine shallows is fine. Six miles out of Road Bay is the scrubby **Prickly Pear Cays**, great for diving and the beach on the eastern island is dreamy. Just off Anguilla's east end is **Scrub Island**, large enough to explore for a day (there's the ruins of a resort and an abandoned airstrip, in addition to a fine, wild beach). Day charters can be easily arranged through your hotel—bring plenty of sunblock.

Saint Martin/Sint Maarten, where evening lights beckon invitingly just across the sea, is a good daytrip for shopping, sightseeing, dining, or even gambling in the casinos that dot the Dutch side. Frequent ferry service (see "Getting Around," below) makes the trip a breeze.

City Celebrations

Carnival   ★★★

Various locations.

To celebrate Emancipation Day, or "August Monday" when the slaves were freed, Anguillans throw a week long party each year that begins the first week of August. Festivities include boat races—the island's national sport—cultural events and general acts of merriment.

Historical Sites

Wallblake House   ★★

Crossroads, The Valley, ☎ *(264) 497-2405.*

This plantation house, circa 1787, can be toured only by appointment, but even if you just get to see the outside, it's worth a look. Great tales of intrigue, murder, a

French invasion and dysfunctional family history surround the place, which is now owned by the Catholic Church. While you're here, check out the newer church next door with its open-air side walls. The best time to come is Saturday mornings in the winter, when local artisans display their works on the grounds.

Museums and Exhibits

Heritage Collection ★★★

East End, ☎ *(264) 497-4440.*
Hours open: 9 a.m.–5 p.m.

Anguilla's first privately owned museum houses historian and author Colville Petty's collection of Anguillian artifacts, old records and photos tracing the history of the island from the Arawak age to the present. Conch shell tools and pottery fragments from the Fountain Cave depict the simple life of the island's first inhabitants, but more contemporary items like a late-'60s-era Anguillian car license plate have their own unique story. The "CN" on the plates stood for St. Christopher (Kitts) and Nevis—Anguilla, which was part of the three-island independence alliance carved up by England in 1967, was not even recognized. The third-class status led to the bloodless rebellion, and Anguilla's eventual return to the safety of British colonial status. General admission: $5.

Tours

Sandy Island ★★★

Off the northwest coast, near Sandy Ground, ☎ *(264) 497-6395.*

This tiny flat of sand, which measures just 650 by 160 feet, is surrounded by a living reef with depths to 10 feet—miraculously it somehow survived Hurricane Luis, though it lost its palm trees and the beach bar had to be rebuilt. Besides the obvious snorkeling possibilities, the real treat is to beach yourself for an epiphany: a world of nothing more than sun, sea and sand. The snack bar is open from 9 a.m. to 4 p.m., and a ferry to the island leaves from Sandy Ground (near the pier) every 30 minutes. Snorkeling equipment is available on the island, but bring anything else you'll need, like sunblock and a hat. The ferry is $8 per person, round-trip.

Fielding Tip:

Learn the language of land directions in Anguilla, inspired by the winds. East is "up." West is "down." And both north and south are "over."

Sports

Watersports are the dominant physical activity on Anguilla (unless you count turning over every half-hour for the perfect tan). Nearly all hotels have a good watersports center; if not, check out the two centers listed below. Snorkeling and diving are excellent with intact wrecks, reef systems and walls to be explored. **Chocolat Catamaran Cruises** ☎ *(264) 497-3394* offers ocean excursions, as does **Wildcat Services** ☎ *(264) 497-2665*, which also arranges fishing trips, horseback riding and historical tours. Boat racing is the national sport and occurs during virtually every holiday and festival. The island's easterly breezes average between 10 and 20 miles per hour and are best in August, when the majority of races take place. The competing sailboats are all wooden, hoist a jib and mainsail from a single spar and range in size from 15 to 28 feet. Tennis players will have no problem finding courts at the major hotels, but duffers are out of luck, as Anguilla has no golf course.

Bicycling

Two locations.

Anguilla is relatively flat and the main roads can be explored in a relaxing day or two. One of the quietest areas is the eastern tip, beyond Island Harbour. Carry plenty of water and sunscreen; a patchkit will come in handy if you do any off-road riding since stickers can be a nuisance. **Multiscenic Tours** in George Hill ☎ *(264) 497-5810* is your best bet for rentals.

Horseback Riding

Hop on a horse and take a beach or trail ride through gorgeous scenery. **El Rancho del Blues** offers beach rides daily at 9 a.m. and 2 p.m., while trail rides leave at 11 a.m. and 4 p.m. One-hour rides cost $25; two hours go for $45. One-hour private beach rides and full-moon beach rides are also available for $45. English and Western saddles are available, as are riding lessons. ☎ *(264) 497-6164*

Watersports

Anguilla has two watersports centers. **The Dive Shop** (formerly Tamariain Water Sports) ☎ *(264) 497-2020* is a full-service PADI dive facility that also rents Sunfish sailboats and hosts water-skiing excursions. Also offering watersports is **Anguillan Divers** ☎ *(264) 497-4750*, including snorkeling and deep sea fishing trips.

Where to Stay

Fielding's Highest Rated Hotels in Anguilla

★★★★★	Cap Juluca	$290–$770
★★★★★	Malliouhana Hotel	$240–$630
★★★★	Cinnamon Reef Resort	$150–$400
★★★★	Covecastles	$425–$995
★★★★	Sonesta Beach Resort	$200–$450
★★★	Anguilla Great House Beach Resort	$120–$230
★★★	Carimar Beach Club	$140–$440
★★★	Frangipani Beach Club	$165–$450
★★★	Paradise Cove Resort	$155–$385
★★★	Shoal Bay Villas	$142–$295

Fielding's Most I-Think-I've-Landed-in-the-Mediterranean-By-Accident Hotels in Anguilla

★★★★★	Cap Juluca	$290–$770
★★★★	Covecastles	$425–$995
★★★★★	Malliouhana Hotel	$240–$630
★★★	Frangipani Beach Club	$165–$450
★★★★	Sonesta Beach Resort	$200–$450

Fielding's Best Value Hotels in Anguilla

★★★	Anguilla Great House Beach Resort	$120–$230
★★	Allamanda Beach Club	$77–$165
★★★★	Cinnamon Reef Resort	$150–$400
★★★	La Sirena	$110–$315

ANGUILLA

Anguilla is almost as famous for its posh resorts as it is for its luminous beaches. Exotic Mediterranean vernacular architecture—from the clean white lines of turrets and cupolas at **Cap Juluca** to ornate Moroccan tilework at **Sonesta Beach Resort**—is part of the show at several spots. However, expect to pay top, top dollar to stay at these bastions of luxury, particularly during high season when residents of the U.S. northeast lose their reasoning and can think of nothing beyond an Anguillan escape from winter's icy grip. Fortunately, at the best hotels, service is professional, rooms are beautifully decorated, and every little amenity is at hand. At **Malliouhana**, this means repeat guests are pampered with perks like clothes storage between trips—the day before check-in, your island wardrobe is pulled out of storage, cleaned, and folded into the drawers of your room.

A few hotels took a beating during Hurricane Luis in 1995, but are back in shape as we go to press. **Cap Juluca** spent millions to restore storm-ravaged Maundays Bay and overhaul their rooms, while the Casablanca became the **Sonesta Beach Resort**, and Pineapple Beach Club changed its name back to **Anguilla Great House**; the latter pair abandoned their all-inclusive policies. **Mariner's** was taken over by an American couple who promise to substantially upgrade a property whose West Indian charms had increasingly been compromised by skimpy upkeep. In other resort news, **Coccoloba** has been sold to the Montreaux Group, a group of doctors who will greatly expand the hotel and reopen it as a health-oriented resort with spa facilities in 1998 (a large portion of the property will also be leased to an Italian touring company).

Hotels and Resorts

Cap Juluca is the big favorite with the money set, popular enough to regularly land in the top five of best Caribbean resorts in the annual *Conde Nast Traveler* readers poll, while tony **Malliouhana Beach** appeals to jet-setters who want everything just so. The austere, one-of-a-kind architecture of **Covecastles** is a turn-off to some, and catnip to others, including celebrities who revel in its isolation. Note than a number of properties add a per-night surcharge during the busy Christmas season.

Anguilla Great House Beach Resort $120–$230   ★★★

Rendezvous Bay, ☎ *(800) 583-9247, (264) 497-6061, FAX (264) 497-6019.*
Website: www.erols.com/gafaxa/aghbr.htm. E-mail: flemingw@zemu.candw.com.ai.
Single: $120–$185. Double: $120–$230.

Located smack dab in the middle of Anguilla's longest beach, this sweetie is a solid choice for those watching their pocketbooks. The horseshoe-shaped array of one-story bungalows use traditional West Indian decor, with verandas, trellises and whimsical gingerbread trim. Rooms are nicely done in hand crafted mahogany furnishings from Jamaica, with both ceiling fans and air conditioning. Not much within walking distance (beyond the spectacular beach), but pleasant poolside dining and lots of resident bunnies and turtles scampering about. There are more luxurious resorts on the island, but this unpretentious spot has its own very lovely charm and a wonderfully friendly staff. 27 rooms. Credit cards: A, D, MC, V.

Cap Juluca $290–$770   ★★★★★

Maundays Bay, ☎ *(800) 323-0139, (264) 497-6666, FAX (264) 497-6617.*
Single: $290–$770. Double: $290–$770. Suites Per Day: $555–$1920.
A Moorish fantasy of domes, turrets and parapets, Cap Juluca is the epitome of swank Caribbean resort living. Guestrooms are housed in striking whitewashed villas that poke out of the seagrape trees along a sublime beach that unfurls like a magic carpet for three-quarters of a mile. Each two-story villa (which contains a maximum of six units) surrounds a courtyard where continental breakfast is served. Awash in white and beige, rooms are exquisitely decorated and boast giant walk-in closets, walnut louvered doors, Italian-marbled bathrooms and huge patios lined with Turk's head cactus. Rooms come in three main categories ranging up to 1100 square feet, while suites include roof terraces, private pools or solariums; the latter, replete with a lusty bathtub for two and floor-to-ceiling windows, send jaws dropping. When you return from dinner, you'll find maids have left flickering candles when they turned down the beds—indeed, the Arabian Nights are alive and well. The imaginatively landscaped, 179-acre grounds include scenic lagoons for bird-watching, two restaurants, three tennis courts with a resident pro, a croquet court and a fitness center. There's entertainment four nights a week, and room service is available through most of the day. More laid-back and casual than its chief competitor, Malliouhana, but Cap Juluca is undeniably top-drawer all the same. 98 rooms. Credit cards: A, MC, V.

Cinnamon Reef Resort $150–$400   ★★★★

Little Harbour, ☎ *(800) 222-2530, (264) 497-2727, FAX (264) 497-3727.*
Website: www.cinnamon-reef.com. E-mail: cinnamon-reef@cinnamon-reef.com.
Closed Date: September and October.
Single: $150–$400. Double: $150–$400.
Pleasantly informal is the atmosphere at this intimate 35-acre resort, long heralded for its unpretentious luxury and owner-managers who care. Accommodations are in whitewashed villas set on the beach or perched on a bluff; each has living and dining rooms (no kitchen), a raised bedroom, patio complete with hammock, and tiled sunken showers. Most of the villas are unattached and appropriately private. For recreation, there's a huge pool (40 by 60 feet), three tennis courts and all kinds of complimentary nonmotorized watersports. Located on a secluded part of Anguilla's southern coast, this excellent resort's only downfall is a relatively small beach, though its protected waters make for great windsurfing and snorkeling. Rates include a continental breakfast. 22 rooms. Credit cards: A, MC, V.

Covecastles $425–$995   ★★★★

Shoal Bay West, ☎ *(800) 223-1108, (264) 497-6801, FAX (264) 497-6051.*
E-mail: Caribisles@aol.com.
Closed Date: September.
Single: $425–$995. Double: $425–$995.
This breathtaking, ultra-modern interpretation of Mediterranean villa living may take some getting used to at first, but these futuristic white structures are a noncon-

formist's delight, designed (and owned) by architect Myron Goldfinger. The accommodations are in individual, two-story villas with up to three bedrooms, or in one and two-bedroom beach houses—their unmistakable outline is visible from St. Martin, five miles away. Interiors vaunt more traditional trappings of refined luxury—raw silk cushions and oversized custom rattan sofas beneath soaring ceilings and skylights. All units have cable TV, CD players, VCRs, a well-stocked and modern kitchen, living and dining rooms, elegant bathrooms, and a covered beachfront veranda with a hammock; bicycles, tennis, kayaks and sunfish sailing are available. There's an acclaimed restaurant on the premises and limited room service, but otherwise few traditional resort amenities like a pool or bar, and little within walking distance. Still, for those looking for austere escapism and discrete exclusivity on a voluptuous beach, Covecastles can't be beat. 14 rooms. Credit cards: A.

Fountain Beach $100–$280   ★ ★

Shoal Bay East, ☎ (264) 497-3491, FAX (264) 497-3493.
Closed Date: September.
Single: $100–$280. Double: $100–$280.

Set on a scrumptious beach along the rural north coast, this homey and secluded inn appeals to those who like privacy and calm. Accommodations are in oversized studios and one- and two-bedroom suites with Caribbean artwork, colorful rattan and wicker furniture, large marble baths and full kitchens. The grounds include a well-liked restaurant and a nice pool. Decent digs for the price, but note that room quality varies from one unit to the next. 12 rooms. Credit cards: A, D, MC, V.

Malliouhana Hotel $240–$630   ★ ★ ★ ★ ★

Meads Bay, ☎ (800) 835-0796, (264) 497-6111, FAX (264) 497-6011.
Closed Date: September–October.
Single: $240–$630. Double: $240–$630. Suites Per Day: $395–$1400.

Every little detail is in place at this impeccable 25-acre resort, set atop a limestone bluff that bisects two beaches—one a sprawling strand that unfurls for a mile, the other a petite cove. The lush Haitian artwork in the lobby continues into the oversized guestrooms, which are beautifully decorated with rattan and bamboo furniture, marble bathrooms with copious tubs and patios or balconies (four fabulous corner units have wraparound balconies, available by request). A new three-unit villa contains a one-bedroom, two-bath suite with a private pool and two suites with private Jacuzzis. There are four tennis courts, three pools, complimentary watersports (windsurfing and waterskiing lessons are extra) and an open-air exercise pavilion with lovely ocean views to keep you motivated. Live music is offered each night during the winter (and three times a week in the summer), and parents can leave the little ones in free supervised programs. The staff can be a bit cool and the overall atmosphere a bit reserved, but Malliouhana retains its place as one of the Caribbean's very best splurges. 56 rooms.

Mariners $150–$325   ★ ★

Sandy Ground, ☎ (800) 848-7938, (264) 497-2671, FAX (264) 497-2901.
E-mail: Mariners@candw.com.ai.
Single: $150–$325. Double: $150–$325.

A true West Indian-style resort, complete with charming gingerbread cottages and handcrafted lattice, but undergoing much needed improvements for the '98 season as we go to press. The best accommodations are in cottages with pitched ceilings, wicker furniture painted in pastels, and modest bathrooms; a few also boast living rooms and kitchenettes, but not all have air conditioning. A pool, sailing and tennis are available. Mariners is situated at one end of Anguilla's busiest beach, and a few restaurants and bars are within walking distance. Ideally, Mariners' charm and character will survive intact while the numerous kinks are ironed out—it's a spot with real potential. 61 rooms. Credit cards: A, D, MC, V.

Rendezvous Bay Hotel   **$90–$250**   ★★

☎ *(800) 274-4893, (264) 497-6549, FAX (264) 497-6026.*
Single: $90–$250. Double: $90–$250.
The island's first resort, Rendezvous draws lots of repeat customers for its quirky charm and magnificent beach, though the simple original rooms do show their age (1961). But they're priced well, even accounting for the lack of amenities—no pool or air conditioning, for example. The 24 newer villa units are either spacious one-bedroom suites or studios with full kitchens and air conditioning; they start at $120 (low season). There are two tennis courts, a game and TV room and, best of all, a local celebrity—the octogenarian owner and Anguillan revolutionary, Mr. Jeremiah Gumbs, who regales guests with stories about the pretourism era mixed in with a dose of his homespun aphorisms. 45 rooms. Credit cards: A, MC, V.

Sonesta Beach Resort   **$200–$450**   ★★★★

Rendezvous Bay West, ☎ *(800) 766-3782, (264) 497-6999, FAX (264) 497-6899.*
Single: $200–$450. Double: $200–$450. Suites Per Day: $385–$825.
An ornate Moroccan lobby—filled with dazzling tiled mosaics, hand-carved artwork and seductive arches—is the eye-popping introduction to Anguilla's youngest resort. Acquired by the Sonesta Corporation in 1996 and occupying a prime locale between two terrific beaches, the pink and green buildings of this $20-million, 60-acre resort are a somewhat incongruous sight, even on architecturally-adventurous Anguilla. Guestrooms are more subdued, but still nicely appointed with a melange of exotic stenciled patterns in pastel tones; all have original contemporary artwork, and deluxe units and suites have large marble baths. Rates include nonmotorized watersports, tennis, and exercise room and afternoon tea. Note that the original creators made one tragic design error: the resort's tallest building sits closest to the beach, blocking much of the spectacular view for rooms in the rear. Otherwise, the setting is splendid and Sonesta has overcome the rocky birth this contender originally encountered by toning down the cacophony, polishing the service, and establishing a somewhat more moderate rate card. 100 rooms. Credit cards: A, MC, V.

Apartments and Condominiums

Independent-minded folks with time on their hands will enjoy the villa life in Anguilla, though cooking with limited resources isn't exactly a snap—the outdoor market across from the Anglican Church in The Valley (daily except Sunday) has a pretty narrow selection of fruits and vegetables. For an extended stay, stocking up in St. Martin is a better plan, though prices will be higher than at home. Villa rentals are provided by **Anguilla**

Connections ☎ *(264) 497-4403* and **Easy Corner Villas** ☎ *(800) 223-9815* or ☎ *(264) 497-6433.*

Allamanda Beach Club   **$77–$165**   ★★

Shoal Bay East, ☎ *(264) 497-5217, FAX (264) 497-5216.*
E-mail: allamanda@offshore.com.ai.
Single: $77–$165. Double: $77–$165.
The best value on luminous Shoal Bay East, Allamanda is a three-story apartment complex located a few hundred feet off the beach. All units have smallish kitchens and the decor is not the sharpest, but the staff is pleasant, the pool fine, the beach perfect. The new restaurant, Zara's, is eliciting some raves. Low season rates include tax and service charge. 16 rooms. Credit cards: A, D, MC, V.

Carimar Beach Club   **$140–$440**   ★★★

Meads Bay, ☎ *(800) 235-8667, (264) 497-6881, FAX (264) 497-6071.*
Website: www.carimar.com. E-mail: carimar@candw.com.ai.
Single: $140–$350. Double: $140–$440.
A small, charming complex on a terrific beach, these comfortable one- and two-bedroom apartments are condos rented out when the owners aren't using them. The villas are Mediterranean style and nicely done with wicker and rattan furniture, TVs, full kitchens, large living rooms, dining areas and balconies or patios; tennis is across the street. Most rooms offer only partial views of the beach, but the tropical grounds are tended by a gardener who obviously takes great pride in coaxing color and life and out of the Anguillan limestone. There's no pool, restaurant or bar on-site, but the complex is within walking distance of several good facilities. Pricey in winter, but a good summer value. 24 rooms. Credit cards: A, MC, V.

Frangipani Beach Club   **$165–$450**   ★★★

Meads Bay, ☎ *(800) 892-4564, (264) 497-6442, FAX (264) 497-6440.*
Single: $165–$450. Double: $165–$450.
This lovely Spanish-style pink stucco and red-tile roof oasis offers guest rooms and one- to three-bedroom suites on gorgeous Meads Bay Beach. All units have air conditioning, full kitchens, natural rattan furnishings and a patio or balcony; some boast Jacuzzis as well (be sure to request a sea view room, which is priced the same as the garden or parking lot view). The on-site restaurant is quite good (and expensive); open for breakfast, lunch and dinner daily. Watersports and other activities are extra and there is no pool, but a professional staff with a familial embrace are attributes of this attractive spot. 21 rooms. Credit cards: A, MC, V.

La Sirena   **$110–$315**   ★★★

Meads Bay, ☎ *(800) 331-9358, (264) 497-6827, FAX (264) 497-6829.*
Single: $110–$190. Double: $145–$315. Villas Per Day: $200–$530.
Accommodations at this split-personality property are in two distinct sections. Twenty are in a three-story, Spanish-style stucco building that wraps around gardens and a nice pool area. These units are nicely done with rattan furnishings, ceiling fans and Caribbean pastels, a tad cozy (only upper rooms boast a sea view) and most have air conditioning. A stone pathway leads to a hamlet of five, two- and three-bedroom villas with a second pool. These are great for either families or couples, with full kitchens, a veranda or sundeck, and one has air conditioning. There

is a formal restaurant and casual poolside cafe—the gorgeous beach is a five-minute walk through a grove of sea grape trees (the same beach Malliouhana's customers pay twice the price for). Not the most dynamic spot, and "perhaps the management has acquired too much serenity," said one guest, but a good value for the rates, particularly for singles. 25 rooms. Credit cards: A, MC, V.

Paradise Cove Resort   **$155–$385**   ★★★

The Cove, ☎ *(264) 497-6603, FAX (264) 497-6927.*
Website: www.mrat.com/paradise/index.ht. E-mail: para-cove@candw.com.ai.
Single: $155–$270. Double: $155–$385.
An intimate, romantic hideaway nestled among palm trees and lush tropical gardens just a five-minute walk from beautiful Cove Beach. Centrally air-conditioned one- and two-bedroom units are quite spacious and elegantly furnished and include telephones, private laundry facilities, huge bathrooms, cable TV, high beamed ceilings, two large balconies and fully-equipped kitchens—hire a private cook and indulge. This is one of Anguilla's few locally owned properties, and it's a winner, despite its slightly off the beach locale. The grounds include a barbecue area, a large but plain pool, two Jacuzzis, a restaurant that serves breakfast and lunch and a playground for the kids. Request an end unit for more privacy. 14 rooms. Credit cards: A, MC, V.

Shoal Bay Villas   **$142–$295**   ★★★

Shoal Bay East, ☎ *(800) 722-7045, (264) 497-2051, FAX (264) 497-3631.*
Single: $142–$295. Double: $142–$295.
Contemporary villa-style condominiums located on prime Shoal Bay East. The one- and two-bedroom units have kitchenettes and painted rattan furniture, but no air conditioning. The pool in back is lovely, the palm-studded beach in front is a tropical dream. There's a restaurant and bar on-site with occasional live music, with other spots nearby that are a big draw on weekends. 13 rooms. Credit cards: A, D, MC, V.

Low Cost Lodging

If a low-cost vacation is your goal, Anguilla should not be the first island on your list. But if its powdery sands call to you incessantly, there are a few budget options, providing you visit during the low season—generally mid-April through mid-December. Note that a number of the moderately priced hotels above have reduced rates in the summer for guests who book a five- or seven-night stay.

Lloyd's Guest House   **$60–$80**   ★

Crocus Hill, ☎ *(264) 497-2351, FAX (264) 497-3028.*
Single: $60. Double: $80.
A quaint, traditional West Indian guesthouse, operational since 1959. Rooms are small but sweet and clean at this family-run outfit; all have private bath and fan (no air conditioning), and a balcony out back overlooks The Valley. The only drawback is that the beach is a mile and a quarter away, down a steep hill (leave some energy for the return trip). No discount during low season, but pretty fair rates for the winter, and note that the price includes breakfast. 14 rooms.

Where to Eat

Fielding's Highest Rated Restaurants in Anguilla

★★★★★	Koal Keel	$22–$35
★★★★★	Malliouhana	$27–$37
★★★★	Eclipse	$20–$32
★★★★	Gorgeous Scilly Cay	$25–$45
★★★★	Hibernia	$18–$30
★★★★	Palm Court	$22–$26
★★★	Barrel Stay	$23–$32
★★★	Mango's	$17–$28
★★★	Paradise Cafe	$19–$25
★★★	Roy's	$16–$33

Fielding's Most Romantic Restaurants in Anguilla

♥♥♥♥♥	Eclipse	$20–$32
♥♥♥♥♥	Koal Keel	$22–$35
♥♥♥♥♥	Malliouhana	$27–$37
♥♥♥♥	Hibernia	$18–$30
♥♥♥♥	Palm Court	$22–$26

Fielding's Best Value Restaurants in Anguilla

★★★	Ferryboat Inn	$7–$26
★★★★★	Koal Keel	$22–$35
★★★	Ripples	$10–$25
★★★★	Palm Court	$22–$26
★★★★	Hibernia	$18–$30

Those with enough money for an Anguillan vacation demand the best, and island chefs work hard to keep customers happy, usually with excellent results. French and Continental cuisine have been popular for some time—often prepared elegantly—but Thai and other Asian influences are increasingly accenting the local palate. The British connection means fish and chips and other pub-style foods are found at a few places, but with a price tag higher than almost any in London. Seafood is an island mainstay, of course, and you can count on fresh lobster, crayfish, red snapper, whelk and conch. Because local produce is limited to pigeon peas, corn, pumpkin and potatoes, almost everything else used to create Anguilla's highfalutin gourmet cuisine has to be imported, frequently from the U.S., at great expense (a hydroponics farm recently opened and may revolutionize the local fresh produce industry). Otherwise, visitors on any kind of reduced budget should stick to local specialties, like pigeon pea soup or grilled chicken and fish, and keep your eyes out for roadside grills like **Rafe's**, overlooking Sandy Ground from South Hill, where barbecued ribs or chicken are succulent and cheap.

Barrel Stay $$$ ★★★

Road Bay, ☎ *(264) 497-2831.*
Lunch: 11 a.m.–3 p.m., entrées $8–$23.
Dinner: 6:30–9:30 p.m., entrées $23–$32.

The name refers to the old rum barrels and disassembled barrel stays that used to comprise much of this Sandy Ground restaurant, but then Luis whipped through and a new construction houses this local favorite. Tasty seafood is dressed in a variety of sauces, while Porterhouse and U.S. prime Black Angus steaks are popular—you can also special order a robust seafood bouillabaisse for two the day before. Some say the food is overpriced, but the French wines are reasonable and the outdoor terrace is quite pleasant. Credit cards: A, MC, V.

Dunes $ ★★★

Rendezvous Bay, ☎ *(264) 497-6699.*
Lunch: 12:30–4 p.m., entrées $10–$19.

First of all, you'll need a sturdy car to get to this unique beach spot on fabulous Rendezvous Bay. As they say, follow the funky signs and don't give up as you bump and grind down a dirt path that barely deserves to be called a road. It's worth it once you get here, for The Dunes is owned and run by Bankie Banx, a Anguillan reggae star. Lunch is a barefoot affair—barbecue chicken, ribs, grilled snapper and salads—appealing enough. But the setting, above a windswept beach amid a clatter of driftwood, flotsam and jetsam, is fantastic. And don't miss the open-mike Friday and Sunday nights, when Bankie and friends let the music rip, or better yet, the monthly Moonsplash Nights.

Eclipse $$$ ★★★★

Maundays Bay, ☎ *(264) 497-6755.* Associated hotel: *Cap Juluca.*
Dinner: 6–10 p.m., entrées $20–$32.

Long one of the most magical restaurant settings in all the Caribbean, the former Pimm's has been taken over by Hollywood's Eclipse for "cuisine of the sun."

Roughly translated, this means California-meets-Provence by way of the Caribbean, with bright seafood offerings like flash grilled ahi tuna, roasted wahoo with an almond-orange zest crust, and grilled salmon filet on asparagus; there's also a few pasta dishes and meats. But it's the scene—candle-lit tables in a Moorish palace looking across the water to Cap Juluca—that makes this place work. The food and service are quite good, but they aspire for higher ground and the experience is priced to match. Still, Eclipse has the potential to blossom into something quite special. Live music several nights a week. Credit cards: A, MC, V.

Ferryboat Inn $$ ★★★

Cul de Sac Road, ☎ (264) 497-6613.
Lunch: Noon–2:30 p.m., entrées $7–$26.
Dinner: 7–10 p.m., entrées $7–$26.
Set on the beach near the Blowing Point Ferry Pier, this romantic spot specializes in French/Caribbean dishes. Wonderful soups like French onion and black bean; lobster thermidor is the house favorite. The Ferryboat is especially inviting at night, with the lights of St. Martin weaving an enchanting spell. Credit cards: A, MC, V.

Gorgeous Scilly Cay $$$ ★★★★

Scilly Cay, Island Harbour, ☎ (264) 497-5123.
Lunch: Noon–3 p.m., entrées $25–$45. Closed: Mon.
An Anguillan institution since 1987, the restaurant that occupies Scilly Cay, a coral outcrop a few hundred feet off Island Harbour, is quite a scene—particularly when the beautiful people from St. Martin helicopter over for an afternoon of live music (Wednesday, Friday and Sunday) and attitude. Wonderful (but extremely expensive) fresh lobster, crayfish and marinated chicken make up the brief menu, all served with spicy pasta salad and fresh fruit over sea grape leaves. Scilly was scalped by Luis but rebuilt, and the complimentary lounge chairs and snorkeling are as appealing as ever. To hail a free ride over, wave from the pier in Island Harbour and the boatman will pick you up. Credit cards: MC, V.

Hibernia $$$ ★★★★

Island Harbour, ☎ (264) 497-4290.
Lunch: Noon–2 p.m., entrées $17–$30.
Dinner: 7–9 p.m., entrées $18–$30. Closed: Mon.
There are just 10 tables at this lovely, perennially popular spot, set in a West Indian-style cottage with a wide porch, on the island's northeast corner. Chef Raoul Rodriguez combines French and Asian (with a dash of Anguillan) for scintillating results: a house-smoked fish, spicy Tom Yam (a Thai coconut-milk soup), and duck magret from Perigord, all enhanced with local ingredients. They whip up their own breads and ice cream daily. Closed September and October. Credit cards: A, MC, V.

Koal Keel $$$ ★★★★★

The Valley, ☎ (264) 497-2930.
Dinner: 6:30–10:30 p.m., entrées $22–$35.
This lusty spot is situated in the Warden's Place, a beautifully restored, 18th-century plantation great house. Although the breezy outdoor setting brims with the ambiance of that era, a few contemporary notions have been incorporated, most notably The Bed, a white lace and mahogany affair that sits provocatively at the entryway.

The cuisine is Euro-Carib, embellishing the simple provisions of Anguilla with sophisticated flair: smoked mahi mahi on a pumpkin risotto pancake, puree of pigeon peas and sweet potatoes, rack of lamb with polenta. Fresh breads and roast meats are prepared in a large rock oven, and a wine cellar, located 17 feet below sea level, has a 25,000-bottle capacity—desserts are appropriately sinful. The restaurant provides tours of the grounds after dinner, and you'll be invited to sample a few of the 30 different rums they sell in their cigar room. There's also a tea and pastry shop upstairs that is open from 7 a.m. daily. Credit cards: A, MC, V.

Malliouhana   **$$$**   ★★★★★

Meads Bay, Road Bay, ☎ *(264) 497-6111.*
Lunch: 12:30–3 p.m., entrées $11–$30.
Dinner: 7–10:30 p.m., entrées $27–$37.
Set in a magnificent open-air pavilion on a rocky promontory overlooking the sea, Malliouhana's candle-lit dining terrace is wonderfully elegant, with gracious service, fine china and crystal. But, amazingly, unlike many hotel restaurants, the food manages to live up to the surroundings. Under the auspices of Paris chef Michel Rostang (who supervises the rotating menu of more than 50 dishes), Alain Laurent and his staff labor affably over mahi mahi with marmalized celery, a saddle of lamb in puff pastry with spinach and pilaf, or Black Angus tenderloin capped with a dollop of foie gras. Yes, many of the offerings are heavy (and save room for the fine desserts, at $11 a pop), but Malliouhana delivers one of the Caribbean's great dining experiences. Also worth noting is the wine cellar, which stocks some 25,000 bottles—possibly the region's best cache. Credit cards: A, MC, V.

Mango's   **$$$**   ★★★

Barnes Bay, ☎ *(264) 497-6479.*
Dinner: 6:30–9 p.m., entrées $17–$28. Closed: Tue.
Make reservations far in advance to get into this newer hot spot, which has two seatings for dinner, at 6:30 and 8:30 p.m. Partners Dave and David use the freshest ingredients for their grill-cooked meats and fish, including sesame snapper filet, lobster cakes and some tasty vegetarian selections; they also make their own bread, desserts and ice cream daily. This well-run bistro continues to draw raves from locals in the know, and the beachfront setting can't be topped—though a few note that the staff can be haughty. Credit cards: A, MC, V.

Old House, The   **$$**   ★★

George Hill, The Valley, ☎ *(264) 497-2228.*
Lunch: Noon–5 p.m., entrées $5–$12.
Dinner: 6–11 p.m., entrées $16–$20.
Yes, this eatery really is situated in an old house, set on a hill overlooking the airport. The decor is simple but the food's just fine, drawing a number of local businessmen at lunch for hefty burgers, steaks and barbecue. West Indian specialties are featured at dinner, including conch, local lamb, curry goat and Anguillan pot fish. It's nice to sit on the porch and watch the planes come and go. Also open for good, cheap breakfasts from 7-11:30 a.m. (try the fruit pancakes). Credit cards: A, MC, V.

Palm Court   **$$$**   ★★★★

Little Harbour, ☎ *(264) 497-2770.* Associated hotel: *Cinnamon Reef.*

Lunch: Noon–2:30 p.m., entrées $12–$18.
Dinner: 7–9 p.m., entrées $22–$26.

Haitian furniture, colorful murals and huge picture windows overlooking the sea make this out-of-the-way place special. The nouvelle Caribbean food is good too, with favorites like grouper encased in toasted pumpkin seeds, seafood in a ragout of lima beans, barbecued rabbit with an onion-and-apple cole slaw. Lunch is more casual, with good salads, soups and sandwiches. Save room for the mango puffs in caramel sauce. Credit cards: A, MC, V.

Paradise Cafe $$$ ★★★

Shoal Bay West, ☎ (264) 497-6010.
Lunch: Noon–2:30 p.m., entrées $8–$14.
Dinner: 7–9:30 p.m., entrées $19–$25. Closed: Mon.

Ocean breezes set many windchimes tinkling, a soothing backdrop to tasty dishes with French and Asian influences. Try the richly-endowed West Indian bouillabaisse, a pan-seared grouper in an almond crust, designer pizzas or the catch of the day. Lunches are simpler: burgers, salads and an only-in-Anguilla club sandwich made with lobster, bacon, lettuce and tomato. Reservations are suggested—the rich and famous have discovered Paradise. Closed in September. Credit cards: A, MC, V.

Ripples $$ ★★★

Sandy Ground, ☎ (264) 497-3380.
Lunch: Noon–midnight, entrées $10–$25.
Dinner: Noon–midnight, entrées $10–$25.

"Everyone comes here sooner or later," says congenial Jacquie Ruan, the ex-pat proprietress (with her husband Roland) of this time-honored local stand-by. Menu offerings include spicy equatorial tastes: Ginger-braced Thai salad, cold Mexican gazpacho, oven-roasted Jakarta chicken, along with pub food like fish and chips, cottage pie and pastas. Reserve to dine on the porch, and stick around 'til late when the bar gets lively. Be sure to ask Jacquie how she named the restaurant (and stand back when Tom Jones comes through the sound system). Credit cards: A, MC, V.

Riviera Bar & Restaurant $$$ ★★

Sandy Ground, ☎ (264) 497-2833.
Lunch: 11 a.m.– 3 p.m., entrées $11–$22.
Dinner: 6–9:30 p.m., entrées $18–$38.

This bistro terrace on the beach complements its French and Creole dishes with distinctive Asian accents—oysters sauteed in sake and soy sauce, and sashimi in wasabi mustard, for instance. A three-course prix fixe menu is available for $23-37. There's live music on Saturdays at this casual site, and the daily happy hour, 6–7 p.m., is happening. Cigar lovers are in heaven—manager Didier is a local rep for Havana's finest. Credit cards: A, D, MC, V.

Roy's $$$ ★★★

Crocus Bay, ☎ (264) 497-2470.
Lunch: Noon–2 p.m., entrées $4–$16.
Dinner: 6–9 p.m., entrées $16–$33.

Two British expatriates set up this little slice of their homeland, and they got it right, all the way down to the English beers (thankfully served cold) and dart board.

But everyone comes for the fresh catch, and don't overlook the decent steaks, crisp fish and chips, and fine key lime pie—all served al fresco on the veranda with nice sea views. Fridays are a scene, when the generous happy hour (two-for-one meals) draws in a big crowd. Credit cards: MC, V.

Shops are almost as rare on Anguilla as rainfall; if you're really looking to hit the stores, head for St. Martin right across the water (a 20- to 30-minute ferry ride). Otherwise, you'll find some goods in the upscale shops at the major hotels. For fashions, try **Caribbean Fancy** *(George Hill, ☎ [264] 497-3133)* and the **Riviera** *(Sandy Ground, ☎ [264] 497-2833)*, where they also have a good selection of wine.

Perhaps the best local wares to shop for are original artworks as the island is home to a small but thriving art colony. **Lucia Butler** *(☎ [264] 497-4259)* paints scenes of village life and wooden house plaques. **Marj Morani** *(☎ [264] 497-4259)* specializes in hand-thrown pottery and tiles and **Anne Saunders** *(☎ [264] 497-4087)* offers her hand-crafted fabrics, murals, paintings and sculptures. **Devonish Art Gallery** *(George Hill, ☎ [264] 497-2949)* showcases many local artists, including Lynne Bernbaum, a watercolorist who depicts island life, and Courtney Devonish, a sculptor and potter who owns the studio. **Cheddie's Carving Studio** *(The Cove, ☎ (264) 497-6027)* showcases the work of self-taught Cheddie Richardson, who works with driftwood, alabaster and coral.

Anguilla Directory

Arrival and Departure

There is talk of a new and expanded runway, but for now, all flights arrive at Anguilla's Wallblake Airport, just outside The Valley. **American Airlines** offers the only connecting service to the island from North America, via San Juan, using **American Eagle** for the one-hour hop to Anguilla. When seats are hard to come by, you can also fly American, **Continental** or **USAirways** to Dutch Sint Maarten's Juliana Airport, where flights to Anguilla are available on **Winair**, **LIAT** or Anguilla's own **Tyden Air** ☎ *(800) 842-0261* or *(264) 497-2719* and **Air Anguilla** ☎ *(264) 497-2634*. Tyden Air and Air Anguilla also provide limited service to the island from St. Thomas. Or use the frequent **ferry** service from Saint Martin/Sint Maarten to the Blowing Point ferry dock on Anguilla (see "Getting Around," below).

Departure tax is $10 for those leaving by air, $2 by ferry.

Business Hours

Most stores open Monday–Saturday 8 a.m.–5 p.m. or 6 p.m. Banks open 8 a.m.–3 p.m. Monday–Thursday and until 5 p.m. Friday.

Climate

Anguilla has one of the driest climates in the region—a bane to farmers, but a boon to sunseekers. As a result, vegetation is short and sparse, with few palm trees. With the lowest average annual rainfall in the Leeward Islands, Anguilla receives only 35 inches annually.

Current

Most outlets are 110 AC, as in the U.S.

Documents

Visitors must show ID with a photo, preferably a passport, and an ongoing ticket. Departure tax is $10 at the airport and $2 at the ferry port.

Getting Around

There is no bus service on Anguilla, though hitchhiking is safe and accepted. Taxis are available at Wallblake Airport and the Blowing Point dock; rates are established for most major destinations, and an island tour is $40 for two persons. Renting a car for at least a portion of your trip is the ideal way to see the island; roads are decent, speeds are reduced, though driving is on the left. You'll need to procure a local drivers license for $6, available through rental agencies or at the Traffic Department in The Valley. Reliable agencies include **Triple K**, a Hertz affiliate, ☎ *(800) 654-3131* or *(264) 497-2934*, **Maurice Connors** ☎ *(264) 497-6410*, and **Island Car Rentals** ☎ *(264) 497-2723*.

Daytrips to Saint Martin/Sint Maarten are easy by 20-minute ferry from Blowing Point. Ferries to Marigot leave as they fill, about every 30 minutes from 7:30 a.m. to 6:15 p.m.; out of Marigot, service is from 8 a.m. to 7 p.m. The trip is $10 one way, $12 in the evening. **Link Ferry** ☎ *(264) 497-2231* is considered the most dependable of the various outfits, and also offers service several times a day between Blowing Point and Juliana Airport for $15. Carry a valid passport or ID to show at both ends of your trip. It's also possible to fly over to Sint Maarten, but not quite worth the extra expense for the few minutes saved (see "Arrival and Departure," above).

Language

The official language is English spoken with a West Indian lilt.

Medical Emergencies

For serious problems, head for a hospital in Puerto Rico. The small Prince Alexander hospital at Stoney Ground is suitable for minor problems only.

Money

Official currency is the Eastern Caribbean dollar (EC), which is pegged to the U.S. dollar, $2.70 to $1 U.S. Before you shell out any dough, however, make sure the price is not referring to American dollars. Traveler's checks and American dollars are also readily accepted everywhere.

ANGUILLA

Telephone

The new area code for Anguilla is *(264)*. From the U.S., dial *1 + (264)*, then the seven-digit local number. To save money when calling home from Anguilla, go to the Cable and Wireless office and purchase a phone card.

Time

Anguilla is on Atlantic standard time, one hour ahead of Eastern standard time in winter (that means 1 p.m. in New York, 2 p.m. in Anguilla). During the summer, it's the same time.

Tipping and Taxes

Ten percent service charges and an 8 percent government tax are usually included in hotel bills; 10 percent service on all food and beverage tabs (no tax on food). Waiters and waitresses appreciate tips, but don't expect any. If a young boy carries your bag at the airport, one dollar per bag will put a smile on his face. More often, your taxi driver will tote them.

Tourist Information

Contact the **Anguilla Tourist Board** ☎ *(800) 553-4939* or *(264) 497-2759; Old Factory Complex, The Valley, Anguilla*. They can assist with general information and accommodations.

Web Site

www.candw.com.ai/~atbtour

When to Go

Anguilla Day is celebrated by a huge boat race on May 30, and the **Queen's Birthday** is feted by events in the month of June. But the island's biggest event is the annual **Carnival**, held in early August, which includes boat races, arts festivals, dancing, beach barbecues and special pageants.

ANGUILLA HOTELS	RMS	RATES	PHONE	CR. CARDS
★★★★★ Cap Juluca	98	$290–$770	(800) 323-0139	A, MC, V
★★★★★ Malliouhana Hotel	56	$240–$630	(800) 835-0796	
★★★★ Cinnamon Reef Resort	22	$150–$400	(800) 222-2530	A, MC, V
★★★★ Covecastles	14	$425–$995	(800) 223-1108	A
★★★★ Sonesta Beach Resort	100	$200–$450	(800) 766-3782	A, MC, V
★★★ Anguilla Great House Beach Resort	27	$120–$230	(800) 583-9247	A, D, MC, V
★★★ Carimar Beach Club	24	$140–$440	(800) 235-8667	A, MC, V
★★★ Frangipani Beach Club	21	$165–$450	(800) 892-4564	A, MC, V
★★★ La Sirena	25	$110–$315	(800) 331-9358	A, MC, V
★★★ Paradise Cove Resort	14	$155–$385	(264) 497-6603	A, MC, V
★★★ Shoal Bay Villas	13	$142–$295	(800) 722-7045	A, D, MC, V
★★ Allamanda Beach Club	16	$77–$165	(264) 497-5217	A, D, MC, V

ANGUILLA

ANGUILLA HOTELS	RMS	RATES	PHONE	CR. CARDS
★★ Fountain Beach	12	$100–$280	(264) 497-3491	A, D, MC, V
★★ Mariners, The	61	$150–$325	(800) 848-7938	A, D, MC, V
★★ Rendezvous Bay Hotel	45	$90–$250	(800) 274-4893	A, MC, V
★ Lloyd's Guest House	14	$60–$80	(264) 497-2351	

ANGUILLA RESTAURANTS	PHONE	ENTRÉE	CR. CARDS
Asian Cuisine			
★★★★ Hibernia	(264) 497-4290	$17–$30	A, MC, V
Continental Cuisine			
★★★★★ Koal Keel	(264) 497-2930	$22–$35	A, MC, V
★★★ Barrel Stay	(264) 497-2831	$8–$32	A, MC, V
French Cuisine			
★★★★★ Malliouhana	(264) 497-6111	$11–$37	A, MC, V
★★★ Ferryboat Inn	(264) 497-6613	$7–$26	A, MC, V
★★ Riviera Bar & Restaurant	(264) 497-2833	$11–$38	A, D, MC, V
Nouvelle Cuisine			
★★★★ Eclipse	(264) 497-6755	$20–$32	A, MC, V
Regional Cuisine			
★★★★ Gorgeous Scilly Cay	(264) 497-5123	$25–$45	MC, V
★★★★ Palm Court	(264) 497-2770	$12–$26	A, MC, V
★★★ Dunes, The	(264) 497-6699	$10–$19	
★★★ Paradise Cafe	(264) 497-6010	$8–$25	A, MC, V
★★★ Ripples	(264) 497-3380	$10–$25	A, MC, V
★★ Old House, The	(264) 497-2228	$5–$20	A, MC, V
Seafood Cuisine			
★★★ Mango's	(264) 497-6479	$17–$28	A, MC, V
★★★ Roy's	(264) 497-2470	$4–$33	MC, V

ANGUILLA

ANTIGUA

Some 200 boats from 25 countries pour into Antigua's English Harbour for Sailing Week in late April. It's the Caribbean's premier yachting event.

With its trove of dazzling beaches, ideal and historic sailing anchorages, and a clutch of upmarket resorts, one thing is clear: tourism is big business in Antigua. It has been for years. When it became apparent in the late 1960s that sugar production could no longer support the island, Antigua (pronounced An-*tee*-gah) began a very successful full-scale launch into tourism. The island has grown into one of the region's major destinations with almost a half-million visitors annually, mostly from North America and England. The island attracts a broad-based range of tourists, and though a few of the resorts are clearly aimed at a clientele carrying a few Swiss bank accounts in their back pocket, there is plenty for the mid-range traveler. Those looking for a budget destination should be forewarned that although a few hotels and restaurants are less expensive, hidden charges add up quickly on this island. Still, the attractions of Antigua are not to be denied. The beaches are stunning and the larger bays contain idyllic sailing anchorages. The island's rich naval and sugar history is on display in several areas, with Nelson's Dockyard and Betty's Hope being among the best historical sights in the region. And Antigua seems positively dedicated to serious festivities: International yachting fans congregate in late April for Antigua Sailing Week—the premiere nautical event of the Caribbean—and color and music explode in late July/early August when Carnival comes to the island, filling the air with calypso competitions and the streets with fanciful costumes. Since flying is the easiest way to reach the Caribbean, it doesn't hurt that Antigua is one of the better connected islands to North America.

Antigua received the full brunt of Hurricane Luis' force, but the island rebuilt surprisingly quickly and, although a few hotels were still closed at press time, most visitors will see little if any of the storm's impact. The beaches have been combed and cleaned, and a few are actually bigger than they were before the 1995 hurricane.

BEST BETS FOR...

Bird's-Eye View

Sprawling over about 108 square miles, Antigua is the largest and the most developed and heavily visited of the British Leewards. Antigua is well-positioned as a hub between a number of islands, with Guadeloupe to the south, Montserrat to the southwest, and St. Kitts-Nevis to the west. Together with Barbuda (28 miles to the north) and an uninhabited rocky islet named Redonda, the three islands form the independent nation of Antigua and Barbuda, within the Commonwealth of Nations. The capital is St. John's, which has a population of about 36,000 and is located at the mouth of one of the island's natural harbors. There are actually quite a few of these bays, inlets and coves scalloping the coastline, creating excellent sailing anchorages and a surfeit of beaches. Antigua's interior is somewhat drier in appearance than the more mountainous islands to the south—the one truly verdant spot is the southwest portion of the island where Boggy Peak rises to 1319 feet, luring a few rain-producing clouds to its slopes and down into a valley known as

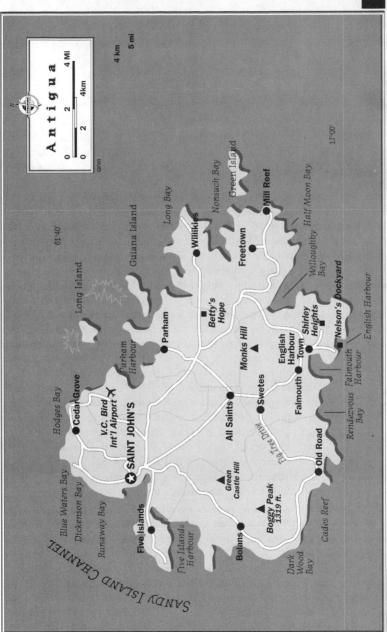

Fig Tree Drive. In the northeast, the terrain is flatter, with scrub and occasional cactus for vegetation. Otherwise, Antigua is generally remembered for its irregular coastline and the scenic harbors and coves of sand it creates.

History

The Siboney Stone people were the first to graze the terrain of Antigua with settlements dating back to 2400 B.C. Arawaks lived on the islands between A.D. 35 and 1100. Columbus discovered the island on his second voyage in 1493, naming it Santa Maria de la Antigua. The absence of freshwater springs persuaded French and Spanish colonists to sail on, but by 1632, the English had successfully established colonization. Apart from a brief French invasion in 1666, the three islands of Antigua, Barbuda and Redonda have all remained British. The first large sugar estates were established in Antigua in 1674 by Sir Christopher Codrington, who convinced the natives on Barbuda to raise provisions for the plantations. As production increased, forests were cleared for cultivation and African slaves were imported by the boatloads. Today many Antiguans trace the lack of rainfall to this early forest devastation. A vicious cycle of drought led eventually to barren lands, testimony of which can be seen in the ruined towers of sugarcane throughout the island. Abolition arrived in 1834, but the former slaves found they could barely subsist due to a lack of surplus farming and an economy that was based on agriculture and not manufacturing. Poor labor conditions and growing violence led to the organization of unions in 1939. A strong political Labor Party emerged seven years later, catapulting Antiguans into the 20th century. During World War II, Antigua was selected as a military base and American servicemen arrived in droves. Until 1959, Antigua and Barbuda was administered as part of the Leeward Islands, until attaining associated status with full self-internal government in 1967. The sugarcane industry fell off by 1972, and although some light farming persists, tourism was pegged early on as the machine to drive the island's future economy.

Since independence, island politics have been firmly in the hands of the Bird family. Vere C. Bird was Antigua's first prime minister, but charges of election fraud and corruption dogged his administration until retirement in 1994, at the age of 84. Although Bird's two sons had long rivaled to be next in line for his seat, in 1990 Vere Bird Jr., then minister of public works and communication, became the focus of judicial inquiry for his involvement in an arms smuggling scheme that used Antigua as a trans-shipment point between Israel and the Medellin drug lords in Colombia (there was no prison sentence). Lester Bird was elected as Prime Minister in 1994, though corruption still taints the island's politics. In 1995, another son, Ivor, was found carrying a 25-pound shipment of cocaine as he boarded a plane at the airport named after his father (he was fined $75,000). In addition to tourism, off-shore banking is another big industry, though a lack of regulation has allowed its banks to be used for money-laundering. Today, Antigua's opposition party is headed by Tim Hector, an outspoken critic of the government in the pages of his newspaper, the *Outlet*.

Antigua is visited by more than 400,000 annually, with about 55 percent of that total coming from cruise ship arrivals.

People

Antigua's population is 67,000; 85 percent are of African descent, although there is also a small minority of English, Portuguese, Lebanese and Syrian inhabitants. Many islanders, particularly those working in the tourism sector, come cloaked with a British frostiness that is off-putting. If you can crack the facade of formality, a warm, generous character surfaces. Almost half of the population lives in St. John's, while the remainder are spread throughout the island, in 40 small towns and villages. Most Antiguans own some kind of property, even if it is just a small shack in the countryside. Because the island has an excellent harbor and relatively easy access to the outside world, its people are quite used to traveling and are well aware of current events.

For another glimpse into Antigua and its character, read Jamaica Kinkaid's devastating, bitter profile of the island, its people and the effect of tourism, *A Small Place* (1988).

Beaches

While the government's claim to possessing 365 beaches is laughably insupportable, you could indeed spend more than one vacation exploring the dozens ringing Antigua. Beginning in St. John's and working around the island clockwise, the first you'll encounter is **Fort Bay**, popular with locals and tourists alike, and recently developed with a bar, restaurant and performance stage—it remains busy well into the evening, and particularly when a cruise ship has docked. Just a little farther up the coast are **Runaway Bay** and **Dickenson Bay**, both of which have seen extensive resort growth over the past cou-

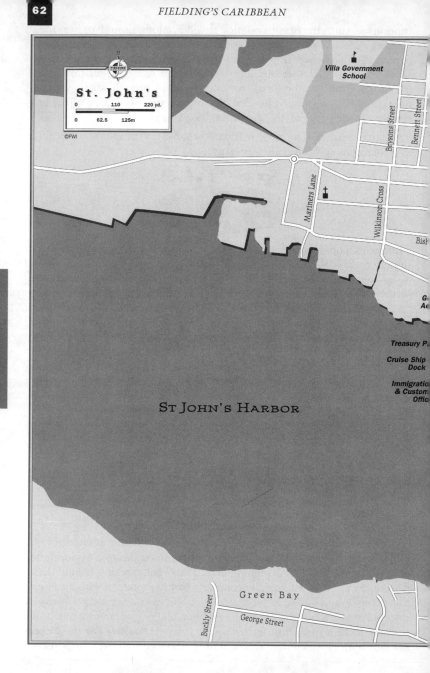

St. John's

0   110   220 yd.

0   62.5   125m

©FWI

Villa Government
School

Brysons Street

Bennitt Street

Marmers Lane

Wilkinson Cross

Bish

G
A

Treasury P

Cruise Ship
Dock

Immigratio
& Custom
Offic

St John's Harbor

Green Bay

Buckly Street

George Street

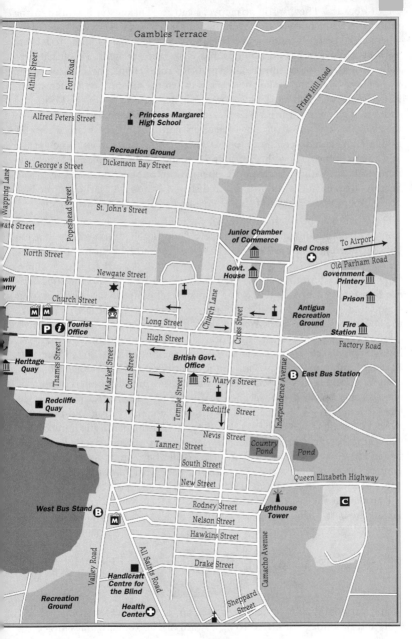

ANTIGUA

ple of decades. They're still attractive; head for Dickenson if you're in the mood for watersports and a lively beach scene, or to Runaway next door where crowds aren't quite as overwhelming. Hodges Bay is home to **Jabberwock Beach**, which has no facilities, but is a quiet spot with a reef that provides protection for swimmers and sights for snorkeling. There's little in the way of accessible sand along the coast between the airport and Indian Point, but at **Long Bay**, Hurricane Luis generously deposited tons of sand onto the shore to make one of the island's nicest beaches. **Half Moon Bay** takes the cake for sheer variety; most of it has been left natural, and there are waves for body surfing and quieter areas for swimming. The calm lagoon beach at the St. James Club comes with security guards and all the trappings of exclusivity, but as all Antigua beaches are open to the public, you may use it too. Several coves lie in the embrace of English and Falmouth Harbours, the best being quiet **Pigeon Beach**, on the peninsula that divides the two harbors.

The coast that curls west and north away from English Harbour is a succession of one stunning and usually undeveloped beach after another, starting with secluded **Rendezvous Bay**, which is best reached by boat or on foot; the road to it begins in the village of Falmouth (you'll need to ask for directions). The western foot of Fig Tree Drive is met by lovely, palm-lined **Carlisle Bay**, while just past the Curtain Bluff Hotel is **Morris Bay**, another long strand that is pleasant to walk and fine for swimming. A little farther is one of the most spectacular, **Dark Wood Beach**, a Caribbean Shangri-La where a small beach bar and restaurant is located. Continuing north, you may pass lovely **Fryes Beach** without seeing the turnoff, but there's no missing **Jolly Beach**, a long strand with two mammoth resorts to provide watersports, bars, restaurants and plenty of people. By contrast, few make it out to ominously named **Leper Colony Beach**, reached by four-wheel-drive road out of the village of Jennings—it's a small cove with excellent snorkeling and protected by rocky headlands on each end. Heading out on the peninsula immediately west of St. John's, you'll pass **Deep Bay**, which has the monstrous Royal Antiguan Hotel as a signpost, then attractive **Galley Bay**, which is used by surfers January through March, and we finish our tour with **Hawksbill**, which is not one, but four beaches. They all face a landmark rock in the shape of a hawksbill turtle, but the last of the four, reached by a 10-minute trail past the resort, is the best—it's also known as the island's clothing-optional spot.

Similar in topography to nearby St. Martin, the coral reef surrounding Antigua and Barbuda—estimated to be upward of 1000 square miles in size—is part of a giant, sloping underwater platform. As such, there are no real wall dives, although the area below Shirley Heights does offer relatively sheer drop-offs exceeding 100 feet; most dive spots tend to be shallow in nature, typically bottoming out at 60 feet or so. The best sites line the south and west coasts, though the area just northeast of the airport is now being explored. Underwater visibility is somewhat limited, averaging 70 to 80 feet due primarily to the healthy plankton growth, which thrives over the shallow reefs. Additionally, the government doesn't actively enforce the fishing ban within national parks, meaning that marine life can be skimpy, even at the island's best sites (such as Cades Reef). The island's massive, offshore reef structure provides many underexplored areas; some of the charted sites lie several miles off the coastline, requiring long boat rides but, in the words of *Undercurrent Magazine*, these dives are "well worth it." Snorkelers can head to the remains of the *Andes*, in shallow water off Deep Bay in front of the Royal Antiguan Hotel; it's one of the few Caribbean wrecks that's easily accessible from shore (though not particularly interesting for divers).

Advanced divers head for 122-foot deep Sunken Rock.

Dive Shops

Dockyard Divers

English Harbour; ☎ *(268) 460-1178.*

Dockyard specializes in the south coast surrounding Shirley Heights, with most dives 10–15 minutes from the shop. Resort course available. Groups average 5-10 divers; two-tank dive $63.

Dive Antigua

Dickenson Bay; ☎ *(268) 462-3483.*

Boasts a logbook containing more than 200 dive sites, many of which are "exclusive, proprietary locations." Integrates marine biology orientation into all dives. Oldest shop on the island (since 1970), featuring PADI and NAUI courses to assistant instructor. Resort courses, $85 (including a reef dive). Two-tank dive $70.

On Foot

Antigua has heard the green-backed cry of the eco-tourism monster and is now attempting to mine its hillsides and coasts for trails and exploration possibilities. The island may be playing catch-up with the ecological advances made on other islands, but it's the thought that counts. Much of Antigua's interior, once covered in sugarcane, is dry and unappealing, which limits the hiking opportunities available. But the National Trust claims to be trying to identify trails, primarily in the southern region between Boggy Peak and English Harbour, and may have finally produced a hiking brochure by the time you visit. Or, join the Hash House Harriers on their fortnightly jog/walk/stroll through the Antiguan countryside. They meet on Saturday afternoon at a predetermined location ☎ *(268) 462-0132.*

What Else to See

Although portions of St. John's, the capital of Antigua, look a bit ragged these days, there are areas being developed for tourism and worthy of a stroll. **Redcliffe Quay** is a picturesque district full of historical buildings, duty-free stores, souvenir shops and restaurants. Cruise ship passengers tend to crowd into **Heritage Quay**, off the harbor, where there is also a casino and satellite reception for a big screen TV. If you're looking for a cool interior to escape from the sun, dip into **St. John's Cathedral**, rebuilt several times due to earthquakes—no matter where you stand in town, you can see the twin towers.

Outside St. John's, several places are worth driving to, but note that although there is always road work in progress, driving conditions overall are quite shoddy (locals note, however, that roads leading to the residence of the prime minister or his cronies are always in good shape). Start with the coastline south of Jolly Harbour, lined by one gorgeous beach after another—after passing through the town of Old Road, you'll head in to Antigua's most verdant region, **Fig Tree Drive**, a rainforest with cow pastures and a variety of fruit trees (in Antigua, bananas are known as figs). **Nelson's Dockyard** in English Harbour is one of the region's most important historical sites—a secure port and hurricane hole that was used by Admiral Horatio Nelson as the regional facility for repairs to the British Royal Navy. Take the footpath that leads around the bay to **Fort Berkeley** for a great view you'll share with grazing goats. Nearby, the future King William IV spent his nights in Antigua at Clarence House when he served in the navy during the 1780s. Overlooking English Harbour, at **Shirley Heights**, are the ruins of 18th-century fortifications, with a million-dollar view over English and Falmouth harbors and extending to Montserrat and Guadeloupe in the distance. For a less historic, considerably more upbeat experience, visit Shirley Heights on Sunday afternoon, when steel bands play at the lookout point bar, the Battery—be prepared for loud music and a raucous atmosphere that draws hordes of locals, ex-pats and tourists alike.

There's a multimedia museum at Shirley Heights, the **Dow's Hill Interpretation Center**, which provides a Disney-ish explanation of the island's former slave economy. For a much more interesting, if decidedly more low-tech, account of the sugar plantation story, head to **Betty's Hope**, an award-winning historical site where a mill has been restored to working condition to help foster a better understanding into Antigua's history. The northeast coast of the island is quieter and flatter than the rest of Antigua; charming **Parham** is the island's oldest village, while **Devil's Bridge** is a natural bridge carved by the crashing Atlantic—it's not worth a substantial side trip.

City Celebrations

Antigua Sailing Week ★★★★★

English Harbour, ☎ *(268) 462-8872*
One of the region's biggest parties as well as the Caribbean's premiere yachting event, Antigua Sailing Week celebrates its 31st year in 1998. Some 200 boats from 25 countries pour into English Harbour for a series of races over five days—the last blowout of the season before the yachts head north for summer. Landlubbers are kept happy with food vendors, beach dancing and above all, lots of partying (and a bazillion cops to keep things from getting out of hand). For $30 you can dress up and attend Lord Nelson's Ball at the Admiral's Inn, but those in the know say it's a bit too stuffy compared to the unabashed goings-on elsewhere. Held in late April.

Carnival ★★★★

St. John's, ☎ *(268) 462-4959.*
What began some 20 years ago as a celebration to welcome Queen Elizabeth II has become a full-fledged annual festival with 11 days of art shows, parades and partying. The main event is "J'Ouvert," when hundreds of locals dance behind steel and brass bands. Held in late July and early August, you can pick up a full program once on the island.

Historical Sites

Betty's Hope ★★★★★

Pares, ☎ *(268) 462-4930.*
Hours open: 10 a.m.–4 p.m.

Originally developed in the late 1600s and for many years one of the island's most prosperous sugar estates, Betty's Hope is now the site of a groundbreaking restoration project. Antiguans banded together after the plantation was designated as a historic landmark in 1990—the communal effort helped rebuild the mill with the old sugar crushing machinery and the site now boasts the only operational windmill in the Caribbean (the sails are stowed during hurricane season for safekeeping). The Betty's Hope Trust won the *Islands* magazine Ecotourism Award in 1996. Future plans entail restoring the old boiling house and excavating the adjacent village—the first dig of a slave village ever in the Caribbean.

Nelson's Dockyard National Park ★★★★★

Nelson's Dockyard, English Harbour, ☎ *(268) 460-1053.*
Hours open: 8 a.m.–6 p.m.

This beautiful spot is the only Georgian-style naval dockyard left in the world. It has a rich history as home base for the British fleet during the Napoleonic Wars and was used by Admirals Nelson and Hood. The area includes colonial naval buildings, nice beaches, ancient archeological sites and lots of nature trails. Short dockyard tours, nature walks of varying length and boat cruises are offered daily. Check out the Admiral's House, a lovely inn and museum of colonial history, then have a drink at their popular bar. Children under 16 admitted to the park for free. General admission: $3.

St. John's Cathedral ★★

Newgate Street and Church Lane, St. John's, ☎ *(268) 462-4686.*

This Anglican cathedral has a sorrowful history. Originally built of wood in 1683, it was replaced by a stone building in 1745, then destroyed by an earthquake in 1843. Replaced in 1847, it was once again heavily damaged by an earthquake in 1973. Restoration continues as funds are available. The figures of St. John the Baptist and St. John the Divine were taken from a French ship in the early 19th century, and the iron railing entrance dates back to 1789.

Museums and Exhibits

Dow's Hill Interpretation Center ★★

Shirley Heights, English Harbour.
Hours open: 9 a.m.–5 p.m.

The observation platforms at Shirley Heights yield stellar views of English and Falmouth Harbours, Antigua's southern coastline and, on a clear day, Guadeloupe and Montserrat—bring your camera. The museum's multimedia presentation of Antigua's six periods of history, from Amerindians to slavery to independence, is unusually polished, and perhaps the most upbeat "interpretation" of slavery you'll ever witness. $2 for kids under 16. General admission: $4.

Museum of Antigua and Barbuda ★★★

Church and Market Street, St. John's, ☎ *(268) 462-1469.*

Hours open: 8 a.m.–4 p.m.

Worth a look if you're in the neighborhood, this small museum in a one-time courthouse spotlights Antigua's geological and political past. Some interesting exhibits include a lifesize Arawak house, a wattle and daub house, models of sugar plantations and Arawak and pre-Columbian artifacts. There's also a decent giftshop selling local arts and crafts, books and historic artwork. Donation requested.

Best View:

Even Antiguans still flock to the top of the Shirley Heights installations to view the fabulous sunsets. You can see the English and Falmouth harbors in the foreground and the hills and coast of Antigua in the distance. On a clear day you can see as far as Redonda, Montserrat and Guadeloupe.

Antigua Sailing Week is one of the region's major sailing events, held annually in late April at Nelson's Dockyard. It's a great time for drinking, music, socializing and more drinking. There are also a number of sailing events, including races, and the presence of multimillion-dollar yachts from around the world. Landlubbers who want to try their hand at the sport through the rest of the year can contact the **Antigua School of Sailing** ☎ *(268) 462-2026*. Other watersports are found at the major resorts, particularly those in the Dickenson Bay area. Windsurfing is easiest on western shores, most challenging on the eastern shores or in Half Moon Bay, with Windsurfing Antigua at the Lord Nelson Beach Hotel being a great hub for the activity. Tennis is found at several of the major resorts, led by the St. James Club, which has seven courts; rates for balls and courts are exorbitant. Golfers will find a decent 18-hole course at the Cedar Valley Golf Club, located between St. John's and the airport. Horseback riding is available at the St. James Stables, part of the **St. James Club** ☎ *(268) 463-1430*, or can be arranged through your hotel—the southeast countryside is rife with trails and a great half-day trek can be made to Monks Hill. **Tropikelly Trails** provides off-road 4 x 4 tours of the island with hiking for $55 per person ☎ *(268) 461-0383*.

Bicycling

Two locations.

The ride from English Harbour to St. John's, by way of Fig Tree Drive and the west coast, is terrific. You'll pass one breathtakingly white beach after another, but be wary of traffic when entering busy St. John's (about 25 miles one way, but allow the whole day for beach sampling). Mountain biking through the former cane fields is also fun, but carry a patch kit for the ever-present stickers. Dimples and Noreen handle rentals, sales and repairs at **Cycle Krazy** in St. John's; they're also in charge of many of the local bike events ☎ *(268) 462-9253*. Also check with **Sun Cycles** in Hodges Bay for rentals ☎ *(268) 461-0324*.

Golf

Two locations.
Hours open: 8 a.m.–6 p.m.
The island has only two golf courses, so it won't be hard to make your choice. At **Half Moon Bay Hotel** ☎ *(268) 460-4300* there are nine holes (2410 yards, par 34), with more challenging conditions at **Cedar Valley Golf Club** ☎ *(268) 462-0161*. Their 18-hole, par-70 course has some lovely views of the north coast. Green fees are $20 and cart rental is an additional $25.

Watersports

If it involves getting wet, they have it on Antigua. Diving, snorkeling, sailing and more are concentrated primarily in the Dickenson Bay area. Among the island's vendors are **Shorty's** ☎ *(268) 462-6066*, **Halycon Cove Watersports** ☎ *(268) 462-0256* and, on the other side of the island, **Long Bay Hotel** ☎ *(268) 463-2005*.

Windsurfing

Here's your chance to try this sport. The **Windsurf Shop** at the Lord Nelson Beach Hotel overlooks a prime wind zone; they guarantee you'll be whisking around on your own after $50 and a two-hour lesson. If you don't, they also provide radio-assisted rescues ☎ *(268) 462-3094*.

Where to Stay

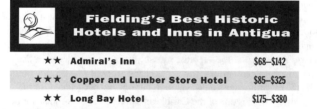

Fielding's Highest Rated Hotels in Antigua

★★★★★	Curtain Bluff	$425–$875
★★★	Club Antigua	$101–$306
★★★	Copper and Lumber Store Hotel	$85–$325
★★★	Galley Bay	$320–$620
★★★	Hawksbill Beach Resort	$155–$385
★★★	Inn at English Harbour, The	$105–$410
★★★	Pineapple Beach	$290–$490
★★★	Sandals Antigua	$497–$660
★★★	Siboney Beach Club	$130–$290
★★★	St. James Club	$235–$335

Fielding's Best Historic Hotels and Inns in Antigua

★★	Admiral's Inn	$68–$142
★★★	Copper and Lumber Store Hotel	$85–$325
★★	Long Bay Hotel	$175–$380

Fielding's Best Value Hotels in Antigua

★★	Lord Nelson's Beach Hotel	$60–$115
★★	Admiral's Inn	$68–$142
★★	Rex Blue Heron Beach Hotel	$87–$128
★★	Sunset Cove	$100–$160

Antigua offers an enormous array of resorts, all-inclusives and self-catering accommodations. The government opted long ago to cater specifically to the upmarket clientele, meaning less-expensive lodgings are few and far between. Construction is a constant reality, but conservation groups are taking the issue in hand to preserve the coastline. Most properties are close to St. John's, either along Runaway and Dickenson Bays just to the north, or out on the Five Islands peninsula that juts west of St. John's; another cluster of accommodations is found around English Harbour on the south coast of Antigua. A few hotels will close in September and/or October to spruce up for the winter season. Howard and Chelle Hulford add something new to Curtain Bluff every year—this year it's a pool. If you arrive on Antigua without a reservation, the tourist office at the airport (next to baggage claim, before customs) will help you book a room.

Hotels and Resorts

Antigua's most posh resort, **Jumby Bay**, closed unexpectedly in early 1997 (financial problems were the main issue), and so the island's luxury haven is **Curtain Bluff**, a dreamy vision perched on a bluff along the island's quiet southwest coast. A little lower on the price scale, secluded and inviting **Hawksbill Beach Resort** has added new club rooms.

Curtain Bluff   **$425–$875**   ★★★★★

Morris Bay, ☎ *(888) 289-9898, (268) 462-8400, FAX (268) 462-8409.*
Closed Date: Mid May–Mid October.
Single: $425–$775. Double: $525–$875. Suites Per Day: $775–$1655.

For almost four decades Antigua's most famous and remarkable resort, Curtain Bluff lies on a spectacular bluff above a shimmering cove of sand. In addition to the dreamy setting, the hotel earned its reputation through lavish accommodations and excellent service. Extras like fresh flowers daily, bidets and plush robes accent the spotless rooms and suites. The best bets are the striking bluffside split-level suites, which offer up great views from two balconies. The all-inclusive rates include all watersports—even scuba—tennis, squash, fitness center, deep-sea fishing, putting green, fine meals and drinks (the wine cellar is stocked with 25,000 bottles). It used to be the only thing missing was a pool, but one has been added for the '97-'98 season. Curtain Bluff is one of the Caribbean's prettiest resorts—ideal for honeymooners, and offering enough diversions to keep the active set happy. But with a jacket required for gents at dinner (in high season) and a loyal, chummy clientele, the atmosphere can be a bit too refined for laid-back types. 63 rooms. Credit cards: A.

Hawksbill Beach Resort   **$155–$385**   ★★★

Five Islands, ☎ *(800) 223-6510, (268) 462-0301, FAX (268) 462-1515.*
Single: $155–$305. Double: $220–$385.

Named after a turtle-shaped rock formation that juts out of the water, this lively spot is frequented by Europeans and young babyboomer couples. The atmosphere is nicely informal, and accommodations are in West Indian-style cottages near the main beach with nice lawns; all have tropical decor, pleasant furnishings and modern baths. There's also a Colonial-style Great House with three bedrooms and a kitchenette that rents for $1300-1800 per night. The 37 acres include an old sugar mill that has been transformed into a boutique, tennis, watersports and not one but four beaches, one where you can shuck your bathing suit. Expensive, but well run and quite pleasant. 99 rooms. Credit cards: A, DC, MC, V.

Rex Blue Heron Beach Hotel   **$87–$128**   ★ ★

Johnson's Point, ☎ *(800) 255-5859, (268) 462-8564, FAX (268) 462-8005.*
Single: $87–$128. Double: $87–$128.

This very basic beach hotel appeals to Europeans on a budget, and received a much-needed facelift and expansion following the 1995 hurricane. The best units are right on the beach and have balconies; the least expensive rates are for the few without air conditioning or a sea view—all are simply furnished with wood and formica. Watersports are free, and there's a nice beach bar. Nothing quaint or especially charming here, and the location is miles from other tourist facilities but if all you want is a quiet beach to crash on, it's a good budget option. 64 rooms. Credit cards: A, D, MC, V.

Rex Halcyon Cove   **$130–$380**   ★ ★

Dickenson Bay, ☎ *(800) 255-5859, (268) 462-0256, FAX (268) 462-0271.*
Single: $130–$380. Double: $130–$380.

Lots of group tours from the U.S. and Europe congregate at this busy spot, made even more crowded by cruise passengers who spend the day at its beach. The expansive complex includes several restaurants, four bars and a nightclub, a casino, a pool, and extensive watersports including scuba, water skiing and glass-bottom boat rides. Of the six room types, standard units are barely adequate with simple furnishings and ceiling fans only; the beachside rooms are quite small but open right onto the beach. Not bad if you want that resort experience, but you'll probably be happier in one of the higher room categories. 210 rooms. Credit cards: A, D, MC, V.

Royal Antiguan   **$120–$410**   ★ ★

Five Islands, ☎ *(800) 345-0356, (268) 462-3733, FAX (268) 462-3732.*
Single: $120–$360. Double: $150–$410.

Built in 1987 to the horror of many residents, this eight-story high-rise is the island's most American-like resort. It does a bang-up business, though, by offering modern conveniences like direct-dial phones, TV and air conditioning—rooms are otherwise quite standard. There are also a dozen cottages with more plush accommodations. Set on 150 acres, there's a lot to keep visitors occupied, including a full casino and an enormous pool with swim-up bar; tennis, non-motorized watersports and a supervised children's program are included in the rates. A meal and beverage plan is also available. It's a few minutes' walk to the beach, which is frequented by local artists displaying their wares. Previously run by the Ramada chain, it became part of the Pineapple and Galley Bay operation in 1996. 282 rooms. Credit cards: A, DC, MC, V.

St. James Club   **$235–$335**   ★ ★ ★

Mamora Bay, ☎ *(800) 274-0008, (268) 460-5000, FAX (268) 460-3015.*
Single: $235–$335. Double: $235–$335. Suites Per Day: $325–$460.

Set on 100 acres a couple miles east of English Harbour, this nice resort does not quite live up to its reputation as a playground for the rich and famous. Nevertheless, this amenity-heavy spot has two pretty beaches, an attractive European-style casino, tony boutiques and a lively disco. Rooms are beautifully furnished, and the two-bedroom hillside villas are wonderful; an all-inclusive plan is also available. Guests can choose from watersports, horseback riding, working out in the gym, playing tennis or frolicking in three pools. Little true glamour perhaps, but lots of glitz anyway. Ask about off-season discounts. 178 rooms. Credit cards: A, DC, MC, V.

All-Inclusives

All-inclusive resorts are an extensively developed option on Antigua. In addition to **Sandals Antigua**, part of the region's largest chain of all-inclusive resorts, there's **Pineapple Beach**, **Club Antigua**, **Galley Bay** and several others. A few hotels (like the **Royal Antiguan** and **St. James Club**), offer a choice of all-inclusive or regular European Plan. There are also a couple of properties that are really all-inclusive, but don't quite fit with the rest of this crowd: sumptuous **Curtain Bluff** and quaint **Long Bay**.

Club Antigua $101–$306   ★★★

☎ *(800) 777-1250, (268) 462-0061, FAX (268) 462-4900.*
Single: $101–$149. Double: $194–$306.
This huge resort, set on 40 acres with a half-mile beach, received a $2 million post-hurricane renovation. It hums with action and attracts mainly young people who don't mind the busy beach—lined with vendors hawking everything from jewelry to joints—and noisy nightlife. Lots to do, including four restaurants, six bars, a slot casino, happening disco, watersports (scuba introductory course), eight tennis courts and, for the kids (and their parents), a supervised children's club. The cheapest rooms, called minimums, are just so and come without air conditioning. Definitely a mass-market operation, but decent value. 476 rooms. Credit cards: A, MC, V.

Galley Bay $320–$620   ★★★

Five Islands Village, ☎ *(800) 345-0356, (268) 462-0302, FAX (268) 462-4551.*
Single: $320–$520. Double: $420–$620.
Battered by Hurricane Luis, this unique resort was doubled in size following an extensive renovation, and a pool was added. The resort is set on 40 lovely acres adjacent to a bird sanctuary. Accommodations are on the beach in Polynesian thatched huts or in modern cottages; all lack air conditioning but do have coffee makers, robes and hair dryers. The best rooms are built around a salt pond and coconut grove; request the "Gauguin Cottage" units for the Tahitian experience. The beach is great and the hotel offers non-motorized watersports as well as tennis, a restaurant, bar and the very popular afternoon tea. This spot is popular with Europeans who aren't looking for much of a nightlife, though a new open-air movie theater plays movies at night—popcorn provided. 61 rooms. Credit cards: A, MC, V.

Pineapple Beach $290–$490   ★★★

Long Bay, ☎ *(800) 345-0356, (268) 463-2006, FAX (268) 463-2452.*
Single: $290–$430. Double: $350–$490.
This 25-acre all-inclusive resort flanks a beautiful white sand beach on the remote eastern tip of the island. Pineapple is one of the nicest of the island's large resorts, a good spot for those who want all-inclusive amenities without sacrificing an arm or leg at check-out time. Most accommodations front the ocean and are of average size with wicker furniture, local artwork, large balconies and Mexican tile floors; less-expensive rooms face the pleasant garden. This busy place teems with action throughout the day, with folks running from tennis to croquet to windsurfing (non-

motorized watersports included in the rates). Two restaurants, several bars and a small casino stocked with one-armed bandits. 135 rooms. Credit cards: A, MC, V.

Sandals Antigua   **$497–$660**   ★★★

Dickenson Bay, ☎ *(800) 726-3257, (268) 462-0267, FAX (268) 462-4135.*
Double: $497–$660. Suites Per Day: $660–$757.

Only heterosexual couples are allowed at this all-inclusive resort, set on a narrow, lively beach lined with palms and local vendors. Most accommodations are in motel-like units that are small but adequate; the 17 rooms in rondovals are better. There are five pools scattered through the property, four restaurants, tennis courts, a fitness center, and more. There's tons going on here at all hours, and the staff will cheerfully badger you to participate—despite an ad campaign to the contrary, this is not the spot for discreet liaisons. Most of the couples are young, and many are honeymooning. 189 rooms. Credit cards: A, MC, V.

Apartments and Condominiums

Antigua boasts of a number of self-catering complexes that work well for vacationers, particularly for families or for extended visits. If you plan to cook at home to save money, note that food staples are expensive and not always worth the time and trouble to uncover. Otherwise, options range from simply furnished studio apartments (some right on a beach), to glorious homes rented by the owner. Booking is usually done through the central office number.

Antigua Village   **$95–$245**   ★★

Dickenson Bay, ☎ *(800) 447-7462, (268) 462-2930, FAX (268) 462-0375.*
Single: $95–$245. Double: $95–$245.

This rambling complex of two-story red-roof condominiums is located on a peninsula along a busy beach. Choose from spacious studios or one- and two-bedroom units, all with kitchenettes, bright tropical decor, air conditioning and daily maid service; a few have TVs. Watersports are free, and there's a restaurant, bar and on-site mini-market. Reliable, but nothing too exciting. 100 rooms. Credit cards: MC, V.

Dickenson Bay Cottages   **$142–$199**   ★★

Dickenson Bay, ☎ *(268) 462-4940, FAX (268) 462-4941.*
Single: $142–$199. Double: $142–$199.

Attractive, well-kept apartments in a residential area overlooking the island's busiest beach. One-, two- and three-bedroom units, some quite spacious with full kitchens—all overlook a pleasant garden with a small pool. The beach is a ten-minute walk down the (steep) hill, and guests are welcome to use the facilities at the Rex Halcyon resort there, including the tennis courts. 12 rooms. Credit cards: A, DC, MC, V.

Falmouth Harbour Beach Apartments   **$68–$142**   ★

English Harbour, ☎ *(800) 223-5695, (268) 460-1027, FAX (268) 460-1534.*
Single: $68–$102. Double: $90–$142.

A low-frills property with reasonable rates and a good location next door to English Harbour, this small apartment complex houses guests on or near a small beach. Rooms have ceiling fans, a full kitchen, and little else. In addition to the sand the rooms overlook, another nice beach is a five-minute walk, limited watersports are nearby, as are a number of restaurants and a market. A good bet for the price. 22 rooms. Credit cards: MC, V.

Marina Bay Beach Resort $80–$200   ★★

Runaway Bay, ☎ *(268) 462-3254, FAX (268) 462-2151.*
Single: $80–$200. Double: $80–$200.

A basic, but pleasant spot, with spacious and bright studios and one- and two-bedroom villas. All have air conditioning, cable TV, full kitchens and Italian-tiled baths. Located on Corbinson Point, right between two of the island's best beaches with watersports available nearby. There's no restaurant on-site, but several within an easy walk. 27 rooms. Credit cards: A, DC, D, MC, V.

Siboney Beach Club $130–$290   ★★★

Dickenson Bay, ☎ *(800) 533-0234, (268) 462-0806, FAX (268) 462-3356.*
Single: $130–$270. Double: $155–$290.

This three-story all-suite property, enhanced by a cornucopia of palms and other greenery, is right on Dickenson Bay, a beautiful but busy beach. The 12 one-bedroom suites are nicely furnished with rattan, kitchenettes and ceiling fans; there's also a cozy treehouse studio peeking through the bamboo and palms. A maid tidies things up and limited room service is available. An idyllic freshwater pool is in back, and a trademark British red phone booth sits on the beach if you get homesick. There's a lovely restaurant and entertainment most nights at the bar; extensive watersports including excursions via catamaran or glass-bottom boat are available. The service is very friendly at this small, well-run spot. 12 rooms. Credit cards: A, DC, MC, V.

Sunset Cove $100–$160   ★★

Runaway Bay, ☎ *(268) 462-3762, FAX (268) 462-2684.*
Single: $100–$160. Double: $100–$160.

A cute little apartment complex with good rates for a beachside property, Sunset Cove offers a selection of one- and two-bedroom studios with full kitchen or standard rooms with kitchenette. All are clean and tidy and wrap around a small garden. There's a small pool and bar on the property, not much else. But the beach is grand. 33 rooms. Credit cards: A, MC, V.

Yepton Beach Resort $125–$245   ★★

Five Islands Village, ☎ *(800) 361-4621, (268) 462-2520, FAX (514) 843-4783.*
Website: www.world-traveler.com/antigua/yepton.html.
Single: $125–$245. Double: $125–$245. Suites Per Day: $190–$385.

This condominium resort is located outside St. John's Harbour and consists of Mediterranean-style white stucco buildings with nice views of the beach and lagoon. All units have air conditioning, and studios and suites include Murphy beds and kitchenettes; there are also one- and two-bedroom apartments. All line the excellent beach where complimentary windsurfing and sunfish sailing await—tennis, a pool and lawn croquet are also available. There's a restaurant and bar with live music three nights a week, with other eating choices within a short drive. 38 rooms. Credit cards: A, MC, V.

Inns

Inns on Antigua provide charming ambiance and down-home hospitality. The most authentically historic is the **Admiral's Inn**, set in an 18th-century building and overlooking Nelson's Dockyard. But the **Copper and Lumber Store** next door has plenty of bona-fide naval roots to deliver a history-tinged vacation. In either case, you might be sleeping in the vicinity of billionaire yachties who occasionally tie up in English Harbour. A nice compromise that delivers both the rustic ambiance and a beach location is **Long Bay Hotel**.

Admiral's Inn $68–$142   ★★

English Harbour, ☎ *(800) 223-5695, (268) 460-1027, FAX (268) 460-1534.*
Closed Date: September 1–October 18.
Single: $68–$102. Double: $82–$142.

Housed in a Georgian brick building dating back to 1788, this intimate inn has a nautical theme and is loaded with distinctive charm. Rooms are small with beam ceilings and antiques; some have air conditioning and patios. Each is unique in decor—the least expensive are in the attic, with room 6 the best of the mid-range rooms (minimal view), and rooms 1 and 4 the choice bets in the superior category (room 1 suffers a bit from foot traffic and bar noise). Four rooms in a one-story annex next door are pleasant, with room A the biggest and best positioned. There's also a two-bedroom apartment with full kitchen, the "Joiner's Loft," that is priced $130–$220 for two. Admiral's Inn is a tourist attraction in its own right, and can get crowded with folks coming through to take a look. Management transports guests to two nearby beaches. In addition to the on-site restaurant (decent pub food, lovely terrace setting for breakfast or lunch), other restaurants are a short stroll away. A great spot if you don't mind sacrificing resort amenities for quaint atmosphere in the lap of history—and a bargain at that. 13 rooms. Credit cards: A, MC, V.

Copper and Lumber Store Hotel $85–$325   ★★★

English Harbour, ☎ *(268) 460-1058, FAX (268) 460-1529.*
Single: $85–$325. Double: $85–$325.

This charming inn is housed in a restored Georgian brick warehouse, dating back to 1782, which overlooks the marina at English Harbour. All named after Lord Nelson's ships, rooms are either studios or duplex suites, but the higher-priced rooms in each category have authentic or reproduction 18th-century furnishings, oil paintings and charts, canopy beds, brass chandeliers and hand-stenciled floors; all have kitchenettes. No air conditioning, but ceiling fans provide a breeze, and no beach or pool—guests are whisked via ferry to nearby Galleon Beach. There is both a restaurant and pub for dining, and other eateries are a short stroll away. We've received word of operational problems recently, but otherwise, a wonderful historic spot with the sound of clattering rigs against the masts of yachts for a soundtrack. 14 rooms. Credit cards: A, MC, V.

Inn at English Harbour, The $105–$410   ★★★

English Harbour, ☎ *(800) 223-6510, (268) 460-1014, FAX (268) 460-1603.*
Closed Date: September–mid October.
Single: $105–$330. Double: $140–$410.

Set on ten acres of beach and hillside overlooking colorful Nelson's Dockyard, this small inn has rooms in cottage-style buildings on the beach or atop a breezy hill with views. All are nicely done with island-style rush rugs, wicker and modern furniture and ceiling fans. There are two restaurants and bars, and rates include Sunfish sailing, windsurfing and a free shuttle to Nelson's Dockyard two minutes away. The clientele is mostly English. 28 rooms. Credit cards: A, DC, D, MC, V.

Long Bay Hotel   **$175–$380**   ★ ★

Long Bay, ☎ *(800) 225-4255, (268) 463-2005, FAX (268) 463-2439.*
Closed Date: June–September.
Single: $175–$300. Double: $255–$380.

This intimate resort, run by the Lafaurie family, is set far out on Antigua's northeast tip overlooking a tranquil bay. The 20 guest rooms, situated in motel-style wings, are large but simple; rates include breakfast and dinner. Six cottages are also available, with gabled ceilings, nice artwork and small but fully equipped kitchens—quite pleasant ($255-450 per night without meals). For recreation, there's a tennis court, watersports (scuba and waterskiing are extra), a library and a great beach next door. This is an authentic Caribbean retreat, not some corporation's idea of one—best exemplified by the newsletter that goes out to guests keeping everyone posted on the status of local birds, staff and island news. Lots of American families are attracted by the warm and friendly atmosphere. 26 rooms. Credit cards: A, MC, V.

Lord Nelson's Beach Hotel   **$60–$115**   ★ ★

Dutchman's Bay, ☎ *(268) 462-3094, FAX (268) 462-0751.*
Single: $60–$90. Double: $70–$115.

This small and informal inn is the oldest on the island, built in 1954 by an American couple who run it today with their son-in-law. It has lots of lived-in beachcomber ambiance, but could use a renovation to bring it into the '90s. Rooms are simple but newer units have balconies, and there's a restaurant and bar on-site. There's a dive shop and other watersports, but this breezy spot is particularly loved by windsurfers—the staff of the on-site shop is eager to share the sport. There is no pool and the beach is adequate if unspectacular. Located on a rather isolated spot on the northeast coast near the airport, there's essentially nothing within walking distance, so you'll need a rental car. 17 rooms. Credit cards: A, MC, V.

Low Cost Lodging

Locating a budget room on Antigua is not impossible. A good source is the *Guide to Small Hotels and Guest Homes* provided by the Tourist Office. Of course, no money pays for no ambiance; most low-cost lodgings are in modern, stucco buildings with only basic furnishings, and a beachside location is rare. As such, you'll probably need to throw your savings into renting a car. The **Island Inn** provides 10 clean, simple rooms with full kitchen and a small pool for around $75 a night year-round; the location is half-way between St. John's and Dickenson Bay (you're one mile from the nearest beach) ☎ *(268) 462-4065.* If you don't mind staying in St. John's (more than one mile from a beach), **Joe Mike's** is a small downtown hotel with acceptable budget rooms and a good restaurant for $65 a night ☎ *(268) 462-1142.*

Where to Eat

	Fielding's Highest Rated Restaurants in Antigua	
★★★★	Coconut Grove	$18–$43
★★★★	Julian's	$18–$27
★★★★	Le Bistro	$22–$34
★★★	Alberto's	$18–$27
★★★	Le Cap Horn	$13–$20
★★★	Redcliffe Tavern	$10–$23

	Fielding's Most Romantic Restaurants in Antigua	
♥♥♥♥	Admiral's Inn	$10–$25
♥♥♥♥	Coconut Grove	$18–$43
♥♥♥♥	Le Bistro	$22–$34
♥♥♥♥	Warri Pier	$12–$30
♥♥♥	Colombo's	$22–$32

	Fielding's Best Value Restaurants in Antigua	
★★★	Redcliffe Tavern	$10–$23
★★★	Le Cap Horn	$13–$20
★★★★	Julian's	$18–$27
★★★★	Le Bistro	$22–$34
★★★	Alberto's	$18–$27

ANTIGUA

Antigua has rarely suffered for lack of good restaurants, but additions are always cropping up. Unfortunately, the island lost its best, **La Perrouche**, to Hurricane Luis. The best scene on the island remains the Sunday barbecue at **Shirley Heights Lookout**, housed in a restored, 18th-century fort with memorable views of English Harbour and the southern coastline. In Dickenson

Bay, **Warri Pier** is a great setting for a sunset cocktail, while the island's most romantic spot may be beachside **Coconut Grove**. Elsewhere, prices for a top-class dinner aren't cheap; expect to fork over at least $100 for two in the best places. Spices, influenced by East Indian and Creole cooking, are liberally added and tend to run on the hot side. Look for local specialties such as banana and cinnamon pancakes with Antiguan rum syrup at breakfast, pepper-pot stew with fungi (a cornmeal dumpling), sea urchin flan, and lump crabmeat with avocado and lemongrass.

Admiral's Inn $$ ★★

Nelson's Dockyard, ☎ *(268) 460-1027.* Associated hotel: *Admiral's Inn.*
Lunch: Noon–2:30 p.m., entrées $10–$25.
Dinner: 7-9:30 p.m., entrées $10–$25.
Like the Copper and Lumber Store Hotel alongside it, the Admiral's Inn is so long on atmosphere and history, the food doesn't have to be good to be worth a visit. But thankfully, that is not the case here, especially for a silky pumpkin soup and a fresh pan-fried snapper that draw raves. Some never get as far as the restaurant, preferring to stay in the dark bar or sit under the old trees outdoors, looking out at the convoys of ships in the harbor. Those so inclined can eat here three times a day, and breakfast, served daily from 7:30-10 a.m., is a terrific deal. Closed September–mid October. Credit cards: A, MC, V.

Alberto's $$$ ★★★

Willoughby Bay, ☎ *(268) 460-3007.*
Dinner: entrées $18–$27. Closed: Mon.
Locals rave about the Italian specialties served in Alberto's spacious gazebo that is wrapped in bougainvillea and features walls lined with Italian ceramics. The menu changes seasonally, but frequent offerings include osso buco, braised rabbit with polenta, farfalla with salmon, cream and vodka, and baked fish with a pinenut crust. For dessert, try the baked pears in marsala with creme fraiche. The loquacious and genial Alberto draws diners from English Harbour and St. James area to his rather isolated south coast location just outside Bethesda.

Big Banana Holding Co. $ ★★

Redcliffe Quay, St. John's, ☎ *(268) 462-2621.*
Lunch: Noon–4 p.m., entrées $6–$30.
Dinner: 4 p.m.–midnight, entrées $6–$30. Closed: Sun.
A lot of locals and tourists homesick for pizza flock here at all hours. The pies in question are rather pricey and not very exciting, but the location, in the interesting and trendy Redcliffe Quay shopping center, helps. All in all it's considered very proper to sit under the whirring fans and just sip a cool tropical drink (these are bright, frothy and potent). Salads, seafood dishes and fruit plates are also available. Big Banana's best asset may be that its other, newly remodeled and expanded location at V.C. Bird Airport, is a truly welcome respite for those who are island-hopping via Antigua. Credit cards: A, DC, MC, V.

Calypso $$ ★★

Redcliffe Street, St. John's, ☎ *(268) 462-1965.*

Lunch: 10 a.m.–4 p.m., entrées $8–$25. Closed: Sun.
This open-air, lunch-only spot jumps weekdays, and is an accessible, friendly location to try West Indian specialties. These often include fresh seafood, sauteed or
prepared in batter, washed down with local fruit juices. Homey stews and soups
with pumpkin or okra satisfy; the less adventurous can chow down on burgers and
sandwiches. Credit cards: A, DC, MC, V.

Chutneys $ ★★
Fort Road, St. John's, ☎ *(268) 462-2977.*
Dinner: entrées $10–$19. Closed: Mon.
One of the few East Indian restaurants in the West Indies with an authentic tandoori oven, Chutneys is the best spot on the island for curry, roti, and other spice-
enhanced dishes (you can request hot or mild for most). The restaurant also has a
"non-curry lovers menu" with steak, lobster and chicken kebabs. But most come for
the specialties cooked in the clay Tandoori oven—the lamb tikka is succulent.
Located on the outskirts of St. John's en route to the Dickenson Bay area; ideal for
takeout. Credit cards: MC, V.

Coconut Grove $$$ ★★★★
Dickenson Bay, ☎ *(268) 462-1538.* Associated hotel: *Siboney Beach Club.*
Lunch: 11:30 a.m.–3 p.m., entrées $9–$29.
Dinner: 6:30–10 p.m., entrées $18–$43.
A lovely beachfront spot surrounded by tall coconut palms swaying in the breeze,
this eatery is a choice spot for privacy, moonlight and amore. The lobster is caught
fresh daily and prepared grilled, in a sandwich (for lunch), thermador, and other
succulent ways. Chicken, hearty chops, creative pastas, tangy curry and salads are
also available. The location, at the south end of Dickenson Bay and right on the
water, is unbeatable—so are the daily drink specials, like mango daiquiris. Credit
cards: A, DC, MC, V.

Colombo's $$$ ★★
Galleon Beach, ☎ *(268) 460-1452.* Associated hotel: *Galleon Beach Club.*
Lunch: 12:30–2:30 p.m., entrées $22–$32.
Dinner: 7–10 p.m., entrées $22–$32.
Only in the Caribbean can one eat spaghetti Bolognese or carpaccio in a thatched-
roof hut and dance to a reggae band (Wednesday nights) on the beach. Though this
was the first Italian eatery on Antigua, regulars note that the food has gone downhill
yet the service is still amiable. There are daily specials and a variety of wines. Credit
cards: A, DC, MC, V.

Copper and Lumber Store, The $$$ ★★
Nelson's Dockyard, ☎ *(268) 460-1058.* Associated hotel: *Copper and Lumber Store.*
Lunch: 11:30 a.m.–4:30 p.m., entrées $8–$25.
Dinner: 6–11 p.m., entrées $18–$30. Closed: Wed.
Old Antigua hands will be pleased with the new face given the 18th-century Copper
and Lumber Store Hotel in Nelson's Dockyard. Others should come at least once
to savor the Georgian atmosphere and nautical prints at the Wardroom, and eat
adequate, if unspectacular food at rather high prices. But American-style or English
lunches and cool drinks are within most everyone's reach at the hotel's pub, the

Mainbrace, where fish and chips, shepherd's pie and draft beers are offered. Reservations recommended. Credit cards: A, MC, V.

Hemingway's $$ ★★
St. Mary's Street, St. John's, ☎ *(268) 462-2763.*
Lunch: 11:30 a.m.–4:30 p.m., entrées $7–$15.
Dinner: 4:30–11 p.m., entrées $9–$23. Closed: Sun.
Not very far from the sea Ernest Hemingway once wrote about is this 1829-era, gingerbread-trimmed Victorian house with a restaurant on the second floor. There's a lot of activity on Heritage Quay below and people-watching opportunities on the porch, where frothy tropical drinks can be sipped. Nibble on lobster, salads, burgers and spicy chicken. Vegetarian specialties are also available and the pumpkin soup is tops. An only-in-the-Caribbean treat, and a good value. Credit cards: A, MC, V.

Julian's $$$ ★★★★
Church Street and Corn Alley, St. John's, ☎ *(268) 462-4766.*
Dinner: 7–10 p.m., entrées $18–$27. Closed: Mon.
A handsomely redecorated 18th-century Colonial house in the heart of St. John's is now home to this delightful eatery that provides both al fresco dining in a sheltered courtyard out back or in the lovingly-appointed interior awash in white walls with green accents. Proprietor Julian Waterer does the cooking, preparing pan-seared veal sweetbreads, rich lamb casserole, escallops of fresh salmon and dangerous desserts, while Marie manages the friendly staff. Closed for lunch Sunday.

Le Bistro $$$ ★★★★
Hodges Bay, ☎ *(268) 462-3881.*
Dinner: 6:30–10:30 p.m., entrées $22–$34. Closed: Mon.
Le Bistro, on the island's north shore, caters to residents with expensive villas in the area, but anyone with a fancy for fine cuisine can repair here for classic French dishes crafted with care. Lobster (prepared six ways) and red snapper are always available, and made with cream, white wine and fresh herb sauces, or invest in the rack of lamb for two. Operated by the husband-and-wife team of Raffaele and Philippa Esposito since 1981, the dining room is inviting and plant-filled, and a great setting for crepes suzette or bananas flambé after all. Credit cards: A, MC, V.

Le Cap Horn $$ ★★★
Falmouth Harbour, ☎ *(268) 460-3336.*
Lunch: Noon–6:30 p.m., entrées $10–$13.
Dinner: 6:30–11 p.m., entrées $13–$20.
A popular Argentinian and French restaurant in a verdant outdoor setting en route to Nelson's Dockyard. Snacks, wood-fired pizza or more substantial meat dishes are available for decent prices. Dine early or late on the greenery-embraced porch on daily specials for under $20. Credit cards: A, MC, V.

Lemon Tree $$$ ★★
Long and Church Streets, St. John's, ☎ *(268) 462-1969.*
Lunch: 10 a.m.–4 p.m., entrées $15–$25.
Dinner: 4–11 p.m., entrées $15–$25. Closed: Sun.
The atmosphere here is very South Seas, with a lot of wicker and wooden blinds, good for a cool-off drink or air-conditioned meal after a visit to the Museum of

Antigua and Barbuda nearby. Graze Caribbean-style from a long menu of finger foods, Tex-Mex items and the usual lobster and chicken dishes, which vary in quality. Unfortunately, with a cruise crowd in attendance, service can be rushed, but it's good for music in the evening. Credit cards: A, DC, MC, V.

Lobster Pot $$$ ★★

Runaway Bay, ☎ *(268) 462-2856.* Associated hotel: *Runaway Beach Club.*
Lunch: entrées $7–$12.
Dinner: entrées $15–$25.
Even picky diners will find something to their liking at this airy eatery in Runaway Bay that does creative things with chicken and lobster at prices that won't leave you breathless. In addition to the titular item, the substantial menu runs the gamut from hearty breakfasts to leafy salads, sandwiches and fresh local fish and shellfish. Commune with nature at tables on the seaside veranda; come early for these or reserve a seat. Credit cards: DC, MC, V.

Miller's by the Sea $$ ★★

Fort James Beach, ☎ *(268) 462-9414.*
Lunch: 11 a.m.–5 p.m., entrées $8–$18.
Dinner: 5 p.m.–2 a.m., entrées $10–$25.
Formerly the happening spot of Dickenson Bay, in 1996 Tenniel Miller moved his booming restaurant and car rental business to the beach just northwest of St. John's, to near-overnight success. Food is pretty basic, with garlic or curried conch, grouper creole and grilled rock lobster being the prime offerings; steak, pork and lamb chops round out the selection. Miller's draws people for reasons other than the food: it's the only spot on this beach (frequented by cruise ship passengers and locals alike), the music is strong, and the food pours out of the kitchen later than any other on the island. The weekend scene is quite merry with live bands Friday and Saturday at 10 p.m. Credit cards: MC, V.

Redcliffe Tavern $$ ★★★

Redcliffe Quay, St. John's, ☎ *(268) 461-4557.*
Lunch: 11:30 a.m.–3 p.m., entrées $7–$20.
Dinner: 7–11 p.m., entrées $10–$23. Closed: Sun.
Begin or end a shopping tour at the charming Redcliffe Quay complex in St. John's harbor with lunch or dinner or a snack at the dependable Redcliffe Tavern. It's one of a handful of vintage structures that have been restored for commercial usage. Once an old warehouse, the Tavern sports island machinery from a pumping station for decor, and the staff serves good burgers or barbecue or pastas and freshly caught lobster. Architecture buffs and Anglophiles should find the surroundings especially appealing. Credit cards: A, MC, V.

Shirley Heights Lookout $$$ ★★

Shirley Heights, ☎ *(268) 460-1785.*
Lunch: 9 a.m.–4 p.m., entrées $15–$26.
Dinner: 4–10 p.m., entrées $15–$26.
Something festive is always happening in this two-story pub/restaurant amidst the ruins of Fort Shirley—especially on Sunday, when there's dancing and live bands that play for free from mid-afternoon on (steel bands play on Thursday afternoons,

but it hasn't quite yet become the same tradition). Barbecued meats at decent prices accompany the tunes, and the views behind the Lookout are superb. The rest of the week, eat in peace upstairs or downstairs for breakfast, lunch or dinner. The second-floor dining room is a very intimate trysting spot. Credit cards: AE, MC, V.

Warri Pier   **$$$**   ★★

Dickenson Bay, ☎ *(268) 462-0256.* Associated hotel: *Rex Halcyon Cove.*
Regional cuisine. Specialties: Seafood linguine, marlin.
Lunch: Noon–6 p.m., entrées $7–$30.
Dinner: 6–10:30 p.m., entrées $12–$30.

Dine on marlin—"warri" is the local name—on a private pier belonging to the Rex Halcyon Cove Resort. This is a lovely setting poised above the sea like a great wooden bird on the northern edge of Dickinson Bay. It's an excellent perch from which to observe the setting sun, though the food doesn't live up to the staging. Light meals of chunky fruit salads or burgers and seafood soups are fine at lunch; dinner gets somewhat fancier with grilled lobster, steaks and the like and elaborate desserts. Reservations recommended. Credit cards: A, MC, V.

Where to Shop

ANTIGUA

The bulk of Antigua's shops are concentrated in St. John's at **Redcliffe Quay** and **Heritage Quay**, both within easy access of the main cruise ship dock. Go to Redcliffe for local shops and color, head for Heritage for duty-free international shopping. There are other good shops clustered on St. Mary's Street or High Street. Duty-free products are omnipresent, and there are also some special Antiguan items such as rum, silk-screened fabrics, native straw work and curios made from shells. Hot new clothing stores have also sprung up or expanded in the wake of Hurricane Luis. Check easy-to-wear cotton and cotton/lycra styles for men, women and children at **Base** (the flagship store for the Caribbean clothier). Also in Redcliffe is the chic **Debra Moises** boutique, which carries husband-and-wife-designed sensations in flowering gauze and one-of-a-kind hair accessories (carried by Bergdorf's and Saks in Manhattan). Heritage houses **Caribelle Batik**, a store filled with one-of-a-kind batik clothing and art pieces made in St. Kitts with sea island cotton. Check out the Saturday fruit and vegetable market at the West Bus Station on Independence Avenue. There is usually a good selection of local handicrafts. For some strange reason, some shops close Thursday at noon.

Antigua Directory

Arrival and Departure

Antigua is connected to North America via several carriers. **American Airlines** has both jet and commuter service out of its hub in San Juan, Puerto Rico, daily. **Air Jamaica** has service from New York's JFK, and via their hub in Montego Bay, Jamaica several times a week. **Continental** has several flights a week out of Newark. **BWIA** has several flights a week from both Miami and JFK. Within the Caribbean, Antigua serves as the hub for **LIAT**, with non-stop or direct flights to Anguilla, Barbados, Barbuda, Dominica, Grenada, Guadeloupe, Martinique, Montserrat, Nevis, St. Croix, St. Kitts, St. Lucia, Sint Maarten, St. Thomas, St. Vincent, San Juan and Tortola. V.C. Bird Airport, 4.5 miles east of St. John's, receives all air traffic.

The departure tax is $12.

Business Hours

Shops open Monday–Friday 8:30 a.m.–4 p.m. and Saturday 8 a.m.–noon or 3 p.m. Banks open Monday–Thursday 8 a.m.–2 and Friday 8 a.m.–4 p.m.

Climate

The Antiguan climate is one of the best in the Caribbean, with so little rainfall at times that water shortage sometimes becomes a problem. Constant sea breezes and trade winds keep the air fresh and the temperatures hovering around 81 degrees F, except in the hot season (May-November), when temperatures can rise to 93 degrees F. The mean annual rainfall of 40 inches is slight for the region.

Documents

U.S. and Canadian citizens must show a passport or proof of citizenship (birth certificate, or voter's registration) plus a photo ID, and an ongoing or return ticket.

Electricity

The majority of hotels use 220 volts, 110 AC. Some shaver outlets are 110-volt. Hotels generally have adapters.

Getting Around

Because there is no single, well-maintained primary route around the island, sightseeing on Antigua is time-consuming. If you want to rent a car, you must procure a local driver's license for the exorbitant sum of $20, available at the local police stations or through the car rental agency by showing your license from home. Be forewarned that Antiguan roads are infamous for gaping potholes, crumbling shoulders, poor signage and stray dogs; fortunately, outside St. John's, they are generally free of congestion. Antiguan drivers are about as courteous as French ones, so drive defensively... on the left! Several U.S.-based rental firms are represented on the island including **Avis**, **Budget**, **Dollar** and **National**, as well as a host of local outfits, many of which are represented at a bustling desk you'll pass immediately after leaving customs at the airport.

ANTIGUA

Given the overall price and aggravation of renting a car for a day, you might be better off hiring a guide, and some of the best are taxi drivers. The main taxi stand is across from the market in St. John's and is open 24 hours. It's also possible to take the inexpensive local buses: In St. Johns, the West Bus Station on South Street (opposite the market) serves as the departure point for the west, south and English Harbour areas; the East Bus Station on Independence Avenue serves the north and east. The buses do not leave until they're jammed full—they connect St. John's with outlying residential or business areas, not necessarily the tourist sights such as Dickenson Bay or Shirley Heights (nor do they stop at the airport); check before boarding. To go to St. John's, head for one of the main roads leading to town and flag a bus down as it passes.

Daytrips to **Barbuda** can be arranged through Barbara Jappal at Caribrep for $125 per person, including airfare, lobster lunch and drinks, a visit to the bird sanctuary and beaches ☎ *(268) 462-3884*. **Montserrat** is a 15-minute flight away; **Nevis** and **Guadeloupe** are slightly farther. **Carib Aviation** arranges charters for five to nine passengers, which can work out to be less expensive if you fill the plane; they work out of V.C. Bird Airport ☎ *(268) 462-3147*.

Language

English is the official language, though the special Antiguan lilt may make some words indistinguishable.

Medical Emergencies

Holberton Hospital, on the outskirts of St. John's, is a 220-bed facility. Serious medical emergencies are flown off the island to San Juan or Miami.

Money

The official currency is the Eastern Caribbean dollar, commonly referred to as "E.C." The exchange rate is pegged to the U.S. dollar, $2.70 for one American dollar. You'll get the best exchange rate at banks, though most establishments will accept either currency. Make sure you note which currency is being used for your bill at restaurants or hotels, particularly smaller establishments.

Telephone

The area code for Antigua and Barbuda is *(268)*. From the U.S., dial *1 + (268)*, then the seven-digit local number.

Time

Atlantic standard time.

Tipping and Taxes

In addition to an 8.5 percent hotel tax, most hotels and restaurants add a 10 percent service charge. When not included, tip 10–15 percent for waiters, $1 per room per day for maids, and 50 cents per bag for bellhops.

Tourist Information

The government tourist office is located at Long and Thames Street in St. John's. You can also find an information counter at the airport, in the baggage claim area (before customs). For more information ☎ *(268) 462-0480*, or call the New York office: ☎ *(212) 541-4117*.

Web Site

www.interknowledge.com/antigua-barbuda

When to Go

Antigua Sailing Week takes place in late April and draws sailors and spiffy yachts from all over the region for the last big blowout of the season. **Carnival** is held during the week before the first Monday and Tuesday in August. **Independence Day** is Nov. 1.

ANTIGUA HOTELS		RMS	RATES	PHONE	CR. CARDS
★★★★★	Curtain Bluff	63	$425–$875	(888) 289-9898	A
★★★	Club Antigua	476	$101–$306	(800) 777-1250	A, MC, V
★★★	Copper and Lumber Store Hotel	14	$85–$325	(268) 460-1058	A, MC, V
★★★	Galley Bay	61	$320–$620	(800) 345-0356	A, MC, V
★★★	Hawksbill Beach Resort	99	$155–$385	(800) 223-6510	A, DC, MC, V
★★★	Inn at English Harbour, The	28	$105–$410	(800) 223-6510	A, CB, D, DC, MC, V
★★★	Pineapple Beach	135	$290–$490	(800) 345-0356	A, MC, V
★★★	Sandals Antigua	189	$497–$660	(800) 726-3257	A, MC, V
★★★	Siboney Beach Club	12	$130–$290	(800) 533-0234	A, DC, MC, V
★★★	St. James Club	178	$235–$335	(800) 274-0008	A, DC, MC, V
★★	Admiral's Inn	13	$68–$142	(800) 223-5695	A, MC, V
★★	Antigua Village	100	$95–$245	(800) 447-7462	MC, V
★★	Dickenson Bay Cottages	12	$142–$199	(268) 462-4940	A, DC, MC, V
★★	Long Bay Hotel	26	$175–$380	(800) 225-4255	A, MC, V
★★	Lord Nelson's Beach Hotel	17	$60–$115	(268) 462-3094	A, MC, V
★★	Marina Bay Beach Resort	27	$80–$200	(268) 462-3254	A, D, DC, MC, V
★★	Rex Blue Heron Beach Hotel	64	$87–$128	(800) 255-5859	A, D, MC, V
★★	Rex Halcyon Cove	210	$130–$380	(800) 255-5859	A, D, MC, V
★★	Royal Antiguan	282	$120–$410	(800) 345-0356	A, DC, MC, V
★★	Sunset Cove	33	$100–$160	(268) 462-3762	A, MC, V
★★	Yepton Beach Resort	38	$125–$245	(800) 361-4621	A, MC, V
★	Falmouth Harbour Beach Apartments	22	$68–$142	(800) 223-5695	MC, V

ANTIGUA RESTAURANTS	PHONE	ENTRÉE	CR. CARDS
Continental Cuisine			
★★★★ Julian's	(268) 462-4766	$18–$27	
★★★ Le Cap Horn	(268) 460-3336	$10–$20	A, MC, V
French Cuisine			
★★★★ Le Bistro	(268) 462-3881	$22–$34	A, MC, V
Indian Cuisine			
★★ Chutneys	(268) 462-2977	$10–$19	MC, V
International Cuisine			
★★★★ Coconut Grove	(268) 462-1538	$9–$43	A, DC, MC, V
Italian Cuisine			
★★★ Alberto's	(268) 460-3007	$18–$27	
★★ Colombo's	(268) 460-1452	$22–$32	A, DC, MC, V
Regional Cuisine			
★★★ Redcliffe Tavern	(268) 461-4557	$7–$23	A, MC, V
★★ Admiral's Inn	(268) 460-1027	$10–$25	A, MC, V
★★ Big Banana Holding Co.	(268) 462-2621	$6–$30	A, DC, MC, V
★★ Calypso	(268) 462-1965	$8–$25	A, DC, MC, V
★★ Copper and Lumber Store, The	(268) 460-1058	$8–$30	A, MC, V
★★ Hemingway's	(268) 462-2763	$7–$23	A, MC, V
★★ Lemon Tree	(268) 462-1969	$15–$25	A, DC, MC, V
★★ Lobster Pot	(268) 462-2856	$7–$25	DC, MC, V
★★ Miller's by the Sea	(268) 462-9414	$8–$25	MC, V
★★ Shirley Heights Lookout	(268) 460-1785	$15–$26	AE, MC, V
★★ Warri Pier	(268) 462-0256	$7–$30	A, MC, V

ANTIGUA

ARUBA

Windsurfing is Aruba's most popular sport.

Long one of the Caribbean's most popular destinations, Aruba is, appropriately enough, the "A" in the so-called ABC Islands (Bonaire and Curacao make up the trio) in the Netherlands Antilles—although Aruba is now considered a separate entity within the "Kingdom of the Netherlands." Some half-million tourists descend on the small island each year to hang out in its posh resorts, gamble in its numerous casinos, dine in a sampling of its 100 restaurants and shop for duty-free bargains in an endless array of stores.

Located just 15 miles off the coast of Venezuela, Aruba is sated with 28 luxury hotels lining its southwestern shore, near the capital city of Oranjestad. It is not a particularly pretty island; it's desertlike and the land is tough and scrubby, punctuated by cacti and the wind-sculpted Watpana (divi divi) trees. Nonetheless, thousands of tourists converge on the island each year, drawn by its unparalleled watersports and friendly, welcoming residents. The island has tourism down pat, with a sophisticated infrastructure evidenced by its large, modern airport that services many direct flights linking it to the United States and South America, popular cruise port, guest-pleasing hotels and resorts and thriving casinos and nightlife. When it comes to food, expect to pay sky-high prices, but packages can help you out on the hotel and airfare side. Aruba only has a handful of museums and other man-made attractions, but obviously the island is doing something right. Today's visitor will find it hard to believe that, back in 1499, it was officially declared an *isla inutil* (useless island) upon its discovery by the Spanish.

BEST BETS FOR...

Bird's-Eye View

Aruba is located in the southern Caribbean, 15 miles off the coast of Venezuela, a two-and-a-half hour flight from Miami. It measures 19.6 miles long by six miles wide, for a total of 70 square miles. The island receives just 24 inches of rain each year, and the desert countryside is marked by dramatic rock formations, cacti as tall as a man, and wind-bent divi divi trees bent at a 45° angle thanks to the constant trade winds. Tiny bright red flowers called fioritas provide one of the few splashes of natural color—besides, of course, the ever-changing hues of the crystalline sea. The southwest coast, where most resorts are located, has seven miles of palm-fringed beaches of white sand, while the northeast coast is rugged, punctuated by coral cliffs and pounding surf. Because it is so close to the Equator, the median temperature for day to night and summer to winter varies by just 3.6 degrees. Daytime temperature hovers around 82° with little humidity. The scant rain that falls on Aruba occurs mainly in short spurts during the months of November and December. The island lies completely outside the hurricane belt.

Oranjestad, the capital city, is a real Dutch charmer with its gabled, pastel buildings. Shopping is popular along the pretty streets of Nassaustraat and Wilhelminastraat. Arubans are in the midst of an $800 million plan to transform one-fourth of the island into a national park (adding to the existing Arikok National Park), develop the area of San Nicolas, the island's largest

ARUBA

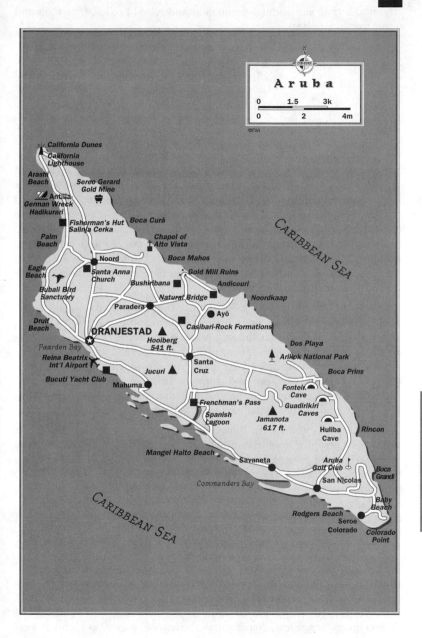

city, into a civic and cultural destination and rebuild roads, bike trails and water treatment plants.

History

When Spanish explorers arrived in the 15th century, the Caiquetios, a tribe of Arawaks, may have already been living on Aruba for more than 4500 years, having migrated there from their ancestral homes in Venezuela. The Spanish exiled most of them in 1513, though more immigration occurred around 1640, when the Dutch permitted the Indian population to live a free—if difficult—life in Aruba. Though the last full-blooded natives died out in 1862, remains of their villages, workshops and cemeteries can be glimpsed throughout the Aruban countryside. Many place names still retain their Indian origins, such as Arashi, Daimari, Jamanota and perhaps the name Aruba itself, which some think is Arawak for "guide." Even the faces of modern Arubans—with their high cheekbones and tawny complexions—strongly reflect their native ancestry.

After being discovered by the Spanish explorer Alonso de Ojeda in 1499, Aruba was deemed useless along with its sister island Bonaire and Curaçao, and ignored for years. After the Spanish shipped off the resident male Indians to work the salt mines of Hispaniola, they began a limited colonization, turning the dusty mote into a large ranch and introducing horses, donkeys, sheep, dogs, goats, pigs, cats and chickens. In 1636, the Dutch took over and continued ranching. The English and the Spanish duked it out from 1792-1816, though the Dutch remained in control.

In 1824 a lowly goat herder discovered the first gleaming nuggets of gold and started a tropical gold rush. Smelters were built and miners flooded the island. When the going got rough, major smelters shut down in 1914, but today some still find nuggets. The real gold of Aruba became aloe vera, brought over from North America via Jamaica in the mid-19th century, a hardy succulent that adapted well to the climate. By 1900 Aruba had become the largest exporter of aloe vera, earning itself the nickname of Island of Aloe, for producing more than 90 percent of the world's supply. Today every Aruban home boasts its own small crop, using it as a natural laxative and wound-healer.

In 1924, oil refining arrived, ushering in an unprecedented era of prosperity. By 1985 the oil boom had gone bust, and the country's biggest employer Exxon went home, leaving the country its worst crisis, with 60 percent of the foreign exchange lost, 70 percent of the harbor space empty, and 40 percent of the population unemployed. In 1986, Aruba separated from its sister islands of the Netherlands Antilles (Curaçao, Bonaire, Sint Maarten, Saba and Statia), but still remained part of the Dutch Kingdom. This move was favored by Arubans, and forced the island to totally depend on tourism. Government guarantees were given to the Hyatt, Sheraton and Holiday Inns—a plucky move that worked. Today tourism is Aruba's biggest industry, employing about half the population, and the island is viewed by its neighbors as the rich, distant cousin.

People

Expect to find some Dutch customs and windmills on Aruba.

Aruba is known for its welcoming, friendly people, and indeed, such warm hospitality is one of the prime draws for so many repeat visitors. The island has more than 81,500 residents who represent 43 nationalities, mainly Dutch, South American, North American, European and Chinese. Native Arubans have a mix of Dutch, Spanish and Arawak Indian ancestry. While Dutch is the official language and Papiamento the local dialect (a lilting blend of Spanish, Dutch, Portuguese, Indian, English and French), most everyone speaks excellent English and Spanish. The education system is Dutch and high standards are the norm; fully 24 percent of the island's budget is devoted to education. English, Spanish, French and German are taught in the schools starting at age 10. Students who wish to pursue higher education

ARUBA

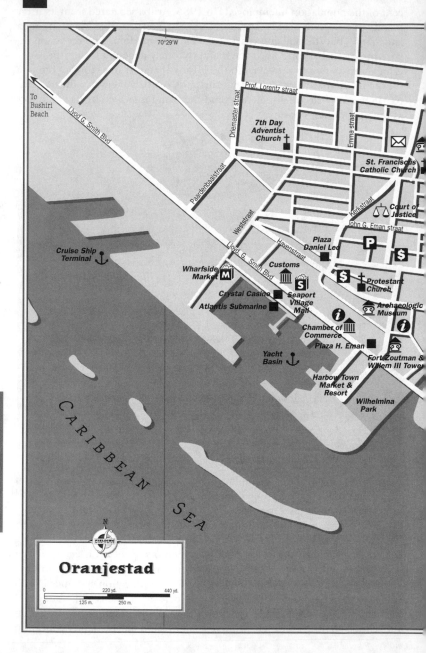

ARUBA

12°32'N

De la Salle straat

A. van Leeuwenhoek straat

umismatic
useum

Hospitaal straat

Malanchi River

Nassaustraat

To
Santa
Cruz

Cava G F (Betico) Croes

Wilhelminastraat

Adriaf. Laclé Blvd

Vondeljaan

Ferguson straat

Beth Israel
Synagogue

Wilhelmina
Stadium

Methodist †
Church

Stadion Weg

To Queen Beatrix
International
Airport

attend Aruba's law school, teacher college or Hospitality Trades Training Center.

Aruba became a separate entity within the Kingdom of the Netherlands on July 1, 1986 (*prior to that it was part of the Netherlands Antilles*). The island has a democratic, Dutch form of government, with an appointed governor, parliament, council of ministers and elected prime minister. Arubans enjoy a high standard of living and live up to the line in their national anthem that proclaims, "The greatness of our people is their great cordiality."

Several yachts and catamarans offer cruises along Aruba's coast.

Of the three ABC Islands, Aruba has the most beautiful beaches. All are open to the public free of charge. Avoid swimming on the east side because the surf can get dangerously rough. **Palm Beach**, considered by some to be one of the 10 best beaches in the world, is the hub of Aruban beach life—interpret that as *crowded*—but it is also excellent for swimming and other watersports. **Fishermen's Hut**, north of the hotel strip, is the favorite hangout of the windsurfing crowd. Here you'll see a lovely view of neon sailboats bobbing madly in the wind. **Rodger Beach** is notable for its lovely palm trees, and **Baby Lagoon** on the west is unusually calm. A truly wondrous wide stretch of strand, **Manchebo Beach** seems to magically inspire women to fling their tops off. Other good beaches are **Bachelor's Beach** and **Boca Grandi** in the east, also good for windsurfing.

Perpetually consigned to the impressive shadow cast by Bonaire and Curacao, Aruba will never attain premier status as a dive destination. A decent barrier reef extends between Oranjestad and the southern tip, but with all dive operators located a long boat ride away, visitors don't always hear about it. One does need to be wary of a brisk current, but lovely sites along this reef (two of them below) are worthy of exploration. Visibility varies from 50–100 feet depending on current and plankton bloom. Shore diving is possible, but a maze of cuts and channels must be negotiated in order to access the main reef; the current also allows for some drift dives, but these, too, can be difficult to locate. If you really want to experience the island's limited reef and wall diving, your best bet is to hook up with a dive shop that knows this area. What the island does offer is a bevy of wrecks—rated only behind Bermuda by "Rodale's Scuba Diving" readers, including one of the Caribbean's finest, the **Antilla**, a WWII remnant which sits close enough to the surface to be explored by snorkelers. There's also a tug, a 200-foot freighter, a pair of rusting airplanes and, off the rugged northern tip, the remains of the **California**, which is notorious as the ship that didn't respond to the *Titanic's* S.O.S. signals. The best area for snorkeling is probably **DePalm Island**, a small resort served by a free ferry every half-hour. A new guide to dive sites is available from the Aruba Tourism Authority.

Dive Shops

Aruba Pro Dive

Costa Linda Beach Resort, Oranjestad; ☎ *(297) 8-25520; FAX (297) 8-37723.*
Explores the south coast area between Spanish Lagoon and Seroe Colorado via shore dives; wreck dives in the afternoon. Four-hour resort courses taught from beach $70; single tank dive $35 from boat or shore. Keeps groups limited to 10 and does underwater photography. PADI, NAUI, SSI and IDD. Snorkel trips to Antilla and two reefs $45 with lunch.

Red Sail Sports Aruba

Palm Beach; ☎ *(800) 255-6425, (297) 8-61603; FAX (297) 8-66657;*
e-mail: redsail@setarnet.aw; website: www.redsail.com.
One-tank dive, $30, two-tanks, $54, plus rental equipment. Two dives scheduled daily, focuses on wrecks; resort courses daily in pool $77. PADI and NAUI, training to Divemaster. High-volume operation with huge boats.

Scuba Aruba

Noord; ☎ *(297) 8-66690; FAX (297) 8-61066.*

One-tank dive, $30; two-tank dive $55, including equipment. Caters to beginners (resort courses, $50). Maximum group size 16. All-Caribbean staff.

With an average annual rainfall of only about 20 inches, Aruba's interior is scraggly and desolate, with a series of low rolling hills that snuggle against the middle part of the northern coast. The island's highest elevation is **Ya-manota Hill**, a rise of 617 feet near the center of Aruba. Its summit can be reached by car, and a series of trails trickle down the slopes, but hikers should be cautious in their explorations as a unique, venomous rattlesnake inhabits this rugged territory. **Arikok National Park** encompasses a triangle of land be-tween San Fuego and Boca Prins (on the eastern coast); a group of short trails surround the park's focal point, **Mt. Arikok**, Aruba's second-highest summit. Also worth on-foot investigation is **California Point**, the island's northern tip, where sand dunes reach toward the sea and brown pelicans nest.

Wind-bent divi-divi (watpana) trees are a common sight on Aruba.

What Else to See

You won't find a slew of historical and man-made attractions on Aruba, but some places are well worth checking out. The **Natural Bridge**, located on the jagged northern coast, is the Caribbean's largest. The gaping coral bridge is a favorite stop for every tour bus on the island, so come early to avoid the crowds. The old indian caves known as Guadirikiri and Fontein have painted petroglyphs on the walls and ceilings, though some wags say they were actually painted for an Italian film years ago. San Nicolas, Aruba's oldest settlement and its largest city with a population of 25,000, is located on the southwestern tip. It's best known for the Exxon refinery that was attacked by German U-Boats in World War II. The refinery closed down in 1986 after 60 years in operation, and today San Nicolas is the target of an ambitious revitalization effort that will add a Caribbean Cultural Center, sports park, market square and waterfront park.

Festivals

Carnival   ★★★★

Various locales around Aruba, Oranjestad, ☎ (800) 862-7822.
This yearly party starts two weeks before Lent (usually in February). Don't miss the Grand Parade, held on the Sunday before Lent. Other festivities include a children's carnival, street dancing and the crowning of the Carnival Queen.

Historical Sites

Fort Zoutman/Willem III Tower   ★★★

Off Lloyd G. Smith Boulevard, Oranjestad.
The fort, built in 1796, is the island's oldest building and the site of a Bonbini Festival every Tuesday from 6:30–8:30 p.m. with arts crafts, local foods and drinks, folkloric music and dances. The Willem III tower was added in 1868 and served as a lighthouse for decades. On the grounds is Museo Arubano, a historical museum in an 18th-century home that displays relics and artifacts found around Aruba. General admission: $1.

Museums and Exhibits

Archeological Museum   ★★★

Zoutmanstraat 1, Oranjestad, ☎ (297) 8-28979.
Hours open: Mon.–Fri. 8 a.m.–noon, 1–4 p.m. Closed weekends.
Artifacts from the precolonial period—including some skeletons 2000 years old—are on exhibit at this small museum.

De Man's Shell Collection   ★★★

Morgenster 18, Oranjestad, ☎ (297) 8-24246.

ARUBA

The De Mans are proud owners of one of the world's largest private shell collections. Call ahead and if they're free, they'll let you check it out.

Numismatic Museum ★★

Zuidstraat 27, Oranjestad, ☎ *(297) 8-28831.*
Hours open: Mon.–Fri. 7:30 a.m.–noon, 1–4:30 p.m. Closed weekends.
More than 30,000 historic coins and currency from 400 countries—including Aruba—are on display.

Tours

Atlantis Submarines ★★★

L.G. Smith Boulevard 82, Oranjestad.
Hours open: 10 a.m.–3 p.m.
Not for the claustrophobic, but a great excursion for everyone else in a modern submarine that goes as deep as 150 feet below the sea to observe coral and fish in the Barcadera Reef Marine Park, the Mi Dushi shipwreck or the Sonesta airplane wrecks. Trips depart every hour on the hour, and reservations are essential. The fee for the narrated one-hour dive is $69 for adults, $32 under age 16; children under four not permitted. This attraction has won the island award for "Most Outstanding Tourist Attraction" for five years running. General admission: $69.

De Palm Tours ★★★

L.G. Smith Boulevard 142, Oranjestad, ☎ *(297) 8-24400, FAX: (297) 8-23012.*
If it involves showing tourists around Aruba, they're happy to oblige at De Palm. On- and off-road excursions start at $49.95 and include lunch and snorkeling; three-hour treks for hikers cost $25; deep-sea fishing starts at $220; horseback rides are $30 for two hours. They also do boat tours and snorkel excursions, with prices starting at $22.50.

BEST VIEW:

Schooner Harbor is a great photo op for its colorfully docked sailboats and open market where fishermen and boatpeople hawk their wares in open-stall markets.

Sports

Aruba's remarkably clear and temperate waters are the island's chief attraction, and most visitors come for the plethora of excellent watersports that await. Windsurfing conditions are ideal, thanks to constant trade winds. Fisherman's Hut is a good spot for beginners, while those more advanced flock to the high waves of Boca Grandi and Manchebo Beach, which has small, choppy waves. The smooth sea of the south and west coasts is good for both water- and jet-skiing; though the latter is restricted in certain areas.

ARUBA

A pair of golf courses awaits duffers, including the **Tierra del Sol**, the island's first championship links. Tennis courts can be found at virtually every major resort, or contact **Aruba Racquet Club** ☎ *(297) 8-60215* in Palm Beach, which boasts eight lighted courts, an exhibition center court, a fitness center and pool, open from 8 a.m.–9 p.m.

Biking

Aruba's flat landscape makes it ideal for road or mountain bike riding. However, the ferocious heat and sunlight can make the sport less than pleasant unless you prepare carefully. Take plenty of water, a good map and apply sunscreen generously. A circuit of the island is roughly 50 miles. The divi divi trees—winds keep them pointed southwest—serve as a compass of sorts. **Pablito Big Rental** (☎ *(297) 8-78655* in Oranjestad) rents Taiwanese mountain bikes for a full day $12. Hourly and weekly rates are available, too. **Tri Bike Aruba** (☎ *(297) 8-50609)* in Santa Cruz features mountain bikes rented by Olympian triathlete Gert Van Vliet.

Golf

Aruba Golf Club *(Golfweg 82, San Nicolas,* ☎ *(297) 842-0006)* This desert course has nine holes. Trade winds, oiled sand greens and an occasional live goat keep things interesting. It is located on the island's southeastern part, and open to non-members only on weekdays. Greens fees are $7.50 for nine holes, $10 if you want to go around twice. **Tierra del Sol Golf Course** *(☎ (297) 8-60978; FAX (297) 8-60671; near the California Lighthouse on the northwest coast)* brought the island its first championship golf course, designed by the Robert Trent Jones II Group in January 1995. The 18-hole, par-71 course totals 6811 yards in length, with the highest tee 98 ft. above sea level. Fifteen of its holes offer sea views, and many of them are rooted at the base of coral rock formations, bordered by wind-shaped divi-divi trees. A clubhouse, pro shop, locker rooms, swimming pool and restaurant with panoramic view are on site. Greens fees are $85 including a cart and access to the driving range; $57 after 3 p.m. Golfers can arrange tee-times with their resort or hotel. During the high season (Oct.–March), getting a tee time can be difficult.

Horseback riding

Aruba's topography offers many exotic locations for riding: from challenging sand dunes to desert-like plains. **Ponderosa Ranch** *(☎ (297) 8-25027; Papaya 30)* is located at an abandoned gold mill. **Rancho Del Campo** *(☎ (297) 8-20290; Sombre 22 E)* and **Rancho Diamari** *(☎ (297) 8-60239)* offer rides to the Natural Pool. For rides through the countryside and on the coast, contact **Rancho El Paso** *(☎ (297) 8-63310; Washington 44)*.

Watersports

Deep-sea fishing in Aruba's warm, plankton-rich waters can be a treat with Atlantic game fish caught year around. An annual championship event is held each October at the **Aruba Nautical Club** *(☎ (297) 8-53022)*. **De Palm Tours** *(☎ (297) 8-24545)* can arrange a full-day or half-day of fishing or contact the fishing boat captain of your choice: **Amira Darina** *(☎ (297) 8-33424)*; **Dorothy** *(☎ (297) 8-23375)*; **Driftwood** *(☎ (297) 8-32512)*; **La Tanga** *(☎ (297) 8-46825)*; **Monsoon**

(☎ (297) 9-33311). Aruba's cruise and sailing operators offer a myriad of options, too. Here are some of them: **Andante** *(☎ (297) 8-47718)* **Mi Dushi** *(☎ (297) 8-23513);* **Pelican Watersports** *(☎ (297) 8-31228);* **Wave Dancer** *(☎ (297) 8-25520);* **Windfeather Charters** *(☎ (297) 8-65842);* **Red Sail Sports** *(☎ (800) 255-6425 or (297) 8-61603).* Each November a catamaran regatta—with catamarans from North and South America as well as Europe—takes place in front of the hotels on Palm Beach.

Windsurfing   ★★★★★

Aruba's perfect trade winds and smooth waters attract the best windsurfers in the world. Each June it hosts the **Aruba Hi-Winds Amateur World Challenge** (call coordinator Julie Renfro at ☎ *(297) 8-60440*), which attracts windsurfers from 30 countries. Aruba also inaugurated the Caribbean's first Windsurfing Festival in June 1997, which featured live island music, a food festival on the beach and a trade show for the windsurfing industry. Numerous windsurfing shops can offer instruction for beginners as well as equipment for hard-core sailors. Here are some to try: **Divi Winds** *(☎ (297) 8-24150);* **Happy Surfpool** *(☎ (297) 8-66288);* **Pelican Watersports "Velasurf"** *(☎ (297) 8-63600);* **Red Sail Sports** *(☎ (800) 255-6425 or (297) 8-61603; e-mail: infor@redsail.com; or http://www.redsail.com);* or **Roger's Windsurf Place** *(☎ (297) 8-61918).*

ARUBA

Where to Stay

Fielding's Highest Rated Hotels in Aruba

★★★★★	Aruba Sonesta Resort & Casino at Seaport Village	$145–$330
★★★★★	Hyatt Regency Aruba Resort & Casino	$190–$495
★★★★	Aruba Marriott Resort & Stellaris Casino	$150–$550
★★★	Americana Aruba Beach Resort & Casino	$200–$400
★★★	Aruba Palm Beach Resort & Casino	$125–$235
★★★	Bushiri "All Inclusive" Beach Resort	$210–$380
★★★	Costa Linda Beach Resort	$290–$489
★★★	Divi Aruba Beach Resort	$175–$370
★★★	Playa Linda Beach Resort	$220–$350
★★★	Wyndham Aruba Beach Resort & Casino	$205–$375

Fielding's Best Programs for Children in Aruba

★★★★★	Aruba Sonesta Resort & Casino at Seaport Village	$145–$330
★★★★★	Hyatt Regency Aruba Resort & Casino	$190–$495
★★	Holiday Inn Aruba Beach Resort & Casino	$170–$220
★★★	Bushiri "All Inclusive" Beach Resort	$210–$380
★★	Casa del mar Beach Resort	$120–$400

Fielding's Best Value Hotels in Aruba

★★★	Amsterdam Manor Beach Resort	$110–$170
★★★★★	Aruba Sonesta Resort & Casino at Seaport Village	$145–$330
★★★	Aruba Palm Beach Resort & Casino	$125–$235
★★★★★	Hyatt Regency Aruba Resort & Casino	$190–$495
★★	Best Western Manchebo Beach Resort	$110–$190

ARUBA

Most of Aruba's major properties are situated along J.E. Irausquin Boulevard on Palm Beach and L. G. Smith Boulevard just west of Oranjestad. As you would expect, prices in the resorts are quite high during wintertime; families looking to economize are best off in one of the island's many condominium units, though note that most are located in modern, somewhat sterile buildings. Many resorts have Las Vegas-style casinos attached—a trend that started in 1959 when the Aruba Caribbean Hotel and Casino opened its doors, so finding things to do after dark is never a problem. Some of the top casinos are the Alhambra Bazaar—an 8000 sq. ft. playground for adults—and Royal Cabana Casino, the largest in the Caribbean. Be sure to inquire about package deals; active types who plan to golf and pursue watersports can often save big by paying for everything at once. And during the summer months, several hotels have offered incredible packages for families with children.

Gambling is a major attraction on Aruba and there are many casinos.

Hotels and Resorts

If you have a taste for the Vegas life, stay in one of Aruba's many top-class resorts that will serve your every need; between the health club, the casino, the lagoon-style pool and the full deck of restaurants, you'll never have to leave the premises. High-rises, of course, give you a better view of the sea; low-rises seem more intimate and are usually planted around fabulous gardens. The Sonesta offers some of the best shopping malls on the island.

Americana Aruba Beach Resort & Casino $200–$1060   ★★★

Oranjestad, ☎ (800) 203-4475, (297) 8-64500, FAX (297) 8-63191.
Website: www.ameruba.com. E-mail: ameruba@aol.com.
Single: $200–$400. Double: $200–$400. Suites Per Day: $335–$1060.

Situated directly on Palm Beach with its own full casino and showroom with live entertainment, this well-managed property consists of twin high-rise towers. A social hostess ensures that guests—most are from the U.S. and Canada—stay extremely busy. Accommodations are decent if not spectacular, with air conditioning, bamboo and wood furniture, cable TV and hair dryers; balconies overlook the sea. Some overlook the free-form swimming pool with waterfalls and Jacuzzis. Red Sail Sports has a facility here. It also has three restaurants, four bars, tennis courts and a shopping area. A great spot for kids with special supervised activities, though not exactly teeming with island flavor. You can go either with the European plan or all-inclusive. 421 rooms. Credit cards: A, MC, V.

Amsterdam Manor Beach Resort   **$110–$170**   ★★★

Eagle Beach, ☎ *(800) 766-6016, (297) 8-71492, FAX (297) 8-71463.*
E-mail: ambrmgt@mail.setarnet.aw.
Associated Restaurant: *The Waterfall Restaurant.*
Single: $110–$170. Double: $110–$170.
This complex is marked by its authentic Dutch style, with gabled roofs and inner courtyards. Accommodations range from studios to two-bedroom apartments, all with pinewood furniture and full kitchens or kitchenettes, and oceanview balconies or terraces. A restaurant and mini-market are on-site. The nice pool with a bar is set right on the road and lacks privacy. Eagle Beach is across the street, and guests can arrange watersports at various nearby properties. Not a top choice, but decent enough for the price. Lots of Europeans here. 72 rooms. Credit cards: A, DC, MC, V.

Aruba Marriott Resort & Stellaris Casino   **$150–$750**   ★★★★

Oranjestad, ☎ *(800) 223-6388, (297) 8-69000, FAX (297) 8-60649.*
Associated Restaurant: *La Vista/Tuscany's.*
Single: $150–$550. Double: $150–$550. Suites Per Day: $250–$750.
Opened in May 1995, this new Marriott is a smashing full-service resort, with a magnificent free-form pool with swim up bar, huge casino, spiffy health spa, tennis and all the usual watersports.Bars, restaurants and shopping on-site keep visitors happy, though as with all these mega-resorts, genuine island atmosphere is scarce. Oversized guestrooms face the ocean and each has 100 sq. ft. balconies. Golf is available nearby. 413 rooms. Credit cards: A, MC, V.

Aruba Palm Beach Resort & Casino   **$125–$295**   ★★★

Palm Beach, ☎ *(800) 345-2782, (297) 8-63900, FAX (297) 8-61941.*
Associated Restaurant: *Seawatch Restaurant.*
Single: $125–$235. Double: $125–$235. Suites Per Day: $175–$295.
This eight-story, Moorish-style beachfront hotel is set amid exquisitely landscaped tropical grounds with palm trees and exotic birds. Rooms are spacious with walk-in closets and come with all the usual amenities, though their balconies are quite small, and not all have an ocean view. This hotel offers all the expected recreational diversions, from three tennis courts, a dive shop, Olympic-size pool and full casino. A choice spot. 187 rooms. Credit cards: A, DC, D, MC, V.

Aruba Sonesta Resort & Casino
at Seaport Village   **$145–$480**   ★★★★★

Oranjestad, ☎ *(800) 766-3782, (297) 8-36000, FAX (297) 8-34389.*

ARUBA

Associated Restaurant: *L'Escale.*
Single: $145–$330. Double: $145–$330. Suites Per Day: $285–$480.
The Aruba Sonesta Suites and Casino ($205-$400 a night) adds 250 one-bedroom suites each with kitchenette and balcony to this sprawling complex. No beach, but boats depart every 20 minutes to take guests of both resorts to a private island seven minutes away which features six private beaches, tennis, fitness room and Red Sail Sports, a dive operation with other watersports offerings. Located in the heart of Oranjestad in the Seaport Village complex, which offers 120 shops and restaurants, a marina, three cinemas and De Palm Tours activities desk in the resort lobby. After entering through an impressive atrium lobby, guests are brought to their nice rooms, which have all the usual amenities plus minibars and tiny balconies. The new Tierra del Sol Golf Course is ten minutes away and Sonesta guests have access to it through the hotel. The children's program (ages 5–12) is free and highly rated, and the two casinos are happening. The Seaport Conference Center, managed by Sonesta, just opened with 22,000 sq. ft. of meeting and function space next door. A great spot, but only for those who don't mind being well off the beach. 300 rooms.
Credit cards: A, DC, D, MC, V.

Best Western Manchebo Beach Resort $110–$190   ★★

Manchebo Beach, ☎ *(800) 223-1108, (297) 8-23444, FAX (297) 8-32446.*
Associated Restaurant: *Bistro Aruba Restaurant.*
Single: $110–$175. Double: $125–$190.

This sprawling lowrise, located on one of Aruba's best beaches and popular with Europeans, has guest rooms that are comfortable if unexciting; each has a minifridge and coffeemaker. Friendly, personal attention in a relaxed atmosphere. It hosts theme nights in one of its three restaurants, and has a freshwater pool and dive shop. A casino is adjacent. 71 rooms. Credit cards: A, DC, MC, V.

Bucuti Beach Resort $120–$260   ★★

Manchebo Beach, ☎ *(297) 8-31100, FAX (297) 8-25271.*
Website: www.bucuti.com. E-mail: int1233@mail.setarnet.aw.
Associated Restaurant: *The Pirate's Nest.*
Single: $120–$200. Double: $155–$260.
This casual, three-story, red-tiled roof resort occupies a prime spot on Aruba's largest white sand beach. Next door is the Alhambra Casino, and several restaurants and shops are within easy walking distance. An exercise room and mini-market is on the property as well as a fine dining restaurant. The oversized rooms of this owner-managed hotel have sitting areas, sofa beds, large balconies or patios, as well as microwave ovens, coffee makers, mini bars, hairdryers and ironing boards. 63 rooms.
Credit cards: A, MC, V.

Caribbean Palm Village $115–$215   ★★

Noord, ☎ *(800) 992-2015, (297) 8-62700, FAX (297) 8-62380.*
Associated Restaurant: *Valentino's.*
Single: $115–$215. Double: $115–$215.
Located a mile from Palm Beach, this luxury hotel with red-tile roof and lushly landscaped grounds has two pools and Jacuzzis. Besides the regular rooms, one- or two-bedroom suites with two baths, living and dining areas and kitchens are also

available. Valentino's, a gourmet Italian restaurant is on-site. It also has supervised programs for the kiddies. 170 rooms. Credit cards: A, DC, MC, V.

Costa Linda Beach Resort $290–$1075 ★★★

Eagle Beach, ☎ *(800) 223-6510, (297) 8-38000, FAX (297) 8-36040.*
Associated Restaurant: *Sun Club Restaurant.*
Single: $290–$489. Double: $290–$489. Suites Per Day: $625–$1075.
This attractive beachfront resort on Eagle Beach consists of nicely appointed two- and three-bedroom suites with Roman tubs and separate showers, full kitchens, private ocean-view balconies and two TVs. (King-size beds are available on request). Two lit-tennis courts, a large tropical pool with plenty of palms for shades, whirlpool spas, fitness center, shopping arcade, game room, three restaurants and bars with nightly entertainment round out the facilities. Supervised children's activities are offered during high season, and it has a children's pool and playground as well. 155 rooms. Credit cards: A, MC, V.

Divi Aruba Beach Resort $175–$600 ★★★

Eagle Beach, ☎ *(800) 554-2008, (297) 8-23300, FAX (297) 8-34002.*
Associated Restaurant: *Red Parrot.*
Single: $175–$370. Double: $175–$370. Suites: $275–$600.
Located on glorious Druif Beach, this popular lowrise is nicely casual and very friendly. Standard accommodations are in motel-like wings and feature tile floors, ceiling fans (as well as air), and small balconies. Concrete casitas offer more privacy. Other rooms front the ocean and have tiled patios and larger bathrooms, while the newer Divi Dos rooms include refrigerators and Jacuzzis. Lots of honeymooners at this spot, which comes highly recommended more for the excellent beach than for the property itself. 203 rooms. Credit cards: A, DC, MC, V.

Holiday Inn Aruba Beach Resort & Casino $170–$220 ★★

Palm Beach, ☎ *(800) 462-6868, (297) 8-63600.*
Website: www.ArubaResort.com.
Single: $170–$220. Double: $170–$220.
It's a Holiday Inn, after all, so don't come looking for anything special. Rooms— air-conditioned and color satellite TV— are acceptable but could really use a refurbishing, but the outdoor gardens are quite nice. It has beginning windsurfers and SCUBA clinics, six tennis courts, horseback riding, a large pool, fitness and activities/games center and, of course, the ubiquitous casino. It also has a supervised children's activities program. If you have children (ages 2–11), consider this hotel's "Stay, Eat & Play Free" program, which runs from June through Oct. 31. It now offers all-inclusive packages through Bounty Vacations. 600 rooms. Credit cards: A, DC, MC, V.

Hyatt Regency Aruba Resort & Casino $190–$1000 ★★★★★

Palm Beach, ☎ *(800) 233-1234, (297) 8-61234, FAX (297) 8-65478.*
Associated Restaurant: *Ole/Ruinas Del Mar.*
Single: $190–$495. Double: $190–$495. Suites Per Day: $430–$1000.
Set on 12 acres fronting Palm Beach, this $52 million resort—rooms, expansion of the casino and Camp Hyatt were recently refurbished with $4 million—features a $2.5 million three-level pool, waterpark and 5000 sq. ft. lagoon, a trademark of

Hyatt resorts. The opulent nine-story, Mediterranean-style complex (built in 1990) with an open-air lobby is flanked by two wings with four and five stories. If you are the active type, but don't enjoy the circus-like atmosphere that sometimes plagues hotels that pedal numerous activities, this well-managed resort makes a top-notch choice. While it offers watersports through top-of-the-line operator Red Sail Sports; golf at the island's first and only 18-hole championship course; gambling at a 12,500 sq. ft., carnival-themed casino with night entertainment; workouts at its health and fitness center (sauna, steam and massage, of course); tennis on its two, newly resurfaced courts; and splashing about at its own waterpark, you never feel crowded or pulled. The other big plus: Camp Hyatt offers award-winning supervised activities and special programs for children ages 3–12. Especially fun: Papiamento lessons. The camp is open daily, year around unlike those of many on-island competitors. This Hyatt boasts five restaurants and four bars with 24-hour room service. If nothing suits, you can always call the concierge for help. The rooms have electronic locks, voice mail, new furnishings and carpeting, cable TV, French balconies, hairdryers, ironing boards, juice bars, coffee makers, and mini-safes. 360 rooms. Credit cards: A, DC, MC, V.

Wyndham Aruba Beach Resort & Casino $205–$375   ★★★

Palm Beach, ☎ *(800) 996-3426, (297) 8-64466, FAX (297) 8-68217.*
Associated Restaurant: *Havana Tropical/Pago Pago.*
Single: $205–$375. Double: $205–$375.

Wyndham lavished $42 million on this former Concorde Hotel. Nicely decorated accommodations are in a high-rise with all the modern touches and—best of all—balconies with full ocean views. The grounds include a new watersports center, two pools (one for kids), nice public spaces, a fitness center and spa, two tennis courts and a full casino. Splurge on the VIP floors if your budget allows for a bit more space and more amenities. This place has four restaurants—one with a dinner show—and two bars. 444 rooms. Credit cards: A, DC, D, MC, V.

All Inclusives

Bushiri "All Inclusive" Beach Resort $210–$380   ★★★

Oranjestad, ☎ *(297) 8-25216.*
Associated Restaurant: *Steak Ranch/Al Fresco Terasa.*
Single: $210–$260. Double: $320–$380.

Aruba's first all-inclusive resort is physically nondescript, but excellent service (it's attached to a training school for budding hoteliers) makes up for the lack of atmosphere and explains the heavy number of repeat guests. Young clientele favor this busy property, which has an activity director who helps guide guests in their choices of watersports, sightseeing excursions, tennis and more. Good for families, thanks to its comprehensive, year-round kids' program from 9 a.m.–5 p.m. Air-conditioned rooms front the sea and a spectacular beach. A pool, hot tub and fitness center have been added. 155 rooms. Credit cards: A, MC, V.

Tamarin Aruba Beach Resort $130–$185   ★★

Eagle Beach, ☎ *(800) 554-2008, (297) 8-24150, FAX (297) 8-24002.*

This all-inclusive resort is a sister property to the Aruba Divi Beach Resort, with golf carts whisking guests to and fro. The Dutch-style architecture consists of two-story townhouse-style oceanfront units with the typical furnishings and amenities inside. The grounds include a pool, two tennis courts, five restaurants and four bars, beginners windsurf and watersports center, fitness area and mountain bikes. Guests can get free admittance and transport to the Alhambra Casino. Lots of honeymooners here. Also packages for families (kids' camp included) and golfers. 236 rooms. Credit cards: A, CB, MC, V.

Apartments and Condominiums

Families and couples will find the best bargains in this section—except during the off-season when the big hotels kick in incredible freebies for kids. Some complexes even throw in a rental car; if you don't plan on driving, make sure you are near an accessible bus route. Some of the most inexpensive deals can be found in the Malmok district.

Dutch Village   **$120–$415**   ★

Eagle Beach, ☎ *(800) 367-3484, (297) 8-32300.*
Single: $120–$414. Double: $120–$415.

This three-story complex built in 1987 consists of time-share studios and apartments of one- to three bedrooms, all with full kitchens, satellite TV and Jacuzzis. It has three pools. Meal plans and activities are available from the Tamarin Aruba Beach Resort, which is in front of it on the beach. Several shops and additional restaurants are within walking distance. 97 rooms. Credit cards: A, DC, MC, V.

Mill Resort   **$85–$350**   ★ ★

Palm Beach, ☎ *(800) 992-2015, (297) 8-67700, FAX (297) 8-67271.*
Associated Restaurant: *O Sole Mio.*
Single: $85–$160. Double: $128–$235. Suites Per Day: $170–$350.

This condominium hotel is 300 yards from Palm Beach. The white-washed, lowrise complex consists of studios and one- to two-bedroom suites all with Jacuzzis and air conditioning. Suites have fully-equipped kitchens. A restaurant is poolside (there's a pool for kids, too), and the lushly-landscaped resort offers tennis, sauna and exercise room. Complimentary beach access is across the street at the Wyndham. 200 rooms. Credit cards: A, DC, D, MC, V.

Playa Linda Beach Resort   **$220–$675**   ★ ★ ★

Palm Beach, ☎ *(800) 346-7084, (297) 8-61000, FAX (297) 8-63479.*
Associated Restaurant: *Le Bistroquet.*
Single: $220–$350. Double: $220–$350. Suites Per Day: $420–$675.

This snazzy time-share complex has a great location on Palm Beach, tucked between the Hyatt and the Holiday Inn. Accommodations are in studios and one- and two-bedroom apartments, tropically decorated. The one- and two-bedroom apartments have full, modern kitchens and private verandas. The centerpiece of the activity here is the lagoon-style swimming pool complete with falls and whirlpools. Downstairs is a shopping area with mini-mart and a TCBY. If you aren't a member of a time-share company, you can only rent the apartments by the week. 194 rooms. Credit cards: A, DC, MC, V.

ARUBA

Where to Eat

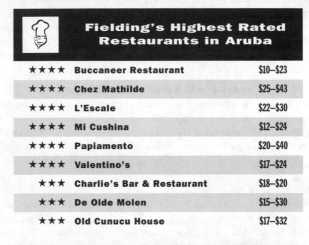

Fielding's Highest Rated Restaurants in Aruba

★★★★	Buccaneer Restaurant	$10–$23
★★★★	Chez Mathilde	$25–$43
★★★★	L'Escale	$22–$30
★★★★	Mi Cushina	$12–$24
★★★★	Papiamento	$20–$40
★★★★	Valentino's	$17–$24
★★★	Charlie's Bar & Restaurant	$18–$20
★★★	De Olde Molen	$15–$30
★★★	Old Cunucu House	$17–$32

Fielding's Most Romantic Restaurants in Aruba

♡♡♡♡♡	Chez Mathilde	$25–$43
♡♡♡♡♡	L'Escale	$22–$30
♡♡♡♡♡	Papiamento	$20–$40
♡♡♡♡	Buccaneer Restaurant	$10–$23
♡♡♡♡	Mi Cushina	$12–$24

Fielding's Best Value Restaurants in Aruba

★★★★	Buccaneer Restaurant	$10–$23
★★★★	Mi Cushina	$12–$24
★★★	Que Pasa?	$10–$18
★★★★	Valentino's	$17–$24
★★★	Charlie's Bar & Restaurant	$18–$20

ARUBA

Arubans enjoy the people-to-people contact tourism has brought them.

Aruba may be small in size, but it boasts more than 100 restaurants offering just abut every type of cuisine imaginable. Its chefs have consistently won medals at "A Taste of the Caribbean" competition held annually in Puerto Rico. Be sure to try some authentic Aruban cuisine at Mi Cushina and Brisas del Mar, with dishes such as *sopi di yuana* (iguana soup, which tastes a lot like chicken soup), *pan bati* (griddle bread made with cornmeal) and *funchi* (cornmeal bread), *pastechi* (cheese or meat-filled turnovers) and *carbito stew* (a traditional seasoned goat meat dish). Those hankering for good old spaghetti and meatballs or cheeseburgers will have no problem in hotel coffeeshops; but expect a hefty check.

Boonoonoonoos **$$$** ★★

Wilhelminastraat 18A, Oranjestad, ☎ (297) 831888.
Lunch: 11:30 a.m.–5 p.m., entrées $4–$15.
Dinner: 5:30–10:30 p.m., entrées $15–$34.
No, the eyes do not deceive, there are four pairs of oo's in this downtown restaurant's name, which means "extraordinary" in Jamaican patois. Located in a restored colonial home that's been brightly splashed with paint, cuisine covers the Caribbean in a nutshell as conceived by Austrian owners Kurt and Jacky Biermann. Signature dishes include Jamaican jerk ribs and a silky pumpkin cream soup; hungry diners will be more than satisfied with the Carib Combo platter, groaning with eight or nine dishes representing several Caribbean islands. The service is as good as the food. No lunch is served on Sunday. Reservations recommended. Credit cards: A, DC, MC, V.

Brisas del Mar **$$** ★★★

Savaneta 22A, ☎ (297) 847718.
Lunch: Noon–2:30 p.m., entrées $5–$20.

ARUBA

Dinner: 6:30–9:30 p.m., entrées $10–$29. Closed: Mon.

Bustling and jammed with locals, especially on music-filled weekends, Brisas del Mar is about 20 minutes away from downtown Oranjestad, but well worth the trek for spanking fresh seafood and some of the finest local dishes on the island. Reservations at this folksy beach shack—hung with fisherman's nets and with a terrific view of the sea—are required because there are only 10 tables. A recurring special is a flavorful fish stew, loaded with whatever's fresh, in a tasty broth. Groups can order the Aruban special, a potpourri of lightly fried fish cakes, spiced minced shark, hot relishes, plenty of rice and corn pancakes. Reservations required. Credit cards: A, MC, V.

Buccaneer Restaurant $$ ★★★★

Gasparito 11-C, Oranjestad, ☎ (297) 866172.
Dinner: 5:30–10 p.m., entrées $10–$23. Closed: Sun.

Moderately priced and expertly prepared seafood generally satisfies the crowds of diners who come back again and again to this cozy restaurant located just a short jog from the large hotel strip in Noord. Most tables have their own aquariums. If you don't want to eat, there's a popular bar, and plenty of swimming marine life at which to gaze. European-style meat dishes are also available for seafood-hating companions. No lunch is served on Mondays. Credit cards: A, DC, D, MC, V.

Charlie's Bar & Restaurant $$$ ★★★

Main Street 56, San Nicolas, ☎ (297) 845086.
Lunch: 11:45 a.m.–4 p.m., entrées $18–$20.
Dinner: 4–9:30 p.m., entrées $18–$20. Closed: Sun.

You too can become a part of history by hanging a hankie or old tennis shoe to join the hundreds of other artifacts on the ceiling of this 50-plus-year-old bar. It's located in the once-thriving ghost town of San Nicolas, former headquarters of The Standard Oil Company. Charlie's served as a watering hole for workers (no women were allowed then) and it now overflows with locals, artists, writers and musicians. Meals are simple: fresh seafood or steak. Overseeing all this activity is Guus Dancker, who has manned the circular bar for more than 40 years.

Chez Mathilde $$$ ★★★★

Havenstraat 23, ☎ (297) 834968.
Lunch: 11:30 a.m.–2:30 p.m., entrées $17–$25.
Dinner: 6–10:30 p.m., entrées $25–$43.

Every Caribbean island must have a bastion of haute cuisine, and this elegant and intimate beauty in a 19th-century town house—one of the few left in its original state on the island—is Aruba's offering. Dishes are prepared in the classic French style by Ronad van Hasenbroek, who won a gold medal for "Chef of the Show" in the 1996 "A Taste of the Caribbean" Culinary Competition. Seafood and beef dishes are highly recommended, especially the thick, juicy veal chops, bouillabaisse, tournedos with peppercorns or lobster thermidor. The romantic setting comes complete with candlelight, fine tableware and classical music. No lunch is served on Sunday. Reservations required. Credit cards: A, DC, D, MC, V.

De Olde Molen $$$ ★★★

L.G. Smith Boulevard 330, Oranjestad, ☎ (297) 866300.
Dinner: 6–9:30 p.m., entrées $15–$30. Closed: Sun.

Until the brisk winds that blow on the islands threatened to ruin them, this authentic Dutch windmill among the high-rise hotels in Palm Beach sported real sails. Reassembled from an 1800s-era mill that was shipped over from the old country, this tourist attraction-cum-restaurant serves international food with Aruban touches. Shrimp is often featured, prepared in a savory cheese sauce, as is pepper steak and liqueured ice cream desserts. Credit cards: A, DC, MC, V.

L'Escale $$$ ★★★★

☎ *(297) 836000.* Associated hotel: *Aruba Sonesta Resort.*
Dinner: 6:30–11 p.m., entrées $22–$30.
Overlooking Oranjestad Harbor, this elegant restaurant specializes in romance. Couples are serenaded by a violin trio while they dine on tropical seafood, French fare or traditional classics prepared by Executive Chef Fernand "Ferry" Zievinger. A native of Aruba, Zievinger has won multiple awards at the "Taste of the Caribbean" Culinary Competition for two years running. He carefully pairs wines with all of his entrées. Dinner starts with inspired appetizers—jerk quail or Caribbean escargot, for example—then treat yourself to either lobster bisque or one of his salads. Wilted spinach and cashews is especially good. For the main course, the Aruban seafood fiesta satisfies even the hungriest seafood lover. Or try the tropical duckling—slow roasted and flamed tableside—or crystal veal, sauteed medallions with chunks of crabmeat and asparagus topped with bearnaise sauce. Sides (stuffed christophine, broccoli, asparagus) are $4.50–$6.75 extra. On Sundays an expansive brunch ($24.95 a person: $4.95 a person) features seven stations with salads, seafood, smoked fish and caviar, steaks, and, of course, a kids' buffet. Credit cards: A, DC, MC, V.

Mi Cushina $$ ★★★★

Noord Cura Cabai 24, ☎ *(297) 848335.* Associated hotel: *La Quinta Beach Resort.*
Lunch: Noon–2 p.m., entrées $12–$24.
Dinner: 6–10 p.m., entrées $12–$24. Closed: Tue.
This cozy restaurant serves home-style Aruban cuisine. Mi Cushina, or owner Wijke Maduro's "kitchen" and family museum, has a ceiling decorated with coffee bags, light fixtures made from old wagon wheels, and walls dotted with family photographs. The tiny museum has a display on the processing of aloe vera that was done on island until the 1930s. Occasionally, Maduro serves iguana soup or goat stew, but usually fresh fish like grouper or shark served lightly fried in cake form called *funchi* or minced with tangy sauce, is central to the menu. A specialty is *bestia chiquito stoba*, or lamb stew in a Creole sauce. Entrees are reasonably priced because of the hearty portions, which include some of the best *pan bati* (pancake) on the island. Reservations are advised. Credit cards: A, DC, MC, V.

Old Cunucu House $$$ ★★★

Palm Beach 150, Oranjestad, ☎ *(297) 861666.*
Dinner: 6–10 p.m., entrées $17–$32. Closed: Sun.
Experience the Aruba of bygone days in this 1920s-style dwelling with a restaurant whose name means "old country" house. Tasty seafood is featured, as well as New York steaks and a few Aruban specialties. The atmosphere here is very relaxed and informal, amidst modern high-rise hotels that dwarf it. Happy hour is held at the rustic bar 5–6 p.m. daily with live and local entertainment on weekends. On Satur-

days the restaurant has an all-you-can-eat special for $16.95. Reservations recommended. Credit cards: A, DC, MC, V.

Papiamento $$$ ★★★★

Washington 61, Oranjestad, ☎ *(297) 864544.*
Dinner: 6–10:30 p.m., entrées $20–$40.

One of Aruba's "don't miss" experiences if only for the exquisite surroundings of a gracious private home. Lenie and Eduardo Ellis design their own handwritten menus, garnish their Continental dishes with fresh garden herbs, and have decorated the various dining areas with distinctive plantings and antiques. You can dine outside on the terrace by the pool or request a single honeymoon table. The continually changing menu usually contains favorites like chateaubriand for two, jumbo shrimp and Caribbean-style lobster. Pastry chef Lenie won a silver medal as "Pastry Chef of the Show" in "A Taste of the Caribbean" Culinary Competition. Reservations required. Credit cards: A, MC, V.

Que Pasa? $ ★★★

Schelpstraat 20, Oranjestad, ☎ *(297) 833872.*
Dinner: 6 p.m.–2 a.m., entrées $10–$18.

Hang with the locals at this funky cafe/art gallery in an eclectic Dutch house. The imaginative menu features dishes from all over the world—especially good are the seafood specialties and fresh fish. The portions are huge and the service friendly. The walls are adorned with colorful Haitian art; if one strikes your fancy, you can buy it on the spot. This fun spot is a real winner. Credit cards: MC, V.

Valentino's $$$ ★★★★

Palm Beach Road, ☎ *(297) 864777.* Associated hotel: *Caribbean Palm Village.*
Dinner: 6:30–8:30 p.m., entrées $17–$24. Closed: Sun.

Arubans like to come here to celebrate special occasions along with residents and guests at the chic Caribbean Palm Village Resort in Noord. The reason is delicious pastas—especially fettuccini with salmon—intimate tables and gracious, friendly service. Before dining, patrons can unwind with drinks, then ascend to the second-story courtyard restaurant overlooking the pool and cooled by evening breezes. Reservations required. Credit cards: A, DC, MC, V.

Aruba's duty-free status means great shopping, and the island has hundreds of stores offering everything from liquor to designer fashions. Most shops are open from 8 a.m. until 6 p.m., with a lunch hour from noon to 2 p.m. Stores in malls and shopping centers are open from 9:30 a.m. to 6 p.m. When cruise ships are in port, many stores open on Sunday and holidays. The capital city of Oranjestad is a shopper's haven, with many stores and boutiques lining the main streets. Savings of 20 to 30 percent can be found on items such as electronics, crystal, china, perfumes, liquor, designer fashions and jewelry; you'll find brand-names such as Gucci, Cartier, Waterford, Baccarat and Tiffany's. For arts and crafts, try the street Art Gallery held the last Saturday of the month from May to October in downtown Oranjestad (between the Protestant Church and The Cellar), and The Watapana "One Cool Festival," held each Thursday from 6:30–8 p.m., again from May to October, at the parking lot in front of Parliament in Oranjestad. American travelers are allowed up to $400 in duty free goods.

Aruba Directory

Arrival and Departure

American Airlines flies nonstop to Aruba's Queen Beatrix International Airport from New York's JFK Airport and Miami daily. The flight takes about 4.5 hours from NYC. **ALM**, **United** and **Air Aruba** fly nonstop from Miami to Aruba. If you book recommended accommodations and flights at the same time through American, you can receive substantial discounts. You can also save money by reserving your flight 14 days in advance, as well as flying Monday through Thursday. The Venezuela airline **VIASA** flies three times a week from Houston. Aruba's national carrier Air Aruba flies from Newark, Baltimore, Tampa and Miami. **Air Canada** offers flights from Toronto or Montreal to either Miami or New York, and then transfer to American or ALM. Aruba is also served by charters from Boston, Chicago, Cleveland, Detroit, Hartford, Los Angeles, Minneapolis, Philadelphia and Pittsburgh.

The departure tax is $10.

Business Hours

Shops open Monday–Saturday 8 a.m.–6 p.m. Alhambra Shopping Bazaar is open 5 p.m.–midnight. Banks open Monday–Friday 8 a.m.–noon and 1:30–4 p.m.

Climate

Dry and sunny, Aruba boasts average temperatures of 82 degrees F, though trade winds make the heat seem gentler. Mosquitoes get pesky in July and August, when it is less windy.

Documents

U.S. and Canadian citizens need to show some proof of citizenship—birth certificate, passport or voter's registration plus a photo ID; driver's license is not accepted. You must also show an ongoing or return ticket.

Electricity

Current runs at 110 volts, 60 cycles, as in the United States.

Getting Around

Taxis are plentiful, but the lack of meters requires firm negotiations with the driver before you take off. Drivers often know the city as well as private guides. Ask your hotel to recommend one. A dispatch office is also located at **Alham-**

bra Bazaar and Casino ☎ *(297) 8-21604.* You can also flag down taxis from the street. All Aruban taxi drivers are specially trained guides; an hour's tour will run about $30.

Arubans drive on the right-hand side of the road. Cars are easily rented on the island; you will need a valid U.S. or Canadian driver's license to rent a car; but according to the agency, you must be at least 21–25 years of age. You will save money if you rent from a local agency rather than from one of the well-known agencies. Among the best are **Hedwina Car Rental** ☎ *(297) 8-26442* and **Optima** ☎ *(297) 8-36263.* Avis, Budget and Hertz are all available at the airport.

Scooters are the best vehicle to tool around the island and are the most economical. You'll save money renting for two days or longer. **Ron's** ☎ *(297) 8-62090* and **George's** ☎ *(297) 8-25975* will deliver to the airport.

Inexpensive and reliable buses run hourly between the beach hotels and Oranjestad. The main terminal is located in South Zoutmanstraat, next to Fort Zoutman. A free Shopping Tour Bus departs hourly from 9:15 a.m.–3:15 p.m., starting at the Holiday Inn and making stops at all the major hotels on the way toward Oranjestad.

Language

Arubans are pleasantly multilingual. The official language is Dutch; also spoken are English, Spanish, Portuguese and the local dialect called Papiamento. French and German are also common.

Medical Emergencies

Horacio Oduber Hospital ☎ *(297) 8-74300* is a modern facility near Eagle Beach, with an efficient staff. Ask your hotel about doctors and dentists on call.

Money

The official currency is the Aruban florin (also called the guilder), written as Af or Afl. American dollars are accepted at most establishments, but it might be cheaper to pay in florins.

Telephone

To call Aruba from the U.S., dial ☎ *011+297+8* followed by the five-digit number. Forget calling home from your hotel—surcharges can hike the price of an overseas call to exorbitant levels. Instead, head for SETAR, the local company, with several locations in Oranjestad and near the high-rise hotels in Palm Beach. You can make phone calls using a card you purchase, and also send and receive faxes. Or you can buy a phone card, good at phone booths throughout the island.

Time

Aruba is on Atlantic standard time, year round.

Tipping and Taxes

Aruban custom is to charge a 10–15 percent service charge and 6 percent government tax. The total of these two charges is usually written into the "tax" slot on credit cards. If you want to give more for service, feel free, but it is not expected.

Tourist Information

Aruba Tourism Authority, *A. Shuttestraat 2, Oranjestad, Aruba, N.A.* ☎ *(297) 8-23777*, FAX *(297) 8-34702*. From the U.S. call ☎ *(800) 862-7822*.

When to Go

New Year's is celebrated with an explosion of fireworks set off by the hotels and serenaded by strolling musicians and singers. Carnival is a blowout event, which starts two weeks before Lent, and culminates with a Grand Parade on the Sunday preceding Lent. National Anthem and Flag Day on March 18 is celebrated by displays of national dancing and folklore. A weekly Bonbini show in the courtyard of the Fort Zoutman museum on Tuesdays from 6:30–10:30 p.m. also presents island folklore, song, and dance. The International Theatre Festival is an annual event; contact the tourist board for exact dates.

ARUBA HOTELS		RMS	RATES	PHONE	CR. CARDS
★★★★★	Aruba Sonesta Resort & Casino at Seaport Village	300	$145–$330	(800) 766-3782	A, D, DC, MC, V
★★★★★	Hyatt Regency Aruba Resort & Casino	360	$190–$495	(800) 233-1234	A, DC, MC, V
★★★★	Aruba Marriott Resort & Stellaris Casino	413	$150–$550	(800) 223-6388	A, MC, V
★★★	Americana Aruba Beach Resort & Casino	421	$200–$400	(800) 203-4475	A, MC, V
★★★	Amsterdam Manor Beach Resort	72	$110–$170	(800) 766-6016	A, DC, MC, V
★★★	Aruba Palm Beach Resort & Casino	187	$125–$235	(800) 345-2782	A, D, DC, MC, V
★★★	Bushiri "All Inclusive" Beach Resort	155	$210–$380	(297) 8-25216	A, MC, V
★★★	Costa Linda Beach Resort	155	$290–$489	(800) 223-6510	A, MC, V
★★★	Divi Aruba Beach Resort	203	$175–$370	(800) 554-2008	A, DC, MC, V
★★★	Playa Linda Beach Resort	194	$220–$350	(800) 346-7084	A, DC, MC, V
★★★	Wyndham Aruba Beach Resort & Casino	444	$205–$375	(800) 996-3426	A, D, DC, MC, V
★★	Best Western Manchebo Beach Resort	71	$110–$190	(800) 223-1108	A, DC, MC, V
★★	Bucuti Beach Resort	63	$120–$260	(297) 8-31100	A, MC, V
★★	Caribbean Palm Village	170	$115–$215	(800) 992-2015	A, DC, MC, V
★★	Holiday Inn Aruba Beach Resort & Casino	600	$170–$220	(800) 462-6868	A, DC, MC, V
★★	Mill Resort, The	200	$85–$235	(800) 992-2015	A, D, DC, MC, V

ARUBA

ARUBA HOTELS	RMS	RATES	PHONE	CR. CARDS
★★ Tamarin Aruba Beach Resort	236	$130–$185	(800) 554-2008	A, CB, MC, V
★ Dutch Village	97	$120–$415	(800) 367-3484	A, DC, MC, V

ARUBA RESTAURANTS	PHONE	ENTREE	CR.C ARDS
American Cuisine			
★★★ Charlie's Bar & Restaurant	(297) 8-45086	$18–$20	
★★★ Talk of the Town	(297) 8-23380	$8–$50	A, DC, MC, V
French Cuisine			
★★★★ Chez Mathilde	(297) 8-34968	$17–$43	A, D, DC, MC, V
★★★★ L'Escale	(297) 8-36000	$22–$30	A, DC, MC, V
International Cuisine			
★★★ De Olde Molen	(297) 8-66300	$15–$30	A, DC, MC, V
Italian Cuisine			
★★★★ Valentino's	(297) 8-64777	$17–$24	A, DC, MC, V
★★★ La Dolce Vita	(297) 8-65241	$12–$38	A, D, MC, V
Regional Cuisine			
★★★★ Mi Cushina	(297) 8-48335	$12–$24	A, DC, MC, V
★★★★ Papiamento	(297) 8-64544	$20–$40	A, MC, V
★★★ Old Cunucu House	(297) 8-61666	$17–$32	A, DC, MC, V
★★ Boonoonoonoos	(297) 8-31888	$4–$34	A, DC, MC, V
Seafood Cuisine			
★★★★ Buccaneer Restaurant	(297) 8-66172	$10–$23	A, D, DC, MC, V
★★★ Brisas del Mar	(297) 8-47718	$5–$29	A, MC, V
★★★ Que Pasa?	(297) 8-33872	$10–$18	MC, V

ARUBA

BARBADOS

Barbados lives up to its island paradise reputation.

Barbados at first glance is deceiving. From the air, the rolling fields of sugarcane seem to unfurl for miles with little to break the visual monotony. Your drive out of the airport lands you immediately on zipping roads bustling with traffic—Barbados is the second most populous island in the Eastern Caribbean. A pass through Bridgetown, as everyone does sooner or later, reminds you that this is a major commercial center and port within the Caribbean. Since none of these characteristics exactly shouts *island vacation*, it takes a few hours to adjust to the rhythms and nuances of this sophisticated, yet welcoming destination.

And adjust you probably will. It may be a particular stretch of sand that calls to you (the island seems positively girdled with beaches tucked into every possible limestone cove), or just the sight of the roiled and windblown Atlantic coastline at Bathsheba. It could be when you settle into a seat at one of Barbados' many fine dining establishments for a grand meal, or tuck into bed at one of the island's handful of exclusive hotels. Or it might simply be when you get lost in your rental car on the lattice of roads, pull over to reconnoiter with a map, and a Bajan pulls up alongside to offer directions (it happens every time). Despite independence in 1966, this friendly isle is veddy British—at least as much as it is West Indian—reflected in the afternoon tea served at many of the better resorts, in the passion for cricket and polo, in the prim respect for tradition and formality. Barbados even looks a bit like the English countryside. It's a dressy community—a light jacket and tie for men and a cocktail dress folded into a ladies' wardrobe may come in handy, unless it's Christmas or New Year's, in which case black tie is preferred at finer hotels.

The island has been cultivating tourists since the 1700s, and they've practiced the art long enough to get it right within the grand scheme of things. George Washington visited Barbados in 1751 with his tubercular brother Lawrence (the island's pure air gave it the title of "sanitarium of the West Indies" in the 19th century). Today, Barbados does a big business with conventions and cruise ship passengers, but vacationers—whether overnighting in the posh resorts of St. James or in the more moderate blocks of apartment-style hotels of Christ Church—are the priority. It's not an inexpensive island, and keeping up with the living standards at Bajan hotels, restaurants and sites can give a frugal traveler ulcers. Although the number of visitors to Barbados has been gradually increasing, American arrivals have been on a downswing for the past decade, and since 1994 are eclipsed by the number of UK arrivals for the first time. But, as one North American tourist who has visited Barbados 17 times said, "I don't come here to save money. I come because I'm guaranteed sun and warmth, a good beach and a clean room." Indeed, what many visitors like about Barbados is that the island delivers a reliable, hassle-free and polished vacation product, just as it has for so many years.

BEST BETS FOR...

Barbados (166 square miles) is the easternmost island of the Caribbean, positioned farther out in the Atlantic than its fellow Windwards; St. Vincent

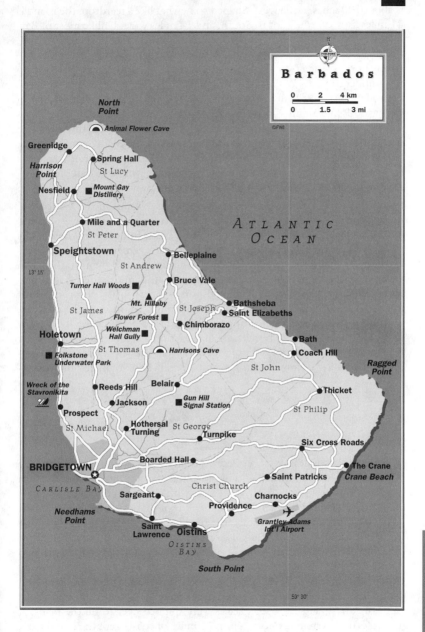

Barbados

0 2 4 km
0 1.5 3 mi

©FWI

North Point

Animal Flower Cave

Greenidge

Spring Hall

Harrison Point

St Lucy

Nesfield

Mount Gay Distillery

Mile and a Quarter

St Peter

Speightstown

St Andrew

Belleplaine

A T L A N T I C
O C E A N

13° 15'

Turner Hall Woods

Bruce Vale

Mt. Hillaby

St Joseph

Bathsheba
Saint Elizabeths

Flower Forest

Chimborazo

Welchman Hall Gully

Holetown

St James

St Thomas

Harrisons Cave

Bath

Coach Hill

Ragged Point

Folkstone Underwater Park

St John

Wreck of the Stavronikita

Reeds Hill

Belair

Thicket

Prospect

Jackson

Gun Hill Signal Station

St Philip

St Michael

Hothersal Turning

St George

Turnpike

Six Cross Roads

BRIDGETOWN

Boarded Hall

CARLISLE BAY

Christ Church

Saint Patricks

The Crane
Crane Beach

Needhams Point

Sargeant

Charnocks

Providence

Saint Lawrence

Oistins

Grantley Adams Int'l Airport

OISTINS BAY

South Point

59° 30'

is about 100 miles to the west. Shaped somewhat like a teardrop, the island is 21 miles from North Point to South, and 14 miles wide. Unlike most of Barbados' neighbors, this is a limestone massif rather than a volcanic island, pockmarked with caves and collapsed sinkholes that have formed in the relatively porous stone over the years (the island's water needs are pumped up from underground). With a highest point of just 1116 feet above sea level, the rolling terrain is gentle, making the Bajan climate more temperate than many (no lofty summits to lure rain-producing clouds). Most of Barbados was cleared of its forests for sugarcane production long ago, though some deep ravines contain dense pockets of mature trees. The slow erosion of the limestone has produced the island's fine beaches, and a number of scenic vistas, particularly in the area of Bathsheba, where the wind and water has crafted abrupt cliffs and turrets, engulfed by sand and waves.

Barbados is one of the most densely populated islands in the Caribbean, though the most intense development has been focused on the western and southern coasts, and at the junction of these areas, Bridgetown, the island's capital and one of the Caribbean's major business centers. The island is divided into 11 parishes, and since most establishments use them (rather than a town) for location, it helps to have a map that identifies their position as you explore the island. The two that visitors will particularly come into contact with are St. James, which occupies the middle portion of the western, Caribbean coast (also known as the Gold Coast, and not because of the color of the sand), and Christ Church, which takes up the southern coast between Bridgetown and the airport. Within these two parishes are more than 90 percent of Barbados' accommodations, and a good chunk of its restaurants.

History

When the Portuguese explorer Pedro a Campos discovered Barbados in the 17th century, he found the island uninhabited. As the sailor took in the lush tropical surroundings, he spotted fig trees with clumps of bushy roots hanging from branches that resembled beards. From that came the name Barbados, which in Portuguese means "the bearded ones." Long before the first European contact, Arawak Indians were said to be living on the island, but they were long gone by the time of the first British expedition in 1625. Two years later, 80 British settlers under the leadership of Captain John Powell settled at Jamestown (later renamed Holetown). Soon, conditions proved highly favorable for tobacco, cotton and sugarcane production, and thousands of African and European slaves were shipped over to till the fields. A strong fortress system (26 forts along 21 miles of coast) kept the island from

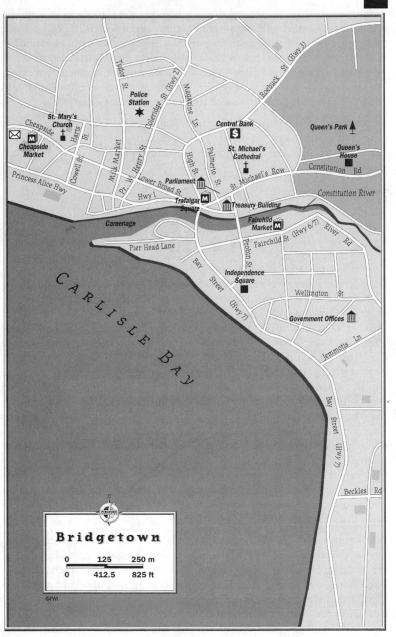

Bridgetown

| 0 | 125 | 250 m |
| 0 | 412.5 | 825 ft |

©FWI

invasion, and Barbados became the only island in the Caribbean to be under uninterrupted British rule for more than three centuries. In 1937, economic problems caused by the fluctuating price of sugar led to demonstrations in Bridgetown, which resulted in the establishment of a British Royal Commonwealth to the West Indies—a gesture that proved instrumental in bringing about social and political reform, including universal adult suffrage in 1951. Fifteen years later, Barbados received its full sovereignty.

Today Barbados is a British Commonwealth nation with a parliamentary system of government headed by an appointed governor-general and an elected prime minister. British influence extends to the courts, laws, language and place names.

People

Barbados' population totals some 265,000 people, most descended from West Africa (slavery was abolished here in 1834), with a generous sprinkling of descendants from Great Britain. It is home to more centenarians than any other Caribbean island. Though about 100 religions are represented on the island, the population is primarily Anglican. Despite independence since 1966 (Barbados is officially a British Commonwealth nation), the Queen of Great Britain still serves as the Queen of Barbados, and government is a democratic parliamentary system headed by an appointed governor-general and an elected prime minister. Many locals retain a more British accent than West Indian, and continue to embrace English customs like afternoon tea and a love for cricket and polo. The literacy rate—more than 98 percent—is among the highest in the world, yet citizens possess a fresh mix of Caribbean informality and British manners. The population is truly friendly and unassuming and will patiently answer a tourist's questions while throwing in a bit of sincere hospitality at the same time. However, note that many natives are familiar only with the area of the island that they were raised in—for instance, it's not uncommon to meet an adult from Christ Church who has never been to the north of the island.

Although Barbados boasts a much higher standard of living than is common within the region, and a large population of middle-class blacks, there are racial divisions that run deeper than the casual eye might discern. Though sugar production and light manufacturing are important, more than 10,000 Bajans are directly employed by tourism, the island's biggest industry—Barbados hosts more than 400,000 overnight visitors annually, and almost a half-million cruise ship passengers. But in many ways, sugar, and its by-product, is still the life blood of the island. It is said that when the prime minister identifies himself with a particular rum, for a Bajan to drink that brand is to show support for the party. But mostly, rum is tradition, and this is an island built on its past—the word *rum* even originated here. Everyone knows the world's oldest brand, Mount Gay, but slip into one of Barbados' thousand-or-so tiny rum shops and knock back a few shots of the local favorite, Barbados Gold, and you'll take in a real Bajan experience.

Beaches

All Bajan beaches are open to the public, including those abutting the high-priced hotels. Much of the Christ Church coastline east of Bridgetown is a continuous ribbon of sand, but the best spots include **Accra Beach** (aka Rockley), which is frequented by many locals, has a car park and gentle waves. A short distance east is **Sandy Beach**, at the hotel of the same name, a photogenic cove of calm water that is good for families. Just past the South Point Lighthouse is **Silver Sands**, a velvety stretch of sand that usually provides ideal windsurfing conditions. Past the airport, the beaches become more dramatic. **Foul Bay** is a long spread of sand, usually uncrowded and with no facilities, while a little farther is **Crane Beach**, one of the island's most photographed spots, backed by dramatic bluffs that are foundation to an old hotel. The hotel charges a day-use fee to enter the beach from its stairs, so proceed just past it to the small road that leads down to the beach (parking can be a problem). The beaches at Sam Lord's Castle are good, and just beyond is **Bottom Bay**, a real looker with waves, palms and limestone cliffs. The island's Atlantic coastline has a number of attractive beaches, but most are not considered safe for swimming. The most picturesque is the several-mile stretch along windswept **Bathsheba**, where the rugged coast is lined with both sand and improbable limestone towers—though you'll see surfers in winter months, check around before entering the water for a swim.

The island's Caribbean coast is famous for calm, placid waters that are ideal for bathing. Starting in Bridgetown, a local favorite is **Carlisle Bay**, with lots of yachties and snorkeling (or diving) over several wrecks. Heading north, **Paynes Bay** is right next to the road with watersports and eating facilities nearby; you can walk to the beach at Sandy Lane from here. Just past Holetown is the St. James Church and **Church Point**, where activities and food are available from hotels. A little further up the coast is **Mullins Bay**, with outdoor showers and a good non-hotel restaurant/bar (parking is in the lot across the road). Just beyond Speightstown is busy **Heywoods Beach**, backed by the

Fielding

THE CARIBBEAN

BEST OF BARBADOS

Known as the "Gateway to the West Indies," Barbados retains an aura of British civility. This tiny island encompasses only 166 square miles but offers an array of sights, including military garrisons, rum factories and lush gardens, as well as caves, mahogany forests, and panoramic hilltop views.

North Point

Farley Hill Park

Near the Wildlife Reserve, Farley Hill is home to the ruins of a once-grand plantation house. From the crest of the hill, you can see much of the east coast.

St. Lucy

Mount Gay

Speightstown

St. Peter

Turner's Hall Woods

St. Andrew

Mullins Bay

St. Joseph

The Barbados Wildlife Reserve

Observe the Barbados green monkey in its native habitat while exploring this protected section of mahogany forest near Farley Hill Park. Also look for iguanas, Cayman tortoises and shy Brockett deer.

St. James

Cane Field

St. Thomas

Mount Gay Visitors Centre

Barbados-produced rum is world-renowned. At the Mount Gay Rum Visitors Centre near Bridgetown, you can tour the rum-making facilities, then sample some of the famous "liquid gold" for yourself.

St. Michael

Bridgetown

From St. Michael's Cathedral to the statue of Lord Nelson in Trafalgar Square, this historic area is testimony to British influence. The castle-like Parliament Buildings are constructed of coral-stone. Stroll beneath the dramatic Independence Arch.

BARBADOS

Welchman Hall Gully

Part of the same cave system as Harrison's Cave, this collapsed cavern was planted with exotic flowers and greenery beginning in 1860. Today, the one-mile gully is home to bamboo, ferns, citrus and spice trees. Limestone formations create a dream-like backdrop.

Harrison Cave

Nearly a mile long, this limestone cave was first mentioned in records in 1796, but remained undisturbed until 1976, when it was "rediscovered." Bring along your camera (flash photography permitted) and ride on an electric tram to see the shimmering cave formations and the 40-foot subterranean waterfall.

Gun Hill

Serving as a military lookout since 1697, this 700-foot high hill offers visitors a bird's eye view. Climb the stone-built Signal Station, then admire the huge stone lion, carved from a single block of rock in 1868.

St. John

Francia Plantation House

One of the best examples of a Caribbean plantation house, this elegant mansion is decorated with antique European furnishings, china and silver. The surrounding gardens feature terraces, fountains and "ferneries."

St. George

Grantley Adams International Airport

Bridgetown

Oistins

South Point

The Garrison

Carlisle Bay

First fortified in 1705, the Garrison includes the former military prison, built around 1815, now the home of the Barbados Museum. Don't miss the outdoor exhibit of cannons, which includes a rare Commonwealth gun made in 1650.

Almond Beach Resort, and the last good beach on this coast; you can enter it from a small road at the end of town.

Industrious Barbados has long been preoccupied with maintaining its commercial needs, sometimes at the expense of the marine life lying just off its shores. Pollution, dynamite fishing and anchors have taken their toll on the inner reefs, so it should be no surprise that the best underwater attractions the island offers are of the unnatural kind: wrecks. Fortunately, a "Rescue the Reefs" program was instituted by an association of local dive shops in 1994 and their efforts are bearing fruit: permanent moorings and a marine park in Carlisle Bay are among the initial successes. There are rolling plains of coral along the west and south coasts, and the outer reefs are intact, but divers should not expect extensive formations or marine life. Barbados' coral structures tend to lie flat, rather than producing the caves and caverns found on other islands.

But, if you come for the wrecks, there are a number to hold your interest, including the massive *Stavronikita*, a freighter now developing a forest of black coral on its decks. Visitors who come to the island in fall may be able to dive the pristine and beautiful northern coast, which is otherwise fairly inaccessible due to rough water. Sharks are rare, island-wide, and this includes at misnamed Shark Reef. The inner fringe reef averages 40 to 60 feet deep and provides decent breeding ground, particularly along the southern coast, while some of the best diving (and snorkeling) lies right off Bridgetown in **Carlisle Bay**. Barbados has a recompression chamber available at St. Anne's Fort. Snorkelers can visit the *Pamir*, a 150-foot vessel resting in shallow waters, easily visible from the shoreline near Mullins Bay.

Dive Shops

Coral Isle Divers

Bridgetown; ☎ *(246) 434-8377 or (800) 513-5840.*
PADI-affiliated with courses through Divemaster, but serves many beginners. Dives inner and outer reefs from a 40-foot catamaran with full amenities; north and east coast dives in fall as weather permits. Two-tank dive, $70, including tanks and weights.

Dive Boat Safari

Bridgetown; ☎ *(246) 427-4350.*
PADI five-star facility; provides free introductory classes in the Hilton pool; resort courses, $45 (including easy wreck dive). Three dives daily and snorkeling trips to Carlisle Bay. Two-tank dive, $50; snorkeling trips, $15.

The Dive Shop

Aquatic Gap; ☎ *(246) 426-9947.*
PADI- and NAUI-affiliated and the oldest shop on the island (since 1965). Dives Carlisle Bay, where divers can pick up 18th-century bottles, as well as bigger wrecks and reefs. Resort course, $50. Two-tank dive $55.

Exploresub

St. Lawrence; ☎ *(246) 435-6542.*
Island's only PADI five-star facility, includes an Instructor Development Center. Organizes underwater weddings, providing staff as witnesses. Dives south coast reefs and wrecks. One-tank dive $35; two-tank dives $70.

Hightide Watersports

Sandy Lane Hotel, Holetown; ☎ *(246) 432-1311, ext. 264.*
Works with smaller groups of six to eight, focusing on the northern half of the west coast. PADI facility teaching most specialty courses including underwater photography; uses a 36-foot-long dive boat with full amenities. Two-tank dive, $65. Resort course, $70.

Walking is a beloved pastime for many locals. Indeed, the activity may remind visitors of country excursions in England: rolling green hills and breezy coastlines with regularly scheduled walking tours. Thigh-challenging hikes are at a minimum; the island is one of the most densely populated countries in the world, its fields extensively cultivated and, owing to the limestone-based topography, the hillsides slope gently toward the muted summit of **Mount Hillaby** (1116 feet). Be sure to connect up with the National Trust ☎ *(246) 426-2421*, which organizes free Sunday walks. These depart at 6 a.m. and 3:30 p.m. year-round, average three hours and provide visitors a chance to mingle with locals. The excursions are so well attended they break up the group into three speeds, from casual (termed "stop and stare," and guided with an educational p.o.v.) to breakneck. Several dedicated forest reserves (that charge admission) provide Barbados' most scenic natural environments, although solitude is probably best located on the broad east coast.

The capital city of Bridgetown is a major free port, which means shopping, and lots of it, along bustling Board Street, where prices are often 30 to 50

percent below those in the States in the tony, well-tended stores and boutiques. The city—and it is indeed one—is also home to several historic structures, including **St. Michael's Cathedral**, said to have been visited by George Washington. Dotted among Bridgetown's many modern buildings are Victorian Gothic structures and small colonial buildings with fanciful wrought-iron balconies. While in the city, check out the **Barbados Museum**, a former military prison turned into a fascinating look at island life in the 19th century.

Morgan Lewis Mill, Barbados

Beyond Bridgetown, Barbados provides a multitude of sightseeing opportunities. A driving tour of the island can be accomplished in one day, but this will allow little time for sightseeing; it's better to spread your island tour over two or three relaxed days. Renting a car is the easiest way to experience the island's museums, gardens and historical sights, and if you are planning an extensive tour of **Barbados National Trust** properties, most of which are listed below, you may want to consider a Heritage Passport. The full passport provides a 50 percent discount to the 16 National Trust sites for $35, or a mini passport to five sites is available for $12, plus tax (children under 12 are admitted free); the passports are available from any of the individual sites. From January through April, the National Trust also has a weekly open house program, allowing visitors to tour some of the private homes of historical importance; Wednesdays from 2:30 to 5:30 p.m. ☎ *(246) 426-2421.*

Barbados' limestone foundation has created several caves of note. **Harrison's Cave** is the most famous, and visitors experience the cave via a 20-minute electric tramride that winds down into the cave's depths. Spelunkers may be happier with nearby **Coles Cave** which, though well-explored, has not been turned into a ride and allows for a more personal experience. Bring a flashlight; ask for directions to Cole's at the Harrison gift shop. Finally, an underground experience of a different nature is provided at the **Animal Flower Cave** at the northern tip of Barbados. The caves are at sea level and the titular animals are wispy sea plumes that are found at water level throughout the caverns. Wear shoes with good tread as the rocks inside the cave are slippery.

Historical Sites

Francia Plantation   ★★★
Near Gun Hill, St. George, ☎ *(246) 429-0474.*
Hours open: 10 a.m.–4 p.m.
This family estate, still home to descendants of the original owner, has been designated a house of architectural interest by the Barbados National Trust. It provides an authentic look at old Barbados, particularly with its blend of European and Caribbean styles; the gardens surrounding the house are worth exploring. Also check out the **Sunbury Plantation Home** in St. Philip ☎ *(246) 423-6270,* a 300-year-old great house filled with fine antiques. General admission: $4.

Grenade Hall Signal Station   ★★★
Farley Hill, St. Peter, ☎ *(246) 422-8826.*
Hours open: 10 a.m.–5 p.m.
Built in the early 1800s, Grenade Hall is one of six towering signal stations that were erected around Barbados to relay intelligence information and other messages via arm signals with flags. Restored by the Barbados Wildlife Reserve in 1992, the tower now houses detailed exhibits on the historical signaling system. Upstairs are wonderful panoramas and telescopes that give line of sight views to the other towers. Don't leave without exploring the surrounding forest, where a coral stone walkway winds languidly through trees and rock outcrops. A visit to Grenade Hall can easily be combined with the Barbados Wildlife Reserve, a short stroll away.

Gun Hill Signal Station   ★★★
Highway 4, St. George, ☎ *(246) 429-1358.*
Hours open: 9 a.m.–5 p.m.
This 1818 signal station was the central hub of communications used by the British Army when semaphores—visual signaling by hand-held flags—were the Ma Bell of their day. Even if you're not into military history, the views from atop the highland are worth the trip; if the site appeals to you, also visit Grenade Hall Signal Station, inland from Speightstown in the north. Also check out the lion carved out of stone, at the base of Gun Hill—it's meant to represent the strength of Great Britain circa the mid-19th century. General admission: $4.

Morgan Lewis Sugar Windmill   ★★★★
Highway 2, St. Andrew, ☎ *(246) 426-2421.*
Hours open: 9 a.m.–5 p.m.
This historic spot, owned by Barbados' National Trust since 1963, provides a splendid example of the windmills used to process sugarcane—it ground cane until 1944, the last mill on the island to cease operation. It is also the region's last fully intact mill, and in 1996 the World Monuments Fund selected 200-year-old Morgan

Lewis as one of the 100 Most Endangered Sites in the world; a restoration project began in 1997. Nice views of the Scotland District. General admission: $3.

Old Synagogue

Synagogue Lane, Bridgetown, ☎ (246) 426-5792.
Hours open: 9 a.m.–4 p.m.
Built by Jews from Brazil in 1654, this synagogue is the second oldest in North America. It was partially destroyed by hurricane and rebuilt to its present state in 1833. The grounds include a cemetery, still used today, with graves of early Jewish settlers from as far back as the 1630s.

St. Nicholas Abbey ★★★

Cherry Tree Hill, St. Peter, ☎ (246) 422-8725.
Hours open: 10 a.m.–3:30 p.m.
This Jacobean mansion is one of Barbados' oldest structures, dating back to 1650, though it was actually an abbey only in the mind of a former owner, who dubbed it so in the 1800s. Two hundred acres of sugarcane surround the great house of wood and stone. General admission: $3.

Museums and Exhibits

Barbados Museum

St. Ann's Garrison, St. Michael, ☎ (246) 427- 201.
Hours open: 9 a.m.–5 p.m.
This unusually fine museum, housed in a former military prison, traces the island's history from prehistoric times to the present. Good exhibits on natural history, West Indian maps and arts and the slave trade. The grounds also include a decent gift shop and an excellent cafe. General admission: $5.

Parks and Gardens

Andromeda Gardens ★★★

Bathsheba, on boundary of St. Joseph and St. John, ☎ (246) 433-9384.
Hours open: 9 a.m.–5 p.m.
This unique spot encompasses eight acres of private gardens set into oceanfront cliffs; the name Andromeda comes from the way the house and gardens are "chained" to the rock, like the Greek maiden of legend. The emphasis is on unusual plants from around the world, and they have those aplenty, hundreds of orchids, hibiscus and palm varieties—plus a babbling brook winding throughout. General admission: $6.

Barbados Wildlife Reserve ★★★★

Farley Hill, St. Peter, ☎ (246) 422-8826.
Hours open: 10 a.m.–5 p.m.
Located in a four-acre mahogany forest, this reserve is a project of the Barbados Primate Research Centre, which focuses on the conservation of the Barbados Green Monkey. But there are lots of animals that roam the grounds in freedom (though the large resident python is, happily for visitors, caged). Among the attractions are caimans, mongoose, otters, Brocket deer, iguana, hyrax, tortoises and a number of bird species in the walk-in aviary. There's an Information and Education Centre and snackbar, and feeding time for the animals is 4 p.m. daily. General admission: $10.

Farley Hill Park ★★★

Farley Hill, St. Peter.
Hours open: 8:30 a.m.–6 p.m.
Very rugged grounds, splendid trees and the ruins of a once-grand plantation house mark this picturesque national park. A great place for a picnic following a visit to the Wildlife Reserve and Grenade Hall Signal Station next door. General admission: $2.

Flower Forest

Highway 2, St. Joseph, ☎ *(246) 433-8152.*
Hours open: 9 a.m.–5 p.m.
Set on an old sugar plantation in the scenic Scotland District, this park encompasses 50 acres of flowering trees and shrubs growing wild—visitors are encouraged to step off the pathways for up-close observations. General admission: $6.

Welchman Hall Gully ★★★

Highway 2, St. Thomas, ☎ *(246) 438-6671.*
Hours open: 9 a.m.–5 p.m.
A peaceful oasis owned by the Barbados National Trust, with acres of labeled trees and flowers, and a green monkey or two. The gully itself is a collapsed portion of the Harrison Cave system, and now shelters huge older trees at its base and a thriving forest of bamboo. The breadfruit trees are said to be descended from seeds brought by Captain Bligh. It's a serene place to cool off. General admission: $5.

Tours

Animal Flower Cave ★★★

North Point, St. Lucy, ☎ *(246) 439-8797.*
Hours open: 9 a.m.–4 p.m.
The small sea anemones that inhabit this shoreside cave are known locally as animal flowers—they look like pretty flowers, until you touch them and they blink shut. The atmospheric cave formed through sea erosion at the junction of two layers of coral: one 126,000 years old, the other almost a half-million years old. A guide will take you down to see the delicate creatures. General admission: $3.

Atlantis Submarines ★★★

The Shallow Draught, Bridgetown, ☎ *(246) 436-8929.*
Hours open: 9 a.m.–6 p.m.
The perfect way to see the world below, without getting wet, is aboard an Atlantis submarine, which takes its passengers in air-conditioned comfort some 150 feet beneath the water's surface. Fifty minutes of the two-hour excursion are underwater, and the highlight is the sighting of a shipwreck. Recommended for everyone but the claustrophobic, though the price is quite steep: $80 for adults, $40 for children. Atlantis also offers a less expensive surface excursion aboard the Seatrec, which has underwater viewing windows to observe a shallow reef structure ($35 for adults, $17.50 for children).

Banks Brewery Tour ★★

Bridgetown, ☎ *(246) 429-2113.*
A tour of one of the region's major beer producers is offered by the Banks Breweries. You'll see the computerized brewing facility and its huge stainless steel vats, the bottling hall that fills up to a quarter-million bottles per day and, of course, a sam-

pling room. Tours conducted on Tuesday and Thursday only; call ahead for reservations. General admission: $3.

Guided Tours

Various locations.

If you're itching to see Barbados but would rather leave the driving to someone else, contact one of these tour operators. **Highland Outdoor Tours** ☎ *(246) 438-8069* provides a plantation tour in a tractor-drawn, open-air jitney, as well as eco-adventures on horseback, mountain bike or foot. **Margaret Leacock** ☎ *(246) 425-0099* offers customized tours, while **VIP Tour Services** ☎ *(246) 429-4617* gives tailor-made tours in air-conditioned Mercedes Benz cars.

Harrison's Cave   ★★★★

Highway 2, St. Thomas, ☎ *(246) 438-6640.*
Hours open: 9 a.m.–4 p.m.

Barbados' biggest tourist attraction, these extensive limestone caverns are unique to the Caribbean. Although the caves were discovered 200 years ago, they weren't really explored until their rediscovery in 1970. Discreet lighting illuminates the mile-long passages, which include slowly forming stalactites and stalagmites (quick—do you remember which drops from the ceiling and which rises from the floor?). Don a hard hat (more for drama than necessity) and ride an electric tram through the immense caverns, replete with waterfalls and streams. Reservations are recommended. General admission: $8.

Mount Gay Rum Tour   ★★

Spring Garden Highway, Bridgetown, ☎ *(246) 425-9066.*
Hours open: 9 a.m.–4 p.m.

Immerse yourself in the history and production secrets of Caribbean rum. A short audio-visual presentation is followed by a 45-minute tour. Complimentary rum tastings conclude the experience. General admission: $5.

Sports

As on most Caribbean islands, watersports reign supreme; Barbados is especially good for windsurfing between November and May, when the trade winds make for perfect conditions along the south coast; Silver Sands is particularly challenging for intermediate to advanced surfers. Contact the **Barbados Windsurfing Club** at ☎ *(246) 428-6001* for details. With big swells landing on the east coast almost year-round, Barbados is one of the few legitimate surfing destinations in the Eastern Caribbean. The best action is found in **Bathsheba** (where the Barbados International Surfing Championship is held early November), although **South Point** and **Needham's Point** (just outside Bridgetown) are also good spots. Waves die down for the summer, with winter providing the best rides.

Bicycling

With more than 800 miles of paved roads, Barbados presents a multitude of cycling options off the busy west and south coasts—the area around Bathsheba provides beautiful coastal hills and vistas of rugged Atlantic beaches. Barbados has a dedicated cycling club and world-class riders; contact Mario or Larry Williams at **M.A. Williams Rentals** in Hastings for more information ☎ *(246) 427-3955*. Other rental outfits include **Club Mistral** in Maxwell, Christ Church (aka Windsurf Village) ☎ *(246) 428-7277* and **Sunshine Bikes** in Husbands, St. James ☎ *(246) 438-2783;* the latter also provides island tours by bike.

Golf

Golfers have a choice of links to choose from, offering all levels of play, scenery and price. The best is the new **Royal Westmoreland Golf and Country Club**, a championship course offering 18 holes on 290 manicured acres designed by Robert Trent Jones II. A succession of spectacular "feature holes," grand ocean views, and a high level of upkeep makes this one of the region's finest, against a backdrop of the island's newest mansions. Greens fees, which include a cart and unlimited use of the driving range, range from $75 to $90 in the off season, $110–$145 in the winter; you must be staying at a resort that has access to tee times ☎ *(246) 422-4653*. Also noteworthy is **Sandy Lane Golf Course**, a par 72, 18-hole course with its famous short 7th hole (the green drops 100 feet in 135 yards that face the Caribbean). Sandy Lane is open to guests of other hotels; $120 for a round of 18 holes ☎ *(246) 432-4563*. Two nine-hole courses at a pair of all-inclusive resorts are also available to non-guests: **Almond Beach Village** ☎ *(246) 422-4900* and **Club Rockley** ☎ *(246) 435-7873*.

Horseback riding

Trail rides from 75 minutes to four hours on handsome horses are available from **Caribbean International Riding Centre** ☎ *(246) 433-1453*, while **Brighton Riding Stables** in St. Michael specializes in beach rides and other scenic excursions ☎ *(246) 425-9381*.

Windsurfing

Rent a windboard from the **Silver Sands Resort** (near the airport) for $20 an hour, $40 per half day, or partake in a lesson ☎ *(246) 428-6001*. Also check out **Windsurf Village** in Welches, an entire hotel devoted to the sport ☎ *(246) 428-9095*.

Where to Stay

Fielding's Highest Rated Hotels in Barbados

★★★★★	Glitter Bay	$235–$475
★★★★★	Royal Pavilion	$275–$615
★★★★★	Sandy Lane	$525–$1290
★★★★	Cobblers Cove Hotel	$170–$800
★★★★	Coral Reef Club	$135–$1020
★★★★	Sandpiper, The	$145–$800
★★★	Colony Club Hotel	$320–$704
★★★	Settler's Beach Villa Hotel	$175–$500
★★★	Tamarind Cove Hotel	$290–$636
★★★	Treasure Beach Hotel	$160–$650

Fielding's Rooms With a View in Barbados

★★	Crane Beach Hotel	$100–$270
★★★★★	Royal Pavilion	$275–$615
★★	Kingsley Club	$79–$101
★★★	Barbados Hilton	$139–$285

Fielding's Best Value Hotels in Barbados

★★	Woodville Beach Apartments	$65–$150
★★★	Casuarina Beach Club	$90–$215
★★★	Sam Lord's Castle	$130–$225
★★	Kingsley Club	$79–$101
★★	Beachcomber Apartments	$70–$160

With about 5600 rooms to choose from, Barbados offers both a handful of the Caribbean's finest resorts, along with a generous sampling of mid-range properties (frequently apartment complexes that have been turned into hotels). Almost all of the island's rooms can be found in one of two general areas: the Gold Coast that runs up the Caribbean side from north of Bridgetown to Speightstown, and the south coast of the island, between Bridgetown and the airport. Barbados' very finest accommodations are located along the chic Gold Coast, as well as many of the better restaurants. Less expensive rooms are generally found on the south coast, in the parish of Christ Church (each hotel listing provides the name of the community the hotel is located in, followed by its parish); this is also where many of the nightlife and watersports activities are concentrated. There are a few places that don't fall into these two areas: **Sam Lord's Castle** and **Crane Beach Hotel**, both a few miles northwest of the airport, and the **Kingsley Beach Club**, located amid the splendor of Bathsheba.

Virtually every hotel on Barbados lies on or within a few hundred feet of a beach. Also note that on Barbados, where nonmotorized watersports are included in rates, this usually means waterskiing as well (though not scuba).

Hotels and Resorts

If the very best is a priority, Barbados can provide it—the only question is what style of luxury you want to be enveloped by. **Glitter Bay** and its sibling **Royal Pavilion** are large resort facilities with fabulous gardens and provide well for Americans, while the starched glory of European decadence shines at **Sandy Lane** (it also flaunts what is perhaps the single heftiest rate card in the Caribbean). Three smaller properties deliver more personalized attention and considerably more Bajan charm: **Cobbler's Cove**, **Sandpiper Inn** and **Coral Reef Club** are lovely island retreats, each with its own unique identity—the latter will undergo a major renovation during summer 1998. These hotels, plus **Settler's Beach**, have their own exclusive umbrella organization, the **Elegant Resorts of Barbados**, and a central reservation number ☎ *(800) 535-3426*.

Note that a number of the more expensive properties have a mandatory MAP package in the winter, locking you in to their meal plan. The more generous hotels will provide a dine-around option that allows you to sample the food at other comparable hotels. Also noteworthy is that, at some hotels, the month of January is not considered high season, but a mini-shoulder period of sorts, with somewhat reduced rates (compared to Christmas and the February–March time frame).

Barbados Hilton　　　　　　　　　**$139–$285**　　　　　　★★★

Needhams Point, Bridgetown, ☎ *(800) 445-8667, (246) 426-0200, FAX (246) 436-8946.*

Single: $139–$269. Double: $163–$285. Suites: $284–$520.

A fairly safe choice—but don't expect much Caribbean flavor at this six-story business hotel just outside Bridgetown. Surrounded by nice beaches and near an oil refinery, this busy spot has the modern conveniences you'd expect from a Hilton-managed property—plus lots of conventioneers running around in nametags. The pool and beach are excellent, and there's a health club and tennis courts on-site, as well as an old British fort for exploring. Accommodations are tasteful if a bit frumpy, and service is professional. 184 rooms. Credit cards: A, MC, V.

Cobblers Cove Hotel $170–$1500   ★★★★

Speightstown, St. Peter, ☎ *(800) 890-6060, (246) 422-2291, FAX (246) 422-1460.*
E-mail: cobblers@caribsurf.com.
Single: $170–$470. Double: $220–$800. Suites Per Day: $640–$1500.

Built on the site of a former British fort, this lovely and intimate all-suite hotel keeps guests pampered, earning its reputation as one of the island's treasures. The beautifully decorated suites come with a wet bar, a living area and balcony or patio—among the most livable "standard" guest rooms we've seen. The *creme de la creme* is a pair of immense, fantasy suites—Camelot and Colleton—that are positioned above the restaurant/bar area. These deluxe units are decorated in an English style with marble floors and rich, colorful fabrics; each has a private sun terrace with a plunge pool (one of which is roof-top). The lush tropical grounds include a tennis court, pool and a fine beach; nonmotorized watersports and waterskiing are included in the rates. The restaurant is one of Barbados' best, and helped the hotel secure membership in the Relais and Chateaux organization. Children under 12 welcome, except mid-January through mid-March; winter rates reflect mandatory MAP (dining exchange program is available). 40 rooms. Credit cards: MC, V.

Colony Club Hotel $320–$704   ★★★

Porters, St. James, ☎ *(800) 223-6510, (246) 422-2335, FAX (246) 422-0667.*
Single: $320–$647. Double: $378–$704.

The priciest of the four hotels operating under the St. James banner, Colony Club is comprised of a series of two- and three-story buildings with several architectural styles. Rooms and junior suites have standard-issue tropical decor, with balcony or patio, minibar and air conditioning. The centerpiece for the resort is an ambling series of free-form swimming pools that lead from a waterfall at one end of the resort down to the beach—patios of the ten Luxury Poolside rooms each have their own access to these channels. Non-motorized watersports are complimentary, as is tennis, a fitness center and the shuttle that runs guests into town or to the other three hotels. A nice, quiet spot located between Holetown and Glitter Bay on the toniest stretch of the Gold Coast. The mandatory MAP rate is shown, and includes VAT and service; children under 12 not permitted in February. 98 rooms. Credit cards: MC, V.

Coral Reef Club $135–$1020   ★★★★

Holetown, St. James, ☎ *(800) 223-1108, (246) 422-2372, FAX (246) 422-1776.*
Website: www.barbados.org/hotels/coral.htm. E-mail: coral@caribnet.net.
Closed Date: April 25–October 10, 1998.
Single: $135–$680. Double: $205–$1020.

Flawlessly run by the O'Hara family for four decades, this fine favorite is made up of small but spacious cottages scattered about 12 acres of lovingly landscaped gardens. The cottages come equipped with refrigerators, hair dryers, a small library of paperbacks and air conditioning. A newer two-story wing holds sumptuous junior suites with expansive bathrooms. Non-motorized watersports are included, two pools and tennis courts are a short stroll from your room; no children under 12 in February. Winter rates reflect mandatory MAP (a fine restaurant, and a dine-around option is offered). Long one of Barbados' very best, the hotel will be undergoing a major renovation in 1998. 71 rooms. Credit cards: A, MC, V.

Crane Beach Hotel $100–$270 ★★

Crane Beach, St. Philip, ☎ *(246) 423-6220, FAX (246) 423-5343.*
Single: $100–$270. Double: $100–$270. Suites Per Day: $175–$425.
Set on a sheer bluff overlooking a gorgeous beach, the Crane has the Hollywoodish feel of a private estate, though as Barbados' oldest resort, a facelift is in order. All rooms are studded with antiques (only two have air conditioning); most have kitchenettes. The Roman-style pool and a statue-punctuated courtyard add a delightfully regal touch, particularly considering the dramatic beach backdrop. There's one restaurant on property, otherwise everything else is a bit of a drive. Novice swimmers beware: the surf can be rough. 18 rooms. Credit cards: A, DC, D, MC, V.

Discovery Bay Hotel $130–$360 ★★★

Holetown, St. James, ☎ *(800) 223-6510, (246) 432-1301, FAX (246) 432-2553.*
Single: $130–$325. Double: $185–$360.
This plantation-style hotel, set on four tropical acres just beyond Holetown, consists of two-story structures around an attractive courtyard. Accommodations are spacious and modern, if undynamic, and there's also a three-bedroom villa for those who don't mind splurging. The grounds include a restaurant, two tennis courts and a pool, and a watersports facility is on the beach. The location is very convenient to Holetown's restaurants and shopping. 88 rooms. Credit cards: A, DC, D, MC, V.

Glitter Bay $235–$475 ★★★★★

Porters, St. James, ☎ *(800) 223-1818, (246) 422-4111, FAX (246) 422-1367.*
Single: $235–$475. Double: $235–$475. Suites Per Day: $275–$615.
One of Barbados' newer bastions of luxury, this uncluttered, 30-acre beachfront resort wraps around an elegant coral stone villa, providing a graceful aura of tradition to the modern, four-story accommodations. Rooms are primarily suites and feature air conditioning, kitchenettes, marble baths, bidets, living rooms and great views of the sprawling, manicured gardens from your balcony or terrace—a few sport ocean views for the same price. The five-bedroom beach house has individual suites that front the sand—or rent it all for a family party (in fact, despite the name, Glitter Bay is probably the most family-oriented of Barbados' deluxe properties). A large free-form pool with a waterfall, tennis, a well-equipped fitness center and all non-motorized watersports (plus waterskiing) are part of the package; guests can also use the facilities at Royal Pavilion next door. 83 rooms. Credit cards: A, DC, D, MC, V.

Royal Pavilion $275–$615 ★★★★★

Porters, St. James, ☎ *(800) 223-1818, (246) 422-4444, FAX (246) 422-0118.*
Single: $275–$615. Double: $275–$615.
This elegant Spanish Mission-style enclave is a top choice on Barbados, with gorgeous grounds brimming with hibiscus and other flowers as you navigate through archways and pergolas to your quarters. The rooms are in a pair of three-story buildings that sit at sand's edge—each are junior suites with unfettered marble floors,

king beds, lovely furnishings and ocean views from your terrace. Two lighted tennis courts and nonmotorized watersports are part of the rates, as is afternoon tea. The beach is fine and guests can use facilities at Glitter Bay, which is a bit more informal but shares the 30-acre spread (both are part of the Princess Hotels group). The excellent Royal Westmorland Golf Club is almost across the street. A terrific choice for those who want luxury without attitude. 75 rooms. Credit cards: A, DC, D, MC, V.

Sam Lord's Castle $130–$225   ★★★

Long Bay, St. Philip, ☎ *(888) 765-6737, (246) 423-5918, FAX (246) 423-6361.*
Single: $130–$225. Double: $130–$225.
This former Marriott property takes its name from the 1820 great house built by Samuel Hall Lord, known as the "Regency Rascal" for his penchant for tricking ships to his jagged shore, then looting the smashed cargo. Today's resort is set among 72 acres with formal gardens and a long list of amenities and activities—which is good since not much is nearby. Accommodations are varied; choose one of the quaint cottages if possible. The beach is great to look at, but surf can be unpredictable. All ran smoothly under the Marriott name, but upkeep started to slide at the end of their tenure. The abundance of conventioneers can leave individual travelers feeling forgotten and overwhelmed. 234 rooms. Credit cards: A, DC, D, MC, V.

Sandpiper, The $145–$800   ★★★★

Holetown, St. James, ☎ *(800) 223-1108, (246) 422-2251, FAX (246) 422-1776.*
Website: www.barbados.org/hotels/sand.htm. E-mail: coral@caribnet.net.
Single: $145–$545. Double: $195–$800.
There's a real island feel to this charming, yet upmarket hotel, set right on the beach among coconut trees. Accommodations are in standard rooms or spacious suites with kitchens, one or two bedrooms, air conditioning and nice local artwork (book the few overlooking the beach early—for the same price as a garden view). A respected restaurant, small pool and free non-motorized watersports round out the picture. Well-run by the O'Hara family that operates Coral Reef Club just up the beach. High appeal to the British, who return again and again. 44 rooms. Credit cards: A, MC, V.

Sandy Lane $525–$1290   ★★★★★

Holetown, St. James, ☎ *(800) 223-6800, (246) 432-1311, FAX (246) 432-2954.*
Website: www.sandyland.com.
Single: $525–$1290. Double: $525–$1290. Suites Per Day: $630–$1705.
Pretentious. Old Money. Snooty. Yes, Sandy Lane is all that, and yet this is a resort that manages to roll out the extravagance and glamour unlike any other Caribbean hotel. Rooms are lavishly decorated in acres of marble and antiques, and a surfeit of amenities like two phones and an ottoman—many have furnished terraces inviting enough to spend the night upon. The three restaurants and 24-hour room service are other areas where Sandy Lane struts its stuff. Though rates are undeniably steep, they include some generous extras: in-room breakfast daily, golf on the excellent championship course, waterskiing and Hobie Cat sailing; tennis, a large free-form pool, fitness center and the languid beach round out the menu. Sandy Lane is a haven for Europeans, the nip-and-tuck set, and a few stray honeymooners—families swoop in for Christmas, Easter and summer. Casual types will be happier (and spend

lots less) elsewhere, but for those who want every ounce of pampering luxury the Caribbean has to offer, you're not likely to find a more generous allotment than is provided here. 121 rooms. Credit cards: A, DC, MC, V.

Southern Palms Beach Club $90–$270 ★★

St. Lawrence Gap, Christ Church, ☎ *(800) 223-6610, (247) 428-7171, FAX (246) 428-7175.*
Single: $90–$245. Double: $115–$270.
Set on six acres surrounding a three-story plantation-style house, Southern Palms attracts a fun-loving set. The resort sits on a nice beach with a variety of buildings of different influence, including Italian, Spanish and West Indian styles. Lots of organized activities keep guests busy, from miniature golf tournaments to steel band dances. All the usual watersports are free, and accommodations are pleasant— the best are loft-style. 92 rooms. Credit cards: A, DC, D, MC, V.

Treasure Beach Hotel $160–$650 ★★★

Paynes Bay, St. James, ☎ *(800) 223-6510, (246) 432-1346, FAX (246) 432-1094.*
Single: $160–$650. Double: $160–$650.
This nice, intimate hotel underwent a renovation in 1996, though the ambiance and lovely beach remain. All accommodations are in suites done with pleasant tropical art and furnishings; all have a sitting room with a balcony or terrace (request an upper unit for more privacy). Wet bars, toasters and kettles are standard in all rooms. The grounds are cozy and the small pool is a drawback, but otherwise a solid choice that draws a number of repeat visitors. No children under 12 in winter. 29 rooms. Credit cards: A, DC, MC, V.

Inns

True island inns are a rarity in Barbados, in part because many of the smaller properties have expanded their amenities and service to accommodate a very upmarket crowd that wouldn't be caught dead staying at something less than a resort.

Kingsley Club $79–$101 ★★

Bathsheba, St. Joseph, ☎ *(246) 433-9422, FAX (246) 433-9226.*
Single: $79–$92. Double: $84–$101.
This remote, peaceful spot just north of scenic Bathsheba appeals to Bajans and others who savor a true island experience. Rooms in the historic house are simple but clean, and the views are spectacular. The optional meal plan features West Indian and European cuisine. It's best not to tempt the very strong surf, although the beach, right across the street, is glorious. 7 rooms. Credit cards: A, MC, V.

All-Inclusives

Despite the rich panoply of dining experiences offered outside the resorts, Barbados is increasingly delving into the all-inclusive business. However, the island has a more relaxed approach to the concept, and couples-only properties are nonexistent. One British-owned company, **St. James Beach Hotels**, is turning three of its four properties into all-inclusives for 1998, and staying at any of the three allows guests to water taxi between all four of their Gold Coast hotels for meals and activities; their **Colony Club** (see "Hotels and Resorts") will continue with what they term an "all embracing" package, a kind of a glorified MAP. **Almond Beach** has two locations: one called Club that is just south of

Holetown and positioned more for adults, the other called Village that welcomes families. The latter, with its pleasant beach and expansive property, is the more appealing choice (the St. James people hope to add to their empire by acquiring the Almond Beach hotels, but this deal is stalled as we go to press). Meanwhile, the long-pondered debut of a Barbados **Sandals** appears unlikely to happen anytime soon.

Almond Beach Club $300–$630   ★★★

Vauxhall, St. James, ☎ *(800) 425-6663, (246) 432-7840, FAX (246) 432-2115.*
Website: www.almondresorts.com. E-mail: vacation@iag.net.
Single: $300–$530. Double: $400–$630.

This all-inclusive is refreshingly free of pressure to join in activities, but if you're game, there's a slew of stuff going on, from island tours to shopping trips to watersports—just about everything shy of scuba. The accommodations are in three- and four-story buildings that wrap around a pleasant pool area; choices include standard units, junior suites and one-bedroom suites, all with straightforward island decor and a choice of pool or ocean views (most have balconies). The grounds include tennis and squash, two restaurants, and a free shuttle to Almond Beach Village, where other activities and dining options await. Of the two, Village is the nicer option, but adults may appreciate the 16-and-up age policy at the Club. The beach is narrow for a property of this size, but better ones are close by. Rates include all tax and service charges. 161 rooms. Credit cards: A, MC, V.

Almond Beach Village $320–$660   ★★★

Speightstown, St. Peter, ☎ *(800) 425-6663, (246) 422-4900, FAX (246) 422-0617.*
Website: www.almondresorts.com. E-mail: vacation@iag.net.
Single: $320–$560. Double: $420–$660.

Barbados' largest resort is a well-run all-inclusive located away from all other hotels, just north of Speightstown, on a lovely beach. Rooms are in three-story buildings that sprawl along the 32-acre site, with a variety of sizes and views available. A nine-hole golf course provides entertainment for duffers; tennis, squash, an exercise center, an array of swimming pools and extensive watersports (except scuba) are included in the rates. Children—no charge for the first one sharing your room—are welcomed with a bevy of activities. Dining options range from delightful West Indian at Enid's to atrocious make-believe Italian at the resort's Fine Dining Restaurant; other food possibilities here and at the sister property, Almond Beach Club, which is reached by free shuttle. The location is fine if you are planning to stick around the resort for most of your stay, but some distance from most sightseeing and island activities. A good pick for young families. Rates include all tax and service charge. 288 rooms. Credit cards: A, MC, V.

Coconut Creek Hotel $226–$496   ★★★

Derricks, St. James, ☎ *(800) 223-6510, (246) 432-0803, FAX (246) 432-0272.*
Single: $226–$388. Double: $278–$496.

Set on a beautifully landscaped limestone bluff overlooking a tiny cove of sand, this charming all-inclusive resort is the least expensive of the slick St. James Hotels operation. Accommodations are smallish but very clean and attractive, with tropical decor, air conditioning, and walk-in closets; the best units are the Ocean View rooms—cute cottages perched at the edge of the bluff. A drawback: the secluded beach can almost disappear during high tide, and the pool is none too large. The rates include all meals, drinks, non-motorized watersports (including sailing and waterskiing), and evening entertainment—even room service. Transportation via water taxi or bus takes you to the other three hotels in this chain, where you may use their restaurants and sports facilities (including tennis and exercise rooms). Overall, a pretty good value when all is accounted for. Rates shown include VAT and service. 53 rooms. Credit cards: MC, V.

Crystal Cove   **$258–$584**   ★★★

Appleby, St. James, ☎ *(800) 223-6510, (246) 432-2683, FAX (246) 432-8290. Single: $258–$532. Double: $312–$584. Suites Per Day: $366–$610.*

Set above a small beach, this St. James Hotel includes a mix of standard rooms, junior suites and one-bedroom suites; all have minifridge, air conditioning and are decorated with bright tropical furnishings. The focal point of the property is a tiered swimming pool with a roaring waterfall and, behind it, a "cave bar." Non-motorized watersports (including sailing and waterskiing) and tennis are included, along with live entertainment most evenings; a beach bar provides a barbecue. The facilities and restaurants at the other three hotels in this chain are available to guests. Rates shown include VAT and service. 88 rooms. Credit cards: MC, V.

Tamarind Cove Hotel   **$290–$636**   ★★★

Paynes Bay, St. James, ☎ *(800) 223-6510, (246) 432-1332, FAX (246) 432-6317. Single: $290–$653. Double: $346–$636. Suites Per Day: $426–$680.*

Nestled among coconut trees and soft sand, this attractive resort does a booming business with British families. Guest rooms, junior suites and one-bedroom suites are nicely furnished if unspectacular, with air conditioning, minifridge and balcony or patio. The newer suites have Roman tubs and bidets, while a pair of honeymoon suites have a private plunge pool. Five pool areas enhance the grounds, but the beach is excellent. Nonmotorized watersports are complimentary, including sailing and waterskiing. There's lots of nightlife here, including a Barbadian revue and boisterous barbecues; rates include all meals and drinks. Guests may use the tennis courts, restaurants and facilities of the three other resorts in this chain. Prices shown include VAT and service. 166 rooms. Credit cards: MC, V.

Apartments and Condominiums

Self-contained accommodations, most of them concentrated along the southern coast, are very popular on Barbados. The plethora of choices can be confusing, particularly since the properties seem to regularly consume each other with abandon—so, what was Bougainvillea last year is now part of Sand Acres next door, etc. There's plenty provided at the local supermarkets, so feasting at home shouldn't be a problem for make-do types. Many additional units, usually under $100 a night, are available through some of the island's assorted rental agencies; try **Cacrabank** ☎ *(246) 435-8057*, **Homar Rentals** ☎ *(246) 432-6750*, or **St. Lawrence East and West** ☎ *(246) 435-6950.*

Beachcomber Apartments   **$70–$160**   ★★

Paynes Bay, St. James, ☎ *(800) 223-6510, (246) 432-0489, FAX (246) 432-2824. Single: $70–$160. Double: $70–$160.*

This small beachfront complex of basic apartments provides good value on the Gold Coast. Six are spacious two-bedroom units ($175-370 per night), that are great for families or a pair of couples. But there is also a pair of cozier studios with beach views, and a one-bedroom unit off the beach with even lower rates. All are air-conditioned with full kitchens and quite comfortable—the beach is terrific, and the location is posh (just down from Sandy Lane). No pool or restaurant, but a good deal nonetheless. 9 rooms. Credit cards: MC, V.

Casuarina Beach Club　　　　　　$90–$215　　　　★★★

St. Lawrence Gap, Christ Church, ☎ *(800) 822-7223, (246) 428-3600, FAX (246) 428-1970.*
Website: www.bajan.com. E-mail: casbeach@bajan.com.
Single: $90–$215. Double: $90–$215.
Set on seven acres of well-tended tropical palms and shrubs, this family-owned hotel has air-conditioned studios and apartments of one or two bedrooms, all with kitchenettes and spiffy accessories. Resort-style amenities include two tennis courts, squash, two pools, a few bars and a restaurant. Nice beach, too, but the choppy water isn't for everyone. The lush gardens are reason enough to enjoy this very fine spot; another are the reasonable prices. 160 rooms. Credit cards: A, D, MC, V.

Sand Acres Hotel　　　　　　　$87–$238　　　　★★

Maxwell Coast Road, Christ Church, ☎ *(800) 822-7223, (246) 428-7141, FAX (246) 428-2524.*
Single: $87–$238. Double: $87–$238.
Accommodations at this beachfront property are in studios or one-bedroom apartments with kitchenettes, many of them time-shares. The grounds include a simple restaurant, standard pool and a beach bar, as well as tennis and non-motorized watersports. The beach is nice, but service can be harried. Now encompasses the former Bougainvillea Beach Resort next door. 101 rooms. Credit cards: A, MC, V.

Sandridge Beach Hotel　　　　　$75–$175　　　　★★

Speightstown, St. Peter, ☎ *(800) 223-6510, (246) 422-2361, FAX (246) 422-1965.*
E-mail: bernmar@caribsurf.com.
Single: $75–$160. Double: $75–$175. Suites Per Day: $120–$230.
This apartment hotel on the edge of charming Speightstown has standard rooms, or studios and one-bedroom units with air conditioning, kitchenettes and TVs. Room decor is dated, but in good shape; the one-bedroom units are quite spacious. There's a pool and restaurant, plus a few watersports, but little else. Still, a good choice for families or those who don't mind being away from the action. 58 rooms. Credit cards: A, DC, MC, V.

Sandy Beach Island Resort　　　$85–$295　　　　★★

Worthing, Christ Church, ☎ *(800) 822-7223, (246) 435-8000, FAX (246) 435-8053.*
Single: $85–$295. Double: $85–$295.
This informal all-suite hotel offers both hotel-style units and one- or two-bedroom apartments; the latter have kitchens, and all feature satellite TV and air conditioning. There's a pool and restaurant on-site, and watersports can be arranged for an additional fee. The beach is big and pleasant. A good value. 129 rooms. Credit cards: A, DC, D, MC, V.

Sea Breeze Beach Hotel   **$75–$155**   ★★
Maxwell Coast Road, Christ Church, ☎ *(800) 822-7223, (246) 428-2825, FAX (246) 428-2872.*
Website: www.sea-breeze.com. E-mail: seabreez@caribnet.net.
Single: $75–$150. Double: $80–$155.
Located at the junction of two good beaches, this apartment complex has air-conditioned studios with kitchenettes and balconies overlooking gardens or the beach. There are also three 2-bedroom units for those who need the space. A restaurant, snack bar and two pools complete the scene. Not much to distinguish this from all the other apartment/condo conglomerates that pepper the coast, but competitive rates. 79 rooms. Credit cards: A, DC, D, MC, V.

Settler's Beach Villa Hotel   **$175–$500**   ★★★
Holetown, St. James, ☎ *(800) 223-6510, (246) 422-0840, FAX (246) 432-2147.*
E-mail: altman@caribnet.net.
Single: $175–$500. Double: $175–$500.
Settler's Beach offers accommodations in bi-level townhouses or cottages, each with large living/dining areas, kitchens, one or two bedrooms and spacious terraces; all are bright, sunny and pleasantly decorated, and a few have a private courtyard. The well-tended grounds include a small pool and a restaurant, and the beach is grand. The rates are valid for groups of up to five, so expect to see lots of families. 22 rooms. Credit cards: A, MC, V.

Woodville Beach Apartments   **$65–$150**   ★★
Hastings, Christ Church, ☎ *(246) 435-6693, FAX (246) 435-9211.*
E-mail: wdville@caribsurf.com.
Single: $65–$150. Double: $65–$150.
Accommodations at this oceanfront complex range from studios to one- and two-bedroom units, each with full but tiny kitchens, though only some have air conditioning. They are rather basic, but clean and comfortable. The beach is mostly coral; better bathing is found at Rockley, a five-minute walk. The family-run property has a pool, a small bar and restaurant and weekly parties where guests can mingle. There's lots within walking distance. A good value. 36 rooms. Credit cards: A, MC, V.

Worthing Court   **$65–$120**   ★
Worthing, Christ Church, ☎ *(800) 822-7223, (246) 435-7910, FAX (246) 435-7374.*
E-mail: wcourt@ndl.net.
Single: $65–$110. Double: $75–$120.
A cute little apartment hotel across the street from the beach, Worthing offers studios both with and without kitchenette, and one bedroom apartments with a full kitchen. Decor is colorfully tropical, there's a poolside bar and restaurant. The beach is two minutes away, and a number of restaurants are within walking distance. Credit cards: A, DC, MC, V.

Yellow Bird Apartments   **$60–$80**   ★
St. Lawrence Bay, Christ Church, ☎ *(246) 435-8444, FAX (246) 435-8522.*
Single: $60–$80. Double: $60–$80.
Situated across the street from the bay at St. Lawrence Gap and a five-minute walk from a good beach, this apartment complex offers air-conditioned studios with kitchenettes and ocean-view balconies. There's a poolside bar and restaurant, and

the location is close to several good eating spots. Nice management. 21 rooms.
Credit cards: A, D, MC, V.

Low Cost Lodging

Barbados is no backpacker's haven, but a few options can be ferreted out for the undemanding. Also check out **Homar Rentals** ☎ *(246) 432-6750*, which offers one-bedroom apartments within a short walk from Holetown for about $75 per night, and the **Sugar Cane Club** ☎ *(246) 422-5046*, which provides simple rooms in the countryside near Speightstown from $40 a night. You can also request a copy of the rates pamphlet for hotels and guest houses from the New York office of the **Barbados Tourism Authority** ☎ *(800) 221-9831* or ☎ *(212) 986-6516*.

Little Paradise Hotel   **$50–$78**   ★

Paradise Beach Drive, St. Michael, ☎ *(246) 424-3256, FAX (246) 424-8614.*
Single: $50–$71. Double: $55–$78.

Located three miles north of downtown Bridgetown, this recently renovated hotel is a smart choice for budget travelers—it draws a number of Europeans. Most units have a balcony or patio, are simply furnished and surround a pleasant garden. There's a pool and Jacuzzi, and a restaurants for light meals. Little Paradise overlooks an abandoned hotel development (a would-be Sandals), but its beach is lovely, and little used. 18 rooms. Credit cards: A, DC, D, MC, V.

Pink Coral Inn   **$35–$60**   ★

Hastings, Christ Church, ☎ *(246) 435-3151, FAX (246) 435-3151.*
Single: $35–$45. Double: $50–$60.

Canadian artist Patricia Morris runs this charming little pink guest house on the Hastings Main Road. She decorates the two-story house with her delightfully quirky oils and watercolors, and serves a full breakfast to all who stay (included in the rates). Each of the six rooms have their own sink, but share one of four bathrooms; there's no air conditioning. The Hilton's beach is a 10-minute walk, and a fair number of restaurants are also within walking distance. A simple but upbeat spot.

Windsurfing Village   **$35–$75**   ★

Maxwell Main Road, Christ Church, ☎ *(246) 428-9095, FAX (246) 428-2872.*
Single: $35–$75. Double: $35–$75.

An upbeat, youthful atmosphere prevails at this budget inn dedicated to windsurfers—Club Mistral Windsurfing is located on property and non-takers will feel a bit out of place. Some accommodations are almost spacious but still bare-bones; the least expensive rooms are cozy, but everyone's always out zipping along the surf, anyway. They'll teach you how, too, but most who come here are already pretty good. A 40-room expansion was planned for 1998. 18 rooms. Credit cards: MC, V.

Where to Eat

Fielding's Highest Rated Restaurants in Barbados

★★★★★	Carambola	$21–$50
★★★★★	Cliff	$26–$40
★★★★	Bagatelle Great House	$7–$42
★★★★	La Maison	$19–$42
★★★★	Mews	$21–$38
★★★★	Pisces	$18–$38
★★★	Ile de France	$18–$38
★★★	Koko's	$16–$22
★★★	Raffles	$20–$27

Fielding's Most Romantic Restaurants in Barbados

♥♥♥♥♥	Carambola	$21–$50
♥♥♥♥♥	Cliff	$26–$40
♥♥♥♥	Bagatelle Great House	$7–$42
♥♥♥♥	Fathoms, The	$15–$32
♥♥♥♥	Pisces	$18–$38

Fielding's Best Value Restaurants in Barbados

★★	Atlantis	$12–$15
★★★	David's Place	$12–$30
★★★	Koko's	$16–$22
★★★★	Pisces	$18–$38
★★★	Brown Sugar	$15–$35

"There's no good dining in the Caribbean" is oft-heard, but these gripers probably haven't been to Barbados lately. The island caters to an upmarket clientele that isn't interested in setting aside swank dining habits when they go on vacation. A team of Bajan chefs was a big winner at the 1996 "Taste of the Caribbean" culinary competition held in Puerto Rico. Barbados has almost 2000 acres of land under cultivation for fruits and provisions; beef from Red Pol cattle and fresh chicken are also local, all of which contributes to the healthy dining scene. But the signature item is flying fish, little darlings that flit over the ocean and onto the menu of virtually every island restaurant in more preparations than you can imagine: fried, smoked, pated, slapped into a sandwich, swaddled in creamy sauce, et al. Flying fish are found off many islands, but their local popularity is, in part, due to the uniquely Bajan ability to debone the little suckers—they top out at about nine inches long—a talent celebrated at the annual deboning competition during the Oistins Fish Festival (a dozen fish in about 18 minutes lands you in the running).

Refreshingly, Bajan influences creep onto the menu at many of the posh eateries, but for a true sampling of local fare, it's best to stick with the places that celebrate it without the Euro varnish. **Brown Sugar** in Bridgetown and Sunday Brunch at the Atlantis Hotel in Bathsheba are island institutions, **Ragamuffins** in Holetown uses local chefs to prepare its menu of West Indian favorites. But keep your eyes out for spots like the **Chicken Barn** and **Carib Beach Bar**, simple and cheap snack stands that serve fried chicken and seafood for Sandy Beach-goers. Even the local **KFC** gets into the action with black pudding and souse—sweet potato sausage and pigs feet marinated in lime. Other West Indian specialties to watch out for include pepperpot (a slowly simmered meat stew made with the juice of the cassava), oil down (a stew of breadfruit and pork), conkies (a mash of cornmeal, coconut and pumpkin steamed in a banana leaf), and cou-cou (a baked cornmeal pudding, sometimes spiced with slivers of okra or pepper).

Otherwise, Barbados delivers a wide variety of international tastes, particularly French, with polished results. And, no surprise, the island's British heritage creeps onto a number of menus, with fish and chips, bangers and mash, and roast beef and Yorkshire pudding waving the flag for the sizable contingent of UK visitors. Dining is not inexpensive here, and a few of these establishments request long pants for gents. For many of the restaurants, reservations are essential in season, but if you get caught without, head to Holetown, the island's unofficial restaurant row, where more than a dozen worthy spots are clustered into the space of a couple blocks.

Atlantis   **$**   ★ ★

Bathsheba, St. Joseph, ☎ (246) 433-9445. Associated hotel: *Atlantis Hotel*.
Lunch: 11:30–3 p.m., prix fixe $12.
Dinner: 7–9 p.m., prix fixe $15.

You might go without a full meal for a week after the enormous Sunday brunch at the Atlantis Hotel, a traditional hostelry with breathtaking sea views. Although this dining room operated by owner Enid Maxwell serves set lunches and dinners daily at very reasonable prices, Sunday is when everyone (including tour groups) blows in—reservations are essential for this $18 feast. The tables groan with authentic Bajan specialties, including pepper pot stew (assorted meats in a rich broth, simmered for days), breadfruit, flying fish and rice and peas (no dinner served on Sunday). If lines are overwhelming, try the Edgewater Hotel dining room nearby ☎ *(246) 433-9902*. Reservations recommended. Credit cards: A.

Bagatelle Great House $$$ ★★★★

Highway 2A, St. Thomas, ☎ *(246) 421-6767.*
Lunch: entrées $7–$12.
Dinner: 7–9:30 p.m., prix fixe $42.
Part of the Barbados National Trust, the Bagatelle Great House is located within the former residence of the first governor of Barbados. Operating "since 1645," the restaurant is one of the island's more elegant dining experiences, with stellar service—though some carp that the food is less distinguished than the surroundings. The three-course prix fixe menu is pretty good deal if lobster is your fancy, or try the Caribbean butterfly shrimp in coconut with tamarind dip, or smoked dorado with fennel and pink peppercorns. Guests can wander through the lovely art gallery before or after dining. Reservations recommended. Credit cards: A, MC, V.

Boatyard, The $ ★★

Bay Street, Bridgetown, ☎ *(246) 436-2622.*
Lunch: Noon–3 p.m., entrées $9–$16.
Dinner: 7–10 p.m., entrées $10–$20.
Eclectic fare centered around traditional pub food comprises the menu at this Bridgetown hot spot, right on the tasty beach at Carlisle Bay. So, on one hand you've got chicken satay, lamb souvlaki and crab backs, and on the other is fish and chips, bangers and mash, or a simple ploughman's lunch. The Boatyard draws lots of yachties throughout the day (the restaurant will do their laundry or assist with boat repairs!), while at night, the bar comes alive with live music (Tuesday, when there's a cover charge, and weekends), and copious drinking. Quite a scene—the bar stays open 'til 12:30, or as late as 5 a.m. if things are jumpin'. Credit cards: A, MC, V.

Brown Sugar $$$ ★★★

Aquatic Gap, Bridgetown, ☎ *(247) 426-7684.*
Lunch: Noon–2:30 p.m., prix fixe $18.
Dinner: 7–9:45 p.m., entrées $15–$35.
One of the most popular restaurants among died-in-the-wool Bajans is this lush, terraced, tropical-style restaurant located a few miles south of Bridgetown. Smart businesspeople and others in the know dine here at lunch on weekdays when a West Indian buffet is available for $17. There are various soups, salads and stews to choose from, including pepper pot. Other offerings include flying fish, jerk chicken and pork and luscious desserts. Dinner is more of a Continental affair, with international touches added to local ingredients, like broiled pepper chicken or curried lamb. No lunch on Saturdays. Reservations recommended. Credit cards: A, DC, MC, V.

BARBADOS

Carambola   **$$$**   ★★★★★

Derricks, St. James, ☎ (246) 432-0832.
Dinner: 6:30–9:30 p.m., entrées $21–$50. Closed: Sun.

This longtime favorite is still wowing both islanders and visitors, who ooh and aah over the spicy French-Caribbean cuisine served along a rambling cliffside dining terrace, with the sea lapping 10 feet below. Among the delicacies pouring forth from the kitchen are a seared yellow fin tuna in a potato crust, blackened dolphin served with a drunken watermelon salsa, and a grilled Thai spiced pork tenderloin. It's too bad that only dinner is served, because the view is spectacular. In fact, Carambola's one-of-a-kind setting is easily one of the Caribbean's most romantic—the only thing that could top it is coming on a moonlit night. No shorts policy. Reservations recommended. Credit cards: A, MC, V.

Cliff, The   **$$$**   ★★★★★

Derricks, St. James, ☎ (246) 432-1922.
Dinner: 6–9:30 p.m., entrées $26–$40.

A 1995 addition to the Barbados dining scene, the Cliff is one of the region's very finest and most romantic restaurants. The terraced dining area is like a theater, and vaults out of St. James' limestone bluffs above a tiny swatch of silvery sand just big enough for a pair of imaginary lovers—lighting this stage are five percolating torches, and perhaps moonlight over the shimmering, writhing sea. Amazingly, the food lives up to the lusty scenery: grilled tuna served rare and warmed by a gentle brace of pink peppercorns in cream, or a chicken breast receiving royal treatment on braised cabbage with a fricassee of mushrooms. Those who must seen dining here coo and preen on the lower, open terrace (just try to get one of these seats!), but those who really want to take in the setting nest on the more intimate second terrace. Reservations recommended. Credit cards: A, MC, V.

David's Place   **$$$**   ★★★

St. Lawrence Main Road, Christ Church, ☎ (246) 435-9755.
Dinner: 6–10 p.m., entrées $12–$30. Closed: Mon.

Wear loose clothing to eat this delicious Bajan food in a pretty cottage beside St. Lawrence Bay, where every table has an ocean view. A spicy fried chicken named in honor of the Baxter Street food vendors is a specialty, as is pepperpot and pumpkin soup. Huge helpings of rice and peas, cheese bread, potatoes and vegetables come with all the entrées, but you can't stop there. Make room for the delicious coconut cream pie if you can. Reservations recommended. Credit cards: A, MC, V.

Fathoms, The   **$$$**   ★★★

Paynes Bay, St. James, ☎ (246) 432-2568.
Lunch: Noon–3 p.m., entrées $8–$14.
Dinner: 6:30–10 p.m., entrées $15–$32.

An idyllic beachfront restaurant serving offbeat seafood dishes and Caribbean specialties are the hallmark of outdoor dining terrace on Paynes Bay, just south of Holetown. Local rock lobster simmered in herbs and white wine, fillet of red snapper with a curried pecan topping, or dorado in a Tanzanian coconut milk curry are among the varied seafood offerings; rack of lamb and jerk barbecue ribs are for the land-lubbers. Lunch is Bajan casual—a lighter fare of salads, sandwiches and smaller fish portions. The candlelight and crashing waves are best at night, when Fathoms becomes enchanting and romantic. Reservations recommended. Credit cards: A, MC, V.

Ile de France $$$ ★★★
Hastings, Christ Church, ☎ *(246) 435-6869.*
Dinner: 6:30–10 p.m., entrées $18–$38. Closed: Mon.
An innovative French restaurant, Ile de France brings Gallic intensity to its slower-paced, old-fashioned surroundings. Many classic dishes are represented, including a definitive foie gras and ballotine de canard (one of the owners is from Toulouse), escargots de Bourgogne, and crepes flambeed at tableside. The atmosphere is sublime and unobtrusive, with candlelight, subtle lighting and music. Reservations recommended. Credit cards: MC, V.

Koko's $$ ★★★
Prospect House, St. James, ☎ *(246) 424-4557.*
Dinner: 6:30–10 p.m., entrées $16–$22. Closed: Mon.
The chef here is a talented saucier, creating a symphony of flavors that accentuate the freshly caught shellfish and game garnishing the colorful plates. The beach setting is pretty, with tables set on the patio of a traditional Bajan house on the west coast. The food is island-style, with pepper pot soup often on hand, as well as lightly fried shellfish cakes in a tangy citrus and mayonnaise sauce. Credit cards: MC, V.

La Maison $$$ ★★★★
Balmore House, St. Peter, ☎ *(246) 432-1156.*
Dinner: 6:30–10 p.m., entrées $19–$42. Closed: Mon.
Comfortably positioned in a coral stone Great House on the St. James coast, La Maison has been wowing visitors and residents alike since it opened with sophisticated, French-inspired seafood. Tables are set in a courtyard exposed to ocean breezes and views. The ever-changing menu may feature pan fried dorado with aubergine tagliatella and tomato vinaigrette, filet of flying fish on a red peppercorn cream sauce, or simply grilled lobster tail; a few meat dishes round out the menu, but this is a place for the fruits of the sea, richly prepared. The requisite desserts follow, including a beloved chocolate souffle. Reservations required. Credit cards: MC, V.

Mews, The $$$ ★★★★
Second Street, Holetown, ☎ *(246) 432-1122.*
Dinner: 7–10 p.m., entrées $21–$38. Closed: Sun.
One of two new restaurants opened by award-winning Austrian chef Josef Schwaiger, founder of the popular Josef's in St. Lawrence Gap. The menu changes nightly (to take advantage of the fresh catch), but might include a grilled filet of dolphin served on spinach with hollandaise, breast of duck in a balsamic jus with wasabi mash, or even lobster thermador. Seating is in a tiny Mediterranean-style villa with an open-air courtyard, a lover's balcony and other nooks. A reliable favorite. Reservations recommended. Credit cards: A, MC, V.

Olives Bar and Bistro $$$ ★★★
Second Street, Holetown, ☎ *(246) 432-2112.*
Dinner: 6–10 p.m., entrées $11–$33.
Mediterranean flavors with Caribbean flair are the specialty at this newer Holetown spot, popular from the git-go, but probably more for its quaint setting and reason-

able prices (by Bajan standards) than for the food. The restaurant is housed in a traditional West Indian building that sits at the edge of the main road. Starters and
pizzas are a mixed bag (the "zesty" caesar salad is bland), but entrées shine—try the
jerk pork tenderloin with roasted garlic mash, Caribbean shrimp and vegetable curry
served on a dal roti, or the long list of seafood specials. If the wait to get into the
patio or dining room is too long, the menu is served upstairs in the informal bar
area; try for a table on the balcony overlooking the road. Credit cards: A, MC, V.

Peppers $$$ ★★

Second Street, Holetown, ☎ *(246) 432-7549.*
Lunch: 11:30 a.m.–2:30 p.m., entrées $14–$35.
Dinner: until 10 p.m., entrées $14–$35. Closed: Sun.

A breezy and informal terrace houses this Holetown standby. The appetizer list
showcases regional favorites like crab backs, smoked flying fish and pates, while the
entrées further promote Caribbean flavors with a few twists like Dominican shrimp,
Jamaican jerked pork, and even a rack of lamb in provincial herb marinade. For a
spot featuring "local food," the wine and champagne selection is impressive; the
daily happy hour from 5:30 to 6:30 is popular. Credit cards: A, D, MC, V.

Pisces $$$ ★★★★

St. Lawrence Gap, Christ Church, ☎ *(246) 435-6564.*
Dinner: 6–10 p.m., entrées $18–$38.

Flowers, greenery, an oceanfront table and an impeccable reputation for fresh seafood draws visitors to Pisces again and again, though a few locals grumble that all
the acclaim had made service a tad snobbish. Red snapper caribe stuffed with tomatoes and shrimp is an ongoing special, though the long and varied menu also
include a catch of the day, Caribbean crab backs with herbs, or another favorite—
pepper-crusted tuna with papaya and balsamic vinaigrette. There's a refreshing gazpacho and a few meat, chicken and vegetarian dishes. Desserts are luscious: mango
pave, banana galette or the ubiquitous death by chocolate. A lovely, romantic
evening under the bobbing lanterns and moonlight is assured. Reservations recommended. Credit cards: A, MC, V.

Raffles $$$ ★★★

1st Street, St. James, ☎ *(246) 432-6557.*
Dinner: 7–10 p.m., entrées $20–$27. Closed: Wed.

Named after the Raffles Hotel in Singapore and inspired by British colonial exploits
abroad, this intimate restaurant employs a safari theme that starts with the leopard
print pillows as you enter. Chef Adam uses vegetable stocks and reduced fruit juices
for his sautees, including a pan roasted chicken and potted leg of duck with red cabbage and sweet potato, a baked Napoleon of flying fish and seafood mousse, or the
fillet of saltfish roasted with a ragout of dried peas and root vegetables. There's also
a selection of grilled fish and meat items. Fun, but the wait between courses can be
interminable. Reservations recommended. Credit cards: A, DC, MC, V.

Ragamuffins $$ ★★

First Street, St. James, ☎ *(246) 432-1295.*
Dinner: 6–10 p.m., entrées $15–$22. Closed: Mon.

Yet another Holetown delight, Ragamuffins is perhaps the only restaurant housed in an authentic chattel house—with the local food to match. Blackened fish, Caribbean stir fry, jerk chicken salad and West Indian chicken curry are menu highlights, but this colorfully decorated and smoky dive is also great for the live music on Sunday evenings. Come for food or come for beer, but this is one of the island's best scenes. Credit cards: A, MC, V.

Waterfront Cafe $ ★★

The Careenage, Bridgetown, ☎ *(246) 427-0093.*
Lunch: 10 a.m.–2 p.m., entrées $10–$20.
Dinner: 2–10 p.m., entrées $10–$20. Closed: Sun.

The Waterfront Cafe is an inexpensive cool-off eatery on the Careenage, a small inlet for light craft—it's also a great lunch spot for Bridgetown shoppers. It serves Bajan-inspired quick meals like pepper pot soup, a copious appetizer platter and flying fish interspersed with familiar burgers and English pub food. Tuesday nights brings a Caribbean buffet with live steel pan ($17), and on Thursday evenings the joint is jumpin' with Dixieland jazz; an otherwise relaxed bar scene prevails. Seating is either outdoors facing the water or in the dining room—service steps lively when cruise ships are docked. Credit cards: A, MC, V.

Witch Doctor $$$ ★★

St. Lawrence Gap, Christ Church, ☎ *(246) 435-6581.*
Dinner: 6–10 p.m., entrées $13–$31.

You'll think you've landed off the east coast of Africa when dining at this wild, jungle-themed dining room serving spicy, innovative and traditional island and African cuisine. If the decor doesn't get to you, the good food will satisfy, including creamy split pea and pumpkin soup, seafood cocktail and flying fish—the house specialty is a lime-enhanced Mozambican dish, chicken piri piri. Daiquiris in a variety of flavors are another highlight. Credit cards: A, MC, V.

Shopping is a high art form in Bridgetown, where elegant shops and boutiques line crowded Board Street. As a major duty-free port, you'll save as much as 30 to 50 percent on watches, crystal, gold, bone china, cameras, cashmere, tweeds and liquor. It would be a mistake, however, to confine your purchases to such items, as Barbados has a wealth of artisans and craftspeople who create unique mementoes from the island's resources of clay, wood, shells, weaving materials and fabrics. Craft fairs are held throughout the year in addition to the four major annual events: the Holetown Festival Street Market in February, the Oistins Fish Festival Street Market at Eastertime, the Crop Over Bridgetown Market in summer and the Barbados Museum Annual Craft Fair in December.

BARBADOS

Earthworks Pottery ☎ *(246) 425-0223* is a family-owned studio that produces decorative and functional ware, while **Daphne's Sea Shell Studio** ☎ *(246) 432-6180*, located in a 320-year-old plantation house, offers everything from hand-crafted mirrors to jewelry to Christmas ornaments. **Pelican Village**, located on Harbour Road just outside Bridgetown, is a cluster of small shops, galleries and studios where local craftspeople sell their wares. **Articrafts**, which has two locations in Bridgetown ☎ *(246) 427-5767* or ☎ *(246) 431-0044* also offers up Barbadian crafts, as well as the exquisite wallhangings and clay figurines by Roslyn. For an up-close and personal look at the craft of pottery, head for **Chalky Mount**, a village whose inhabitants have been potters for more than 300 years.

Barbados Directory

Arrival and Departure

Barbados travelers are provided fairly comprehensive airline service from North America. **American Airlines** has daily nonstop jet service from both New York's JFK and Miami, along with daily flights from San Juan, Puerto Rico, that allow connections from a number of US gateways. **BWIA** also provides daily service from both JFK and Miami, and **Air Jamaica** has service several times a week out of JFK and daily service out of their hub in Montego Bay, which also allows connections from a number of US cities. **LIAT** provides non-stop or direct service to Antigua, Dominica, Grenada, Guadeloupe, Martinique, St. Kitts, St. Lucia, Sint Maarten, St. Vincent, Tobago, Trinidad and Tortola. **Carib Express**, **Air Martinique** and BWIA also provide inter-island service.

The departure tax is $12.50.

Business Hours

Stores open weekdays 8 a.m.–4 p.m., Saturday 8 a.m.–1 p.m. Banks open Monday–Thursday 8 a.m.–3 p.m. and Friday 9 a.m.–5 p.m.

Climate

Constant northeast trade winds keep temperatures between 75-85 degrees F year-round. The wet season, from June to November, is more humid than at any other time; September and October are the rainiest months. Weather can change quickly—in a cross trip on the island from west to east, you can start out with sunny skies and end up in a raging storm. Rainfall varies from 50 inches on the coast to 75 inches in the higher interior.

Documents

U.S. and Canadian citizens need to show a passport or proof of citizenship (birth certificate or voter's registration card, along with a government-issued photo ID, such as a driver's license). Also required is an ongoing or return ticket.

Electricity

The current is 100 volts, 50 cycles, as in the U.S., though the speed is somewhat slower. Hotels with 220 volts usually provide adapters.

Getting Around

Barbados has an extensive network of roads, most of them in adequate shape, that invite island exploration. The only hitches: driving is on the left, and road signage leaves something to be desired once you leave the main coastal roads. Not to worry—Bajans are courteous, and will stop and assist anyone who they see pull out a map. There are no U.S.-affiliated rental firms on Barbados. You can procure a car at the airport, but most rental agencies will deliver cars anywhere on the island. Local outfits include **Sunny Isle Motors** in Christ Church ☎ *(246) 435-7979*, **P & S Car Rentals** in St. Michael ☎ *(246) 424-7591*, **National Car Rentals** in St. Michael ☎ *(246) 426-0603*, and **Courtesy Rent-a-Car** at the airport ☎ *(246) 431-4160*. When renting a car, you will need to procure a Bajan drivers license from the rental agency for $5.

Taxis are used by many tourists, but relying on this method of transportation during your entire stay will ring up a hefty bill. Rates are established to major destinations and most hotels and restaurants will have taxis positioned at their entrance. The **local bus service** is safe and reliable, with most routes starting or ending in Bridgetown (there is also infrequent service between Speightstown and Bathsheba). For rides up and down the west coast or along the Christ Church coast, they provide an inexpensive and efficient method of transportation between the hours of 6 a.m. and midnight daily. There is an assortment of yellow and blue, public and private buses, but they charge the same fare—75 cents—and work the same routes, so it doesn't really matter which you get on. In Bridgetown, there are two bus stations: **Jubilee Bus Town** (aka Lower Green), providing buses to the north, usually along the main coastal road (ask to make sure), or **Fairchild**, which provides buses along the south coast and to the east, including Bathsheba. If you are riding at peak times (morning or late afternoon), be prepared for buses to be crowded—standing can be difficult if you are carrying packages or luggage.

An **island tour** by taxi is possible, and many of the drivers are experts about their country; plan to spend about $70 for a full day's tour. One individual we liked is **Randy Hallett** ☎ *(246) 230-5890*.

Language

English is the official language, spoken with a pronounced island lilt.

Medical Emergencies

Top-class hotels usually have a doctor on call. The 600-bed Queen Elizabeth Hospital, located on Martinsdale Road in Bridgetown, is the preeminent training hospital in the Caribbean. The island has a decompression chamber in Bridgetown for divers.

BARBADOS

Money

The official currency is the Barbados dollar, which trades at about $1.98 to one U.S. dollar. Most stores will accept American dollars and traveler's checks. However, to get your best rate, it's better to use a credit card, or exchange your American dollars for Bajan ones at a bank.

Telephone

Area code is *(246)*. To call Barbados from the U.S., dial *1 + (246)* and the seven-digit local number.

Tipping and Taxes

The official tax rate for hotel rooms is 7.5 percent; a service charge of 10 percent is also added. The tax for meals is 15 percent, plus a 10 percent service charge. *However*, most restaurants include the tax (also referred to locally as a VAT) and many do not add the service charge to your final bill. When you are presented your dining tab, verify whether service has been included; if not, 10 percent is considered standard.

Tourist Information

The **Barbados Tourism Authority** has an office in New York ☎ *(800) 221-9831* or ☎ *(212) 986-6516*. The island office is in the Harbour Industrial Park on Harbour Road in Bridgetown ☎ *(246) 427-2623*.

Web Site

www.barbados.org OR www.prideofbarbados.com

When to Go

The **Barbados Jazz Festival** will celebrate its fifth year in January, 1998; the festival takes place in historic homes around the island and at the Sir Garfield Sobers Gymnasium. The **Barbados Windsurfing Championships** is held at the Silver Sands in January. A week-long **Holetown Festival** celebrates the arrival of the island's first settlers every February; there are food stands, marching bands and a carnival at the fairgrounds in Holetown. The island's biggest society event is **Holder's Season**, celebrated for most of March, and featuring internationally-acclaimed musicians, opera singers and actors. The April **Oistins Fish Festival** centers around fishing, boat racing and deboning competitions, along with food stands, arts and crafts and road racing. **De Congaline Carnival** is an 11-day street festival held in late April and early May, with a celebration of music, dance and arts and culminating in the formation of the Caribbean's longest congaline. The island's most renowned event is the century-old **Crop Over Festival**, a six week tribute to Bajan arts, food, music and dance; Crop Over starts in late June and runs through early August. During the month of November, the **National Independence Festival of Culture and Arts** is held, celebrating a long list of creative and performing arts; finalists are featured in a gala presentation on Independence Day, November 30. **Run Barbados** is the island's annual 10K run and marathon, held in early December. **Christmas** is a major holiday on the island, with church masses, special holiday meals featuring traditional dishes and drinks, and blooming poinsettias throughout the island. The Christmas-New Year's season is also the busiest time for tourism, with many hotels and restaurants planning special events.

BARBADOS HOTELS		RMS	RATES	PHONE	CR. CARDS
★★★★★	Glitter Bay	83	$235–$475	(800) 223-1818	A, D, DC, MC, V
★★★★★	Royal Pavilion	75	$275–$615	(800) 223-1818	A, D, DC, MC, V
★★★★★	Sandy Lane	121	$525–$1290	(800) 223-6800	A, DC, MC, V
★★★★	Cobblers Cove Hotel	40	$170–$800	(800) 890-6060	MC, V
★★★★	Coral Reef Club	71	$135–$1020	(800) 223-1108	A, MC, V
★★★★	Sandpiper, The	44	$145–$800	(800) 223-1108	A, MC, V
★★★	Almond Beach Club	161	$300–$630	(800) 425-6663	A, MC, V
★★★	Almond Beach Village	288	$320–$660	(800) 425-6663	A, MC, V
★★★	Barbados Hilton	184	$139–$285	(800) 445-8667	A, MC, V
★★★	Casuarina Beach Club	160	$90–$215	(800) 822-7223	A, D, MC, V
★★★	Coconut Creek Hotel	53	$226–$496	(800) 223-6510	MC, V
★★★	Colony Club Hotel	98	$320–$704	(800) 223-6510	MC, V
★★★	Crystal Cove	88	$258–$584	(800) 223-6510	MC, V
★★★	Discovery Bay Hotel	88	$130–$360	(800) 223-6510	A, D, DC, MC, V
★★★	Sam Lord's Castle	234	$130–$225	(888) 765-6737	A, D, DC, MC, V
★★★	Settler's Beach Villa Hotel	22	$175–$500	(800) 223-6510	A, MC, V
★★★	Tamarind Cove Hotel	166	$290–$636	(800) 223-6510	MC, V
★★★	Treasure Beach Hotel	29	$160–$650	(800) 223-6510	A, DC, MC, V
★★	Asta Beach Hotel	67	$60–$130	(800) 466-2526	A, MC, V
★★	Beachcomber Apartments	9	$70–$160	(800) 223-6510	MC, V
★★	Crane Beach Hotel	18	$100–$270	(246) 423-6220	A, D, DC, MC, V
★★	Kingsley Club	7	$79–$101	(246) 433-9422	A, MC, V
★★	Sand Acres Hotel	101	$87–$238	(800) 822-7223	A, MC, V
★★	Sandridge Beach Hotel	58	$75–$175	(800) 223-6510	A, DC, MC, V
★★	Sandy Beach Island Resort	129	$85–$295	(800) 822-7223	A, D, DC, MC, V
★★	Sea Breeze Beach Hotel	79	$75–$155	(800) 822-7223	A, D, DC, MC, V
★★	Southern Palms Beach Club	92	$90–$270	(800) 223-6610	A, D, DC, MC, V
★★	Woodville Beach Apartments	36	$65–$150	(246) 435-6693	A, MC, V

BARBADOS

BARBADOS HOTELS	RMS	RATES	PHONE	CR. CARDS
★ Little Paradise Hotel	18	$50–$78	(246) 424-3256	A, D, DC, MC, V
★ Pink Coral Inn		$35–$60	(246) 435-3151	
★ Windsurfing Village	18	$35–$75	(246) 428-9095	MC, V
★ Worthing Court		$65–$120	(800) 822-7223	A, DC, MC, V
★ Yellow Bird Apartments	21	$60–$80	(246) 435-8444	A, D, MC, V

BARBADOS RESTAURANTS	PHONE	ENTRÉE	CR. CARDS
French Cuisine			
★★★★★ Carambola	(246) 432-0832	$21–$50	A, MC, V
★★★★★ Cliff, The	(246) 432-1922	$26–$40	A, MC, V
★★★★ Bagatelle Great House	(246) 421-6767	$7–$42	A, MC, V
★★★ Ile de France	(246) 435-6869	$18–$38	MC, V
Italian Cuisine			
★★★ Olives Bar and Bistro	(246) 432-2112	$11–$33	A, MC, V
Latin American Cuisine			
★★ Witch Doctor	(246) 435-6581	$13–$31	A, MC, V
Regional Cuisine			
★★★ Brown Sugar	(247) 426-7684	$18–$35	A, DC, MC, V
★★★ David's Place	(246) 435-9755	$12–$30	A, MC, V
★★★ Fathoms, The	(246) 432-2568	$8–$32	A, MC, V
★★★ Koko's	(246) 424-4557	$16–$22	MC, V
★★★ Raffles	(246) 432-6557	$20–$27	A, DC, MC, V
★★ Atlantis	(246) 433-9445	$12–$15	A
★★ Boatyard, The	(246) 436-2622	$9–$20	A, MC, V
★★ Peppers	(246) 432-7549	$14–$35	A, D, MC, V
★★ Ragamuffins	(246) 432-1295	$15–$22	A, MC, V
★★ Waterfront Cafe	(246) 427-0093	$10–$20	A, MC, V
Seafood Cuisine			
★★★★ La Maison	(246) 432-1156	$19–$42	MC, V
★★★★ Mews, The	(246) 432-1122	$21–$38	A, MC, V
★★★★ Pisces	(246) 435-6564	$18–$38	A, MC, V

BARBADOS

BARBUDA

Barbuda features some of the most breathtaking beaches in the Caribbean.

Looking for a truly off-the-beaten-track experience? For an island that turns its desolate, barren landscape into an asset? Barbuda is one of the most unusual Caribbean backwaters, a curious anomaly whose charms almost defy description for its few visitors. Part of the twin-island nation of Antigua and Barbuda, the destination is almost as flat as a pancake and seemingly just as featureless, left to bake at the junction of the Caribbean and Atlantic. What makes this oversized coral atoll worth visiting are its stark isolation, a colony of magnificent frigate birds who proudly display a flashy mating ritual, and some of the most breathtaking beaches in the Caribbean, washed gently by luminous turquoise water. The limestone island is so rich with sand that, on and off through the years, its biggest business has been supplying sand for concrete and, of course, to supplement the beaches at more-deprived destinations. Adding further allure is a pair of ever-so-pricey resorts that draw a posh clientele dripping with money. The late Princess Diana took a winter sojourn at the K Club and so appreciated the escape from shutterbugs that she returned for second and third visits. Another was William F. Buckley, who arrived by yacht and praised the island's loamy sands. But don't come here for star-gazing—exclusivity and privacy are very big on Barbuda.

BEST BETS FOR...

Barbuda is the perfect place to indulge in the "deserted island" experience.

Twenty-eight miles to the north of Antigua, coralline Barbuda is larger than its wafer-like appearance might otherwise indicate. The island encompasses about 62 square miles, and most of it rarely sees footprints or tire tracks. When you fly in, enjoy the view—it's the last elevated perspective you'll have during your visit. Barbuda receives little rain, and therefore vegetation is mostly limited to scrubby greenery that hugs the ground. There's almost no shade above ankle level. The only settlement on the island is Co-

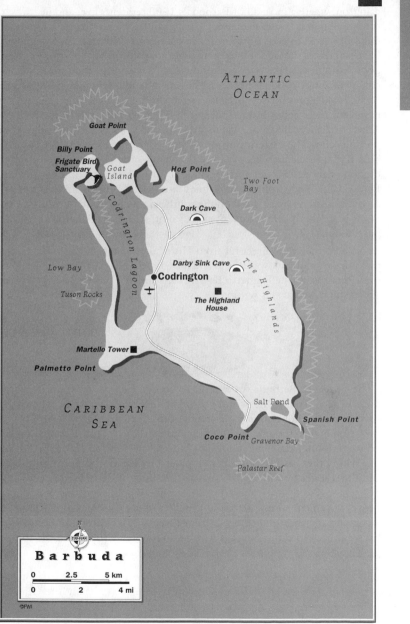

ATLANTIC OCEAN

Goat Point

Billy Point

Frigate Bird Sanctuary

Goat Island

Hog Point

Two Foot Bay

Codrington Lagoon

Dark Cave

Low Bay

Darby Sink Cave

The Highlands

Tuson Rocks

●**Codrington**

The Highland House

Martello Tower ■

Palmetto Point

CARIBBEAN SEA

Salt Pond

Spanish Point

Coco Point *Gravenor Bay*

Palastar Reef

N

Barbuda

0	2.5	5 km
0	2	4 mi

©FWI

drington, where almost all of Barbuda's 1200 residents live, and just west of town is a huge saltwater expanse, Codrington Lagoon, one mile wide and six miles from end to end. About a dozen palm trees offer an oasis along a sand bar that creates the lagoon's western edge. In the northern portion of the lagoon, mangroves take over and provide shelter and breeding grounds to a colony of about 2000 frigate birds. The main road on the island is called the River Road—presumably because it floods during heavy rains—and it is paved for three miles from Codrington south to the ruins of the Martello Tower and the waterfront, where a dilapidated dock is used, mostly for exporting sand. The eastern portion of the island provides whatever physical bulk Barbuda needs to keep it from drowning—the Highlands roll to an elevation of about 150 feet and conclude at the eastern edge of the island with Pigeon Cliff. Aside from a couple guest houses in Codrington, the two main accommodations are situated on the southern tip of Barbuda. Just past Coco Point is another promontory, Spanish Point, where the Atlantic and Caribbean collide.

Barbuda received a direct hit from Hurricane Luis in 1995, but the minimal infrastructure allowed the island's two main resorts to get in shape for the 1996 season (the Palmetto Beach Hotel suffered more extensive damage and is still closed at this writing).

People

The people of Barbuda were never subject to close supervision by plantation owners. Today, the island's 1200 residents are make-do types. They have to be to endure this hardscrabble existence. About 200 work for the two main hotels, though not all of them do so year-round. The next biggest activity is lobster catching and fishing, virtually all of which is shipped to Antigua and other islands. Some are employed by the sand exporting business, and the rest get by with a little farming, hunting or other evanescent activities. There is some resentment toward Antigua's politicians, and an independence movement sprung to life in the '80s—the government responded by increasing the local police force from three to 25. The number has since been cut back to eight individuals, who undoubtedly still have little to do.

Beaches

Barbuda's beaches are, in a word, resplendent. They crawl for miles on end, with sands that are plush and fine and, in one stretch, they have a pink sheen created by a thin layer of tiny shells washed up from the Caribbean. The two main resorts steer the focus to Coco Point, a finger of land that defines the east end of a single unbroken, nine-mile-long sweep of brilliant white sand that eventually reaches Palmetto Point to the west (there is sometimes an undertow present around Palmetto). The ribbon of sand doesn't end at Palmetto, however. It makes a hard right to the north where it continues for another eight miles or so, soon forming the edge of Codrington Lagoon. It is along this expanse that the sand shimmers with a rosy pink hue—a striking photo when set against baby blue skies and aquamarine seas. Midway up this slender isthmus is a sprout of palm trees around an abandoned beach house—this spot (perhaps the only natural shade on the island) is sometimes referred to as Palm Beach. To the east of Coco Point is Gravenor Bay, a three-mile-long curl where the strip of beach is thinner, but the snorkeling is superb. One of the few spots on Barbuda where there is no beach is around the tip of Spanish Point, but just north, and facing the Atlantic, are a series of sand-dune-backed bays with idyllic coves of sand that eventually lead to the bluffs that form The Highlands.

Underwater

Although several excellent reefs can be found in the waters off Barbuda, there is no professional dive facility at present—visitors are strongly advised to have tanks supplied and filled on Antigua, 28 miles away. Visibility is generally limited to 40-50 feet due to the rougher Atlantic weather conditions. There is a 20-mile-long barrier reef fronting the eastern coastline (dangerous for snorkeling), while coral formations off Coco Point swarm with tropical fish and crustaceans. Snorkelers can charter a boat from fishermen to visit Tuson Rock, about three miles west of Codrington; a few other good sites lie just north of here. All told, Barbuda is a challenging, isolated dive frontier for serious adventurers, and is best served by a live-aboard dive boat.

BARBUDA

Barbuda is one of the flattest of all Caribbean islands, peaking at a series of hills, termed The Highlands, rising to about 150 feet in elevation. As such, well-defined trails are basically nonexistent. Dry and unremarkable in appearance, greenery is limited to low-lying scrub, with mangroves fringing the salt-water ponds. But for travelers with a true bushwhacker's zeal, this 14- by 8-mile backwater has abundant exploration possibilities, most of it marginally charted. Beyond the magnificent frigate birds, additional wildlife includes fallow deer, guinea fowl and wild pigs and donkeys.

Most of the island's highlights are seen with the assistance of your hotel or by arranging trips with locals. The nesting area for the magnificent frigate bird, reached by boat from Codrington, is the must-see. You can ask the same boatman to drop you off for a few hours at the "forest" of palms along the west side of the lagoon for a Robinson Crusoe escape.

Tours

Frigate Bird Sanctuary   ★★★★

Codrington Lagoon.

Reached only via small boat, this spot is one of only a few in the world where Fregata Magnificens—the magnificent frigate bird—brood their eggs in mangrove bushes. The impressive birds have eight-foot wingspans and soar to 2000 feet at speeds of up to 100 miles per hour. Mating season, August to November, is the best time to come, when the males puff up a huge bright red sack under their beaks; chicks hatch from December to March and remain in the nest for up to eight months. Also look out for pelicans, warblers, snipes, ibis, herons, kingfishers, tropical mockingbirds and cormorants. The site is visited by several local boatmen—try **Foster Hopkins** ☎ *(268) 460-0212*, who charges $10 per person (minimum of five) for the one-hour excursion from Codrington.

Where to Stay

⚑	**Fielding's Highest Rated Hotels in Barbuda**	
★★★★	**Coco Point Lodge**	$485–$1060
★★★★	**K Club**	$500–$950

Barbuda offers frustratingly little selection when it comes to accommodations. There are two outrageously priced resorts on one end, and a smattering of very basic guest houses in Codrington. After a closure following Hurricane Luis, the **Palmetto Point Hotel** hopes to be open eventually, though last time we checked its rates were pretty lofty for what you get.

Hotels and Resorts

Two resorts dominate the scene here. **Coco Point Lodge** opened in 1961 on a dazzling finger of sand protruding out into the aquamarine water. Built by William Kelly, for years, it was the only hotel on Barbuda and established a reputation as an ultra-exclusive, all-inclusive beach haven for East Coast establishment types. Sometime in the 1980s, the legend goes, a falling out between Kelly and one of his best customers, Mariuccia Mandelli (of the Krizia Italian clothing line), led to Mandelli pulling the ultimate one-upmanship by deciding to build her own resort, the $30 million, 241-acre **K Club**, just down the beach from Coco Point. Today, the two are fortresses for the rich and famous, and although they share many qualities (beyond the same magnificent beach), they are still quite unique. Since its 1989 opening, K Club has had a succession of managers come and go, whereas Coco Point has had the same hands-on family operation for three-and-a-half decades (Mr. Kelly passed away in 1997). K Club is tastefully chic, while Coco Point happily showcases a fashion sense straight out of the '60s. Princess Diana stayed at K Club, the Fortune 500 at Coco Point. Both properties are extravagantly priced.

Coco Point Lodge $485–$1060 ★★★★

Coco Point, ☎ *(212) 986-1416, (268) 462-3816, FAX (268) 464-8334.*
Closed Date: May–October.
Single: $485–$960. Double: $585–$1060.
This secluded resort, set on a spectacular 164-acre peninsula at Barbuda's southern tip, is for those who really do want to get away from it all and don't need the bells and whistles of a traditional hotel. Overlooking a glorious beach, Coco Point accommodates guests in ranch-style villas that are comfortably though very simply furnished; the more expensive units share a common living area with one or two other rooms. The all-inclusive rates include most everything from soup to nuts (and drinks), as well as bonefishing, deep sea fishing, water skiing, tennis and more, but excursions to the frigate bird sanctuary or elsewhere are extra. There's little action at night—people come here to relax and socialize, not party. The plain, retro architecture and decor is a turn-off to some, while others (like Andrew Harper's *Hide-*

away Report) applaud the low-key ambience. Coco Point appeals to clubby establishment types—Wall Street bankers, lawyers, doctors and politicians—some of whom return year after year and are welcomed like family. Interlopers need not apply. The rate includes air transportation from Antigua to Coco's private airstrip. 34 rooms.

K Club $500–$1600   ★★★★

Coco Beach, ☎ *(800) 223-6800, (268) 460-0300, FAX (268) 460-0305.*
Closed Date: September–October.
Single: $500–$950. Double: $500–$950. Suites Per Day: $1100–$1600.

Visually, most everything is perfect at this stylish enclave of 28 white cottages set on a spectacular beach. The bungalows are spacious and beautifully decorated by owner Krizia, the Milanese fashion designer, who oversaw every detail of the opulent development, down to the cotton lounging robes in each room. Units vary from a golf lodge (no air conditioning, but a mere $700 per night in winter), to two-bedroom beach villas; all suites have kitchens, although why this club thinks their guests would want to tackle cooking is strange (the all-inclusive rates include wonderful Italian meals). But, splendid as everything is, it's still absurdly overpriced—beverages, fishing, water skiing and golf at the struggling nine-hole course are not included. The resort draws Europeans and a select few from Hollywood who don't mind paying top, top dollar for a fabulous piece of sand, and true exclusivity. Know that service is not always up to par and management continues on a revolving-door basis. Air transport from Antigua via private plane is $150 round-trip, per person. No children under 12. 39 rooms. Credit cards: A, DC, MC, V.

Low Cost Lodging

There are few options here, and expect little of the creature comforts you might have in a typical budget Caribbean property. The best choice for now is probably **Nedd's Guest House**, a five-room operation above a supermarket and two blocks from the airport in Codrington. Rates are $60 for a double, or $35 for a single, but some negotiating might be possible ☎ *(268) 460-0059*. Other guest houses are located in Codrington, but you may be best off contacting the **Antigua and Barbuda Department of Tourism** for their current recommendations ☎ *(268) 462-0480*. Remember, if you stay in town, you are several miles from the nearest beaches.

Where to Eat

Outside the two main hotels, there are no sit-down restaurants on Barbuda. If you aren't staying at Coco Point or the K Club and want to eat at their restaurants for lunch or dinner, you'll need to phone ahead for reservations (K Club charges a walloping $100 per person for dinner, not including wine). In Codrington, there are a few snack stands that sell fried fish and lobster, and a bakery, but little else. The town also contains a few makeshift bars where fishermen and others congregate for gossip and drink.

Barbuda and Codrington are not designed for shopping. There is a very small gift shop at **Coco Point**, and a duty-free **Krizia Boutique** for upmarket accessories at K Club, but otherwise, you'll need to leave your shopping ambitions at home, or tackle them on Antigua.

Barbuda Directory

Arrival and Departure

All scheduled flights into Barbuda originate in Antigua. The 15-minute flight is made twice daily by **LIAT** ☎ *(800) 468-0482 or (268) 462-0701* making daytrips from Antigua possible. Be aware that LIAT flights out of Barbuda leave as quickly as possible after loading passengers, which usually means flights depart as much as 15 minutes early. **Carib Aviation** also provides limited service to the island ☎ *(268) 462-3147*. The K Club has its own plane to bring in guests, while Coco Point also has its own plane, and delivers guests to a private airstrip near the lodge. Antigua is served from North America by **American Airlines**, **BWIA** and **Continental**. For additional information, see "Arrival and Departure" in "Antigua."

Climate

Average temperatures hover around 75–85 degrees F. year-round.

Documents

U.S. and Canadian citizens need to present a valid passport (or original birth certificate and photo ID), plus an ongoing ticket. British citizens need to show a valid passport.

Electricity

Most of the island uses 220 volts, AC/60 cycles.

Getting Around

Most visitors hire a taxi for island touring. Barbara Jappal at **Caribrep** sets up daytrips (daily except Sunday) from Antigua for $125 per person including airfare, lobster lunch and drinks, and a visit to the bird sanctuary and beaches ☎ *(268) 462-3884*. **George (Prophet) Burton** meets most planes and is a knowledgeable guide, but makes sure all arrangements and prices are very clearly understood; plan on about $75-100 for a day-long tour of the island ☎ *(268) 460-0103*. Car rental is a shaky prospect, and driving on the island's (mostly) dirt and sand roads is not for the timid. **Burton Car Rental** in Codrington has a few vehicles for hire, starting at about $50 per day for a small jeep ☎ *(268) 460-0078*. You'll need to purchase an Antigua/Barbuda driver's license for $20 (or EC$50); there is one tiny gas station in Codrington.

Language

The official language is English.

Medical Emergencies

There is a 10-bed hospital in Codrington. Anything remotely serious should be handled in Antigua or, better yet, Puerto Rico.

Money

Official currency is the Eastern Caribbean dollar, but the two resorts conduct business in American dollars.

Telephone

The new area code for Antigua/Barbuda is *(268)*. To dial Barbuda from the U.S., dial 1 + (268) plus the seven-digit local number.

Tipping and Taxes

In addition to 8 percent room tax, the resorts add 10 percent service charge.

Tourist Information

The **Antigua and Barbuda Department of Tourism** is located in St. John's Box *363, Long and Thames Street, Antigua, W.I.* ☎ *(268) 462-0480; FAX (268) 462-2483.* The country maintains an office in New York ☎ *(212) 541-4717.*

Web Site

www.interknowledge.com/antigua-barbuda.

When to Go

See the calendar in the "When to Go" section of Antigua. Special events in Barbuda are few and far between.

BARBUDA HOTELS	RMS	RATES	PHONE	CR. CARDS
★★★★ Coco Point Lodge	34	$485–$1060	(212) 986-1416	
★★★★ K Club	39	$500–$950	(800) 223-6800	A, DC, MC, V

BONAIRE

Bonaire has one of the largest flamingo colonies in the world. The birds build their mud nests in the salt pans.

Divers have long flocked to Bonaire where shore diving is the lure. You can literally wade just a few feet out in the water at 50 marked sites and see a dazzling array of underwater life inhabiting the pristine coral reefs that are this desert island's crowning glory. But in recent years visitors have come to appreciate the island's natural beauty, and, of course, that has sparked development of new hotels and restaurants to accommodate them. Protected reefs that the island, a nature sanctuary occupies 20 percent of the land, and mangroves and flats serve as nurseries for fish and other wildlife.

Bonaire's Washington-Slagbaai National Park, formerly a plantation of aloe and divi-divi trees, is a 13,500-acre wildlife sanctuary. Birdwatchers flock to Goto Meer, a saltwater lake where you'll find most of the island's famed pink flamingo population at one of their few nesting sites in the world. Over 200 species of birds, including parakeets, parrots and humming-birds, make their home in the park, along with more than a dozen species of Bonaire's only native mammal: the bat.

Long before eco-tourism became the buzzword of the 1990s, Bonaire had the foresight to designate its surrounding waters as a protected marine park. On land, signs extolling all to *"Tene Boneiru Limpi"* ("Keep Bonaire Clean") remind both locals and tourists that litter has no place here. If you love the desert and the water, Bonaire delivers the best of both worlds. It boasts some of the Caribbean's most beautiful turquoise waters, yet, when you are on dry land, you'd almost think you were in Arizona. Its vegetation includes a wide variety of cacti set among odd rock formations. Divi-divi trees are sculptured by the continually blowing tradewinds. If your taste in Caribbean islands runs to those emphasizing gambling and frenetic nightlife, Bonaire isn't for you. But if you bring your sense of discovery, Bonaire's laid-back charm provides the perfect antidote to the hustle-bustle of everyday life.

BEST BETS FOR...

Bird's-Eye View

Located 50 miles north of Venezuela and 86 miles from Aruba, Bonaire is one of the Netherlands Antilles, which includes Curaçao, Saba, Sint Eustatius and Sint Maarten. The island lies outside the hurricane belt and is very dry, with a desert landscape and climate. Rainfall averages just 22 inches each year, mostly occurring in December through March. The average temperature is a balmy 82 degrees Fahrenheit.

Bonaire, which sprawls over 112 square miles, is shaped something like a boomerang. It is 24 miles long and seven miles across at its widest point, small enough that you will feel at ease ambling around the island within days of your arrival. Bonaire was formed from the tip of a 24-mile-long volcanic ridge poking out from the sea. It is surrounded by the fringing reefs and exceptionally clear waters that make Bonaire arguably one of the best diving locales in the Caribbean. Since 1979, all waters around Bonaire have been designated a marine sanctuary, making it illegal to spearfish, collect fish or coral, or anchor on the reefs. The result is one of the richest reef systems in

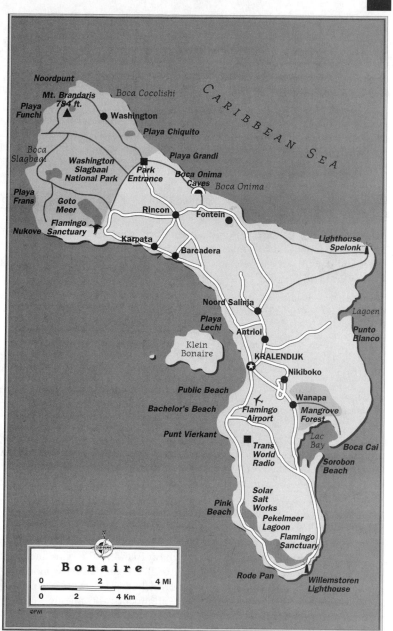

Noordpunt
Boca Cocolishi
C A R I B B E A N
Mt. Brandaris
784 ft.
S E A
Playa
Funchi
Washington
Playa Chiquito
Boca
Slagbaai
Washington
Slagbaai
National Park
Playa Grandi
Park
Entrance
Boca Onima
Caves
Boca Onima
Playa
Frans
Goto
Meer
Rincon
Fontein
Nukove
Flamingo
Sanctuary
Karpata
Lighthouse
Spelonk
Barcadera
Noord Salinja
Lagoen
Playa
Lechi
Antriol
Punto
Blanco
Klein
Bonaire
KRALENDIJK
Nikiboko
Public Beach
Wanapa
Bachelor's Beach
Flamingo
Airport
Mangrove
Forest
Punt Vierkant
Lac
Bay
Boca Cai
Trans
World
Radio
Sorobon
Beach
Solar
Salt
Works
Pink
Beach
Pekelmeer
Lagoon
Flamingo
Sanctuary
Rode Pan
Willemstoren
Lighthouse

B o n a i r e

0   2   4 Mi

0   2   4 Km

©FWI

the West Indies and quite dramatic ones at that, with plunging walls, teeming schools of colorful fish and several shipwrecks—including the notorious *Hilma Hooker*, a 235-foot cargo ship, which was sunk in 1984 after being busted for carrying 25,000 pounds of marijuana.

On land, the crown jewel is Washington—Slagbaai National Park, which was set aside as a sanctuary to iguanas, donkeys, goats and thousands of exotic birds. The island is roughly divided into thirds: the north end is hilly and green, the middle flatter and more arid, and the flat south end punctuated by salt pans, mangrove swamps and sand dunes. It's here that it becomes obvious why Arawak Indians named the island "Bajnaj," meaning low land.

The capital city of Kralendijk (population 2500) is compact and colorful, with Dutch influence that dates to 1636 apparent in the shops and restaurants that line the main drag, J.A. Abraham Boulevard (the name changes to Kaya Grandi in city center).

Klein ("Little") Bonaire, an uninhabited 1500-square-acre island, lies off the west coast about a half-mile offshore and is frequented by divers, snorkelers and day trippers for romantic picnics. Like its larger sister island, it is scrubby and arid.

Note that mosquitoes can be a real problem from October through December, so if you're visiting then, use bug repellant.

History

Ever since the Spanish explorer Amerigo Vespucci discovered Bonaire in 1499, entrepreneurs have been toying with how to exploit it. Failing to discover gold on the island, the Spanish turned to extracting salt from the seas, stripping the forests of hardwoods and dyewoods, and hunting wild goats and sheep. Neither the Dutch, who arrived in 1623 and made it a colony in 1636, nor the British, who briefly wrested control between 1800 and 1816, garnered much success in the many ventures attempted on the island. Slaves were introduced early on to work the salt pans. When the Dutch took control in 1816, they once again harvested salt, and ventured into shipbuilding, brickmaking and stock raising with little success. In recent years, many of Bonaire's natives were forced to find work off-island in the oil refineries of Venezuela, Curaçao and Aruba. As news of Bonaire's natural wonders became disseminated by the emigration, tourists began to trickle onto the island: fishermen who marveled at the abundance of marine life and untouched coral reefs and bird-watchers who were astounded by the glorious flocks of pink flamingos at Goto Meer and Pekel Meer. But it wasn't until the first scuba divers arrived around 1962, when there were only two major hotels, that the island began to discover where its fortune and future lay—right under its crystalline waters.

People

The population of Bonaire is around 14,500, mostly of mixed Arawak, European and African descent. They are a friendly and welcoming people who rely on tourism for their main livelihood, though salt mining, textiles and oil trans-shipment also contribute to the economy. While the official language is Dutch, most everyone speaks Papiamento, a lyrical mixture of Spanish, Dutch, Portuguese, English and French. Tourists, however, will have no problem finding English and Spanish speakers in the hotels, shops and restaurants. Dress is casual but conservative; cover up your beachwear when going into town. Although you'll have no need for jacket and tie or evening dress, don't show up for dinner in a tank top and cut-offs.

Beaches

The gift of Bonaire is shore-diving. The flipside of this equation is that the reefs thrive here because of a lack of sand and silt that would kill them. The wide, long stretches of sandy beach most traditionally associated with the Caribbean are not characteristic of Bonaire. Its beaches lie tucked away in small coves. The best swimming is on the western or leeward side of the island where the waters are calm. Generally, the windward side isn't good for swimming or diving because of the rough seas and strong currents. All the major hotels have a beach, ranging from the man-made lagoon in front of The Plaza Resort, Bonaire, to the aptly-nicknamed **Seven Body Beach** in front of Captain Don's Habitat. The best beaches are on the southwestern shore. To get to **Pink Beach**, south of Kraldendijk, and near the salt works, you cross over sand dunes to see Bonaire's longest stretch of beach, palm-fringed and adjacent to startlingly blue waters. Another popular stop is **Boca Slagbaai**. Snorkel its waters to cool off after your hike in the park. At **Boca Cai** on Lac Bay, you'll find small dunes made of conch shells, a remnant of a bygone era.

Underwater

Simply put, Bonaire offers one of the world's great dive locations, possibly the best in the Caribbean. The island is well outside the hurricane belt. which plagues most other Caribbean islands. That stroke of nature combined with the protection since 1971 of Bonaire's fringing coral reef has allowed it to thrive and provide a dynamic playground. Although big creatures are few and far between, reef fish are in good supply (almost 300 species have been identified) and 84 species of coral are gloriously showcased (it's a perfect destination for photo enthusiasts). The reef on the leeward shore of Bonaire and along Klein Bonaire, usually starts right at the shoreline right under the surface, rather than be separated from shore by a lagoon area as is commonly the case for fringing reefs. A shallow and narrow reef terraces gently, slopes to 30 ft. and then drops steeply to depths of 130 ft. or more. Rain averages 12 inches a year; visibility is reliable from 60 to 80 feet, but sometimes reaches 140 feet. Currents are almost nonexistent—one diver referred to the whole leeward coast as "like a big lake"—but diving on the choppy windward side is rare (limited to occasional calm days in the fall). Shore diving enthusiasts simply hop in the car and look for one of the painted yellow stones that mark the island's 50 or so "official" shore dive locations. You could park and dive for two weeks without visiting the same spot twice. Bonaire isn't known for wall diving, but Tom van't Hof, a marine biologist integral to establishing the Bonaire Marine Park and author of the locally available and excellent *New Guide to the Bonaire Marine Park*, suggests you try Carl's Hill, Cliff, Small Wall, Rapel, Las Dania's Leap and Wayaka.

Bonaire has a leg up on the competition because it has long been a leader in marine conservation. Island native Captain Don Stewart, the founder of diving on Bonaire, successfully lobbied to ban spearfishing in 1971. He also introduced permanent moorings to prevent reef damage from anchors. Because these practices have been in effect for decades here, the island is years ahead of most other Caribbean locales in terms of a genuinely protected undersea environment. When you arrive at your dive shop, you'll pay a $10 annual admission fee to the **Bonaire Marine Park**, established in 1979. A few of the park's more than 80 named and marked sites are currently off-limits to divers; these areas were overdived and local operators are giving them time to rejuvenate. For overachievers, a recompression chamber is available at the island's San Francisco Hospital.

You'll find outstanding snorkeling all along the west coast. In April 1996, the government debuted Bonaire's guided snorkeling program, becoming one of the first islands to offer one. The program has a series of one-half hour slide shows (12 in all) with a mini-lecture to orient snorkelers to what they will see at each of the program's 12 designated snorkeling areas in the Bonaire Marine Park. Twelve resorts have adopted the program and offer it daily. **Klein Bonaire** is terrific, particularly Jerry's Jam (where the coral grows up to the surface) and **Leonora's Reef**, famed for its Boulder star and brain corals, ochre fire and yellow pencil corals, as well as its abundance of French and Queen Angelfish, parrotfish, damselfish and butterfly fish. Other great sites on the main island are **Thousand Steps**, **Nukove**, **Playa Funchi** and **Windsock** (so named because it lies at the foot of Bonaire's airport runway). One other, albeit unpredictable, snorkeling possibility occurs for a few days each year (usually late summer or early fall) when krill swarm the placid Bonaire waters, followed by whale sharks and mantas which feed gleefully on the red crab larvae.

Don't limit yourself to this selection of dive sites; make sure you see some of the island's other great spots. For further information (and more sites), pick up a copy of the *Diving and Snorkeling Guide to Bonaire* by Jerry Schnabel and Suzi Swygert.

Dive Shops

Bruce Bowker's Carib Inn

Kralendijk; ☎ *(5997) 8819.*

One of the smallest shops on Bonaire is a unique operation that opened in 1980. Single-tank boat dive, $25 (not including equipment); second dive the same day, $19. A PADI five-star facility and SSI-affiliated, with a nine-room inn popular among divers. Huge repeat business means rooms are booked up months in advance.

Captain Don's Habitat

Kralendijk; ☎ *(5997) 8290.*

A PADI five-star facility with courses through instructor (also handles NAUI referrals). In operation since 1975, but Captain Don started diving in 1962. Tanks available 24 hours. Single-tank boat dive $33; includes unlimited shore dives the same day; unlimited shore diving $14, or $44 for two boat dives and unlimited shore dives (all plus 10% service charge). Rodale's Scuba Diving survey named Captain Don's as its reader's favorite resort/operator in the Caribbean.

Sand Dollar Dive and Photo

Kralendijk; ☎ *(5997) 5252.*

Open since 1986 and now the largest on the island with 15 instructors and an extensive photo/video department, this shop is PADI, NAUI, SSI affiliated; courses through instructor. Arranges two-tank, all-day trips to sites off Washington/Slagbaai National Park, $65. Single-tank boat dive, $28 (plus 10% service charge); shore dives, $8 per tank. Runs four or five boat dives per day, and scheduled Wednesday night boat dives. Good choice for families.

Fielding   **THE CARRIBEAN**

BOUNTIFUL BONAIRE

A mecca for nature lovers, whether on land or under water, boomerang-shaped Bonaire has rocky hills, salt ponds, freshwater lakes and fabulous dive spots off-shore from its sandy beaches.

Washington

Mount Brandaris

Washington-Slagbaai National Park

Rincon

Fontein

Gotomeer

Washington-Slagbaai National Park

Encompassing a former plantation site, this 13,500-acre park has hiking trails that lead past wind-sculpted divi-divi trees and cacti to caves and rocky coasts. If you have a four-wheel-drive vehicle, take either a 15- or 21-mile road tour.

Rincon

Originally a Spanish settlement, Bonaire's oldest village is filled with red-tiled buildings and steepled churches . Look for petroglyphs on the rock faces near the roadside leading to Fontein east of Rincon.

1000 Steps Beach

Located opposite the Bonaire Caribbean Club, this limestone staircase carved out of the cliff leads to a beach that offers superb snorkeling and scuba diving. The 67 steps feel like 1000 when you hike back up!

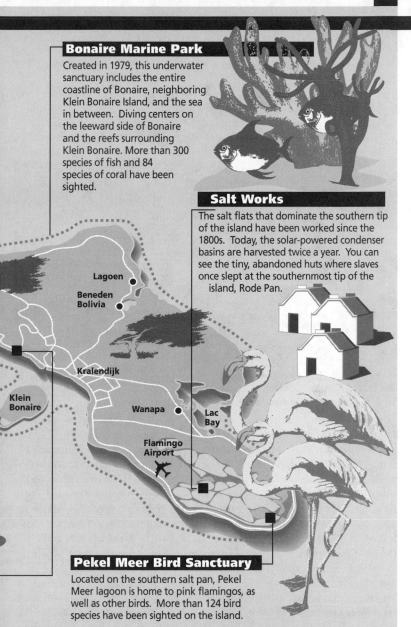

Bonaire Marine Park

Created in 1979, this underwater
sanctuary includes the entire
coastline of Bonaire, neighboring
Klein Bonaire Island, and the sea
in between. Diving centers on
the leeward side of Bonaire
and the reefs surrounding
Klein Bonaire. More than 300
species of fish and 84
species of coral have been
sighted.

Salt Works

The salt flats that dominate the southern tip
of the island have been worked since the
1800s. Today, the solar-powered condenser
basins are harvested twice a year. You can
see the tiny, abandoned huts where slaves
once slept at the southernmost tip of the
island, Rode Pan.

BONAIRE

Lagoen

Beneden
Bolivia

Kralendijk

Klein
Bonaire

Wanapa

Lac
Bay

Flamingo
Airport

Pekel Meer Bird Sanctuary

Located on the southern salt pan, Pekel
Meer lagoon is home to pink flamingos, as
well as other birds. More than 124 bird
species have been sighted on the island.

Sunset Beach Dive Center

Kralendijk; ☎ *(5997) 8330.*

PADI five-star facility; NAUI and SSI referrals. Single-tank boat dive and unlimited shore diving (the same day), $33. Six days of unlimited shore dives, $109. Several other combination packages available.

Some Bonaire tours include the huts where salt mine slaves lived.

Bonaire's environmental awareness extends to the **Washington—Slagbaai National Park**, which occupies most of Bonaire's northern end. The 13,500-acre wildlife sanctuary is laced by dirt roads, and on-foot exploration is easy, as long as you're equipped with sun block and plenty of water. Once a plantation, which produced aloe, charcoal and goats, it was turned over to the government in 1967. After paying your $5 entry fee, you'll be handed a map detailing three treks: the yellow route is a 22-mile circuit of the park, while the green route is a shorter, 15-mile track through the center (the two routes overlap at points). A dotted green trek ascends **Brandaris Hill**, Bonaire's 784-foot high point; allow two hours round trip. Another area which deserves impromptu exploration is the solar salt pans—visible from the road—that loom mysteriously on the horizon, south of Kralendijk. On the southern end of the island, next to 150-year-old salt pans lined by slave huts, is **Pekel Meer Lagoon**, a 135-acre flamingo sanctuary and breeding ground that serves as a home to as many as 15,000 greater flamingos. Because flamingos are shy birds, sensitive to noise, you are prohibited from entering the sanctuary directly. From a safe distance, though you are allowed to photograph and admire them through binoculars. An additional option is exploring Bonaire's honeycomb of caves on its coasts—most of which have only been discovered in the past decade.

What Else to See

The capital city of Kralendijk is laid-back and casual (though strolling around in swimwear is not appropriate). Colorful, Dutch Colonial low-rise buildings are easily navigated by foot. The Fish Market, located on the waterfront and surrounded by Romanesque stone arches, is great for people-watching. Rincon, tucked away in the center of Bonaire, is the island's oldest village; nearby is Boca Onima, a 50-foot volcanic cliff with shallow caves where ancient petroglyphs can be viewed. Snorkelers, divers and kayakers frequent Klein Bonaire, a small uninhabited island with nice beaches.

Caves near Barcadera, Bonaire

BONAIRE

Museums and Exhibits

Bonaire Art Gallery ★★

Kaya L.D. Gerharts #10, Kralendijk, Bonaire.

Artist Bonnie Kerr galvanized the local art community and opened this gallery to represent Bonaire's small but prolific group of artists. From impressionistic oils to underwater photography, the common thread is reverence for the island's natural beauty.

Parks and Gardens

Bonaire Marine Park ★★★★★

To keep its world-famous reefs intact, this government-run park, which includes the entire coastline of Bonaire and neighboring Klein Bonaire, enacted strict rules for snorkelers and divers long before its neighboring islands did. You may not step on or collect the coral; anchors and spear fishing are forbidden; and you can't wear diving gloves (helps discourage touching). Patrolling marine police see that the rules are enforced. The undersea world includes some 80 species of colorful coral and 270 species of fish. The Visitors Center offers brochures, slide shows and lectures. The $10 annual fee goes to maintain the park.

Washington—Slagbaai National Park ★★★★★

Hours open: 8 a.m.–5 p.m.

This 13,500-acre national park, dedicated to preserving the island's natural landscape, is well worth a visit. Opt for the short route (15 miles and marked with green arrows) or the longer version (22 miles and yellow arrows); if you're driving, a four-wheel drive is essential for navigating the dirt roads. Once a plantation of divi-divi trees and aloe plants, the park has been a wildlife sanctuary since 1967, with additional acreage added in 1978. The roads take you past dramatic seascapes, freshwater lakes and lowland forest that is home to 150 species of birds (bring your binoculars) and a few mammals like donkeys and goats. A small museum is at the gatehouse. General admission: $5.

Tours

Bonaire Sightseeing Tours ★★★

If you prefer exploring Bonaire in the hands of professional guides, contact either **Baranka Tours** *(☎ (5997) 2200)* or **Bonaire Tours** *(☎ (5997) 8778)*. Excursions, via jeep or minivan, are offered to the northern coast, the low-lying south or Washington/Slagbaai National Park. Prices range from $16 to $48.

Getting wet is the order of the day here and the reason most tourists visit Bonaire. It is also a haven for fishers, with great bonefishing and angling for tarpon, permit and snook. Sea kayaking is relaxing along the leeward side and Klein Bonaire; on the windward side, paddle over to Lac Bay, a lagoon that is a nursery for fish life. Bonaire's steady trade winds make it ideal for windsurfing, popular all year round in Lac Bay and on the leeward side, where the winds are especially strong December through August. Trekking through the national park is a lovely way to soak up the serene landscape, but be sure to bring plenty of water. Mountain biking has grown in popularity on the island in recent years, too. For horseback riding, contact the **Kunuku Warahama Riding Academy** (☎ (09) 607324 or (5997) 2500).

Biking

Bonaire yields fantastic terrain for mountain bikers. **Cycle Bonaire** (☎ (5997) 7558) maintains top-notch equipment with great service and offers packages combining biking with scuba diving, snorkeling and/or ocean kayaking. **Discover Bonaire** (☎ (5997) 5252), which specializes in nature tours on Fridays, also has bike rentals and guided excursions at reasonable prices.

Birdwatching

Bonaire's place in the migration path between North and South America coupled with its variety of topography from freshwater lakes to dry salt flats make it a birdwatcher's paradise. Some 150 species of birds—a few unique to Bonaire—have been sighted. Besides flamingos, Bonaire is inhabited by a large number of parrots and parakeets. Contact the **Tourism Corporation of Bonaire** (☎ (5997) 8322).

Boating and Sailing

Most hotels and resorts offer boat charters. A popular trip is right at sunset when the sun drops into the sea producing an odd "green flash." Sailing every day except Sundays from the Harbour Village Marina, the **Bonaire Dream** (☎ (5997) 4514), the island's only glass-bottom boat, offers day and night trips through Bonaire Marine Park. **The Samur** (☎ (5997) 5592) is an authentic, beautiful Siamese sailing junk offering everything from full moon sails to seven-course, Thai dinners and snorkel trips. **Woodwind** (☎ (5997) 8285 or 09-607055) is a 37-foot trimaran with an open bar to make snorkel trips a little more jolly. **Seawitch Charters** (☎ (5997) 5433 or 09-607449) offers a 56-ft. Pilot House Ketch for everything from daytrips to mini-cruises to Curacao. Mid-October Bonaire hosts an international sailing regatta that draws a myriad of vessels. **Sail Oscarina** (☎ (5997) 8290) charters a 42-ft. deep water sailing yacht for private parties, snorkeling trips to Klein Bonaire, a sunset champagne cruise or sunset dinner sail. **Sunset Sailing Bonaire** (☎ (5997) 2050) sports its own sailing school and rents sailboats. **Triad Boat Rental** at Club Nautico Bonaire (☎ (5997) 5800) rents boats for both fishing or diving.

Deep-Sea Fishing

Sailfish, marlin, wahoo and tuna are the stars of deep-sea fishing in Bonaire's waters. **Big Game Sportfishing** (☎ (5999) 6500) features a 29-ft. cabin cruiser. Captain Chris Morkos offers bill-to bone fishing with his **Piscatur Fishing** (☎ (5997) 8774). On his 42 ft. twin diesel sportfisherman, he will cook your catch on board. For reef fishing, try the 15 ft. skiff. Or Morkos will aid you in walking the salt flats, attempting to hook the skittish bone fish. **Club Nautico** (☎ *(5997) 5800)* offers fishing charters, as does the Ocean Breeze (☎ *(5997) 5661)*.

Guided Snorkeling

This unique program, launched in 1996 in conjunction with the government, hotel association, *Skin Diver* magazine and individual dive operators, is aimed at the many tourists who visit Bonaire but don't dive. Participants are taught all about snorkeling, with a half-hour slide presentation on underwater life and what to expect at each of the 12 official sites and a guided snorkel tour. Virtually every hotel and dive shop on the island participates in the program, which costs $25 a person. You can reserve a spot with your travel agent before reaching Bonaire.

Kayaking

Kayaking though the calm waters that surround much of the island is as relaxing as it gets. Or explore Lac Bay, a peaceful lagoon punctuated by mangroves. **Jibe City Kayaking** (☎ *(5997) 7363)* will set you up with half- or full-day rentals.

Scuba Diving

Many outfits offer lessons, equipment rentals and excursions. Best known is **Captain Don's Habitat Dive Center** (*Kaya Gobernador N. Deprot,* ☎ *(5997) 8290)*, a PADI five-star training facility. Also check out: **Dive I** and **Dive II** (Divi Flamingo Beach Resort, ☎ *(5997) 8285)*; **Bonaire Scuba Center** (Black Durgon Inn, ☎ *(5997) 8978)*; **Sand Dollar Dive and Photo** (Sand Dollar Condominiums, ☎ *(5997) 5252)*; **Neil Watson's Bonaire Undersea Adventures** (Coral Regency Resort, ☎ *(5997) 5580)*; **Great Adventures Bonaire** (Harbour Village Beach Resort, ☎ *(5997) 7500)*; and **Bruce Bowker's Carib Inn Dive Center** (Carib Inn, ☎ *(5997) 8819)*. Personalized tours for twosomes are offered by **Dee Scarr's Touch the Sea** (☎ *(5997) 8529)*.

Tennis

Tennis buffs will find courts—most lighted—at Sunset Beach Hotel, Divi Flamingo Beach, Harbour Village, Sand Dollar, Tennis Club Bonaire and Plaza Resort Bonaire.

Windsurfing

Lac Bay

In recent years, windsurfing has soared in popularity on Bonaire, thanks to its gentle trade winds. In Lac Bay, the waist-deep, clear water and 2 1/2 miles of undisturbed waters make it a perfect spot for beginners ($40 for an hour-long session). You can rent boards or get lessons at **Jibe City** (☎ *(5999) 607363*; closed in September); **Bonaire Windsurf Place,** (☎ *(5999) 607495)*; **Windsurfer's Castle** (☎ *(5999) 8198);* and **Bonaire Windsurfing School** (*[599]9-2500)* at Plaza Resort, the only center located on Kralendijk Bay.

Where to Stay

Fielding's Highest Rated Hotels in Bonaire

★★★★★	Harbour Village Beach Resort	$275–$705
★★★★	Plaza Resort Bonaire	$125–$400
★★★	Captain Don's Habitat	$145–$440
★★★	Club Nautico Bonaire	$220–$450
★★★	Divi Flamingo Beach Resort	$84–$240
★★★	Lion's Dive Hotel Bonaire	$160–$440
★★★	Port Bonaire Resort	$185–$385

Fielding's Most Diver-Friendly Hotels in Bonaire

★★★	Captain Don's Habitat	$145–$440
★★★	Divi Flamingo Beach Resort	$84–$240
★★	Sand Dollar Condominium Resort	$155–$360
★★	Carib Inn	$69–$149

Fielding's Best Value Hotels in Bonaire

★★★	Divi Flamingo Beach Resort	$84–$240
★★	Carib Inn	$69–$149
★★★★	Plaza Resort Bonaire	$125–$400
★★	Buddy Beach & Dive Resort	$93–$232

Many of Bonaire's hotels and resorts cater to divers, and one, the Sorobon, is for nudists. Hotel development continues with three recent hotels—the Plaza Resort, Port Bonaire and Club Nautico—added since late 1994. If you're looking to save money, consider staying in one of the many condominium and apartment complexes, but note that hotel prices are reasonable anyway, and local food prices so high the savings from cooking it yourself may be negligible.

Hotels and Resorts

All hotels face the sea. All you need to do is choose whether you want to stay in town or in the countryside. Perhaps the liveliest hotel is **Captain Don's Habitat**, due to the wildcat personality of its owner, Don Stewart, who has been rumored to shoot a mosquito with a pistol. **Divi Flamingo Beach Hotel** has the best restaurants, the Chibi-Chibi and the Calabash Terrace, plus a casino that draws crowds. **Sorobon Beach Resort** is infamous for its clientele who like to take advantage of the nearby "clothes optional" beach.

Captain Don's Habitat $145–$440   ★ ★ ★

☎ *(800) 327-6709, (5997) 8290, FAX (5997) 8240.*
Single: $145–$440. Double: $145–$440.

The clientele at this casual spot is mostly scuba divers and the facilities cater to them well, with instruction, seven boats and an underwater photo shop. Landlubbers are kept happy, too, in two-bedroom cottages with kitchens or oceanfront rooms or villas. The beach is tiny, but the pool is nice. The atmosphere here is informal and fun, especially on Tuesday nights when Captain Don, who pioneered scuba diving on the island, stops by to spin tall tales. 93 rooms. Credit cards: A, MC, V.

Divi Flamingo Beach Resort $84–$240   ★ ★ ★

☎ *(800) 367-3484, (5997) 8285, FAX (5997) 8238.*
Single: $84–$240. Double: $84–$240.

Despite the need for at least a fresh coat of paint, the Divi remains a popular choice due to its friendly staff and lively atmosphere. The original buildings housed German prisoners of war during World War II, but from that dubious start the resort has grown into a funky but hip hangout. Accommodations are merely adequate, but the grounds are nice with tennis (including a resident pro), extensive dive facilities (with boat dives twice daily and special programs for the handicapped), a casino and after-dark entertainment. 145 rooms. Credit cards: A, DC, D, MC, V.

Harbour Village Beach Resort $275–$705   ★ ★ ★ ★ ★

☎ *(800) 424-0004, (5997) 7500, FAX (5997) 7507.*
Single: $275–$705. Double: $275–$705.

This Iberian village-style complex offers the poshest digs on the island, though you still won't have to dress up here. The word is casual elegance. Both traditional guestrooms and condos with kitchens are spacious, nicely decorated and have air conditioning. The beach is wide by Bonaire standards, and the diving facilities are choice. A spiffy spa and fitness center offer pampering treatments. Use of the tennis center, 60-slip marina, pool and traditional watersports are included in the rate. Lush landscaping belies its desert isle locale. Guest receive a daily posting of activities, ranging from birdwatching to stargazing. 72 rooms. Credit cards: A, DC, MC, V.

Plaza Resort Bonaire $125–$400   ★ ★ ★ ★

☎ *(800) 766-6016, (5997) 2500, FAX (5997) 7133.*
Single: $125–$400. Double: $125–$400. Suites Per Day: $200–$400.

Located right on the beach five minutes from Kralendijk and opened in summer of 1995, the Plaza adds another upscale option on Bonaire. Accommodations are in suites or one- and two-bedroom villas with fully equipped kitchens. Facilities include the requisite dive shop and other watersports, pool, fitness center, three restaurants and three bars, a mini-market and four tennis courts. It also sports the island's second—and largest—casino. 200 rooms.

Apartments and Condominiums

One- and two-bedroom apartments are often chosen by visitors who want to save a little money, but you may empty your wallet anyway if you stock up on staples in Bonaire; the prices can be exorbitant. In most cases, you may need a car. For more information about housekeeping units, contact **Hugo Gerharts** *(Kralendijk, Bonaire, N.A.;* ☎ *(5997) 8300)* or **Harbourstown Real Estate** *(Kaya Grandi 62, P.O. Box 311;* ☎ *(5997) 5539, FAX (5997) 5081).*

Buddy Beach & Dive Resort   **$93–$232**   ★★

☎ *(800) 359-0747, (5997) 5080, FAX (5997) 8647.*
Single: $93–$232. Double: $93–$232.
Accommodations vary from small apartments with no air conditioning to newer and more spacious units with air conditioning and kitchens. Primarily serving divers, this no-frills complex provides clean towels daily, but maid service only once a week. There's a pool and bar, but no restaurant. A decent choice for those who don't mind fending for themselves and are seeking budget quarters. 40 rooms. Credit cards: A, DC, MC, V.

Club Nautico Bonaire   **$220–$450**   ★★★

☎ *(800) 359-0747, (5997) 5800.*
Single: $220–$450. Double: $220–$450.
Opened in the fall of 1994, this property, popular with sailors and yachters, offers colonial-style one-, two- and three-bedroom apartments by the sea. Each unit is beautifully appointed and comes with rattan furniture, garden tubs, plantation shutters, full kitchen, and air conditioning in the bedroom and living room. It boasts a restaurant, bar, pool, private pier and marina. The one drawback: A road lies between it and the marina. Don't book here expecting a beach. Inquire about money-saving dive packages. 24 rooms. Credit cards: A, MC, V.

Lion's Dive Hotel Bonaire   **$160–$440**   ★★★

☎ *(800) 786-3483, FAX (5997) 5680.*
Single: $160–$440. Double: $160–$440.
This time-share resort puts up guests in studios and one- and two-bedroom suites with ocean views in two-story buildings arranged around a free-form pool. Units are attractive with large sitting areas, air and full kitchens. It has a recreation center and dive shop, as well as a bar and restaurant—but no beach. 31 rooms. Credit cards: A, DC, MC, V.

Port Bonaire Resort   **$185–$385**   ★★★

☎ *(800) 766-6016, (5997) 2500, FAX (5997) 7133.*
Single: $185–$385. Double: $185–$385.

This condo resort, opened in late 1994, is adjacent to the lightly-trafficked airport on the waterfront. Lodging is in one- and two-bedroom apartments, a penthouse and a two-bedroom beach house; all have fully equipped kitchens, cable TV, direct-dial phones, patios and other modern amenities. On-site facilities include a pool, private dock, playground, dive shop and coffee shop.A sister property to the Plaza Resort Bonaire, guests can use both facilities. 26 rooms. Credit cards: A, MC, V.

Sand Dollar Condominium Resort $155–$360   ★★

☎ *(800) 288-4773, (5997) 8738, FAX (5997) 8760.*
Associated Restaurant: *The Green Parrot.*
Single: $155–$360. Double: $155–$360.

Accommodations at this beachfront condominium complex include studios and apartments from one to three bedrooms, all with private balconies or terraces, air conditioning, full kitchens and contemporary furnishings. Each is differently done as these units are individually owned. It has an excellent on-premise dive center, as well as two tennis courts, supervised children's programs during high season, a restaurant and a tiny beach strollable only during low tide. A good choice for families. 85 rooms. Credit cards: A, MC, V.

Sorobon Beach Resort $145–$215   ★

Lac Bay, ☎ *(5997) 8080, FAX (5997) 6080.*
Single: $145–$215. Double: $145–$215.

Bonaire's only "naturalist" resort means that clothes are optional—and many guests take advantage of it. Accommodations on Lac Bay are in cabin-like structures and consist of one-bedroom units with small kitchens and simple furnishings. The grounds include a small family-style restaurant, bar and private beach. A simple spot for the carefree set who don't mind forgoing air conditioning. 30 rooms. Credit cards: D, MC, V.

Inns

These inns are dedicated to serving the committed diver. Furnishings are usually very basic and require a no-nonsense attitude.

Carib Inn $69–$149   ★★

☎ *(5997) 8819, FAX (5997) 5295.*
Single: $69–$149. Double: $69–$149.

This intimate scuba inn, founded and operated by U.S. diver Bruce Bowker, attracts those who love the sport and are seeking simple lodgings. Most units have their own kitchen; all are air-conditioned. You'll have to cook in or walk to a nearby restaurant to be sated. The inn has daily maid service and a pool. Bowker's place has lots of repeat guests, so reserve early. His dive center is excellent. 13 rooms. Credit cards: A, MC, V.

Low Cost Lodging

To save money in Bonaire, travel with several people and share the cost of an apartment or condominium. The tourist board can also supply names of private homes that rent out individual rooms. Travel during low season (mid-April through mid-December), when rates are slashed 20 to 40 percent.

Where to Eat

Fielding's Highest Rated Restaurants in Bonaire

★★★★	Richard's Waterfront	$13–$35
★★★	Beefeater Garden Restaurant	$14–$38
★★★	Chez Truus	$11–$25
★★★	Chibi-Chibi Restaurant	$11–$19
★★★	Den Laman Seafood Restaurant	$12–$35
★★★	Green Parrot	$12–$28
★★★	Jardin Tropical Restaurant	$20–$20
★★★	Mona Lisa Bar & Restaurant	$16–$23
★★★	Old Inn	$10–$30
★★★	Rendez-Vous Restaurant	$14–$26

Fielding's Most Romantic Restaurants in Bonaire

♥♥♥♥♥	Beefeater Garden Restaurant	$14–$38
♥♥♥♥♥	Richard's Waterfront	$13–$35
♥♥♥♥	Chibi-Chibi Restaurant	$11–$19
♥♥♥♥	Jardin Tropical Restaurant	$20–$20
♥♥♥	Old Inn	$10–$30

Fielding's Best Value Restaurants in Bonaire

★★★	Chibi-Chibi Restaurant	$11–$19
★★★★	Richard's Waterfront	$13–$35
★★★	Chez Truus	$11–$25
★★★	Rendez-Vous Restaurant	$14–$26
★★★	Old Inn	$10–$30

Food prices are high on the island because virtually everything besides fresh fish is imported. Among native specialties are wahoo, dolphin, conch, goat stew, red snapper, Dutch cheeses and fungi (a thick pudding made from cornmeal). Many hotels offer theme nights, including the popular Indonesian cuisine with rijstaffel, the traditional rice table. A new restaurant worth checking out includes Jardin Tropical Restaurant, located in Kralendijk 's tallest building, a whopping three stories with an elevator. For nightlife, try your luck at the gaming hall at the Divi Flamingo Resort, billed as the world's first "barefoot" casino; or the island's largest casino at the Plaza Resort. Popular nightspots include Fantasy Disco and Karel's Beach Bar.

BONAIRE

Beefeater Garden Restaurant $$$ ★★★

Kaya Grandi 12, Kralendijk, ☎ *(5997) 7776.*
Dinner: 4:30–10:30 p.m., entrées $14–$38.

The expansive tropical garden behind this traditional Bonaireian house centered in Kralendijk is the focal point of this 80-seat restaurant. Despite its size, the plants and lighting combine to provide a sense of seclusion, inviting romance and lingering. Don't be fooled by its name. The menu is heavily skewed toward local fish and traditional Bonaireian favorites like *cabrito stoba* (goat stew), as well as a wide range of choices for the vegetarian set. The fish calypso is especially tasty, as well as its homemade ice cream. The walls are decorated with original art for sale by locals. On Sunday, live music is the lure. Reservations recommended. Credit cards: A, MC, V.

Chez Truus $$ ★★★

Kaya C.E.B. Hellmund 5, Kralendijk, ☎ *(5997) 8617.*
Dinner: 6:30–10 p.m., entrées $11–$25. Closed: Tue.

Bonaire has a number of old homesteads, but Chez Truus, with a red London phone booth as its landmark and mascot, roosts in one of the oldest and coziest. Near the market and across the road from the sea, it produces solid French cuisine— duck à la orange, poached salmon in Bearnaise sauce—with a hint of local cooking worked into the menu for good measure. Freshly-brewed coffee is service in a pot left at your table, along with French cognac, a nice accompaniment to the rich chocolate mousse or warm goat cheese in puff pastry drizzled with honey and pinenuts. Reservations recommended. Credit cards: A, MC, V.

Chibi-Chibi Restaurant $ ★★★

J.A. Abraham Boulevard, Kralendijk, ☎ *(5997) 8285.* Associated hotel: *Divi Flamingo Beach Resort.*
Dinner: 2–11 p.m., entrées $11–$19.

Chibi-Chibi—named for a tropical bird—is positioned prettily over the water on stilts. If you like the cool, breezy feel of a treehouse, this spot is for you. At night the sea is lit by floodlights and is visible from this open-air restaurant. Steak, shrimp and chicken figure prominently on the continental menu, which changes nightly. But the food isn't the main attraction for the crowds who flock to soak up the atmosphere and admire the reef fish below. Reservations strongly recommended. Credit cards: A, DC, MC, V.

China Garden $$ ★

Kaya Grandi 47, Kralendijk, ☎ *(5997) 8480.*
Lunch: 11:30 a.m.–2 p.m., entrées $5–$24.
Dinner: 4–10 p.m., entrées $5–$24. Closed: Tue.
Located downtown in a restored home, China Garden is notable for its Cantonese dishes with island staples like goat and conch figuring heavily on its expansive menu. The decor is uninspired and the service pedestrian, but no one can fault the generous portions sure to satisfy the most voracious appetite. Black bean sauce dishes are delicious. Credit cards: A, MC, V.

Den Laman Seafood Restaurant $$$ ★★★

Kaya Gobernador Debrot 77, Kralendijk, ☎ *(5997) 8955.*
Dinner: 6–11:30 p.m., entrées $12–$35. Closed: Tue.
Tucked between the Sunset Beach Hotel and The Sand Dollar Condominium Resort is this open-air, garden terrace restaurant, specializing in seafood from conch to grouper and guaranteeing four different types of freshly-caught, local fish daily. Or you can choose your dinner from the lobster tank on the patio. High ceilings and a large saltwater aquarium add to the relaxed mood. Every Saturday night, live entertainment is featured at this 105-seat gathering place. Credit cards: A, MC, V.

Green Parrot $$$ ★★★

Kaya Gobernador, Kralendijk, ☎ *(5997) 5454.* Associated hotel: *Sand Dollar Condominiums.*
Lunch: 11a.m.–3 p.m., entrées $7–$10.
Dinner: 4:30–10 p.m., entrées $12–$28.
On Saturday night, the Green Parrot holds a barbecue buffet with a local popular trio jamming for the crowd. This casual eatery, known for its juicy burgers, is located over the water and boasts a terrific view of the sunset. The frosty tropical drinks during its daily Happy Hour (5–7 p.m.) put the crowd in a good mood. It's the sort of place where the characters populating Jimmy Buffet's songs would fit right in. Breakfast is served from 8–10:30 a.m., and the staff will gladly pack picnic baskets for daytrippers, too. Reservations recommended. Credit cards: A, MC, V.

Jardin Tropical Restaurant $$ ★★★

Kaya Grandi, Kralendijk, ☎ *(5997) 5718.*
Dinner: 6–10 p.m., prix fixe $20.
Jardin Tropical resides on the top floor of Kralendijk's tallest building: a whopping three stories high, adorned with flamingos and painted bright yellow. Take the elevator, which moves in typical island-style: leisurely. The restaurant overlooks Bonaire's leeward side and the sea. Creamy lobster soup is a nice starter, followed by *rouleau de poisson tri-color* (fresh sole and salmon roll). Finish with either cheeses or a chocolate parfait. The bar area is cozily tucked away down the hall where patrons retire for after-dinner drinks. Credit cards: MC, V.

Mona Lisa Bar & Restaurant $$$ ★★★

Kaya Grandi 15, Kralendijk, ☎ *(5997) 8718.*
Lunch: Noon–2 p.m., entrées $12–$23.
Dinner: 6–10 p.m., entrées $16–$23. Closed: Sat., Sun.
Absorb local color in this lively, in-town bar and restaurant, where the Dutch-born chef personally oversees each table. The Mona Lisa bar, decorated with a profusion

BONAIRE

of hometown knick-knacks, is a riot of activity. Copious snacks are served there until late. The pretty restaurant wears a more demure face, with a diverse menu of Indonesian, Dutch and French favorites. An ongoing special is pork satay (tenderloin marinated with garlic, sesame oil, soy and other spices) served with peanut sauce, and smoked Dutch eel and smoked salmon on an apple and onion salad. Reservations recommended. Credit cards: A, MC, V.

Oasis Bar & Grill $$$ ★★

Kaminda Sorobon 64, Kralendijk, ☎ *(5997) 8198.* Associated hotel: *Lac Bay Resort.*
Lunch: 10 a.m.–2 p.m., entrées $4–$6.
Dinner: 7–10 p.m., entrées $12–$32. Closed: Mon.

An energetic young couple manages this 32-seat restaurant as well as the Lac Bay Resort. Hummingbirds in the garden out front greet you as you enter this small place with high ceilings and abundant windows facing the peaceful lagoon on Bonaire's windward side. Most diners opt for patio dining. The atmosphere is one of contentment. Juicy burgers compare to the stateside's best. The specialty is "chicken haze," a chicken breast stuffed with herbs, feta, spinach, wrapped in hickory-smoked bacon, then grilled. Reservations recommended. Credit cards: A, MC, V.

Old Inn $$$ ★★★

J.A. Abraham Boulevard, Kralendijk, ☎ *(5997) 6666.*
Dinner: 5–10 p.m., entrées $10–$30.

This international menu is peppered with Dutch, French and Indonesian specialties, and the Indonesian chef excels at the typical Indonesian banquet—called rijstaffel—for two or more gourmands. Indonesian dishes (meats, fish, chicken, eggs, fish paste and vegetables) are laced with a myriad of fresh spices from ginger root to tamarind. Dishes are accompanied by fried rice, bami and spicy sambal. Archways, pale coral walls painted monochromatically with Indonesian scenes and comfortable seating unite with the thoughtful menu to give this place a pulled-together air sometimes missing in far-reaching outposts. Credit cards: MC, V.

Rendez-Vous Restaurant $$$ ★★★

Kaya L.D. Gerharts 3, Kralendijk, ☎ *(5997) 8454.*
Lunch: Noon–2 p.m., entrées $8–$16.
Dinner: 6–10:30 p.m., entrées $14–$26. Closed: Sun.

Although, like most island eateries, Renzdez-Vous has an open-air terrace, opt for the air-conditioned dining room. The terrace is adjacent to one of the town's busier intersections. Green linen tablecloths grace the tables; original photographs taken around the island hang on the walls; and the bar attracts lingerers for espresso or liqueurs. Rendez Vous has added a charcoal grill and well-stocked salad bar. Reservations recommended. Credit cards: A, MC, V.

Richard's Waterfront $$$ ★★★★

J.A. Abraham Boulevard 60, Kralendijk, ☎ *(5997) 5263.*
Dinner: 6:30–10:30 p.m., entrées $13–$35. Closed: Mon.

Opened since 1991, this waterfront charmer quickly set the high-mark for dining on Bonaire. Boston-born owner Richard Beaty attentively mingles with guests, while Chef Benito turns out steaks and deliciously fresh island fish dishes. Lush tropical gardens and a popular coral bar, a favorite spot from which to watch the magnificent sunset, add to the jovial mood here. The daily menu, designed around what's freshest, is presented on a chalkboard brought to your table. The wait staff gives detailed descriptions and top-notch service. Reservations recommended. Credit cards: A, MC, V.

Zeezicht Restaurant $$ ★

Kaya Corsow 10, Kralendijk, ☎ *(5997) 8434.*
Lunch: Noon–4 p.m., entrées $5–$9.
Dinner: 4–11 p.m., entrées $12–$25.

This waterfront eatery with a front porch at the water's edge serves a good American breakfast starting at 7:30 a.m. Lunch is usually local fish and conch sandwiches. Indonesian specialties, including a mini-rijstaffel for those who can't handle the usual 16-dish feast, are on the dinner menu. Service can be slow at peak times. Credit cards: A, MC, V.

Where to Shop

Though you can find some bargains in the duty-free stores of Bonaire, the island is hardly the shopper's paradise of St. Thomas or Aruba. Most stores are located in Kralendijk, whose four narrow, picturesque streets offer up the typical T-shirt shops, boutiques and jewelry stores. Native art is available at the **Bonaire Art Gallery** *(Kaya L.D. Gerharts #10; for opening hours* ☎ *(5997) 7120)*, which also provides custom framing. **Caribbean Arts & Crafts** *(38A Kaya Grandi,* ☎ *(5997) 5051)* has black coral crafts, as well as Mexican onyx, wall tapestries and other local wares; the government-sponsored **Fundashon Arte Industri Bonairiano** *(next to the post office in Kralendijk on J.A. Abraham Blvd.)* is also a good source for coral jewelry and other crafts.

Bonaire Directory

Arrival and Departure

ALM offers daily flights to Bonaire from Miami and Atlanta (twice a week). **Air Aruba** has direct flights from Newark, New Jersey, three times a week (these flights first touch down in Aruba before flying onto Bonaire). **American Airlines** flies daily to Curaçao from Miami, allowing passengers to make immediate transfers to Bonaire, usually on ALM, which makes 4–5 daily nonstop flights to Bonaire from Curaçao. American also flies daily from New York via Aruba. A plus for flying on American Airlines is that you can sometimes receive a discount if you book your hotel at the same time you make your flight reservation.

The departure tax is $10 and an inter-island departure tax of $5.65.

Business Hours

Stores open Monday–Saturday 8 a.m.–noon and 2–6 p.m. Banks open weekdays 8:30 a.m.–4 p.m.

Climate

Temperatures average 82 degrees F and vary only 6 degrees between summer and winter. Water temperatures range from 76–80 F. Bonaire gets less than 22 inches of rainfall per year. Bonaire is well below the Hurricane Belt and is rarely bombarded by storms or heavy seas.

Documents

U.S. and Canadian citizens need show only proof of citizenship (passport, original or notarized birth certificate, valid driver's license or voter's registration with photo ID), and an ongoing or return ticket.

Electricity

Current runs 127/120 volts, 50 cycles. American appliances will work slower; best to bring an adapter.

Getting Around

Expect to take a taxi from the airport to your hotel—about $10. Rates are established by the government, and most honest drivers will show the list of prices if you ask. Note that rates are higher (25 percent) after 8 p.m., and from 11–6 a.m. (50 percent).

Driving in Bonaire is on the right side of the road. Unless you are an experienced driver, tooting around Bonaire in a scooter or moped can be dangerous since roads are often strewn with rocks or full of holes. The best way to see the Washington—Slagbaai National Park is in a Jeep, van or automobile. To rent a car, you must be a minimum of between ages 21–26 depending on the rental company's policy, and you will need to show a valid U.S., British or Canadian driver's license that you've had for two years or more.

Avis, **Budget**, **Dollar Rent a Car** and **Hertz** all have booths at the airport. The government charges a $3 daily car rental tax.

Language

Papiamento is the unofficial island language, Dutch the official. English is almost universally spoken. Spanish is also well known.

Medical Emergencies

St. Francis Hospital in Kralendijk ☎ *8900* is run by well-trained doctors who studied in the Netherlands. Divers will be happy to know it is equipped with a decompression chamber.

Money

Official currency is the Netherlands Antilles florin or guilder, written as NAf or Afl. Most establishments list prices in guilders, but will accept dollars (giving change in guilders). U.S. dollars and traveler's checks are accepted everywhere.

BONAIRE

Telephone

From the U.S. dial *011* (international code), plus *5997* (country code), plus the four-digit local number. In recent years cell phones have proliferated. These numbers bounce to Curaçao. Few lodgings have room phones, so most people head down to the Landsradio office in Kralendijk. The airport also has telephones.

Time

Bonaire is on Atlantic standard time.

Tipping and Taxes

Most hotels and restaurants add a 10–15 percent service charge. The government also requires hotels to add a $6.50-per-person daily room tax. Feel free to tip more for especially good service.

Tourist Information

The tourist office is located at *Kaya Libertador Simon Bolivar 12* in Kralendijk; ☎ *(5997) 8322 (or 8649) or FAX (5997) 8408*. For information in the U.S., contact the Bonaire Tourist Office at ☎ *(800) 266-2473 or FAX (212) 956-5913*.

Water

Tap water is safe to drink since it comes from distilled seawater.

When To Go

Carnival takes place in February. Coronation Day is April 30. St. John's Day is June 24. St. Peter's Day is celebrated in Rincon on June 28. Bonaire Day is Sept. 6. Annual Sailing Regatta are a series of races celebrated with a festive air in mid-October.

BONAIRE HOTELS		RMS	RATES	PHONE	CR. CARDS
★★★★★	Harbour Village Beach Resort	72	$275–$705	(800) 424-0004	A, DC, MC, V
★★★★	Plaza Resort Bonaire	200	$125–$400	(800) 766-6016	
★★★	Captain Don's Habitat	93	$145–$440	(800) 327-6709	A, MC, V
★★★	Club Nautico Bonaire	24	$220–$450	(800) 359-0747	A, MC, V
★★★	Divi Flamingo Beach Resort	145	$84–$240	(800) 367-3484	A, D, DC, MC, V
★★★	Lion's Dive Hotel Bonaire	31	$160–$440	(800) 786-3483	A, DC, MC, V
★★★	Port Bonaire Resort	26	$185–$385	(800) 766-6016	A, MC, V
★★	Buddy Beach & Dive Resort	40	$93–$232	(800) 359-0747	A, DC, MC, V
★★	Carib Inn	13	$69–$149	(5997) 8819	A, MC, V
★★	Sand Dollar Condominium Resort	85	$155–$360	(800) 288-4773	A, MC, V
★	Sorobon Beach Resort	30	$145–$215	(5997) 8080	D, MC, V

BONAIRE

BONAIRE RESTAURANTS	PHONE	ENTREE	CR.C ARDS
Chinese Cuisine			
★ **China Garden**	(5997) 8480	$5–$24	A, MC, V
Continental Cuisine			
★★★ **Chibi-Chibi Restaurant**	(5997) 8285	$11–$19	A, DC, MC, V
★★★ **Green Parrot**	(5997) 5454	$7–$28	A, MC, V
★★ **Oasis Bar & Grill**	(5997) 8198	$4–$32	A, MC, V
★ **Zeezicht Restaurant**	(5997) 8434	$5–$25	A, MC, V
French Cuisine			
★★★ **Chez Truus**	(5997) 8617	$11–$25	A, MC, V
★★★ **Jardin Tropical Restaurant**	(5997) 5718	$20–$20	MC
International Cuisine			
★★★ **Mona Lisa Bar & Restaurant**	(5997) 8718	$12–$23	A, MC, V
★★★ **Old Inn**	(5997) 6666	$10–$30	NoneMC, V
★★★ **Rendez-Vous Restaurant**	(5997) 8454	$8–$26	A, MC, V
Regional Cuisine			
★★★ **Beefeater Garden Restaurant**	(5997) 7776	$14–$38	A, MC, V
Seafood Cuisine			
★★★★ **Richard's Waterfront**	(5997) 5263	$13–$35	A, MC, V
★★★ **Den Laman Seafood Restaurant**	(5997) 8955	$12–$35	A, MC, V

BRITISH VIRGIN ISLANDS

On Virgin Gorda huge boulders form a natural swimming pool and underwater caves known as The Baths.

With countless pristine coves and dozens of minimally or uninhabited islands peppering the Caribbean horizon in every direction, it's no wonder the British Virgin Islands can refer to themselves as Nature's Little Secrets, and get away with it. The combination of these precious elements have long conspired to create a sailor's paradise. However, until relatively recently, the country has never sought nor desired mass tourism, preferring to let the discerning or curious traveler discover it over time. There are no direct flights from the continental U.S. to Tortola (you fly a puddle jumper from San Juan, or ferry over from St. Thomas), and heading to Virgin Gorda or the other BVIs requires an additional effort that no doubt scares off many customers in search of a fast, easy vacation. But the extra hassle has a payoff, for when compared against the frantic pace of St. Thomas next door, the BVIs are positively laid-back and friendly.

Friendliness and charm are one sales point, and although the BVI government is gradually expanding the tourism infrastructure, it's reassuring to note they recognize that a chief lure for current and future visitors is the untrammeled nature of these outposts. For the moment, cruise ships are limited to the medium-size variety and the behemoths are kept out of BVI waters. Though there are a number of pricey resorts, high-rise accommodations are nowhere to be found. What nightlife there is typically focuses on the lively beach bars—on tiny Jost Van Dyke, there's a bar for every 17 residents, though the island somehow still remains serene and unspoiled. And though crime has become an everyday concern for both locals and tourists on other nearby islands, in the BVIs, many of the smaller hotels still don't bother with room keys.

Instead, the sailing ambiance predominates, as it has for centuries. Norman Island is reputed to be the setting for Robert Louis Stevenson's *Treasure Island*, and stories of buried treasure in the holds of the many sunken galleons still percolate among the yachting set. Today, bare-boat charterers define much of the BVI character, most of them lured by the secluded bays and fine anchorages. There are special beaches sprinkled throughout the chain, good diving and snorkeling along the Sir Francis Drake Channel, and delightful short hikes in Gorda Peak and Mount Sage National Parks. But don't overlook the pleasure of island-hopping during your visit—most of the islands are a short ferry or charter boat ride away from Tortola.

BEST BETS FOR...

Bird's-Eye View

Lying 60 miles east of Puerto Rico and just a few miles northeast of St. John, more than 50 islands, crags and cays make up the complex referred to as the British Virgin Islands. Sixteen of the islands are inhabited, the most important being Tortola, where more than four-fifths of the 17,000-strong population lives, and where the archipelago's capital, Road Town, is posi-

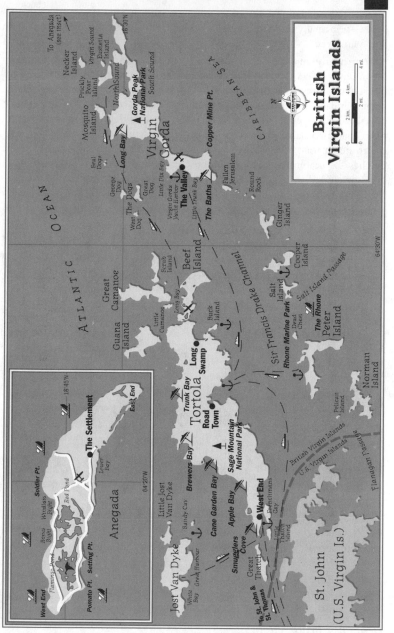

tioned. The remaining 3500 or so residents are scattered among the other islands—principally on Virgin Gorda, with 170 living on Anegada and 150 on Jost Van Dyke.

From nearly any vantage point on Tortola, the sublime view is that of seemingly endless tropical islands stretching off into the horizon. The topography of these islands—all but Anegada volcanic in origin—ranges from sloping mountains cloaked with verdant green growth to scrub and cactus-covered hills layered with massive rounded boulders. Long stretches of palm-shaded beaches border much of Tortola's perimeter, while offshore, rough-hewn rock formations poke their heads out of the water to provide perches for seabirds. Tortola's highest point is 1780-foot Mount Sage, a peak enveloped by a small rainforest, even though the summit receives less than 100 inches of rain annually.

Devil's Bay, British Virgin Islands

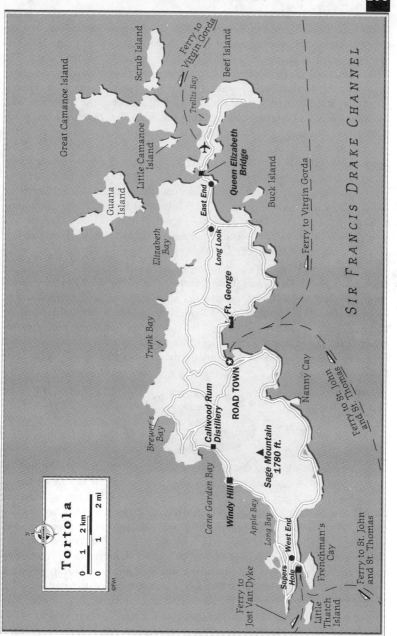

BRITISH VIRGIN ISLANDS

Seven miles long and mirroring the outline of a lopsided bat in flight, **Virgin Gorda** has a similar crest at its center, 1370-foot Virgin Gorda Peak, and another claim to fame—the unforgettable Baths, a group of giant boulders strewn along the beach in Devil's Bay, at the island's southern wing. The rocks are a geological mystery, but remain a supremely photogenic location for swimming and snorkeling, except when cruise ships have called. There's also sweet **Jost Van Dyke**, where a four-room inn caters to the lucky few who overnight here and discover the origin of the Painkiller. Further afield is 15-square-mile **Anegada**, a coralline outpost about 15 miles northwest of the other islands out in the Atlantic. Sometimes referred to as a drowned island, Anegada's highest point above sea level is 28 feet, and mariners have found the coral shelf that surrounds it treacherous—more than 300 ships are estimated to have been sent to their grave off the island's shores. Scattered among these four are the other, sparsely inhabited British Virgins, including what we refer to as the **Resort Islands**—a handful of islets that are home to a single resort or special inn—from fabulously expensive Necker Island to fabulously unpretentious Cooper Island.

Cutting through the BVIs, and protected yearlong from the brunt of tradewinds, is the **Sir Francis Drake Channel**, one of the world's great sailing passages. On either side of the channel are a series of pristine anchorages, many of them next to uninhabited islands. Below the water, particularly on the south side of the Drake passage, are the archipelago's best dive sites, including the *RMS Rhone*, a magnificently encrusted steamer that went down in a hurricane in 1867—it is probably the Caribbean's most popular and treasured wreck.

History

The Virgin Islands were discovered by Christopher Columbus on his second voyage in 1493. Fascinated by the exquisite natural beauty of the islands, he named them *Las Once Mil Virgines* (the 11,000 Virgins) in honor of St. Ursula and her followers. The truth is, Columbus was the not the first human to set forth on the island. Prior to the European invasion, these islands had been populated by successive waves of Indian tribes migrating north from the Orinoco region of South America. Unfortunately, the arrival of the Europeans spelled the end of the native population; within a generation, there was not a trace of them. The occupation of the island by the Spanish and other Europeans followed a pattern similar to that of other Caribbean islands. For two centuries, control of the island was passed from one country to another while the islands remained mostly uninhabited. Many of those who balked at directly challenging the Spanish chose instead the path of piracy and pirateering, the most famous of whom were Sir John Hawkins, Henry Morgan, Jost Van Dyke and Edward Teach, better known as Blackbeard. These islands provided a secluded and safe anchorage for these brigands. Even today the legacy of piracy survives in the names of many islands and in the ever-persistent legends of buried treasure. Control of the Virgin Islands finally equalized with the Danish taking control of the western islands, now known as the U.S. Virgin Islands, while the British controlled the eastern set—so-named the British Virgin Islands. In fact, Tortola (BVI) is separated from St. John (USV) by less than two miles. From the 1700s to the mid-1800s, a plantation economy supported these islands. The remnants of the sugar industry can still be seen in the ruins of sugar mills hidden in the bush. In 1967, the BVI became a self-governing member of the British Commonwealth.

People

Because of generous economic assistance received from Great Britain, islanders enjoy considerable enthusiasm for, and strong identification with, their mother country. As a group, the people have a reputation for being extraordinarily friendly and will naturally extend you greetings as you stroll down the street. In fact, an islander will be hurt if you don't return the salutation. At the same time, Gordians and Tortolans are said to be somewhat retiring and are not exactly prone to inviting travelers into their homes. Those who live in the interior mountains definitely tend to be shyer, but their lifestyle is also comparatively less pressured by touristic demands; these are older people in the hillside communities who still ride donkeys, make their own charcoal and harbor age-old superstitions about "duppies" or spirits. As tourism has blossomed due to the efforts of established black families as well as spunky outsiders, some of the island's women have become renowned for their cooking skills. Mrs. V. Thomas was decorated by the Queen of England for her guava jelly and mango chutney. As construction demands have risen, traditional island occupations such as stonemasonry and gardening have begun returning, and sailors in the old school of sloops are finding another kind of work in more progressive boating.

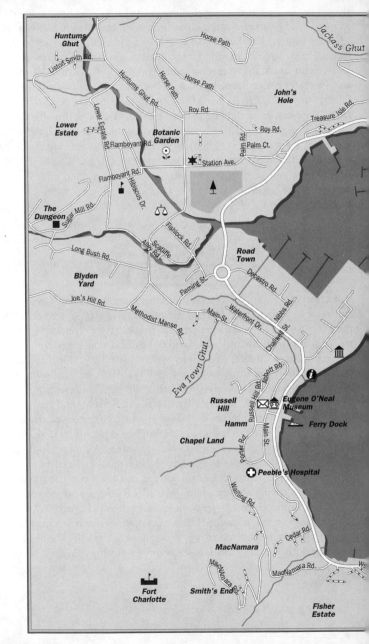

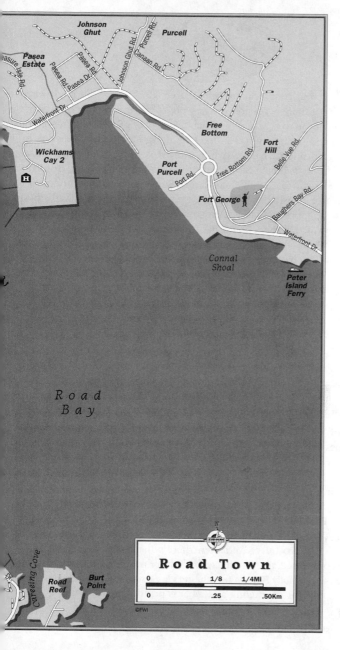

On Tortola, all the best beaches are located along the scalloped north shore, a number of them accessible only by boat (remember, this is a sailor's island). Starting at the west end of the island, **Smuggler's Cove** is often void of fellow bathers, and features good snorkeling along its length, while nearby **Long Bay** is a near-mile of narrow white sand that invites romantic sunset strolls. Surfers head for **Apple Bay** during the day, while at night, Bomba's Shack is the beach bar to end all. **Cane Garden Bay** is a popular anchorage for boaters, while its expansive curl of sand attracts visitors for the island's best collection of watersports activities. Another large cove, **Brewers Bay**, is ideal for snorkeling, while **Elizabeth Beach** has only recently become accessible by road, thanks to a new condo development. Beef Island, which is connected to Tortola by bridge, has **Long Bay** and **Trellis Bay**, both nice pieces of real estate, but for the regular activity in and out of the airport.

As on Tortola, Virgin Gorda's best beaches are on the north side of the island, beginning with one of the most unique and picturesque swimming locations anywhere in the region, **The Baths**. Alas, the spot, scattered with massive boulders that create enchanting grottoes, is a hot ticket on cruise ship itineraries—visit before 9 a.m. or after 4 p.m. Next door is **Spring Bay**, a good place to duck over to when the crowds get thick at The Baths, and just beyond is glistening **Trunk Bay**, reached by a rough path through private lands from Spring Bay. Two other Gorda beauties are **Savannah Bay** and **Mahoe Bay**, with long, gentle curves of sand for sunning and swimming.

A number of excellent beaches are found away from the two main BVIs. Perhaps the best for a day trip is Peter Island's idyllic **Deadman's Bay**, an isolated, palm-lined strand that has grown a beach bar and grill. Mountainous Jost Van Dyke has a beautiful sandy beach at **White Bay**, another at **Great Harbour Bay**, and lively bars at both. An uninhabited scrub-covered islet just off Jost Van Dyke, **Sandy Cay**, has a velvety swatch of radiant white sand, and little else. **Prickly Pear Island** (opposite the Bitter End Yacht Club), has a long shelf of sand, **Vixen Point**, which sometimes has a beach bar and watersports center when things are busy. And then there's flat Anegada, which could practically be considered a beach in itself. If you're making the trip to remote Anegada, head for **Loblolly Bay**—a few shelters are provided from the sun, the offshore reef is nice for snorkeling and a bar is positioned at each end.

In the British Virgin Islands, all beaches are public, including those on the private resort islands.

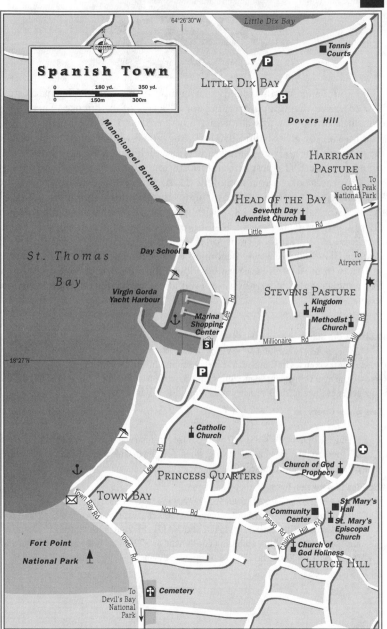

Spanish Town

0   180 yd.   350 yd.
0   150m   300m

Little Dix Bay

Tennis Courts

P

LITTLE DIX BAY

P

Dovers Hill

HARRIGAN PASTURE

To Gorda Peak National Park

HEAD OF THE BAY

Seventh Day Adventist Church †

Little   Rd

Manchioneel Bottom

Day School ■

St. Thomas Bay

To Airport

STEVENS PASTURE

Kingdom Hall ■

Methodist Church †

Virgin Gorda Yacht Harbour

Marina Shopping Center

S

Millionaire Rd

Crab   Hill   Rd

Lee   Rd

P

—18°27'N

† Catholic Church ■

Church of God † Prophecy

PRINCESS QUARTERS

St. Mary's Hall ■

Community Center ■

St. Mary's † Episcopal Church

Lee   Rd

Passo   Rd

Church   Hill   Rd

TOWN BAY

North   Rd

Town Bay Rd

Tower Rd

Church of God Holiness ■

CHURCH HILL

Fort Point

National Park

To Devil's Bay National Park

† Cemetery

Underwater

The abundance of tiny islands that compose the British Virgins create a host of varied diving opportunities for all levels of experience. The islands offer little in the way of wall diving, but wrecks and reefs are plentiful, and visibility can top a crystalline 130 feet. Anegada is off limits to boat dives for the moment due to over-fishing (and shore diving is not easy); the snorkeling is fine. The BVI's best is found mostly among the small, uninhabited islands southeast of Tortola including the spectacular 310-foot steamer, the **RMS *Rhone***, the Caribbean's most famous wreck, which sunk theatrically off the rocks of Salt Island in 1867 with most of its 300 passengers on board. There's also the *Chikuzen*, a 246-foot refrigeration ship, and a newer wreck, the *Inganess*, a 120-foot transporter ship with crane that went down off Cooper Island and is slowly becoming encrusted. Diving is more expensive here than in most of the Eastern Caribbean, but the British Virgins feature a nice concentration of worthy sites, even after one has taken in the must-see *Rhone*.

Dive Shops

Baskin in the Sun

Prospect Reef Resort and Sopers Hole Wharf; ☎ *(800) 233-7938 or (284) 494-5854.*
Features courses in Caribbean reef ecology and historical shipwrecks. Two-tank dive $80 if you bring your own equipment. The shop at Sopers Hole on the West End accesses dives in the sleepier waters around Jost Van Dyke.

Blue Water Divers

Nanny Cay, Tortola; ☎ *(284) 494-2847.*
PADI facility, handles SSI referrals; courses to instructor in September. Utilizes a 47-foot catamaran with full diving amenities. Two-tank dive including all equipment, $80. Resort course, $95.

Kilbrides Underwater Tours

Bitter End Yacht Club; ☎ *(800) 932-4286, (284) 495-9638.*
The oldest shop on the island, situated in a quiet location at Gorda's North Sound Bay (closest to the *Chikuzen*). PADI and NAUI affiliated, with courses to Divemaster. Two-tank dive $80, including equipment or $72 if you bring your own BC and regulator (or $90 for the Chikuzen trip, usually on Thursdays). Resort courses, $95.

On Foot

Quiet and uncrowded, well-tended yet off-the-beaten track, the natural environments of the British Virgin Islands are a lot of things their U.S. counterparts aspire to, but only attain on protected St. John, which lies a scant two miles off Tortola's southern coast. There are almost 60 islands in the BVIs, but almost all are uninhabited, which allows the option to travel to an island for a day of private exploration and contemplation. There are delightful, mostly short trails on the main islands, while the outer destinations boast a wealth of unmarked possibilities.

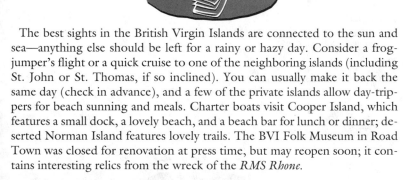

What Else to See

The best sights in the British Virgin Islands are connected to the sun and sea—anything else should be left for a rainy or hazy day. Consider a frog-jumper's flight or a quick cruise to one of the neighboring islands (including St. John or St. Thomas, if so inclined). You can usually make it back the same day (check in advance), and a few of the private islands allow day-trippers for beach sunning and meals. Charter boats visit Cooper Island, which features a small dock, a lovely beach, and a beach bar for lunch or dinner; deserted Norman Island features lovely trails. The BVI Folk Museum in Road Town was closed for renovation at press time, but may reopen soon; it contains interesting relics from the wreck of the *RMS Rhone*.

Parks and Gardens

Baths, The (Devil's Bay Nat'l Park) ★★★★★

Lee Road, Virgin Gorda.

Gigantic house-size boulders strewn about create luminous seawater grottoes, and a geological mystery: The stones are granite, which is not usually found south of the Carolinas. Are they the product of ancient volcanoes or were they carried south by glaciers during the ice age? No matter. The cave-like passages lead to seductive hidden pools and the snorkeling here is unique. A step and ladder system through the boulders leads to a gorgeous, protected swimming area, Devil's Bay. This is by far the island's most-visited spot, a big stop for cruise ship passengers—come early in the morning or late in the afternoon to avoid the crowds.

Gorda Peak National Park ★★★★

North Sound Road, Virgin Gorda.

The "peak" in the name rises some 1370 feet, making it Virgin Gorda's highest point. This 265-acre preserve is home to indigenous and exotic plants and has been reforested with mahogany trees. Hike to the top, then catch your breath at the observation tower, though foliage obscures the view.

J.R. O'Neal Botanical Gardens ★★★

Road Town, Tortola, ☎ (284) 494-4557.
Hours open: 8 a.m.–4 p.m.

Indigenous and exotic plants are beautifully showcased at this four-acre garden, which includes an herb garden and hothouses for orchids and ferns. A must for flower lovers.

Sage Mountain National Park ★★★★

Ridge Road, Tortola.

Located on the slopes of Tortola's once-volcanic summit, this 92-acre national park protects the remains of a primeval rain forest—most, alas, was cut down over the years. A graveled path will take you to the top, some 1780 feet up, the highest elevation in the British and U.S. Virgin Islands. A nice morning trip on clear days and a snack bar at the base of the trail is available for refreshment.

Tours

Travel Plan Tours ★★★

Waterfront Plaza, Tortola, ☎ (284) 494-2872.

Half-day tours of Tortola in surrey buses or vans and include all the hot spots. $50 per person.

Virgin Gorda Tours Association ★★★

Fischers Cove Beach Hotel, Virgin Gorda, ☎ (284) 495-5252.

Ferrying over for the day and want to see Virgin Gorda without renting a set of wheels? They'll shuttle you about, taking in all the high points, from the Baths to North Sound, for $50. Two tours are offered daily; call for a schedule.

Sports

When the sea is as inviting as it is in the BVIs, who needs other activities? Bare boat or crewed yacht charters are available from **Moorings** and a number of other outfits. It's probably the biggest local activity—navigation is not difficult and the weather is usually so clear you can't get lost, though the numerous inlets and rippled coastlines can give navigators a run for their money (note that bare-boaters aren't allowed around Anegada due to the dangerous reefs and prohibition against anchoring). If you're not an educated sailor, try a few classes at the **Nick Trotter Sailing School** at the Bitter End Yacht Club on Virgin Gorda (see "Where to Stay" in Virgin Gorda, below). Snorkeling is generally excellent throughout the BVIs. Several outfits provide snorkeling day trips aboard boats, and some of the dive operators will allow snorkelers to join them as they head off to some of the remote destinations; the *RMS Rhone* is close enough to the surface to be appreciated by snorkelers, and nearby Norman Island is an excellent spot. Windsurfing has become popular, and sea kayaking—sometimes between the U.S. and British islands with camping equipment stashed aboard—has developed quite a following.

Bicycling

Although many roads on Tortola are too steep for riding, much of the south coast makes for pleasant touring, and it's worth checking into a daytrip over to Virgin Gorda where cycling is a little easier. **Last Stop Sports** rents Gary Fishers for $20 per day and invites visiting cyclists to join the biweekly races put on by the BVI bicycling club; also hike/bike tours for $23–$40 per person ☎ *(284) 494-0564*.

Horseback Riding

Hop aboard a horse at **Shadow's Ranch** and venture along the beach or through the countryside to Sage Mountain National Park. Prices start at $25 per hour ☎ *(284) 494-2262*.

Watersports, Tortola

Various locations.

Sailing is the big activity, and quite a few individuals charter their boats for daytrips or longer. The bigger companies include **Moorings** ☎ *(800) 535-7289* or *(284) 494-2501*, **Sun Yacht Charters** ☎ *(800) 772-3500* or *(284) 494-5538*, and **Virgin Island Sailing** ☎ *(800) 382-9666* or *(284) 494-3658*; all three specialize in multi-day hires, but also offer day sails. **Cat PPALU** offers a day sail to the Baths and Norman Island aboard a 75-foot catamaran ☎ *(284) 496-7716*. Kuralu provides day sails on a 50-foot cat to Jost Van Dyke and Green Cay for $75 ☎ *(284) 495-4381*. **Boardsailing BVI** provides kayaks, catamarans, and one-hour windsurfing lessons for $20 (hourly, daily and weekly board rentals available); two locations: Trellis Bay (Beef Island) ☎ *(284) 495-2447* and Nanny Cay ☎ *(284) 494-0422*, or *(800) 880-7873*. Beginner to advanced sailing courses are provided by **Thomas Sailing** at Nanny Cay ☎ *(284) 494-0333*. Sportfishing is available from two sources: **Pelican Charters** at Prospect Reef Harbour ☎ *(284) 496-7386*, and **Tamarin Charters** at Seabreeze Marina, East End ☎ *(284) 495-9837*. Snorkeling trips are offered by **Caribbean Images Tours**, with full-day trips to Virgin Gorda or Jost Van Dyke for $60, and half-day trips to the Indians or the Rhone for $40 ☎ *(284) 494-1147*.

Watersports, Virgin Gorda

Various locations.

The Bitter End Yacht Club leads the way when it comes to activities for water babies, including the renowned **Nick Trotter Sailing School** ☎ *(800) 872-2392* or *(284) 494-2746*. **Leverick Bay Watersports** provides catamaran, sunfish and kayak rentals as well as waterskiing and parasailing ☎ *(284) 495-7376*. **Captain Dale** arranges sport fishing trips ☎ *(284) 495-5225*.

Where to Stay

	Fielding's Highest Rated Hotels in British Virgin Islands	
★★★★★	Biras Creek Resort	$250–$695
★★★★★	Guana Island	$440–$675
★★★★★	Little Dix Bay	$250–$700
★★★★★	Necker Island	$12,000–$18,000
★★★★★	Peter Island Resort	$295–$895
★★★★	Drake's Anchorage	$398–$690
★★★	Bitter End Yacht Club	$320–$610
★★★	Fort Recovery Estates	$135–$240
★★★	Long Bay Beach Hotel	$85–$360
★★★	Sugar Mill Hotel	$135–$265

	Fielding's Best Deserted Island Escapes in the British Virgin Islands	
★★★★★	Guana Island	$440–$675
★★★★	Drake's Anchorage	$398–$690
★★	Cooper Island Beach Club	$75–$155
★★	Sandcastle	$85–$175
★★★★★	Biras Creek Resort	$250–$695

	Fielding's Best Value Hotels in British Virgin Islands	
★★★	Treasure Isle Hotel	$80–$170
★★★	Olde Yard Inn	$90–$195
★★★	Prospect Reef Resort	$90–$210
★★	Ole Works Inn	$50–$170
★★	Leverick Bay Resort	$100–$125

Where to Stay—Tortola

Accommodations in the British Virgin Islands are the antithesis of the big-island resort; for the most part they are intimate and casual and reflect the style of the owner/management, frequently husband-and-wife teams. Although the islands are rarely overrun with tourists, even in peak season, travelers seeking maximum solitude will want to pick up a copy of *Intimate Inns and Villas*, a free pamphlet with color pictures covering a couple dozen small properties on the four main islands; it's available from the **British Virgin Islands Tourist Board** in New York ☎ *(800) 835-8530* or *(212) 696-0400*.

Claiming roughly half of the archipelago's rooms, Tortolan accommodations tend to cater to moderate budgets and the yachting set and a number of the hotels are situated in and around bustling Road Town. If you're seeking luxury, Tortola is probably the one BVI you'll want to steer away from, but if nightlife or a social scene is important, Tortola is as close as it comes in this chain. It also makes a convenient base from which to explore the other islands on day trips.

Hotels and Resorts

Tortola's lead property is **Long Bay Beach Hotel**, which also acts as the unofficial social hub of the island. It and several other hotels mix standard room accommodations with villas and condos; if the property you are considering mixes these room types, check to make sure the rate you're quoted includes maid service (which is sometimes a mandatory additional charge).

Long Bay Beach Hotel   **$85–$360**   ★ ★ ★

Long Bay, ☎ *(800) 729-9599, (284) 495-4252, FAX (284) 495-4677.*
Single: *$85–$340.* Double: *$145–$360.*
Situated on a 52-acre estate that slopes down to a powdery, narrow mile-long beach, Long Bay offers a variety of rooms with good summer rates for singles. Some units are located along a hillside (great views)—others, including charming cabanas, are right on the beach. All come equipped with air conditioning, ceiling fans, refrigerators, wet bars, hair dryers and phones, while the most expensive units also boast full kitchens, VCRs and huge decks. Active types are kept happy with the complimentary pitch-and-putt golf course, pool, and tennis courts. The restaurant is housed in an old sugar mill and offers live music most nights. Villas also available, and dwellers can arrange to have a chef prepare a private dinner—nice! 72 rooms.
Credit cards: A, D, MC, V.

Maria's Hotel   **$70–$125**   ★

Road Town, ☎ *(284) 494-2595, FAX (284) 494-2420.*
Single: *$70–$105.* Double: *$85–$125.*
A new waterfront hotel in Road Town, Maria's is a well-run local operation that appeals to business-people, but has decent winter rates for those who don't mind the in-town locale. Rooms are generously-sized, with rattan furnishings, kitchenette and balcony or patio. There's a nice pool and a good West Indian restaurant on the premises. 20 rooms. Credit cards: MC, V.

Prospect Reef Resort $90–$210   ★★★

Road Town, ☎ *(800) 356-8937, (284) 494-3311, FAX (284) 494-5595.*
Single: $90–$210. Double: $90–$210.

Set on lush oceanside grounds (but lacking a beach), the choices here range from standard guest rooms to studios to townhouses and villas (that sleep up to four), some with kitchenettes, some with air conditioning. Accommodations are uninspired, but a 1997 spruce-up left things looking fresh. Lots going on, including six tennis courts, a pitch-and-putt golf course and a fitness center; three restaurants and three bars are on hand. Two pools including one that is junior-Olympic sized, plus two sea enclosures for bobbing or snorkeling. A nice selection of children's activities, day sails are available at the small harbor, and an excellent dive shop is on property. 15-minute walk to Road Town. 130 rooms. Credit cards: A, MC, V.

Sebastian's on the Beach $65–$190   ★

Apple Bay, ☎ *(800) 336-4870, (284) 495-4212, FAX (284) 495-4466.*
Website: www.britishvirginislands.com/sebastians. E-mail: sebhotel@caribhotel.com.
Single: $65–$180. Double: $75–$190.

Set on the gorgeous beach at Apple Bay, this small hotel is split in two by a road; request a room on the beach side for obvious reasons, but you'll pay a premium. The "tropical yard units" on the other side of the road are cheapest, but a bit tatty. Just eight have air conditioning; the rest make do with ceiling fans. The slender beach is just fair for swimming and sunning, but lovely to look at. There's a bar and restaurant, a fun weekly barbecue on Sunday, and Bomba's Shack is a few hundred feet away. 26 rooms. Credit cards: A, D, MC, V.

Treasure Isle Hotel $80–$170   ★★★

Road Town, ☎ *(800) 223-1108, (284) 494-2501, FAX (284) 494-2507.*
Single: $80–$155. Double: $95–$170. Suites Per Day: $125–$230.

All the air-conditioned rooms at this pretty hotel overlook the harbor and marina, and include tropical art and pleasant rattan furniture. Situated on 15 acres of hillside, the grounds feature a festive free-form, porthole-lined pool and a good restaurant, the Lime and Mango. Complimentary transportation to one of Tortola's beaches daily. The management is friendly, and guests here are kept happy with lots of evening entertainment for the partying set. A full dive shop is across the street featuring a selection of water sports. 43 rooms. Credit cards: A, MC, V.

Village Cay Marina Hotel $77–$165   ★★

Road Town, ☎ *(284) 494-2771, FAX (284) 494-2773.*
Single: $77–$138. Double: $99–$165. Suites Per Day: $225–$440.

This small hotel is located downtown in the Village Cay Marina Complex. Rooms are air conditioned and have cathedral ceilings, Oriental rugs and cable TV; a laundry facility is available. There's a restaurant and bar on site, as well as a small pool and watersports. The clientele is largely comprised of yachtsmen, and there's lots to do within walking distance. Note that the usual 10 percent service charge is included in the rates (consider a tip for the staff). 19 rooms. Credit cards: A, MC, V.

Apartments and Condominiums

Yacht owners and vacationers prepared to settle in for a long stay take advantage of the many private homes rented by owners during high season. Apartments and condos also offer the opportunity for independent living, especially if you want to do your own cooking (bring staples from home since prices on Tortola run high). There are many brokers on the island; check with the **BVI Tourist Board** ☎ *(800) 835-8530* or *(212) 696-0400* for an up-to-date list. Rates for a simple condo start as low as $500 per week and sometimes accommodate six or eight guests comfortably; winter rates start closer to $850 per week and soar heavenward from there. Luxury rentals are offered by **McLaughlin Anderson Villas** at ☎ *(800) 537-6246* or *(284) 776-0635*. For provisioning your villa with the best, head straight to **Fort Wines Gourmet**, where pates, Parisian chocolates, fine coffee and tea and, of course, wines from the U.S. and Europe are stocked; it's on Main Street in Road Town ☎ *(284) 494-3036*.

Fort Recovery Estates$135–$240★★★

Freshwater Pond, ☎ *(800) 367-8455, (284) 495-4354, FAX (284) 495-4036.*
Website: www.1travel.com/fortrecovery/. E-mail: FTRHotel@caribsurf.com.
Single: $135–$240. Double: $135–$240.

The stone tower is all that remains of this 17th-century Dutch fort, today a small group of attractive one- and two-story villas. All have TVs, full kitchens and air-conditioned bedrooms, while the cozy new penthouse units have cathedral ceilings of pickled pine. Larger parties can rent two- to four-bedroom facilities that sleep up to eight ($215–$640 per night). Continental breakfast is included in the rates and—a nice touch—a complimentary dinner is served in your room for each seven-night stay. Nice pool, and the small beach makes for good swimming and snorkeling, or unwind with a yoga class or massage. The grounds are littered with colorful flowers, the informal atmosphere is pleasant. 17 rooms. Credit cards: A, MC, V.

Frenchman's Cay Resort$120–$220★★

Frenchman's Cay, ☎ *(800) 235-4077, (284) 495-4844, FAX (284) 495-4056.*
Website: www.frenchmans.com. E-mail: fmchotel@caribsurf.com.
Single: $120–$200. Double: $130–$220.

Set on the scenic tip of Frenchman's Cay and connected via bridge to Tortola, this small enclave of villas has nice views of the channel and neighboring islands. There are just nine one- and two-bedroom villas, each with a full kitchen, ceiling fans (no air conditioning), and island art. The small beach is good for snorkeling, but rocks make wading difficult. There's also a small pool, hammocks meant for snoozing, a tennis court and an open-air restaurant; the marina and Pusser's is a 15-minute walk. A nice, quiet spot. 9 rooms. Credit cards: A, D, MC, V.

Nanny Cay Resort$70–$195★★

Nanny Cay, ☎ *(800) 742-4276, (284) 494-2512, FAX (284) 494-3288.*
Single: $70–$145. Double: $119–$195.

Set on a 25-acre islet on Sir Francis Drake Channel, Nanny Cay houses guests in studio apartments with kitchenettes, West Indian decor, ceiling fan and air conditioning. Lots of yachtsmen come here, lured by the 180-slip marina, and beach-lovers will want to look elsewhere. Extras include two restaurants and bars, a pair of pools and tennis. Service can be uneven. 42 rooms. Credit cards: A, MC, V.

Inns

Ole Works Inn   **$50–$170**   ★★

Cane Garden Bay, ☎ (284) 495-4837, FAX (284) 495-9618.
Single: $50–$130. Double: $60–$170. Suites Per Day: $110–$265.

This atmospheric inn sits behind the sea grape trees above beautiful Cane Garden Bay. Clustered around a 300-year-old sugar mill, rooms are a jumble of modern, sometimes curious additions. Most are in good shape, but each is a little different, and there are some suites and a "honeymoon tower" room. Service can be spotty, but the great location includes happening beach bar, Quito's Gazebo. Excellent summer discounts. 18 rooms. Credit cards: MC, V.

Sugar Mill Hotel   **$135–$265**   ★★★

Apple Bay, ☎ (800) 462-8834, (284) 495-4355, FAX (284) 495-4696.
Website: www.sugarmillhotel.com. E-mail: sugmill@caribsurf.com.
Closed Date: August-September.
Single: $135–$250. Double: $150–$265. Suites Per Day: $195–$585.

The dining room is housed in an old sugar mill and rum distillery, hence the name. The lushly landscaped estate features accommodations in simple cottages scattered about a hillside. Furnishings are adequate, but colorful; some have kitchens and most now have air conditioning. A two-bedroom villa is also available, complete with a full kitchen, large balcony and spacious stone terrace. There's a small pool for those who don't want to cross the street to the compact beach, where a bar and restaurant is located. The property is owned by an American couple who used to write about travel and food—they oversee great meals, and wonderful service to match. Just the spot for those who want to get away from it all but don't want all the trappings of a full resort. 21 rooms. Credit cards: A, MC, V.

Low Cost Lodging

Budget accommodations are now available on Tortola, usually in a decent location that won't require you to rent a car. **Sea View**, a popular local restaurant, added rooms (with a view) to its property ☎ *(284) 494-2483*, while the **Cane Garden Bay Hotel** is a good place to meet local yacht owners ☎ *(284) 495-4639*. The **Fort Burt Hotel** is located on the outskirts of Road Town ☎ *(284) 494-2587*. All three of these properties have rooms for under $100 a night during the winter season, but don't forget about apartments and condos—these offer savings by accommodating larger groups of people or through cooking your own meals. Camping is available at **Brewer's Bay**.

Where to Eat

Fielding's Highest Rated Restaurants in British Virgin Islands

★★★★★	Brandywine Bay	$20–$28
★★★★	Sugar Mill	$17–$26
★★★	Bath and Turtle Pub, The	$11–$30
★★★	Big Bamboo's	$12–$23
★★★	Capriccio di Mare	$6–$13
★★★	Mrs. Scatliffe's	$20–$27
★★★	Olde Yarde Inn	$18–$30
★★★	Pusser's Leverick Bay	$13–$24
★★★	Skyworld	$16–$30
★★★	Virgin Queen	$8–$16

Fielding's Most Romantic Restaurants in British Virgin Islands

♡♡♡♡♡	Brandywine Bay	$20–$28
♡♡♡♡	Sandcastle	$30–$30
♡♡♡♡	Skyworld	$16–$30
♡♡♡♡	Sugar Mill	$17–$26
♡♡♡	Mrs. Scatliffe's	$20–$27

Fielding's Best Value Restaurants in British Virgin Islands

★★★	Pirate's Pub & Grill	$5–$7
★★★	Capriccio di Mare	$6–$13
★★★	Virgin Queen	$8–$16
★★★★★	Brandywine Bay	$20–$28
★★★	Pusser's Leverick Bay	$13–$24

Where to Eat—Tortola

With at least 65 restaurants currently in business—about one for every 200 residents—Tortola boasts one of the Caribbean's most extensive food scenes. Credit the yachties, who obviously prefer jumping into the dinghy for the evening meal over assembling it at sea. From the inexpensive pepper- and chutney-laden rotis of **Roti Palace** in Road Town, to the romantic splurge proffered at the Florentine **Brandywine's**, there is a wide variety to choose from, with West Indian cuisine the front-and-center specialty. There's even a mini-chain, **Pusser's**, a popular trio of pub-style restaurants spread between the British Virgin's largest settlements. However, most BVI dining prices are extravagant and even the informal settings can give New York tabs a run for their money. A majority of restaurants are located in and around Road Town; this is also where the island's few bargains are found.

West Indian food is found throughout the British Virgins, but home-cooked meals have become increasingly popular on Tortola, led by the justifiably famous **Mrs. Scatliffe**, who serves guests out of her tin-roofed home at Carrot Bay—and may serenade you with gospel music for dessert (though we wonder about that rumor that Mr. Scatliffe is buried in the front yard). Other restaurants serving home-style native selections are **The Apple**, **Oliver's** and the **North Shore Shell Museum**. Reservations at these and other small eateries are a good idea, particularly during the busy winter season. The local drink is the **Painkiller**, made with Pusser's Rum (a BVI product), orange and pineapple juice and a splash of coconut creme. It's tasty, but more than one visitor has found the drink's name a double-edged sword.

Speaking of drinking, **Bomba's Shack** at Cappoons Bay near West End is a rum-soaked institution visited regularly by the region's best reggae bands. The monthly full moon parties at the plywood-and-nails beach hut draw callers from neighboring islands for raucous revelry 'til dawn. Another spot worth checking into is **Quito's Gazebo** at Cane Garden Bay (below the Ole Works Inn). Tortolan Quito Rymer plays reggae and more on Tuesday, Thursday, Friday and Saturday. Both spots are noteworthy for drawing an enthusiastic cross-section of locals, yachties and land-lubbing visitors.

Apple, The $$$ ★★

Zion Hill Road; Little Apple Bay, West End, ☎ (284) 495-4437.
Dinner: 6:30–9:30 p.m., entrées $15–$35. Closed: Mon.

An enterprising and talented Tortolan, Liston Molyneux, has opened a restaurant in his home in Apple Bay, preparing local dishes like whelks (a sea snail), and the more familiar conch. Lunches are varied and include curried chicken rotis (West Indian burritos), or crepes. An interesting Sunday barbecue of West Indian treats is also offered from 7-9 p.m., and Friday nights come alive with a fish fry. Coconut chips and conch fritters are served at happy hour from 5 to 7 p.m. daily. Reservations recommended. Credit cards: A, MC, V.

Bing's Drop Inn Bar   **$$**   ★★
Fat Hog's Bay, East End, ☎ (284) 495-2627.
Dinner: 7 p.m.–midnight, entrées $10–$20. Closed: Mon.
Do drop in to Bing's—and you'll probably make a local friend or two. Tasty home-style conch fritters and fish stew are specialties and more elaborate lobster, chicken and steak dishes are served as well. Come to dance and kibitz here after a meal else-where; it's a very unpressurized environment that stays open for snacks and drinks until midnight. Credit cards: A, MC, V.

Brandywine Bay   **$$$**   ★★★★★
Blackburn Highway, Brandywine Bay, ☎ (284) 495-2301.
Dinner: 6:30–9 p.m., entrées $20–$28. Closed: Sun.
For a special occasion, drive out a little east of Road Town to this hillside peninsular spot owned by Cele and David Pugliese for Florentine food that's widely praised. Whether it's local fish simply grilled with home-grown fresh herbs or an elaborately sauced roast duckling, everything is superb—the menu changes daily based on fresh ingredients. Dining is on the terrace outside the once-private home that overlooks the Sir Francis Drake Channel. Hostess Cele will personally describe each entree on the menu while David prepares and arranges everything picture-perfectly (he's a former fashion photographer). Closed August-October. Reservations recom-mended. Credit cards: A, MC, V.

Capriccio di Mare   **$**   ★★★
Waterfront Drive, Road Town, ☎ (284) 494-5369.
Lunch: 8 a.m.–9 p.m., entrées $6–$13.
Dinner: 8 a.m.–9 p.m., entrées $6–$13.
A welcome taste treat for seafood-dominated Tortola. A little sister operation to the popular Brandywine Bay, a bastion of cucina fiorentina, Capriccio di Mare is an informal Italian cafe—a place to sit and sip espresso or cappuccino and nibble past-ries or sandwiches on foccacia bread. Pizzas with a choice of vegetable or meat top-pings are also available, as well as pastas. Fresh pastries and cappuccino are delightful for breakfast at this sidewalk cafe. Credit cards: A, D, MC, V.

Fish Trap, The   **$$$**   ★★
Columbus Centre, Road Town, ☎ (284) 494-3626.
Lunch: 11:30 a.m.– 3 p.m., entrées $8–$14.
Dinner: 6:30–11 p.m., entrées $16–$30. Closed: Sun.
An informal, open-air terrace restaurant in Wickham's Cay that always has some good-value meals happening, the Fish Trap features barbecues on Saturdays and Sundays, prime rib on Sundays and local fish, shellfish, teriyaki chicken and other hearty, honest food the rest of the week. Reservations required. Credit cards: A, MC, V.

Mrs. Scatliffe's   **$$$**   ★★★
Carrot Bay, ☎ (284) 495-4556.
Dinner: 7–9 p.m., entrées $20–$27.
Una Scatliffe, a native Tortolan, operates this West Indian restaurant on the deck of her home, a yellow-and-white, tin-roofed building across from the primary school in Carrot Bay. Diners come for the set meal of four courses, which are prepared with fruits and vegetables from her own garden. Popular starters are fresh fruit daiquiris,

followed by soup, home-baked bread, chicken in a coconut shell or curried goat, and fresh fruit in imaginative ice cream desserts. Entertainment follows, usually a family sing-out with a live fungi band. Reservations essential. In light of all the acclaim, Scatliffe's daughter, Mona Donovan, has opened her own eatery down the road, the North Shore Shell Museum. A one-of-a-kind Tortolan experience.

Pusser's Landing $$ ★★

Sopers Hole, Frenchmans Cay, ☎ *(284) 495-4554.*
Lunch: 11:30 a.m.–2:30 p.m., entrées $5–$9.
Dinner: 6:30–9:30 p.m., entrées $13–$25.

Diners can look out to the lights of St. Thomas from this waterfront restaurant in Tortola's West End, a fancier link in the Pusser's chain, serving black bean soup, West Indian ribs, roasted half-chicken in guava sauce and the signature Pusser's dishes, Beef Wellington with Bearnaise sauce and mud pie for dessert. Special events include dancing under the stars to a live band on Saturdays and all-you-can-eat shrimp dinners on Tuesday nights for $17.95. The potent Pusser's Painkiller may cure what ails you, but don't quaff too many or you'll be back in pain in the morning. Credit cards: A, D, MC, V.

Pusser's Pub $ ★★

Waterfront Drive, Road Town, ☎ *(284) 494-3897.*
Lunch: 11 a.m.–10 p.m., entrées $6–$10.
Dinner: 11 a.m.–10 p.m., entrées $6–$10.

The Outpost upstairs is gone, but you can still enjoy pub food with the yachting set in this second link in the Pusser's (local rum) chain of eateries. The downstairs pub offers the namesake libation, accompanied by fish and chips, shepherd's pie, sandwiches and snacks amid a boisterous atmosphere. Later, if you have room, down Pusser's famous mud pie. Credit cards: A, MC, V.

Skyworld $$$ ★★★

Ridge Road, ☎ *(284) 494-3567.*
Lunch: 11 a.m.–3 p.m., entrées $6–$15.
Dinner: 5–8 p.m., entrées $16–$30.

A perfect remembrance of a Tortola visit is dining or having a drink before sunset and watching a technicolor movie in the sky at this dining room perched some 1000 feet above sea level. Dinner is semi-formal with regional specialties given international flair: beautifully grilled local fish, filet mignon or lobster. The lunch menu is simpler—burgers, fried shrimp, grilled dolphin—but don't miss a soursop or banana daiquiri while casting an eagle eye on neighboring islands in the distance. Credit cards: A, MC, V.

Spaghetti Junction $$ ★★

Waterfront Drive; Road Town, Road Town, ☎ *(284) 494-4880.*
Dinner: 6–11 p.m., entrées $10–$21. Closed: Sun.

Boasting a chef who's cooked for not one but two American presidents, Spaghetti Junction is the spot for Italian, located upstairs in a small blue building. Favorites include fruiti di mari, penne arrabbiata, veal and chicken (Picatta or Marsala style), and eggplant Parmigiana and other vegetarian dishes. The Caesar salad, served with sun-dried tomatoes, isn't bad, either. Formerly a bar that overlooked the water, it is now separated from the ocean by new roads and office buildings—all in the name of progress. Yachties and others like it for its infectious grooves. Daily chalkboard specials and desserts. Credit cards: A, MC, V.

Sugar Mill   **$$$**   ★★★★
Apple Bay, ☎ *(284) 495-4355.* Associated hotel: *Sugar Mill Estate.*
Lunch: Noon–2 p.m., entrées $6–$12.
Dinner: 7–8:30 p.m., entrées $17–$26.
Bon Appetit columnists Jefferson and Jinx Morgan spent a lot of years cooking and writing about food and wine before they decided to buy a 300-year-old sugar mill in Apple Bay, converting it to an atmospheric inn and restaurant, decorated in Haitian paintings. The Morgans have wisely kept their menu small, rotating it nightly and allowing them to concentrate on the details of each dish, which might include a soup with local provisions and fresh fish in banana leaves with herbs from the Mill's own garden. A popular entree is Cajun oysters with shrimp etouffee. Leave room for a scrumptious banana bread pudding with rum sauce when it's available. Reservations recommended. Credit cards: A, MC, V.

Virgin Queen   **$**   ★★★
Fleming Street; Road Town, ☎ *(284) 494-2310.*
Lunch: 11 a.m.–2 p.m., entrées $7–$12.
Dinner: 6 p.m.–midnight, entrées $8–$16. Closed: Sun.
The Queen's pizza has been nominated for best in the islands, but it's also great finger food for sailors and other active types who like to quaff a few, throw darts at a board and shoot the breeze. There's a TV for background noise to go with the other fare offered—mostly English pub and West Indian food like bangers and mash, saltfish and shepherd's pie.

Virgin Gorda

Where to Stay—Virgin Gorda

Notwithstanding a brief gold rush in the 17th century, this idyllic island lay undiscovered until Laurance Rockefeller cruised by in the 1950s and decided to build **Little Dix Bay**. The island whose shape reminded Christopher Columbus of a "fat virgin"—hence the name—can be roughly divided into three sections. The central, heftiest land mass is lorded over by Virgin Gorda Peak, which is surrounded by a National Park and a few short trails. The flatter southwest wing of the island is the most populated and developed, and the location of Little Dix Bay and several smaller inns. Boats and ferries from Tortola regularly dock here at The Valley (aka Spanish Town), while flights from Tortola and St. Thomas land at a small airstrip just beyond. A road connects Spanish Town to Virgin Gorda's second town, Gun Creek. Below it is a great sailing anchorage, North Sound, and beyond, the northeast wing where two fine resorts accessible only by boat are located amid the dollops of scalloped land leading to the Atlantic Ocean. A tiny island facing the Bitter End Yacht Club, **Saba Rock**, is home to a lively bar accessed by dinghy or brief swim. Beyond a number of fine pieces of sand, the biggest attraction on the island is **The Baths**, but don't miss **Gorda Peak National Park**.

Hotels and Resorts

Little Dix Bay, a sister property to Caneel Bay on St. John, remains the island's premiere lodging facility, though a renovation and new management at **Biras Creek** makes this smaller property on the other end of the island a very close second. For sailors and wannabes, the popular **Bitter End Yacht Club** is a one-of-a-kind resort for those who want to charter a boat but don't want to do the dishes.

Biras Creek Resort $250–$695   ★★★★★

Biras Creek, ☎ *(800) 223-1108, (284) 494-3555, FAX (284) 494-3557.*
Single: $250–$595. Double: $350–$695.

Following a change of ownership and multi-million-dollar renovation in 1995, Biras Creek is better than ever. Located on a 140-acre estate and accessible only by boat, all of the accommodations at this first-class tropical retreat are in suites with colorful decor and open-walled showers; there's also a two-bedroom villa ($600–795). The rooms are each positioned for complete privacy and now have expanded terraces, air conditioning and phones, with tasteful new furnishings and fabrics. The beach is rather grassy, so most guests opt for sunning at the pool, tiled in Italian marble. Surrounded by water on three sides (the best swimming is at Deep Bay, a five-minute walk), Biras Creek is a true escape, and guests are appropriately pampered. The rates include all meals and most watersports (water skiing and diving are extra); a bicycle is provided to each guest for exploring the property. The restaurant is highly regarded, and the beach barbecues are themselves worth the trip. One of the Caribbean's great small resorts. 33 rooms. Credit cards: A, MC, V.

Bitter End Yacht Club $320–$610   ★★★

North Sound, ☎ *(800) 872-2392, (284) 494-2746, FAX (284) 494-4756.*
Single: $320–$510. Double: $420–$610.

This lively all-inclusive yacht club and cottage colony houses guests in hillside or beachfront villas with tropical decor and wraparound porches draped with hammocks. Visitors can also opt to stay in three Freedom-30 sailboats. The resort is accessible only by boat (transfer price included in week long stays), so room keys are unnecessary. There's lots going on at all times; landlubbers seeking a luxury island hideaway may be happier elsewhere. All kinds of watersports are for the taking (scuba is extra), and the Nick Trotter Sailing School is highly touted as among the Caribbean's best (Course 101 is included in the daily rates); a three-and-a-half day learn-to-sail package is available. The food still takes a drubbing from some guests who note that drinks aren't included in the steep rates. 94 rooms. Credit cards: A, MC, V.

Little Dix Bay $250–$1300   ★★★★★

Little Dix Bay, ☎ *(800) 928-3000, (284) 495-5555, FAX (284) 495-5661.*
Website: www.rosewood-hotels.com.
Single: $250–$700. Double: $250–$700. Suites Per Day: $650–$1300.

Built in 1964 by Laurance Rockefeller, Little Dix is one of the standard-bearers in Caribbean luxury resorts—a gem that curls around a half-mile of sparkling sand. The resort is now run (along with Caneel Bay) by Rosewood Hotels, which has worked to build a new following for this classic while maintaining its exclusive cache among the Ivy League set that made it famous. Set amid a 500-acre estate, Little Dix has formal gardens, seven tennis courts, and a fleet of boats to whisk you to the beach of your choice. The several styles of accommodations include wood-frame cottages on stilts, hexagonal hillside bungalows, or fieldstone-walled beach bungalows with peaked roofs sporting exposed beams; there are also four suites priced at $450–$1100 per night. The 1993 makeover added color and panache—bamboo and wood decor embracing a southeast Asian aura; about half the units now have air conditioning. Telephones were also added (anathema to some long-timers) and refrigerators are now positioned in each room, but the TVs were kept out. The resort's food is improved and nightly live entertainment is featured. There's no pool, but ample watersports are available. Little Dix still draws Old Money in the winter, while the summer season blossoms with honeymooners. Some consider the spot a tad pretentious, while the rest of those who can afford it are happy to sign up for the full-court treatment. 98 rooms. Credit cards: A, DC, MC, V.

Apartments and Condominiums

Self-catering cottages and villas are available; try **Virgin Gorda Villa Rentals** for houses with one to five bedrooms ☎ *(800) 848-7081* or *(284) 495-7421*, **Diamond Beach Villas** ☎ *(800) 871-3551* or *(284) 495-5452*, or **Kakana Property Management** for villas accommodating six persons ☎ *(284) 495-5201*. Otherwise, **Guavaberry Spring Bay** claims one of the island's best locations, a brief stroll from The Baths.

Fischer's Cove Beach Hotel $90–$285 ★★

The Valley, ☎ *(800) 621-1270, (284) 495-5252, FAX (284) 495-5820.*
Single: $90–$285. Double: $100–$285.

This simple cottage enclave overlooks St. Thomas Bay, in Spanish Town. Accommodations are in eight stone cottages with one or two bedrooms and a kitchenette (one minute from the beach), or in a 12-room hotel building. There are two bars and a restaurant, a nice beach with snorkeling nearby, but little else in the way of diversions. Also be aware that cruise ships dock nearby several times a week and tender boats come in to use this beach. 20 rooms. Credit cards: A, DC, D, MC, V.

Guavaberry Spring Bay $95–$142 ★★

Spring Bay, ☎ *(284) 495-5227, FAX (284) 495-5283.*
Single: $95–$142. Double: $95–$142.

Situated among 20 acres of towering boulders and lush foliage, Guavaberry is a unique colony of hexagonal or round cottages, perched on stilts less than a 10-minute walk from The Baths. The one or two bedroom units are simply furnished and feature a sitting room, modern bath and full kitchen—there's a decent commissary for light meals (frozen chicken and pizzas, snacks, beer and wine). All of the cottages have their own resident cat, rooster and lizard (guard your barbecue!). The location a mile from The Valley means you'll want a car for exploring. Guavaberry isn't for everyone—a rustic campground ambiance predominates—but those that love it come back again and again. 19 rooms.

Leverick Bay Resort $100–$125 ★★

North Sound, ☎ *(800) 848-7081, (284) 495-7421, FAX (284) 495-7367.*

Website: www.britishvirginislands.com/leverickbay. E-mail: leverick@caribsurf.com.
Single: $100–$125. Double: $100–$125.

A charming hillside villa complex with 16 standard guest rooms, with air-conditioning, cable TV and balconies with views over the North Sound. Rooms are simple, but have a small fridge and coffee-maker; rates include daily maid service. The resort also features four two-bedroom condos ($1175-1600 per week). There's an outdoor pool and 44-slip marina, as well as tennis, a dive shop, beauty salon, grocery store and restaurant. 20 rooms. Credit cards: A, MC, V.

Inns

Olde Yard Inn   **$90–$340**   ★★★

The Valley, ☎ *(800) 633-7411, (284) 495-5544, FAX (284) 495-5986.*
Website: www.travelxn.com/oldeyard. E-mail: oldeyard@caribsurf.com.
Single: $90–$145. Double: $110–$195. Suites Per Day: $180–$340.

Situated atop a hill in a beautifully maintained garden overlooking Handsome Bay, this charming inn puts guests up in a two-story building with simple island furniture, tile floors and roomy baths. Five rooms are air-conditioned and a two-bedroom suite is also available. Most of the rooms are too dark, but regional and other artwork helps lighten the mood. Though the nearest beach is a mile, a reading and video library keeps visitors contented, and the staff happily accommodates those with special interests, arranging day sails and the like and shuttling guests to the beach. Recent additions include a luscious pool, Jacuzzi, poolside bar and open-air health club. The hotel's owners pride themselves on an ecologically balanced operation. 13 rooms. Credit cards: A, MC, V.

Low Cost Lodging

Best bargains will be found outside the winter season. Try **Bayview Vacation Apartments** near The Valley ☎ *(284) 495-5329,* or also in The Valley is **The Wheelhouse** which has 12 rooms in a recently renovated property ☎ *(284) 495-5230.*

Where to Eat—Virgin Gorda

For such a tiny island, the cuisine on Virgin Gorda can be excellent, especially at **Little Dix Bay**, where the hotel's distinctive Pavilion Restaurant offers splendid views from the dining terrace for candlelight dinners of West Indian dishes presented with French flair, or afternoon teas complete with scones and clotted cream. At **Biras Creek**, the hotel dining is romantic, perched on the resort's hilltop, and the wine list is among the region's best. **Pusser's Leverick Bay** branch is the spot for Sunday brunch, served in a delightful pub at North Sound. If you're visiting the Baths, stop by **Mad Dog**, a bar set amongst the rocks that provides sandwiches until around sunset.

Bath and Turtle Pub, The   **$$$**   ★★★

Yacht Harbour, North Sound, ☎ *(284) 495-5239.*
Lunch: 11:30 a.m.– 5 p.m., entrées $7–$15.
Dinner: 5–10 p.m., entrées $11–$30.

A convivial bar-tavern, The Bath and Turtle has two happy hours a day, one mid-morning, and another one before sundown. Drinks are usually fruity and tropical, accompanied by good pizzas (Mexican crabmeat, veggie and special of the day), a West Indian chicken sandwich with spicy local seasonings, filet mignon, lobster and burgers. The location is fine too, in a tropical garden next to shopping and the local lending library. The Pub is open for breakfast from 8 a.m. and Sunday brunch runs 8:30 a.m.–3 p.m. Live entertainment on Wednesday and Sunday nights. Reservations recommended. Credit cards: A, MC, V.

Olde Yarde Inn   **$$$**   ★★★
The Valley, ☎ *(284) 495-5544.* Associated hotel: *Olde Yarde Inn.*
Dinner: 6:30–8:30 p.m., entrées $18–$30.
The ambience is lovely at this garden restaurant in the Olde Yarde Inn, and the French-Continental food enhances the experience. Inn guests and others can dine here all day, starting with a breakfast menu that commences at 8 a.m. Lunch is served at the Slip and Dip Grill and includes burgers, fish and sandwiches. But the real draw is dinner, where classics like escargot with garlic butter or caesar salad for two can be paired with local fish of the day, or Caribbean lobster with lemon butter sauce. Soups and desserts are all homemade and change frequently. Sunday night barbecue. Reservations recommended. Credit cards: A, MC, V.

Pirate's Pub & Grill   **$**   ★★★
Saba Rock, ☎ *(284) 495-9537.*
Lunch: 10 a.m.–10 p.m., entrées $5–$7.
Dinner: 10 a.m.–10 p.m., entrées $5–$7.
Located on Saba Rock, a minuscule outcrop within shouting distance of the Bitter End Yacht Club, Pirate's is one of the world's few bars most easily accessed by dinghy. It can get wild and woolly here some nights when the booze flows, but this informal pub is kind to the pocketbook, serving a small menu of hefty sandwiches, ribs and chicken with all the trimmings for under $10. Patrons are expected to drink their desserts here, downing such delights as raspberry pound cake and strawberry short cake blended at the bar. Entertainment is in the form of darts, or impromptu jam sessions with whomever washes up. Credit cards: A, MC, V.

Pusser's Leverick Bay   **$$**   ★★★
Leverick Bay; North Sound, ☎ *(284) 495-7369.*
Lunch: 11:30 a.m.–6 p.m., entrées $6–$10.
Dinner: 6–10 p.m., entrées $13–$24.
The Virgin Gorda branch of the popular Pusser's chain is located in a boisterously colored Victorian house, where familiar and tasty stateside favorites like nachos with guacamole and jalapeno pepper and cheddar fries are served with drinks. The chain's filet of beef Wellington is a specialty, served with fresh mushrooms and encased in pastry. There's also lobster, and pasta with vegetables, and Friday brings all-you-can-eat Cajun shrimp. Desserts are huge and sweet, like mud pie with mocha ice cream and cookie crust, or the Mud Head, a chocolate and Pusser's rum concoction with gooey cream on top. Credit cards: A, MC, V.

Jost Van Dyke

Named after a Dutch pirate, three-square-mile Jost Van Dyke (pronounced "yost") pursues a Robinson Crusoe atmosphere, though electricity finally came to the island in 1991. Most of Jost Van Dyke's 150 residents live in **Great Harbour**, a picturesque collection of wooden houses along a sandy beach, lined with palm trees and funky bars—the island is very popular among the yachting set and with tent-pitching landlubbers. Rastas happily trade in ganja and mushrooms at the island's numerous bars. **White Bay**, the island's nicest beach, previously could be reached only by boat, but a road to it was completed in March 1996; be sure to stop by the **Soggy Dollar Bar**, where the Painkiller was invented (the bar was named after the condition of payment after a swim in from a boat). A mile offshore from Great Harbour is uninhabited **Sandy Cay**, with another spellbinding beach, and a path through the outcrop's interior.

Transportation to Jost Van Dyke is by water (there is no airstrip); a ferry serves the island from St. Thomas and St. John, or you can take a water taxi from Tortola. There is a sandy road around the island, and a couple cars, but most people get around on foot or by boat. Eight island villas are rented by **Sandy Ground Estates** with rates starting at about $980 per week in the summer season ☎ *(284) 495-9466*. Budget accommodations are provided by **Abe's By the Sea** in Little Harbour ☎ *(284) 495-9329*, or Rudy's Mariner Inn in Great Harbour ☎ *(284) 495-9282*. Campsites and cabins with showers rent for $35–$40 per night at the **White Bay Campground**, ☎ *(284) 495-9358*; call ahead to reserve a space, particularly in the busy winter season.

Where to Stay—Jost Van Dyke

Inns

Sandcastle　　　　　　　　　　**$85–$175**　　　　　　　　　　★★

White Bay, ☎ (284) 495-9888, FAX (340) 775-3590.
Single: $85–$150. Double: $95–$175.

"The water is clearer, the beach is whiter and the stars are brighter" says the brochure, and it's no exaggeration. This tiny inn consists of four octagonal cottages set among tropical gardens next to an idyllic cove—other than a dirt road, there isn't a trace of civilization within view. The four rooms are rustic and simple, and there's no air conditioning (electricity only arrived in 1996). Sandcastle is not for everyone, but those who don't mind roughing it just a little love the peace and serenity—this is a real barefoot hideaway you'll probably be sharing with less than a dozen people (including the small staff). Dinner is by candlelight and a two-meal-a-day plan (almost unavoidable) is available for $40 per person. Arrive in your own boat, or the hotel will arrange for pickup in Tortola in a private launch. A couple more rooms are on the drawing board for 1998. Be forewarned that smaller cruise ships have begun to use White Bay occasionally for *their* promised escape—this is when you explore Jost Van Dyke on foot or plan a day sail. 4 rooms. Credit cards: MC, V.

Where to Eat—Jost Van Dyke

Several of the BVI's more legendary beachside dining experiences can be found on Jost Van Dyke, not the least of which is **Foxy's**, a beach bar and grill that draws the yachting crowd in droves throughout the year. Against a steady reggae beat, the aforementioned Painkiller is served here in a plastic milk carton; the bar also sells its own rum—Foxy's Firewater. Foxy himself provides much of the music—impromptu ditties composed on the fly (be careful what you tell him—it's likely to wind up in a song). Also worth checking into are **Happy Laurry** on the beach at Great Harbour (pig roast and barbecue on Friday evenings) and in Little Harbor, **Sidney's Peace and Love** where you keep your own bar tab, and **Harris'**, where a "no-wait" lunch program is offered. On the other hand, on Jost Van Dyke, what's your hurry?

Abe's By the Sea **$$$** ★★

Little Harbour, ☎ *(284) 495-9329.*
Lunch: 11:30 a.m.–3 p.m., entrées $8–$25.
Dinner: 7–9:30 p.m., entrées $12–$30.

Abe's is a swinging place to try fresh fish, lobster and conch on a waterfront terrace in Little Harbour. Bright coral and fish nets decorate this popular hangout for yachtspeople and tourists who drop in morning, noon and night. An American breakfast with sausage, ham, bacon and eggs and juice is a good buy for $5. Lunches and dinners are substantial and served with rice and peas, coleslaw or green salad and corn on the cob; sandwiches are also available. There's a traditional pig roast Wednesdays. Credit cards: MC, V.

Club Paradise **$$$** ★★

Great Harbour, ☎ *(284) 495-9267.*
Lunch: 10:30 a.m.–4 p.m., entrées $4–$8.
Dinner: 6–9 p.m., entrées $15–$25.

There are many nice touches that make this simple open-air restaurant in Great Harbour a good place to alight. There's a delicious Barbados-style flying fish sandwich available for lunch for $5, served on home-baked bread. At dinner, patrons can pick a lobster from the tank, try a whole cornish game hen with honey-glazed carrots and garlic, or dine on sauteed grouper. Bushwhackers are a specialty. Credit cards: A, MC, V.

Foxy's **$$$** ★★

Great Harbour, ☎ *(284) 495-9258.*
Lunch: Noon–2:30 p.m., entrées $6–$9.
Dinner: 6:30–9 p.m., entrées $15–$30.

Don't expect luxury at this famous beach bar presided over by the delightful Philicianno "Foxy" Callwood—only unabashed camaraderie and excellent grilled meat and seafood. An institution for close to 30 years, Foxy's Tamarind Bar draws an amazing yachting crowd for New Year's Eve, clogging Great Harbour with an overflow of boats and frenzied folks. The rest of the year it's calypso, reggae or soca (soul and calypso) music with burgers, rotis and killer rum punches. Lunch is served Monday–Friday only; the real closing time at Foxy's varies wildly. Credit cards: MC, V.

Anegada

With a population barely topping three digits, a flat and scrubby rather than mountainous interior, and positioned 15 miles from the nearest other BVI, Anegada proudly goes its own way in the archipelago. Most of the 170 residents live in **The Settlement**, a tranquil community positioned near the south shore of this 12-mile-long outpost—they share this curve of coral with some fierce-looking, endangered iguanas that grow up to five feet in length (they're rarely seen). A small colony of flamingos was donated by Bermuda in hope of reintroducing the species to the BVIs—the species has not nested here since the 1950s, but in 1995 hatched the first of the next generation.

The best beach is **Loblolly Bay**, where several informal restaurants, bars and sun shelters are found. The fishing here is excellent, and enough vessels have sunk on the craggy coral reefs to create some fine wreck dives; unfortunately, they're currently off limits since anchoring on Anegada's reefs is prohibited. Snorkelers can find deep satisfaction exploring caverns and ledges just off the shore in the coral reefs, where they may see shoals of neon-colored fish, rays, turtles and barracudas. Otherwise, on an island where a few dozen tourists is a crowd, activities are decidedly low-key in nature. Over the years, Anegadians have been the victim of several development schemes that have left them suspicious, not to mention poorer, but they remain friendly to the few travelers who make the trip. If you rent a jeep (there are a couple), it's likely there won't be any rental agreement to sign. Although there is no regular boat ferry, day trips to the island are possible via Anegada's small airstrip.

The 16-room **Anegada Reef Hotel**, located five miles west of The Settlement and the airport, is the island's main tourist facility. However, **Neptune's Treasure Guest House** ☎ *(284) 495-9439* has some budget rooms and tents, a couple of smaller guest houses can be found in town, and the **Anegada Beach Campground** provides rustic tent facilities ☎ *(284) 495-9466*.

Where to Stay—Anegada

Hotels and Resorts

Anegada Reef Hotel   **$150–$250**   ★★

Setting Point, ☎ *(284) 495-8002, FAX (284) 495-9362.*
Single: $150–$200. Double: $200–$250.

Located in a remote setting on remote Anegada, this small hotel appeals to those who truly want to get away from it all. The air conditioned, bungalow-style accommodations are simple, but tastefully decorated and comfortable, and the couple that runs the place goes out of their way to please. The hotel owns its own fishing boat for deep-sea or bone fishing excursions, and tank rentals and air fills are available for divers, but most guests stick to renting the bicycles, kayaks, snorkeling and beach chairs (though the beach isn't too spectacular). Lots of people return for more, lured by Anegada's laid-back nature, but this is not a spot for people who want amenities or luxe living. Three meals a day are included with room rate; this property adds a 15 percent service charge to the final bill. 16 rooms. Credit cards: MC, V.

Low Cost Lodging

Neptune's Treasure $45–$85 ★

Setting Point, ☎ *(284) 495-9439, FAX (284) 495-9439.*
Single: $45–$55. Double: $70–$85.
A half-mile west of Setting Point is this rustic but cute, four-unit cottage complex on a fair beach. Rooms are cozy and simply furnished, but clean; rooms can be hot since there's no air-conditioning, and showers are solar heated. There are also eight tents set up—$15 single or $25 double per night including linens and foam mattresses. Pam's Kitchen in back serves delectable brownies and chutneys. Away from it all, to the nth. 4 rooms.

Where to Eat—Anegada

A small collection of restaurants is found in Anegada—though food is mostly limited to West Indian cooking, particularly lobster and conch. The **Anegada Reef Hotel**'s restaurant is informal and pleasant, with a reliable menu served beachside, though food prices throughout the island edge well past "moderate." **Big Bamboo's**, amid the dunes of Loblolly Bay, might be the unlikeliest place for star-gazing, but both Ted Kennedy and the late Princess Diana are said to have stopped by while on sojourn at nearby Necker Island. The fresh lobster you dine on here and elsewhere is usually sitting out in the water when you order it; go for a snorkel while you're waiting for it to be brought in and cooked.

Big Bamboo's $$ ★★★

Loblolly Bay, ☎ *(284) 495-2019.*
Lunch: Noon–6 p.m., entrées $12–$23.
Situated below the sea grape tress amid the sand dunes of Loblolly Bay, informal Big Bamboo's is just far enough off the beaten track that it pulls in the occasional celeb from nearby Necker Island, but you can eat there, too. The popular conch is topped with red and green sweet peppers, garlic and onions, but some call the lobster that owner Avbrey Levons grills the best around. Or you can try the fresh catch, which might be triggerfish, snapper or grouper; sometimes there's home-made brandy made from the sea grapes. Anegada native Levons opened his simple picnic-table restaurant in 1984, but he's about to start taking credit cards—a sure sign he's been found out. Lunch hours vary, but he'll stay open "as long as we're having a good laugh"; dinner by reservation only.

Resort Islands

Peter Island Resort in the British Virgin Islands is located on its own private island south of Tortola. Luxury and privacy are the bywords here.

Beyond Tortola and Virgin Gorda, the islands that seduce most visitors to the British Virgins, beyond even the escape found on Jost Van Dyke and Anegada, are a series of privately owned resort islands—seductive frontiers with just one hostelry for accommodation and few or no permanent residents. The prices range from modest to absurd, and the resorts vary substantially in how they accommodate guests—Necker Island is a one-villa hinterland housing up to 24 guests for $12,000 per night (and up), while Peter Island possesses a 50-room resort that can be visited by Tortola daytrippers. It will take an extra effort to get to these resorts (private ferry, boat taxi or perhaps helicopter), but all you need do is ask the management to take care of arrangements when you make the reservation. What you get in return are places that take full advantage of their natural surroundings and provide true sanctuary from the demands of civilization.

Where to Stay—Resort Islands

Hotels and Resorts

Cooper Island Beach Club   **$75–$155**   ★ ★

Cooper Island, ☎ *(800) 542-4624, (413) 863-3162, FAX (413) 863-3662.*
E-mail: info@cooper-island.com.
Single: $75–$115. Double: $95–$155.

Situated between Peter Island and Virgin Gorda is a one-and-a-half by half-mile outpost called Cooper Island. It's not a privately owned isle like Peter and its ilk, but since the number of permanent residents doesn't even top double-digits, we're content to tuck this happy little surprise in among the swank joints. Cooper is reached by a ferry from Road Town. Rooms are in six spacious cottages with a kitchenette (propane stove and fridge), a semi-outdoor shower and rattan furnishings. A small dive center is next to the dock and snorkeling is fine right off the beach; hiking around the island provides additional diversion. There's a small restaurant on site that caters to the few guests and assorted daytrippers, but make no mistake, this is a simple, generator-powered backwater with sparse amenities, and the activities are geared more for the do-it-yourself set. But if escape is paramount, Cooper Island may be just your ticket. 12 rooms.

Drake's Anchorage $398–$690 ★★★★

Mosquito Island, ☎ *(800) 624-6651, (284) 494-2254, FAX (617) 969-5147.*
Closed Date: August–September.
Double: $398–$690.

Located on private, 125-acre Mosquito Island just off Virgin Gorda's North Sound, this low-key resort has four beaches, one just big enough for a snuggling couple. The accommodations are in separate cottages lining a narrow beach and feature Haitian art, red-tile floors and modern baths; ceiling fans keep things cool. Each has a terrace for private sunbathing, or there is also a pair of villas with even more privacy. Drake's popular restaurant draws the yachting set for five-course meals; breakfast, lunch and dinner are included for hotel guests (drinks are extra, from an honor bar). Rates also include windsurfing, kayaks, bicycles, use of a 19-foot sailboat, and a motorized dinghy to explore nearby islands; the snorkeling and coral life is good enough to lure Jean-Michel Cousteau's marine study group eight years in a row. Drake's is not a deluxe resort by the usual measure—ambiance and location are the selling point at this laid-back and unpretentious spot. The service charge added here is 15 percent. 10 rooms. Credit cards: A, MC, V.

Guana Island $440–$675 ★★★★★

Guana Island, ☎ *(800) 544-8262, (284) 494-2354, FAX (914) 967-8048.*
Website: www.guana.com.
Closed Date: September–October.
Single: $440–$600. Double: $515–$675.

Situated on a pristine 850-acre island, this hideaway was formerly a sugar cane plantation and is now a nature sanctuary. Guana is marvelously untouched, and boasts extremely diverse wildlife for its size. Accommodations are in white stone cottages arranged along a hilltop with smashing views of neighboring islands. The rooms are simple but lovely and lack real-world distractions like phones, televisions and air conditioners. A secluded, one-bedroom house is located on North Beach and goes for $925-1290. Rates include all meals, and groups of 30 can rent the entire island—the perfect spot for a family reunion or wedding ($8700–$11,000 per day). There's great hiking, bird watching, tennis and watersports, but Guana is not a high-amenity resort, nor does it dole out luxurious pampering. It's a tranquil and lovely retreat where evenings might be spent trading travel stories with fellow guests, counting stars, or fussing over a game of Scrabble. 15 rooms.

Necker Island $12,000–$18,000   ★★★★★

Necker Island, ☎ *(800) 557-4255, (284) 494-2757, FAX (212) 689-1598.*

Got a wad of thousand dollar bills burning a hole in your pocket? Need room to spread out? Don't fret—simply join the list of luminaries who have ponied up at least $12,000 per day to stash their duffle bags on Necker Island, a 74-acre paradise located two miles off Virgin Gorda's North Sound. Among the guests who've stayed are Steven Spielberg, Oprah Winfrey, Princess Diana, Mel Gibson and, of course, the island's entrepreneurial owner Richard Branson (of Virgin Atlantic Airways). The hilltop mansion is draped in brilliant red bougainvillea and furnished in Balinese textures of elephant bamboo and plush batiks. In addition to a living room that sports a 360-degree view of the sea, this main villa has 10 of the 12 bedrooms, each with a private bathroom containing stone grotto showers; the master bedroom has its own Jacuzzi. There's also a pair of cottages—Bali Hi and Bali Lo, each with their own private pool—for your guests who deserve even more seclusion. Otherwise, Necker is a world unto itself. Activities are endless, and include tennis, snorkeling, sailing, waterskiing, swimming, windsurfing and just lazing about on the beach. The professional staff of 22 includes a full-time chef, and a boatman to whisk you off to neighboring islands. The year-round daily rates start at $12,000 and go all the way up to $18,000—based on the number of people in your group (the rooms accommodate 24), plus 2.5 percent service charge (the hotel tax is already included); rates include food, drinks and virtually all possible activities. Or, there's a nifty feature at Necker called Celebration Weeks, which are held four times per year. During these weeks you and your mate can share the island with 11 other couples, at an all-inclusive rate of just $10,000 for seven days. What a deal!

Peter Island Resort $295–$895   ★★★★★

Peter Island, ☎ *(800) 346-4451, (284) 495-2000, FAX (284) 495-2500.*
Website: www.peterisland.com. E-mail: 2090598@mcimail.com.
Single: $295–$810. Double: $380–$895.

Located on its own island four miles south of Tortola, this smashing resort shuttles guests over by boat. Everything is quite luxurious, and the beaches—five total—are perfect. Accommodations are beautifully done and include standard guest rooms and a trio of villas with two to four bedrooms ($585-$4280 per night). The resort takes up about half of the 1800-acre island, and the extensive grounds include a gorgeous free-form pool, four tennis courts (pro on hand during high season), a dive shop, a yachting marina and extensive trails for walking or mountain biking. The food is great and the service impeccable (two meals a day are included in the rates). The resort completed a full makeover in late 1997—the dock was rebuilt, the lobby redesigned, garden view units have been expanded and all rooms are redecorated. And lovers can still spend the day at their own private beach with a picnic lunch. 50 rooms. Credit cards: A, MC, V.

The British Virgin Islands don't give American citizens the same duty-free break as do the U.S. Virgins, so you'll want to save serious shopping for a stopover in bustling St. Thomas on your way home. Additionally, there's not much to rave about here in terms of quality. In Road Town, the unofficial shopping hub is located on Main Street beginning with Sir Olva Georges Plaza. **Pusser's Rum** ("the Official Drink of the Royal British Navy") is one of the big island buys, available at the company store on Main Street. An aromatic excursion to the **Sunny Caribee and Spice Company** won't be time wasted, especially if you want to pick from the best selection of Caribbean spices and handicrafts on the island. Stop next door at **Sunny Caribee Gallery**, which features fine artwork by islanders as well as handpainted furniture and wood carvings. If you need to supplant your vacation wardrobe, there are several boutiques in the Abbot Building, including **Sea Urchin** and **Kids in De Sun**, which specializes in tropical attire for children.

On Virgin Gorda, boutiques at Little Dix Bay and the Bitter End resorts carry the proverbial casual wear and souvenir merchandise. Along the Yacht Harbour on Virgin Gorda you'll find another bevy of shops, including a few handicraft stores. Most of the work is imported from other islands, though you can find interesting buys on homemade preserves and spices. A local artist, Aragon, sells hand-painted shirts for $15 to $20 around the boat-dock at Trellis Bay near the Beef Island airport.

British Virgin Islands Directory

Arrival and Departure

There is no airport in the British Virgin Islands big enough to accommodate jets and, accordingly, there is no direct service between North America and the BVIs. All of the international flights enter the BVIs through the airport on Beef Island, which is connected to Tortola by the Queen Elizabeth Bridge. **American Eagle** provides up to ten flights per day out of San Juan, Puerto Rico. Other companies that fly to Beef Island include: **CaribAir** (daily service from San Juan), **Air St. Thomas** (daily from St. Thomas), **Sunaire** (daily from St. Thomas and St. Croix), and **Winair** (weekends from St. Maarten). **LIAT** offers direct or nonstop service from Anguilla, Antigua, San Juan, St. Kitts, St. Maarten and St. Thomas. Air transport to Virgin Gorda usually via Beef Island, but Air St. Thomas flies from both San Juan and St. Thomas to Virgin Gorda (see "Getting Around" below for more information on how to get to the other BVIs). Because government regulation forbids anyone to rent a car at the Beef Island airport, taxis are omnipresent when a plane arrives. Some hotels will arrange to meet you.

Another option that can sometimes save a few dollars is to **ferry** over to the British Virgins from the U.S. Virgins. This plan makes particular sense if a flight from North America to St. Thomas is significantly cheaper than a connection into Tortola (not uncommon). Two companies offer several ferries daily from Charlotte Amalie or Red Hook on St. Thomas, to West End or Road Town on Tortola: **Smith's Ferry Services** ☎ *(284) 495-4495* and **Native Son** ☎ *(284) 495-4617*. Prices are $19 one-way. **Inter-Island Boat Services** connects Cruz Bay, St. John with West End, Tortola three times daily ☎ *(284) 495-4166*. **Speedy's** plies the route between St. Thomas and Virgin Gorda daily ☎ *(284) 495-5240*. Additional ferry information is provided under "Getting Around," below.

Departure tax from the British Virgin Islands is $10 by air, $5 by sea.

Business Hours

Stores open Monday–Saturday 9 a.m.–5 p.m. Banks open Monday–Thursday 9 a.m.–2:30 p.m. and Friday 9 a.m.–2:30 p.m. and 4:30–6 p.m.

Climate

Little rain falls on these islands, with temperatures hovering between 75 degrees F and 85 degrees F year-round. The constant trade winds keep the humidity low. Even during the rainy season, rain usually arrives in 10-minute bursts that stop as fast they start.

Documents

Customs officials prefer visitors to bring passports, but will accept proof of citizenship (birth certificate or voter's registration, plus driver's license or other photo identification). Travelers must also possess an ongoing or return ticket.

Electricity

Current runs 110 volts, 60 cycles, as in the U.S.

Getting Around

There is no real bus service in the BVIs, and although hitching is fairly common, most visitors rent a car for at least some of their trip to see Tortola and Virgin Gorda. Car rentals can be exorbitant during high season when demand is high. As such, it's best to reserve a car before you arrive. Rates seem to change daily based on availability, so reconfirm your quoted rate at least two days before your anticipated pick-up. Expect to pay upwards of $50 per day, but sometimes a better rate is negotiated on the spot when demand is low. To rent a car, you must obtain a BVI drivers license from the rental agency by presenting your valid hometown license and shelling out $10. There are numerous local agencies with slightly lower prices, but it's easier to reserve a car with the American firms (and easier to rectify billing errors after-the-fact). Based on Tortola are agencies for **Avis** ☎ *(800) 331-1212* or *(284) 494-3322*, **Budget** ☎ *(800) 527-0700* or *(284) 494-2639*, **Hertz** ☎ *(800) 654-3131* or *(284)*

495-4405, and **National** ☎ *(800) 227-7368* or *(284) 494-3197*. On Virgin Gorda, try **Speedy's Car Rental** ☎ *(284) 495-5235*. On Anegada, the **Anegada Reef Hotel** has a small selection ☎ *(284) 495-8002*.

Transportation between islands is fairly comprehensive, though primarily by sea. From Tortola's Beef Island airport, only two of the other BVIs are served by air. **Virgin Islands Airways** offers daily flights to Virgin Gorda ☎ *(284) 495-1972*, and **Gorda Aero Services** provides flights to Anegada on Monday, Wednesday and Friday ☎ *(284) 495-2271*. Otherwise, transportation between the islands is by ferry or water taxi.

At least four companies offer ferry service from Tortola to Virgin Gorda. **Speedy's** offers up to six trips daily out of Road Town ☎ *(284) 495-5240*. **Smith's Ferry Services** provides three to five trips daily from Road Town with some service originating out of West End, Tortola ☎ *(284) 495-4495*. **Williams & Williams Car Ferry Service** provides two trips daily from Beef Island to Virgin Gorda ☎ *(284) 494-2627*. **North Sound Express** operates four times daily between Beef Island and North Sound, Virgin Gorda ☎ *(284) 495-2271*. The large resorts on Virgin Gorda each have their own private ferry service, though prices are generally higher than on the public ferries.

The ferry *When* (you'll get the name soon enough) provides service to Jost Van Dyke from West End, Tortola with four departures daily (three on Sunday); contact **Jost Van Dyke Ferry Service** ☎ *(284) 494-2997*. The resort on **Peter Island** operates their own private ferry out of Road Town; officially, it's only for guests of the resort, but it's available during the evening to non-resort guests who want to try Peter Island's restaurant ☎ *(284) 494-2561*. **Cooper Island** is reached by a private ferry originating from the Prospect Reef Resort on Wednesday and Saturday ☎ *(284) 494-3311*. There is no ferry service to Anegada; other islands, such as Ginger, Norman and Salt, are reached only by private water taxi. For information about ferry and air transportation to the US Virgin Islands, see "Arrival and Departure," above.

Language

British English is spoken with a West Indian accent.

Medical Emergencies

The Peebles Hospital, Porter Road, Road Town; ☎ *(284) 494-3497* is a fully functioning facility with lab and X-ray machines. Hotels usually have a list of doctors on-call in Tortola. Serious emergencies require airlift to St. Thomas or San Juan.

Money

The American dollar is used exclusively.

Telephone

The new area code for the British Virgin Islands is *(284)*. To reach the islands from North America, dial *1 + (284)*, and the seven digit local number.

Time

Atlantic standard time throughout the year.

Tipping and Taxes

Most hotels and restaurants customarily add a 10 percent service charge to bills (though a few bump it to 15 percent); a seven percent room tax is also in effect. Feel free to tip more for special service. There is no sales tax on merchandise purchased.

Tourist Information

The **British Virgin Islands Tourist Board** on Tortola is located in Road Town ☎ *(284) 494-3134.* In the United States an office in New York is set up for sending out brochures and providing tourist information ☎ *(800) 835-8530* or ☎ *(212) 696-0400.* An additional office is based in San Francisco ☎ *(415) 775-0344.*

Web Site

www.bviwelcome.com

When to Go

BVI residents throw parties at the drop of a hat, most notably once a month at Bomba's Surfside Shack, where the **Full Moon Parties** have become a regional lure for serious merrymaking. Not to be outdone, Foxy's on Jost Van Dyke holds an annual **New Year's Eve Party** that draws a slew of yachties into the small harbour—this traffic jam is not for the timid. The annual BVI calendar also includes the **Emancipation Festival**, a two-week-long event held in Road Town in late July-early August, with calypso, fungi and steel band music, local food and drinks, and native arts and crafts. **Sailing events** are frequently scheduled at the various resorts, but particularly at the Bitter End Yacht Club, which holds a Women's Sailing Week, a First-Timer's Week and other events ☎ *(284) 494-2746.* For more information on the many sailing events organized by the BVI Yacht Club, call ☎ *(284) 494-3286.*

BRITISH VIRGIN ISLANDS HOTELS	RMS	RATES	PHONE	CR. CARDS
Tortola				
★★★ Fort Recovery Estates	17	$135–$240	(800) 367-8455	A, MC, V
★★★ Long Bay Beach Hotel	72	$85–$360	(800) 729-9599	A, D, MC, V
★★★ Prospect Reef Resort	130	$90–$210	(800) 356-8937	A, MC, V
★★★ Sugar Mill Hotel	21	$135–$265	(800) 462-8834	A, MC, V
★★★ Treasure Isle Hotel	43	$80–$170	(800) 334-2435	A, MC, V
★★ Frenchman's Cay Resort	9	$120–$220	(800) 235-4077	A, D, MC, V
★★ Nanny Cay Resort	42	$70–$195	(800) 742-4276	A, MC, V
★★ Ole Works Inn	18	$50–$170	(284) 495-4837	MC, V
★★ Village Cay Marina Hotel	19	$77–$165	(284) 494-2771	A, MC, V
★ Maria's Hotel	20	$70–$125	(284) 494-2595	MC, V
★ Sebastian's on the Beach	26	$65–$190	(800) 336-4870	A, D, MC, V

BRITISH VIRGIN ISLANDS

BRITISH VIRGIN ISLANDS HOTELS	RMS	RATES	PHONE	CR. CARDS
Virgin Gorda				
★★★★★ Biras Creek Resort	33	$250–$695	(800) 223-1108	A, MC, V
★★★★★ Little Dix Bay	98	$250–$700	(800) 928-3000	A, DC, MC, V
★★★ Bitter End Yacht Club	94	$320–$610	(800) 872-2392	A, MC, V
★★★ Olde Yard Inn	13	$90–$195	(800) 633-7411	A, MC, V
★★ Fischer's Cove Beach Hotel	20	$90–$285	(800) 621-1270	A, D, DC, MC, V
★★ Guavaberry Spring Bay	19	$95–$142	(284) 495-5227	
★★ Leverick Bay Resort	20	$100–$125	(800) 848-7081	A, MC, V
Jost Van Dyke				
★★ Sandcastle	4	$85–$175	(284) 495-9888	MC, V
Anegada				
★★ Anegada Reef Hotel	16	$150–$250	(284) 495-8002	MC, V
★ Neptune's Treasure	4	$45–$85	(284) 495-9439	
Resort Islands				
★★★★★ Guana Island	15	$440–$675	(800) 544-8262	
★★★★★ Necker Island		$12,000–$18,000	(800) 557-4255	
★★★★★ Peter Island Resort	50	$295–$895	(800) 346-4451	A, MC, V
★★★★ Drake's Anchorage	10	$398–$690	(800) 624-6651	A, MC, V
★★ Cooper Island Beach Club	12	$75–$155	(800) 542-4624	

BRITISH VIRGIN ISLANDS RESTAURANTS	PHONE	ENTRÉE	CR. CARDS
Tortola			
English Cuisine			
★★★ Virgin Queen	(284) 494-2310	$7–$16	
★★ Pusser's Landing	(284) 495-4554	$5–$25	A, D, MC, V
★★ Pusser's Pub	(284) 494-3897	$6–$10	A, MC, V
International Cuisine			
★★★★ Sugar Mill	(284) 495-4355	$6–$26	A, MC, V
★★★ Skyworld	(284) 494-3567	$6–$30	A, MC, V
Italian Cuisine			
★★★ Capriccio di Mare	(284) 494-5369	$6–$13	A, D, MC, V

BRITISH VIRGIN ISLANDS RESTAURANTS	PHONE	ENTRÉE	CR. CARDS
★★ Spaghetti Junction	(284) 494-4880	$10–$21	A, MC, V
Regional Cuisine			
★★★★★ Brandywine Bay	(284) 495-2301	$20–$28	A, MC, V
★★★ Mrs. Scatliffe's	(284) 495-4556	$20–$27	
★★ Apple, The	(284) 495-4437	$15–$35	A, MC, V
★★ Bing's Drop Inn Bar	(284) 495-2627	$10–$20	A, MC, V
Seafood Cuisine			
★★ Fish Trap, The	(284) 494-3626	$8–$30	A, MC, V
Virgin Gorda			
English Cuisine			
★★★ Bath and Turtle Pub, The	(284) 495-5239	$7–$30	A, MC, V
★★★ Pusser's Leverick Bay	(284) 495-7369	$6–$24	A, MC, V
International Cuisine			
★★★ Olde Yarde Inn	(284) 495-5544	$18–$30	A, MC, V
Regional Cuisine			
★★★ Pirate's Pub & Grill	(284) 495-9537	$5–$7	A, MC, V
Jost Van Dyke			
American Cuisine			
★★ Foxy's	(284) 495-9258	$6–$30	MC, V
International Cuisine			
★★ Sandcastle	(284) 690-1611	$5–$30	MC, V
Seafood Cuisine			
★★ Abe's By the Sea	(284) 495-9329	$8–$30	MC, V
★★ Club Paradise	(284) 495-9267	$4–$25	A, MC, V
Anegada			
International Cuisine			
★★ Anegada Reef Hotel	(284) 495-8002	$7–$30	MC, V
Regional Cuisine			
★★★ Big Bamboo's	(284) 495-2019	$12–$23	

CAYMAN ISLANDS

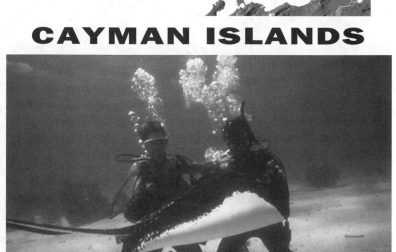

Divers in Sting Ray City, Cayman Islands

The trio that makes up the Cayman Islands has long been regarded world over as the spot for diving. Grand Cayman, the largest, has more than 130 dive sites, many less than a half-mile from shore, and visibility of 100 to 150 feet is common. Cayman Brac is known for its spectacular drop-offs and fascinating coral gardens in both shallow and medium depths. And Little Cayman—where the drop-off begins at 18 feet and plunges to 1000 feet, with visibility often reaching up to 200 feet—was voted the top Caribbean dive destination by the readers of *Rodale's Scuba Diving* magazine in 1997.

Obviously, diving and watersports are the lure of the Caymans. The British colony is not especially picturesque, and while you can score some deals in the shops, peruse a few museums and enjoy world-class accommodations, the whole idea of a Cayman sojourn is getting wet. And just because most of the attraction lies underwater, don't expect your Caymans vacation to be cheap. In fact, especially on Grand Cayman, you'll pay—and pay and pay. Apparently that is not a problem for the island's tourist-based economy; visitors outnumber residents each year by 10 to one. Recognizing a good thing, the government is aggressively protecting its natural resources with far-sighted programs to keep pristine land free from development.

BEST BETS FOR...

Bird's-Eye View

Located 480 miles south of Miami, the Caymans consist of three islands: Grand Cayman, Cayman Brac and Little Cayman. As the name suggests, Grand Cayman is the largest, coming in at just 22 miles long by eight miles wide. Despite the fact that half of its 76 square miles is swampland, Grand Cayman is by far the most populated and developed of the trio. The hub of tourism is West Bay Beach, a fantastic strand along the western shore. North Sound, a large bay to the west, is surrounded by a huge and colorful coral reef. Good shopping and restaurants are found in the capital city of George Town, where cruise ships frequently dock.

Cayman Brac, 89 miles to the northeast (a 20-minute flight), is a 12-mile island of low-lying land that rises to a 140-foot bluff, from which the island takes its name (brac means "bluff" in Gaelic). Besides great diving all around the coastline—with more than 50 designated sites—the island has several large caves and sinkholes that are a spelunker's joy. Protected woodlands are home to native cacti, thatch palms, rare orchids, frigate birds, peregrin falcons, brown boobies and the rare Cayman Brac parrot.

Little Cayman, sitting just seven miles away from Cayman Brac, totals just 12 square miles and about 100 residents. Diving reigns supreme at **Bloody Bay Wall**, whose 1200 foot vertical plunge makes it one of the world's standout dive spots A handful of small lodges cater to divers on the island but nightlife is nil. Visitors retreat here to really get away from it all, commune with nature and keep an eye peeled for the resident West Indian whistling birds, wild iguanas, egrets, herons and red-footed boobies.

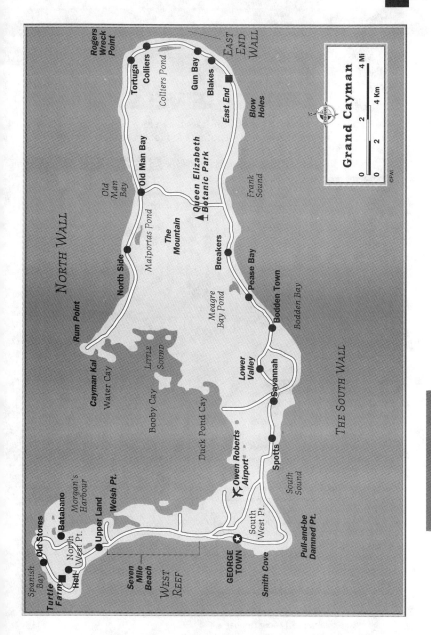

Fielding WORLDWIDE **GRAND CAYMAN DELIGHTS**

A TRIO OF CROWN JEWELS

Although best-known for the 544 offshore banks located in George Town, Grand Cayman holds treasures of another kind for those who enjoy history, diving, and bird-watching.

Turtle Farm

Where else can you hold a live green sea turtle? Tour the farm and see eggs, hatchlings, yearlings, and the full-grown breeding adults. Loggerhead, hawksbill and Ridley sea turtles also are on exhibit.

Stingray City

This dive spot just inside the barrier reef near Rum Point is known for the large stingrays that populate the shallow, 12-foot-deep waters. Divers can touch, feed and photograph these strange-looking, graceful creatures.

Hell

The post office in this tiny village perched on the rocky "ironshore" beach will postmark your letters from "Hell." The T-shirts and souvenirs are all rather tacky but what the—? Inspect the rugged black rocks from a boardwalk trail.

Treasure Museum

This museum is operated by a professional salvage-operation firm. View dioramas and exhibits of relics retrieved from shipwrecks—don't miss the chance to heft the bar of gold to test its weight. (345) 947-5033.

Cayman Island National Museum

Located in George Town, the museum is housed in the white-painted Old Courts Building, constructed 150 years ago. Exhibits include displays of rare coins and a 14-foot catboat.

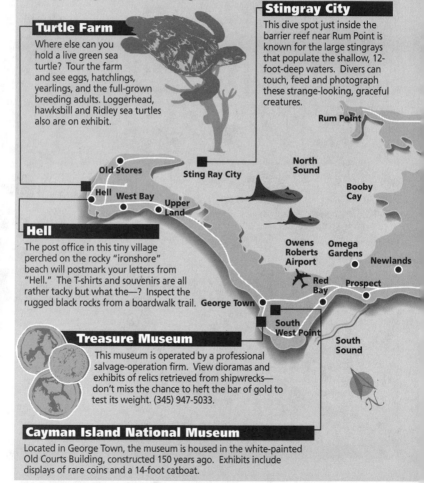

Rum Point

Old Stores

Hell   West Bay

Upper Land

Sting Ray City

North Sound

Booby Cay

Owens Roberts Airport

Omega Gardens

Newlands

Red Bay

Prospect

George Town

South West Point

South Sound

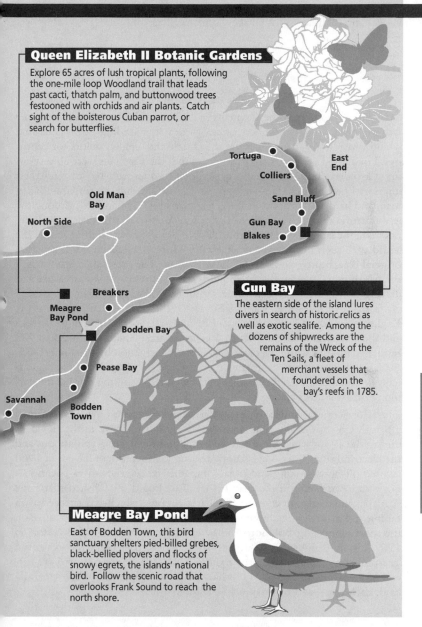

Queen Elizabeth II Botanic Gardens

Explore 65 acres of lush tropical plants, following the one-mile loop Woodland trail that leads past cacti, thatch palm, and buttonwood trees festooned with orchids and air plants. Catch sight of the boisterous Cuban parrot, or search for butterflies.

Tortuga

East End

Colliers

Old Man Bay

Sand Bluff

North Side

Gun Bay

Blakes

Breakers

Gun Bay

The eastern side of the island lures divers in search of historic relics as well as exotic sealife. Among the dozens of shipwrecks are the remains of the Wreck of the Ten Sails, a fleet of merchant vessels that foundered on the bay's reefs in 1785.

Meagre Bay Pond

Bodden Bay

Pease Bay

Savannah

Bodden Town

Meagre Bay Pond

East of Bodden Town, this bird sanctuary shelters pied-billed grebes, black-bellied plovers and flocks of snowy egrets, the islands' national bird. Follow the scenic road that overlooks Frank Sound to reach the north shore.

Just offshore Little Cayman is tiny Owen Island, whose welcoming sign ("Private Property—Visitors Welcome—Please Help Keep This Island Clean") pretty much sums up the Caymans all around.

History

Columbus discovered the Caymans in 1503 and dubbed them *Las Tortugas* for the enormous numbers of sea turtles surrounding the islands that would provide sustenance to English, Dutch and French sailors for centuries. For a good 150 years after being sighted, the Caymans were almost entirely avoided. They were remote, perilous to approach by sea, and their interiors were inhospitable—swampy and mosquito-infested in Grand Cayman, and hard and scrubby on Little Cayman and Cayman Brac. Among the few creatures that thrived here were tropical American crocodiles, called *caymanas* in the language of the Carib Indians. For a time the critters shared the island with such buccaneers as Sir Henry Morgan and Edward Teach (the original Blackbeard) who hid out in the islands while preying on Spanish and French ships. (Cayman history abounds with stories of sunken treasure and derring-do.) But the first real settlers didn't arrive until 1655, when deserters from Oliver Cromwell's army abandoned their platoon in Jamaica as the English were taking it from the Spanish. In 1670, Spain ceded both Jamaica and the Caymans to Great Britain. A century later, Grand Cayman had 933 residents, most of whom were slaves. After emancipation by Britain in 1835, the island became home to many other freed slaves; their descendants gradually intermingled with the families of the island, paving the way for the harmony that still exists today.

Just 36 years ago Jamaica chose independence, but the Caymans remained a British Crown Colony. The first tourists started to arrive in the Caymans during the 1950s while the roads were still bad, the insects voluminous and the electrical supply iffy. Legislation creating tax-investment havens in 1966 favored offshore banking and trust companies whose executives began seeing vacation promise in the islands. A tourist board, established that same year, began strictly supervising hotel inspections, which has succeeded in raising and maintaining a high standard of service. It began to capitalize on the sport pioneering Bob Soto had begun to introduce to island visitors in 1957: diving. Laughs Soto: "Hotel owners used to try to keep me away from guests. They were afraid I'd drown them." Nowadays Soto is touted as a legend in the world of diving. About half a million people visit the Cayman Islands each year—and the majority are divers.

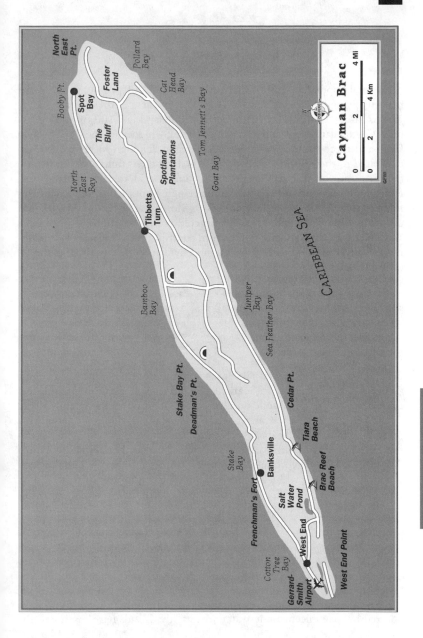

Cayman Brac

People

The total population of the Cayman Islands is 21,000 people, with the vast majority living on Grand Cayman—a quarter of them in the capital, George Town. About 1300 souls live on Cayman Brac and just 100 on Little Cayman. Caymanians enjoy a high quality of living—highest in the Caribbean in fact—and there is little crime or racial tension. Though locals are well off compared to their Caribbean counterparts, life here is simple and nonmaterialistic. A mix of African, Welsh, Scottish and English descent, natives speak with a lilting brogue and are known for being exceptionally polite and helpful. Caymanians are well-educated, with a literacy rate of more than 97 percent. The Cayman Islands are a British colony with an appointed governor and elected Executive Council. Tourism contributes the most to the economy, followed by banking. Indeed, Grand Cayman is home to more than 500 offshore banks.

Beaches

The beaches of the Caymans can be described in a few short words—powder-fine white strands. **Seven Mile Beach** is considered one of the most fantastic beaches in the Caribbean, marked by a beautiful crescent shape and clear turquoise blue waters. Public buses operate hourly down the strand. North of the Holiday Inn, where most of the watersports facilities are based, is a public beach with small cabanas and tables and chairs. Most memorable sunsets can be seen from the beach at **Rum Point**, at the northeastern tip of North Sound, a sleepy little community of private homes and condos. **Little Cayman** is known for its long white beaches with nary a footprint to mar their beauty. For some reason, locals don't use the beaches much for sunbathing or swimming, so most of the strands are exquisitely private.

Underwater

Make no doubt about it, diving is an industry in the Cayman Islands. Spurred by magnificent underwater scenery, the islands have captivated the

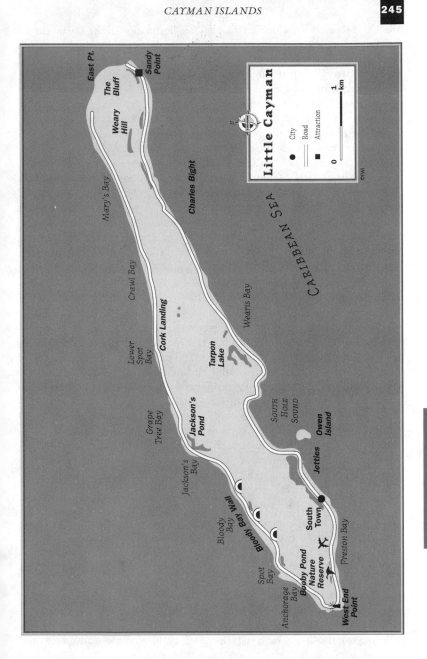

press, and secured a position as the top dive destination in the Caribbean. A series of immense walls, dropping to 6000 feet or more, line the islands and create ideal diving conditions in waters 80–84°F. Another big plus are the numerous wrecks surrounding the islands. The downside is that dive operators are frequently accused of running a cattle show; as the number of shops on the island has increased over the last decade, competition has heated up and operators have begun using larger boats to increase their efficiency. Groups of 15 or 20 are the rule, but some operators will carry more, particularly when cruise ships dock. Some more-experienced divers, unaccustomed to crowded dive sites and stringent safety rules, disparagingly refer to the Caymans as "the McDonald's of dive destinations." Nonetheless, the diving, with 119 permanent mooring sites off Grand Cayman alone, and with visibility sometimes approaching 200 feet, is still among the world's best. Indeed, for the past five years, an off-season program called Cayman Madness held at the end of October has broken records for attracting divers from around the world. Halving the price of the dive vacation helped.

The structure of the Cayman Reef formation is relatively simple. Each of the islands represent the (possibly volcanic) summits of immense mountains which rise thousands of feet from the floor of the Caribbean Sea. Leading out from the shoreline, the first region is a gentle sloping plane of sand, usually covered in turtle grass, which leads to a fringing reef of elkhorn or staghorn corals. The next section is a moderate incline of alternating channels of patch reef and sand, referred to as a spur-and-groove system, which leads to a steeper drop-off. With the exception of Little Cayman's wall (which starts at only 20 or 30 feet), the sheer escarpment usually begins about 50 or 60 feet below the surface (diving on Cayman Brac and Little Cayman is discussed in more detail below). As a rule, depth approaches a staggering 6000 feet less than a mile offshore, continuing down on the south side of the islands to the Cayman Trench, 24,720 feet below the surface—the deepest part of the Caribbean. Divers are kept to a firm depth limit of 110 feet by shops who are members of the Cayman Islands Watersports Operator's Association (CIWOA), which regulates universal safety standards for the plethora of dive shops on the islands.

Four separate walls, named after the compass points, surround Grand Cayman. The **West Reef** structure stretches along **Seven Mile Beach** and offers the best visibility and access, and some of the most famous dives. Since the majority of dive operators and tourist accommodations are located along this beach, its sites are more heavily trafficked than most of the others on the island. The vast **North Sound** is the breeding ground for Grand Cayman, which in turn spills into the Caribbean at low tide, attracting bigger fish to the **North Wall** (on the flip side, the rich effluent can sometimes decrease visibility, however); the diving here is exciting and somewhat more advanced, and

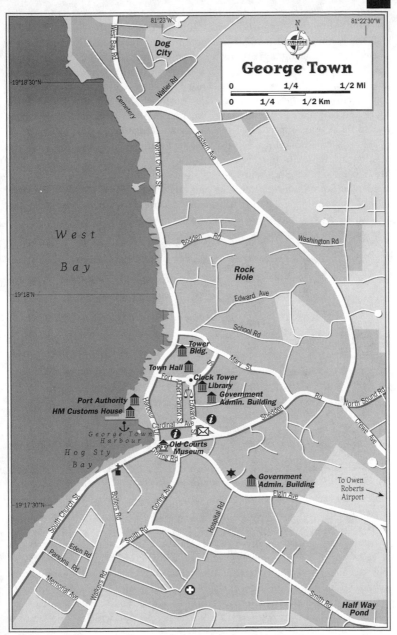

CAYMAN ISLANDS

summer months draw Caribbean reef and hammerhead sharks to the area for breeding. Sometimes referred to as "the last frontier," the rugged **East End Wall** has some of the island's most pristine, and least-visited dives—56, by one count—featuring a great concentration of tunnels and caves. The main drawback is that the eastern reef is a solid two-hour boat ride from **West Bay** dive shops, but that's also its attraction. It's also worth noting that winds usually approach the island from the southeast, making the walls on the south and east sides somewhat more weather dependent. Several noteworthy wrecks lie at opposing ends of the island; the ***Ridgefield***, on the eastern tip, offers excellent snorkeling. It's possible to locate good snorkeling locations off almost any beach, but the south end of West Bay provides a number of sites close to shore. Snorkeling the channels which lead through reefs fringing North Sound, along Sand Cay and at Pedro Point is possible, but they should be approached with caution due to unpredictable currents (check around locally before visiting these areas).

The Cayman Islands provide many thrills for divers.

There are currently around 40 dive operators on Grand Cayman alone. The competition makes two-tank dive prices reasonable by Caribbean standards; single-tank dives, however, priced anywhere from $5 to $20 less than two tanks, are not generally a good deal by comparison. The operations we've listed (plus a live-aboard) are those which consistently crop up favorably in reader surveys and local recommendations. It is by no means a comprehensive list of the only decent shops on the island. Given the variety of services and differing styles of operation available, your best bet is to shop around and solicit more opinions to make the selection which works best for you; it's worth inquiring if they are a member of the CIWOA. Finally, if a quieter atmosphere stirs your diving fantasies, head east to **Cayman Brac** or **Little Cayman**. The sites on these smaller islands frequently rival those of Grand Cayman, yet they exist off the shores of remote backwaters which have thus far not been overrun.

FIELDING'S CHOICE:

Stingray City, the world-famous dive site, in North Sound, is less than an hour's catamaran ride from the Hyatt Regency's dock. The surprise is that you can actually scuba and snorkel with a large family of stingrays, who, years ago, learned to bump a diver's mask so the diver would drop his bag of squid.

Dive Shops

Bob Soto's Diving Ltd.

George Town; ☎ *(800) BOB-SOTO, (345) 949-2022, FAX (345) 949-8731, e-mail: BobSotos@cayman.org.*

Oldest operation on the island (since 1957) is also the oldest in the world. PADI five-star development center, also NAUI and SSI affiliated. Two-tank dive, $60 daily. Maximum group size, 20. Runs an East End "safari" via bus, $70 (including lunch and two dives). Night dives scheduled Tuesday and Saturday, $55. Unlimited shore diving.

Cayman Aggressor III

☎ *(800) 348-2628, (345) 949-5551.*

Popular, all-inclusive live-aboard boats; $1495 for the seven-day trips, which feature five-and-a-half days of diving (up to five dives daily including a night dive). Generally sticks to the less-visited East End Wall of Grand Cayman but, weather permitting, will also swing over to Little Cayman. The boat sleeps 16 and operates 52 weeks a year, departing every Saturday afternoon. Instructor available on all trips and beginners may obtain certification over the course of the week.

Don Foster's Cayman Ltd.

George Town; ☎ *(800) 833-4837, (345) 949-7181, FAX (345) 949-5133, e-mail: dfdus@airmail.net.*

One of the island's better-established outfits, with groups limited to 20, custom-built diving boats. PADI, NAUI and SSI affiliated; courses to divemaster. Two-tank dive, $60, snorkeling trips $25.

Parrots Landing Watersports Park

George Town; ☎ *(800) 448-0428, (345) 949-7884, FAX (345) 949-0294, e-mail: splash@parrotslanding.com.*

Refers to itself as an "elite" dive operation, Parrots opened in 1988 and is PADI, NAUI and SSI affiliated. Maximum group size, 20. Two-tank dives, $60. Night dives Tuesday and Friday, $50.

Sunset Divers

George Town; ☎ *(800) 854-4767, (345) 949-7111, e-mail: susets@candwky.*

A 23-year-old operation, PADI, NAUI, SSI affiliated, courses to divemaster. Two-tank dive, $65. Computer diving available on all boats, with regular trips to remote east-end sites. Group size, 50 maximum, but also has smaller boats.

Cayman Brac—Underwater

Although many residents consider Brac the loveliest of the three Caymans topside, the island's dive sites—which would be rated excellent most anywhere else in the world—are always compared against the glories of Grand and Little Cayman. Yet Cayman Brac's wall, which starts at a depth of 50 to 60 feet, actually offers drama comparable to the better known Bloody Bay Wall. Tunnels and crevices abound throughout many sites, and fine diving is found on both sides of the island. Winter winds from the northwest can sometimes play havoc, but year-round visibility is roughly comparable to the 100+ foot average found on the sister islands. At popular **East Chute**, a small 1986 wreck sits placidly on the sand floor near the lip of the wall and has begun to develop soft corals and sponges on her hull. **Bert Brothers Boulders**, on the less-dived eastern tip of the island, is a spur-and-groove reef structure featuring beautiful swim-throughs and gorges. **Windsock Reef**, off the island's western tip, offers excellent snorkeling among forests of elkhorn and pillar coral, while the nearby barrier reef also provides good snorkeling possibilities.

Dive Shops

Dive Tiara

Stake Bay, Cayman Brac; ☎ *(800) 367-3484, (345) 948-1553, e-mail: steve@candw.ky.* A 10-year-old operation, PADI, NAUI and SSI affiliated. Two-tank dive, $66. Tiara also runs trips to Little Cayman four times a week (40–50 minutes to Bloody Bay Wall).

Little Cayman—Underwater

From the air, an almost insignificant 11-mile strip of sand, Little Cayman anchors what is possibly the single most spectacular wall in the Caribbean. The top of the formation starts at only 20 or 25 feet below the surface on the northern coast of the island, then plunges to a pulse-quickening depth of more than 6000 feet, sometimes at a dead-vertical, or even inverse, angle. The three-mile stretch actually encompasses two areas that are slightly different near the crest; **Bloody Bay Wall**, to the west, is a sheer drop from 20 or 30 feet down, whereas the **Jackson Bay Wall** (on the east) is more typical of the spur-and-groove structure found on Grand Cayman. One unique aspect about Little Cayman is that virtually all sites along the cascading wall are accessible for beginners, weather and depth permitting. Although visibility averages 100 feet year-round, conditions are better from spring through fall, and can secure visibility approaching 200 feet in the placid summer months. Shore diving is possible from a number of points but, with very limited medical services no closer than Cayman Brac, local operators frown on it. The

Bloody Bay Wall is also a spectacular setting for snorkelers, with coral heads rising to within 10 feet of the surface at some spots.

As if to literally portray the difference between Grand and Little Cayman diving, the noted animal show here is not a slew of southern stingrays, but a single, graceful manta named Molly who sports a 10-foot wingspan. Molly does not inhabit the Jackson Bay area year-round, but dive shops claim that she puts in an appearance about 95 percent of the time during their summer night dives. Molly is attracted by dive lights—which seduce a rich bounty of plankton for her to feed on—and she swoops, circles and plays with divers in appreciation. The local operators are protective of Molly, who has been interacting with them since 1991, and she in turn has established a bond, allowing them to sever nets and ropes she became entangled in on two separate occasions.

A few years ago, few divers made it to Little Cayman, primarily due to transportation and accommodation considerations. However, airline service has increased and several new resorts have opened with a keen eye toward accommodating dive business. The government has stepped up the conservation effort at the island and limits each shop to a strict maximum of 14 weekly boat trips to the Jackson/Bloody Bay area, with no more than 20 divers on board each boat. So far, a backlash has not occurred, but the potential for disappointed visitors certainly exists. Still, with barely a hundred year-round residents on the substantially uninhabited island, this is a remote dive destination with an extraordinary payoff.

Dive Shops

Paradise Divers

Little Cayman; ☎ *(800) 450-2084, (345) 948-0001, e-mail: iggy@candw.ky.*
The island's only independent outfit, Paradise keeps groups to a maximum of 16. PADI affiliated. Two-tank dive, $69. Shore dives, $35.

Reef Divers

Little Cayman; ☎ *(800) 327-3835, (345) 948-1033, FAX (345) 948-1040, e-mail: refz79a@prodigy.com.*
Tied in to Little Cayman Beach Resort, Reef Divers is the island's busiest and largest outfit with three dive boats working the shoreline; PADI affiliated. Two-tank dive, $63.

On Foot

Cayman Islands Governor Michael Gore is an ardent bird-watcher, which has helped ensure protection for the island's 180 species. Some of the better known are the snowy egret, the bananaquit, many species of heron and, of course, the Cayman parrot. There are a series of mosquito control dikes on the peninsula at West Bay which are explored (repellent well in hand) by keen birders and there is a book, *Birds of the Cayman Islands*, available locally for die-hards. Trails on Grand Cayman are limited, but the Ordnance Survey map sold at the Land and Survey Department in George Town details the starts and stops of a number of possibilities. Among them are sporadic paths along the north shore, an area inhabited by the nearly extinct Cayman iguana. There is also an interpretive nature trail, just under a mile long, that tours wetlands, logwood swamp, air plant woodland and a cactus thicket; this trail is located in the **Queen Elizabeth Botanic Park** (admission $3 for adults). A newly restored 200-year-old footpath also explores the woodlands at the heart of Grand Cayman. The two-mile trail can only be done with a wildlife guide, **Albert Hines**, who offers a 2.5-hour tour Monday through Friday at 8:30 a.m. and 3 p.m., Saturdays at 8:30 a.m. only; the price of the excursion is $30 and profits are used to maintain the path *(reservations required: ☎ (345) 949-1996)*.

Cayman Brac's 180-acre Brac Parrot Reserve is home to 500 rare parrots.

Cayman Brac—On Foot

Brac distinguishes itself among the Caymans by having the most interesting interior landscape. In particular, a limestone bluff (a "brac" in Gaelic) rises to an elevation of about 140 feet—the highest point in the Caymans—and provides the islands' best hike. The 180-acre **Brac Parrot Reserve** is located on the bluff and serves as home to about 500 of the rare birds, a unique subspecies of the Amazon parrot. Also located on the bluff is a series of caves, which are said to have once held pirate treasure. Most vehicular traffic is concentrated along the paved coastal roads, however, a dirt track follows the island's spine (between the north and south coasts) and provides secluded walking potential. Hikers should be on the alert for the maiden plum prevalent around the bluff, which can cause a skin rash if brushed against.

Little Cayman—On Foot

The smallest of the Caymans is a mostly undistinguished flat of sand accented by scrub and mangroves. Just past South Town is the 200-acre **Booby Pond Nature Reserve**, nesting grounds for roughly 3500 mating pairs of red-footed boobies; the island is also home to great blue herons, black-necked stilts and even some magnificent frigatebirds. The truly adventurous can head east along the island's coastline for solitude and exploration, or two simpler paths depart from the airport just outside town; one heads west to the lighthouse, while the other, referred to as **The Nature Trail**, crosses the island to the northwest and leads to **Spot Bay** (allow an hour round-trip for either of these walks).

What Else to See

A turtle from the Cayman turtle farm

No one in the know comes to the Caymans for its man-made or historic attractions, but for their wonderfully translucent water and colorful reefs. Even so, a morning or afternoon spent exploring the capital city of George Town is well worth the time. Though town center is dominated by modern office

CAYMAN ISLANDS

buildings, a few historic gems are here, including the Grand Caymans National Museum, housed in an 1833 building formerly used as a jail, courthouse and even dance hall. Also worth checking out is the Treasure Museum which has some good exhibits on shipwrecks and pirate folklore. At the north end of West Bay Beach, a formation of blackened coral rock that rises like petrified flames has the dubious name of Hell; stop at the nearby post office and your postcards back home will bear the postmark "Hell, Grand Cayman." On Cayman Brac, the chief on-land activities are birdwatching and spelunking among a half-dozen caves and sinkholes, while birdwatching is good on Little Cayman.

City Celebrations
Grand Cayman

Pirates' Week　　　　　　　　　　　　　　　　　　　★★★★

☎ *(345) 949-5078.*

To celebrate its history as a pirate haunt, this island-wide festival, held in late October, brings out the buccaneer in locals with costume parades, fishing tournaments, treasure hunts and the ever-popular kidnapping of the governor. Lots of ho-ho-hoing, and more than a few bottles of rum.

Historical Sites
Grand Cayman

Pedro St. James Historic Site

Castle Road.

This National Historic Site, the oldest existing structure on the Caymans, has undergone a three-year, $6.25-million major restoration. Formerly known as Pedro Castle, the building was constructed in 1780 as a great house, and, in 1831, was the meeting site of residents who formed the first democratically elected legislative assembly of the islands—which also held its first meeting here. It was destroyed by fire in 1877. Considered the birthplace of democracy of the Caymans, it is the islands' largest restoration project, with the original house accurately reconstructed, the addition of small Caymanian houses from the 19th century, a visitor center with a multimedia display, restaurant and botanical gardens.

Museums and Exhibits
Cayman Brac

Cayman Brac Museum　　　　　　　　　　　　　　　　　　★★

Stake Bay, ☎ *(345) 948-2622*
Hours open: 9 a.m.–4 p.m.

This small museum exhibits local antiques and relics from shipwrecks.

Grand Cayman

Cayman Islands National Museum　　　　　　　　　　　　　★★★

Harbour Drive, George Town, ☎ *(345) 949-8368.*
Hours open: 9 a.m.–5 p.m.

Housed in an 1833 West Indian building on the waterfront—which in previous incarnations was a jail, courthouse and dance hall—this museum exhibits more than

2000 items detailing the history of the islands and its peoples. Students & Seniors $2.50. General admission: $5.

Treasure Museum ★★★

West Bay Road, George Town, ☎ *(345) 949-5033.*
Hours open: 9 a.m.–5 p.m.

This small museum specializes in recovered artifacts from shipwrecks, with lots of pieces from the Maravillas, a Spanish galleon that sank in 1656. Among the exhibits are a seven-pound gold bar, dioramas of the islands' seafaring history and an animated Blackbeard the Pirate, who regales visitors with long-ago tales that may or may not be true. General admission: $5.

Parks and Gardens
Grand Cayman

Queen Elizabeth II Botanical Park

center of the island, ☎ *(345) 947-9462*
Hours open: 7:30 a.m.–5:30 p.m.

This new interpretive woodland trail is less than a mile long, but packs a lot in a relatively small space. The trail passes through more than a dozen Caymanian landscapes, from wetlands to cactus thicket, logwood swamp to woodland and mahogany trees. There's also an iguana habitat partially funded by the World Wildlife Fund that is home to the endangered native blue iguanas, a crocodile swamp with 300-year-old fossil bones and a pond housing small freshwater turtles found only in the Caymans. Birdwatchers may spot Grand Cayman parrots, Northern Flicker woodpeckers, Vitelline warblers, Zenaida doves and Bananaquits. The Botanic Park is the first of several ambitious projects to protect the Caymans' environment, and new additions include a visitor center, lake and Heritage Garden. General admission: $3.

Little Cayman

Booby Pond Nature Reserve

The National Trust for the Cayman Islands continues in its quest to protect its natural resources with improvements to this nature reserve, which consists of a saltwater pond and surrounding mangrove habitat that is a natural rookery. Some 3500 nesting pairs of red-footed boobies and 100 pairs of frigate birds call the reserve home. A new visitor center, built to resemble a Cayman-style house, includes a reference library, observation deck with high-powered telescope and information center. This is the first tract of land on Little Cayman to become owned and protected by the National Trust, which is now working to acquire the remaining 67 acres of privately owned land that surrounds the area.

Tours
Grand Cayman

Atlantis Submarines Cayman ★★★

Goring Avenue, George Town, ☎ *(345) 949-7700.*

Not for the claustrophobic but memorable for everyone else, this modern submarine seats 46 people in air-conditioned comfort. It travels along the Cayman Wall at depths of up to 90 feet, giving nondivers a taste of the fascinating underwater sights.

Night dives are especially recommended. Prices range from $79-$90; half that for kids under 12 (children under four are not permitted). Atlantis also operates two research subs that go as deep as 800 feet and carry just two passengers at a time. This trip costs $275 per person; a highlight is the wreck of the cargo ship Kirk Pride. Tours last one and half hours.

Cayman Turtle Farm   ★ ★ ★

West Bay, ☎ *(345) 949-3893.*
Hours open: 8:30 a.m.–5 p.m.

The island's most-visited tourist attraction houses more than 12,000 green turtles, from hatchlings to giant specimens weighing 600 pounds. It's the world's only green sea turtle farm, and while it supplies turtle meat to local restaurants, it also strives to replenish their numbers in the wild. You can taste turtle dishes at the cafe, but skip the gift shop: U.S. citizens can't import anything made of these endangered critters. Children 6–10 are half price and under 6 are free. General admission: $5.

"He Hath Founded It Upon the Seas" is the official motto of the Cayman Islands—but perhaps it should read in the seas, since that's the main reason so many tourists flock here. Windsurfing is coming on strong here; it's best along the four miles of reef-protected shallows off East End where prevailing winds from November to March are a hefty 15-25 miles per hour. Para-sailing has also reached new heights in popularity. Deep-sea fishers search for blue marlin, yellowfin tuna, wahoo, dorado (dolphin) and barracuda year-round, and because the ocean floor drops off sharply as close as a quarter-mile offshore, you won't have to travel for hours to hook up. Light tackle and flyfishers angle for bonefish tarpon and permit, but note that fishing for these creatures is catch and release. Little Cayman is the best for such action year round.The annual Million Dollar Month International Fishing Tournament, held each year throughout the month of June, has a top prize of $250,000 for the first angler to break the Caymans' All-Tackle records for yellowfin tuna, wahoo and dolphin. Finally, those who don't want to get wet but do want to see what all the excitement is about can book a ride on the Atlantis Submarine, which drops to 150 feet, or the even more dramatic Research Submersibles sub, which carries just two passengers and descends to depths of up to 800 feet along a wall. If you're worried about claustrophobia, try a semi-submarine or glass-bottom-boat ride instead.

Biking

With a maximum elevation of only 60 feet above sea level riding on Grand Cayman is easy. From George Town to Rum Point is a 55-mile round trip. Or you can cycle around Hell and the Turtle Farm. **Cayman Cycle Rentals** (☎ *(345) 945-4021;* credit cards accepted) in George Town has Huffy 10-speeds for $15 a day. Scooters are available for $25 a day. On Little Cayman, **McLaughlin Rentals** (☎ *(345) 948-1000)* rents bikes for $7.50 a day.

Grand Cayman

Deep-Sea Fishing

Several outfits offer charters and excursions for deep-sea, reef, bone and fly fishers: **Crosby Ebanks** (☎ *(345) 945-4049)*, **Capt. Eugene's Watersports** (☎ *(345) 949-3099)*; **Charter Boat Headquarters** (☎ *(345) 945-4340)*, and **Island Girl** (☎ *(345) 947-3029)*. Serious fishermen and women should plan to visit Grand Cayman in June, when the Million Dollar Month fishing tournament is held, featuring international competitors and cash prizes. For details, contact **Cayman Islands Department of Tourism** (☎ *(345) 949-0623)*.

Golf

The island's newest course is the **Links at Safehaven** (☎ *(345) 947-5988;* $90 for greens fees and a cart), a par-71, 6519-yard championship course designed by Roy Case. Duffers can also tee off at **Hyatt Regency's Britannia**, designed by Jack Nicklaus, which includes a nine-hole regulation course, an 18-hole executive course, and a Cayman course, in which special short-distance balls are used. Green fees are $65–$80; ☎ *(345) 949-8020*.

Mastic Trail

Frank Sound Road, ☎ *(345) 949-1996.*

This restored 200-year-old footpath winds through a two-million-year-old woodland at the island's heart. Reopened in 1995, the trail is located west of Frank Sound Road, a 45-minute drive east from George Town. The two-mile trail showcases the Mastic Reserve's scenic wonders, including a mangrove swamp, woodland area, and traditional farms. Birders should be on the lookout for the Grand Cayman parrot, Caribbean dove, West Indian woodpecker, Cuban bullfinch, smooth-billed Ani and Bananaquit. The nonprofit reserve now numbers 200 acres, with the plan of adding 800 more acres as funds become available. Guided tours, which are not recommended to children under six, the elderly or the infirm, last 2.5 hours and are limited to eight people, so reservations are essential. They are available Monday through Friday at 8:30 a.m. and 3:00 p.m. and on Saturday at 8:30 a.m. Admission price includes a guide. General admission: $30.

Windsurfing

Chances are good your hotel can set you up for windsurfing, but if it lacks facilities, try **Cayman Windsurf** (☎ *(345) 947-7492;* FAX *(345) 949-8492)* or **Sailboards Caribbean** (☎ *(345) 949-1068)*.

CAYMAN ISLANDS

Where to Stay

Fielding's Highest Rated Hotels in Cayman Islands

★★★★★	Hyatt Regency Grand Cayman	$190–$385
★★★★	Marriott Grand Cayman Resort	$165–$390
★★★★	Westin Casuarina Resort	$205–$446
★★★	Beach Club Colony	$113–$265
★★★	Caribbean Club	$175–$440
★★★	Conch Club	$300–$400
★★★	Holiday Inn Grand Cayman	$178–$328
★★★	Indies Suites	$170–$305
★★★	Lacovia Condominiums	$175–$715
★★★	London House	$275–$900

Fielding's Best Hotels for Divers in Cayman Islands

★★★★★	Hyatt Regency Grand Cayman	$190–$385
★★★★	Westin Casuarina Resort	$205–$446
★★★	Morrit's Tortuga Club	$145–$350
★★	Divi Tiara Beach Resort	$95–$200
★★★	Beach Club Colony	$113–$265

Fielding's Best Value Hotels in Cayman Islands

★★★	Ambassadors Inn	$60–$80
★★	Spanish Bay Reef Resort	$205–$257
★★★	Beach Club Colony	$113–$265

Many of Grand Cayman's lodging choices are along Seven Mile Beach, a glorious strand considered one of the Caribbean's best. The Hyatt Regency Grand Cayman and new Westin Casuarina Resort are known for their outstanding dive operations. You aren't even expected to hoist your own gear. West Bay is also a good spot for a home away from home as it is within an easy walk to shops and restaurants. About half of the island's accommodations are found in condominium units (almost 50 at last count) for do-it-yourselfers; note, however, that food prices in the markets can be quite high. There are more than 2000 hotel rooms on the islands with 24 hotels.

Hotels and Resorts

The big chain hotels, including **Holiday Inn**, **Radisson** and **Ramada**, give good service here and particularly lean toward providing package tours, some specifically for divers. The **Hyatt Regency**, luxurious and lushly landscaped, is known for being the hub of lively social activities, especially at night. (Hyatt's private villas come with their own pool, Jacuzzi and cabaña.) The **Spanish Bay Reef**, the first all-inclusive property on Grand Cayman, rates as the island's most secluded—a true dive hotel. **Pirates Point Resort** is run by a Cordon-Bleu educated-chef. The Beach Club Colony should be avoided if you don't care for your personal beach space to be invaded by loads of cruise passengers.

Cayman Brac

Brac Reef Beach Resort $100–$115 ★

West End Point, ☎ *(800) 327-3835, (345) 948-1323, FAX (813) 323-8827.*
Double: $100–$115.
This casual hotel has become a favorite with divers who like its dive packages. The rooms are basic but at least air cooled, and recent renovations have added decks or patios as well as new carpeting and wallpaper. A pool and tennis court round out the facilities. 40 rooms. Credit cards: A, MC, V.

Divi Tiara Beach Resort $95–$200 ★★

Stake Bay, ☎ *(800) 367-3484, (345) 948-1553, FAX (345) 948-1316.*
Single: $95–$165. Double: $100–$200.
Set on a fine beach, this pleasant hotel appeals to those who want to avoid crowds. Rooms are typical but do offer air conditioning; a few have Jacuzzis to boot. There's a pool and tennis court, and most meals are served buffet-style. Good service. The dive center is excellent. 58 rooms. Credit cards: A, D, MC, V.

Grand Cayman

Beach Club Colony $113–$265 ★★★

Seven Mile Beach, ☎ *(800) 482-DIVE, (345) 949-8100, FAX (809) 945-5167.*
Single: $113–$240. Double: $125–$265.
Dating back to the 1960s (making it one of the island's oldest resorts), the Beach Club resembles a colonial plantation villa. Accommodations are strung along the beach and include standard and unexciting guest rooms and villas. Watersports cost extra, but a great dive shop is on-site. Lots of cruise passengers converge here when their ship is in port, so don't expect tranquility. 41 rooms. Credit cards: A, DC, D, MC, V.

Clarion Grand Pavilion $160–$350 ★★★

Seven Mile Beach, ☎ *(345) 947-5656, FAX (345) 945-5353.*
Single: $160–$350. Double: $160–$350.
This spot was reopened in February 1994 by new Cayman owners after extensive refurbishing. Accommodations are tasteful and well-appointed; all have central air

and such extras as coffeemakers, minibars, even a trouser press (do you really need creases in the Caribbean?) and hair dryers. It also offers 24-hour room service and in-room safes. The pool is found in a lovely garden courtyard complete with lush foliage and a cascading waterfall. The hotel has two restaurants and two bars. Other facilities include a fitness center, tennis courts, a 24-hour business center, jeep rentals and nearby watersports, plus a supervised kids' program all year round. 93 rooms. Credit cards: A, DC, D, MC, V.

Holiday Inn Grand Cayman $178–$328   ★★★

Seven Mile Beach, ☎ *(800) 421-9999, (345) 945-4444, FAX (345) 945-4213.*
Single: $178–$328. Double: $178–$328.
Guestrooms at this busy, but pleasant hotel are air-conditioned and nicely done, though only some boast views. The hotel has a full-service dive shop, twice-weekly barbecues by the great pool and all sorts of watersports (though prices are a tad high). Its best asset is its prime spot on Seven Mile Beach. It's not too close to the cruise ship port, so guests are not overrun with day-trippers. Not a lot of island flavor—this is, after all, a Holiday Inn—but the lodgings are dependable and the two restaurants, two bars and a comedy club keep guests hopping. On the other hand, for this kind of dough why not splurge and go for the much nice Hyatt Regency also on Seven Mile Beach. 213 rooms. Credit cards: A, DC, MC, V.

Hyatt Regency Grand Cayman $190–$825   ★★★★★

Seven Mile Beach, ☎ *(800) 233-1234, (345) 949-1234, FAX (345) 949-8528.*
Associated Restaurant: *Garden Loggia/Hemingway's.*
Single: $190–$385. Double: $190–$385. Suites Per Day: $440–$825.
Unquestionably Grand Cayman's finest resort, this Hyatt Regency—where part of *The Firm* was filmed—boasts accommodations in British Colonial-style buildings surrounding a central courtyard. These fabulous digs are replete with expensive furnishings, original art, air conditioning (of course), Italian marble baths, voice mail and the long list of amenities travelers have come to expect from a place like this. It has 101 nonsmoking rooms, 10 suites and 50 villas with one-to-four bedrooms and full kitchens. Lush landscaping—English gardens line the paths to the beach—gives a sense of privacy despite the crowds. Guests can choose from four restaurants, four bars, four pools (one has a whirlpool covering one-third of an acre), four lighted tennis courts, fitness center and spa with jogging paths, a private marina, daily ferry to Rum Point Beach and the Britannia Golf Club with 18 holes of golf designed by Jack Nicklaus. One of the prime assets is Red Sail Sports, a top of the line watersports center that has helped this resort achieve well-deserved acclaim among divers. A room here also entitles you to a spot on one of the most desirable stretches of Seven Mile Beach. Camp Hyatt offers supervised activities for children including trips to the nearby Turtle Farm and snorkeling lessons. At presstime, the resort was making a $15 million addition: 53 beachfront suites with keyed elevator access, its own concierge and fax machines. Each also has a microwave and stove. Hyatt was also building a new Red Sail Sports watersports center, a landscaped pool complex with three pools, coffee bar and ice cream cafe, rooftop sundeck, and a new health club. 296 rooms. Credit cards: A, MC, V.

Marriott Grand Cayman Resort   **$165–$390**   ★★★★

Seven Mile Beach, ☎ *(800) 228-9290, (345) 949-0088, FAX (345) 949-0288.*
Single: $165–$240. Double: $165–$390.

Set on a scenic spread of beach, this five-story hotel, which opened in 1990, has newly-renovated, comfortable and contemporary guest rooms. Marriott took over in June 1997; the hotel used to be a Radisson. The open lobby area and lounge has views of the interior courtyard with a terrace surrounding the waterfall. A deck houses a pool, bar and Jacuzzi surrounded by potted plants. All the usual watersports, plus a dive shop, fitness center, and 2336 sq. ft. of retail space keep guests busy. A truly pleasant and elegant spot. 309 rooms. Credit cards: A, DC, MC, V.

Sleep Inn   **$105–$215**   ★★

Seven Mile Beach, ☎ *(800) 753-3746, (345) 949-9111, FAX (345) 949-6699.*
Single: $105–$185. Double: $105–$185. Suites Per Day: $215.

This modern hotel, set right on the beach, has air-conditioned guest rooms with all the typical amenities. Eight suites have kitchenettes. The grounds are basic, with just a pool and Jacuzzi for recreation, but watersports can be found nearby. 115 rooms. Credit cards: A, CB, DC, D, MC, V.

Sunset House   **$105–$243**   ★★

☎ *(800) 854-4767, (345) 949-7111, FAX (345) 949-7101.*
Single: $105–$135. Double: $110–$145. Suites Per Day: $195–$243.

Great diving and snorkeling right offshore, but there's no beach to speak of at this casual hotel that dates back to the late 1950s. Accommodations are in standard guest rooms and two efficiencies; all are nicely done and air-cooled. Two pools help make up for the lack of beach, and there's a full-service dive shop, with a fleet of six boats, on-site. A really nice spot. Dive and non-divers packages available. 59 rooms. Credit cards: A, D, MC, V.

Treasure Island Resort   **$160–$260**   ★★★

☎ *(800) 203-0775, (345) 949-7777, FAX (345) 949-8489.*
Single: $160–$260. Double: $160–$260.

One of the island's largest resorts, this former Ramada fronts the beach and situates its guest rooms around a courtyard with two pools, a Jacuzzi and a gurgling waterfall. Accommodations are larger than usual and nicely done with minibars and sitting areas. There's live music in the nightclub six nights a week, and by day lots to keep busy with, including two tennis courts, a dive shop and all watersports. A good choice for those who like a lot of action. 280 rooms. Credit cards: A, DC, MC, V.

Westin Casuarina Resort   **$205–$1650**   ★★★★

Seven Mile Beach, ☎ *(800) 228-3000, (345) 945-3800, FAX (345) 949-5825.*
Website: www.westin.com.
Single: $205–$446. Double: $205–$446. Suites Per Day: $850–$1650.

Opened in December 1995, this $50-million Westin is the largest resort in the Cayman Islands. The eight-acre, beachfront property includes a dive shop, tennis courts, two freshwater pools, two whirlpools, a swim-up bar and fitness center. The spacious guestrooms are done in Caribbean-style and feature oversized bathrooms with hair dryers and French doors opening onto balconies. The Links at SaveHaven are nearby for duffers. 343 rooms. Credit cards: A, MC, V.

CAYMAN ISLANDS

Little Cayman

Little Cayman Beach Resort   **$120–$350**   ★★

Blossom Village, ☎ *(800) 327-3835, (813) 323-8727, FAX (813) 323-8827.*
Single: $120–$180. Double: $120–$180. Suites Per Day: $300–$350.

Opened in 1993, this resort on the southern end of the island has a nice sandy beach off a reef-protected bay. Air-conditioned guest rooms are a cut above the competition on the island and attractively furnished. Two-bedroom condos are also available. Guests keep busy diving (it has an excellent shop), hanging out by the pool or in the Jacuzzi, working out at the new fitness center, playing tennis, riding bikes, or playing pick-up volleyball games. The bar and restaurant are good and popular with locals. Guests can choose from a variety of packages that include all meals and diving. A week during high season would be $1514; during low, $1386. 40 rooms. Credit cards: A, MC, V.

Pirates Point Resort, Ltd.   **$135–$200**   ★★★

Preston Bay, ☎ *(345) 948-1010, FAX (345) 948-1011.*
Associated Restaurant: *Pirates Point.*
Single: $135–$150. Double: $185–$200.

Most accommodations are in air-conditioned rooms with private baths; there are also four cottages overlooking the sea. The best reason to come, however, is mealtime: owner Gladys Howard is a graduate of Paris' Cordon Bleu, and judging from the food, she passed with flying colors. The rates include meals, and dive packages are also available. A friendly, peaceful spot. No kids under five. 10 rooms. Credit cards: MC, V.

All Inclusives
Cayman Brac

Spanish Bay Reef Resort   **$205–$257**   ★★

West Bay Road, ☎ *(800) 482-DIVE, (345) 949-3765, FAX (345) 949-1842.*
Single: $205–$257. Double: $205–$257.

Situated on a private coral reef on the island's isolated northwest tip, this resort houses guests in air-conditioned rooms with Caribbean decor. Popular with divers, it offers good facilities for scuba, as well as other watersports and the typical resort pool. The rates include all meals and activities. The atmosphere is nicely casual, but service is not always up to par. 50 rooms. Credit cards: A, MC, V.

Little Cayman

Southern Cross Club   **$280–$330**   ★★★

South Hole Sound, ☎ *(800) 899-2582, (345) 948-1099, FAX (345) 948-1098.*
Website: www.southerncrossclub.com. E-mail: scc✫candw.ky.
Associated Restaurant: *Loggerhead Bar.*
Single: $280–$330. Double: $280–$330.

This cottage resort, built in 1958 and renovated in 1995, sits on a pretty, white-sand beach on a protected lagoon. Bungalows are basic Caribbean-style with a sitting reading area, lots of windows, beamed ceilings with fans and newly-added air conditioning. It also has a freshwater swimming pool with a deck and an extension of the indoor bar. The basic rates include three family-style meals a day, airport transfers, use of beach towels, bicycles and kayaks and the 10% government room tax and service charge. Most who come are into deep-sea fishing and diving with the hotel providing on-site dive facilities and guided fishing programs for additional fees. The bar attracts lots of tale-swapping fishermen and women. Weddings are often performed on deserted Owen Island about 500 yards offshore. But with only 23 locals on the entire island, this spot appeals strictly to those looking for a getaway. 10 rooms. Credit cards: not accepted.

Apartments and Condominiums

Visitors who come to the Caymans seek rough and rugged adventure underwater, so they're used to taking care of themselves. Not surprisingly, more self-catering accommodations are appearing every year. The downside is that if you plan to cook for yourself, food costs are extremely high; though the markets are at least getting better stocked. Amid the action on Seven Mile Beach, a short walk from restaurants and a supermarket, are **Pan Cayman** in the Caribbean Club; here you'll find a better beach and a lot more peace and quiet. Golfers congregate in the **Britannia Villas**, which is part of the Hyatt complex, at the golf course. The **Indies Suites** are a good bargain for travelers who spend most of their time underwater and shut their eyes the minute their head hits the pillow (one plus is the free breakfast).

Grand Cayman

Beachcomber Condos   **$195–$425**   ★

Seven Mile Beach, ☎ *(800) 327-8777, (345) 945-4470, FAX (345) 945-5019.*
Single: $195–$425. Double: $195–$425.
This condo complex has two-bedroom, two-bath units with air conditioning, fully equipped kitchens and a balcony or patio with ocean views. Several units have dens that can convert into a third bedroom if needed. There's a pool on-site, and maid service is available, but you'll have to dine elsewhere. 24 rooms. Credit cards: A, MC, V.

Caribbean Club   **$175–$440**   ★★★

Seven Mile Beach, ☎ *(800) 327-8777, (345) 945-4099, FAX (345) 945-4443.*
Single: $175–$440. Double: $175–$440.
This colony of villas includes one- and two-bedroom units (only six are actually on the beach) in a secluded atmosphere. The pink cottages are air-conditioned and include large living/dining areas, full kitchens and attractive, comfortable decor. The restaurant is popular with visitors as well as locals. There's a tennis court, but no pool. No kids under 11 during the winter season. 18 rooms. Credit cards: A, MC, V.

Cayman Kai Resort   **$140–$180**   ★★

Northside, east of Rum Plantation, ☎ *(800) 223-5427, (345) 947-9055, FAX (345) 947-9102.*
Single: $140–$180. Double: $140–$180.
Situated in a 20-acre grove along the secluded north shore beach, this secluded resort houses guests in one- and two-bedroom lodges and villas, all with kitchens but only some with air conditioning. The beach is not great for swimming, but the snorkeling is great. The property caters primarily to divers, but is a bit more formal than the island's other dive resorts. A restaurant, bar and three tennis courts keep nondivers occupied. 20 rooms. Credit cards: A, MC, V.

Christopher Columbus Apartments   **$190–$390**   ★★

Seven Mile Beach, ☎ *(345) 945-4354, FAX (345) 945-5062.*
Single: $190–$390. Double: $190–$390.
Popular with families, this condominium resort offers individually decorated two-bedroom, two-bath units with air conditioning, small but complete kitchens and light, tropical furnishings. As expected, the penthouse units are by far the nicest (and most expensive). No restaurant or bar, so guests congregate at the pool, tennis courts and sandy beach. 30 rooms. Credit cards: A, MC, V.

Colonial Club   **$280–$468**   ★

West Bay Road, ☎ *(345) 945-4660, FAX (345) 945-4839.*
Single: $280–$468. Double: $280–$468.
Built in Bermudian-style with a pink and white exterior, this condo complex has comfortable two- and three-bedroom units with central air, complete kitchens and maid service. Located on an especially nice stretch of beach, extras include a pool and lighted tennis court. No restaurant on-site, so you'll have to cook in or venture out. 15 rooms. Credit cards: A, MC, V.

Discovery Point Club   **$220–$360**   ★★

Seven Mile Beach, ☎ *(345) 945-4724, FAX (345) 945-5051.*
Single: $220–$360. Double: $220–$360.
Located on the north end of Seven Mile Beach, this well-appointed resort offers one- and two-bedroom condos with all the modern conveniences, including air and full kitchens. There are also studios sans cooking facilities. A pretty pool and two tennis courts are on-site, but no restaurant or bar. 45 rooms. Credit cards: A, MC, V.

George Town Villas   **$160–$420**   ★

Seven Mile Beach, ☎ *(345) 949-5172, FAX (345) 949-0256.*
Single: $160–$420. Double: $160–$420.
A condominium community with two-bedroom units that come equipped with two baths, full kitchens, air conditioning, living and dining areas and washer/dryers. There's a pool and tennis court, and shopping and restaurants are nearby. 54 rooms. Credit cards: A, MC, V.

Grand Bay Club   **$160–$390**   ★★★

Seven Mile Beach, ☎ *(800) 825-8703, (345) 945-4728, FAX (345) 945-5681.*
Single: $160–$390. Double: $160–$390.
All units at this modern complex are suites, ranging from studios that lack kitchens to one- and two-bedroom units with cooking facilities. Maids keep things tidy. The site includes a large pool, Jacuzzi and tennis. No restaurant, but many are within walking distance. Packages available. 21 rooms. Credit cards: A, MC, V.

Harbour Heights   **$185–$335**   ★★

Seven Mile Beach, ☎ *(800) 327-8777, (345) 945-4295, FAX (345) 945-4522.*
Single: $185–$335. Double: $185–$335.
This three-story condominium overlooks the pool and seafront along Seven Mile Beach. Two-bedroom suites are attractive, with living/dining areas, complete kitchens, air conditioning and balconies. The grounds are nicely landscaped, and the beach is good for swimmers. Restaurants are nearby. 46 rooms. Credit cards: A, MC, V.

Indies Suites $170–$305 ★★★

West Bay Road, ☎ *(800) 654-3130, (345) 945-5025, FAX (345) 945-5024.*
Single: $170–$305. Double: $170–$305.
This comfortable and attractive property houses guests in nicely furnished one- and
two-bedroom suites with full-size kitchens, satellite TV, telephones and a private
balcony or patio. Kids under 12 stay free with their parents. Facilities include a large
pool and Jacuzzi and a dive shop. There's no restaurant, but guests can grab snacks
at the pool bar, and the daily complimentary continental breakfast is a nice touch.
The beach is across the street, a liability when so many similar properties lie directly
on the sand. Nevertheless, this family-owned and operated property is a good
choice. 40 rooms. Credit cards: A, MC, V.

Island Pine Villas $115–$227 ★

Seven Mile Beach, ☎ *(800) 223-9815, (345) 949-6586, FAX (345) 949-0428.*
Single: $115–$227. Double: $115–$227.
This two-story condo complex is within walking distance of shops and restaurants.
Units are quite comfortable, with one or two bedrooms, air conditioning, kitchen-
ettes and patios or balconies. No pool or restaurant, but a good value nonetheless.
40 rooms. Credit cards: A, DC, D, MC, V.

Lacovia Condominiums $175–$715 ★★★

Seven Mile Beach, ☎ *(800) 223-9815, (345) 949-7599, FAX (809) 949-0172.*
Single: $175–$715. Double: $175–$715.
Stylish and tasteful, this condo complex surrounds a free-form pool and clubhouse
with sauna and games. Units, with daily maid service, have one to three bedrooms
with separate living/dining areas, full kitchens and Spanish-style balconies; most
also boast oversized tubs. The nicely landscaped grounds include a tennis court for
working up a sweat. 55 rooms. Credit cards: A.

London House $275–$900 ★★★

Seven Mile Beach, ☎ *(800) 423-4095, (345) 945-4060, FAX (345) 945-4087.*
Single: $275–$290. Double: $275–$900.
This mission-style complex has well-maintained accommodations, a freshwater
pool, and snorkeling gear for rent. A dive boat picks up at its beach. Units have one
or two bedrooms with patios or balconies overlooking the beach and the ocean,
daily maid service, and full kitchens with dishwasher and microwave. A penthouse is
available by request. Ceiling fans supplement the air conditioning, and each room is
equipped with satellite TV. George Town is five minutes away. 22 rooms. Credit
cards: A, MC, V.

Morrit's Tortuga Club $145–$350 ★★★

East End, ☎ *(800) 447-0309, (345) 947-7449, FAX (345) 947-7669.*
Single: $145–$350. Double: $145–$350.
This plantation-style condo complex is situated on eight beachfront acres near some
of Grand Cayman's best diving sites. Three-story buildings house comfortable one-
and two-bedroom units with full kitchens. Built on the site of the former Tortuga
Club, today's resort is a far cry from that hideaway spot, but it remains popular with
divers. In addition to a pool, there's a decent restaurant and both windsurfing and
diving schools. 121 rooms. Credit cards: A, D, MC, V.

CAYMAN ISLANDS

Pan Cayman House   **$165–$370**   ★★

Seven Mile Beach, ☎ *(800) 248-5115, (345) 947-4002, FAX (345) 947-4002.*
Single: $165–$370. Double: $165–$370.

A popular apartment complex with 10 units ranging from two to three bedrooms, all with two baths, air conditioning, full kitchens and maid service. Great views from the private balconies or patios. 10 rooms. Credit cards: MC, V.

Plantana Condominiums   **$175–$425**   ★★

Seven Mile Beach, ☎ *(345) 945-4430, FAX (345) 945-5076.*
Single: $175–$425. Double: $175–$425.

One- and two-bedroom condominiums are arranged on three floors, with the ones higher up offering the best views. All are individually decorated and have full kitchens and screened balconies or patios; most also have washer/dryers. A pool supplements the sea for splashing about. One of the nicer condo complexes on the island. 49 rooms. Credit cards: A, MC, V.

Plantation Village Beach Resort   **$175–$460**   ★

Seven Mile Beach, ☎ *(800) 822-8903, (345) 949-4199, FAX (345) 949-0646.*
Single: $175–$460. Double: $175–$460.

Set on four acres of Seven Mile Beach, this condo complex popular with families has individually decorated two- and three-bedroom units with two baths, complete kitchens, central air and screened lanais. It has daily maid service, two pools, a Jacuzzi, a tennis court and a playground for the kids. 70 rooms. Credit cards: A, MC, V.

Silver Sands   **$205–$440**   ★★★

Seven Mile Beach, ☎ *(800) 327-8777, (345) 949-3343, FAX (345) 949-1223.*
Single: $205–$440. Double: $205–$440.

Set amid tropical gardens, this casual complex—at the end of Seven Mile Beach where it is a bit rockier—has air-conditioned, two and three bedroom units with all the modern amenities. This place, with its extra-large pool, gazebo, two tennis courts, has a nice resort feel. Only downside: The closest watersports are available at the Westin. 42 rooms. Credit cards: A, MC, V.

Tarquynn Manor   **$185–$345**   ★★

Seven Mile Beach, ☎ *(800) 223-9815, (345) 945-4038, FAX (345) 945-5060.*
Single: $185–$345. Double: $185–$345.

At least one bedroom in these two- or three-bedroom units fronts the beach. The modern units have air conditioning, kitchens and patios or balconies. A concierge handles special requests. There's an outdoor pool and games room to keep kids occupied. 20 rooms. Credit cards: MC, V.

Victoria House   **$137–$415**   ★★

Seven Mile Beach, ☎ *(800) 327-8777, (345) 945-4233, FAX (345) 945-5328.*
Single: $137–$415. Double: $137–$415.

These Caribbean-style apartments front the ocean and are far from the crowds. Units are air-conditioned and come in a variety of configurations, from studios to penthouses; some have gardens and barbecues out back. All are comfortable with full kitchens. There's no pool on-site, but watersports are available nearby. It has a tennis court. Sea turtles frequent the quiet, sandy beach in the early mornings. 26 rooms. Credit cards: A, MC, V.

Villas of the Galleon   **$200–$430**   ★★
West Bay Beach, ☎ *(800) 235-5888, (345) 947-4433.*
Single: $200–$430. Double: $200–$430.
Facing a private beach, this condo complex offers units with one or two bedrooms, all with air conditioning, modern kitchen, small baths and balconies; maids tidy up daily but take Sundays off. Most folks here are staying for a long time. Request an upper floor unit for the best sea views. 75 rooms. Credit cards: A, MC, V.

Little Cayman
Conch Club   **$300–$400**   ★★★
☎ *(813) 323-8727, FAX (813) 323-8827.*
Single: $300–$400. Double: $300–$400.
These new luxury townhouses are rented out when the owners are off-island. Accommodations consist of two- and three-bedroom oceanfront units, each with a patio downstairs and a balcony up above, fully equipped kitchen and spacious living and dining areas. There's a dock, pool and Jacuzzi on site, and meals can be taken at the nearby Bird of Paradise restaurant at the Little Cayman Beach Resort, which also has a full-service dive shop. Credit cards: A, MC, V.

Low Cost Lodging
One way to save money in the Caymans is to cram a lot of people into a multi-bedroom apartment. But individuals can find single rooms for rent in guest houses (don't hesitate to ask the tourist board). The nightclub keeps things hopping at **Windjammer Hotel**, where rooms are also air-conditioned and come with kitchenettes. Diving is the main topic of conversation at these lodgings, especially at the **Ambassadors Inn**, which attracts the diehards.

Grand Cayman
Ambassadors Inn   **$60–$80**   ★★★
☎ *(800) 648-7748, (809) 949-7577, FAX (809) 949-7050.*
Single: $60–$70. Double: $70–$80.
Located a mile from George Town and some 200 yards and across the street from the beach, this casual spot appeals to divers on a budget. Rooms are basic but do offer air conditioning and private baths. There's a pool on site. 18 rooms. Credit cards: A, MC, V.

Windjammer Hotel   **$100–$155**   ★
☎ *(809) 947-4608, FAX (809) 947-4391.*
Single: $100–$155. Double: $100–$155.
Located at the Cayman Falls Shopping Plaza, across from Seven Mile Beach, this small hotel offers air-conditioned rooms with kitchenettes. There are two restaurants, a bar and a nightclub, and this place does do a good after-dark trade. 12 rooms. Credit cards: A, MC, V.

Where to Eat

★★★★★	Hemingway's	$17–$23
★★★★★	Lantana's	$20–$40
★★★★	Chef Tell's Grand Old House	$20–$34
★★★★	Crow's Nest, The	$12–$19
★★★★	Ottmar's Restaurant	$12–$27
★★★	Garden Loggia Cafe	$16–$34
★★★	Pirate's Point Resort	$37–$37
★★★	Ristorante Pappagallo	$15–$29
★★★	Wharf, The	$20–$40
★★★	Cracked Conch By the Sea	$12–$30

Fielding's Most Romantic Restaurants in Cayman Islands

♡♡♡♡♡	Chef Tell's Grand Old House	$20–$34
♡♡♡♡♡	Crow's Nest, The	$12–$19
♡♡♡♡♡	Lantana's	$20–$40
♡♡♡♡♡	Ottmar's Restaurant	$12–$27
♡♡♡♡♡	Wharf, The	$20–$40

Fielding's Best Value Restaurants in Cayman Islands

★★★★★	Hemingway's	$17–$23
★★★★	Crow's Nest, The	$12–$19
★★★★	Ottmar's Restaurant	$12–$27
★★★★★	Lantana's	$20–$40
★★★★	Chef Tell's Grand Old House	$20–$34

Not surprisingly, seafood is a staple in a Cayman diet; nearly everything else is imported and, as a result, food prices are sky high—though portions are generally generous. Turtle is a local specialty—they are specially bred to be eaten—and lobster is especially good from August through January. **Hemingway's**, at the Hyatt Regency, is considered the best place for seafood and turtle steak, while **Benjamin's Roof**, off West Bay Road, is known for the blackened alligator tail that lures those who must try everything at least once. For a special night, splurge at **Lantana's** or **The Wharf** where giant tarpon are fed each evening. If you're hankering for good old American food, try the **Hog Sty Bay Cafe**, a casual American-English style pub. Grand Cayman offers more than 100 establishments. Restaurants are limited on Cayman Brac and Little Cayman—it's the diving that attracts tourists, not the cuisine.

Cayman Brac

Edd's Place   **$$**   ★★

West End, ☎ (345) 948-1208.
Lunch: 8 a.m.–4 p.m., entrées $6–$15.
Dinner: 4 p.m.–midnight, entrées $10–$25.
A nice change from resort cookery on Cayman Brac is this restaurant that's open early for breakfast and later on serves American, as well as local, favorites all day and late into the evening. Reservations recommended. Credit cards: A, D, MC, V.

Grand Cayman

Almond Tree, The   **$$$**   ★★

North Church Street, George Town, ☎ (345) 949-2893.
Dinner: 5:30–10 p.m., entrées $13–$26. Closed: Tue.
An informal and reliable restaurant located just north of George Town, the Almond Tree is a good place to try turtle steak. Less adventurous diners will find all types of seafood, including conch, lobster, and fish filets. It's dramatically lit with tiki torches at night. Starting Oct. 1–April 15, lunch is served from 11 a.m. until 5 p.m. Reservations recommended. Credit cards: A, DC, MC, V.

Benjamin's Roof Seafood   **$$$**   ★

George Town, ☎ (345) 945-4080.
Dinner: 3:30–10:30 p.m., entrées $12–$30.
Greenery abounds in this cool spot in the Coconut Place retail center with a bar dispensing strong libations, a pianist in the corner and spicy blackened-cajun style fish and seafood, with barbecued ribs, lamb and pastas to round out the menu. Desserts are also notable for their richness. Reservations required. Credit cards: A, MC, V.

Chef Tell's Grand Old House   **$$$**   ★★★★

George Town, ☎ (345) 949-9333.
Lunch: 11:45 a.m.–2 p.m., entrées $13–$32.
Dinner: 6–10p.m., entrées $20–$34. Closed: Sun.
This lovely, 100-year-old gingerbread house once served as a hospital, Sunday school and private home. Its current incarnation is the base of jolly, red-cheeked TV celebrity Chef Tell Erhardt. Inside for dinner, tables are softly lit by candlelight and sconces. Fans hum, suspended from the soaring ceilings. Outside the oceanside

deck is lit by lanterns and the moon. The savory cuisine relies on the chef's liberal use of herbs, curries and sauces. German specialties—spaetzle and sauerkraut—are offered from time to time, reflecting the chef's heritage, but the menu is a hodge-podge of Caribbean, Californian, European, Indian and Oriental influences. Closed May through October. Reservations required. Credit cards: A, MC, V.

Cracked Conch By the Sea $$$ ★★★

Grand Cayman, ☎ *(345) 945-5217.*
Lunch: 11 a.m.–4 p.m., entrées $6–$9.
Dinner: 5–10 p.m., entrées $12–$30.

This landmark, established in 1980 and relocated in 1996, is tucked into a spot designed to look old. Plank floors came from the wreckage of a pirate ship. Mirrors are made from original shutters and doors of an Old Cayman house. Bob Soto, the father of diving on the island, has donated original hard hat diving helmets for display. The food, especially conch, served 14 ways including the local favorite stewed, is smashing. Shrimp is served eight ways and lobster prepared six different styles. Stumped? Try the fisherman's platter, which has cracked conch, sauteed fish filet, conch fritters, turtle steak and shrimp. The menu also features lobster, pasta, fish, mango chicken and filet mignon. For lunch, you can order a salad, sandwich or soup. Friday nights, locals and tourists mingle at the bar and dine on the outdoor terrace, which seats 70, to catch the sunset. On Sundays check out the Caribbean-style brunch from 11:30 a.m.–3 p.m. This eatery offers a kids' menu, too. Reservations recommended. Credit cards: A, MC, V.

Crow's Nest, The $$ ★★★★

George Town, ☎ *(345) 949-9366.*
Lunch: 11:30 a.m.–2 p.m., entrées $7–$12.
Dinner: 5:30–10 p.m., entrées $12–$19.

This exquisitely funky little eatery on the south point of the island has been transformed from a Caymanian-style home to a seaside delight. Diners on the expansive, screened in deck, right beside the ocean, have a view of Sand Cay. At night the beach is lighted and twinkling lights glimmer in the palm trees. The West Indian chef whips out tasty, spicy dishes like grilled red snapper with mango salsa and coconut fried shrimp. Noted for its homemade key lime and banana toffee pie. It's hard to believe that George Town is only two miles away. Reservations required. Credit cards: A, D, MC, V.

Garden Loggia Cafe $$$ ★★★

George Town, ☎ *(345) 949-1234.* Associated hotel: *Hyatt Regency Grand Cayman.*
Lunch: 7 a.m.–11:30 a.m, entrées $9–$16.
Dinner: 7–10:30 p.m., entrées $16–$34.

This top-rated, indoor-outdoor cafe facing an elegant expanse of greenery with birds flitting about is noted for its daily breakfast buffet (7 a.m.–11:30) and Sunday brunch (11:30 a.m.–2:30 p.m.) replete with champagne and roast suckling pig. Tuesday night Caribbean-style food is the main attraction. Otherwise, the menu changes nightly. No lunch. Reservations required. Credit cards: A, DC, D, MC, V.

Golden Pagoda $ ★★

☎ *(345) 949-5475.*

Lunch: 11:30 a.m.–2:30 p.m, prix fixe $8.
Dinner: 6–10 p.m., entrées $7–$21.
The oldest Chinese restaurant on the island—started in 1977—this family-owned charmer dishes out Hakka-style food (sans MSG) with a few menu items from the Szechuan and Mongolian regions as well. Handily located across the road from the Marriott and known for its popular and reasonably-priced lunch buffet, this spot is popular with locals. In the evenings you can go à la carte or try Chinese owner Cicily Delanpenha's four-course dinner for $17.50 for one. Credit cards: A, MC, V.

Hemingway's $$$ ★★★★★

George Town, ☎ *(345) 949-1234.* Associated hotel: *Hyatt Regency.*
Lunch: 11:30 a.m.–2:30 p.m., entrées $10–$17.
Dinner: 6–10 p.m., entrées $17–$23.
Spectacular Seven Mile Beach and its teal waters only add to the strong appeal of the Hyatt Regency Grand Cayman's luxury dining room. Executive Chef David Brown's nouvelle Caribbean dishes like grouper stuffed with roasted corn and crab mousse with Scotch bonnet pepper sauce and coconut and almond shrimp with orange-ginger dipping sauce make terrific use of local ingredients. Cocktails are creative, the wine list is extensive (heavy on California wines with a touch of Australia and Chile) and service is attentive. Reservations required. Credit cards: A, DC, MC, V.

Hog Sty Bay Cafe $$$ ★★

George Town, ☎ *(345) 949-6163.*
Lunch: 11:30 a.m.–5 p.m., entrées $5–$12.
Dinner: 5:30–10 p.m., entrées $12–$29.
A good, casual American-English style pub in George Town Harbor, this brightly-painted bungalow is a relaxing perch for burgers and sandwiches or fish and chips. It hums inside with a crowd of regulars who come for the sunset views and happy hour drinks. Breakfast (8-11:15 a.m.) is also served, with all the usual offerings plus Mexican-style eggs for added zing. Reservations required. Credit cards: A, MC, V.

Lantana's $$$ ★★★★★

West Bay Road, George Town, ☎ *(345) 947-5595.* Associated hotel: *The Caribbean Club.*
Dinner: 5:30–10 p.m., entrées $20–$40.
Lantana's, one of the island's most prestigious dining establishments, has garnered well-deserved acclaim from *Gourmet, Bon Appetit* and several other food and wine publications. As soon as you take the first bite of Chef Keith Griffin's New Caribbean-American cuisine, you'll understand. This air-conditioned, two-story restaurant, casually decked out with local art and stuffed fish, features a menu that changes daily according to what fish and sea delicacies are the freshest. Try crab and shrimp cake with field greens and chipolte tartar sauce for a starter, followed by roasted garlic soup.

The chef has a special talent with seafood, but if you're in the mood for meat, you can't lose with his rack of lamb or spicy Jamaican jerked pork tenderloin with rice and mango salsa. The wine list is nicely matched to the well-herbed food with smart selections from California and South Australia. The dessert specialty is warm, upside down apple pie "gaby" with caramel sauce and mango ice cream, or you can wind up the evening with a cognac or port. Some of the partners here also own The

Wharf nearby. Upstairs can be reserved for special parties. Reservations required.
Credit cards: A, DC, D, MC, V.

Lobster Pot $$$ ★★
George Town, ☎ *(345) 949-2736.*
Lunch: 11:30 a.m.–2:30 p.m., entrées $6–$13.
Dinner: 5–10 p.m., entrées $14–$31.
When the Hog Sty Bay Cafe is busy, this upper-level pub facing West Bay fits the
bill. The Lobster Pot manages an intimate atmosphere despite its popularity and the
tendency of servers to rush diners through their meals. Nevertheless, the food is
good, particularly the lobster, salads and frozen tropical drinks. A dart board offers
diversion. Reservations required. Credit cards: A, D, MC, V.

Ottmar's Restaurant $$$ ★★★★
☎ *(345) 945-5879.* Associated hotel: *Grand Pavilion.*
Dinner: 6–11 p.m., entrées $12–$27.
Another excellent dining room run by German expatriate, Ottmar's proffers classi-
cal-French cuisine like bouillabaisse and then turns around and offers a Dutch-Jav-
anese rijstaffel (a spicy feast with eight condiments surrounded by steamed rice).
You'll be welcomed like royalty by Maitre' D Tony to the elegant and spacious
room, where conversations are carried on unheard by diners at neighboring tables.
And Ottmar has assembled a strong wine list. Reservations required. Credit cards: A,
MC, V.

Ristorante Pappagallo $$$ ★★★
West Bay, ☎ *(345) 949-1119.*
Dinner: 6–10:30 p.m., entrées $15–$29.
Set in the midst of a 14-acre bird sanctuary, this pleasant restaurant serves Northern
Italian cuisine in a series of thatched-roof huts facing a lagoon, surrounded by palm
trees and wooden bridges. Interior dining rooms are air-conditioned, or you can
dine on the patio. Chattering macaws in cages deliver lively background music, and
the food—homemade pastas and breads—is well prepared, with veal and seafood
predominating. Even if you don't come to eat, it's a relaxing spot for a cocktail. Reservations required. Credit cards: A, MC, V.

Wharf, The $$$ ★★★
West Bay Road, ☎ *(345) 949-2231.*
Lunch: Noon-2:30 p.m., entrées $15–$20.
Dinner: 6–10 p.m., entrées $20–$40.
Dine under the stars on this huge terrace (seats 120) overlooking the waterfront.
Austrian Executive Chef Tony Egger likes to pair fresh local seafare with Caribbean
touches. Start with the seared tuna carpaccio, try the turtle pepper pot soup and put
yourself in Egger's hands for the main course. For example, Caribbean lobster can-
nelloni baked in puff pastry with roasted shallot mayonnaise, or the marinated
queen conch served with onions, peppers and spices that will bring tears to your
eyes. Service is terrific, and this lively place has become popular with honeymooners.
Except on Sunday when live music is banned, a harpist and guitarist rove from table
to table, and calypso bands play in the attached popular bar. At 9 p.m. nightly the
draw is the feeding of the giant tarpons off the rear dock beside the bar. Closed for

lunch during the summer months. Reservations recommended. Credit cards: DC, D, MC, V.

Little Cayman

Pirate's Point **$$$** ★★★

☎ *(345) 948-1010.* Associated hotel: *Pirate's Point Resort.*
Lunch: prix fixe $20.
Dinner: prix fixe $37.
Owner Gladys Howard, trained at Paris' Cordon Bleu and owner of an international cooking school/gourmet catering service for 20 years, whips up wonderful seafood dishes most nights, supplemented by fruits and vegetables flown in. Lunch is a casual affair under the seagrape trees, but this chef/caterer serves dinner in the air-conditioned dining room with the works: fresh cut flowers gathered daily around the island, crystal stemware and linen napkins. You can recreate some of her dishes back home by buying one of her award-winning cookbooks. She recently recruited two chefs from San Francisco. On Saturday nights Howard's native Tex-Mex food is featured with fajitas and green enchiladas; on Mondays traditional-style Caymanian food stars. All meals are fixed-price (breakfast goes for $12); dinner includes wines selected by Howard, who has owned this spot since 1986. Reservations are a must. Reservations required. Credit cards: MC, V.

Shopping is not the reason to visit the Caymans, though George Town has a decent selection of boutiques and stores with duty- and sales-tax-free items such as Irish linen, French perfumes, china, crystal, silver and British woolens. Do not buy any products made of turtle; you will not be able to get such a purchase past customs in the United States. Art lovers should venture to **Pure Art Gallery and Gifts** (☎ *(345) 949-9133*), which features local works and Caribbean collectibles. For jewelry head to the **Jewelry Centre** *(George Street,* ☎ *(345) 949-0070)*, for the island's biggest selection. For crafts, try **Viking Gallery** *(South Church Street, George Town,* ☎ *(345) 949-4090)*, the nearby **Caymandicraft** (☎ *(345) 949-2405)* and **Heritage Crafts Shop** (☎ *(345)949-7093)*, near the harbour in George Town. Jewelry made from black coral is popular but controversial, because the species is rare, though you can legally bring it back home. Stamp and rare coin collectors should check out **Artifacts Ltd.** *(Harbour Drive, George Town* ☎ *(345) 949-2442)*, which boasts an excellent collection, as well as antique prints and maps.

Cayman Islands Directory

Arrival and Departure

Grand Cayman is serviced by **Cayman Airways** ☎ *(800) 422-9626)* from Miami (three non-stop direct flights daily), Tampa, Atlanta and Houston; by **American Airlines** ☎ *(800) 433-7300* from Miami and Raleigh-Durham; by Delta Airlines from Atlanta; by **USAir** ☎ *(800) 428-4322* from Charlotte, NC, Baltimore-Washington; and by **Northwest Airlines** ☎ *(800) 447-4747* from Detroit, Minneapolis and Memphis via Miami. Caymanian-owned **Island Airways** ☎ *(800) 922-9626* is also the only airline that services Little Cayman and Cayman Brac.

A taxi from the airport to central Seven Mile Beach is $8–$12, Seven Mile Beach to George Town is about $8, taxi rates are set by law.

Departure tax is $10.

Business Hours

Shops open Monday–Saturday 9 a.m.–5 p.m. Banks open Monday–Thursday 9 a.m.–2:30 p.m. and on Friday 9 a.m.–1 p.m. and 2:30–4:30 p.m.

Climate

With an average temperature of 79 degrees, the Caymans are pleasant year-round. High season runs from mid-December to mid-April, but July and August, when waters are clearest, are the prime times for diving.

Documents

U.S. and Canadian citizens may show either a valid passport or proof of citizenship (voter registration or birth certificate with photo ID) and an ongoing or return ticket.

Electricity

The current runs 110 volt, 60-cycles, as in the United States.

Getting Around

Taxis and locally-owned minibuses are omnipresent whenever a plane arrives, and rates are officially fixed. Since the islands are small and flat, bicycling and walking are pleasant alternatives to walking. Autos, are nevertheless, easy to rent (except you must be at least age 21). Major U.S. firms are here as well as local ones, such as **Just Jeeps** ☎ *(345) 949-7263*. Motorcycles and motor-scooters are for hire at **Soto's** ☎ *(345) 945-2424*.

Driving is on the left side of the street.

Language

English is the main tongue, though the accent is a highly musical mélange of Irish, Welsh, Scottish and West Indian lilts.

Medical Emergencies

George Town Hospital ☎ *(345) 949-8600* is the only facility on Grand Cayman, and has an emergency room recompression chamber and 60 beds. Cayman Brac has a 16-bed facility called **Faith Hospital** ☎ *(345) 948-2243*.

Cayman Dental Services ☎ *(345) 947-4447* has two dental surgeons on call 24 hours a day.

Money

The official currency is the Cayman Islands dollar, unique to the islands. Most tourist establishments accept U.S. dollars and credit cards. Local banks will cash traveler's checks. Keep track which dollars (American or Cayman) are being quoted on menus, etc. If quoted in Cayman dollars, the price will look a lot cheaper than it actually is. The fixed exchange rate with U.S. currency is CI$1 equals US$1.25.

Telephone

Area code is *345*. International calls can be made 24 hours a day. Local calls now use 7 digits (as opposed to 5 digits in the past).

Time

Eastern standard time all year long, with no change during the northern shift to daylight savings.

Tipping and Taxes

Service charges are not standardized among hotel establishments and can range from 5 percent at condos to 15 percent at top hotels. Always check your bill before adding your own tips. Taxi drivers generally expect tips especially when you've exhausted them with huge trunks. Bellboys expect 50 cents per bag.

Tourist Information

The **Cayman Islands Department of Tourism** is located in the Harbour Centre in George Town ☎ *(345) 949-0623*. Tourist information booths can also be found at the pier and at the airport. In the U.S. call ☎ *(213) 738-1968* or *(212) 682-5582* or *(305) 266-2300*.

When to Go

Pirates Week Festival in the last week of October is celebrated with parades, songs, contests and games; even businessmen arrive at the office dressed in costume. Million Dollar Month in June brings anglers from all over the world to compete in one of the world's biggest big-fish contests. Batabano, the weekend before Easter, is the island's cultural carnival weekend. Queen Elizabeth's birthday in mid-June is celebrated with a full-dress uniform parade, marching band and 21-gun salute.

CAYMAN ISLANDS HOTELS	RMS	RATES	PHONE	CR. CARDS
Cayman Brac				
★★ Divi Tiara Beach Resort	58	$95–$200	(800) 367-3484	A, D, MC, V
★ Brac Reef Beach Resort	40	$100–$115	(800) 327-3835	A, MC, V

CAYMAN ISLANDS

CAYMAN ISLANDS HOTELS

		RMS	RATES	PHONE	CR. CARDS
	Grand Cayman				
★★★★★	**Hyatt Regency Grand Cayman**	296	$190–$385	(800) 233-1234	A, MC, V
★★★★	**Marriott Grand Cayman Resort**	309	$165–$390	(800) 228-9290	A, DC, MC, V
★★★★	**Westin Casuarina Resort**	343	$205–$446	(800) 228-3000	A, MC, V
★★★	**Ambassadors Inn**	18	$60–$80	(800) 648-7748	A, MC, V
★★★	**Beach Club Colony**	41	$113–$265	(800) 482-DIVE	A, D, DC, MC, V
★★★	**Caribbean Club**	18	$175–$440	(800) 327-8777	A, MC, V
★★★	**Clarion Grand Pavilion**	93	$160–$350	(345) 947-5656	A, D, DC, MC, V
★★★	**Grand Bay Club**	21	$160–$390	(800) 825-8703	A, MC, V
★★★	**Holiday Inn Grand Cayman**	213	$178–$328	(800) 421-9999	A, DC, MC, V
★★★	**Indies Suites**	40	$170–$305	(800) 654-3130	A, MC, V
★★★	**Lacovia Condominiums**	55	$175–$715	(800) 223-9815	A
★★★	**London House**	22	$275–$900	(800) 423-4095	A, MC, V
★★★	**Morrit's Tortuga Club**	121	$145–$350	(800) 447-0309	A, D, MC, V
★★	**Pan Cayman House**	10	$165–$370	(800) 248-5115	MC, V
★★★	**Silver Sands**	42	$205–$440	(800) 327-8777	A, MC, V
★★★	**Treasure Island Resort**	280	$160–$260	(800) 203-0775	A, DC, MC, V
★★	**Cayman Kai Resort**	20	$140–$180	(800) 223-5427	A, MC, V
★★	**Christopher Columbus Apartments**	30	$190–$390	(345) 945-4354	A, MC, V
★★	**Discovery Point Club**	45	$220–$360	(345) 945-4724	A, MC, V
★★	**Harbour Heights**	46	$185–$335	(800) 327-8777	A, MC, V
★★	**Plantana Condominiums**	49	$175–$425	(345) 945-4430	A, MC, V
★★	**Sleep Inn**	115	$105–$185	(800) 753-3746	A, CB, D, DC, MC, V
★★	**Spanish Bay Reef Resort**	50	$205–$257	(800) 482-DIVE	A, MC, V
★★	**Sunset House**	59	$105–$145	(800) 854-4767	A, D, MC, V
★★	**Tarquynn Manor**	20	$185–$345	(800) 223-9815	MC, V
★★	**Victoria House**	26	$137–$415	(800) 327-8777	A, MC, V
★★	**Villas of the Galleon**	75	$200–$430	(800) 235-5888	A, MC, V
★	**Beachcomber Condos**	24	$195–$425	(800) 327-8777	A, MC, V

CAYMAN ISLANDS

CAYMAN ISLANDS HOTELS	RMS	RATES	PHONE	CR. CARDS
★ Colonial Club	15	$280–$468	(345) 945-4660	A, MC, V
★ George Town Villas	54	$160–$420	(345) 949-5172	A, MC, V
★ Island Pine Villas	40	$115–$227	(800) 223-9815	A, D, DC, MC, V
★ Plantation Village Beach Resort	70	$175–$460	(800) 822-8903	A, MC, V
★ Windjammer Hotel	12	$100–$155	(809) 947-4608	A, MC, V

Little Cayman

	RMS	RATES	PHONE	CR. CARDS
★★★ Conch Club		$300–$400	(813) 323-8727	A, MC, V
★★★ Pirates Point Resort, Ltd.	10	$135–$200	(345) 948-1010	MC, V
★★★ Southern Cross Club	10	$280–$330	(800) 899-2582	None
★★ Little Cayman Beach Resort	40	$120–$180	(800) 327-3835	A, MC, V

CAYMAN ISLANDS RESTAURANTS	PHONE	ENTREE	CR.C ARDS

Cayman Brac

	PHONE	ENTREE	CR.C ARDS
★★ Edd's Place	(345) 948-1208	$6–$25	A, D, MC, V

Grand Cayman

Chinese Cuisine

	PHONE	ENTREE	CR.C ARDS
★★ Golden Pagoda	(345) 949-5475	$8–$21	A, MC, V

English Cuisine

	PHONE	ENTREE	CR.C ARDS
★★ Hog Sty Bay Cafe	(345) 949-6163	$5–$29	A, MC, V

International Cuisine

	PHONE	ENTREE	CR.C ARDS
★★★★★ Hemingway's	(345) 949-1234	$10–$23	A, DC, MC, V
★★★★ Chef Tell's Grand Old House	(345) 949-9333	$13–$34	A, MC, V
★★★★ Ottmar's Restaurant	(345) 945-5879	$12–$27	A, MC, V
★★★ Garden Loggia Cafe	(345) 949-1234	$9–$34	A, D, DC, MC, V

Italian Cuisine

	PHONE	ENTREE	CR.C ARDS
★★★ Ristorante Pappagallo	(345) 949-1119	$15–$29	A, MC, V

Regional Cuisine

	PHONE	ENTREE	CR.C ARDS
★★★★★ Lantana's	(345) 947-5595	$20–$40	A, D, DC, MC, V
★★★★ Crow's Nest, The	(345) 949-9366	$7–$19	A, D, MC, V
★★★ Wharf, The	(345) 949-2231	$15–$40	D, DC, MC, V

CAYMAN ISLANDS

CAYMAN ISLANDS RESTAURANTS	PHONE	ENTREE	CR.C ARDS
Seafood Cuisine			
★★ **Almond Tree, The**	(345) 949-2893	$13–$26	A, DC, MC, V
★★★ **Cracked Conch By the Sea**	(345) 945-5217	$6–$30	A, MC, V
★★ **Lobster Pot**	(345) 949-2736	$6–$31	A, D, MC, V
★ **Benjamin's Roof Seafood**	(345) 945-4080	$12–$30	A, MC, V
Little Cayman			
International Cuisine			
★★★ **Pirate's Point Resort**	(345) 948-1010	$20–$37	MC, V

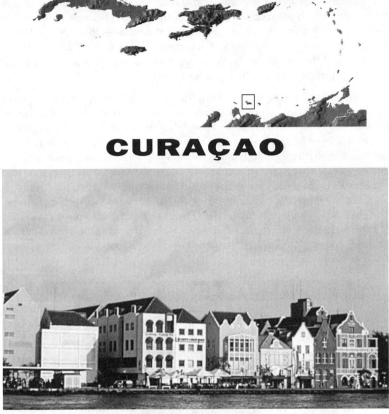

CURAÇAO

Handelskade in Curaçao is lined with striking yellow and red brick houses.

The C in the ABC Dutch islands known as the Netherlands Antilles, Curaçao (pronounced CURE-a-sow) lies between the A (Aruba, 42 miles to the west) and B (Bonaire, 30 miles to the east). Like its better known siblings, it is a hilly island that is quite dry and desertlike, with little chance of rain to ruin your vacation. But Curaçao combines a generous portion of its siblings' best attributes: Aruba's nightlife and casinos and Bonaire's terrific diving. This island has the added charm of being the most important architecturally in the entire Caribbean, thanks to Willemstad, a Dutch colonial city dating from 1634 that also boasts the largest natural harbor in the Caribbean. That harbor has proven a boon to Curaçao, which has thrived as a duty-free port since the time that the Dutch West India Company set up shop here. The island became a cultural crossroads, attracting immigrants from around the world. Today that cosmopolitan air serves Curaçao well as it is beginning to attract sophisticated travelers from the U.S. eager to visit the Caribbean islands that have largely been ignored. Because Curaçao has long been such a favorite vacation spot of Europeans—especially the Dutch and Germans—it has a plethora of accommodations from which to choose and offers all the amenities travelers expect with few of the kinks that occur on islands just grappling with expanding tourism.

The fact that it remains an unknown quantity with most Americans acts as a double-edged sword. Curaçao stands out as a curiosity in the Caribbean landscape, so tourists often don't know what to expect. Those who crave an understanding of Caribbean history should put Curaçao high on their must-see list. Highlights include Curaçao's Mikve Israel-Emanuel, built in 1728 and the oldest synagogue in continuous use in the Western hemisphere, and the island's eight forts. Frenetic adventurers will find plenty to see on the island, from restored *landhuises* (Dutch for land houses) to secluded sugar-sand beaches to craggy cunucu (the countryside), reminiscent of the desert Southwest in the U.S., to the bustling shopping areas of downtown Willemstad. Of course, Curaçao's protected, crystalline waters offer great options for watersports as well.

BEST BETS FOR...

Bird's-Eye View

Curaçao lies 35 miles north of Venezuela and is the largest of the five islands composing the Netherlands Antilles. It is one of the Caribbean's southernmost islands, located just 12 degrees above the equator and 1710 miles south of New York (a four-hour flight). Considered to be below the hurricane belt, it has avoided the traumatic lashings endured by many of its northern neighbors. The dry, hilly landscape—of volcanic origin—receives less than 23 inches in annual rainfall. (November and December are the rainiest months.)

The highest point on the 180-sq.-mile island is **Mount Christoffel** at 1239 feet, located in the midst of the 4500 acre **Christoffel National Park** where scores of iguana and the rare Curaçao white-tailed deer roam. Year round the

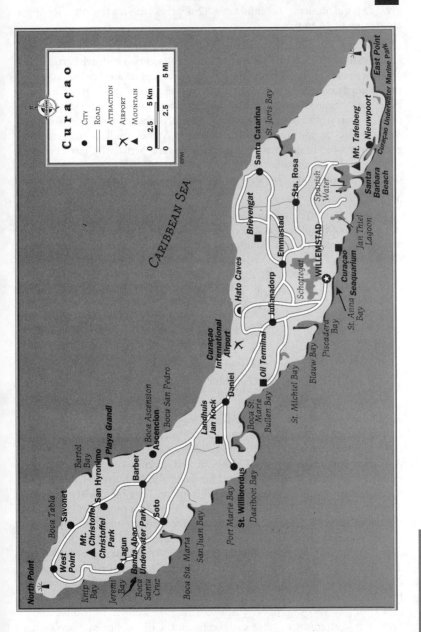

Curaçao

CITY
ROAD
ATTRACTION
AIRPORT
MOUNTAIN

0   2.5   5 Km
0   2.5   5 Mi

CARIBBEAN SEA

North Point
West Point
Boca Tabla
Savonet
Bartol Bay
Knip Bay
Jeremi Bay
Mt. Christoffel
Christoffel Park
San Hyronimo
Playa Grandi
Lagun
Banda Abao Underwater Park
Boca Santa Cruz
Barber
Soto
St. Willibrordus
Boca Sta. Maria
San Juan Bay
Port Marie Bay
Boca St. Marie
Daaiboci Bay
Boca San Pedro
Boca Ascension
Ascension
Landhuis Jan Kock
Daniel
Curaçao International Airport
Oil Terminal
Bullen Bay
St. Michiel Bay
Blauw Bay
Piscadera Bay
St. Anna Bay
Hato Caves
Julianadorp
Emmastad
Schottegat
WILLEMSTAD
Curaçao Seaquarium
Brievengat
Santa Catarina
St. Jorts Bay
Sta. Rosa
Spanish Water
Jan Thiel Lagoon
Mt. Tafelberg
Nieuwpoort
Santa Barbara Beach
Curaçao Underwater Marine Park
East Point

average temperature is a comfortable 82 degrees with tradewinds blowing at an average of 16 m.p.h.

Willemstad, the world's second busiest port and the capital of the Netherlands Antilles, is sliced by the Santa Ana Bay into two distinct parts: Punda and Otrabanda, connected by the Queen Emma pontoon bridge. Several of the original colonial to Victorian buildings lining the bay on the Punda side have been beautifully restored, and in the past year the business and shopping districts of Otrabanda have gotten a much-needed facelift. In addition, shops and restaurants now line the Waterfort Arches, built in 1634, and several shops were under construction at presstime across the bay at Riffort, which guards the entrance of the harbor. A number of cruise lines now call on Curaçao throughout the year: Crystal, Costa, Norwegian, Regent and Cunard.

One of the island's most popular attractions is the **Hato Caves**, a 50,000 sq. ft. network of chambers, and coral fossils, located near the airport. Near the caves you'll see ancient Indian petroglyphs—the only ones of this type in the Caribbean.

History

When Alonso de Ojeda landed on Curaçao in 1499 he promptly deported the native Caquetio Indians, a seafaring tribe that was closely related to the Arawaks, to work the prosperous mines of Hispaniola. Finding no gold or arable land, he declared Curaçao an "isla inutil" (useless island) and moved on. The Spanish briefly established a colony on the island almost 30 years later, but unceremoniously abandoned it a century later. The Dutch West Indies Company, recognizing the value of the wide natural harbor at Queen Anna Bay (the largest in the Caribbean and seventh largest in the world), claimed it in 1634 for Holland and busily established a colonial base there for neighboring possessions, Aruba and Bonaire. They built Fort Amsterdam with thick walls around Willemstad, which proved an important move since the island's strategic location quickly attracted the attention of the English and French, who were largely unsuccessful in their many attempts to wrest it from Dutch control. Ships sailed to and from South America, the West Indies, Holland and the North American colonies, carrying cash crops through the duty-free port adding to the coffers of the Dutch West Indies Company. In 1642, Peter Stuyvesant became the island's governor; three years later he took over governorship of New Amsterdam, now known, of course, as New York. While attempts to grow cash crops on the island's plantations weren't terribly fruitful, Curaçao thrived on profits from goods in transit. One historian in 1778 noted, that though the island was so barren that it couldn't support life for more than 24 hours, its inhabitants actually lived better than anywhere else in the West Indies. In the 18th century, Portuguese Jews immigrated from Holland where they had settled after being persecuted during the Inquisition. These prominent merchants became an integral part of society.

Until the Dutch abolished slavery in 1863, Curaçao was known as the major selling and transfer depot for human cargo in the Caribbean. In 1918, the Royal Dutch Shell Company erected the world's largest oil refinery near Willemstad to process oil discovered in Venezuela, drawing even more immigrants from 70 nations, resulting in the melting pot that Curaçao is today. The island continued to prosper throughout World War II, when virtually all the fuel for the Allied Forces came from its refinery. Curaçao's social and political climate has been largely devoid this century of the unrest that has roiled other islands. However, one incident sullied that record. In 1969—just as some major hoteliers began eying Curaçao—some of the working class rioted, burning parts of Otrabanda, and looting Willemstad to protest cutbacks at the refinery. Calls for labor power resulted in positions in government, political parties and high levels of the private sector being open to Curaçaoans of non-European descent for the first time. Unfortunately, interest in making Curaçao more of a tourist destination fizzled. Indeed, the island has yet to attract a major hotelier from the U.S. The next bump for Curaçao occurred when Shell pulled out in 1985. Venezuelan investors eventually leased the oil refinery. Willemstad remains the capital of the Netherland Antilles, which includes Bonaire, Saba, St. Eustatius and St. Martin.

People

About 144,00 people—known as Curaçaoans—live on the island, most around the capital city of Willemstad. The people represent more than 55 nationalities, but are mostly of African or mixed African and European descent. The official language is Dutch, but most people actually speak Papiamento, a Creole language that is a lively blend of African, Portuguese, Dutch, English, French and Arawak Indian. It is unique among the Creole languages in that it's the only one widely used by all classes. In 1987, the first school opened to specifically teach Papiamento, and some hotels offer classes for guests. English speakers are common, and tourists should have no problem communicating.

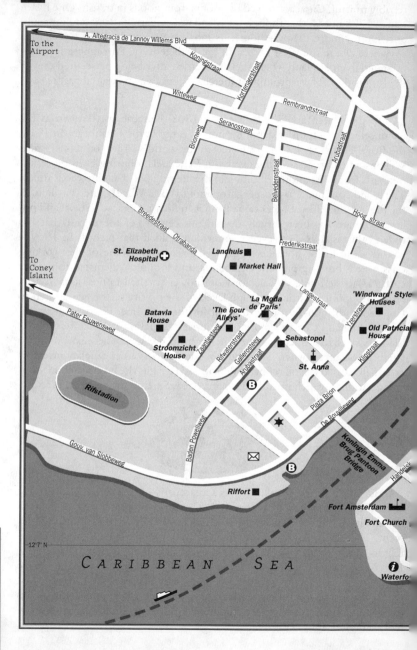

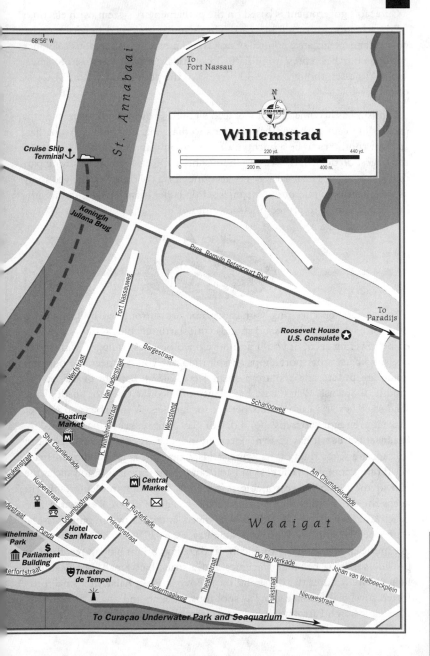

Curaçao's government is based on the parliamentary system, with elections held each spring, every four years. The island is governed by an executive council and a legislative council. Curaçao is known for its religious tolerance and has churches representing faiths from Judaism to Mormonism to Jehovah's Witnesses, though some 80 percent of the population is Roman Catholic.

Tourism has become one of Curaçao's fastest growing industries, but it is proceeding cautiously and has no plans to mass-market the way Aruba has. Its port continues to be a linchpin of its economy and its harbor is home to the largest drydock in the western hemisphere. Oil also remains a strong part of the economy. Financial services accounts for a solid part of the economy as well, because numerous companies set up paper branches in Curaçao during World War II to protect their holdings.

Beaches

Thirty-eight beaches ring Curaçao: some are surrounded by giant cliffs, others are secluded white-sand strands with startlingly blue waters surrounded by towering cacti, or you'll find developed beaches equipped with showers, snackbars, watersport shops and all the buzz you'd expect at a hotspot. Some are private and require a small fee ($2–$5). **Barbara Beach**, at the mouth of Spanish Water Bay, has plenty of coconut trees for shade, wide sand stretches and calm waters perfect for families. A snackbar and shower make it even more attractive for a day of play. On weekends locals crowd in. **SeaAquarium Beach** has grown extremely popular in recent years. You can snorkel and scuba right off its white sands, Curaçao's largest and palm-shaded. It offers complete facilities, and you can get a terrific fruit smoothie at the end of the beach for reasonable price. Most evenings free entertainment keeps the crowds there long after the sun has gone down. **Westpunt**, a free beach, is known for huge cliffs where divers entertain by jumping into the waters below. South of Westpunt, **Knip Bay**, especially busy on Sundays with live music and dancing, is notable for its dazzling, bright blue water. Parasols provide shade. It has toilet facilities and a snack bar. Small, but beautiful, **Knip Chikitu** features tiki huts, and locals love it. **Playa Kalki**, in a small protected cove, makes a nice getaway spot for snorkelers and divers. Since 1989, Curaçao's Beach Patrol watches over swimmers at all beaches on the western part of the island.

Klein Curaçao, a small, uninhabited island off East Point, makes a nifty day excursion; many charter boats and dive operators offer packages with lunch included.

The independent spirit will be well-served on Curaçao, where shore diving from rugged cliffs is a chief attraction. The island is encircled by calm waters and a fringing reef, which features several dozen excellent sites along its southern (leeward) side; there are more than 40 permanent mooring buoys established and over 100 recognized dive sites. Typically, the shallow reef drops gently to 50 feet followed by a second slope 200 to 300 feet from shore; the terrain in-between is frequently undulating and surreal with visibility of up to 150 ft. Because diving did not become established here until the 1980s, the reefs are in good shape and new sites await discovery. Local marine biologists claim that Curaçao actually possesses a greater diversity of hard and soft corals and sponge life than the reefs of famed Bonaire. However, heavily populated Curaçao has depleted much of the fish life existing on the reefs. Otherwise, while not always as convenient or accessible as the diving available on its sibling to the east, many of Curaçao's sites are genuinely comparable to the best dives on Bonaire. And like Bonaire, Curaçao is taking a progressive approach to protecting its reefs. Each year Reef Care organizes volunteer divers to document coral and sponge spawning, and quarterly the organization sponsors underwater cleanups.

In recent months Curaçao has boosted awareness among divers by introducing its "We Want You Back...Diving" promotion. Through December 20, 1998, Curaçao invites lapsed or inactive SCUBA divers to rediscover the sport. Curaçao's top resorts and dive operators are offering specially priced packages ranging from $308 to $534 for four night stays, and $481 to $896 for seven night stays, all per person, double occupancy. (For information, ☎ *(888) 848-3287*). All packages include accommodations, breakfast, unlimited use of tanks, weights and belts, free unlimited airfills, tax and service charges, round-trip airport transfers (except in the case of Lion's Dive), as well as free scheduled shuttle service to and from Willemstad. Night and wreck diving offers vary by hotel. Participating hotels and their related dive operators are the Lion's Dive Hotel/Underwater Curaçao; Habitat Curaçao; Curaçao Caribbean Hotel & Casino/Curaçao Seascape; Holiday Beach Hotel & Casino/Eden Roc Dive Center; the Crown Plaza Princess Beach Resort & Casino/Peter Hughes Princess Divers, and the Plaza Hotel & Casino/Toucan Diving. Certified but inactive divers simply book a vacation in Curaçao of at least four nights and get a free refresher dive course at any participating dive operator. In addition, they receive a 15% discount on all dive equipment rental during their stay. Non-diving traveling companions are not left out — they can enjoy either a 50% savings on the cost of a dive resort course, or use of rent-free snorkeling equipment.

Curaçao's underwater attractions are just beginning to generate press in the United States, and American divers are still substantially outnumbered by their European counterparts, who have been coming here for years. **Banda Abao Underwater Park** is home to some of Curaçao's most adventurous diving and occupies much of the island's northern half; the **Central Underwater Park** lies north of Willemstad. The island's original marine reserve, the **Curaçao Underwater Park**, situated along the 12.5-mile shoreline east from the Princess Beach Hotel to the tip of the island, offers good diving and a snorkeling trail (in front of the Jan Thiel Lagoon). The south coast, from Newport east to the lighthouse, is private property and diving must be accessed by boat. *Take the Plunge* by Cynthia Mulder-Cudmore is one of the most recent books written about Curaçao's dive sites and provides detailed information for snorkelers, beginning and advanced divers on the sites. A locally available *Guide to the Curaçao Underwater Park* by Jeffrey Sybesma and Tom van't Hos, provides additional information about dive sites, and the *Complete Guide to Landside Diving and Snorkeling Locations in Curaçao* by Jeffrey Sybesma and Suzanne Koelega, features maps and road directions to shore sites. Among a number of good snorkeling areas are **Playa Lagoon**, a beach tucked between two outsized rocks formations, and the **Jan Thiel Reef**, located just outside the bay and snorkeling trail. Two decompression chambers—the Caribbean's largest—are available at the island's St. Elizabeth Hospital.

Dive Shops

Eden Roc Dive Center

Holiday Beach Hotel; ☎ *(800) 444-5244; (5999) 462-8878; e-mail: edenroc@ibm.net*
Located on the private beach of Holiday Beach, this PADI-5 star facility and SCUBAPRO dealer specializes in day trips to Klein Curaçao and drift dives over the "Superior Producer," which is five minutes from the shop. It also offers a helicopter dive for those with adventurous tastes. A two-tank dive is $58; a helicopter dive is $69; night dive is $25; and housereef dive is $20.

Habitat Curaçao

Southwest Coast; ☎ *(800) 327-6709 or (5999) 464-8800; FAX (305) 438-4220*
A top-flight, PADI-5 star training and instructor development center, Habitat Curaçao offers courses from beginner level to specialty like night, deep, wreck and computer diving. The three-story dive shop offers dive equipment, classrooms, dive-gear storage, video and photo equipment rental, film processing, underwater video and photographic instruction. This dive center boasts dive freedom with a choice two-tank morning or afternoon boat dives, unlimited shore diving and snor-

keling on its fringing reefs. A guided, two-tank dive is $44; a week of unlimited shore diving, $108.

Peter Hughes/Princess Divers Diving

Willemstad; ☎ *(5999) 465-8991.*

A full PADI five-star facility with courses to PADI divemaster. Resort course (M, W, F) $55, taught in the nearby lagoon. Two-tank boat dive, $55; one-tank night boat dive, $38.50, including taxes (Tues. and Thurs.). Uses three custom dive boats. Boat and/or shore dive packages available. Snorkeling trips (Tues. and Thurs.).

Underwater Curaçao

Willemstad; ☎ *(5999) 461-8100; (888) 546-6734.*

One of the island's larger operations, established in 1987 and part of the Lion's Dive Hotel. PADI five-star facility, with courses to assistant instructor.; 24-hour dive service at house reef; two 40-ft. custom boats; photo and video equipment. Two-tank boat dive, $60. Single-tank boat dives, $33. Shore dive, seven days unlimited $145.

Although most of Curaçao's arid interior is composed of rocky hills or flat scrublands, as one heads northwest on the island's two main roads, a bumpier topography of chalky mountains and relatively greener valleys emerges. The terrain, including a flat-topped mesa, will remind some visitors of the rugged beauty found in the American Southwest. **Christoffel National Park** occupies 4500 acres, much of Curaçao's northern tip, and is home to eight trails, each color-coded for easy identification, including a path that ascends 1238-foot Christoffel itself, the highest point on the island. They crawl through a varied and interesting landscape, between century plants (which bloom only once every hundred years), wind-sculpted divi divi trees, and fields of oversize cactus; keen eyes will also spot the several species of orchids growing on the hillsides. Inhabitants include roughly 150 species of birds, as well as the tiny, indigenous Curaçao deer, a subspecies of the more common white-tailed deer. Two small slitherers inhabit the park, whipsnakes and silver snakes, but neither are poisonous. The park administration office can provide you with detailed maps, or you can purchase the in-depth *Excursion Guide to the Christoffel Park,* by Peer Reijns. The park is open between 8 a.m.–5 p.m. (6 a.m.–3 p.m. on Sundays). There are, however, occasional guided walks at dawn or dusk; additional information may be obtained by calling the park at ☎ *(5999) 464-0363.*

What Else to See

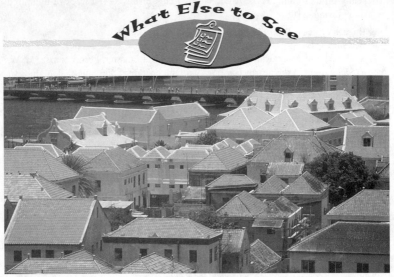

Willemstad, capital of Curaçao, features Dutch-inspired architecture.

Willemstad, the capital city, is a little slice of Denmark right in the southern Caribbean. A walk around the pristine city makes it quickly obvious why Curaçao is a favorite port for cruise ships. Split in two by Santa Ana Bay, the city has two districts: Punta and, on the other side, Otrabanda (literally "the other side"). Otrabanda is mostly residential, while Punta is for tourists, with a good variety of shops and restaurants. To get from one side to the other, you can catch the free ferry, take a cab over Juliana Bridge or walk across the Queen Emma Pontoon Bridge, a 700-foot floating pedestrian bridge that swings open up to 30 times a day to allow ships to pass through. Known as "the swinging old lady," it was designed by American consul Leonard B. Smith in 1888, who made a fortune charging tolls. Today, it's free.

Just a few minutes' walk from the Queen Emma, on the Punda side, is the Floating Market, where you'll easily use up an entire roll of film capturing the colorful sights. Each day schooners from Venezuela, Columbia and other West Indian islands tie up alongside the canal to sell clay pottery, bird cages, fresh fish, fruits, produce and spices. If you can bear to get up early on your vacation, come at 6:30 a.m. as owners set up shop under colorful canopies. The action takes place most of the day if you'd rather sleep in.

Willemstad, with its red tile rooftops and curly white gables atop sometimes shockingly colorful buildings, invites walking. Stroll along the Handelskade, a string of Dutch facades and rococo curlicues lining the bay. Head to the Waterfort Arches for shopping and a quick lunch, or have lunch at one of the

CURAÇAO

many outdoor cafes in Punda. Plan to spend at least a day exploring the colonial city—a 1989 monument act identified and protected all its historic landmarks and buildings and about 70% have been restored. After a trip to the Mikve Israel Emmanuel Synagogue, stroll through Scharloo, where well-to-do Jewish merchants built lavish neo-classical and Palladian-style homes in the late 19th century. On the Otrabanda side—built 150 years after Punda—several buildings have been renovated, especially along Koral Agostini and Porto Paseo. Recently some interesting new art galleries have come on the scene. You can't miss the Kas di Alma Blau (House of Blue Soul), in a restored century-old mansion painted a bright Indigo blue. This stunning structure is visible from several vantage points around town. The Riffort, at the end of the waterfront, contains one of the island's best restaurants, Bistro Le Clochard, which has a terrace perfect for watching the giant ships glide past.

Outside the city limits, you're best off renting a car to take in other sites. Distances aren't bad, but the heat makes biking or hiking inadvisable. The roads are well-marked and decently maintained. The Curaçao Ostrich and Game Farm makes a fun morning outing. Close by is Den Paradera, a small botanical garden where you can get a nice history lesson and learn about herbal cures. History buffs could easily spend a day exploring Curaçao's landhuises; many have been restored and opened to the public.

BEST VIEW:

A spectacular view of the sunset is available at Fort Nassau, on one of the highest hills in the city.

Children's Activities

Curaçao Ostrich and Game Farm   ★★★

Groot St. Joris West.
Hours open: 8 a.m.–5 p.m.
This 200-acre ostrich farm is the largest one outside of Africa and is operated by a native South African who grew up in the business. The fastest living animals on two legs, ostriches were nearly extinct at the turn of the century when they were hunted for their feathers. A tour of the operation allows you to view the bird's eggs and see the chicks through adulthood. A snack bar and gift shop featuring—what else—painted ostrich eggs, feathers and other products from these creatures has recently been added. Several island restaurants have put ostrich on their menus. General admission: $6.

Historical Sites

Hato Caves   ★★

F.D. Rooseveltweg, Willemstad.
Hours open: 10 a.m.–4 p.m.
Some of Curaçao's few underground caverns open to the public, these three-level limestone caves—once used as a hideout by runaway slaves—are imbedded with fos-

sil coral formations. Guided tours start on the hour and take you into several dramatically lit caverns and past active stalagmites and stalactites, an underground waterfall and colonies of bats. Indian petroglyphs—1500 years old—are outside along the cliffs. General admission: $6.

Landhuis Brievengat   ★★

Brievengat, Willemstad.

This plantation house built in 1730—one of the first to be restored—has 18-inch-thick walls, watchtowers and period antiques. The last Sunday of each month at 5:30 p.m. a folkloric dance show takes place. After hours it has become a popular nightspot and features live music and dancing several nights a week. Happy hour starts on the terrace around 5 p.m. Wednesday, Friday and Sunday. Located about 15 minutes out of Willemstad. General admission: $1.

Museums and Exhibits

Curaçao Museum   ★★★

Van Leeuwenhoestraat, Willemstad.

A former military quarantine hospital for those with yellow fever on the western side of Otrabanda, this two-story 1853 building serves as the island's largest museum with permanent exhibits of antiques—including 18th century mahogany pieces—as well as paintings by the island's best-known artists. The shady grounds include a garden with specimens of all the plants and trees of Curaçao and a small Children's Museum of Science where kids are encouraged to touch. Special exhibitions are organized regularly. General admission: $3.

Curaçao Seaquarium   ★★★★★

Bapor Kibra, Willemstad.
Hours open: 8:30 a.m.–10 p.m.

Don't miss this marvelous aquarium, opened in 1984, which showcases more than 40 species of fish and other sea creatures collected by marine biologists from local waters. Plankton-rich water is pumped directly into the tanks from the sea, creating miniature reefs. Kids like the touch tank, shark pond and sea lion channel. Displays are well-marked, and the staff here is dedicated to reef protection. Special discovery days can be arranged for children. The truly daring can try the "Animal Encounters" in which divers feed lemon and nurse sharks and sea turtles by hand through holes in a Plexiglas™ wall ($30–$50; must reserve 24 hours in advance). A professional underwater video of your adventure makes a nice memento. You can also snorkel in a natural tidal pool with eagle rays, angelfish, horse-eyed jacks, grouper and other locals hoping for a handout—or just watch the fun from the underwater observatory. Plan to spend the better part of your day here, since it is also adjacent to one of the island's best beaches. The complex is expanding to include a larger touch tank, library, museum, shell displays, marine life videos and a dolphin breeding program. General admission: $6.

Gallery Eighty-Six   ★★

Trompstraat z/n, Punda, Willemstad.
Hours open: 10 a.m.–5 p.m.

This gallery on the Punda side is tucked away on the third floor overlooking the Santa Ana Bay. The traditional and contemporary artists represented here are some of the region's best. The Dutch owner often features artists from her homeland as well. Even if you aren't an art lover, come for the view.

Mikve Israel-Emanual Synagogue & Jewish Historical ★★

Hanchi di Snoa No. 29, Willemstad.

This synagogue, dedicated in 1732, is the oldest continuously operating in the Western Hemisphere. Located in two traditionally Dutch buildings constructed in 1728, the synagogue and neighboring museum, both undergoing restoration, exhibit Torah scrolls, Hanukkah lamps and other ceremonial and cultural objects from the 17th and 18th centuries used by this Jewish community. Open Sundays when large cruise ships are in port. Men and boys are required to wear a head covering inside the synagogue. General admission: $2.

Parks and Gardens

Christoffel Park ★★★

Savonet, West Point.
Hours open: 8 a.m.–4 p.m.

Avid nature lovers should put this 4500-acre nature preserve high on their list. Located on the island's highest point, crowned by 1239-ft.-high Mt. Christoffel, the highest point in all the Dutch Leewards, reserve a half day for the park, but come early to avoid the stifling late-afternoon heat. A 20-mile network of roads winds through the hills and past breathtaking views. Eight marked hiking trails meander past rare orchids, cacti, divi-divi trees, rare sabal palms, lots of birds, rabbits, wild goats and donkeys. A small museum has nature-related exhibits on Curaçao's geology. Also on the grounds is Landhuis Savonet, one of the island's oldest plantation houses. Special activities include bird and Curaçao deer watching (4 p.m.–6:30 p.m.), cave excursions, guided tours and, occasionally, full moon walks. General admission: $9.

Den Paradera ★★

Seru Grandi Kavel 105 A.

This one-acre, organic herb garden features life-size rag dolls in small huts that explain the island's slave culture and rural life. The owner has lovingly catalogued local plants and explains their traditional use for folk medicine. She'll tell you how to cure everything from stomach ulcers to headaches. A small shop sells Dinah's special concoctions from aloe juice to natural perfumes. General admission: $3.

Tours

Old City Tours ★★

De Ruyterkade 53, Willemstad.

Interesting walking tours of Willemstad, which has the most important architecture in the western Caribbean, are sometimes led by owner Anko van der Woude, a local expert on the island's history. The two- to three-hour trek costs $15. General admission: $15.

Senior Curaçao Liqueur Factory ★★★★

Salina, Willemstad.

Hours open: 8 a.m.–5 p.m.

The orange-flavored liqueur is still produced in a 17th-century landhuis (land house) and has been since 1896. The Senior Curaçao Liqueur Factory still distills and distributes the drink, which resulted from a failed agricultural experiment, using the original 19th century recipe and distilling equipment. Witness the process and sample the results. If you visit on Tuesday or Thursday, head over to the Amstel Brewery at 10 a.m. for a tour and tasting. The beer is made from desalinated seawater.

Tours of Curaçao

Willemstad

This company conducts solid tours of Curaçao's highlights. Thursday is an all-day excursion that takes you to Landhuis Brievengat, Hato Caves, Boca Tabla National Park, Cunucu House Museum, Kudushi Cliff Resort, Playa Kalki and Christoffel Berg and the surrounding countryside. Saturday afternoon introduces visitors to the eastern side of the island: the Ostrich Farm, Herb garden, Jan Thiel, Caribbean handicrafts and Fort Nassau. General admission: $37.

Willemstad Trolley Train Tour ★★★

Shorex International at Caribbean Hotel, Willemstad.

This tour takes visitors on open-sided trolley cars through Dutch colonial Willemstad. The tour commences in Scharloo, a formerly residential neighborhood line with picturesque homes built by wealthy merchants in the 1880s. Bolo di Bruid, nicknamed the "wedding cake" house," is the old city's most photographed site and now houses the Central Historical Archives. Next is the Floating Market where Venezuelan merchants come by boat to sell fresh fish, vegetables, pottery, bird cages and more, followed by the Mikve Israel Emmanuel Synagogue and Waterfort Arches, an imposing fortress once the site of the Wilhelm III Barracks. The finale is Fort Amsterdam, built in 1635 to guard the harbor's entrance from enemy ships. The hour and a half trolley tour takes place only on Mondays at 11 a.m. and Wednesdays at 4 p.m. The cost is $15 per person, $10 for children 2–12. General admission: $15.

Sports

Thanks to the constant trade winds that breeze over the island, Curaçao has become big with windsurfers, with year-round winds of 13 to 25 knots. The Curaçao Open International Pro-Am Windsurfing Championship, which attracts serious competitors from around the world, is held each year on the southeast coast between Jan Thiel and Princess beaches. If you're new to the sport, try the calmer and more protected waters at Spanish Water lagoon. These winds are also the delight of sailors, and you'll have no problem finding places to rent a hobie-cat or sunfish. Deep-sea fishing for sailfish, marlin, tuna and wahoo is good; each March, the island hosts an international blue marlin tournament. Duffers are limited to the "greens" at the nine-hole Curaçao Golf & Squash Club—though those greens are actually made of tightly packed sand.

Cruises

Willemstad.

Take to the high seas aboard a variety of vessels. **Taber Tours** (☎ *(5999) 737-6637; E-mail Tabertrs@Cura.Net)* offers sunset cruises with wine and munchies and snorkel trips to Point Marine. The **Seaworld Explorer** (☎ *(5999) 462-8833;* $29 adults, $19 for children ages 2–12), an air-conditioned "semi-submarine" has a hull five feet below the water's surface and was developed in Australia for use on the Great Barrier Reef. It's a good way for non-divers and non-snorkelers to view Curaçao's waters, which teem with marine life. The 129-foot **Insulinde** (☎ *(5999) 560-1340)*, a two-masted schooner built in 1931 and restored in 1987, offers day sails and weekend trips to neighboring Bonaire and the Bounty islands off Venezuela. Another choice is the **Bounty** (☎ *(5999) 560-1887)*, a 90-ft. traditional wooden gaff-rigged schooner, which offers daytrips from Friday to Monday, as well as private charters. **Sail Curaçao** (☎ *(5999) 767-6003)*, owned by Hank van Gent, a former Olympic sailor for the Netherlands, operates the cozy, 36-ft. Vira Cocha, a twin-masted gaff yawl hand-built in Norway. The restored boat goes on day-sails (starting at $39) from the SeaAquarium, travels the scenic south coast and ends up at Caracas Bay for swimming and snorkeling. To avoid disappointments, book as early as possible.

Curaçao Golf & Squash Club ★★★

Wilhelminalaan, Emmastad.
Hours open: 8 a.m.–12:30 p.m.

Non-members can golf on this nine-hole course only from 8:00 a.m.–noon Fridays through Wednesdays, and Thursdays from 10 a.m. to 4 p.m. What makes it unique is that the greens are actually firmly packed sand. Trade winds add to the challenge. The roughs are more sand and cactus. Greens fees are $20 for nine holes. General admission: $20.

Horseback riding

Christoffel Park yields great trails for riders. **Rancho Christof** (☎ *(5999) 864-0363;* $49–$100) offers three rides with personal guides along 300-year-old treks, ranging from 2 1/2 hours to 6 hours. Especially nice October-December, when you ride through breeding grounds for many bird species. Or for a ride through the cunucu or on a beach, call **Ashari's Ranch** (☎ *(5999) 869-0533;* $40 for two hours), which has sleek, small and well-tended horses. Both require reservations.

Watersports

Willemstad.

Many outfits offer a myriad of watersports; chances are good your hotel has facilities, or try the following: **Coral Cliff Diving** (☎ *(5999) 464-2822)* for sailing and windsurfing; **Seascape Dive and Watersports** (☎ *(5999) 462-5000)* for deep-sea fishing, water-skiing and glass-bottom boat rides; and **Curaçao High Wind Center** (☎ *(5999) 461-4944)* at the Princess Beach Hotel for windsurfing lessons and rentals.

Where to Stay

Fielding's Highest Rated Hotels in Curaçao

★★★★★	Sonesta Beach Resort & Casino	$180–$365
★★★★	Avila Beach Hotel	$90–$225
★★★	Habitat Curaçao	$165–$220
★★★	Kadushi Cliffs	$295–$295
★★★	Lion's Dive Hotel & Marina	$135–$195
★★★	Plaza Hotel Curaçao	$105–$165
★★★	Princess Beach Resort & Casino	$140–$230
★★	Coral Cliff Resort & Casino	$115–$195
★★	Curaçao Caribbean Resort & Casino	$150–$200
★★	Otrabanda Hotel & Casino	$105–$105

Fielding's Best Hotels to Try Lady Luck in Curaçao

★★★★★	Sonesta Beach Resort & Casino	$180–$365
★★	Curaçao Caribbean Resort & Casino	$150–$200
★★★	Princess Beach Resort & Casino	$140–$230
★	Holiday Beach Hotel & Casino	$100–$180

Fielding's Best Value Hotels in Curaçao

★★★★	Avila Beach Hotel	$90–$225
★★	Otrabanda Hotel & Casino	$105–$105
★★★	Plaza Hotel Curaçao	$105–$165
★★★	Princess Beach Resort & Casino	$140–$230

Many of Curaçao's hotels—large and small—boast casinos and the accompanying nightlife. Curaçao's newest additions is Habitat Curaçao, a new dive hotel at **Rif St. Marie**, west of the capital. Wing additions have also been added to venerable Avila Beach Hotel. Choice Hotels at presstime announced construction of a $15 million Comfort Inn Resort, which will add 206 rooms to the southwestern part of the island. Unlike many other Caribbean islands, the pickings are rather slim for self-catering holidays at apartments or condominiums, though Tropic Resorts Marketing (☎ *(5999) 7372328*) can probably set you up in style. Note that most properties charge a 12 percent service charge (so extra tipping is not necessary) and a government tax of 7 percent, usually above and beyond the quoted room rate.

Hotels and Resorts

Hotel choices in Curaçao range from the classy **Sonesta Beach Hotel & Casino** to the funky, but terrific **Lion's Dive Hotel & Marina** where divers rule to the **Avila Beach Hotel**, which has been known to entertain royalty. One of the few choices outside the city area is the new **Habitat Curaçao**, which brings to mind adobe lodges from Arizona. Unfortunately, the largest number of hotels were built in that rather bland architectural phase of the 1950s and 1960s and appear caught in somewhat of a time-warp. Curaçao offers relatively little in the way of inns, and right now none of the landhuises are offering lodgings.

Avila Beach Hotel	**$90–$430**	★ ★ ★ ★

Penstraat 130, ☎ *(800) 448-8355, (5999) 461-4377, FAX (5999) 461-1493.*
Associated Restaurant: *Belle Terrace.*
Single: $90–$215. Double: $100–$225. Suites Per Day: $230–$430.
Lush, tropical landscaping envelops this burnished-yellow, historic hotel, centered around the former Governor's Mansion dating from 1780. A modern extension was added in 1991, and another cluster of 25 rooms built out over the water debuted in December 1996. Despite the uneven transition from the old to the new, this hotel and its accompanying restaurants and bars are charmingly eccentric and attract a lively mixture of local professionals, as well as business and leisure travelers. Its new nightclub, Blues, built on a pier, has become the happening scene Thursday and Saturday nights. One of the few beachfront hotels in Willemstad proper, this European-style gem is where Holland's royal family stays when in town (Queen Beatrix's portrait hangs in the grand lobby). Although the guestrooms in the original mansion have a certain appeal, opt instead for the more spacious rooms in the Blues wing over the water. Decorated with prints of jazz greats, each has a Jacuzzi and shower, cream tile floors with blonde wood ceilings. Some have kitchenettes. Room #291 at the end is especially romantic. All units have air conditioning, cable TV and phones (deluxe rooms have fax lines). The one drawback: no pool and small beaches. 110 rooms. Credit cards: A, DC, MC, V.

Coral Cliff Resort & Casino	**$115–$235**	★ ★

Santa Martha Bay, ☎ *(800) 223-9815, (5999) 864-1610, FAX (5999) 864-1781.*
Single: $115–$195. Double: $115–$195. Suites Per Day: $195–$235.

A favorite with Europeans, this three-story beachfront hotel—traditional Curaçao architecture—is situated on a bluff overlooking Santa Martha Bay and a 600-ft. natural beach. Surrounded by 18 acres of cliffs and desert mountains, this place appears peaceful even though it has a casino and dive shop on-site. Other activities include tennis, watersports, and miniature golf. It now has its own open air restaurant. Babysitting (a playground is available), waterskiing and horseback riding can also be arranged. A daily shuttle transports guests to the restaurants and shopping of Willemstad, some 25 minutes away. 46 rooms. Credit cards: A, DC, MC, V.

Curaçao Caribbean Resort & Casino $150–$850 ★★

Piscadera Bay, ☎ *(800) 223-9815, (5999) 462-5000, FAX (5999) 462-5846.*
E-mail: Montoo@ibm.NET.
Associated Restaurant: *Pirates/Garuda.*
Single: $150–$160. Double: $160–$200. Suites Per Day: $285–$850.

Located at the site of historic Fort Piscadera, five minutes from downtown Willemstad, this five-story hotel—built in 1967—overlooks a tiny beach. Despite updated interiors, the dull architecture dates it. (Think back to the opening scenes of "Hawaii Five-O.") However, it remains a jumping spot—especially with big groups—with the island's busiest casino, organized parties, theme nights and dance lessons. Business people also like it because of its proximity to the International Trade Center. A free bus takes you on the 10-minute trip into town. Facilities include a dive shop, four restaurants and two bars, two tennis courts, a playground and a pool. 194 rooms. Credit cards: A, DC, MC, V.

Habitat Curaçao $165–$220 ★★★

Coral Estate, Rif St. Marie, ☎ *(800) 327-6709, (5999) 864-8800, FAX (5999) 864-8464.*
Associated Restaurant: *Rum Runners at the Reef.*
Single: $165–$220. Double: $165–$220.

Catering to divers, this smashingly-designed property, built on the rocky bluffs near Rif St. Marie, hits the mark. From the welcome area with vaulted ceilings and original island art, you know you've picked a gem. The coral-red adobe, two-bedroom cottages and junior suites—each with a kitchenette, two queen-sized beds, air conditioning, phone, and balcony or patio facing the sea—look like something you'd find in New Mexico. The pool—alas, no shade yet since it's new—appears to spill off into the sea, where snorkeling and shore diving await several steps below. Opened in September 1996, Habitat Curaçao is located 20 minutes west of Willemstad in a heretofore undeveloped part of the island. The open air, artfully decorated Rum Runners restaurant adjacent to the multi-tiered pool area encourages hanging out. As you'd expect, the PADI Five-star Instructor Development Center is well-stocked and well-managed. On premises are a dive and photo shop, convenience store, boutique, tennis, watersports, and a minuscule beach. It also offers mountain bike rentals. Seven-night and honeymoon packages are also available. 78 rooms. Credit cards: A, MC, V.

Holiday Beach Hotel & Casino $100–$180 ★

Otrabanda, ☎ *(800) 444-5244, (5999) 462-5400, FAX (5999) 462-4397.*
Website: www.hol-beach.com.

Single: $100–$150. Double: $110–$180.

Located on a nice swath of Coconut Beach and noted for one of the Caribbean's largest casinos, this former Holiday Inn still brings to mind, well, a Holiday Inn. Guest rooms—with air-conditioning, cable TV and private balconies—are decent but only a few have ocean views. Within walking distance of Willemstad, the hotel—popular with European divers—has lighted tennis courts, watersports and a PADI-Five Star facility, supervised children's activities, a lively beach bar, organized tours and a large pool. On an island known for its restaurants, the fact that this hotel trumpets its 24-hour Denny's restaurant speaks volumes. 200 rooms. Credit cards: A, DC, D, MC, V.

Hotel & Casino Porto Paseo   **$95–$125**   ★

Otrabanda, ☎ *(5999) 462-7878, FAX (5999) 462-7969.*
Associated Restaurant: *Bon Bini.*
Single: $95. Double: $95–$125.

This rather pedestrian-looking hotel, which opened in 1993, has little curb appeal with a ho-hum lobby and small rooms. But it is perched on Otrabanda's waterfront overlooking the postcard-perfect, red-roof Dutch buildings across the Santa Ana Bay. It also offers surprising amenities if you get past the first impression: a dive center, two-story casino, an unpretentious restaurant that's a good place to mingle with locals and Dutch guests, a decent pool with lush tropical landscaping and garden courtyards with lamp-lit walkways. Rooms—beige decor—are air-conditioned and have refrigerators, cable TV, coffee makers and phones. The good rates make this place a favorite with Dutch and Germans, who like lengthy stays once they've made it to Curaçao. 44 rooms. Credit cards: A, DC, MC, V.

Kadushi Cliffs   **$295–$295**   ★★★

Westpunt, ☎ *(800) 523-8744, (5999) 864-0200, FAX (5999) 864-0282.*
Single: $295. Double: $295.

This luxury resort—a small cluster of villas—sits perched on a cliff overlooking Playa Kalki, a small cove with a white sandy beach. This place appeals more to the traveler who wants a getaway. The 45-minute trek to Willemstad tends to restrict shopping excursions and sightseeing. Each two-story villa has two air-conditioned bedrooms, two baths, a living room, dining room, kitchen, sundeck, terrace and Jacuzzi. An open-air restaurant, swimming pool and dive shop round out the offerings. The flat rate includes service charges. Credit cards: A, MC, V.

Lion's Dive Hotel & Marina   **$135–$195**   ★★★

Seaquarium Beach, ☎ *(800) 223-9815, (5999) 461-8100, FAX (5999) 461-8200.*
Single: $135–$180. Double: $150–$195.

Located next to the Seaquarium complex on one of the island's most popular and developed beaches, this rustic, Caribbean-style spot specializes in the scuba diving trade. Its PADI five-star dive center, Underwater Curaçao, is superb. Resort courses are taught in the large pool. Serious athletes will find the island's best fitness center here as well along with aerobic classes, a professional windsurfing school and massage. The air-conditioned guest rooms are standard but fine—especially if you are the always-on-the-go vacationer like most others who choose Lion's Dive. Guests get to visit the aquarium for free; the shuttle that runs back and forth to nearby town is also complimentary. A busy but fun pick for couples when one person doesn't dive. 72 rooms. Credit cards: A, DC, MC, V.

Otrabanda Hotel & Casino   **$105–$105**   ★★

Otrabanda, ☎ *(800) 223-9815, (5999) 462-7400, FAX (5999) 462-7299.*
Associated Restaurant: *Bay Sight Terrace.*
Single: $105. Double: $105.
Located in the historic Otrabanda section of Willemstad, the hotel boasts the best view of the much-photographed Dutch gabled architecture across the harbor. It's handy to the business and shopping district next to Queen Emma Bridge for pedestrians. Some of its small, air-conditioned guest rooms have great harbor views. Its new restaurant or small pool area also provide grand vistas of the ships and boats cutting a swath through the city's heart. The casino on-site is relatively busy and local business people tend to like this facility. A new nightclub might make peace and quiet harder to come by, so ask for an upper floor room, which yield the best views anyway. 45 rooms. Credit cards: A, DC, D, MC, V.

Plaza Hotel Curaçao   **$105–$185**   ★★★

Punda, ☎ *(800) 766-6016, (5999) 461-2500, FAX (5999) 461-6543.*
E-mail: vdvalk@ibm.net.
Single: $105–$185. Double: $130–$165. Suites Per Day: $150–$185.
Its 12-story tower sticks out like a sore thumb in quaint Willemstad and the nearest beach is a 15-minute drive away. Nonetheless, stunning harbor views make this hotel, built in the walls of a 17th-century fort, a decent choice. The central city location attracts working travelers who are catered to with secretarial and business services. In November 1996, its restaurant on top of the building opened, but it's Caribbean-formal without the special cuisine to recommend it. Guestrooms are merely adequate, but the great views of passing ships make a lot forgivable. There's a full casino and pool on site, but no health club. Shopping is convenient at Waterfort Arches. The hotel offers a 24-hour babysitting service for infants to age eight. 253 rooms. Credit cards: A, MC, V.

Princess Beach Resort & Casino   **$140–$550**   ★★★

Seaquarium Beach, ☎ *(800) 992-2015, (5999) 736-7880, FAX (5999) 461-7205.*
Website: www.holiday-inn.com.
Associated Restaurant: *L'Orangerie.*
Single: $140–$230. Double: $140–$230. Suites Per Day: $300–$550.
This Holiday Inn Crowne Plaza property is not affiliated with its namesake cruise line. Sprawling directly in front of the National Underwater Park on a palm-lined beach near the Seaquarium, the hotel—Curaçao's largest—offers spacious guest rooms with all the modern comforts including dataports on phones. The lobby and bar area were recently updated with poor results, but two new wings were added, all rooms with ocean views. The grounds are nicely landscaped and include two restaurants, five bars, a happening casino, two pools, a well-designed and shaded playground, a tennis court and a new Peter Hughes full-service, PADI five-star dive center. If you're looking for a family-friendly resort and can't afford Sonesta, this resort should be the next call. Children under 19 stay free in your room. 341 rooms. Credit cards: A, DC, D, MC, V.

Sonesta Beach Resort & Casino   **$180–$965**   ★ ★ ★ ★ ★

Piscadera Bay, ☎ (800) 766-3782, (5999) 736-8800, FAX (5999) 462-7502.
Associated Restaurant: *Portofino/Emerald Grille.*
Single: $180–$365. Double: $180–$365. Suites Per Day: $380–$965.

Handsomely constructed in Dutch Colonial style in 1992, this $41 million resort brought a new level of elegance and top-notch service to Curaçao. Lush landscaping and contemporary island artwork collected by the owner of the Sonesta chain lend the touches that help the resort ascend the cookie-cutter feel that sometimes mars this type of experience. From the grand entrance at the circular driveway to the oversized, beautifully-designed pool—one of the prettiest in the Western Caribbean—this Piscadera Bay resort strives to dazzle. It manages to do what few hotels can: live up to the expectations of a broad audience. Honeymooners love the terrace rooms that have areas for private sunbathing and Jacuzzis. Families love the complimentary kids program (kids up to age 12 stay free). (One tiny complaint: the lack of shade on the playground makes it virtually unusable). Vacationers love the myriad of offerings: updated and expanded health club with massage, full casino, two gourmet restaurants, shops, tennis and watersports. It also offers 3000 ft. of meeting space for business travelers. All the guest rooms have a patio or balcony and at least a partial ocean view. 248 rooms. Credit cards: A, DC, MC, V.

Where to Eat

Fielding's Highest Rated Restaurants in Curaçao

★★★★★	Bistro Le Clochard	$21–$32
★★★★★	De Taveerne	$18–$32
★★★★★	Emerald Grille, The	$18–$27
★★★★	Curnonsky	$13–$15
★★★★	L'Orangerie	$16–$45
★★★★	Portofino Restaurant	$12–$34
★★★★	Rysttafel Indonesia	$15–$22
★★★★	Seaview	$15–$30
★★★★	Wine Cellar, The	$20–$35
★★★	Fort Nassau	$22–$28

Fielding's Most Romantic Restaurants in Curaçao

♡♡♡♡♡	Bistro Le Clochard	$21–$32
♡♡♡♡♡	De Taveerne	$18–$32
♡♡♡♡♡	L'Orangerie	$16–$45
♡♡♡♡♡	Portofino Restaurant	$12–$34
♡♡♡♡♡	Wine Cellar, The	$20–$35

Fielding's Best Value Restaurants in Curaçao

★★★★	Curnonsky	$13–$15
★★★★★	Emerald Grille, The	$18–$27
★★★★	Rysttafel Indonesia	$15–$22
★★★★★	De Taveerne	$18–$32
★★★★★	Bistro Le Clochard	$21–$32

Curaçaoans love to dine out and typically dress for the occasion. Unless you're dining alfresco, consider taking a sweater or light wrap because the air conditioning is usually set on high. The fact that the population is such a mixed bag means a wealth of choices for diners that is almost unparalleled in the Caribbean. You can get terrific Indonesian, Dutch, Antillean, French, Creole, South American, Swiss and Italian cuisine. Perhaps due to its heavy ties to Europe—its youths often study abroad for several years—many of its chefs trained at some of Europe's highly acclaimed hospitality schools and restaurants. The Indonesian influence is strong with *nasi goreng* (bean sprouts sauteed with chunks of meat and chicken) and satay (skewered meat with peanut sauce) often showing up on menus. Local food relies on the Creole influence: stewed goat, fried fish, chicken served with peas and rice and funchi, a boiled cornmeal paste that resembles polenta. For an inexpensive local meal, try **Jannchie's** near Westpunt. At holidays *keshi yena* (stuffed Edam cheese) is the main dish, a nod to the Dutch.

Prices are typically 50 percent more than you'd pay in the U.S. for a comparable meal, but, if you stick to our recommendations, you'll steer clear of the sometimes unimaginative food you'll find on other islands. The 18th-century **De Taverne** landhuis, replete with stunning antiques, makes a romantic night out. **Bistro Le Clochard** tucked in the corner of the Riffort allows a grand opportunity to sample history while dining from the dynamite French/Swiss menu. Wine connoisseurs will be delighted to find broader choices at most restaurants than are available on many of the Caribbean islands. Dinner tends to be a languorous affair. Afterwards diners head to casinos featuring poker, black jack, roulette, craps and slot machines for nightcaps or to the new Blues at Avila to listen to jazz.

Bay Sight Terrace   **$$$**   ★

Hoek Breedesstraat, Willemstad, ☎ *(599) 462-7400.* Associated hotel: *Otrabanda.*
Lunch: 11a.m.–4 pm, entrées $3–$22.
Dinner: 4–10 p.m., entrées $16–$37.
On the second floor of the Otrabanda Hotel, the open air terrace offers one of the city's best views of quaint Willemstad's famed architecture across the bay. Although the food is more diner-style, this spot, adjacent to the Queen Emma Bridge for pedestrians, is a good place to rest your feet and grab a bit after a day of shopping and exploring. Especially nice at dusk when the lights come on across the way. Credit cards: MC, V.

Belle Terrace   **$$$**   ★★★

Penstraat 130, Willemstad, ☎ *(5999) 461-4377.* Associated hotel: *Avila Beach Hotel.*
Lunch: Noon–3 p.m., entrées $10–$22.
Dinner: 7–10 p.m., entrées $16–$28.
Tucked away in a 200-year-old mansion, the former home of Curaçao's governor, Belle Terrace lets you dine by candlelight under the cool of an ancient flamboyant tree within earshot of the sea. Fish is smoked on the premises. Sometimes cuisine,

which features several Danish favorites, can be less than stellar, but with a setting like this, who cares? Wednesday evening is Antillean night; Saturday night brings a barbecue with steelband or mariachis. Breads and ice creams are homemade. Cigars, specialty coffees and cognacs bring the meal to a leisurely end. Reservations required. Credit cards: A, DC, MC, V.

Bistro Le Clochard $$$ ★★★★★

Rif Fort, Willemstad, ☎ *(5999) 462-5666.*
Lunch: Noon–2 p.m., entrées $21–$32.
Dinner: 6:30–11 p.m., entrées $21–$32. Closed: Sun.

Opened in 1978 by Curaçaon native Freddy Berends, who studied at a famed hotel school in Lucerne, Switzerland, Bistro Le Clochard occupies the prime corner of the 18th century Rif Fort, which formerly guarded the city. Berends, a convivial host, has transformed the fort's prison into a cozy and romantic gourmand's delight. One of the most unique dishes prepared by the talented Swiss chef is *la potence*—skewered beef served on a hot steel globe, which looks like it would have been used by knights. The beef comes with a variety of tasty sauces. Fondues, of course, are a specialty on the menu, which also includes several veal, seafood and steak entrées. The wine list—impressive for the Caribbean—is a good selection of Chilean, Italian, French and South African wines. Although you'll likely be full by the time dessert arrives, sample the Swiss chocolate mousse. While you wait for a table inside, have a drink on the harbour-side outdoor terrace at the mouth of the Santa Ana Bay for a panoramic view of the ships going by and the fish gliding through the waters below, illuminated by lights from the restaurant. The terrace is open for dinner, too. Lunch isn't served on Saturdays. Reservations recommended. Credit cards: A, DC, MC, V.

Blues $$$ ★★★

Penstraat 130, Willemstad, ☎ *(5999) 461-4377.* Associated hotel: *Avila Beach Hotel.*
Dinner: 5 p.m.–1 a.m., entrées $15–$28. Closed: Mon.

At the end of a pier this happening restaurant and jazz bar makes a great choice for late-night dining or drinks at sunset for happy hour. You can construct your own three-course meal for fixed price $28, or order à la carte. The menu is centered around seafood: blue mussels in wine sauce, smoked bluesy salmon with vegetables in basil cream, sole fillet stuffed with scallops. The main event is Thursday (6-9 p.m.) and Saturday (10 p.m-midnight) nights when live jazz is played. Reservations strongly recommended. Credit cards: MC, V.

Cockpit, The $$ ★★

F.D. Rooseveltweg 524, Willemstad, ☎ *(5999) 868-8044.*
Lunch: entrées $12–$27.
Dinner: entrées $12–$27.

Sample Dutch fare by the pool at the Hotel Holland located on the highway to the airport. The former 'T Kokkeltje (meaning cockles) serves marinated mussels when available. Other specialties to savor are split-pea soup, pickled herring and salads. There is also a dimly lit dining room for those who prefer it. Food is served from 7 a.m. to 10:30 p.m. Credit cards: A, MC, V.

Curnonsky $ ★★★★

Root Santu 620, ☎ *(5999) 747-1066.*
Dinner: 6–11 p.m., entrées $13–$15.
About 20 minutes drive from town on the way to Caracasbaai, you'll discover one
of the hot new restaurants in Curaçao. Curnonsky, which offers romantic dinners
outside, has drawn raves from locals as well as those tourists lucky enough to find it.
The Dutch chef changes the wildly eclectic menu every five weeks, but the presentation and flavor are an art form. Oven-poached Scottish salmon with wild spinach,
mustard cream and tomato-basil vinaigrette is a delight. Another winner is the pan-
fried curry-oil jumbo shrimp served with mango chutney and tamarind sauce. The
three-course meal (without wine) runs about $40. Adventurous souls should spring
for the chef's five-course surprise menu. Desserts are a don't miss treat—although,
again, they tend to be unusual concoctions like a champagne pastry with candied
rhubarb and cloves ice cream. Credit cards: A, MC, V.

De Taveerne $$$ ★★★★★

Landhuis Groot Davelaar, Willemstad, ☎ *(5999) 736-7936.*
Lunch: Noon–2 p.m., entrées $12–$19.
Dinner: 7–11 p.m., entrées $18–$32. Closed: Sun.
The owners of this innovative restaurant in the Salina residential area have stylishly
renovated a traditional old octagonal country mansion—the Landhuis Groot Dave-
laar, built in the early 18th century by a South American revolutionary. French and
international haute-cuisine—Dutch Chef Kees van Santen changes the menu every
five weeks—is served in the cool cellar, amidst period antiques. For casual elegance
choose the Brasserie upstairs with soaring ceilings and polished marble floors, or the
garden terrace for snacks and cocktails. Between courses peek upstairs at the new art
gallery, featuring local artists. You'll have plenty of time, because the meal is served
at a European pace. Dessert—especially the terrine of white and brown chocolate
mousse—is worth the wait. Closed for lunch on Saturdays. Reservations required.
Credit cards: A, DC, MC, V.

Emerald Grille, The $$$ ★★★★★

Willemstad, ☎ *(5999) 736-8800.* Associated hotel: *Sonesta Beach.*
Dinner: 6–11 p.m., entrées $18–$27.
Evening light filters through the ceiling-to-floor, sea-foam colored sheers that give
privacy to this intimate steakhouse—decorated with dark woods and tapestries—
across from Sonesta's casino. A jazz pianist serenades those having cocktails on the
small terrace overlooking the cascading fountain and awaiting a table. Attentive
waiters and an exacting chef make certain your steak is prepared to your liking.
From appetizers—try the blackened tuna carpaccio—to the caesar side for two prepared table-side and beyond, the food here is an experience. You can finish with a
choice Dominican cigar and a single-malt scotch whiskey if you like. Be forewarned,
however, everything—even the sauce for your steak—has an ala carte charge, making it easy to run up a whopping bill on this pricey island.

Fort Nassau $$$ ★★★

Fort Nassau, ☎ *(5999) 461-3450.*
Lunch: Noon–3 p.m., entrées $22–$28.

Dinner: 6:30–11 p.m., entrées $22–$28.
Perched like an eagle's nest above Willemstad and overlooking Santa Anna Bay since 1796, this fort—used by the Dutch in the late 18th century and by Americans in World War II—became a restaurant in the 1950s. Often billed as a must-see by other publications, the views here scarcely compensate for the bored, inattentive waitstaff and overly-ambitious cuisine. The picture-perfect dishes, which run the gamut from Asian to Italian, utilize fresh fish, pasta and game in combination with local tropical fruits. But the flavors rarely gel, and the main dining area primarily overlooks the industrial part of the island. The extensive wine list features Chilean, South African, European and American wines. For a better view, consider having a cocktail during happy hour (6–7 p.m.) on the open-air terrace, which overlooks the harbor. Live piano music on weekend evenings. No lunch served on weekends. Reservations recommended. Credit cards: A, DC, MC, V.

Fort Waakzaamheid $$$ ★★

Seru di Domi, Willemstad, ☎ *(5999) 462-3633.*
Dinner: 5–11 p.m., entrées $15–$45. Closed: Tue.
An alternative to the often-crowded Fort Nassau, which gets inundated with cruise-ship passengers, this hilltop aerie in the Otrabanda was held captive many moons ago by the notorious Captain Bligh, probably in part because he was spellbound by the view. No need to dress up for dinner at this American-style tavern and bar. Popular with families, the extensive menu features several steak choices, fish (Curaçao-style or pan-fried in butter), duckling, chicken and shrimp, as well as a nine-item salad bar. A three-course, early bird dinner is available from 5-7 p.m. Credit cards: A, MC, V.

Jaanchie's $ ★★

West Point 15, ☎ *(5999) 864-0126.*
Lunch: 11:30 a.m.–3 p.m., prix fixe $15.
This ultra-casual seaside pavilion—opened in 1936 and owned by father and son—stands out as a pleasant stop when you are touring the Westpunt area or diving from Kadushi Cliffs. Banana quits flit around the outskirts of the restaurant, attracted by the sugar set out for them. Seafood—conch, shrimp, wahoo—and regional favorites like goat stew are the specialties here. The adventurous try the local favorite: iguana stew, which is quite tasty, but you have to watch out for the small bones. Jaanchie will keep the place open past lunch time for you if you call ahead and bring some friends. Credit cards: MC, V.

L'Orangerie $$$ ★★★★

Dr. Martin Luther King Boulevard, Willemstad, ☎ *(5999) 465-5955.* Associated hotel: *Princess Beach Resort.*
Dinner: 6–10 p.m., entrées $16–$45. Closed: Mon.
High ceilings, chandeliers, sparkling marble floors and crisp linen tablecloths lend a chic—and unexpected—elegance to this restaurant inside the Princess Beach's sprawl. A formally dressed, snap-to-it waitstaff quickly gets your meal off to a pleasant start. The talented chef comes up with some interesting marriages of flavors—his menus veer toward international cuisine with a nod to the Caribbean—but they usually work. For example, take the grilled rib-eye with gratinated turnips and a

white Curaçao liqueur sauce or the red seabass tart with a confit tomato and green mango dressing. The thoughtful wine list yields plenty of fine choices to round out your meal. Call after 4 p.m. for reservations. Credit cards: V.

La Pergola Italian Restaurant $$$ ★★

Waterfort Arches, Willemstad, ☎ *(5999) 461-3482.*
Lunch: Noon–2 p.m., entrées $25–$35.
Dinner: 6:30–10:30 p.m., entrées $30–$35. Closed: Sun.
A seaside, Northern Italian eatery offers the best lunch option in the trendy Waterfort Arches shopping center. La Pergola serves pastas, veal, steak, fresh fish and desserts with a light hand—no heavy tomato or gloppy cream sauces here. Take your seat on the lovely terrace facing wrap-around windows and watch the wavy action below, and feast on the likes of grouper Sicilian-style with a puttanesca sauce and conclude with an airy tiramisu. Closed for Sunday lunch. Reservations recommended. Credit cards: A, DC, D, MC, V.

Mambo Beach $ ★★★

Willemstad, ☎ *(5999) 461-8999.*
This new beach club on the palm-lined Seaquarium Beach has quickly become the hot spot for Curacaoans and tourists alike. Every Friday and Sunday it's the site of happy hours and a barbecue with live bands playing. A wooden dance floor has been constructed to make dancing better. The surprisingly expansive menu offers sandwiches, spicy soups, fish, beef and pastas, as well as a short wine list. Snacks include Dutch bitterballen, fried calamari and spicy local meatballs. You can also order breakfast here. Credit cards: MC, V.

Pirates Seafood Restaurant $$$ ★★

Piscadera Bay, Willemstad, ☎ *(5999) 462-5000.* Associated hotel: *Curaçao Caribbean Hotel.*
Lunch: entrées $15–$35.
Dinner: entrées $15–$35.
Famous for theme-night parties, Pirates—one of the restaurants at the city-within-a-city Curaçao Caribbean—specializes in seafood prepared in a myriad of styles and served by a waitstaff in nautical garb. Like the hotel, this 24-table place is caught in a serious time warp. Yo-ho-ho-hum. Reservations recommended. Credit cards: A, DC, MC, V.

Portofino Restaurant $$$ ★★★★

Willemstad, ☎ *(5999) 736-8800.* Associated hotel: *Sonesta Beach.*
Lunch: 11 a.m.–2 p.m., entrées $12–$25.
Dinner: 6–10:30 p.m., entrées $12–$34.
This dramatic restaurant captures an airy feel with a ceiling that soars two stories, floor to ceiling glass windows that look out onto the tropical landscape and giant palm-frond fans attached to a trapeze overhead that gently stir cool. Hand-painted tiles adorn the pink stucco walls. Plush booths and comfy chairs invite lingering over the northern Italian cuisine. Nightfall renders the scene especially romantic, although there are no cozy alcoves in which to tuck away. Couples may want a candle-lit table on the terrace screened from the pool area by lush tropical gardens. The inventive salads and antipastos launch you into a surprisingly authentic Italian meal.

(Caution, though, request your pasta al dente.) Oven-roasted salmon with sauteed escarole, pine nuts, white wine and fresh tomato vinaigrette is a standout. On Sundays an elaborate Sunday brunch ($25 a person) is presented. Credit cards: MC, V.

Rysttafel Indonesia $$ ★★★★

Mercuriusstraat 13-15, Willemstad, ☎ *(5999) 461-2999, (5999) 461-2606.*
Lunch: Noon–2 p.m., prix fixe $10–$17.
Dinner: 6–9:30 p.m., entrées $15–$22.

A carry-over of Dutch colonial days, rijsttafel—which means rice table—is a banquet of up to 25 spicy and savory Indonesian-Javanese dishes surrounded by a mound of steaming rice. To eat here, get a group together and book a table several days ahead for a 16-to-25 dish feast that includes *bami goreng* (fried noodles, shrimp, meat and vegetables) and *krupuk oedang* (gigantic shrimp chips). Vegetarian and a la carte dishes are also available. Batik fabrics, wajang dolls, copper pots and pans, along with intricately designed wallpapers add to the atmosphere. No lunch on Sundays. Reservations recommended. Credit cards: A, DC, MC, V.

Tentaboka Restaurant $ ★★

Schottegatweg (0)185, Willemstad, ☎ *(5999) 465-7678.*

For the food of the people, head to this simple restaurant where main dishes are heavy and hearty, like goat stew and fried fish patties. Sweet polenta with black-eyed peas, pumpkin fritters, fried plantains and rice and beans make tasty accompaniments. A centerpiece of the menu is *keshi yena*, a gouda cheese stuffed with chicken, capers and raisins that rates high with Curacaoans. This complicated dish is a holiday favorite. Okra soup with its slimy texture is an acquired taste. Credit cards: MC, V.

Wine Cellar, The $$$ ★★★★

Concordiastraat, Willemstad, ☎ *(5999) 461-2178.*
Lunch: Noon–2 p.m., entrées $20–$35.
Dinner: 5–11 p.m., entrées $20–$35. Closed: Mon.

Connoisseurs of fine wines repair here to master sommelier and rotisseur of the Chaine de Rotisseur's Nico Cornelisse's lair, a traditional and comfortable Dutch home. Handsomely decorated with original art and Victorian antiques, this expanded restaurant, near the cathedral in downtown Willemstad, remains cozy despite the addition, which brought it to 29 seats. Cornelisse served as the caterer to the Dutch royal family on their recent visit to Curaçao. His voluminous wine list consists of vintages from the Alsace region of France, as well as Germany and Italy. To complement these refined labels are some hearty dishes to warm the blood, including filet of beef with goat cheese sauce and roasted filet of hare with cherry sauce. More delicate appetites will appreciate light seafood salads and well-prepared fish dishes. Service is attentive and personable. Reservations are a must during high season. Reservations required. Credit cards: A, MC, V.

Unlike the other two islands that make up the ABCs, Curaçao is great for shoppers, with trendy boutiques and upscale shops in picturesque Willemstad, where two of the main shopping streets are pedestrian malls. Because it has no duty or sales tax, good deals can be found on imported cameras, china, crystal, electronics, linens, jewelry and perfume. As always, if you plan on doing some serious dropping of cash, check the prices back home first to see if you're really saving enough to justify the hassle of transporting your purchases and obtaining refunds or repairs if necessary. For name-brand make-up, perfume and Tommy Hilfinger menswear, check out **Penha & Sons** *(Heerenstraat 1,* ☎ *(5999) 612266),* housed in a 1708 building; **Little Switzerland** *(Breedesstraat 44, Punda,* ☎ *(5999) 612111),* and **Boolchand's** *(Heerenstraat,* ☎ *(5999) 616233).* For handicrafts by local artisans, check out **Fundason Obra di Man** *(Bargenstraat 57,* ☎ *(5999) 612413).* Heerenstraat and Mardurostraat have been made pedestrian malls, closed to traffic. When major cruise ships are in port, merchants organize a **Bon Bini** (welcome) marketplace in Punda. Small shopping malls outside the city center are **Bloempot**, **Salina Galleries**, **Promenade** and the **77 complex** on Jan Noorduynweg. Good souvenirs include ceramic replicas of local buildings; hanging planters made from old tires and painted like tropical birds (trust us, more attractive than they sound); handmade dolls in folklore costumes; Chilean wine; Curaçao liqueur; South American hammocks; and wheels of Dutch cheese. Most shop employees are fluent in English. Though stores usually close for a lunch hour and on Sundays, they stay open during those times when cruise ships are in port.

Curaçao Directory

Arrival and Departure

> **American Airlines** *(☎ (800) 433-7300)* provides daily nonstop flights to Curaçao from Miami. American also offers flights to Aruba from New York, Miami, and San Juan, Puerto Rico, where you can make an easy transfer to Curaçao. American also offers discounts if its agent makes your hotel reservation at the same time as your air passage. **ALM** *(☎ (800) 327-7230),* the national carrier of Curaçao, also flies 13 times a week from Miami to Curaçao (three nonstop) and four times a week from Atlanta and twice out of Ft. Lauderdale. **Air Aruba** *(☎ (800) 882-7822)* serves Curaçao out of Newark, Baltimore, Miami and Tampa with a stop on Aruba. **Guyana Airways** *(☎ (800) 242-4210)* also flies from New York to Curaçao several times a week. Departure tax is $12.50.

Business Hours

Shops open Monday–Saturday 8 a.m.–noon and 2–6 p.m. Banks open Monday–Friday 8:30 a.m.–noon and 1:30–4:30 p.m.

Climate

Like Bonaire and Aruba, its neighbors, Curaçao is to the south of the Hurricane Belt, making storms an extremely unusual occurrence. The island is constantly refreshed by trade winds blowing from 10–20 miles per hour and the temperature stays constant all year round, seldom fluctuating out of the mid-80s. Summer can be a few degrees hotter and winter a little cooler. Light, casual clothing is the rule. Hotels and casinos are air-conditioned so you may wish to bring fancier clothes, or a sweater.

Documents

U.S. and Canadian citizens need to show proof of citizenship (passport, birth certificate, or voter's registration) plus a photo ID, and an ongoing or return ticket beyond the Netherlands Antilles.

Electricity

Current is 110–130 volts AC, 50 cycles. Outlets are American-style. Converters are not needed for American appliances, but hotels have supplies.

Getting Around

Inquire whether your hotel has a free shuttle service to the shopping district of Willemstad. If not, yellow city buses stop at Wilhelmina Plein, near the shopping center, and travel to most parts of the city. Buses stop when you hail them.

Taxi rates are regulated by the government. Charges after 11 p.m. go up by 25 percent. You'll find taxis waiting for passengers on the Otrabanda side of the floating bridge. Tip 10 percent of the fare. If you want to make a tour by taxi, expect to pay about $20 per hour (up to four passengers allowed).

Rental cars are represented by **Avis** toll-free ☎ *(800) 331-1084*, **Budget** toll free ☎ *(800) 527-0700* and **Hertz** toll-free ☎ *(800) 654-3001*. Check your credit card to see if you can obtain insurance just by charging. To save money, reserve the car from the States before you arrive. Do note that all driving is on the right.

Language

The native language is Papiamento, the official language Dutch, but most everybody speaks some form of English, as well as Spanish.

Medical Emergencies

The 550-bed St. Elizabeth Hospital is the main facility of the island.

Money

Official currency is the Antillean guilder (Netherlands Antilles florin), noted as NAf. One U.S. dollar equals 1.78 NAf. U.S. dollars and credit cards—except Discover—are accepted unilaterally.

Telephone

Country code is *5999*. From the States, dial *011* (international access code), *5999* (country code) + local number. If you are calling from another Caribbean island, check to see if the same code applies. Within Curaçao itself, use only the seven-digit number.

Time

Atlantic standard time all year long.

Tipping and Taxes

Ten percent service charge is added to restaurant bills, but waiters appreciate an extra five to 10 percent. Hotel tax is seven percent with a ten percent service charge.

Tourist Information

The **Curaçao Tourist Board** has an office at *19 Pietermaai* ☎ *466-1600* where you can obtain brochures, maps and have questions answered by English-speaking staff. A kiosk is also at the airport ☎ *466-8678* (open daily 8 a.m.–10 p.m.). In the U.S. call ☎ *(800) 332-8266; e-mail: curaçao@ix.net-com.com.*

Water

Tap water, distilled seawater, is safe to drink.

Website

www.curaco-tourism.com

When to Go

Carnival takes place in January, an unrestrained revel complete with costumes, parades and street parties. The height of celebrations is the weekend right before Ash Wednesday. The International Sailing Regatta is held in March. The 11th Annual Curaçao Jazz Festival will take place Oct. 2 and 3, 1998.

CURAÇAO HOTELS		RMS	RATES	PHONE	CR. CARDS
★★★★★	Sonesta Beach Resort & Casino	248	$180–$365	(800) 766-3782	A, DC, MC, V
★★★★	Avila Beach Hotel	110	$90–$225	(800) 448-8355	A, DC, MC, V
★★★	Habitat Curaçao	70	$165–$220	(800) 327-6709	A, MC, V
★★★	Kadushi Cliffs		$295–$295	(800) 523-8744	A, MC, V
★★★	Lion's Dive Hotel & Marina	72	$135–$195	(800) 223-9815	A, DC, MC, V
★★★	Plaza Hotel Curaçao	253	$105–$165	(800) 766-6016	A, MC, V
★★★	Princess Beach Resort & Casino	341	$140–$230	(800) 992-2015	A, D, DC, MC, V
★★	Coral Cliff Resort & Casino	46	$115–$195	(800) 223-9815	A, DC, MC, V
★★	Curaçao Caribbean Resort & Casino	194	$150–$200	(800) 223-9815	A, DC, MC, V
★★	Otrabanda Hotel & Casino	45	$105–$105	(800) 223-9815	A, D, DC, MC, V

CURAÇAO HOTELS	RMS	RATES	PHONE	CR. CARDS
★ Holiday Beach Hotel & Casino	200	$100–$180	(800) 444-5244	A, D, DC, MC, V
★ Hotel & Casino Porto Paseo	44	$95–$125	(5999) 462-7878	A, DC, MC, V

CURAÇAO RESTAURANTS	PHONE	ENTREE	CR.CARDS
Asian Cuisine			
★★★★ Rysttafel Indonesia	(599) 961-2999	$10–$22	A, DC, MC, V
Continental Cuisine			
★★★★★ Emerald Grille, The	(5999) 736-8800	$18–$27	
★★★★ Curnonsky	(5999) 747-1066	$13–$15	A, MC, V
★★★★ L'Orangerie	(5999) 465-5955	$16–$45	V
★★★ Fort Nassau	(5999) 461-3450	$22–$28	A, DC, MC, V
★★★ Mambo Beach	(5999) 461-8999		MC, V
★★ Fort Waakzaamheid	(5999) 462-3633	$15–$45	A, MC, V
★ Bay Sight Terrace	(5999) 462-7400	$3–$37	MC, V
French Cuisine			
★★★★★ Bistro Le Clochard	(5999) 462-5666	$21–$32	A, DC, MC, V
★★★★★ De Taveerne	(5999) 736-7936	$12–$32	A, DC, MC, V
★★★★ Wine Cellar, The	(5999) 461-2178	$20–$35	A, MC, V
International Cuisine			
★★ 'T Kokkeltje		$12–$27	A, MC, V
Italian Cuisine			
★★★★ Portofino Restaurant	(5999) 736-8800	$12–$34	MC, V
★★ La Pergola Italian Restaurant	(5999) 461-3482	$25–$35	A, D, DC, MC, V
Regional Cuisine			
★★ Jaanchie's	(5999) 864-0126	$15–$15	MC, V
★★ Tentaboka Restaurant	(5999) 465-7678		MC, V
Scandinavian Cuisine			
★★★ Belle Terrace	(5999) 461-4377	$10–$28	A, DC, MC, V
Seafood Cuisine			
★★★★ Seaview	(5999) 461-6688	$15–$30	A
★★★ Blues	(5999) 461-4377	$15–$28	MC, V
★★ Pirates Seafood Restaurant	(5999) 462-5000	$15–$35	A, DC, MC, V

DOMINICA

Bananas, coconuts, grapefruit, limes and passionfruit are important to Dominica's economy.

Your first sight of Dominica is likely to be memorable. From the air, the island appears like a chunky, verdant emerald swathed in clouds. Rivers plunge wildly down precipitate slopes and lavish foliage envelopes the terrain to shelter seemingly impenetrable jungle. Dominica could be the one Caribbean outpost that Columbus might recognize today. Although the island has grown up since 1493, there are still no McDonald's, no casinos, no duty-free stores, no luxury resorts and precious little nightlife. There is also a noticeable absence of white-sand beaches, a "setback" that stalled Dominica from being tamed for tourists when other islands were busy paving over their mangrove swamps for bigger airstrips.

Ah, but what a silver lining this setback has yielded, for Dominica has riches of an increasingly rarer nature. The island is home to one of the world's last ocean rain forests, a flooded and boiling volcanic fumarole said to be the second-largest anywhere, a lake covered with purple hyacinths, and so many species of trees that one of them is actually called "no-name." Here is an earth of striking, lava-formed landscapes, of vine-draped forests so dazzlingly accented with flowers you could believe you're in the Garden of Eden. Dominica receives so much rain—up to 250 inches a year in the mountains—that literally hundreds of rivers cascade down the valleys. Fortunately, sunshine makes regular appearances, sometimes in shafts of light that radiate through the evanescent drizzles of mist wafting over the green (liquid sunshine, they call it here). Beyond the shoreline, Dominica's underwater world is equally spectacular and highlighted by dives into pristine submarine craters that percolate with invertebrate life and through simmering volcanic vents.

A vacation to Dominica is, quite simply, a different one than is offered on any other Caribbean isle. The Dominica experience is about trudging up muddy mountain paths, diving around underwater pinnacles, and tracking the flight of the rare, endangered *sisserou*, a parrot whose numbers were counted in the dozens only a few years ago. In sum, Dominica is not for the faint-hearted, and those who are in shape will be rewarded the most. Although mining, hydro-electric and other ecologically reckless projects have been called into question, the government will continue its pursuit of eco-tourism dollars, primarily because there are few short-term alternatives and the banana exporting business is increasingly slippery. However, if the island's politicians can protect their environment and keep the tourism infrastructure small and manageable, Dominica will continue to reward adventurous visitors with a one-of-a-kind Caribbean experience.

BEST BETS FOR...

Bird's-Eye View

Wai'tukubuli, the Carib Indians called it: "tall is her body." Not to be confused with the much larger Dominican Republic, the Commonwealth of Dominica (pronounced Dom-en-*ee*-ka) sprawls over a mountainous, 29- by 16-mile territory, lying between Guadeloupe to the north and Martinique to the south. Like the two French islands, 290-square-mile Dominica is part of

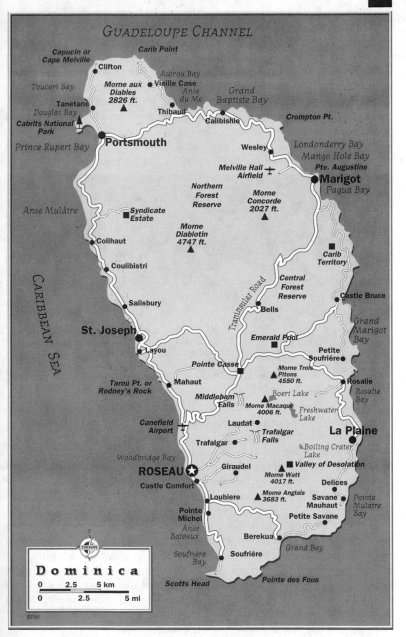

GUADELOUPE CHANNEL

Capucin or
Cape Melville
Carib Point
Clifton
Autrou Bay
Morne aux
Diables
2826 ft.
Vieille Case
Anse
du Me
Grand
Baptiste Bay
Toucari Bay
Thibaud
Tanetane
Douglas Bay
Calibishie
Crompton Pt.
Cabrits National
Park
Portsmouth
Wesley
Londonderry Bay
Mango Hole Bay
Prince Rupert Bay
Melville Hall
Airfield
Pte. Augustine
Marigot
Pagua Bay
Northern
Forest
Reserve
Morne
Concorde
2027 ft.
Anse Mulâtre
Syndicate
Estate
Colihaut
Morne
Diablotin
4747 ft.
Carib
Territory
Coulibistri
Transinpular Road
Central
Forest
Reserve
Salisbury
Castle Bruce
St. Joseph
Bells
Grand
Marigot
Bay
Layou
Emerald Pool
Pointe Casse
Petite
Soufrière
Tarou Pt. or
Rodney's Rock
Mahaut
Morne Trois
Pitons
4550 ft.
Rosalie
Boeri Lake
Rosalie
Bay
Middleham
Falls
Morne Macaque
4006 ft.
Freshwater
Lake
Canefield
Airport
Laudat
Trafalgar
Falls
La Plaine
Woodbridge Bay
Trafalgar
Giraudel
Boiling Crater
Lake
ROSEAU
Valley of Desolation
Castle Comfort
Morne Watt
4017 ft.
Delices
Loubiere
Morne Anglais
3683 ft.
Savane
Mauhaut
Pointe
Mulâtre
Bay
Pointe
Michel
Anse
Bateaux
Petite Savane
Berekua
Soufrière
Bay
Soufrière
Grand Bay
Scotts Head
Pointe des Fous

CARIBBEAN SEA

Dominica

0   2.5   5 km
0   2.5   5 mi

©FWI

the Caribbean's chain of volcanoes, with a jagged terrain born from the violence of past eruptions. The northern half of the island is dominated by a single peak, Morne Diablotins, which rises to 4747 feet—its slopes are uninhabited except along the shoreline. This is also the location of the vast Northern Forest Reserve, and the habitat of the island's two indigenous and endangered parrots: the brown and green sisserou (or Imperial), the largest and perhaps rarest Amazon species in the world, and the jaco (or rednecked), a more colorful bird. Successful conservation efforts have helped re-establish their population numbers in the wild—the sisserou is now estimated to number about 300 and the jaco is approaching 1000. Dominica's second-largest town, Plymouth, population 5000, lies in a large bay near the northwest tip.

Dominica's small Emerald Pool waterfall attracts hordes of tourists.

The center portion of the island is less mountainous, with its small Central Forest Reserve and plantations of lime and banana, but rising above Pont Casse, a crossroads near the middle of the island, is steep Morne Trois Pitons, the island's second-highest point at 4403 feet. The deeply indented valleys and soaring peaks south of here allow primal rain forests to grow unfettered, and waterfalls to tumble into ravines. On the slopes of Morne Nicholls is the Boiling Lake, a rain-choked volcanic crater that bubbles with temperatures ranging from simmering to torrid—next to the crater is the Valley of Desolation, a basin filled with vivid geothermal activity. Roseau is the prototypical West Indian port, as many appeared a few decades ago—it is slightly ragtag in spots, but a fair number of older structures are intact and provide much charm. Though large cruise ships now dock and modern buildings have sprung up, the town still rings of the authentic bustle of island trade. About a third of Dominica's 71,000 residents live in and around Roseau. The rest reside in smallish communities that dot the coastline on both the Caribbean and wilder Atlantic coasts.

History

Dominica was first settled by Arawaks and then Carib Indians. During the 17th and 18th centuries, control for the island was hotly contested between the British, the French and the native tribes. The British finally prevailed and Dominica formed part of the Leeward Islands federation until 1939. In 1940 it was transferred to the Windward Islands and remained attached to that group until the federal arrangement was ended in 1959. Under a new constitution, effective from January 1960, Dominica achieved a separate status with its own administrator and an enlarged legislative council. In 1967, it became one of the West Indies Associated States, gaining full autonomy in internal affairs with the United Kingdom retaining responsibility for defense and foreign relations. Following a decision in 1975 by the Associated States to seek independence separately, Dominica became an independent republic within the Commonwealth in 1978.

Dominica has long been one of the least prosperous islands in the neighborhood, but conditions are getting better. Dame Eugenia Charles was the island's prime minister from 1980 until her retirement in 1995 at the age of 76. She had some measure of success by embracing the U.S., particularly during the 1983 Grenada intervention when she represented the region during a press conference with President Reagan (Dominica also supplied troops for the incursion). But with U.S. and other aid shrinking, and the fields of banana harboring an uncertain future, the island is looking for other areas to boost the economy. Tourism has climbed dramatically in recent years: the new cruise ship pier in Roseau lured 290 ships with 193,484 visitors to Dominica in 1996, and overnight arrivals are also up, to 63,259 in 1996, due in part to the recent debut of American Eagle service from San Juan. There is concern over the impact of the increased tourism, particularly the cruise ship passengers. Fortunately the success of the "Nature Island" image has meant that most of the overnight tourists who come are those who are looking for a rustic vacation, rather than the high-spending resort crowd that frequent other Caribbean islands. However, although the island pursues eco-tourism, the government also takes actions that make environmentalists cringe. Dominica passed a controversial mining bill in 1996 that gave the government mineral rights to all public and private land, and an Australian mining firm performed exploratory drilling to determine the extent of island's copper deposits—public outcry has stalled further action. In 1997, Prime Minister Edison James announced his country's support in the

United Nations fro Japan's pro-whaling position. presumably in exchange for financial aid from Japan.

People

Almost all Dominicans profess Christianity and about 80 percent are Roman Catholics. There is a community of about 3000 Carib Indians on the east coast, one of the last in existence, though very few are pure-blooded and almost none speak the Carib language (Chief Irvince Auguiste is attempting to revive usage of the language). In part of the northeast, an English dialect known as *cocoy* is spoken by the descendants of freed slaves originally from Antigua. The French influence is notable here—Dominica was part of the French empire for many years, and a third of the tourist arrivals are visitors from nearby Martinique and Guadeloupe; there is a thriving Alliance Francaise outlet. For now, farming remains the principal industry, heavily dependent on the banana, with citrus and coconuts other agricultural exports. The island has historically been one of the region's poorest, but conditions are improving. The amiable population is almost 98 percent black, and have not been hardened to outsiders in the way that residents of more heavily trammeled islands have been. As such, what hotels and restaurants may lack in efficiency and amenities is made up by friendly, generous nature. Novelist Jean Rhys was born here, and wrote about Dominica memorably in *Wide Sargasso Sea* (made into a panting 1992 movie shot in Jamaica), while contemporary author Lennox Honeychurch has documented the island's history in *Our Island Culture* and other books.

Beaches

Dominica has only a few beaches of note, and many will happily point to the rivers as the best place for swimming. The west coast has some decent strands, particularly the long cove just south of Portsmouth at the **Picard Estate**. Farther south at **Mero**, just south of Salisbury, the sand is black but well kept at the Castaways Beach Hotel. The best beach near Roseau is at **Scott's Head**, a 20-minute drive south of the capital to lovely Soufriere Bay. Light sand beaches can be found on the north coast, such as **Woodford Hill** (near the Melville Hall airport) and **Hampstead** but currents are tricky all along the Atlantic coast. The sand is a beautiful golden color at **Point Baptiste**.

Diving on Dominica was an insider's secret only a few years ago, but the island has quietly emerged as one of the four or five best dive locations in the Eastern Caribbean. The underwater terrain looks much like the mountains above: walls drop for hundreds of feet but are still manageable for beginning-to-intermediate divers. Visibility, despite frequent rain run-off, averages a respectable 75 feet; sediment is quickly carried to plunging depths (the mountain soil actually contributes to the underwater scene far more than it detracts by supplying nutrients to the reef's many filter feeders). Most of the diving is concentrated in Soufriere Bay, a submerged volcanic crater a mile wide, that drops to nearly a thousand feet in its center; pinnacles are scattered liberally along the sheer lip and invertebrate life is superbly displayed. A series of 18 permanent moorings were installed in 1997—they help protect the pristine underwater environment, as well as provide better access to the sites on the Atlantic side of Scotts Head. There is also good diving in Douglas Bay just north of Portsmouth. Snorkelers will enjoy the inside of Scott's Head and should not miss the singular sparkle of Champagne.

Dive Shops

Anchorage Hotel and Dive Center

Castle Comfort; ☎ *(767) 448-2638.*

PADI outfit open since 1987 with courses to the divemaster level; uses small groups under eight. Two-tank dive $65. Whale-watching trips, with a proclaimed 95 percent success rate spotting pilot and sperm whales (up to 65 feet) off the western coast November through March; a recent law now bans divers from swimming with the creatures.

Dive Dominica

Castle Comfort; ☎ *(767) 448-2188.*

The island's oldest outfit (established in 1984), PADI and NAUI affiliated, this shop features three boats including a huge 47-foot catamaran (accommodating up to 60 snorkelers when cruise ships dock) but keeps dive groups to 8 or 10. Two-tank dive $75. Also schedules whale-watching trips October through April, $50.

Nature Island Dive

Soufriere; ☎ *(767) 449-8181.*

Three-year-old outfit in advantageous Soufriere Bay location overlooks island's best dive spots. Two-tank dive $63. Resort course, $84. Also sea kayak rentals ($42 full day, $26 half-day; stick to the coast rather than heading straight out) and mountain bikes (see "By Pedal").

Fielding DOMINICA

A THOUSAND SHADES OF GREEN

Unspoiled and untamed, this 290-square mile island has 365 rivers—enough to provide you one to explore every day for a year! This is a land of extremes, from towering mountains, huge tree ferns and giant-size insects to vast stands of tall trees and misty waterfalls that stream down jagged cliffs. Conservation efforts have preserved the wilderness, as well as the culture of the Carib Indians.

Morne Diablotins Hike

At 4747 feet, this is the island's highest peak. A rigorous, three-hour (one-way) hike can take you to the summit. If you hire a guide and start by 4 a.m., you'll reach the peak at sunrise, the best time to see and hear the island's rare imperial parrots or the more common red-necked parrot.

Colihaut

Trafalgar Falls

A short car drive from Roseau takes you to the trailhead leading to Trafalgar Falls. Called "mother" and "father" by the locals, the "mother" falls are cold, while the "father" falls are fed by warmer water from orangish sulfuric springs.

Canefield Airport

Mahaut

Roseau

Morne Trois Pitons National Park

The Boiling Lake

This challenging hike for serious trekkers leads from Laudat through the Valley of Desolation, where sulfur fumes waft up from the rough volcanic crust to Boiling Lake. This hike requires a guide and an early start to make the all-day six-mile round trip. If you're in good shape, you'll be rewarded with the sight of the boiling lake—the world's second largest.

Fort Chchacrou

Cabrits National Park

Just north of Portsmouth, this 1300-acre park encompasses ruined fortifications that once covered an entire hillside. Fort Shirley, which also houses a small museum, is the most impressive site.

Portsmouth

Northern Forest Reserve

Marigot

Snorkeling & Diving

Snorkeling and diving spots are less developed in the north, but if you like to snorkel, try Douglas Bay, which has a large reef located 180 feet off-shore. Rodney's Rock, accessible by land or water has canyon-like features offshore that make the area a good diving site.

Indian River Tours

South of Portsmouth, local guides take visitors on boat rides up the Indian River. The river is lined with mangroves, palms and other tropical plants. The ride ends at a bamboo hut that serves as a bar—try the home-made punch.

Central Forest Reserve

Carib Territory

This region occupies the northeast portion of the island and it serves as home to the island's Carib Indians. The reservation itself contains 3700 acres. While the Caribs have embraced modern civilization as fishermen and farmers, you can buy samples of their traditional skills—woodcarvings and hand-woven baskets are offered for sale in little thatched-roof huts that line the road.

Castle Bruce

Emerald Pool

North of Roseau, this short walk brings hikers to the Emerald Pool, a favorite bathing place. Along the way to the pool, you'll see breathtaking views of the windward (Atlantic) coast. The pool is ringed with bright green ferns and fed by a 50-foot waterfall.

Waterfalls tumbling past wild orchids, slender ridges leading to mist-blown peaks, and three crater lakes—cool or boiling, take your pick. If there's a better adventure destination in the Caribbean than Dominica, step forward now. For the most part, the government has protected its natural resources admirably, and in 1997 instituted a fee to visit the island's National Parks ($5 per day or $2 per site, collected at the Tourist Office at the cruise ship dock, at the Botanical Gardens, or at the sites themselves). Time will tell how the moneys generated will be spent, but why wait and see? Your visit to the verdant forests and volcanic innards of this out-of-the-way destination will be nothing less than memorable.

Guides are available for all excursions, but are not absolutely necessary for experienced hikers tackling the Freshwater and Boeri lakes or Trafalgar Falls trails. Visitors do become lost, however, and the trek to the Boiling Lake, in particular, should not be attempted without a guide. Dominica's regular and heavy rainfall works against trails in two ways: paths become washed out or engulfed with mud, and the forest never stops growing, enveloping the trails in green with lightning speed. Guides almost always carry a machete and can frequently be seen maintaining trails even when they're not leading hikes. In addition to the outfit listed below, guides of varying ability are available at many trailheads, or the management of Papillote Wilderness Retreat (see "Where to Stay") can help set you up. Two other worthy treks are **Morne Diablotins**, the country's highest point and home to the endangered sisserou and jaco parrots, and **Morne Trois Pitons**, where heavy rain inspires ribbons of water to cascade from its sheer north face; neither are terribly long trips, but both require the services of a qualified guide.

Trekking Tours

Ken's Hinterland Adventure Tours
Roseau; ☎ (767) 448-4850.
Van and hiking tours; guide for group of up to four people to Boiling Lake or Morne Diablotin, $160; for Syndicat and parrot watching, $100.

What Else to See

In Roseau, all the sights are within walking distance of each other. Many of the attractive older buildings are standing, even after the devastation of 1979's Hurricane David, though newer structures increasingly dominate the scene. Dawbiney Market Plaza is chock-full of art exhibits, handicrafts and local fruits and vegetable stands—the big market day is Saturday morning. On the outskirts of town, heading toward Trafalgar Falls, is the 40-acre **Botanical Gardens**, which houses an orchid collection and also a breeding program for the sisserou and jaco parrots. Several roads out of Roseau snake high into the mountains, leading to the trailheads that access the lush **Morne Trois Pitons National Park** (see "On Foot"). The easiest trail is the 15-minute hike to **Trafalgar Falls**—stop by Papillote Wilderness Retreat on the way back to your car for lunch or a sip of their fine rum punch. The road south from Roseau passes through the quaint village of **Soufriere** on the way to **Scotts Head**, a promontory jutting into the Caribbean. Views of Martinique can be excellent, and snorkeling in Soufriere Bay, a submerged volcanic crater whose debris has been located as far away as Grenada, is excellent.

The main road circuiting the island is in pretty good shape, and a rental car is the best way to tour the major sights, but even though there's only one traffic light on the island, be sure to allow more than one day. The west coast of Dominica is spectacular, a succession of tiny fishing villages perched at the mouths of steep river valleys. The island's second largest town is **Portsmouth**, which isn't anything special, but it lies next the **Indian River**, where it is possible to take a one-hour cruise by paddle up the peaceful, mangrove-fringed river. Just north of Portsmouth is **Cabrits National Park**, a double-peaked peninsula that defines the north edge of **Prince Rupert Bay**, lovely natural harbor watched over by Morne Diablotins. Cabrits contains the ruins of **Fort Shirley**, a British fort dating back to the mid-1700s. Heading east out of Portsmouth, one passes coconut plantations and scenic beaches en route to the village of **Calibishie**, and Almond Beach Restaurant, a good lunch stop; farther down the coast is another good rest stop, Floral Gardens in Concord. This is **Carib Indian Territory**. You can drive through the 3700-acre reservation, but a guide will provide a better appreciation of the area. Continuing toward Pont Casse (a rotary near the center of the island), you'll soon reach a turnoff for **Emerald Pool**, where a 50-foot waterfall plunges into a basin surrounded by dense forest. The trail is short, and the falls are nice, but avoid the spot if a cruise ship tour has invaded.

Parks and Gardens

Cabrits National Park ★★★

Portsmouth, ☎ *(767) 448-2401*

Located on the northwestern coast, this gorgeous peninsula encompasses 1313 acres of tropical forests, swampland, beaches, coral reefs and various ruins. The most notable structure is Fort Shirley, a military complex built in 1770 that has been undergoing restoration and includes a small museum. Good for birding.

Morne Trois Pitons National Park ★★★★★

South-central region, ☎ *(767) 448-2733.*

The 25-square-mile slice of nature, named after Dominica's second-highest peak, is a primordial rainforest high in the mountains above Roseau. Most of the park is reached on foot only, and guides are a good idea. The highlight is the Boiling Lake, a bubbling mass of muddy water that's seen only by the hardy—it takes six to seven strenuous hours to hike there and back. The Valley of Desolation you pass through to get to the Boiling Lake is another area of geothermal activity. Shorter trails include one to Freshwater and Boeri Lakes, which were once one body of water until a younger volcano, Morne Micotrin, sprouted and split them in two. Another trail goes to the thundering Middleham Falls; see "On Foot" for more hiking information. The day-use fee for the National Park is now $5, or $2 per site.

Tours

Carib Territory ★★★

Salybia.

A drive into the 3700-acre Carib reservation, established in 1903 by the British government, is free to anyone—the main road passes through it six miles north of Castle Bruce. The Caribs were Amerindians who originated in South America's Amazon Basin and journeyed in dugout canoes to the Caribbean in the 14th century. When the Caribs encountered the peaceful native Arawaks, the tribes warred on various islands, and Caribs were the usual victors. Throughout the region, the Caribs developed a somewhat exaggerated reputation as cannibals, and soon lost out to the invasion of the Europeans, who slaughtered most tribes and shipped others off to the island of Roatan, in the western Caribbean. About 3400 descendants of Dominica's original Carib population live in the territory today, the only such reserve in the world, and another 2000 live in other parts of Dominica (a few Caribs live in St. Vincent and Guyana but Dominica is home to the largest concentration). Very few of the modest and humble Caribs still speak their native tongue, but 35-year-old elected Chief Irvince Auguiste is making a determined effort to preserve the language, as well as the culture. There are plans to develop a Carib Village to depict the lifestyle prior to Columbus, but for now you can see the territory's thatch roof huts and the wares of its talented weavers; also stop by the reservation's Catholic Church, where a dugout canoe serves as an altar. The **Bionics Guest House** ☎ *(767) 445-7167* is a women's cooperative with a crafts store and pre-school, and can help with very simple accommodations or a guided tour of the territory.

Guided Tours

Various locations, Roseau.

A number of outfits will take you on driving tours around Dominica, from the city sights of Roseau to the rainforest, Trafalgar Falls to Portmouth: **Wilderness Adventure Tours** ☎ *(767) 448-2198*, **Rainbow Rover Tours** ☎ *(767) 448-8650*, **Dominica Tours** ☎ *(767) 448-2638*, **Emerald Safaris** ☎ *(767) 448-4545*, **Mally's Tour Service** ☎ *(767) 448-3114*, and **Sun Link Tours** ☎ *(767) 448-2552*, which also offers sea excursions. Prices are generally in the $30–$50 range for half- or full-day driving tours. **Anchorage Dive Center** ☎ *(767) 448-2638* and **Dive Dominica** ☎ *(767) 448-2188* offer whale-watching trips along the Dominica coast for $50–$65. There are a number of good hiking guides on the island: **Ken's Hinterland Adventure Tours** is a good bet ☎ *(767) 448-4850*. Other hiking guides for Morne Trois Pitons National Park typically hang out in the villages of Laudat and Trafalgar. The going rate for a guide to the Boiling Lake is $100–$120 for up to four people; Middleham Falls $75–$80.

Indian River   ★★★

Portsmouth.

Avoid the sputtering motor-powered boats and climb aboard a hand-powered and colorfully painted rowboat for a relaxing "cruise" up the Indian River. The journey begins at a seaside bridge at the mouth of the river, just south of Portsmouth, and continues about a mile through mangrove swamp. As the flowers and vegetation increase, the waterway gradually narrows, winding up at a surprising outpost in the jungle—a bar and restaurant that pipes in *zouk* from a Guadeloupe radio station. International flags painted on coconuts dangle from the canvas roof and the Dynamite Rum Punch is, well, just that. The guided boat trip is $10 per person; rum drinks are extra.

Hiking and diving predominate in Dominica. **Tennis** can be played at two hotels: Reigate Hall in Roseau and Castaways Beach in Mero. A **squash court** is found at the Anchorage Hotel in Castle Comfort. **Game fishing** is provided by Dominica Tours in Castle Comfort ☎ *(767) 448-2638*.

Bicycles and Kayaks

Biking on Dominica is not for the faint-hearted. Yet those who are up to its steep and winding roads will discover numerous possibilities. **Nature Island Dive** in Soufriere has mountain bikes available for rent. Full day rental is $32, half day $23. Also offers biking tours that start from Pont Casse (elevation: 2000 feet) and head downhill through scenic and less-visited areas. $84 per person for a group of two or three, $68 for four or five, including transport, bike and lunch. Nature Island also rents kayaks, and the Soufriere Bay area in front of their shop is a terrific place for beginners; $23 for a half day, $42 for a full day ☎ *(767) 449-8181*.

Where to Stay

Fielding's Highest Rated Hotels in Dominica

★★★	Exotica	$132–$161
★★★	Fort Young Hotel	$95–$135
★★★	Garraway Hotel	$95–$130
★★★	Petit Coulibri Guest Cottages	$115–$225
★★★	Sutton Place Hotel	$75–$135

Fielding's Best Mountain Escapes in Dominica

★★★	Petit Coulibri Guest Cottages	$115–$225
★★★	Exotica	$132–$161
★★	Papillote Wilderness Retreat	$70–$100
★	Springfield Plantation	$45–$80

Fielding's Best Value Hotels in Dominica

★★	Hummingbird Inn	$55–$65
★★★	Sutton Place Hotel	$75–$135
★★★	Garraway Hotel	$95–$130
★★★	Fort Young Hotel	$95–$135
★★	Castaways Beach Hotel	$82–$130

Those in need of serious pampering best head elsewhere, as Dominica is not the spot for luxury resorts—for now. A high-amenity resort in Layou Valley began construction in 1996, but was abandoned halfway through; its completion might dramatically alter the clientele visiting the island, which has so far favored those inclined to "rough it" on vacation. Yes, air conditioning is a rarity. Otherwise, the low price of accommodations here may surprise you, particularly if you're used to the inflated ones on other Caribbean islands. All of the hotels are small (the largest has 43 rooms), most are locally owned, and there is an extensive selection of properties with rooms under $100 per night. Most properties are clustered around Roseau—a few are on the coast near Layou or around Plymouth. Other choice spots around like **Petit Coulibri** and **Exotica** take advantage of the natural surrounding in supremely remote hideaways; inquire about transportation logistics, as some of these may be reached only by four-wheel drive.

Hotels and Resorts

Fort Young Hotel, on the site of the erstwhile fort at the edge of Roseau, gets high marks for historical charisma and civilized service. Fort Young is the best full-service hotel on the island, though **Garraway Hotel** lays on the modern conveniences in a new waterfront building with all the personality of a hospital. The closest thing to a beach resort is provided at **Castaways Beach Hotel**.

Anchorage Hotel   **$65–$110**   ★★

Castle Comfort, ☎ *(800) 223-6510, (767) 448-2638, FAX (767) 448-5680.*
E-mail: anchorage@mailtod.dm.
Single: $65–$80. Double: $85–$110.
Located about a mile south of Roseau, this casual hotel appeals mainly to divers. Accommodations are basic, and the older rooms need refurbishment, so be sure to book one of the newer units. There's a good-sized pool, restaurant, dive center and watersports, which cost extra. Though it's located on the water, there is no beach, but this spot remains popular for its friendly, family-run service. 32 rooms. Credit cards: A, DC, D, MC, V.

Castaways Beach Hotel   **$82–$130**   ★★

St. Joseph, ☎ *(888) 227-8292, (767) 449-6244, FAX (767) 449-6246.*
Website: www.delphis.dm/castaways.htm. E-mail: castaways@mail.tod.dm.
Single: $82. Double: $130.
Situated on the edge of a rain forest along a lovely, palm-lined black-sand shoreline, Castaways is essentially Dominica's only beach resort. Accommodations are in a two-story wing running along the beach; only a few have air conditioning, but all are pleasant and comfortable. Recreational pursuits include a full dive shop, tennis and watersports. Nothing fancy, but a well-run property with a friendly staff and the sunsets can be memorable. MAP plan available (little else is nearby). 26 rooms. Credit cards: A, MC, V.

Evergreen Hotel   **$78–$118**   ★★

Castle Comfort, ☎ *(767) 448-3288, FAX (767) 448-6800.*
Website: www.delphis.dm/evergreen.htm.
Single: $78–$88. Double: $103–$118.
Plenty of local hospitality at this well-run, family-owned hotel a mile south of Roseau. The original two-story house overlooks a rocky beach. Accommodations are comfortable and bright and have air conditioning; the newer units are more polished, the original rooms have more character. All have phones and cable TV, and a full breakfast is included in the rates. There's a pool and good restaurant, and they'll help arrange watersports. 16 rooms. Credit cards: A, DC, D, MC, V.

DOMINICA

Fort Young Hotel $95–$160   ★★★

Roseau, ☎ *(800) 223-6510, (767) 448-5000, FAX (767) 448-5006.*
Single: $95–$115. Double: $115–$135. Suites Per Day: $155–$160.

Built within the ruins of old Fort Young, which dates back to the 1770s, this is Dominica's best hotel, though business travelers keep it bustling through the day. Nicely accented with antique art, rooms are air-conditioned and look out over the harbor. The three suites are beautifully done, filled with antiques, and well worth the extra splurge. The pool is decent, too. A fine in-town spot, with more rooms planned for 1998. 33 rooms. Credit cards: A, D, MC, V.

Garraway Hotel $95–$170   ★★★

Roseau, ☎ *(767) 449-8800, FAX (767) 449-8807.*
E-mail: garraway@tod.dm.
Single: $95–$105. Double: $110–$130. Suites Per Day: $135–$170.

The newest hotel on the island, Garraway is housed in a modern five-story building on the waterfront offering great views extending to Scotts Head at the southern tip of the island. It was a big deal that Garraway brought the first elevator to Dominica, yet it's delightfully uncooperative! Rooms are attractive if unoriginal, with air-conditioning, king size beds (or two doubles), rattan furnishings and floral print fabrics. Geared more to business travelers, but the Garraway family lives next door and keeps the atmosphere cordial. 31 rooms. Credit cards: A, DC, MC, V.

Sutton Place Hotel $75–$135   ★★★

Roseau, ☎ *(800) 544-7631, (767) 449-8700, FAX (767) 448-3045.*
Website: www.delphin.dm/sutton.htm. E-mail: sutton2@tod.dm.
Single: $75–$105. Double: $95–$135.

A 1995 addition to the island, Sutton Place is a small Roseau hotel that caters to both business and leisure travelers with attractive, air-conditioned rooms decorated with lovely antiques; a few have four-poster beds. Three suites are also available and feature a kitchenette. The cozy cellar bar is a real gathering spot for local movers and shakers. Rates include a continental breakfast. A good value if you don't mind the in-town location. 8 rooms. Credit cards: A, D, MC, V.

Apartments and Condominiums

Dominica has a handful of self-catering places for rent, but don't expect to find modern shopping facilities or anywhere near the variety you're used to at home. If you want to stay someplace long-term, come to the island and snoop around to find exactly what you want. Prices are sometimes negotiable, depending on the length of your stay. Those interested in a villa should consider **Pointe Baptiste**, a house and cottage (rented separately) set near a beach at the north coast village of Calibishi ☎ *(809) 445-7322.*

Coconut Beach Hotel $55–$150   ★

Picard Beach, Portsmouth, ☎ *(767) 445-5393, FAX (767) 445-5693.*
Single: $55. Double: $65. Suites Per Day: $150–$150.

Located just south of Portsmouth on a decent beach, this is an enclave of cottages and apartments with kitchenettes; furnishings are simple and basic, and some units have air conditioning. There's a restaurant on site if you're not up to cooking, and the nearby medical school is usually bustling with students. Activities include watersports, river tours and hiking; there's no pool. Bashed by hurricanes recently, but should be functioning at full speed for 1998. 22 rooms. Credit cards: A, D, MC, V.

Exotica $132–$161   ★★★

Morne Anglais, ☎ *(800) 544-7631, (767) 448-8839, FAX (767) 448-8829.*
Single: $132. Double: $161.
Looking for a mountain hideaway where no one can find you? Exotica is perched at the 1200-foot elevation above Roseau, where a series of quaint one-bedroom cottages, each with full kitchen, living room and porch, overlook an organic farm, with views down the lush valley to the sea below. The facility is new and surprisingly polished; a small restaurant prepares meals. Proprietors Fae and Athie Martin want to create a real (rather than contrived) eco-center. There's nothing but lush wilderness surrounding the spot, but if retreat is what you want, Exotica delivers. 8 rooms. Credit cards: A, D, MC, V.

Lauro Club $73–$140   ★★

Salisbury, ☎ *(767) 449-6602, FAX (767) 449-6603.*
Single: $73–$100. Double: $105–$140.
Situated on a small cliff about 12 miles north of Roseau, this complex of rustic villas is fine for make-do types. The larger units sleep four and offer separate living rooms and a kitchen on the large veranda; smaller units sleep two, but still have a kitchen. All are cooled by ceiling fans. There's a nice pool and the restaurant is fine; guests may use tennis courts at Castaways. The beach is a ten-minute walk and snorkeling is good just below the bluff. You'll want a car as Lauro is rather remote, but that's also its appeal. The clientele is mostly European. 10 rooms. Credit cards: A, DC, MC, V.

Petit Coulibri Guest Cottages $115–$225   ★★★

Soufriere, ☎ *(767) 446-3150, FAX (767) 449-8182.*
Website: www.delphis.dm/petit.htm. E-mail: barnard@tod.dm.
Single: $115–$225. Double: $115–$225.
You can thank a glut of aloe for the inspiration to build Petit Coulibri. The Barnard family abandoned aloe farming when they could no longer compete on the world market—and a cottage industry was born. Located atop a remote ridge on Dominica's drier southern tip, high enough above sea level to afford views of Martinique across the channel, Petit Coulibri offers three two-bedroom cottages and two charming studios, all made of stone and wood. The cottages are of generous size (adequate for a family or two couples) and have full kitchens, but the much-cheaper studios are a better value if you don't need a kitchen; all are beautifully appointed. The Barnards and their staff cook breakfast and dinner on request ($10 and $25 per person, respectively), otherwise there's little but Mother Nature within walking distance (the town of Soufriere is two miles away). The swimming pool and view are idyllic enough to have landed on the cover of *Condé Nast Traveler* in 1997. Praise be to aloe! 5 rooms. Credit cards: A, MC, V.

Picard Beach Cottage Resort $100–$140   ★★

Picard Beach, Portsmouth, ☎ *(800) 223-6510, (767) 445-5131, FAX (767) 445-5599.*
E-mail: picard_beach@tod.dm.
Single: $100–$120. Double: $120–$140.

Set on a former coconut plantation at the foot of Morne Diablotin, these eight simply furnished cottages are designed in 18th-century Dominican style. Surrounded by lush gardens, the rustic, all-wood units are dark, but each has a kitchenette and veranda; ceiling fans help cool things off (four have air conditioning). There's a bar and restaurant, and guests can use the pool at the Portsmouth Beach Hotel (which is now used for medical students) next door, or the decent black-sand beach is at your doorstep. Pleasant, if a little pricey. 8 rooms. Credit cards: A, D, MC, V.

Inns

Papillote Wilderness Retreat is a unique mountain hostelry nestled against a steep hillside brimming with orchid-laced waterfalls. Developed in the late 1960s (before the term "eco-tourism" existed) by Floridian Anne Grey and her Dominican husband Cuthbert Baptiste, the inn helped to shape the hotel industry Dominica has.

Hummingbird Inn $55–$110   ★★

Morne Daniel, ☎ (767) 449-1042, FAX (767) 449-1042.
Single: $55. Double: $65. Suites Per Day: $110–$110.

Located just up the hill from Canefield Airport, this sweet guest house is perched on a cliff and surrounded by all manner of wildlife, including enough hibiscus and wild ginger to keep the hummingbirds and iguanas happy. Rooms are simple but attractive, with hand-woven local quilts for color, and ceiling fans. There's also a honeymoon suite with a four-poster bed, kitchenette and veranda. Road noise can be a little annoying, but the views up the coast are fine. Roseau is two miles away; a fair beach is 10 minutes downhill on foot. 10 rooms. Credit cards: A, D, MC, V.

Papillotte Wilderness Retreat $70–$100   ★★

Trafalgar, ☎ (767) 448-2287, FAX (767) 448-2285.
Website: www.delphis.dm/papillot.htm. E-mail: papillote@tod.dm.
Single: $70–$100. Double: $80–$100.

This small family-owned inn is set right in a lush valley, 1000 feet above sea level and some 20 minutes from Roseau. The location, in a cool rain forest amid hot mineral pools, gardens and waterfalls, can't be beat. Standard rooms are simple and basic and without air conditioning, but individually decorated with local art and pretty weavings; there's also a two-bedroom, two-bath cottage with a kitchen and a private waterfall laced with orchids. Meals are served on an outdoor terrace with lots of fresh fruits and vegetables—the food is delicious (the hotel's meal plan at $30 per day is a good idea). The flit of hummingbirds and butterflies through the gardens, meticulously cared for by Anne Baptiste, will keep you enthralled; a soak in one of the three hot mineral baths is terrific after a long day of hiking. Daytrippers visiting Trafalgar Falls can be a nuisance, and the new hydroelectric facility nearby is unfortunate, but otherwise, this is a very special escape, far removed from the "luxuries" of city life. 8 rooms. Credit cards: A, D, MC, V.

Springfield Plantation $45–$80   ★

Springfield Estate, ☎ (767) 449-1401, FAX (767) 449-2160.
Website: www.tod.dm/DolphinSoft/sceptre. E-mail: Springfield@tod.dm.
Single: $45–$80. Double: $55–$80.

The foundation of this mountain plantation inn dates back to 1840—today it is known as the Springfield Centre for Environmental Protection, Research and Education, and hosts visiting scientists and students (who receive a discount). Located a couple miles up from Canefield Airport at an elevation of 1200 feet, Springfield is sometimes inundated with students, while at other times you might be the only guest—the operation can be inconsistent. Like the wooden structure itself, accommodations have plenty of character, including four-poster beds with mosquito netting, huge wooden armoires and other antiques. There's a protected river pool for splashing about, nature trails for hiking and safari tours, or rub shoulders in the herbarium with the resident scientist. The creaking inn is a bit worn these days, but nature lovers will find plenty to enjoy—those put off by rustic atmosphere will be happier at a more commercial establishment. 11 rooms. Credit cards: A, MC, V.

Low Cost Lodging

Inexpensive guest houses are abundant, though the quality varies considerably. You may be best off beginning your vacation with one of the spots listed above, then switching to a lower priced guest house after you've had a chance to personally inspect it. The island's **National Development Corporation** publishes a free accommodations directory with prices that may help you select the place you want ☎ *(767) 448-2351*. One historic Roseau spot, **Vena's**, was the childhood home of novelist Jean Rhys—rooms are just $25 a night, but somewhat gloomy ☎ *(767) 448-3286*. Another is the **Cherry Lodge**, a rustic six-room hotel downtown that oozes with character for $35 a night ☎ *(767) 448-2366*. Other guest houses are situated in the mountains and valleys well away from Roseau.

Continental Inn   **$30–$70**   ★
Roseau, ☎ (767) 448-2214, FAX (767) 448-7022.
Single: $30–$55. Double: $45–$70.
This hotel in the heart of Roseau has small, air-conditioned rooms, but only some have a private bath. The restaurant serves Creole dishes. Mainly used by regional business travelers and backpackers—sufficient for anyone counting pennies. 11 rooms. Credit cards: A, MC, V.

Where to Eat

Fielding's Highest Rated Restaurants in Dominica

★★★★	La Robe Creole	$11–$26
★★★	Balisier	$15–$30
★★★	Crystal Terrace	$8–$22
★★★	De Bouille	$13–$25
★★★	Papillotte Wilderness Retreat	$12–$19
★★★	Pearl's Cuisine	$13–$17

Fielding's Most Romantic Restaurants in Dominica

♡♡♡	La Robe Creole	$11–$26
♡♡♡	De Bouille	$13–$25
♡♡♡	Papillotte Wilderness Retreat	$12–$19

Fielding's Best Value Restaurants in Dominica

★★★★	La Robe Creole	$11–$26
★★	Orchard Restaurant	$8–$19
★★★	Pearl's Cuisine	$13–$17
★★★	Crystal Terrace	$8–$22

Although the island is sandwiched between Martinique and Guadeloupe, French cuisine has not invaded Dominica, though Creole can be found. Flavors tend to lean toward English (meaning basic and/or bland), and the quantity of budget-minded travelers hasn't pushed the quality upscale. The major exception by all accounts is **La Robe Creole**, where rich soups, stuffed crab backs, and local delicacies tempt diners. Many visitors dine at their hotel more often than not, particularly those staying outside Roseau. A few hotel restaurants are pretty good, particularly **Papillote Wilderness Retreat**, where souk, a local river shrimp, is a tasty treat in season. "In season" is an important concept on Dominica because mountain chicken (the legs of frogs that burrow in the woods), land crabs and freshwater crayfish are to be obtained

September through February only; restaurants serving them out of that period should not be supported.

Balisier $$$ ★★★

Bay Street, Roseau, ☎ *(767) 449-8800.* Associated hotel: *Garraway Hotel.*
Lunch: Noon–2:30 p.m., entrées $15–$28.
Dinner: 6:30–10 p.m., entrées $15–$30.
Located in a modern, five-story hotel on the oceanfront in Roseau, Balisier offers views of the sea from the first floor, serving competently prepared local fish, curries, steaks and lobster newburg. All come with heapings sides of provisions, and the pies are home-baked and tasty. What Balisier lacks in atmosphere it makes up for in professional staff. Credit cards: A, MC, V.

Callaloo Restaurant $ ★★

66 King George V Street, Roseau, ☎ *(767) 448-3386.*
Lunch: 11:30 a.m.– 2:30 p.m., entrées $6–$14.
Dinner: 6:30–10 p.m., entrées $6–$14.
Chefs at Callaloo present home-style cooking on a terrace overlooking downtown Roseau. Like its namesake, the hearty soup made from the omnipresent dasheen (a spinach-like green) is made from scratch daily. There are daily specials, which often include conch prepared in a number of different ways, and crayfish or mountain chicken (when in season).

Castaways Beach Hotel $$ ★★

Mero, ☎ *(767) 449-6244.* Associated hotel: *Castaways Beach Hotel.*
Lunch: Noon–2 p.m., entrées $12–$18.
Dinner: 7–9 p.m., entrées $12–$18.
Dine informally by the ocean at this hotel restaurant popular for good breakfasts, tropical rum punches and the ubiquitous national dish of crapaud, or frog legs. Sometimes there is crab and conch, and although most of the food is freshly prepared, it varies in quality. Credit cards: MC, V.

Coconut Beach $$ ★★

Picard Beach, ☎ *(767) 445-5393.* Associated hotel: *Coconut Beach Hotel.*
Lunch: Noon–2:30 p.m., entrées $10–$15.
Dinner: 6:30–10:30 p.m., entrées $10–$25.
A casual sandwich and seafoodery right on the beach located two miles south of Portsmouth, the Coconut Beach serves as a yacht and boat stop as well as a watering hole for students from the university almost next door. It's also a good place to try rotis, or flatbread rolled around curried meat or vegetables. Credit cards: A, DC, MC, V.

Crystal Terrace $$ ★★★

Castle Comfort, ☎ *(767) 448-3288.* Associated hotel: *Evergreen Hotel.*
Lunch: Noon–2:30 p.m., entrées $8–$22.
Dinner: 7–9 p.m., entrées $8–$22.
One of the island's most convivial spots, the Evergreen Hotel's terrace dining room is open to non-guests for a sunset meal by the shore. The always evolving menu might include a spry house salad of watercress and cucumber, curried conch, entrées of chicken, frogs' legs (in season) and lamb, and always an assortment of local side

DOMINICA

dishes, like green banana pie. The owners, the Winston family, run a tight ship, with generally excellent service. Credit cards: A, MC, V.

De Bouille $$$ ★★★

Victoria Street, Roseau, ☎ *(767) 448-5000.* Associated hotel: *Fort Young Hotel.*
Lunch: Noon–2:30 p.m., entrées $5–$14.
Dinner: 7–10 p.m., entrées $13–$25.

A baronial and stately restaurant serving a varied cuisine, De Bouille is ensconced in an old fort, now one of Roseau's best hotels. Nothing earth-shattering on the menu, but diners can feel history in the stone walls, which add plenty of atmosphere to go along with the pumpkin soup, seafood and steaks served here. A good place to spot local movers and shakers. Credit cards: A, MC, V.

La Robe Creole $$$ ★★★★

3 Victoria Street, Roseau, ☎ *(767) 448-2896.*
Lunch: 11 a.m.–3:30 p.m., entrées $7–$26.
Dinner: 3:30–9:30 p.m., entrées $11–$26. Closed: Sun.

Long regarded as Dominca's best restaurant, the 23-year-old La Robe Creole occupies a cozy, stone- and brick-walled building near the harbor. Named after the native madras costume, it serves a sublime vegetarian callaloo soup with coconut, and tasty creole octopus. There's also Dominican favorites like freshwater shrimp and crayfish or mountain chicken (in season), and tropical fruit and coconut pies— we love the short but potent rum punch. Patrons are prominent Dominicans who come to see and be seen in air-conditioned luxury. Settle in for a wonderful evening. A snackette downstairs, the Mouse Hole, is a good spot for short order sandwiches and roti throughout the day. Reservations recommended. Credit cards: D, MC, V.

Orchard Restaurant $ ★★

31 King George V Street, Roseau, ☎ *(767) 448-3051.*
Lunch: 8 a.m.–3 p.m., entrées $8–$19.
Dinner: 3–10 p.m., entrées $8–$19. Closed: Sun.

Hearty, complete meals for under $20 draw patrons to this informal downtown eatery, which also has a popular bar. Entrees like conch (called lambi here) are served with trimmings, which in this case involve rice, relishes, salads and whatever the chef has on hand. Those wishing to eat lighter can order a la carte sandwiches and soups, or get food to go. No dinner is served on Saturdays. Credit cards: A, MC, V.

Papillotte Wilderness Retreat $$ ★★★

Trafalgar Falls Road, ☎ *(767) 448-2287.* Associated hotel: *Papillote Wilderness Retreat.*
Lunch: Noon–3 p.m., entrées $8–$19.
Dinner: 7–8 p.m., prix fixe $12–$19.

Paradise awaits in this garden of eden near Trafalgar Falls, a haven for nature lovers; amateur botanists will be in seventh heaven. The Retreat's restaurant is now open to nonguests for dinner, and some selections from the small menu, like river shrimp and flying fish, are rarely available elsewhere. Under the eye of den mom Anne Grey Jean-Baptiste, the menu leans to healthy and fresh selections using much of the produce grown locally—there's a barbecue on Wednesday nights. A gushing hot springs pool invites daytrippers for a dip before or after meals. The Rudy Rooster rum punch is awesome. Reservations recommended. Credit cards: A, MC, V.

Pearl's Cuisine   **$$**   ★★★

    50 King George V Street, Roseau, ☎ *(767) 448-8707.*
    Lunch: Noon–5 p.m., entrées $10–$12.
    Dinner: 6:30 p.m. until..., entrées $13–$17.

    A rewarding evening is assured at this downtown establishment run by Pearl Pinard.
    The setting is perfect: a gingerbread-fringed house with a tiny balcony that sits
    above the rustic street. The menu changes nightly, but heaps of tasty local food are
    reliable—baked chicken in creole sauce, grilled fish, T-bone steaks are common
    items, all accompanied by sides of rice, veggies, salad and plantains. Pearl has a way
    with garlic bread, which might be one reason everyone comes here sooner or later.

World of Food   **$$**   ★★

    48 Cork Street, Roseau, ☎ *(767) 448-3286.* Associated hotel: *Vena's Guest House.*
    Lunch: Noon–3 p.m., entrées $9–$22.
    Dinner: 6–10:30 p.m., entrées $9–$22.

    Literary lions will delight in the fact that this restaurant is located at the site of
    author Jean Rhys' birthplace. Owner Vena McDougal has turned it into a patio res-
    taurant that brims with office workers at cocktail hour. Diners can sit under a
    spreading mango tree and partake of local fish cakes, souse (black pudding) or rea-
    sonably priced sandwiches and soups; steaks, rabbit, pork chops and lobster tail
    make up the entree list. Service can be abrupt.

Local arts and crafts will take some effort to uncover, but since most are
found in Roseau, you can usually locate them on foot. Look for the locally
produced after shave and body lotion, Bay Rum, while Macoucherie is the
local drinking rum. **Tropicrafts** on Turkey Lane sells sturdy, hand-woven
grass mats, pottery, and baskets and hats produced by Carib Indians (another outlet is on Bay Street in Plymouth). **Cotton House Batiks** on Kings Lane
designs batik clothing, napkins and wall hangings, while **Artwear Gallery** on
King George V Street sells handpainted T-shirts and other garments. A small
business complex on Great Marlborough Street has additional shops selling
local goods. In Laudat, **Papillote Wilderness Retreat** has a nice gift store selling local arts and crafts.

Dominica Directory

Arrival and Departure

    Dominica cannot be reached directly from the United States, but **American
    Eagle** began serving the island daily from San Juan, Puerto Rico, in 1996, al-
    lowing connecting service from a number of North American departure points

on American and other airlines. Otherwise, the predominant carrier for the island is **LIAT**, which offers nonstop or direct service from Anguilla, Antigua, Guadeloupe, Martinique, St. Lucia and St. Maarten. A Dominica-based outfit, **Cardinal Airlines** provides service from Antigua, Barbados and Sint Maarten ☎ *(767) 449-0322*, and **Air Guadeloupe** provides connections from Martinique and Guadeloupe ☎ *(767) 448-2181*. There are two airports on the island: The larger airstrip is **Melville Hall**, used by American Eagle and LIAT, but it is located on the northeast coast, a one-hour drive from Roseau and most island hotels. For most visitors, **Canefield Airport**, about three miles north of Roseau, is the more convenient entry point, but it is served only by smaller aircraft (including most of the LIAT flights). Scheduled ferry service connects Dominica with Martinique and Guadeloupe: **Caribbean Express** ☎ *(767) 448-2181* and **Madikera** ☎ *(767) 448-6977*.

The departure tax is $8.

Business Hours

Stores open weekdays 8 a.m.–1 p.m. and 2–4 p.m. and Saturday 8 a.m.–1 p.m. Banks open Monday–Thursday 8 a.m.–3 p.m. and Friday 8 a.m.–5 p.m.

Climate

The climate is tropical, though tempered by considerable rain, heaviest July through October. Average temperature is 80 degrees, with little seasonal variation. Rainfall is heavy especially in the mountainous areas, where the annual average is 250 inches compared with 70 inches along the coast.

Documents

Visitors will need a passport, or proof of citizenship in conjunction with a photo ID, as well as a return or ongoing ticket.

Electricity

The current is 220 volts/50 cycles, which means you must have a transformer with the proper adapters. Rechargeable strobes and lights should be charged on the stabilized lines most dive operators have available for his purpose.

Getting Around

Taxis and buses are plentiful, but renting a car is your best way to explore the island. Although most main roads are in good shape, they are narrow, twisting and steep; driving is on the left. There are a number of rental outfits on the island, including two American-based firms, **Avis** and **Budget**. If you are flying in to Melville Hall, the shared taxi to Roseau will be about $16 per person; to Portsmouth, about $12. For now, there are no car rental firms at Melville Hall, though the outfits based in Roseau will usually pick you up if you arrange it in advance. From Canefield Airport, a taxi to Roseau is $8 (up to four passengers); to Papillote, $18; to Portsmouth, $43. Most of the island's bus routes start or end in Plymouth—the main bus station in town is at the West Bridge, near the market. Fares are based on distance; from Roseau to Canefield or Trafalgar is less than a dollar, to Portsmouth is about $3, etc.

Language

English is the official language, but a local French patois, or Creole, is widely spoken.

Medical Emergencies

There are two main hospitals at Roseau and Portsmouth, with 242 and 50 beds, respectively. Serious emergencies require airlift to San Juan.

Money

The official currency is the Eastern Caribbean dollar, which is pegged to American currency at about $2.70 to one U.S. dollar. However, U.S. dollars are accepted virtually everywhere.

Telephone

The new area code for Dominica is *(767)*. To call Dominica from the U.S., dial *1 + (767)* and the seven-digit local number. Calling home from your hotel can be expensive—to save money, call from the Telecommunications of Dominica office in Roseau.

Time

Atlantic standard time, one hour later than New York.

Tipping and Taxes

Hotels collect a 5 percent government tax; restaurants collect a 3 percent sales tax. A 10 percent service charge is added to your bill by most hotels and restaurants. If you feel inclined to leave more for service, do so.

Tourist Information

For more information, write to the **Dominica Tourist Office** *10 East 21st Street, Suite 600, New York, NY 10010,* ☎ *(212) 475-7542*. The island's **Division of Tourism** can be reached through the National Development Corporation: *P.O. Box 293, Roseau, Commonwealth of Dominica* ☎ *(767) 448-2045*. A **Tourist Information Office** is also maintained at the Cruise Ship Berth in Roseau. All mail to the island should be addressed to the "Commonwealth of Dominica" to avoid the common problem of mail being mis-routed to the Dominican Republic.

Web Site

www.dominica.dm

When to Go

Carnival takes place in February, on the Monday and Tuesday preceding Ash Wednesday; street parades, costumes and calypso competitions dominate the festivities, which also feature Lap Kabwit bands (goat skin drums). **Domfesta**—Dominica Festival of the Creative Arts—is a one-week event held in June and celebrating music, dance, drama, fine arts, culture, cuisine and literary arts. Dominica's **Independence Day** is November 3, and a one-week celebration honors the island's history and culture and also features the **World Zouk-Cadence Festival**, which showcases zouk music, the Caribbean beat popularized in the French West Indies.

DOMINICA

DOMINICA HOTELS	RMS	RATES	PHONE	CR. CARDS
★★★ Exotica	8	$132–$161	(800) 544-7631	A, D, MC, V
★★★ Fort Young Hotel	33	$95–$135	(800) 223-6510	A, D, MC, V
★★★ Garraway Hotel	31	$95–$130	(767) 449-8800	A, DC, MC, V
★★★ Petit Coulibri Guest Cottages	5	$115–$225	(767) 446-3150	A, MC, V
★★★ Sutton Place Hotel	8	$75–$135	(800) 544-7631	A, D, MC, V
★★ Anchorage Hotel	32	$65–$110	(800) 223-6510	A, D, DC, MC, V
★★ Castaways Beach Hotel	26	$82–$130	(888) 227-8292	A, MC, V
★★ Evergreen Hotel	16	$78–$118	(767) 448-3288	A, D, DC, MC, V
★★ Hummingbird Inn	10	$55–$65	(767) 449-1042	A, D, MC, V
★★ Lauro Club	10	$73–$140	(767) 449-6602	A, DC, MC, V
★★ Papillotte Wilderness Retreat	8	$70–$100	(767) 448-2287	A, D, MC, V
★★ Picard Beach Cottage Resort	8	$100–$140	(800) 223-6510	A, D, MC, V
★ Coconut Beach Hotel	22	$55–$65	(767) 445-5393	A, D, MC, V
★ Continental Inn	11	$30–$70	(767) 448-2214	A, MC, V
★ Springfield Plantation	11	$45–$80	(767) 449-1401	A, MC, V

DOMINICA RESTAURANTS	PHONE	ENTRÉE	CR. CARDS
Regional Cuisine			
★★★★ La Robe Creole	(767) 448-2896	$7–$26	D, MC, V
★★★ Balisier	(767) 449-8800	$15–$30	A, MC, V
★★★ Crystal Terrace	(767) 448-3288	$8–$22	A, MC, V
★★★ De Bouille	(767) 448-5000	$5–$25	A, MC, V
★★★ Papillotte Wilderness Retreat	(767) 448-2287	$8–$19	A, MC, V
★★★ Pearl's Cuisine	(767) 448-8707	$10–$17	
★★ Callaloo Restaurant	(767) 448-3386	$6–$14	
★★ Castaways Beach Hotel	(767) 449-6244	$12–$18	MC, V
★★ Coconut Beach	(767) 445-5393	$10–$25	A, DC, MC, V
★★ Orchard Restaurant	(767) 448-3051	$8–$19	A, MC, V
★★ World of Food	(767) 448-3286	$9–$22	

DOMINICAN REPUBLIC

The best place to tee off in Santo Domingo is the course at Casa de Campo.

The Dominican Republic isn't for everyone. Poverty is rampant, crime high in the city of Santo Domingo, power blackouts common. But that's just the black lining around this silver cloud of the Caribbean, which brims with history, lush scenery, vibrant people, pulsating nightlife and glorious beaches—all at a fraction of the cost of a typical Caribbean holiday.

The Dominican Republic is the Western Hemisphere's oldest European settlement, the spot where Christopher Columbus first landed upon journeying to the New World. The capital city of Santo Domingo dates back to 1496 and was established by Columbus' brother, after a few disastrous attempts by the more famous sibling at earlier colonization. Though it has had a particularly bloody history, with many revolutions, coups and tyrannical leaders, the nation has been fairly stable since the 1970s, and Americans are warmly welcomed—though tourists should exercise more than the usual caution associated with most of the Caribbean.

Tourism didn't start to come on strong here until after the 1961 assassination of Generalissimo Rafael Leónidas Trujillo, the ruthless dictator who ruled the nation for more than 30 years. But by the mid-1970s, interest in the country as a vacation destination was strong, and today's Dominican Republic attracts some 2 million tourists each year; only about 18 percent are from the U.S.

The Dominican Republic boasts literally thousands of beaches, soaring mountain ranges, fertile valleys, dense jungles and the Caribbean's lowest inland spot—a million-year-old lake the size of Manhattan. This island attracts adventurous outdoors types who revel in the ample opportunities for diving, trekking, deep-sea fishing and boating. At the other extreme, swank resorts lure those who like spending their holiday being pampered and sun-kissed. However, Type As who go ballistic when they encounter problems should probably steer clear. Islanders are laid-back. Even getting a room rate quoted can be a challenge.

BEST BETS FOR...

Bird's-Eye View

Sprawling over two-thirds of the island of Hispaniola (Haiti comprises the rest), the Dominican Republic is located some 800 miles south of Florida and lies between Cuba and Puerto Rico. On the north is the Atlantic Ocean, to the south the Caribbean Sea. The island is much larger than most of its Caribbean counterparts, totaling 48,422 square kilometers, and more geographically diverse. Besides its literally thousands of miles of unspoiled beaches, it has tropical rainforests, dense jungles, mangrove swamps and the Caribbean's highest mountains. National parks comprise more than 10 percent of the island's territory, and more than 5600 species of flora have been identified. Mountain ranges run down the backbone of the country, including Pico Duarte at 10,400 feet, the highest mountain in the Caribbean. At the other extreme, the Dominican Republic also lays claim to the Caribbean's lowest point, a large salt-water lake called Lago Enriquillo, whose 125

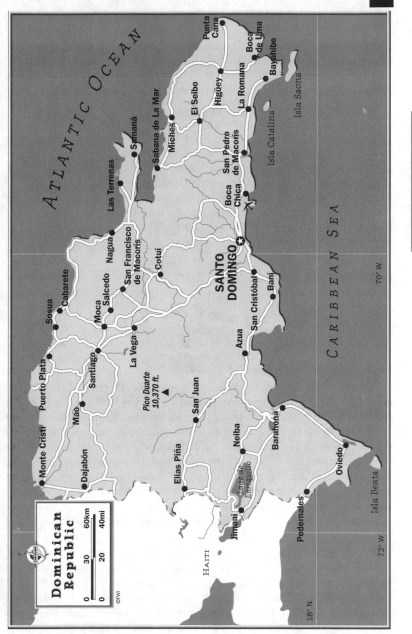

square miles is home to endangered crocodiles, rhinoceros., variegated shell turtles and pink flamingos.

The opening scene of the film *Jurassic Park,* which shows DNA being extracted from an insect trapped in amber, was shot in the Dominican Republic, with good reason, as it is a prime source of the ancient substance. You'll find many samples of the translucent substance in jewelry stores, but fakes are plentiful.

The city of Santo Domingo, home to some two million souls, is the oldest capital in the New World, and history buffs will go crazy inspecting all its treasures in the Zona Colonial (Colonial Zone). Along the north coast, the highway runs closely along the path laid out by Christopher Columbus, winding through fishing villages, cattle farms and sugar plantations. Puerto Plata, where many of the tony resorts hug the coast, is a particular charmer with its gingerbread structures. Tourists also flock to the resort area of Punta Cana on the far eastern end and the 7000-acre resort community of La Romana, east of Santo Domingo.

The average temperature island-wide is 77 degrees Fahrenheit, with August the warmest month and January the coolest, though the difference is only about 10 degrees or so.

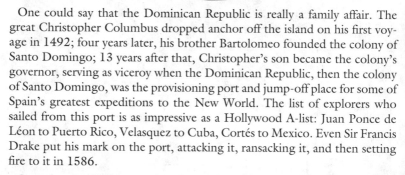

History

One could say that the Dominican Republic is really a family affair. The great Christopher Columbus dropped anchor off the island on his first voyage in 1492; four years later, his brother Bartolomeo founded the colony of Santo Domingo; 13 years after that, Christopher's son became the colony's governor, serving as viceroy when the Dominican Republic, then the colony of Santo Domingo, was the provisioning port and jump-off place for some of Spain's greatest expeditions to the New World. The list of explorers who sailed from this port is as impressive as a Hollywood A-list: Juan Ponce de Léon to Puerto Rico, Velasquez to Cuba, Cortés to Mexico. Even Sir Francis Drake put his mark on the port, attacking it, ransacking it, and then setting fire to it in 1586.

Over the next 300 years, the island changed hands among France, Spain and Cuba, and for a time it was even self-ruled in a phase called "Ephemeral Independence." Since winning its independence from Spain in 1821 and from Haiti in 1844, the Dominican Republic has been plagued by recurrent domestic conflicts and foreign intervention; between 1916 and 1924 it was occupied by U.S. forces. In 1930 the country entered into a 30-year dictatorship led by General Rafael Leónidas Trujillo Molina, who ruled personally until 1947 and indirectly thereafter until his assassination in 1961. His death gave rise to renewed political turmoil, and an election in December 1962 led to the inauguration of Juan Bosch Gaviño, a left-of-center democrat, as president in February 1963. In the same year, Bosch was overthrown by a military coup; subsequently the military installed a civilian triumvirate that ruled until April 1965, when civil war erupted. Military forces intervened on April 28, 1965, and imposed a truce while arrangements were made to establish a provisional government and prepare for elections. For the next 12 years the country was run by a moderate, Dr. Joaquin Balaguer, who returned after one term for another two consecutive ones. Presently there are at least 10 political parties representing diverse ideological viewpoints, including the Social Christian Reformed Party of 80-year-old Dr. Balaguer to the Dominican Revolutionary Party, a left-democratic grouping, to the right-wing Quisqueyan Democratic Party, the Dominican Communist Party (a traditionally pro-Moscow party), and the Dominican Popular Movement, which is pro-Peking. The current president is Leonel Fernandez, who is pro-tourism and has unveiled an aggressive plan to increase hotel rooms to 80,000 over the next 15 years.

People

The population of the Dominican Republic is a hefty 9 million. Spanish is the official language, but at the major tourist areas you'll find English, French and even German speakers as well. Dominicans are polite and friendly and have a great passion for music and dancing, particularly the merengue. Islanders are informally broken into four categories: *blanco* (white), *indio claro* (mixed white and black), *indio oscuro* (black, but not 100 percent so) and *negro* (100 percent black). The island's chaotic history and sometimes-corrupt political structure leads to occasional violent strikes and demonstrations. Because the country has so much poverty, crime is prevalent, and tourists should be extremely cautious—never leave cameras unattended at the beach, for instance, and hold tight to your wallet or purse when walking about. Pickpockets are desperate and brazen, often not backing off even when confronted face-to-face. Some 80 percent of Dominicans are Roman Catholic, with a small minority of Jewish and Protestant communities. Despite their often hard lives, locals are a wonderfully friendly bunch—virtually everyone smiles and is quite outgoing. Americans will be surprised to find that many Dominicans know a lot about the United States—be prepared for impromptu conversations and lots of questions.

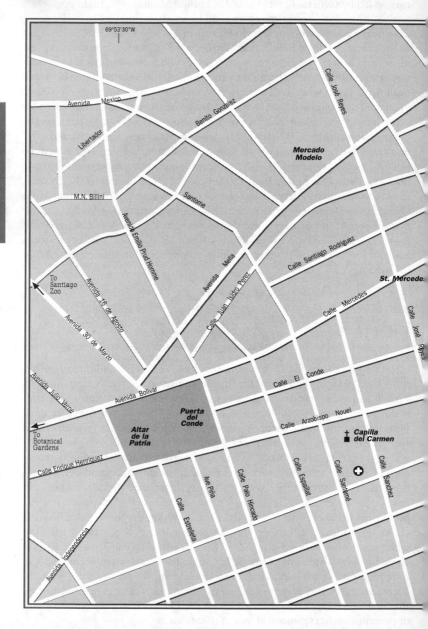

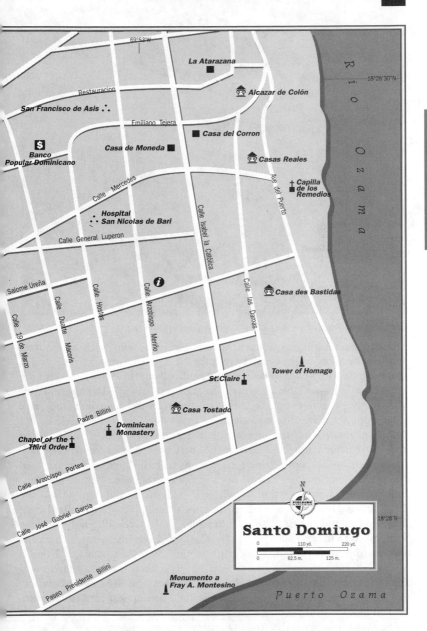

69°53'W

La Atarazana

18°28'30"N

Restauracion

Alcazar de Colón

San Francisco de Asis

Emiliano Tejera

Casa del Corron

Casa de Moneda

Casas Reales

Banco
Popular Dominicano

Calle Mercedes

Capilla
de los
Remedios

Ave del Puerto

Hospital
San Nicolas de Bari

Calle General Luperon

Calle Isabel la Católica

Salome Ureña

Calle las Damas

Casa des Bastidas

Calle 19 de Marzo

Calle Duarte

Calle Hostds

Calle Maconis

Calle Arzobispo Merino

Tower of Homage

St. Claire

Casa Tostado

Padre Billini

Dominican
Monastery

Chapel of the
Third Order

Calle Arzobispo Portes

Calle José Gabriel Garcia

N

Santo Domingo

| 0 | 110 yd. | 220 yd. |
| 0 | 62.5 m. | 125 m. |

18°28'N

Paseo Presidente Billini

Monumento a
Fray A. Montesino

Puerto Ozama

Rio Ozama

Beaches

The Dominican Republic is known for its beautiful beaches.

A whopping 1000 miles of beaches await visitors, who often have a hard time just deciding which beach to pick for the day. Unfortunately, the beach closest to the city—**Boca Chica** (about 21 miles from the capital)—is also the most crowded, a veritable zoo on the weekends as locals and tourists alike invade the vanilla-white strands. In the past five years the fine white sands have gone from nearly deserted to a clutter of pizza huts, plastic beach tables and lounge chairs, and rental cottages full of screaming babies. The one thing that has remained protected here are the coral reefs, which serve to keep dangerous marine life from getting too close. As such, feel free to walk out in to the sea. Twenty minutes east of Boca Chica is **Juan Dolio**, with its powdery white beach. Here you'll find the Villas del Mar Hotel and the Punta Garza Beach Club. Other excellent beaches are the thumbprint-sized **Minitas** beach and lagoon, and the palm-fringed **Bayahibe**, only accessible by boat. This area, called **La Romana**, also houses the Casa de Campo Resort, which means it is usually crowded. The island's pride and joy is **Punta Cana**, a 20-mile sprawl (though it seems longer for its beauty), lined with shady trees and 300,000 coconut palms. Here is located **Club Med**, the **Melia Punta Cara** and the **Bavaro Beach Resort**. Primitive is the only description for **Las Terrenas**, tucked into the north coast of the Samaná peninsula. You'll be hard-pressed to find anything here other than tall palms, sea, mountains and sand. **Sosúa**

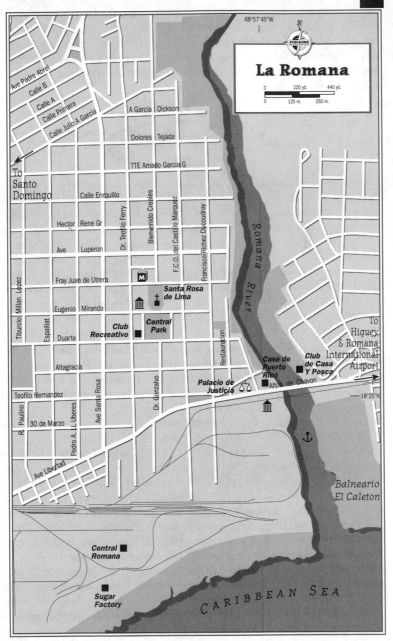

could be pleasant since the waves are gentle and the sand white and soft, but the scene is marred by camping tents and hawkers selling cheap trinkets. The beach of the future is **Puerto Plata**, on the north Amber Coast, where there are excellent reefs for snorkeling and the horizon hasn't yet been marred by civilization. Windsurfers and water-skiers particularly love the conditions, and many fishing expeditions take off from here.

Diving in the Dominican Republic is an activity undergoing a slow evolution. There have always been a number of good diving possibilities off the island's extensive coastline. Unfortunately, with few exceptions, the island's fish population is substantially depleted, even in the so-called marine parks which have been set up to counteract the shortage of fish life. Extensive spear fishing has also hurt the reefs themselves along the coastline; they are battered and trashed within swimming distance from many shores. Most of the coral off **Barahona** is dead; even the reefs ringing remote **Monte Cristi** are said to be largely destroyed. Artificial wrecks (see below) are slowly helping to boost the marine creatures, but the entire island, sadly, will never be the first-class dive destination it might have been a few decades ago.

Some of the island's best diving lies off the **Pedernales Coast**, near the southern border with Haiti, but access to this part of the island is through a distant, forbidding frontier, requiring a sort of mini-expedition to reach. The seclusion is the key to its beauty and serious dive visitors will want to inquire about a multi-day trip. A number of the Dominican Republic's better sites are located off the South Coast at **Boca Chica**, where two small islands within **La Caleta Marine Park**, provide some diversion. Visibility is limited, by Caribbean standards, to an average of 50 to 60 feet, though it can hit 75 feet on good days. There is a wall (15 to 100 feet) and reef on the north side of **Catalina Island**, an outpost just off the coast from Romana—"real Caribbean-style diving," says one local diver—but plans for a cruise ship pier may wreck havoc. Farther east, at **Bayahibe**, a small fishing village approaching tourism with a cautious eye, there is also good diving. At the eastern tip of the island, off **Punta Cana**, where the Atlantic Ocean and Caribbean Sea meet; there are nice reefs and several interesting wrecks, but dive shops are based only out of the all-inclusive resorts for now. At **Las Terrenas**, on the Samana Peninsula, dive shops have started springing up, but visibility here can be hampered by freshwater runoff from the lush forests. Those who enjoy wrecks can be occupied by several sites. Among the major finds are two 17th-century Spanish galleons, the ***Tolosa*** and the ***Guadeloupe***, both located near the entrance to

Samana Bay. La Caleta Marine Park has two artificial reefs for diving; the wreck of the 140-foot steel-hulled *Hickory* sits on a slope which drops to 60 feet, while the wooden 90-foot patrol boat *Capitan Alcina* is wedged in a canyon, 126 feet down. The north coast reefs off Monte Cristi, near the Haitian border, are a graveyard for a number of pirate ships, although the wooden hulls are long gone.

Outside the major resorts, Dominican dive shops have mixed reputations and tend to change hands with alarming frequency. Although most of the Dominican Republic's visitors are European, the outfit listed below caters to Americans. It's also possible to contact the major coastal resorts and arrange a day or two of diving with them. There is a recompression chamber located in Santo Domingo.

Dive Shops

Treasure Divers

> Boca Chica; ☎ *(809) 523-5320; FAX (809) 523-4819.*
> Walter and Peter Horst are the German owners of this seven-year-old PADI and CMAS facility, offering courses to assistant instructor. Single-tank dive, $40 including all equipment (or $37 if you bring your own); packages also available. Night dives, $55. Resort course (in pool), $75. Arranges multi-day trips to the Pedernales coastline off Cabo Rojo, as well as whale-watching ($1000 for a week) January–April.

On Foot

Supporting one of the most diverse eco-systems in the Caribbean basin, the Dominican Republic is an explorer's paradise. Cresting at a majestic 10,370 feet, **Pico Duarte** represents the highest point in the Caribbean basin, high enough to attract a delicate mantle of snow a few times each winter. Physically, the island's major summits—almost a dozen rising higher than 8000 feet—do not look anything like the craggy Sierras or Rockies, but actually more resemble the gentle terrain found in the Adirondacks of New York. The country features 5500 species of flowering plants and ferns. The **Armando Bermudez National Park**, which encompasses most of the island's highest points, is a prime destination for visitors inclined toward outdoor activities.

The Cordillera Central, the island's highest mountain range, slices through the island's interior from the northwest toward the capital. This beautiful range contains the Caribbean's highest peak, Pico Duarte (10,420 ft.). Lower mountains are covered with majestic royal palms. Constanza and Jarabacoa, towns in the lower hillsides, are popular escapes for those seeking cooler weather. The area also boasts magnificent waterfalls.

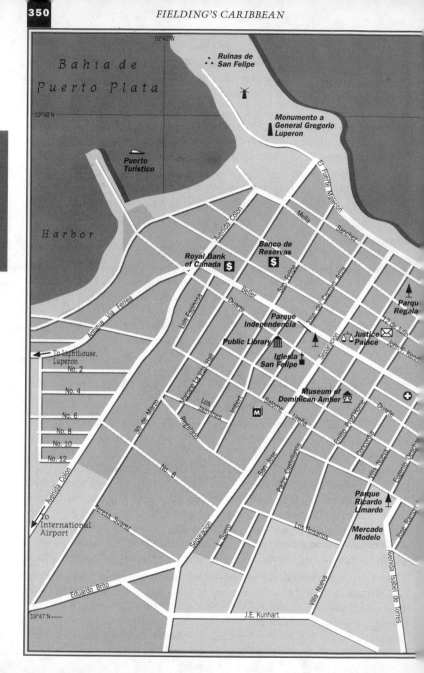

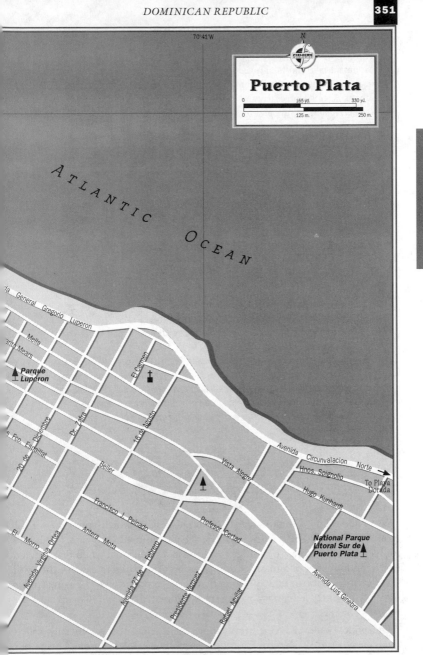

Puerto Plata

ATLANTIC OCEAN

70°41'W

N

0   165 yd.   330 yd.
0   125 m.   250 m.

la   General   Gregorio   Luperon

Melta

arita Mears

Parque
Luperon

El Carmen

s. Fco. Espaillat

20 de Diciembre

Dr. Zafra

16 de Agosto

Beller

Vista Alegre

Avenida   Circunvalacion   Norte

Hnos. Spignolio

Hugo Kunhardt

To Playa
Dorada

Francisco J. Peinado

Profesor Certad

El   Morro

Avenida Virgina Ortea

Antera Mota

Avenida 27 de   Febrero

Presidente Vazquez

Rafael Aguilar

National Parque
Litoral Sur de
Puerto Plata

Avenida Luis Ginebra

Bike Rental Shops

Iguana Mama

Cabarete; ☎ *(800) 849-4720; (809) 571-0908; FAX (809) 571-0734.*

Mountain bike and hiking venture shop run by an enthusiastic American woman determined to make the Dominican Republic the mountain bike capital of the Caribbean. Also assembles day and overnight adventure tours that combine elements of cycling, hiking, rafting and more. The outfit is an excellent resource on nonresort exploration.

FIELDING'S CHOICE:

From January to late February, whales can be seen at the mouth of the Samaná Bay. There are organized excursions, AND local boatmen will arrange trips, though permission must be obtained from the Naval Station in advance. From late December to early March, 3000 migrating humpback whales come to mate in Silver Bank, a marine sanctuary located 50 miles off the coast, directly north of Cabrera. Occasional expeditions by scientists are taken to the site, which run about 7–12 hours. To join an expedition, contact the National Parks Office in Santo Domingo.

BEST VIEW:

The panoramic sweep of the island, seen from the top of the Pico Duarte mountain, is spectacular. At almost 11,000 feet, it's a climb only the truly fit should attempt. It's best to go with a guide. Beginning in late fall 1994, Eco-turisa, in partnership with Occidental Hotels, began offering five-day packages, blankets, flashlights, guides, mules and meals. Part of the climb is covered on muleback, the rest on foot. During December and January, frost glazes the tropical landscape and intensifies the grandeur of the view.

What Else to See

Santo Domingo's **Zona Colonial** (Colonial Zone), which sprawls over 12 blocks, is a must. The narrow cobbled streets, jammed with cars, locals and tourists alike, wind past buildings that look just as they did when first erected nearly 500 years ago, and an ongoing restoration program assures they will stay historically accurate. It's odd and exciting to walk down the same streets traveled by such legendary explorers as Ponce de Leon, Cortés and Sir Frances Drake.

The wide boulevard that runs along the oceanfront is officially called Avenida George Washington, though locals call it **The Malecon**. This is the place to be during the annual carnival, when a frantic mass of merengue dancers will have even the most inhibited tourist swinging along.

Along the north coast are the world's richest deposits of amber and a fast-growing tourist region called **Puerto Plata**. The area's Fort of San Felipe heralds back to 1540.

The city of Sousa, also in the north, was built in 1939 as a model community by European Jewish refugees fleeing the impending Holocaust. (Dominicans are justifiably proud of the fact that they welcomed Jewish refugees with open arms during World War II.) Pedro Clisante, its main street, has a humble synagogue and a newer museum that chronicles the settlement.

Traveling east from Santo Domingo, you'll encounter **Les Tres Ojos de Agua** (the Three Eyes of Water), a huge open cave that contains three translucent, spring-fed lagoons. This luscious area, called the **Costa Sur**, is home to the luxurious resort of **Casa de Campo**, and, further east, **Altos de Chavon**, which houses an exact reproduction of a 15th-century Spanish village, a good spot to pick up locally crafted works of art.

Rent a car to visit the Dominican Republic's central region, where verdant valleys, towering mountains and fields of tobacco and sugarcane conjure up images not usually associated with the Caribbean. The town of **Santiago** is considered the birthplace of merengue music and is a good place to learn of the island's centuries-old traditions.

Finally, you won't want to miss **Lago Enriquillo**, the lowest inland point in all the Caribbean. This 125-square-mile lake, which sits some 130 feet below sea level, has brackish waters and an island that's usually off-limits to all but scientists. Access to this ecologically sensitive area is limited, so join one of the occasionally offered photo safaris for a glimpse of the world's largest surviving population of American crocodiles and endangered rhinoceros iguana and variegated-shell turtles. Birders may add pink flamingoes, herons, ibis, parrots and spoonbills to their lists.

Historical Sites

Alcazar de Colon ★★★

Calle Las Damas, Santo Domingo, ☎ *(809) 687-5361.*
Hours open: 9 a.m.–5 p.m.

Situated on the bluffs of the Ozama River, this castle belonged to Don Diego Colon, Christopher Columbus' son, who was the colony's governor in 1509. Built in 1514 and reconstructed, after years of neglect, in 1957, the 22-room house has 40-inch-thick limestone walls and 22 rooms filled with 16th-century antiques. General admission: $1.

Capilla de los Remedios ★★★★

Calle Las Damas, Santo Domingo.
Hours open: 9 a.m.–6 p.m.

The Chapel of Our Lady of Remedies was built in the 17th century in the Castilian-Romanesque style. Sunday masses begin at 6 a.m.

Cathedral Santa Maria la Menor ★★★

Calle Arzobispo Merino, Santo Domingo.
Hours open: 9 a.m.–4 p.m.

This is the first cathedral built in the Americas, begun in 1514 and completed three decades later. The Spanish Renaissance-style building has a gold coral limestone facade and houses an impressive art collection and a high altar of beaten silver. Sunday masses begin at 6 a.m.

El Faro a Colon ★★★★

Av Espana, Santo Domingo.
Hours open: 9 a.m.–4 p.m.

The Columbus Memorial Lighthouse was completed in 1992 to celebrate the 500th anniversary of his "discovery" of the Dominican Republic. The impressive pyramid shaped monument houses six museums on the explorer and the early days of the New World. It also reportedly contains the remains of Columbus. Several institutions around the world make similar claims. At night, the monument projects a huge cross on the clouds above that can be seen as far away as Puerto Rico.

Fort San Felipe ★★★

Puerto Plata

This, the oldest fort in the New World, dates back to 1564. You can explore its small rooms and eight-inch-thick walls and be glad you weren't a prisoner here during Trujillo's rule. Lots of sidewalk vendors lend a tawdry air. General admission: $1.

National Pantheon ★★★

Calle Las Damas, Santo Domingo.
Hours open: 10 a.m.–5 p.m.

This Spanish-American colonial-style building dates back to 1714 and was once a Jesuit monastery. A mural of Trujillo's assassination is on the ceiling above the altar, and the ashes of martyrs who tried to oust him in 1959 are preserved here.

Santa Barbara Church ★★★★

Av Mella, Santo Domingo.
Hours open: 8 a.m.–midnight

This combination church and fortress, unique to the city, was built in 1562 and is worth a gander if you're in the neighborhood. Sunday masses begin at 6 a.m.

Torre del Homenaje ★★★

Paseo Presidente Belini, Santo Domingo.
Hours open: 8 a.m.–7 p.m.

The Tower of Homage in Fort Ozama was built in 1503, and was the place where condemned prisoners awaited execution. General admission: $1.

Museums and Exhibits

Museo de la Familia Dominicana ★★★★

Calle Padre Bellini, Santo Domingo, ☎ *(809) 689-5057.*
See how wealthy Dominicans lived during the 19th century. General admission: $1.

Museo de las Casas Reales ★★★

Calle Las Damas Esq. Mercedes, Ciudad Colonial Santo Domingo, ☎ *(809) 682-4202.*
Hours open: 9 a.m.–6 p.m.
Two 16th-century palaces house the Museum of the Royal Houses, which spotlights Dominican history from 1492–1821. Exhibits include antiques and artwork, Indian artifacts, relics from two galleons sunk in 1724, pre-Columbian artwork, and replicas of Columbus' ships. General admission: $2.

Museum of Dominican Amber ★★★

Calle Duante 61, Puerto Plata, ☎ *(809) 586-3910.*
Hours open: 9 a.m.–6 p.m.
A beautiful mansion houses exhibits on amber, the country's national stone. You can buy amber pieces and jewelry at the giftshop. Guided tours are conducted in English daily. General admission: $2.

Plaza de la Cultura ★★

Av Maximo Gomez, Santo Domingo.
This large, modern complex includes a theater, the national library and museums of Dominican man, natural history and modern art—each well worth a look. Guided tours of the complex are offered in English on Tuesday and Saturday afternoons at 2:30 p.m.

Parks and Gardens

Jardin Botanico Nacional ★★★

Altos de Gala, Santo Domingo.
Hours open: 10 a.m.–6 p.m.
The largest botanical garden in the entire Caribbean, with 445 acres of orchids, Japanese plants and trees, colorful flowers and 200 varieties of palms, was established in 1976 to honor Dr. Rafael M. Moscoso, the first to catalog the island's flora. You can tour it via foot, boat, train or horse-drawn carriage. General admission: $0.

Los Haitises National Park ★★

Samana, Santo Domingo.
A natural rainforest, pristine and primitive, with mangrove swamps, lakes and caves with Indian petroglyphs.

Tours

Acuario Nacional ★★★

Av de las Americas, Santo Domingo.
Hours open: 10 a.m.–6 p.m.
The Caribbean's largest aquarium park, established in 1990, emphasizes scientific and educational programs with exhibits on the main species of the salt and fresh water flora and fauna of the island. It is surrounded by gardens. General admission: $1.

Parque Zoologico Nacional ★★★

Av Arroyo Salado, Santo Domingo, ☎ *(809) 562-3149.*
Hours open: 9:30 a.m.–6 p.m.
Lions, tigers, hippos and antelopes roam in relative freedom at this 320-acre national zoo overlooking the Isabela River on the north. Opened in 1975, it also

features an aquatic bird lake, a pond teeming with crocodiles, a snake pit and a large aviary. General admission: $2.

The country has a national passion for baseball; in fact, Dominican Republicans outnumber all other Latin American nations with the most players on North American Major League teams. Most U.S ballclubs have academies or camps in the Dominican Republic, with games played at Quisqueya Stadium in Santo Domingo and other stadiums in Santiago, San Pedro de Macoris and La Romana. The professional season runs from October to the end of January; if you're on island then, inquire at your hotel about a schedule. Other spectator sports include professional basketball from June though late August, and boxing, both at Palacio de los Deportes. Horse and dog racing are popular, and, unfortunately, the cruel "sport" of cock fighting.

All the typical watersports associated with the Caribbean can be enjoyed in the Dominican Republic; your hotel can usually arrange all equipment rentals right on site. If your hotel lacks a watersports center, you're usually welcome at a large resort, for a fee of course. Scuba diving and snorkeling are good, as is fishing in the deep sea for marlin and wahoo. Tennis players will have no problem finding courts at virtually every hotel and resort. Windsurfing is good year round, but especially from June to October at **Cabarete Beach**, with wind speeds of 20–25 knots and three- to 15-foot waves.

Golf

The best place to tee off is at one of the two public championship courses, designed by Pete Dye, at **Casa de Campo** (☎ *523-3333 ext. 8115* to reserve or *ext. 3187* for the pro shop) in La Romana: greens fee at Links is $85 ($60 after 2:30 p.m.) and $135 at Diente de Perro ("Teeth of the Dog"). Hours are 7:30 a.m. to 5:30 p.m. In Puerto Plata, the Robert Trent Jones, Jr.-designed Playa Dorada offers a challenge. Santo Domingo's only course is private, but if you're staying at one of the better hotels, they can arrange to get you in on weekdays.

Watersports

Your hotel will probably offer all you need in the way of aqua activity, and you would be wise to follow management's suggestions about reliable operators. Make certain times of pick-up and return are crystal clear—-and then be prepared to run behind schedule. The best deep sea fishing is found off the northwest coast of the island at Cabeza de Toro, Boca de Yuma and Montecristi. Snorkelers will find good spots at Cabo Rojo in Pedernales, Bahia Escocesa, and Samana Bay.

Where to Stay

Fielding's Highest Rated Hotels in Dominican Republic

★★★★★	Casa de Campo	$180–$240
★★★★	Renaissance Jaragua Hotel and Casino	$150–$220
★★★★	Barcelo Bavaro Beach Resort	$120–$220
★★★★	Capella Beach Resort	$135–$380
★★★★	Dominican Fiesta Hotel	$100–$200
★★★★	Dorado Naco Suite Resort	$80–$145
★★★★	El Embajador Hotel	$105–$115
★★★★	Hotel Santo Domingo	$125–$150
★★★★	Melia Bavaro Resort	$77–$179
★★★★	Sheraton Santo Domingo	$125–$155

Fielding's Best Bets to Keep You Busy in Dominican Republic

★★★★★	Casa de Campo	$180–$240
★★★★	Melia Bavaro Resort	$77–$179
★★★	Punta Cana Beach Resort	$105–$200
★★★	Club Med Punta Cana	$110–$230
★★★	Allegro's Jack Tar Village Puerto Plata	$120–$235

Fielding's Best Value Hotels in Dominican Republic

★★	Hotel Sosua	$35–$65
★★★★	El Embajador Hotel	$105–$115
★★★★	Dorado Naco Suite Resort	$80–$145
★★★★	Sheraton Santo Domingo	$125–$155
★★★	Hotel Gran Bahia	$100–$200

The Dominican Republic has more rooms than any other destination in the Caribbean, with some 33,000 rooms scattered around the island, as well as the lowest room price. Luxury resorts, virtually all situated on fine, sprawling beaches, are centered around Punta Cana on the east coast, Puerto Plata on the far north coast, and Playa Juan Dollio, Boca Chica and La Romana on the south coast. Those into a vibrant city life and lots of history should consider a stay in the capital city of Santo Domingo, which has several fine European-style hotels. One drawback to a Dominican vacation: Few restaurants are usually within walking distance from the large hotels, so you're better off signing up for a full meal plan at your property.

Hotels and Resorts

The trend among resorts on the Dominican Republic is toward the all-inclusive program. Always check your contract to make sure what your particular program includes, but most include all meals and sports activities. The hotels in Santo Domingo, at least 30 minutes by car from any acceptable beach for swimming, often provide excellent views of the sea. (In contrast, hotels in Playa Dorado that are not situated on a beach offer a shuttle bus service that takes you to a suitable strand.) Among the top hotels in Santo Domingo are the **Ramada Renaissance Jaragua** resort, with its splashy Vegas-type casino, luxurious bedrooms and bathrooms that belong on a Hollywood set. **Barcelo Gran Hotel Lina** is known island-wide for its excellent restaurant and the nearby casino, which can be exciting if you pick the right day (depends on the traffic). Hotel Santo Domingo retains both the elegance and the tropical feel of the island, and its views of the sea from many of the rooms are stellar.

Puerto Plata

Caribbean Village Club on the Green   **$120–$330**   ★★
☎ *(800) 858-2258, (809) 320-1101, FAX (809) 320-5386.*
E-mail: EVASQUEZ@cvclongr.allegroresort.com.
Single: $120. Double: $190–$330.
What is it with swim-up bars? Does anyone really use them? In any event, you'll find another one at this all-inclusive resort with accommodations in two-story buildings in a landscaped garden setting. The health club is excellent, and there are 18 holes of golf and seven tennis courts for the active set. Guests can choose from three restaurants, and there's nightly entertainment. The beach is a good 10-minute walk, or you can catch the free shuttle. 336 rooms. Credit cards: A, MC, V.

Flamenco Beach Resort   **$120–$150**   ★★
☎ *(800) 545-8089, (809) 320-5084, FAX (809) 320-6319.*
Single: $120. Double: $120–$150.
Spanish-style in appearance, this resort is on a nice beach and has lushly landscaped grounds. Accommodations, scattered about the property, are spacious and nicely decorated. All the standard diversions, including two pools and tennis courts, watersports and daily entertainment. Not bad. 582 rooms. Credit cards: A, DC, MC.

Heavens   **$95–$155**   ★★
☎ *(800) 835-7697, (809) 321-5250, FAX (809) 320-4733.*
Single: $95–$135. Double: $95–$135. Suites Per Day: $115–$155.
This resort has a casual environment and tons of activities to keep guests busy. Rooms are pleasant and all have air conditioning, but the ones closest to the disco—

which hops—can be noisy. You can choose to eat at a few restaurants, and for an added fee, dine at its upscale Italian restaurant. 150 rooms. Credit cards: A, MC, V.

Playa Dorada Hotel $95–$155 ★★

Puerto Plata, ☎ *(800) 545-8089, (809) 320-3988, FAX (809) 320-1190.*
Single: $95–$155. Double: $95–$155.
This contemporary beach resort, located two minutes out of town, has nice accommodations, most with balconies. Like many of the other properties in the area, the pool has a swim-up bar, and there are three tennis courts for working up a sweat. Watersports and 18 holes of golf complete the scene. 254 rooms. Credit cards: MC, V.

Villas Doradas Beach $95–$270 ★★★

☎ *(800) 545-8089/(800) 424-5192, (809) 320-3000, FAX (809) 320-4790.*
Single: $95–$185. Double: $190–$270.
Situated in a lush tropical setting, all accommodations at this resort are a short walk to the semi-private beach, which provides plenty of shade and has 24-hour security. The first hour of horseback riding and golf are free; after that you pay extra. An inviting spot. 207 rooms. Credit cards: A, MC, V.

Punta Cana

Barcelo Bavaro Beach Resort $120–$220 ★★★★

Punta Cana, ☎ *(305) 374-0045, (809) 686-5797, FAX (809) 686-5859.*
E-mail: bavaro@codetel.net.do.
Single: $120–$220. Double: $120–$220.
Located on Bavaro Beach at the northern end of the 20 mile long beach at Punta Cana, this sprawling resort consists of five low-rise hotels. Accommodations vary from standard guest rooms to apartments; all are air-conditioned and pleasant. The facilities are varied and ample, with a mind-boggling 14 restaurants; 18 bars; discos featuring international, merengue and salsa; live entertainment; 18 holes of golf; nine tennis courts; horseback riding; watersports and organized tours. Supervised programs keep kids just as active. Tight security, too. A fun and busy complex. 1955 rooms. Credit cards: A, MC, V.

Hotel Riu Taino $77–$305 ★★★★

Punta Cana, ☎ *(809) 221-2290, FAX (809) 686-5917.*
Single: $77–$117. Double: $77–$117. Suites Per Day: $305.
Sitting right on a lovely beach, this hotel has pretty tropical gardens surrounding Dominican-style, white two-story bungalows with pleasant, air-conditioned rooms. The usual pool, tennis courts and watersports are on hand; those looking to dance head to sister property Riu Naiboa's disco next door. If you're torn between the two, choose this one—it's nicer all around. 360 rooms. Credit cards: A, DC, MC, V.

Hotel Riu Naiboa $101–$277 ★★★

☎ *(809) 221-7515, FAX (809) 686-6077.*
Single: $101–$277. Double: $101–$277.
It's a five-minute walk to the beach—no big deal, but all the other hotels in the area are right on the sand. This newer (1992) property has pretty guest rooms done up in pink and gray. The lagoon-style pool has a sandy area for those who don't feel like hoofing it to the real thing. There's also tennis and a disco, and lots of activities for children, making this primarily a family resort. 372 rooms. Credit cards: A, DC, MC, V.

Melia Bavaro Resort   **$77–$179**   ★★★★

☎ *(800) 336-3542, (809) 221-2311, FAX (809) 686-5427.*
Website: www.solmelia.es.
Associated Restaurant: *Chopin Restaurant.*
Single: $77–$179. Double: $77–$179.

Built in 1992 on 96 beachfront acres, this smashing, all-suite resort is the only one in the Dominican Republic to receive an official title of "Ecological Hotel." It houses guests in split-level suites with high-quality furnishings and impressive touches or in bungalows with kitchenettes and platform beds. Fountains and ponds dot the grounds, and some 50 species of tropical birds and peacocks roam freely around the palms and mangrove forests. A shuttle takes guests back and forth to the beach, where two large, free-form pools await those who don't want to get sandy. Seven restaurants, fully equipped health, spa and fitness center with two saunas, two Jacuzzis and massage, four tennis courts, mini-zoo, horseback riding and water sports center with diving, snorkeling, deep-sea fishing, sailing, jet-skis, banana boats, sea bikes, windsurfing and kayaks more than keep guests entertained. The beach stays crowded even during the off-season. Full-day and night entertainment program for children. 766 rooms. Credit cards: A, DC, MC, V.

Punta Cana Beach Resort   **$75–$280**   ★★★

☎ *(800) 972-2139, (809) 221-2262, FAX (809) 687-8745.*
E-mail: puntacanabr@codetel.net.do.
Associated Restaurant: *Mamma Venezia/La Cana.*
Single: $75–$165. Double: $100–$280.

Situated on a white sandy beach a few miles from Punta Cana's international airport, this palm-shaded, pale pink and turquoise low-rise resort manages to bridge the gap between the mega-resorts that dominate and the hideaway for which you hope. A nature reserve of 1555 acres of virgin forests lies next door. Management sponsors nature walks through the forest, which will delight birders. Lagoons and a tropical fruit garden delight the senses. The fronds of the cana palm, indigenous to this island, were used in the roof of the beachside, open-air restaurant. Ocean-view rooms directly on the beach have queen-sized beds. All rooms are air conditioned with balconies or terraces. The mood here is relaxed and casual despite the many activities from which to choose. Four restaurants, a pizzeria, two bars, live music and a disco keep most guests on the property. Horseback riding, scuba and night tennis require additional charges. 400 rooms. Credit cards: A, DC, MC, V.

Santo Domingo

Barcelo Gran Hotel Lina & Casino   **$105–$173**   ★★★

☎ *(800) 942-2461, (809) 563-5000, FAX (809) 682-2801.*
Single: $105–$110. Double: $110–$150. Suites Per Day: $173–$173.

This Spanish-style downtown highrise steps from the Colonial Zone in downtown Santo Domingo, is stylish, though guest rooms are disappointingly basic and only some have terraces. The public spaces are grand, though, with lots of colorful modern art and elegant touches. The gym is well equipped, and the hotel also has a large pool, sauna, masseuse, hairdresser, boutiques, a casino and several restaurants and bars, including the elegant Restaurante Lina. It is frequented by both tourists and business travelers. The latter often prefer the Executive Floor, where you get private check-in, continental breakfast, tea and tropical fruit, and concierge service. Guest rooms have cable TV, minibar, direct dial telephone and safety deposit box. 217 rooms. Credit cards: A, DC, MC, V.

Casa de Campo $180–$240 ★★★★★

La Romana-Bayahibe, ☎ *(800) 856-5971, (809) 523-3333, FAX (809) 523-8548.*
Website: www.ccampo.com.do.
Single: $180–$240. Double: $180–$240.
A true mega-resort set on 7000 acres, a two-hour drive east of Santo Domingo, this amazing place represents the country's best resort—in fact, it's one of the best in the entire Caribbean. The resort is essentially its own town—you can even fly directly into its own airstrip—with 16 bars and nine restaurants, seven pools, polo, 13 tennis courts, 36 holes of golf and beaches. *Golf* magazine ranks the resorts "Teeth of the Dog" course as one of the world's best. The accommodations, designed by Oscar de la Renta, are in two-story villas with plush furnishings and kitchenettes. You'll hate to leave. 750 rooms. Credit cards: A, MC, V.

Dominican Fiesta Hotel $100–$400 ★★★★

☎ *(800) 782-1340, (809) 562-8222, FAX (809) 562-8938.*
Single: $100–$200. Double: $110–$200. Suites Per Day: $250–$400.
Located opposite Paseo de los Indios Park, this full-service resort and convention hotel has nice guest rooms with original artwork, refrigerators and balconies. The extensive grounds include a huge pool with swim-up bar, eight tennis courts, basketball, volleyball, a gym and casino. A great spot for those seeking all the bells and whistles of a large resort, but heavily used by business travelers. 331 rooms. Credit cards: A, DC, MC, V.

El Embajador Hotel $105–$115 ★★★★

☎ *(800) 457-0067, (809) 221-2131, FAX (809) 532-9444.*
Single: $105–$115. Double: $105–$115.
Dating to 1956, this downtown hotel was built as dictator Rafael Trujillo's showplace. Guest rooms are oversized and done in French provincial style; each has a large balcony with sea or city views. You'll be busy here: Olympic-size pool, four tennis courts, three restaurants (including an Italian one), three bars, a disco, gym, basketball courts, a casino, and even a Turkish bath. 300 rooms. Credit cards: A, DC, MC, V.

Hispaniola Hotel and Casino $135–$195 ★★

☎ *(800) 877-3643, (809) 221-1511, FAX (809) 535-0876.*
Single: $135–$195. Double: $135–$195.
Located in the heart of the city and certainly one of its better bargains, this older (1956) hotel has nicely appointed guest rooms with hand-crafted pine furniture, large walk-in closets and tiled balconies. A restaurant, bar, elegant casino and disco are on-site, and guests can use the tennis courts at sister property Hotel Santo Domingo. Seasonal and off-seasonal packages are available. The rates make this one worth a look. 165 rooms. Credit cards: A, MC, V.

Hotel Santo Domingo $125–$150 ★★★★

☎ *(809) 221-1511, FAX (809) 535-4050.*
Single: $125–$150. Double: $125–$150.

This elegant resort is appreciated especially by business travelers—the true jet set can land right on the helipad and then check in. Accommodations are beautifully done with handsome furnishings, large modern baths, and good views. Three tennis courts and a pool offer recreational diversion. Located some 15 minutes from downtown, tourists may be happier in the historic district or on the beach, but this place is a winner. 220 rooms. Credit cards: A, DC, MC, V.

Hotel V Centenario Intercontinental $150–$375   ★★★

☎ *(800) 214-1024, (809) 221-0000, FAX (809) 221-2020.*
Single: $150–$270. Double: $150–$270. Suites Per Day: $360–$375.
This Inter-Continental highrise, opened in 1992, has spacious guestrooms with marble accents, original art and minibars; only the suites, alas, have balconies. Facilities include two restaurants, three bars, a casino, pool, tennis, squash, and racquetball. 200 rooms. Credit cards: A, DC, MC, V.

Metro Hotel & Marina $75–$115   ★★

San Pedro, ☎ *(809) 526-2811, FAX (809) 526-1307.*
Single: $75–$115. Double: $75–$115.
Situated on Juan Dolio Beach, this modern hotel houses guests in adequate, if unexciting, standard rooms. Two restaurants and two bars keep people sated; activities range from watersports to a lively disco. It has two pools and two tennis courts. 180 rooms. Credit cards: A, DC, MC, V.

Renaissance Jaragua Hotel and Casino $150–$2000   ★★★★

☎ *(800) 468-3571, (809) 221-2222, FAX (809) 686-0528.*
Associated Restaurant: *Lotus/Figaro/Latino/Manhattan. Closed Date: 0.*
Single: $150–$220. Double: $150–$220. Suites Per Day: $450–$2000.
Located on the Malecon, Santo Domingo's seaside boulevard, this elaborate, 10-story hotel flanked by two-story buildings is situated on 14 garden acres with lagoons and waterfalls facing the Caribbean, minutes from the historic Colonial Zone. Step into the soaring pink marble lobby with skylights and you know you've landed in the Caribbean-gone-Vegas. The resort includes a 20,000 sq. ft. casino with more than 50 gaming tables and a 16,000 sq. ft. European Spa featuring exercise equipment, massage and saunas. Penthouse suites have Jacuzzis with skylights. All rooms featuring subdued tones with white wicker decor, have air-conditioning, direct-dial telephones, mini-bar and refrigerator, color cable TV hair dryers, and 24-hour room service. La Fiesta Showroom presents performers in Las Vegas-style revues. Other offerings include a tennis center with a pro and four, lighted tennis courts with an 800-seat stadium, an Olympic-sized pool and a disco featuring dance, salsa, reggae and oldies. Five specialty restaurants give you lots of evening options. Golf facilities are 20 minutes from the hotel. Packages available. Resort lovers need look no further. And if you can't stand to be disconnected from your office, this place has just added a state-of-the-art business center with Internet connections, Federal Express service, and the Renaissance Club, which offers additional amenities. 300 rooms. Credit cards: A, DC, MC, V.

Sheraton Santo Domingo $125–$155   ★★★★

☎ *(800) 325-3535, (809) 221-6666, FAX (809) 687-8150.*

Website: www.sheraton.com.

Single: $125–$145. Double: $135–$155.

This highrise, overlooking the sea, offers stylish rooms with the typical extras. A casino, two restaurants, disco and a few bars provide nightlife. It's equipped with a large pool and two tennis courts. Kids under 17 stay free with an adult. 258 rooms. Credit cards: A, DC, MC, V.

Talanquera Country and Beach Resort   **$75–$125**   ★★

San Pedro, ☎ *(809) 541-1166, FAX (809) 541-1292.*
Single: $75–$115. Double: $85–$125.

One-half mile from Juan Dolio Beach, where kayaking and scuba diving are the main draw, this well-landscaped resort has four pools and atypical activities like shooting and archery. Accommodations run the gamut from standard rooms to junior suites in cabanas; only some have balconies. Four bars and a disco keep things interesting once the sun goes down. 328 rooms. Credit cards: A, DC, MC, V.

Sosua

Hotel Sosua   **$35–$65**   ★★

☎ *(809) 571-2683, FAX (809) 571-2180.*
Single: $35–$50. Double: $50–$65.

Set five minutes from the beach in a suburban neighborhood, this budget, three-story hotel has basic but clean rooms that rely on ceiling fans to keep things cool. Three apartments offer kitchenettes. There's a pool and restaurant, but not much else in the way of extras. Good value for the money, though. 39 rooms. Credit cards: A, MC, V.

La Esplanada   **$90–$225**   ★★

☎ *(809) 571-3333, FAX (809) 571-3922.*
Single: $90. Double: $150–$225.

Located 25 minutes from Puerto Plata and the beach, this resort, built in 1991, has light and airy air-conditioned guest rooms, some with a balcony. It also has 12 apartments for those who like to spread out. The grounds include a few restaurants and bars, a pool and two tennis courts. Decent. 210 rooms. Credit cards: A, DC, MC, V.

All Inclusives
Puerto Plata

Allegro's Jack Tar Village Puerto Plata   **$120–$235**   ★★★

Playa Dorada, ☎ *(800) 999-9182, (809) 320-3800, FAX (809) 320-4161.*
Associated Restaurant: *Elaine's/La Yola/Papaya.*
Single: $120–$165. Double: $170–$235. Suites Per Day: $190–$225.

Situated on rambling grounds eight miles from Puerto Plata International Airport, this all-inclusive resort offers accommodations in Mediterranean-style, air-conditioned villas with one to three bedrooms. Each also has a phone, color cable TV, and a view of the pool, garden or partial ocean view. Rates don't include air fare or transfers, but include all meals, drinks, snacks and most activities. You'll pay extra for golf, night tennis and diving. It has five restaurants, two bars and a disco open until 2 a.m. All the usual amenities: three tennis courts, two pools, watersports, horseback riding and 18 holes of golf. Poolside aerobics, volleyball and archery goes on daily, too. And you get one free massage. These resorts have been bought out throughout the Caribbean and were undergoing extensive renovations at presstime. No guests under age 18 are allowed. 283 rooms. Credit cards: A, DC, MC, V.

Boca Chica Resort $60–$80   ★★

Boca Chica, ☎ *(809) 563-2200, FAX (809) 523-5236.*
Single: $60. Double: $80.

Located near but not on the beach, this property offers decent accommodations and resort amenities like watersports and tennis. The all-inclusive rates cover all activities, meals and drinks. 273 rooms. Credit cards: A, MC, V.

Paradise Beach Club $110–$330   ★★

☎ *(800) 752-9236, (809) 320-3663, FAX (809) 320-4858.*
Single: $110–$150. Double: $220–$330.

Another of the area's many all-inclusive resorts, Paradise is stylish, with pretty architecture lending an elegant touch. Accommodations run the gamut from standard rooms to two-bedroom suites on two levels; all are pleasant and comfortable. Guests can dine in five restaurants and toss some back in another five bars. The lushly landscaped grounds include an artificial river, large pool, two tennis courts, watersports and a disco. Nice. 436 rooms. Credit cards: A, MC, V.

Puerto Plata Beach Resort & Casino $130–$290   ★★★

Puerto Plata, ☎ *(809) 586-4243, FAX (809) 586-4377.*
E-mail: amhsacodetel.net.do.
Single: $130. Double: $210. Suites Per Day: $290–$290.

Victorian-style in design, all accommodations are in suites with limited kitchenettes. All the typical resort amenities, including a pool, three tennis courts, sauna and watersports. The tiny beach is across the road and not especially good for swimming, but its two restaurants and casino are nice. Generally a good choice. 216 rooms. Credit cards: A, DC, MC, V.

Punta Cana

Club Med Punta Cana $110–$230   ★★★

☎ *(800) 258-2633, (809) 686-5500, FAX (809) 685-5287.*
Website: www.clubmed.com.
Associated Restaurant: *Hispaniola/La Cana.*
Single: $110–$230. Double: $110–$230.

This all-inclusive vacation village appeals to families and fun lovers who spend beads in lieu of cash. Accommodations are in dorm-like structures clustered above palm-fringed, sugar white Punta Cana Beach, which happens to be one of the island's best. Once you get over the shock of the room's sparseness (each at least has its own shower and bathroom) you'll realize that you are rarely there anyway. That's the whole point at Club Med: to spend your time dashing from tennis to waterskiing to archery to circus workshops (even adults like the trapeze). Watersports are the focus at this resort. The hot thing in the Caribbean is bragging rights to the best children's program. This place lives up to its claims for toddlers through the teenage years. Club Med has three restaurants, two bars, a disco, 10 hard clay courts (half are lit), windsurfing and waterskiing, kayaking and sailing. Instruction from archery to the circus is tops. If you tire of the resort, it offers numerous excursions like horseback riding, nature walks and trips to Santo Domingo. The company charges a one-time $30 initiation fee plus a $50 per year membership fee, on top of the rates. Over the next several months, the property is going through several phases of renovation but will remain open. 334 rooms. Credit cards: A, MC, V.

Paradisus Punta Cana All-Inclusive Resort $225–$503 ★★★

☎ *(800) 336-3542, (809) 687-9923, FAX (809) 687-0752.*
Associated Restaurant: *El Romantico/Antojitos.*
Double: $225–$503.

Opened December 1995 on 96 acres on famed Bavaro Beach in Punta Cana, this all-inclusive resort takes the concept to a new level. It has five restaurants, a lobby bar, disco pub, swim-up bar and entertainment bar. If you tire of the casino, you can always learn merengue on the beach. The resort also hosts painting classes, theme dinners, fiestas and beach parties. Water lovers take full advantage of the snorkeling, sea bikes, beach volleyball, beach football, water aerobics, windsurfing, sailing and scuba diving (beginner's courses available). Believe it or not, the list goes on: horseback riding, tennis, archery, table tennis, badminton, shuffleboard, darts and giant chess. After all that, if you have any energy left, you can burn it off at the fully-equipped fitness center. Bungalow rooms and a lake-style swimming pool were designed to blend with the surrounding natural beauty. The split-level rooms have living areas downstairs and sleeping quarters upstairs with a furnished terrace, air conditioning, ceiling fans, oversized bathroom and king or double beds. A remote-control satellite TV, refrigerator and direct telephone round out the offerings. Kids ages 4–12 are welcomed, too, at the daily club, which has a playground, playhouse and counselors. 434 rooms. Credit cards: A, MC, V.

Santo Domingo

Capella Beach Resort $135–$635 ★★★★

Villas del Mar, ☎ *(809) 526-1080, FAX (809) 526-1088.*
Associated Restaurant: *I Capellini/El Pescador.*
Single: $135–$160. Double: $210–$380. Suites Per Day: $195–$635.

This beachfront, pale yellow gem of a resort in the newly developed town of Villas del Mar, about 45 minutes from Santo Domingo, delivers all the luxury amenities resort guests expect. It's just 20 minutes from the new International Airport of the Americas. Built in 1994 to resemble an Andalusian town in Southern Spain, its architecture reflects the rustic intimacy of that region. Grounds include three restaurants, a private and picturesque beach, excellent health club, two free-form pools with the ubiquitous swim-up bar and a waterslide, a watersports center, two lit tennis courts, boutique shops, billiard and game room and a disco. New are the children's program, offered 9 a.m.–5 p.m. for ages 5–12, and a golf course nearby. Guestroom decor is floral prints, with local paintings, terra-cotta pottery and hardwood furniture. Each room comes equipped with satellite TV, individually controlled air conditioning, direct-dial telephones, safes and hairdryers. Thirty-five are nonsmoking rooms, and the resort also offer handicapped facilities. Six honeymoon suites feature Jacuzzis and wraparound decks. The 17-acre site is lushly landscaped. The hotel also has its own 46-foot yacht available for private charters. 283 rooms. Credit cards: A, DC, MC, V.

Caribbean Village Decameron   **$100–$300**   ★★

Juan Dolio, ☎ *(800) 223-9815, (809) 526-2009, FAX (809) 526-1430.*
Single: $100–$200. Double: $200–$300.
This all-inclusive resort—20 minutes east of Boca Chica outside of Santo Domingo—has one- and two-bedroom suites. It also has horseback riding, disco dancing, tennis, volleyball, bike rides, and a casino. This place appeals mostly to a young crowd. 292 rooms. Credit cards: A, MC, V.

Samana

Gran Bahia Beach Hotel   **$100–$200**   ★★★

Samana, ☎ *(800) 457-0067, (809) 538-3111, FAX (809) 538-2764.*
Single: $100. Double: $200. Suites Per Day: $200.
Set on a bluff near a mountainside rain forest, this Victorian-style hotel appeals to lovers of all ages. Wonderful views abound. Guest rooms are spacious and comfortably done; request a suite when you reserve and you'll get one for no extra cost if they are available. The rocky shore below has sandy inlets for sunbathing, and there's also a pool. A good spot for whalewatching. Packages are available. 110 rooms. Credit cards: A, DC, MC, V.

Hotel Cayo Levantado   **$100–$200**   ★★

☎ *(800) 424-5192.*
Single: $100. Double: $200.
This simply decorated, all-inclusive hotel is on a small island called Cayo Levantado just off the coast of Samana. You reach the island via a quick ferry ride. Rooms are simply decorated with local art. All are air-conditioned. No pool, but the beaches are magnificent and the grounds are lush. Perfect for those seeking solitude and no TV. 44 rooms. Credit cards: A, MC, V.

Sosua

Punta Goleta Beach Resort   **$85–$140**   ★★

Sosua, ☎ *(809) 571-0700, FAX (809) 571-0707.*
Single: $85–$140. Double: $85–$140.
Fifteen minutes from the airport at Puerto Plata and set on 100 acres across the street from a beach known for good windsurfing, this resort has large rooms with air conditioning and Victorian-style balconies. All the typical amenities, including a pool and two tennis courts, as well as two restaurants and four bars. Some rooms come with Jacuzzis. You can also easily arrange mountain hikes and horseback riding from here. 252 rooms. Credit cards: A, MC, V.

Apartments and Condominiums

In general, few of the self-catering units available in the Dominican Republic are anything to write home about, except for the luxury villas at Casa de Campo. If you don't speak good English, you will have a real adventure trying to communicate your needs to the management. Boca Chica and Juan Dolio boast more modern apartments; kitchens are usually fully furnished. For units in the cityscape, contact **ARAH** (*194 Avenida 27 de Febrero, Santo Domingo, R.D.* Another source is the **Villa, Condo and Apartment Rental Service**, *Box 30076, Pedro Henriques Urena 37, Santo Domingo, R.D.,* ☎ *(809) 686-0608.*

Puerto Plata

Dorado Naco Suite Resort   **$80–$145**   ★★★★

☎ *(888) 339-6226, (809) 320-2019, FAX (809) 320-3608.*
Single: $80–$145. Double: $80–$145.
All accommodations are in one- and two-bedroom suites with full kitchens and bal-
conies at this Spanish Caribbean-style hotel. The beach is a short stroll away.
There's live entertainment nightly around the pool and two restaurants and three
bars for after-dark diversions. Kids are kept occupied in supervised programs year-
round. Guests can also use the facilities at the adjacent Playa Naco. 175 rooms.
Credit cards: A, DC, MC, V.

Low Cost Lodging

In a country where hotel rates start low (comparatively for the Caribbean), the cheapest rooms are not going to be impressive, or even acceptable according to some Western
standards of cleanliness. However, deals can be found, especially among hotels geared to
Dominican businessmen and Dominican tourists, which are always lower than the European and American-owned hotels and resorts. Figure out beforehand if you are really saving any money, since you will no doubt have to rent a car to get around. Also be careful
you have not stumbled upon a front for a brothel or pay-by-the-hour-room rate.

Where to Eat

Fielding's Highest Rated Restaurants in Dominican Republic

★★★★	Casa del Rio	$7–$29
★★★★	Chopin	$7
★★★★	Restaurant Lina	$10–$30
★★★	El Alcazar	$10–$25
★★★	El Conuco	$8–$15
★★★	Meson de la Cava	$25–$40
★★★	Pez Dorado	$18–$30

Fielding's Most Romantic Restaurants in Dominican Republic

♡♡♡♡♡	Casa del Rio	$7–$29
♡♡♡♡♡	Chopin	$7
♡♡♡♡♡	Restaurant Lina	$10–$30
♡♡♡♡	Fonda La Aterazana	$20
♡♡♡♡	Meson de la Cava	$25–$40

Fielding's Best Value Restaurants in Dominican Republic

★★★★	Chopin	$7
★★	El Don Camillo	$8–$8
★★★	El Conuco	$8–$15
★★★★	Casa del Rio	$7–$29
★★★★	Restaurant Lina	$10–$30

Though restaurants generally open around 6 p.m. for dinner, you'll find that most locals don't venture out until 9 or 10 p.m.—and they make a real occasion of their evening out. Though tourists can get away with casual clothing just about anywhere, you may want to dress up for dinner, as locals do. Some local dishes to try include *bollito de yucca* (a tiny hors d'oeuvre made of ground yucca root and cheese), *sancocho* (a thick stew of at least five different meats), *platanos* (plantains), *chicharrones* (fried pork rinds), *galletas* (flat, biscuit crackers) and *tortilla de jamon* (spicy ham omelette). Save room for dessert, maybe a *majarete* (cornmeal custard) or a simple *añejo* (dark aged rum over ice). Don't despair if your palate is conservative—you'll be able to find American-style fixings in most of the hotel coffee shops.

While meals are generally quite reasonably priced, note that all wine is imported, so tends to be pricey.

After dinner, join the many locals who stroll along Santo Domingo's **Malecon**. Check out **Las Palmas** in the Hotel Santo Domingo *(Av. Independencia,* ☎ *809-535-1511)* for dancing to local merengue bands; the younger crowd flocks to **Alexander's** *(Av. Pasteur 23,* ☎ *809-685-9728).* The island's many casinos, which open at 3 p.m. and don't close till 4 a.m., provide the chance to test lady luck; note that you must be at least 18 to enter, and jackets are required for men.

DOMINICAN REPUBLIC

Puerto Plata

Pez Dorado   **$$$**   ★★★

43 Calle el Sol, ☎ *(809) 582-2518.*
Lunch: 11 a.m.–3 p.m., entrées $18–$30.
Dinner: 6 p.m.–midnight, entrées $18–$30.
If you visit the historical town of Santiago de los Caballeros, an hour and half away from Puerto Plata, this restaurant serving seafood Chinese or Creole-style in a posh, comfortable room is one of the best dining choices in town. Afterwards, you can wend your way to a local dance club—after all, this is the birthplace of the merengue. Reservations recommended. Credit cards: A, MC, V.

Roma II Restaurant   **$**   ★★

Calle Beller, ☎ *(809) 586-3904.*
Lunch: 11 a.m.–2:30 p.m., entrées $6–$15.
Dinner: 2 p.m.–midnight, entrées $6–$15.
This plain but comfortably air-conditioned bistro with charming service serves an excellent array of pizzas, plain or fancy—cheese or perhaps shrimp, made on dough baked fresh daily. The octopus, a specialty here, served with a vinaigrette sauce, or with fresh tomatoes, or on pasta is tasty. Steaks and filets are also on the menu. Credit cards: A, MC, V.

Punta Cana

Chopin   **$**   ★★★★

Playas de Bavaro, ☎ *(809) 221-2311.* Associated hotel: *Melia Bavaro.*
This wonderfully romantic open-air restaurant at the equally romantic Melia Bavaro resort is reached via a short stroll through the rainforest. The restaurant offers a different cuisine as a buffet each night or you can choose between two entrées and two desserts featured on the gala menu. Other nights you may find smoked salmon, paella or Spanish ham. After dinner, you're senenaded from a gondola on the

lagoon by a quartet from the Symphony Orchestra of Belgrade playing classical tunes. The bill for hotel guests is included in the room rate, while the fee for non-guests is $7. Reservations should be made before noon of the day you'd like to come. Reservations recommended. Credit cards: A, DC, MC, V.

Santo Domingo

Cafe del Sol   **$**   ★

Altos de Chavon Village, ☎ *(809) 523-3333.*
Lunch: Noon–3 p.m., entrées $8–$10.
Dinner: 6–11 p.m., entrées $8–$10.

This pretty rooftop cafe in the artists' colony of Altos de Chavon makes a perfect stop for a light repast of pizza or salad. Credit cards: A, MC, V.

Casa del Rio   **$$**   ★★★★

Altos de Chavon Village, ☎ *(809) 523-3333.*
Dinner: 6–11 p.m., entrées $7–$29.

One of the island's pricier restaurants (and the chicest), Casa del Rio is just the place for resort dwellers at the nearby Casa de Campo to go for a night on the town, but some fans have no compunction about driving the 100 miles from Santo Domingo to eat here. The tower room where you dine glows with candlelight, overlooking the Chavon River. French chef Philippe Mongereau likes a challenge, and constantly experiments with Asian and Caribbean spices to dress up shellfish, meats and poultry. Reservations required. Credit cards: A, MC, V.

El Alcazar   **$$**   ★★★

Avenida Independencia, Esquina Abraham Lincoln, ☎ *(809) 221-1511.* Associated hotel: *Hotel Santo Domingo.*
Lunch: Noon–3 p.m., prix fixe $14.
Dinner: 6 p.m.–1 a.m., entrées $10–$25.

The noonday lunch buffet at the El Alcazar is an exotic, reasonably priced dining adventure, with a bevy of international dishes and succulent seafood items available daily. World-renowned couturier (and local hero) Oscar de la Renta designed the interiors of the chic hotel-restaurant on a grand North African theme, with gorgeous fabrics, shells and mirrors for accents. Evenings the mood turns formal, and the kitchen turns out an interesting blend of Creole, Dominican, American and continental dishes. Reservations recommended. Credit cards: A, DC, MC, V.

El Conuco   **$**   ★★★

Calle Casimiro de Moya #152 Gazcue, ☎ *(809) 686-0129.*
Lunch: Noon–3 p.m., entrées $8–$15.
Dinner: 7 p.m.–midnight, entrées $8–$15.

This comically hokey but fun restaurant—the name means farmer— is situated in an ersatz, large thatched-roof house, where hanging artifacts from former diners ensure lively conversation. A favorite spot for Dominicans to take visiting friends for a taste of hearty, county cooking, El Conuco delivers on its promise. Fill up on Creole-style rice and kidney beans, stews, cod and crunchy fried chicken bits while hammy waiters turn into musicians and/or dancers at the drop of a sombrero. Reservations recommended. Credit cards: MC, V.

El Don Camillo $ ★★

74 Esquinas Las Damas, ☎ *(809) 687-0023.*
Lunch: 9:30 a.m.–4 p.m., entrées $8.
Dinner: 4 p.m.–midnight, entrées $8.
French meets the Dominican Republic in the kitchen of this restored home in the Old City area of Santo Domingo. Specialties include choice cuts of ranch-style beef fillets or steaks, fish, lobster served with salads. Desserts are rich and French. Colorful decor and a lively atmosphere add to the casual feel of this spot. Reservations recommended. Credit cards: MC, V.

Fonda La Aterazana $$ ★★

Calle Aterazana 5, ☎ *(809) 689-2900.*
Feel like a Spanish dandy in this whitewashed-stone building in the Aterazana section of the Colonial Zone, sharing seafood or crunchy fried Dominican chicken strips (spicy and delicious) with someone special. This bright and festive spot comes alive with folkloric musical groups and merengue dancers. Dominicans dress for a night on the town and you should, too. Credit cards: A, DC, MC, V.

La Terraza $$$ ★

Avenida Sarasota 65, ☎ *(809) 221-2131.* Associated hotel: *Hotel Embajador.*
Lunch: 7 a.m.–12 p.m., entrées $12–$22.
Dinner: Noon–midnight, entrées $12–$30.
This small restaurant in a beautifully decorated room in the imposing Hotel Embajador serves international cuisine for breakfast, lunch and dinner buffet style. Reservations recommended. Credit cards: A, DC, MC, V.

Meson de la Cava $$$ ★★★

Avenida Mirador del Sur #1, ☎ *(809) 533-2818.*
Lunch: Noon–4 p.m., entrées $25–$30.
Dinner: 6 p.m.–midnight, entrées $25–$40. Closed: Mon.
In order to eat here, diners must descend to a cavern way below ground (some 50 feet), reached via a scary staircase. What's down under is some rollicking entertainment from a live band (contemporary and merengue) that encourages patrons to dance. Locals as well as tourists frequent this hopping place for the simply prepared but delicious seafood. Reserve way in advance, and dress fashionably. Reservations required. Credit cards: A, DC, MC, V.

Neptuno's Club $$ ★★

Boca Chica Beach, ☎ *(809) 523-4703.*
Lunch: Noon–2 p.m., entrées $10–$15.
Dinner: 2–10 p.m., entrées $10–$25.
Calm and warm waters and a short (about 45 minute) drive from the capital make Boca Chica Beach, where this little hut is located, popular with daytrippers. A romantic little spot, Neptuno's has a good reputation for fish stews and sauteed kingfish. Reservations recommended. Credit cards: A, MC, V.

Palace of Jade $$$ ★★

Calle Jose Maria #6, ☎ *(809) 686-3226.*
Lunch: Noon–3 p.m., entrées $8–$30.
Dinner: 7 p.m.–midnight, entrées $8–$30.

A favorite with locals, this formal Chinese restaurant has well-prepared Chinese dishes from the most popular regions of that country. It also has karaoke for those who want to ham it up. Reservations recommended for groups.

Reina de Espana $$ ★★

Avenida Cervantes 103, ☎ *(809) 685-2588.*
Lunch: Noon–4 p.m., entrées $12–$20.
Dinner: 4 p.m.–midnight, entrées $12–$25.

In a city where Spanish food is treated with respect, Reina de Espana, located in a restored home not far from the sea between the Hotel Cervantes and the Sheraton, manages to present more than just the average paella or seafood stew for discriminating diners. The menu traverses each region of Spain, with roast quail or suckling pig prepared as specials from time to time. But the old favorites like gazpacho are all represented and rarely disappoint. A pianist entertains on Thursday and Saturday nights. Reservations required. Credit cards: A, DC, MC, V.

Restaurant Lina $$$ ★★★★

Avenida Maximo Gomez 27, ☎ *(809) 563-5000.* Associated hotel: *Barcelo Gran Hotel Lina.*
Lunch: Noon–4 p.m., entrées $10–$25.
Dinner: 6:30 p.m.–1 a.m., entrées $10–$30.

A cut above most hotel restaurants, this grand dining experience features a thoughtful continental menu. Many of the appetizers reflect a Spanish influence—the restaurant was, after all, named after the personal chef of long-reigning President Rafael Trujillo, the late Chef Lina Aguado, who was noted for her Spanish cooking—Madrid-style tripe, Andalusian-style fried squid. The soups are shellfish, garlic with egg, onion or asparagus. Simple salads are offered, too, followed by Italian pastas. For the main course, grilled red snapper or grouper, Creole prawns, lobster thermidor or a mixed grill of fish and seafood please seafood fans. More hearty eaters might opt for filet mignon, veal medallions or chicken served grilled or prepared cordon bleu. Desserts are brought to your table by trolley to tempt you. Reservations required. Credit cards: A, DC, MC, V.

Vesuvio I $$$ ★★

Avenida G. Washington #1521, ☎ *(809) 221-3333.*
Lunch: Noon–2 p.m., entrées $8–$25.
Dinner: 2 p.m.–1 a.m., entrées $8–$30.

The Bonarelli family from Naples has been running this boisterous restaurant on the Malecon—the main strip—since the 1950s. They are not content to rest on past laurels: Every visit brings a new specialty or improvements on old favorites. The voluminous menu—a good mix of French, Italian and American-influenced dishes—features seafood and plenty of it, including crayfish with garlic, although veal scaloppine with fresh herbs is worth noting. Management has also put together a good wine list, not always easy to find in the Caribbean. Decor is contemporary, with plenty of colorful marine life painted on the walls. Credit cards: A, DC, MC, V.

Because exchange rates between the U.S. dollar and Dominican peso are usually extremely favorable, the Dominican Republic can be a real bargain. Among the best souvenirs are cigars (best purchased at the end of a tour of a cigar factory near Santiago); pieces of translucent amber with a leaf or insect embedded inside (think *Jurassic Park*); rum, fashions by native son Oscar de la Renta; and wood carvings. Note, however, that while legal, it's best not to purchase items made from mahogany, because buying it only encourages the destruction of the rainforest. Haiti-influenced local artwork is also popular, but usually is of poor quality compared with the far-superior work put out by Haitians. Duty-free zones are in Santo Domingo and Puerto Plata.

Bargaining is standard practice throughout the country and it's all a big game, so join in the fun and hold out for a good price, which will often be less than half of what you were first quoted. While street vendors who work the stalls at Plaza Criolla El Mercado Modelo (Santo Domingo's huge covered market) expect you to haggle, they also are slow to give up—you will have to be firm in your refusals if you decide against the item after all.

Besides El Mercado, the main shopping areas in Santo Domingo are in La Atarazana and along Calle El Conde and Calle Duarte in the Colonial Zone.

Dominican Republic Directory

Arrival and Departure

Travelers to the Dominican Republic use two major international airports: Las Américas International Airport, 25 miles outside Santo Domingo, and La Unión International Airport, about 25 miles east of Puérto Plata on the north coast. **American Airlines** offers the most flights to the island, with nonstops from New York to Santo Domingo. **American**, **Continental**, **TWA** and **Pan Am** also fly nonstop from New York to Puerto Plata. Continental Airlines offers connecting service to both Santo Domingo and Puerto Plata from San Juan, Puerto Rico; and **American Eagle** has two flights a day from San Juan to La Romana. Punta Cana Airport and La Romana Airport have both seen increased activity of late. Ask about flights here, which can significantly slash travel time to your resort.

For inter-island service, ALM flies from Santo Domingo to St. Maarten and Curaçao. Limited domestic service is available from Maria Montez Airport in Barahona and La Herrera Airport in Santo Domingo to smaller airfields in La Romana, Samana and Santiago.

Be cautious in both airports with regard to your luggage and personal valuables. Luggage theft is a common occurrence, and general confusion can often lead to "lost" luggage. Try to carry your own luggage, or prepare to be royally hassled for service by porters. The island is famous for *buscones*, who offer you assistance and then disappear with your belongings. If you have arranged for transport by your hotel, the representative should be awaiting you in the immigration hall.

You'll also love to pay a $10 departure tax. Be prepared to pay it twice due to unscrupulous agents eager for U.S. dollars.

Business Hours

Stores open weekdays 8 a.m.–12:30 p.m. and 2:30–5 p.m., and Saturday 8 a.m.–noon. Banks open weekdays 8:30 a.m.–4:30 p.m.

Climate

The climate is subtropical; with an average annual temperature of 77 degrees. Summer temperatures range from 80° to 95°F and in winter, from 75° to 90°F. The west and southwest of the country is arid. Hispaniola lies in the path of hurricanes.

Documents

In order to purchase a $10 tourist card, good for 90 days, visitors must present a valid passport or other proof of citizenship (birth certificate, voter's registration card, with an official photo ID such as driver's license). Cards may be purchased upon arrival, or through the consulate.

Electricity

Current is 110 volts, 60 cycles, as in the United States.

Getting Around

Taxis are available at the airports, and the 25-minute ride into Santo Domingo averages about U.S.$20. There is no bus service, but fellow travelers are usually open to sharing a taxi.

Buses in Santo Domingo are called *públicos*, small blue-and-white or blue-and-red cars that run regular routes, stopping to let passengers on and off. The fare is two pesos. There are also *conchos* or *coléctivos* (privately owned buses) whose drivers tool around the major thoroughfares, leaning out the window and trying to seduce passengers onboard. (For this inconvenience you get to pay a peso less.) Privately owned air-conditioned buses make regular runs to Santiago, Puerto Plata and other destinations. Avoid night travel because the country is rife with potholes.

Cars can be rented in the airports and at many hotels. The top names are **Avis** ☎ *(800) 331-1084* or *(809) 532-9295*; **Budget** ☎ *(800) 527-0700* or *(809) 562-6812*; **Hertz** ☎ *(800) 654-3131* or *(809) 586-0200* and **National** ☎ *(800) 227-7638* or *(809) 562-1444*. Driving is on the right side of the street, but drivers here are maniacs, often driving down the middle of the road and passing dangerously whenever they feel like it. They are nice enough, however, to flash their light on when they know the highway patrol is lurking about—the 50 mph (80 kph) limit is strictly enforced. (Police have been known to stop drivers on the pretext of some violation and insinuate the need for a bribe.) If you must drive around the unilluminated mountain roads at night, drive with utmost caution since many cars do not have headlights or taillights, cows stand in the middle of the road, and bicycles are rarely well lit. Gas stations are few and far between. Short distances can take several hours.

Motorbikes, called *motoconchos*, are a popular and inexpensive way to tool around the island, especially in such places as Puerto Plata, Sosúa and Jaraba-coa. Bikes can be flagged down on the road and in town.

Language

The official language is Spanish, so do as much as you can to bone up on Span-ish before you go. Supposedly everyone involved in tourism speaks English, but it is often an odd version and many people have trouble understanding English. Waitresses in coffee shops may simply drop their jaws when you speak to them in English. In the outlying areas, it is absolutely necessary to speak Spanish. Bring along a phrase book and keep it handy.

Medical Emergencies

The island has numerous hospitals and clinics; that is not say that you should pursue any medical attention with enthusiasm. The biggest and most revered is **José Maria Cabral y Baez**; ☎ *(809) 583-4311* on Central, near the church in the town of Santiago. You'll find a number of American medical students working here since the national medical school uses the facilities. Hospitals in Santiago tend to be crowded and harassed. Hospital Marion in Santo Domin-go is known for its cardiovascular center. Bring your Spanish phrase book, par-ticularly if you get stuck in a hospital for any length of time. Do your best to fly home to the States. Remember to bring any medications you need from home, with a copy of the prescription and a letter from your doctor that you have been medically directed to take them. The U.S. Consulate ☎ *(809) 221-2111* may be of some help in extreme cases.

Money

Official currency is the Dominican peso. Most hotels and shops welcome American dollars as well as major credit cards and traveler's checks. Try to spend your pesos rather than exchange them into dollars before you leave.

Telephone

The country code is *809*. To call the Dominican Republic from the United States, dial *011* (international access), the country code *(809)* and the local number. Connections from the U.S. are generally made with ease and are clear. Calling from the Dominican Republic can become a headache—fast. It has a direct-dial system, but you should feel extraordinarily blessed to have it work right. Try dialing 1, then the area code, followed by the number.

Time

Atlantic standard time year-round.

Tipping

Hotels and restaurants add a whopping 23 percent government tax (which includes a 10 percent service charge) to all bills. It is customary to leave a dollar or two per day for the maid; if you balk, just imagine her income status in such a poor country. In restaurants and nightclubs, an extra 5–10 percent above the service charge included on the bill will be greatly appreciated by the waiters and waitresses. Taxi drivers expect a 10 percent tip; tip more if you arrive alive. Skycaps and hotel porters expect at least 10 pesos per bag.

Tourist Information

The **Dominican Tourist Information Center** is located at the corner of *Avs. México and 30 de Marzo;* ☎ *221-4660* or *00-752-1151.* Information booths are in Santiago *(City Hall Av. Duarte;* ☎ *582-5885)* and in Puerto Plata Av. Hermanas Mirabel ☎ *586-3676.* You can also find a booth at the airport open daily. In the U.S. call ☎ *(212) 575-4966, FAX (212) 575-5448* or write *1501 Broadway, Suite 410, New York, NY 10036.*

When to Go

Merengue Festival explodes in late July in Santo Domingo, the island's biggest rum-filled festival dedicated to the national dance. **Carnival** is held the week before Ash Wednesday. The **Cabarete World Cup**, a PBA-sanctioned international windsurfing championship is staged in June.

DOMINICAN REPUBLIC HOTELS	RMS	RATES	PHONE	CR. CARDS
Puerto Plata				
★★★★ **Dorado Naco Suite Resort**	175	$80–$145	(888) 339-6226	A, DC, MC, V
★★★ **Allegro's Jack Tar Village Puerto Plata**	283	$120–$235	(800) 999-9182	A, DC, MC, V
★★★ **Puerto Plata Beach Resort & Casino**	216	$130–$210	(809) 586-4243	A, DC, MC, V
★★★ **Villas Doradas Beach**	207	$95–$270	(800) 545-8089	A, MC, V
★★ **Boca Chica Resort**	273	$60–$80	(809) 563-2200	A, MC, V
★★ **Caribbean Village Club on the Green**	336	$120–$330	(800) 858-2258	A, MC, V
★★ **Flamenco Beach Resort**	582	$120–$150	(800) 545-8089	A, DC, MC
★★ **Heavens**	150	$95–$135	(800) 835-7697	A, MC, V
★★ **Paradise Beach Club**	436	$110–$330	(800) 752-9236	A, MC, V
★★ **Playa Dorada Hotel**	254	$95–$155	(800) 545-8089	MC, V
Punta Cana				
★★★★ **Barcelo Bavaro Beach Resort**	1955	$120–$220	(305) 374-0045	A, MC, V
★★★★ **Hotel Riu Taino**	360	$77–$117	(809) 221-2290	A, DC, MC, V

DOMINICAN REPUBLIC

DOMINICAN REPUBLIC HOTELS	RMS	RATES	PHONE	CR. CARDS
★★★★ Melia Bavaro Resort	766	$77–$179	(800) 336-3542	A, DC, MC, V
★★★ Club Med Punta Cana	334	$110–$230	(800) 258-2633	A, MC, V
★★★ Hotel Riu Naiboa	372	$101–$277	(809) 221-7515	A, DC, MC, V
★★★ Paradisus Punta Cana All-Inclusive Resort	434	$225–$503	(800) 336-3542	A, MC, V
★★★ Punta Cana Beach Resort	400	$105–$200	(800) 972-2139	A, DC, MC, V

Santo Domingo

	RMS	RATES	PHONE	CR. CARDS
★★★★★ Casa de Campo	750	$180–$240	(800) 856-5971	A, MC, V
★★★★ Capella Beach Resort	283	$135–$380	(809) 526-1080	A, DC, MC, V
★★★★ Dominican Fiesta Hotel	316	$100–$200	(800) 782-1340	A, DC, MC, V
★★★★ El Embajador Hotel	300	$105–$115	(800) 457-0067	A, DC, MC, V
★★★★ Hotel Santo Domingo	220	$125–$150	(809) 221-1511	A, DC, MC, V
★★★★ Renaissance Jaragua Hotel and Casino	300	$150–$220	(800) 468-3571	A, DC, MC, V
★★★★ Sheraton Santo Domingo	258	$125–$155	(800) 325-3535	A, DC, MC, V
★★★ Barcelo Gran Hotel Lina & Casino	217	$105–$150	(800) 942-2461	A, DC, MC, V
★★★ Hotel V Centenario Intercontinental	200	$150–$270	(800) 214-1024	A, DC, MC, V
★★ Caribbean Village Decameron	292	$100–$300	(800) 223-9815	A, MC, V
★★ Hispaniola Hotel and Casino	165	$135–$195	(800) 877-3643	A, MC, V
★★ Metro Hotel & Marina	180	$75–$115	(809) 526-2811	A, DC, MC, V
★★ Talanquera Country and Beach Resort	328	$75–$125	(809) 541-1166	A, DC, MC, V

Samana

	RMS	RATES	PHONE	CR. CARDS
★★★ Gran Bahia Beach Hotel	110	$100–$200	(800) 457-0067	A, DC, MC, V
★★ Hotel Cayo Levantado	44	$100–$200	(800) 424-5192	A, MC, V

Sosua

	RMS	RATES	PHONE	CR. CARDS
★★ Hotel Sosua	39	$35–$65	(809) 571-2683	A, MC, V
★★ La Esplanada	210	$90–$225	(809) 571-3333	A, DC, MC, V
★★ Punta Goleta Beach Resort	252	$85–$140	(809) 571-0700	A, MC, V

DOMINICAN REPUBLIC RESTAURANTS	PHONE	ENTRÉE	CR.C ARDS
Puerto Plata			
Chinese Cuisine			
★★★ **Pez Dorado**	(809) 582-2518	$18–$30	A, MC, V
Regional Cuisine			
★★ **Roma II Restaurant**	(809) 586-3904	$6–$15	A, MC, V
			Punta Cana
Continental Cuisine			
★★★★ **Chopin**	(809) 221-2311	$7	A, DC, MC, V
Santo Domingo			
Chinese Cuisine			
★★ **Palace of Jade**	(809) 686-3226	$8–$30	
Continental Cuisine			
★★★★ **Restaurant Lina**	(809) 563-5000	$10–$30	A, DC, MC, V
★★ **Vesuvio I**	(809) 221-3333	$8–$30	A, DC, MC, V
★ **La Terraza**	(809) 221-2131	$12–$30	A, DC, MC, V
Creole Cuisine			
★★ **Fonda La Aterazana**	(809) 689-2900	$20	A, DC, MC, V
French Cuisine			
★★★★ **Casa del Rio**	(809) 523-3333	$7–$29	A, MC, V
★★ **El Don Camillo**	(809) 687-0023	$8–$8	MC, V
International Cuisine			
★★★ **El Alcazar**	(809) 221-1511	$14–$25	A, DC, MC, V
Italian Cuisine			
★ **Cafe del Sol**	(809) 523-3333	$8–$10	A, MC, V
Regional Cuisine			
★★★ **El Conuco**	(809) 686-0129	$8–$15	MC, V
Seafood Cuisine			
★★★ **Meson de la Cava**	(809) 533-2818	$25–$40	A, DC, MC, V
★★ **Neptuno's Club**	(809) 523-4703	$10–$25	A, MC, V
Spanish Cuisine			
★★ **Reina de Espana**	(809) 685-2588	$12–$25	A, DC, MC, V

GRENADA

St. George's, Grenada's picturesque capital

Grenada doesn't snuggle up to the Spice Island moniker casually. Walk along the Carenage, the classic curl of waterfront tucked into the island's capital, St. George's, and you'll see dozens of turbaned black ladies hawking their fragrant cloves, allspice, cinnamon, turmeric and nutmeg with a merry song and a spiel. Stroll onto the estate of Morne Fendue or another fine plantation home and your feet trample the nutmeg shells recycled as driveway gravel, stirring their sweet scent into the air. Aroma, it seems, takes on a seductive, almost musical quality on this sweet island, though color plays perhaps an equally important role in defining Grenada's sensory appeal. From the lush green of its dense forests, to the pearly bright sand of Grand Anse, to the neatly ironed burgundy dresses of giggling schoolgirls in Sauteurs. The full artist's palette greets buyers at the festive market square.

The island's rich panoply of natural wonders completes a delightful package that American tourists are now discovering 15 years after U.S. troops quelled a Marxist-based coup. Things are relatively quiet now on the local political front and, although the Reagan-initiated intervention undoubtedly (and unnecessarily) scares some potential visitors away, it has also worked in the island's favor, keeping tourist development to a reasonable scale. From rum shop to fishing village to market place, Grenada celebrates the Caribbean the way it was—the way the region operated before the American *cultural* invasion of KFC and Coke began to replace the roti and maubi of old. But if Grenadians sometimes refer to Reagan's intervention in ambivalent terms today, Americans are always welcomed warmly, albeit more for their touristic impulses than for militaristic pursuits.

The independent, three-island nation is officially called Grenada, Carriacou and Petit Martinique—the latter two isles are part of the necklace of Grenadines that stretch between Grenada and St. Vincent. Charming Carriacou makes a fine daytrip, or it can be visited as part of a voyage along the exquisite sailing passage through the Grenadines. But Grenada itself is hardly short on sights and activities to fill a vacation. Beyond Grand Anse, the island's regal one-and-a-half-mile long beach, travelers can hike rain forest trails riddled with cascading rivers, seek out some of the more than 450 flowering plant species and 150 varieties of birds, or dive into the depths to reach the *Bianca C*, a luxury liner that went down in 1961 and is called The Titanic of the Caribbean. In the end, Grenada is that rare commodity: an easy, rewarding adventure, awaiting your discovery.

BEST BETS FOR...

Bird's-Eye View

Sixty miles southwest of St. Vincent, 90 miles north of Trinidad, Grenada (pronounced Gre-*nay*-da) lies at the southern end of the Windward Islands, and is one of the smallest nations in the Western Hemisphere. The oval-shaped island is 12 miles wide at its center, 21 miles in length, and volcanic in origin, with extinct Mt. St. Catherine rising to 2757 feet. The nation also includes Carriacou and Petit Martinique, as well as a quantity of uninhabited islands winding north toward the Grenadines (which are politically connected

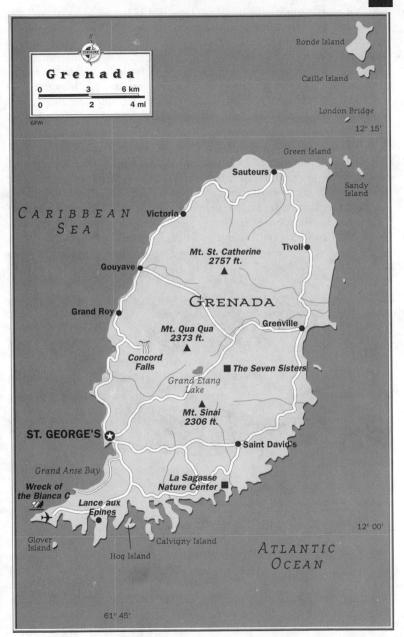

Grenada

0   3   6 km
0   2   4 mi

©FWI

Ronde Island

Caille Island

London Bridge

12° 15'

Green Island

Sauteurs

Sandy Island

CARIBBEAN SEA

Victoria

Tivoli

Mt. St. Catherine 2757 ft. ▲

GRENADA

Gouyave

Grand Roy

Grenville

Mt. Qua Qua 2373 ft. ▲

Concord Falls

■ The Seven Sisters

Grand Etang Lake

Mt. Sinai ▲ 2306 ft.

ST. GEORGE'S ✪

Saint David's

Grand Anse Bay

La Sagasse Nature Center ■

Wreck of the Bianca C

Lance aux Epines

Glover Island

Calvigny Island

12° 00'

Hog Island

ATLANTIC OCEAN

61° 45'

to St. Vincent), bringing the total land mass to 133 square miles (there's also an island-to-be in the form of an undersea volcano, intriguingly named Kick 'em Jenny, that's rapidly building its way to the surface between Grenada and Carriacou). Inhabited by mona monkeys and armadillos, the interior of Grenada is mountainous and lush, and the fertile volcanic soil inspires vegetation so thick that the island looks as if it were upholstered in deep green velvet. You'll spot residents carrying machetes, as though the path they cleared yesterday is once again overgrown with green tangles today.

It's difficult to imagine a prettier Caribbean town than Grenada's capital, St. George's, with its pedestrian walkway, the Carenage, that hugs the horseshoe-shaped, postcard-perfect harbor. Several lofty lookouts—Fort George with cannons aimed seaward, Fort Frederick and Cemetery Hill—present splendid views of the town clambering up the slopes from the waterfront. Although a number of restaurants are located here, the majority of the island's hotels are concentrated to the south of St. George's—primarily near the sweep of sand at Grand Anse, and on a south-facing peninsula, L'Ance aux Epines.

GRENADA

On Grand Anse, no development may be taller than a coconut palm.

History

Grenada was sighted by Columbus on his third voyage in 1498. The French built Grenada's first settlement, first appeasing and then battling the native Carib Indians, the last of whom leaped to their death from Morne de

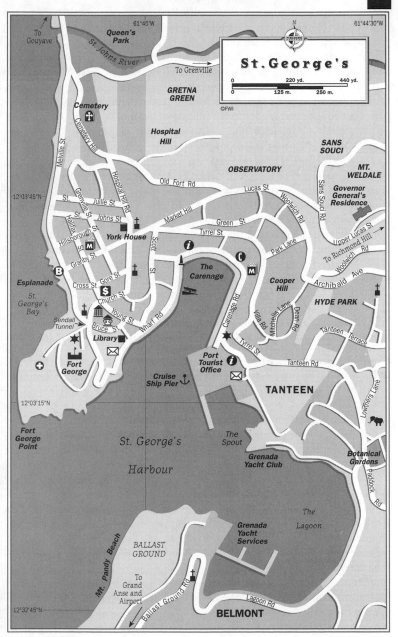

St.George's

0   220 yd.   440 yd.
0   125 m.   250 m.

©FWI

To Gouyave

Queen's Park

St. Johns River

To Grenville

61°45'W

61°44'30"W

N

GRETNA GREEN

Hospital Hill

Cemetery

Melville St

Cemetery Hill

Hospital Hill Rd

Old Fort Rd

OBSERVATORY

Lucas St

SANS SOUCI

MT. WELDALE

Governor General's Residence

Sans Souci Rd

12°03'45"N

St.

Grenville St

Juille St

St.

Halifax St

Johns St

Market Hill

Green St

Tyrrel St

Woolwich Rd

Upper Lucas St

To Richmond Hill

Woolwich Rd

Park Lane

Hillsborough St

Granby St

York House

Scott St

The Carenage

Cooper Hill

Archibald Ave

HYDE PARK

Cross St

Gore St

Church St

Young St

Wharf Rd

Carenage Rd

Mitchell's Lane

Villa Rd

Dean Rd

Tanteen Terrace

Lowther's Lane

Esplanade

St. George's Bay

B

Sendall Tunnel

Library

Bruce St

Fort George

Port Tourist Office

Tyrrel St

Tanteen Rd

TANTEEN

12°03'15"N

Cruise Ship Pier

Fort George Point

St. George's

Harbour

The Spout

Grenada Yacht Club

Botanical Gardens

Paddock Rd

The Lagoon

Grenada Yacht Services

Mt. Pandy Beach

BALLAST GROUND

To Grand Anse and Airport

Ballast Ground Rd

Lagoon Rd

BELMONT

12°32'45"N

Sauteurs, a rock promontory in the island's north coast, in 1651. Over the next century, Grenada was a battlefield between the French and British until the island was declared British under the Treaty of Versailles in 1783. Soon after, the island experienced the first rebellion led by a French plantocrat, Julien Fedon, resulting in the murder of 51 British colonists. (Fedon, who was never captured, remains a legend today in Grenada.) In 1838, the Emancipation Act freed Grenada's African slaves, forcing plantation owners to import indentured laborers from India, Malta and Madera. The descendants of this cultural stew live on today in the multiethnic cuisine, the French-African lilt to the language, and the British and French village names. Until 1958, the island remained a British colony, when it joined the abortive Federation of the West Indies. In 1967 it became a member of the West Indies Associated States, with Britain retaining responsibility. Many Grenadians were opposed to self-rule under Eric Gairy, the first prime minister, who was often compared to Haiti's Papa Doc Duvalier. Nevertheless, Gairy became a champion of the poor overnight, though he gained an irreverent reputation for some strange actions—for example, marching a steel band through an opponent's meeting and lecturing the U.N. about UFOs. In the early '70s, Maurice Bishop, a charismatic lawyer, just back from his studies in England, earned popular support as a human-rights activist when his New Jewel Movement convicted Gairy of 27 crimes in a mock trial that called for his resignation. Bishop, along with other members of his party, was mercilessly beaten by Gairy's police and thrown into jail for the night.

Such was the climate when Grenada (and its two dependencies, Carriacou and Petit Martinique) gained independence from the British Commonwealth in 1974. By the late 1970s, Gairy's economy was a shambles and his support diminished, even among the poor. On March 13, 1979, Bishop staged the first modern coup in the English-speaking Caribbean while Gairy was off-island. The economy improved and countries around the world accepted Bishop and the New Jewel Movement as a governing force. Still, free elections were never held. Bishop fostered ties with Cuba and the Eastern Bloc countries, and as his friend Fidel Castro granted Grenada aid and labor to build a larger airport at Port Salines in the south, U.S. ties began to unravel. In 1983 Bishop was ousted by a more Marxist/Leninist member of his own party, Bernard Coard, who placed Bishop under house arrest and imprisoned some of his followers. At a rally to support the release of Bishop, members of the People's Revolutionary Army fired into the throng; today no one is sure how many men, women and children were killed. Using the subsequent brutal execution of Bishop as pretext, the U.S. government landed 7000 troops on October 26, 1983, on Grenada, accompanied by the military forces of other neighboring islands. Ostensibly the invasion was to protect democracy and defend the lives of some 1000 Americans residing there, mostly medical students at St. George's University. The American troops were welcomed with open arms by most Grenadians who called the mission not an invasion, but an "intervention."

The aftermath of what is considered a bad dream by Grenadians resulted in new bridges, a retrained police force, and a renewed sense of democracy. Americans put the finishing touches on the Point Salines Airport and American Airlines began a daily run in 1990. But some islanders look back on the period when American cash flowed thick and fast as a missed opportunity, that more could have been done with the money to build the island's infrastructure (U.S. aid plunged from $225 million in 1985, to $26 million a decade later). Surprisingly, under the tenure of current Grenadian Prime Minister Dr. Keith Mitchell, the island is flirting with Cuba again. Fidel Castro is helping fund construction of a new stadium just outside St. George's, and political ties between the two countries are increasingly friendly—a visit from Castro is planned for some time in 1998. Says Mitchell, "We're taking all the aid we can get." For the moment, Washington turns a blind eye, while Grenada holds its democratic elections every five years.

People

The nation's three-island population is about 96,000 (of whom 87,000 live on Grenada), many of whom live off the land or sea. Grenada is a youthful country and more than half of the population is under 30 years of age, though unfortunately, unemployment is a substantial problem to be reckoned with. In addition to supplying roughly one-quarter of the world's nutmeg, 120-square-mile Grenada also grows bananas, sugar cane, cocoa, breadfruit and most of the other fruits and vegetables it consumes. Agriculture still employs a number of people, but the fragility of the global market was shown when the price of nutmeg plummeted from $2.60 a pound in the 1980s to about 40 cents today; the future of banana exports is also shaky. As a result, the government is increasingly committed to tourism as a long-term solution to economic woes, and in 1996 announced a $75 million commitment to upgrade and expand the current infrastructure.

Like other recently created Caribbean countries freed from colonial ties, Grenadians are politically aware and fascinated by foreigners. Warm and witty, islanders are insatiably curious, often quizzing tourists on Clintonomics or the latest about Michael Jackson. Grenadians are very pro-American, and still grateful to the U.S. and Ronald Reagan for the military intervention of 1983. They receive visitors with open arms, though like many in the region, they prefer to be asked before you snap their picture, particularly at the (very photogenic) market square in St. George's. An innovative "People to People" program invites visitors to experience Grenada through the eyes of a local for a few hours, whether at church, during a game of golf, or over a meal. Call **New Trends Tours** *(473) 444-1236.*

Grenada has a number of fine beaches, though some are accessible only by boat and, as with most of the islands in this part of the Caribbean, the Atlantic side comes equipped with an undertow that can make swimming tricky. The most famous and popular is **Grand Anse**, a mile-and-a-half stretch that begins just south of St. George's and is a center for watersports, beach peddlers and hair-braiders. When cruise ships dock, daytrippers tend to gather at the western end (where most of the accommodations are clustered); otherwise there's almost always room to spread out on this excellent beach. The best of the rest are also on the southwest end of the island. Just west of Grand Anse is **Morne Rouge**, a quiet cove with a small snack bar. A little further, the Rex Grenadian overlooks **Magazin Beach**, and just beyond is tranquil **Pink Gin Beach**, at LaSource. East of the Point Salines Airport is **L'Ance aux Epines**, a peninsula with several coves lining Prickly Bay. Along the deeply scalloped southern shore are other beaches, most reached by boat or four-wheel drive vehicle. More accessible is **La Sagesse**, where a placid grey-sand cove is backed by cow pastures and a nature preserve. Untrammeled **Levera Beach**, at the northern tip of the Grenada, overlooks several islets at the point where the Atlantic and Caribbean meet; it's quite a beauty, and might be devoid of footprints or towels when you visit, but the government is discussing a possible hotel development. **Bathway Beach** just south of here is also nice, with a natural "swimming hole" formed by coral that protects bathers from the rougher Atlantic surf. Carriacou's best beaches are **Sandy Island**, reached by five-minute boat ride off Hillsborough, **Anse la Roche** at the foot of High North Peak and reached by a 20-minute path from the Caribbee Inn, and **Tyrrel Bay** on the southwest coast.

Diving is a low-key, comfortable pursuit in Grenada, free of much of the hustle and crowding prevalent at better-established locations. Part of this can simply be attributed to the newness of the sport here. In the rush to attract visitors and develop a tourism infrastructure in the years following the excitement of 1983, it took awhile to recognize that the island boasted attractive dive sites. Most are located at **Moliniere Point**, a 10- to 15-minute boat ride north from the Grand Anse area, where the dive shops are based. The *Bianca C*, easily the Caribbean's largest wreck, is a very dramatic dive which will thrill sunken ship enthusiasts. Farther afield, the pristine area off Carriacou should not be overlooked. Snorkelers looking for shore dives should check out the cliffs at the south end of **Grand Anse** or nearby **Point Salines**; boat trips will take snorkelers to Moliniere or to Boss Reef off Grand Anse Bay.

Dive Shops

Dive Grenada

Grand Anse; ☎ *(800) 329-8388, (473) 444-1092.*
Grenada's first dive shop opened in 1989. Believes scuba should be a low-impact sport and attempts to locate drift dives whenever possible. PADI courses (up to assistant instructor). Two-tank dive, $50.

Grand Anse Aquatics

Grand Anse; ☎ *(473) 444-1046.*
New retail store makes this a PADI five-star facility. Single-tank dives, $40. Weekly runs up to Isle de Ronde; two dives, $90, including lunch.

Scuba World

Grand Anse; ☎ *(473) 444-4371.*
Friendly staff and good equipment. PADI courses up through divemaster. Separate location at the Rex Grenadian on Point Salines. Two-tank dive, $65, or an all-day trip (with lunch) to north coast areas, $110. Snorkeling trips.

Silver Beach Diving

Carriacou; ☎ *(473) 443-7337.*
An independent operator, the only one based on Carriacou. PADI facility with courses to assistant instructor on request. Single-tank dive, $40. Also offers half-day snorkel trips to Sandy Island and Anse La Roche, $23.

On Foot

For a bantam destination, the rumpled topography of Grenada provides splendid opportunities, making the island one of the better hiking destinations in the Eastern Caribbean. As you trek through Grenada's gentle range of mountains amid wafts of the local nutmeg and cloves, the term "spice island" will float through your senses. A variety of fruits and vegetables are also grown here, and contribute to Grenada's interior appeal. The truly ambitious can combine **Mount Qua Qua**, **Fedon's Camp** and **Concord Falls**, which are relatively close to each other, for a vivid all-day trek. Less grandiose ambitions can be sated in the coves and hills surrounding **La Sagesse Nature Center**; the owners will eagerly point you toward several trails, particularly if you stay for lunch. Several of the island's bigger hikes invite a guide's familiarity for uncomplicated navigation. But it's worth noting that escorts are available for anything harder than getting out of your car, which means you are in the awkward position of evaluating your physical stamina and Caribbean route-finding abilities—always carry a good map—vs. the leadership and amiable banter of a knowledgeable tour guide. If in doubt, spring for the local help; but, although tracks divide, cross and converge with maddening frequency, it's hard to get lost for long on this cozy island.

Trekking Tours

Henry's Safari Tours

St. George's; ☎ (473) 444-5313.

The very pleasant Denis Henry manages a group of guides who handle the island's hikes as well as driving tours. The trek to the Seven Sisters is $70 for a solo traveler, $45 each for a pair.

What Else to See

Grenada is full of natural wonders, but begin your tour by strolling through the narrow streets and cobbled alleys of **St. George's**, the superbly picturesque capital, established in 1705 by the French, though English Georgian architecture predominates. The town surrounds a tiny harbour, the **Carenage**, where the French careened their ships—it was once a volcanic crater (easy to appreciate from above). The local tourist board offers a helpful pamphlet, *Historic Walking Tour of St. George's*, which will add to your explorations. But the sightseeing opportunities aren't limited to static ones: the crisply-uniformed, white-gloved traffic officers at the intersection of Young and Church Streets and at the top of Scott Street are delightful. There are centuries-old churches to explore and you can even walk through **Fort George**, where Maurice Bishop et al were assassinated in 1983, precipitating the American intervention (today it houses the police headquarters). Despite the sorrowful setting, the fort provides excellent views of St. George's and the southern coastline. Stop by the **National Museum**, once a French garrison, where an antique rum still, wildlife specimens and even personal effects of Josephine Bonaparte—including the marble tub she used as a child—are kept. Though almost any is lively, the best day to take in St. George's **market square** is Saturday, when the plaza bustles with the brightest aromas and colors of the Caribbean as vendors set out their fruits, vegetables and spices. For a few dollars, you can come home laden with baskets of cocoa sticks (to make tea), sorrel, tannia, yams, limes, mangoes and papayas.

Outside St. George's stick to the sensory theme by heading up the Caribbean coast to the **Dougaldston Spice Plantation** outside the town of Gouyave, where you can explore the secrets of nutmeg cultivation. Afterward, a dollar will get you into the **Nutmeg Processing Plant**, where the nuts and mace are separated and graded by hand, then loaded into huge burlap bags for shipping. In the center of the island is the lush **Grand Etang Forest Reserve**—an idyllic lake nestled in the bowl of a volcanic crater. The east coast of Grenada is riddled with winding roads, inviting you to lose your way en route to **Grenville**, the island's second-largest town, a fishing village typical of an earlier era, and also home to a Saturday morning market. Further north, a small side road takes you to one of Grenada's nine remaining rum factories, the **Rive Antoine Rum Distillery**—notable as one of the last factories of any kind in the Western Hemisphere powered by water wheel. The men who work the machinery will provide a brief, impromptu tour, though the rum they produce is true firewater. The river that supplies the distillery's power comes from **Lake Antoine**, also an extinct volcano—a road leads up to the verdant crater lip, while the lake below is just 20 feet above sea level.

Historical Sites

Fort George   ★ ★

Church Street, St. George's.
Built by the French in 1705 on a promontory to guard the entrance to the harbor, this old fort has lots of small rooms and four-inch-thick walls, and excellent views of St. George's. But it is most famous for its more recent history—Fort George is the site where Maurice Bishop et al were killed, precipitating the American intervention of Grenada. The fort is now used as police barracks; the nondescript basketball court is where the assassinations took place.

HEAVENLY HIKES THROUGH GRENADA

Volcanic crater lakes, rain forests, dramatic mountains, and soaring seaside cliffs—the diverse topography of Grenada is a walker's paradise. Hire a guide to lead you on the more strenuous treks.

Petit Martinique

Windward

Camp Fedon

This challenging, five-hour (one-way) walk over an ancient Carib Indian path begins at the top of Concord Falls. The trail passes giant mahogany trees, teak trees and huge ferns and leads to a cave once used as a hide-out by Grenadian rebel Julian Fedon in 1795.

Hillsborough

Carriacou

St. Mark Bay

Mt. Granby

Concord Falls

The first stage of the falls lies close to the road and is popular with swimmers. A footpath across slippery rocks leads to the second-stage falls, a moderately strenuous 45-minute hike (faster coming back). The third stage, Fountainbleu Falls, is a challenging hike that requires three hours for a round trip from the second-stage falls.

Annandale Falls

The most accessible falls on Grenada, Annandale Falls can be reached via a set of cement steps. Enjoy a picnic or a swim beneath the falls. Nearby, an herb and spice garden provides an up-close look at the island's main crops.

Moliniére Pt.

Bay Gardens

Winding paths of crushed nutmeg shells lead strollers through more than three acres planted with 3000 tropical species. Situated on the site of an old sugar mill, Bay Gardens also features fish ponds and a turtle aquarium.

Pt. S

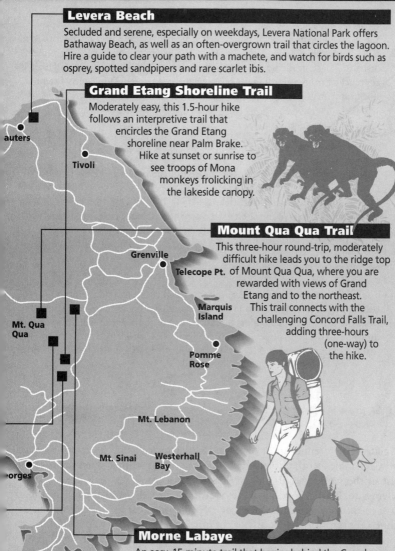

Levera Beach

Secluded and serene, especially on weekdays, Levera National Park offers Bathaway Beach, as well as an often-overgrown trail that circles the lagoon. Hire a guide to clear your path with a machete, and watch for birds such as osprey, spotted sandpipers and rare scarlet ibis.

Grand Etang Shoreline Trail

Moderately easy, this 1.5-hour hike follows an interpretive trail that encircles the Grand Etang shoreline near Palm Brake. Hike at sunset or sunrise to see troops of Mona monkeys frolicking in the lakeside canopy.

Mount Qua Qua Trail

This three-hour round-trip, moderately difficult hike leads you to the ridge top of Mount Qua Qua, where you are rewarded with views of Grand Etang and to the northeast. This trail connects with the challenging Concord Falls Trail, adding three-hours (one-way) to the hike.

Morne Labaye

An easy, 15-minute trail that begins behind the Grand Etang Forest Park Visitor's Center and leads to a look-out point to view the east coast and Mount Sinai. A brochure explains 12 points of interest.

auters

Tivoli

Grenville

Telecope Pt.

Marquis Island

Mt. Qua Qua

Pomme Rose

Mt. Lebanon

Mt. Sinai

Westerhall Bay

orges

GRENADA

Museums and Exhibits

Grenada National Museum   ★★★

Monckton Street, St. George's, ☎ (473) 440-3725.
Hours open: 9 a.m.–4:30 p.m.

Set in the foundations of an old French army barracks and prison dating back to
1704, this small museum has some interesting exhibits on the island's natural and
historical past, right up to and including the 1983 intervention, which is
approached from a refreshingly level-headed viewpoint. Don't miss Josephine
Bonaparte's marble bathtub. General admission: $2.

Parks and Gardens

Grand Etang National Park   ★★★★★

Main Interior Road, St. George's, ☎ (473) 442-7425.
Hours open: 8:30 a.m.–4 p.m.

This rainforest and bird sanctuary, located in the island's interior between St.
George's and Grenville, has lots of gorgeous, unspoiled scenery. Several trails wind
throughout for easy to difficult treks (see "On Foot"). Don't miss Grand Etang
Lake, whose 13 acres of cobalt blue waters are nestled in the crater of an extinct volcano—the shoreline is canvassed by mona monkeys. General admission: $1.

Tours

Nutmeg Processing Plant   ★★

Gouyave

You'll never again take this little spice for granted after a half-hour tour of the processing plant. Nutmeg is Grenada's largest export and smells sweet, too. Just inland
from the plant is the **Dougaldston Estate**, where some of the island's spices are
grown. This is a good place to buy Grenadian coffee, which is not exported off the
island. General admission: $1.

Sports

Sailing is the premier sport on Grenada, particularly the classic trip through
the Grenadines to the north, with conditions sometimes referred to as the
best in the world. Seagoing travelers always come back with great tales of
derring-do, hidden coves, and the occasional near-disaster (the south-bound
passage is usually considered easier). Numerous charter operations can arrange programs of any length or for any vessel (rates are about 30 percent
lower in the off-season). The **Carriacou Regatta**, held the first weekend in August, attracts seamen from all over the world who thrive on the ferocious
competition. Hobie cats, sailfish, sunfish and other small boats can be rented
on Grand Anse for short excursions. **Sportfishing** is excellent November
through May; a few operators offer four-hour or longer charters. Several ho-

tels have **tennis courts**, including Calabash, Coral Cove, LaSource, Secret Harbour, Spice Island Inn and the Grenada Renaissance.

Bicycling

Casual rides through the gentle hills south of St. George's, through L'anse Aux Epines and Point Saline, are pleasant, while stronger riders should investigate the main east coast road from Gouyave to Sauteur. **Ride Grenada** in Grand Anse (next to Green Grocer) rents Raleigh 15- and 18-speeds ☎ *(473) 444-1157.*

Golf

Grenada Golf and Country Club, Grand Anse, ☎ *(473) 444-4128.*

Not the greatest golf course in the world, but since it's the only one on the island, it'll do. The nine-hole course has some nice views. Greens fees are a reasonable $20 and club rentals are available.

Watersports

Various locations.

Grand Anse is the headquarters for most watersports activities. In addition to the Scuba outfits (see "Underwater"), check out the following for snorkeling: **Sanvics Scuba and Watersports** ☎ *(473) 444-4271* offers trips aboard their 32-foot pirogue; **Captain Peters' Water Taxi** ☎ *(473) 440-1349* provides daytrips to Calivigny and Hog Islands; **Aquarium Beach Club** ☎ *(473) 444-1410* offers kayaks and snorkeling equipment from a spot right near the airport. A number of charter boat companies sell day or extended sailing trips: **Seabreeze Yacht Charters** ☎ *(473) 444-4924*, **The Moorings** ☎ *(473) 444-4439* and **Footloose Yacht Charters** ☎ *(473) 440-7949* are the biggest outfits. For deep-sea fishing: **Evans Chartering Services** ☎ *(473) 444-4422* or **Bezo Charters** ☎ *(473) 443-5477*. A major fishing tournament is held each January.

FIELDING'S CHOICE:

Every other Saturday a bunch of Grenadians known as the Hash House Harriers get together, split into teams, and set off on chases through glorious countryside on trails that always end up at Rudolf's, a bar next to the Carenage in St. George's. It's a great way to meet and mingle with those Grenadians not in good enough shape for the triathlon.

Where to Stay

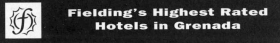

Fielding's Highest Rated Hotels in Grenada

★★★★	Calabash Hotel	$205–$545
★★★★	LaSource	$275–$630
★★★★	Spice Island Beach Resort	$260–$725
★★★	Blue Horizons Cottage Hotel	$105–$180
★★★	Caribbee Inn	$90–$250
★★★	Coyaba Beach Resort	$80–$175
★★★	Renaissance Grenada Resort	$129–$246
★★★	Rex Grenadian	$115–$275
★★★	Secret Harbour Resort	$130–$230
★★★	Twelve Degrees North	$130–$195

Fielding's Most Ideal Hideaways in Grenada

★★★★	Calabash Hotel	$205–$545
★★	La Sagesse Nature Center	$50–$95
★★★	Caribbee Inn	$90–$250
★★★	Secret Harbour Resort	$130–$230
★★★	Twelve Degrees North	$130–$195

Fielding's Best Value Hotels in Grenada

★★	La Sagesse Nature Center	$50–$95
★★★	Secret Harbour Resort	$130–$230
★★★	Coyaba Beach Resort	$80–$175
★★★	Blue Horizons Cottage Hotel	$105–$180
★★	Siesta Hotel	$60–$135

La Sagesse Nature Center is located in a remote setting near hiking and bird-watching trails. It's a favorite with nature lovers.

More than 85 percent of Grenada's hotels are owned by Grenadians; their personal stake in tourism is somewhat unique in the Caribbean. But a new era is dawning—the success of the **Rex Grenadian** and **LaSource** properties that opened in late 1993 caused a significant jump in tourism arrivals. In 1996, the government announced an initiative to substantially increase the number of rooms from 1600 to 2500 (by the year 2006). One of the first to participate in this new boom is expected to be the **Ritz-Carlton** chain, which has grand plans for a resort on Hog Island (off L'Anse aux Epines) and golf course, with construction slated to begin in late 1997. The ripples from this project are only just beginning to be felt.

Most of Grenada's accommodations are found along or near Grand Anse, with other properties scattered around the southern tip of the island, between Point Salines and L'Anse aux Epines. These are not high-rise hotels, but mostly small, intimate inns and self-catering complexes (by law, no hotel can be more than three stories). The variety of accommodations, from budget guest houses to luxury establishments and everything in between, is excellent, providing rooms for virtually any type of Caribbean traveler. The **Grenada Hotel Association** produces an accommodations directory listing all properties on the three islands; they also act as a booking service for smaller hotels and can be reached toll-free from the U.S. ☎ *(800) 322-1753.* See "Carriacou" and "Petit Martinique" below for accommodations on those islands.

Hotels and Resorts

The last decade has brought a surfeit of new hotels and renovations to Grenada. The newest additions to the island are **LaSource**, an all-inclusive 100-room resort with a spa and a nine-hole, non-regulation golf course, and the **Rex Grenadian**, the island's largest hotel at the edge of a three-acre lagoon. Both hotels benefit from their own white sandy beaches. A new hotel slated to open on Grand Anse for the 1998 season is the **Grand Anse Beach Club**, next to the Coyaba Beach Resort; winter rates will start at about $149 for a garden view unit ☎ *(473) 444-4646.*

Calabash Hotel   **$205–$545**   ★★★★

L'Anse aux Epines, ☎ *(800) 528-5835, (473) 444-4334, FAX (473) 444-5050.*
Closed Date: June.
Single: $205–$510. Double: $235–$545.
A lovely and soothing escape, accommodations at Calabash are arranged in a horse-shoe around a garden of coconut palms and bougainvillea on an eight-acre estate fronting a placid cove. The rooms are suites housed in two-story stone and wood cottages—some have private plunge pools in back, others Jacuzzis but all are bright and cheery. One of the hotel's best features is that a maid prepares breakfast in your room each morning, to be served on the patio (she'll avoid disturbing your slumber via a separate entrance). There are three bars and an excellent restaurant, a pool, non-motorized watersports and tennis, frequent live entertainment and wonderful, attentive service by a staff that seems proud to be part of the operation (rather than offering stiff servitude). You've got to admire management cheeky enough to depict their "busy sales office" as down on the beach, laptop and phone in hand, and a bucket of champagne just within reach. Calabash is known for Old Money and honeymooners, but privacy prevails, making the resort a haven for anyone longing for gracious retreat. 30 rooms. Credit cards: A, MC, V.

Coyaba Beach Resort   **$80–$175**   ★★★

Grand Anse, ☎ *(473) 444-4129, FAX (473) 444-4808.*
Single: $80–$125. Double: $100–$175.
Set on the site of an ancient Arawak Indian village, this recently expanded, family-run hotel puts guests up in tropically decorated rooms just off the sands of Grand Anse. The accommodations are a bit motel-like and the amenities are pretty simple, but there's tennis courts, an appealing pool with the island's only swim-up bar, and the beach is terrific. Sunfish sailing and windsurfing are included in the rates. 70 rooms. Credit cards: A, DC, D, MC, V.

Flamboyant Hotel   **$80–$150**   ★★

Grand Anse, ☎ *(800) 223-9815, (473) 444-4247, FAX (473) 444-1234.*
Website: www.cpscaribnet.com/ads/flambo/flambo.html. E-mail: flambo@caribsurf.com.
Single: $80–$115. Double: $90–$130. Suites Per Day: $100–$150.
Great views are the calling card for this popular property, set up on a hillside that slopes gently down to the southern end of Grand Anse. Most rooms are fairly standard, but there are one-bedroom suites with kitchenettes and two-bedroom cottages; most have sweeping views. The good location makes this a relative bargain, and the friendly staff keeps guests happy. There's a restaurant, pool and free snorkel equipment; the beach is less than five minutes from most rooms. An expansion was planned for late 1997. 41 rooms. Credit cards: A, DC, D, MC, V.

LaSource   **$275–$630**   ★★★★

Pink Gin Beach, Pt. Saline, ☎ *(800) 544-2883, (473) 444-2556, FAX (473) 444-2561.*

Single: $275–$380. Double: $420–$630.

Grenada's sole all-inclusive resort is situated along a half-mile beach on Grenada's southwest tip. Accommodations are lovely, with Persian rugs, mahogany furniture, four-poster beds and original artwork by Canute Calliste (of Carriacou); some upstairs units have terrific cathedral ceilings. The price is steep, but includes all meals, drinks, watersports (including scuba, water-skiing and sailing) and—best of all—pampering treatments in the spa (one a day included in the rates). When you're not being spoiled by a massage, you can play tennis or a short nine holes of golf, work out in the gym, swim in the ocean, or try one of the more eclectic offerings like a class in fencing, archery or yoga. All in all, one or the more relaxed and pleasant all-inclusive properties in the region. 100 rooms. Credit cards: A, DC, D, MC, V.

Renaissance Grenada Resort $129–$376   ★★★

Grand Anse, ☎ *(800) 228-9898, (473) 444-4371, FAX (473) 444-4800.*
Single: $129–$246. Double: $129–$246. Suites Per Day: $376–$376.
This complex has a prime location—right on Grand Anse and across from a good shopping complex—but lacks island flavor; in 1997 the resort was just starting a much-needed spruce-up. Accommodations in two-story buildings are comfortable but on the small side, and the motel-like furnishings are generic. On the plus side, the resort offers a complete range of amenities, from watersports to tennis courts to yacht charters, and attracts families with its supervised children's programs (on holidays); the resort attracts occasional conventions. The two-and-a-half mile beach is terrific. 195 rooms. Credit cards: A, DC, D, MC, V.

Rex Grenadian $115–$600   ★★★

Magazine Beach, Pt. Saline, ☎ *(800) 255-5859, (473) 444-3333, FAX (473) 444-1111.*
E-mail: grenrex@caribsurf.com.
Single: $115–$275. Double: $115–$275. Suites Per Day: $240–$600.
A 1993 addition to Grenada and the island's biggest hotel, this Rex property offers most of the bells and whistles resort lovers expect. Set on 12 acres that open onto two beaches, the hotel houses guests in blandly decorated standard rooms, or pay a little extra for air conditioning, a bigger bathroom with a tub, or perhaps a view of the nice beach. A couple of restaurants provide dining choices (the location is a bit isolated), there's a pleasant, elevated pool area, and the usual watersports, exercise room and tennis are available. There's a lagoon stretching over two acres at the entrance. Decent value for the bucks, but expect occasional business groups, along with a predominantly British clientele. 212 rooms. Credit cards: A, MC, V.

Siesta Hotel $60–$135   ★★

Grand Anse, ☎ *(800) 742-4276, (473) 444-4645, FAX (473) 444-4647.*
E-mail: siesta@caribsurf.com.
Single: $60–$115. Double: $80–$135.
Located inland from Grand Anse, this small hotel has air-conditioned rooms with comfortable furnishings; some have kitchens. The upbeat property is very clean and casual, with friendly, helpful management. There's a bustling pool and restaurant (no alcohol served); the rates for the least expensive units include breakfast. The beach is a five-minute walk. Good value for the price, and the owners are opening their Grand Anse Beach Resort for 1998. 37 rooms. Credit cards: A, D, MC, V.

Spice Island Beach Resort　　　　$260–$725　　　★★★★

Grand Anse, ☎ *(800) 223-9815, (473) 444-4258, FAX (473) 444-4807.*
Website: www.cpscaribnet.com/ads/spice/spice.html. E-mail: spiceisl@caribsurf.com.
Single: $260–$490. Double: $295–$725.

Set on eight tropical acres on a beautifully maintained stretch of Grand Anse, all accommodations at this island institution are in suites. All have whirlpool tubs and all are simply but comfortably furnished with huge, pampering bathrooms. A renovation a few years ago added private plunge pools—a generous 16 by 20 feet—to the sunny patios of 17 units (four now also have their own sauna and exercise bike). These rooms are perfect hideaways from the world, though there's no reason to escape Grenada—the Spice Island grounds are nicely done with lots of flowers and trees, and the beach is lovely. Rates are MAP, and include non-motorized watersports (kayaks, sunfish and snorkeling), bicycles, tennis, a gym and breakfast and dinner daily. 56 rooms. Credit cards: A, DC, D, MC, V.

Inns

Grenada's inns are run and owned by devoted families who make their personalities known in every detail. **True Blue Inn** is commendable for modern kitchen facilities in the one-bedroom apartments and cottages, and the attractive seaside restaurant (see "Apartments and Condominiums"). An umbrella organization, **Grenada Inns and Beach Clubs**, represents a block of smaller properties all over the island; they will send brochures for the various inns if you request it in writing: *P.O. Box 73, St. George's Grenada.*

La Sagesse Nature Center　　　$50–$95　　　★★

La Sagesse, St. David's, ☎ *(473) 444-6458, FAX (473) 444-6458.*
Website: www.caribbean-connexion.com/hotels/lsnature-html. E-mail: lsnature@carib-surf.com.
Associated Restaurant: *La Sagesse.*
Single: $50–$95. Double: $50–$95.

Located in a remote, unspoiled cove a half-hour drive from the airport, this small, family-run guesthouse offers nine rooms. Five are in the rebuilt old manor house; a few have full kitchens, all have ceiling fans (the American owners added air conditioning in one to keep his mother happy when she visits). A newer cottage has two units, one with a jacuzzi, and a pair of budget rooms in back are fine for the unfussy. The atmosphere is pleasantly informal—you might have to interrupt their daughter's math lesson to order a beer—but go with the flow and it works. The restaurant is reliable, and the surrounding area is lovely: banana fields, cow pastures, a deserted beach, with hiking and bird-watching opportunities nearby. A special discovery for nature lovers. 6 rooms. Credit cards: A, MC, V.

Secret Harbour Resort　　　$130–$230　　　★★★

L'Anse aux Epines, ☎ *(800) 334-2435, (473) 444-4548, FAX (813) 530-9747.*
Single: $130–$230. Double: $130–$230.

Overlooking Mount Hartman Bay on Grenada's southernmost tip, this attractive hotel consists of Mediterranean-style brick and stone villas in which each unit is a suite. They're decorated with four-poster beds, local art, trouser presses, large balconies and capacious Italian-tiled bathtubs. The original creators (1970) definitely had a soft spot for lovers, and the Moorings charter yacht company (that acquired the place a few years ago) has done a good job keeping the pace relaxed and intimate (children under 12 are discouraged). There's a marginal beach where watersports await, but the generous pool with sweeping views is more appealing. A three-night minimum stay, or special packages allow guests to spend a few nights aboard one of their many yachts. Either way, count on a soundtrack of creaking boats and rippling sails to lull you to sleep. 20 rooms. Credit cards: A, DC, MC, V.

True Blue Inn   **$90–$195**   ★ ★

True Blue, Point Saline, ☎ *(800) 742-4276, (473) 444-2000, FAX (473) 444-1247. Website: www.cpscaribnet.com/ads/trueblue/trueblue.html. E-mail: trueblue@caribsurf.com.*

Single: $90–$195. Double: $90–$195.

Accommodations at this south coast property are in one-bedroom apartments and two-bedroom cottages, all with air conditioning and full kitchens. There's no beach, but you can swim from the dock or a small pool is available; bicycles are provided for tooling about and a scuba shop handles divers. A nice, unpretentious atmosphere, and the restaurant, Indigo's, is well-liked. 7 rooms. Credit cards: A, DC, D, MC, V.

Apartments and Condominiums

Grenadians are leaders in the Caribbean self-catering business, and the variety of fresh tropical fruits and vegetables available here is almost unsurpassed. **Villas of Grenada** represents several dozen properties on the island, with rates starting as low as $115 per night in summer, $143 in winter ☎ *(473) 444-1896.*

Blue Horizons Cottage Hotel   **$105–$180**   ★ ★ ★

Grand Anse, ☎ *(800) 223-9815, (473) 444-4592, FAX (473) 444-2815. Website: www.cpscaribnet.com/ads/blue/blue.html. E-mail: spiceisl@caribsurf.com.* Associated Restaurant: *La Belle Creole.*

Single: $105–$170. Double: $110–$180.

Set on a terraced hillside some 300 yards from Grand Anse, accommodations are in comfortable one-bedroom cottages and duplex suites of various sizes, each air-conditioned and sporting kitchenettes. There's a restaurant and two bars on hand, as well as a pool and Jacuzzi. Watersports are at the nearby sister property, the Spice Island Inn (one hour of free non-motorized per day). The beach is a ten-minute walk, but that's what keeps the rates reasonable. 32 rooms. Credit cards: A, DC, D, MC, V.

Cinnamon Hill Hotel   **$85–$160**   ★ ★

Grand Anse, ☎ *(473) 444-4301, FAX (473) 444-2874.*

Single: $85–$130. Double: $85–$160.

This Spanish-style villa complex of several buildings scattered over a steep hillside overlooking Grand Anse. Accommodations are in very spacious one- and two-bedroom apartments with kitchens and balconies; decor is a bit frumpy, but comfortable, and most of the units are split-level. There's a restaurant and pool on-site, with watersports available on the public beach, five minutes away on foot. 20 rooms. Credit cards: A, D, MC, V.

Coral Cove Cottages   **$75–$145**   ★ ★

L'Anse aux Epines, ☎ *(473) 444-4422, FAX (473) 444-4718.*

Single: $75–$145. Double: $75–$145.

Situated on a peaceful cove with nice views six miles from St. George's, this small outfit offers one- and two-bedroom Spanish-style apartments and cute cottages with kitchenettes and terraces. There's a tennis court and small pool, but no dining facilities; the beach is fair and a jetty extends to a snorkeling area. Out of the way and informal, but a well-run little operation. 11 rooms. Credit cards: A, MC, V.

Gem Holiday Beach Resort $55–$120   ★

Morne Rouge Bay, ☎ *(800) 223-9815, (473) 444-4224, FAX (473) 444-1189.*
Single: $55–$110. Double: $60–$120.

Located on a less-known beach a mile south of Grand Anse, this apartment hotel houses guests in one- and two-bedroom units that are air-conditioned and have full kitchens. Room decor is dated; no pool, but the beachside location is fine for the price. There's a restaurant and bar, and a happening disco next door. You'll probably want a rental car to get around. 18 rooms. Credit cards: A, DC, D, MC, V.

No Problem Apartments $55–$85   ★

True Blue, Point Saline, ☎ *(473) 444-4634, FAX (473) 444-2803.*
Single: $55–$75. Double: $65–$85.

Located near the airport, this Mediterranean-style complex has clean and well-kept air-conditioned suites with full kitchens. A free shuttle takes you to town and Grand Anse (a five-minute drive), but there's little within walking distance. There's a restaurant and pool, and a sparsely stocked mini-mart. Decent for the price. 20 rooms. Credit cards: A, D, MC, V.

Twelve Degrees North $130–$195   ★★★

L'Anse aux Epines, ☎ *(800) 322-1753, (473) 444-4580, FAX (473) 444-4580.*
Website: www.cpscaribnet.com/ads/twelved/twelved.html. E-mail: 12degrsn@carib-surf.com.
Single: $130–$195. Double: $130–$195.

Now here's a special property with a unique concept. Located on the southeast coast and facing the sea, you'll find just eight self-contained apartments positioned on a hill. While bathrooms are a tad small and furnishings are lived-in rather than stylish, they're adequate to make you feel right at home—ceiling fans keep things cool. You've got a full kitchen with a stocked refrigerator on arrival, and a pleasant and semi-private deck, but soon you'll notice how well-kept your apartment is. This is because each unit has its own housekeeper who takes care of it (and you) unobtrusively through the morning. She will prepare breakfast, and your lunch and dinner if you like, before leaving at 1 p.m.—she'll keep your kitchen stocked with food (at market prices), do laundry during your stay, even packing you for home with clean clothes! Below the apartments is a lovely pool and a shoreline where kayaks and sunfish await—tennis is across the street. Twelve Degrees North offers a vacation like no other and the "no kids under 15" policy keeps the atmosphere sedate. 8 rooms. Credit cards: not accepted.

Low Cost Lodging

Grenada is stocked with inexpensive guest houses in and near Grand Anse. The quality of accommodations varies considerably, but a clean, decent double for under $50 a night is definitely possible. Try **Mamma's Lodge**, affiliated with Mamma's Restaurant and within walking distance of both St. George's and Grand Anse ☎ *(473) 440-1623*. Peace and quiet relaxation is the business at **Morne Fendue**, the rustic private home of a native Grenadian that is still full of her family antiques ☎ *(473) 442-9330*.

Tropicana Inn   **$35–$60**   ★

Lagoon Road, St. George's, ☎ *(473) 440-1586, FAX (473) 440-9797.*
Single: $35–$50. Double: $45–$60.

If a pool or beach location is not a priority and you don't mind being close to the main road into St. George's, this newer hotel is a great deal. Rooms in front overlook the lagoon (and traffic) with a small porch; rooms in back are a little larger, but lack a view (despite being called garden view). All have air conditioning and cable TV, and simple but adequate and clean furnishings. The Carenage is a five-minute walk; a decent restaurant is downstairs. 20 rooms. Credit cards: A, DC, D, MC, V.

Wave Crest Holiday Apartments   **$40–$65**   ★

Above Grand Anse, ☎ *(800) 223-3463, (473) 444-4116, FAX (473) 444-4847.*
Single: $40–$60. Double: $45–$65.

Grand Anse is a 10-minute walk (on a busy road) from this small property on a hillside in a residential area. You can choose from one- and two-bedroom apartments with air conditioning, verandas and kitchens; a few have a nice view. Pleasant and attentive management, but not much else. 20 rooms. Credit cards: A, D, MC, V.

GRENADA

Where to Eat

Fielding's Highest Rated Restaurants in Grenada

★★★★	Canboulay	$29–$42
★★★	Coconut Beach	$13–$28
★★★	La Belle Creole	$35–$35
★★★	La Sagesse	$6–$21
★★★	Morne Fendue	$15–$15

Fielding's Most Romantic Restaurants in Grenada

♥♥♥♥	Canboulay	$29–$42
♥♥♥♥	Coconut Beach	$13–$28
♥♥♥	La Belle Creole	$35–$35
♥♥♥	La Sagesse	$6–$21
♥♥♥	Morne Fendue	15–$15

Fielding's Best Value Restaurants in Grenada

★★★	La Sagesse	$6–$21
★★★	La Belle Creole	$35–$35
★★★	Coconut Beach	$13–$28
★★★★	Canboulay	$29–$42
★★	Nutmeg, The	$5–$21

Few West Indians have mastered the art of adapting local fruits, vegetables, seafood and spices to Continental-style recipes as well as Grenadians have. The restaurant scene, which traditionally centered around the island's hotels, now includes newcomers that have added not only spice but variety to island cuisine. The national dish, oil down, concocted with breadfruit and salt pork wrapped in dasheen leaves and steamed in coconut milk, is delicious. Don't miss tasting callaloo soup (made with the spinach-like leaves of the dasheen), christophene au gratin, pepperpot stew, and nutmeg ice cream. All options are possible, however, when you dine at famous **Mamma's**, where possum and armadillo are but a few of the native dishes prepared for you during an elaborate, 20-or-so-course feast. **Canboulay** is arguably the island's best dining experience, overlooking Grand Anse, while **Morne Fendue** is an island institution hosted by a woman who cooked five Thanksgiving turkeys and 40 pumpkin pies for U.S. troops in 1983. A good bakery and coffee shop is located in **Le Marquis Complex**, in the Grand Anse district.

Bird's Nest $$ ★★

> *Grand Anse,* ☎ *(473) 444-4264.*
> *Lunch: 9:30 a.m.–3 p.m., entrées $6–$10.*
> *Dinner: 3-11 p.m., entrées $8–$25.*
> A no-surprises, pleasant Chinese restaurant that also serves good sandwiches for lunch, Bird's Nest roosts opposite the supermarket in Grand Anse. Specialties include sweet and sour chicken or fish, served with tasty fried rice, or you may splurge on various lobster preparations. Take-out is available. The restaurant is open on Sunday for dinner only, from 6-11 p.m. Credit cards: A, D, MC, V.

Canboulay $$$ ★★★★

> *Morne Rouge,* ☎ *(473) 444-4401.*
> *Lunch: 11:30 a.m.– 2:30 p.m., entrées $7–$20.*
> *Dinner: 6:30-10 p.m, entrées $29–$42. Closed: Sun.*
> For a grand night out in a casual setting, choose this festive restaurant with a view of the lights of St. George's across the bay. The decor and the tropical cuisine reflect the heritage of Trinidad-born owners Erik and Gina-lee Johnson, where spices, heady scents and Carnival are a way of life. Though they tell people the food is free— they just charge for the stellar view, the Johnsons really shine in the kitchen, blending African, Asian and Caribbean elements gracefully. Try the Prawn Possey— shrimp poached in a puree of papaya and wine, or pumpkin ravioli filled with sweet potato served over creamy pesto with frizzled eggplant and chive. Desserts are equally memorable. Entree prices include starter course, salad and dessert. Reservations recommended. Credit cards: A, MC, V.

Coconut Beach $$$ ★★★

> *Grand Anse,* ☎ *(473) 444-4644.*
> *Lunch: 12:30–6 p.m., entrées $6–$28.*
> *Dinner: 6–10 p.m., entrées $13–$28. Closed: Tue.*
> Plant your feet in the sand of Grand Anse while you dine in high style under palm-frond shelters, or in the dining room of a spiffy, native house with an open kitchen where the chefs deftly saute the catch of the day in gleaming cookware. French flair takes over with lobster in various butter sauces or lambi (conch) curry; other mouth-watering choices are ribs, chicken or steak. A good lunch menu of crepes, salads or sandwiches offers most dishes for under $10 (the conch salad is delicious). Credit cards: A, DC, D, MC, V.

Cot Bam $$ ★

Grand Anse, ☎ *(473) 444-2050.*
Lunch: *9 a.m.–2 p.m., entrées $5–$13.*
Dinner: *2–11 p.m., entrées $12–$23.*

Savory, quick meals and a cold brew draw guests to this tin-roofed bar and grill after a hard day at the beach. Since it's within strolling distance of all hotels on Grand Anse, why settle for room service? Snacks and meals include West Indian rotis, salads, shrimp and chips, etc. The cheerless service is perfunctory, on its best days. Live entertainment on Thursday, Friday and Saturday. Credit cards: A, D, MC, V.

Delicious Landing $ ★★

The Carenage, St. George's, ☎ *(473) 440-9747.*
Lunch: *10:30 a.m.–2 p.m., entrées $5–$9.*
Dinner: *6:30–11:30 p.m., entrées $8–$20. Closed: Sun.*

Although a few Grenadian eating establishments boast enviable views, Delicious Landing has the best one of the Carenage, situated right on the water's edge on the second floor. Despite the diner-like ambiance, decently prepared seafood and fish is featured, as well as local specialties, like conch stew, barbecue chicken, oil down (by request), lambi steak, all at reasonable prices. Try the fish pando—fresh catch in coconut cream and callaloo bargi, or a cinnamon daiquiri. Credit cards: MC, V.

La Belle Creole $$$ ★★★

Grand Anse, ☎ *(473) 444-4316.* Associated hotel: *Blue Horizons.*
Lunch: *12:30–2:30 p.m., entrées $5–$13.*
Dinner: *7–9 p.m., prix fixe $35.*

Creative West Indian dishes are served in this airy terrace restaurant on the grounds of the Blue Horizons Cottages. For many years "Mamma" Audrey Hopkin cooked up a reputation as the best home Creole chef in town, and now her sons have carried the torch. Real men (and women) eat quiche here, which is an unusual combo of callaloo (dasheen leaf) and lobster or shrimp; there's also veal Creole, spiced ginger pork chops, and a tasty fish mousse. Desserts are imaginative—try the unique farine pudding—however they, like the entrées, can be surprisingly heavy and rich (as is the service). The rotating fixed-price menu covers a five course meal. Reservations suggested. Credit cards: A, DC, D, MC, V.

La Sagesse $ ★★★

Eastern Main Road, ☎ *(473) 444-6458.* Associated hotel: *La Sagesse.*
Lunch: *11 a.m.–3:30 p.m., entrées $6–$21.*
Dinner: *6:30–9 p.m., entrées $6–$21.*

This charming restaurant by the sea is part of La Sagesse Nature Center, formerly the home of a cousin of Queen Elizabeth, now a rustic guest house at the edge of a banana plantation. Fittingly, patrons get a nice selection of vegetables and blended tropical fruit drinks. Other dishes include seafood, pastas, sandwiches and burgers (red meat is otherwise scarce)—all fresh and nicely prepared. The calm waters here are about 30 minutes from St. George's. A great lunch spot. Credit cards: A, MC, V.

Mamma's $$ ★★

Lagoon Road, St. George's, ☎ *(473) 440-1459.*
Dinner: *7:30–11 p.m., prix fixe $19.*

Yes, eating here is like Sunday dinner at Mamma's—if she was West Indian. But no one has to wait until the end of the week to dine here; Mamma's daughter Cleo and other family members set out a groaning buffet of some 20-plus local dishes in a friendly, boardinghouse atmosphere every day of the week. The menu features the overwhelming bounty of this verdant isle, including christophene stuffed with crab, oil down (breadfruit, meats, callaloo in coconut milk), curries and some pretty exotic fare like stewed armadillo and iguana. It's not really a fine culinary experience, but plenty of fun. Reservations suggested.

Morne Fendue $$ ★★★
St. Patrick's, near Sateurs, St. George's, ☎ (473) 442-9330.
Lunch: 12:30–3 p.m., prix fixe $15. Closed: Sun.
Lunch at this history-laden plantation home under owner Betty Mascoll, who has been holding court here for many years (and is well into her 80s), is an island institution. So come while you can, and reserve a place at this traditional West Indian buffet, making friends with the repeat visitors and a faithful staff that prepares peas and rice, stewed chicken and island vegetables every afternoon except Sundays and holidays. Mrs. Mascoll says the original pepper pot was "killed off by the communists in '83," but the current version has been brewing since January 1984. The house itself, built of native stone and decorated with family keepsakes, is a national treasure. Located near the north end of Grenada—make it part of your island tour. Reservations suggested.

Nutmeg, The $ ★★
The Carenage, St. George's, ☎ (473) 440-2539.
Lunch: 11:30 a.m.–11 p.m., entrées $5–$21.
Dinner: 4–11 p.m., entrées $5–$21.
This well-known and widely visited restaurant with a view of seagoing vessels in St. George's Carenage features the namesake spice in a few specialties, including a nutmeg ice cream and a fine rum punch. Otherwise, for a few dollars, sample local dishes like callaloo soup, roti, curried lambi or fish sandwiches and fries, washed down with Carib beer. The scenery is great, and the restaurant is popular with local yachties and cruise ship passengers alike. Breakfast is served Monday–Saturday from 8 a.m.; open Sunday from 2:30 p.m. on. Credit cards: A, MC, V.

Portofino $$ ★★
The Carenage, St. George's, ☎ (473) 440-3986.
Italian cuisine. Specialties: Pizza, Pstas.
Lunch: 11 a.m.–3 p.m., entrées $8–$23.
Dinner: 3–11 p.m., entrées $8–$23.
A comforting plate of pasta plus a harbor view make this upper-level Italian charmer an unbeatable draw. A good variety of pizzas and pastas, most under $12, plus lobster and veal dishes. Jazz often plays in the background, putting everyone in a relaxed mood. Open Sundays for dinner only, from 5 p.m. Credit cards: A, MC, V.

Red Crab, The $$$ ★★
L'Anse aux Epines, St. George's, ☎ (473) 444-4424.
Lunch: 11 a.m.–2 p.m., entrées $10–$31.
Dinner: 6–11 p.m., entrées $10–$31. Closed: Sun.

This place should have been named the Plush Cow, because although it serves seafood, old-timers roll in here for the beefsteaks, which are among the best on the island. Curried lambi and shrimp crepes under the pines are also reliable. It's located in posh L'Anse aux Epines, which draws in many of the island's upper crust for live music on Mondays and Fridays (in season). Credit cards: A, D, MC, V.

Rudolf's   **$$**   ★

The Carenage, St. George's, ☎ *(473) 440-2241.*
Lunch: 10 a.m.–3 p.m., entrées $8–$19.
Dinner: 3 p.m.–midnight, entrées $8–$19. Closed: Sun.
Although it's got a humming bar scene with yacht owners, Rudolf's features a large selection of seafood and steak dishes for those who want to eat here. It also helps that this pub-style eatery with a harbor view has some of the best prices in town—many dishes are under $10. There are daily specials, usually lobster or conch (highly recommended), as well as sandwiches, salads and fish and chips. Stick with these and other traditional favorites and you'll have a decent meal. Credit cards: MC, V.

Where to Shop

Shopping isn't duty-free on Grenada, but bargains do exist. Special buys to bring home are spice baskets or coconut shells full of native-grown nutmeg, cinnamon, cloves, coriander and others—perfect for Christmas gifts or spicing the eggnog. At St. George's market square there are spice vendors who stroll up and down the streets barking their prices (don't be shy about bargaining). You can find other shopping centers on the Esplanade side of Fort George, and on Melville Street, facing the harbor. Grenada shops open and close with their own schedules, but usually cater their hours to cruise ship arrivals. The best time to visit market square on Granby Street is on Saturday mornings.

Carriacou

Blessed with an Amerindian name that means "island of many reefs," 13-square-mile Carriacou (pronounced *Carry*-a-coo) is the largest of the Grenadines, the chain of tiny islands that pepper the 70-mile-long channel between Grenada and St. Vincent. Unlike the other Grenadines, this postage-stamp paradise (and Petit Martinique, below) is politically connected to Grenada, though the occasional call for secession rises up now and again as Carriacou carves out its own identity. But many overlook the island, including the U.S. marines that landed on Grenada on October 25, 1983—it is said they weren't aware of Carriacou and didn't reach the smaller island until

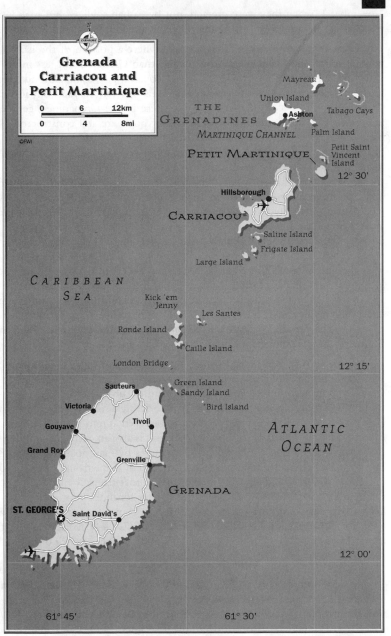

Grenada
Carriacou and
Petit Martinique

| 0 | 6 | 12km |
| 0 | 4 | 8mi |

©FWI

Mayreau

Union Island

THE

GRENADINES

●Ashton

Tabago Cays

MARTINIQUE CHANNEL

Palm Island

PETIT MARTINIQUE

Petit Saint
Vincent
Island

12° 30'

Hillsborough

CARRIACOU

Saline Island

Frigate Island

Large Island

CARIBBEAN
SEA

Kick 'em
Jenny

Les Santes

Ronde Island

Caille Island

London Bridge

12° 15'

Green Island

Sandy Island

Sauteurs

Bird Island

Victoria

ATLANTIC
OCEAN

Gouyave

Tivoli

Grand Roy

Grenville

ST. GEORGE'S

Saint David's

GRENADA

12° 00'

61° 45'

61° 30'

GRENADA

November 1, when they were greeted, not by Cuban soldiers, but islanders who had been patiently awaiting their arrival with soft drinks and beer.

The seat of government is Hillsborough, where a portion of the island's population of 8000 lives. Carriacou is drier than Grenada, and less mountainous (the highest point is 955 feet), with coconut palms and almond trees lining the beaches. Since the cotton and sugar plantations died out in the 18th century, the economy here, as elsewhere in the Grenadines, centers around fishing and boatbuilding. The sturdy boats are still constructed by hand in the hamlet of Windward (which claims Scottish descendants), though far fewer are launched today than a few years ago. Inter-island trading is an off-the-books revenue source. Monday is a big day on Carriacou, when the local market sputters to life with fruits and vegetables brought in from Grenada and nearby Union Island, and mail from the twice-weekly mail boat is distributed. Shops in town have charmingly direct signage: the Variety Store, the Industrious Store, the Novelty Store. There's a tiny museum, the **Carriacou Historical Society**, with a collection of Amerindian and European artifacts. One of the region's best artists lives here—**Canute Calliste**, whose paintings are exhibited at his house and gallery in L'Estere. A unique local tradition called **Big Drum**, a vibrant dance directly linked to African tribal roots, is performed at weddings, boat launches and house warmings. An old-fashioned **Carnival** is celebrated the week prior to Ash Wednesday in February, but the island's big event is the **Carriacou Regatta**, a four-day bash in August that lures sailors and fine yachts from around the region.

Carriacou is so far untouched by big developments, though smaller cruise ships call on the island a few dozen times a year now, and there's talk of developing more accommodations than the handful currently available. It's refreshingly laid-back, with cows and goats wandering aimlessly about, and an airstrip so bantam that the main island road bisects it at mid-point and planes can only land during daylight hours. Carriacou is also an excellent jumping-off point for exploring the northern Grenadines by mail boat. Located 23 miles north of Grenada, you can reach Carriacou by plane from Grenada (20 minutes), Union Island or St. Vincent, or via boat from Grenada (two to three hours). See "Arrival and Departure" below for more information. **Caribbean Horizons** provides daytrips to Carriacou from Grenada three days a week for $150, including airfare and lunch ☎ *(473) 444-1555*, or contact **Osprey Lines** ☎ *(473) 407-0470*, the island's new ferry service, for daytrips.

Where to Stay

Lodging is humble on Carriacou, but not without grace. The **Caribbee Inn** is easily the best choice—a simple but very special island inn. A small selection of villas and apartments are available from **Down Island, Ltd**. ☎ *(473) 443-8182*. There are at least a dozen informal guest houses and apartment units available; for rates and more information, obtain the **Grenada Accommodations Directory** from the Board of Tourism ☎ *(800) 927-9554.* The restaurant scene won't exactly give New York a run for its money, but again, the one at **Caribbee** leads the pack while **Gramma's Place** on Main Street is the island's unofficial meeting place and serves breakfast and snacks.

Hotels and Resorts

Silver Beach Resort   **$70–$120**   ★

Hillsborough, ☎ *(800) 225-5463, (473) 443-7337, FAX (473) 443-7165.*
Single: $70–$90. Double: $85–$120.
Set on a quiet beach on the edge of Hillsborough, this family-run hotel has comfortable rooms with ceiling fans; five face the beach with pleasant balconies. Four two-unit cottages off the beach provide a little more room and a kitchenette, but no view. Activities include fishing and boating to nearby Sandy Island, and watersports through the dive shop on property. What it lacks in character or charm it makes up for in location, but a tad expensive for the digs. 18 rooms. Credit cards: A, D, MC, V.

Inns

Caribbee Inn   **$90–$250**   ★★★

Prospect, ☎ *(473) 443-7380, FAX (473) 443-8142.*
Single: $90–$250. Double: $90–$250.
When you arrive at the Caribbee, a small sign suggests you take off your shoes to enter the lobby—a simple request that sets the tone for a relaxed hideaway. Each of Caribbee's six suites are unique, with personality to spare—American indian weavings, old pottery, Haitian-style fretwork, four-poster beds, jalousie windows to let the breeze. Four simpler rooms with lower rates round out the facility. A two-minute trail scampers down to the tiny beach below where you can snorkel or loll in the gently writhing sea, or a 20-minute trek takes you to Anse la Roche, one of the Caribbean's last undiscovered beauties. The management is attentive, the restaurant is the best on the island, and macaws swoop in for breakfast and dinner (bring nuts from home if you want to make friends). That pretty much sums up the action here. Maybe it's nice just knowing you don't have to put your shoes back on until you leave, but Caribbee is the ideal place for a barefoot holiday—one of the truly special inns of the Caribbean. 10 rooms. Credit cards: MC, V.

Low Cost Lodging

Cassada Bay Hotel   **$45–$70**   ★

Belmont, ☎ *(473) 443-7494, FAX (473) 443-7672.*
Single: $45–$55. Double: $55–$70.
Located on a scrawny bluff on the sparsely inhabited south side of Carriacou, Cassada Bay is a little beacon of unrealized potential. The somewhat rustic accommodations are in attractive wooden cabins with ceiling fans, each set on a hillside sloping down to the water. Wonderful views, particularly from the lobby/dining area at the top, plus a boat can be hired for the 10-minute trip to mirage-like White Island—otherwise, a fair beach is a 10-minute walk. Sunsets are stunning with miscellaneous Grenadines trailing off into the distance. 16 rooms. Credit cards: MC, V.

Petit Martinique

A tiny burp in the sea two-and-a-half miles northeast of Carriacou and the third member of Grenada's troika, 586-acre Petit (pronounced *petty*) Martinique is inhabited by about 900 people of primarily French descendancy who live at the base of a 738-foot volcanic cone. There are less than a dozen cars, and only a mile or two of road, so most residents use speedboats to get around. Officially, the economy is similar to Carriacou's—fishing and boat-building—but there's essentially no tourism, which makes it hard to understand how the island could be one of the wealthiest per-capita in the Windwards. In fact, Petit Martinique has never quite eclipsed its age-old reputation as a pirate's den, and contraband from Martinique, St. Martin and elsewhere—liquor mostly, but also cigarettes, clothes, televisions, refrigerators—has long flowed freely through the island.

That may be about to change. In 1997, U.S.-funded construction began on a Coast Guard base that will help bolster the U.S. drug-fighting presence in the southern Caribbean. The Petit Martiniquians are furious at the intrusion—the island has always been crime-free, they claim, and drugs do not cross their shores. While most of the anger is being directed at Grenadian Prime Minister Dr. Keith Mitchell (who says the base will be Grenada-managed and staffed), there's also resentment toward the Americans overseeing the construction. The tension may eventually dissipate, or it could worsen if islanders feel their lifestyle is further threatened.

There's a bank that opens for a few hours, three days a week (it is rumored that the average deposit is $20,000). Though most everyone has electricity and appliances, the island maintains a few traditions seemingly left over from another century—the weekly arrival of produce sellers from St. Vincent is announced with the blowing of a conch shell. A beach curves around the west and north coast of the island, but it is littered and unkempt. To reach Petit Martinique, you'll need to hop on a mail boat or hire a water taxi from the dock at Windward on Carriacou (there's no airport), or check with the folks at **Osprey Lines**, the new ferry service to the island from Carriacou and Grenada ☎ *(473) 407-0470.* A scruffy, five-room guest house, the **Sea Side View Holiday Cottages**, is available for $35 a night for a double; they will help arrange transfer from Carriacou ☎ *(473) 443-9210.*

Grenada Directory

Arrival and Departure

The opening of Point Salines Airport in 1984, exactly one year after the arrival of American troops, has made flying to Grenada much easier. American Airlines offers daily jet service to Grenada from its hub in San Juan, Puerto Rico, with connecting service available from a number of North American cities. **BWIA** has twice-weekly service to the island from New York's JFK and Miami. **LIAT** provides non-stop or direct service to Grenada from Antigua, Barbados, St. Lucia, Sint Maarten, St. Vincent, Tobago, Trinidad and Union Island.

Carriacou is reached via daily **LIAT** service out of Grenada or St. Vincent, as well as by **Airlines of Carriacou** ☎ *(473) 444-1475*, and **Region Air** ☎ *(473) 443-7337*. A 21-day round-trip excursion ticket from Grenada is about $55 (a daytrip is slightly less). One may also use the **inter-island boats** that ply the Grenadines five days a week. The standard three-and-a-half hour crossing is about $7.50 one-way; $12 round-trip. Confirm exact departure times and days with the Tourist Office. Other boats continue the route north from Carriacou to Union Island, Bequia and St. Vincent. **Osprey Lines**, a new and faster ferry service between Grenada and its siblings started in 1997. Osprey makes the run from Grenada twice daily during the week and once on Saturday and Sunday mornings, arriving in Carriacou about 90 minutes after departure, arriving in Petit Martinique 45 minutes later. Round-trip fare is $28, or an "all-inclusive" day tour of one of the islands is $80 ☎ *(473) 407-0470*.

The departure tax is $14. A $4 surcharge is levied when departing Carriacou.

Business Hours

Shops are generally open Monday through Friday from 8 a.m. to noon, and 1 to 4 p.m., and Saturdays from 8 a.m. to noon. Many stores in St. George's will open on Sunday if a cruise ship is docked. Banking hours are 8 a.m. to 1:30 or 2 p.m. Monday through Friday, as well as 2:30 to 5 p.m. on Fridays.

Climate

June through November is the rainy season, December through May is dry. Showers tend to be frequent, but brief during the summer and fall, with the total annual rainfall can be as little as 40 inches at the airport to as much as 170 inches at Grand Etang. The temperature hovers around 80 degrees with cooling trade winds reliable year-round.

Documents

U.S. citizens must present a valid passport or proof of citizenship (birth certificate or voter's registration card), plus a photo ID and an ongoing or return ticket.

Electricity

The current is 220 volts, 50 cycles, AC.

Getting Around

Driving is on the left, though somewhat tumultuous for the constant flow of goats and pedestrians onto roadways, and the twisting and winding roads are poorly maintained in some areas of the island. A dearth of appropriate signage can make sightseeing a challenge, though if you carry a good road map, you won't get lost for long. There are three American-based car rental outfits represented on the island: **Avis**, **Budget** and **Dollar**. Local firms include **Y&R Rent-**

als ☎ *(473) 444-4984* and **C. Thomas and Sons** ☎ *(473) 444-4384*. On Carriacou, contact **Barbra Gabriel** ☎ *(473) 443-7574*. You will need to obtain a local driver's license for $10, available from rental agencies.

Taxis are easily obtained at the airport, at the Carenage, and at most major hotels. Rates for frequently driven routes are fixed, but confirm the cost of a particular destination. The price from the airport to St. George's is $12; from St. George's to Grand Anse, $7, etc. Outside the southern area rates are $1.60 per mile for the first 10 miles, $1.35 per mile thereafter. The hourly rate to hire a taxi is $15. Taxi rates on Carriacou are also fixed, and average $6–$8 to most destinations. A two-and-a-half hour tour of Carriacou can be arranged at the airport with one of the taxi drivers for about $60.

Many visitors use the frequent and cheap local minibus service. Most routes, including to Grand Anse, start or end at St. George's market square; fare for the longest ride is about $2. The traditional, wooden-seat buses of old primarily stick to the east coast of the island around Grenville.

Language

Since Grenada was formerly under the British throne, natives speak English with a beautiful lilt. A local dialect mixes French with African slang.

Medical Emergencies

The General Hospital in St. George's has limited facilities; you might find better advice at the Grenada School of Medicine, a privately owned, U.S.-managed school of medicine in **True Blue** ☎ *(473) 444-4271*. Serious emergencies may warrant airlift to San Juan, Puerto Rico. The 36-bed hospital in Carriacou is for minor problems only.

Money

The official currency is the Eastern Caribbean dollar, commonly referred to as "E.C." The exchange rate is tied to the U.S. dollar, and currently trades at $2.70 for one American dollar. Prices are usually quoted in E.C., but you should always ask to make sure. Traveler's checks and credit cards are widely accepted. If you plan to pay by cash, you will usually receive a slightly better exchange rate by converting your money to E.C. at a bank.

Telephone

The new area code for Grenada is *(473)*. To call Grenada from the U.S., dial *1 + (473)* and the seven-digit local number. To save money, head for the Grenada Telecommunications, Ltd., in St. George or use a special phone card on other telephones.

Time

Atlantic standard time, which is one hour earlier than New York time half of the year, the same for the rest of the year.

Tipping and Tax

The hotel tax is 8 percent. Expect a 10 percent service charge to be added to hotel and restaurant bills; no need to tip help further.

Tourist Information

The **Grenada Board of Tourism** is located next to the cruise ship dock in The Carenage, St. George's ☎ *(473) 440-2001* and will answer questions, offer brochures and maps. Stop here if you are traveling on to other Grenadine islands. In the United States call ☎ *(800) 927-9554*.

Web Site

www.interknowledge.com/grenada

When to Go

Grenada's **Carnival** is held in early August, a four-day-to-night blowout of calypso songs and steel bands, and the traditional "jump-up" parades. Carriacou comes alive in early August for the annual **Carriacou Regatta**. Also check out the ninth annual **International Triathlon**, usually held in January. Competitors come from as far away as Australia and Norway and it takes place along and near Grand Anse.

GRENADA HOTELS		RMS	RATES	PHONE	CR. CARDS
★★★★	Calabash Hotel	30	$205–$545	(800) 528-5835	A, MC, V
★★★★	LaSource	100	$275–$630	(800) 544-2883	A, D, DC, MC, V
★★★★	Spice Island Beach Resort	56	$260–$725	(800) 223-9815	A, D, DC, MC, V
★★★	Blue Horizons Cottage Hotel	32	$105–$180	(800) 223-9815	A, D, DC, MC, V
★★★	Coyaba Beach Resort	70	$80–$175	(473) 444-4129	A, D, DC, MC, V
★★★	Renaissance Grenada Resort	195	$129–$246	(800) 228-9898	A, D, DC, MC, V
★★★	Rex Grenadian	212	$115–$275	(800) 255-5859	A, MC, V
★★★	Secret Harbour Resort	20	$130–$230	(800) 334-2435	A, DC, MC, V
★★★	Twelve Degrees North	8	$130–$195	(800) 322-1753	None
★★	Cinnamon Hill Hotel	20	$85–$160	(473) 444-4301	A, D, MC, V
★★	Coral Cove Cottages	11	$75–$145	(473) 444-4422	A, MC, V
★★	Flamboyant Hotel	41	$80–$130	(800) 223-9815	A, D, DC, MC, V
★★	La Sagesse Nature Center	6	$50–$95	(473) 444-6458	A, MC, V
★★	Siesta Hotel	37	$60–$135	(800) 742-4276	A, D, MC, V
★★	True Blue Inn	7	$90–$195	(800) 742-4276	A, D, DC, MC, V
★	Gem Holiday Beach Resort	18	$55–$120	(800) 223-9815	A, D, DC, MC, V
★	No Problem Apartments	20	$55–$85	(473) 444-4634	A, D, MC, V
★	Tropicana Inn	20	$35–$60	(473) 440-1586	A, D, DC, MC, V
★	Wave Crest Holiday Apts.	20	$40–$65	(800) 223-3463	A, D, MC, V

GRENADA

GRENADA HOTELS	RMS	RATES	PHONE	CR. CARDS
Carriacou				
★★★ Caribbee Inn	10	$90–$250	(473) 443-7380	MC, V
★ Cassada Bay Hotel	16	$45–$70	(473) 443-7494	MC, V
★ Silver Beach Resort	18	$70–$120	(800) 225-5463	A, D, MC, V

GRENADA RESTAURANTS	PHONE	ENTRÉE	CR. CARDS
Chinese Cuisine			
★★ Bird's Nest	(473) 444-4264	$6–$25	A, D, MC, V
International Cuisine			
★★ Red Crab, The	(473) 444-4424	$10–$31	A, D, MC, V
★ Rudolf's	(473) 440-2241	$8–$19	MC, V
Italian Cuisine			
★★ Portofino	(473) 440-3986	$8–$23	A, MC, V
Regional Cuisine			
★★★★ Canboulay	(473) 444-4401	$7–$42	A, MC, V
★★★ Coconut Beach	(473) 444-4644	$6–$28	A, D, DC, MC, V
★★★ La Belle Creole	(473) 444-4316	$5–$35	A, D, DC, MC, V
★★★ La Sagesse	(473) 444-6458	$6–$21	A, MC, V
★★★ Morne Fendue	(473) 442-9330	$15–$15	
★★ Delicious Landing	(473) 440-9747	$5–$20	NoneMC, V
★★ Mamma's	(473) 440-1459	$19–$19	
★★ Nutmeg, The	(473) 440-2539	$5–$21	A, MC, V
★ Cot Bam	(473) 444-2050	$5–$23	A, D, MC, V

GRENADA

GUADELOUPE

Guadeloupe's Ste.-Anne offers white sand beaches and crystal-clear water.

Opposing themes quickly announce their presence on Guadeloupe. In its food, its people, its landscapes, this is an island that wears cultural and geographic diversity proudly on its sleeve. Unvarnished Creole cuisine is rolled out in restaurants, but so is French. Cool streams pour down the slopes of a gently smoldering volcano, while black sand beaches are almost as common as white. And Guadeloupe's crowded, busy resort area—the long coast that beelines east from Pointe-a-Pitre—finds polarity in a canefield countryside just inland where life proceeds at an ox-driven pace mimicking provincial France. This succession of split personalities enhances Guadeloupe's well-developed vacation package that now lures more than one million cruise ship and overnight visitors annually to its shores.

Shaped much like a lop-sided butterfly, the island is actually two, connected by a bridge over a three-mile-long saltwater channel. Grande-Terre, the eastern wing, is relatively flat and robed in sugarcane, and its south coast is home to most of the island's accommodations; Basse-Terre, the western half, boasts a mountainous topography lush with forests, that climaxes at La Soufriere, a steaming volcanic summit. And Guadeloupe offers not just a two-for-one island destination, but several enchanting offshore outposts, including Les Saintes and Marie-Galante. Though Pointe-a-Pitre is the busy commercial hub, there is also Basse-Terre the city, the center of government for not only Guadeloupe, but St. Barthelemy and French St. Martin as well (nearby Martinique is a different *region* of France).

Guadeloupe is an adventurous destination for non-French-speaking Americans. If you're not fluent you'll want a phrasebook close at hand, for most island residents do not speak English (though a number of those who work in the major hotels do). The island's cruise ship arrivals have dramatically increased in the last three years, yet many American passengers who unload into the less-than-dynamic clutter of Pointe-a-Pitre come away from Guadeloupe unimpressed or even scornful (even though the beloved Big Mac is now obtainable). But for those who take the time to peel away the modern veneer of the island's extensive, French-oriented tourism infrastructure, a rich cultural stew and superb hiking opportunities step to the fore. They make distinct highlights for any Caribbean connoisseur looking to discover something different.

BEST BETS FOR...

Bird's-Eye View

Sprawling over 530 square miles and encompassing two distinct land masses, Guadeloupe is the region's sixth-largest island (after Trinidad). The two sides—Basse-Terre to the west and Grand-Terre to the east—are barely severed by a narrow seawater channel, the Riviere Salee. But Guadeloupe is no separated-at-birth story. Mountainous Basse-Terre was born through eons of volcanic turmoil, and its high point, La Soufriere, still steams away and sends shudders through the island whenever something underground disturbs its tenuous dormancy. On the other hand, Grand-Terre is a relatively

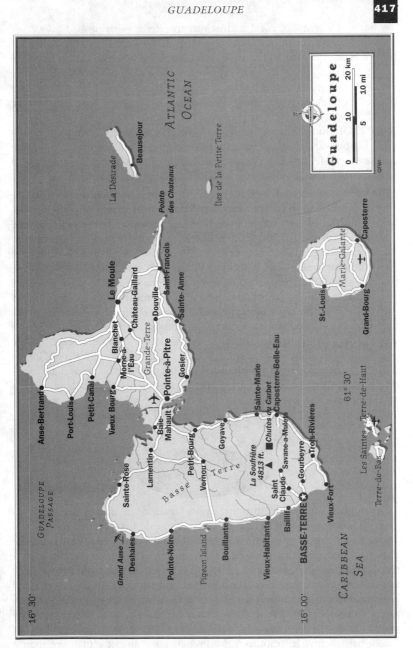

flat heap of limestone, coral formations that have been pushed above sea level through the centuries. The terrain of the two sides isn't the only contrast of note. The lofty summits of Basse-Terre lure enough clouds to create deep green rainforests that crawl up steep valleys carved by towering waterfalls—the dominant crop is bananas. Grand-Terre is drier, almost dusty, and cloaked in fields of sugarcane—it's also where the white sand beaches are found, as well as most of the resorts. The population of the two halves is 408,000. Although the city of Basse-Terre (on the western shore of Basse-Terre) is the capital, it's densely populated Pointe-a-Pitre on Grand-Terre that serves as the bustling commercial center of Guadeloupe. Little French Creole charm remains—the city is charitably described as serviceable.

Just offshore are Guadeloupe's satellites, which have been the focus of increased promotion in recent years. **Les Saintes** are a group of eight tiny islands south of Basse-Terre; only Terre-de-Haut and Terre-de-Bas are inhabited, with about 1500 residents each, most of whom are white descendants of the original Breton fishermen. Four-mile-long Terre-de-Haut gets all of the daytrippers—it's a photogenic outcrop with a scalloped coastline yielding hidden beaches. Encompassing 60 square miles, sweetly innocent **Marie-Galante** is much larger, and similar in terrain to Grand-Terre, just to the north. Accordingly, sugarcane and its products remain the primary industry for the 13,000 residents, and windmills are everywhere, but although visitors are starting to discover this old-fashioned backwater and its fine beaches, accommodations are still rustic. Lying off the eastern tip of Grand-Terre is seven-mile-long **La Desirade**. With just 1600 residents and an economy centered around fishing, sheep-rearing and a few crops, La Desirade has been comparatively overlooked by tourists for the moment. The satellite islands are connected to Guadeloupe by regular ferry and plane service.

History

Christopher Columbus stumbled upon Guadeloupe during his 1493 excursions, dubbing it Santa Maria de Guadeloupe de Estremadura in honor of a Spanish monastery with which he had close ties. Some 143 years later, the French landed, peopling the island with settlers who had to work in indentured conditions for three years to pay off their sea passage from France. Unfortunately, many proved to be unskilled and unacquainted with tropical farming, and the island soon fell into disrepair while nearby Martinique continued to prosper. The French Revolution inspired the settlers to revolt; they eventually declared themselves independent and even solicited the help of the British enemy. In response, the French government sent more than a

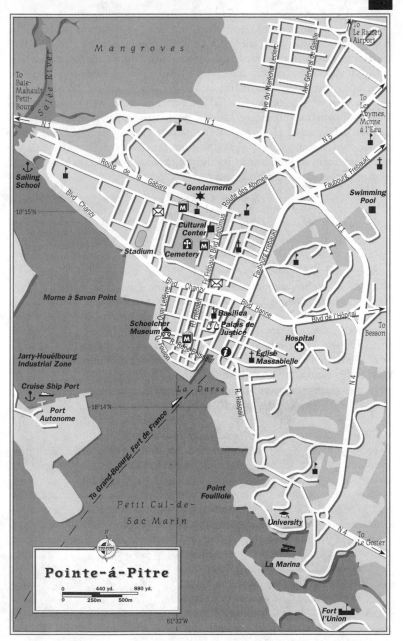

Mangroves

To Le Raizet Airport

To Baie-Mahault, Petit-Bourg

Salée River

N1

N1

Ave du Maréchal Leclerc

Ave Général de Gaulle

N5

To Les Abymes, Morne à l'Eau

Route de la Gabare

Route des Abymes

Faubourg Frebault

Gendarmerie

Sailing School

16°15'N

Blvd Chanzy

Cultural Center

Fr Frebault Blvd Legitimus

Faubourg Frebault

N1

Swimming Pool

Stadium

Cemetery

Morne à Savon Point

Blvd Chanzy

Fr Frebault

Blvd Hanne

Blvd de l'Hôpital

To Besson

Schoelcher Museum

Q. Foulon

Rue Pelsseur

Basilica

Palais de Justice

Hospital

Jarry-Houëlbourg Industrial Zone

Cruise Ship Port

Église Massabielle

N4

Port Autonome

16°14'N

La Darse

R. Raspail

To Grand-Bourg, Fort de France

Point Fouillole

Petit Cul-de-Sac Marin

University

N4

To Le Gosier

La Marina

Pointe-á-Pitre

| 0 | 440 yd. | 880 yd. |
| 0 | 250m | 500m |

Fort l'Union

61°32'W

thousand soldiers to whip the settlers into shape, expelling the British and executing more than 4000 Guadeloupian rebels on guillotines set up in the main squares. Under the Napoleonic reign, slavery was reinstated. In 1810 the British successfully reinvaded the island, handing it over to Louis XVIII during the Restoration, and returning when Napoleon came to power; the Brits finally surrendered the island for the last time when the French emperor was exiled to St. Helena in 1815. Since then, Guadeloupe has retained its distinct French flavor combined with a spicy West Indian allure. In September 1989, Hurricane Hugo struck the islands, causing widespread devastation and leaving about 12,000 people homeless. But by the mid-1990s the banana industry and the tourist industry had recovered and the majority are looking forward to prosperous years.

People

Guadeloupe is a *departement* owned by France, and language is the major influence from the mother land—although shops do close, European-style, for a long lunch complete with fine wine. Locals are a blend of European, African and East Indian origin; the majority are Christians, with a large contingent of Roman Catholics. A love of music is a major characteristic of Guadeloupans, so be sure to tune in the radio at every opportunity, as you'll be regaled with the supercharged rhythms of *zouk*, a beat born in the French West Indies (and quite popular in the mother country, too).

Bananas are the largest export for Guadeloupe.

Many residents are employed in agriculture; sugarcane and bananas are the primary crops, though the island also exports melons (introduced in 1984) and yams. Though most Guadeloupans are black, the population on Les Saintes is virtually all white; since the climate prohibited sugarcane production, no slaves were ever brought there. Locals are a generally superstitious lot. *Quimboiseurs*, described as "half witch-doctor, half bone-setter" are frequently consulted to concoct potions, cast a spell or provide numbers for the lottery. Most houses are not painted, due to the local superstition that dictates that a coat of paint prevents the good spirits from entering.

Guadeloupe has a wide variety of beaches, though a surprising number of those on the south coast of Grand-Terre are handcrafted and carefully manicured by resorts. The idyllic, palm-fringed beaches celebrated on postcards are the exception, not the rule here. But there are a number of genuine beauties awaiting the dedicated explorer. On the resort-lined south coast of Grand-Terre, there is a public beach in **Gosier** and just offshore is the tiny **Ilet du Gosier** with a scenic lighthouse; the boat ride over is about $2. **Ste. Anne** has a long stretch of sand and plenty of watersports activities, but just west of town is **Caravelle**, backed by the Club Med operation; it's one of the island's most attractive beaches, and it's open to the public if you access it via the shore from town—one section (near the point) is *au naturel*. **St. Francois** has several beaches, one of them swallowed up by the huge Le Meridien operation, but just east of town, a narrow finger of land points toward the Atlantic. On the south coast of this peninsula is a fairly unbroken stretch of sand, one part of which is called **Anse Kahouanne** and popular with locals, while individual coves are found on the north side, including tiny **Plage Tarare**, the island's official nude beach. The small beach at the tip, **Pointe des Chateaux**, is scenic, but the surf is dangerous. On the north end of Grand-Terre, a long white-sand beach is found just east of **Le Moule**, another just outside **Port-Louis**, and a treasure is **Anse Laborde**, tucked into a cove just north of Anse-Bertrand (watch for tricky currents).

Though the white sand is found primarily on Grand-Terre, what is arguably Guadeloupe's finest beach, **Grand Anse**, is on Basse-Terre, just north of the fishing village, Deshaies. The beach is almost two miles of rosy-golden sand backed by palms and there is little development beyond a good Creole restaurant and a few snack bars. Just north of here is another scenic spot, **Anse de la Perle**, but currents are unreliable (check around locally). The other beaches on Basse-Terre are mostly black or gray sand, but quite a few dot the west coast all the way down to the capital. On Terre-de-Haut, beaches are small and quiescent, but two of the lovelies are **Plage de Pompierre** and **Plage de Crawen**, the island's nude beach. Marie-Galante has excellent white sand beaches, including **Vieux-Fort** on the north coast and **Capesterre** and **Petite Anse** on the south, as does undeveloped La Desirade.

When the late Jacques Cousteau named a destination one of the top 10 dive spots in the world, you can expect that a sizable industry will spring up around it. In reality, Cousteau placed **Pigeon Island** on his top ten list some years ago, when many areas of the undersea world were still waiting to be explored, so the designation is of a qualified nature today. Still, the locally named **Reserve du Commandant Cousteau** at Pigeon Island is a marvelous dive location, and at least one Guadeloupe operator paves the way for American visitors to experience its lush depths. Beginners will find a number of easier sites surrounding Pigeon, although one must remember that French dive tables and apparatus are different from those used by most American-run operations. Visibility off Pigeon often exceeds 100 feet, although showers will carry mountain silt down to the reefs surrounding Basse-Terre; usually this settles in a matter of hours. Unfortunately, crowded boats are a common complaint from many visitors at this busy location, and avid divers should also try to explore other portions of the expansive west coast, sometimes referred to as "the Kingdom of Sponges." It's worth noting that, unlike most other Caribbean islands, Guadeloupe shops price their dives based on the distance traveled from shore, creating a diverse price structure. The **Iles des Saintes** also offer pristine diving, centered around a reef plateau, which offers relatively shallow depths. In addition to the western face of Pigeon Island, snorkeling is good in the coral garden below the bluffs just north of the harbor at **Deshaies**, off the **Ilet du Gosier** (the tiny island with a lighthouse facing Gosier), at **Anse a la Barque** (small cove six miles north of Basse Terre), and in the reefs surrounding **Ilet a Fajou** (north of the Riviere Salee).

Dive Shops

Aqua-Fari Club

Gosier; ☎ (590) 84-26-26.

Convenient to the main resort area, Aqua-Fari dives the Ilet du Gosier as well as the Ilet a Fajou (in the northern bay between Grande- and Basse-Terre). Single-tank dive in the Gosier area, $37; more for longer trips, which includes Pigeon Island (one hour by car from Gosier).

Les Heures Saines

Bouillante; ☎ *(590) 98-86-63.*

The oldest, and perhaps biggest, operator on the island, Les Heures Saines offers "baptisms" and some of their instructors speak English. Uses PADI, NAUI and all European dive systems, including CEDIP. Four divers per moniteur, with a maximum dive group of 25. One-tank dive $45; Baptism, $51. Snorkeling, $21 for two-hour trip. Night dives on Fridays, wreck dive Sunday mornings.

Plongee Club De L'autre Bord

Moule; ☎ *(590) 93-97-10.*

Very small operation (maximum number of divers is four), concentrates on "the other beach," the north coast area. PADI affiliated, with most sites close to shore; beginner dives conducted in the lagoon. $41 for a single-tank dive. Small size allows flexible schedule and operation.

Centre Nautique Des Saintes

Terre-de-Haut; ☎ *(590) 99-54-25.*

Only dive shop in Les Saintes, 10 years in existence. $41 for a one-tank dive; $52 to Le Sec Pate. Handles PADI and NAUI referrals. Two boats, accommodating groups of up to 30 divers; all sites are within 20 minutes. Snorkeling trips organized on request. English-speaking staff.

Guadeloupe is second only to Martinique for maintaining the best and most extensive trail system in the Caribbean. From easy walks approaching tall waterfalls to a fierce traverse of the island's volcanic spine, there is no shortage of trails to keep active travelers engaged. The island's geologic focus, Soufriere in the vast **Parc National**, is one of the region's more recently troubled summits—a series of eruptions in 1976–1977 were exciting enough to occasion the evacuation of Basse-Terre—and, ironically, it's probably the most visited. Almost every day, dozens of hikers gamely ascend the moderate path to its moonlike crown, the highest in the Eastern Caribbean. Because island trails are so well-maintained, guides are generally unnecessary. A guidebook containing routes within the Parc National is available from the **Bureau des Guides de Moyenne Moutagne** *(☎ (590) 81-24-83);* they also conduct guided walks in English.

What Else to See

The city of **Point-a-Pitre**, on Grand-Terre, is one of the Caribbean's busiest, and though it's doubtful you'll want to spend your vacation here, it's worth a visit of at least a few hours. Though some French colonial structures still remain, the city is basically modern and quite hectic, with 80,000 residents. The **Tourist Office**, at Place de la Victoire, is a good place to pick up maps and brochures on the area's attractions. Lots of nearby local vendors sell everything from kitchenware to underwear, and unlike on some other islands, they'll let you stop and browse without being persistent about making a sale. The same is true at the local **Marketplace**, located between the streets of St. John Perse, Freebault, Schoelchen and Peynier, where women in brightly colored madras sell fresh fruits and vegetables. The ferry port bustles with activity as locals and tourists jostle to buy tickets and catch the boats that travel to and from Marie-Galante, Les Saintes and La Desirade. For some reason, all the competing ferries leave for the exact same destinations at the exact same time.

Outside Pointe-a-Pitre, **Grand-Terre** boasts two distinct personalities: a resort atmosphere is found along the south coast, while just inland is the provincial countryside. Virtually all tourists come into contact with the former, but surprisingly few take the time to explore the scenic northern area where sugar cane is still hauled by ox-driven carts and bucolic fishing villages dot the rocky coastline. The eastern-most tip of the island, **Pointe des Chateaux** has picturesque bluffs that meet the crashing Atlantic, while an oddly serene bay is created by the **Porte d'Enfer** (Gate of Hell), dramatic cliffs that break the incoming waves as they roll into a deep gully. In the middle of Grand-Terre, the town of **Morne-a-l'Eau** has a beautiful cemetery set in an amphitheater, with tombstones and crypts embellished in black and white tiles. The cemetery becomes a fairyland the first two nights of November—All Saints Night—when hundreds of candles light up the grounds.

Basse-Terre, the other wing of Guadeloupe's butterfly, has the lion's share of the scenery, including the 74,100-acre **Parc National**, which by itself offers more than a day's worth of exploration possibilities. Start by driving the lush **Route de la Traversee**, a 16-mile-long passage through the center of Basse-Terre. Along the way, you'll encounter the **Cascade aux Ecrevisses**, a waterfall just off the road, and just beyond is the **Parc Bras-David**, which offers easier strolls into the verdant canopy and the **Parc Zoologique et Botanique**, a zoo and botanical garden with a restaurant that offers great views from its perch

1500 feet above sea level. You can tour a working sugar factory at the **Compagnie Fermiere de Gross Montagne**, or learn about the rum-making process at the **Musee du Rhum**. The west coast of Basse-Terre is dotted by gray and black sand beaches, backed by fishing villages relatively unfettered by tourism. The capitol **Basse-Terre** has little in the way of museums or activities, but it retains a measure of West Indian charisma missing in Pointe-a-Pitre, and offers excellent views up the flanks of La Soufriere.

A special treat for Guadeloupe visitors is a daytrip to the offshore islands of **Les Saintes**, **Marie-Galante** or **La Desirade**, each of which can be reached by ferry from Pointe-a-Pitre (and elsewhere) or plane. These charmers are appealing enough that you'll want to bring an overnight bag, just in case.

Historical Sites
Basse-Terre

Parc des Roches Gravees ★★

Trois-Rivieres
Hours open: 9 a.m.–5 p.m.
At this peaceful archeological site near the wharf, displays interpret the rock engravings of animal and human figures by Carib Indians that date back to 300 or 400 A.D.

Museums and Exhibits
Basse-Terre

Musee du Rhum ★★★

Bellevue, Ste. Rose.
Hours open: 9 a.m.–5 p.m.
The Rum Museum showcases three centuries of sugarcane history, including a display of machetes from around the world, colonial money from Guadeloupe and more. After a brief tour and 20-minute video (in English or French), you may taste the potable and, of course, buy a bottle to take home. But every bit as interesting as the rum tour is "La Galerie des Plus Beaux Insectes du Monde" upstairs, where you can marvel at more than 5000 critters—from beautiful butterflies to spiders, roaches, and other huge creepy-crawlies. General admission: $7. Those interested in the rum-making process may also want to check out the nearby **Domaine de Severin** in Ste. Rose ☎ *(590) 28-91-86*. This distillery still functions with a paddle wheel, and a guided tour takes you though each step of production.

Grand-Terre

Musee Edgar Clerc ★★

La Rosete, Le Moule.
This small museum displays artifacts from the Carib and Arawak Indians found on the islands of the Eastern Caribbean. Closed Wednesday afternoons and Tuesdays.

Musee Schoelcher ★★★

24 Rue Peynier, Pointe-a-Pitre.
Displays highlight the personal papers and belongings of Victor Schoelcher, who, in the 19th century, worked to abolish slavery in the French West Indies.

Musee St. John Perse ★★★

Achille Rene-Boisneuf Rue, Pointe-a-Pitre.

Hours open: 9 a.m.–5:30 p.m.

This museum in a restored colonial house contains the works of St. John Perse, a local boy made good who won the Nobel Prize in Literature in 1960.

Parks and Gardens
Basse-Terre

Le Domaine de Valombreuse ★★★

Cabout, Petit-Bourg.

Hours open: 9 a.m.–5 p.m.

This Eden-like spot on the east coast of Basse-Terre is a must-see for flower enthusiasts. Numerous shady valleys house 300 species and 200 sub-species of flowers and a slew of exotic birds. The Park Restaurant is open daily for lunch, and there's a playground on site for little tykes. General admission: $5.

Parc Naturel de la Guadeloupe ★★★★★

Basse-Terre.

Covering 74,100 acres with 200 miles of trails, this national park has something for everyone: waterfalls, thick vegetation, nature walks and the centerpiece, La Soufriere, a smoldering volcano that last erupted in 1977. Stop by the Maison de la Foret for a look at the park's history (only, alas, in French) and a booklet on hiking trails. Wear rain gear, as this area gets some 250 inches per year.

Zoological and Botanical Park ★★★★

Route de la Traversee.

Hours open: 9 a.m.–4:30 p.m.

Located high in the hills of Basse-Terre, this reserve is home to myriad trees, bushes, and creepers that lots of critters like mongoose, iguana, land turtle, and raccoon call home. Great views abound at Le Ti-Raccoon restaurant (open daily for lunch except Mondays), which serves solid Creole cuisine. General admission: $5.

Tours
Grand-Terre

Aquarium de la Guadeloupe ★★

Place Creole, Marina Bas-du-Fort.

Hours open: 9 a.m.–7 p.m.

This is the Caribbean's largest aquarium and considered to be one of France's most important. Good exhibits feature everything from tiny fish to giant sharks. While in the area, check out the 18th-century Fort Fleur d'Epee, complete with dungeons and spectacular views. General admission: $7.

Watersports reign supreme on Guadeloupe, with the most popular sites at Pigeon Island off the west coast. Snorkeling is especially good at St. Francois reef and Ilet du Gosier, as well as Pigeon Island. Deep-sea fishers hunt for barracuda and kingfish from January to May, and tuna, dolphin and bonito from December to March. Strong currents and good winds make yachting popular; *Boating Magazine* calls Bas du Fort's Port de Plaisance marina one of the finest in the Western Hemisphere.

Golfers are limited to the island's sole course, the 18-hole Golf de St. Francois, designed by Robert Trent Jones Sr. Tennis courts are plentiful at the major hotels and resorts. Cycling is a major passion with locals, and each August the island hosts the Tour de la Guadeloupe, a 10-day race that draws international competitors.

Bicycling

A winter home to a lucky few French racers, Guadeloupe was established as a leading cycling destination in the Caribbean years before most other islands thought about the sport. Navigating the busier roads can be a challenge—stick to the northern part of Grand-Terre and you'll be rewarded with gently rolling hills and most of the traffic will be limited to farm equipment. The 10-day Tour de la Guadeloupe is a big regional biking event, held in August. For rentals, try **MM** ☎ *(590) 88-59-12* or **Easy Rent** ☎ *(590) 88-76-27*, both in St. Francois, or **Dingo Location** in Pointe-a-Pitre ☎ *(590) 83-81-19*. The local mountain bike group is the **Association Guadeloupeenne de VTT** ☎ *(590) 82-82-67*.

Golf

Guadeloupe offers the **Golf de St. Francois**, an 18-hole Robert Trent Jones Sr. course that offers windy challenges for duffers, and an English-speaking pro. It is located in St. Francois, and greens fees for the 6755-yard, par-71 course are about $45. ☎ *(590) 88-41-87*.

Watersports

Most hotels have an array of watersports, or you can check out the following. For windsurfing: **Callinago** ☎ *(590) 84-25-25* and **UCPA Hotel Club** ☎ *(590) 88-64-80*. Deep-sea fishing: **Caraibe Peche** ☎ *(590) 90-97-51*, **La Rocher de Malendere** ☎ *(590) 98-70-84*, **Evasion Exotic** ☎ *(590) 90-94-17*, and **Fishing Club Antilles** ☎ *(590) 86-73-77*. Boat rentals: **Soleil et Voile** ☎ *(590) 90-81-81*, **Vacances Yachting Antilles** ☎ *(590) 90-82-95*, and **Locaraibes** ☎ *(590) 90-82-80*.

GUADELOUPE

Where to Stay

	Fielding's Highest Rated Hotels in Guadeloupe	
★★★★	Auberge de la Vieille Tour	$136–$390
★★★★	Hamak	$200–$400
★★★★	Le Meridien la Cocoteraie	$273–$618
★★★★	Plantation Ste. Marthe	$110–$218
★★★	Anse des Rochers	$132–$204
★★★	Club Med Caravelle	$138–$372
★★★	La Toubana	$109–$237
★★★	Le Jardin Malanga	$176–$320
★★★	Le Meridien St. Francois	$132–$291
★★★	Marissol Hotel	$110–$255

	Fielding's Most Romantic Hotels in Guadeloupe	
★★★	Le Jardin Malanga	$176–$320
★★★★	Hamak	$200–$400
★★★★	Le Meridien la Cocoteraie	$273–$618
★★★	La Toubana	$109–$237
★★	Relais du Moulin	$80–$131

	Fielding's Best Value Hotels in Guadeloupe	
★★★	Village de Menard	$60–$100
★★★	Auberge les Petits Saints	$65–$127
★★★	Hotel St. Georges	$93–$120

Guadeloupe boasts more than 5000 accommodations, yet variety is not a buzzword. There are perhaps a few too many cookie-cutter chain properties dotting the southern coast of Grand-Terre, home to more than 80 percent of the rooms on the island. These hotels are popular with the French, who fill them during winter months and in late summer, but few offer the personality and character intrepid Americans may be looking for. The Gosier/Bas du Fort area in particular is densely developed, while Ste. Anne and St. Francois are a little less cluttered (and have better beaches).

An important note: most of the hotels have two rate cards—one in American dollars and one in French francs. However, the exchange rate between the two currencies changes daily. At press time, the franc was trading at its lowest rate in years and, as a result, a number of hotels did not raise their *dollar* rate card for the 1998 season. The situation may have changed by the time you read this, and if the franc has further declined, you'll want to negotiate your room rate carefully to make sure you are obtaining the best price. For hotels that did not provide prices in dollars, we have used an exchange rate of 5.5 francs for one U.S. dollar.

Hotels and Resorts

In sifting through the many hotel options available on Guadeloupe, it helps to establish a few priorities. If a high-amenity luxury vacation is paramount, **Hamak**, **Auberge de la Vieille Tour** and **La Cocoteraie** should deliver the goods. If an English-language staff is important, **Plantation Ste. Marthe**, **Canella Beach** and **La Toubana** lead the list, though a number of the larger properties will also do their best to assist you. If you want your activities and meals packaged up front, you may want to consider the island's **Club Med**, situated on one of the best beaches, and welcoming to both Americans and singles.

Basse-Terre

Hotel St. Georges	$93–$162	★★★

St. Claude, ☎ *(590) 80-10-10, FAX (590) 80-30-50.*
Single: $93. Double: $120. Suites Per Day: $153–$162.

This strangely generic facility opened in 1996, in the town of St. Claude, between the capitol of Basse-Terre and the summit of La Soufriere. What St. Georges lacks in rustic country charm, it makes up with sleek, tasteful modernity, with rooms that are clean and spare but with attractive mahogany furnishings; there are two elegant suites. The pool is splendid, there's a fitness room, an air conditioned squash court, and a restaurant serving gastronomique cuisine. Well-run St. Georges was probably designed more for Basse-Terre business visitors than vacationers, but it's a good location for those wanting to explore the Parc National and winter rates are reasonable. 40 rooms. Credit cards: A, MC, V.

Grande-Terre

Anse des Rochers	$132–$204	★★★

Just west of St. Francois, ☎ *(800) 322-2223, (590) 93-90-00, FAX (590) 93-91-00.*
Single: $132–$192. Double: $144–$204.

A collection of pastel-colored Creole buildings trimmed with white gingerbread are the core of this upscale resort three miles west of St. Francois. Guests are accommodated in nicely furnished rooms, or in 34 villas on the hillside. Each is air conditioned and has a terrace, refrigerator and direct-dial phones. The expansive grounds include several restaurants, an immense free-form swimming pool, tennis, and a reef-protected beach that's nice for lolling about in shallow water. There's a disco and various theme evenings each week, but little else within walking distance. As the largest hotel on the island, this Anchorage property caters primarily to the French market, but it's a good bet for Americans seeking a resort atmosphere on a nice beach. 356 rooms. Credit cards: MC, V.

Auberge de la Vieille Tour $136–$390   ★★★★

Gosier, ☎ *(800) 763-4835, (590) 84-23-23, FAX (590) 84-33-43.*
Single: $136–$315. Double: $169–$390.

This esteemed Sofitel property is set on a five-acre estate surrounding the tower of an 18th-century sugar mill. Accommodations are richly drawn with colonial-style teak furnishings and brightly colored fabrics—the best rooms are the deluxe units which have a glass-walled bathroom that faces the sea (some have more privacy than others); these rooms come with other amenities that make them worth the bump in price (about $100 extra). There is tennis and a pool—the beach is small, with water-sports available nearby, or have the hotel boat you over to the nearby Ilet du Gosier. The resort finished a refurbishing in 1996 that redesigned the lobby, restaurants and bar and spruced up the rooms. One thing remains unchanged: the hotel's signature restaurant is possibly the island's best. 181 rooms. Credit cards: A, MC, V.

Club Med Caravelle $138–$372   ★★★

Ste. Anne, ☎ *(800) 258-2633, (590) 85-49-50, FAX (590) 85-49-70.*
Website: www.clubmed.com.
Single: $138–$233. Double: $225–$372.

Sprawling along one of Guadeloupe's best beaches and dotted by coconut palms, this Club Med has a small percentage of American visitors who appreciate that most of the GOs (the gentils organisateurs responsible for guest activities) speak English. However, the principal clientele is from France, and most socializing is in the home tongue. The all-inclusive rates cover just about everything on property, from tennis to watersports, circus workshops to a lively night scene (lots of singles)—a good thing since the less expensive rooms are puny by any standard. Rates don't include excursions around Guadeloupe or drinks other than what is consumed at meal time. The *tres* '60s lobby decor and architecture is reminiscent of the TWA terminal at JFK—swooping, airy and deliciously retro. No pool; the east end of the fine beach is nude. 329 rooms. Credit cards: A, MC, V.

Hamak $200–$400   ★★★★

St. Francois, ☎ *(590) 633-7411, (590) 88-59-99, FAX (590) 88-41-92.*
Closed Date: August 29-October 3.
Single: $200–$370. Double: $250–$400.

Set on five acres facing a reef-protected lagoon, this lushly landscaped property is elegant and exclusive—it was the site of a summit meeting with President Carter in 1979. The accommodations are dappled about the property in smartly designed bungalows embraced by greenery. Each has a living area that opens onto a terrace, a full bathroom, and a bedroom that leads to a private, enclosed sun patio with an outdoor shower; the total area covers 650 square feet. The rooms are tasteful and comfortable, with beautiful wood furnishings. There's no pool and the man-made beach isn't much, propped up by a seawall that prevents guests from shuffling directly into the water. But relaxation is still the theme, with lazy *hamaks* yawning freely on every terrace, urging guests to sway in the breeze. Strong service, a well-heeled atmosphere, and the idyllic garden setting make Hamak a little oasis of serenity on busy Guadeloupe. Rates include a full American breakfast; a 15 percent tax/service charge is added to the bill. 54 rooms. Credit cards: A, MC, V.

La Creole Beach Hotel   **$87–$299**   ★★★

Gosier, ☎ *(800) 322-2223, (590) 90-46-46, FAX (590) 90-46-66.*
Single: $87–$219. Double: $93–$299.
Once three separate hotels crowded onto a 10-acre estate on Pointe de la Verdure, La Creole, Residences Yucca and Mahogany now share one front desk and one not-terribly-large beach. There's a bevy of air-conditioned options here, with Yucca representing the least-expensive and least-appealing section—rooms are worn and basic, with kitchenettes on the terrace. La Creole section rooms are nicely furnished in wood, but lack balconies. Entertainment nightly and the beach offers watersports; there is also a pool, tennis, a gym, and the casino is nearby. If you want a full-on resort, La Creole provides one, in the heart of the Gosier development. 321 rooms. Credit cards: A, DC, MC, V.

La Toubana   **$109–$237**   ★★★

Ste. Anne, ☎ *(800) 322-2223, (590) 88-25-78, FAX (590) 88-38-90.*
Single: $109–$177. Double: $139–$237.
Spectacularly perched above the south shore of Grande Terre, this charming complex boasts views of the raging sea from its splendid pool which spills over the edge of the cliff. Guests stay in sweet, red-roofed *toubanas* (an Arawak word for little houses) with air conditioning, kitchenettes and gardens overflowing with flowers and views. Each bungalow is the same size, but some have a second bedroom instead of a terrace. The grounds include a tennis court, bar and reliable restaurant, and a path leads down the steep hill to a small beach where watersports await; you'll want a car for exploring. A delightful find. 32 rooms. Credit cards: A, DC, MC, V.

Le Meridien St. Francois   **$132–$509**   ★★★

St. Francois, ☎ *(800) 543-4300, (590) 88-51-00, FAX (590) 88-40-71.*
Single: $132–$209. Double: $155–$291. Suites Per Day: $273–$509.
Located near the eastern tip of Grand Terre's southern shore, this five-story contemporary resort sits on one of the better beaches. The property is self-contained, with lots going on in the protected lagoon and on the tennis courts, in the marina and on the archery range; the pool is large and inviting with a Jacuzzi burbling away next door. Guest rooms feel a bit tired, but have balconies, comfortable tropical furnishings and English-language stations on the TV. A casino and the municipal golf course are nearby. One of the island's few resorts where Americans won't feel out of place. 265 rooms. Credit cards: A, DC, MC, V.

Le Meridien la Cocoteraie   **$273–$618**   ★★★★

St. Francois, ☎ *(800) 543-4300, (590) 88-79-81, FAX (590) 88-78-33.*
Closed Date: August 25–October 25.
Single: $273–$618. Double: $273–$618.

GUADELOUPE

An all-suite resort for well-heeled Europeans that debuted in 1992, La Cocoteraie contains what are probably Guadeloupe's poshest rooms, which dot the small property in two- and three-story bungalows. Each suite is decorated in vivid tropical colors, with an elaborate minibar and terrace or balcony, and two bathrooms, one with an elevated octagonal tub surrounded by windows; request an upper unit for the appealing cathedral ceilings. The beach is quite small but guests may use the facilities next door at Le Meridien St. Francois, including a marina and watersports. Otherwise, tennis courts are on site, a golf course is across the street, and the bungalows surround a large pool decorated with clusters of ornate Chinese vases just waiting to be toppled. The hotel's restaurant offers refined dining. La Cocoteraie is stuffy and elegant, pretentious and lovely—not for all tastes, but probably the island's best pick for someone expecting a high level of pampering. 50 rooms. Credit cards: A, MC, V.

Marissol Hotel   **$110–$255**   ★★★

Bas du Fort, ☎ *(800) 221-4542, (590) 90-84-44, FAX (590) 90-83-32.*
Single: $110–$175. Double: $134–$255.

Facing the bay at Point-a-Pitre, this resort complex shares its nice beach with the Fleur d'Epee Novotel—actually the two are practically joined at the hip, and share many facilities. Accommodations range from standard guest rooms to bungalows, all air-conditioned and with balconies overlooking the pleasant gardens. Several restaurants, a pool, tennis and a large array of watersports provide other diversions; a marina is nearby. Like many of its competitors, this one attracts mostly young and casual Europeans. 195 rooms. Credit cards: A, DC, MC, V.

Plantation Ste. Marthe   **$110–$218**   ★★★★

St. Francois, ☎ *(800) 333-1970, (590) 93-11-11, FAX (590) 88-72-47.*
E-mail: Tmcauban@ix.netcom.com.
Single: $110–$164. Double: $148–$218.

Set on a hill with sweeping views and surrounded by 15 acres of fields and gardens, this is a great value for those who don't mind being off the beach. The strange ruins of sugar-crushing equipment are at one end, while guests are put up in three-story Louisiana-style buildings with standard rooms and nice junior suites, all with air conditioning and extras like room service, mini bars, and hair dryers. Shuttles transport beach-lovers to the sand, one mile away. There's a luscious pool and fitness center on site; 18 holes of golf are next door. Built more for the meeting trade, but fine if you're not sharing it with a big group. 120 rooms. Credit cards: MC, V.

Tropical Club Hotel   **$82–$113**   ★★

Le Moule, ☎ *(800) 322-2223, (590) 93-97-97, FAX (590) 93-97-00.*
E-mail: ath@wanadoo.fr.
Single: $82–$113. Double: $82–$113.

Built up against an untamed bluff lush with yucca trees, this family-friendly hotel has rooms with a queen bed and, on a small alcove, bunk beds for the little tykes. The pretty blonde furnishings are enhanced by gaily colored fabrics; the resort received a makeover in 1997. Other features include a kitchenette on the terrace, air conditioning and ceiling fans, TV, telephones, and small shower-only baths (request a unit on the second or third floor for the best sea views). The grounds include a nice pool area, fitness room, a couple restaurants, watersports center, beach bar, and a long, reef-protected white sand beach. The location is not central, but the rates make Tropical a good value for beach aficionados. 96 rooms. Credit cards: A, MC, V.

Les Saintes

Auberge les Petits Saints   **$65–$127**   ★★★

La Savane, ☎ *(800) 322-2223, (590) 99-50-99, FAX (590) 99-54-51.*
Single: $65–$118. Double: $73–$127.

Lovely views abound from this charming and eccentric hotel, run by a pair of artists and perched on a hill about a 10-minute walk from the port. You could spend hours poking through the lobby, a glorious hodge-podge of antiques from around the world (many of the items are for sale). All rooms are air conditioned and individually decorated with antiques and artwork by the owners and others. Our favorite is Room 12, which is outside the main house and has a large stone wall, queen bed, and large balcony. Note that four units share a pair of bathrooms. The grounds include an excellent restaurant, a small but pretty pool, and a sauna. This unique spot is a real winner, and matches perfectly with the offbeat nature of Terre-de-Haut. 10 rooms. Credit cards: MC, V.

Hotel Bois Joli   **$64–$181**   ★★★

Anse a Cointe, ☎ *(800) 322-2223, (590) 99-50-38, FAX (590) 99-55-05.*
Single: $64–$181. Double: $68–$181.

Set above a small, scenic cove, this decent hotel is the island's oldest, dating back to the 1960s. Guestrooms are simply furnished, but were upgraded recently so that all have air conditioning and private baths. The new bungalows are lovely; each comes with white wooden furniture, twin beds in the master bedroom, bunk beds in the second bedroom, modern baths, refrigerators, and a large patio overlooking the sea. There's a nice restaurant and bar as well. With its cute bridge adding a touch of atmosphere, the pool is pleasant; the nude beach is 10 minutes away on foot. This is the island's only full-service hotel, but its remote location—two miles from Bourg—is a plus or a minus depending on your needs. The management speaks no English, but may try to rope you into an MAP setup. 31 rooms. Credit cards: MC, V.

Marie Galante

Village de Menard   **$60–$100**   ★★★

Menard, ☎ *(590) 97-09-45, FAX (590) 97-15-40.*
Single: $60–$100. Double: $60–$100.

This peaceful spot is located on the site of an old rum factory, with stone ruins dotting the grounds. Accommodations are in air-conditioned bungalows with one or two bedrooms (the second one has bunk beds and a twin) and complete kitchenettes. The more deluxe units are well worth the small bump in price and feature tile floors, high beamed ceilings, telephones, and TV. Save for an inviting pool, there's nothing on site and not much in the immediate area—a car is a good idea. The beach is a 15-minute walk. 7 rooms. Credit cards: MC, V.

Apartments and Condominiums

Since eating out is an art in Guadeloupe, having a unit with your own cooking facilities may seem a bit superfluous, but the big advantage of preparing some of your meals at home is a greatly reduced dining bill that may allow you to splurge on a few restaurant meals without needing to calculate prices at each sitting. It doesn't hurt that the local supermarkets are stocked with fine French cheese, pate, bread and wine, as well as an array of local produce to make stocking your kitchen easy. You may also want to contact the **Gites de France**, an organization that oversees more than 400 homey lodgings options on Guadeloupe. Many are simple apartments or bungalows, but larger homes and villas are also available. Rates for the least expensive properties start at about $240 per week, but make sure you understand the rental contract and all the pertinent details about the property (up to and including whether it has running hot water). The Gites are represented by the local tourist office ☎ *(590) 82-09-30.*

Inns

Inns on Guadeloupe are often defined as a lodging with fewer than 50 rooms. Such accommodations are handled through a local association of hotels called **Relais Créoles**. The best combine high ceilings and mansionlike elegance with the tropical breeziness. The smaller the hotel, the more necessary it is to speak French well; although hosts can be congenial, don't expect too much in the way of room service.

Basse-Terre

Auberge de la Distillerie   **$68–$160**   ★★

Tabanon, ☎ *(800) 322-2223, (590) 94-25-91, FAX (590) 94-11-91.*
Single: $68–$105. Double: $102–$160.

This sweet French-style country inn in a residential area near the national park appeals to nature lovers. Guest rooms are simple but comfortable with air conditioning and television sets. The Creole restaurant and bar are popular with locals, and there's also a pool on site. The owners will happily direct you to the Trace Merwat and other sites within the park, but you may feel left out if *vous ne parlez pas Francais.* 15 rooms. Credit cards: A, DC, MC, V.

Le Jardin Malanga   **$176–$320**   ★★★

Trois Rivieres, ☎ *(800) 322-2223, (590) 92-67-57, FAX (590) 92-67-58.*
Single: $176–$248. Double: $240–$320.

You'll need to persevere to locate it, there's no beach within walking distance, and nightlife is miles away—and that's exactly why one travels to Le Jardin Malanga, a 1996 addition to the southern hillsides of Basse-Terre. The inn is a plantation house tucked into a verdant valley community above the town of Trois Rivieres, on a six-acre property overflowing with bananas and other fruits. The rooms in the main house are spare and chic, with beautiful woodwork and colonial antiques throughout. A trio of two-story, air-conditioned cottages occupies the back of the property, each with a sleek bathroom lined by a one-way picture windows. The centerpiece is a pool that pours over a lip toward Les Saintes in the distance—a sublime sight. There is a small restaurant and bar, but services are limited, which lead to one caveat: the stiff rate card is excessive. Daytrips to Les Saintes are easy (the dock is a 10-minute drive), and hikes to La Soufriere and the Chutes du Carbet are nearby. But once you've checked in, it will take such wonderful options as those to lure you away from the gardens and pool deck of this special inn. 5 rooms. Credit cards: MC, V.

Grand-Terre

Relais du Moulin   **$80–$131**   ★★

Chateaubrun, ☎ (800) 742-4276, (590) 88-23-96, FAX (590) 88-03-92.
Closed Date: September.
Single: $80–$120. Double: $89–$131.

Located on an old sugar plantation amid tropical gardens, this charming inn is
somewhat isolated, set in cattle-grazing countryside just west of St. Francois.
Accommodations surround the beautifully restored windmill in air-conditioned
bungalows with kitchenettes and patios complete with hammocks. Tennis, archery,
horseback riding and a cool swimming pool await—the beach is not too far to walk.
The restaurant is very good and great views reward those who climb the windmill.
40 rooms. Credit cards: A, DC, MC, V.

Low Cost Lodging

Although moderate-priced rooms are common on Guadeloupe, inexpensive lodgings
are surprisingly hard to come by. In addition to the choices below, consider **Serge-Helene**
in Gosier *(590) 84-10-25*, **Carmelita's Village Caraibe** in St. Felix *(590) 84-28-28*, **Al-
gues** in Ste. Anne *(590) 88-30-37*, and the **Relais des Sources** above Lamentin *(590)
25-31-04*. Your accommodations will be very basic at any of these spots, and expect little
if any exchange in English. Also note that room prices are much lower on Marie-Galante
and Terre-de-Haut.

Basse-Terre

Le Rocher de Malendure   **$64–$64**   ★

Bouillante, ☎ (590) 98-70-84, FAX (590) 98-89-92.
Single: $64. Double: $64.

A nest of 14 cottages on a rock overlooking Pigeon Island and the town of Bouil-
lant. Units are strictly functional with rustic ambiance, but have air conditioning
and balconies with kitchenettes that face the sea. Road noise can be a problem in the
evening, but a delightful lobster restaurant is on the property and the owners will
help set you up for the best diving on the island. 4 rooms.

Grand-Terre

Mini Beach Hotel   **$54–$127**   ★★

Ste. Anne, ☎ (590) 88-21-13, FAX (590) 88-19-29.
Single: $54–$127. Double: $54–$127.

This small, family-run spot on Ste. Anne's pretty beach provides lots of appealing
guest house touches to make visitors feel at home—our favorite is the Tuesday
evening classical piano recitals that accompany dinner in the veranda. Accommodation upstairs are in air-conditioned guestrooms with colonial-style decor; all have
private bath (though #3's is across the hall). There are also three bungalows for
those needing more room or a kitchenette. The on-site restaurant serves up tasty
Creole and French fare daily, and *petit dejeuner* is included in the rates. Watersports
are easy to locate; town is a five-minute walk. 9 rooms. Credit cards: MC, V.

Where to Eat

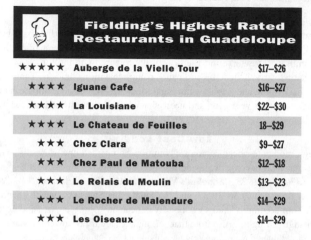

Fielding's Highest Rated Restaurants in Guadeloupe

★★★★★	Auberge de la Vielle Tour	$17–$26
★★★★	Iguane Cafe	$16–$27
★★★★	La Louisiane	$22–$30
★★★★	Le Chateau de Feuilles	18–$29
★★★	Chez Clara	$9–$27
★★★	Chez Paul de Matouba	$12–$18
★★★	Le Relais du Moulin	$13–$23
★★★	Le Rocher de Malendure	$14–$29
★★★	Les Oiseaux	$14–$29

Fielding's Most Romantic Restaurants in Guadeloupe

♥♥♥♥♥	Auberge de la Vielle Tour	$17–$26
♥♥♥♥	Iguane Cafe	$16–$27
♥♥♥♥	La Louisiane	$22–$30
♥♥♥♥	Le Chateau de Feuilles	$18–$29
♥♥♥♥	Le Karacoli	$12–$27

Fielding's Best Value Restaurants in Guadeloupe

★★★	Victoria	$9–$18
★★★	Chez Paul de Matouba	$12–$18
★★★★	Iguane Cafe	$16–$27
★★★	Le Rocher de Malendure	$14–$29

A trip to Guadeloupe provides an immersion into the heart of Creole cooking. Only Martinique can compete for the sheer variety and quality of the experience, and since little genuine Creole food makes its way into the United

States, you'll want to sample some of the many specialties, like **boudin**, a soft sausage made with breadcrumbs, herbs, spices and either blood or milk; **blaff**, a fragrant broth of fish poached in wine and spiced with lime, garlic and spices; **colombo**, a curry of chicken or other meats similar to East Indian curries; or simple **accras**, precious cod-spiked fritters. Seafood is a mainstay island-wide, and such exotics as **sea urchins**, **octopus** and **crayfish** are among the delicacies found on menus. All this comes with a steep price, but note that Creole food is generally less expensive than French. Watch for restaurants with fixed price, or "tourist" menus and pick up a copy of **Ti Gourmet**, a handy free booklet with descriptions and prices for several dozen establishments—a free drink is usually offered to those carrying the book. Prices are calculated at 5.5 French francs to one U.S. dollar.

Basse-Terre

Chez Clara   **$$**   ★★★
Ste. Rose, ☎ *(590) 28-72-99.*
Lunch: Noon–2:30 p.m., entrées $9–$27.
Dinner: 7–10 p.m., entrées $9–$27. Closed: Wed.
Like the jazz she once danced to, native chef Clara Lesueur's culinary improvisations are realized by years of perfecting basic techniques. Guests who patronize Clara's chez on Ste. Rose's seafront are fans of long-standing, guaranteeing a bit of a wait, but refreshing rum drinks at the bar help ease the pain. Go easy on the cocktails so you can enjoy the Creole specials of lambi with lime and peppers, crayfish and crab backs. No dinner is served Sundays. Credit cards: MC, V.

Chez Paul de Matouba   **$$**   ★★★
Riviere Rouge, ☎ *(590) 80-29-20.*
Dinner: entrées $12–$18. Closed: Mon.
Enjoy a refreshing country lunch in this Creole restaurant in Matouba, formerly a Hindu settlement, in the mountains above Basse-Terre. The ambience here is similar to a fishing lodge, where diners enjoy a veritable marketplace of local greens and fresh seafood while a river runs outside. Specialties include *accras* (codfish fritters) with an incendiary sauce, or grilled *ouassous* (crayfish). Fixed-price meals under $20 are available. Credit cards: MC, V.

Le Karacoli   **$**   ★★★
Grand Anse, ☎ *(590) 28-41-17.*
Lunch: Noon–3 p.m., entrées $12–$27.
Named after the jewel worn by the Arawak and Carib indians, Le Karacoli is the pearl in the string of restaurants that lie just behind the rosy sand of Grand Anse. The food lives up to the setting, with traditional Creole specialties prepared Basse-Terre style—boudin, crab farci, chicken colombo or scallops in West Indian spices. The fixed price menu is $15, or the three-course lobster menu is $80 for two. It's a family-run affair, and Lucienne Salcede is the charming hostess; her brother Robert oversees the kitchen. A great place for a beach lunch. Credit cards: MC, V.

Le Rocher de Malendure   **$$$**   ★★★
Malendure Beach, ☎ *(590) 98-70-84.*

Lunch: Noon–3:30 p.m., entrées $14–$29.
Dinner: 6–9 p.m., entrées $14–$29. Closed: Sun.

The vista from this eatery perched on a bluff above Malendure Beach is Pigeon Island, a top diving locale and underwater reserve. If you can keep your eyes from the scenery, you'll be drawn to the delectable Creole treats on the fixed-price lunch that runs under $20—accras, barbecued chicken, crayfish in sauce and a beverage. Dinners are served Fridays and Saturdays only. Credit cards: DC, MC, V.

Sucrerie du Comte $$$ ★★

Comte de Loheac, Sainte-Rose, ☎ (590) 28-60-17.
Lunch: Noon–3 p.m., entrées $13–$35.
Dinner: 7–9:30 p.m., entrées $13–$35.

This pretty open-air restaurant, built of Brazilian woods and volcanic rock, is on the site of a former sugarcane factory and a small hotel that bears the same name. It's open all day for salads and sandwiches and offers such evening specialties as Tahitian fish with coconut milk, fish stew, mahi in parchment paper, and fresh fruit crepes. A good wine list accompanies the tasty dishes, many accented with local spices. On Sundays, the menu features traditional Creole dishes. Credit cards: MC, V.

Grand-Terre

Auberge de la Vielle Tour $$$ ★★★★★

Gosier, ☎ (590) 84-23-23. Associated hotel: *Auberge de la Vielle Tour.*
Dinner: 7–10 p.m., entrées $17–$26.

With other stars having moved on, the Auberge de la Vielle Tour is probably Guadeloupe's finest dining room. The view alone, of the Ilet du Gosier and its lighthouse in the distance, is worth the high tariff (tables facing the wraparound windows are the most sought after—request one in advance). The menu is split between traditional French continental cuisine with a smattering of polished Creole dishes. Typical offerings include red snapper served with exotic fruit butters, court-bouillon with crayfish and lemon grass, or lamb loin beautifully roasted with herbs. A prix-fixe menu is also available for about $38. Thursdays are Creole night, with folk dancing. Reservations recommended. Credit cards: A, DC, MC, V.

Folie Plage $$ ★★

Anse Laborde, ☎ (590) 22-11-17. Associated hotel: Chez Prudence.
Lunch: Noon–3 p.m., entrées $13–$24.
Dinner: 7–10 p.m., entrées $13–$24.

Also known as Chez Prudence, local families flock to this terrace restaurant and guesthouse at Anse Laborde, one mile north of Anse Bertrand, on the striking north coast of Grand-Terre. The offerings are simple from Prudence: beach-combing and swimming (beware the tricky undertow), grilled fish, accras, court bouillon and chicken curry. It's nothing fancy and the food is strictly average, but the setting is one of the most beautiful on the island. Credit cards: A, DC, V.

Iguane Cafe $$$ ★★★★

Route de la Pointe des Chateaux, ☎ (590) 88-61-37.
Dinner: 7:30–11 p.m., entrées $16–$27.

If you've had your fill of Creole cuisine, saunter over to this polished new restaurant, located just past the airstrip in St. Francois. Creative touches are rampant, though not at the expense of simple delights like a cold tomato soup with olive oil and herbs. Entrees include the ever-popular crayfish ravioli, foie gras marbre and rock lobster sauteed in aged rum, and roasted pork filet mignon. The ambiance makes the most of its viewless setting, and Sunday brunch is popular. Credit cards: MC, V.

La Creole $$$ ★★

Perinette Gosier, ☎ (590) 84-10-34.
Lunch: Noon–3:30 p.m., entrées $13–$27.
Dinner: 7:30–11 p.m., entrées $13–$27.
Formerly Chez Violetta and still one of the best-known tourist establishments in Guadeloupe, this restaurant serves traditional Creole specials in a room resplendent with baroque trappings. A mecca for delicacies like accra (cod fritters) and lambi (conch) and still going strong, despite the passing of its creator Violetta Chaville. This is a good introduction to Creole for first-time visitors. Credit cards: A, DC, MC, V.

La Louisiane $$$ ★★★★

Quartier Ste. Marthe, ☎ (590) 88-44-34.
Lunch: Noon–2 p.m., entrées $22–$30.
Dinner: 7–10 p.m., entrées $22–$30. Closed: Mon.
Located just inland from St. Francois in Ste. Marthe, this bloom-filled hillside colonial house has established a fine reputation for creative French-Antillean cuisine. Dinner for two can get pricey, but the experience is worth the splurge—specialties include shark prepared in a saffron sauce and pate of sea urchin roe. Credit cards: MC, V.

Le Chateau de Feuilles $$$ ★★★★

Campeche, ☎ (590) 22-30-30.
Lunch: 11 a.m.–3 p.m., entrées $18–$29. Closed: Mon.
If you pass the remains of a crumbling old sugar mill in off-the-beaten-path Anse Bertrand, you're close to your goal—a fabulous culinary landmark in an unlikely location—a farm owned by chef-hosts Jean-Pierre and Martine Dubost. The atmosphere is like a house party, with a pool to swim in after lunch and a breathtaking choice of 20 flavors of rum (a sort of Baskin-Robbins for adults). If you had a hard time finding the restaurant, don't indulge too much or you may never make it home. Reservations required. Credit cards: MC, V.

Le Relais du Moulin $$ ★★★

Chateaubrun, ☎ (590) 88-23-96. Associated hotel: *Relais du Moulin.*
Lunch: 12:30–2:30 p.m., entrées $13–$23.
Dinner: 7:30–9:30 p.m., entrées $13–$23.
Le restaurant at the village-style Relais du Moulin serves Antillean-French dishes with flair in an elegant dining room facing the inn's pool. Reasonably priced a la carte offerings include grilled lobster with herbs, blaff (fresh seafood in a spicy infusion) and red snapper; the fixed-priced menu is $40. Stroll the grounds before dinner—the old mill (moulin) dating back to the inn's plantation days makes a picturesque photo opportunity. Reservations recommended. Credit cards: A, DC, MC, V.

Les Oiseaux $$$ ★★★

Anse des Rochers, ☎ (590) 88-56-92.
Lunch: Noon–3 p.m., entrées $14–$29.
Dinner: 7–10:30 p.m., entrées $14–$29. Closed: Sun.

It's easy to imagine that you're in the South of France while dining on the terrace of this stone structure facing the sea, located a few miles east of Ste. Anne. The talented chef is a whiz with seafood, attesting to the popularity of his cassoulet de fruits de mer, and a cheeseless fondue of various fish and shellfish cooked with aromatic oils. Jazz pours out of the kitschy attic bar from 10 p.m. nightly (except Monday). Closed for lunch in low season. Reservations recommended. Credit cards: MC, V.

Victoria   **$**   ★★★

Le Moule, ☎ *(590) 23-78-38.* Associated hotel: *Cottage Hotel.*
Lunch: Noon–2 p.m., entrées $9–$18.
Dinner: 7–10 p.m., entrées $9–$18.

Sandrine and Isabelle are the sweet proprietors of this pretty open-air cafe across from the beach at la Moule. Choose from imaginative meat, chicken, and fish dishes are prepared with Antillean flair; the goat cheese salad is wonderful. Tasty food and a good wine list, plus reasonable prices. Also open for breakfast from 7–9:30 a.m. daily; lunch hours can vary. Closed Thursday in low season. Credit cards: A, MC, V.

Where to Shop

Shopping is not high on the list of things that makes Guadeloupe worth a visit, though you'll have no problem finding ways to spend your French francs. The Juan Perse Cruise Terminal in Point-a-Pitre is a nicely done mall with some two dozen shops catering to upscale shoppers. Other shopping areas in the city are the streets of rue Frébault, rue Schoelcher and rue de Nozieres. In Bas-du-Fort, check out the Cora Shopping Center and the Marina. Duty-free goods can be found at Poles Caraibes Airport.

Some stores offer a 20 percent discount on purchases paid with traveler's checks or major credit cards—it's always worth asking. Bargains are generally limited to items form the motherland of France, including perfumes, fashions, china, crystal and scarves. For rum—always a popular souvenir—try the **Musée du Rhum** or **Distillerie Severin**, both in Sainte-Rose. Haitian handicrafts and artworks can be found at **Artisans Caraibes in Saint-Francois** *Avenuede l'Europe,* ☎ *(590) 90-87-28;* for local handiworks such as wood carvings, intricate lace and brightly costumed dolls, try **L'Imagerie Creole** in Bas-du-Fort ☎ *(590) 90-87-28* and **Mariposa** in Saint-Francois 13, *Galerie du Port.* **Domaine de Valombreuse** *Petit-Bourg,* ☎ *(590) 95-50-50* ships tropical flowers and gift packages all over the world. Shops are generally open from 9 a.m. to 1 p.m. and 3–6 p.m. weekdays, as well as on Saturday mornings.

Guadeloupe Directory

Arrival and Departure

The new **Pole Caraibes** airport terminal just outside Pointe-a-Pitre is one of the region's most modern facilities. **American Eagle** flies nonstop from San Juan to Guadeloupe twice daily, allowing easy connections with **American Airlines** flights from major cities in the United States. **Air France** has twice-weekly jet service to Guadeloupe out of Miami. Inter-island service is also available, with **LIAT** providing nonstop or direct flights to Guadeloupe from Antigua, Dominica, Martinique, St. Lucia and St. Vincent, and **Air Guadeloupe** providing service to the French islands. Daily ferry service to Guadeloupe is available from Martinique and Dominica on **Express des Iles** ☎ *(590) 83-12-45*.

There is no departure tax when leaving Guadeloupe.

Business Hours

Stores open weekdays 9 a.m.–1 p.m. and 3–6 p.m. Banks open weekdays 8 a.m.–noon and 2–4 p.m. Some shops and banks are open Saturday mornings.

Climate

The climate is tropical with an average temperature of 79 degrees F. The more humid and wet season runs between June and November.

Documents

If you're staying up to three weeks, you need show only a current or expired passport (five years old or less) or proof of citizenship (voter's registration, birth certificate and official photo ID), as well as an ongoing or return ticket. Longer stays require a valid passport.

Electricity

Current is 220 volts, AC, 50 cycles. Adapters for U.S. appliances are needed.

Getting Around

With more than 1200 miles of paved roads to explore, you'll want to rent a car for at least part of your trip. Roads are good by Caribbean standards, though traffic is swift, particularly around Pointe-a-Pitre (it helps to have a navigator with a good map). When you pick up your car at the airport, note carefully the location of the car rental firms—they're on the *opposite* side of the runway at the old terminal. Along with a host of local outfits, four American firms are represented on the island—**Avis**, **Budget**, **Hertz** and **Thrifty**—with daily rates starting at about $35 per day (lower rates apply for weekly rentals); there's a 9.5 percent local tax, plus an $11 surcharge for rentals at the airport.

Taxis are common transportation, though most drivers do not speak English and the cost will add up quickly. Samples fares: from the airport to Gosier, about $11; from the airport to St. Francois, $32. Fares go up 40 percent from 9 p.m. to 7 a.m. and all day Sunday. Cabs are available at most major hotels and restaurants, or call ☎ *(590) 20-74-74* or *(590) 82-96-69* to have a car dispatched. The Guadeloupean **bus** system is comprehensive, but an involved option for those not fluent in French. Most routes start or end in Pointe-a-

Pitre and operate from 5 a.m. to 7:30 p.m. Fares are based on distance; about $5 from Pointe-a-Pitre to St. Francois, or $7 to the capitol of Basse-Terre. They are, however, a true French Antillean experience: music is played, and the faster the *zouk* beat, the faster they go.

Ferry service to Guadeloupe's satellite islands, as well as to Martinique, Dominica and St. Lucia are frequent. **Terre-de-Haut** is served by Express des Isles ☎ *(590) 83-12-45* and Brudey Freres ☎ *(590) 90-04-48*, which leave from Pointe-a-Pitre harbor daily at 8 a.m.; the trip takes 45 minutes and departs for the return trip at 4 p.m. Round-trip fare is about $31. The island is also reached from Trois-Rivieres by the *Princess Caroline* ☎ *(590) 86-95-83*; the boat leaves Trois-Rivieres daily at 8 a.m. and 4 p.m., and leaves Terre-de-Haut at 6 a.m. and 3 p.m. More limited service is also available out of St. Francois and the town of Basse-Terre.

The 45-minute trip to Grand-Bourg on **Marie-Galante** is also served daily by Express des Isles and Brudey Freres out of Pointe-a-Pitre harbor, daily at 8 a.m.; round-trip fare is about $31. Express des Isles and Amanda Galante ☎ *(590) 83-12-45* have limited service from St. Francois. The 45-minute crossing to **La Desirade** is handled by Socimade ☎ *(590) 83-32-67* and Sotramade ☎ *(590) 20-02-30* daily from St. Francois; round-trip fare is about $22. There is also service to La Desirade from Pointe-a-Pitre on Wednesdays.

Ferry crossings are sometimes rough; anyone prone to seasickness should seriously consider flying to the outer islands. All three islands are served by air from Guadeloupe's Pole Caraibes airport; round-trip fare is about $75.

Language

The official language is French. African-influenced Creole is spoken by nearly everyone. Only some people speak English, so bring a French phrase book.

Medical Emergencies

There are five hospitals and 23 clinics in Guadeloupe. Your hotel or the tourist office can assist you in finding an English-speaking physician.

Money

The official currency is the French franc. The exchange rate we have used to calculate hotel and restaurant prices provided to us in francs is 5.5 to one U.S. dollar. If the dollar has further strengthened, you may find lower prices on the island than what we have quoted. Dollars are accepted in tourist establishments, but paying in francs will usually get you a better rate. Credit cards are accepted by most businesses, and plastic frequently yields a better rate than is available through island banks.

Telephone

The international dialing code for Guadeloupe and its outer islands is *(590)*; to call from the U.S., dial 011 + *(590)* plus the six-digit local number. The cheapest way to call the U.S. from Guadeloupe is to purchase a *telecarte*, sold at post offices and other outlets marked "Telecarte en Vente Ici." The cards can be used in any phone booth marked "Telecom."

Time

Guadeloupe is one hour later than Eastern standard time.

Tipping

Restaurants and bars are required by law to add a 15 percent service charge. Most taxi drivers don't expect tips, especially if they own their own cars. Room maids should be tipped $1–$2, bellboys 50 cents–$1 a bag.

Tourist Information

In the U.S., information can be obtained through the **Guadeloupe Tourist Office** ☎ *(888)* 4-*GUADELOUPE*. On island, the **Office Départemental du Tourisme** is open Monday–Saturday from 8 a.m. to 5 p.m.; it is located at *5, Square de la Banque in Pointe-a-Pitre* ☎ *(590) 82-09-30*. There are additional offices in Basse-Terre and on Marie-Galante.

When to Go

Leave it to the French to celebrate their food, which they accomplish in inimitable fashion during the **Fete des Cuisinieres**—the Festival of Women Chefs, held every August. The origins of the celebration date to 1916, and it climaxes with a five-hour feast of exotic Creole specialties. And, just as mainland France loves bicycling, so do the French West Indies, which hold a 10-day **Tour de la Guadeloupe**, also in August. A new addition to the island's calendar of events is the **Intercontinental Kite Challenge**, a week-long competition held in St. Francois in May. **Carnival** is celebrated in grand style during the five days leading up to Ash Wednesday in February.

GUADELOUPE HOTELS	RMS	RATES	PHONE	CR. CARDS
Basse-Terre				
★★★ Hotel St. Georges	40	$93–$120	(590) 80-10-10	A, MC, V
★★★ Le Jardin Malanga	5	$176–$320	(800) 322-2223	MC, V
★★ Auberge de la Distillerie	15	$68–$160	(800) 322-2223	A, DC, MC, V
★★ Sucrerie du Comte	50	$50–$85	(590) 28-60-17	MC, V
★ Le Rocher de Malendure	4	$64–$64	(590) 98-70-84	
Grande-Terre				
★★★★ Auberge de la Vieille Tour	181	$136–$390	(800) 763-4835	A, MC, V
★★★★ Hamak	54	$200–$400	(800) 633-7411	A, MC, V
★★★★ Le Meridien la Cocoteraie	50	$273–$618	(800) 543-4300	A, MC, V
★★★★ Plantation Ste. Marthe	120	$110–$218	(800) 333-1970	MC, V
★★★ Anse des Rochers	356	$132–$204	(800) 322-2223	MC, V
★★★ Club Med Caravelle	329	$138–$372	(800) 258-2633	A, MC, V
★★★ Fleur d'Epee Novotel	190	$105–$225	(800) 221-4542	A, DC, MC, V
★★★ La Creole Beach Hotel	321	$87–$299	(800) 322-2223	A, DC, MC, V
★★★ La Toubana	32	$109–$237	(800) 322-2223	A, DC, MC, V

GUADELOUPE

GUADELOUPE HOTELS	RMS	RATES	PHONE	CR. CARDS
★★★ Le Meridien St. Francois	265	$132–$291	(800) 543-4300	A, DC, MC, V
★★★ Marissol Hotel	195	$110–$255	(800) 221-4542	A, DC, MC, V
★★ Mini Beach Hotel	9	$54–$127	(590) 88-21-13	MC, V
★★ Relais du Moulin	40	$80–$131	(800) 742-4276	A, DC, MC, V
★★ Tropical Club Hotel	96	$82–$113	(800) 322-2223	A, MC, V

Les Saintes

	RMS	RATES	PHONE	CR. CARDS
★★★ Auberge les Petits Saints	10	$65–$127	(800) 322-2223	MC, V
★★★ Hotel Bois Joli	31	$64–$181	(800) 322-2223	MC, V

Marie-Galante

	RMS	RATES	PHONE	CR. CARDS
★★★ Village de Menard	7	$60–$100	(590) 97-09-45	MC, V

GUADELOUPE RESTAURANTS	PHONE	ENTRÉE	CR. CARDS

Basse-Terre

Creole Cuisine

	PHONE	ENTRÉE	CR. CARDS
★★★ Chez Clara	(590) 28-72-99	$9–$27	MC, V
★★★ Chez Paul de Matouba	(590) 80-29-20	$12–$18	MC, V
★★★ Le Karacoli	(590) 28-41-17	$12–$27	MC, V
★★ Sucrerie du Comte	(590) 28-60-17	$13–$35	MC, V

French Cuisine

	PHONE	ENTRÉE	CR. CARDS
★★★ Le Rocher de Malendure	(590) 98-70-84	$14–$29	DC, MC, V

Grande-Terre

Creole Cuisine

	PHONE	ENTRÉE	CR. CARDS
★★★ Le Relais du Moulin	(590) 88-23-96	$13–$23	A, DC, MC, V
★★★ Victoria	(590) 23-78-38	$9–$18	A, MC, V
★★ Folie Plage	(590) 22-11-17	$13–$24	A, DC, V
★★ La Creole	(590) 84-10-34	$13–$27	A, DC, MC, V

French Cuisine

	PHONE	ENTRÉE	CR. CARDS
★★★★★ Auberge de la Vielle Tour	(590) 84-23-23	$17–$26	A, DC, MC, V
★★★★ Iguane Cafe	(590) 88-61-37	$16–$27	MC, V
★★★★ La Louisiane	(590) 88-44-34	$22–$30	MC, V
★★★★ Le Chateau de Feuilles	(590) 22-30-30	$18–$29	MC, V
★★★ Les Oiseaux	(590) 88-56-92	$14–$29	MC, V

GUADELOUPE

JAMAICA

Bamboo rafts on the Rio Grande River take tourists past magnificent scenery.

If Jamaica competed in a beauty pageant lined up against her competitors—the 30-some-odd other Caribbean islands—she'd be a standout: stunningly exotic and exquisitely beautiful, cultured yet wild with a penchant for shocking the judges. This island inspired Ian Fleming to create the ultimate man of mystery and impeccable taste: James Bond. Indeed, since before the turn of the century, Jamaica has been attracting a myriad of travelers, and it has emerged as a favorite with honeymooners, adventurers, nature-lovers and jet-setters, movie stars and rock icons looking for hideaways. Jamaica's unparalleled natural beauty—wild flower-blanketed mountains, roaring waterfalls, colonial great houses, stunning beaches, tropical jungles—coupled with its sports offerings—world-class golf, horseback riding, tennis, fishing and watersports galore—add up to a smorgasbord that allows you to design your own ideal vacation.

In recent years, Jamaica's tourism trade suffered amidst growing concern about safety on the island. The high-pressured hustlers who harangued visitors from the moment they landed on the island, hawking everything from ganja to t-shirts, set many tourists on edge. Plus, Kingston's unsavory reputation as a Caribbean crime hotspot didn't help. Neither did the armed guards at checkpoints along Negril's Seven Mile Beach. However, over the past few years the government has actively pushed a campaign to discourage such aggressive salesmanship and make tourists feel much safer. Though Kingston retains its big-city problems, murders are largely drug-related and primarily occur in gang-controlled areas. As long as you use the same precautions you'd employ when visiting a city like New York, you should be fine. On a recent visit, walking Negril's streets alone was no problem. Merchants only spoke when asked about a product. Apparently, the new push is working: Tourism from the U.S. was up 11 percent from June 1995 to June 1997, primarily from the Southeast.

"Mo Bay," Jamaica's most popular resort area, has all the modern resort amenities, some of Jamaica's notable great houses, restaurants, watersports, golf courses, shopping and decent beaches—but note that the area has become so touristy it has an almost generic feel. Edenic Ocho Rios—home of fine accommodations, historic plantations and the famous, 600-foot-high Dunn's River Falls—has emerged as a favorite with more sophisticated travelers. With its high crime rate and lack of architectural charm, the capital of Kingston rarely attracts mainstream tourists, with the exception of Bob Marley devotees, businesspeople, adventurers and those drawn by its vibrant nightlife. However, since it sits at the base of the Blue Mountains, it has become a departure point for those who want to hike the area. Historic and oh-so-British Mandeville is a mountain-lover's delight complete with historic buildings, mineral baths, bird-watching tours and the island's oldest golf course. Mountainous Port Antonio, called the most exquisite port on earth, is an interesting mix of well-heeled resorts and an unassuming village that belies the fact that this place is frequented by the rich and famous. Unfortunately, the word is out on funky Negril, long considered Jamaica's best-kept secret. A haven for hippie-types and Rastafarians since the 1970s, the beach-front village has been transformed into one of Jamaica's prime tourist destinations, though it still oozes with laid-back charm. But it hasn't quite lost the edginess that made it so appealing. Meanwhile, Treasure Beach, on the Southwest Coast, has been anointed as the next Negril.

The island has more than 20,400 guestrooms, enabling tourists to book exactly what they want. The popular concept of all-inclusive resorts was born here and, as it rapidly spreads throughout the Caribbean like whitecaps on a windy day, Jamaica continues to refine the concept to ever-higher levels, with all-inclusives catering to couples, singles and families. You'll also find

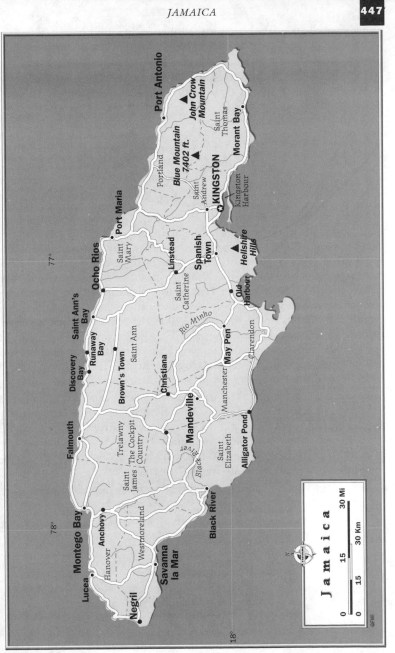

formal, British-style five-star resorts, affordable, low-frills hotels, hedonistic spa-resorts and small country inns.

BEST BETS FOR...

Bird's-Eye View

   Roughly the size of the state of Connecticut, Jamaica is the Caribbean's third-largest island (after Cuba and Puerto Rico), totaling 4411 square miles. It is located 1551 miles from New York, a nearly four-hour flight. The island is 146 miles long, with widths varying from 22 to 51 miles, and quite mountainous; almost half of the island lies 1000 feet above sea level. The highest point is Blue Mountain Peak, which rises up 7402 feet. Jamaica's lush terrain has valleys, cliffs, caves, bays, coves and mineral springs. Another notable feature is its wealth of rivers—120 in all, unusual in the Caribbean. Floating downstream on bamboo rafts is a lovely way to spend a day; at night, some routes are romantically lit with tiki torches. The island boasts 150 miles of beach where you can laze away the day. Its southwest coast is drier. In places, you might think you were in the plains of Africa.

   The average temperature is 82 degrees Fahrenheit, and average rainfall is 78 inches, mostly occurring from October through November and May through June. Don't despair if you're coming during the rainy season, though—usually the rain falls in big, quick bursts, then the clouds move away to let the sun shine through. In the high mountains of the east, temperatures can drop as low as 40 degrees Fahrenheit.

   Much of the island is limestone, sporting a variety of underground caves and offshore reefs that are the delight of divers and snorkelers.

   Kingston, the capital city, has more than 800,000 residents, making it one of the Caribbean's largest cities.

History

   Named for its Arawak word "Xamayca," which means "land of wood and water," Columbus first glimpsed the north coast of Jamaica in May 1494.

When he returned nine years later, stormy weather crippled two of his ships and he was forced to anchor at St. Ann's Bay, where he and his men were shipwrecked until the governor of Hispaniola retrieved them. In 1510, a permanent Spanish settlement was finally established under the orders of Don Diego, the son of Columbus, who was then governor of the West Indies, based in Santo Domingo. A new capital was erected in 1935 at Villa de la Vega (the Town on the Plain), now known as Spanish Town. In 1655, Britain, under Oliver Cromwell, challenged Spain's claim on the island, ultimately triumphing and establishing a head base at Port Royal, across the harbor from what is now Kingston. Port Royal became the hub of some of the most nefarious activities on the high seas, under the direction of the buccaneer Henry Morgan, whose sacking of the Spanish colony in Panama clinched England's claim to Jamaica. A massive earthquake in 1692 actually shook half the town into the sea.

The multi-ethnic, though black-based, population of Jamaica began to grow over the next centuries as sugarcane farming took root. After Jamaica's slave population rose to 300,000 at the end of the 18th century, the ratio of blacks to whites was a staggering 15 to one. Included in the mix were "free coloureds," the offspring of white men and slave women, and Maroons, descendants of free slaves. (For more information about the Maroons, see below under "People.") The planters, too, were rebellious. When the 13 American colonies declared independence, the Jamaica House of Assembly voted to join them—a daring but impotent gesture. Slave revolts became a common occurrence in Jamaica. The largest, bloodiest conflict was led by "Daddy" Sam Sharpe, a Baptist preacher whose oratory and convictions led the way to the abolishment of slavery in Jamaica in 1838. Emancipation, however, led directly to the fall of the sugarcane industry since the labor pool was no more. The condition of the freed blacks was further worsened by drought and unsteady economic conditions, leading to another revolt in 1865, which resulted in the murder of a government official. Shortly thereafter, the island was designated a British Crown Colony in 1866, which it remained until 1944, when full adult suffrage was granted.

A British colony from 1655–1962, Jamaica developed a two-party system before World War II. A considerable measure of self-government was introduced in 1944, but full independence was delayed by attempts to set up a wider federation embracing all or most of the Caribbean Commonwealth territories. Jamaica joined the now-defunct West Indies Federation in 1958, but withdrew in 1961 because of disagreements over taxation, voting rights, and location of the federal capital. Sir Alexander Bustaments, one of the original founders of the two-party system, became the nation's first prime minister when Jamaica gained independence in 1962. Under the 1962 constitution, the Queen is the titular head of state. Her representative, a governor general, is advised in areas bearing on the royal perogative, by a six-member privy council. Jamaica is divided into 13 parishes and the Kingston and St. Andrew Corporation, a special administrative entity encompassing the principal urban areas.

Jamaica's national flag—black for the people, green for the land, and gold for the sun—was proudly displayed. The newly independent nation was relatively prosperous following independence, thanks to the mining of bauxite. The tide shifted, however, with the rise to power of Michael Manley, son of the previous prime minister, in 1972. He enraged the United States with his socialist leanings and by sympathizing with Cuba. Western companies began abandoning Jamaica in droves, toppling the economy. The 1980 elections brought the most violence since 1865's rebellion: 700 were killed, primarily in Kingston. Manley's successor, Edward Seaga, a Harvard-educated economist, severed ties with Cuba much to the delight of the Reagan White House. Economic recovery planted the seeds for Jamaica's emerging middle class. Then in 1988, Hurricane Gilbert—the first to strike since 1951—devastated the island, leaving one-quarter of Jamaicans homeless and wreaking $300 million worth of damage. It also severely damaged Seaga's popularity with the people, leaving an open door for Manley to return to power in 1989. He resigned for health reasons a few years later and was eventually succeeded by Percival James Patterson, Jamaica's first black prime minister. Elections for prime minister are coming up in 1998; unfortunately almost half the population, according to a recent survey, expects them to be surrounded by violence. The Jamaican dollar, once equivalent to the U.S. dollar in 1962, at press time traded at JA $37 to US $1.

People

The country's motto, "Out of Many, One People," is certainly appropriate for Jamaica. The population of 2.5 million is a racial mix of African, European, Afro-European, East Indian, Afro-East Indian, Chinese and Afro-Chinese. A visible minority follows the religion Rastafarianism, characterized by dreadlocks and a great love of marijuana, locally called *ganga*. Rastas believe the late Emperor Haile Selassie was a divine being who believed God would lead the blacks from oppression to the Promised Land. However, relatively few rastas continue to embrace the notion of living peacefully, eschewing city life and its "soul pollution." The "rastas" most visitors encounter are more likely urbanites sporting the dreadlocked hair but not the attitude of nonviolent rastas who tend to stick to the countryside and live commune-style. True believers call these interlopers "wolves." Other religions include

Protestant (the majority belong to the Church of Jamaica, formerly the Church of England), Roman Catholic, Judaism, Seventh Day Adventists, Pentecostals, Muslims, Hindus and Quakers.

Another interesting minority lives in the rugged Cockpit country, Port and St. Mary. The Maroons—derived from a Spanish word that means "wild"—are descendants of escaped slaves who eluded capture for some 100 years, and their modern leaders are believed to have spiritual powers. Chances are you won't encounter any Maroons—they live autonomously under a treaty from 1739, in the hill country in villages barely reached by road.

Jamaicans are a cheerful, outgoing group with a great sense of humor and a fierce national pride. The reply to any statement or query will invariably be "no problem, mon," and it's not sarcasm, but a truly held belief that things will work out. You'll also hear a lot of *"irie"* (EYE-ree), which means "everything's okay." English is the official language, spoken in a charming musical lilt, and many also speak Patios, a blend of English and African.

To really know Jamaica, sign up for the Meet the People program; you'll be matched with a volunteer Jamaican family with similar interests. Arrange far in advance by calling the **Jamaica Tourist Board** at ☎ *(800) 233-4582.*

Tourism remains the most important contributor to the island's economy, followed by mining bauxite and exporting bananas. The drug trade is still vigorous, although the Jamaican government has enlisted help from the U.S. government and regularly burns marijuana fields.

Another major export is Jamaica's indigenous music—reggae—made famous by the late Bob Marley, who touched the hearts of many with the driving rhythms and his lyrics about freedom. In 1972, Marley joined forces with fellow Jamaican Chris Blackwell and his Island Records. Blackwell produced some of Marley's greatest works and gave him refuge at his home at Strawberry Hill in 1976 after Marley was wounded during an attempt on his life on the eve of the elections. Marley died at age 36 of brain cancer in 1981, but his musical legend has continued to grow. Today Jamaican deejays dub their own lyrics over music—a music form that evolved into dance hall, Jamaica's answer to rap. Dance hall with its heavy baseline is the current music of the people.

Beaches

Trying to pick a favorite beach in Jamaica is somewhat akin to being asked to pick your favorite child: they are each different and have their own attributes. Many of the best beaches are inaccessible to the public, reserved for the tourists who pay a pretty price to loll in the sun on that particular strand. Don't worry, you'll have more beautiful spots than you can possibly see on one trip anyway. Montego Bay has three public beaches in town—**Cornwall**, **Doctor's Cave** and **Walter Fletcher**. The first two are frequented more by tourists, while the latter is favored by locals. None are stunningly beautiful, but they are handily close to the airport and shopping. Sandals Montego Bay arguably staked out Jamaica's best private beach. If you're willing to pay for the privilege, you can get a day pass ($55) to **Rose Hall Beach Club**, giving you access to one of Montego Bay's better beaches. Native fig trees, hung with hammocks, offer shelter after you snorkel the reef. Every Thursday (11 a.m.- 4 p.m.) an all-inclusive beach party is held here, offering guests watersport equipment and instruction, lunch at the new Pavilion and live calypso music. Negril has long-held the claim on the island's best beach. Watersports are abundant, and it remains a good spot for snorkelers. Its **Seven Mile** beach is a stunner, but it has been blighted somewhat by the fact that you have to sign books as you pass through sections of it under watchful eyes of guards making certain you don't belly up to the bar at one of the many all-inclusives sprawled along beach. If you are looking for a beach-party atmosphere, though, you can't miss in Negril. At **Turtle Beach**, fronting the harbor in the center of Ocho Rios, you'll find plenty of watersports. Lawmakers are considering banning jet skis at both Negril and Turtle Beach, because of several accidents and their use in the drug trade. But for now it can get noisy. Lush, romantic Port Antonio not surprisingly boasts some of the choice spots for lovers. Head to **Frenchman's Cove** or **San San Beach**, white sand wisps offering ultimate seclusion. The white sands of nearby **Long Bay** beach remain undeveloped due to its large waves and the undertow which make swimming inadvisable. But the setting is gorgeous. Those who want to veg out should go south. The sand may be gray, but the locals are colorful around Treasure Beach. Snorkeling and swimming are popular in the calm waters of Great Bay. You'll also find plenty of fishermen willing to take you out, or you can lie in a hammock and listen to the sea. At the southeastern tip of the parish near Southfield is Lover's Leap, a precipice where mountains meet the sea. Two young slave lovers leapt 1600 feet to their death rather than be separated by the young girl's jealous master who wanted her for himself.

Although the deep Cayman Trench lies off Jamaica's north coast, one unfortunate trade-off on a densely populated Caribbean island is that every shoreline is a potential fishing area. Hard-core divers would not put Jamaica high on their list—indeed, much of its coral reefs collapsed in 1992, the result of overfishing—but its sites are a good adjunct. The many all-inclusives can also make a good starting point for novices. Divers will find most of Jamaica's touristy north coast overfished and barren, despite having attractive reef architecture and well-developed sponge life once greatly admired by the late Jacques Cousteau. The island's main exception is **Negril**, situated on the west coast, and more protected from the wind and currents that sometimes play havoc with the rest of the island. Negril's 10-mile reef parallels the beach and encircles nearby Booby Cay, and features more than 40 known dive sites at all levels of ability. **Montego Bay** is the location of Jamaica's first marine park, established in 1990. Unfortunately all sites close to shore are well-trammeled and contain few fish. However, it does feature some wall dives; curiously, one of the best is **Airport Reef**, notable for its coral caves, tunnels and canyons. The **Falmouth/Runaway Bay** area represents the best north coast diving; fish life is a little better developed, and the reef structure features good wall and canyon diving. The name Ocho Rios translates to eight rivers, which come pouring down from the mountains and can create less-than-stellar underwater visibility after wet weather. Otherwise, north coast diving visibility averages 60 to 100 feet, soaring to 150 feet on occasional summer days.

The dive frontier of Jamaica lies on the largely unvisited south coast, where offshore cays, wrecks and walls, await more extensive exploration. One of the Caribbean's most unusual underwater locations is a veritable sunken Pompeii lying in Kingston Harbor, **Port Royal**. The current (above-ground) fishing village of the same name bears little resemblance to its former self: a pirate lair was once referred to as "the wickedest city in Christendom," which succumbed to a devastating earthquake in 1692 by sinking, literally, into the bay. Old Port Royal has been frozen in time over the ensuing 300 years, collecting silt and rust from the harbor; unfortunately, the government has closed the site to sport diving while it contemplates how best to salvage the site. Other locations to enjoy, include **Wreck Reef**, a shallow bank of coral off the Hellshire Hills which has proven a disastrous magnet for many ships. Visibility off Kingston is limited by harbor traffic and turbulent waters, but averages 50 to 70 feet which allows divers to see the reef. In addition to the dive shops listed below, a number are based out of the all-inclusive resorts. A recompression chamber is in Discovery Bay.

Dive Shops

Buccaneer Scuba Club
> Port Royal; ☎ (876) 967-8061.
> Four-year-old shop visits Wreck Reef, the cays off Kingston Harbor and a site known as the Edge. PADI affiliated. Two-tank dive, $50; resort course, $80 (in pool at Morgan's Harbour Hotel). Mostly local clientele.

Negril Scuba Center

Negril; ☎ *(800) 818-2963 or (876) 957-4425.*

Situated near the harbor, this shop is the only one not directly tied to a resort and boasts a multilingual staff. Open since 1983, a PADI and SSI facility, with courses through assistant instructor. It offers dive tours to the Throne Room. Two tank dive, $55; night dives scheduled regularly, $40.

Resort Divers

Ocho Rios; ☎ *(876) 974-5338.*

Probably Jamaica's largest dive operation (since 1986), with shops set up in Ocho Rios, Runaway Bay, Falmouth and Montego Bay. PADI five-star outfit with training to assistant instructor. Two-tank dive, $65, all equipment included; night dives, $60, but this price seems negotiable based on group size. Free hotel transfer from nearby resorts included in dive price.

Sundivers of Jamaica

Negril; ☎ *(876) 973-2346.*

Two Negril Beach locations, plus a Discovery Bay branch; an Instructor Development Center and PADI five-star facility. Two tank dive, $60; resort course, $75. Free "discover scuba" program.

JamAqua Limited

Runaway Bay; ☎ *(876) 973-4845; FAX: (876) 973-4875;*
e-mail: jamaqua@infochan.com; Web-site: http://www.inforchan.com/jamaqua

Located at Club Caribbean, approximately 18 miles from Ocho Rios, this PADI 5-star diving facility has four instructors who offer courses from beginner to assistant instructor in four languages. It serves 20 divesites: coral reef gardens, wall and canyon dives, small cave dives, an underwater island, Spanish anchor and a plane crash. Its dive boats carry eight and ten divers. A two-tank dive costs $35; night dive, $52.

A local saying has it that "you can walk anywhere in Jamaica, " but hiking in Jamaica is no small adventure. The 14- or 27-mile trek to the 7402-foot summit of the **Blue Mountains** takes the better part of two days. Nighttime temperatures can drop to freezing in this magnificent mountain range, the second-highest in the Caribbean. Several areas of the country are rarely traveled, and at least one range, the **John Crow Mountains**, north of Kingston, has been uncharted since a major British expedition explored in 1819. Shorter trails are few and far between, although goat paths and unmarked foot trails that appeal to intrepid walkers abound. In sum, the wilds of Jamaica are truly spectacular, but are best ventured in the company of a qualified guide.

The island features a great diversity of flowering plants—about 3000—and among the species, 827 are found only on Jamaica as well as 550 types of fern. Jamaica's wildlife is also a chief asset in the island's first tentative steps toward developing eco-tourism. An endemic lizard, the Jamaican iguana, was thought to be extinct for several decades, but a family made an appearance in 1990 in the **Hellshire Hills** southwest of Kingston, an uninhabited area that local conservationists are now trying to protect. The Jamaican boa grows to eight feet and also lives in these gentle hills of dry scrub and cactus. Several species of snake are on the island; none are poisonous. A rare native butterfly, *Papillio homerus*—one of the world's largest—can sometimes be glimpsed in the foothills of the John Crow Mountains. Several places outside the rugged Blue Mountains invite birdwatching: the Kingston foothills and nearby Clydesdale National Park (near Hardwar Gap), Marshall's Pen (a nature reserve three miles outside Mandeville), Jamaica's largest extant marshland Black River Great Morass, the mangrove swamps of Falmouth Lagoon, and on the trails surrounding the Rockland Bird Sanctuary, west of Montego Bay. A 1990 book, *Birds of Jamaica: A Photographic Field Guide* by Audrey Downer and Robert Sutton, can be located in some stores and will aid in identifying the island's many species.

Another ambitious hike is one which traverses the mysterious **Cockpit Country** to **Windsor Caves** (nine miles each way); the muggy area can only be visited on foot, but reveals a strange landscape of limestone karst formations and a reclusive community of ex-slaves, the Maroons. Both of these rewarding treks should be undertaken only with a guide. A simpler excursion for those wanting to experience the Blue Mountains without the commitment of an overnight adventure are the paths which climb above Jack's Hill to Peter's Rock (two hours) and nearby points. **Catherine's Peak** (5060 feet) can be attained via a short military track out of Newcastle; other nearby trails are maintained by the forestry department, which has an office in Hollywell. When hiking below 3000 feet and near cow pastures, you'll need to be prepared for ticks, particularly during February and March; in swampy areas, mosquitoes are combated with repellent. The topographical map is the best resource for heading off the beaten track, and is available at the Land and Survey department in Kingston on Charles Street; unfortunately, black-and-white reproductions are all that are available at this writing.

Trekking Shops
Sense Adventures

Jack's Hill; ☎ *(876) 927-2097.*

President of the Jamaican Alternative Tourism, Camping and Hiking Association, Peter Bentley oversees this guide company that specializes in two-day treks to Blue Mountain Peak, $125 per person including ground transportation to the Penlyne Castle hostels (or $75 per person if hiking from Mavis Bank). Other itineraries include day-trips in the Newcastle area, iguana tours, raft and canoe trips and "clothes optional recreation." Bentley's operation is based out of the Maya Lodge overlooking Kingston.

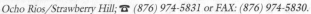

Touring Society of Jamaica

Ocho Rios/Strawberry Hill; ☎ *(876) 974-5831 or FAX: (876) 974-5830.*

TSOJ is a licensed tour operator that specializes in custom tours of Jamaica with an insider's eye—called "keeping company" by islanders. Tours include hikes to Alex Twyman's The Old Tavern Blue Mountain Coffee Estate, night crawls through Kingston's music scene, tours of Jamaica's gardens and more.

Treasure Tours

Calabash Bay, St. Elizabeth; ☎ *(876) 965-0126;*
web-site http://www.ultranet.com/~usrbw.

Rebecca Wiersma has lived in Treasure Beach for five years and loves to show off her new stomping ground. She can arrange for tours to Black River, where more than 300 crocodiles make their home, horseback rides of the backcountry, fishing expeditions or whatever you can think of to do in this remote area.

Valley Hikes

Port Antonio; ☎ *(876) 993-3881.*

Experience the rich, green beauty of Portland Parish with Valley Hikes, which offers hikes of varying difficulty throughout the Rio Grande Valley. The paths parallel bubbling streams and waterfalls, climb mountains or meander through fern-covered valleys. Treks include Scatter Waterfalls, Foxes Caves, the Nanny Fall and the soon-to-be-built Maroon Museum in Moore Town.

What Else to See

Most tourists start their Jamaica trip at **Montego Bay**, which features some excellent Georgian architecture on the Northwest Coast. The second largest city on the island and the most touristy, Montego Bay's Gloucester strip is known for its discos and bars. The heart of the city is **Sam Sharpe Square**, named in honor of the slave who led the bloody "Christmas Rebellion" of 1831, which ultimately expedited emancipation. Outside the city, you'll see the area's many great houses. The **Greenwood Great House**, **Belvedere Estate**, **Barnett Estate** and recently restored, opulent **Rose Hall Great House** (haunted by its cruel mistress) are grand examples of the colonial era when Jamaican landowners made fortunes from the sugar trade.

Thirty miles east, Falmouth, a small 18th century port town is easily explorable in a half-hour on foot. Nearby is the **Good Hope great house**, an 18th century estate of John Thorpe, one of the richest Jamaican planters. You'll also find **Rafter's Village**, where you can take a bamboo raft down the Martha Brae River.

Continue on the north coast to **Discovery Bay**, reputedly where Columbus first landed in 1494. The lush beauty of this part of Jamaica is the main attraction. You'll find **Columbus Park** in Discovery Bay, an open-air museum with an eclectic collection related to the sugar trade and Columbus. **Runaway Bay**, site of the first planned resort development on Jamaica, will soon come into view. In tiny Runaway Bay you can mix and mingle with the locals in the casual rum houses where playing dominoes is serious business.

Ocho Rios, an enchanted garden that decorates the northeast coast, has become a magnet for the elite. Cruise ships dock nearly daily and some of the island's best resorts are here. Although admittedly touristy, one of the top must-sees is **Dunn's River Falls**, a stair-step of waterfalls shaded by a rainforest until they make the 600-ft. descent down to the beach. Expect a crowd, and go with a guide. Nature lovers should take a trip to **Coyaba River Garden**, the Arawak word for paradise, and **Shaw Park Gardens**, a tropical wonderland. Famed playwright Noel Coward made his home at a modest estate called **Firefly**, which has been restored by entrepreneur Chris Blackwell. Native son Blackwell has taken the small town of **Oracabessa**, 13 miles east of Ocho Rios, under his wing and has been quietly funding the restoration of its fretwork storefronts. This small town gives a window on what a 19th-century fishing village looked like.

Goldeneye, the 15-acre beachfront estate of novelist Ian Fleming, who penned the James Bond series, has likewise been purchased by Blackwell, and at presstime was scheduled to be opened to overnight guests in 1998.

Nearby is **Port Antonio**, a sleepy, miniature island port built around two picturesque harbors. Since the 1920s, the bay has attracted stars like Ginger Rogers, Bette Davis and Clara Bow, as well as financial powerhouses like J.P. Morgan and William Randolph Hearst to its tropical beauty. In his later years Errol Flynn made his home here and noted that Port Antonio was "more beautiful than any woman I've ever seen." Indeed, the town boasts some of the best architecture on the island, and many of the Victorian mansions have been converted to guest houses. The mysterious 282-foot deep lagoon called the **Blue Hole** was the site of filming for Brooke Shields' *Blue Lagoon*. At the **Caves of Nonsuch**, visitors can view fossilized sea sponges and the remains of a Taino Indian community. The **Athenry Gardens** merit a stop, too. From Port Antonio, you can easily stage a hike into the **Blue Mountains**, so called because they are often shrouded in mist. Much of the year, these mountains are covered with wildflowers.

Over the mountains to the southeast lies Kingston, much of which is grimy, traffic-clogged and low on the list of grand Caribbean places. However, this teeming city also serves as a cultural breeding ground for Jamaica's music, dance and theatre. With a population of almost 1 million, it is the largest English-speaking city south of Miami. New Kingston, laid out in 1962 to celebrate Jamaica's independence, has palm-lined avenues lined with new buildings. Its chief attraction is **Devon House**, the preserved 19th-century home of George Stiebel, one of the Caribbean's first black millionaires. Another highlight is the **Bob Marley Museum**, which has recently been upgraded.

Across the harbor are the ruins of **Port Royal**, once the island's premier 17th century buccaneer city. Henry Morgan, the British pirate who controlled Jamaica for many years, called Port Royal home until it was toppled into the sea in 1692 by an earthquake.

Further to the west of Kingston is **Spanish Town**, which served as the capital from 1534 to 1872. When the English conquered Jamaica in the 17th century, its buildings were razed and replaced with those of English design.

Traveling to the Southwest Coast and Central Highlands will take you to Jamaica at its most laid-back. **Treasure Beach**, dubbed the new Negril, offers a terrific escape. From Black River, the first town to have electricity on the island, you can take a boat tour on Jamaica's longest river, the Black River Great Morass and see the area wildlife and waters still inhabited by crocodiles. **YS Falls**, a mere 15 minute hike away and located on a plantation, is gloriously unspoiled.

A 50-minute drive from Treasure Beach leads to **Mandeville**, founded in 1816 and Jamaica's most prosperous town. Set on the gently rolling farmland of south-central Jamaica, Mandeville looks like a typical, small British town with its Georgian courthouse and stone parish church beside the village green, which has been transformed into a market.

On the West Coast, Negril, once a mecca for hippies, escapists and artists, awaits. Off West End, the **Negril Lighthouse Park**, erected in 1894, still shines. Nudists head to the beach at **Bloody Bay** at the opposite end of town. On Tuesday, Friday and Sunday nights, **Alfred's Ocean Palace** features live bands playing dancehall and reggae. Here you'll find a heady mix of colorful locals. **Booby Cay**, a small coral island, named for the blue-footed booby birds who nest there, used to be a favorite spot for picnics. However, most recently, the raucous clientele of the Hedonism resort has virtually laid claim to it, threatening the bird population and causing others to steer clear as well.

Historical Sites
Montego Bay

Greenwood Great House   ★★

> Highway A1, Montego Bay.
> Hours open: 9 a.m.–6 p.m.
> One of Jamaica's finest great houses, this structure belonged to the Barrett family, of which Elizabeth Barrett Browning is a descendant. The early 19th-century mansion is filled with antiques, unusual musical instruments, rare books, custom-made china, and portraits of the family. General admission: $8.

Rose Hall Great House   ★★★

> Rose Hall Highway, Montego Bay, ☎ (876) 953-2323.
> Hours open: 9 a.m.–6 p.m.

Not as architecturally impressive as Greenwood, this great house from the 1700s is filled with tales of murder and intrigue. Mistress Annie Palmer seduced slaves and bewitched her three husbands eventually murdering them all, one-by-one. Her story has been fictionalized in several books, which you'll find in the giftshop. Annie's Pub in the basement features witch's brew. General admission: $10.

Ocho Rios

Firefly ★★★

Grants Pen, St. Mary, ☎ (876) 997-7201.
Hours open: 9 a.m.–5 p.m.

The modest, hillside home of Sir Noel Coward, who spent the last 25 years of his life in Jamaica, was donated to the Jamaican government upon his death in 1973. Restored by admirer Chris Blackwell to the exact state it was in when Coward lived there, guided tours take you through his bedroom with period furnishings and paintings by Coward. He was buried at the far end of the garden. A cafe and gift shop are on-site. Special events like the moonlight tour offer a terrific view of Port Marie. Continue your literary tour at **Goldeneye** *(☎ (876) 974-5833)*, located on the outskirts of Oracabessa, 20 miles east of Ocho Rios. This 15-acre beachfront estate was the winter home of Ian Fleming, creator of the James Bond books. He penned 14 of the popular novels here, five set in Jamaica. The house is even more modest than Firefly, but the grounds are gorgeous. General admission: $10.

Kingston

Devon House ★★

26 Hope Road, ☎ (876) 929-7029.
Hours open: 9:30 a.m.–4:30 p.m.

This 1881 mansion is filled with period furnishings and has an excellent crafts shops, two restaurants and an ice cream shop famed for its homemade treats. General admission: $4.

Museums and Exhibits
Ocho Rios

Harmony Hall ★★★

Highway A3, Tower Isle, ☎ (876) 460-4120.
Hours open: 10 a.m.–6 p.m.

This late 19th-century great house is now a gallery displaying high-quality paintings and arts and crafts by Jamaican artists.

Kingston

Bob Marley Museum ★★★★

56 Hope Road, Kingston 6, Jamaica, WI, Kingston, ☎ (876) 927-9152.
Hours open: 9:30 a.m.–4:30 p.m.

The national hero's clapboard house was his home and recording studio for many years. A new addition to the collection is the awards room. A guided tour takes about one hour; reggae fans will appreciate the collection of Marley memorabilia and consider this a five-star attraction. General admission: $10.

Institute of Jamaica ★★★

12-16 East Street, Kingston, ☎ (876) 922-0620.

Fielding
WORLDWIDE

JAMAICA

RESTORATIONS AND RUINS

Jamaica's historical heritage lives on in its myriad architectural styles—Spanish-, English-, and French-colonial buildings are scattered across the island. From mysterious castles to graciously appointed plantation great halls, Jamaica offers a wealth of architectural sights.

Plantation Ruins

Throughout the island, ruins of the great plantations attest to the greedy vigor of colonists. Stone aqueducts march across the land in southern parishes, while at Orange Valley, the shell of the plantation hospital stands in solemn silence.

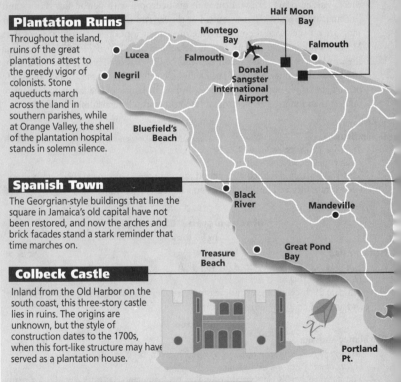

Half Moon Bay

Montego Bay

Falmouth

Lucea

Falmouth

Negril

Donald Sangster International Airport

Bluefield's Beach

Black River

Mandeville

Treasure Beach

Great Pond Bay

Portland Pt.

Spanish Town

The Georgian-style buildings that line the square in Jamaica's old capital have not been restored, and now the arches and brick facades stand a stark reminder that time marches on.

Colbeck Castle

Inland from the Old Harbor on the south coast, this three-story castle lies in ruins. The origins are unknown, but the style of construction dates to the 1700s, when this fort-like structure may have served as a plantation house.

Vale Royal

Home to the prime minister, this building was constructed in the 1700s as a plantation house. The lookout tower enabled residents to watch the ships entering the harbor.

Rose Hall Great House

Considered one of the grandest restored plantation great houses, Rose Hall is steeped in grisly legend—its second mistress, Annie Palmer, allegedly murdered three husbands and one lover on the premises.

Devon House (Kingston)

This 19th-century great house has been restored and furnished with period antiques. The stables have been converted to rather touristy craft and souvenir shops.

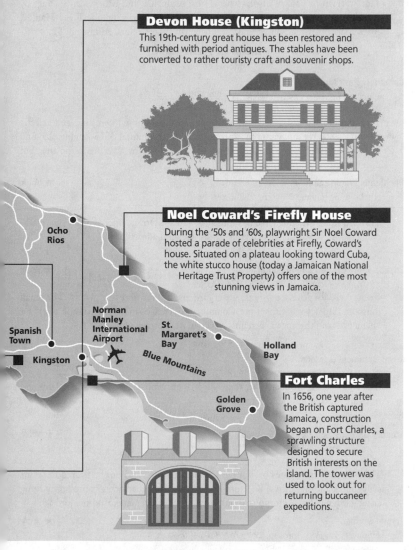

Noel Coward's Firefly House

During the '50s and '60s, playwright Sir Noel Coward hosted a parade of celebrities at Firefly, Coward's house. Situated on a plateau looking toward Cuba, the white stucco house (today a Jamaican National Heritage Trust Property) offers one of the most stunning views in Jamaica.

Ocho Rios

Norman Manley International Airport

St. Margaret's Bay

Holland Bay

Spanish Town

Kingston

Blue Mountains

Fort Charles

In 1656, one year after the British captured Jamaica, construction began on Fort Charles, a sprawling structure designed to secure British interests on the island. The tower was used to look out for returning buccaneer expeditions.

Golden Grove

Hours open: 9 a.m.–5 p.m.

This museum houses the national library and has excellent exhibits on the island's history, including some impressive old charts and almanacs.

National Gallery ★★

12 Ocean Boulevard, Kingston, ☎ (876) 922-1561.

Hours open: 11 a.m.–4:30 p.m.

This waterfront gallery displays paintings, sculpture and other works of art by Jamaica's most famous artist, Kapo. Other artists' works include Edna Manley, Alvin Marriott, Isaac Belisari and Augustine Brunias. General admission: $2.

Parks and Gardens
Montego Bay

Columbus Park Museum ★

Queens Highway, Discovery Bay, ☎ (876) 973-2135.

Hours open: 9 a.m.–5 p.m.

This outdoor park, studded with pimento trees, has some interesting and eclectic exhibits: 18th-century cannons, a stone cross, a large mural of Columbus' landing in 1494, and displays on the history of sugarcane. Stop by if you're in the area, but don't bother making a special trip.

Rocklands Wildlife Station ★★★

Anchovy, St. James, ☎ (876) 952-2009.

Hours open: 2–5 p.m.

This privately owned reserve is a must for birders. Doves, finches and other feathered creatures eat right out of your hands. General admission: $4.

Ocho Rios

Coyaba River Garden and Museum ★★★

Shaw Park, Ocho Rios, ☎ (876) 974-6235.

Come here for lovely gardens, watergardens, a river and fish ponds. The small museum displays relics from pre-Columbian days. Coyaba is the Arawak word for "paradise" and this spot is certainly a slice of it. General admission: $5.

Kingston

Royal Botanical Gardens ★★★

Hope Road, Kingston, ☎ (876) 927-1257.

A peaceful refuge from city life, these gardens encompass 50 acres. Most plants and trees are marked for identification.

Port Antonio

Athenry Gardens and Cave of Nonsuch ★★★

Portland, ☎ (876) 993-3740

Hours open: 9 a.m.–4 p.m.

The Nonsuch Cave dates back some 1.5 million years, and can be toured to see its stalagmites and stalactites. Back on ground level are great views at the pretty flowering gardens. Port Antonio is about 20 minutes away. General admission: $5.

Crystal Springs ★★★

Highway A2, Port Antonio, ☎ (876) 996-1400.

This former sugar plantation is a privately-owned estate covering 158 acres. A peaceful spot to while away the hours, it has more than 15,000 orchids, many hummingbirds and other feathered friends. Bring binoculars. General admission: $2.

Theme/Amusement Parks
Negril

Anancy Family Fun & Nature Park   ★★★
☎ *(876) 957-4100.*
This small theme park consists of three acres of miniature golf, a fishing pond, paddle boating, a carousel, a miniature train that travels by Jamaica Avenue (a living history display), go-carts and nature trails. Geared toward kids. General admission: $10 adults; $5 children.

Tours
Montego Bay

JUTA Tour Company   ★★
Claude Clarke Avenue, ☎ *(876) 952- 813.*
This well-established tour company has offices all over Jamaica; it will take you river rafting, on sea cruises, through great houses, and into Kingston.

Ocho Rios

Dunn's River Falls   ★★★★
Highway A3, ☎ *(876) 974-2857.*
Hours open: 9 a.m.–5 p.m.
These much-photographed falls cascade down some 600 feet into the sea. The best way to experience them is to hire a guide and make a human chain that climbs right up the slippery rocks. Wear sneakers, and don't forget to tip your guide. You can stop along the way to dip in pools and be massaged by the tumbling water. There's a path on dry land for the less daring. Touristy but fun. General admission: $3.

Prospect Plantation   ★★★
Highway A3, St. Ann, ☎ *(876) 974-2058.*
Located just east of Ocho Rios, this working plantation with gorgeous scenery can be toured via jitney. Many trees were planted by famous folks, including Noel Coward and Charlie Chaplin. General admission: $10.

Touring Society of Jamaica
c/o Island Outpost, P.O. Box 118, Ocho Rios, St. Ann, ☎ *(876) 974-5831.*
This licensed tour operator specializes in custom tours with an insider's view of the island. Itineraries focus on Jamaica's cultural heritage found in the arts, architecture, music, epicurean delights, garden and natural history. Prices start at $250 for a full day tour. Recent offerings included: Jamaica's Historic Gardens; Bird-watcher's Jamaica Tour; Jamaican Art & Fine Craft Fair; and Alex Twyman's The Old Tavern Blue Mountain Coffee Estate.

Negril/Southwest Coast

Milk River Mineral Baths   ★★
Milk River, Clarendon, ☎ *(809) 924-9544.*

Arthritis acting up? Rheumatism got you down? Liver ailing? Come for a half-hour soak in what is reportedly the world's most radioactive supposedly curative mineral waters. A bit rundown, but it's funky fun. The baths are private and tepid at 90 degrees. General admission: $2.

Somerset Falls　　　　　　　　　　★★★

Highway A4, Hope Bay, ☎ *(876) 926-2950.*
Hours open: 9 a.m.–5 p.m.
On your way to Port Antonio, stop by for a gondola ride to these scenic falls, located in a deep grove and surrounded by tropical rainforest. Wear your swimsuit so you can take a dip in the refreshing pools. General admission: $2.

Kingston

Port Royal　　　　　　　　　　★★

Near Kingston.
Hours open: 9 a.m.–5 p.m.
This port used to be known as the "wickedest city in the world" because of its buc-caneering past and frequent visits by Blackbeard. That all changed in 1692 when it was destroyed by an earthquake. The buildings to visit today include St. Peter's Church; the Archaeological and Historical Museum; a small maritime museum housed in the former British naval headquarters; Fort Charles, which dates back to 1656 and is the port's only remaining fort; and the Giddy House, permanently tilted after the earthquake.

Sports

For an active vacation, Jamaica makes a marvelous choice. When it comes to watersports, the island's facilities are hard to beat. Sailboats and cruisers can be rented by the day or week from almost any town on the north coast and around Kingston as well. Every two years in the spring Montego Bay hosts the Pineapple Cup for yachters and annual Easter regatta.

Anglers love Jamaica with its deep-water game fish that run year-round through "marlin alley." Port Antonio's waters offer some of the best game fishing. Freshwater fishing hasn't caught on with visitors yet, although locals make good use of the island's 120 rivers. Water-skiing and jet-skiing are popular in resort areas, but jet-skiing has come under fire from local govern-ments in Negril and Ocho Rios. Parasailing is popular at the latter's Jamaica Grande beach. Scuba and snorkeling are not strong in Jamaica because many of its reefs collapsed earlier this decade due to overfishing, which destroyed the delicate balance of the reef system. About the only decent spot for surf-ing is off Boston Beach near Port Antonio. Near Kingston, Morgan's Har-bour is the headquarters for watersports.

Sports that are extremely popular with visitors are golf (Jamaica has ten 18-hole courses and has been a regular stop for the PGA, LPGA and PGA Senior tours), hiking (see Hiking section above) and horseback riding, which offers a great way to explore the island. Horseback riding is particularly popular in Ocho Rios and in the countryside around Negril. Biking has yet to attract great interest, largely because navigating the roadways can prove hazardous. Tennis is available at virtually every resort.

Polo enthusiasts can watch matches at the Kingston Polo Club, Drax Hall and Chukka Cove. Cricket is considered the national sport. The best competitions are held at Sabina Park in Kingston and Jarrett Park in Montego Bay throughout the year. Track is also extremely popular in Jamaica, which has regularly produced stars in the sport over the years. Each February the Carib Cement International Marathon takes place in Kingston. Triathalons are held in Negril in January and Treasure Beach in April.

Biking

Biking hasn't taken hold in Jamaica, probably because of the high rate of traffic accidents. Trying to bike here takes a certain fortitude. If you are determined, try **Montego Bike Rentals** (☎ *(876) 952-4984)* on Walter Fletcher Beach in Montego Bay. It rents Diamond Back and other mountain bikes for $10 per day. **Rusty's X-cellent Adventures** (☎ *(876) 957-0155)* in Negril rents mountain bikes—full suspension and hard tails—and does terrific trips (bed & breakfast and group rates available) through the back country surrounding Negril (virgin trails, cross country, by waterfalls, cliff jumps and more). **Blue Mountain Tours** (☎ *(876) 974-7075)* based in Ocho Rios does mass tours—catering to the all-inclusive Sandals crowd—to the Blue Mountains. The six-hour ride costs $78 and includes brunch and transportation up the mountain.

Cruises

Sailing and cruising the waters around Jamaica's secluded bays, coves and protected waters has proven popular. Several events are scheduled in Montego Bay in the spring, starting with the annual Easter Regatta. Montego Bay: the **Calico** (☎ *(876) 952-5860)*, **Sandals' Mary Ann** (☎ *(876) 953-2231)*, and the **Rhapsody** (☎ *(876) 979-0104)*. Ocho Rios: **Heave-Ho Charters** (☎ *(876) 974-5367)* and Red Stripe (☎ *(876) 974-2446)*. Negril: **Aqua Nova Water Sports** (☎ *(876) 957-4323)*. Treasure Beach: **Treasure Tours** (☎ *(876) 965-0126/http://www.ultranet.com/usrbw)*. Excursions range from snorkel trips to catamaran sails to booze cruises with live bands.

Golf

Golf in Jamaica ranks as some of the Caribbean's best. At some courses, caddies carry golf bags on their heads. At most courses, hiring a caddy is required. Carts are available at most courses, too. Greens fees vary from $13–$140. The best by far are the links at **Tryall Golf Club** (☎ *(876) 952-5110)* in Montego Bay, a PGA tour-approved, par-71 course that is considered one of the world's best. Also in the Montego Bay area are the **Half Moon Golf Club** (☎ *(876) 953-2280)*, a spacious,

JAMAICA

par-72 course designed by Robert Trent Jones; **Ironshore Golf and Country Club** (☎ *(876) 953-2800)*, is a par 72 and known for its many blind holes; and **Wyndham Rose Hall Country Club** (☎ *(876) 953-2650)*, is a par-72 course on the historic Rose Hall estate with an imaginative layout. In Kingston, try **Caymanas Golf Club**, (☎ *(876) 922-3386)*, a par 72 known for its challenging 12th hole; and **Constant Springs** (☎ *(876) 924-1610)*, a par-70 course. The oldest golf course in the Caribbean is the **Manchester Country Club** (☎ *(876) 962-2403)* in Mandeville, built over 100 years ago not long after the game was invented in Scotland. In Negril: try **Negril Hills Golf Club** (☎ *(876) 957-4638)*. In Ocho Rios: **Sandals Golf and Country Club** (☎ *(876) 975-0181)* is tucked 700 feet up into the mountains.

Horseback Riding

Several operations offer horseback riding. Ocho Rios: **Richmond Landovery/Chukka Cove Farm** (☎ *(876) 972-2506; e-mail:chukka@infochan.com)*, $30 per hour; $40 for 2 hours; and **Prospect Plantation** (*reserve in advance at* ☎ *(876) 994-1058)*, $20 per hour. Montego Bay: **Rocky Point Stables** (☎ *(876) 953-2212; FAX (876) 953-9489)*, where 1.5-hour rides start at $40. Negril: **Horseman Riding Stables** (☎ *(876) 957-4474)*, $25 for two hours.

River Rafting

Jamaica's many rivers make for great float trips, usually on a bamboo raft that holds just two and is piloted by a character who spins tales of local lore. Several outfits offer trips that last an hour or so and cost about $36 per couple. Highly recommended! In the Montego Bay area, try **Martha Brae's Rafting Village** (☎ *(876) 952-0889)* or **Mountain Valley Rafting** (☎ *(876) 952-0527)*. Near Port Antonio, **Rio Grande** is the oldest and most famous operator. In Ocho Rios, call **Calypso Rafting** (☎ *(876) 974-2527)*. From Treasure Beach, contact **Treasure Tours** (☎ *(876) 965-0126)*.

Watersports

Most hotels offer a variety of watersports. Jet skiing, waterskiing and kayaking are popular around Negril and Treasure Beach, although talk was strong about banning jet skis in Negril. Check the following operations. Runaway Bay: **JamAqua Watersports** (☎ *(876) 973-4845; e-mail jamaqua✩infochan.com)* and **Sun Divers Jamaica** (☎ *(876) 973-2346)*. Negril: **Negril Scuba Centre** (☎ *(876) 957-4425)* and Sun Divers Jamaica (☎ *(876) 957-4069)*. Ocho Rios: **Sea and Dive Jamaica** (☎ *947-5762)*. Montego Bay: **Seaworld** (☎ *(876) 953-2180)* and **Sandals Beach Watersports** (☎ *(876) 949-0104)*. Port Antonio: **Lady Godiva** (☎ *(876) 993-3281)* and **Aqua Action** (☎ *(876) 993-3318)*. In addition to the above, **Resort Divers** (☎ *(876) 974-0577)* has six locations around the island. For deep-sea fishing, you can reach deep waters in 15 minutes. Your likely catch would be blue and white marlin (mainly off the North Coast and Port Antonio), tuna, dolphin and wahoo. Check out **Grand Lido Sans Souci** (☎ *(876) 974-2353)*. Port Antonio holds a fishing tournament each October. You must reserve a charter 24 hours in advance. Expect to pay $300–$350 for a half day.

Where to Stay

Fielding's Highest Rated Hotels in Jamaica

★★★★★	Half Moon Golf, Tennis & Beach Club	$265–$600
★★★★★	Jamaica Inn	$200–$475
★★★★★	Round Hill Hotel & Villas	$160–$420
★★★★★	Trident Villas & Hotel	$365–$800
★★★★	Boscobel Beach Hotel	$415–$995
★★★★	Grand Lido Sans Souci	$544–$640
★★★★	Plantation Inn	$300–$999
★★★★	Sandals Dunn's River Golf Resort & Spa	$420–$560
★★★★	Strawberry Hill	$195–$450
★★★★	Swept Away	$450–$625

Fielding's Hot Spots for Honeymooners in Jamaica

★★★★	Grand Lido Sans Souci	$544–$640
★★★★	Strawberry Hill	$195–$450
★★★★★	Half Moon Golf, Tennis & Beach Club	$265–$600
★★★★★	Jamaica Inn	$200–$475
★★★	Rockhouse	$80–$100
★★★	The Caves	$295–$600

Fielding's Best Value Hotels in Jamaica

★★★	Rockhouse	$80–$100
★★	Hibiscus Lodge	$93–$115
★★	Natania's Guest House	$50–$60
★★★	Xtabi On the Cliffs	$50–$145
★★★	H.E.A.R.T. Country Club	$55–$75

No matter what kind of traveler you are, you'll find something to please in Jamaica. From gargantuan all-inclusives to fully-staffed villas to colonial great houses to funky beachside cottages, the choices are mind-boggling. New construction in 1997 and 1998 is adding more rooms to the 20,400 on the island, and several of the island's most notable properties have recently undergone renovations.

At presstime, **Goldeneye**, the home of the late author Ian Fleming, was rumored to be opening its doors in the spring of 1998 for guests. Famed **Frenchman's Cove**, a cluster of luxurious villas once favored by Elizabeth Taylor in Port Antonio, reopened after renovation. Three new inns were also scheduled to open there: **Paradise Inn** *(☎ (876) 993-5169);* **Tim Bamboo** *(☎ (876) 993-2049)* and **Blue Beyond Villa** *(☎ (876) 990-3051).* Both of Sandals' Ocho Rios properties have been renamed to reflect golf privileges. **Breezes Runaway Bay** also added "Golf and Beach Resort" to its name and was adding 60 new suites with Jacuzzis. SuperClubs Super-Inclusive Resorts acquired **Braco Village Resort**, which was renamed **Grand Lido Braco** and added 52 new luxury suites. Sans Souci Lido was renamed **Grand Lido Sans Souci** and added another 36 beachfront suites.

In Montego Bay, **Half Moon Golf, Tennis & Beach Club** has upgraded and expanded its spa facilities. Its main building, which was damaged by fire in the summer of 1997, has been completely restored. **Round Hill Hotel & Villas** now offers a family program in the summer that includes free accommodations for children in the Pineapple House in adjoining rooms with parents, as well as complimentary nanny service. **Tryall Club Resort & Villas** transformed its hotel rooms into one and two-bedroom villas.

In Negril, **Couples Negril** is slated to open in June 1998 with 240 guest rooms and suites. **Beaches Negril**, the newest Sandals resort in Jamaica opened in May 1997. Set on 20 acres, it caters to families, couples and singles. The boutique resort **Rock House** is doubling its thatched-roof studios by early 1998. Chris Blackwell's Island Outpost added **The Caves**, a collection of one and two-bedroom cottages on the western cliffs of Negril, to its growing stable of boutique properties.

Kingston has seen its first major hotel in many years go up: **The Crowne Plaza Kingston**.

Jamaica is the birthplace of the all-inclusive concept. Kingston-born Butch Stewart launched it with Sandals Montego Bay in 1981. The concept, where one price pays for a room, all meals, drinks, most watersports, nightly entertainment, tips and other activities, has rapidly grown in popularity. Indeed, his resorts regularly enjoy an occupancy rate of 90 percent year-round. Most recently, all-inclusives have been scrambling in a competitive market to beef up restaurant facilities, add spas and upgrade exercise and sports offerings.

Some are also upgrading accommodations, which some patrons have found too plain-vanilla, even bunkerlike. Sandals Resort is lavishing $25 million on its couples only properties to meet demands of patrons. As you are comparing rates, make certain that you are clear on exactly what is included in the price. For divers, for instance, that sport often entails an additional cost. Or your beverages may only include nonalcoholic libations.

At some of these all-inclusives, you'll scarcely see outside the walls and, thus, miss the real Jamaica. And if you don't like crowds, you should avoid them at all costs.

For luxury, Jamaica boasts a plethora of villas, which often come with maid, cook, gardener and laundress. This style of vacationing hearkens back to the old days when Noel Coward used to entertain his peers on a small stage at Round Hill.

If you are on a budget, you'll find that Jamaica isn't out of reach. Especially on the South Coast around Treasure Beach, you can find reasonable accommodations.

Where to Stay in Montego Bay

Hotels and Resorts

Coyaba Beach Resort & Club   **$140–$326**   ★ ★ ★
☎ *(800) 237-3237, (876) 953-9150, FAX (876) 953-2244.*
Associated Restaurant: *The Vineyard.*
Single: $140–$326. Double: $140–$326.
"Coyaba" is the Arawak word for "a kind of heaven where time is passed feasting and dancing," and that's the atmosphere this plush, family-built and managed resort strives for. The young couple who owns the place, Joanne and Kevin Robertson, warmly welcome guests. Plantation-style, airy guestrooms in three pale-yellow, tiled-roof buildings each have air conditioning, ceiling fans, TVs and French doors leading to oversized private balconies. The deluxe oceanview rooms—which fetch the highest rate—are quite large and have mahogany four-poster beds, dining alcoves and sitting areas decorated with Queen Anne and Chippendale reproductions. Facilities include two restaurants and a bar, a private beach with watersports, a fitness room and a tennis court. It also has a piano bar, volleyball, croquet and bocce, as well as massage. Rates include airport transfers, a welcome basket with fresh banana bread, day tennis, watersports and afternoon tea. 50 rooms. Credit cards: A, MC, V.

Doctors Cave Beach Hotel   **$80–$160**   ★ ★
☎ *(800) 223-6510, (876) 952-4355, FAX (876) 952-5204.*
E-mail: dcbh@toj.com.
Single: $80–$145. Double: $105–$160.
Set on four acres of tropical gardens in the heart of the resort district, this informal hotel is across the street from Doctor's Cave Beach and convenient to area shopping. Guest rooms, decorated in rattan and air-conditioned, are comfortable. Facilities include a pool, Jacuzzi, three restaurants, watersports across the street and a

weight room. The atmosphere is lively, with special events like crab races and rum parties. 90 rooms. Credit cards: A, MC, V.

Half Moon Golf, Tennis & Beach Club   **$265–$1400**   ★★★★★

☎ *(800) 626-0592, (876) 953-2211, FAX (876) 953-2731.*
Website: www.halfmoon.com.jm. E-mail: hmoonres@infochan.com.
Associated Restaurant: *Seagrape Terrace.*
Single: $265–$300. Double: $320–$600. Suites Per Day: $550–$1100.

Located on 400 acres with its own mile-long, crescent-shaped beach, this posh, Georgian Colonial-style resort—seven miles east of Montego Bay and opened in 1954—is simply outstanding in every way. Just ask Queen Elizabeth II, Bishop Desmond Tutu, Princess Stephanie, Paul Newman or George Bush, to name a few of the resort's guests. The luxurious accommodations are in suites, cottages, and villas, all with bright Jamaican paintings, Queen Anne antique mahogany reproductions, sitting areas, and patios or balconies with sea views. One-bedroom suites have full kitchens and spacious living areas, while the villas offer ample space on two levels. Two main swimming pools are open to all guests, plus 17 other pools are shared among the white-washed villas, which have five to seven bedrooms and are each staffed with a chef, gardener and chambermaid. By Sunrise Beach, drinks are doled out from beneath a pavilion in case you break a sweat on the croquet lawn or on the new 18-hole putting course. Other amenities include an equestrian center, shopping plaza (40 shops plus a disco and the newly-opened The Bob Marley Experience), bicycles,13 tennis courts, four squash courts, all kinds of watersports with an on-site dive center, a children's center with duck pond, horse shoe court, sand boxes and more. If you still aren't motivated, you can always order in your own personal trainer at your villa for a quick 45-minute workout ($35). A big draw for guests, of course, is the Robert Trent Jones-designed, par-72, 18-hole golf course (resort guests get 50% off greens fees). Aerobics classes and a cardio theater are available in the fitness center, as well as sauna, body wraps, beauty treatments and massage. Three restaurants (two Jamaican, one Italian) are on the property as well as a wine cellar. The resort also has a program that allows its guests to dine at several nearby properties' restaurants. Half Moon won the Green Hotelier award for environmental practices (from composting to water conservation) in 1995–1996 from the Caribbean Hotel Association. Most recent additions: a cigar room and piano bar. Hold onto your pocketbook though: During peak season a seven-bedroom villa rents for $11,550 for a week; from mid-April through mid-December rates drop to a mere $7700. Like its cousins, Half Moon offers several packages. Whatever the price, this place is a knockout. 424 rooms. Credit cards: A, MC, V.

Holiday Inn SunSpree Resort   **$120–$270**   ★★

☎ *(800) 352-6731, (876) 953-2485, FAX (876) 953-2840.*
Associated Restaurant: *Mo Bay Festival/Vista's.*
Single: $120–$190. Double: $120–$190. Suites Per Day: $220–$270.

Located on 12-landscaped acres fronting a half-mile of private beach and part of the historic Rosehall Sugar Plantation Estate, this second-largest resort in Jamaica lives up to the dependable, if unexciting, Holiday name (a $13 million renovation ensured that). Rooms and suites have air-conditioning, cable TV, direct dial phones

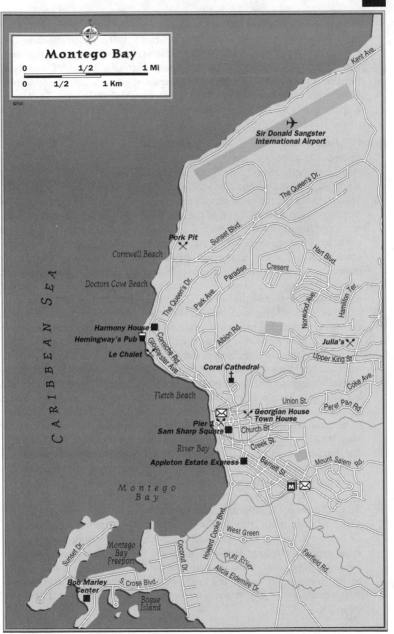

Montego Bay

0   1/2   1 Mi
0   1/2   1 Km

©FWI

Sir Donald Sangster International Airport

Kent Ave.

The Queen's Dr.

Sunset Blvd.

Hart Blvd

Pork Pit

Cornwell Beach

Paradise

Cresent

Norwood Ave.

Hamilton Ter.

Doctors Cove Beach

Park Ave.

The Queen's Dr.

Harmony House

Albion Rd.

Julia's

Hemingway's Pub

Corniche Rd.

Gloucester Ave.

Upper King St.

Le Chalet

Coral Cathedral

Coke Ave.

Fletch Beach

Union St.

Georgian House

Peter Pan Rd.

Pier 1

Town House

Sam Sharp Square

Church St.

Creek St.

River Bay

Barnett St.

Appleton Estate Express

Mount Salem Rd.

C A R I B B E A N   S E A

M

*M o n t e g o
B a y*

West Green

*Montego
Bay
Freeport*

Howard Cooke Blvd.

Pies River

Fairfield Rd.

Sunset Dr.

Coconut Dr.

Alicia Eldemire Dr.

**Bob Marley
Center**

S. Cross Blvd.

*Boque
Island*

and private balconies or patios, but many lack water views. Organized activities and entertainment (crab races, anyone?) are continuous. The complex also boasts tropical freshwater pools, sports bar with a big-screen TV, golf at nearby Ironshore Golf Course, electronic gaming parlor, a disco, a fitness center with Nautilus equipment, four lighted tennis courts, a watersports center, basketball and volleyball courts, two restaurants and three bars. Good security keeps non-guests at bay. The resort now offers formal kids programs for children from 6 months through teens. The nursery is open from 9 a.m. to 9 p.m. It just began offering all-inclusive packages, too. 523 rooms. Credit cards: A, MC, V.

Round Hill Hotel & Villas $160–$730   ★★★★★

☎ *(800) 972-2159, (876) 956-7050, FAX (876) 956-7505.*
Website: www.elegantresort.com. E-mail: roundhill@toj.com.
Single: $160–$360. Double: $220–$420. Suites Per Day: $310–$730.

Set on a lush green peninsula with a private, crescent beach eight miles west from Montego Bay and thankfully off of the busy airport's flight pattern, this exclusive resort encompasses 98 acres of what was formerly a pineapple plantation. Accommodations are in the Pineapple House, the main oceanfront, British Colonial-style building that has become particularly popular with young families, or in privately-owned villas dotting the tropical garden hillside. Some villas have private pools and all offer the pampering of your own maid, gardener and cook. Supposedly the higher you are on the hill, the better you rate. But before you jump at the chance to stay in a villa owned by a duke, understand that some veer toward shabby chic. After all, the resort, founded by Jamaican entrepreneur John Pringle, has been around since 1952. Even subtle changes are handled slowly, admits Josef Forstmayr, the resort's Austrian managing director, and the audience here likes it that way. Here ladies and gentlemen still dress up for dinner on the terrace beneath the stars. Ralph Lauren, who owns a villa on the property, recently redesigned the main dining and bar area where afternoon tea is formally presented. Happily, Lauren gave it star treatment, complete with black and white photos taken of guests over the years. Indeed, the rich and famous turn out in droves—especially during the holidays when bookings are handled years in advance—perhaps enthralled with the magic that once drew Noel Coward, Grace Kelly, Clark Gable, honeymooners JFK and Jackie and other glitterati. The upside is that all the offerings of this venerable resort can be had relatively inexpensively, especially during the off-season when Americans typically don't think to go to Jamaica. But be prepared: Although the service is stellar, you'll hand out tips, tips and more tips. Activities include jogging and walking paths, five tennis courts (two lit), fitness center, a pool, watersports (Sunfish, paddle-boats, water-skiing, snorkeling, scuba diving, and glass-bottom boat rides), and a kids' program, which includes five hours of free nanny services a day. Guests have greens privileges at the Tryall Club, one of the Caribbean's best golf courses. A beauty salon is on-site, as well as a small but excellent art gallery filled with works from Jamaican artists. Inquire about meal plans and all-inclusive rates. 110 rooms. Credit cards: A, MC, V.

Tryall Club Resort & Villas, The   **$375–$1543**   ★★★★

☎ *(800) 238-5290, (876) 965-5660, FAX (876) 956-5673.*
Associated Restaurant: *The Beach Restaurant.*
Single: $375–$650. Double: $465–$1000. Suites Per Day: $772–$1543.

The news here is that an additional 15 villas have replaced the guest rooms once located in the shingle-roofed Great House (Georgian-style circa 1834). Each features oversized marble bathrooms, wooden jalousie doors opening onto expansive terraces and a dining room, as well as a full staff. Set on 2200 acres of rolling hills and gardens that were once a sugar plantation estate 12 miles west of Montego Bay, this deluxe resort has a true country club feel. All of the original privately-owned villas—ranging in size from one to six bedrooms, each with a separate bath and vaulted ceilings—come with a private pool, cook, maid, laundress, and gardener. The resort's centerpiece is the 18-hole PGA championship golf course—par 71 with a slope of 128—designed by Ralph Plummer that stretches 6920 yards along the sea and palm-lined fairways. Nine Laykold tennis courts, massage and salon services, two restaurants, a private beach (not spectacular), and watersports including snorkeling, windsurfing, pedal boats and glass bottom boat rides are available. Diving can be arranged. Cannons that once repelled invaders still guard the beach. Lovely and grand. 69 rooms. Credit cards: A, DC, MC, V.

Wyndham Rose Hall Golf & Beach Resort   **$145–$740**   ★★★★

☎ *(800) 996-3426, (876) 953-2650, FAX (876) 953-2617.*
Website: www.wyndham.com.
Associated Restaurant: *Ambrosia.*
Single: $145–$230. Double: $145–$230. Suites Per Day: $320–$740.

Set on the 400-acre Rose Hall Plantation fronting a 1000-ft. stretch of beach, this stylish property, undergoing a $5.6 million renovation to be completed by the end of 1997, has large, newly-redone guestrooms accented by nice artwork, good lighting and quality furnishings. The hotel has added electronic keys for guestrooms, too. Guests can choose from 18 holes of golf on a par-72 course, six lighted tennis courts—freshly resurfaced—with a pro on hand, an air-conditioned fitness center with outdoor Jacuzzi, steam baths, sauna, three interconnected swimming pools and an extensive watersports center, including scuba. Five restaurants—including Ambrosia, an award-winning Mediterranean gourmet restaurant—offer a plethora of dining options, too. Parents can enroll little ones in the supervised Kid's Klub (ages 5-12) for no charge. Kids 12 and under stay and eat free when sharing with adults. Rates quoted are European plan; all-inclusive packages are available. 489 rooms. Credit cards: A, CB, DC, MC, V.

All Inclusives

Grand Montego Beach Resort   **$135–$300**   ★★

☎ *(800) 999-9182, (876) 952-4340, FAX (214) 363-9825.*
Website: www.allegroresorts.com.
Associated Restaurant: *Starlight.*
Single: $135–$150. Double: $270–$300.

Located a mile from downtown Montego Bay, this resort is perched right on the beach, albeit, a narrow one. A $2.2 million upgrade in 1996 gave guest rooms a needed facelift. The resort also renovated its lobby, Starlight restaurant, and added a 2500 sq. ft. pool with swim-up bar, a beach-side snack bar, a second private beach and new remote-controlled TVs in the guest rooms. The rates include all meals, drinks (three bars vs. one restaurant indicates the priorities of the guests who frequent this spot) and activities, including four tennis courts, volleyball, watersports, and nightly entertainment. You'll pay extra for scuba (a PADI five-star facility is onsite) and jet skiing, but a daily massage and sauna are complimentary. Golfers get a 25% discount on greens fees at the nearby Ironshore golf course, designed by Robert Trent Jones. Parents will like the "Kids Klub" for ages 3–12 (children under six stay and eat free during high season; during low season children 6–12 get that deal). Those who book far in advance are rewarded with lower rates. 132 rooms. Credit cards: A, MC.

Sandals Inn $330–$390 ★★

☎ *(800) 726-3257, (876) 952-4140, FAX (305) 284-1336.*
Website: www.sandals.com.
Double: $330–$390.

Open only to heterosexual couples, this small, less expensive resort is hampered by its location across from, not on, the beach. Guest rooms are colonial-themed and large, but the sea is only visible from the more expensive units and it's close to the airport. Compulsive shoppers will like the location, though. Couples keep busy with a large courtyard pool, tennis, a gym and watersports. Guests can hop a free shuttle to the area's other two larger Sandals, or visit the others on the island, too. A seven night stay starts at $2340 per couple. 52 rooms. Credit cards: A, MC, V.

Sandals Montego Bay $403–$931 ★★★

☎ *(800) 726-3257, (876) 952-5510.*
Associated Restaurant: *Oleander Room/Cuccina Romana.*
Double: $403–$494. Suites Per Day: $517–$931.

The largest—and priciest—of Montego Bay's three Sandals couples-only resorts and its flagship property, this one has its own private, white sand beach and 26 acres of tropical gardens. The downside is being close to the busy airport (flights stop at 11 p.m.). Honeymooners who like the Sandals concept would likely be more satisfied at one of the chain's Negril, Ocho Rios or Dunn's River properties. At the least request a room at the outer fringes of this property. Avoid the few noisy rooms over the dining room if you can help it. This resort offers 243 guest rooms and suites in nine categories (top of the line is the prime minister suite). The all-inclusive rates cover all meals, drinks, entertainment and facilities. The atmosphere at this spot can be frenetic; good for those who like to go, go, go. Diversions include four bars, a disco, two pools, two tennis courts, a gym, all watersports, exercise classes, and several Jacuzzis. Dining options range from Jamaican to Asian to Italian in gourmet restaurants. One bonus: free, regularly-scheduled shuttles give you free access to the other two Montego Bay resorts. The above nightly rates are based on a seven-night stay; rates for the (minimum) two-night stay start at $940. 243 rooms. Credit cards: A, MC, V.

Sandals Royal Jamaican **$220–$640** ★★★

☎ *(800) 726-3257, (876) 953-2231, FAX (305) 284-1336.*
Website: www.sandals.com.
Associated Restaurant: *Bali Hai/Pavilion.*
Single: $220–$270. Double: $290–$300. Suites Per Day: $440–$640.
This heterosexual couples-only resort has several guest rooms that open right onto the beach. This link in the popular chain sports a Georgian-style great house and a slightly more upscale feel on 17 acres. Here you'll find all the bells and whistles associated with this popular and efficient spot, which has become famed for packing in folks determined to have a good time without ever having to leave the complex and those who really could care less whether they're in Jamaica. Here you get continental breakfast in bed and afternoon tea. You have a choice of four restaurants—the Bali Hai is on Kokomo, a private offshore island—and four bars, three pools, three tennis courts, a good health club, all watersports (waterskiing, snorkeling and scuba diving are popular), and organized activities and entertainment. This resort is suited to travelers who simply want guaranteed, hassle-free fun in the sun and shopaholics who will enjoy the heavy concentration of stores in Montego Bay. Seven nights for a couple starts at $3060. 190 rooms. Credit cards: A, MC, V.

Inns

Breezes Montego Bay **$415–$1380** ★★

Doctor's Cave Beach, ☎ *(800) 859-7873, (809) 940-1150.*
This brand-new property, part of the SuperClubs chain, opened in the fall of 1995. The $13-million resort sits on Doctor's Cave Beach and has two restaurants, a beach grill, disco, piano bar, and watersports. There's also nightly entertainment, theme nights and a pool. Open to couples and singles aged 16 and over. Rates for three nights (minimum stay) are single: $415–$740, double: $830–$1380. Rates include all meals, drinks and activities. 124 rooms. Credit cards: A, MC, V.

Richmond Hill Inn **$75–$220** ★★

☎ *(876) 952-3859.*
Associated Restaurant: *Richmond Hill.*
Single: $75. Double: $90. Suites Per Day: $168–$220.
Set high on a hill with stunning views, the main building of this casual inn dates from the 1700s. Guest rooms are simple but comfortable, and a few suites with kitchenettes are available for those who prefer to cook in. A pool offers daytime diversions; the piano bar and open-air restaurant noted for its lobster specialties help fill evening hours. Be forewarned, you may encounter tour groups from the cruise ships trooping through to check out the view. Doctors Cave and Cornwall beaches are within walking distance. 20 rooms. Credit cards: A, MC, V.

Apartments and Condominiums

Montego Bay Club Resort **$50–$155** ★★

☎ *(800) 223-9815, (876) 952-4310.*
Associated Restaurant: *Top of the Bay.*
Single: $50–$155. Double: $55–$155.
Overlooking the bay, across from Doctor's Cave Beach (a free shuttle is provided), this high-rise resort offers tastefully furnished studios and one-bedroom apartments

with fully-equipped kitchens. A pool, two tennis courts and a restaurant on the top of the building are the main attractions. 51 rooms. Credit cards: A, MC, V.

SeaCastles $90–$290   ★★★

☎ *(800) 752-6824, (876) 953-3250, FAX (212) 924-8038.*
Single: $90–$135. Double: $90–$135. Suites Per Day: $145–$290.
This modern complex has one- to three-bedroom, air-conditioned apartments, all with colorful tropical furnishings, kitchenettes, and private balconies. Combining the convenience of apartment living with the amenities of a hotel, it offers turndown service and limited room service. It has a pool, two lighted tennis courts, an age-appropriate kids program (ages 0-12) and playground, nonmotorized watersports, and a private, though small, beach. Nice, especially for families who don't mind the somewhat remote location. European or all-inclusive packages available. Rates quoted are for the European plan. 198 rooms. Credit cards: A, MC, V.

Where to Stay in Ocho Rios/ Discovery Bay/Runaway Bay

Hotels and Resorts

Ambiance Jamaica $70–$138   ★★

Ste. Anne, ☎ *(800) 523-6304, (876) 973-4705, FAX (876)973-2066.*
Associated Restaurant: *The Renaissance.*
Single: $70–$138. Double: $138.
Set on a small private beach, this laid-back hotel—catering to divers—offers good rooms (air-conditioned with private balconies or terraces) and services. It has Sun-Divers on-site (a PADI five-star instructor development center), a pool, gym, gourmet French restaurant, coffee shop, Jacuzzi, and disco. Offers all-inclusive packages. 80 rooms. Credit cards: A, MC.

Eaton Hall Beach Hotel $135–$299   ★★★

Runaway Bay, ☎ *(809) 973-3503.*
Single: $135–$299. Double: $185–$299.
A former 18th-century Georgian-style slave station has become an all-inclusive resort that caters to a predominantly young crowd. Guests stay in standard rooms, suites, or villas with kitchenettes; all comfortable, but showing their age. No beach to speak of, but there are two pools, as well as tennis, watersports, glass-bottom boat rides, and organized activities. 52 rooms. Credit cards: A, CB, MC, V.

H.E.A.R.T. Country Club $55–$75   ★★★

Runaway Bay, ☎ *(809) 973-2671.*
Single: $55. Double: $75.
This plantation-style country club is staffed by people learning the hotel business (it stands for Human Employment and Resource Training), so you can count on enthusiastic service. Set on a hillside with nice views, guest rooms are nice and bright. There's a decent restaurant and pool, golf next door, and they'll shuttle you to a small private beach. Really good for the rates. 20 rooms. Credit cards: A, MC.

Plantation Inn $300–$999   ★★★★

Ocho Rios, ☎ *(800) 752-6824, (876) 974-5601, FAX (876) 974-5912.*
Associated Restaurant: *Bougainvillea Terrace.*

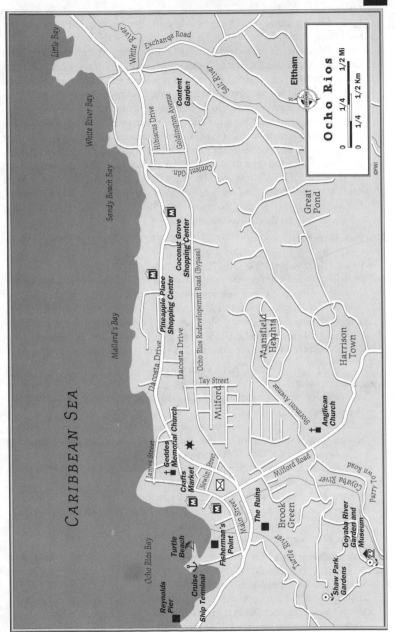

Ocho Rios

CARIBBEAN SEA

Caribbean Sea

Little Bay

White River

Exchange Road

White River Bay

Sandy Beach Bay

Mallard's Bay

Ocho Rios Bay

Reynolds Pier

Cruise Ship Terminal

Turtle Beach

Fisherman's Point

Salt River

Content Garden

Eltham

Hibiscus Drive

Goldington Avenue

Content Gdn.

Great Pond

Dacosta Drive

Pineapple Place Shopping Center

Coconut Grove Shopping Center

Ocho Rios Redevelopment Road (Bypass)

Mansfield Heights

Harrison Town

Tay Street

Milford

Stormont Avenue

Anglican Church

James Street

Geddes Memorial Church

Crafts Market

Newlin

Brey

Main Street

The Ruins

Brook Green

Milford Road

Coyaba River

Parry Town Road

Turtle River

Coyaba River Garden and Museum

Shaw Park Gardens

©FWI

Double: $300–$999.

Located on eight acres of tropical hillside gardens near Prospect Plantation, this antebellum mansion-style hotel has a country club atmosphere that draws a predominantly conservative (and rich) crowd. Croquet lawns get a workout here. Two guest room wings span the beachfront affording good views of the ocean. All rooms have private balconies, air-conditioning and walk-in closets. The upper rooms have the best views. Junior suites, two penthouse suites and two villas with private pools are available for those who hate to be cramped. The grounds include two beaches (reached via a steep walk down the hill), two tennis courts, two restaurants and a bar, a small pool, watersports, a gym, as well as massage and beauty services. Not quite as snazzy as the neighboring Jamaica Inn, and a tad more casual, though you're still required to dress up at night. Watersports are available here, too, and the resort offers childrens' activities. Like many of the more exclusive properties in Jamaica, Plantation Inn now offers two all-inclusive plans: standard and platinum. The latter gives you daily golf, daily scuba, one 90-minute horseback riding session and a tour of Ocho Rios. 80 rooms. Credit cards: A, DC, MC, V.

Shaw Park Beach Hotel $168–$582   ★★

Cutlass Bay, Ocho Rios, ☎ (876) 974-2552.
Single: $168. Double: $182. Suites Per Day: $582.

Set on a private though narrow beach, this Georgian-style resort has adequate but simple guest rooms; the two-bedroom suites with kitchens are much nicer, but also much pricier. Standard recreational activities include two tennis courts, a pool, watersports, and exercise classes. Nights are kept busy with three bars, a lively disco and organized entertainment. Decent, but aging in a not particularly graceful fashion. All-inclusive packages are available. 118 rooms. Credit cards: A, MC, V.

All Inclusives

Boscobel Beach Hotel $415–$995   ★★★★

Ocho Rios, ☎ (800) 467-8737, (876) 975-3330, FAX (954) 925-0334.
Double: $415–$995.

Set on the beach, this resort, part of the SuperClubs group, caters to families. Accommodations range from spacious guestrooms to suites, all newly refurbished and some with sunken tubs. The grounds include a large playground, two theaters showing films, a disco and two pools, one in the adults-only section. Four tennis courts, watersports (a new boat has been added to its fleet) and a healthclub with a new treadmill round out the action. Kids are kept busy with supervised programs, and for an additional fee, will be assigned by their own private nanny. If you have more than two children, you'll find this spot a better buy than the Franklyn D. Resort. 228 rooms. Credit cards: A, MC.

Breezes Golf & Beach Resort $240–$439   ★★★★

Runaway Bay, ☎ (800) 467-8737, (876) 973-2436, FAX (876) 973-2352.
Single: $240–$319. Double: $330–$439.

Encompassing 214 acres opening onto a wide, sandy beach, this super all-inclusive resort (formerly Jamaica Jamaica) near Ochos Rios does just about everything right. Accommodations are bare-bones, but everyone's too busy with organized activities to notice. The resort boasts an excellent golf course with a golf school, four lighted tennis courts (with resident pros), diving (for a minimal fee), two beaches (one nude), two pools and three Jacuzzis, classes in Jamaican handicrafts, all watersports, horseback riding, and a full health club with aerobics classes. It has four bars and three restaurants. Toga and pajama parties, reggae and mixology classes, steel bands, afternoon tea, body painting contests—well, you get the idea. Besides, the disco hops and the snorkeling offshore is great. Even weddings are complimentary. All visits are a three-night minimum. By May 1998, a new clubhouse adjacent to the golf course was to open. Also planned: 69 new beachside suites with Jacuzzis, as well as a new beach bar and pool. All guests must be age 16 or older. 238 rooms.

Credit cards: A, MC, V.

Ciboney Ocho Rios $400–$800 ★★★★

Ocho Rios, ☎ *(800) 333-3333, (876) 974-1027, FAX (876) 974-5838.*
Associated Restaurant: *Manor/Orchids/Marketplace.*
Double: $400–$424. Suites Per Day: $420–$800.

Set just outside of town on 45 hillside acres, this stylish and impressive resort and spa offers top-flight amenities with free massage, manicure and pedicure, an aerobics studio and gym. It has 90 swimming pools (several attached to the villas), 20 whirlpools, six tennis courts, one squash court, golf at two 18-hole courses, croquet, jogging trail, library, six restaurants and cafes, piano bar and nightclub. Most accommodations are in villas with full kitchens, semi-private pools, and personal attendants who unpack and pack for you, do laundry and cook breakfast. On the beach after 10 p.m., you'll find moonlight, champagne and strolling minstrels. Great spot for honeymooners and romantics. No children under 16. 282 rooms.

Credit cards: A, MC, V.

Club Caribbean/Alamanda Inn $125–$295 ★★

Runaway Bay, ☎ *(800) 223-9815, (876) 973-4030, FAX (876) 973-5195.*
Single: $125–$395. Double: $215–$295.

Guests are put up in octagonal cottages with ceiling fans (no air conditioning) and kitchenettes on this 10 acres of tropical gardens. Typical organized activities like crab races, volleyball games and the like. Jamaica Water Sports, a Canadian owned and operated five-star PADI dive center, is on-site. Two tennis courts, disco, bicycles, a swim-up bar in the pool with a thatched roof bar set out over the water. Instead of stools, you sit on swings. Alamanda Inn is behind Club Caribbean and has 15 apartments for adults only. 128 rooms. Credit cards: A, MC, V.

Club Jamaica Beach Resort $180–$290 ★★

Ocho Rios, ☎ *(800) 423-4095, (876) 974-6642.*
Single: $180–$235. Double: $220–$290.

Located on Turtle Beach near the crafts market, the property has comfortable guestrooms. Themed buffets at poolside, nightly entertainment, a disco, watersports (including diving for an extra fee) and activities keep guests busy. Transfers are not included in the price. No kids under twelve. 95 rooms. Credit cards: A, MC, V.

Couples Jamaica $410–$540 ★★★

Ocho Rios, ☎ *(800) 423-4095, (876) 975-4271.*
Double: $410–$540.

Guestrooms are modern and comfortable, with king beds, cable TV and CD players (pack your own discs)—though showers sometimes run out of hot water. The beach is small but great. This busy resort has nightly entertainment, five tennis courts with pros, free lessons for all watersports and a windsurfing school. Guests can dine at any of the three restaurants, which all have live entertainment at mealtime. You'll also get sunset sails, scuba lessons, and optional day trips. If you get carried away by romance, Couples will marry you for free. 172 rooms. Credit cards: A, MC, V.

Enchanted Garden $140–$450 ★★★

Ocho Rios, ☎ *(800) 554-2008, (876) 974-1400, FAX (876) 974-5823.*
Single: $140–$170. Double: $280–$340. Suites Per Day: $320–$450.

Set in the foothills of the former estate of one-time Jamaica's Prime Minister, Edward Seaga, the many gardens and waterfalls lend a truly exotic feel to this resort. Accommodations range from standard rooms to villas with kitchens and one to three bedrooms, all nicely done. You can swim in two pools or 14 natural ponds with waterfalls. Dining features ethnic choices at five restaurants as well as spa cuisine. Two tennis courts, a fully equipped health spa that specializes in aromatherapy, and an aviary are also on site. The resort takes you to the beach or into town for free. 113 rooms. Credit cards: A, D, MC, V.

Franklyn D. Resort $280–$1400 ★★★★

Runaway Bay, ☎ *(888) 337-5437, (876) 973-4591, FAX (876) 973-3071.*
Website: www.fdrholidays.com. E-mail: fdr@infochan.com.
Associated Restaurant: *Teeto's Italian/Verandah.*
Single: $280. Suites Per Day: $560–$1400.

This beachfront, Georgian-style resort, opened in 1990 and geared to families, offers spacious suites with one to three bedrooms, kitchens, and a "Girl Friday" to cook clean and look after the kids by day (an extra charge for night-time babysitting applies). It was one of four resorts worldwide to win the Seal of Approval from The National Parenting Center for "exceptional value, service and programming for family travelers." Air conditioners are only in the bedrooms. Kids under 16 stay and eat free, which means the resort is heavily populated with the younger set. The 600-ft., white sand beach attracts adults, while kids head to their own private "kids' safe" beach protected by two shallow sand banks. The resort has two pools (one for kids), tennis, exercise room, and myriad organized activities for both kids and their parents. At the supervised kids' program (ages 2-11), kids get computer, snorkeling and photography/videography training, a learning center on Jamaican culture and language, Nintendo, donkey rides, picnics, arts and crafts. It also has supervised daily teen programs. The rates include everything from nightly dancing to a Dunn's River tour to a family picnic at Puerto Seco to hotel taxes to transfers from Montego Bay Airport (45 miles away). A great spot for watersports, too. Inquire about weekly rates, and special packages for couples who want to get married with their children in tow, and a program where a grandparent can stay free with your family. Note that rates quoted are for two people per night in the one-bedroom suite to five adults per night, the minimum required to reserve the three-bedroom suite. 76 rooms. Credit cards: A, MC, V.

Grand Lido Sans Souci   **$544–$640**   ★★★★

Ocho Rios, ☎ *(800) 467-8737, (876) 974-2353, FAX (954) 925-0334.*

Associated Restaurant: *Terrace.*

Double: $544–$640.

This elegant resort—noted for its Charlie's Spa—has smashing digs and all are suites with one or two bedrooms, some with Jacuzzis and kitchens. All the veranda suites have ocean views. Set on a lush, steep hillside, the resort spills down to the sea where the beach is accessed via an elevator or steep walkways. It has five tennis courts, two outdoor pools, mineral baths, a jogging track, watersports, and a new clothing-optional beach. Another 36 suites are being added. No children under age 16. 105 rooms. Credit cards: A, MC, V.

Renaissance Jamaica Grande Resort   **$320**   ★★★★

Ocho Rios, ☎ *(800) 468-3571, (876) 974-2201, FAX (876) 974-5378.*

Associated Restaurant: *Dragons/L'Allegro/Mallard's.*

Single: $320. Double: $320.

At first glance, this resort feels a little like Disney does Jamaica. Indeed, its free-form pool dubbed "Fantasy" is modeled after the island's famed Dunn's River Falls. Of course, the resort has thrown in caves, bridges, Jacuzzis and a swim-up pool bar. Tennis lovers have four championship courts lit for night play; fitness buffs have a center with aerobics classes, free weights, steam, sauna and Swedish massage. The grandiose resort has its own casino with 80 slots and electronic blackjack, and it has its own shopping arcade. Live entertainment runs nightly here. The Grande even has its own "Jump Up Carnival," and its disco is an island favorite. Like most Renaissance properties, the rooms are tastefully, if rather blandly done; each has air conditioning, satellite TV, in-room safes and radios. Meanwhile, for children 12 and under, it has a club and children's center, which has picnics, beach parties, an ecology awareness program and more. 720 rooms. Credit cards: A, MC, V.

Sandals Dunn's River Golf Resort & Spa   **$420–$620**   ★★★★

Ocho Rios, ☎ *(800) 726-3257, (876) 972-1610.*

Website: www.sandals.com.

Associated Restaurant: *Windies/Ristorante d'Amore.*

Double: $420–$560. Suites Per Day: $560–$620.

Set on 25 tropical acres fronting a North Coast beach near Ocho Rios, this couples-only resort is among the chain's best. The open-air, Italian palazzo-style lobby with marble columns and Oriental carpets scattered about is your first clue. Spacious guest rooms in the Mediterranean-style buildings come in seven categories and are generally pleasant and comfortable. Gourmet restaurants include Windies; Ristorante d'Amore and Tappanyaki. Other amenities include a new, full-service spa, daily complimentary golf clinics with Andy Gorman (a PGA-qualified pro) at Sandals Golf & Country Club (a championship, 18-hole, par 71 course), seven bars, frequent live entertainment, Jamaica's largest pool (complete with a waterfall) and another smaller one, four tennis courts, a gym, all watersports, and a free trip to Dunn's River Falls. A free shuttle runs from the resort to Sandals Ocho Rios and the golf course. A bit more sophisticated than its siblings. Rates range from $3340 to

$5220 per couple per week. Please note that all Sandals properties are open to heterosexual couples only. 256 rooms. Credit cards: A, MC, V.

Sandals Ocho Rios Resort & Golf Club $420–$4380   ★★★★

Ocho Rios, ☎ *(800) 726-3257, (876) 974-5691, FAX (305) 284-1336.*
Website: www.sandals.com.
Associated Restaurant: *Michelle's/Arizona/Reef Terrac.*
Double: $420–$560. Suites Per Day: $600–$4380.

Nestled among 15 acres of tropical, beachfront gardens, this couples-only resort boasts verdant grounds replete with fragrant jasmine and babbling brooks by which to stroll. Top-notch service makes this spot even more terrific. Rates cover all meals, drinks and activities, including nightly entertainment, all watersports, a gym with exercise classes, two tennis courts and nearby golf on a championship 18-hole course. Mediterranean-style accommodations are in five categories; rooms open onto furnished balconies, most with sea views. Dining is varied with three restaurants: one Northern Italian, one Southwestern and one offering Jamaican cuisine. Four bars and a disco offer additional entertainment. A free shuttle transports guests to the golf course or to Sandal's Dunn's River Golf Resort & Spa, where guests also have complimentary privileges. A weeks' stay starts at $3080 per couple. 237 rooms.
Credit cards: A, MC, V.

Inns

Hibiscus Lodge $93–$115   ★★

Ocho Rios, ☎ *(876) 974-2676.*
Associated Restaurant: *Almond Tree.*
Single: $93–$115. Double: $93–$115.

Situated in a quiet tropical garden fronting the sea, this intimate Jamaican-style inn has no beach, but it does have a pool. Guest rooms are spacious and comfortable, but only a few have air conditioning. Tennis and a well-regarded restaurant are on site, as well as a bar built into the cliffs. 26 rooms. Credit cards: A, CB, MC, V.

Jamaica Inn $200–$800   ★★★★★

Ocho Rios, ☎ *(800) 837-4608, (876) 974-2514, FAX (876) 974-2449.*
Associated Restaurant: *Jamaica Inn.*
Single: $200–$475. Double: $250–$475. Suites Per Day: $325–$800.

Tucked in a cove with a 700-ft. private white sand beach and surrounded by six acres, this intimate, family-owned and operated inn—painted Wedgwood blue—two miles east of Ocho Rios' town center has retained the classic appeal that brought Winston Churchill to its White Suite in 1950. The Morrow family, who has owned the inn for more than 35 years, requires guests to dress up in the evening—the better to dance on the terrace under the stars to the small orchestra that plays nightly. Time stands almost still here. Indeed, bills are still hand-written upon checkout. The rooms were recently upgraded with new phone systems, bathrooms, curtains and lighting fixtures. Each is thoughtfully decorated with Jamaican antiques, writing tables, large sofas, plush armchairs, and local artwork. The living-room size verandahs overlooking the flowering gardens are a beautiful place to lounge. Amenities are Crabtree and Evelyn toiletries, fresh-cut flowers daily, robes and champagne. The Cowdray Suite on the second floor sports a large bedroom with a dressing room and spectacular views of the sea; the 2000 sq. ft. White Suite is on a private peninsula. Its marble bathroom and private terrace opening onto a private pool epitomize posh. For a real splurge, request the Blue Cottage, a one-bedroom hideaway right on the beach. The exercise room has Life Fitness equipment. The beach has a reef ideal for snorkeling. Guests also have a choice of croquet, the pool, kayaks, and sailing. Skiing and diving are available at nearby Shaw Park, where guests can also play tennis free. Golf and horseback riding are easily arranged, and the Touring Society of Jamaica provides private eco-tours into the surrounding areas. The hotel's elegant restaurant, featuring New Jamaican cuisine, has been featured on the cover of *Gourmet*, and in several other top-drawer publications. Airport transfers are provided for guests on plans; à la carte guests take taxis ($80 one-way). No kids under 14 at this spot catering to an affluent, conservative crowd. 45 rooms. Credit cards: A, MC, V.

Apartments and Condominiums

Portside Villas & Condos   **$75–$250**   ★★

Discovery Bay, ☎ *(876) 973-2007.*
Single: $75. Double: $75. Suites Per Day: $85–$250.
Located 20 minutes outside of Ocho Rios at Discovery Bay, this complex has studios and suites of one to five bedrooms, all with air conditioning and ceiling fans. For an extra $15 a day you can have your own private cook. The complex has a game room, tennis court, two swimming pools and a wading pool, Jacuzzi, and restaurant/bar. The private beach is small, but offers non-motorized watersports. 15 rooms. Credit cards: A, MC, V.

Where to Stay in Negril

Hotels and Resorts

Caves, The   **$295–$600**   ★★★

Lighthouse Road, ☎ *(800) 688-7678, (876) 957-0270, FAX (876) 957-4930.*
Website: www.islandlife.com.
Single: $295–$360. Double: $295–$360. Suites Per Day: $340–$600.
This intriguing property—another pearl in the Island Outpost necklace—was conceived, built and is operated by Jamaican artists Bertram and Greer-Ann Saulter, who moved their brood to Negril when it was still a hippie enclave. Perched on 10 acres atop the honeycomb cliffs on the western tip of Jamaica's coast near the old Negril Lighthouse, The Caves combines cleverly designed thatched-roof and wood cottages—each beautifully decorated with hand-made wood furniture and one-of-a-kind Jamaican art pieces—that mesh with the sea caves and natural beauty of this tranquil spot. Access to good snorkeling over the coral reefs is easy via the coral stairways carved into the cliffs, ladders, or you can jump from Hopper's Hop (named for Dennis). Or if you tire of swimming in the sea, you can take a dip in the small saltwater pool, then sprawl in the hot tub or take a sauna. The couple has integrated the wild tropical landscape to ensure guests' privacy. Sunshine, a two-bedroom, two-story cottage with a terrific view of the sea, rates as tops for romance. Outdoor showers, king-size beds, candles, CD/cassette stereos and the discreet but caring staff make this spot a terrific choice for honeymooners and romantics. Its

whimsical charm and remote feel—a feat since it is, after all, in Negril—have also made it a hot spot for models, rock stars and beautiful people. Suffice it to say that one of the options is helicopter transfer from the airport. Breakfast, lunch, juices and cocktails (included in the rates) are served from a small kitchen connected to a terrace under a thatched roof. The cuisine is traditional Jamaican, prepared with a sure hand and plenty of spices; the Saulters have long owned and operated a nearby restaurant specializing in Rasta food. The couple is in the process of adding another restaurant on the property, as well as an outdoor Aveda spa. Exquisite for those seeking something beyond the typical. 8 rooms. Credit cards: A, MC, V.

Chuckles $75–$260 ★★

☎ *(876) 957-4250, FAX (876) 957-9150.*
Single: $75–$260. Double: $90–$260.
Located on a hill above the commercial center, this Mediterranean-style resort is peaceful and quiet. Guest rooms are nicely done with ceiling fans, air-conditioning, cable TV and room safes; two-bedroom villas have kitchens. Facilities include two lighted tennis courts, a large free-form pool, table tennis room, volleyball, gym, Jacuzzi, a Jamaican restaurant and two bars. The public beach is down the hill. A golf course and disco are both nearby. 73 rooms. Credit cards: A, MC, V.

Drumville Cove Resort $40–$100 ★★

☎ *(800) 423-4095, (876) 957-4369.*
Single: $40–$100. Double: $45–$100.
Set on the side of a cliff overlooking the sea, this complex is 2.5 miles from town. Accommodations are in cottages, some with kitchenettes. There's nightly entertainment, a weekly barbecue, restaurant and bar. 20 rooms. Credit cards: A, MC, V.

Foote Prints on the Sands $85–$255 ★

☎ *(876) 957-4300, FAX (876) 957-4301.*
Associated Restaurant: *Robinson Crusoe.*
Single: $85–$145. Double: $85–$145. Suites Per Day: $115–$255.
This family-run hotel sits right on Seven Mile Beach. Guest rooms are in the low-slung concrete buildings that proliferated after this area was hard-hit by a hurricane about a decade ago. Rooms are nice and comfortable, and a few have whirlpool tubs. Four kitchenette suites are also available, as well as two-bedroom units. There's no TV in the rooms. No pool, but it has a Jacuzzi deck, and plenty of watersports. A beach barbecue is held twice a week. 33 rooms. Credit cards: A, MC.

Negril Beach Club Hotel $77–$185 ★★

☎ *(800) 526-2422, (876) 957-4220, FAX (876) 957-4364.*
Single: $77–$185. Double: $77–$185.
Informal, this complex is especially popular with divers. Negril Scuba Centre is based here (night dives are a specialty) and Aqua Nova Water Sports is also on-site. The hotel has a restaurant, coffee shop, game room, bar, small pool, health club and two tennis courts, but most activity centers around the beach, where most sunbathers are topless. 100 rooms. Credit cards: A, MC.

Negril Cabins $110–$190 ★★

Bloody Bay, ☎ *(800) 382-3444, (876) 957-4350.*
Single: $110–$162. Double: $130–$190.

Set on 10 lushly forested acres across from Bloody Bay beach, this complex of two-bedroom log cabins on stilts offers rustic accommodations; each has a tree-level balcony overlooking a garden. If you want air conditioning and satellite TV, book a superior room for about $20 more per night. There are s two restaurants, one bar and occasional live entertainment. It's under new management. Families like the supervised children's program and the fact that kids under 16 stay free. A nice alternative to the cookie-cutter beach hotels. 50 rooms. Credit cards: A, MC.

Negril Gardens $165–$370 ★★

Seven Mile Beach, ☎ *(800) 752-6824, (876) 957-4408, FAX (876) 957-4374.*
Associated Restaurant: *Orchid Terrace.*
Single: $165–$370. Double: $165–$370.
This resort is cut in two by Negril's main road, meaning that some accommodations are on Seven Mile Beach; the remainder are situated in a tropical garden across the road. All are air-conditioned, with satellite TV, safes, ceiling fans and either two double beds or a queen. The resort has two bars, a tennis court, swimming pool, gift shop and restaurant. Note that during high season rates are all-inclusive, while during low season the European Plan is included in the rates. 65 rooms. Credit cards: A, MC, V.

Negril Tree House Resort $85–$330 ★★

☎ *(800) 634-7451, (876) 957-4387, FAX (876) 957-4386.*
Single: $85–$150. Double: $85–$150. Suites Per Day: $145–$330.
Set right on Seven Mile Beach, this unusual spot accommodates guests in two-story octagonal "tree house" cottages and oceanfront suites with either garden or ocean views. Nicely done with rattan furniture and air-conditioning, ask for a room on the second floor; they have better views and more atmosphere. They are all air-conditioned and have ceiling fans. You get daily maid service, too. Twelve suites offer one or two bedrooms, full kitchens and wide verandas. Amenities include a pool, Jacuzzi, games, watersports, two bars, a Monday night beach party and twice-weekly island picnics. Locals often hang out at the restaurant perched in a mango tree. Very nice, if you don't mind rustic. 70 rooms. Credit cards: A, MC, V.

Rockhouse $80–$165 ★★★

West End Road, ☎ *(876) 957-4373, FAX (876) 957-4373.*
Associated Restaurant: *Rock House Restaurant & Bar.*
Single: $80–$100. Double: $80–$100. Suites Per Day: $100–$165.
Take a team of energetic, young Aussies, add a 20-something, rustic tropical paradise, blend with a cutting-edge architectural firm and garden designers, and you've got a recipe for one of the hippest resorts to hit Negril in a long time. If you eschew the all-inclusives crowding Seven Mile Beach, and long for the good old days when Negril was yet undiscovered, check out the new and greatly improved Rockhouse, set on coral outcroppings. Its Australian management team completely renovated the existing cottages. New digs are in octagonal, thatched-roof cottages of wood and stone with wraparound terraces and enclosed outdoor showers. Pencil post beds are draped with mosquito netting. Think of Polynesian meets Caribbean. The new owners were also busy doubling the number of rooms at the resort at presstime after winning a long battle to build its own water supply. (Water shortages have

plagued hotels in the area in recent years.) Other changes include a new cliffside, freshwater pool, though some may still prefer to take their dips in the aptly-named Pristine Cove, above which the resort perches. The grounds have been landscaped, but the wildness that fans of the old admired remains. Another welcome addition is a jazzy new restaurant and bar that deservedly attracts young lovers. This place is a terrific buy. 28 rooms. Credit cards: A, MC, V.

All Inclusives

Beaches Negril $480–$620   ★★★

☎ *(800) 726-3257, (876) 000-, FAX (305) 284-1336.*
Website: *www.sandals.com.*
Associated Restaurant: *Seville/Tappanyaki.*
Double: $480–$620. Suites Per Day: $620–$2760.

Located at Long Bay on Negril's Seven Mile Beach, this represents Sandals' foray into the burgeoning family market. This 20-acre resort offers rooms in seven categories up to a two-bedroom beachfront suite. Rooms are air-conditioned and have ceiling fans, TV, in-room safe, and king-size beds. Amenities include an amphitheater, five gourmet restaurants, beach bandstand, disco, theatre bar, piano bar and lobby bar, beauty salon, two freshwater pools, three whirlpools and a toddlers pool. It also has a fully-equipped fitness center with sauna/steam and massage. Water sports are scuba diving, water-skiing, paddle-boating, snorkeling, and windsurfing. The resort also offers tennis, beach volleyball, and board games. Children under age two are free; those under 16 are charged $60 a night. 225 rooms. Credit cards: A, MC, V.

Grand Lido Negril $350–$600   ★★★★

☎ *(800) 467-8737, (876) 957-4010, FAX (876) 957-4317.*
Associated Restaurant: *Piacere/Cafe Lido/La Pasta.*
Single: $350–$390. Double: $500–$600.

Glamorous and elegant, this resort is open only to adults, though it's a lot less of a meat market than its neighbor, Hedonism II. Set on 22 acres, the Mediterranean-style property wows guests with a dramatic entrance, personalized check-in, and the *M.Y. Zein,* a 147-ft. yacht given by Ari Onassis as a wedding gift to Princess Grace and Prince Rainier. Accommodations are in wings that run parallel to the beach, all with sea views. They are beautifully done with tasteful decor, large baths, sitting areas, and such niceties as stereos. Room service operates 24-hours a day. The resort has a 24-hour clubhouse with Jacuzzis and music and laser karaoke. Four restaurants, disco, six bars, two pools, four tennis courts, a full health club, cruises aboard the yacht, a beauty salon, and on and on and on. The large beach is divided in two for those who wear suits and those who don't. Service, of course, is superb. This place, part of the SuperClubs group, is really special for those who like to splurge and be in the company of equally monied people. No one under age 16 allowed. At press time, the resort was building an eight one-bedroom and two presidential suites, outdoor aerobics floor, satellite massage areas and mini-spa. 200 rooms. Credit cards: A, MC, V.

Hedonism II $205–$376   ★★★

Seven Mile Beach, ☎ *(800) 467-8737, (876) 957-4200.*
Single: $205–$260. Double: $305–$376.

This resort, open only to those over 18, is aptly named, as it is dedicated to the pursuit of pleasure—and partying. Lots of singles are mixed in with the couples, and it is a meat market. Set on 22 acres at the northern end of Seven Mile Beach, it houses guests in uninspired rooms where phones have recently been added; the whole point is to be out frolicking, anyway. Rates include all meals, drinks (drinking is a big pastime), and activities; tips are forbidden. Two restaurants, five bars, a pool and two Jacuzzis, six tennis courts, all watersports, a gym, and nightly entertainment in the disco. The beach is divided for "prudes" and "nudes." On the clothing-optional side a new pool with swim-up-bar, beach grill, oversized Jacuzzi and misting pool with waterfall have been added. An additional 80 suites with Jacuzzis are being added, and the beach pool and disco are being enlarged. 280 rooms. Credit cards: A, MC.

Negril Inn $115–$145   ★

☎ *(876) 957-4209.*
Single: $115–$145. Double: $115–$145.
A nice alternative to the larger and livelier all-inclusives, this small resort—largely appealing to Italians and Germans—offers everything for one price in a more peaceful setting. Guest-rooms are simple but pleasant with private patios or balconies. Most meals are served buffet style. The resort has two bars and nightly entertainment. Recreational facilities include two tennis courts, bicycles, horseshoes, a pool and gym. No kids under 16. 46 rooms. Credit cards: A, MC, V.

Poinciana Beach Resort $155–$179   ★★★

Seven Mile Beach, ☎ *(800) 468-6728, (876) 957-4100.*
Associated Restaurant: *Paradise Plum.*
Single: $155–$179. Double: $155–$179. Suites Per Day: $195–$264.
Set on six tropical acres on a prime spot on Seven Mile Beach, this resort—owned by a Jamaican-born opthamologist and his wife—strives to attract couples, families and singles and generally successfully meets their needs. Rumor has it that this resort was where the author of the novel *How Stella Got Her Groove Back* was inspired. Guests are housed in a mix of standard rooms, studios, and one- and two-bedroom villas (each with a Jamaican valet and some with whirlpool baths). Rooms are vibrantly decorated with tropical colors and green rattan furnishings, original art, oriental rugs, white tile floors and Murphy beds. Fresh orchids add class. It has a watersports center, which offers PADI certification for divers. Three restaurants (Paradise Plum specializes in "New World" cuisine), two tennis courts, a gym open 24 hours a day, rental bikes, heated Jacuzzi, two pools and a disco make it good for the active set. A masseuse is on site if you overdo. Families love the extensive children's program (open from 9 a.m.–10 p.m. daily), creative playground, teen disco and the nature theme park across the street; exceptionally friendly babysitters and staff here know how to treat tykes. 130 rooms. Credit cards: A, MC.

Sandals Negril Beach Resort & Spa $480–$580   ★★★

☎ *(800) 726-3257, (876) 957-4216.*
Website: www.sandals.com.
Associated Restaurant: *The 4 C's/Kimonos/Sundowner.*
Double: $480–$580. Suites Per Day: $600–$740.

Another of the chain's couples-only resorts, this well-run operation is set on a narrow stretch of Negril's palm-studded, Seven Mile Beach. A boat shuttles guests to a small island where they can tan in the buff. Rooms—in six categories—are comfortable at this laid-back spot, but only the more expensive units have balconies and sea views. Honeymooners will likely favor the beachfront, one-bedroom loft suites. All kinds of activities (plus meals and drinks) are covered in the rate, including three tennis courts, watersports, two gyms, two pools, diving, a racquetball center and a newly-opened, full-service spa. Four gourmet restaurants give a choice of international, Caribbean or Teppanyaki-style Oriental cuisine. A few bars and a disco provide nighttime fun. Appeals mainly to the young and in love, and it's far more subdued than Hedonism II, which though cheaper is geared more toward heavy partiers. Rates are $3220 (a deluxe room) to $5140 (beachfront honeymoon loft) per couple per week. 219 rooms. Credit cards: A, MC, V.

Swept Away   **$450–$625**   ★★★★

Seven Mile Beach, ☎ *(800) 545-7937, (876) 957-4061.*
Associated Restaurant: *Feathers.*
Double: $450–$625.

Open only to couples, this special spot puts an emphasis on sports and fitness. Accommodations are in attractive two-story villas near the beach and are beautifully decorated in a minimalist style with Mexican tile floors, white canvas sailcloth furniture, clay lamp sconces and masks. Each has a large veranda surrounded by lots of plants, adding to the secluded feel. The centerpiece lies across the road away from the beach—an excellent fitness center, which has a gym, lap pool, ten tennis courts, and squash and racquetball. Swept Away has all the usual watersports, plus you can do laps in a lagoon-style pool. Alcohol is available, but the clientele here leans toward juice and veggie bars. 134 rooms. Credit cards: A, MC, V.

Inns

Charela Inn   **$80–$170**   ★★★

☎ *(800) 423-4095, (876) 957-4648, FAX (809) 957-4414.*
Associated Restaurant: *Charela Inn Restaurant.*
Single: $80–$150. Double: $96–$170.

This small Spanish hacienda-style inn has lush inner gardens and is set right on Seven Mile Beach. Guest rooms exude charm with four-poster beds and balconies. Request the upper floor for the best views. There's a pool and free sunfish, sailboards and kayaks, and a good restaurant serving French and Jamaican cuisine (a nightly, five-course table d'hote). Live shows are presented Thursday and Saturday nights at 7:30 p.m. This family-run inn is peaceful and friendly. Babysitting is available. 39 rooms. Credit cards: MC, V.

Apartments and Condominiums

Beachcomber Club   **$100–$325**   ★★★

☎ *(800) 423-4095, (876) 957-4171, FAX (876) 957-4097.*
Associated Restaurant: *Gambino's Italian.*
Single: $100–$150. Double: $100–$325.

Set right on Seven Mile Beach, this Georgian-style condominium complex has standard rooms, studios and one- and two-bedroom units with attractive furnishings, full kitchens, and large covered verandas with ocean views. Some sport four-poster beds. Hotel-like touches include room service and nightly turndowns. It also has an Italian restaurant, bar, tennis, watersports, a pool, Benetton Shop, and supervised programs for children year-round. Wedding packages are available. 45 rooms. Credit cards: A, MC.

Point Village $100–$230 ★★★

☎ *(800) 752-6824, (876) 957-5170, FAX (876) 957-5351.*
Associated Restaurant: *Village Connection.*
Single: $100–$200. Double: $125–$230. Suites Per Day: $210–$412.
Set on 14 acres of Rutland Point between Hedonism II and Grand Lido, this village-style resort has tropically decorated studios and one-to-three bedroom suites with kitchens; all have satellite TV, in-room phone, balcony/patio with ocean or garden view. A house band entertains nightly; theme nights are frequent. By day, it has a restaurant and two eateries, three bars, a freshwater pool and Jacuzzi, two natural salt water rock pools, private beach with watersports, volleyball and tennis. This resort heavily promotes its age-appropriate supervised kids' program (0–3 years; 4–7 years; and 8–12 years). All-inclusive, European and MAP plans are available. Quoted rates are based on European plan. Booking early yields additional discounts. 256 rooms. Credit cards: A, MC.

Xtabi On the Cliffs $50–$145 ★★★

☎ *(876) 957-4336, FAX (876) 957-0121.*
Associated Restaurant: *Restaurant Xtabi.*
Single: $50–$145. Double: $50–$145.
Perfect for nature lovers and just plain lovers, this resort on the West End demonstrates Negril's original funky charm, housing guests in octagonal cottages set on rugged cliffs or across the road in a garden setting. All are simply furnished and have small kitchens and enclosed outdoor showers, but no air conditioning. The popular cliffside restaurant specializes in seafood. The grounds are wild and natural, with dense foliage, five sea caves and dramatic sunsets. Spiral stairs lead down though a cave to a tiny beach, where great snorkeling awaits; it has a pool for cooling off where sunbathers often lounge nude. 26 rooms. Credit cards: A, MC.

Low Cost Lodgings

Hotel SamSara $35–$115 ★★

Light House Road, ☎ *(876) 957-4395, FAX (876) 957-4073.*
Associated Restaurant: *Chez Maurice.*
Single: $35–$115. Double: $70–$115.
Perched on low cliffs overlooking the sea, this small hotel has no beach, but is a great value for the money if you don't mind a few rambunctious folks ambling about. Cottages are spacious (all but 10 have oceanviews), but sparsely decorated. Only some are air-conditioned. Relaxed and informal, the place hops during the Monday night reggae concerts, starting at 10 p.m. The sports bar (with satellite TV) has a happy hour daily from 4-7 p.m. and it has a disco. There's also a tennis court, game room, dive center (good snorkeling from here), pool with a water slide that will dunk you right into the ocean. 52 rooms. Credit cards: A, MC.

Where to Stay in Treasure Beach/ Mandeville (Southwest Coast)

Inns

Astra Country Inn   **$60–$115**   ★★

Mandeville, ☎ (876) 962-3265.
Single: $60–$115. Double: $60–$115.

Set high up, some 2000 feet above sea level in the mid-island hills, this informal inn is in a former home. Guest rooms are comfortable, though not air-conditioned. There's a pool and sauna on-site, as well as horseback riding. Great for birders and nature lovers. 22 rooms. Credit cards: A, MC.

Jake's   **$75–$250**   ★★

Calabash Bay,Treasure Beach, ☎ (800) 688-7678, (876) 965-0552.
E-mail: jakes@toj.com.
Single: $75–$95. Double: $75–$95. Suites Per Day: $115–$250.

In a word: quirky. Jake's has been constructed with an artist's sensibilities and eccentricities on a private cove of sleepy Treasure Beach. Artist and owner Sally Henzell has cheerfully mixed rustic Caribbean, adobe, Moroccan and Cape Town Dutch exteriors in building cottages, four double rooms and a three-bedroom, two-story villa dubbed "Abalone." The proprietors will happily arrange a tour up the nearby Black River or a fishing trip with locals. Each room is sparsely furnished with Jamaican antiques, local artwork, and CD/cassette players with a good selection of CDs. Cooling fans spin lazily overhead and mosquito nets aren't just for aesthetics. You'll need them. Showers are outdoors, but don't worry, modest folks have plenty of coverage. This place has the feel of a hippie commune where no one cares any-way, which brings us to one complaint: When trouble arises—a toilet stops up, a mosquito net doesn't cover adequately—don't expect a rush to fix the problem. Ahhh well, sitting by the saltwater pool, adorned with colored mosaic tiles, you'll soon forget the minor annoyances and be charmed by Duggie, the convivial bar-tender, who nightly holds court with a cast of characters: locals, Peace Corps volun-teers and the artistic souls who have christened this spot their new favorite hangout. The chef serves up some of the island's best Jamaican cuisine like saltfish and ackee, perfectly-spiced pumpkin soup, escovitch fish and banana flambé. No phones or TV. 10 rooms. Credit cards: A, MC, V.

Mandeville Hotel   **$60–$200**   ★★

Mandeville, ☎ (876) 962-2460.
Single: $60–$200. Double: $60–$200.

This mountain hotel on four acres has traditional guest rooms, some with air con-ditioning, as well as suites with kitchen facilities. Rooms have been refurbished and have four-poster, mahogany beds. Favored by the mature market, it offers commu-nity experience tours. It also has two restaurants, two bars, a pool and horseback riding. Guests can golf at the nearby Manchester Club. 60 rooms. Credit cards: A, MC.

Natania's Guest House   **$50–$60**   ★★

Little Culloden, ☎ (800) 330-2332, (876) 963-5342, FAX (876) 963-5342.
Single: $50–$60. Double: $50–$60.

Natania's is located on Jamaica's south coast (probably the next area marked for development; a Sandals is opening here soon), 37 miles from Montego Bay. This unassuming little inn is on 2.5 acres of private, waterfront tropical gardens, with a beach, swimming pool, bar and restaurant on-site. Each pleasant room has a private bath and ceiling fans. The lounge has satellite TV for those who need their daily fix of CNN. Friendly and charming. 8 rooms.

Where to Stay in Kingston/ Blue Mountains

Hotels and Resorts

Crowne Plaza Kingston   **$129–$500**   ★★★★

☎ *(800) 618-6534, (876) 968-0936, FAX (876) 920-1276.*
Associated Restaurant: *Isabella's.*
Single: $129–$139. Double: $129–$149. Suites Per Day: $350–$500.
Marking the first major new hotel development in the island capital in two decades, the Crowne Plaza opened in January 1997 in an affluent suburb at the edge of town in view of the Blue Mountains and Kingston Harbor. It's four miles from the business center, New Kingston. If you need high-tech during your Jamaica visit, head for this hotel which has dual-line telephones with voicemail and dataports with on-line capability. Throughout the hotel you'll find one of the finest collections of Jamaican artists' work. Rooms are decorated with island furniture hand-produced at Strawberry Hill and by another native craftsman. On the Club floors, guests get in-room faxes, private key access and registration, a private concierge, and complimentary breakfasts. Rooms have all the top-drawer amenities business travelers expect, including a business center; the hotel also offers a pool, tennis, squash and a fitness center with sauna and Jacuzzi. A shopping plaza and 18-hole golf course are minutes away. 135 rooms. Credit cards: A, CB, DC, MC, V.

Jamaica Pegasus Hotel   **$180–$564**   ★★★

☎ *(876) 926-3690, FAX (876) 929-5855.*
E-mail: jmpegasus@toj.com.
Single: $180–$564. Double: $185–$564.
Located in New Kingston, three miles north of downtown, this high-rise hotel offers a sophisticated atmosphere that attracts lots of business travelers and conventioneers. Guest rooms are nice, with extras like coffeemakers and large balconies. There's a large pool, two restaurants, shopping arcade, business center, two tennis courts, and a jogging track. The top five floors of the 17-story building, the Executive Club, have added amenities. An excellent choice for the business traveler, though tourists may feel out of place. 350 rooms. Credit cards: A, DC, MC, V.

Morgan's Harbour Hotel   **$98–$150**   ★★

☎ *(876) 967-8075, FAX (876) 967-8073.*
Single: $98–$130. Double: $116–$150.
Downtown Kingston is 20 minutes away from this waterfront, colonial-style hotel. Completely rebuilt after devastating Hurricane Gilbert, it houses guests in extra-nice rooms with luxurious furnishings, good artwork, and wet bars. The pleasantly landscaped grounds include a restaurant, fresh-water pool, a marina that attracts lots

of yachters, a disco and a dive shop. Perfect for those who need to be near Kingston but want the resort feel of a waterfront property. 45 rooms. Credit cards: A, MC, V.

Strawberry Hill　　　　　　　　**$195–$525**　　　　　★★★★
Irish Town, ☎ *(800) 688-7678, (876) 944-8400, FAX (876) 944-8408.*
Website: www.islandlife.com. E-mail: strawberry@toj.com.
Associated Restaurant: *Strawberry Hill.*
Single: $195–$350. Double: $275–$450. Suites Per Day: $315–$525.

Located 50 minutes from the Kingston airport, this villa resort—opened in December 1994—is designed in the style of 19th-century Jamaican architecture. Hand-carved fretwork decorates the doorways, original island art and photographs personalize each villa. Handmade island furniture—reproductions of island antiques made on the property—invites lolling, and wrap-around wooden verandahs deliver stunning views of the surrounding Blue Mountains. Nestled on 26 acres of a former coffee and strawberry plantation established in 1780 at an altitude of 3100 feet, the resort offers simple, but elegant studio, one-, two-, and three-bedroom accommodations. These white-washed, paneled rooms include four-poster beds with goosedown bedding and heated mattress pads, mosquito netting, ceiling fans, terra cotta baths and, in the larger units, modern kitchens. The signature touch of owner Chris Blackwell, founder of Island Records—CD players with a terrific selection and cordless phones with answering machines—is a nod to the hip crowd that frequents this escape. In the evenings, a fire blazes in the bar area. The terrific restaurant makes good use of its chef who specializes in New Jamaican cuisine. Stroll along the garden paths—a staff botanist has transformed the grounds into an 18th century showplace. Blackwell is adding an Aveda spa and salon to the current offerings (a plunge pool and sauna). Romantics should request Birdshill, which comes with a private Jacuzzi just off its terrace. Special long-term rates are available. 14 rooms. Credit cards: A, MC, V.

Wyndham Kingston Hotel　　　　**$160–$575**　　　　★★★
☎ *(800) 996-3426, (876) 926-5430, FAX (876) 929-7439.*
Single: $160–$575. Double: $160–$575.

Situated in the business center on 7.5 acres, this towering hotel was recently redone, with good results. Primarily appealing to business travelers and conventioneers, it offers modern accommodations in the 16-story tower or older and funkier cabana units. Two tennis courts, a pool and a fully equipped health club, as well as several bars and restaurants. Decent, but the Pegasus remains superior. 384 rooms. Credit cards: A, DC, MC, V.

All Inclusives

Grand Lido Braco　　　　　　　**$270–$360**　　　　★★★★
Rio Bueno, ☎ *(800) 467-8737, (876) 973-4882, FAX (876) 954-0020.*
Single: $270–$360. Double: $190–$280. Suites Per Day: $270–$360.

Opened in spring 1995 and formerly called Braco Village Resort, this village is located one mile west of Rio Bueno, 38 miles east of Montego Bay and 30 miles west of Ocho Rios. The village reflects Jamaica's various architectural styles, from Georgian to gingerbread. The centerpiece is the Town Square, with several restaurants, bars, and artists in residence creating and exhibiting their work. The idea is to make the village as authentically Jamaican as possible, while still spoiling guests with the resort amenities. Facilities include an Olympic-size pool, four tennis courts, a soccer field, 85 acres of jogging and hiking trails, a fitness center, and all watersports, including scuba and kayaking. Guests are also treated to manicures and pedicures. Each guestroom has a unique feature such as a gazebo, balcony, or love seat, as well as direct-dial telephone, satellite TV, 24-hour room service, valet and laundry. Golfers have a choice between SuperClubs' 18-hole, PGA-quality course at Breezes in Runaway Bay, or Braco's own nine-hole course. The 2000-ft. beach has a clothing-optional section. 284 rooms.

Where to Stay in Port Antonio

Hotels and Resorts

Bonnie View Plantation   **$60–$98**   ★★

 (876) 993-2752.
Single: $60–$72. Double: $88–$98.
Sweeping views are the draw at this small hotel perched atop a hill and set on a farm. Guest rooms are quite simple, but a bargain. It has a pool, restaurant and bar, and a free shuttle to the beach four miles away. 20 rooms. Credit cards: A, MC, V.

Dragon Bay   **$96–$246**   ★★

☎ *(800) 423-4095, (876) 993-8514, FAX (876) 993-3284.*
Single: $96–$132. Double: $96–$132. Suites Per Day: $198–$246.
Set on 55 hillside acres with its own private, protected cove, this villa-style resort is adjacent to the Blue Lagoon. Accommodations are pleasant and run the gamut from single rooms to three-bedroom villas (comfortable for up to six). One even has its own pool. Two restaurants and bars, a helicopter pad, weekly reggae concerts, a pair of pools and tennis courts, fitness center, and all the usual resort amenities. A bit off the beaten track, so you'll want a rental car. Portions of the movies *Lord of the Flies* and *Cocktail* were filmed here. 86 rooms. Credit cards: A, MC, V.

Fern Hill Club   **$145–$230**   ★★

Mile Gully Road, ☎ *(876) 993-7374.*
Single: $145. Double: $230.
Set on 40 acres, this hillside retreat offers fabulous views over San San Beach, accessible by shuttle or a hike. Popular with Canadians and honeymooners, this spot offers all-inclusive rates and has an exercise room, pools, tennis courts, a hilltop restaurant and bar. 31 rooms. Credit cards: A, MC, V.

Hotel Mocking Bird Hill   **$95–$140**   ★★★

Near Frenchman's Cove, ☎ *(876) 993-3370, FAX (876) 993-7133.*
Associated Restaurant: *Mille Fleurs.*
Single: $95–$140. Double: $95–$140.
This tiny hotel—owned by artist Barbara Walker and Shireen Aga—offers prettily decorated rooms, blue and white fabrics, bamboo furniture and ceramic tiles, on seven, lushly landscaped acres in the foothills of the Blue Mountains. Some 15 minutes from the center of Port Antonio, the spacious units have double or twin beds and a balcony or patio, most with sea views. Facilities include a restaurant serving family recipes using local produce and a bar with spectacular views. An on-site art

gallery features Walker's works along with those of other local artists. 10 rooms.
Credit cards: MC, V.

Jamaica Palace Hotel   **$130–$325**   ★★★
☎ *(800) 423-4095, (876) 993-2020.*
Single: $130–$325. Double: $130–$325.
Set on five well-manicured acres, this colonial-style mansion draws mainly European
guests. The elegant guest rooms are quite nice with antiques, Oriental rugs, and
marble floors. There's no beach nearby, but you can take a dip in the 114-foot pool,
which is shaped like Jamaica. Elegant and refined, but a bit too out of the way for
some folks. 80 rooms. Credit cards: A, MC.

Navy Island Marina Resort   **$50–$180**   ★★
Navy Island, Port Antonio Harbour, ☎ *(800) 423-4095, (876) 993-2667.*
Single: $50. Double: $100. Suites Per Day: $180–$180.
Comprising 64 acres on a 17th-century British naval station, this secluded resort
later acted as Errol Flynn's personal hideaway. Like the name implies, it is located
on its own small island a quarter-mile off the coast. Accommodations are in oceanfront villas with sun decks and kitchens, but no air-conditioning. One of the three
beaches is clothes optional. There's also a pool, tennis and watersports. 21 rooms.
Credit cards: A, MC, V.

Trident Villas & Hotel   **$365–$800**   ★★★★★
☎ *(800) 423-4095, (876) 993-2705.*
Single: $365–$500. Double: $385–$800.

One of Jamaica's most luxurious resorts, set on 14 lush acres fronting the sea, it is
two miles east of town. Guest rooms and villa suites are exquisitely furnished with
antiques, plush decor, and ocean views. Only some are air-conditioned, but constant trade winds keep everything cool. The lovely grounds include a small private
beach, flowering gardens, pretty walkways, and two pools. Dinner is a formal affair
that includes white-glove service; you'll have to dress up for the occasion. Service,
of course, is outstanding. Truly elegant. 28 rooms. Credit cards: A, MC, V.

Apartments and Condominiums
Goblin Hill Villas   **$1350–$2135**   ★★★
Port Antonio, ☎ *(800) 423-4095, (876) 925-8108.*
Suites Per Week: $1350–$2135.
Situated on 12 tropical acres of a hill above San San Beach, this complex has Georgian-style villas perfect for families. All have locally-made furniture and artwork,
kitchens, and air-conditioned bedrooms. Each comes with a maid and cook. Guests
enjoy are two lighted tennis courts, the beach down the hill, a pool and watersports,
a bar and restaurant. 28 rooms. Credit cards: A, MC.

Where to Eat

Fielding's Highest Rated Restaurants in Jamaica

★★★★★	Evita's	$10–$24
★★★★★	Strawberry Hill	$18–$27
★★★★★	Trident Hotel Restaurant	$50–$50
★★★★	Blue Lagoon Jamaican Restaurant	$12–$22
★★★★	Blue Mountain Inn	$24–$30
★★★★	Hungry Lion	$8–$20
★★★★	Jamaica Inn	$15–$30
★★★★	Norma's at the Wharfhouse	$26–$34
★★★★	Sugar Mill	$14–$39
★★★	Almond Tree	$12–$26

Fielding's Most Romantic Restaurants in Jamaica

♥♥♥♥♥	Blue Mountain Inn	$24–$30
♥♥♥♥♥	Ivor	$40–$27
♥♥♥♥♥	Jamaica Inn	$15–$30
♥♥♥♥♥	Strawberry Hill	$18–$27
♥♥♥♥♥	Trident Hotel Restaurant	$50–$50

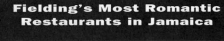

Fielding's Best Value Restaurants in Jamaica

★	Hot Pot, The	$3–$7
★★★★★	Evita's	$10–$24
★★★	Reading Reef Club	$10–$22
★★	Pork Pit	$3–$10
★★★★	Hungry Lion	$8–$20

The motto "Out of many, one people" applies to politics as well as cuisine in Jamaica—for the influences that have gone into the *dutchie*, or cast-iron cooking pot, to create Jamaican menus, are many—the barbecuing techniques of the Arawaks, the African meat-preserving techniques in the country's best known dish, jerk pork; Spanish marinades meet New World vegetables in twice-cooked *escovitch* fish. British *cornish pastries*, which are meat-and-potato-filled pastries, have become Jamaican spicy beef patties. And the spices of Asia come together in dishes such as curried goat. Today nouvelle Jamaican cuisine is also dressing up traditional ingredients in trendy resort restaurants along the North Coast. Rastafarianism—Jamaica's contribution to 20th-century religion—has created a cuisine all its own called I-Tal, which places the accent on nature's bounty. Rastas don't drink alcohol, eat meat or use salt, but their vegetarian cooking is delicious, including hearty vegetable stews with ingredients such as *callallo* (a spinach-like vegetable), *chocho* (a pear-shaped squash), pumpkin and yams. Johnnycakes—flat, dense, unleavened breads—were a slave adaptation of British breads, while *bammie* was the Amerindian cassava bread that Columbus wrote about in his journals. One of the foundations of Jamaican cooking is "poor folk's food," such as codfish, stewed peas and roast breadfruit. But those travelers with adventurous palates may even learn to like boiled green bananas as a breakfast dish.

Other Jamaican specialties include some that are reportedly aphrodisiacs, including *cowfoot soup* (a spicy stew of cow feet and vegetables) and *mannish water* (goat meat and vegetable soup flavored with white rum and hot peppers). If you're not brave enough for either, stick to *bun* (a dark fruitcake served with cheese), *matrimony* (orange and star apple pulp in cream), *Solomon gundy* (spiced pickled herring) and *rundown* (mackerel or codfish boiled in coconut milk and served with ashed onions and peppers).

In the Blue Mountains high above Kingston, Sunday brunch is special at Strawberry Hill, where you can linger on the terrace, watching the streamer-tailed hummingbirds (dubbed the doctor bird) flit among the jade vines. You'll be served the region's Blue Mountain coffee while you indulge in fluffy yellow *ackee*, a Jamaican-grown tree vegetable, whose custardy flesh tastes and looks somewhat like scrambled eggs. *Ackee* is largely unknown in the U.S., because it has to be prepared immediately after it ripens. Eaten at the wrong time, *ackee* is poisonous. This mixture of the savory *ackee* and salt fish hearkens back to the days of slavery when feeding the slaves cheaply was a major concern for plantation owners.

Jerked cooking is a method of barbecue using well-seasoned meat, said to have originated with the Maroons, the fierce, escaped slaves who retreated to the mountains of Cockpit Country and kept the British at bay for more than a century. They would roast pork over hot coals in earthen pits that were covered with branches of green pimento or allspice wood. The smoking wood along with an incendiary mix of island-grown ingredients—scotch bonnet pepper, pimento seeds, thyme and nutmeg—is what provides the unique seasoning. At Boston Beach today, pit men such as Vasco "Kojak" Allen at Front Line #1 are famous for their grill-work, which includes jerked pork, the classic dish, as well as jerked chicken, sausage, and fish.

Near Montego Bay, the restaurant at the four-bedroom hostelry called **Norma's** at the Wharfhouse in Reading is a treasurehouse of Jamaican nouvelle cuisine designed by celebrated chef Norma Shirley, who has received acclaim from *Bon Appetit* and *Food & Wine*. Desserts run the course between plantain turnover with brandied whipped cream or a vine-ripened papaya, with a drizzle of island grown ortanique (cross between an orange and a tangerine).

You won't know the I-tal vegetarian cuisine of the Rastas until you make a stop at Negril's **Hungry Lion**. To experience a special Jamaican breakfast feast stop at **The Three Sisters** on the road from Sheffield to Negril. At Treasure Beach locals flock to the funky **TransLove Café** where the owner serenades the guests and talks to her two pet parrots while she serves your food.

FIELDING'S CHOICE:

If you want to learn more about Jamaica's famed Blue Mountain coffee, book a hike with the Touring Society of Jamaica (see Trekking Shops above) to Alex Twyman's The Old Tavern Blue Mountain Coffee Estate. After a long fight, estates have finally gotten permission from the Jamaican Coffee Board to label their coffees by estate rather than under generic Blue Mountain labels. Twyman was one of the pioneers on this issue and will gladly give you a tour and explain what makes Blue Mountain coffee so special. At the end of the journey, you'll be offered a steaming, freshly-brewed cup and a chance to buy the coffee.

Where to Eat in Montego Bay

Julia's Italian $$$ ★★

Bogue Hill, ☎ *(876) 952-1772.*
Dinner: *6–10:30 p.m., prix fixe $35.*
Take this mountaintop restaurant's offer of a private van to pick you up at your door. Negotiating the steep road that leads to this estate above MoBay (800 feet or thereabouts) can be hazardous. Once ensconced in your seat, relax and enjoy dinner served by an attentive staff, while the lights of the bay and the city glitter below. The Italian entrées of veal (usually Parmesan), chicken, or fish include a salad, pasta, dessert and choice of beverage. Reservations required. Credit cards: A, MC, V.

Norma's at the Wharfhouse $$$ ★★★★

☎ *(876) 979-2745.*
Lunch: *Noon–2:30 p.m., entrées $26–$34.*
Dinner: *7:30–10:30 p.m., entrées $26–$34. Closed: Mon., Tue., Wed.*

The finest restaurant on the island may be this historical dockside beauty created by Norma Shirley, Jamaica's most famous chef who launched Jamaican nouvelle cuisine. Dine with influential Jamaicans and visiting celebrities while watching the action at a table set on the wharf of this 300-year-old warehouse, or in an antique-filled salon. Shirley, who owned a restaurant in New York, utilizes the rich bounty of the region to spectacular effect; the menu, which changes daily, often includes succulent smoked marlin with papaya or grilled deviled crab backs. The elegantly-dressed plates are a treat. Reservations recommended. Credit cards: MC, V.

Pork Pit $ ★★
Gloucester Avenue, ☎ *(876) 952-1046.*
Lunch: 11 a.m.–4:30 p.m., entrées $3–$10.
Dinner: 4:30–11 p.m., entrées $3–$10.
Fiery jerk pork, chicken, sausage or spare ribs picnic-style on benches open to the sea breeze are the draw at this pitstop, which offers a decent introduction to Jamaica's trademark dish. Common accompaniments include local cornbread (called festival), yams, rice and peas and Red Stripe beer. Located across from Walter Fletcher Beach and five minutes from the airport, Pork Pit is a popular stop for hungry travelers headed to points beyond, like Negril.

Reading Reef Club $$ ★★★
Bogue Lagoon, Montego Bay, ☎ *(876) 952-5909.*
Lunch: Noon–3 p.m., entrées $10–$22.
Dinner: 7–10 p.m., entrées $10–$22.
Located in a discreet, small (21-room) hotel in Reading Square, this Caribbean-influenced Italian restaurant reflects the tastes of the hotel's owner, JoAnne Rowe, a New York-born expatriate. A unique combination of pasta served with ginger works quite well. Crayfish, lobster and shrimp are served curried or Jamaican thermidor. Entrees are paired with local produce. And you get ocean views to boot. From November to April, reggae bands entertain diners. Reservations required. Credit cards: A, MC, V.

Sugar Mill $$$ ★★★★
Rose Hall, ☎ *(876) 953-2228.*
Lunch: Noon–2:30 p.m., entrées $14–$39.
Dinner: 7–10 p.m., entrées $14–$39.
Chef Alex Radakovitz of Austria dishes out New Jamaican cuisine in historic Rose Hall. Its terrace overlooks the ocean and the golf course of the Half Moon Club, which is across the road. The emphasis here is on creative use of Jamaican ingredients with an international flair. Marlin, a specialty catch of the area, is often smoked and served with pasta. Even if you're just passing through, come for a look at an antique sugar wheel. For romantics, request a private table out by the waterfall. Reservations required. Credit cards: A, MC, V.

Town House $$$ ★★
16 Church Street, ☎ *(876) 952-2660.*
Lunch: 11:30 a.m.–2:30 p.m., entrées $13–$30.
Dinner: 6–10 p.m., entrées $13–$30.

This grand, 300-year-old Georgian building makes a fun outing, especially in its art-filled, brick-walled cellar room, which is a novel change from the favored practice of dining alfresco. But that can also be achieved here on an outdoor terrace. Jamaican cooking with spicy curried dishes and steaks are the mainstays. Reservations recommended. Credit cards: A, DC, MC, V.

Where to Eat in Ocho Rios/ Discovery Bay/Runaway Bay

Almond Tree $$$ ★★★

87 Main Street, Ocho Rios, ☎ *(876) 974-2813.* Associated hotel: *Hibiscus Lodge.*
Lunch: Noon–2:30 p.m., entrées $12–$26.
Dinner: 6–9:30 p.m., entrées $12–$26.

If you can stop swinging in the unique chairs suspended from the ceiling in the bar of this small inn on a cliff overlooking the sea, you'll find the food in the restaurant to be good. The menu is expansive, but on the pricey side. The Almond Tree has a real tree growing through its roof, a diverse clientele (rock stars have been known to dine here) and roast suckling pig on the menu. Soups are divine, especially the pumpkin. Drop in at the piano bar on the hotel grounds for some good tunes to accompany after-dinner drinks in a more subdued atmosphere. Reservations recommended. Credit cards: A, DC, MC, V.

Evita's $$ ★★★★★

Eden Bower Road, Ocho Rios, ☎ *(876) 974-2333.*
Lunch: 11 a.m.–4 p.m., entrées $8–$24.
Dinner: 4–11 p.m., entrées $10–$24.

Don't cry for Evita—in this instance, restaurateur Eva Myers—who has no trouble drawing in pasta lovers and others craving Italian food to this 1860s-era gingerbread house perched over Mallard's Bay. One of the few restaurants on the island to be granted membership into the exclusive Chaine de Rottisseur, Evita's offers terrific sunset views from the terrace and a voluminous menu with all the traditional courses associated with Italian dining—hot and cold appetizers, soups, salads, pastas, entrées and, of course, a lengthy dessert menu. Half orders of pasta are cheerfully doled out. Reservations recommended. Credit cards: A, MC, V.

Jamaica Inn $$$ ★★★★

P. O. Box 1, Ocho Rios, ☎ *(876) 974-2514.*
Lunch: Noon–2 p.m., entrées $10–$15.
Dinner: 7–9 p.m., entrées $15–$30.

Jamaican-born chef Wilbert Mathison prepares beautiful meals that match the romantic setting of the dining terrace at Jamaica Inn. His obvious love affair with food translates to his guests and has gotten rave reviews, even making the cover of *Gourmet*. Start with his sauteed shrimp and conch, move to the cold avocado soup and for the main dish, go with the poached fillet of yellowtail arranged on a plate with steamed mussels and tomato concasse. Choose from the ample desserts, or you can end with Jamaican coffee and a piece of homemade fudge. After dinner, couples dance under the starlight and the warm glow of lamplights, or slip off to the loggia where the sound of the waves competes with the small orchestra. Jacket and tie requested. Credit cards: MC, V.

Where to Eat in Negril

Cosmo's $ ★★

Norman Manley Boulevard, ☎ *(876) 957-4330.*
Lunch: 11 a.m.–4 p.m., entrées $5–$12.
Dinner: 4–10 p.m., entrées $5–$12.

Seafood is pretty much the focus here, but what seafood! Owner-character Cosmo Brown specializes in conch, either stewed, curried or in a generous vat of soup. Since this chewy gastropod appears more often in other Caribbean islands, this is a good spot to try it. Otherwise, a grilled or baked escovitch (well-marinated in spices) whole fish is a popular choice. Cosmo's is situated in an informal, thatched-roof hut on a sparsely-populated East End beach. Credit cards: MC, V.

Hungry Lion $$ ★★★★

West End Road, ☎ *(876) 957-4486.*
Dinner: 5–10:30 p.m., entrées $8–$20.

The verdant, colorful setting at this 40-seat popular restaurant, where the bar is hand-painted by the owner using bright flowers and tropical birds as inspiration, gives a hint of the I-tal vegetarian treats and well-prepared seafood that you are in for. This restaurant evolved because owners Greer Ann and Bertram, who are also partners in The Caves and who moved here more than two decades ago, wanted good food for their own eight children to eat. (The extended family lives in a compound that used to be rental cottages behind the restaurant.) The couple adopted many of the rules of the Rastafarians in their cooking: I-tal means all natural ingredients, no salt and no dairy. Last year marks the first time they've ever even had chicken on the menu. The menu changes nightly according to which fish and other ingredients are the freshest. Coconut milk is often used in recipes here. If you dine outside by the fish pond, you'll be surrounded by a greenhouse of flowering plants. Inside, the dining room is a living canvas. During the day only light fare and all-natural fruit juices are served. Terrific for a taste of true Jamaican cuisine at its freshest in Negril's hippest restaurant. Credit cards: A, MC, V.

Rick's Cafe $$ ★

West End Road, ☎ *(876) 957-4335.*
Lunch: Noon–4 p.m., entrées $11–$28.
Dinner: 4–10 p.m., entrées $11–$28.

This famous (circa 1974) bar-restaurant-hangout is a scene and a place to be seen. One of the many draws here is a concept imitated from the La Quebrada divers in Acapulco—locals and visitors plunge some 25 feet into the sea from the cliffs at Rick's before emerging (it's hoped) for a papaya daiquiri. A tamer ritual takes place just before sunset when crowds of tanned and buffed young people pack the rock-encrusted, palm-fronded terrace for fun and frolic and a last glimpse of old sol. You can also come here for lunch or brunch, but for that you can go anywhere. Credit cards: MC, V.

Tan-ya's   **$$**   ★★

Norman Manley Boulevard, ☎ *(876) 957-4041.* Associated hotel: *SeaSplash Resort.*
Lunch: 8 a.m.–3 p.m., entrées $5–$15.
Dinner: 6:30–11p.m., entrées $10–$19.

This oceanside restaurant at the SeaSplash Resort is where you can go if you want
to dress up (just a little) for French-inspired seafood and a creative way with lobster.
The new chef calls his work Nouvelle Jamaican: for example, he pairs ackee with
lobster in an appetizer. Delivery can be uneven, however, and the hours kept have
been irregular in recent months. Call ahead first. Reservations recommended. Credit
cards: A, MC, V.

Where to Eat in Kingston/ Blue Mountains

Blue Mountain Inn   **$$$**   ★★★★

Gordon Town Road, ☎ *(876) 927-1700.*
Dinner: 7 p.m.–until late, entrées $24–$30.

One of Jamaica's most elegant dining experiences, set in an old coffee plantation
house overlooking the Mamee River, located about half an hour from Kingston,
Blue Mountain inn provides a good excuse for women to air out a little black dress
and men a jacket (ties are not required). Sample stuffed lobster or filet mignon
impeccably prepared and served by a gracious staff. On Sundays the chef whips up a
lavish brunch. Reservations recommended. Reservations required. Credit cards: A, DC,
MC, V.

Chelsea Jerk Centre   **$**   ★

97Chelsea Avenue, ☎ *(876) 926-6322.*
Lunch: 11 a.m.–4 p.m., entrées $3–$11.
Dinner: 4–11 p.m., entrées $3–$11.

The Jerk Centre proffers blazingly hot barbecued chicken or pork that's been mar-
inating for hours in a medley of incendiary spices that are a closely-guarded secret.
Most dishes here are under $5 and come with sides of rice and peas (white rice with
red beans). A half-chicken or pork slab can be packaged to go. Credit cards: not
accepted.

Devon House Restaurant   **$**   ★★

Devon House, ☎ *(876) 929-6602.*
Lunch: 10 a.m.–4 p.m., entrées $6–$16.
Dinner: 4 p.m.–midnight, entrées $6–$16. Closed: Sun.

This former colonial mansion turned restaurant/coffee house/craft emporium is
one of Kingston's most-visited tourist sites. An incredible Jamaican breakfast is
served on the breezy Coffee Terrace every day except Sunday. Diners saunter to a
long table topped with red-checked country cloths for a buffet of beautifully carved
fresh fruit, ackee and saltfish, cod fish balls and breads. Blue Mountain coffee and
exotic juices are included. If you have room, pop into the adjoining I-Scream for a
frozen concoction of soursop or mango. Reservations recommended. Credit cards: A,
MC, V.

Gap Cafe, The   **$$**   ★★

Hardwar Gap, ☎ *(876) 997-3032.*

Lunch: 10 a.m.– 5 p.m., entrées $12–$15.
Dinner: entrées $17–$22.

A visit to the Gap Cafe, located on a former mule path to Newcastle and built in the late 1930s, is a journey to another Jamaica—one where a fireplace may be glowing all year round, understandable at a height of 4200 feet. Gloria Palomino welcomes guests to sip fresh-brewed, aged Blue Mountain coffee—the latest thing, trust me, and it's heavenly—and savor some of the best pastries on the island, served at lunch and at high tea on Sundays. Lunch is a simple affair: *bammy*, chicken breast stuffed with callaloo or rasta pasta with vegetables. Native guavas are used in the cheese-cake, as well as soursop and passionfruit for the cakes and mousses. The Cafe, a cozy, flower-filled charmer decked out in tones of maroon and blue, offers a few tables on a terrace, overlooking the misty, wild flower-dotted mountainside. Hummingbirds busily flit around attracted by feeders and agapanthus lilies and other flowers that surround the small cafe. The gift shop on premises carries island coffee and food products, as well as a few crafts, but prices are usually higher than what you'll find elsewhere. Reservations recommended. Credit cards: A, MC, V.

Hot Pot, The $ ★

2 Altamont Terrace, ☎ (876) 929-3906.
Lunch: 8 a.m.–4 p.m., entrées $3–$7.
Dinner: 4–10 p.m., entrées $3–$7.

A dandy place to try Jamaican specialties is this informal joint behind the Wyndham Hotel. The decor isn't much, but the authentic dishes are cheap and filling. The Hot Pot serves three meals a day, including the legendary saltfish and ackee (a vegetable brought over by Captain Bligh of Bounty fame) for breakfast. Credit cards: MC, V.

Ivor $$$ ★★★

Jacks Hill, ☎ (876) 702-0276. Associated hotel: *Ivor Guest House.*
Lunch: entrées $23–$27.
Dinner: prix fixe $40.

This cozy, century-old guest house/dining room on a hill high above Kingston boasts a million dollar view (at 2000 feet). The chef prepares dishes with a Jamaican flair. The menu changes nightly but always includes an appetizer, soup, salad, choice of three entrées and a dessert. The price also includes wine. The open terrace of this small colonial inn is a popular spot for high tea and cocktails. On a clear night, the distant city lights make for a breathtaking vista. Reservations required. Reservations required. Credit cards: A, MC, V.

Strawberry Hill $$$ ★★★★★

IrishTown, ☎ (876) 944-8400.
Lunch: Noon–4 p.m., entrées $18–$24.
Dinner: 6–10 p.m., entrées $18–$27.

The spectacular setting alone would be enough to merit a trip up the mountain from Kingston to this fabulous place. The bar area stars a crackling fire in the fireplace, unusual walls that took workmen weeks to finish, clay masks by a Kingston artist. Book a table right at sunset and watch the twinkling lights of Kingston below. You can dine on the second-floor, wrap-around verandah, where an English garden is on one side and the city and the mountain slope is on the other. Or on a chilly night, dine at a table in the great house, which has soaring ceilings with custom-made, wrought iron chandeliers. Black and white photos of music greats decorate the wall reminding you of owner Chris Blackwell's musical connections. James Palmer, the native Jamaican chef, has become renowned for his new Jamaican cuisine. He takes native specialties and conjures up his own riffs: Irish Town potato cakes with passionfruit sauce and mango relish, grilled jumbo shrimp brushed with Jamaican rum and molasses on a bed of pineapple-papaya salsa. Creme Carmel with a dash of Grand Marnier provides a perfect punctuation point to the meal. Sunday Brunch has become a hot ticket. Service comes at a leisurely pace, but when you're sitting this close to heaven, relax and enjoy. Credit cards: DC, MC, V.

Where to Eat in Port Antonio

Blue Lagoon Jamaican Restaurant   **$$**   ★ ★ ★ ★
☎ *(876) 993-8491.*
Regional cuisine. Specialties: Jerk chicken, pork, sausage and lobster.
Lunch: entrées $8–$15.
Dinner: entrées $12–$22.
Near the famed Blue Hole, tucked into a rustic, old stone house with wooden decks (and a raft in case you suddenly want to play Tom Sawyer) is a restaurant that does wonders with Jamaica's fiery jerk meat. Austrian chef Ernst Forstmayr marinates the meats in the traditional manner but cooks over pimento wood after covering them with fresh pimento leaves. The results are a succulent delight. Don't miss the incredible rum cake. Credit cards: MC, V.

De Montevin Lodge   **$$**   ★ ★ ★
21 Fort George Street, ☎ *(876) 993-2604.*
Latin American cuisine.
Lunch: 12:30-2 p.m., prix fixe $11–$20.
Dinner: 7–9 p.m., prix fixe $11–$20.
Errol Flynn's chef used to rule the kitchen at this veddy British Victorian-style inn on Titchfield Hill (I don't think he paid much attention to what he was eating) but the food served here now is unadulterated Jamaican, prepared home-style; the number of courses that arrive depend on what you pay—the cheaper menus are just a tad over $10. Dishes include pumpkin soup, fricassee chicken, dessert and coffee. Reservations recommended.

Trident Hotel Restaurant   **$$$**   ★ ★ ★ ★ ★
☎ *(876) 993-2602.* Associated hotel: *Trident Villas & Hotel.*
International cuisine.
Lunch: Noon–2:30 p.m., entrées $25–$35.
Dinner: 8–10 p.m., prix fixe $50.
Even if you aren't staying at this bastion of subdued luxury, it's a memorable experience to dine in the high-ceilinged restaurant of this 14-acre hotel. Here five course dinners are served on the terrace or in the main dining room by white-gloved waiters; the only sounds you hear are gentle murmurings from fellow guests and the softly-whirring ceiling fans above. Once in a while the stillness is broken by the shrill cries of the tame peacocks that live on the property. Reservations required. Credit cards: A, MC, V.

Where to Shop

More than 100 duty-free shops make Jamaica a great place for bargain hunters. Each U.S. citizen is entitled to $600 worth of duty free merchandise. It is especially good in Montego Bay, Ocho Rios and Kingston. If you plan to do serious shopping on luxury items, check prices before you leave the States. You will generally find good buys on Swiss watches, electronic equipment, gold jewelry, South American emeralds, European crystal, china, French perfumes, British woolens, liquor and cigarettes. Carry identification to get duty-free prices. Local goods that make great souvenirs include Blue Mountain Coffee, Tia Maria (coffee liqueur), Jamaican rum and handmade Macanudo cigars.

Craft markets are common, and a good place to pick up fine wooden carvings (amazingly cheap), straw work, colorful silk-screened resort wear and silk batiks sold by the yard. Be warned: Merchants at the craft markets are sometimes overly aggressive but, thanks to a national campaign, the pressure on tourists has eased of late with craft merchants being forced into sanctioned markets.

Art lovers should head to Betty McGann's Design Centre on Montego Bay's main road westward toward Round Hill. Here you'll find hand-made furnishings using indigenous materials like mahogany and woven banana and plantain. Strawberry Hill has launched a shop where unique, island-style furniture is handcrafted. The Gallery of West Indian Art on Church Street and another smaller outlet at Round Hill features the works of some of Jamaica's great intuitive artists. The Art Gallery in the Wyndham Kingston and another on Garelli Avenue has a range of original paintings by top artists. For antiques, rare books and maps, try the Bolivar Bookshop and Gallery in Kingston. Other good spots include the Contemporary Art Center in Spanish Town, Harmony Hall in Ocho Rios and the Grosvenor Gallery, which showcases the art of emerging Jamaican artists.

For Bob Marley mementoes, try the new Bob Marley Experience, which opened in Half Moon Shopping Village in Montego Bay.

Jamaica Directory

Arrival and Departure

American Airlines and **Air Jamaica** both fly nonstop from New York; **Air Jamaica** also flies nonstop from Miami and has service from Atlanta, Baltimore,

Chicago, Los Angeles, Newark, Orlando and Philadelphia. As of June 15, 1997, Air Jamaica (☎ *(800) 523-5585)* began using Montego Bay airport as its hub, servicing nine U.S. gateways with connections to Barbados, St. Lucia, Antigua, Grand Cayman, Nassau and Turks & Caicos with more than 200 flights a week. **BWIA** flies from San Juan. **Continental** flies in daily from Newark. US Airways flies from Charlotte and Philadelphia. **Northwest Airlines** flies in daily from Minneapolis and Tampa and **Aeroflot** flies in from Havana. **Air Canada** offers service from Toronto and Montreal in conjunction with **Air Jamaica**, and both **British Airways** and **Air Jamaica** fly to London.

Donald Sangester International Airport in Montego Bay is the best place to arrive if you are headed for Montego Bay, Round Hill-Tryall, Ocho Rios, Runaway Bay and Negril. Montego Bay's airport has recently undergone much-needed renovations, and the hustlers that used to make it so unpleasant have largely been banned. If you are staying in Port Antonio, the Blue Mountains, or Kingston, the capital, it's best to land at Norman Manley Airport in Kingston. **Air Jamaica Express** ☎ *(876) 922-4661* offers a shuttle service.

In general, there is no public transportation to and from the airports. Taxi rates are not fixed, but sample fares to popular destinations are usually posted in public places. Negotiate beforehand. All-inclusive resorts provide free transfers from the airport, as do many small hotels when you have booked a package. Sometimes a hotel will throw it in for free if you ask in advance. If transfers are included in your package, you will normally be given a voucher with the name of the operator, and a company representative will meet you at the airport. If not, it's a good idea to ask your travel agent to reserve space in advance. **JUTA** (Jamaica Union of Travellers Association) offers taxis that hold up to five people and run from the nearest airports to hotels in Negril, Ocho Rios and Port Antonio. Runs to Montego Bay and Kingston, which are much closer, are much cheaper. If you are heading beyond Montego Bay (and you have time to spare), you'll save lots of money if you book one of Tropical Tours' air-conditioned minibuses at their desk just outside the luggage area of **Sangster Airport** ☎ *(876) 953-1111*. Tropical Tours runs to Ocho Rios and Negril and charge a per-person fare. Unfortunately, you won't be able to leave until the bus is at least half full.

Business Hours

Stores open weekdays 9 a.m.–5 p.m. and Saturday 9 a.m.–6 p.m. Banks open weekdays 9 a.m.–5 p.m.

Climate

Jamaica has a tropical climate with considerable variation. High temperatures on the coast are usually mitigated by sea breezes, while mountain areas enjoy cooler and less humid conditions. Jamaica lies in the hurricane zone, so always check weather reports before you come (even before you book). Rainfall is plentiful throughout Jamaica; the heaviest season is in May and from August–November. In Kingston temperatures range from 60 degrees Fahrenheit in January to 81 degrees Fahrenheit in July.

Documents

U.S. citizens need either a passport or other proof of citizenship (birth certificate, voter's registration) and a photo ID. All others need a passport. Departure tax is U.S. $15.

Electricity

Current is not consistent throughout the island. Some hotels feature 110, some 220. Adapters and converters for those who need them are supplied by hotels. Ask at your hotel.

Getting Around

Taxis are best taken for short trips. At the airport you can always find a JUTA taxi and coach, as well as at most resorts. If you're planning an out-of-the-way excursion, particularly for dinner, arrange for the driver to pick you up afterwards and negotiate a round-trip fare. Most taxis are unmetered; if you seem to be having trouble with the driver, enlist the help of your hotel's concierge or doorman. When in doubt, ask to see the rate sheet, which all cabs are supposed to carry. After midnight, a 25 percent surcharge is added, though that is often negotiable, particularly if you have arranged for a round-trip deal or if your destination is especially far away.

Buses prove to be a cheap way to toot around the Kingston and Montego Bay areas; they run often but they are often unbearably overcrowded, hot and dirty. Kingston bus fares range from $6 JDS to $15 JDS (about 30 cents to 75 cents in American currency) at press time. The fee depends on the distance traveled. Minibus jitneys also travel around the island, but they are unscheduled and you may have to flag them down in the street—not a reliable way to get somewhere on time. As a result, most people cave in and rent cars or hire a cab.

Car rentals are a good idea on Jamaica since most of the roads are decent and your own car will allow you to conduct your sightseeing at your own pace. You must be able, however, to handle that "British thing" of driving on the left—which takes getting used to—so be careful the first few days. However, be warned that Jamaica has one of the highest accident rates in the world. In 1996, 380 people died in car accidents. Indeed, Jamaica is one of the few places where American Express has withdrawn its car-rental coverage for card holders.

About a dozen agencies on the island offer rentals; among the best are **Avis** ☎ *(800) 331-1084* or *(876) 926-1560*; **Budget** ☎ *(800) 527-0700* or *(876) 952-1943*; and **Hertz** ☎ *(800) 654-3131*. **Island Car Rentals** *(*☎ *(876) 926-8861)* is the island's largest local car rental company. In Ocho Rios you'll find **Sunshine Car Rental** ☎ *(876) 974-2980*. In Port Antonio try **Eastern Car Rental** ☎ *(876) 993-3624*. Major international chains accept bookings through stateside toll-free *(800)* numbers. Always ask for a written confirmation (a fax will do) and be sure you bring it along. There have been numerous cases of lost reservations, and supply often runs low, despite the presence of

2800 rental cars on the island. Be prepared for sticker shock. Also remember to add the cost of gas to your expenses and a 10 percent government tax. Valid U.S. and Canadian licenses are acceptable, but many agencies have a 25-and-over age limit (ask before you book). **Vacation Network**, an agency in Chicago ☎ *(800) 423-4095* offers a special "Fly-Drive Jamaica/The Great Escape Package," which combines a rental car with air transportation and overnight accommodations. Vouchers that come with the package allow you to use them at 50 participating small hotels and inns; the package comes with a guidebook geared for drivers as well as road maps.

Language

The official language is English. The unique Jamaican dialect, used by natives, is patois, a blend of English, Spanish, French and African.

Medical Emergencies

The most efficient and advanced medical facilities are in Kingston, where you will find the country's largest hospital.

Money

The official currency is the Jamaican dollar, which has proven to be quite unstable in relation to the U.S. dollar. However, U.S. dollars are widely-quoted and often accepted in most establishments, but exchange rates will vary (also make sure when you are quoted a price, that you know which "dollar" is being used). All airports have exchange houses; best rates are found at banks. Major credit cards are accepted by most hotels and many restaurants, as are traveler's checks. When changing money, be sure you keep the receipt so you can change the money back before you leave.

Security

Crime in Jamaica is lower per capita than in most large U.S. cities, but the city of Kingston is rife with incidents. However, violent crime typically occurs in Kingston's ghettoes, far from the tourist centers. Crime against tourists is usually garden variety stuff like pickpocketing, and a national program to stamp out crimes against visitors initiated in 1994 has drastically reduced the number of incidents. Still, be aware of your surroundings and carry your valuables in a pouch under your clothing. Do not flash cash in the markets. Use your in-room safe. Take the same precautions you would in any big-city hotel stateside. Don't open your room door unless you called for room service and the person has proper identification. If you are renting a villa, make sure security is provided, because there have been some terrible incidents where it was not. Marijuana is common on the streets of Jamaica, and you can almost bet you'll be approached at some point during your stay; however, Jamaican drug laws are strict and severe. If you buy drugs, you may find yourself arrested by an undercover agent, and Jamaican jails are what you would expect to find in an impoverished nation. Trying to smuggle anything out of the country is absolutely foolhardy. At Montego Bay's airport most recently, departing passengers had to go through not one but two checkpoints, both involving drug-sniffing dogs.

Telephone

The area code is *(876)*. Direct telephone, telegraph, telefax and telex services are all available.

Time

Eastern Standard Time throughout the year.

Tipping

Most Jamaican hotels and restaurants add a service charge of 10 percent; always check first to see if it's included. If not, tip waiters 10–15 percent, depending on the service. Hotel maids should receive about $1–2 per person per day. Airport porters and hotel bellhops should be tipped 50 cents per bag (but not less than a $1). It's not necessary to tip taxi drivers, although 10 percent of the fare is usually appreciated.

Tourist Information

The Jamaica Tourist Board has six offices on the island and throughout major cities in the U.S.; contact ☎ *(800) 233-4582 or (876) 929-9200)*.

When to Go

Carnival is a recent addition to Jamaica, held oddly at Easter time. An annual reggae festival called **Sun Fest** is usually held in the beginning of August in Montego Bay at the Bob Marley Centre. **Reggae Sunsplash Festival** will he held in Ocho Rios Feb. 5–8, 1998. The **Independence** celebrations *(☎ (876) 926-5726)*, also held for a week in August, are colorful blowout bashes (beginning usually on Independence Day, August 1). In October, the annual **International Marlin Tournament** at Port Antonio attracts fishermen from all over the world and includes festivals other than fishing. Contact the Tourist Board for a twice-yearly calendar of events covering a wide spectrum of sports and arts festivals.

JAMAICA HOTELS	RMS	RATES	PHONE	CR. CARDS
Montego Bay				
★★★★★ **Half Moon Golf, Tennis & Beach Club**	424	$265–$600	(800) 626-0592	A, MC, V
★★★★★ **Round Hill Hotel & Villas**	110	$160–$420	(800) 972-2159	A, MC, V
★★★★ **Tryall Club Resort & Villas, The**	69	$375–$1000	(800) 238-5290	A, DC, MC, V
★★★★ **Wyndham Rose Hall Golf & Beach Resort**	489	$145–$230	(800) 996-3426	A, CB, DC, MC, V
★★★ **Coyaba Beach Resort & Club**	50	$140–$326	(800) 237-3237	A, MC, V
★★★ **Sandals Montego Bay**	243	$403–$494	(800) 726-3257	A, MC, V
★★★ **Sandals Royal Jamaican**	190	$220–$640	(800) 726-3257	A, MC, V
★★★ **SeaCastles**	198	$90–$135	(800) 752-6824	A, MC, V
★★ **Breezes Montego Bay**	124	$415–$830	(800) 859-7873	A, MC, V

JAMAICA

JAMAICA HOTELS		RMS	RATES	PHONE	CR. CARDS
★★	Doctors Cave Beach Hotel	90	$80–$160	(800) 223-6510	A, MC, V
★★	Grand Montego Beach Resort	132	$135–$300	(800) 999-9182	A, MC, V
★★	Holiday Inn SunSpree Resort	523	$120–$190	(800) 352-6731	A, MC, V
★★	Montego Bay Club Resort	51	$50–$155	(800) 223-9815	A, MC, V
★★	Richmond Hill Inn	20	$75–$90	(876) 952-3859	A, MC, V
★★	Sandals Inn	52	$330–$390	(800) 726-3257	A, MC, V

Ocho Rios

		RMS	RATES	PHONE	CR. CARDS
★★★★★	Jamaica Inn	45	$200–$475	(800) 837-4608	A, MC, V
★★★★	Boscobel Beach Hotel	228	$415–$995	(800) 467-8737	A, MC
★★★★	Breezes Golf & Beach Resort	238	$240–$439	(800) 467-8737	A, MC, V
★★★★	Ciboney Ocho Rios	282	$400–$424	(800) 333-3333	A, MC, V
★★★★	Franklyn D. Resort	76	$280–	(888) 337-5437	A, MC, V
★★★★	Grand Lido Sans Souci	105	$544–$640	(800) 467-8737	A, MC, V
★★★★	Plantation Inn	80	$300–$799	(800) 752-6824	A, DC, MC, V
★★★★	Renaissance Jamaica Grande Resort	720	$320	(800) 468-3571	A, MC, V
★★★★	Sandals Dunn's River Golf Resort & Spa	256	$420–$560	(800) 726-3257	A, MC, V
★★★★	Sandals Ocho Rios Resort & Golf Club	237	$420–$560	(800) 726-3257	A, MC, V
★★★	Couples Jamaica	172	$410–$540	(800) 423-4095	A, MC, V
★★★	Eaton Hall Beach Hotel	52	$135–$299	(809) 973-3503	A, CB, MC, V
★★★	Enchanted Garden	113	$140–$340	(800) 554-2008	A, D, MC, V
★★★	H.E.A.R.T. Country Club	20	$55–$75	(809) 973-2671	A, MC
★★	Ambiance Jamaica	80	$70–$138	(800) 523-6304	A, MC
★★	Club Caribbean/ Alamanda Inn	128	$125–$295	(800) 223-9815	A, MC, V
★★	Club Jamaica Beach Resort	95	$180–$290	(800) 423-4095	A, MC, V
★★	Hibiscus Lodge	26	$93–$115	(876) 974-2676	A, CB, MC, V
★★	Portside Villas & Condos	15	$75–$75	(876) 973-2007	A, MC, V
★★	Shaw Park Beach Hotel	118	$168–$182	(876) 974-2552	A, MC, V

JAMAICA

JAMAICA HOTELS	RMS	RATES	PHONE	CR. CARDS
Negril				
★★★★ Grand Lido Negril	200	$350–$600	(800) 467-8737	A, MC, V
★★★★ Swept Away	134	$450–$625	(800) 545-7937	A, MC, V
★★★ Beachcomber Club	45	$100–$325	(800) 423-4095	A, MC
★★★ Beaches Negril	225	$480–$620	(800) 726-3257	A, MC, V
★★★ Caves, The	8	$295–$360	(800) 688-7678	A, MC, V
★★★ Charela Inn	39	$80–$170	(800) 423-4095	MC, V
★★★ Hedonism II	280	$205–$376	(800) 467-8737	A, MC
★★★ Poinciana Beach Resort	130	$155–$179	(800) 468-6728	A, MC
★★★ Point Village	256	$100–$230	(800) 752-6824	A, MC
★★★ Rockhouse	28	$80–$100	(876) 957-4373	A, MC, V
★★★ Sandals Negril Beach Resort & Spa	219	$480–$580	(800) 726-3257	A, MC, V
★★★ Xtabi On the Cliffs	26	$50–$145	(876) 957-4336	A, MC
★★ Chuckles	73	$75–$260	(876) 957-4250	A, MC, V
★★ Drumville Cove Resort	20	$40–$100	(800) 423-4095	A, MC, V
★★ Hotel SamSara	52	$35–$115	(876) 957-4395	A, MC
★★ Negril Beach Club Hotel	100	$77–$185	(800) 526-2422	A, MC
★★ Negril Cabins	50	$110–$190	(800) 382-3444	A, MC
★★ Negril Gardens	65	$165–$370	(800) 752-6824	A, MC, V
★★ Negril Tree House Resort	70	$85–$150	(800) 634-7451	A, MC, V
★ Foote Prints on the Sands	33	$85–$145	(876) 957-4300	A, MC
★ Negril Inn	46	$115–$145	(876) 957-4209	A, MC, V
Treasure Beach/Mandeville				
★★ Astra Country Inn	22	$60–$115	(876) 962-3265	A, MC
★★ Jake's	10	$75–$95	(800) 688-7678	A, MC, V
★★ Mandeville Hotel	60	$60–$200	(876) 962-2460	A, MC
★★ Natania's Guest House	8	$50–$60	(800) 330-2332	
Kingston				
★★★★ Crowne Plaza Kingston	135	$129–$149	(800) 618-6534	A, CB, DC, MC, V
★★★★ Grand Lido Braco	284	$270–$280	(800) 467-8737	
★★★★ Strawberry Hill	14	$195–$450	(800) 688-7678	A, MC, V

JAMAICA HOTELS		RMS	RATES	PHONE	CR. CARDS
★★★	Jamaica Pegasus Hotel	350	$180–$564	(876) 926-3690	A, DC, MC, V
★★★	Wyndham Kingston Hotel	384	$160–$575	(800) 996-3426	A, DC, MC, V
★★	Morgan's Harbour Hotel	45	$98–$150	(876) 967-8075	A, MC, V

Port Antonio

★★★★★	Trident Villas & Hotel	28	$365–$800	(800) 423-4095	A, MC, V
★★★	Goblin Hill Villas	28	$1350–$2135	(800) 423-4095	A, MC
★★★	Hotel Mocking Bird Hill	10	$95–$140	(876) 993-3370	MC, V
★★★	Jamaica Palace Hotel	80	$130–$325	(800) 423-4095	A, MC
★★	Bonnie View Plantation	20	$60–$98	(876) 993-2752	A, MC, V
★★	Dragon Bay	86	$96–$132	(800) 423-4095	A, MC, V
★★	Fern Hill Club	31	$145–$230	(876) 993-7374	A, MC, V
★★	Navy Island Marina Resort	21	$50–$100	(800) 423-4095	A, MC, V

JAMAICA RESTAURANTS		PHONE	ENTREE	CR.C ARDS

Montego Bay

Italian Cuisine

★★★	Reading Reef Club	(876) 952-5909	$10–$22	A, MC, V
★★	Julia's Italian	(876) 952-1772	$35–$35	A, MC, V

Regional Cuisine

★★★★	Norma's at the Wharfhouse	(876) 979-2745	$26–$34	MC, V
★★★★	Sugar Mill	(876) 953-2228	$14–$39	A, MC, V
★★	Pork Pit	(876) 952-1046	$3–$10	
★★	Town House	(876) 952-2660	$13–$30	A, DC, MC, V

Ocho Rios

Italian Cuisine

★★★★★	Evita's	(876) 974-2333	$8–$24	A, MC, V

Regional Cuisine

★★★★	Jamaica Inn	(876) 974-2514	$10–$30	MC, V
★★★	Almond Tree	(876) 974-2813	$12–$26	A, DC, MC, V

JAMAICA

JAMAICA RESTAURANTS	PHONE	ENTREE	CR.C ARDS
Negril			
Continental Cuisine			
★★ Tan-ya's	(876) 957-4041	$5–$19	A, MC, V
Regional Cuisine			
★★★★ Hungry Lion	(876) 957-4486	$8–$20	A, MC, V
Seafood Cuisine			
★★ Cosmo's	(876) 957-4330	$5–$12	MC, V
★ Rick's Cafe	(876) 957-4335	$11–$28	MC, V
Kingston			
Continental Cuisine			
★★ Devon House Restaurant	(876) 929-6602	$6–$16	A, MC, V
International Cuisine			
★★★★ Blue Mountain Inn	(876) 927-1700	$24–$30	A, DC, MC, V
★★★ Ivor	(876) 702-0276	$23–$27	A, MC, V
Latin American Cuisine			
★ Hot Pot, The	(876) 929-3906	$3–$7	MC, V
Regional Cuisine			
★★★★★ Strawberry Hill	(876) 944-8400	$18–$27	DC, MC, V
★★ Gap Cafe, The	(876) 997-3032	$12–$22	A, MC, V
★ Chelsea Jerk Centre	(876) 926-6322	$3–$11	None
Port Antonio			
International Cuisine			
★★★★★ Trident Hotel Restaurant	(876) 993-2602	$25–$50	A, MC, V
Latin American Cuisine			
★★★ De Montevin Lodge	(876) 993-2604	$11–$20	
Regional Cuisine			
★★★★ Blue Lagoon Jamaican Restaurant	(876) 993-8491	$8–$22	MC, V

MARTINIQUE

Mt. Pelée towers above St. Pierre village in northern Martinique.

Martinique is a little bit of foie gras in the middle of the Caribbean. From the cuisine to the chic style of the women, to the lilt of the language, Martinique exudes the charm of its mother country—France. But add to that a decidedly West Indian cachet and shopping values that would make a Parisian's jaw drop open, and you have a tiny island nation waiting to be loved. Rising from beaches to rainforest to the heights of a volcanic mountain that wiped out an entire city in 1902, Martinique is rife with opportunities to dive, trek, sail, surf, parasail and pursue just about any other sport imaginable—from mountain biking to deep-sea fishing in some of the clearest waters in the Caribbean. Despite a population of 389,000, the island has stayed ecologically pure enough to still boast good sightings of many birds in the mangroves, including the yellow-breasted sandbird, a symbol of the island. Best of all, tourism is just beginning to snap at the heels of this nearly forgotten island and locals are still green enough—businesswise—to have escaped becoming jaded. Of course, on an island such as this one, there will always be a few cases of French snoots, but try to ignore them and concentrate on the natural beauties.

BEST BETS FOR...

Bird's-Eye View

Fifty miles long and 22 miles wide, Martinique covers 425 square miles. Of its neighboring islands, Dominica lies to the north and St. Lucia to the south; Miami is 1470 miles away. San Juan, Puerto Rico, is only 425 miles away. Martinique comes from volcanic origins, and today the 4575-foot Mount Pelée in the Parc Naturel Régional de la Martinique is the only active volcano, situated in the northwest corner of the island. Most of the island is mountainous. In the center of the island lie the Pitons du Carbet, and the Montagne du Vauclin is in the south. The capital city of Fort-de-France, built like an amphitheater around the yacht-filled harbor, is backed by luxurious mountains and is one of the more picturesque settings in the Caribbean. The north of the island is covered by an enormous rainforest; banana and pineapples are cultivated there, while sugarcane dominates the rest of the island. Black sandy coves are found throughout the north and along the rugged coast open to the Atlantic, white and gray sands characterize the beaches facing the Caribbean and in the south. Salines Beach, on the southernmost tip of the island, looks as if it is straight out of a beautiful postcard. On the east coast, the peninsula of Caravelle, the oldest volcanic formation of the island, stretches into the rough Atlantic, boasting a mangrove swamp lined with a coral reef. Along the Caravelle coastline are a large number of picturesque coves and bays. Fort-de-France is situated on the western coast, while the burgeoning town of Lamentin is inland. The new International Fort-de-France Lamentin Airport has been a boon for the local tourist industry. Located adjacent to the old terminal at Lamentin, it is 10 minutes away from Fort-de-France. Martinique's climate is mild, averaging 79°F. Breezes known as *les alizés* blow in from the east and northeast, constantly cooling the air.

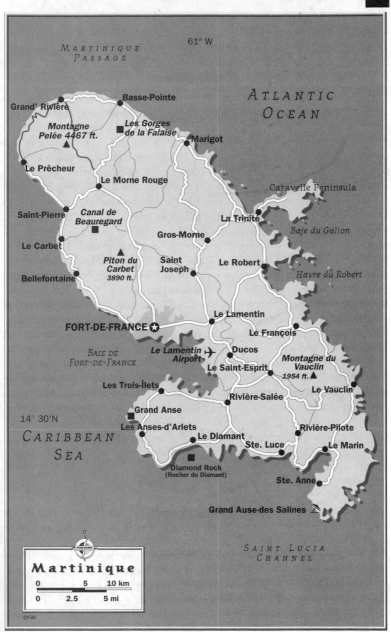

MARTINIQUE PASSAGE

61° W

ATLANTIC OCEAN

Grand' Rivière

Basse-Pointe

Montagne Pelée 4467 ft. ▲

Les Gorges de la Falaise

Marigot

Le Prêcheur

Le Morne Rouge

Caravelle Peninsula

Saint-Pierre

Canal de Beauregard

La Trinité

Baie du Galion

Le Carbet

Gros-Morne

Piton du Carbet 3890 ft. ▲

Saint Joseph

Le Robert

Bellefontaine

Havre du Robert

Le Lamentin

FORT-DE-FRANCE ✪

Le François

BAIE DE FORT-DE-FRANCE

Le Lamentin Airport ✈

Ducos

Le Saint-Esprit

Montagne du Vauclin 1954 ft. ▲

14° 30'N

CARIBBEAN SEA

Les Trois-Îlets

Rivière-Salée

Le Vauclin

Grand Anse

Les Anses-d'Arlets

Le Diamant

Ste. Luce

Rivière-Pilote

Le Marin

Diamond Rock (Rocher du Diamant) ■

Ste. Anne

Grand Ause-des-Salines

SAINT LUCIA CHANNEL

N

Martinique

0   5   10 km

0   2.5   5 mi

©FWI

History

Columbus was stunned when he chanced upon Martinique—historians can't decide whether it was 1493 or 1502—but phrases like "the most fertile, the softest...the most charming place in the world" leave no doubt regarding his true feelings. Carib Indians were the resident locals on Martinique when Columbus happened by. Martinica was the name Columbus bestowed on the volcanic island, in honor of St. Martin. The Caribs called it *madinina*, meaning "island of flowers." The Caribs proved too hostile for the Spaniards who moved on to other shores, but they continued to fight the French who settled on the island in 1635. Twenty-five years later the French signed a treaty with the Caribs who agreed to stay on the Atlantic side of the island; nevertheless, they were soon exterminated. The next 200 years was a struggle between the Brits and the French. In 1762 the Brits took control, only to pass it over in exchange for Canada, Senegal, the Grenadines, St. Vincent and Tobago. France remained with Guadeloupe and Martinique because they were knee-deep in the sugarcane. The English took over again between 1794 and 1802, at the request of plantation owners who needed assistance in the face of growing dissent among slaves. Slavery was abolished in 1848 by the French but not before a major slave rebellion occurred in 1879, encouraged by the French Revolution. Eventually, a new wave of immigrant workers from India began to change the dominant color of skin in the island's population. Martinique finally became a French Department in 1946 and a region in 1974.

People

There are about 359,000 people in Martinique, about half of whom live in the capital of Fort-de-France. A racially mixed batch of Africans, East Indians, Caucasians and others, they are all considered citizens of France, and governed by a general council and a Régional Council elected locally. There is also a prefect (governor), appointed by the French Government. Unemployment is quite high; about a third of the people have no jobs. About a quarter of those employed are in tourism. To get a good glimpse of social life, hang out in the Savane, a 12-acre park of lawn, shade trees, footpaths and benches where families relax and children play, and old men play serious

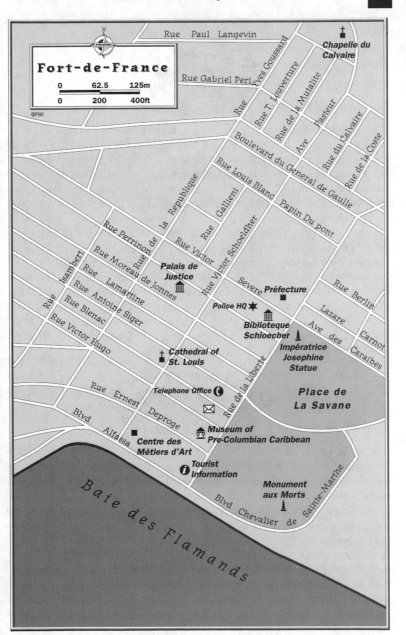

Fort-de-France

games of dominoes. Locals are called Martiniquais, the women Martiniquaises.

You will find magnificent, palm-fringed **Grande Anse des Salines** at the island's southern tip. It is less visited by tourists than the beaches at Pointe du Bout, although it can get more crowded on weekends. Nearby is the petite pretty village of **Anse d'Arlets**. **Diamant Beach**, just south of Anse d'Arlets, is a paradisiacal stretch of 2.5 miles along the south coast dominated by the **Diamond Rock**, a famous volcanic rock that stands about a mile out to sea where the English stationed cannons in the 18th century (British ships still passing it salute her Majesty's "Ship Diamond Rock"). The beach is nearly deserted and fringed with coconut palms and almond trees. It is not advised for swimming since the currents are strong. From the town of Le Marin south, you'll find long white sand beaches with palm trees and calm, clear seas. **Ste. Anne**, where the Club Med is, has its own fine beach, adjacent to the public one, where you can see a terrific view of the southwest coast. There are many places for shade on Ste. Anne under trees that sometimes overhang into the sea. There are lots of bars and restaurants here. There's a family beach on the road heading east from Marin called **Cap Chevalier**.

Walls and caves, reefs and wrecks, Martinique offers a little of everything for divers. Sites are situated along the western coast, north and south of Fort-de-France, with the scalloped coastline between Pointe du Bout and Le Diamant noteworthy for its abundance of smaller reef fish and colorful coral life, particularly Cap Salomon and nearby Anses d'Arlets. Because the island is so densely populated, many of the reefs are overfished and some of the coral is damaged. However, the bay off St. Pierre provides one of the Caribbean's most unusual wreck sites, a veritable graveyard created by the eruption of Mt. Pelée in 1902. There are over a dozen dive companies on Martinique, and most provide the French "baptism" dive for first-timers, priced only slightly more than a single-tank dive; many resorts also provide underwater initiation in a hotel pool at no charge. Two-tank boat trips are not generally offered in the French West Indies; it is *de rigueur* to share a casual meal between dives. A medical certificate must be produced before diving, and although PADI and NAUI instructors can be found, it's helpful to be familiar with French dive standards before heading out on a boat.

Dive Shops

Espace De Plongee Meridien

> *Pointe du Bout;* ☎ *(596) 66-01-79.*
> Primarily serves clientele of the Meridien, but welcomes non-guests. Groups limited to 15; there is one PADI instructor on staff, as well as English-speaking staff. One tank dive, $41; Baptism, $52. Half-day snorkeling trips on dive boats, $10.

Tropicasub

> *St. Pierre;* ☎ *(596) 78-38-03.*
> Lionel and Françoise Lafont have been operating this shop for ten years. Two dives daily, 9:30 and 3; closed Monday. One tank dive $41; Baptism, $45. Maximum group size, 10, including instructors. Snorkel trips available. English language staff.

Showcasing a variety of trails through a surprisingly diverse selection of landscapes and climate regions, Martinique is truly a hiker's paradise. All of this coexists in relatively close proximity to the island's fast-paced and cosmopolitan lifestyle, creating a breathtaking juxtaposition, even by Caribbean standards, where contrasting environments are the spice of life. The island's population and tourist center is heavily concentrated in and around Fort-de-France, leaving Martinique's outlying forests well-visited, but comparatively unscathed by development. Hikers must beware the rare fer de lance, a poisonous snake found predominantly in the drier areas to the south (see "On Foot" introductory chapter). The hikes listed below are merely the *crème de la crème* of a rich and impressive lot. An excellent trail guidebook, *Guide des Sentiers Pedestres à la Martinique*, (in French) is available in local bookstores, and the tourist maps of the island mark many of the major trails.

Trekking Tours

Parc Naturel Régional de La Martinique

> *Fort-de-France; (596-64-42-59).*
> Provides an assortment of guided hiking tours within the park. $12 per person. They also sell a fine guide to the best hikes, *Les Plus Belles Balades de la Martinique.* (in French); $34.

MARTINIQUE

What Else to See

The capital of Martinique, **Fort-de-France**, is one of the most appealing cities in the Caribbean to see on foot. Among the first sites to check out is the city's architectural pride and joy, the **Bibliothèque Schoelcher**, or Schoelcher Library, a Romanesque Byzantine treasure constructed a century ago for the Paris Exposition of 1889, then dismantled and shipped to Martinique piece by piece. It sits close to **La Savane**, the city's central park, full of exotic flora; it's a lovely place to stroll and eavesdrop on locals. La Savane's gardens boast two impressive statues: one of Pierre Belain d'Esnambuce, the French nobleman who claimed the island for France in 1635; the other of Marie Josephe Rose Tascher de la Pagerie, who was born in Trois Ilets across the bay and made history as Napoleon's Empress Joséphine. Narrow streets with beautiful balconies overhanging sidewalks filled with shops and restaurants lead you to another must-see: the **Cathedral of Saint-Louis**. Nearby is the **Palais de Justice** with its statue of Victor Schoelcher. The **Musée Departemental de la Martinique** presents archaeological finds from prehistoric Martinique. The **Jardin de Balata** (Balata gardens) is a tropical botanical park around a restored Créole house. It's a good place for browsing and relaxing. By the **Rivière Madame** (Madame River) you'll find the bustling fish markets. If you want a guided tour, excellent ones are offered by **Azimut** ☎ *(596) 60-16-59.*

North along the coast, you'll discover **St. Pierre**, considered the Paris of the West Indies until 1902 when Mount Pelée erupted and spilled ash and gas, Pompeii-style, all over it. You can see the full extent of the tragedy in the exhibits of the museum there. To get there with style, take the little train called **Cyparis Express**, which presents one-hour tours during the week and half-hour tours on the weekend. The drive from Fort-de-France is less than an hour, but make time to stop at such atmospheric fishing villages as **Case-Pilote** and **Bellefontaine**, as well as **Carbet**, where Columbus landed in 1502; Gauguin lived and painted there in 1887. A museum featuring his work is found in Carbet.

In the north, a dazzling route through the rainforest, called **La Trace**, is lush with banana and pineapple plantations, avocado groves, cane fields and lovely inns such as **Leyritz** and **Habitation Lagrange**. Le Prêcheur, the last village along the northern Caribbean coast, is known for hot springs of volcanic origin as well as the **Tomb of the Carib Indians**. Ajoupa-Bouillon is an enchanting flower-lined town with a nature trail called **Les Ombrages**.

Rum is king on Martinique and most visitors enjoy sampling the island-brewed wares at distilleries. The St. James Distillery at Sainte-Marie in the north operates the **Musée du Rhum**. Nearby is a straw-weaving center called **Morne des Esses**. The **Fonds Saint Jacques**, a historically important 17th-century sugar estate in the north, attracts visitors with its museum, Musée du Père Labat. A modern museum devoted to sugar and rum, the **Maison de la Canne**, is just outside Trois Ilets. Also near Trois Ilets is Joséphine Bonaparte's birthplace, **La Pagerie**, and a museum filled with her mementos.

Martinique is often known as the Isle of Flowers and there are numerous floral gardens to visit. **Morne Rouge**, a pretty town with a cool climate, is the site of **MacIntosh Plantation**, a renowned cultivator of Martinique's best known flower, the anthurium. Near La Pagerie is **Parc des Floralies**, a peaceful and pretty botanical park. One of the most beautiful is the **Jardin de Balata** on the Route de La Trace in the suburbs north of the capital. A short drive from here is the **Sacré Coeur de Balata**, a replica of the well-known basilica that dominates Montmartre in Paris. Other attractions south of Martinique include the H.M.S. *Diamond Rock*, a kind of Rock of Gibraltar Caribbean-style rising 600 feet from the sea as used by the British in 1804 as a sloop of war. Anyone not venturing into the depths of the sea with a dive tank should really take a ride on the thrilling **Aquascope**, a semi-submersible craft that makes about an hour tour. One is located at the Marina Pointe du Bout ☎ *(596) 68-36-09* and the other at Le Marin ☎ *(596) 74-87-41*.

Martinique has two **gambling casinos**. Located in the Meridien and the La Batelière hotels, they are open nightly from 9 p.m. to 3 a.m. Both feature American and French roulette and blackjack. Proof of identity in the form of a passport, driver's license or other photo ID is required. The legal gambling age is 18. Dress is casual and an entrance fee of $12 is charged. There is no fee to play the slot machines, which are located just outside the casinos.

There are about a dozen good nightspots in Fort-de-France featuring Latin music or jazz, a few piano bars and late night discos in the larger hotels. The legal drinking age is 18. Any town celebrating a *fête patronale* will feature street dancing where you are welcome to participate.

Museums and Exhibits

Maison de la Canne   ★★★

> *Trois-Ilets.*
> *Hours open: 9 a.m.–5:30 p.m.*
> You've probably always taken sugar for granted, but won't any more after touring this museum dedicated to the history and production of sugarcane. Signage is in both French and English. Really quite interesting General admission: $15.

Musée Departementale de Martin   ★★★

> *9 Rue de la Liberte, Fort-de-France.*

Decent exhibits on the history of slavery, clothing and furniture from the colonial period and artifacts from the pre-Columbian eras of the Arawak and the Carib indians. General admission: $15.

Musée Paul Gauguin   ★★★

Anse-Turin, Le Carbet.
Hours open: 10 a.m.–5 p.m.

Famed artist Paul Gauguin lived in Martinique in 1887. This museum pays homage to that period, with reproductions of works he created while here, letters and other memorabilia pertaining to his life. The museum also displays the works of other noted artists and changing displays by local artists. General admission: $10.

Musée Vulcanologique   ★★★★

St. Pierre.
Hours open: 9 a.m.–5 p.m.

American Frank Perrot established this museum in 1932, an homage to St. Pierre, the island's oldest city and a bustling one at that, until a devastating eruption of volcano Mt. Pelee on May 8, 1902. The entire town was buried in minutes and some 30,000 residents perished, all except for a prisoner whose underground cell saved him. (He later joined Barnum and Bailey's circus as a sideshow oddity.) Residents had been warned of the imminent danger but city fathers played it down because of an upcoming election. St. Pierre today is a modest village, but you can get a feel for its former glory days at the museum, which exhibits photographs and documents from the period. General admission: $10.

Musée de Poupees Vegetales   ★★★

Leyritz Plantation, Basse-Pointe.
Hours open: 7 a.m.–5:30 p.m.

Certainly the only one of its kind in Martinique (or possibly the world for that matter), this small museum displays sculptures made entirely of leaves and plants, designed to look like famous women in French history. It is located at the scenic Leyritz Plantation, which is detailed in the lodging section. General admission: $15.

Musée de la Pagerie   ★★★★

Trois-Ilets, Fort-de-France.
Hours open: 9 a.m.–5 p.m.

Located on the grounds of the birthplace of Josephine, Napoleon's wife and empress of France from 1804-1809, this museum is housed in a stone building that was formerly the kitchen (the rest of the estate was destroyed by hurricane). Memorabilia of her life, her childhood bed, and a passionate love letter by Napoleon are among the interesting exhibits. General admission: $15.

Musée du Rhum   ★★★

Ste. Marie.
Hours open: 9 a.m.–6 p.m.

The St. James Distillery owns this monument to rum, located on a sugar plantation in an old creole house. After a guided tour showing the history and production of rum, you can taste-test the product yourself.

Parks and Gardens

Jardin de Balata   ★★★

> *Route de Balata, Balata.*
> *Hours open: 9 a.m.–5 p.m.*
> This tropical park, located on a hillside some 1475 feet above sea level, has stunning views and more than a thousand varieties of trees, flowers and plants. A lovely spot to while away the afternoon exploring winding walkways, lily pond, and breathtaking overlooks. General admission: $30.

Tours

Martinique Aquarium   ★★★

> *Boulevard de Marne, Fort-de-France.*
> *Hours open: 9 a.m.–7 p.m.*
> This large aquarium has more than 2000 fish and sea creatures representing some 250 species. Of special interest are the shark tank and piranha pool. General admission: $38.

Zoo de Carbet   ★★★

> *Le Coin, Le Carbet.*
> *Hours open: 9 a.m.–6 p.m.*
> Also called the Amazona Zoo, this park showcases 70 species from the Amazon Basin, including birds and big cats. General admission: $15.

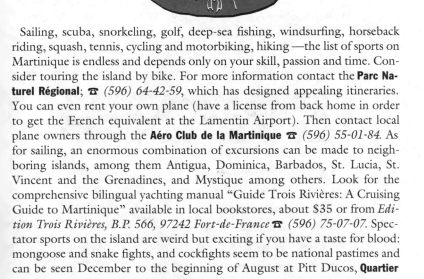

Sailing, scuba, snorkeling, golf, deep-sea fishing, windsurfing, horseback riding, squash, tennis, cycling and motorbiking, hiking —the list of sports on Martinique is endless and depends only on your skill, passion and time. Consider touring the island by bike. For more information contact the **Parc Naturel Régional**; ☎ *(596) 64-42-59*, which has designed appealing itineraries. You can even rent your own plane (have a license from back home in order to get the French equivalent at the Lamentin Airport). Then contact local plane owners through the **Aéro Club de la Martinique** ☎ *(596) 55-01-84*. As for sailing, an enormous combination of excursions can be made to neighboring islands, among them Antigua, Dominica, Barbados, St. Lucia, St. Vincent and the Grenadines, and Mystique among others. Look for the comprehensive bilingual yachting manual "Guide Trois Rivières: A Cruising Guide to Martinique" available in local bookstores, about $35 or from *Edition Trois Rivières, B.P. 566, 97242 Fort-de-France* ☎ *(596) 75-07-07*. Spectator sports on the island are weird but exciting if you have a taste for blood: mongoose and snake fights, and cockfights seem to be national pastimes and can be seen December to the beginning of August at Pitt Ducos, **Quartier**

Brac ☎ *(596) 56-05-60* and **Pitt Marceny**. Horse racing can be found at the Carère racetrack in Lamentin ☎ *(596) 51-25-09*.

Bicycling

Cycling is the unofficial sport of the French West Indies, celebrated annually in July with the Tour de la Martinique, a sort of mini Tour de France with palm trees. The **Parc Naturel Régional** has created some interesting itineraries ☎ *(596) 64-42-59*. For mountain bike rentals, check with **V.T. Tilt** in Pointe du Bout ☎ *(596) 66-01-01*, **Basalt** in Bellefontaine ☎ *(596) 55-01-84*, both of which provide cycling tours.

Golf

Trois-Ilets, near Pointe du Bont.

Martinique's only course, the **Golf de Imperatrice Josephine**, was designed by Robert Trent Jones Sr. The 18-hole, par-71 course covers 150 acres and is quite scenic.

The grounds include a pro shop (English-speaking), restaurant, and three tennis courts. Greens fees are about $49; guests of some hotels receive a discount.

Horseback Riding

Various locations, Martinique.

Several outfits offer trail rides: **La Cavale** ☎ *(596) 76-22-94*, **Ranch Jack** ☎ *(596) 68-37-67*, **Black Horse Ranch** ☎ *(596) 68-37-80*, and **Ranch Val d'Or** ☎ *(596) 76-70-58*.

Watersports

Various locations, Fort-de-France.

Most hotels offer watersports. If not, try one of the following. Boating and sailing: in Pointe du Bont try **Soleil et Voile** ☎ *(596) 66-09-14* or **Captains Shop** ☎ *(596) 66-06-77*, **Ship Shop** in Fort-de-France ☎ *(596) 71-43-40*, **Carib Charter** in Schoelcher ☎ *(596) 73-08-80*, **Caraibes Nautique** in Trois-Ilets ☎ *(596) 66-06-06*, and **Cercle Nautique** in Schoelcher ☎ *(596) 61-15-21*. For snorkeling: **Aquarium** in Fort-de-France ☎ *(596) 61-49-49*.

Where to Stay

★★★★★	**Fielding's Highest Rated Hotels in Martinique**	
★★★★★	**Sofitel Bakoua Hotel**	$122–$530
★★★★	**Habitation Lagrange**	$220–$365
★★★★	**Le Meridien Trois-Ilets**	$132–$327
★★★	**Fregate Bleue**	$100–$225
★★★	**La Bateliere Hotel**	$135–$400
★★★	**Leyritz Plantation**	$68–$148
★★★	**Novotel Diamant**	$110–$375

Fielding's Most Romantic Hotels in Martinique

★★★★★	Sofitel Bakoua Hotel	$122–$530
★★★★	Habitation Lagrange	$220–$365
★★★	Leyritz Plantation	$68–$148
★★	Diamont les Bains	$76–$120

Fielding's Best Value Hotels in Martinique

★★	Victoria Junior	$45–$64
★★	Martinique Cottages	$53–$62
★★	Rivage Hotel	$45–$73
★★★	Leyritz Plantation	$68–$148
★★	St. Aubin Hotel	$55–$105

Accommodations on Martinique run from the 300-room resort to the inn with 10 rooms. You can choose between resorts happily ensconced on the seashore to guesthouses run by congenial families, part of the "Relais Creoles" organization. Prices range from expensive to modest. All of the larger hotels have sports facilities, a choice of restaurants and evening entertainment. All beachfront hotels offer a full watersports program. Some hotels have kitchenette studios.

An important note: most of the hotels have two rate cards—one in American dollars and one in French francs. However, the exchange rate between the two currencies changes daily. At press time, the franc was trading at its lowest rate in years and, as a result, a number of hotels did not raise their U.S. *dollar* rate card for the 1998 season. The situation may have changed by the time you read this, and if the franc has further declined, you'll want to negotiate your room rate carefully to make sure you are obtaining the best price. For hotels that did not provide prices in dollars, we have used an exchange rate of 5.5 francs for one U.S. dollar.

Hotels and Resorts

Sofitel Bakoua Hotel, perched on a hillside, is the leading resort, retaining a distinct local feel in the historical plantation-style surroundings. **La Bateliere Hotel**, with its recent renovations, comes in second for style, service and location.

Balisier $56–$77 ★

Fort-de-France, ☎ (596) 71-46-54, FAX (596) 71-46-54.
Single: $56–$77. Double: $67–$77.

Set in the heart of Fort-de-France, this budget property offers small and simple rooms with narrow beds. There are also three apartments with kitchenettes. There are no dining or recreation facilities on-site, but many within walking distance. The view of the port is nice; street noise can be a problem. 27 rooms. Credit cards: A, MC.

Diamant les Bains $76–$120 ★★

Diamant, ☎ (800) 823-2002, (596) 76-40-14, FAX (596) 76-27-00.
Closed Date: September.
Single: $76–$95. Double: $109–$120.

Set on a sandy beach overlooking Diamond Rock, this family-run property accommodates guests in the main house or in small, rustic bungalows with refrigerators. Bungalow decor is nice: local art, rattan furnishings and wood ceilings—these rooms are right on the beach. There's a pool ringed by flowers and a restaurant, with watersports nearby. Service is cheerful and caring. 24 rooms. Credit cards: MC, V.

Domaine de Belfond $132–$244 ★★

Ste. Anne, ☎ (800) 322-2223, (596) 76-92-32, FAX (596) 76-91-40.
Single: $132–$232. Double: $144–$244.

A favorite with Europeans and now part of the Anchorage chain, this recently renovated village-style resort is perched on a hillside near the sea. Accommodations are in country French-style buildings, each with its own check-in and swimming pool. Rooms are very nicely done with lovely furnishings, high ceilings and comfortable appointments. All have kitchenettes either inside or on the balcony. The fabulous beach at Salines is a 10-minute walk. 186 rooms. Credit cards: A, MC, V.

L'Imperatrice Village $107–$175 ★★

Anse Mitan, ☎ (596) 66-08-09, FAX (596) 66-07-10.
Single: $107–$127. Double: $135–$175.

Set on tropical grounds across the bay from Fort-de-France, this resort houses guests in standard rooms, studios, and bungalows with kitchens. All are on the modest side, but pleasant enough. A bit off the beaten path, so you'll want to rent a car. On-site features include a restaurant and bar, pool and games like billiards and ping-pong. 59 rooms. Credit cards: A, MC, V.

La Bateliere Hotel $135–$400 ★★★

Schoelcher, ☎ (800) 223-6510, (596) 61-49-49, FAX (596) 61-70-57.
Single: $135–$400. Double: $135–$400.

Located on 6.5 acres on a bluff overlooking the sea, this five-story hotel opened as a Hilton, but has recently been refurbished. Guest rooms are spacious, with all the modern amenities. For recreation, there are eight lighted tennis courts and a pro, all watersports, a pool, excursions in a cabin cruiser, and a fine, sandy beach. Several restaurants, a disco, and the island's new casino are around the corner. Dependable service. 199 rooms. Credit cards: A, MC, V.

La Dunette $55–$125 ★

Ste. Anne, ☎ (596) 76-73-90, FAX (596) 76-76-05.
Closed Date: Two weeks in July.

Single: $55–$100. Double: $73–$125.
Located in a fishing village, this three-story hotel offers simple rooms, some with plant-lined balconies, all with air conditioning. There is a bar and charming dining room, but no pool—the fabulous beach at Grande Salines is a short distance away. 18 rooms. Credit cards: MC, V.

La Pagerie-Mercure   **$83–$182**   ★★
Pointe du Bout, ☎ *(800) 221-4542, (596) 66-05-30, FAX (596) 66-00-99.*
Single: $83–$139. Double: $99–$182.
This informal hotel faces the marina across the bay from Fort-de-France. Guest rooms are spacious if a bit worn; some have kitchenettes while others have only refrigerators. Located in a high-density hotel area, there is little on-site besides a pool, but plenty within walking distance, including Anse Mitan. Guests may also use the facilities at the nearby Carayou, which has tennis and watersports. 98 rooms. Credit cards: A, MC, V.

Le Meridien Trois-Ilets   **$132–$509**   ★★★★
Pointe du Bout, ☎ *(800) 543-4300, (596) 66-00-00, FAX (596) 66-00-74.*
Single: $132–$327. Double: $145–$327. Suites Per Day: $272–$509.
Located across the harbor from Fort-de-France, this seven-story property shows its age, and attracts both individuals and convention groups. Rooms are smallish but comfortable. There's lots to do at this busy resort, including complimentary watersports, a pool, health club, two tennis courts and a 100-slip marina. The man-made beach is small and gets crowded. There's also a casino and nightly entertainment during high season. A ferry transports passengers to Fort-de-France. Decent for its wide range of facilities, but perhaps best suited to the group market. 295 rooms. Credit cards: A, CB, MC, V.

Les Alamandas   **$105–$162**   ★★
Anse Mitan, ☎ *(800) 223-9815, (596) 66-01-39, FAX (596) 66-05-05.*
Single: $105–$147. Double: $143–$162.
Located right in the heart of the tourist region and within walking distance of the beach, this small hotel accommodates guests in studios, some with kitchens. There's not much here in the way of diversions, but you'll find watersports, shopping and restaurants nearby. The MAP rates include two meals daily—a drawback if you want to sample some of the island's fine cuisine. 54 rooms. Credit cards: MC, V.

Novotel Carayou   **$121–$375**   ★★
Pointe du Bout, ☎ *(800) 322-2223, (596) 66-04-04, FAX (596) 66-00-57.*
Single: $121–$260. Double: $147–$375.
Located on Fort-de-France Bay, this hotel has been completely renovated for 1998. Accommodations are quite nice, with large, modern baths that include bidets. All units have a balcony. The small beach is found in a sheltered cove, and beautiful Ste. Anne beach is a quarter mile away. There's also a large pool, two tennis courts, archery, a driving range and watersports. The disco is popular during high season. 201 rooms. Credit cards: A, DC, MC, V.

Novotel Diamant   **$110–$375**   ★★★
Diamant, ☎ *(800) 221-4542, (596) 76-42-42, FAX (596) 76-22-87.*
Single: $110–$260. Double: $134–$375.

Bordered by white sand beaches near a fishing village, this hotel houses guests in comfortable rooms in three-story buildings on a private peninsula facing the sea and Diamond Rock. There's a pool, table tennis, a floating barge on which to sun, two tennis courts and supervised programs for children. A handful of bars and restaurants complete the scene. Popular with both families and honeymooners, who love the unique setting. 181 rooms. Credit cards: A, MC, V.

Sofitel Bakoua Hotel $122–$530   ★★★★★

Trois Ilets, ☎ *(800) 763-4835, (596) 66-02-02, FAX (596) 66-00-41.*
Single: $122–$340. Double: $157–$530.

Located in a garden setting on a bluff above a private beach, this deluxe hotel is probably Martinique's best. Accommodations are on the hillside or the beach; all quite nice but some are on the small side. There are two lighted tennis courts, a lovely pool, all watersports and a nearby golf course. The service is tops, and most of the French staff speaks at least some English. The beach is fine. Worth the splurge— and a full American breakfast is included. 139 rooms. Credit cards: A, CB, MC, V.

Apartments and Condominiums

The **Villa Rental Service** of the Martinique Tourist Office ☎ *(596) 71-56-11* can arrange vacation home rentals. Among the choices are apartments, studios, or villas. Most of the properties are located in the southern sector, near good beaches. Rentals can be arranged for the week or month.

Les Ilets de l'Impératrice are two tiny islands off Le François on the windward coast, each with a 19th-century vacation house, beach, watersports, full-time maid and cook. Ilet Thierry's house has six double bedrooms; Ilet Oscar's has five. All-inclusive rates (airport pickup, lodging, food and drink, and sports, etc.) runs $200 per person per day year round. Contact Jean-Louis de Lucy ☎ *(596) 65-82-30.*

Martinique Cottages $53–$62   ★★

Lamentin, ☎ *(596) 50-16-08, FAX (596) 50-26-83.*
Single: $53. Double: $62.

Located in a residential area 15 minutes from Fort-de-France and near the airport, this small operation is popular, especially with business travelers. Accommodations are in bungalows nestled among the trees. Each is nicely done with small kitchens and verandas. The beach is 15 minutes away by car; if that's too far, you can relax by the free-form pool. There's also a superb restaurant and bar. This family-owned spot is peaceful and pleasant. 8 rooms. Credit cards: A, CB, DC, D, MC, V.

Rivage Hotel $45–$73   ★★

Anse Mitan, ☎ *(596) 66-00-53, FAX (596) 66-06-56.*
Single: $45–$73. Double: $55–$73.

With all the personality of an outdated motel, this small, family-run operation nonetheless offers great deals. The clean and spacious rooms have a kitchenette and balcony (no views); if you want a TV, you'll pay extra. There's a bar and pool, and lots of diversions within walking distance, including Anse Mitan, across the road. 20 rooms. Credit cards: MC, V.

Inns

For those seeking a more intimate island experience, an inn may be the best choice. The **Fregate Bleue** is one with breakfast included in the price.

Fregate Bleue $100–$225 ★★★

Le Francois, ☎ *(800) 633-7411, (596) 54-54-66, FAX (596) 54-78-48.*
Single: $100–$200. Double: $120–$225.
Set on a hillside overlooking the sea, this gingerbread-trimmed inn is positively charming. All accommodations are in spacious studios with kitchenettes, armoires, four-poster beds and antiques. Breakfast is complimentary each morning, but you'll have to cook in or venture off-site for other meals. There's a pool for those too relaxed to walk three minutes to the beach. Elegant and gracious, this lovely inn is best suited to those not seeking a lot of action. 7 rooms. Credit cards: A, MC, V.

Habitation Lagrange $220–$365 ★★★★

Marigot, ☎ *(800) 633-7411, (596) 53-60-60, FAX (596) 53-50-58.*
Closed Date: closed June and September.
Single: $220–$365. Double: $220–$365.
This 18th-century Creole mansion was refurbished and opened as an inn in 1991. Some guest rooms are suites in the great house, the former headquarters of a sugar factory, and a pair are in the renovated stable. The others are found in new two-story buildings tucked into the lush gardens. All are elegantly decorated with canopy beds, antique furnishings, minibars, plus a few modern comforts like air conditioning. For recreation, there's a putting green, pool and tennis courts, plus exploring the ruins of the former plant; the nearest beach is a 30-minute drive, but lots of explorations by car through some of the island's best scenery are possible. Lagrange exudes the romance of a bygone era. 18 rooms. Credit cards: A, MC, V.

Leyritz Plantation $68–$148 ★★★

Basse-Pointe, ☎ *(596) 78-53-92, FAX (596) 78-92-44.*
Single: $68–$143. Double: $93–$148.
Set on the grounds of a 230-acre banana plantation, this winsome inn arranges guests in a variety of lodgings: in a converted 18th-century great house, in the former guardhouse and slave quarters, as well as in bamboo and stone cottages. All are air-conditioned, antique-filled, have four-poster beds and loads of charm. The most atmospheric rooms are in the main house with its high ceilings, dormer windows, and thick walls. The soothing ambiance of running water—produced by the stone canals that run through the property—is wonderful. The north coast location is remote: the beach is a full half-hour away, but there's a pool, a tennis court, and you can spend hours exploring the ruins of the former plantation. Note that a major drawback are the hordes of tourists trouping through on organized tours (the mid-day lunch hour is worst, but evenings are quiet). Nonetheless, this picturesque and unique spot is hard to leave. 67 rooms. Credit cards: A, MC, V.

St. Aubin Hotel $55–$105 ★★

Trinite, ☎ *(800) 823-2002, (596) 69-34-77, FAX (596) 69-41-14.*
Single: $55–$65. Double: $76–$105.
This colonial-style inn, a former private residence, sits on a sugarcaned hillside with nice views of the Atlantic coast. An old-fashioned porch wraps around the building

on two floors; you'll spend a lot of time on it reading or just taking in the view. Each room is individually decorated with modern amenities, but a little spare. The grounds include a pool and good dining room serving French and creole fare. You'll need a car to explore beyond this remote spot. 15 rooms. Credit cards: A, MC, V.

Low Cost Lodging

Martinique has more than 200 **Gites de France** ☎ *(596) 73-67-92*, which are apartments, studios and guest rooms in private homes. **Logis Vacances Antilles** ☎ *(596) 63-12-91* also offers rooms in private homes, as well as holiday studios and houses. Camping can be done—in the mountains, forest, and on many beaches, although indiscriminate camping is not permitted. **Tropicamp** at Gros Raisins Plage, Ste. Luce ☎ *(596) 62-49-66* is one of several companies with full services, including hot showers. Other comfortable camps with showers and toilets are **Nid Tropical** at Anse-a-l'Ane near Trois Ilets ☎ *(596) 68-31-30*; one at **Vauclin** on the southeast Atlantic coast ☎ *(596) 74-45-88*; an another at **Pointe Marin** near the public beach of Ste. Anne ☎ *(596) 76-72-79*. A nominal fee is charged for facilities. For details, contact the **Office National des Dorês**, 3.5 km, route de Mouette, Fort-de-France; ☎ *(596) 71-34-50*.

The trend these days is to rent a camping car, which allows you opportunity to discover many of the treasures along Martinique's 300-mile roadway. One recommended camping-car operation is **West Indies Tours**, whose campers are outfitted with beds for four, refrigerator, shower, sink, 430-gallon water tank, dining table, stove and radio/cassette player. Contact Michel Yula, **West Indies Tours**, Le François; ☎ *(596) 54-50-71*; or **Wind Martinique**, Anse Mitan; ☎ *(596) 66-02-22*.

Auberge de l'Anse Mitan $51–$95   ★

Anse Mitan, ☎ *(800) 223-9815, (596) 66-01-12, FAX (596) 63-11-64.*
Single: $51–$75. Double: $55–$95.
This casual French-style inn is within walking distance of the beach in Anse Mitan. Accommodations include standard rooms in the three-story main building and six studios with kitchenettes. All are air-conditioned and have private baths and telephones. There's a bar and restaurant serving French and creole fare, but little else in the way of extras. Friendly and cheerful service at this family-run establishment. 20 rooms. Credit cards: A, DC, MC, V.

Victoria Junior $45–$64   ★ ★

Fort-de-France, ☎ *(596) 60-56-78, FAX (596) 60-00-24.*
Single: $45–$55. Double: $58–$64.
Located on a hillside in a residential neighborhood with views, this colonial-style hotel offers good value for its reasonable rates, and attracts mainly business travelers. Accommodations are comfortable, some with TVs and others with kitchenettes. There's a French restaurant and a pool on site. 36 rooms. Credit cards: MC, V.

Where to Eat

Fielding's Highest Rated Restaurants in Martinique

★★★★	La Fontane	$47–$56
★★★★	Leyritz Plantation	$36–$50
★★★	Athanor	$11–$30
★★★	Au Poisson d'Or	$25–$30
★★★	Chez Mally Edjam	$11–$29
★★★	La Mouina	$15–$30
★★★	La Villa Creole	$14–$18
★★★	Le Colibri	$18–$27
★★★	Le Coq Hardi	$18–$36
★★★	Les Filets Bleus	$13–$30

Fielding's Most Romantic Restaurants in Martinique

♡♡♡♡	La Fontane	$47–$56
♡♡♡♡	Leyritz Plantation	$36–$50
♡♡♡	Au Poisson d'Or	$25–$30
♡♡♡	Le Colibri	$18–$27
♡♡♡	Le Coq Hardi	$18–$36

Fielding's Best Value Restaurants in Martinique

★★★	Le Second Souffle	$8–$12
★★★	La Villa Creole	$14–$18
★★	Le Marie Sainte	$8–$15
★★	La Dunette	$6–$20
★★★	Athanor	$11–$30

Perhaps it's the irrepressible French dedication to cuisine, but chefs in Martinique seem to take special care with their menus, overseeing both the preparation and the service. Throughout the island you will generally find one of two cuisines: traditional French or island Creole; many restaurants combine the two on their menus. Fresh seafood dishes are omnipresent, among the tastiest are *chatrou* (octopus), *langouste* (small clawless lobster), *lambi* (conch), and *cribiches* (large river shrimp). Red snapper is served in a variety of ways. *Coquille de lambi* (minced conch in creamy sauce served in a shell) is an island must; the *blaff de poisson* (steamed fish in local spices) is excellent at Le Mareyeur. Another island specialty, *pâté en pot*, is a thick creole soup made with mutton. A good afternoon drink to cool you off is *les planteurs*—a planter's punch in a sweet fruit juice base. Hearty islanders tend to chug down *décollage*—aged herbal rum with a fruit juice chaser. Most restaurants have excellent selections of French wines. Prices per person for a three-course meal without wine range from $30–$45 and up. The French & English booklet *Ti Gourmet*, available from the Tourist Office, will give out more information about where and what to eat.

Athanor $$$ ★★★

Rue de Bord de Mer, ☎ *(596) 76-72-93.*
Dinner: 7–10 p.m., entrées $11–$30.

This popular and informal eatery located one block from the beach in Ste. Anne prepares tasty brick-oven baked pizzas, sea urchin tart, salads and other casual meals from a large menu. Diners can choose a few fancier items including the specialty, grilled lobster, which is delicious. There's a choice of seating in a garden behind the restaurant or in a greenery-draped dining room indoors. Credit cards: MC, V.

Au Poisson d'Or $$$ ★★★

Anse Mitan, ☎ *(596) 66-01-80.*
Lunch: Noon–2:30 p.m., prix fixe $25–$30.
Dinner: 7–10 p.m., prix fixe $25–$30. Closed: Mon.

This is a casual roadside seafood eatery set between the beach cities of Anse Mitan and Pointe du Bout. Tropical greenery and a bamboo ceiling make you feel like you're dining on an isle in the South Seas. A fixed-price meal for $25 is a good buy for an array of Creole specialties including a lime-marinated conch appetizer and an elegant dessert. Reservations recommended. Credit cards: MC, V.

Chez Mally Edjam $$$ ★★★

Route de la Cote, Basse Pointe, ☎ *(596) 78-51-18.*
Lunch: Noon–3 p.m., prix fixe $11–$29.

It's a very pleasant drive to get to this home-style restaurant run by stellar cuisiniere Mally Edjam and her family. The surrounding landscape en route is dotted with pineapple plantations, and trees hung heavily with boughs of green bananas. That's just a prelude to the symphony of flavors on the fixed-price lunches served here, which may include pork colombo (local curry), conch and fabulous desserts. Don't miss the homemade preserves made from local fruits. Dinners may be arranged by appointment. Reservations recommended. Credit cards: A, MC, V.

MARTINIQUE

Diamant Les Bains $$ ★★

Le Diamant, ☎ *(596) 76-40-14.* Associated hotel: *Diamant Les Bains.*
Lunch: Noon–2:30 p.m., entrées $16–$20.
Dinner: 6:30–10:45 p.m., entrées $16–$20.
Good local fare is served in a motel-like hostelry in Le Diamant, a cozy beach town whose claim to fame is the imposing Diamond Rock, majestically rising from the deep to an almost 600-foot height. The beach it fronts is nothing special, but it's a nice spot to dine on blaff (fish cooked with thyme, peppers, clove and other spices), boudin and coconut flan. Credit cards: MC, V.

La Dunette $ ★★

Ste. Anne, ☎ *(596) 76-73-90.* Associated hotel: *La Dunette.*
Lunch: 12–3 p.m., entrées $6–$20.
Dinner: 7–10 p.m., entrées $6–$20.
La Dunette is like a lot of pleasant seaside restaurants on the island that serves seafood specialties. Dine inside or out in a tropical garden facing the sea on poached sea urchins, curries or grilled fish. Connected to a pleasant, intimate hotel where you might consider staying if you're in the area, which is noted for gorgeous beaches and fine weather. Credit cards: MC, V.

La Fontane $$$ ★★★★

Rue de Balata, Fort-de-France, ☎ *(596) 64-28-70.*
Lunch: entrées $47–$56.
Dinner: entrées $47–$56. Closed: Mon., Sun.
A highly-regarded French-Creole restaurant, La Fontane is located in a restored gingerbread house—peaceful and surrounded by fruit trees. The service is formal, the interior is antique-filled and tasteful, with exotic carpets on the floors. Popular dishes include crayfish salad with fruit, noisettes of lamb and mango, poached sea urchins and lobster stew with basil. Reservations recommended. Credit cards: A.

La Mouina $$$ ★★★

Route de Redoute, Fort-de-France, ☎ *(596) 79-34-57.*
Lunch: Noon–4 p.m., entrées $15–$30.
Dinner: 7:30–9:30 p.m., entrées $15–$30. Closed: Sat., Sun.
This is suburbia, Fort-de-France style—fine dining in a typical upper-class home in Redoute, high above the capital below. Guests are made welcome in a dining salon on a balcony with a garden view. The smart set likes to make La Mouina a regular stop for luncheons of stuffed crab backs, tournedos and crayfish, and avocado sherbet—it was the site of a Bush-Mitterrand summit meal in 1991. Dinners are served by candlelight. Reservations recommended. Credit cards: MC, V.

La Villa Creole $$ ★★★

Anse Mitan, ☎ *(596) 66-05-53.*
Lunch: Noon–2 p.m., entrées $14–$18.
Dinner: 7–10 p.m., entrées $14–$18. Closed: Sun.
A friendly and warm atmosphere permeates this gingerbread house with tables set on a seaside terrace in Anse Mitan, a beach resort famed for low-key, moderately priced hotels. There are several prix-fixe meals to choose from, from plain to fancy, but all feature a bevy of side dishes, vegetables and dessert. The owner sometimes gives impromptu song and dance performances. Credit cards: A, DC, MC, V.

Le Cantonnais $$ ★★

La Marina, ☎ *(596) 66-02-33.*
Dinner: 6:30–11 p.m., prix fixe $14–$20. Closed: Tue.

Guests staying at the large resort hotels near the marina in Pointe du Bout can take a break from French-creole cuisine at this Chinese foodery serving a voluminous menu of unusual dishes including broiled shark's fin and bird's nest soup. Vegetarians also have a choice of several meatless entrées. Credit cards: A, MC, V.

Le Colibri $$$ ★★★

Allee du Colibri, ☎ *(596) 69-91-95.*
Lunch: Noon–3 p.m., entrées $18–$27.
Dinner: 7–11 p.m., entrées $18–$27. Closed: Mon.

A family-run operation overlooking Marigot, Le Colibri (The Hummingbird) could be named for the friendly bustling about hither and tither of Mme. Palladino and her daughters, who serve succulent Creole meals to weekenders from Fort-de-France. These denizens fill the veranda of the house for conch pie, roast suckling pig, fish stew and a dreamy coconut flan. Come early to nab these choice seats or you'll be seated inside facing the open kitchen (not so bad an idea). Credit cards: A, DC, MC, V.

Le Coq Hardi $$$ ★★★

Rue Martin Luther King, Fort-de-France, ☎ *(596) 63-66-83.*
Lunch: Noon–2 p.m., entrées $18–$36.
Dinner: 7–11 p.m., entrées $18–$36. Closed: Wed.

Red meat is god here, prepared au bleu (very rare) which is the French way. Master charcutier Alphonse Sintive regularly imports the choice cuts of T-Bone, filet mignon and entrecote from France. After you choose your own steak, it's cooked over an open wood fire. An old-fashioned tournedos rossini is prepared with foie gras and truffles, and is a favorite. If you still have room after the huge portions served, there's still a wide selection of scrumptious desserts and sorbets. Reservations recommended. Credit cards: A, MC, V.

Le Marie Sainte $ ★★

160 rue Victor Hugo, Fort-de-France, ☎ *(596) 63-82-24.*
Lunch: 8 a.m.–3 p.m., entrées $8–$15.
Dinner: 7–10 p.m., entrées $8–$15.

An inexpensive introduction to Creole cuisine is offered by this pleasant, family-style restaurant popular with locals. Shrimp in coconut milk, chicken fricassee, conch and other shellfish are the specialties, or stop by for a hearty Creole-style breakfast. Credit cards: A, MC, V.

Le Second Souffle $ ★★★

27 rue Blenac, Fort-de-France, ☎ *(596) 63-44-11.*
Lunch: Noon–3 p.m., entrées $8–$12.
Dinner: 7:30–10 p.m., entrées $8–$12. Closed: Sat., Sun.

A treat for the body and soul is a cleansing visit to this pleasant vegetarian restaurant after a tour of the Byzantine Saint Louis Cathedral nearby. This bright spot dishes up a salad of seasonal fruits with honey sauce, vegetable Creole curries, or a meatless plat du jour, which may include a christophene or callaloo souffle. And to those who ask where's the first souffle?—this is it, and a new branch recently opened in Lamentin ☎ *(596) 57-14-28.* Credit cards: MC, V.

Les Filets Bleus $$$ ★★★

Point Marin, ☎ *(596) 76-73-42.*
Lunch: 12:30–2:30 p.m., entrées $13–$30.
Dinner: 7:30–9:30 p.m., entrées $13 $30. Closed: Mon.

A restaurant of many contrasts—although Filets Bleus charges haute cuisine prices, the place is so casual you can come here in a beach cover-up after a swim in the briny which is in full view of the tables. Also, dishes are mostly hearty West Indian dishes like *chatrous* (octopus) with red beans and rice, hardly justifying the stiff tab. Still, what you're served is usually very good, and the ambience is friendly and intimate.
Credit cards: MC, V.

Leyritz Plantation $$$ ★★★★

Basse Pointe, ☎ *(596) 78-53-92.* Associated hotel: *Plantation Leyritz.*
Lunch: 12:30–2 p.m., entrées $27–$40.
Dinner: 7:30–9 p.m., entrées $36–$50.

Dining at one of Martinique's prime tourist attractions sounds like a recipe for disaster, but surprisingly, the Creole cuisine remains first rate. Guests also get a lot of food for their francs, especially a set luncheon of stuffed crab, blood pudding, an entrée (sometimes conch), rice and vegetables and dessert. The million-dollar setting amidst an 18th century sugar plantation is a fond postcard memory. Although lunch is the preferred time, come for dinner when the tour bus pandemonium becomes practically nonexistent. Reservations recommended. Credit cards: MC, V.

Yva Chez Vava $$$ ★★

Boulevard de Gaulle, Grand-Riviere, ☎ *(596) 55-72-72.*
Lunch: Noon–5 p.m., entrées $18–$27.

This *chez* on the northern tip of the island is the domain of local legend Vava and her daughter Yva, who now continues the tradition of cooking family-style Creole meals in their own residence near a river. As Grand Riviere is a fishing village, seafood appears prominently on the menu. Specialties include *accras* (cod fritters), chicken colombo and *z'habitants* (crayfish prepared Martinique style). After lunch, you might want to visit the fish market where your food originated, or stroll on the black sand beach. Reservations recommended. Credit cards: DC, MC, V.

Where to Shop

"Go French" is the password when trying to decide what to buy in Martinique, a place where you can find the best bargains among French imports—perfumes, cosmetics, clothes, china, and crystal—at prices 25-40 percent lower than in the U.S. If you pay in traveler's checks, you'll often receive an additional 20 percent discount. Either way, you will never find these prices in France. Don't miss picking up a few bottles of Martinique-brewed rum.

Craft buys range from folk-styled appliqué wall hangings to the Martiniquais doll dressed in the national costume, which can be seen in nearly every store and in every size imaginable. Paintings and sculptures by native-born Martiniquais or artists who have moved to the islands can be found at galleries in Fort-de-France and at some hotels. A conical bakoua straw hat does nicely as a sun-stopper. Madras, long popular in traditional folk costumes, is available in shops on every street for $6–$12 a meter. If you're interested in the bright gold Creole jewelry found around many women's necks, ears and wrists, you will be joining a long-standing cultural tradition. The special "convict's chain" called *chaîne forçat*, and the *tremblants*, gold brooches with special adornment, can be found in several stores, where you should be able to judge authenticity by the price. Among the most reputable are **Cadet Daniel**, **Bijouterie Onyx** and **Emile Mothie's** workshop in Trenelle. (The latter is for serious fans who want to observe his work.) For delicious French delicacies, wines, foie gras and chocolates, head for **Boutique Michel Montignac**. Gourmet chefs will find a plethora of exotic spices in many of the open air markets. To pick up the latest in island music, try **Hit Parade** on Rue Lamartine. Boutiques like *La Chamade* on rue Victor Hugo in Fort de France carry Cote d'Azur designers and fashions from Paris. Other shops on or near rue Victor Hugo are *Georgia, Kookai, Alain Moanoukian* and *Ah!Nana*. Others, like *Mounia* on rue Perrignon, carry top names such as Claude Montana, Dorothee Bis and Yves St. Laurent. Young Martinique designers are also now presenting their own collections in shops like *Anacaona*, featuring designs by Paul-Herve Elisabeth.

Martinique Directory

Arrival and Departure

The new **Lamentin Airport** terminal just outside Fort-de-France is one of the region's most modern facilities. **American Eagle** flies nonstop from San Juan to Fort-de-France twice daily, allowing easy connections with **American Airlines** flights from major cities in the United States. **Air France** has twice-weekly jet service to Fort-de-France out of Miami. Inter-island service is also available, with **LIAT** providing non-stop or direct flights to Martinique from Antigua, Barbados, Dominica, Grenada, Guadeloupe, St. Lucia, St. Vincent and Trinidad. **Air Martinique** ☎ *(596) 60-00-23* flies in from Antigua, Barbados, Dominica, St. Lucia, St. Martin, St. Vincent and the Grenadines, and San Juan, and **Air Guadeloupe** ☎ *(596) 55-33-00* provides service to the other French islands. Daily ferry service to Martinique is available from Guadeloupe, St. Lucia and Dominica on **Caribbean Express** ☎ *(596) 63-12-11*.

There is no departure tax when leaving Martinique.

MARTINIQUE

Business Hours

Stores open weekdays 8:30 a.m.–6 p.m. and Saturday 8:30 a.m.–1 p.m. Bank hours vary but are generally open weekdays 7:30–noon and 2:30–4 p.m.

Climate

Martinique's temperatures stay temperate all year long, hovering around 79 degrees F, with only a five-degree difference between seasons. The air is cooled by constant wind currents (east and northeast); trade winds are called *les alizés*.

Documents

For stays up to three weeks, U.S. and Canadian citizens traveling as tourists must show proof of citizenship in the form of a valid passport, or a passport that expired no more than five years ago, or other proof in the form of a birth certificate or voter's registration card with a government-authorized photo ID. For stays of more than three weeks, or for nontourist visas, a valid passport is necessary. All passengers must show an ongoing or return ticket.

Electricity

Current is 220 AC, 50 cycles. American and Canadian appliances require a French plug, converter and transformers.

Getting Around

With an extensive network of paved roads to explore, you'll want to rent a car for at least part of your trip. Roads are good by Caribbean standards, though traffic is swift, particularly around Fort-de-France (it helps to have a navigator with a good map). Along with a host of local outfits, four American firms are represented on the island—**Avis**, **Budget**, **Hertz** and **Thrifty**—with daily rates starting at about $35 per day (lower rates apply for weekly rentals); there's a 9.5 percent local tax, plus an $11 surcharge for rentals at the airport.

Taxis are common transportation, though most drivers do not speak English and the cost will add up quickly. Samples fares: from the airport to hotels in Pointe du Bout, about $27; from the airport to Fort-de-France, $11. Fares go up 40 percent from 8 p.m. to 6 a.m. Cabs are available at most major hotels and restaurants, or call ☎ *(596) 63-63-62* to have a car dispatched. The Martinique bus system is comprehensive, but an involved option for visitors if you're not fluent in French. Most routes start or end in Fort-de-France and operate from 5 a.m. to 7:30 p.m. Fares are based on distance; about $5 from Fort-de-France to Ste. Anne, for instance.

Language

The languages of the isle are French and Creole. You'll find some English spoken in most hotels, restaurants and tourist facilities, but you'll be happy if you remember to bring along a French phase book and pocket dictionary.

Medical Emergencies

There are 20 hospitals and clinics on the island, many well equipped; the best is **La Meynard** ☎ *(596) 55-20-00*. Ask the Tourist Office to assist you in securing an English-speaking physician.

Money

The official currency is the French franc. The exchange rate we have used to calculate hotel and restaurant prices provided to us in francs is 5.5 to one U.S. dollar. If the dollar has further strengthened, you may find lower prices on the island than what we have quoted. Dollars are accepted in tourist establishments, but paying in francs will usually get you a better rate. Credit cards are accepted by most businesses, and plastic frequently yields a better rate than is available through island banks.

Telephone

The international dialing code for Martinique is *(596)*; to call from the U.S., dial *011 + (596)* plus the six-digit local number. The cheapest way to call the U.S. from Guadeloupe is to purchase a *telecarte*, sold at post offices and other outlets marked "Telecarte en Vente Ici." The cards can be used in any phone booth marked "Telécom."

Time

Martinique is one hour later than New York (Eastern Standard Time). Time is related on the 24-hour schedule; i.e., 1 p.m. is 13:00 hours.

Tipping and Taxes

Some hotels add a 10 percent service charge or 5 percent government tax to the bill. At restaurants, check your bill carefully and avoid adding on an extra service charge. If there is no charge added, a 10–15 percent tip is appreciated by waiters and waitresses.

Tourist Information

In the U.S., information can be obtained through the **Martinique Promotion Bureau** ☎ *(800) 391-4909*. On island, the **Office Departemental du Tourisme** is located at Boulevard Alfassa, on the waterfront in Fort-de-France; hours are 7:30 a.m.–5:30 p.m. Monday through Friday (closed 12:30–2:30) and 8 a.m.–noon on Saturday ☎ *(596) 63-79-60*. There is an English-speaking staff, and they can provide maps and touring suggestions. There is also an office at the airport.

Web Site

www.nyo.com/martinique AND www.martinique.org

When to Go

La Fete des Rois, or **Epiphany**, is celebrated on January 5 with feasting, dancing and a cake known as *galette des rois*. **Carnival** is in February, during the five days leading up to Ash Wednesday; all business comes to a halt and streets spill over with parties and parades. In May, **Le Mai de St. Pierre** is a month-long program of theater, dance, music, art exhibitions and other cultural events commemorating the famed city's past. In July, the **Tour de la Martinique** is held, a week long bike-race around the island. On July 14, **Bastille Day** is celebrated with parades. In August, the week-long **Tour des Yoles Rondes** is held—a beautiful spectator sport as traditional yawls sail around the island. On November 1, **All Saints Day** is marked by cemeteries being illuminated with candles. In early December, the ten-day **International Jazz Festival** is held with concerts, classes and competitions.

MARTINIQUE HOTELS		RMS	RATES	PHONE	CR. CARDS
★★★★★	Sofitel Bakoua Hotel	139	$122–$530	(800) 763-4835	A, CB, MC, V
★★★★	Habitation Lagrange	18	$220–$365	(800) 633-7411	A, MC, V
★★★★	Le Meridien Trois-Ilets	295	$132–$327	(800) 543-4300	A, CB, MC, V
★★★	Fregate Bleue	7	$100–$225	(800) 633-7411	A, MC, V
★★★	La Bateliere Hotel	199	$135–$400	(800) 223-6510	A, MC, V
★★★	Leyritz Plantation	67	$68–$148	(596) 78-53-92	A, MC, V
★★★	Novotel Diamant	181	$110–$375	(800) 221-4542	A, MC, V
★★	Diamant les Bains	24	$76–$120	(800) 823-2002	MC, V
★★	Domaine de Belfond	186	$132–$244	(800) 322-2223	A, MC, V
★★	L'Imperatrice Village	59	$107–$175	(596) 66-08-09	A, MC, V
★★	La Pagerie-Mercure	98	$83–$182	(800) 221-4542	A, MC, V
★★	Les Alamandas	54	$105–$162	(800) 223-9815	MC, V
★★	Martinique Cottages	8	$53–$62	(596) 50-16-08	A, CB, D, DC, MC, V
★★	Novotel Carayou	201	$121–$375	(800) 322-2223	A, DC, MC, V
★★	Rivage Hotel	20	$45–$73	(596) 66-00-53	MC, V
★★	St. Aubin Hotel	15	$55–$105	(800) 823-2002	A, MC, V
★★	Victoria Junior	36	$45–$64	(596) 60-56-78	MC, V
★	Auberge de l'Anse Mitan	20	$51–$95	(800) 223-9815	A, DC, MC, V
★	Balisier	27	$56–$77	(596) 71-46-54	A, MC
★	La Dunette	18	$55–$125	(596) 76-73-90	MC, V

MARTINIQUE RESTAURANTS		PHONE	ENTRÉE	CR. CARDS
Chinese Cuisine				
★★	Le Cantonnais	(596) 66-02-33	$14–$20	A, MC, V
Creole Cuisine				
★★★★	La Fontane	(596) 64-28-70	$47–$56	A
★★★★	Leyritz Plantation	(596) 78-53-92	$27–$50	MC, V
★★★	Au Poisson d'Or	(596) 66-01-80	$25–$30	MC, V
★★★	Chez Mally Edjam	(596) 78-51-18	$11–$29	A, MC, V

MARTINIQUE RESTAURANTS	PHONE	ENTRÉE	CR. CARDS
★★★ La Villa Creole	(596) 66-05-53	$14–$18	A, DC, MC, V
★★★ Le Colibri	(596) 69-91-95	$18–$27	A, DC, MC, V
★★★ Les Filets Bleus	(596) 76-73-42	$13–$30	MC, V
★★ Diamant Les Bains	(596) 76-40-14	$16–$20	MC, V
★★ Le Marie Sainte	(596) 63-82-24	$8–$15	A, MC, V
★★ Yva Chez Vava	(596) 55-72-72	$18–$27	NoneDC, MC, V
French Cuisine			
★★★ Athanor	(596) 76-72-93	$11–$30	MC, V
★★★ La Mouina	(596) 79-34-57	$15–$30	MC, V
★★★ Le Coq Hardi	(596) 63-66-83	$18–$36	A, MC, V
★★★ Le Second Souffle	(596) 63-44-11	$8–$12	MC, V
Seafood Cuisine			
★★ La Dunette	(596) 76-73-90	$6–$20	MC, V

MONTSERRAT

Many of Montserrat's quaint buildings sit empty as residents wait for volcano activity to subside. Hopefully the island can soon return to normal.

Long one of the most peaceful and friendly communities of the Caribbean, Montserrat, the Emerald Isle, benefited from an interior sculpted by ancient volcanic activity that invited hikers to explore its peaks and *ghauts* (ravines), and mountain bikers to toil gamely through its forests. An increasing number of Americans were building retirement homes on the 39-square-mile island, delighting in the 11-hole golf course at the base of the Belham River Valley, happy to live somewhere that felt truly safe. Although tourist arrivals had been on the upswing in the early 1990s, the island was in no imminent danger of becoming oversaturated, and the local tourist board could honestly call Montserrat, "the way the Caribbean used to be." The slogan now has another meaning.

In July 1995, a fissure opened up in English Crater beneath volcanic Chances Peak and spewed ash over the surprised residents of Plymouth, the island's quaint capital. Being the first signs of real volcanic activity on Montserrat in 300 years, the gesture was dramatic enough to send vulcanologists from the United States and England scurrying to the Caribbean for evaluation and monitoring. A gradual increase in activity, marked by the growth of a glowing lava dome in the crater, pyroclastic flows that added new acreage to the island, and ash eruptions that reached at least 30,000 feet into the air, caused scientists to eventually recommend the evacuation of the southern third of the island, including Plymouth. Although some left Montserrat in 1996 to resettle in England or other Caribbean islands, the rest of the residents from the south moved to the north, many of them staying in hastily created shelters. Islanders tried to go about their business, despite a number of obstacles. Although the activity was concentrated on the undeveloped eastern slope of the volcano, many of the island's accommodations were in the designated unsafe zone and closed, so tourist arrivals slowed to a trickle. Also problematic was that Montserrat's most fertile soil lay on the northern slopes of the volcano—an area not directly affected by the early eruptions, and a number of farmers defied the evacuation order and tended their fields.

Then 23 months after the start of the activity, the volcano had a marked increase in activity. With a lava extrusion rate estimated at 3.5 cubic meters per second, the sheer dome had grown to a height 300 feet taller than Chances Peak (previously the island's highest point) and was increasingly unstable. An inflation/deflation cycle of the dome was measured and the number of hybrid earthquakes rose from a few a day to hundreds. Scientists renewed their call for evacuation of the unsafe zone. At 12:55 p.m. on June 25, 1997, the dome collapsed and pyroclastic avalanches of superheated ash, rock and gas swept down the north eastern slopes of the volcano, flattening everything in their path—an estimated four to five million cubic meters of the dome was unloaded in the eruption. Nineteen people died in a matter of minutes, eight villages were damaged or destroyed, and 200 homes were ruined. The flows blanketed an area that extended from Windy Hill to Bethel and as far away as the airport. Other eruptions over the following months deposited a layer of sizzling ash on both Plymouth and the airport, rendering both unusable for the foreseeable future. The island's "bread basket" immediately north of the volcano—the name for the once-verdant saddle where most of Montserrat's diverse bounty of produce was grown—is now an ashen wasteland.

What sounds like an environment fit for Dante is not deterring about 3500 intrepid souls who want to sit out the activity and hope to put their island back in order. For most residents and even the ex-pats who have remained, this is not just a case of defiantly holding on to a house or property, but a

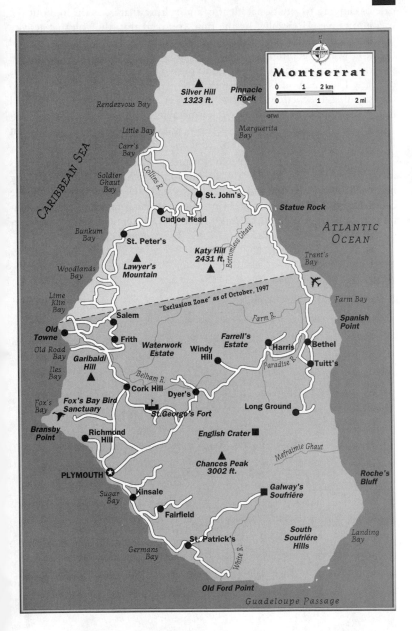

MONTSERRAT

Montserrat

| 0 | | 1 | | 2 km |
| 0 | | 1 | | 2 mi |

©FWI

Rendezvous Bay

▲ **Silver Hill**
1323 ft.

Pinnacle Rock

CARIBBEAN SEA

Little Bay

Marguerita Bay

Carr's Bay

Soldier Ghaut Bay

Collins R.

● **St. John's**

● **Cudjoe Head**

Statue Rock

ATLANTIC OCEAN

Bunkum Bay

● **St. Peter's**

▲ **Katy Hill 2431 ft.**

Bottomless Ghaut

Trant's Bay

Woodlands Bay

▲ **Lawyer's Mountain**

"Exclusion Zone" as of October, 1997

Farm Bay

Lime Klin Bay

● **Salem**

Farm R.

Spanish Point

Old Towne ●

● **Frith**

Waterwork Estate

Windy Hill

Farrell's Estate

● **Harris**

● **Bethel**

Old Road Bay

Iles Bay

▲ **Garibaldi Hill**

Belham R.

● **Cork Hill**

● **Dyer's**

Paradise R.

● **Tuitt's**

Fox's Bay

Fox's Bay Bird Sanctuary

⚓ **St.George's Fort**

Long Ground ●

Bransby Point

● **Richmond Hill**

English Crater ■

Mefraimie Ghaut

Roche's Bluff

▲ **Chances Peak 3002 ft.**

☆ **PLYMOUTH**

Sugar Bay

● **Kinsale**

■ **Galway's Soufriére**

● **Fairfield**

Germans Bay

● **St. Patrick's**

White R.

South Soufriére Hills

Landing Bay

Old Ford Point

Guadeloupe Passage

case of clinging to a national identity and culture that is, as throughout the region, unique. Hopefully, by the time you read this, the volcanic activity will have settled down and residents will be putting the turmoil behind them. However, geologists are wary about laying out a long-term prognosis—the activity could stop as we go to press, or might continue for months or years. The situation as of October 1997 is that the only transportation to the island is via scheduled ferry or helicopter service from Antigua, but all hotel accommodations including the venerable Vue Pointe are closed indefinitely. Before planning travel to the island, call the Montserrat Tourist Board for the latest information: ☎ *(664) 491-2230.*

We hope to be able to devote a full chapter in Fielding's Caribbean to this lovely island again in the not-too-distant future, when volcano sightseeing may be viable and accommodations are re-opened. Until then, you can make donations to the Montserrat Red Cross through the American Red Cross International Response Fund: ☎ *(800) HELP-NOW.* Or mail a check to *International Response Fund, P.O. Box 37243, Washington, D.C. 20013.*

NEVIS

St. John's Fig Tree Church in Nevis contains interesting memorials to Admiral Nelson and his wife, Fanny Nisbet.

Approaching Nevis by ferry from St. Kitts, one cannot help but be compelled by the swooning, near-perfect shape of conical Nevis Peak, which sits on the sea like a giant Hershey's Kiss, mistakenly wrapped in a mantle of greenery rather than foil. As you cross the channel that separates the two islands, you can pick out Pinney's Beach, a Caribbean Shangri-La backed by a former coconut plantation. The topographical grandeur is stately and formal, which fits nicely, for Nevis offers a taste of the old Caribbean. Sister to St. Kitts, Nevis is the quiet child, shunning the hustle of Kittian casinos for the leisure of a quiet drink on the veranda of 200-year-old inns. There are a few patches of sand, and a volcanic summit that protrudes splendidly into the clouds, but the character of Nevis is defined by genteel plantation inns, five in all, that recall an earlier, slower-paced era. With the exception of the 1991 debut of a Four Seasons resort on Pinney's Beach, which contains more rooms than all other Nevis properties combined, nothing aggressive is being done about tourism. This makes the island a good hang-out for celebrities—but also for travelers in search of genuinely hospitable people—about 9,000 of them—willing to share in the quiet charm and history of their tiny island.

There's a Nevisian independence movement afoot. Its roots are said to lie in politics and the island's status as an off-shore tax haven, but a bigger reason may simply be that the strong local economy is seeing too much of its revenue head across the channel to St. Kitts. But don't hold your breath for overnight or dramatic changes. No one seems to move faster than a ceiling fan in Nevis, and following a lavish gourmet dinner in a history-filled plantation home, your dreams may well be about the luscious array of tropical fruits that will grace your breakfast buffet in the morning. Despite the laid-back nature of the island, however, locals have not remained lax in regard to ecology. For that reason, the hundred or so cruise liners that stopped in Charlestown last year did little to upset the island's ideal ecological balance. Hurricane Hugo damaged Nevis badly in 1989, and Luis grazed it in 1995, but the island quickly recovered from each. Nevis is as deep green and lush as ever, beckoning well-heeled travelers for a slice of the Caribbean at its most sedate and civilized.

BEST BETS FOR...

Bird's-Eye View

Separated from St. Kitts by a two-mile channel, the Narrows, Nevis is a 36-square-mile island about six or seven miles across with a classic volcanic cone named Nevis Peak rising out of its center. At 3232 feet, this high point is usually shrouded in clouds and mist, which inspired Columbus to name the island "Las Nieves." Two smaller rises, Round Hill in the north and Saddle Hill in the south, create a watershed between the east and west sides of the island. The northern half of Nevis is drier and covered in scrub in the lower elevations, but the southern portion has an exuberant rampage of trees, creepers and giant ferns that appear the moment you head east out of the sleepy capital of Charlestown. This portion of Nevis is where the round-island road climbs to 800 feet above sea level (before descending to the undeveloped east coast), and it is also the most-densely inhabited part of the is-

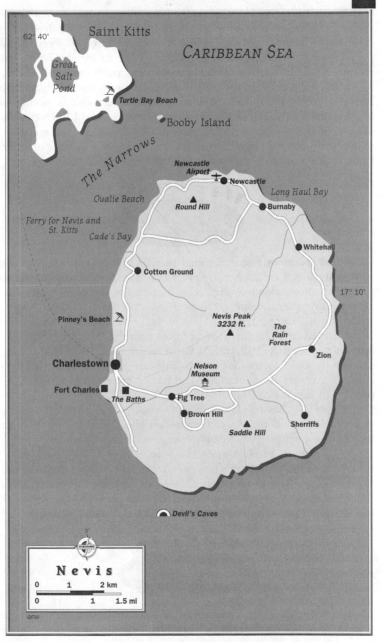

land, with small enclaves nestled on the hillside. A number of plantations lie in this region of the peak's flanks. The plantations include gardens lovingly cultivated by islanders. Above 1300 feet, evergreen tropical forest blankets the increasingly steep slopes of Nevis Peak, while its summit holds dense, mossy jungle with clutches of orchids peeking through the vines. Throughout the higher elevations, the gregarious vervet monkey is the chief inhabitant—the combined simian population of St. Kitts/Nevis outnumbers humans almost three to one. Charlestown, home to about 1200 Nevisians, is a laconic sprawl of pastel walls, tin roofs and shady gardens, and remains one of the best-preserved towns in the West Indies. As on a number of other islands, regulations prohibit any building taller than a palm tree.

History

Nevis has had a long history for such a small island. After spotting an island and naming it St. Christopher (later nicknamed St. Kitts) for his patron saint, Columbus spied a cloud-covered conic island rising out of the water during his second voyage, dubbing it "Nuestra Señora de las Nieves," or "Our lady of the Snows," since it reminded him of the snow-capped Pyrenees. British troops arrived in 1623, first joining forces with the French to conquer the Spanish and decimate the resident Carib Indian tribes, then later duking it out with the Gallic forces for the next 150 years. The British used St. Kitts as a base to colonize Nevis, Antigua, Barbuda, Tortola and Montserrat, while the French dominated Martinique, St. Martin, Guadeloupe, St. Barts, La Désirade and Les Saintes. The Treaty of Versailles in 1783 ceded the islands to Britain. Known as the "Queen of the Carribbees" in the late 18th century for its thriving sugar trade, Nevis later saw its fortunes decline with the abolition of slavery in 1834. Almost 150 years later in 1983, Nevis, with St. Kitts, became the Caribbean's newest independent country, with the establishment of the federation of St. Kitts-Nevis. Recently, another independence movement—to allow Nevis to secede from St. Kitts—is growing. The split would make Nevis the smallest nation in the Western Hemisphere.

People

Perhaps a key reason Four Seasons chose Nevis for its first Caribbean resort is due to the caliber of the island's work force—about 700 are now employed by the hotel firm. On the surface, Nevisians are as laid-back and friendly as residents in most of the region, but the island also claims one of the highest literacy rates in the Western Hemisphere—98 percent of Nevisians read and write with ease. To savvy insiders, the island was a prime candidate for a posh resort, and yet the rhythm of life is gentle and noninvasive, much quieter than on St. Kitts. Many local people are still imbued with age-old superstitions; door frames are painted blue to keep "jumby" spirits out in accordance with ancient *obeah* voodoo customs. Many people still use herbal cures and some retain their respect for the mystical powers of the big, fat native toads called *crappos*. Social interaction has both written and unwritten rules. Of the former, note that the use of profanity in public is prohibited by law, and it is an offense to splash water on pedestrians while driving. This small community also embraces customs long gone from most parts of "civilized" society: because most Nevisians are related in some way, conversations typically begin with a caring inquiry into the health or well-being of one another. And when there is a death on the island, it is not uncommon for hundreds to pay their respect at multi-hour church services that can tie up the road with traffic for hundreds of yards.

Beaches

Nevis isn't usually thought of as a beach destination, and yet it has several luxuriant strips of velvety sand curling around its waist—the best are on the west and north coasts, facing St. Kitts. The most famous is **Pinney's Beach**, a narrow four-mile shore that starts at the edge of Charlestown and winds north, passing the Four Seasons on its languid course to the ruin of Ashby Fort and the site of the former colony, Jamestown. Although the sand is gray rather than pearly white, it is fine, and bordered by whispering surf on one side and rows of coconut trees on the other; extensive watersports activities are proffered by the Four Seasons, along with bars and beachside restaurants. Continuing north, Mosquito Bay is home to **Oualie Beach**, one of the island's few coves—a quiet spot ideal for swimming, snorkeling, windsurfing and more. Just before reaching the airport is an infrequently visited outpost below **Round Hill**, and just past Newcastle is **Nisbet Plantation**, where a fine white shoreline provides good swimming and snorkeling lies on the nearby reef.

NEVIS

The waters off Nevis have yet to become a high-profile destination for divers. However, a diverse selection of interesting sites are available, including a unique ride through long-dormant underwater lava tubes. The relative paucity of dive business means that Nevis' reefs are in better shape than a number of other islands; visibility averages 80 to 100 feet. The channel between St. Kitts and Nevis, **The Narrows**, contains many of the best dives, including **Nag's Head** (see "Underwater" in "St. Kitts"); these sites are shared by the operators on both islands. **Redonda Reef** off the remote southern coast offers a little-visited wilderness where hammerheads and whales sometimes tarry (calm seas are required for diving). Many visiting divers inquire about the mysterious settlement of **Jamestown**, rumored to lie underwater off the island's west coast. One story goes that the village submerged dramatically as a result of a cataclysmic earthquake, while others say a tidal wave or hurricane washed it out to sea. Consumed in myth and folklore, the reality may be simply that the village was abandoned and overgrown by marshland. Historic records are conveniently contradictory, but local fishermen say that one can hear the church bells ringing near the ruins of Jamestown. Experienced snorkelers should head for **Longhaul Bay**, southeast of Newcastle, where a protected inner reef is hidden just past the last jetty southeast of the main reef; novices will enjoy the shallows around the jetty. Snorkeling is good at the north end of **Oualie Beach**, and around the reefs off **Nisbet Plantation**.

Dive Shops

Scuba Safaris

Oualie Beach; ☎ *(869) 469-9518.*

Locally born Ellis Chaderton is Nevis' long-time dive operator who uses two 32-foot dive boats to visit sites around Nevis and southern St. Kitts. Resort courses and PADI certification through Divemaster. Two-tank dive, $80 (not including gear). Half-day snorkel trips, $35.

Life on Nevis is wrapped, literally, around the island's classically shaped volcanic cone. For adventurous visitors, hiking the steep slopes of **Nevis Peak** is the main trek on the island, completed by relatively few intrepid outsiders, which leaves the trail overgrown and difficult to follow in some sections. However, walking is still a way of life for some islanders. Nevis is small enough and vehicular traffic light enough that many locals continue to use foot travel between the small villages. Join them in their informal method of transportation, even along the 20-mile road circling the island, for an inviting glimpse into a slower Caribbean life-style. The Upper Round Road, a nine-mile path built in the late 1600s to link the island's plantations to one another, is scheduled to be re-opened. The trail extends from Nisbet on the north coast around the flanks of the mountain to Golden Rock, much of it above the 1000-foot elevation. Completion is anticipated in summer 1998.

What Else to See

The history of Nevis is found behind the shutters and porches of its great **plantation houses**, five of them now playing host to fine hotels. A taste of the Colonial era can still be experienced at any of them, all of which provide brochures that detail tidbits about their individual pasts. **Charlestown**, the island's capital, is a tropical rainbow of pastel storefronts, tin roofs and palm shaded gardens—good for strolling and lingering. Many visitors will be surprised to discover that Nevis was once the home of a thriving Jewish community, and their restored **cemetery** lies just behind Charlestown. A *mikvah*, or ritual bath, was discovered in 1992, and excavation continues to determine if the adjacent foundation ruins are what remains of the earliest known synagogue in the Caribbean (potentially dating back to 1650). Just south of town, the crumbling **Bath Hotel** sits above mineral hot springs where, until recently, guests could soak in the rejuvenating waters. The hotel has been closed for over a century and currently houses the Nevis police force, but there is hope of restoring it.

Continuing around the island in a clockwise direction, the **St. Thomas Anglican Church** dates to 1643 making it the oldest church in Nevis, and possibly the oldest still standing in the British Leewards. Nearby is the community of **Cotton Ground** and **Nelson Spring**, where Captain Nelson obtained fresh water for his troops in the 1780s, and just past the spring is the ruin of **Ashby Fort**, one of the oldest on the island. Along the shore here is the site of **Jamestown**, a community that was protected by the fort, but is said to have perished in an earthquake or tidal wave around 1680. Just before reaching the Newcastle Airport and off the road is the **Cottle Church**, the first church in the Caribbean where slaves were allowed to worship with their master—in this case John Cottle, owner of the 980-acre Round Hill Estate. Just past Newcastle is the **St. James Anglican Church**, built in the late 1600s,

Fielding NEVIS

THE QUEEN OF
THE CARIBBEAN

Famed for its historic ties to Lord Nelson as well as its natural
beauty, Nevis is a close neighbor to its sibling, St. Kitts. Sugarcane
brought colonists to the island, but the mineral baths attracted
the first tourists. Today, the plantation great houses have been
transformed into intimate inns, and tourists come to hike,
swim, horseback ride and snorkel. You can reach
Nevis by plane or ferry from St. Kitts.

Mosquito
Bay

Pinney's Beach

Located on the west side north of
Charlestown, this four-mile beach has acres
of soft, golden sand and a line of
picturesque palm trees. The palm-shaded
lagoon is a perfect place to relax.

Cotton
Ground

Nevis Peak

Pinney's
Beach

Hamilton Museum

Alexander Hamilton was born in a
waterfront house on Nevis. Today, the
house is filled with exhibits about the
American statesman, as well as artifacts
reflecting the island's history.

Charlestown

Fort Charles

Begun in 1690, Fort Charles
was a military stronghold by
1790. Today, you can visit its
ruins.

Fig
Tree

Saddl
Hill

St. John's Anglican Church

This venerable stone church is situated
in the village of Fig Tree. Dating
back to 1680, the church displays
Lord Nelson's marriage certificate
verifying his union with Frances
Nisbet.

Dogwood
Pt.

NEVIS

Newcastle

Watch the potters at work and buy colorful souvenirs at Newcastle Pottery.

Newcastle Airport

Newcastle

Eden Brown

Gingerland

Red Cliff

Sugar Plantations

Several of the island's historic plantations have been converted into inns and hotels. At the Golden Rock Estate, guests can stay the night in the restored sugar mill. Also visit the government-owned Eden Brown Estate, now in ruins, but built in 1740. Eden Brown is rumored to be haunted by the ghost of Miss Julia Huggins.

Stamps

Many stamp collectors seek out the colorful stamps issued by Caribbean nations. The first Nevis stamps were issued in 1879. Since 1980, Nevis has produced four issues a year, and the stamps often reflect the island's flowers and animal life. The Philatelic Bureau is in Charlestown.

Nevis

Nevis

Horatio Nelson Museum

This museum features one of the largest privately owned collections of Lord Nelson's furniture, documents and other mementos.

NEVIS

and one of only three churches in the region that contains a black crucifix. After passing what's left of the **Eden Brown Estate**, you'll begin a climb onto a prominent shoulder of Nevis Peak, passing four plantation homes that have been turned into inns. Any of the four make an excellent stop for lunch, an afternoon tea, or leisurely stroll. On the way down into Charlestown, keep an eye out for **St. John's Fig Tree Anglican Church**, where Admiral Nelson and Fanny Nisbet's marriage certificate is on display.

Historical Sites

Eden Brown Estate ★

Near Huggins Bay.

This government-owned estate house was built in 1740. It is said to be haunted by the ghost of Julia Huggins, who was about to be married in 1822. But the night before the wedding, the groom and best man got drunk, argued and ended up killing each other in a duel. Poor Julia became a recluse and is said to still hang around the house. The estate includes other stone ruins from the plantation.

Museums and Exhibits

Hamilton Birthplace and Museum of Nevis ★★★

Low Street, Charlestown, ☎ *(869) 469-5786.*
Hours open: 8 a.m.–4 p.m.

This Georgian-style house is actually a replica of Alexander Hamilton's childhood home, which was built in 1680 and destroyed by a hurricane in the 19th century. Hamilton was born on Nevis in 1755 (the ruins of his birthplace are immediately behind the museum), later emigrated to the fledgling United States, and was appointed by George Washington as the first Secretary of the U.S. Treasury. He died in a duel with Aaron Burr. The building contains memorabilia of his life, as well as photographs and exhibits on the island's history, dating from the 17th century. The Nevis House of Assembly is on the second floor. General admission: $2.

Nelson Museum, The ★★★

Bath Road, Charlestown, ☎ *(869) 469-0408.*
Hours open: 8 a.m.–4:30 p.m.

This small museum commemorates the life of Lord Nelson, who met and married local girl "Fanny" Nisbet at the Montpelier Estate in 1787. Reproductions of paintings, engravings, costumes and replicas of the furniture from his flagship recall the bravery of England's great naval hero. General admission: $2.

Water-skiing, windsurfing, sport fishing, golf, tennis and horseback riding are all prime activities on Nevis, and if your hotel can't arrange it there are several agencies that will. A number of **watersports** are concentrated at the Four Seasons, but Oualie Beach also has its share, with **windsurfing** leading the bill. **Sport fishing** takes advantage of a good supply of wahoo, tuna, king-fish and dorado, and seasoned skippers will guide you to the best waters. The 18-hole Four Seasons **golf course** is spectacular, with narrow, difficult fairways that snake up the slopes of Nevis Peak; it's one of the two or three best courses in the Caribbean. Several hotels have **tennis courts**, though the Four Seasons' leads the pack, with 10 beautifully maintained hard surface and clay courts and managed by Peter Burwash International. The latest craze on Nevis is **horse racing**, which is sponsored by the Nevis Turf and Jockey Club at a ramshackle track near White Bay. The races are generally held on holidays, such as Easter Monday, Whit Monday, Boxing Day, the first Sunday of August, and Independence Day. Admission is $4. Or you can trot off on your own by **renting a horse** at one of the island's several stables.

Bicycling

Nevis' perimeter road is ideal for pleasant, casual riding, although those seeking to conquer the entire 20-mile circuit should be advised that steep hills, climbing to over 800 feet above sea level, lie in the several-mile section east of Charlestown. The east side of the island (south of the airport), is the quietest stretch. For rentals, check with **Carlton Mead** at the Meadville Guest House, just outside Charlestown. Rentals are $10 per day ☎ *(869) 469-5235.*

Golf

Four Seasons Resort, Pinney's Beach, ☎ *(869) 469-1111.*
Designed by Robert Trent Jones, Jr., this is one of the Caribbean's most scenic and challenging courses. It encompasses 18 holes and provides tremendous views up the slopes of 3232-foot Nevis Peak and down to palm fringed shoreline—concentrating on your game can be a tad difficult. The 15th hole, a 660-yard par five, is a whopper. Greens fees are $110 for 18 holes if you are staying at the hotel, otherwise it is $135. Celebrate the 19th hole at one of the resort's posh watering holes.

Horseback Riding

Hop on a horse and ride into the sunset at one of three outfits: **Nisbet Plantation** ☎ *(869) 469-9325* ($45 for two hours), **Nevis Equestrian Centre** in Cole Hill ☎ *(869) 469-2638,* and **Garner Estate's** ☎ *(869) 469-5528* ($35 for two hours).

Watersports

A number of companies offer aqua activity. For general watersports equipment and boating, try **Newcastle Bay Marina** ☎ *(869) 469-9373* or **Captain Julian Rigby** at Oualie Beach ☎ *(869) 469-9735.* For deep-sea fishing, contact **The Lady James** ☎ *(869) 469-1989* or **Jans Travel Agency** ☎ *(869) 469-5578.* Windsurfing can be arranged through **Winston Cooke** ☎ *(869) 469-9615.*

NEVIS

Where to Stay

NEVIS

Fielding's Highest Rated Hotels in Nevis

★★★★★	Four Seasons Resort Nevis	$275–$650
★★★★	Montpelier Plantation Inn	$175–$295
★★★★	Nisbet Plantation	$191–$525
★★★	Golden Rock Estate	$110–$200
★★★	Hermitage, The	$160–$410
★★★	Mount Nevis Hotel and Beach Club	$130–$270
★★★	Old Manor Estate and Hotel	$125–$250

Fielding's Best Plantation Inns on Nevis

★★★★	Montpelier Plantation Inn	$175–$295
★★★	Hermitage, The	$160–$410
★★★★	Nisbet Plantation	$191–$525
★★★	Golden Rock Estate	$110–$200

Fielding's Best Value Hotels in Nevis

★★★	Golden Rock Estate	$110–$200
★★★★	Montpelier Plantation Inn	$175–$295
★★★	Old Manor Estate and Hotel	$125–$250
★★★	Mount Nevis Hotel and Beach Club	$130–$270

Until the 1991 opening of the Four Seasons, Nevis was known primarily for its intimate old plantation inns, five of which flourish today. They are rich in history and color, though they aren't the spot for visitors who crave tremendous luxury and air conditioning. For this, look no further than the Four Seasons, a 196-room resort plopped down smack in the middle of the island's best beach. The debut of this hotel has changed the character of the island dramatically, but all shared in the pride when the hotel was awarded five diamonds by AAA.

Hotels and Resorts

The **Four Seasons Nevis** dominates the scene in most every way. In addition to a four-mile stretch of beach, the resort offers superb tennis and golf facilities and will arrange almost any other island activity you can think of.

Four Seasons Resort Nevis   **$275–$3800**   ★★★★★

Pinney's Beach, ☎ *(800) 332-3442, (869) 469-1111, FAX (869) 469-1112.*
Single: $275–$650. Double: $275–$650. Suites Per Day: $500–$3800.
Scattered over 350 choice acres, this scene stealer occupies a picturesque former coconut plantation along Pinney's Beach. The hotel's attractive hub is a cluster of buildings that house reception, a restaurant and other common area facilities overlooking the pool. The two-story guest wings extend down the beach and draw some gripes; admittedly they don't make the most of the very Caribbean surroundings, and have all the personality of a ski lodge. But the standard guest rooms themselves—big enough to qualify as junior suites—are undeniably fine. Palatial bathrooms with cool planes of marble in every direction are tops; Persian rugs, mahogany and rattan furnishings, and fresh plants and flowers are among the luxe trappings. Most rooms face the sea (the beach is not quite within view) but you can snare a golf view with, in our opinion, a more prodigious canvas to behold—the swoop of Nevis Peak—for a few dollars less. There is also an assortment of one- two- and three-bedroom suites, and a series of villas sprinkled above on the slopes, some with a private pool ($700-$3800 per night). The championship golf course is justly praised for its quiet grandeur, but the grounds also include 10 tennis courts, two pools, an exercise room, and all manner of watersports (non-motorized are included in the rates). Families are welcome, and parents can relax after putting their kids in various supervised programs. Otherwise, as befits a stiff rate card, the atmosphere here is a tad formal; you'll want to dress for dinner. Despite the terrific setting, posh rooms and pampering amenities, at the end of the day what really makes the Four Seasons stand out is a near-unassailable staff—they and the hotel's management understand well the line between prim and amiable, formal and graceful, and toe it splendidly. 196 rooms. Credit cards: A, MC, V.

Mount Nevis Hotel and Beach Club   **$130–$270**   ★★★

Newcastle, ☎ *(800) 756-3847, (869) 469-9373, FAX (869) 469-9375.*
Website: www.mountnevishotel.com. E-mail: mountnevis@aol.com.
Single: $130–$270. Double: $130–$270.
Located on the drier northern slopes of Mt. Nevis, this family-run property includes air-conditioned guest rooms with VCRs (videos are loaned to guests) and private patios with great views of St. Kitts. Junior suites also have full kitchens, as do the two-bedroom suites. Facilities include a good, expensive restaurant, bar, pool, and a beach club a mile away (free shuttle). A bit lonely in the off season, but a good alternative if the rustic nature of Nevis' inns is a turn-off. Five minutes from the Nevis airport. 32 rooms. Credit cards: A, MC, V.

Oualie Beach Hotel   **$100–$255**   ★★

Oualie Beach, ☎ *(800) 682-5431, (869) 469-9735, FAX (869) 469-9176.*
E-mail: oualie@caribsurf.com.
Single: $100–$215. Double: $140–$255.

Located right on the beach, this small family-run property accommodates guests in charming gingerbread-style duplex cottages that are pleasant and comfortable. Only some have air conditioning and kitchens, but all sport screened verandas with nice views of St. Kitts. There's a dive shop on-site that also handles most watersports including windsurfing. This is one of the few Nevis hotels without a pool, but also one of the few with a beach, and a pretty one at that. 22 rooms. Credit cards: A, D, MC, V.

Apartments and Condominiums

The focus on Nevis is on plantation-style inns, but **Hurricane Cove** is a good choice if cooking at home is on your agenda. Villa rentals are available from the **Four Seasons Nevis** ($700 per night and up) ☎ *(869) 469-1111,* while **Oualie Realty** has a few less-pricey options ☎ *(869) 469-9817.* **Super Foods**, a well-stocked grocery store that caters to the ex-pat and villa community, is located in Charlestown on Main Street. **Nevis Bakery**, on Happy Hill Drive in Charlestown, sells fresh breads, buns, pastries and cakes.

Hurricane Cove Bungalows $95–$265   ★★

Oualie Beach, ☎ *(869) 469-9462, FAX (869) 469-9462.*
Single: $95–$265. Double: $95–$265.
Set on a steep hill with glorious views, this small complex consists of one- to three-bedroom bungalows with ceiling fans, complete kitchens and covered porches. There's a shared splash pool on-site, but most of the units have their own small pool. The beach is at the foot of the hill, five minutes away on foot. Rustic, but one of Nevis' better buys. 10 rooms. Credit cards: MC, V.

Inns

Plantation inns are a particular specialty on Nevis. For many visitors who enjoy a few basic luxury perks amid rustic atmosphere, the inns are still a top choice. One, the **Montpelier Plantation Inn**, provided enough of a chic retreat to keep the late Princess Diana happy a few years ago. Another, **The Hermitage**, is possibly the oldest wooden plantation house extant in the West Indies. Four of the five inns are located on the southern slopes of Nevis Peak, around 800 feet above sea level, which allows them to get away without air conditioning. The nearest beach is a 10-minute drive from each of these four, though all have a pool for relaxing. **Nisbet Plantation**, on the other hand, has a manicured lawn with rows of palms that extend from the great house past the cottage accommodations to a nice curl of sand—it's located on the north end of the island, a short drive from the Nevis airport. Note that all of the plantations have a quantity of stairs to navigate and do not work well for those who are physically challenged.

Golden Rock Estate $110–$200   ★★★

Gingerland, ☎ *(800) 223-9815, (869) 469-3346, FAX (869) 469-2113.*
Single: $110–$185. Double: $130–$200. Suites Per Day: $165–$235.
Set high on the slopes of Nevis Peak, sugar is no longer the product of this 18th-century plantation estate, an environmentally sound inn is the new focus. Run by Pam Barry, the great-great-great granddaughter of the man who built the main house in 1815, it oozes character. Accommodations are in a series of spacious cottages, all with mahogany furnishings, island art, canopied king beds, large verandas and ceiling fans in lieu of air conditioning. The prize is a two-story bridal suite located inside a converted old stone windmill—perfect for honeymooners or a fam-

ily of four. The estate is surrounded by lush rainforest, with a good hiking trail starting at the property. The tropical grounds include a spring-fed pool, a tennis court and views of ash-spouting Montserrat in the distance. Free transportation to the beach or into town is provided. 15 rooms. Credit cards: A, MC, V.

Hermitage, The $160–$410 ★★★

Fig Tree, ☎ (800) 223-9832, (869) 469-3477, FAX (869) 469-2481.
E-mail: nevherm@caribsurf.com.
Single: $160–$410. Double: $160–$410.
Set on a 250-year-old plantation up in the hills, this charming property accommodates guests in colorful restored cottages that are nicely done with Oriental rugs, pitched ceilings, canopied four-poster beds or twin beds, large verandas with hammocks and antiques. Some also have full kitchens. A gorgeous two-bedroom house set on two private acres with its own pool, oversized baths, full kitchen and antique canopy beds is also available ($620 nightly). The terraced grounds include stables for horseback riding, a small pool, tennis and a plantation-style restaurant in an antique-filled room. Hermitage's charisma is that of creaking floors and fluttering ceiling fans, producing a delightful ambiance with a reputation for luring Hollywood writers and others spurred to creativity by the retreat. Rates include a full American breakfast. 14 rooms. Credit cards: A, D, MC, V.

Montpelier Plantation Inn $175–$295 ★★★★

Fig Tree, ☎ (800) 223-9832, (869) 469-3462, FAX (869) 469-2932.
Website: www.stkitts-nevis.com/montpelier. E-mail: montpinn@caribsurf.com.
Single: $175–$265. Double: $195–$295. Suites Per Day: $245–$345.
Set on a shoulder of Nevis Peak high above the sea, this former sugar plantation was the site of Admiral Nelson and Fanny Nisbet's wedding in 1787. The event blessed the lush, 60-acre estate with a romantic atmosphere that continues to this day. Accommodations are in cottages and of good size; all are nicely done with large private patios that take in a sea view—ceiling fans keep things cool. There's a brilliant blue pool (perhaps the largest on the island) and tennis court, and they'll shuttle you to their section of Pinney's Beach, about 25 minutes away. Rates include continental breakfast, and afternoon tea is served daily poolside on request. The fine restaurant is acclaimed for its English-Mediterranean fusion cuisine, using the harvest of the estate's organic garden and orchard. Children under 8 not allowed. 17 rooms. Credit cards: MC, V.

Nisbet Plantation $191–$525 ★★★★

Newcastle, ☎ (800) 742-6008, (869) 469-9325, FAX (869) 469-9864.
Website: www.nisbetplantation.com. E-mail: nisbetbc@caribsurf.com.
Single: $191–$394. Double: $255–$525.
This well-run property combines the charm of an 18th-century plantation with the services of a resort. Set on 30 acres fronting a decent mile-long beach, this is the former home of Fanny Nisbet, though it's grown quite a bit since then. The signature vista is of a regal avenue of coconut palms that unfurls from the great house, where meals are served, for several hundred yards down to the sea. Accommodations are on either side of the lawn, generally in cottages decorated in white and wicker with tropical accents—most with screened-in porches that greet the sunrise.

Facilities include two restaurants, two bars, a tennis court, pool, small library and croquet. Complimentary laundry service and evening turndown are nice perks, and the staff will help arrange activities. MAP rates include breakfast and dinner in Nisbet's fine dining room, and traditional English tea. 38 rooms. Credit cards: A, MC, V.

Old Manor Estate and Hotel   **$125–$250**   ★★★

Gingerland, ☎ *(800) 892-7093, (869) 469-3445, FAX (869) 469-3388.*
Closed Date: August.
Single: $125–$250. Double: $125–$250.

Perched high in the hills, this converted plantation house dates back to 1832 and is unique because, in contrast to the windmills that powered most sugar factories, Old Manor used steam energy. The rusting equipment sits evocatively among stone ruins like beacons from another era—one can almost hear their whistling and clattering jangle! Guest rooms in the Georgian buildings are nicely done and spacious, with marble floors, high ceilings, canopied beds, verandas and ceiling fans (no air conditioning). A renovation under the property's new manager/owners has provided a much-needed sprucing up with new furnishings and linens. Facilities include a bar, excellent restaurant and a pool that gazes up at Nevis Peak. They'll shuttle you back and forth to their beach bar at Pinney's. 12 rooms. Credit cards: A, MC, V.

Low Cost Lodging

Nevis is one of the Caribbean's more expensive destinations, and low-priced bunks are few and far between. The Mead family makes the **Meadville Cottages** the friendliest option ☎ *(869) 469-5235,* while **Yamseed** is a cute guest house on a quiet beach near the airport ☎ *(869) 469-9361.* **Paradise Guest House** outside Cotton Ground is another possibility ☎ *(869) 469-1195,* while the spartan **Sea Spawn Guest House** will do in a pinch ☎ *(869) 469-5239.* **Pinney's Beach Hotel** was formerly a budget option, but its location (at the end of Pinney's Beach, a half-mile from the Four Seasons) has gone to their head and the edging-toward-moderate rates are unreasonable for its well-worn rooms ☎ *(869) 469-5207.*

Where to Eat

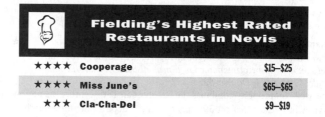

	Fielding's Highest Rated Restaurants in Nevis	
★★★★	Cooperage	$15–$25
★★★★	Miss June's	$65–$65
★★★	Cla-Cha-Del	$9–$19

	Fielding's Most Romantic Restaurants in Nevis	
♡ ♡ ♡ ♡	**Cooperage**	$15–$25
♡ ♡ ♡	**Miss June's**	$65–$65

	Fielding's Best Value Restaurants in Nevis	
★★★★	**Cooperage**	$15–$25
★★★	**Cla-Cha-Del**	$9–$19
★★	**Eddy's**	$9–$12
★★	**Unella's**	$5–$21
★★	**Muriel's Cuisine**	$12–$18

Driven by the island's up-market accommodations, and because there is little in the way of an agricultural economy, dining on Nevis is expensive. The best restaurants are located in the plantation inns and at the **Four Seasons**, but plan on spending at least $50 per person for dinner. Although dress is casual (long pants for men), the atmosphere in each is such that romantic dinners are embellished by hauling out your best resort duds. Many visitors make a nightly ritual of stopping at each of these spots over the course of a four- or five-night visit; **Nisbet Plantation** also proffers a fine afternoon tea. But don't miss a trip to one of the island's smaller eateries for local fare. Here, such Nevisian delicacies as jerk chicken, curried goat, salt-fish casserole, johnnycakes, breadfruit salad and piles of steamed squash and rice 'n' peas may be heaped onto your plate. There's also **Miss June's**, which provides a long meal rich in traditional West Indian fare. A popular beach bar, **Tequila Sheila's**, serves brunch on Sunday.

Callaloo　　　　　　　　**$$$**　　　　　　　　★★

Main Street; Charlestown, ☎ *(869) 469-5389.*
Lunch: 10 a.m.–4 p.m., entrées $5–$7.
Dinner: 4–10 p.m., entrées $15–$22. Closed: Sun.
This unprepossessing place on Main Street in Charlestown is the place to come for everything from tasty charbroiled burgers to grilled lobster ($22). West Indian specialties abound, and you have a choice of seating at little tables on a sidewalk patio or in an air-conditioned dining room. Callaloo offers a wide variety of dishes from pizza to pastries. Bring your own wine or beer. Credit cards: A, MC, V.

Cla-Cha-Del　　　　　　　**$$**　　　　　　　★★★

Cade's Bay; ☎ *(869) 469-9640.*

Lunch: 11 a.m.–4 p.m., entrées $7–$19.
Dinner: 6 p.m. until..., entrées $9–$19. Closed: Thur.
Cade's Bay, on the north end of Pinney's Beach, is home to the Pinney family's eatery, Cla-Cha-Del. Named after siblings Claudina, Charlie and Delroy, this West Indian dining spot showcases the family's ties to the local fishing industry. Try parrotfish, conch or lobster, or drop in on Saturday for goat water, a stew with Irish origins. Burgers, soups and sandwiches are also available. Credit cards: MC, V.

Cooperage $$$ ★★★★

Old Manor Estate, ☎ *(869) 469-3445.* Associated hotel: *Old Manor Hotel.*
Dinner: 6:30–9:30 p.m., entrées $15–$25.
The historical setting and solid food help make for a fine meal—you might get lucky and have views of Montserrat rumbling away across the channel. Located in a restored, 17th-century plantation inn, the stone-walled dining room once reverberated with the sounds of coopers making barrels for the sugar mill. Of the island's major restaurants, this is one of the few with an a la carte menu—for under $20 you can have chicken, shrimp or veal scallopini. For a splurge, the green-pepper soup served with complete meals is delicious. A plantation-style buffet is held on Fridays in season. Reservations recommended. Credit cards: A, MC, V.

Courtyard, The $$ ★★

Main Street, Charlestown, ☎ *(869) 469-5685.*
Lunch: 8 a.m.–3 p.m., entrées $4–$10.
Dinner: 5–11 p.m., entrées $12–$20. Closed: Sun.
This popular downtown spot is known for fresh-from-the-oven pumpkin or ginger-infused sweets. Ferry passengers who alight near here come for the hearty breakfasts; others might drop in for lunch or dinner when the menu is either burgers, salads, curries or seafood specials. Dine indoors or in the tree-shaded garden restaurant known as the Courtyard Cafe. Credit cards: A, MC, V.

Eddy's $ ★★

Main Street, Charlestown, ☎ *(869) 469-5958.*
Lunch: Noon–3 p.m., entrées $2–$7.
Dinner: 7:30–9:30 p.m., entrées $9–$12. Closed: Thur., Sun.
Ever had a flying fish sandwich? Don't let it get away from you at this informal, second-story patio restaurant that's an ideal vantage point for tourist-watching. Inside the warmly decorated old wood townhouse, the crowd tends to be dominated by repeat visitors and permanent residents. Eddy's has a jumpin' bar with potent drinks and a well-attended Wednesday happy hour. Credit cards: A, MC, V.

Miss June's $$$ ★★★★

Jones Bay, ☎ *(869) 469-5330.*
Dinner: 7:30 p.m., prix fixe $65.
Several evenings a week, Trinidadian June Mestier serves a bountiful buffet groaning with delectable dishes to a couple dozen lucky individuals. The meals are served in her home, but strictly by reservation. There's one seating—at 7:30 p.m., when guests assemble for cocktail hour. The buffet tables are filled with some 25 or 30 different items (depending on what's fresh at the market), but regular favorites include lamb in an orange and chanteuse sauce, and baby ribs cooked in mauby, a

NEVIS

local aphrodisiac (it's the dish fourth from the left). After dinner, everyone adjourns to a parlor for aperitifs and anecdotes. The price is high, but includes all alcohol, before, during and after your huge meal, until the last guest leaves. A Nevis institution. Reservations required. Credit cards: MC, V.

Muriel's Cuisine   **$$**   ★★

Upper Happy Hill Drive; Charlestown, ☎ (869) 469-5920.
Lunch: 8:30 a.m.–4 p.m., entrées $5–$7.
Dinner: 4–10 p.m., entrées $12–$18. Closed: Sun.
Miss Muriel's establishment is fast becoming a choice spot to dine in Charlestown, especially for her substantial West Indian buffet lunches served on Wednesdays ($8). This talented lady can't offer a sea view, but the food is rib stickin', especially the variety of curries (chicken, goat, sometimes seafood) served with local vegetables, which may include christophene (chayote), plantain and rice and peas; the jerk chicken is always tasty. Breakfast is served Monday through Saturday, and features salt fish and eggs with bacon, ham or cheese. Credit cards: A, MC, V.

Shopping on Nevis pursues simple pleasures as a rule, but several spots are worth a stop. **Island Hopper** carries the full line of Caribelle Batik fashions. Swimsuits and cotton handmade dresses can be picked up at **Amanda's Fashions**. **Knick Knacks** has artwork and souvenirs and is located just behind the Bank of Nevis on Main Street. An excellent array of souvenirs, crafts, guava jelly, gooseberry or soursop jam, banana chutney and fruit wines are available at **Nevis Handicraft Co-Op**. Nevis and St. Kitts are known throughout the world for their issued stamps, and the **Nevis Philatelic Bureau** provides a wide assortment. The commemorative stamps of September 19, 1993, which celebrate the 10th anniversary of the federation's independence, are considered collectibles. All of these stores are located in Charlestown, and the local market is held on Saturdays.

The **Eva Wilkin Gallery**, located in a sugar mill at the **Clay Ghaut Estate** (opposite the Old Manor Hotel) commemorates the work of a now-deceased elderly lady artist whose evocative pastels and watercolors of Nevis life were beloved by islanders. Today the gallery, which also sells postcards and other contemporary Nevis art, is run by a Canadian couple and is open to the public. Photo needs and one-hour processing can be served at **Rawlins Photo Color Lab and Studio** in Fig Tree or **Pemberton's** on Main Street in Charlestown.

Nevis Directory

Arrival and Departure

As we go to press, the small air strip in Newcastle is being extended to handle larger planes, with completion expected in 1998. Though jets still won't be able to land in Nevis, the larger runway may lure **American Eagle** to schedule service from San Juan, Puerto Rico, allowing connections to Nevis from most North American gateways. Until then, you have several options, all of which require a little extra effort.

Most air service into Nevis originates in St. Kitts (see "Arrival and Departure" in "St. Kitts"). From St. Kitts, three carriers make the ten-minute hop to Nevis: **LIAT** and two local airlines, **Air St. Kitts-Nevis** ☎ *(869) 469-9241* and **Nevis Express** ☎ *(869) 469-3346*. Alternatively, if you are not planning to visit St. Kitts during your vacation, it may be easier to fly to Nevis through one of the other islands these three commuter airlines serve, including Antigua, Sint Maarten, St. Thomas, St. Croix or Puerto Rico, all of which can be reached by jets from North America. Have your travel agent investigate which routing works best for you from both a time and monetary standpoint.

Guests of the **Four Seasons** typically fly into St. Kitts, where they are met at the airport by a van and transferred to a private ferry out of Basseterre for a 30-minute trip to the resort's beachside dock (visitors not staying at the Four Seasons may use this ferry for the same $25 one way fee on a space-available basis). **Public ferry** service, aboard the *Caribe Queen* or the *Spirit of Mount Nevis*, makes the 45-minute crossing between Charlestown and Basseterre one to three times daily for $4 one way ☎ *(869) 469-9373*.

The departure tax is $10.

Business Hours

Shops open Monday–Saturday 8 a.m.–noon and 1–4 p.m. Most close earlier on Thursday. Banks open Monday–Thursday 8 a.m.–3 p.m. and Friday 8 a.m.–5 p.m.

Climate

As on St. Kitts, average temperatures hover between 78 and 85 degrees Fahrenheit, during the day; nighttime temperatures can drop to 68 degrees Fahrenheit. Trade winds keep it breezy, though the humidity can rise during the summer. Downpours are quick but heavy between mid-June through mid-November, which is considered the rainy season.

Documents

U.S. citizens need to present a passport or proof of citizenship (drivers license, voter's registration card and birth certificate), along with a return or ongoing ticket.

Electricity

The current is 220 volts, though some hotels have 110 volts. Bring a transformer and adapter just in case.

Getting Around

Taxis are available in both Charlestown and at the Newcastle Airport. From the airport to the Four Seasons, figure $12; to the plantation inns west of Charlestown, it will be $15–17. From Charlestown to the Four Seasons, the price is $6; to the plantation inns, $11–12; to Nisbet Plantation, $14. Three- to four-hour island tours are common; try **All Seasons Streamline Tours** which has comfortable, air conditioned vans ☎ *(869) 469-1138*. **Minibus** service around the island is fairly reliable and cheap—about $1 to almost anywhere—although there's less service on Thursday and Sunday. All routes originate in Charlestown; one usually heads north and around to Newcastle, the other heads west and up to Newcastle, but service is largely dependent on the needs of local riders, not sightseers. Rental cars start at $35 per day, or $65 if the Four Seasons arranges it for you. You'll need to shell out $12 for a Nevis drivers license, and don't forget to drive on the left. Daytrips to St. Kitts are possible either via air or ferry; see "Arrival and Departure" above.

Language

English is the official language, spoken with a rhythmic lilt. Natives also speak a local patois.

Medical Emergencies

Alexandra Hospital in Charlestown ☎ *(869) 469-5473* operates a 24-hour emergency room service. Serious emergencies should be handled in San Juan, Puerto Rico.

Money

The official currency in St. Kitts-Nevis is the Eastern Caribbean dollar, or EC, the exchange rate for which is about $2.70 to one American dollar. U.S. currency is accepted island-wide, but you'll get a better rate by exchanging travelers checks at a bank or by paying with a credit card.

Telephone

The area code is *869*, for both St. Kitts and Nevis. To call Nevis from the U.S., dial 1 + (869) and the seven-digit local number. Telegrams can be sent from the **Cable & Wireless office** on Main Street in Charlestown ☎ *(869) 469-5000*. You can also make international telephone calls from this office, which will save you a lot of money. The Cable & Wireless office is open from Monday–Friday 8 a.m.–6 p.m., and on Saturday from 8 a.m.–noon. The office is closed on Sunday and on public holidays.

Time

Atlantic Standard Time, which is one hour later than New York time, except during Daylight Saving Time, when it is the same.

Tipping and Taxes

Expect your hotel to add a 10 percent service charge. Check restaurant bills before adding your own 10–15 percent service tip. If a taxi driver hasn't added the tip himself, 10–15 percent is considered standard.

Tourist Information

The **Nevis Tourist Office** is located on Main Street in Charlestown ☎ *(869) 469-1042*. You can pick up brochures and maps, and they can assist with budget accommodations. It's open Monday through Saturday. A St. Kitts/Nevis tourism office is also operated in New York ☎ *(800) 582-6208 or (212) 535-1234*.

Web Site

www.interknowledge.com/stkitts-nevis

When to Go

Culturama, a popular and festive event, celebrates the island's history, folklore and arts with presentations, talent shows, beauty pageants, calypso contests and West Indian delicacies. It is held in late July.

NEVIS HOTELS	RMS	RATES	PHONE	CR. CARDS
★★★★★ Four Seasons Resort Nevis	196	$275–$650	(800) 332-3442	A, MC, V
★★★★ Montpelier Plantation Inn	17	$175–$295	(800) 223-9832	MC, V
★★★★ Nisbet Plantation	38	$191–$525	(800) 742-6008	A, MC, V
★★★ Golden Rock Estate	15	$110–$200	(800) 223-9815	A, MC, V
★★★ Hermitage, The	14	$160–$410	(800) 223-9832	A, D, MC, V
★★★ Mount Nevis Hotel and Beach Club	32	$130–$270	(800) 756-3847	A, MC, V
★★★ Old Manor Estate and Hotel	12	$125–$250	(800) 892-7093	A, MC, V
★★ Hurricane Cove Bungalows	10	$95–$265	(869) 469-9462	MC, V
★★ Oualie Beach Hotel	22	$100–$255	(800) 682-5431	A, D, MC, V

NEVIS RESTAURANTS	PHONE	ENTRÉE	CR. CARDS
Regional Cuisine			
★★★★ Cooperage	(869) 469-3445	$15–$25	A, MC, V
★★★★ Miss June's	(869) 469-5330	$65–$65	MC, V
★★★ Cla-Cha-Del	(869) 469-9640	$7–$19	MC, V
★★ Callaloo	(869) 469-5389	$5–$22	A, MC, V
★★ Courtyard, The	(869) 469-5685	$4–$20	A, MC, V
★★ Eddy's	(869) 469-5958	$2–$12	A, MC, V
★★ Muriel's Cuisine	(869) 469-5920	$5–$18	A, MC, V
★★ Unella's	(869) 469-5574	$4–$21	D, MC, V

PUERTO RICO

Watersports of all kinds are available at Sun Bay.

Puerto Rico makes a great introduction to the Caribbean. Indeed, its cosmopolitan capital, San Juan, with its treasure trove of colonial historic sites, idyllic beaches and bustling casinos and nightlife, has emerged as the region's most popular destination. This U.S. Commonwealth yields the niceties to which U.S. natives are accustomed while delivering a spicy culture and exotic scenery to make it intriguing.

Part of the reason Puerto Rico does so well is due to its accessibility. Many carriers that service the Caribbean use San Juan's Luis Munoz Marin International Airport as a hub; if you're not into the hassle of laying over and changing planes, there's no reason not to just stay put in Puerto Rico. The island's well-developed tourism infrastructure makes vacations a breeze, whether you're seeking the newest, plushest accommodations or the charming country inns, called *paradors*, that dot the countryside. Some of Puerto Rico's resorts number among those pearls much beloved by travel sophisticates. And gourmands won't be disappointed by the food—especially if they sample the haute cuisine coming from some of the restaurants based in the highest rated hotels. Puerto Rico hit a record 1.5 million hotel and inn registrations for the period July 1, 1996 to June 30, 1997, and for the first six months of 1997 visitors were up 9.4 percent.

Although you could easily spend your entire vacation in San Juan, most tourists like to use it as a base and make day trips to Puerto Rico's natural wonders such as the impressive rain forest or the magnificent web of caves. Just a 90-minute drive takes you to the town of Ponce, founded in 1692 and reminiscent of Barcelona with a blend of neoclassical, art deco and Creole architecture. Even the sidewalks are edged with local pink marble.

Remember that the island is large—you'll definitely want to rent a car if you're staying for any length of time. Birdwatchers and nature lovers should head east to Fajardo and Humacao. The Caribbean National Forest and Las Cabezas Nature Reserve are handy, and the area is notable for good scuba diving as well. On the west coast, the third largest town, Mayaguez, awaits those who collect local crafts and arts. You'll find good shopping in downtown amidst its Victorian and Baroque storefronts. Mayaguez and nearby Rincon both make launching points for mountain hikes in the area.

If your idea of the perfect vacation involves decking out at night, eating gourmet meals and shopping til you drop, at least part of your time should include San Juan. Travelers looking for more of an idyllic, casual vacation would do better heading for Puerto Rico's out islands, Culebra or Vieques. While most Caribbean islands are best suited to one type of vacationer or another, Puerto Rico stands as one of the few that satisfies almost every taste.

This year may prove a milestone in Puerto Rico's history: in 1998 the Puerto Rican people will once again vote on the issue of statehood. The last time it came up for vote, those voting to keep the status quo narrowly won and a small minority voted for independence. If you want to stir up a lively conversation, mention this political hot potato. Regardless of whether it joins the union or not, Puerto Rico will undoubtedly retain the Spanish-flavored charm that has made it so popular.

PUERTO RICO

BEST BETS FOR...

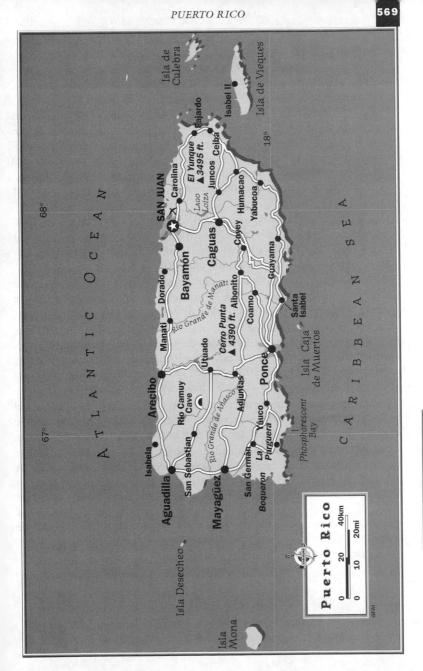

Located in the Greater Antilles some 1045 miles from New York, Puerto Rico is surrounded by the Atlantic Ocean to the north and the Caribbean Sea to the south. The island measures 110 by 35 miles (about the size of Connecticut) and has a variety of ecosystems, including more than 200 miles of coastline, old volcanic mountains, a sprawling cave system and 20 designated forest reserves, including the famed 28,000-acre El Yunque rainforest near San Juan.

San Juan, the capital city whose metropolitan area stretches some 300 square miles, draws the lion's share of tourists who flock to the excellent beach resorts in Condado and Isla Verde and the beautifully preserved historic section called Old San Juan, the oldest city under the U.S. flag.

The north coast, known as karst country, is named for its limestone, and the region is pocked with hills, holes and one of the world's largest river cave systems, called Río Camuy Cave Park, a 300-acre network.

The city of Ponce, called the "pearl of the south," is a coastal city 70 miles from San Juan and founded by Ponce de Léon's great-grandson in 1692. Fronting the Caribbean Sea it is noted for its distinctive architecture dating from the mid-1800s to the 1930s. Ponce has restored more than 600 of its 1000 historic buildings in a 40-by-80 block area.

Because of its agriculturally intense past, less than one percent of the island today is virgin forest. Coffee and bananas are grown in the mountains, while coastal farmers produce sugarcane and pineapples.

Two of Puerto Rico's nearby islands are inhabited: Culebra, located off the west coast half-way between the mainland and St. Thomas; and Vieques, six miles east of Fajardo. The former is actually an archipelago of one main island and 20 surrounding cays—most of which comprise the Culebra National Wildlife Refuge. On Vieques, horses run wild, cattle graze on the hills and tree frogs (called *coqi*) are the nosiest residents. Its Mosquito Bay on the south shore is one of the world's few remaining bioluminescent bays. Tourist facilities on both islands are decidedly casual.

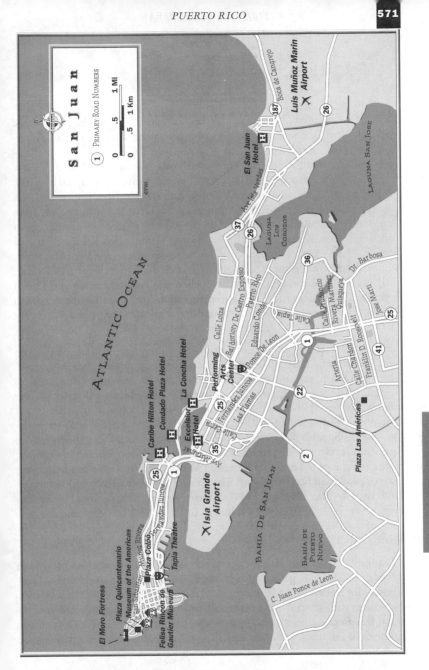

History

In 1493, Columbus arrived on the island of Puerto Rico in the company of Ponce de León, who named the island for his patron saint, San Juan. The island, however, already had a name—*Borinquen*—a Taino Indian nomenclature and one that is still lovingly used today by native Puerto Ricans. Caparra, inland and across the bay, was the first choice for a capital in 1508. With the permission of supreme cacique Agueybana, Juan Ponce de León (the island's first governor) and his men first scouted the island of San Juan Bautista. Eventually de León set off on his journey to discover eternal youth and never actually resided in the handsome home, Casa Blanca, that had been built for him. Thirteen years later, settlers decamped for the drier, windier islet fronting the Atlantic, where they permanently settled. During early years of colonization, the city repelled the British, French and Dutch corsairs. La Fortaleza, now the governor's mansion, and El Morro and San Cristóbal forts were built during those times with the specific aim of keeping marauders at bay.

By the early 1800s, the era of Caribbean piracy was finally brought to a halt. At the same time, Spain threw open her doors to immigration; subsequent increase in economic prosperity coupled with new aesthetic influences from abroad were soon reflected in the island's architectural styles. It was during this period that Old San Juan developed the colonial/neoclassic look that predominates today—all within the urban grid pattern envisioned by the original Spanish planners. In 1897 the island gained independence from Spanish rule. On July 25, 1898, however, Spanish troops landed in Guánica, in the middle of the Spanish-American War, and disturbed whatever modicum of peace had been achieved. The Treaty of Paris of 1899 handed the island over to the U.S. In 1917, Puerto Ricans were granted American citizenship; in 1952, the island achieved unique status by becoming the only member of the commonwealth to receive its own constitution and government.

During the early 20th century, a burgeoning population brought growth beyond the Old City gates and soon after, the destruction of substantial sections of its massive walls. Today, Old San Juan boasts only 5000 residents. No longer the financial hub, it still pulls 5000 workers to offices and government buildings, eateries and shops. A seven-block enclave that boasts a large number of art studios, florists, doctor's offices, and galleries is considered one of the more desirable spots to live on the island.

People

The total island population is 3.7 million, with some one million living in the San Juan metropolitan area. Puerto Rico is the Caribbean's most industrially developed island, and annual income is the highest in Latin America. Education is good, and more than a third of high school students go on to higher learning. Since the 1950s, U.S. businesses doing business in Puerto Rico have received tax breaks, a policy now being phased out. Besides tourism, which represents just six percent of the gross national product, Puerto Rico is a major producer and exporter of manufactured goods, pharmaceutical (producing 90 percent of the drugs sold in the U.S.) and high-tech equipment. Some 83 percent of the rum sold in the United States comes from the territory.

Freedom of faith is guaranteed by the Commonwealth Constitution, though the majority of islanders are Roman Catholic. Spanish and English are both official languages; the former is predominant, but since English is taught from kindergarten to high school in public schools, communication is rarely a problem, especially around San Juan. Some officials are currently attempting to make English the language used in schools.

American media have a huge influence on Puerto Ricans, who, paradoxically, have a fierce national pride, and, for some, a longing for independence from the United States. On the eve of its 100th anniversary as a U.S. Commonwealth, a bill is pending in U.S. Congress that would allow islanders to choose in 1998 whether to become the 51st state. Public sentiment is heavily divided on that topic. In 1993, 48 percent voted for commonwealth status, 46 percent wanted statehood, and independence advocates had 4.4 percent of the votes. Islanders are generally a friendly lot, but note that crime around the cities can be high, so use the typical precautions and discretion in displaying cash, cameras and valuable jewelry. Avoid deserted beaches both day and night.

Beaches

All the beaches on the island are public with one exception—the artificial beach at the Caribe Hilton in San Juan. Many hotels are situated right on the beach; if they aren't, they are but a short walk away. Hotels that do not enjoy such proximity usually provide a shuttle to the beach free of charge. **Luquillo Beach** is probably the best beach on the island for swimming. The waters are calm, and the coral reefs protect the pristine lagoon from the stronger waves of the Atlantic. Picnic tables are available as well as camp facilities. Also suitable for swimming is **Seven Seas**, a long strand with compacted sand. Trailers may be parked nearby and campers can pitch tents. Watersports of all kinds can be arranged at **Sun Bay**, a sugar-white beach on Vieques. Vessels for sailing also can be rented. One of the most famous beaches is **Condado Beach**, along Ashford Avenue in San Juan. It's a beauty-watcher's delight, especially for those who want to see the latest trend in swimwear and the prettiest island girls. Within walking distance are the long beaches of **Rincón**, **Cabo Rojo** and **Paguera**. Surfers claim that the best waves are along the Atlantic coastline from Borinquén Point south to Rincón. The surf is best from October through April. In summer, La Concha and Aviones have the best curls. All these beaches have board rentals nearby.

The best beaches near San Juan, are at Isla Verde in front of the major hotels.

Many knowledgeable divers regard Puerto Rico as little more than a hub for changing planes en route to Bonaire. The undersea reality is quite different. Some of the Caribbean's best and least exploited diving can be found in Puerto Rico. Water temperatures hover around 78°F and underwater visibility can exceed 100 feet. Why isn't it more famous? One reason may be that San Juan and the island's biggest resort area lie on the long northern coast, which offers none of Puerto Rico's prime diving. You have to venture away from the tourist mecca—to **Fajardo**, Dorado, Humacao, tiny **Parguera**, or the offshore islands—to experience the most succulent reefs and walls. Additionally, as happens on some other regional islands with a substantial variety of top-side activities, diving frequently takes a back-seat to a diversified vacation. So, to whet your appetite, pack up the car for a front-row tour of Puerto Rico's coastline.

When combined with **Culebra**, which has 50 dive sites and whose cays and islets are part of a national wildlife refuge, the east coast offers the island's greatest concentration of dive sites. Mini-walls, spur-and-groove formations, small caverns and plenty of marine life are available, as well as a wide variety of reef topographies to sample; at **Red Hog**, for instance, the abrupt wall drops from 80 to 1160 feet. If you want convenient diving, stick to the reefs off **Humacao** with 24 sites in a five-mile radius off shore or quiet La Parguera, where sites are closer to shore. Visibility varies more than wildly, but averages 75 feet or more, and can extend to 150 feet on really good days; the east coast sites can be impacted by freshwater runoff more than the other areas. Puerto Rico's dramatic wall comes close to shore at Guánica, a 20-minute boat ride from shore. Rays, turtles and moray eels are common here. Day trips from San Juan are possible (it's less than an hour drive to Fajardo or Humacao) while offshore Culebra, in particular, has several outstanding dives. Diving on the sprawling south coast is found on the stretch between Ponce and tiny **La Parguera** where hotels are low-key and swamps of mangrove replace beaches, deterring a number of would-be visitors. But the dive shops overlooking the patch reefs of La Parguera with 50 dive sites will proudly stack their precipitate wall—which is 22 miles long and plunges from 60–120 ft. to 3000 feet—against any other in the Caribbean. Black coral, now rare in the Caribbean, is healthy here. Throw in a stunning phosphorescent bay (you'll swim, not dive) and you have a sparkling marine experience. Salinas is one of the newest dive destinations in this region. Its Cayo Media Luna is good for snorkelers and beginning divers. Manatees are often seen feeding along the little-explored, shallow mangrove coast. Circling around to Puerto Rico's choppy west coast, there are lightly visited patch reef sites between Boqueron and Aguadilla, and attractive underwater caves near **Isabela**. But the best is found around two offshore destinations, **Desecheo** and **Mona Islands** where visibility is sometimes in triple digits and which yield a spectacular glimpse of what Caribbean diving might have been like a few decades ago, before overfishing and coral destruction began to take their toll. The latter has been called the Caribbean Galapagos and more than 270 fish species have been spotted here. These two islands (and Culebra) illustrate one local problem: many of the best sites are an hour or more away from a dock.

Long ignored, environmental concerns have finally become a front burner issue for local divers. The government has not instituted a permanent mooring system, which means a number of reefs in heavily traveled cruising locations are anchor-damaged; the busy Fajardo area is one abused spot. The dive operations will apparently have to undertake this project on their own. Although there are more than two dozen dive shops on the island, the three listed below are the standouts. Some of the other operations are not environmentally oriented and others have shown inconsistent ownership. Watch for this to change in coming years as dedicated divers focus more attention on Puerto Rico as a legitimate underwater destination. Dive style is friendly and casual, and it's not uncommon to be diving with the actual owners of the shops, which tend to be generally smaller outfits than typically found in the Caribbean.

Dive Shops

Aquática Underwater Adventures

Aguadilla; ☎ *(787) 890-6071.*

This small, but full service PADI dive center, opened in 1985 and specializes in underwater photo/video training. One tank dive $45–$65. Two tank dive, $65 in immediate area, or $85 to Desecheo; shore dives $45–$85. U.S. Coast Guard-certified boats hold 14 and supply each diver with a dive computer. Can arrange charters to Mona.

Coral Head Divers

Palmas del Mar Resort, Humacao; ☎ *(800) 635-4529 or (787) 850-7208.*

One of the island's more firmly established operations (since 1978) operated by and founded by Jim Abbott, a PADI and NAUI outfit with training to instructor/divemaster. Requires computers on all dives (included in price if you don't have your own); two tank dive, $95 (including equipment). Resort course, $45. All sites within 30 minutes from dock.

Culebra Dive Shop

Culebra; ☎ *(787) 742-3555.*

Handles over 50 sites of Culebra. PADI and NAUI affiliated. Two-tank dive $75 (equipment rental $20); resort courses $65. Owner Gene Thomas specializes in small groups for night diving, wrecks and underwater photography.

Parguera Divers

La Parguera; ☎ *(787) 899-4343 ext. 131.*

Smaller operation affiliated with Parador Posada Por la Mar, but owner and 25-year veteran Efra Figueroa is respected islandwide, plus he pioneered most of the Parguera sites. PADI and NAUI affiliated. Two-tank dive, $73, including lunch ($85 if you didn't bring your equipment). All Parguera dives within 30 minutes or less.

On Foot

It speaks well of Puerto Rico and its visitors that **El Yunque National Forest** remains the single most popular day trip outside San Juan, drawing upward of one million visitors annually. Thirteen trails of varying length cover 23 miles of the park's verdant terrain. It may surprise you to discover that most of these paths are paved to help prevent erosion (the summits receive up to 240 inches of rain a year), but the pavement may also be a slight concession to taming the wilds for city dwellers and tourists. With the exception of the longer **El Toro** and **El Yunque** trails, most of these hikes will take no more than an hour or two. The 28,000-acre El Yunque preserve covers four different types of forest, and is home to 240 species of tropical trees, flowers and wildlife, including 20 varieties of orchids and 50 types of ferns. A quarter-sized tree frog, the *coquí*, exists only on Puerto Rico and has become a local mascot, while the island's extremely rare Puerto Rican parrot—only a couple dozen left by the mid-'70s—is making a gradual comeback in the El Yunque forests.

Trails are not limited to those found in El Yunque; it's worth investigating some of the 19 other existing forest preserves sprinkled around the island. The bat-filled **Río Camuy Cave** features the third-largest subterranean river in the world. **Pinones Forest**, just east of San Juan, contains the island's biggest thicket of mangroves, and several other preserves line the island's scenic **Panoramic Route**. A few snake species inhabit the island, but none are poisonous; one, the Puerto Rican boa constrictor grows long enough to be intimidating—as long as seven feet—but it's considered harmless to humans.

Trekking Tour Groups

Encantos Ecotours

San Juan; ☎ *(787) 272-0005.*

This diversified outdoor touring organization, visits a different part of the island each day of the week, and offers manatee encounters, El Yunque walks, biking excursions, river swims, Culebra trips, kayaking, etc. Groups are limited to 20 people; $89–149, including lunch and transportation costs; percentage of fee goes to local conservation foundations. Three-day Mona Island trips are scheduled once a month, $599. Whale-watching trips are offered in winter. Stump Jumper mountain bike rentals, $30 per day; $100 per week.

What Else to See

Puerto Rico is so diverse that renting a car and getting out into the countryside is highly recommended. Two hours west of San Juan is the town of **Arecibo**, which dates to 1556, and the **Arecibo Observatory**, the world's largest radar/radio telescope. Operated by Cornell University and the National Science Foundation, the facility monitors radio emissions from outer space. SETI, the Search for Extraterrestrial Intelligence, is based here as well, but don't expect the people working there to share any secrets. The center is open for self-guided tours Tuesday through Friday from 2–3 p.m. and on Sundays from 1–4 p.m. Call ☎ *(787) 787-2612* for information.

On the island's southwest corner, the quaint town of **San German** retains much of its original Spanish architecture. The town's **Porta Coeli Church**, built in 1606, is the oldest church still intact under the U.S. flag.

Just 45 minutes from San Juan is **Las Cabezas de San Juan Nature Reserve** ☎ *(787) 722-5834)*, just opened in 1991. Its 316 acres house a 19th-century working **lighthouse**, called El Faro, and seven different ecological systems, including forest, mangroves, beaches, lagoons and offshore coral reefs.

Those interested in the long-gone Taino Indian way of life can check out two well-preserved ceremonial sites. **Tibes Indian Ceremonial Park**, near Ponce, has seven ceremonial ball courts, two dance grounds and a recreated Taino Indian village, as well as a museum displaying artifacts from the era. **Caguana Indian Ceremonial Ball Park**, in Utuado, was built by the Taino Indians some 800 years ago, and includes 10 ball courts and stone monoliths, some etched with petroglyphs.

The **LeLoLai VIP Program** offers discounted sightseeing tours and savings at participating shops, restaurants and sports operators, as well as free performances showcasing Puerto Rico's Indian, Spanish and African heritage. For information, call ☎ *(787) 723-3135* or *(787) 723-3136* during business hours on weekdays.

Puerto Rico's free tourist publication, *Que Pasa*, has many good ideas for sightseeing and tours.

What Else to See in San Juan

Historical Sites

Capilla de Cristo   ★

   Calle del Cristo, Old San Juan, ☎ *(787) 721-2400.*
   Hours open: 10 a.m.–3:30 p.m.

The Christ Chapel was built in 1753 after a horse rider's life was supposedly spared after a tragic accident. (Historical records say the youth did, indeed, die.) In any event, the small silver altar is dedicated to the Christ of Miracles.

Casa de los Contrafuertes ★★

Calle San Sebastian 101; P.O. Box 4184, Old San Juan, ☎ (787) 724-5477.
Hours open: 9 a.m.–4:30 p.m.
Called the House of Buttresses (for obvious reasons once you see it), historians assert that this house is the oldest residence left in Old San Juan, dating back to the early 18th century. Inside, a museum holds a 19th-century pharmacy.

Cathedral de San Juan ★★

Calle del Cristo 151; P.O. Box 9022145, Old San Juan, ☎ (787) 722-0861.
Hours open: 9 a.m.–5 p.m.
The San Juan Cathedral was built in 1540, destroyed by hurricane in 1529, and damaged by another hurricane in 1615. Today it holds the remains of Ponce de Leon and the relic of San Pio, a Roman martyr. Saturday mass is at 7 p.m., and Sunday masses begin at 11 a.m.

Convento de los Dominicos ★★

Plaza de San Jose, Old San Juan, ☎ (809) 724-5949.
Puerto Rico's first convent, started in 1523, was home to Dominican friars until 1838, when it became barracks for the United States Army. Inside you'll find the old chapel, art exhibits and a fine gift shop.

El Morro Fortress ★★★

Calle Norzagaray, Old San Juan, ☎ (787) 729-6960.
Hours open: 9 a.m.–5 p.m.
The oldest of the two great forts, commonly known as El Morro, guards the entrance to San Juan Bay. The Spaniards started construction in 1539, but it wasn't until 1787 that the fort was deemed complete. Now run under the auspices of the National Park Service, the six-level fort can be explored via guided tours or on your own. The dramatic fort contains dungeons, lookouts, barracks and vaults, as well as a small museum on its history. The Asiolo de Beneficencia, at one corner of El Morro's entrance, dates from 1832 when it operated as an indigents' hospital. It is now the new home of the Institute of Puerto Rican Culture.

Fort San Cristobal ★★★

Calle Norzagaray 501, Old San Juan, ☎ (787) 729-6960.
Hours open: 9 a.m.–5 p.m.
This massive fort protected land approaches to Old San Juan and dates back to 1634. Its walls rise 150 feet above sea level, and it sprawls 27 acres. Now run under the auspices of the National Park Service, the site includes a restoration of 18th-century Spanish troop barracks. Free tours are given daily from 10:00 a.m.–4:00 p.m.

Fort San Jeronimo ★

Next to the Caribe Hilton, Cordado Bay, ☎ (787) 724-5949.
This tiny fort was attacked by the British in 1797, 11 years after it was built. Now run by the Institute of Puerto Rican Culture, it houses a small military museum.

HISTORY & CULTURE IN OLD SAN JUAN

Founded in 1521 by Ponce de León, San Juan reigns as one of the Caribbean's most cosmopolitan cities. Take time to see the seven-square-mile historic area known as "Old San Juan." Enjoy the busy action at the port, wander through European-style public squares and explore the massive forts.

Fuerte San Felipe del Morro

A San Juan icon, this large, thick-walled fort was constructed by the Spaniards between 1450-1783. The six-level complex towers 140 feet above the breakers. Explore the dungeons and climb the towers.

Casa Blanca

Although the original frame house was destroyed in a 1623 hurricane, this is the site of Ponce de León's home. Rebuilt by the explorer's son-in-law, the present masonry house sheltered Ponce de León's decendants for 250 years.

Sir Francis Drake tried to capture La Fortaleza

La Fortaleza

The oldest executive mansion in the Western Hemisphere, La Fortaleza sits on a hill overlooking the harbor. Built on the remains of a 16th-century fort, the structure's architecture combines many styles. Don't miss the guided tour to see the splendid furnishings on the second floor.

Casa del Libro

Rare books that date back as far as 2000 years are on display in this museum, housed in an 18th-century building. The museum collection includes more than 5000 books.

Morro

Monjas

Virtud

San Sebastián

San José

Hospital

San Juan

Paseo de la Princesa

Recinto Oeste

Cristo

Presidio

Dominican Convent

Built in 1523, the convent often served as a shelter during Carib Indian attacks. Completely restored, the building contains a beautiful 18th-century altar, along with rare manuscripts and religious artifacts.

San Juan Museum of Art and History

Built in 1855, this building contains displays highlighting Puerto Rican art and culture. The large courtyard is the site of frequent concerts.

Pablo Casals Museum

This museum celebrates the world-famous cellist, who spent the last 16 years of his life in Puerto Rico. Displays include the musician's favorite cello, as well as manuscripts, photographs and recordings of his works.

San Juan Cathedral

This important shrine traces its beginnings to the 1520s, when worshippers gathered in a thatch-roof wood structure. The famous cathedral you see today was built in 1540. The remains of Ponce de León are kept in a marble tomb near the trancept.

Norzagaray

Acosta

Sol

Luna

San Francisco

Plaza de Colón

La Capilla

Fort San Cristobal

Even larger than "El Morro", this sprawling fortress was known as the "Gibraltar of the West." Designed with an intricate series of tunnels, this 17th-century fort is a masterpiece of military architecture.

Plaza de San José

San Justo

Fortaleza

Cruz

Tetuán

Sur Recinto

Tanca

Comercia

La Marina

Puntilla

Paseo de la Princesa

Pier 3 is where the cruise ships dock, but once you pass Plazoleta del Puerto, where local artisans sell their wares, you can stroll the Paseo de la Princesa, which is planted with trees and flower beds.

Pier 3

PUERTO RICO

Governor's Mansion

Recito Oeste Street, Old San Juan, ☎ *(787) 721-2400.*
Hours open: 9 a.m.–4 p.m.

Built in 1540, La Fortaleza is the office and residence of Puerto Rico's governor and lays claim to being the oldest executive mansion in continuous use in the New World. Now a U.S. National Historic Site, the mansion can be toured in the mornings, with tours of the gardens running all day.

San Jose Church   ★★★

Plaza de San Jose, Old San Juan, ☎ *(787) 725-7501.*
Hours open: 8:30 a.m.–4 p.m.

The San Jose Church, the second-oldest in the Western Hemisphere, dates to 1532 and represents a rare New World example of Gothic architecture. Originally a Dominican chapel, it was the family church of Ponce de Leon's descendants, many of whom are buried here. Highlights are the explorer's crucifix, oil paintings by Jose Campeche and Francisco Oller, and ornate processional floats. Sunday mass is at 12:15.

Museums and Exhibits

Casa Blanca Museum   ★★

Calle San Sebastian 1, Old San Juan, ☎ *(787) 724-4102.*

The land on which the "White House" sits was given to explorer Ponce de Leon by the Spanish Crown. He was fatally struck by an Indian's arrow in Florida before the house was built in 1521, but his descendants lived there for some 250 years. In 1779, it was taken over by the Spanish military, then taken over in 1898 by the United States as a residence for military commanders. In 1967 the mansion was declared a National Historic Monument. It has gardens and two museums, one on the Taino Indians and one on colonial life in the 16th and 17th centuries. General admission: $2.

La Casa del Libro   ★★★

Calle del Cristo, Old San Juan.
Hours open: 11 a.m.–4:30 p.m.

Exhibits on printing and bookmaking are displayed at this 19th-century house. Noteworthy are pages from the Gutenberg Bible, a decree signed by Ferdinand and Isabella concerning Columbus' second voyage, and other pre-16th century examples of the art.

Museo de Arte y Historia   ★★★

Calle Norzagaray 150; mailing: P.O. Box 9024100, Old San Juan, ☎ *(787) 724-1875.*

This center for Puerto Rican arts and crafts displays works by local artists. It was a marketplace in 1857. Audio-visual shows in English or Spanish on the city's history are shown daily.

Pablo Casals Museum   ★★★

Calle San Sebastian 101, Old San Juan, ☎ *(787) 723-9185.*
Hours open: 9:30 a.m.–5:30 p.m.

The famed Spanish cellist, who died in 1973 but had the Casals Festival in his honor since 1957, spent his last years in Puerto Rico, where his mother and wife were born, leaving behind a collection of memorabilia from his long and distinguished career. The 18th-century house displays his cello, manuscripts and photos from his life, as well as videotaped performances, shown on request. General admission: $1.

Theater

Centro de Ballas Artes   ★★

De Diego and Ponce de Leon avenues, San Juan.
This fine arts center is the largest in the Caribbean. Enquire at your hotel about events—from operas to plays.

Teatro Tapia   ★★

Avenue Ponce de Leon, San Juan.
Dating back to 1832, one of the Western Hemisphere's oldest theaters is named after Puerto Rican playwright Alejandro Tapia y Rivera. Check with your hotel concierge for scheduled plays and cultural events.

Tours

Bacardi Rum Plant   ★★★

Route 165, Km. 2.6, Int. 888, Catano, ☎ *(787) 788-8400.*
Across the bay from Old San Juan (a short hop ferry), this plant offers 45-minute tours. More than 2 billion cases have been produced here since this site opened in 1936; the Bacardi family started producing rum in 1862. You'll see the six-story tall distillery and bottling plant, and get to judge the results yourself in a Pavilion, which has an impressive view of Old San Juan. A gift shop sells samples.

Caribbean National Forest   ★★★★★

Hwy 191 Km 4.4, Palmer ☎ *(787) 887-2875.*
Known simply as El Yunque, this pristine preserve encompasses 28,000 acres of virgin tropical rainforest—the only one in the United States—with some 240 species of tropical trees. Rare creatures like the Puerto Rican boa, which grows to seven feet; the greenish blue, red-fronted Puerto Rican parrot, and 26 other species found nowhere else make their home here. El Yunque contains more than 20 kinds of orchids, over 200 varieties of ferns, and millions of tiny tree frogs called Coqui, who serenade visitors. Stop at the new El Portal Tropical Forest Center at the park's entrance to peruse 10,000 sq. ft. of exhibits and pick up a map. Numerous hiking trails traverse the park, leading to waterfalls, natural pools and the peak of El Toro, but bring raingear. You can also camp overnight with a 50 cent permit *(☎ (787) 723-1718).*

Río Camuy Cave Park   ★★★★★

Road 129, Arecibo, ☎ *(787) 898-3100.*
Hours open: 8 a.m.–4 p.m.
Located near Arecibo in Northwest Puerto Rico, 2.5 hours from San Juan, is one of the world's largest cave networks at 300 acres. Sixteen entrances have been found and seven miles of passages explored so far. A trolley spirals down into a sinkhole, where you get out and walk through a 170-ft. high Cueva Clara de Empalme, passing sinkholes, one of the world's largest underground rivers, and giant stalagmites and stalactites. Another tram shuttles you to a platform overlooking Tres Pueblos Sinkhole, measuring 65 feet in diameter and 400 feet deep. A spiral sinkhole

recently opened where a 205-step descent leads to another spiral cave. The Taino Indians, believed to be Puerto Rico's first inhabitants, also explored the cave. Reservations are essential, as this place is understandably popular. Guided tours last 45 minutes. A cafeteria, picnic area, gift shop, walking trails, exhibition hall and theater are on the grounds. General admission: $10.

What Else to See in Fajardo

Parks and Gardens

Cabezas de San Juan Nature Reserve ★★★★

Route 987, Fajardo, ☎ *(787) 722-5882.*

Located on a peninsula, this nature reserve encompasses 316 acres and 124 acres of lagoons. It contains all of Puerto Rico's ecosystems except for the rainforest. A two-hour guided tour (reservations essential) will take you through a half-mile-long coral reef, mangrove swamps, beaches, a dry forest, and beds of turtle grass *(thalassia)*. A highlight is El Faro, a lighthouse built in 1880 and still used by the U.S. Coast Guard. The small nature center in the lighthouse, which is a designated National Historic Place, has touch tanks, aquariums, and an observation deck. Bilingual tours are at 9:30, 10:00, 10:30; the one at 2:00 is in English only. Well worth a visit. General admission: $5.

What Else to See in Ponce

BEST VIEW:

A terrific perspective of the surrounding countryside and town of Ponce can be seen from the 100-foot-tall El Vigía, an observatory tower, next to Castillo Serrallés.

Historical Sites

Hacienda Buena Vista ★★

Route 10; Km. 16.8/ c/oThe Conservation Trust of Puerto Rico, PO Box 4747, Ponce, ☎ *(787) 722-5882.*

From 1833 to the 1950s, this thriving plantation at the edge of a subtropical forest produced corn, yams, citrus fruits and coffee. Since 1984 Puerto Rico's Conservation Trust has owned it and carefully restored the farm to its late 19th century state. Reservations are required for 1.5-hour tours; on weekends call ☎ *(787) 848-7020.* The grounds include the manor house with authentic period pieces, former slave quarters, a 60-foot water slide, and working water wheel, corn and coffee mills. The original machinery is significant because few such iron items of the era remain; most were converted for use during the two world wars. Reservations required. Open to groups Wednesday and Thursday; to the general public Friday thru Sunday. General admission: $5.

Tibes Indian Ceremonial Park ★★

Route 503, KM 2.7, Ponce, ☎ *(787) 840-2255.*

Hours open: 9 a.m.–4 p.m.

Just outside town lies the oldest known burial ground in the Antilles, with some 200 skeletons unearthed from A.D. 200 and seven ancient Igneri and pre-Taino Indian ballcourts and two dance grounds from A.D. 700. A new exhibition displays ceremonial objects, pottery and jewelry. General admission: $2.

Museums and Exhibits

Ponce History Museum ★★★
Calle Isabel, Ponce, ☎ (787) 844-7071.
Hours open: 10 a.m.–5 p.m.
Ponce's history is traced from the time of the Taino Indians to present. Interactive displays help visitors orient themselves. The museum, inaugurated on Dec. 12, 1992, has a conservation laboratory, a library, souvenir and gift shop and cafeteria, all in Casa Salazar. The house, an architectural wonder built in 1911, combines neo-classic with Moorish styles. It also displays many of the details you'll notice in the town's architecture: stained glass windows, mosaics, pressed-tin ceilings, fixed jalousies, porch balconies and interior patios. General admission: $3.

Ponce Museum of Art ★★★★
Las Americas Avenue 25, Ponce, ☎ (787) 848-0511.
Designed by Edward Durell Stone, architect of New York's Museum of Modern Art, this fanciful museum exhibits the most extensive collection in the Caribbean of European painting and sculpture of the last five centuries. Especially noted for its late Renaissance and Baroque works and pre-Raphaelite canvases. General admission: $3.

Serralles Castle Museum ★★★
El Vigia Hill17, Ponce, ☎ (787) 259-1774.
Hours open: 10 a.m.–5:30 p.m.
This Spanish-Revival mansion, Ponce's largest building, dates back to the 1930s and is the former home of the Serralles family, producers of Don Q rum. Today the airy, multi-level house is a museum exhibiting elegant furnishings, the history of the local rum industry and a cafe. The lavishly landscaped grounds are a treat, and the views up here are breathtaking. General admission: $3.

What Else to See in Mayagüez/Rincon

Parks and Gardens

Puerto Rico Zoological Gardens ★★★
Route 108, Mayagüez, ☎ (787) 834-8110.
Hours open: 9 a.m.–5 p.m.
Check out the birds and beasts—500 in all—at this tropical zoo spread over 45 acres. General admission: $1.

Sports

With more than 200 miles of coastline, rest assured that Puerto Rico has all the watersports you could desire—including surfing, something many Caribbean islands, with their calm seas, lack. The Puerto Rico Water Sport Federation sets standards for member-operators who offer diving, snorkeling, sailing, deep-sea fishing, windsurfing and other aquatic activities; stick with a member-company to be assured of good service.

Deep-sea fishing for white and blue martin, allison tuna, mackerel, tarpon, sailfish and wahoo is excellent year-round. Some 30 world records have been broken in some of the island's many deep-sea fishing tournaments held each year. Lake fishers can try for largemouth bass, peacock bass, sunfish, catfish and tilapia. For details, contact the Department of Natural Resources at ☎ (787) 722-5938.

The best beaches for catching a wave, especially October through April, are along the Atlantic coastline from **Rincón** north to **Borinquen Point**. In the summer, try **Casa de Pesca** in Arecibo and **La Concha** in San Juan. All good surfing beaches have surf shops nearby for lessons and equipment rentals.

For spectator sports, check out **thoroughbred races** at 2:30 p.m. each Sunday, Wednesday, Friday and holiday at **El Comandante** at Canovanas ☎ (787) 724-6060). The professional baseball season runs from October through April, with games held at stadiums in San Juan, Ponce, Caguas, Santurce, Mayagüez and Arecibo. For a schedule, contact Professional Baseball of Puerto Rico at ☎ (787) 765-6285. The dubious "sport" of **cockfighting** takes place from November through August in Isla Verde at the Coliseo Gallistico.

Duffers have nine **golf courses** from which to choose, while more than 100 **tennis courts** dot the island. If your hotel doesn't have one, you can rent one of 17 courts at San Juan Central Park ☎ (787) 722-1646, or Club Riomar in Rio Grande ☎ (787) 887-3964, which has 13 clay courts.

Fishing

Several communities in Puerto Rico offer big game fishing: a new harbor opened in Aguadilla where fishing is about 45 minutes out; Fajardo has excellent fishing from marlin to dorado about 30 minutes from the dock; Parguera features big game fishing about 30 minutes out; Ponce sports small trolling boats that will take you to seldom fished waters; and the main center for big game fishing is San Juan, where fish are just 15 minutes from the harbor. **Carib Aquatic Adventures in Miramar** (☎ (787) 724-1882) and **Dorado Marine Center** (☎ (787) 796-4645) does light-tackle to deep-sea fishing excursions. For deep-sea fishing, try: **Benitez Fishing Charters** (San Juan, ☎ (787) 723-2292), **Makaira Hunter** (Miramar, ☎ (787) 397-8028), **Parguera Fishing Charters** (☎ (787) 899-4698) **Western Tourist Services** (Mayaguez, ☎ (787) 834-4008) or **Tropical Fishing Charters** (☎ (787) 863-1000). **Southern Witch** (Miramar, ☎ (787) 721-7335) does tarpon and reef fishing with light tackle or fly fishing.

Golf

Unlike most of the Caribbean islands, which have only a handful of golf courses (if any), Puerto Rico boasts 15 courses, including 10 championship links designed by golf's most famous names: Greg Norman, Jack Nicklaus, Gary Player, Robert Trent Jones Sr., George Fazio, Reese Jones and Arthur Hills. Another three are scheduled to be added by 1998. All are 18-hole courses unless otherwise noted. Only 19 miles from San Juan, **Westin Rio Mar Beach Resort and Country Club** *(☎ (787) 888-8811)* has two world-class courses. Rio Grande: **Bahia Beach Plantation** *(☎ (787) 256-5600; FAX (787) 256-1035* $60 greens fees 7 a.m.–1 p.m.) where 13 holes have water hazards is the closest public course to San Juan hotels. **Berwind Country Club** *(☎ (787) 876-3056; FAX (787) 256-5030,* $50 including. cart, non-member only on weekdays) has three of the toughest finishing holes on the island. Fajardo: **El Conquistador Resort** *(☎ (787) 863-6784; FAX (787) 860-1144;* $75 greens fees, 7 a.m.–7 p.m.) has Arthur Hills Golf Course, a 6700 yard, par-72 course featuring ocean views from almost all holes and set against the El Yunque Rain Forest. Dorado: **Hyatt's Dorado and Cerromar** *(☎ (787) 796-8961; FAX (787) 796-5562;* hotel guests $75, non-guests $110 including cart) resorts each have two courses, all designed by Robert Trent Jones, Sr. Jack Nicklaus rates the East Course's 13th hole as one of the top 10 holes in the world. Humacao: **Palmas del Mar Resort** *(☎ (787) 852-6000;* greens fees and cart, $79 resort guests, $119 outside guests) designed by Gary Player is a par-72, 6690-yard course. Near Ramey on west coast: public course **Punta Borinquen** *(☎ (787) 890-2987; FAX (787) 868-1196,* $18 green fees weekdays, $20 on weekends) is noted for its long, windy fairways. Check at your hotel or call **Luiz Ortiz Golf Packages** *(☎ (787) 786-3859;* $95–$150 depending on the course) for access and transportation to courses all over the island. Most tee-times start at 7 a.m.

Horseback Riding

For $20 an hour, hop on a horse and ride off into the sunset, along the beach or through the rainforest at **Hacienda Carabali** *(☎ (787) 889-5820).* The love of horses runs deep in Puerto Rico. Indeed, this island has its own unique breed: the Paso Fino, with 7000 registered. The best competitions are in February and March. Polo has emerged as an up-and-coming sport, too. The Ingenio Polo Club is located just outside of Carolina.

Sailing and Cruising

The best sailing departures tend to be from Fajardo for the islands of Icacos, Lobos, Palomino, Culebra and Vieques. From Ponce most sail west to Salinas or you can sign up for harbor or sunset cruises in San Juan. **Caribbean School of Aquatics, Inc.** *(☎ (787) 728-6606)* offers all-day, $69 boat trips to small islands from San Juan; **Spread Eagle** *(☎ (787) 863-1905;* $55 for a day trip) specializes in snorkel trips from Rio Grande; **Erin Go Braugh** *(☎ (787) 860-4401)* in Puerto Real specializes in small, personalized sails (10 a.m.–5 p.m.) for $75 per person including a barbecue lunch. It also offers day trips, overnights, dinner and sunset sails; **Fajardo Tours, Inc.** *(☎ (787) 863-2821),* does all day trips for $55 per person.

Where to Stay

Fielding's Highest Rated Hotels in Puerto Rico

★★★★★	El Conquistador Resort & Country Club	$330–$545
★★★★★	El San Juan Hotel & Casino	$180–$495
★★★★★	Horned Dorset Primavera	$150–$380
★★★★★	Hyatt Dorado Beach Resort & Casino	$205–$515
★★★★★	Hyatt Regency Cerromar	$205–$435
★★★★	Caribe Hilton & Casino	$215–$380
★★★★	Westin Rio Mar Beach Resort	$205–$475
★★★★	Wyndham Palmas del Mar Resort & Villas	$166–$269
★★★	Condado Plaza Hotel & Casino	$265–$355
★★★	Gran Hotel El Convento	$190–$1200

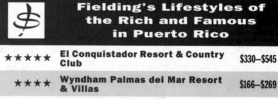

Fielding's Lifestyles of the Rich and Famous in Puerto Rico

★★★★★	El Conquistador Resort & Country Club	$330–$545
★★★★	Wyndham Palmas del Mar Resort & Villas	$166–$269
★★★★★	Hyatt Dorado Beach Resort & Casino	$205–$515
★★★★★	Horned Dorset Primavera	$150–$380
★★★★★	Hyatt Regency Cerromar	$205–$435

Fielding's Best Value Hotels in Puerto Rico

★★	Sea Gate Guest House	$40–$60
★★	Parador Banos de Coamo	$60–$70
★★	Harbour View Villas	$50–$95
★★	Parador Vistamar	$69–$90

Puerto Rico offers a broad range of accommodations from huge, self-contained resorts to condominiums and villas to government-sponsored *paradores puertorriqueños*, which are country inns generally situated in historic buildings or particularly scenic sites. These family-run lodgings are usually quite affordable. To book one, call ☎ *(800) 443-0266.*

One of our favorites in the San Juan area is the **El San Juan Hotel & Casino**, which has an Old-World opulent lobby and upscale casino perfect for whiling away the hours. It's a great place to kill time if you find yourself with a long layover at the airport; it's just a five-minute taxi ride away from the terminal.

Several hotels opened in 1996 and 1997, including the **Westin Rio Mar Beach Resort & Country Club**, **Embassy Suites Hotel & Casino** in Isla Verde, **Colony San Juan Beach Hotel** in Isla Verde and **Hampton Inn** also in Isla Verde. The **Ritz-Carlton San Juan Hotel & Casino** is scheduled to open early in 1998 to the tune of $131.5 million. It will feature a full service spa. **Wyndham Old San Juan Hotel & Casino**. For details, see the following individual listings. The venerable **El Convento Hotel** reopened in January 1997 restored to its original glory.

Where to Stay in San Juan and Condado Area

Running around the Atlantic between Ocean Park and Miramar, the Condado area, now returning to its glitzy rep of years gone by, is now one of the main areas for hotels and resorts. The **Condado Plaza Hotel & Casino** is practically a planet unto itself, with a full range of eateries, casinos, Vegas-type shows, its own shopping mall and top American furnishings. One of the closest to the airport is **El San Juan Hotel & Casino**, also a luxury property of top proportions, features an enormous pool that inspires a lot of social climbing. A good moderate option is **Carib Inn**, near the airport, but a mere short walk to the beach. In Isla Verde, east of San Juan/ Santurce, is the U.S.-run **TraveLodge**, with comfortably large beds, modernized bathrooms and an acceptable pool.

Hotels and Resorts

Atlantic Beach Hotel   **$90–$125**   ★★

Condado, ☎ *(787) 721-6900, FAX (787) 721-6917.*
Single: $90–$125. Double: $90–$125.
This modest hotel, a member of the International Gay Travel Association, caters mostly to gays, though anyone is welcome (except for children). Rooms are spartan but comfortable and air-conditioned; not all have private baths, so be sure to request one if that's important to you. The beach is footsteps away. There's no pool but the Jacuzzi offers pleasant soaking. The restaurant serves only breakfast and lunch, with dinner options within walking distance. A complimentary continental breakfast is served daily on the roof sundeck. 37 rooms. Credit cards: A, D, MC, V.

Best Western Pierre   **$126–$173**   ★★

☎ *(800) 528-1234, (787) 721-1200, FAX (787) 721-3118.*
Single: $126–$173. Double: $136–$173.

Located in the heart of the Santurce business district, four blocks from Condado, this Best Western appeals to business travelers on a budget. Facilities are limited to a restaurant, bar, and pool. 184 rooms. Credit cards: A, CB, DC, D, MC, V.

Carib Inn Tennis Club $105–$320   ★★

☎ *(800) 548-8217, (787) 791-3535, FAX (787) 791-0104.*
Single: $105–$120. Double: $110–$320.

A 10-minute taxi ride from the airport and one block from the beach, this resort caters to tennis players, with eight courts, a ball machine, and video playback. The tennis theme continues with a pool shaped like a racquet. Accommodations are adequate but cry out for renovation. A workout gym features massage, sauna and steam bath. There are a few restaurants and bars on-site, and the salsa bands on Friday and Saturday nights are popular. 225 rooms. Credit cards: A, CB, DC, D, MC, V.

Caribe Hilton & Casino $215–$380   ★★★★

☎ *(800) 468-8585, (787) 721-0303, FAX (787) 722-2910.*
Single: $215–$360. Double: $220–$380.

This behemoth, celebrating its 50th anniversary, does a huge business with meetings and conventions, so you'll be sharing facilities with folks wearing name tags. Nevertheless, this smashing resort, centrally located on 17 tropical acres between the new and Old San Juan, features the island's only private beach, a putting green, six tennis courts, a health club with air-conditioned racquetball and squash courts, spa, supervised programs for kids, six restaurants, and three bars, one with live entertainment. Snorkel and scuba equipment can be found on the small beach. Guest rooms are housed in two towers, one 10 stories, the other 20. The rooms are newly renovated, and most have dramatic ocean views. Business travelers are catered to on three executive levels. Fort San Jeronimo, which dates back to the 16th century, is footsteps away. The $40 million that Hilton poured into the resort a few years back really shows. Claim to fame? The piña colada was supposedly invented here. 670 rooms. Credit cards: A, CB, D, MC, V.

Condado Beach Hotel $190–$430   ★★★

☎ *(800) 468-2822, (787) 721-6090, FAX (787) 724-7222.*
Single: $190–$430. Double: $190–$430.

The Spanish Colonial-style hotel dates back to 1919, when it was built by the Vanderbilt family. Guestrooms are elegant and tastefully done with nice furnishings and original art. The grounds include a few restaurants and bars, a casino and a pool. It has an upscale disco, two restaurants, and live entertainment in one of the two bars. The "beach" in the title is quite narrow. Steps away from terrific boutiques and restaurants. Popular with conventioneers. 245 rooms. Credit cards: A, CB, DC, D, MC, V.

Condado Plaza Hotel & Casino $265–$1160   ★★★

☎ *(800) 624-0420, (787) 721-1000, FAX (787) 722-4613.*
Associated Restaurant: *Laguna Grill.*
Single: $265–$335. Double: $265–$355. Suites Per Day: $1160–$1160.

This modern, full-service resort, which attracts many business travelers, fronts a small public beach on the Atlantic Ocean and the Condado Lagoon, but most guests hang out at one of three pools. The five-acre property was last renovated in

1993. Accommodations are housed in two towers, though only some have sea views. Those shelling out extra for a Plaza Club room enjoy added amenities, snap-to-it service and the use of a lounge. The grounds include two lighted tennis courts, a fitness center, air-conditioned squash and racquetball courts, a business center, concierge services and Puerto Rico's largest casino, as well as five restaurants (including 24-hour room service), bars and a hopping disco. It also has supervised kids activities and babysitting services. Horseback riding or golf at one of six nearby courses is easily arranged. 395 rooms. Credit cards: A, CB, D, MC, V.

El San Juan Hotel & Casino　　　　　**$180–$2500**　　　★ ★ ★ ★ ★

Isla Verde, ☎ *(800) 468-2818, (787) 791-1000, FAX (787) 253-0178.*
Website: www.WilliamsHosp.com.
Associated Restaurant: *Aquarela/Back Street Hong Kong.*
Single: $180–$470. Double: $205–$495. Suites Per Day: $575–$2500.
Opulence dominates at this venerable resort, which just had $72 million worth of improvements pumped into it. The beautiful, 600 ft. beach and the well-designed, Olympic-size pool area with whirlpools, waterfall and swim-up bar would be enough to draw many. Fifty-six luxury suites were scheduled to open by August 1998 along the beach with private terraces, Jacuzzis and private concierge service. Current accommodations are luxurious, with VCRs, CD players, TVs in the bathroom, minibars and modern art. Some have sitting areas, while others have sunken baths, whirlpools, or private garden spas. Try to book away from the airport side, however. Extensive facilities coupled with excellent service keep repeat guests coming. The grounds include five restaurants, eight bars (one for cigar lovers with private humidors lining the back wall), 22 retail shops, children's center, babysitting services, a cranking disco, a top-flight casino (featured in James Bond films), and three lighted tennis courts. Off the Old World lobby, you can get Chinese fare housed in a pavilion from the 1964 New York World's Fair; a new sushi restaurant has recently been added, as well as a nouvelle Puerto Rican restaurant, Aquarela, that is drawing raves. The active set will find all watersports including diving and waterskiing, a modern health club, and a pool for the kiddies. A stay here is an experience you won't soon forget. 392 rooms. Credit cards: A, CB, MC, V.

Gran Hotel El Convento　　　　　**$190–$1200**　　　★ ★ ★

Old San Juan, ☎ *(800) 468-2779, (787) 723-9020, FAX (787) 721-2877.*
Website: www.elconvento.com.
Associated Restaurant: *Tapas Bar.*
Single: $190–$345. Double: $220–$375. Suites Per Day: $550–$1200.
Once a Carmelite convent, this grand hotel, owned by local investors, reopened in January 1997 after an extensive, $15 million, two-year-long renovation. The National Historic Registry building, dates back 350 years; construction was authorized in 1636 by Spain's King Philip IV and was designed and built by the Spanish Army. Transformed into a hotel by the Woolworth family by 1963, the hotel in the heart of Old San Juan retains its authentic 17th-century Spanish style; its interior courtyard with arches and balconies has been reopened to the sky. Handmade tiles have been uncovered, handcrafted furnishings from Spain have been restored. Facilities include a plunge pool and Jacuzzi on the fourth floor with stunning harbor

views, fitness center with massage, business center, tapas bar, small casino and garden terrace for breakfasts. Complimentary continental breakfast and wine and cheese receptions are both served daily. The Spanish decor guestrooms—four are suites—are equipped with extras like a fax machine, two phones, in-room safe, VCR, stereo, iron/ironing board, robes, honor bar and hairdryer. Views are of the city or harbor. A good mix of both leisure and business travelers here. A gourmet restaurant and new shopping arcade on the second floor have yet to be completed. 59 rooms. Credit cards: A, CB, DC, D, MC, V.

Parador El Guajataca $77–$95 ★★

Quebradillas, ☎ *(800) 964-3065, (787) 895-3070, FAX (787) 895-3589.*
Single: $77–$83. Double: $80–$95.

Set on a bluff overlooking the Atlantic Ocean, this small hotel 70 miles west of San Juan has many resort amenities at an unbeatable price. Accommodations are comfortable and modern. Guests can enjoy the nice beach, play tennis on two courts, or swim in the Olympic-size pool. The restaurant serves Creole cuisine, and there's entertainment in the bar on weekends. 38 rooms. Credit cards: A, CB, DC, D, MC.

Radisson Ambassador Plaza $200–$320 ★★★

Condado, ☎ *(800) 333-3333, (787) 721-7300, FAX (787) 723-6151.*
Single: $200–$310. Double: $200–$320.

Set on the Condado strip and 10 minutes from Old San Juan, this glitzy hotel—renovated to the tune of $40 million-plus—consists of an older hotel and an all-suite tower. Accommodations vary, but all are pleasant, though only some have ocean views. As expected, the tower suites offer the plushest digs and feature concierge services well-suited to business travelers. Facilities include a roof-top swimming pool and Jacuzzi, fitness center, business services center, health club, supervised children's programs, casino, and three restaurants and two bars, one with entertainment nightly. This place has come a long way from its Howard Johnson roots. 233 rooms. Credit cards: A, CB, D, MC, V.

Radisson Normandie $195–$490 ★★★

☎ *(800) 333-3333, (787) 729-2929, FAX (787) 729-3083.*
Single: $195–$220. Double: $195–$220. Suites Per Day: $490–$490.

In a landmark art deco building that dates back to 1940, this hotel on the outskirts of Old San Juan features spacious guest rooms, most with working and sitting area and sun-room—and decorated with art deco touches. Facilities include a health club, a lounge and two restaurants, an outdoor pool, concierge desk and a small beach on the Atlantic Ocean. 177 rooms. Credit cards: A, CB, DC, D, MC, V.

Sands Hotel & Casino $210–$305 ★★★

Carolina, ☎ *(800) 544-3008, (787) 791-6100, FAX (787) 791-7540.*
Closed Date: =.
Single: $210–$290. Double: $210–$305.

Situated on five acres fronting three miles of sandy beach, this luxurious property—in the midst of renovation in the fall of 1997—is next door to the splashier El San Juan. Accommodations are generally plush with extras like minibars and floor to ceiling windows. All have balconies but not all have an ocean view. Ask for a beach view; the noise on the airport side can be deafening. The extensive grounds include five restaurants, three lounges, a huge casino, daily activities, and a large freeform pool with a waterfall and swim-up bar. Nice, but the El San Juan is better, and the rates are comparable. 410 rooms. Credit cards: A, CB, DC, D, MC, V.

Westin Rio Mar Beach Resort   **$205–$475**   ★★★★

Rio Grande, east of Luquillo Beach, ☎ *(800) 474-6627, (787) 888-6000, FAX (787) 888-6600.*
Website: www.westin.com.
Associated Restaurant: *Carnaval, Marbella, Patio.*
Single: $205–$475. Double: $205–$475.

This resort—Puerto Rico's first to be built from scratch in 15 years—opened in August 1996 and marks Westin's first foray into the Caribbean. The seven-story hotel is situated on 481 lush acres hemmed in by a one-mile beach on the island's northeast coast and the Caribbean National Forest. Guestrooms come in six categories, all including private balconies or patios, voice mail, electronic security locks, in-room safes, 24-hour room service, cable TV and mini-bars. A concierge level has added amenities on the seventh floor. Facilities of the $178.5 million property include 12 restaurants and lounges, a Las Vegas-style casino, 36 holes of golf (Tom and George Fazio's Rio Mar Ocean Course and River Course by Greg Norman), a 35,000-square-foot clubhouse, 13 tennis courts and a tennis clubhouse, a fitness center and spa, business center, and watersports (scuba diving and deep sea fishing are especially popular with guests). A children's program ($35 a day per child) and babysitting ($5 an hour) are available. A thoroughbred track is also nearby. 600 rooms. Credit cards: A, CB, DC, MC, V.

Apartments and Condominiums

Local Puerto Ricans with luxury apartments or villas often rent their homes during high season, especially those located near the Hyatt Dorado Beach resort. Condominiums in high-rise buildings are also popular for tourist rentals; even rooms in hotels that have kitchenettes can be rented. Among the latter are ESJ Towers, the Regency, and the Excelsior. Shopping is easy because supermarkets tend to boast traditional mainland products along with more Latin-flavored spices, vegetables and fruits.

Inns

Puerto Rico is famous for its network of charming country inns called *paradores puertorriqueños.* Established in 1973, the network offers superb accommodations and the ideal location for exploring the island's diverse attractions. Several privately owned and operated guest houses also serve as quiet and quaint accommodations far from the maddening crowds. What makes the *paradores* so special is they are each situated in a historic place or site of unusual scenic beauty. Prices range from $38–$96 per night, double occupancy, and *paradores* are located from mountains to sea. Most have swimming pools and all offer the island's tantalizing cuisine. Many are even within driving distance from San Juan. Perhaps one of the most special sites is that of the **Parador Baōs de Coamo**, situated on the site of America's oldest thermal springs, once believed to be Ponce de Leon's "fountain of youth." Even FDR took advantage of the medicinal waters, praised by the Indians for more than three centuries. Just a half-hour away is Ponce, the island's second largest city and home to the Caribbean's most extensive art museum.

El Canario by the Sea $65–$99 ★

Condado, ☎ *(800) 533-2649, (787) 722-8640, FAX (787) 725-4921.*
Website: www.infinityclub.com.
Single: $65–$88. Double: $75–$99.

Located one and a half blocks from the beach in the heart of Condado, this small, three-story, Spanish villa-style inn suits low-key, casual travelers looking for a friendly atmosphere. Modest rooms are furnished with wicker, have air-conditioning, ceiling fans, direct dial phones and cable TV. A complimentary continental breakfast is served daily in the courtyard. A lobby bar and a tour desk are the only on-site amenities but it is close to dive shops and yacht charters. 25 rooms. Credit cards: A, MC, V.

Low Cost Lodging

During low season, mid-April through December, expect the most expensive hotels to drop rates to a moderate range. Other hotels give special packages for low season. It doesn't hurt to bargain a little, just do it tactfully. The Puerto Rico Tourism Company currently recognizes 35 camping areas throughout the island, from El Yunque National Forest to Luquillo Beach and many of the public beaches around the island. Camping facilities in Puerto Rico come with a broad definition, including cottages, pup tents, huts, lean-tos and even trailer homes. Fees range from $5–$12. Don't always count on finding hot water or toilets. Another option is renting rooms in locals' houses. The tourist board can put you in touch with interested parties.

Arcade Inn $40–$90 ★

Condado, ☎ *(787) 728-7524.*
Single: $40–$90. Double: $50–$90.

This family-oriented guesthouse is within walking distance to the beach. Rooms are modest but air-conditioned and with private baths; a few efficiencies are also available. A bar is on the premises, but you'll have to venture out for meals, but much is within an easy walk. 19 rooms. Credit cards: A, MC, V.

Where to Stay in Dorado

Dorado, a sleep spot on the northwest coast about 20 miles from San Juan off Route 693, is the closest town to the Hyatt Regency Cerromar Beach and the Hyatt Dorado Beach hotels. A few hours can be whiled away at its shopping center and the handful of arts and crafts stores on the main streets. If you are staying at one of the resorts, a limousine will be sent to pick you up at San Juan's International Airport, about a 45-minute drive. The hotels also use a small airstrip a few minutes away from their front doors.

Hotels and Resorts

Hyatt Dorado Beach Resort & Casino $205–$1785 ★★★★★

☎ *(800) 233-1234, (787) 796-1234, FAX (787) 796-2022.*
Website: www.hyatt.com.
Associated Restaurant: *Su Casa/Surf Room/Ocean Terrac.*
Single: $205–$405. Double: $205–$515. Suites Per Day: $365–$1785.

Located on a 1000-acre estate 22 miles west of San Juan and shared with its sister property, the Hyatt Regency Cerromar, this deluxe operation aims to please—and succeeds. Superior to its sibling, it has extensive facilities, all world-class. Plush accommodations are in 14 two-story buildings (no taller than the coconut trees). Roomy and romantic with plantation furnishings, terra cotta tiles, each room has a balcony or terrace, minibar and marble bath. Two or three bedroom casitas line the fairway. Recreational options are the best on the island, with two 18-hole golf courses designed by Robert Trent Jones Sr., a club house, two pools (one Olympic sized), a spa and beauty center with aerobics classes, eight tennis courts, oceanside in-line skating and jogging trails, a windsurfing school and a private beach with watersports. Dining options range from four formal restaurants to the casual beach bar to theme night dinners; the food is high priced and sometimes mediocre. A shuttle bus takes you to the casino and other facilities (two more golf courses) at the neighboring Hyatt Regency Cerromar. If you're torn between the two, keep in mind that the Dorado has nicer rooms, a better beach and appeals to an older crowd, while the Cerromar has a better pool and a younger clientele and renowned children's program. 298 rooms. Credit cards: A, CB, D, MC, V.

Hyatt Regency Cerromar   **$205–$435**   ★ ★ ★ ★ ★

☎ *(800) 233-1234, (787) 796-1234, FAX (787) 796-4647.*
Website: www.hyatt.com.
Associated Restaurant: *Medici.*
Single: $205–$435. Double: $205–$435.
Sister property to the above-mentioned Hyatt Dorado and sharing its 1000 acres, this plush resort, voted one of the world's best family resorts by 30,000 travel agents, centers around a seven-story, Y-shaped hotel. Guest rooms are decorated in an island theme and have minibars, spacious baths and balconies. The hotel boasts of having the world's largest riverpool, which comes in at 1776 feet, complete with whirlpools, a Jacuzzi grotto, a swim-up bar, 14 waterfalls, five separate swimming areas and an impressive, three-story water slide. Or an Olympic-size pool appeals to the more sedate crowd. Guests stay busy at the spa, which has aerobics and water aerobics classes; morning tennis clinics on 14 tennis courts; waterskiing or snorkeling at the beach; a windsurfing school; supervised children's activities; bicycle and jogging trails; nature walks; water volleyball and basketball; and 36 holes of golf on Robert Trent Jones Sr.-designed courses. Guests can choose from four restaurants—one serving sushi, a rarity in Puerto Rico—or hop the shuttle to try the food at the Hyatt Dorado. For nightlife, try the casino disco, or three bars. Excellent all the way; expect to see a fair amount of business travelers and families. 506 rooms. Credit cards: A, D, MC, V.

Where to Stay in Farjardo and Humacao

Full of small-town spirit, the seaport of Fajardo lies but five miles south of Las Cabezas on Route 3. The lifestyle is slower-paced than in San Juan, and you can take morning and afternoon ferries to Culebra and Vieques. Treks can be made to the **Caribbean National Forest**, of which El Yunque Mountain is a part (see "Treks" above) and Losquillo Beach. Special expeditions can be arranged through **Las Cabezas Nature Reserve** (see "Treks" above) which could last all day, especially if you are interested in bird-watching. Native sloops set sail for **Iacos** where you will find fine snorkeling and swimming conditions. Deep-sea fishing and other watersports can be arranged at the **Puerto del Rey Marina**.

The region has a fine 18-hole golf course and myriads of opportunities for scuba (see "Dive Sites" above.) Also see "Sports" above for more information.

The island's southeast coast can be reached by rental car or taxis (expensive from the international airport), by small planes that land at the airport of Palmas del Mar, near Humacao; or by ferry boat (the cheapest at $2.50).

Two hotels/resorts command the region with their enormous facilities. The patron saint of resorts, **El Conquistador**, has an amazing 16 restaurants and lounges—if you want to avoid the conventioneer crush, you should probably stay elsewhere. **Candelero**, near the beach at Palmas del Mar in the south, is more intimate, and less demanding socially, with activities geared for the athletic, including golf, tennis and artistic performances. You also will find several Puerto Rican *paradores*, intimate inns that reflect the congeniality of the owner/host, as well as numerous cheaper guest houses.

Hotels and Resorts

El Conquistador Resort & Country Club $330–$2290   ★★★★★

Las Croabas, near Fajardo, ☎ (800) 468-5228, (787) 863-1000, FAX (787) 863-5000.
Associated Restaurant: *Stingray Cafe/Ballyhoo.*
Single: $330–$545. Double: $330–$545. Suites Per Day: $500–$2290.
This $250 million enclave crowns a cliff, overlooking the Caribbean on one side and the Atlantic on the other, and consists of a main hotel and three villages occupying 500 acres. Guest rooms are spiffy, with three phones, two TVs, VCRs, stereos, and refrigerators; 88 suites and 176 one-to-three bedroom casitas offer more room and special amenities. You can also get star treatment by opting for "Club Conquistador," which gives you private check-in, all-day snacks, free continental breakfast and access to a private bar. The resort—opened in 1993 and the Caribbean's largest—boasts a casino, six pools, seven tennis courts, pro shop, a health spa, a mind-boggling 16 restaurants and bars, and watersports. Among the gee-whiz attractions is the 6700 yard, par-72 Arthur Hills Golf Course, recognized as one of the Caribbean's finest, an art collection worth a million dollars, a 100-acre private island 10 minutes away where you can spend the day snorkeling, windsurfing and diving, a 55-slip marina, and 22 retail shops. On rare occasions the service or food misses, but complaints are hard to come by when this dazzler comes into conversation. Golfers have nothing but kudos for this incredible resort, but waterbuffs may have a better time where the beach is more handy. 926 rooms. Credit cards: A, CB, D, MC, V.

Wyndham Palmas del Mar Resort & Villas $166–$287   ★★★★

Humacao, ☎ (800) 725-6276, (787) 852-6000, FAX (787) 852-6320.
Website: www.wyndham.com.
Associated Restaurant: *Chez Daniel, Blue Hawaii.*
Single: $166–$253. Double: $179–$269. Suites Per Day: $191–$287.
This sprawling, somewhat isolated enclave on the Southeast Coast, encompasses 2750 acres and fronts three miles of beach. Guests, who don't mind being 45 minutes from San Juan, have a number of lodging options here. The 102-room, Wyndham Hotel has just undergone a $4.5 million renovation (formerly it was called the Candelero). It has spacious rooms with high ceilings and tropical hues of blue and green, and offers the most affordable accommodations replete with elec-

tronic locks and mini refrigerators. It also has nightly entertainment. Also under Wyndham's management is the Palmas Inn, which has 23 opulent suites with large living rooms and combination baths with bidets. You can also book a two- or three-bedroom villa complete with kitchen (though some readers have alerted Fielding that the other accommodations are a better buy). The grounds include a casino, marina, watersports, seven pools, 20 tennis courts (six lighted), a Gary Player-designed golf course, a fitness center with exercise classes, and year-round supervised children's program. A dozen dining outlets include a formal French restaurant and a casual Italian eatery. A free shuttle takes you to and from the action. Inquire about golf and tennis packages that can save you bucks. 102 rooms. Credit cards: A, MC, V.

Inns

Parador La Familia   **$69–$80**   ★

Fajardo, ☎ *(800) 443-0266, (809) 869-5345.*
Single: $69. Double: $80.
Located near Las Cabezas de San Juan Nature Preserve, this family-run inn is three miles from town; you'll definitely want a car for mobility. Rooms are basic but air-conditioned and comfortable. A pool and cozy bar—expect to hear fish tales—are on the premises. A good choice for fishermen and boating enthusiasts. 28 rooms.
Credit cards: A, D, MC, V.

Parador Martorell   **$64–$90**   ★

Luquillo, ☎ *(800) 443-0266, (787) 889-2710, FAX (787) 889-4520.*
Single: $64–$90. Double: $74–$90.
This small family-run inn is located in Puerto Rico's northeast coast. Rooms are small but comfortable; three share a bath and rely on ceiling fans to keep cool. The other seven have private baths and air conditioning, well worth the small bump in rates; a restaurant and pool are on-site, and the beach is just two minutes away. 10 rooms. Credit cards: A, MC, V.

Where to Stay in Ponce

A high-speed road connects Ponce and San Juan, which takes only about 90 minutes to traverse; you can also reach the area by plane from San Juan's International Airport. The historical buildings, such as the stunning Cathedral of Our Lady of Guadeloupe, are masterpieces of construction, as are some 1000 colonial houses that have been designated national historic sites. Nineteenth-century gas lamps illuminate the marble-edged streets with a pink glow; at night the stroll is extremely romantic.

Hotels and Resorts

On the south shore of Ponce, the Hilton is making waves among southern resorts, but it's high-rise modernity takes away from the tropical feel. It does have, however, an extensive watersports program and can make arrangements for treks and other local excursions. Other hotels in the middle of town give you easy access to the historic part of the city, especially at night when Ponce is most atmospheric.

Copamarina Beach Resort   **$135–$155**   ★★★

Guanica, ☎ *(800) 468-4553, (787) 821-0505, FAX (787) 821-0070.*

Website: www.copamarina.com. E-mail: regency✩coqui.net.
Associated Restaurant: *Wilo's Coastal Cuisine.*
Single: $135–$155. Double: $135–$155.

This resort, which dates to the late 1950s, added an additional 36 rooms and a second swimming pool with Jacuzzi, separate kiddie pool and snack bar in 1997. The new rooms have views of the blue Caribbean and have air-conditioning color cable TV, direct dial telephones and spacious balconies. Located 20 minutes south of Ponce, it includes a mile-long, white sand beach, two tennis courts (one lit) and a tennis pro, a complete watersports center and dive operation, a gourmet restaurant serving Puerto Rican nouvelle cuisine, a cafe, and the offshore "Gilligan's Island," a mangrove cay perfect for picnics or snorkeling. Inquire about diving and the new inclusive packages. Nearby a nature trail winds through the Guanica Dry Forest, the largest region of tropical dry coastal forest in the world. Children under 12 sharing with parents stay free. 142 rooms. Credit cards: A, MC, V.

Melia Hotel   **$80–$95**   ★ ★

Ponce, ☎ (800) 742-4276, (787) 842-0260, FAX (787) 841-3602.
Single: $80–$90. Double: $85–$95.

This hotel from 1914 is situated in Ponce's colonial plaza in the historic district. The Spanish-colonial building includes interesting touches such as antiques and old chandeliers. Air-conditioned guest rooms are small and the furnishings dated—not antiques, just old. A decent restaurant serves Puerto Rican cuisine on-site, and guests are treated to a free continental breakfast. Not a top choice by any means, but those who like historic hotels will be satisfied. Light sleepers should request a room in the back, as street noises can be loud. Note that this hotel is not affiliated with the upscale Melia chain, but is named for a prominent local family. 74 rooms. Credit cards: A, MC, V.

Parador Villa Parguera   **$80–$95**   ★

Lajas, ☎ (800) 443-0266, (787) 899-3975, FAX (787) 899-6040.
Single: $80–$90. Double: $90–$95.

Located on the Phosphorescent Bay facing the Caribbean, this parador offers rooms in an older guest house and in more modern wings, all with air conditioning, private baths, and balconies or patios. A restaurant and nightclub on the premises. The pool is filled with saltwater. A beach is nearby. 70 rooms. Credit cards: A, CB, DC, D, MC, V.

Ponce Hilton & Casino   **$160–$375**   ★ ★ ★

La Guancha Beach, Ponce, ☎ (800) 445-8667, (787) 259-7676, FAX (809) 259-7674.
Single: $160–$190. Double: $180–$210. Suites Per Day: $375–$375.

By far the area's nicest hotel, this Hilton sits on 80 garden acres fronting La Guancha Beach. Accommodations are stylish, with high-quality furniture, minibars, bidets, and balconies or patios. Nice public spaces and a good array of recreational facilities, including a large lagoon-style pool, Jacuzzi, four lit tennis courts, gym, games room, watersports on the private beach, five restaurants, an 18-hole golf course added in 1984, disco and a casino. It even has a lit golf practice range. This well-run property does a lot of business with the meetings and convention markets. 150 rooms. Credit cards: A, CB, DC, D, MC, V.

Ponce Hotel Tropicana & Casino   **$105–$110**   ★★
Ponce, ☎ *(787) 844-1200, FAX (787) 841-8085.*
Single: $105–$110. Double: $105–$110.
Perched on a hillside one-mile from the ocean, this hotel—formerly a Holiday
Inn—commands terrific views. Newly renovated guestrooms are comfortable; all
have balconies with that same great view. Nightly entertainment can be found in the
lounge. It also has a disco, casino, pool and restaurant. 116 rooms. Credit cards: A, DC,
D, MC, V.

Inns
Hacienda Gripinas Parador   **$50–$66**   ★★
Jayuya, ☎ *(800) 443-0266, (787) 721-2884, FAX (787) 889-4520.*
Single: $50–$55. Double: $66.
Located on a 20-acre, 18th-century, former coffee plantation, this small country inn
in Puerto Rico's interior mountains is loaded with character. Guest rooms are simple but attractive; most have ceiling fans in lieu of air conditioning. Recreational
facilities include a pool, bar and pool table; note that this area gets a lot of rain. The
dining room serves up three tasty squares a day; Sunday brunch is especially popular.
Not for those seeking a partying holiday, but perfect for relaxing and enjoying the
scenery. 19 rooms. Credit cards: MC, V.

Parador Oasis   **$60–$69**   ★★
San German, ☎ *(800) 223-9815, (787) 892-1175, FAX (787) 892-1175.*
Single: $60–$63. Double: $67–$69.
This Spanish-style mansion, which dates back to 1896, is three blocks from the
Inter-American University. Rooms are in the mansion (the least desirable ones, in
fact) and a newer annex; all are air-conditioned and most are comfortable, though
on the basic side. Facilities include a freshwater pool in a pretty courtyard, weight
room, sauna, restaurant, and two bars. 52 rooms. Credit cards: A, CB, D, MC, V.

Parador Vistamar   **$69–$90**   ★★
Quebradillas, ☎ *(800) 443-0266, (787) 895-2065, FAX (787) 895-2294.*
Single: $69–$90. Double: $69–$90.
Fine views of the Atlantic Ocean from this hilltop inn, which offers air-conditioned
rooms that are comfortable but on the plain side. A small pool and tennis court are
on-site, as well as a restaurant (admitted to the Mesones Gastronomicos program
for its excellence) and a bar with music and dancing on Saturdays. Guajataca beach
is five minutes away. 50 rooms. Credit cards: A, CB, D, MC, V.

Where to Stay in Mayagüez/Rincon
Mayagüez is the island's third-largest town, located on the West Coast about 10 miles
from Rincón on Route 2. Baroque and Victorian buildings make this pretty, bustling port
even more charming. Mayagüez is the launching pad for treks into the western and southwestern interior; routes into the mountains lead to some spectacular climbs (see "Treks")
and can be easily reached by car.

Hotels and Resorts
Best Western Mayagüez Resort & Casino   **$125–$175**   ★★★
Mayagüez, ☎ *(787) 832-3030, FAX (787) 265-3020.*

Single: $125–$150. Double: $135–$175.

Set on 20 landscaped gardens overlooking the harbor, this hotel has a country club feel. Rooms are newly renovated and nicely furnished with all the amenities. The grounds include a casino, nightclub, Olympic-size pool and new river pool, three tennis courts, and a putting green. Children's activities are scheduled during high season. The beach is 20 minutes away, so the hotel caters mainly to a business clientele. Another 100 villas are being built. 140 rooms. Credit cards: A, DC, D, MC, V.

Horned Dorset Primavera   **$150–$380**   ★★★★★

Rincon, ☎ *(787) 823-4030, FAX (787) 823-5580.*
Single: $150–$224. Double: $280–$380.

The name may be odd, but everything else is nearly perfect at this exclusive boutique hotel. Guests are pampered in plush suites with Persian rugs, armoires, four-poster beds, sitting areas, furnished balconies, and large baths. Not a spot bustling with activities. A pool and a library are the only attractions. The idea is to rest and relax in the hands of the excellent staff. The grounds are exquisitely landscaped and open onto the sea. Dinner is a memorable affair with six courses nightly. No kids under 12 permitted, no radios, telephones or TVs. 31 rooms. Credit cards: A, MC, V.

Inns

The *paradores* system offers several choices on the west coast, but be warned that big differences exist in service and surroundings. **Parador Hacienda Gripinas** resonates with the sounds of nature. **Parador Villa Antonio** tends to caters to the older; younger travelers might enjoy the **Parador Perichi** more. Businessmen tend to tuck in at **El Sol**.

Where to Stay in Culebra

Hotels and Resorts

Club Seabourne   **$105–$115**   ★★

☎ *(787) 742-3169, FAX (787) 742-3176.*
Single: $105–$115. Double: $105–$115.

Overlooking Fullodosa Bay, this small complex consists of air-conditioned rooms, villas and cottages, with refrigerators in the larger accommodations. One large cottage has two bedrooms and a full kitchen. A continental breakfast is on the house during the off season. The grounds include a pool, bar and restaurant that is closed on Mondays. 13 rooms. Credit cards: A, MC, V.

Apartments and Condominiums

Several options are available for self-catering, the best being the **Culebra Island Villas**, situated near enough to sea to make sports activities a cinch. Six people can pile into one of two houses that make up the **Harbor View Villas**, a perfect option for a small group of friends or a family who want to do their own thing.

Harbour View Villas   **$50–$95**   ★★

☎ *(787) 742-3855.*
Single: $50–$75. Double: $75–$95.

This small enclave of villas is on the island of Culebra, reached via a 10-minute ferry ride from Fajardo. The town and beach are a quarter-mile stroll. All units are air-conditioned, have kitchens for do-it-yourselfers, and sleep up to six. French doors open onto large balconies overlooking the town and the Vieques Sound. You'll want a car to get around, as there's not much on-site. 8 rooms. Credit cards: MC, V.

Low Cost Lodging

You get what you pay for, and anything cheap in this region tends to run toward the dilapidated and unclean. An exception is the **Coral Island Guest House,** which is mostly used by divers.

Where to Stay on Vieques

To get to the island, you can either take a small plane from San Juan's Isla Grande airport, or a ferry boat from Fajardo—a two-hour sojourn. (As mentioned above, getting to Fajardo is the difficulty here, since taxi rides from San Juan and its airports can be enormously expensive.)

Inns

Sea Gate Guest House $40–$60 ★★

☎ *(787) 741-4661.*
Single: $40. Double: $60.
High on a hill overlooking the harbor town of Isabel Segunda and the sea beyond, Sea Gate offers a private, lush tropical setting. Most rooms are efficiencies with kitchenettes. A small pool is on the premises, and the friendly owners will take you to the beach and arrange watersports. 17 rooms. Credit cards: not accepted.

Where to Eat

Fielding's Highest Rated Restaurants in Puerto Rico

★★★★★	Horned Dorset Primavera	$56–$88
★★★★★	Ramiro's	$22–$35
★★★★	Back Street Hong Kong	$15–$32
★★★★	La Chaumiere	$22–$37
★★★★	La Compostela	$15–$29
★★★	Amadeus	$9–$22
★★★	Anchor's Inn	$10–$24
★★★	El Ancla	$8–$35
★★★	La Mallorquina	$11–$24
★★★	Parador Villa Parguera	$4–$22

Fielding's Most Romantic Restaurants in Puerto Rico

♥♥♥♥♥	Horned Dorset Primavera	$56–$88
♥♥♥♥	La Compostela	$15–$29
♥♥♥	Anchor's Inn	$10–$24
♥♥	El Ancla	$8–$35
♥♥	La Chaumiere	$22–$37

Fielding's Best Value Restaurants in Puerto Rico

★★★	Amadeus	$9–$22
★★	La Bombonera	$5–$8
★★★	Parador Villa Parguera	$4–$22
★★★	El Ancla	$8–$35
★★★★	La Compostela	$15–$29

Fittingly, the annual Caribbean culinary competition is held on Puerto Rico, which has a plethora of talented chefs who routinely reinvent the cuisine of the region. When it comes to food, Puerto Rico once again stands out in the crowd. Don't make the faulty assumption that hotel food will somehow be lacking the panache and excitement of other dining options. Indeed, an unusually high number of the island's best restaurants can be found tucked away in hotels and resorts. You'll also find that these restaurants are not the domain solely of tourists. Puerto Ricans, who tend to be wealthier than their neighboring islanders, heavily populate these fine restaurants and relish the chance to dress to dazzle. The latest trend on the island is Nuevo Latino cuisine, which has been embraced by some of the hot new chefs, so expect new riffs on old favorites.

Puerto Rican cuisine is a rich blend of Spanish, African and Taino Indian cooking. *Cocina criolla*, or Creole cuisine, began with the Tainos, the island's indigenous people who cultivated *yuca* (yucca), *yautia* (*taniers*) and yams. They also made *casabe*, a flat bread still made today. Spaniards introduced wheat, chick peas, eggplant, cilantro, coconut, onions, garlic and rum, while African slaves brought pigeon peas, okra, plantains, and many coconut dishes.

Favorite appetizers include fritters, especially *tostones* (fried green plantains), *empanadillas* (deep-fried flour turnovers filled with cheese, ground meat or shredded chicken), and *rellenos de papa* (deep-fried stuffed mashed potato balls). Common side dishes are *arroz blanco* (white rice boiled in water and oil), tomato and coriander sauce and beans stewed in *sofrito* (a puree of onions, peppers, cilantro, garlic and salt pork). You can also try *mofongo*, fried green plantains mashed with salt, garlic and salt pork rinds and rolled into a ball; or *amarillos*, long, thin slices of yellow plantains sautéed in butter or olive oil.

Puerto Rico's national soup is *asopao*, a gumbo-like concoction of chicken and rice. Roast sucking pig, another national dish, is traditionally served on holidays. With the Caribbean Sea on one side and the Atlantic Ocean on the other, Puerto Rican chefs produce a wealth of deftly prepared seafood dishes, often with a Spanish flair. Sauces are frequently sofrito-based or *escabeche* (marinated in olive oils, white vinegar and spices). Favorite seafood dishes include, red snapper, shrimp, saltwater crayfish, mussels and spiny lobster. Conch and octopus often show up in salads. The island's national dessert, flan, is a condensed milk and vanilla custard with optional ingredients such as coconut milk, mashed pumpkin, breadfruit or cream cheese. And be sure to try Puerto Rican rum, considered by many to be the best in the world.

Where to Eat in San Juan

Al Dente $$ ★★

> *Calle Recinto Sur,* ☎ *(787) 723-7303.*
> *Lunch: 11:30 a.m.–4 p.m., entrées $12–$17.*
> *Dinner: 4–10 p.m., entrées $12–$17. Closed: Sun.*

This restaurant is a touch of old Palermo in Old San Juan. Located in a historical building in the colonial city's heart, the dining room features fresh pasta, chicken and fish in light sauces, utilizing fresh herbs and spices. The atmosphere is as unstuffy as the food. On Saturday, it offers a buffet from noon until 4 p.m. Reservations recommended. Credit cards: A, MC, V.

Amadeus $$ ★★★

> *Calle San Sebastian,* ☎ *(787) 722-8635.*
> *Lunch: Noon–5 p.m., entrées $9–$22.*
> *Dinner: 5 p.m.–1 a.m., entrées $9–$22. Closed: Mon.*

A name like Amadeus connotes glittering candelabra, spinets and powdered wigs. However, this cafe is as modern as can be. The whimsical chef adds French or Italian flair to native dishes; for example, a combination of caviar and sour cream with green plantain. A version of cassoulet is made here with chorizo and black beans. Some people could make a whole meal from a plate of creative appetizers that a group of four or more can share; a sort of Puerto Rican dim sum. Call in advance to reserve space in the back room. Reservations recommended. Credit cards: A, MC, V.

Back Street Hong Kong $$$ ★★★★

> ☎ *(787) 791-1000.* Associated hotel: *El San Juan Hotel/Casino.*
> *Dinner: 6 p.m.–midnight, entrées $15–$32.*

This place isn't your typical greasy spoon chop-suey. In fact, people like to dress up to eat the savory Chinese food in this well-loved restaurant that recreates the hustle and bustle of Hong Kong. The eclectic dining room was transported piecemeal from a Seattle World's Fair exhibition; it also contains a tropical aquarium that delights young children. After dinner you can meander across the lobby to the Cigar Bar for a late-night smoke. Reservations recommended. Credit cards: A, MC, V.

Butterfly People $ ★★

> *152 Calle Fortaleza,* ☎ *(787) 723-2432.*
> *Lunch: 11 a.m.–4:30 p.m., entrées $5–$9. Closed: Sun.*

Notice to lepidopterists—you will be dazzled at this restaurant and gallery that sells butterflies under glass from one of the most extensive private collections in the world. While the prices for these winged beauties range from moderate to stratospheric, the mostly-Puerto Rican dishes here are fairly reasonable. You can also have a soup (gazpacho is good), or salad on a plant-filled patio. Credit cards: A, DC, MC, V.

El Patio de Sam $$ ★★

> *102 Calle San Sebastian,* ☎ *(787) 723-1149.*
> *Lunch: 11 a.m–11 p.m., entrées $8–$22.*
> *Dinner: 11 a.m.–11 p.m., entrées $8–$22.*

This oft-visited eatery—in business for 54 years— is remarkable for serving the juiciest burgers in town in the oldest building in town. Of course, it proffers a well-balanced menu of lobster tail, steaks, pizza, soups, desserts and tropical fruit libations.

The late-night crowd likes to party here; it stays open till midnight on weekends. Live music tunes up after 7 p.m. every night except Sundays. Credit cards: A, DC, MC, V.

La Bombonera $ ★★
259 Calle San Francisco, ☎ *(787) 722-0658.*
Lunch: 7:30–11 a.m., entrées $2–$8.
Dinner: 11 a.m.–8:30 p.m., entrées $5–$8.
Like its name says, this old-fashioned eatery proffers a plethora of traditional goodies, both sweet and savory. You can have a plate of *calamares en su tinta* (squid in its own ink served with rice), while your youngster sips hot chocolate. This place serves as the corner malt shop and tryst spot for locals who have been flocking to it since 1902. It's great for breakfast (the omelets are muy grande), crowded at lunch, and ideal for tea and snacks. Customers sit in booths or stake out a stool at the counter. Take-out available. Credit cards: MC, V.

La Chaumiere $$$ ★★★★
367 Tetuan Street, ☎ *(787) 722-3330.*
Dinner: 6 p.m.–midnight, entrées $22–$37. Closed: Sun.
This restaurant serves classic French cuisine to a faithful clientele in surroundings that transport guests to the Gallic countryside. It's the kind of place where you can order rarely-found specialties like floating island (merengues in a sauce of creme anglaise) or oysters rockefeller. Perfect for a pre-show supper; it's located behind the famous Tapia Theater. It closes from August until mid-September. Reservations recommended. Credit cards: A, DC, MC, V.

La Compostela $$$ ★★★★
Avenida Condado 106, ☎ *(787) 724-6088.*
Lunch: Noon–3 p.m., entrées $15–$29.
Dinner: 6:30–10:30 p.m., entrées $15–$29. Closed: Sun.
Many repeat visitors recommend this Spanish restaurant with a French touch in a commercial suburb of San Juan. The owner has spent time laboring in the kitchens in both countries; he blends the styles effortlessly, concentrating his efforts on fresh seafood. The wine cellar is amazing: close to 10,000 bottles! Reservations recommended. Credit cards: A, DC, MC, V.

La Mallorquina $$ ★★★
Calle San Justo 207, ☎ *(787) 722-3261.*
Lunch: 11:30 a.m.–3 p.m., entrées $11–$24.
Dinner: 4–10 p.m., entrées $11–$24. Closed: Sun.
This restaurant may be a bit of a tourist trap, but it's still worth visiting for the house special asopao, the Puerto Rican rice gumbolike soup, served with a choice of lobster or chicken. It's one of the oldest restaurants in town, founded in 1848. Service is gracious and attentive. Credit cards: A, MC, V.

Parador Villa Parguera $$ ★★★
Route 307, ☎ *(787) 899-7777.* Associated hotel: *Parador Villa Parguera.*
Lunch: 7:30 a.m.–4 p.m., entrées $4–$22.
Dinner: 4–9:30 p.m., entrées $4–$22.
Simply prepared but fresh seafood is a specialty at this seaside inn (one of the island's touted "paradores") surrounded by coconut palms on Phosphorescent Bay,

on the West Coast. The Parador is an excellent base for viewing the local phenomenon—on dark nights, the bay is "lit" by thousands of tiny organisms called dinoflagellates. Come during the week, because hordes of families crowd the area on weekends. Reservations recommended. Credit cards: A, CB, DC, D, MC, V.

Ramiro's $$$ ★★★★★

Avenida Magdalena 1106, ☎ *(787) 721-9049.*
Lunch: Noon–3 p.m., entrées $8–$20.
Dinner: 6:30–10:30 p.m., prix fixe $22–$35.

Patrons dress up to dine at this cocina fantastica; owner Jesus Ramiro merits kudos as one of the island's most creative chefs. He uses local produce and ingredients to produce incredible meals (lamb and duck are often on the menu). No matter what, save room for dessert. No lunch on Saturdays. Reservations recommended. Credit cards: A, DC, MC, V.

Where to Eat in Farjardo and Humacao

Anchor's Inn $$ ★★★

Route 987, KM 2.7, Fajardo, 738, ☎ *(787) 863-7200.*
Lunch: 11:30 a.m.–4 p.m., entrées $10–$24.
Dinner: 4–10 p.m., entrées $10–$24.

This unpretentious spot by the sea offers a scrumptious seafood paella and an equally appealing view of Fajardo Harbor. In the shadow of El Conquistador resort, this casual seafood restaurant owned by native Joe Cruz dishes out a tasty catch of the day—usually tropical lobster or red snapper—along with a strong dose of enthusiasm about his locale. If you are short on ideas on how to spend your vacation, talk to Cruz. He'll steer you to the nearby rain forest, a fishing boat captain or terrific Beach of the Seven Seas. Reservations recommended during the tourist season. Credit cards: MC, V.

Where to Eat in Ponce

El Ancla $$$ ★★★

9 Hostos Avenue, ☎ *(787) 840-2450.*
Lunch: 11 a.m.–4 p.m., entrées $8–$35.
Dinner: 4–10 p.m., entrées $8–$35.

This established, family-owned restaurant perched over the water in Ponce Beach has long been popular with Poncenos and visitors. The warm welcome is what sets it apart from other restaurants serving seafood, which is the specialty of this eatery. Red snapper stuffed with lobster and shrimp served on a plate heaped with plenty of starchy side dishes is a specialty. The chef also does a nice job with lobster, octopus and fish. Credit cards: A, DC, D, MC, V.

Where to Eat in Mayagüez/Rincon

Horned Dorset Primavera $$$ ★★★★★

☎ *(787) 823-4030.*
Lunch: Noon– 2:30 p.m., entrées $9–$25.
Dinner: 7–9:30 p.m., prix fixe $56–$88.

This plush, whitewashed hotel/restaurant stands alone in its glory in a frontier beachfront location catering to surfers and daytrippers. That isn't to say the area isn't sublimely beautiful; it is. Many visitors make a special trip to dine on the continental cuisine with a Caribbean flair. A recent tasting menu included: smoked duck, tomato and fennel soup, roasted beet salad with goat cheese; fresh fettuccini a la romana, red snapper with lemon pan jus, passion fruit granitee, veal medallions with creamy polenta, martinique cake and tropical fruit soup. Location is six miles northwest of Mayaguez. In the evenings Chef Aaron Wratten pulls out all the stops with either a fixed price dinner of six or 10 courses. Lunch hours vary, call for information. Reservations required. Credit cards: A, MC, V.

Where to Shop

Though Puerto Rico is not a free port, good deals can be found on items such as china, jewelry, and crystal because shopkeepers are quite competitive—be sure to shop around before making a major purchase, and remember, you won't have to pay duty upon entering the U.S. mainland. The island has lots of U.S.-style malls with ubiquitous chain stores; the largest (in the entire Caribbean, in fact) is the upscale 200-store Plaza las Americas, located south of San Juan in the Hato Rey district, just off the Las Americas Expressway.

Locally made crafts are always a good buy, especially the small, hand-craved figurines of saints called *santos*. Carnival masks made from *papier-mache* (in Ponce) or coconut husks (in Loirz, near San Juan) also make good mementos, as do hand-rolled cigars, needlework, ceramics, rum, and paintings by local artisans. Good crafts shops include **Ole**, *San Juan*, ☎ *(787) 724-2445*, and **Puerto Rican arts & Crafts**, *Old San Juan*, ☎ *(787) 725-5596*.

Puerto Rico Directory

Arrival and Departure

All three airports in Puerto Rico have recently undergone extensive and expensive renovation. The **Luis Muñoz Marin** in San Juan is the major hub for international travel. Since 1988 **American Airlines** has spent $260 million tripling the size of its San Juan hub, including the reservation center. The Mercedita Airport is located in Ponce, and the Rafael Hernandez is in Aguadilla. Major airlines including **American, Continental, Delta, Pan Am, TWA, Tower, United** and **U.S. Airways** fly into San Juan from most major U.S. cities. **Carnival Airlines** operates service to Aguadilla and Ponce from New York and Newark. American has made San Juan its hub for all flights from Puerto Rico to other Caribbean destinations, the U.S., Europe and Latin America. American added twice-daily, non-stop flights from Fort Lauderdale in late 1996. American Airlines also operates nonstop service from Miami and New York's JFK to Aguadilla and from Miami to Ponce. International carriers include **British Airways**, **Iberia**, **KLM Royal Dutch**, **Martinair Holland** and **Lufthansa**.

The airport departure tax is included in the price of the airline ticket.

Business Hours

Shops open 9 a.m.–6 p.m. Banks open weekdays 8:30 a.m.–2:30 p.m. and Saturday 9:45 a.m.–noon.

Climate

Coastal weather in Puerto Rico is warm and sunny year-round. During the summer, temperatures average in the mid 80s Fahrenheit; during the winter, they hover in the low 70s to the low 80s. The rainiest months are May to December, generally heavier on the north than the south coast. Temperatures in the mountains tend to be 5–10 degrees cooler.

Documents

Since Puerto Rico is a commonwealth of the United States, no passports are required for U.S. citizens. Visitors do need a valid driver's license to rent a car. If you are a citizen of any other country, a visa is required. Vaccinations are not necessary. U.S. citizens do not need to clear customs or immigration (other citizens do). On departure, luggage must be inspected by the U.S. Agriculture Department, as law prohibits the taking of certain fruits and plants in the U.S. Dogs and cats may be brought to Puerto Rico from the U.S. with two documents: a health certificate dated not more than 10 days prior to departure showing that the animal is certified disease-free by an official or registered veterinarian, and a certificate of rabies vaccination, dated not more than 30 days prior to departure, authenticated by the proper authorities.

Electricity

Current runs A.C. 60 cycles, 110 volts, single phase or 220 volts, three phase.

Getting Around

Taxis, buses and rental cars are available at the airport and major hotels. All taxicabs are metered, but they may be rented unmetered for an hourly rate. There's an additional charge of 50 cents for every suitcase. *Publicos* (public cars) run on frequent schedules to all island towns (usually during daytime hours) and depart from main squares. They run on fixed rates. The *Ruta Panoramica* is a scenic road meandering across the island that offers stunning vistas. San Juan is the largest home-based cruise port in the world. Ferries shuttle passengers to and from Culebra and Vieques at reasonable rates. Car transport is also available. San Juan's harbor can also be crossed by the Catana ferry (50 cents) to the Bacardi Rum plant's free tours.

Language

Spanish and English are both official languages of Puerto Rico. Many speak English—and many people don't, especially older people in outlying rural areas. In San Juan however English is taught from kindergarten to high school as part of the school curriculum.

PUERTO RICO

Medical Emergencies

Officially, the medical community of Puerto Rico meets the same standards as those required on the U.S. mainland. Most physicians on the island are based in San Juan with almost all medical specializations represented. San Juan has 14 hospitals, most districts have at least one. Ask your hotel to recommend a physician on call.

Money

The official currency is the U.S. dollar and credit cards are widely accepted by hotels, restaurants and shops. Several foreign exchange offices are available in San Juan and at the airport.

Telephone

The area code is *787*. Postage stamps are equivalent to those in the U.S. as are mail costs. You can dial direct to the mainland.

Time

Atlantic Standard Time, year-round, which is one hour earlier than New York. During Daylight Saving Time, it is the same.

Tipping and Taxes

All hotels include a six percent government tax on the bill. Gratuities on restaurant bills are not included, but a 15 percent tip is expected.

Tourist Information

For more information about the island, contact the **Puerto Rico Tourism Company**, *P.O. Box 4435, Old San Juan, Station San Juan, PR 00902;* ☎ *(787) 721-2400*. There are offices in New York, Los Angeles, Coral Gables, London, Madrid, Mexico City, Milan, Paris, Stockholm, Toronto and Weisbaden, Germany. In the U.S. ☎ *(213) 874-5991*.

When to Go

January–June the Puerto Rico Symphony Orchestra conducts its season with performances. January 6 is traditional gift-giving day in Puerto Rico, celebrated by island-wide festivals with music, dance, parades, puppet shows and caroling troubadours. First week of January is the **International Folklore Festival** (☎ *(787) 724-4747*), featuring dance groups from around the world. Late February is the **National Coffee Harvest Festival** (☎ *(787) 856-1345*). **Carnival** takes place in February. The **Sugar Harvest Festival** (☎ *(787) 892-5574*) takes place in April. The **Festival Casals** takes place in early June, honoring the late cellist (☎ *(787) 721-7727*). **San Juan Bautista Day** is June 21, celebrating the island's patron saint, as sanjuaneros walk backward into the sea three times at midnight for good luck. The Albonito Flower Festival (☎ *(787) 735-3871*) takes place in late June. The **Barranquitas Artisans Fair** (☎ *(787) 859-0520*) is held July 19–21, the island's oldest crafts fair with 130 local artisans. The **International Light Tackle Tournament** (☎ *(787) 851-8880*) takes place in late September. The **Inter-American Festival of the Arts** (☎ *(787) 721-7727*) takes place in September. The **National Plantain Festival** (☎ *(787) 859-1259*) occurs in late October. The baseball season begins in October. The Festival of Typical Dishes lasts from late November–early December. Old San Juan's White Christmas Festival takes place December–January. Island-wide Christmas festivities with life-size nativity scenes are held December–January. The **Bacardi Artisans Fair** *(☎ (787) 788-1500)* featuring more than 100 craftsmen is in December. Lighting of the Town of Bethlehem occurs for three days in mid-December.

Spring is always a good time to visit San Juan. Old San Juan is less crowded with cruise ship day trippers than during the winter, hotels rates begin to drop, and many hotels offer inexpensive summer packages to lure visitors during the slowest months. Puerto Rico doesn't have extreme seasonal changes so you may see that quintessential Christmas flower, the poinsettia blooming and mangoes ripening in the same gardens. San Juan shuts down for much of Holy Week, but Easter celebrations are plentiful. An annual sunrise Easter service is usually held at **El Morro**.

PUERTO RICO HOTELS	RMS	RATES	PHONE	CR. CARDS
San Juan				
★★★★★ El San Juan Hotel & Casino	392	$180–$495	(800) 468-2818	A, CB, MC, V
★★★★★ Hyatt Dorado Beach Resort & Casino	298	$205–$515	(800) 233-1234	A, CB, D, MC, V
★★★★★ Hyatt Regency Cerromar	506	$205–$435	(800) 233-1234	A, D, MC, V
★★★★ Caribe Hilton & Casino	670	$215–$380	(800) 468-8585	A, CB, D, MC, V
★★★★ Westin Rio Mar Beach Resort	600	$205–$475	(800) 474-6627	A, CB, DC, MC, V
★★★ Condado Beach Hotel	245	$190–$430	(800) 468-2822	A, CB, D, DC, MC, V
★★★ Condado Plaza Hotel & Casino	395	$265–$355	(800) 624-0420	A, CB, D, MC, V
★★★ Gran Hotel El Convento	59	$190–$375	(800) 468-2779	A, CB, D, DC, MC, V
★★★ Radisson Ambassador Plaza	233	$200–$320	(800) 333-3333	A, CB, D, MC, V
★★★ Radisson Normandie	177	$195–$220	(800) 333-3333	A, CB, D, DC, MC, V
★★★ Sands Hotel & Casino	410	$210–$305	(800) 544-3008	A, CB, D, DC, MC, V
★★ Atlantic Beach Hotel	37	$90–$125	(787) 721-6900	A, D, MC, V
★★ Best Western Pierre	184	$126–$173	(800) 528-1234	A, CB, D, DC, MC, V
★★ Carib Inn Tennis Club	225	$105–$320	(800) 548-8217	A, CB, D, DC, MC, V
★★ Parador El Guajataca	38	$77–$95	(800) 964-3065	A, CB, D, DC, MC
★ Arcade Inn	19	$40–$90	(787) 728-7524	A, MC, V

PUERTO RICO HOTELS		RMS	RATES	PHONE	CR. CARDS
★	El Canario by the Sea	25	$65–$99	(800) 533-2649	A, MC, V
Fajardo					
★★★★★	El Conquistador Resort & Country Club	926	$330–$545	(800) 468-5228	A, CB, D, MC, V
★★★★	Wyndham Palmas del Mar Resort & Villas	102	$166–$269	(800) 725-6276	A, MC, V
★	Parador La Familia	28	$69–$80	(800) 443-0266	A, D, MC, V
★	Parador Martorell	10	$64–$90	(800) 443-0266	A, MC, V
Ponce					
★★★	Copamarina Beach Resort	142	$135–$155	(800) 468-4553	A, MC, V
★★★	Ponce Hilton & Casino	150	$160–$210	(800) 445-8667	A, CB, D, DC, MC, V
★★	Hacienda Gripinas Parador	19	$50–$66	(800) 443-0266	MC, V
★★	Melia Hotel	74	$80–$95	(800) 742-4276	A, MC, V
★★	Parador Oasis	52	$60–$69	(800) 223-9815	A, CB, D, MC, V
★★	Parador Vistamar	50	$69–$90	(800) 443-0266	A, CB, D, MC, V
★★	Ponce Hotel Tropicana & Casino	116	$105–$110	(787) 844-1200	A, D, DC, MC, V
★	Parador Villa Parguera	70	$80–$95	(800) 443-0266	A, CB, D, DC, MC, V
Mayaguez					
★★★★★	Horned Dorset Primavera	31	$150–$380	(787) 823-4030	A, MC, V
★★★	Best Western Mayaguez Resort & Casino	140	$125–$175	(787) 832-3030	A, D, DC, MC, V
Vieques Island					
★★	Sea Gate Guest House	17	$40–$60	(787) 741-4661	None

PUERTO RICO RESTAURANTS		PHONE	ENTREE	CR. CARDS
San Juan				
Chinese Cuisine				
★★★★	Back Street Hong Kong	(787) 791-1000	$15–$32	A, MC, V
Continental Cuisine				
★★★★★	Ramiro's	(787) 721-9049	$8–$35	A, DC, MC, V
★★★	Amadeus	(787) 722-8635	$9–$22	A, MC, V

PUERTO RICO RESTAURANTS	PHONE	ENTREE	CR.CARDS
French Cuisine			
★★★★ La Chaumiere	(787) 722-3330	$22–$37	A, DC, MC, V
International Cuisine			
★★ Butterfly People	(787) 723-2432	$5–$9	A, DC, MC, V
★★ El Patio de Sam	(787) 723-1149	$8–$22	A, DC, MC, V
Italian Cuisine			
★★ Al Dente	(787) 723-7303	$12–$17	A, MC, V
Latin American Cuisine			
★★ La Bombonera	(787) 722-0658	$2–$8	MC, V
★★★ La Mallorquina	(787) 722-3261	$11–$24	A, MC, V
★★★ Parador Villa Parguera	(787) 899-7777	$4–$22	A, CB, D, DC, MC, V
Spanish Cuisine			
★★★★ La Compostela	(787) 724-6088	$15–$29	A, DC, MC, V
Fajardo			
Latin American Cuisine			
★★★ Anchor's Inn	(787) 863-7200	$10–$24	MC, V
Ponce			
Seafood Cuisine			
★★★ El Ancla	(787) 840-2450	$8–$35	A, D, DC, MC, V
Mayaguez			
Continental Cuisine			
★★★★★ Horned Dorset Primavera	(787) 823-4030	$9–$88	A, MC, V

SABA

Most of the houses on Saba are painted white with red roofs and green shutters.

An improbable green gumdrop plopped into the sea, Saba is one of the Caribbean's surreptitious treasures. The island is cloaked in an almost fairy-tale aura—as if a piece of the Swiss Alps had broken free and been happily misplaced in the tropics. Dollhouse villages clamber up the sheer slopes of mist-kissed Mount Scenery—a muscular peak that lives up to its name from above, from below, from afar—and a trifle of a road snakes from a toy port on one side of the island to a toy airstrip on the other. Whichever side you land on, as you switch back up the hand-hewn road to your inn, you may have to pinch yourself to determine whether it's all some delightful dream you've slumbered into by accident.

Smallest and least-populated of the troika of islands that make up the Dutch Windwards (Sint Maarten and Sint Eustatius are usually visible in the distance), Saba is best described by that overused sobriquet *charming*. With just 1200 residents and five square miles to its name, the island actually lives up the usual clichés we travel writers keep stuffed in our wallet. Also known as "the Unspoiled Queen," Saba is blissfully pristine—the sweet houses are freshly painted, greenery is orderly yet wild, and even the roadways are free of debris. The roster of activities offered here fall into just two categories: hiking and diving (well, three, if you plunge headstrong into the local hobby of over-the-fence gossip). Explorations on foot into the emerald hills reward with serene escape and triumphant vistas, while Saba's underwater world is deep, fast and exciting, and almost unequaled within the Caribbean. Although nightlife has been reported on the odd Friday or Saturday night at Guido's Pizzeria, there are no beaches, no casinos, no resorts, no fine dining, and no apologies about any of it.

Saba is an island that knows what it is, and (perhaps more importantly) what it isn't, to the point that an inn-building moratorium was put in place when the number of rooms began to approach triple-digits. Although tourism is the major economy today, the government undoubtedly knows that what makes Saba special is its very quaintness.

BEST BETS FOR...

Bird's-Eye View

Tiny little Saba (pronounced *Say*-ba) packs a lot into its five square miles. The island's distinctive apex is Mount Scenery (2855 feet), a dormant volcano that towers gracefully over the panoply of green; a few smaller peaks girder its vertical heft. The vegetation evolves as you ascend into the higher elevations—the summit area is an elfin (or cloud) forest, dripping with moisture. The coastline of the island is primarily cliffs, and as you approach by boat it is interesting to ponder Saba's first inhabitants, who regularly unloaded boats in the tossed surf and hauled their supplies up the sheer slopes. There are two main villages: The Bottom is the capitol of the island, nestled in a valley (*botte* is Dutch for bowl), that drops to the sea at either end, and Windwardside, draped over a narrow shoulder of Mount Scenery and home to most of the lodgings—red roofs and white clapboard walls are the rule. The island's one road, built over 18 years by hand, is a Saba-sized modern-

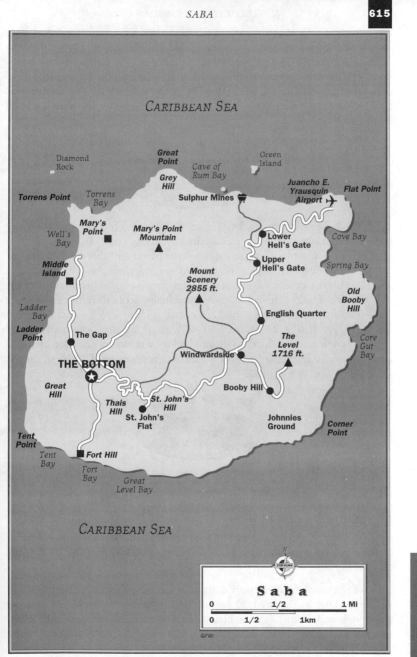

CARIBBEAN SEA

Diamond
Rock

*Great
Point*

Green
Island

*Grey
Hill*

*Cave of
Rum Bay*

*Juancho E.
Yrausquin
Airport* ✈

Flat Point

Torrens Point

*Torrens
Bay*

Sulphur Mines

*Mary's
Point*

*Well's
Bay*

*Mary's Point
Mountain*

▲

Lower
Hell's Gate

Cove Bay

Upper
Hell's Gate

Spring Bay

*Middle
Island*

*Mount
Scenery
2855 ft.*

▲

*Old
Booby
Hill*

*Ladder
Bay*

English Quarter

*Core
Gut
Bay*

*Ladder
Point*

The Gap

*The
Level
1716 ft.*

▲

THE BOTTOM
★

Windwardside

*Great
Hill*

*Thais
Hill*

*St. John's
Hill*

Booby Hill

St. John's
Flat

*Tent
Point*

*Tent
Bay*

Fort Hill ■

Johnnies
Ground

*Corner
Point*

*Fort
Bay*

*Great
Level Bay*

CARIBBEAN SEA

N

FIELDING

Saba

0   1/2   1 Mi

0   1/2   1km

©FWi

day miracle, as previous engineers had deemed such construction impossible on the rugged terrain. It zigzags up and down the slopes, connecting the port on the south end with each of the villages and the airport on the north end. A traffic jam transpires when more than a dozen of Saba's small collection of vehicles collect in Windwardside at the same time. The airstrip was built in 1962 on the only sliver of flat land available—landing here is a thrill in itself.

History

Columbus sighted Saba in 1493, but it took another 129 years for some unlucky Englishman to shipwreck against the rocky coast. In 1665, the English privateer Thomas Morgan captured the island and threw out the original Dutch settlers. Morgan's men stayed behind when he left, a fact that some locals use to claim their ancestors were pirates. Some historians purport that Saba's original British settlers were actually Scottish refugees or exiles from the British civil wars in the 17th century. Until a pier was constructed in 1972, ships had to anchor in Fort Bay, where wooden longboats would transfer people and products to shore in a very wet ride. The island changed hands between European powers a half-dozen times until 1816 when the Dutch took it over for good.

People

With just 1200 souls calling Saba home, everyone knows everyone and all seem to get along quite well. About half the population is black, descended from slaves who toiled on small farms and toted things up and down the mountain. The whites are descendants of Dutch, Scottish and English settlers. An interesting piece of trivia: Nearly half the island's residents—regardless of race—have the surname Hassell. Everyone speaks English, though the official language is Dutch.

Those not involved with tourism make their living farming, fishing, seafaring or working at the medical school, which opened in 1993. As you can imagine, islanders lead a casual lifestyle and visitors can get away with shorts and a T-shirt nearly everywhere, but keep in mind that bathing suits are not appropriate in the villages.

Saba is an autonomous part of the Kingdom of the Netherlands and is self-governing. Crime is virtually unheard of—as the tourist board says, it's "limited to excessive partying or minor traffic violations."

It's no longer news that tiny Saba has emerged as one of the Caribbean's top dive locations. Part of the popularity is its unique underwater layout, which mirrors the above-water topography: sheer. Additionally, the island was one of the first in the Caribbean—close on the heels of eco-sensitive Bonaire—to aggressively protect its marine environment through the use of permanent mooring buoys; the **Saba Marine Park** is currently the only self-supporting underwater reserve in the world. The increasing awareness of Saba's undersea paradise has ballooned the number of divers but, although the island is minute and dives are concentrated into a small area, you'll never feel crowded and the diving is still pristine. Saba remains a somewhat exotic destination, even by Caribbean standards, and the total number of divers visiting the island in 1994 was a mere 5165 (averaging five dives apiece).

The diving is centered off the island's west coast. Black sand covers the sea floor, keeping silt to a minimum and visibility sterling (approaching 125 feet in winter), while dramatic walls and substantial fish and coral life contribute to the vivid underwater environment. With the bottom dropping to more than 1000 feet as close as a half-mile from shore, the diving is serious. This is not a milieu for newcomers; even experienced divers will find the currents and depths challenging. It's also a little more expensive here, but above-water costs tend to balance out the difference; there is also a $3-per-dive fee to help support the Marine Park (you'll save money by booking a dive package). Almost all of the island's 27 primary dive sites are within 10 minutes of the boat dock at Fort Bay, and permanent mooring buoys protect the reefs below. In winter, a north swell will sometimes make snorkeling a little rocky. Weather permitting, **Cove Bay**, near the airport, can also be a good location for snorkeling from shore. Saba has the only decompression chamber in this section of the Caribbean.

Dive Shops

M/V Caribbean Explorer

Phillipsburg, Sint Maarten; (800) 322-3577.
A live-aboard dive boat that originates in Sint Maarten. One-week trips include three-and-a-half days of diving on Saba (up to five dives daily), plus two days on St. Kitts. Year-round, all-inclusive rates are $1195 per person (double occupancy).

Saba Deep Dive Center

Fort Bay; (5994) 63347.

The only shop located on the water, Saba Deep keeps groups under a dozen with three scheduled dives daily: deep, intermediate and shallow. A full PADI and NAUI training facility. Two-tank dive $80, including equipment.

Saba Reef Divers

Windwardside; (5994) 62541.

An offshoot of Wilson's, the first shop on the island, that opened in 1997. The outfit's four owner/managers are from San Diego and PADI-affiliated (one is a Course Director, the highest level of PADI instructor certification), with Saba's only Nitrox equipment. Two tank dives, $80, including transfers to harbor. Snorkeling trips $25; kayak rentals start at $30 for a half-day (guided trips also available).

Sea Saba Dive Center

Windwardside; (5994) 62246.

Two ample 40-foot boats are limited to 12 divers; ask about drift and night dives. Half-day snorkeling trips to Torrens and another site, $25. Resort courses a specialty for the all-instructor staff, with courses to Divemaster. Two-tank dive $90.

Visitors are tempted to call Saba cute—that is, until they climb the stair steps leading up **Mount Scenery**, the island's majestic summit. On second thought, any hiker who spends a few moments observing Saba's imposing outline from an approaching plane or a neighboring island should know what they're getting into: the vacation equivalent of a stairmaster. Trails are discussed not in terms of mileage, but in number of steps (1064 to the top of Mount Scenery, the trailhead sign announces). Nonetheless, this is a walker's island, with a detailed lattice of paths snaking between the villages and peaks. Prior to 1943 when Saba's first (and only) road went into use, transportation was strictly on donkey or foot. But with the import of cars and construction of the airport in 1963, the trails fell into disrepair. In recent years, the tracks have found new fans among the more active tourists drawn to the island and the government now promotes hiking eagerly. A guide is not necessary for anyone reasonably fit, but the verdant valleys offer a diverse ecosystem and trekkers will appreciate the assistance of a knowledgeable guide. Some trails cross private property; stay on the established paths. Stop by the tourist office to pick up a pamphlet outlining island hikes or the walking tour of Windwardside, one of the sweetest villages in the region.

Tours

James Johnson's Guide Service

The Bottom; ☎ *(5994) 63307.*

Offers four-to-six-hour guided hikes to Mary's Point, Troy, and the Sulphur Mine on afternoons and weekends. $40–50 per person depending on itinerary selected.

What Else to See

Saba is not a sightseeing destination in the traditional sense. That is, you won't find much in the way of forts to tour or shopping districts to conquer. But Saba is undeniably eye-filling, particularly for anyone entranced with the sight of Lilliputian villages or the natural environment—the island is photogenic from top to bottom, and most of it can be easily appreciated on foot. You can explore Windwardside in a couple of hours; pick up a copy of the walking tour guide from the Trail Shop (next to the Tourist Bureau)—though most of the spots it guides you to are local businesses (for instance, at Saba Drug, "Vanessa sells anything from aspirin to peanut butter"). As you stroll around, note that a few of the roads are just big enough for a car—you'll need to step out of the road as they pass.

Museums and Exhibits

Saba Museum   ★★

Above Captain's Quarters, Windwardside.

Hours: 10 a.m.–noon and 1–4 p.m.

This small museum is found in the 19th-century cottage of a sea captain. It exhibits antiques from that era including a restored kitchen of the period, and pre-Columbian artifacts found around the island. General admission: $2.

Sports

Two activities steal the spotlight here: hiking and diving. Four-hour **snorkeling** trips aboard dive boats are offered for $25 by Sea Saba ☎ *(5994) 62246* and Saba Reef Divers ☎ *(5994) 62541.* Saba Reef also provides guided **kayaking** trips; $45 per person, or $60 including snorkeling (kayak rentals are also available). **Tennis** can be found at Sunny Valley Youth Centre in The Bottom (and at Willard's, though this court is usually reserved for guests).

Fielding **SABA**
WORLDWIDE

LIFE ON THE ROAD

Only five miles square, Saba (pronounced "Say-ba") is a dormant volcano, ringed by rocky cliffs. Off-the-beaten-track and home to a population of 1200, Saba is ideal for divers and nature lovers. Although there are no beaches, you can dive in the Saba Marine Park or hike the island's scenic trails.

Mt. Scenery

1064 steps lead to the summit of beautiful Mt. Scenery. Despite its difficulty, almost everyone makes the hike during their visit, including Queen Beatrix of the Netherlands, who arrived at the top (in heels, legend has it) and proclaimed: "This is the smallest and highest point in my kingdom!"

The Ladder

This strenuous 30-minute (one-way) 524-step hike down to Ladder Bay begins at the Bottom, located on the island's west side. The hike will give your heart a workout, but your reward is a splendid ocean view.

Saba Marine Park

Created to protect the island's diverse, pristine marine environments, the park's waters encircle the island. Island dive operators make excursions to various moorings, including the Outer Limits, Twilight Zone and Third Encounter, which highlight underwater volcanic pinnacles covered with sponges and inhabited by groupers.

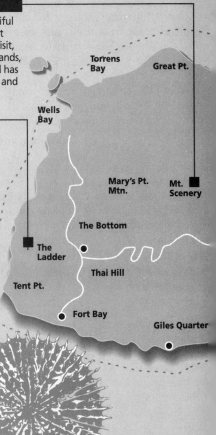

Torrens Bay

Great Pt.

Wells Bay

Mary's Pt. Mtn.

Mt. Scenery

The Bottom

The Ladder

Thai Hill

Tent Pt.

Fort Bay

Giles Quarter

The Road

Corkscrewing into the mountains from the island's eastern side and cresting Mount Scenery, this narrow road is an engineering triumph. Twenty sharp, hairpin curves twist the road between the airport and Hell's Gate. From Mount Scenery, you can look down and marvel at the airport runway—only 1300 feet long, one of the shortest international runways in the world.

Hitch-hiking

In crime-free Saba, this is an acceptable way to travel The Road. To hitch a ride with a friendly driver, you need to stand in the right place. To go from The Bottom, sit on the wall opposite the village's Anglican church. To go from Fort Bay, sit on the wall opposite the Saba Deep Dive Center. From the west side, wait at the Big Rock Supermarket.

Holy Rosary Church

Built in 1919 in Windwardside, this stone church has white fretwork and a red roof.

Juancho E. Yrausquin Airport
Flat Pt.

Hell's Gate

Windwardside

N

Corner Pt.

Saba Lace

Visit the community center in Hell's Gate in the morning to see the island's unique style of lace. Using embroidery techniques brought to Saba in the 1870s, women craft blouses, handkerchiefs and tablecloths. Peggy's Boutique in Windwardside also sells Saban lace. Also try the island liqueur, a potent concoction called "Saba Spice."

Where to Stay

	Fielding's Highest Rated Hotels in Saba	
★★★	Captain's Quarters	$85–$130
★★★	Cottage Club	$94–$136
★★★	Willard's of Saba	$150–$400

	Fielding's Best Rooms With a View on Saba	
★★★	Willard's of Saba	$150–$400
★	El Momo	$30–$35
★★	Gate House, The	$75–$95
★★★	Captain's Quarters	$85–$130
★★	Juliana's	$70–$115

Saba's handful of lodging choices are essentially all small inns, each of which offer an array of money-saving dive packages; for an overview check with **Dive Saba Travel** ☎ *(800) 883-SABA*. There are no luxury resorts here, though **Willard's of Saba** offers the most upscale setting—it is reportedly the highest hotel in the Kingdom of the Netherlands. Another property, **Queen's Garden Resort**, provides high-amenity apartments on a hill above The Bottom, and may be fully operational by the time you read this. In general, rooms are reasonably priced by Caribbean standards.

Apartments and Condominiums

Cottage Club　　　　　　**$94–$136**　　　　　　★★★

Windwardside, ☎ *(5994) 62386, FAX (5994) 62476.*

Website: www.turq.com/cottage-club.

Single: $94–$126. Double: $105–$136.

One of Saba's newer properties, this homey clutch of self-contained and gingerbread-trimmed cottages provide full kitchen, spacious living area, balcony, TV and phone. A pool was added in 1996, but no other facilities are available; town is a few minutes' walk. Great for families. Request unit 1 or 2 for the best views. 10 rooms. Credit cards: MC, V.

Inns

Captain's Quarters   **$70–$135**   ★★★

Windwardside, ☎ *(800) 446-3010, (5994) 62201, FAX (5994) 62377.*
Website: saba-online.com. E-mail: SabaCQ@megatropic.com.
Single: $70–$100. Double: $90–$135.

This delightful inn has long been Saba's best all-around bet. Set high on a hill with
great ocean views, the hotel centers around an old wooden home, built by a sea captain in 1832. Four rooms are in this house, the rest in a newer wing, and there's also
a two-bedroom cottage next door. All are spacious and bright and have four-poster
beds; best of all, each was recently individually decorated by a Saban artist in 1997.
The grounds are nicely landscaped with citrus trees and tropical blooms; there's a
library, swimming pool and a good restaurant. 12 rooms. Credit cards: A, D, MC, V.

Gate House, The   **$75–$95**   ★★

Hell's Gate, ☎ *(5994) 62416, FAX (5994) 62550.*
Single: $75–$85. Double: $85–$95.

Located away from what the owner refers to as Saba's "metropolis" (Windwardside), Gate House is a sweet little inn above the airstrip. Rooms are bright and
cheery with local art; two have kitchens. There's a pleasant pool deck and the restaurant is one of Saba's best. Unless you're an avid hiker, this is one spot for which
you may want a car. Rates include continental breakfast. 6 rooms. Credit cards: MC, V.

Juliana's   **$70–$115**   ★★

Windwardside, ☎ *(800) 223-9815, (5994) 62269, FAX (5994) 62389.*
Single: $70–$90. Double: $90–$115.

Guests can choose from a variety of accommodations at this small property that
caters to dive groups. There are standard guestrooms, apartments with a kitchenette, and 90-year-old Flossie's Cottage, a real sweetie with two bedrooms, a kitchen
and a porch. All are quite decent, and the daily fresh flowers are a nice touch. The
rec room has a TV, VCR, games and books. There's also a small pool and decent
restaurant. 10 rooms. Credit cards: MC, V.

Willard's of Saba   **$150–$400**   ★★★

Booby Hill, ☎ *(5994) 62498, FAX (5994) 62482.*
Single: $150–$400. Double: $200–$400.

Spectacularly situated 1700 feet above sea level and built by the great grandson of
Willard's of Washington, this airy spot offers Saba's best view—a 270-degree panorama of the island. Best accommodations are in four bungalows that clamber up
the cliff into the clouds—each decorated in bright tropical colors; there are other
units in the large main building. All is spacious and in good taste, though the intimate inn's personality is more defined by the owners (and setting). The property
boasts Saba's biggest pool (20 by 40 feet), a tennis court, and breezes cool enough
that air conditioning is almost unthinkable (there's even a fireplace); an edge-of-
the-cliff Jacuzzi is a splashy nook for a sunset cocktail. The food is good, if quite
dear—the overall operation is a sort of fabulous, perhaps overpriced bed-and-breakfast. 7 rooms. Credit cards: A, MC, V.

Low Cost Lodging

El Momo   **$30–$35**   ★

> Booby Hill, ☎ (5994) 62265, FAX (5994) 62265.
> Single: $30. Double: $35.

Located a mile outside Windwardside and at the top of a long flight of stairs, this delightful guest house is a series of rustic, but new wooden cottages, trimmed in gingerbread and perched on a steep hillside. Only one has a bathroom; the others share a two-sided bathroom with sun showers. The grounds are covered in flowers and plants, and a small pool boasts the only bridge in Saba. Best of all are the stellar views of Windwardside, Mt. Scenery and beyond, at sunset or most any other time. Informal and simple, but a back-to-nature bargain for anyone who can handle "roughing it" a little. Credit cards: MC, V.

Where to Eat

	Fielding's Best Value Restaurants in Saba	
★★	Tropics Cafe	$15–$20
★★	Saba Chinese Restaurant	$13–$19
★★★	Brigadoon	$14–$17
★★	Scout's Place	$17–$25
★★	Lollipop's	$26–$26

Don't look for gourmet food on Saba—dining is generally as low-key as the rest of the island. In addition to the selection below, check into the new **Gate House** and **Queen's Gardens**. For meals between diving and other shore-side activities, visit **In Two Deep** at Fort Bay which offers burgers, salads and sandwiches in a pub-style atmosphere. The restaurant at **Captain's Quarters** is receiving a full makeover for the 1998 season that sounds promising. At some meal or another, you'll probably get a whiff of Saba Spice, a local spiced rum that finds its way into most rum-based drinks.

Brigadoon   **$$**   ★★★

> Windwardside, ☎ (5994) 62380.
> Dinner: 6:30 p.m. on, entrées $14–$17.

Brigadoon has developed a healthy reputation for innovative seafood cuisine and boasts the only live lobster tank on the island. Grilled fish with citrus mango sauce, Greg's peanut chicken, salt and pepper shrimp, and a spicy local bouillabaisse are standouts. All are served with fresh vegetables, and lighter fare is also featured. Reservations recommended. Credit cards: A, MC, V.

SABA

Caribake $ ★★

Windwardside, ☎ *(5994) 62539.*
Lunch: 7 a.m.–6 p.m., entrées $6–$8. Closed: Sun.
After picking up some tips and brochures at the tourist office, stop right behind it
for homemade, old-fashioned pastry treats like sticky cinnamon and raisin buns. But
most come for lunch, when pizza, quiche and pork meat pies are unveiled, and perfect supplies for a picnic. Check out the lunch specials for the best buy.

Guido's $ ★

Windwardside, ☎ *(5994) 62230.*
Dinner: 6–11 p.m., entrées $4–$14. Closed: Sun.
Yes, there is nightlife on Saba, contrary to the rumors. It's here at Guido's, which
masquerades as a burger and pizza joint during the week and dons a few sequins as
Mountain High Club and Disco on Saturday evenings. The food is OK, but it's bet-
ter for pool or darts and informal socializing. Credit cards: MC, V.

Lollipop's $$$ ★★

The Bottom, ☎ *(5994) 63330.*
Lunch: entrées $10–$15.
Dinner: prix fixe $26.
Lollipop, or Carmen Hassell (everyone in town is either a Hassell or a Johnson)
offers free pickup to and from her outdoor eatery—she moonlights as a cab driver.
Located in the suburbs of The Bottom, the dining area is on a patio with a view of
the tiny capital, and the food is basic West Indian—curries, seafood, goat, and excel-
lent fish cakes. Credit cards: MC, V.

Saba Chinese Restaurant $$ ★★

Windwardside, ☎ *(5994) 62268.*
Lunch: 11 a.m.–4 p.m., entrées $13–$19.
Dinner: 4 p.m.–midnight, entrées $13–$19. Closed: Mon.
This Chinese restaurant on the north side of Windwardside offers Cantonese and a
few Indonesian dishes. It seems to satisfy a lot of locals, who patronize it often. The
variety of choices is impressive, including an only-in-the-Caribbean conch chop
suey. Credit cards: not accepted.

Scout's Place $$$ ★★

Windwardside, ☎ *(5994) 62295.* Associated hotel: *Scout's Place.*
Lunch: 12:30–2 p.m., entrées $6–$13.
Dinner: 7:30–10 p.m., entrées $17–$25.
Scout's is memorable for its dining room that juts above the hamlet of Windward-
side like the prow of a ship. The restaurant, attached to the hotel of the same name,
is a beloved local hangout. The menu features fresh seafood, and a delicious curried
goat is always available. There's also a bar and a snack shop in front for short-order
meals, snacks and ice cream. Be sure to check out the Saban buffet, rolled out for
special occasions. Credit cards: MC, V.

Tropics Cafe $$ ★★

Windwardside, ☎ *(5994) 63203.* Associated hotel: *Juliana's Apartments.*
Lunch: 12–2:30 p.m., entrées $6–$9.
Dinner: 7–8:30 p.m., entrées $15–$20. Closed: Sun.

The Tropics is a no-frills eatery attached to Juliana's Apartments, but good to know about for the decently priced breakfasts, burgers and sandwiches for under $10 at lunch. The dinner menu includes curried conch or chicken, grouper Creole, shrimp thermidor and steaks. Get them to pack up a picnic basket for you. Credit cards: MC, V.

Don't expect great bargains or streets lined with duty-free shops, but there are a few things to look out for: Saba lace and Saba Spice. Delicate Saba lace has been made on the island for the past 125 years, and it's quite beautiful. You can buy hand-crafted tea towels, napkins, collars and tablecloths at the **Community Center** in Hell's Gate each weekday, and also from the homes of artisans; just look for the signs. Saba Spice is a heady quaff made of 151-proof cask rum, brown sugar, cinnamon, anise and other spices. The village of Windwardside has a number of art galleries.

Saba Directory

Arrival and Departure

There are no direct flights from North America to the tiny airstrip on Saba. The principal gateway is Sint Maarten's Juliana Airport which is served by **American Airlines** nonstop from New York's JFK, Miami and San Juan, Puerto Rico; by **USAir** out of Charlotte and Philadelphia; by **Continental** from Newark; and by several charter operators out of major cities (for additional service see "Arrival and Departure" in "Sint Maarten"). Saba's only airline service is provided by **Winair**, which makes the 20-minute hop several times a day from Sint Maarten (about $88), with additional daily flights from St. Eustatius ☎ *(5994) 22167* or *(800) 634-4907*.

Another way to reach Saba is via high-speed **ferry**. *Voyager* departs from Bobby's Marina on Thursday and (in-season) Saturday at 8:30 a.m. for the 90-minute crossing, leaving for the return trip the same day at 4 p.m. ☎ *(5995) 24096*. *The Edge* is a sleek modern catamaran that makes the trip in 60 minutes on Wednesday, Friday and Sunday, at 9 a.m. from Pelican Marina, returning at 4 p.m. ☎ *(5995) 42640*. Both ferries charge $40 one-way, or $60 round-trip, and reservations are advised. Daytrippers can purchase a lunch/ tour package for an additional $30. Note that inter-island ferry service can be rough, particularly for those with sensitive stomachs. If in doubt fly.

The departure tax is $2 for domestic flights within the Netherlands Antilles, or $10 if you are leaving for home from Saba.

Business Hours

Stores generally open 8 a.m.–5 p.m. Bank (there's only one, in Windwardside) open weekdays 8:30 a.m.–12:30 p.m.

Climate

Temperatures average 78–82 degrees year-round, but since most accommodations are at an elevation higher than 1000 feet above sea level, nights can be brisk and a sweater is handy.

Documents

U.S. and Canadian citizens need to show a current passport or one that expired less than five years ago, or other proof of citizenship (birth certificate or voter's registration plus a photo ID), as well as an ongoing or return ticket.

Electricity

The current is 110 volts, 60 cycles, the same as in the U.S.

Getting Around

From Windwardside, most destinations are within a half-mile, and walking is an agreeable way to experience the island; hitching is not uncommon. Taxis are on-hand to meet most ferry and flight arrivals. A two-hour island tour by taxi runs about $40 (for up to four passengers). Car rentals start at about $40 per day for a manual transmission; try **Scout's Place** ☎ *(5994) 62205* or **Johnson's Rental Car** at Juliana's ☎ *(5994) 62269*. Saba's only gas station is located at Fort Bay (the opposite end of the island from the airport).

Language

The official language is English, though public signs are written in Dutch. English is the spoken language for most.

Medical Emergencies

Emergencies are flown to Sint Maarten; the clinic at The Bottom is limited in facilities. In cases of extreme illness, a chartered flight (one hour) should be arranged to San Juan, Puerto Rico. Saba has a decompression chamber, located at the Marine Park Hyperbaric Facility in Fort Bay ☎ *(5994) 63205*.

Money

The official currency is the Netherlands Antilles *florin*, also called the *guilder* and abbreviated NAf. U.S. dollars are accepted by most businesses.

Telephone

The country code is *(5994)*. To call Saba from the U.S., dial *1 + (5994)*, plus the five-digit local number.

Time

Atlantic Standard Time, one hour ahead of Eastern Standard Time, and the same as Eastern Daylight Saving Time.

Tipping and Taxes

There is a 5 percent room tax; a 10–15 percent service charge is standard at both hotels and restaurants.

Tourist Information

The **Saba Tourist Bureau** is located in Windwardside, open Monday through Friday. For more information, call ☎ *(5994) 62231*, or in the U.S., you may request brochures through the **Saba and Sint Eustatius Tourist Office** ☎ *(800) 722-2394*.

Web Site

www.turq.com/saba

When to Go

Coronation Day and the **Queen's Birthday** are celebrated on April 30, with ceremonies commemorating the Coronation of Queen Beatrix of the Netherlands, and special sports activities and picnics. A week-long **Carnival** celebration is held in late-July early-August with local foods, parades, steel bands, games and competitions. **Saba Days** take place the first weekend of December and feature island-wide festivities, deep-sea fishing events, barbecues, steel band and dance contests. December 26 is **Boxing Day**, a legal holiday.

SABA HOTELS		RMS	RATES	PHONE	CR. CARDS
★★★	Captain's Quarters	12	$70–$135	(800) 446-3010	A, D, MC, V
★★★	Cottage Club	10	$94–$136	(5994) 62386	MC, V
★★★	Willard's of Saba	7	$150–$400	(5994) 62498	A, MC, V
★★	Gate House, The	6	$75–$95	(5994) 62416	MC, V
★★	Juliana's	10	$70–$115	(800) 223-9815	MC, V
★	El Momo	6	$30–$35	(5994) 62265	MC, V

SABA ARESTAURANTS		PHONE	ENTRÉE	CR. CARDS
Chinese Cuisine				
★★	Saba Chinese Restaurant	(5994) 62268	$13–$19	None
Italian Cuisine				
★	Guido's	(5994) 62230	$4–$14	MC, V
Regional Cuisine				
★★★	Brigadoon	(5994) 62380	$14–$17	A, MC, V
★★	Caribake	(5994) 62539	$6–$8	
★★	Lollipop's	(5994) 63330	$10–$26	MC, V
★★	Scout's Place	(5994) 62295	$6–$25	MC, V
★★	Tropics Cafe	(5994) 63203	$6–$20	MC, V

ST. BARTHÉLÉMY

Gustavia Harbor, St. Barts

The Caribbean connoisseur who visits one island after another knows that each is a little different, with commonalities between the culture and people. St. Barthélémy, however, is truly a destination unto itself. With a small population that is almost exclusively white and affluent, cuisine that leans to the French rather than Creole, and a thumb-your-nose attitude toward cruise ship passengers, St. Barts looks, tastes and feels unlike any other island in the region. From the moment you touch down at the hilariously abrupt airstrip, the island subtly begins to work its charms on you, but only if you have a ready wallet, and are willing to embrace the island's chic lifestyle and attitude with full fervor. Thumbprint-sized St. Barts is simply the antithesis of ramshackle outpost, and the luxurious dining and accommodations are the most expensive in the region. Even though you'll discover gorgeous scenery, pristine beaches and a charming harbor, the island remains a place to snooze, to cruise, and to be seen not being seen. In high season, particularly the week following Christmas, St. Barts makes L.A. look limp as celebrities descend. But beyond the hoity-toity glitter is a very special sophistication marked by delightful contrasts. The couple who casually spends three or four hundred dollars a night on their hotel room will happily tool around the island by day in a rattling rental car long past its prime. And while fine food is greatly respected, dressing up at dinner will only make you stick out like a wannabe—the one thing to which you must absolutely not succumb.

As the word began to creep out in the 1980s that St. Barts was *the* in spot, the last decade has seen considerable development on the tiny isle. Fortunately, recent hotel building has been kept relatively small by Caribbean standards, though the newer properties have continued to skew toward the high-end clientele the island prides itself on pleasing. This has made St. Barts a hot day-trip from nearby Sint Maarten/Saint Martin for those who cannot afford the four-star luxe living for more than a few hours, and an even hotter destination for cruise ships, which locals strongly feel threatens their exclusive lifestyle. Sint Maarten/Saint Martin represents a woeful example of an island that became a victim of its success, and it remains firmly within eyesight for St. Barts' long-time residents. The cruise ship backlash that has intensified over the last couple of years—Gustavia shopowners are known to shut down in protest when a big ship comes in—is such that St. Barts will be forced soon to make a few hard choices regarding tourism and its infrastructure. Despite a hurricane that wiped out tourism in late 1995, St. Barts still enjoyed a record number of arrivals—over a quarter-million visitors for the year (including day-trippers and cruise ship passengers). Yes, the island's been discovered. But the good news is that St. Barts is more accessible than ever for the rest of us.

BEST BETS FOR...

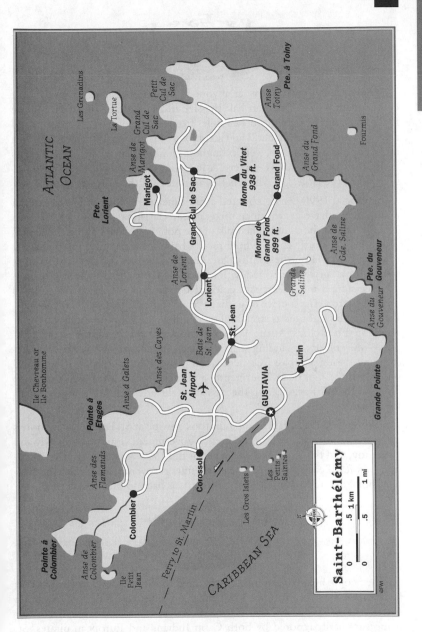

ATLANTIC OCEAN

Les Grenadins

La Tortue

Pte. Lorient

Anse de Margiot

Marigot

Grand Cul de Sac

Petit Cul de Sac

Anse Grand Cul de Sac

Anse Toiny

Pte. à Toiny

Anse du Grand Fond

Fourmis

Morne du Vitet 938 ft.

Grand Fond

Anse de Lorient

Lorient

Morne de Grand Fond 899 ft.

Anse de Gde. Saline

St. Jean

Baie de St. Jean

Grande Saline

St. Jean Airport

Anse des Cayes

Anse à Galets

Pointe à Etages

Ile Chevreau or Ile Bonhomme

Anse des Flamands

Pointe à Colombier

Anse de Colombier

Ile Petit Jean

Colombier

Corossol

Ferry to St. Martin

Les Gros Islets

Les Petits Saintes

GUSTAVIA

Lurin

Anse du Gouveneur

Pte. du Gouveneur

Grande Pointe

CARIBBEAN SEA

Saint-Barthélémy

0   .5 1 km

0   .5   1 mi

GFWI

St. Barthélémy (or St. Barts, as anyone in the know, knows) covers a scant eight square miles—less than half the size of Manhattan. It is a 10-minute flight from Sint Maarten, and 125 miles from Guadeloupe, of which it is still a dependency. Somewhat arid and scrubby, the island has a tropical air and a mountainous appearance, yet its highest point—Morne du Vitet—is less than a thousand feet above sea level. More than 20 islands dot the surrounding waters, the largest of which is Ile Fourchue off the northeast tip.

The official 1990 census counted a full-time population of 5043, though it's bound to have grown since then, and at Christmas, a number closer to 18,000 inhabit the island. The bulk of the population lives along the length of the ruffled north coast, where most of the hotels are, or in the harbor town of Gustavia on the south coast. Gustavia defines quaint—a storybook setting for a fairytale seasoned with million-dollar yachts. The eerily romantic streets are a mix of French, colonial Creole and Swedish styles, and so pristine there's nary a piece of garbage to be spotted. Just over the hill is St. Jean, lined by a gorgeous stretch of sand and peppered by a number of well-established hostelries. At the western terminus of this bay is the island's airport—one end of the landing strip is St. Jean Beach, the other end is a heart-stopping mountain pass. Camera-laden visitors hang out at this absurd photo op, the Col de la Tourmente, and giddily snap away as planes drop down to the runway, clearing the pass at an altitude seemingly close enough for a buzz cut.

In September 1995, Hurricane Luis took a swipe at St. Barts, leaving hotels and restaurants in shambles. The French government responded quickly and efficiently, and the island was in shape for the 1996 season. With the exception of a few beaches that have not yet fully recovered, and several permanent hotel and restaurant closures, St. Barts is back to business as usual.

Some people believe Columbus discovered St. Barthélémy, naming it after his brother, but the island didn't appear on any map until 1523, when a speck of dirt was labeled San Bartoleme by a Spanish cartographer. After being summarily ignored by both Carib Indians and European pirates, St.

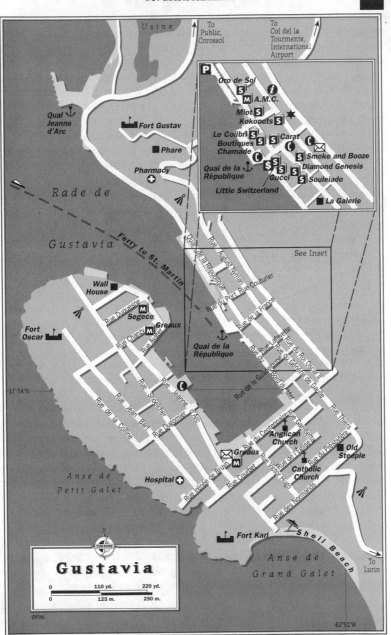

Gustavia

Barts was finally explored in 1637, eight years after St. Kitts was colonized, though some of the first Norman and British settlers were scalped by Carib Indians. Over time, the island became a secret hiding place for pirates, while the culture itself became tenaciously French. When Louis XVI traded the flagging island to the Swedes for some warehouses in Goteborg, St. Barts magically flourished with new management (Thomas Jefferson himself declared the port free of all duties). By 1847, the island had been ravaged by hurricanes, trade competition, fires and piracy, leaving Gustavia, the capital, dirt poor—a fact that convinced the Swedes in 1878 to dump the island back in the lap of the French. Not until 1946 did the French government declare St. Barts a commune in the department of Guadeloupe. In 1947, aviator/hotelier Rémy de Haenen landed the first airplane here on the short, grassy pasture of St. Jean. With the construction of the airport and the island's first runway for STOL (short-takeoff-and-landing) planes, the floodgates of tourism were opened.

People

The first thing one notices is the near-absence of any black islanders. The topography of St. Barthélémy is so rocky it was deemed unsuitable for growing sugarcane, so most slave ships passed the island by. However, during the early 19th century, about 1400 slaves from Africa were used for domestic work and for loading and unloading at the harbor. After emancipation, most of the black population left St. Barts, leaving the islanders to their hard lifestyle. St. Barts also has the unique characteristic of having been the only Caribbean island governed by Sweden—a few reminders of Swedish presence can be seen in the form of architecture, a Swedish cemetery (in Public), the belfry above the harbor, and in the name Gustavia. Today, the most traditional sect of the population are the fiercely independent *grand-meres*—tough old ladies, and thoroughly Caucasian. West Indian by birth and French by heritage, these women single-handedly raised their families in the absence of husbands who frequently had to leave the island to make ends meet. Yes, at one time in the 20th century, everyone on St. Barts was relatively poor. Today, with the influx of well over 1000 ex-pats (most of them French) and thousands of high-class international tourists, the old traditions are slowly dying out. The middle-aged generation is caught in transition while their children are looking solidly into a modernized future.

Anyone anticipating political struggles or racial tension simply won't find them on St. Barts. Instead, an uncommon feeling of unity exists among the locals, though the businessmen who sponsored the building boom of the last decade are observed with some disdain by the two or three thousand residents who have lived here since the 1960s. Crime is almost unheard of, and most everyone is gainfully employed, from fishermen, to builders, to hoteliers and restaurateurs—even the dogs are well-fed. As such, many visitors hitchhike around to see the island, which is also a great way to meet the locals (it is not acceptable behavior to pass up hitchhikers). French is the official language, and a quaint Norman dialect works its way into casual conversation. Much of the population speaks some English (more than on Martinique or Guadeloupe), and language problems are rare at hotels, restaurants or shops. Nonetheless, it's worth bringing a French-English dictionary to ease awkward moments. A note on spelling: the proper French abbreviation of the island's name is St. Barths, but most Americans have dropped the "h," if only as a reminder as to how to pronounce the name.

St. Barthélémy has what might be the finest collection of beaches per square mile of any Caribbean island. The official count is 14, though more can be tallied by the dedicated eye. The most developed is **St. Jean**, with several hotels, a number of restaurants, plentiful watersports and Eden Rock splitting the cove in two. While all of this activity is anathema to those seeking true solitude, it creates a lively social scene throughout the day. **Anse des Flamands** is more quiet—white sand fringed by lantana palms and a residential area where the cluck of chickens provides a charming soundtrack. A trail from the end of the road takes you to **Colombier**, an isolated cove at the island's western tip, accessible only on foot or by boat. On the other end of the north coast, a series of striking coves lies between lush Marigot and Petit Cul-de-Sac. The rugged coastline on the southern slope of Morne du Vitet is the least developed part of St. Barts, with two rugged, little-visited beaches, **Toiny** and **Grand Fond**, but both can be rough for swimming. Nudism is prohibited on St. Barts, though topless is common. There is, of course, an official, unofficial nude beach, **Grande Saline**, a ravishing and undeveloped cove reached via a short path through the brush. It's well-known by now, meaning there's more people with clothes than without—as you enter the beach, hip/gay is to the right, conservative swings to the left. Perhaps the loveliest of all is **Anse du Gouverneur**, reached by a steep road from Lurin and backed by sea grapes over plush sand dunes. Just south of Gustavia is one more beauty, **Shell Beach**, with calm seas and ideal sunset views—it's a five-minute walk from the town harbor. Alas, Shell Beach is the one the cruise-ship passengers flock to, so you may be sharing with a lot of folks in matching shirts and black socks.

St. Jean Beach on St. Barts offers several hotels, restaurants and watersports.

Shallow reefs abound, which makes snorkeling delightful and diving easy, bottoming out at about 80 feet. The best diving is on the southwest coast and around the tiny islets decorating St. Barthélémy's outlying waters, most of it no more than 10 or 15 minutes from the dock at Gustavia. Nearby **Ile Fourchue** is one such possibility, and **Les Petits Saints**, the three rock outcrops just outside the Gustavia harbor, feature pompano and occasional dolphins. **Marigot Bay** offers excellent snorkeling, and a narrow reef stretches into the channel toward the rock offshore, **La Tortue ou l'Ecaille**; winter currents can make this area unsafe, however. The north end of **Anse de Colombier's** beautiful sands yield coral growth over the rocks, which are sprinkled with colorful reef fish and, in calm waters, one can snorkel the rocks past the south end, at **Ile de la Pointe**. **Shell Beach**, **La Petite Anse** and **St. Jean Bay** (northwest of Eden Rock) are other snorkeling possibilities.

Dive Shops

Scuba Club–La Bulle

Gustavia; ☎ *(590) 27-62-25 or 27-68-93.*

Single tank dives, $50 off season, $60 mid-December through mid-April, including all equipment. Three scheduled dives daily, maximum six divers per trip. Not NAUI or PADI at present, but certified by the French Federation. Offers "baptisms," the French diving initiation in 15–20 feet of water, $70.

Marine Service

Gustavia; ☎ *(590) 27-70-34.*
Oldest shop on the island, PADI-affiliated with certification courses through open water. Aims for smaller groups of six to eight, and works with American (as well as French) equipment. Two-tank dive, $83, including gear. Also offers half-day snorkel/sailing tours to Ile Fourchue, $60, or full-day, $100 (including lunch).

On Foot

Physically, St. Barthélémy looks a little more impressive than it does on a map. The island is tiny—just eight square miles—but appears larger due to the hills that rise to a pair of 900-foot peaks on the island's eastern side. The preferred method of visitor transport is the ubiquitous Mini-Moke, but you needn't be hostage to these sputtering upstarts. See St. Barts' compact interior of pastures and charming villages and its scalloped coastline on foot and you'll be experiencing island over attitude. A few beaches hide in coves that are difficult to reach on wheels, while an early morning stroll through Gustavia rewards with bold coffee, fresh croissants and a glimmer of the village that once was—St. Barts before it was overtaken by the chic set. Another fine area for walking is along the southern coastline between Grand Fond and Toiny—although a road exists, it's little traveled and yields the most rugged and undeveloped portion of the island. Similarly, a road climbs the slopes of Morne du Vitet (to within a couple hundred feet of the summit); leave your car at the Hostellerie des Trois Forces for a delightful stroll yielding superlative views of the north and east coasts. Boats can be taken to nearby Ile Fourchue, a half-sunk crater that rises to 340 feet off St. Barts' northwest tip and offers intriguing exploration on foot among cactus and brush across a rocky desert landscape.

What Else to See

St. Barthélémy is blissfully free of tourist traps and boring museums. Anything worth finding will probably be your own special discovery. To find the last threads of traditional life, head for **Corossol**, a tiny fishing village at the

BEAUTIFUL ST. BARTS

Stylish and popular with both international jet-setters and avid snorkelers, St. Barthélémy combines Caribbean lushness with French flair. Unwind on one of the island's many beaches or rent a car to explore the hilly terrain and tiny, sheltered harbors. Snorkelers can explore the island's shallow reefs, which proivide a home for lobsters, sponges and colorful corals.

Inter-Oceans Museum

Ingenu Magras has amassed a collection of more than 7000 varieties of seashells, most of which are on display at this museum in Corossol.

St. Bart's

St. Jean Airport

Corossol

St. Jean

La Baleine Diving

Accessed by boat, this sea-mountain rises up near the surface, attracting barracuda, lobsters and nurse sharks.

Gustavia

Lurin

N

Les Petits Saints Diving

Here, the reef juts above water, and the coral shoals shelter parrot fish, rays and the less commonly seen sea turtles. Popular with charter tours.

Gustavia

Gustavia's harbor is dotted with sleek yachts and sailboats, and its streets are lined with shops and restaurants. Several establishments are housed in Swedish-style buildings that reflects the island's colonial heritage.

Corossol

Village women no longer dress in long skirts and stiff bonnets adapted from Bréton-style clothing popular more than a century ago. Today, the women weave goods from lantana palms, which were introduced to the island 100 years by missionaries. Don't take photographs of the women, but feel welcome to peruse their goods—broad-brimmed hats, purses, satchels and baskets all made from palm fronds.

St. Jean Bay

This mushroom-shaped bay is a favorite with snorkelers, who come to swim in the aquamarine waters. Nearby, from the bay's landmark Eden Rock, a road leads to the Grand Saline, where salt was once mined. From Grand Saline, hike a footpath to reach Anse de Grand Saline, one of the island's best beaches. Watch for kestrels, pelicans and frigatebirds.

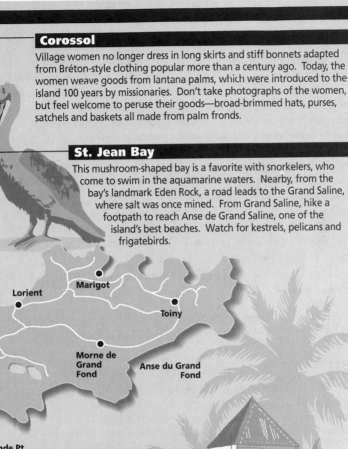

Lorient

Marigot

Toiny

Morne de Grand Fond

Anse du Grand Fond

Grande Pt.

Swedish Belfry

A Gustavia landmark, this green-painted Belfry echoes the architecture of the colonist's far-off homeland of Sweden. Not far away, in La Pointe, the Municipal Museum in the old Wall House has exhibits of paintings and historical documents detailing the island's history.

bottom of a deep valley just northwest of Gustavia. Its population of about 300 is somewhat secluded from the modern St. Barts—the older women still weave handicrafts with *lantana* (palm straw) and wear dresses that recall their French provincial origins. Drive to the mountain-top hamlet of **Colombier**; just a little further up the road and you'll arrive at one of the island's best views, encompassing Sint Maarten/Saint Martin, Saba and Sint Eustatius. Another fine view can be obtained by driving up the steep slopes of **Morne du Vitet** above the community of Vitet—how many beaches can you count from here? No one who comes to the island should miss stopping at the **Col de la Tourmente**, the ridgetop intersection above the head of the landing strip where airplanes drop precipitously over your head during their final approach. Lastly, the dinner prices are sky-high, but so is the view, which makes a stop at the **Carl Gustaf Hotel** for at least a sunset cocktail mandatory—the glittering sight of Gustavia from here is worth a million bucks. Or more.

There are several island tours available, but your money is far better spent on a rental car for a day or two. St. Barts' charms are not the kind that can be pointed out from a passing car, and the island is small enough that it can easily be explored by outsiders.

Museums and Exhibits

Inter-Oceans Museum   ★★

Corossol.

A remarkable collection of some 7000 shells—said to be the second-largest in the world—has been assembled by Ingenu Magras, who has never traveled off the island. General admission: $4.

Musee de St. Barthélémy   ★★★

Le Pointe; Gustavia, Gustavia.

This winsome little museum tells the island's history through costumes, antiques, photos and artwork, including portraits and documents relating to the island's Swedish period. It also has exhibits on St. Barts' vegetation and sea creatures. It's located in the Wall House on the far side of the harbor. General admission: $2.

Sports

Boating is more than a passion on St. Barthélémy—it's a way of life, and sailors are often judged socially by the make of their boat. The location of St Barts, midway between Antigua and the Virgin Islands and next to Sint Maarten—all regional sailing centers—provide sailors with a wide variety of destinations. The island can handle upwards of 500 yachts at anchor—Gustavia has docking facilities and moorings for at least 40 vessels at one time. Other prime locations nearby include Corossol and Public, though other deeply carved bays around the island also provide a number of fine anchorages. Annual **yachting events** include the St. Barts Regatta, celebrated just before Lent, the St. Barts Cup, held in April, and the three-day International Regatta in May.

Deep-sea fishing enthusiasts will want to head for Gustavia, where boat charters with gear can be hired. Snorkeling equipment can be rented at **Marine Service** or purchased at **Loulou's Marine**, both in Gustavia, though a number of hotels will loan their own set to guests. **Windsurfing** has become a big sport on the island, with the bigger bays along the north coast providing ideal locations. **Surfing** can be good at Lorient and Grand Fond, while experts can dare the churn of Washing Machine next door. **Waterskiing** is provided by Stephan Jouany through **Marine Service**, and **parasailing** through Wind Wave Power ☎ *(590) 27-62-73.*

On land, **tennis** is the most accessible sporting activity, with courts provided at a number of hotels, and at the Flamboyant Tennis Club. Pro Yves Lacoste provides tennis lessons at a court in Toiny ☎ *(590) 27-68-06.* The Hotel St. Barts Isle de France has an air-conditioned **squash court**.

Horseback Riding

Laure Nicolas is the person to see at **Ranch des Flamands** for trail rides and other excursions. A two-hour excursion is offered daily at 3:30 p.m. for both beginners and experienced riders. Cost: $40.

Waterskiing in Colombier Bay.

Watersports

Marine Service ☎ *(590) 27-70-34* offers the island's most complete watersports center, with PADI-certified scuba diving, deep-sea fishing, snorkel excursions, and boat rides in the Aquascope from which you see colorful coral, sea creatures, and a submerged yacht wreck. For windsurfing instruction and rentals, try **St. Barts Wind School** ☎ *(590) 27-71-22*, and **Wind Wave Power** ☎ *(590) 27-62-73*. For deep-sea fishing or sailing trips, call **Ocean Must** ☎ *(590) 27-62-25* and Marine Service.

Where to Stay

Fielding's Highest Rated Hotels in St. Barthélémy

★★★★★	Guanahani	$246–$590
★★★★★	Le Toiny	$530–$860
★★★★	Carl Gustaf	$350–$800
★★★★	Christopher Hotel	$260–$450
★★★★	St. Barth Isle de France	$315–$800
★★★	Eden Rock	$220–$680
★★★	El Sereno Beach Hotel	$200–$580
★★★	Le Tom Beach	$260–$530
★★★	Manapany Cottages	$205–$575

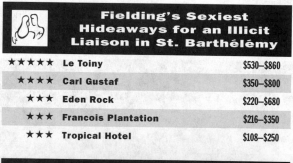

Fielding's Sexiest Hideaways for an Illicit Liaison in St. Barthélémy

★★★★★	Le Toiny	$530–$860
★★★★	Carl Gustaf	$350–$800
★★★	Eden Rock	$220–$680
★★★	Francois Plantation	$216–$350
★★★	Tropical Hotel	$108–$250

Fielding's Best Value Hotels in St. Barthélémy

★★	Hostellerie Trois Forces	$65–$170
★★★	Tropical Hotel	$108–$250
★★★	Yuana Hotel	$137–$250

Don't arrive on St. Barthélémy without your gold card. The island has a deserved reputation as the region's most expensive, and the squeeze begins here. Simply put, you will get more hotel for your money on any other island in the Caribbean. What you won't get, of course, is St. Barts' unique mix of sophistication and charm—an intangible essence exported only in the form of satisfied visitors who always seem to come back for another fix.

Though the choices are extensive, when it comes to hotels, small is big on St. Barts. There are no mega-resorts, all-inclusives, high-rises or properties with extensive meeting facilities. With one exception, the **Guanahani**, all the hotels are under 50 rooms and several of the best have barely a dozen. Except for the **Christopher**, none of the hotels are connected to chains. These are intimate hostelries where you'll get to know the manager rather than a security guard. Privacy is zealously guarded and several hotels vaunt completely private plunge pools with magnificent views, all but a few steps from your bed.

All of this comes with a price, of course. If you're on a budget, we can mention a few options (see "Low Cost Lodging"), but the best advice for penny-pinchers is to avoid the winter season entirely when prices everywhere rocket into the stratosphere. And, one bit of good news: most hotels quote rooms prices with tax and service charge included (verify this when booking your room). If money's no object and a winter sojourn is paramount, book your room well in advance, particularly during the last week of December, when accommodations are typically locked up months beforehand (most properties hike their rates well above the usual high season prices for that one week). Also note that a larger than usual percentage of hotels on this island close for a month or two during the slow, late summer/early fall period.

Hurricane Luis closed several properties either for the short term or indefinitely. The biggest loss was famed mountain-top retreat **Castelets**, for which a rebuilding plan has not been determined. The **Baie des Flamands** is closed indefinitely, while the snobby **Taiwana** was under construction at press time, although a re-opening date was not forthcoming. All other properties listed here are fully operational now.

An important note: most of the hotels have two rate cards—one in American dollars and one in French francs. However, the exchange rate between the two currencies changes daily. At press time, the franc was trading at its lowest rate in years and, as a result, a number of hotels did not raise their *dollar* rate card for the 1998 season. The situation may have changed by the time you read this, and if the franc has further declined, you'll want to negotiate your room rate carefully to make sure you are obtaining the best price. For hotels that did not provide prices in dollars, we have used an exchange rate of 5.5 francs for one U.S. dollar.

Hotels and Resorts

The **Guanahani** is the island's biggest hotel, though with 75 units spread over 16 acres, you probably won't feel crowded or hemmed in. Two very exclusive hotels, the **Carl Gustaf** and **Le Toiny**, provide rooms with their own private plunge pools, while a few properties like **Francois Plantation** and **Hostellerie des Trois Forces** are perched high in the hills and require a car for the trip to the nearest sand. But most of St. Barts' extensive roster of possibilities lie in or near the embrace of its fabled beaches, and there are several favorites. Baie de St. John is the most famous stretch, with the recently re-opened **Eden Rock** positioned on a throne at the center—a number of other properties are on or close to this beach, which keeps it bustling. Anse des Flamands is the sybarite's choice along with the elegant, plantation-themed **Hotel St. Barth Isle de France**.

Baie des Anges Hotel $145–$395   ★★

Baie des Flamands, ☎ *(800) 755-9313, (590) 27-63-61, FAX (590) 27-83-44.*
Closed Date: October.
Single: $145–$395. Double: $185–$395.

Located on a picturesque beach, this small hotel has lots of old-fashioned St. Bartian charm, and is run by an island favorite, Annie Ange. The standard rooms are air-conditioned with a private bath and terrace, as well as bungalows with kitchenettes. A complete post-hurricane makeover spruced up the rooms and added a Creole restaurant, La Langouste, and a pool. Limited facilities, but one of the island's best beaches, Flamands, is right out your door. 9 rooms. Credit cards: A, CB, MC, V.

Carl Gustaf $350–$800   ★★★★

Gustavia, ☎ *(800) 322-2223, (590) 27-82-83, FAX (590) 27-82-37.*
Single: $350–$800. Double: $350–$800.

Named in honor of the king of Sweden, this all-suite hotel is situated on a hillside overlooking Gustavia harbor. Guests are housed in one- and two-bedroom cottages with wooden sundecks and very private plunge pools. The units are quite stylishly done, with high ceilings, marble floors, luxurious furnishings, fax machines, stereos, VCRs, and fully equipped kitchens—the view of Gustavia is stupendous, but be sure to request one of the upper-level rooms. Two-bedroom suites have bunk beds for kids. There's also a honeymoon suite above the rest (sans private pool) with lower rates. Facilities include a gourmet French restaurant, two bars, a fitness center, and a private cabin cruiser for sea and fishing excursions; the restaurant-side pool is for true exhibitionists. It's a five-minute walk down the steep hill into town, or to Shell Beach. Outside the actual rooms, the hotel feels a little tight—primarily in the interest of providing guests ultimate seclusion on their decks. The prices are high, but you're paying for a unique, perhaps unequalled combination of privacy, view and location at this sophisticated resort. 14 rooms. Credit cards: A, MC, V.

Christopher Hotel $260–$980   ★★★★

Pointe Milou, ☎ *(800) 763-4835, (590) 27-63-63, FAX (590) 27-92-92.*
Closed Date: September 1-October 15.
Single: $260–$450. Double: $260–$450. Suites Per Day: $545–$980.

Sleek French Colonial in design, this is St. Barts' only chain hotel, opening in 1993 to great consternation. But the 40 air-conditioned rooms are stylish and quite comfortable, with mahogany furnishings, minibars, and great views from the terrace or balcony; rooms on the second floor have showers in an outdoor patio/garden. Little is within walking distance and the beach is a 10-minute drive, so most guests hang by the fine pool, the island's largest. The site also includes a full-service health spa, two restaurants, three bars, and a concierge to arrange off-premises activities. Service at this Sofitel-managed hotel is reliable. 40 rooms. Credit cards: A, MC, V.

Eden Rock $220–$680   ★★★

St. Jean, ☎ *(800) 322-2223, (590) 27-72-94, FAX (590) 27-88-37.*

Single: $220–$680. Double: $220–$680.

Eden Rock Hotel was the first on St. Barts, built by the first pilot to fly to the island, Remy de Haenen, an adventurer who spent some years as local mayor and made his hotel a swank social hub. After several years of decline while newer, tonier properties were built, Eden Rock was purchased, refurbished and reimagined by a British couple, Jane and David Matthews, who opened its doors in 1996 to fresh acclaim. The romantic rooms on the rock are filled with antiques and four-poster beds—each is unique, and a couple are cramped, but all have charm. A series of tasteful one-bedroom suites have been built on the beach, along with a pool. The original restaurant is top dollar, while a new beach restaurant is another big draw. Perched on a striking promontory in the middle of St. Jean Bay, the location is unmatched, with views extending up and down the beach to the picayune airport and the slap of crashing waves for an endless soundtrack. A true one-of-a-kind hotel. 14 rooms. Credit cards: A, MC, V.

El Sereno Beach Hotel   **$200–$580**   ★★★

Grand Cul de Sac, ☎ *(800) 332-2223, (590) 27-64-80, FAX (590) 27-75-47.*
Closed Date: September 1-October 15.
Single: $200–$580. Double: $200–$580.

Located on the beach 20 minutes from Gustavia, this growing operation consists of a hotel and gingerbread-trimmed villas, each housing three one-bedroom suites with full kitchens and lots of room (these are a great value in winter). There is a new series of beachfront suites with solariums in the bathrooms. The 18 charming standard rooms are not as large, but are comfortable enough and surround a beachfront garden of banana and hibiscus. There's a sexy pool, and a popular restaurant, the West Indies Cafe. A windsurfing school is on site, as well as a glass-walled gym that attracts dedicated body builders. 41 rooms. Credit cards: A, MC, V.

Filao Beach Hotel   **$182–$582**   ★★★

St. Jean, ☎ *(800) 932-3222, (590) 27-64-84, FAX (590) 27-62-24.*
Closed Date: September 6 to October 23.
Single: $182–$582. Double: $182–$582.

Located in the heart of the action on St. Jean Beach, this is a well-run operation, convenient to activities, many restaurants, and the airport. Guest rooms are pleasant, recently refurbished, and located in air-conditioned bungalows with all the modern comforts. They are quite private, but most don't have ocean views (and some of the garden rooms suffer from traffic noise). There's also a large pool, windsurfing and snorkeling, and a good bar and restaurant. The prime location makes Filao a great place to take in the full St. Barts experience. A member of Relais and Chateaux hotel group. 30 rooms. Credit cards: A, CB, DC, D, MC, V.

Francois Plantation   **$216–$350**   ★★★

Colombier, ☎ *(800) 932-3222, (590) 27-78-82, FAX (590) 27-61-26.*
Closed Date: August 15-October 20.
Single: $216–$315. Double: $240–$350.

Positioned on a hilltop overlooking Baie des Flamands amid tropical gardens, this elegant spot consists of 12 charming bungalows. All are very nicely done, with mahogany furniture, four-poster beds, minibars, air conditioning, TVs, and terraces with views of the ocean or gardens. The views everywhere are simply astounding, especially from the pool terrace, which sits atop Le P'tit Morne. Owner Francois Beret is the creator of the bi-annual Gastronomique Festival, and his hotel restaurant and wine cellar is one of the best on the island. But ask about the garden and his eyes sparkle with pride—it bursts with jasmine, impatiens, hibiscus, bougainvillea and more, creating the lushest, most fragrant spot on the island. The beach is a five-minute drive. Rates include full breakfast. 12 rooms. Credit cards: A, MC, V.

Guanahani $246–$938   ★★★★★

Grand Cul de Sac, ☎ *(800) 223-6800, (590) 27-66-60, FAX (590) 27-70-70.*
Website: www.st-barths.com/guanahani.html. E-mail: guana@outremer.com.
Single: $246–$590. Double: $246–$590. Suites Per Day: $530–$938.

Located on 16 beachfront acres at Cul de Sac, this romantic spot is especially popular with couples, who enjoy its intimate atmosphere, amid spacious grounds. Accommodations, in gingerbread-trimmed cottages, are deluxe, swathed in rich, contrasting hues of green, blues, pinks and yellows. The higher-priced studios and one-bedroom suites have full kitchens, as well as whirlpools in the studios and plunge pools with the suites (some have more privacy than others); 24-hour room service is available. The grounds include two restaurants, two tennis courts, two pools, and watersports at not one but two beaches—Marechal and Grand Cul de Sac on either side of the promontory. On an island of small hotels, Guanahani is by far St. Barts' largest property, and some carp that is less personal than most, yet it remains low-key, friendly and very, very chic. 75 rooms. Credit cards: A, MC, V.

Hostellerie Trois Forces $65–$170   ★★

Vitet, ☎ *(590) 27-61-25, FAX (590) 27-81-38.*
Single: $65–$150. Double: $75–$170.

When someone asks "what's your sign?" here it's not just the old come on—each cottage is individually decorated and designed to complement the astrological sign after which it's named. Located up in the mountains above Vitet, this peaceful retreat is run by the island's leading astrologer, who also happens to be a quite decent chef. The gingerbread-trimmed cottages are tiny but nicely done with handmade wooden furnishings and large terraces. Only four are air-conditioned, and none have phones or TV. There's a pool on-site, and this is probably the only hotel in the Caribbean where you can take yoga lessons, have your tarot cards read, and get your chart done. 8 rooms. Credit cards: A, MC, V.

La Banane $150–$480   ★★★

Lorient, ☎ *(800) 932-3222, (590) 27-68-25, FAX (590) 27-68-44.*
Closed Date: September 8 to October 20.
Single: $150–$480. Double: $150–$480.

Located two miles from Gustavia, this small complex consists of nine inviting bungalows, each individually decorated. All are quite nice, with antiques, local artwork, TVs with VCRs, private terraces, and ceiling fans in lieu of air conditioners—the lovely showers are decorated with Mexican tiles. The atmosphere is that of an intimate oasis, with lush gardens surrounding the place, laced by pink and green wooden boardwalks. There's a pool and the beach is within walking distance. Rates include a full American breakfast. 9 rooms. Credit cards: A, MC, V.

Le Toiny   **$530–$860**   ★★★★★

Toiny, ☎ *(800) 932-3222, (590) 27-88-88, FAX (590) 27-89-30.*
Closed Date: September 1–October 20.
Single: $530–$860. Double: $530–$860.

Set on the quiet southeastern coast, this elegant and secluded hotel is sprinkled over a spare hillside dotted by cacti and gaiac trees. The lovely cottage-style accommodations are expansive—almost 1100 square feet—consisting of one-bedroom suites primped with mahogany and teak furnishings and fine Frette linens tucked around four-poster beds. Each unit has a lavish bathroom, full kitchen, and TVs with VCRs, plus a large terrace with a hedonistic 10- by 20-foot pool. With St. Eustatius, St. Kitts and Nevis off in the distance, spectacular views abound, and the villas are cleverly positioned so that maximum privacy is ensured inside and out—well, for everyone except Brad Pitt, who was snared in the buff here by truly ambitious paparazzi! There's a superb open-air French restaurant and a large communal pool as well. The fair beach is a ten-minute walk, and hiking awaits on the undeveloped Pointe a Toiny, but otherwise there's little to distract you from attending to your loved one. Indeed, on an island with at least a dozen seductive options for sexy hideaways, this is the *creme de la creme.* 12 rooms. Credit cards: A, DC, MC, V.

Le Tom Beach   **$260–$530**   ★★★

St. Jean, ☎ *(800) 322-2223, (590) 27-53-13, FAX (590) 27-53-15.*
Single: $260–$530. Double: $260–$530.

Creatively tucked into what seemed like the last whisper of beachfront property available in St. Jean, Le Tom is a complete and successful makeover of the original Tom Beach Hotel, maintaining the original's intimacy and charm. Rooms have tile floors, patios or verandas and four-poster beds; a few guests have noted that some rooms are a little too close to the road. There's a small pool with an arched footbridge and an excellent restaurant. An underground garage (the first on the island) helps make the most of the cozy yet prime location. 12 rooms. Credit cards: A, MC, V.

Manapany Cottages   **$205–$995**   ★★★

Anse des Cayes, ☎ *(800) 932-3222, (590) 27-66-55, FAX (590) 27-75-28.*
Associated Restaurant: Ballahou.
Single: $205–$575. Double: $205–$575. Suites Per Day: $375–$995.

Set in a small cove on the north shore, this property consists of a complex of cottages along a hillside or the beach. Accommodations vary from standard guestrooms to suites with one or two bedrooms and full kitchens. All are fine, but not as luxurious as the rates suggest—some of the hillside cottages are a little tight. The site includes two restaurants, an exercise room, a lovely pool and tennis court. The beach is pretty but tiny, and constantly windy. This operation is quite chic and once attracted a fair share of celebrities, but Manapany may be overshadowed by some of the other luxury properties that were built in its wake. 52 rooms. Credit cards: A, MC.

Sea Horse Hotel   **$80–$295**   ★★

Marigot, ☎ *(800) 932-3222, (590) 27-75-36, FAX (590) 27-85-33.*
Single: $80–$250. Double: $90–$295.

The delightful Sea Horse provides great value in a laid-back setting, a few hundred feet from the beach at Marigot Bay. Two types of rooms, a regular or junior suite are positioned on a hillside with a nice pool. Interiors are tastefully appointed with kitchenettes, air conditioning and tiled terraces. There's also a two-bedroom villa perfect for families. A number of savvy Americans have discovered the relaxed Sea Horse—its young manager, Loic Lecouteller, makes them feel most welcome. 11 rooms. Credit cards: A, MC, V.

St. Barth Isle de France $315–$800   ★★★★

Anse des Flamands, ☎ *(800) 628-8929, (590) 27-61-81, FAX (590) 27-86-83.*
Closed Date: September 1–October 15.
Single: $315–$800. Double: $315–$800.

Set along one of the island's best coves of sand, this newer luxury property houses guests in boardwalk-connected garden cottages or in a plantation-style house that sits above the beach. The spare, marble-floored guest rooms are spacious and furnished with mahogany antiques, plush linens, huge bathrooms (some with whirlpool tubs), refrigerators, and patios or balconies. Nine beachfront rooms have undeniably spectacular views, but are quite expensive—the peaceful garden bungalows are a two-minute walk to the sand and a better value. Facilities include an air-conditioned squash court, tennis court, a pool, and a fitness center; the restaurant is esteemed and provides 24-hour room service. Ultra-tasteful, yet the warm management will make you feel right at home. 28 rooms. Credit cards: A, MC, V.

St. Barth's Beach Hotel $121–$294   ★★

Grand Cul de Sac, ☎ *(800) 621-1270, (590) 27-60-70, FAX (590) 27-75-57.*
Closed Date: September 1–October 8.
Single: $121–$206. Double: $170–$294.

This two-story hotel is right on a nice beach, and received a polish following the hurricane—rooms are still strictly modern and functional, though they have lovely ocean views and a good breeze. All have air conditioning and minibars, and eight have kitchenettes. Other facilities include a saltwater pool, gym and a windsurfing school; the restaurant, Le Rivage, is well-respected. You'll want a rental car, as this spot is fairly isolated. 44 rooms. Credit cards: A, MC.

Tropical Hotel $108–$250   ★★★

St. Jean, ☎ *(800) 322-2223, (590) 27-64-87, FAX (590) 27-81-74.*
Single: $108–$250. Double: $134–$250.

Set a few hundred yards from the beach on a hill overlooking St. Jean Bay, this small country inn-style hotel centers around a ginger bread-trimmed building that houses the reception area, a lounge and bar. Guestrooms are all-white and airy, with evocative mosquito nets and comfortable trappings, and furnished patios overlooking the ocean or lush gardens. There's also a restaurant and pool on-site. 20 rooms. Credit cards: A, MC.

Village St. Jean Hotel $89–$320   ★★★

St. Jean, ☎ *(800) 322-2223, (590) 27-61-39, FAX (590) 27-77-96.*
Associated Restaurant: Le Patio.
Single: $89–$320. Double: $89–$320.

Set on a hillside close to the beach, this well-liked property consists of 21 stone and wood cottages with one or two bedrooms. Each is simply furnished but pleasant enough, with full kitchens and private terraces. Half were refurbished handsomely in 1995 with halogen lights, soft Marseille bedspreads and blue-tiled bathrooms. There are also four standard hotel rooms with twin beds and small refrigerators that go for a bargain $140 a night at peak season. A restaurant, pool and Jacuzzi are on the premises, with lots within walking distance. This friendly operation run by the Charnou family is a very good buy, but note that a 10 percent service charge is added to the rates. 25 rooms. Credit cards: A, MC, V.

Apartments and Condominiums

Self-catering in St. Barts can hardly be termed "roughing it." Prices on villas, usually with fully equipped kitchens and many with private pool, can be extravagant, but the surroundings and convenience are often worth it. The villa leader is **Sibarth**, a real estate agency in Gustavia run by Brook and Roger Lacour. She is a former U.S. citizen who vacationed on the island years ago, fell in love, and married into the St. Barts life. Sibarth rents out 200 island properties that range from modest and quaint (starting at about $900 per week in the low season, $1200 in the winter), to luxurious abodes with three or four bedrooms, a pool, spellbinding views and Hollywood pedigree. All offer a chance to experience the island at its most uncomplicated. Sibarth can be contacted directly on-island ☎ *(590) 27-62-38*, or through its U.S. representative, **WIMCO** ☎ *(800) 932-3222*. Request a copy of Sibarth's comprehensive, 108-page *Vendome Guide* in English ($11). In addition to color photos of most of Sibarth's rentals, the guide also contains information on the island hotels WIMCO represents, as well as restaurants, watersports and other activities. **St. Barth Imoblier** is the other big villa agency on the island, with about 75 properties represented, starting at about $1000 per week in the low season, or $1400 per week in winter ☎ *(590) 27-82-94*, or contacts their U.S. representative, **St. Barth Properties** ☎ *(800) 421-3396*. Another U.S. firm, **French Caribbean International**, handles about 80 properties ☎ *(800) 322-2223*. All three state-side representatives also handle hotel reservations for some of St. Barts' tonier establishments.

| Emeraude Plage Hotel | $118–$535 | ★★★ |

St. Jean, ☎ *(800) 932-3222, (590) 27-64-78, FAX (590) 27-83-08.*
Single: $118–$535. Double: $118–$535.
Ideally situated right on St. Jean Beach and wrapped in sea grape trees, these popular accommodations are in simple yet comfortable bungalows with all the modern conveniences, plus kitchenettes on the patios. Three units qualify as suites, and there's a beachside villa with two bedrooms, two baths and great views. All is kept in tip-top shape by the very friendly staff. There's little in the way of extras, but no one seems to mind. Guests get a discount on watersports at the nearby concession. 28 rooms. Credit cards: MC, V.

| Le P'tit Morne | $108–$160 | ★★ |

Colobier, ☎ *(590) 27-62-64, FAX (590) 27-84-63.*
Closed Date: June.
Single: $108–$145. Double: $114–$160.
Set high in the hills far from the madding crowds, the rates at this family-run apartment complex are quite reasonable. Spare but spacious units are air-conditioned studios with cable TV, minibars, fully equipped kitchens and decks. The premises include a pool and snack bar, which serves breakfast only. The beach is a five-minute

drive down a twisting road. Summer rates usually include car rental. 14 rooms. Credit cards: A, MC.

Yuana Hotel $137–$250   ★★★
Anse des Cayes, ☎ (800) 932-3222, (590) 27-80-84, FAX (590) 27-78-45.
Single: $137–$250. Double: $137–$250.
Set in a lush garden, this hillside hotel has great views but a somewhat awkward location. Guests are put up in spacious studios with full kitchenettes, TVs with VCRs, and comfortable furnishings. The restaurant serves breakfast only; you'll have to cook in or rent a car for other meals. There's a small, shady pool for cooling off. 12 rooms. Credit cards: A, MC, V.

Low Cost Lodging

Affordable accommodations on St. Barts? Say it isn't so! Truly budget lodging is not really found on this most expensive of Caribbean isles, but there are a few lower priced options. In addition to the listings below, seriously consider making your trip during low season, when a few delights like the **Sea Horse** and **Hostellerie des Trois Forces** dip below the triple-digit mark. Beyond the listings below, a few other budget possibilities include **Les Igloos** on Pointe Milou ☎ *(590) 27-56-14*, the **Manoir de St. Barth** in Lorient ☎ *(590) 27-79-27*, and the harborside **Sunset Hotel** in Gustavia ☎ *(590) 27-77-21*.

The cost-conscious visitor to St. Barts should be forewarned that the daily food bill for two can easily outpace your accommodation tab. Unless you're planning on a Cheeseburger in Paradise for breakfast, lunch and dinner daily, be sure to allot a good portion of your budget for food. Finally, though shopping on the island is not inexpensive, make-do types can get by admirably on the fine French cheese, pâte and other items stocked at the **AMC Supermarket** in Gustavia. This opens up one more option, particularly for families—a villa rental. **Sibarth** has a charming group of rustic one-bedroom bungalows with full kitchens where you can step right onto St. Jean beach for $1045 a week in low season. Two-bedroom properties start at about $1400 per week during the summer (see "Apartments and Condominiums" above).

La Presqui'ile $40–$100   ★
Gustavia, ☎ (590) 27-64-60, FAX (590) 27-72-30.
Single: $40–$60. Double: $60–$100.
Built in 1963, La Presqui'ile was the second hotel on St. Barts, and somehow remains a great bargain for those expecting no more than the basics. The bathroom is shared and decor is spartan, but this harborside property will leave a few francs in your pocket for dinner. No pool, but Shell Beach is a ten-minute walk. 10 rooms.

Normandie $45–$76   ★
Lorient, ☎ (590) 27-61-66, FAX (590) 27-98-83.
Single: $45–$63. Double: $58–$76.
This basic, family-run guesthouse offers some of St. Bart's cheapest accommodations. The rooms are quite basic, but immaculate and comfortable. Only two (the most expensive) have air conditioners; the rest rely on ceiling fans. There's a bar, a small pool and garden, but nothing else—the beach is about 10 minutes away on foot. 8 rooms.

Where to Eat

Fielding's Highest Rated Restaurants in St. Barthélémy

★★★★★	Francois Plantation	$16–$50
★★★★★	Le Gaiac	$22–$31
★★★★	Au Port	$19–$28
★★★★	Ballahou	$27–$45
★★★★	Eddy's	$18–$24
★★★★	Le Sapotillier	$47–$47
★★★★	Maya's	$27–$35
★★★	Le Tamarin	$22–$34
★★★	Vincent Adam	$38–$48

Fielding's Most Romantic Restaurants in St. Barthélémy

♥♥♥♥♥	Le Gaiac	$22–$31
♥♥♥♥	Ballahou	$27–$45
♥♥♥♥	Francois Plantation	$16–$50
♥♥♥♥	Le Sapotillier	$47–$47
♥♥♥♥	Vincent Adam	$38–$48

Fielding's Best Value Restaurants in St. Barthélémy

★★	Le Select	$5–$10
★★★	Ines' Ghetto	$12–$17
★★★★	Eddy's	$18–$24
★★★	Vietnam	$14–$18
★★★★★	Le Gaiac	$22–$31

Dining in the Caribbean doesn't come better than on St. Barthélémy. It has to be good to suit persnickety jetsetters who arrive with expectations of gastronomique cuisine on par with what might be found in France. Indeed, unlike on Martinique and Guadeloupe, menus on St. Barts usually steer to the French, often using the spoils of the sea, such as lobster and redfish, though you can find some West Indian restaurants, as well as a smattering of Asian and Italian. Still, French is king here, and celebrated in high style every other April when the biennial **Festival Gastronomique** rolls into town and showcases the best of French food and wine.

Current favorites include the shoreside **Maya's**, which continues to be the hippest celebrity hangout, in large part due to its lack of pretense; the atmosphere is relaxed and the exotic cuisine—from French to creole to Vietnamese—is superb. Equally noteworthy is **Eddy's**, a newer addition to the Stakelborough family that sets fine food against a backdrop of teak and bamboo mementos from Bali, a favorite destination for the affable owner. An estimable wine cellar containing rare and precious vintages tempts diners at **Francois Plantation**, where a young chef works magic in the kitchen—the desserts are memorable. The island's best view is proffered by the spectacular **Carl Gustaf**, though you'll enjoy it even more at lunch or for a sunset cocktail, when Gustavia's panoply of color is fleshed out by the sun.

At the average St. Barts restaurant, expect lunch for two to run $50 to $75, and the dinner check to top $100; these prices don't include a bottle of fancy wine. However, when wallets get low there are a few options. First, seek out the many spots that offer fixed-price menus—the lower price has little relationship to the quality of your meal. A dinner with dessert at one of these restaurants will run $25–35 per person (plus drinks). Next, pick up a copy of *Ti Gourmet*, a free illustrated guide to many island establishments—flash your copy at any of the several dozen restaurants listed in its pages and you will receive a complimentary cocktail. And don't forego a trip to one of the many island rotisseries for tasty and relatively cheap fast food.

Among the more affordable restaurants on the island are the reliable **Repaire** and **Wall House** on the outer end of the harbor in Gustavia. In the heart of Gustavia is **Paradisio** for the island's best Italian and **Vietnam** for splendid Asian. A romantic splurge is safely indulged at the moderately priced and scenic **Marigot Bay Club**. Less expensive still, amid simpler surroundings, are **Brasserie Creole** for West Indian at St. Jean Bay, colorful dive bar **Chez Ginette** in Anse des Cayes which caters to poets with Ginette's famous *Punch Coco*, **Chez JoJo** for burgers and fried chicken in Lorient, **Chez Pompi** for modest meals in Grand Cul-de-Sac, while American food is celebrated at **Santa Fe**, high on the hill above Gustavia. **Le Select** is the island's most famous and down-home bar (a Red Stripe beer is $2), but its adjoining garden and snack stand—**Cheeseburger in Paradise**—sells the titular item for about $6. Several other low-priced eateries in Gustavia compete for the burger-and-sandwich business. Finally, if the wealth of choices begins to seem overwhelming, stop by the real estate office **Sibarth**, where menus from many restaurants are available for browsing.

Au Port $$$ ★★★★

Rue Sadi-Carnot; Gustavia, ☎ *(590) 27-62-36.*
Dinner: 6:30–10 p.m., entrées $19–$28.
Guests navigate a steep staircase to get to the second-floor dining room of this old house above the port. Cuisine is a fanciful blend of traditional French and Creole—witness the popular *colombo* (Creole curry) of prawns or lamb served with seasoned rice. A three-course Creole menu is an excellent value at $36 and might include lamb curry or conch and lobster sausage. There are several foie gras items—it's made on the premises. Reservations recommended. Credit cards: A, MC, V.

Ballahou $$$ ★★★★

Anse des Cayes, ☎ *(590) 27-66-55.* Associated hotel: *Hotel Manapany.*
Lunch: 12:30–4 p.m., entrées $15–$30.
Dinner: 7:30–9:30 p.m., entrées $27–$45.
There's a lot of understandable ballyhoo about this gorgeous restaurant in the sleek Hotel Manapany—architecturally, it seems to blend as one with the rim of the swimming pool. Specialties usually include seafood, but chef Jerome Le Dore's menu changes often. Guests of the hotel and others dine here by candlelight only five months out of the year; it's closed in the warmer months. Manapany's Italian restaurant, Ouanalao, serves lunch and dinner all year round; try the gazpacho and risotto with prawns. Reservations recommended. Credit cards: A, DC, MC, V.

Eddy's $$$ ★★★★

Rue du Centenaire; Gustavia, ☎ *(590) 27-54-17.*
Dinner: 7–10 p.m., entrées $18–$24.
Following the long-running success of Eddy's Ghetto, Eddy Stakelborough (son of island institution Marius, the founder of Le Select), opened a slightly more upscale and eclectic version of his French-meets-West Indian establishment. The decor is Balinese teak and bamboo, while the menu includes Creole curry, a shrimp in Thai-style green curry, and pork tenderloin breaded in fresh coconut and topped with pineapple. Fish dishes are prepared grilled, fried or in parchment. Like the Ghetto (which now operates under the name Ines), Eddy's has no sign—it's across the street from Le Sapotillier. Drop by in person to reserve a table. Credit cards: A, MC, V.

Francois Plantation $$$ ★★★★★

Colombier, ☎ *(590) 27-78-82.* Associated hotel: *Francois Plantation.*
Dinner: 6:30–10 p.m., entrées $16–$50. Closed: Sun.
No one doubts the serene beauty of this place—for exotic plantings, greenery and an interior boasting highly polished woods, and the food, under the watchful eye of owner Francois Beret, lives up to the setting. Lighter versions of traditional French favorites take a front seat, with delicate, unusual spices accenting innovative dishes like lobster taboule, roasted tournedos of ostrich, and home-smoked salmon in a mille-feuilles pastry. Desserts are outstanding, and the island's best cellar produces a wine list some 180 vintages strong. Reservations recommended. Credit cards: A, MC, V.

Ines' Ghetto $ ★★★

Rue du General de Gaulle; Gustavia, ☎ *(590) 27-53-20.*
Dinner: 7–10 p.m., entrées $12–$17. Closed: Sun.

Formerly known as Eddy's Ghetto, when locals go "slumming" they still go to Ines'
for simple grills, salads, ribs, beef ragouts, pumpkin soup, *entrecote* and island
music. The yacht crowd often dominates the wicker- and plant-filled restaurant the
moment it opens at 7 p.m., if the locals haven't gotten there first. The place fills the
need for light meals and provides a casual ambience not found in some of the
island's pricier establishments. You'll need to ask for directions since there's no sign
(it's across from the Sibarth office), but this is one spot everyone can point you to.

L'Entrepont $$$ ★★★

La Pointe; Gustavia, ☎ *(590) 27-90-60.*
Dinner: entrées $25–$33.

Located in a newly fashionable area on the west side of Gustavia's harbor, this Italian restaurant owned by a Neapolitan family is renowned for unusual pizzas. Guests
eat well in a garden setting under coconut trees that's open to the breezes. Other
choices include beef carpaccio, pastas and veal. Credit cards: A, MC, V.

L'Escale $$$ ★★★

La Pointe, Gustavia, ☎ *(590) 27-81-06.*
Dinner: 7 p.m.–midnight, entrées $12–$29. Closed: Tue.

This mostly Italian trattoria on the west side of the harbor has many faithful followers who clamor for the variety of *tagliatelle*, ravioli, lasagna and grilled meats and
seafood. But most come for the delicious pizzas, priced $12–$17. Lately L'Escale
has been facing some competition from other eateries in the area serving similar cuisine, although it swings at night, especially in the hip bar. Reservations required.
Credit cards: MC, V.

L'Iguane $$ ★★★

Carre d'Or mall; Gustavia, ☎ *(590) 27-88-46.*
Lunch: 8 a.m.–5 p.m., entrées $6–$15.
Dinner: 5 p.m.–midnight, entrées $15–$20.

A nice spot in a newer shopping area, L'Iguane serves ice cream, inexpensive crab
and pasta salads and focaccia sandwiches by day. But at night, a sushi menu is rolled
out and served until midnight (daily except Monday)—some say it's the best raw
fish in the islands. A plate for one averages $15-20, while combination platters run
$30–$70.

La Langouste $$$ ★★★

Baie des Flamands, ☎ *(590) 27-63-61.* Associated hotel: *Baie des Anges.*
Dinner: 7–10 p.m., entrées $23–$42.

The island's national crustacean (a clawless lobster) is the star at this pleasant Cre-
ole/French eatery owned by Annie Ange, a member of a St. Barts landowning family (St. Barth's Beach Hotel). The delectable seafood is dependably fresh, and other
offerings include stuffed crabs and *accra de morue* (cod fritters). Reservations recommended. Credit cards: MC, V.

La Mandala $$ ★★★

Rue Thiers; Gustavia, ☎ *(590) 27-96-96.*

Dinner: 5–11 p.m., entrées $11–$25.

La Mandala is the swank creation of Boubou (stepson of Roger Vadim) and his partner Christophe, who have converted the former Hibiscus Hotel into a outdoor restaurant perched on a deck with a fabulous Gustavia view. The menu has a multi-cultural flair (like the eclectic decor), with an emphasis on tapas—appetizer plates priced $7-10. Entrees include beef, chicken, salmon and pasta dishes and there's a sitting table in the rear for small parties. The $34 prix fixe menu is a good value. Credit cards: A, MC, V.

Le Gaiac   **$$$**   ★★★★★

Toiny, ☎ *(590) 27-88-88.* Associated hotel: *Le Toiny.*
Lunch: Noon–2:30 p.m., entrées $12–$28.
Dinner: 7–10 p.m., entrées $22–$31.

This small, very in spot at Le Toiny, a resort on a hilltop above a windswept beach, has quickly developed a new following after bringing in 28-year-old cuisinier Chef Maxime des Champs. The intimate, 30-seat outdoor restaurant features a menu that artfully marries traditional Provencal French with West Indian cuisine. Specialties include yellowtail snapper with curried lentils and squash, a gateau of roast boneless pigeon layered with red cabbage, sweet potato and herbs, and a light monkfish stew with spring vegetables and bacon. Poolside lunch encompasses chilled soups, sandwiches pasta and grilled seafood (reserve early for the $33 Sunday brunch which includes duck and lobster). The name Gaiac comes from the rare trees that dot the property. Reservations recommended. Credit cards: A, MC, V.

Le Sapotillier   **$$$**   ★★★★

Rue Sadi-Carnot; Gustavia, ☎ *(590) 27-60-28.*
Dinner: from 6:30 p.m., prix fixe $47. Closed: Sun.

Some fine chefs have emerged with an appreciative following from the kitchens of this memorable restaurant in a traditional old stone structure in Gustavia, including Le Fregate's Jean-Pierre Crouzette. La Sapotillier's reputation is still stellar, with classic French cuisine served with finesse in a small, dark dining room or alfresco under the branches of a vast sapodilla tree. Specialties include lasagna of escargots in a garlic sauce, foie gras of duck with juniper berry sauce, and veal stew with roquefort and vegetables—many fish dishes are prepared with a Provencal flair. Reservations recommended. Credit cards: MC, V.

Le Select   **$**   ★★

Rue de la France; Gustavia ☎ *(590) 27-86-87.*
Lunch: 10 a.m.–4 p.m., entrées $5–$10.
Dinner: 4–11 p.m., entrées $5–$10. Closed: Sun.

This old favorite (circa 1950) provides a safe haven for ordinary folk seeking refuge from the high prices and over-stuffed, precious atmosphere of some island dining establishments. Besides serving what is probably the best cheeseburger in town at an adjoining snack stand, the scruffy, poster-festooned old warehouse is great for loud reggae, *zouk* or *soca*—Jimmy Buffett schedules impromptu concerts here regularly. Newcomers can't possibly miss Le Select—it sits at a prime location in the middle of town; at night you hear it before you see it. Credit cards: not accepted.

Le Tamarin $$$ ★★★

Plage de Saline, ☎ *(590) 27-72-12.*
Lunch: 11 a.m.–5 p.m., entrées $22–$34. Closed: Mon.

Located a half-mile inland from Grand Saline, perhaps the island's best beach, Le Tamarin is the sole restaurant in the area, with a steady stream of sunbathers seeking nourishment as clientele. The crab, avocado, grapefruit salad is a winner for a lighter meal ($16), or go for the grilled tenderloin embellished with a roquefort or green peppercorn sauce. Desserts are delicious, and owner Cat Cent keeps the atmosphere hip under an ancient tamarind tree. In season, Le Tamarin is open for dinner on weekends. Credit cards: A, MC, V.

Marigot Bay Club $$$ ★★★

Marigot Bay, ☎ *(590) 27-75-45.*
Lunch: entrées $11–$26.
Dinner: entrées $20–$28.

Two giant grilled langoustines appear on your plate here like creatures from Mars— yet they were freshly caught only this morning. Marigot Bay Club is an intimate restaurant offering romance without pretense on a bayside deck. Grilled fish, fillet mignon and duck are offered, but lobster is the specialty, available tucked in ravioli, as a pastry-wrapped stew, with a Creole sauce, in a creamy mushroom and gruyere sauce, etc. Specialties rarely change, which is how most people who eat here like it. Closed for lunch on Monday. Reservations recommended. Credit cards: A, MC, V.

Maya's $$$ ★★★★

Public, ☎ *(590) 27-73-61.*
Dinner: 6–11 p.m., entrées $27–$35. Closed: Sun.

Maya from Martinique serves savory Creole cuisine with some spicy touches to an always appreciative (and expansive) crowd; it's one of the more popular eateries on the island. Fresh seafood and grilled lobster are the focus, but a spicy callallo soup is unlike any other in the islands. The restaurant has a waterfront location in Public (west of Gustavia) with tables on a plant-filled patio. The menu changes frequently, but one thing stays the same—the table-hopping coterie of stars who keep the atmosphere lively night after night. Closed June through October. Reservations recommended. Credit cards: A, MC, V.

Paradisio $$$ ★★★

Rue de Roi; Gustavia, ☎ *(590) 27-80-78.*
Lunch: 11 a.m.–2 p.m., prix fixe $20.
Dinner: 6–11 p.m., entrées $15–$30.

French-inspired Italian food is served at this very popular restaurant in a traditional, historic building in Gustavia. Formerly the site of La Citronelle, the jolly exterior features gingerbread trim, white shutters, tangerine and white railings and a tropical mural. Guests can dine on several different daily pasta offerings in air-conditioned insularity or in a breeze-cooled patio. The menu also features lobster in saffron oil and beef filets, and the variety of carpaccios—beef, lamb, salmon, red snapper and tuna—are well-liked. The fixed-price lunch is a particularly good value for $20. Reservations recommended. Credit cards: MC, V.

Vietnam   **$$**   ★★★

Rue du Roi Oscar II; Gustavia, ☎ *(590) 27-81-37.*
Lunch: prix fixe $12.
Dinner: entrées $14–$18.

Thai, Chinese and Vietnamese dishes are featured on the menu of this inexpensive spot. Seating is in an air-conditioned dining room, or out on a lovely outdoor covered patio overlooking the bustle of Gustavia. The $12 fixed price lunch has to be one of the best deals on the island, while glazed duck, spring rolls and stuffed shrimp are dinner highlights. Angelique and Tuyen are the charming owners. Closed for lunch on Sundays.

Vincent Adam   **$$$**   ★★★

St. Jean, ☎ *(590) 27-93-22.*
Dinner: 6:30–10 p.m., prix fixe $38–$48.

On an island where fabulous eateries come and go, Vincent Adam prevails by proffering a seemingly infinite variety of three-course, prix-fixe dinners for $38; a lobster menu is also available for $48. The wide selection includes filet mignon, lobster tabouli, or filet of pork with a coconut sauce, capped off with creme brulee or other heavenly desserts. The setting is also paradisiacal, high on a hillside with garden and lagoon views; there's art on the walls as well as on the plates. Also known as Adam. Reservations recommended. Credit cards: A, V.

Wall House   **$$$**   ★★★

Gustavia Harbor, ☎ *(590) 27-71-83.*
Dinner: 6:30–10 p.m., entrées $19–$39.

Almost every table in this whitewashed restaurant in the harbor has a lovely view; the wide picture windows in the dining room offer a quayside panorama of swaying palms, small craft, azure waters, and a row of red tile-roofed, gingerbread-trimmed buildings. Diners can also sit outside to be closer to the action. The regular menu is fine, or you may choose from three, three-course fixed-price menus: the $30 and $38 groupings include mahi-mahi in a mint cream, or fillet of lamb in marjoram. A $56 lobster menu features grilled lobster along with a lobster appetizer. Reservations recommended. Credit cards: A, MC, V.

Duty-free reigns supreme in St. Barts. If you're in the market for fine perfumes, china, crystal and liquor, you can find some bargains here. In recent years, several haute couture boutiques have opened on the island, including **Stephane & Bernard**, **Hermes**, **Gucci**, **Polo** and **Cartier**. Some French perfumes, like Chanel, are cheaper here than in Paris. Most name brand shops are located in Gustavia, though a few are scattered through St. Jean, and at La Savane Commercial Center, across the street from the airport. Yacht owners and wannabes tend to congregate at **Loulou's Marine** in Gustavia, where everything you ever needed for a cruise is available—from clothes to rigs, with the canvas tote bags stamped with the store logo a particular favorite.

Beyond the duty-free products, a few local items are unique to St. Barts and have established an international reputation. Skin lotions and tanning oils made from local plants are created by **Belou's P** including beautifully bottled fragrant oils, each named for a different beach—you'll find them at **'Ti Marche**, the open air market in Gustavia. Another line of beauty lotions and suntan products is **Ligne de St. Barth**, sold in Lorient by **Herve Brin**. **M'Bolo** produces delicious rum punch from vanilla, coconut, prune, apricot and other fruits—they are hand-bottled, make lovely gifts, and can be found along with other items at a store in Gustavia's **Carre d'Or** shopping arcade. **St. Barts Pottery**, located just past the Gustavia post office, handles stoneware and terra cotta by Jennifer May, along with a few baskets, paintings and jewelry (open daily, but closed during the summer). To find one of the last vestiges of traditional life, go to the once-isolated fishing village of Corossol, where you can still see older St. Bartian women weaving delicate handicrafts from lantana palm. Magazine spreads to the contrary, the woven, nun-style bonnets called *caleches* or *quichenottes* ("kiss me not") are rarely if ever seen on their heads anymore (the women are notoriously camera-shy). Other local crafts sold in Gustavia include sandals and shell jewelry, as well as paintings and lithographs by island artists. One of the most admired local painters is impressionist Denis Hermenge.

St. Barthélémy Directory

Arrival and Departure

There are no direct flights from North America to St. Barthélémy's tiny airstrip. The principal gateway is Sint Maarten's Juliana Airport which is served by **American Airlines** nonstop from New York's JFK, Miami and San Juan, Puerto Rico; by **USAir** out of Charlotte and Philadelphia; and by **Continental** from Newark. For additional service to Sint Maarten see "Arrival and Departure" in "Saint Martin/Sint Maarten."

The 10-minute flight from Sint Maarten to St. Barts is handled by **Windward Island Airways** ☎ *(800) 634-4907* or *(590) 27-61-01* and **Air St. Barthélémy** ☎ *(590) 27-71-90*, both of which operate 19-seat STOL (Short Takeoff and Landing) aircraft. These small airlines purport to follow a schedule, but the reality is that they tend to leave when their plane fills up—fortunately departures are relatively frequent, particularly during the afternoon when most of the jets land on Sint Maarten. Have patience when you arrive in Sint Maarten; you'll get to St. Barts eventually as long as there's light out (the runway shuts down at dusk). Round-trip fare is about $95. Also from within the Caribbean, **Air St. Barthélémy** ☎ *(590) 27-71-90* and **Air Guadeloupe** ☎ *(590) 27-61-90* each provide service out of San Juan, Guadeloupe and Espérance Airport (on

French St. Martin). **Air St. Thomas** ☎ *(590) 27-71-76* provides flights from San Juan and St. Thomas.

It is also possible to get to St. Barts by boat. **White Octopus**, a 75-foot catamaran, makes the 90-minute crossing from Sint Maarten on Tuesdays and Thursdays. The cat leaves Philipsburg at 9 a.m. and departs Gustavia for the return trip at 4 p.m., allowing just enough time for lunch and a round of shopping. The trip is $25 each way, plus $5 tax (open bar included) ☎ *(5995) 23170.* Several ferry services are also available: **Gustavia Express** plies the route to St. Barts from both Philipsburg and Marigot (on French St. Martin) ☎ *(590) 27-77-24;* **Voyageur** makes the trip from Marigot to Gustavia ☎ *(590) 87-20-78;* and **Bateau Dakar** serves both St. Martin and Guadeloupe ☎ *(590) 27-70-05.* Be advised that the trip to St. Barts via boat can be rough, and is not advised for anyone prone to seasickness.

There is an airport departure tax of about $6.

Business Hours

Shops are open weekdays 8:30 a.m.–noon and 2–5 p.m. (some later) and Saturday 8:30 a.m.–noon. Banks open weekdays 8 a.m.–noon and 2–3:30 p.m.

Climate

St. Barts has an ideal dry climate and an average temperature of 72–86 degrees Fahrenheit.

Documents

For stays of up to three weeks, U.S. and Canadian citizens traveling as tourists must have proof of citizenship in the form of a valid passport or one that has expired not more than five years ago, or a birth certificate (original or copy) or voter's registration accompanied by a government-authorized ID with photo. For stays over three weeks, or for nontourist visits, a valid passport is necessary. A return or onward ticket is also required of all visitors.

Electricity

Current runs at 220 AC, 60 cycles. American-made appliances require French plug converters and transformers.

Getting Around

Car rentals are easy to obtain, but if you are visiting in the winter you may want to ask your hotel to secure one for you in advance. Roads are steep, narrow and winding, and most vehicles have manual transmission. You'll save money by renting for a week (daily rates go as high as $60). The island's two gas stations are not open on Sunday, though a 24-hour pump operated by pre-purchased gas cards is available across from the airport. **Avis**, **Budget** and **Hertz** are among the rental firms represented on the island. **Motorbikes**, **mopeds** and **scooters** are plentiful, but you are required to have a motorbike driver's license to rent one. Rental fees average $28 per day; contact **Denis Dufau's Rent Some Fun** ☎ *(590) 27-70-59.*

Taxis have a flat rate of about $5 for distances of up to 5 minutes, and $4 for each additional 3 minutes; night fares are higher, as are those on Sundays and holidays. Taxis can be obtained by calling ☎ *(590) 27-66-31*. There is no public bus service on St. Barts, though hitchhiking is not uncommon.

For information on boat service to Sint Maarten/Saint Martin, see "Arrival and Departure," above. For information on daytrips to Anguilla, Saba and Sint Eustatius, see "Getting Around" in "Sint Maarten/Saint Martin."

Language

French is the official language, spoken with a quaint Norman dialect. Most people speak English, but a French phrasebook is handy.

Medical Emergencies

Gustavia has a clinic ☎ *(590) 27-60-35*, with eight resident doctors, three dentists, one gynecologist, and specialists in opthalmology, dermatology, etc. There are pharmacies at **La Savane Commercial Center** ☎ *(590) 27-66-61* and in **Gustavia** ☎ *(590) 27-61-82*. Any serious emergencies require airlift to Sint Maarten or San Juan, Puerto Rico.

Money

The official currency is the French franc. The exchange rate we have used to calculate hotel and restaurant prices provided to us in francs is 5.5 to one U.S. dollar. If the dollar has further strengthened, you may find lower prices on the island than what we have quoted. Dollars are accepted virtually everywhere, but paying in francs will usually get you a better rate. Credit cards are more readily accepted on the island than in the past, and credit cards frequently yield a better rate than is available through island banks.

Telephone

The area code for St. Barts is *590*. To call from the U.S. dial *011* (international access code), then *590* plus the six-digit local number. To call St. Barts from Dutch St. Maarten, dial *6* plus St. Barts's local six-digit number. To call St. Barts from other F.W.I. (Martinique, Guadeloupe, and French St. Martin), you can dial direct.

Public phones require the use of *telecartes* that look like credit cards and can be easily purchased at the Gustavia, St. Jean and Lorient post offices and at the gas station near the airport. Both local and international calls can be made from these phones using the card.

Time

St. Barts is one hour ahead of Eastern Standard Time. When it is 9 o'clock in St. Barts, it is 8 o'clock in New York. During daylight saving time, there is no time difference.

Tipping and Taxes

Most hotels include tax and service in their quoted room rates; others add 5–15 percent to the bill. Check at the time of booking to avoid any check-out surprises.

Tourist Information

The **Office de Tourisme** is located on the Quai Général de Gaulle, across from the Capitainerie in Gustavia, open Monday–Friday 8:30 a.m.–6 p.m., and Saturday 8:30 a.m.–noon. From May to October, hours are a bit shorter. *B.P. 113, Gustavia, 97098 Cedex, St. Barthélémy, F.W.I.* ☎ *(590) 27-87-27.*

When to Go

Major island events include the **St. Barts Music Festival**, a two-week series of concerts held in January in Gustavia and Lorient, including jazz, chamber music, opera, ballet and modern dance. **Carnival** is celebrated during the two days leading up to Ash Wednesday in February. Every other April, the **Festival Gastronomique** is held with special events devoted to the cuisine of France (by region) at many island restaurants. Also in April is the **St. Barts Film Fete and Caribbean Cinematheque**, a five-day salute to regional filmmakers. The **Festival of St. Barthelemy** is held in August, and features boat blessing, church bells, a regatta, and wining and dining. Also in August are the **Feast of St. Louis** in the village of Corossol and the **Fete du Vent** in the village of Lorient; each is celebrated with contests, parties, music and dancing.

ST. BARTHÉLÉMY HOTELS		RMS	RATES	PHONE	CR. CARDS
★★★★★	Guanahani	75	$246–$590	(800) 223-6800	A, MC, V
★★★★★	Le Toiny	12	$530–$860	(800) 932-3222	A, DC, MC, V
★★★★	Carl Gustaf	14	$350–$800	(800) 322-2223	A, MC, V
★★★★	Christopher Hotel	40	$260–$450	(800) 763-4835	A, MC, V
★★★★	St. Barth Isle de France	28	$315–$800	(800) 628-8929	A, MC, V
★★★	Eden Rock	14	$220–$680	(800) 322-2223	A, MC, V
★★★	El Sereno Beach Hotel	41	$200–$580	(800) 332-2223	A, MC, V
★★★	Emeraude Plage Hotel	28	$118–$535	(800) 932-3222	MC, V
★★★	Filao Beach Hotel	30	$182–$582	(800) 932-3222	A, CB, D, DC, MC, V
★★★	Francois Plantation	12	$216–$350	(800) 932-3222	A, MC, V
★★★	La Banane	9	$150–$480	(800) 932-3222	A, MC, V
★★★	Le Tom Beach	12	$260–$530	(800) 322-2223	A, MC, V
★★★	Manapany Cottages	52	$205–$575	(800) 932-3222	A, MC
★★★	Tropical Hotel	20	$108–$250	(800) 322-2223	A, MC
★★★	Village St. Jean Hotel	25	$89–$320	(800) 322-2223	A, MC, V
★★★	Yuana Hotel	12	$137–$250	(800) 932-3222	A, MC, V
★★	Baie des Anges Hotel	9	$145–$395	(800) 755-9313	A, CB, MC, V
★★	Hostellerie Trois Forces	8	$65–$170	(590) 27-61-25	A, MC, V
★★	Le P'tit Morne	14	$108–$160	(590) 27-62-64	A, MC
★★	Sea Horse Hotel	11	$80–$295	(800) 932-3222	A, MC, V

ST. BARTHÉLÉMY HOTELS	RMS	RATES	PHONE	CR. CARDS
★★ St. Barth's Beach Hotel	44	$121–$294	(800) 621-1270	A, MC
★ La Presqui'ile	10	$40–$100	(590) 27-64-60	
★ Normandie	8	$45–$76	(590) 27-61-66	

ST BARTHÉLÉMY RESTAURANTS	PHONE	ENTRÉE	CR. CARDS
American Cuisine			
★★ Le Select	(590) 27-86-87	$5–$10	None
Asian Cuisine			
★★★ Vietnam	(590) 27-81-37	$12–$18	
Creole Cuisine			
★★★★ Au Port	(590) 27-62-36	$19–$28	A, MC, V
★★★★ Eddy's	(590) 27-54-17	$18–$24	A, MC, V
★★★★ Maya's	(590) 27-73-61	$27–$35	A, MC, V
★★★ Ines' Ghetto	(590) 27-53-20	$12–$17	
★★★ La Mandala	(590) 27-96-96	$11–$25	A, MC, V
French Cuisine			
★★★★★ Francois Plantation	(590) 27-78-82	$16–$50	A, MC, V
★★★★★ Le Gaiac	(590) 27-88-88	$12–$31	A, MC, V
★★★★ Ballahou	(590) 27-66-55	$15–$45	A, DC, MC, V
★★★★ Le Sapotillier	(590) 27-60-28	$47–$47	MC, V
★★★ La Langouste	(590) 27-63-61	$23–$42	MC, V
★★★ Le Tamarin	(590) 27-72-12	$22–$34	A, MC, V
★★★ L'Iguane	(590) 27-88-46	$6–$20	
★★★ Marigot Bay Club	(590) 27-75-45	$11–$28	A, MC, V
★★★ Vincent Adam	(590) 27-93-22	$38–$48	A, V
★★★ Wall House	(590) 27-71-83	$19–$39	A, MC, V
Italian Cuisine			
★★★ L'Entrepont	(590) 27-90-60	$25–$33	A, MC, V
★★★ L'Escale	(590) 27-81-06	$12–$29	MC, V
★★★ Paradisio	(590) 27-80-78	$20–$30	MC, V

ST. CROIX

Local boys dive off the rocks of St. Croix.

It boasts good beaches, a surprisingly polished array of sports activities, and more than a few relics of true Dutch West Indian architecture, yet St. Croix remains the underappreciated U.S. Virgin. The island's nightlife and shopping opportunities have long been overshadowed by those on frantic St. Thomas, while St. John's National Park steals the show when it comes to tranquil pursuits on miles of undeveloped land. If the USVI's are three siblings, St. Croix is the middle child—often overlooked or misunderstood—and one whose identity was further hampered when 1989's Hurricane Hugo delivered a pummeling that left the island reeling from bad press well into the '90s. No wonder it resembles a Rodney Dangerfield act reinvented as an outpost that desperately craves some respect. The island bounced back in 1996 in an ironic way when Hurricane Marilyn, which walloped St. Thomas and St. John, became a sort of life preserver for St. Croix. Cruise ships diverted itineraries away from storm-ravaged islands, hotels saw their busiest season in years and, once again, St. Croix is quietly reestablishing its presence on the Caribbean tourism map.

Newcomers probably liked what they saw. Though a number of Crucians still wear the yoke of an inferiority complex, what St. Croix offers is a little of the best of the Virgins—a captivating cruise ship port with many of the same shops and deals found in Charlotte Amalie, a peaceful rainforest, and velvety beaches that promise easy escape. Though the presence of KFC and Kmart still imparts more American than Caribbean flair, the Dutch heritage of the Virgins is more obvious here, especially in Christiansted, where the narrow streets are lined with historic buildings painted in colorful pastels and adorned with wooden shutters. Some of the Caribbean's best golf is found here on two excellent 18-hole courses, along with superb diving on the undersea wall that parallels the north coast and plunges 12,000 feet into an oceanic trench. Perhaps one reason the island's superlatives have remained in the shadows is that, unlike its siblings, tourism is not the sole economy—the Hess Oil Refinery located near the airport is the world's second largest (employing 5000 islanders), and the Cruzan Rum Factory is the only rum distillery left in the Virgins. Despite the heavy industry, a nascent environmental movement has sprung up: the award-winning St. Croix Environmental Organization (SEA). The group succeeded in saving Salt River Bay, where Christopher Columbus landed in 1493, from a pre-Hugo building boom— the 912-acre bay is now a National Historic Park and Ecological Preserve, and a candidate for World Heritage Site status.

A major evolution for the island is on the horizon. Developer-friendly legislation was approved in 1995 by voters to build casinos on St. Croix. Although there are currently less than a thousand hotel rooms courting tourists here (compared to more than 4000 on St. Thomas), and while gambling will undoubtedly bring new opportunities and challenges, for the moment, St. Croix is shining its brightest in years.

BEST BETS FOR...

Bird's-Eye View

There are more than 50 U.S. Virgin Islands, but St. Croix—the largest of the archipelago—sits alone, 40 miles to the south of St. Thomas. The island

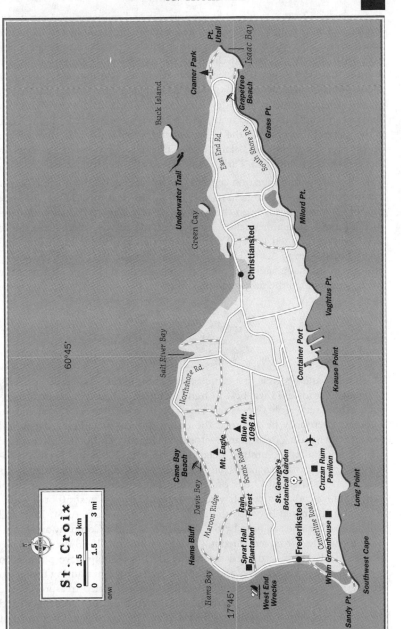

St. Croix

0   1.5   3 km
0   1.5   3 mi

©FWI

17°45'

60°45'

Buck Island

Pt. Utall
Cramer Park
Isaac Bay
Grapetree Beach
Grass Pt.
South Shore Rd.
East End Rd.
Milord Pt.
Underwater Trail
Green Cay
Christiansted
Vaghtus Pt.
Salt River Bay
Container Port
Krause Point
Northshore Rd.
Cane Bay Beach
Davis Bay
Mt. Eagle
Blue Mt. 1096 ft.
Scenic Road
Hams Bluff
Maroon Ridge
Rain Forest
Sprat Hall Plantation
St. George's Botanical Garden
Cruzan Rum Pavilion
Hams Bay
West End Wrecks
Frederiksted
Centerline Road
Whim Greenhouse
Long Point
Southwest Cape
Sandy Pt.

encompasses 82 square miles that support a varied topography along its extended, 23-mile length. A small range of mountains dominates the north coast on the west end of St. Croix, luring enough moisture to create a rain forest that fills the valleys that climb up to the Maroon Ridge—the highest point is Blue Mountain, 1096 feet above sea level. The southern portion of the island is defined by gently rolling hills and sweeping pastures dotted by grazing senepol cattle, a breed developed on St. Croix for hot environments. The eastern end is rocky and drier, and relatively unpopulated—Point Udall is the easternmost point in the United States. One-and-a-half miles off the northeastern coast is Buck Island, a dot of green surrounded by excellent reefs protected by the U.S. Park System as a National Monument.

St. Croix's major population center is Christiansted, on the north coast—a number of hotels are located in or near town, as well as most of the duty-free shopping. A second town on the island's western flank, Frederiksted, dates to 1751 and is sometimes called "Freedom City;" it was where the order to free slaves in the then-Dutch Virgins originated in 1848, anticipating Lincoln's Emancipation Act of 1863. Frederiksted is also the island's cruise ship port, yet is still has a laid-back bohemian charm defined more by artists and entrepreneurs than the disgorged masses.

History

Columbus and his crew first came ashore at St. Croix's Salt River in 1493, but native Caribs did their best to fight them off. In haste he named the island Santa Cruz (Holy Cross) and sailed on to lay claim to St. John and St. Thomas. Eventually he renamed the entire group—including what would become the British Virgin Islands—for the legendary 11,000 followers of St. Ursula. Soon after Columbus' departure, British, Dutch and French colonists began to establish farms on St. Croix, and in 1653, the island was awarded the crusaders' Order of St. John, better known as the Knights of Malta. France took control a few years later, and for the next 50 or so years, possession alternated between the French and the Spanish. As St. John and St. Thomas became acquired by the Danish West India Company and Guinea Company, St. Croix remained in the background. In 1773 the Danes also purchased St. Croix, attracted by its already burgeoning slave population and sugarcane fields. Planters and pirates mingled together during this golden age; some secluded coves are still said to harbor buried treasure. As the sugar beet was introduced to Europe, and the uprisings of slaves threatened the status quo, commercial interest in the island began to flag. Over the past 250 years, seven different conquerors took control of the island, though the

Danish influence has remained the most lasting. During World War I, the Danes, sensing the sugarcane industry had all but dissolved, looked for buyers, and found the U.S. which was seeking a Caribbean base from which it could protect the Panama Canal. Eventually a great deal was struck between the two powers—$25 million for three islands. Though St. Croix was hard hit by Hurricane Hugo in 1989, islanders threw themselves body and soul into renovating the tourist facilities.

People

St. Croix's population stands at about 55,000; the majority are descendants of African slaves who toiled on the many sugar plantations that dotted the island in the 18th and 19th centuries. The sugarcane industry died off in the 1930s—today the island's biggest employer is the Hess Oil Refinery, located on the south coast, just east of the airport. Crucians all speak English—the official language—though Spanish is a common tongue. Music you're apt to hear while out at night includes calypso, reggae and steel pan bands. There's also *quelbe*, a uniquely Crucian musical style that comes from the corrugated gourds scraped for percussion—these scratch bands are found in Frederiksted clubs and during special church events or street fairs. During Carnival and at hotel theme parties, you're likely to spot a Mocko Jumbie, an "elevated spirit" on 10- to 20-foot stilts dressed in bright colors. Despite the festive surroundings, many islanders wear a chip on their shoulders, particularly when the subject of St. Thomas comes up. It's not just because the smaller island is the USVI seat of government, but because Crucians feel it gets favored treatment—from tourists, travel agents, cruise ship operators—you name it. Dare to ask a cabbie about local politics and you'll quickly understand why the unofficial motto of the Department of Tourism is "stop whining."

Beaches

All beaches on St. Croix are public and free of charge, but if you go to a beach that is maintained by the resident hotel, you may have to pay a small fee for facilities. Lying 1.5 miles off northeast St. Croix, **Buck Island**, an 850-acre national monument, has one of the best beaches "on" St. Croix, reachable by boat from Christiansted; the six-mile trip takes 45 minutes to an hour. Some concessionaires that offer sail or motorboat tours also include a picnic lunch and an overland hike to the island's 400-foot summit with terrific views. Turtles also lay their eggs there. **Cane Bay** also has a fine beach on the island's north side. Other beaches can be found at **Protestant Cay**, **Davis Bay**, **Cramer Park** on the east shore, and **Frederiksted Beach** to the north of town. The latter two have changing facilities and showers. Surfing is best on the north coast, and you'll find great shells on the west coast, from **Northside Beach** to **Ham's Bay**, as well as on **Sprat Hall Beach**.

St. Croix offers a splendid, immense wall, a trench that stretches the island's northern coast from Christiansted west past Maroon Ridge and some say rivals similar attractions off Grand Turk and the Caymans. The wall alone makes St. Croix the best dive destination in the U.S. Virgins. In particular, two areas along the northern coast, **Cane Bay** and **Salt River Canyon**, are among the best locations in the Eastern Caribbean; the first is a prime access to the sheer wall (and accessible from shore), the latter is an unusual formation in a sprawling undersea valley. The original **Frederiksted Pier**, famed for its profusion of sea horses and other macro life, is no more. In a controversial decision, it was torn down and replaced by another facility which is better able to accommodate cruise ship needs. Fortunately, sea life, including the delightful seahorses, is slowly regenerating on the new pilings and in a few years it may almost mirror the old site. Although a decent site showcasing four wrecks has been created off Butler Bay, if you're a sunken ship devotee, you'll want to head for St. Thomas or the British Virgins. St. Croix's visibility averages 75 feet year-round but can approach 100 feet in the summer. First-time snorkelers have been delighted for years by the underwater trail at **Buck Island**, just north of St. Croix's eastern tip, but the never-ending crowds can be a bit overwhelming. Additionally, Buck Island's conditions vary, causing jaded snorkelers to shrug off the site if visibility is poor or if fish are percolating elsewhere. Other good snorkeling sites are **Cane Bay**, **Green Cay** (off Chenay Bay), and **Grapetree Beach** (near the eastern tip).

Dive Shops

Anchor Dive Center

> *Salt River Bay;* ☎ *(800) 532-3483 or (340) 778-1522.*
> Centrally located within ten minutes of all wall sites; two-tank dive $65. Nightly excursions to Salt River Canyon for superb nocturnal dives, $55. Limits boats to six divers. PADI Five Star dive center with courses from beginner to instructor.

Cane Bay Dive Shop

> *Cane Bay;* ☎ *(340) 773-9913.*

Shore dives available in front of the shop to St. Croix's wall (two dives, $52.50 including all equipment). Two-tank dive from Zodiacs, $70. PADI affiliated.

Dive Experience PADI

Christiansted; ☎ (800) 235-9047 or (340) 773-3307.
A PADI Five Star and Instructor Development Center. Fish-feeding dives to Chez Barge, which features sociable morays and barracudas. Two-tank dive $70, including all equipment. Custom videos of your dive, $75, or you may rent video equipment.

V.I. Divers

Christiansted; ☎ (800) 544-5911 or (340) 773-6045.
PADI five-star facility (handles NAUI referrals) and the first shop on St. Croix (25 years old), Maximum group size, 12. Two-tank dive, $75. Resort course, $95. Snorkel trips to Green Cay, $35.

On Foot

It doesn't have St. Thomas' cosmopolitan infrastructure nor St. John's well-established National Park system. Neither fish nor fowl, St. Croix embraces a more environmentally conscious use of its interior. But its recently anointed **Salt River Bay National Park** lacks the funds to develop a trail system, and there is, so far, little organization of the paths and dirt roads which lead through the rainforest and hills surrounding **Blue Mountain** (the island's highest, 1096 feet). Interestingly, from afar, the island's fledgling environmental movement seems to be an outgrowth of community concerns, particularly the island's beautification program (originating from Hurricane Hugo) and a new recycling program (due to a landfill approaching capacity). It would appear that the island will soon be diversifying its forest management to include eco-tourism.

Trekking Tours

St. Croix Environmental Association

Christiansted; ☎ (340) 773-1989.
Recently organized nonprofit provides guided nature hikes to East End Beaches, Salt River Bay and the rainforest. Tours average three hours and leave every morning; $20.

What Else to See

St. Croix's two large towns are Christiansted and Frederiksted; most cruise ships dock at the latter. Christiansted, on the north coast, is the more developed of the two. The town is a real charmer with its bright, shutter-accented buildings; even the trash cans are whimsically painted. A walking tour should include a visit to Fort Christiansvaern, built by the Danes in the 1700s, and a stop at the Steeple Building, another 18th century Danish structure with good exhibits on the island's past.

Frederiksted, on the island's western end, also has an impressive fort (Fort Frederik) and an excellent aquarium. The town's shady streets are home to lovely Victorian houses and 19th-century churches.

You won't want to miss a drive along Mahogany Road, which winds through the island's rainforest, home of wild lilies, yellow cedar trees, wild parakeets and mountain doves. At St. Croix Leap, located amidst the forest, craftspeople build fine furniture from mahogany. It's an interesting spot to stop and take a look.

Other don't misses include St. George's Village and the Whim Greathouse, both impressive with their lovely gardens and vintage structures.

Historical Sites

Fort Christiansvaern ★★

Christiansted, ☎ *(340) 773-1460.*
Hours open: 8 a.m.–5 p.m.
This fort was built by the Danes in 1738 and rebuilt after hurricane damage in 1772. Its five rooms are decorated as they were in the 1840s. The admission charge (free for those under 16) includes entry to the Steeple Building. The fort's newest attraction is the St. Croix Police Museum. Created by Lt. Elton Lewis, a 20-year veteran of the St. Croix Police Department, the idea behind the museum is to "promote high morale" and esprit de corps among police officers. Exhibits include weapons, photos, artifacts, and an old police motorcycle from St. Croix's past. General admission: $2.

Fort Frederik ★★

Emancipation Park, Frederiksted, ☎ *(340) 772-2021.*
Hours open: 8:30 a.m.–4:30 p.m.
This fort dates back to 1760, and is now an art gallery and museum. It is best known as the site where on July 3, 1848, Governor-General Peter Von Scholten freed the Danish West Indies slaves, though it may also be the first place that a foreign nation saluted the 13 U.S. states, in 1776.

Steeple Building ★★

Christiansted, ☎ *(340) 773-1460.*
Built by the Danish in 1734, this was their first Lutheran church, called the Church of Lord God of Sabaoth. Deconsecrated in 1831, it served as everything from a bakery to a school, and is now under the auspices of the U.S. National Park Service. Interesting exhibits tell the island's history, with emphasis on Native Americans and African Americans. The entry fee includes admission to Fort Christiansvaern. General admission: $2.

Museums and Exhibits

Estate Whim Plantation Museum ★★★★

Centerline Road, Frederiksted, ☎ (340) 772-0598.
Hours open: 10 a.m.–4 p.m.

This partially restored sugar plantation gives a good look at what life was like in St. Croix in the 1800s. The handsome oblong great house, built of lime, stone and coral and boasting walls three feet thick, is beautifully restored and filled with antiques. Whim is unique in that it is built in a European style (rather than West Indian), with a dry air moat circling its base designed to keep perishables cool in the basement. The grounds also include the cookhouse where you can feast on Johnny cakes ($1 each, but the old woman who cooks them has obviously had her share of camera-laden tourists—she forbids pictures, and charges another dollar for the recipe), a woodworking shop, a windmill, and an apothecary. The giftshop is excellent. Admission for children, $1. General admission: $5.

St. Croix Aquarium ★★

On the waterfront, Frederiksted, ☎ (340) 773-8995.
Hours open: 11 a.m.–4 p.m.

Opened in 1990 by marine biologist Lonnie Kaczmarsky, this aquarium displays some 40 species of marine animals and more than 100 species of invertebrates. What makes it really unique is its "recycling" of sea life—after doing a stint in the tanks, creatures are released back to the open seas. Kaczmarsky is passionate on preserving the ocean environment; this a good place to pick up hints before diving and snorkeling on how to minimize your impact. General admission: $3.

Parks and Gardens

St. George Village Botanical Gardens ★★★

St. George Estate, Kingshill, ☎ (340) 772-3874.
Hours open: 9 a.m.–5 p.m.

Built among the ruins of a 19th-century sugarcane plantation workers' village, this little slice of paradise is not to be missed. The 17 acres were the site of an Arawak settlement dating to A.D. 100. Stop by the Great Hall to pick up a brochure for a self-guided walking tour, then feast your senses on the lovely gardens, which include 850 species of trees and plants. Each ecosystem of St. Croix is represented, from rainforest to desert. The grounds also include restored buildings from the plantation era, including workers' cottages, storehouses and a blacksmith shop. General admission: $5; $1 for children.

Tours

Buck Island Reef National Monument ★★★★★

Buck Island

No trip to St. Croix is complete without a visit to Buck Island, a US National Monument located three miles northeast of the mainland. It's a mile-long volcanic rock comprising some 300 acres with hiking trails, an observation tower, picnic tables, and a picture-perfect beach. The real attraction, however, is its surrounding 550 acres of underwater coral gardens, home to more than 250 species of fish. This is a true snorkelers' paradise, with a marked underwater trail for neophytes to follow.

Fielding   **ST. CROIX**

CRUISING ST. CROIX

Its Danish heritage is on display in the ornate buildings of Christiansted, making St. Croix one of the most picturesque—and in some ways the most European—of the Virgin Islands.

Sandy Point National Wildlife Refuge

This is one of only two nesting grounds for the leatherback turtle in U.S. waters. The 1000-pound females come here from March to June to lay their eggs in the sand.

Frederiksted

Sandy Point

Alexander Hamilton Airport

Fort Frederick

This fort marks the site where the slaves of the Danish West Indies were freed by Governor-General Peter van Scholten in 1848. Today, the fort houses a museum and an art gallery.

Mahogany Road

St. Croix's Route 76 runs through the heart of the island's rain forest, and leads to Ham's Bluff Road (Route 63), a west-coast route that offers water views. You can tour Estate Mount Washington Plantation while on Ham's Bluff Road.

Whim Great House

This restored great house is one of the Caribbean's best. The buildings include a windmill, cook house and the manor, as well as a waterless moat to direct cooler air into the house. Inside the unusual oval-shaped great house, the furnishings reflect the elegance of 18th century colonial life.

Judith's Fancy

The tower once graced a 17th century château where a governor of the Knights of Malta once lived. The name "Judith" was the name of a woman who was buried on the plantation. Today, you can admire the sea views from the ruins.

Buck Island Reef National Monument

This 176-acre, volcanic islet is surrounded by 700 acres of underwater coral gardens. The rocky island serves as pelican rookery. The circular dive trail takes 45 minutes to swim. Signs posted on the ocean floor at various depths identify the types of coral you will see.

Christiansted Harbor

Christiansted

Steeple Building

Christiansted is filled with distinctive, gaily painted Dutch-style buildings. Named a historic landmark, the Steeple Building has a maroon-and-white facade, and houses a national-park museum inside.

Great Pond Bay

East Pt.

Fort Christianvaern

Built by Danish colonists beginning in 1738, the fort protected the harbor, but the structure was severely damaged by a 1772 hurricane. Today, this is considered the best-preserved Danish-built fort in the Caribbean.

St. George Village Botanical Gardens

Set on an old sugar plantation, this 17-acre garden features re-creations of the island's major vegetative zones, including a cactus grove that is home to the unusual "Turk's Head" cactus.

Several operators will take you there as part of their half- and full-day snorkeling trips: **Big Beard's Adventure Tours** ☎ *(340) 773-4482*, **Diva** ☎ *(340) 778-3161*, **Llewellyn's Charter** ☎ *(340) 773-9027*, **Teroro II** ☎ *(340) 773-3161*, and **Mile Mark Water Sports** ☎ *(340) 773-2628*.

Cruzan Rum Factory   ★★

West Airport Road, Frederiksted, ☎ *(340) 772- 0799.*
Hours open: 9 a.m.–4:15 p.m.

Though sugarcane is no longer grown in the Virgins, molasses is imported from other islands for processing into rum at this, the region's largest distillery. The factory tour is moderately informative and you get to sample the wares at its conclusion, but don't count this as one of the island's more interesting sites, particularly if you've toured a rum factory on another island. General admission: $3.

Guided Tours

Various locations, Frederiksted.

If you choose to leave the driving to someone else, these companies provide guided tours of St. Croix's highlights. Be sure to check in advance if admission charges to attractions are included in the rates. **Eagle Tours** ☎ *(340) 778-3313*, **St. Croix Safari Tours** ☎ *(340) 773-6700*, and **Travellers Tours** ☎ *(340) 778-1636*. **St. Croix Environmental Association** offers three-hour island hikes in the rainforest, to Salt River Bay, or along the Estate Mt. Washington beaches ☎ *(340) 773-1989*. For a birds-eye view of the island, call **St. Croix Aviation** ☎ *(340) 778-0090*, which offers sightseeing flights.

Salt River Bay National Historical Park   ★★★

Route 80 near Route 75, Frederiksted.

These 912 tropical acres were added to the national park system under the Bush Administration. The park remains in a pristine condition and is home to many threatened and endangered plant and animal species. It is the largest remaining mangrove forest in the Virgin Islands and a great spot for birdwatching. The site includes an old earthen fort, an Indian ceremonial ball court, and burial grounds. This is also the only documented site on U.S. soil on which Christopher Columbus landed. His ill-fated "discovery" in 1493 led to a skirmish with Carib Indians, with fatalities on both sides.

Sports

St. Croix is a great island for active types—the golf and diving here are among the best in the Eastern Caribbean, but mountain biking, horseback riding and tennis are among the many other offerings rolled out for visitors. For tennis buffs, look no further than the Buccaneer Hotel, which has eight championship courts, with regular round-robin tournaments, matches and instructional clinics. **Snorkeling** is also good, particularly at Buck Island.

Bicycling

Easily the best cycling destination in the Virgins, St. Croix is less hilly and more spread out than its neighbors and, outside Christiansted, road traffic generally moves at a leisurely pace. **St. Croix Bike and Tours** provides excellent tours of the island's west end—including leisurely rides along the coast or more challenging excursions into the rainforest. The well-organized outfit integrates history, ecology and splendid scenery into their enjoyable tours. Half-day tours are $35, all-day rentals run $25 ☎ *(340) 772-2343.*

Golf

Duffers have two excellent choices on St. Croix. **Carambola** is one of the region's finest courses, a gorgeous, par-72 course designed by Robert Trent Jones and located on rolling hills above the Westin Carambola. Greens fees are $78, or $45 after 2 p.m. ☎ *(340) 778-0797.* Just outside Christiansted is the shoreside **Buccaneer's** course, a challenging 18 holes that was upgraded recently; greens fees are $40 ☎ *(340) 773-2100.* The **Reef Club at Tegue Bay** is the nine-hole budget choice; greens fees are $10, or $18 for 18 holes ☎ *(340) 773-8844.*

Horseback Riding

Located just north of Frederiksted, **Paul and Jill's Equestrian Stables** is well-regarded for high-quality horses. The stable takes folks out for two-hour trail rides through the rainforest and past Danish ruins. Jill's family has lived on St. Croix for some 200 years. Two-hour rides are $50, and reservations are essential ☎ *(340) 772-2880.*

Watersports

For deep-sea fishing: **St. Croix Marin** ☎ *(340) 773-7165,* **Captain Pete's Sportfishing** ☎ *(340) 773-1123,* and **Cruzan Divers** ☎ *(340) 772-3701.* For cruises and boating, try **Mile Mark Chaters** ☎ *(340) 773-2628,* **Sundance** ☎ *(340) 778-9650,* **Llwewellyn's Charter** ☎ *(340) 773-9027,* **Bilinda Charters** ☎ *(340) 773-1641,* and **Junie Bomba's** ☎ *(340) 772-2482.* For windsurfing: **Lisa Neuburger Windsurfing Center** ☎ *(340) 778-8312* and **Minstral School** ☎ *(340) 773-4810.*

ST. CROIX

Where to Stay

Fielding's Highest Rated Hotels in St. Croix

★★★★	Buccaneer Hotel	$150–$280
★★★★	Villa Madeleine	$200–$325
★★★★	Westin Carambola Beach Resort	$185–$370
★★★	Club St. Croix	$110–$195
★★★	Hibiscus Beach Hotel	$120–$190
★★★	Hotel on the Cay	$95–$160
★★★	Tamarind Reef Hotel	$145–$180

Fielding's Best Beach Hotels in St. Croix

★★★★	Buccaneer Hotel	$150–$280
★★★	Hibiscus Beach Hotel	$120–$190
★★★★	Westin Carambola Beach Resort	$185–$370
★★	On the Beach Resort	$65–$250
★	Cottages by the Sea	$70–$115

Fielding's Best Value Hotels in St. Croix

★★★	Hotel on the Cay	$95–$160
★★	Hilty House Inn	$70–$110
★	Cottages by the Sea	$70–$115
★★	Pink Fancy Hotel	$65–$120
★★★★	Buccaneer Hotel	$150–$280

Accommodations on St. Croix are varied and inviting. A number of hotels are located in Christiansted but there are no beaches here, other than on tiny Protestant Cay a few hundred feet offshore (where Hotel on the Cay is located). Instead, a couple miles west and east of town are beaches with small hotels—the island's oldest resort, **The Buccaneer**, has no less than three beaches for its guests to enjoy. But a triple-digit rate card is not a prerequisite for easy beach access. Just south of Frederiksted is a long, silky ribbon of sand, and two inexpensive properties—**On the Beach** and **Cottages by the Sea**—that step right onto the sand. A free *St. Croix Planner* is available from the **St. Croix Hotel and Tourism Association**, providing photos and additional information for most island properties ☎ *(800) 524-2026.*

When booking your room, verify what service charge and energy surcharge may be tacked onto your final bill. There is no rule-of-thumb on St. Croix— some properties waive the fees, while others add up to a 10 percent service charge and/or a $3 per person, per night energy surcharge.

ST. CROIX

Hotels and Resorts

Two luxury resorts top the list. **The Buccaneer** is an island institution overseen by the Armstrong family for 50 years—rooms vary greatly but, in terms of service and on-site activities, the Buccaneer is one of the region's best values. The **Westin Carambola** is a well-run operation, but geared more for meeting, incentive and convention trade—however, the wonderful, oversized rooms at this resort are both handsome and plush. At press time, it was announced that the Hugo-bashed former Divi Hotel, the one resort located on the island's south shore (near the eastern tip), will be rebuilt as the 146-room **Grapetree Shores Hotel**, potentially with a casino, for a late 1998 debut.

Anchor Inn $85–$145 ★★

Christiansted, ☎ *(800) 524-2030, (340) 773-4000, FAX (340) 773-4408.*
Single: $85–$130. Double: $95–$145.
This small hotel is set in a quiet courtyard on the waterfront in the heart of Christiansted's National Historic District. Rooms have colorful rattan furnishings, cable TV, refrigerators, air conditioning and telephones; most have porches as well. The on-site restaurant features American and West Indian fare. Other facilities include a lounge, pool and pool bar, tour desk, and watersports facility on the boardwalk. There's lots to see and do within walking distance. 30 rooms. Credit cards: A, MC, V.

Buccaneer Hotel $150–$525 ★★★★

Gallows Bay, ☎ *(800) 255-3881, (340) 773-2100, FAX (340) 778-8215.*
Single: $150–$260. Double: $170–$280. Suites Per Day: $225–$525.
Venerable yet upbeat, the Buccaneer commemorates its 50th anniversary in 1998, making it the longest running family-owned resort in the Caribbean. Set on a landscaped peninsula and encompassing 340 acres with three fine beaches, this comely property is a former sugar estate two miles east of Christiansted. Room style, size and location vary—the least expensive are standard and superior units in the main building (where Alexander Hamilton lived as a child); each is comfortable and newly renovated for 1998. There are family cottages, and a row of lovely oceanfront suites that curl along a bluff between two of the beaches. But the new Doubloon units are choicest of all: a cluster of huge deluxe suites with acres of marble and polished granite, sitting rooms with picture windows, plush fabrics and wide terraces that breathe in the view. One of Buccaneer's calling cards is its wide array of sports

facilities, including an 18-hole championship golf course, eight tennis courts, two pools, a two-mile jogging trail, a health club with sauna, and watersports on the beach. But the resort's best asset is the hands-on family management by ninth-generation Crucians who aren't resting on their laurels. Join Elizabeth Armstrong on one of her weekly nature walks and you'll get a dose of history from a true island insider. Rates include full breakfast daily. 132 rooms. Credit cards: A, D, MC, V.

Frederiksted Hotel $75–$105 ★★

Frederiksted, ☎ *(800) 524-2025, (340) 772-0500, FAX (340) 778-4009.*
E-mail: resortstx@worldnet.att.net.
Single: $75–$95. Double: $85–$105.

This four-story modern inn hotel overlooks the relaxed Frederiksted harbor, and what it lacks in style it makes up for with good rates and a convenient location. All rooms are air-conditioned and comfortable enough, with satellite TV, mini-fridge, microwave and wet bar. The seaview rooms are worth the extra $10 per night. There's a restaurant, bar and pool, and a good beach is within 10-minutes' walk. 40 rooms. Credit cards: A, MC, V.

Hibiscus Beach Hotel $120–$190 ★★★

La Grande Princess, ☎ *(800) 442-0121, (340) 773-4042, FAX (340) 773-7668.*
Single: $120–$180. Double: $130–$190.

This well-run small hotel offers accommodations in two-story buildings that line a palm-studded beach two miles west of Christiansted. All have ocean views off the balcony or patio, and are on the plain side, though comfortable; a couple rooms are handicap-accessible and there are also two-bedroom efficiencies. There's a pretty pool on-site, as well as a restaurant and lounge. The beach is excellent and this property's best feature—watersports are found nearby. Nice and small, with the feel of a mini-resort but not the cost. 37 rooms. Credit cards: A, D, MC, V.

Hotel Caravelle $82–$300 ★★

Christiansted, ☎ *(800) 524-0410, (340) 773-0687, FAX (340) 778-7004.*
Single: $82–$132. Double: $92–$142. Suites Per Day: $225–$300.

This waterfront hotel is in Christiansted's downtown historic district, overlooking the bay. Guestrooms are comfortable and pleasant, with modern furnishings and colorful fabrics. There's a pool on-site and watersports are available nearby. The waterfront restaurant and bar are lively and popular with boaters. A good in-town choice. 43 rooms. Credit cards: A, D, MC, V.

Hotel on the Cay $95–$160 ★★★

Christiansted, ☎ *(800) 524-2035, (340) 773-2035, FAX (340) 773-7046.*
E-mail: hotelonthecay@worldnet.att.net.
Single: $95–$150. Double: $105–$160.

Located on Protestant Cay in Christiansted Harbor, a two-minute ferry ride from the mainland, this imaginatively landscaped hotel offers great seclusion. Guest rooms are comfortable and pleasing, with extras like coffeemakers, TVs, and private terraces with water views. The grounds are dotted with waterfalls, canals, and bridges, lending a tropical feel. Recreational options include a pool and watersports on the small beach. Nice, if you don't mind the isolated location, but the free ferry service into town runs until after midnight. 55 rooms. Credit cards: A, DC, MC, V.

King's Alley Hotel $79–$158 ★★

Christiansted, ☎ *(800) 843-3574, (340) 773-0103, FAX (340) 773-4431.*
Single: $79–$148. Double: $84–$158.

Located at the Christiansted seaplane dock and overlooking the new King's Alley Walk shopping area, this hotel recently added 14 very smart rooms next door to the existing three-story complex of rooms. The older units are being upgraded for 1998—all have ocean-facing balconies, mini-fridge and air conditioning. The new rooms were designed by Twila Wilson (famous for her USVI Olympic costumes, and an Architectural Digest cover) and intermingle Asian elements with West Indian: vivid batiks, mahogany and teak furnishings, and king-size four-poster beds—very attractive. A splash pool is available, or the beach at Protestant Cay is a three-minute ferry ride away. Plenty of shopping and dining within a few minutes' walk. 35 rooms. Credit cards: A, DC, D, MC, V.

Tamarind Reef Hotel $145–$180 ★★★

Green Cay Marina, ☎ *(800) 619-0014, (340) 773-4455, FAX (340) 773-3989.*
Website: www.usvi.net/hotel/tamarind. E-mail: tamarind@usvi.net.
Single: $145–$180. Double: $145–$180.

Located three miles east of Christiansted, this hotel was completely rebuilt in 1993. The atmosphere here is laid-back and friendly, thanks in no small part to the hospitable owners, Dick and Marcy Pelton. Guest rooms have either a patio or balcony and all come equipped with ceiling fan, air conditioners, TV, radio, refrigerators, coffeemakers, hairdryers and bathrobes. The downstairs units have full kitchens; the accommodations on the second floor are larger, but lack the cooking facilities. On-site amenities include tennis, a large pool, watersports, a snack bar, two small beaches and Green Cay Marina, which has slips for 144 boats, a dive shop and a gourmet restaurant. 46 rooms. Credit cards: A, MC, V.

Westin Carambola Beach Resort $185–$370 ★★★★

Davis Bay, ☎ *(800) 228-3000, (340) 778-3800, FAX (340) 778-1682.*
Single: $185–$370. Double: $185–$370.

Situated on a 28-acre spread on St. Croix's north shore, this former Rockresort had a rocky birth, but may finally be hitting its stride a decade later as part of the Westin family. Guestrooms are found in two-story, red-roofed villas dotting the property and surrounded by lush landscaping. The suite-like rooms are dark but quite beautiful, with deep red mahogany tones and Mexican clay tiles, sitting areas, minibars, lavish bathrooms and screened porches; they are among the most attractive "standard" accommodations in the Caribbean. Each unit is essentially identical—the price difference is based on location only, but all are just a minute or two from the sand (second-floor rooms have better views and cathedral ceilings). Facilities include an excellent 18-hole golf course, a pool, four tennis courts, exercise room, three restaurants, two bars and watersports, including a dive shop. Though pretty, the size of the beach is unreliable, and check to see if you'll be sharing the hotel with one of the conventions that swing through regularly. Carambola's remote location is a plus for most, but note that Christiansted is 30 minutes away. 151 rooms. Credit cards: A, D, MC, V.

Apartments and Condominiums

Self-catering is easy on St. Croix, and most properties—from private homes to condos—are available with maid service. Supermarkets are modern and well-stocked, and fresh local fruits and vegetables are easy to obtain. St. Croix has several agents that deal in villa, condo and apartment rentals. **Island Villas** represents 35 island properties; off-season rates in a one-bedroom villa with full kitchen and a private pool start at about $1300 week in low season ☎ *(800) 626-4512* or *(340) 773-8821*. To rent **Horizons**, the four-bedroom private villa located on the grounds of Carambola Beach Resort, call New Jersey-based **The Collection**; the outfit represents a number of island properties in addition to this posh home ☎ *(609) 751-2413*.

Cane Bay Reef Club   **$90–$230**   ★★

Cane Bay, ☎ *(800) 253-8534, (340) 778-2966, FAX (340) 778-2966.*
Single: $90–$230. Double: $90–$230.

This family-run property provides good value for money in a dramatic location atop coral bluffs, about 25 minutes from either Christiansted or Frederiksted. All units are spacious and bright one-bedroom apartments with modern kitchenettes (some are full kitchens), tiled balconies and ceiling fans. There's a bar and good-sized saltwater pool on-site; the beach is a three-minute walk. Although several restaurants are within walking distance, the location is remote enough that you'll appreciate a rental car. 9 rooms. Credit cards: A, MC, V.

Chenay Bay Beach Resort   **$150–$235**   ★★

Estate Green Cay, ☎ *(800) 548-4457, (340) 773-2918, FAX (340) 773-2918.*
Website: www.excursion.com/chenay.
Single: $150–$235. Double: $150–$235.

This cottage colony is located on an isolated 30-acre estate three miles east of Christiansted. The West Indian-style cottages are scattered about well-landscaped grounds; all have kitchenettes and patios, and most are air-conditioned. The grounds, surrounded by a 14-acre wildlife preserve, include a pool, two tennis courts, watersports (snorkeling and kayaking are free), the beach, and a casual restaurant and bar. Nice and relaxing, but you'll want a car to get around. 50 rooms.
Credit cards: A, MC, V.

Club St. Croix   **$110–$195**   ★★★

Christiansted, ☎ *(800) 635-1533, (340) 773-4800, FAX (340) 778-4009.*
E-mail: resortstx@worldnet.att.net.
Single: $110–$195. Double: $110–$195.

This friendly beachfront condominium resort is one mile out of Christiansted. Accommodations include well-furnished junior suites with queen-size murphy beds and one- and two-bedroom apartments, all with full kitchens, cable TV, private balconies, ceiling fans and air conditioning. Recreational choices are good for a condo operation, with three tennis courts, a large pool, Jacuzzi, some watersports, a catamaran and a bar and restaurant. 54 rooms. Credit cards: A, D, MC, V.

Colony Cove   **$140–$195**   ★★

Christiansted, ☎ *(800) 524-2025, (340) 773-9150, FAX (340) 778-4009.*
E-mail: resortstx@worldnet.att.net.
Single: $140–$195. Double: $140–$195.

Set on the beach one mile from Christiansted, this condominium complex offers two-bedroom, two-bath units with full kitchens, individual laundry facilities, private balconies and ocean views. Each is privately owned and decorated, but all can be counted on for clean, comfortable living. The premises includes a restaurant, two tennis courts, a business center and a pool. Watersports await on the wide beach. 60 rooms. Credit cards: A, D, MC, V.

Cottages by the Sea   **$70–$115**   ★

Frederiksted, ☎ (800) 323-7252, (340) 772-0495, FAX (340) 772-1753.
Single: $70–$115. Double: $70–$115.
Located on the western end of the island just outside Frederiksted, this basic complex sits right on the beach. The 20 units are housed in blocky cottages; each is simply furnished and has a kitchenette, patio and air conditioning. Three large patios are situated on the beach for sunning and barbecueing. No children under 8 at this agreeable spot. If instant beach access is paramount and frills are unnecessary, you'll hardly find a better buy in the Virgins. No other facilities—town is a ten-minute walk, but a car is handy. 20 rooms. Credit cards: A, D, MC, V.

Gentle Winds Resort   **$150–$325**   ★ ★

Salt River Bay, ☎ (800) 537-6242, (340) 778-3400, FAX (340) 778-8086.
Website: www.pivar-stcroix.com. E-mail: jeanferry@worldnet.att.net.
Single: $150–$325. Double: $150–$325.
Set on a secluded beach four miles northwest of Christiansted, this contemporary condo complex offers two- and three-bedroom units. All are air-conditioned, have two or three baths, full kitchens, VCRs, telephones, and nice sea views from screened-in porches. There's a pool, two tennis courts, games room, and a beach bar, but you're on your own for meals. Ideal for families. 66 rooms.

On the Beach Resort   **$65–$250**   ★ ★

Frederiksted, ☎ (800) 524-2018, (340) 772-1205, FAX (340) 772-1757.
Single: $65–$250. Double: $65–$250.
The name isn't about the 1959 end-of-the-world movie epic, but in reference to the hotel's prime location, a half-mile south of Frederiksted on a fine ribbon of white sand. On the Beach caters primarily to a gay and lesbian clientele—it is perhaps the Caribbean's only gay-owned beachfront property—and a low-key, amiable atmosphere predominates throughout the day (it is not a pick-up scene for singles). Accommodations are not elaborate, but spacious and tropically furnished; most have kitchenette and some a balcony. Six new villas have one or two bedrooms and complete kitchens, across the street from the beach. The premises include two pools and a Jacuzzi, but little else, so a car is handy (you can walk to Frederiksted in about 10 minutes). Rates include continental breakfast. An excellent beachfront value, and straight-friendly, too. 20 rooms. Credit cards: D, MC, V.

Schooner Bay Resort   **$110–$150**   ★ ★

Christiansted, ☎ (800) 524-2025, (340) 773-9150, FAX (340) 778-4009.
E-mail: resortstx@worldnet.att.net.
Single: $110–$150. Double: $110–$150.
You can walk to downtown Christiansted from this three-story condominium resort, which overlooks the harbor. The two-bedroom units are fairly plush, with

full kitchens, living and dining areas, VCRs, radios, telephones, washer/dryers, and private balconies. There's a pool, Jacuzzi, and tennis court on-site, but you'll have to look elsewhere for meals or a beach. A lot of space for the money. 40 rooms. Credit cards: A, D, MC, V.

Villa Madeleine $200–$325   ★★★★

East End, ☎ (800) 496-7379, (340) 778-7377, FAX (340) 773-7518.
Single: $200–$325. Double: $200–$325.

This deluxe operation is set on a quiet ridge between two beaches, some 15 minutes from Christiansted, with sweeping views of Buck Island and Duggins Reef. Accommodations are in beautiful one- and two-bedroom villas that include sitting rooms, full modern kitchens, four-poster beds and chaise lounges in the bedrooms, two full bathrooms, and—best of all—each has its own small private pool. The on-site restaurant draws raves for its gorgeous decor and smashing food (not open in summer or fall), and there's also a bar, billiards room and tennis court. This is one of St. Croix's more luxurious properties—the only drawback is the distance to the beach, a quarter-mile down the hill. 43 rooms. Credit cards: A, D, MC, V.

Waves at Cane Bay $85–$195   ★★

Cane Bay, ☎ (800) 545-0603, (340) 778-1805, FAX (340) 778-4945.
Single: $85–$195. Double: $85–$195.

Located on the north shore a short walk from Cane Bay Beach, this friendly operation offers large studios with a kitchen or kitchenette, screened porches, ceiling fans and TVs. Only some are air-conditioned, but all are quite comfortable (upper rooms have cathedral ceilings). The pool is a natural sea-fed grotto and the snorkeling is great off the beach. Divers will be in heaven as the Cane Bay Wall is just 100 yards off-shore and the inn has its own dive shop. There's a bar and a popular restaurant (and a couple others nearby), but you'll probably want a car, as this spot is somewhat remote. 12 rooms. Credit cards: A, D, MC, V.

Inns

Inns are a special option on St. Croix—all of them with unique character and attributes. An umbrella organization, **Small Inns of St. Croix**, represents eight owner-managed properties on the island, including some that are listed in "Apartments and Condominiums," and another, **Seaview Farm Inn**, that hopes to open for the 1997–98 season; they can provide brochures and information ☎ (888) INN-USVI.

Hilty House Inn $70–$185   ★★

Christiansted, ☎ (340) 773-2594, FAX (340) 773-2594.
Single: $70–$85. Double: $95–$110. Suites Per Day: $100–$185.

For sheer panache, few Caribbean bed-and-breakfasts can top Hilty House, perched atop a hill a mile outside Christiansted amid the ruins of a 1739 rum distillery. Photos of Hilty's sweeping "great room" with its enormous old-fashioned fireplace have been featured in National Geographic and other magazines. Stunning hand-painted Florentine tiles adorn many of the walls and continue into two of the four standard guest rooms, each individually decorated and with private baths, but no air conditioning. There are also two one-bedroom cottages with kitchenettes. TV can be watched in the library, and there's a 40-foot swimming pool surrounded by deck with lovely views. The rates for standard guest rooms include continental breakfast; there is little within walking distance so a car is a good idea. 6 rooms.

Pink Fancy Hotel   **$65–$120**   ★ ★

Christiansted, ☎ (800) 524-2045, (340) 773-8460, FAX (340) 773-6448.
Website: www.pinkfancy.com.
Single: $65–$90. Double: $65–$120.

Character is what distinguishes this Cruzan classic opened in 1948 by an ex-Ziegfeld Follies girl, and now run by antique lovers specializing in Caribbean collectibles (the good stuff is in their house next door). With one section dating back to 1780 and now listed on the National Historic Trust, the 13 rooms are spread in four hillside buildings surrounding a tiled pool, each named after different estates on the island—Hard Labor and Morning Star are perhaps the nicest. Four "commercial" rooms at street level are less fancy and provide good value; all have simple West Indian decor, air conditioning and a kitchenette. The grounds are brimming with greenery and hammocks. Note that the location on the edge of Christiansted is a bit iffy at night. Rates include continental breakfast and free drinks during the daily happy hour. 13 rooms. Credit cards: A, MC, V.

Low Cost Lodging

Since lodging is based on the scale of the American dollar, not much is to be found in the category of cheap, unless you can bear very small rooms and basic furnishings. Make sure the property is close enough to a beach or stores and restaurants if you can't afford to rent a car. **Danish Manor** takes advantage of its location in the center of Christiansted, although you'll need to take a bus to the beach. Another no-frills operation in town is **Cactus Inn** ☎ *(340) 692-9331.*

Club Comanche   **$36–$108**   ★

Christiansted, ☎ (800) 524-2066, (340) 773-0210, FAX (340) 773-0210.
Single: $36–$86. Double: $36–$86. Suites Per Day: $76–$108.

This downtown hotel dates back to 1948 and it shows—less for its historical charm than because it could really benefit from an overhaul. Guest rooms vary considerably in size, view and furnishings, even within each price category (a few actually have a modicum of character); most have air conditioning and a TV. The least expensive rooms are a fair deal, but check on their condition before you haul your luggage in. The premises include two restaurants and a saltwater swimming pool. 42 rooms. Credit cards: A, MC, V.

Danish Manor Hotel   **$49–$125**   ★

Christiansted, ☎ (800) 524-2069, (340) 773-1377, FAX (340) 773-1913.
Website: www.danishmanor.com.
Single: $49–$115. Double: $59–$125.

This downtown inn consists of an old West Indian-style manor house and a newer three-story addition. The motel-style guestrooms are small and simply furnished, but do have air conditioning, refrigerators and cable television. A pair of budget rooms offer additional savings if you don't mind a shared bathroom. There's a pool, Italian restaurant, and bar on the premises. Good value, and lots within walking distance. Rates include continental breakfast. 34 rooms. Credit cards: A, DC, D, MC, V.

Where to Eat

Fielding's Highest Rated Restaurants in St. Croix

★★★★	Greathouse, The	$18–$26
★★★★	Indies	$17–$23
★★★★	Kendrick's at Quin House	$18–$26
★★★	Blue Moon	$15–$20
★★★	Cafe du Soleil	$16–$23
★★★	Le St. Tropez	$16–$25
★★★	Top Hat	$20–$30
★★★	Waves at Cane Bay, The	$15–$22

Fielding's Most Romantic Restaurants in St. Croix

♡♡♡♡	Greathouse, The	$18–$26
♡♡♡♡	Indies	$17–$23
♡♡♡♡	Kendrick's at Quin House	$18–$26
♡♡♡♡	Le St. Tropez	$16–$25
♡♡♡♡	Waves at Cane Bay, The	$15–$22

Fielding's Best Value Restaurants in St. Croix

★★	Harvey's	$8–$10
★★★★	Indies	$17–$23
★★★★	Kendrick's at Quin House	$18–$26
★★★	Waves at Cane Bay, The	$15–$22
★★★	Blue Moon	$15–$20

St. Croix's dining scene may not aspire to the glamour of St. Thomas, but the variety and quality is still greater than on most Caribbean islands. Local food stays in the background, but callaloo (a spinach-like soup), goat water

(goat stew), and souse (a lime-seasoned pig stew) sneak onto island menus—
Harvey's is perhaps the best spot for West Indian specialties. Christiansted is
home to most of the restaurants, but don't overlook Frederiksted, where
several pleasant options are available. Two newcomers we look forward to re-
porting on for next year are the **St. Croix Chop House and Brew Pub** at King's
Alley Walk in Christiansted and **Bandana's** in Frederiksted.

Antoine's   **$$$**   ★★

58A King Street, Christiansted, ☎ *(340) 773-0263. Associated hotel: Anchor Inn.*
Lunch: 11 a.m.–2:30 p.m., entrées $7–$15.
Dinner: 6:30–9:30 p.m., entrées $14–$32.

Many visitors get their wakeup javas at this second-floor charmer in the Anchor Inn.
The breakfast menu boasts at least a dozen omelets loaded with interesting combi-
nations. But that's not all that's here—later in the day, bartenders proffer tropical
concoctions and a huge selection of beer to a lively crowd. At dinner, hearty and
tasty German and Middle-European food appears on the plates. From the terrace,
there's a great view of seagoing vessels on the wharf below. Credit cards: A, MC, V.

Blue Moon   **$$**   ★★★

17 Strand St., Frederiksted, ☎ *(340) 772-2222.*
Lunch: 11:30 a.m.–2 p.m., entrées $5–$7.
Dinner: 6–10 p.m., entrées $15–$20. Closed: Mon.

Hot jazz and hot food draw folks to this restaurant and club in a cute Victorian
building in the heart of laid-back Frederiksted. The place bustles on Thursdays with
live blues concerts, and on Friday night with jazz concerts (also at Sunday brunch).
The bistro's creative chefs are always experimenting with different cooking styles—
Cajun, Mexican and French-influenced Asian are typical—embellishing steaks, seafood, and pastas. Reservations recommended. Credit cards: A, MC, V.

Cafe du Soleil   **$$$**   ★★★

Strand Street, Frederiksted, ☎ *(340) 772-5400.*
Dinner: 6–10 p.m., entrées $16–$23. Closed: Mon., Tue.

Positioned above a beach used by nesting sea turtles, Cafe du Soleil offers a diverse
dinner menu in a colorful tropical setting. Entrees include a New York fillet stuffed
with gorgonzola and red onions, a tasty blackened tuna and a number of sprightly
pastas. Sunday brunch is a delicious affair, with buttermilk pancakes and a variety of
variations on eggs benedict. A seaside deli downstairs, Turtles, offers inexpensive
soups, salads and sandwiches for lunch, Monday–Saturday. Credit cards: A, MC, V.

Greathouse, The   **$$$**   ★★★★

Estate Teague Bay, ☎ *(340) 773-8141. Associated hotel: Villa Madeleine.*
Dinner: 6–10 p.m., entrées $18–$26.

The crowning glory of the Villa Madeleine, the romantic haven on the east end of
the island, this restaurant recalls a posh plantation house of bygone days. It's all
dolled up in butter-yellow paint, and the patio bursts with bright blooms. The primarily continental cuisine is some of the best on the island, with specialties like lamb
served with rosemary and garlic in a Barolo wine glaze and open ravioli with fresh

lobster in a sauterne sauce. The wine list is excellent. Closed during the summer and fall. Reservations recommended. Credit cards: A, DC, D, MC, V.

Harvey's $ ★★

11 Company Street, Christiansted, ☎ (340) 773-3433.
Lunch: 11:30 a.m.–4 p.m., entrées $8–$10.
Dinner: 4–9:30 p.m., entrées $8–$10. Closed: Sun.

Motherly Sarah Harvey is the chef-owner of this small West Indian dinner house and local hangout. Timid diners won't remain so for long, because Harvey likes to visit at every table, and since there's no real menu, she'll discuss what's cookin' for the evening, then trundle off to prepare it. Usually there's goat water, roast pork, barbecued chicken and ribs, or local seafood in butter sauce, and a mountain of island-grown veggies and starches—lobster runs $23. The decor could be described best as thrift-shop modern: plastic tableware and folding chairs. Open for dinner Thursday-Saturday only. Reservations recommended.

Indies $$$ ★★★★

Christiansted, ☎ (340) 692-9440.
Dinner: 6–10 p.m., entrées $17–$23.

This new favorite continues to lead the pack with adventurous Caribbean flavors spun with California flair. The restaurant is set in a historic and lush 18th-century courtyard. Chef Catherine relies heavily on locally grown produce and fresh fish to churn out mahi mahi in a shrimp-mango-coconut crust with fried rum bananas, grilled wahoo marinated in cumin and lime with tomatillo chutney, and Caribbean stew with fish, mussels, lobster and shrimp in a spicy coconut broth. Fine sushi appears Wednesday and Friday 5–8 p.m. Credit cards: A, MC, V.

Kendrick's at Quin House $$$ ★★★★

51ABC Company St., Christiansted, ☎ (340) 773-9199.
Dinner: 6–9:30 p.m., entrées $18–$26. Closed: Mon., Sun.

Dine among the antiques in the slave quarters of a restored West Indian great house or in the courtyard at one of the island's toniest eating establishments. The nattily attired and well-trained staff keeps wineglasses full and dishes cleared deftly between courses while Chef David prepares island-inspired French Continental cuisine. Highlights include a pecan-crusted roast pork loin with a homemade ginger mayonnaise, rack of lamb marinated with crushed herbs and served with roasted garlic and thyme sauce, or Caribbean lobster served over fettucine with a white wine butter sauce and tomato coulee. Reservations recommended. Credit cards: A, MC, V.

Le St. Tropez $$$ ★★★

67 King Street, Frederiksted, ☎ (340) 772-3000.
Lunch: 11:30 a.m.–2:30 p.m., entrées $8–$14.
Dinner: 6–10 p.m., entrées $16–$25. Closed: Sun.

This amiable bistro is a corner of Gallic charm in the center of the West Indian town of Frederiksted. Familiar favorites like salad Nicoise, croque monsieur and quiche are served at lunch, while the dinner menu focuses on specialties like roast duck, sweetbreads, coq au vin and frog legs served on a terrace or in a romantic dining room. The woodsy bar is a gathering place for locals. Reservations recommended.
Credit cards: A, MC, V.

Tivoli Gardens   **$$$**   ★★
39 Strand, Christiansted, ☎ (340) 773-6782.
Lunch: 11:15 a.m.–2:30 p.m., entrées $6–$15.
Dinner: 6–9:30 p.m., entrées $12–$30.
There's a fairyland of lights and greenery on the spacious porch of this popular saloon facing Christiansted Harbor. A surprising carnival of eclectic treats is prepared with aplomb—but tried and true items like fresh lobster and steak Diane are the highlights. The chocolate velvet cake is wicked on the waistline and heaven on the tastebuds, or try the six flavors of fresh ice cream including lemon cheesecake. Dinner nightly, lunch Monday–Friday. Reservations recommended. Credit cards: A, MC, V.

Top Hat   **$$$**   ★★★
52 Company Street, Christiansted, ☎ (340) 773-2346.
Dinner: 6-10 p.m., entrées $20–$30. Closed: Sun.
Probably the only true Danish restaurant in the USVIs, Top Hat has consistently pleased visitors and residents for more than two decades. The owners—chef Bent Rasmussen and his wife Hanne—run a spic-and-span operation on the top floor of a charming gingerbread trimmed-house. Specialties include crisp roast duck, fillet mignon in cracked black peppercorns, veal saltimbocca and chateaubriand for two. Reservations recommended. Credit cards: A, DC, D, MC, V.

Wahoo Willie's   **$**   ★★
44A Queen Cross, Christiansted, ☎ (340) 773-6585. Associated hotel: *Caravelle Hotel.*
Lunch: 7 a.m.–4 p.m., entrées $7–$9.
Dinner: 4–10 p.m., entrées $7–$19.
Sit surrounded by 18th-century buildings and 20th-century airline and business folk who gather for gossip and low-key deal-making in this open-air eatery known for fresh seafood, burgers and Black Angus steaks; a tank offers lobsters for $1 an ounce. There's also a Blooming Onion—a colossal fried onion that serves a whole table. You don't have to pay high prices here for unsurprising, well-prepared food and a great view of the Christiansted harbor. Credit cards: A, DC, D, MC, V.

Waves at Cane Bay, The   **$$**   ★★★
Cane Bay, ☎ (340) 778-1805. Associated hotel: *Waves at Cane Bay.*
Dinner: 5–9 p.m., entrées $15–$22. Closed: Sun.
Even if you're not staying in the Cane Bay area, this restaurant warrants a trip to the scenic spot—it is beloved by locals for its striking setting and good value. Chef Thomas James is from St. Lucia and he works magic with West Indian-style dishes, including garlic shrimp served over rice or pasta, steak au poivre, and a fresh daily catch served with a Creole sauce or lemon and butter. Credit cards: A, MC, V.

Where to Shop

Not only is St. Croix a duty-free port, but U.S. citizens can bring back $1200 worth of merchandise tax-free to the States—twice that of any other

Caribbean island (except the two other U.S. Virgins). Among the more interesting things to look for are St. Croix's signature hook bracelet, also called a Cruzian bracelet. If you wear the U-shaped hook up, it means you are "taken," if worn upside-down, you're telling the world you're available. Also popular are hurricane bracelets, which symbolize survival.

Straw hats of every style entice shoppers at the market in Christiansted.

Christiansted's quaint downtown is a good spot for shoppers; among the more interesting stores are **Tribal Threadz** *(52A Company Street,* ☎ *(340) 773-2883)*, an upscale boutique with men's and women's fashions; the **Quin House Gallery** *(51 Company Street,* ☎ *(340) 773-0404)* which features Indonesian imports, solid mahogany and hand-carved furniture and other home fashions; and **Jeltrup's Books** *(also on Company Street,* ☎ *(340) 773-1018)*, which has a great selection of works by local authors, tomes on island history and antique, used and new books. For jewelry, check out **Sonya's** *(1 Company Street,* ☎ *(340) 778-8605)*, where the popular hook bracelet originated; the **Natural Jewel** *(Queen Cross Street,* ☎ *(340) 773-3845)*, which specializes in pearl, coral, larimar and semi-precious stones; and **Little Switzerland** *(King Street,* ☎ *(340) 773-1976)*, the chain that offers high-quality pieces. For locally made crafts, try **Folk Art Traders** *(Strand Street,* ☎ *(340) 773-1900)*, **Unique Accents** *(Pan Am Pavilion,* ☎ *(340) 773-7585)*, and **America West Indian Company** *(Strand Street,* ☎ *(340) 773-7325)*.

Frederiksted has fewer shops than Christiansted, but there's some worth checking out: **Frederiksted Gallery** *(King Street,* ☎ *(340) 772-1611)*, which showcases local artists; **Me Dundo's Place** *(Strand Street,* ☎ *(340) 772-0774)*, with a good selection of island-made crafts; and **Yemaya's** *(Inner Passage Court,* ☎ *(340) 773-1169)*, with hand-dyed silks. **Vendors' Plaza**, open on cruiseship days, is an open-air market featuring island-made goods.

The gift shop at **Estate Whim Plantation** (☎ *(340) 772-0598)* is one of the best in the Caribbean and highly recommended, as is the giftshop at the **Westin Carombola Resort** *(Kingshill,* ☎ *(340) 778-1682)*. For high-quality (and dearly priced) mahogany furnishings, try **St. Croix Leap** *(Mahogany Road,* ☎ *(340) 772-0421)*, located in the rainforest.

St. Croix Directory

Arrival and Departure

American Airlines offers daily nonstop service from Miami to St. Croix. American's commuter affiliate, **American Eagle**, provides eight or more flights daily out of San Juan, Puerto Rico, allowing easy connections from throughout North America. American Eagle also has six daily nonstop flights to St. Croix out of St. Thomas. **Delta** provides daily service to St. Croix out of Atlanta, while USAir flies in daily from Philadelphia. **Carnival, Continental, Pan Am, TWA** and **United** fly into San Juan where you may connect to American Eagle.

Interisland service is provided by **LIAT**, which provides nonstop or direct service to St. Croix from Antigua, St. Kitts and St. Maarten, with connecting service from a number of other islands available through Antigua. Among the other regional carriers connecting St. Croix to Caribbean destinations are **Air Anguilla** (Anguilla, St. Thomas, St. Maarten), **Bohlke International Airways** (St. Thomas), and newcomer **Air Sunshine** (San Juan, St. Thomas).

The departure tax when leaving the U.S. Virgin Islands is $3.

Business Hours

Stores open weekdays 9 a.m.–5 p.m., some later in Christiansted. Banks generally open Monday–Thursday 9 a.m.–2:30 p.m. and Friday 9 a.m.–2 p.m. and 3:30–5 p.m.

Climate

Temperatures during the summer, cooled by eastern trade winds, keep the temperature around 82 degrees F. Brief showers also keep things cool. Winter temperatures rise to 77 degrees F. Rainiest months are September–January, and about 40 inches of rain fall per year. A light sweater is needed in winter.

Documents

No passport is required for Americans to enter the U.S. Virgin Islands, but a proof of identity is necessary when departing.

Electricity

Current runs at 110 volts at 60 cycles.

Getting Around

Taxis are expensive, but a round of griping about local politics is usually thrown in at no charge by drivers. A fare structure for the most common routes is set and carried by drivers; if you are traveling between two points that aren't part of the pre-set rates, negotiate firmly ahead of time. Sample rates for one or two passengers are $20 between Christiansted and Frederiksted, $10 from the airport to Christiansted or $8 to Frederiksted, etc. Airport vans are a little cheaper ($5 from the airport to Christiansted, or $4 to Frederiksted), but carry up to eight passengers with several different destinations, dropped off in the order most convenient to the driver. There are also **shared taxi vans** between the two main towns that are more reasonable; you'll need to allow a little more time than the 30 minutes the trip usually requires but the price is right: $1.50 each way, or $2 after 6 p.m. **Buses** between the two towns are less expensive still, with several routes running as frequently as every 30 minutes, for $1.

St. Croix is a bigger island than many visitors expect, and a **car rental** is worth exploring. Rates start at around $40 a day or $240 a week for an economy model; most of the major American firms are represented, with agencies located at the airport, in Christiansted and Frederiksted. **Olympic** is a local firm with good rates ☎ *(800) 344-5776* or *(340) 223-5789*. No special license or permit is required, but driving is on the left.

Ferry service is available to St. Thomas and daytrips are easy and popular. **Virgin Hydrofoil** ☎ *(340) 776-7417* leaves from St. Croix's Gallows Bay marina daily at 9:15 a.m. and 5 p.m. (return trips are 7:15 a.m. and 3:15 p.m.). The 75-minute crossing is $37 one-way or $70 round-trip. Scheduled seaplane service is available from King's Alley in Christiansted to Charlotte Amalie harbor every 30 minutes in the morning and afternoon on **Seaborne Seaplane** ☎ *(340) 777-4491*; $45 one way for USVI residents, or $50 for visitors (reservations necessary).

Language

The official language is English, but the special lilt to the accent is called Crucian. Some locals speak a musical patois called English Creole—a blend of English, African and Spanish. Many people also speak good Spanish.

Medical Emergencies

St. Croix has a 250-bed **hospital** ☎ *(340) 778-6311*, with 24-hour emergency service. Ask your hotel about doctors on call when you check-in.

Money

The official currency is the U.S. dollar.

Telephone

The new area code for the U.S. Virgin Islands is *(340)* and standard intrastate toll charges apply. Since the USVI is an incorporated territory, toll-free *(800)* numbers on the island can be accessed from the mainland. Regular U.S. postage rates also apply.

Time

Atlantic Standard Time, one hour later than New York City; during Daylight Saving Time, it is the same as New York.

Tipping and Taxes

The USVI hotel occupancy tax is 8 percent. Some hotels also add a service charge to your final bill, but between the big resorts, small hotels and guest houses, there's no consistent schedule. For instance, the **Westin Carambola** adds 10 percent, the **Buccaneer** doesn't; **Sprat Hall** tacks on 15 percent, while **Hilty House** adds none. A few others bill an energy surcharge of $2 or $3 per person, per day. To know what you're going to be charged at check-out, verify with the hotel directly at the time of booking. If a service charge is not added to your bill, a tip in the room is appropriate. Restaurant tips are handled as in the U.S.; 15 percent is standard.

Tourist Information

The U.S. Virgin Islands **Department of Tourism** has information booths at the airport, at the Christiansted wharf next to the Old Scale House, and at the cruise ship pier in Frederiksted ☎ *(340) 773-0495* or *(800) 372-USVI*. You may write to the **St. Croix Visitors Bureau** at *P.O. Box 4538, St. Croix, VI 00822*. Local offices for the USVI Department of Tourism are found in Atlanta, Chicago, Los Angeles, Miami, New York and Washington D.C.

Web Site

www.usvi.net OR www.st-croix.com

When to Go

The **St. Croix Blues Heritage Festival** is held in January, and draws name talent for a weekend of island-wide concerts and events. A festive street party, **Christiansted Jump-Ups**, are one-night events held in February, May, July and November, with music, dancing and mocko jumbies. An **LPGA Tournament** is held at the Carambola Golf Course in April. The **St. Croix International Triathlon** is an annual sporting event held in May that draws more than 500 contenders from 32 countries. The **Mumm's Cup Regatta** is an annual boat race around St. Croix to Buck Island, held in November. The **Crucian Christmas Festival** is a month-long, island-wide Carnival-style celebration with poinsettias, Christmas trees and carolers, and climaxes with the **Three Kings Day Parade** in early January.

ST. CROIX HOTELS		RMS	RATES	PHONE	CR. CARDS
★★★★	Buccaneer Hotel	132	$150–$280	(800) 255-3881	A, D, MC, V
★★★★	Villa Madeleine	43	$200–$325	(800) 496-7379	A, D, MC, V
★★★★	Westin Carambola Beach Resort	151	$185–$370	(800) 228-3000	A, D, MC, V
★★★	Club St. Croix	54	$110–$195	(800) 635-1533	A, D, MC, V
★★★	Hibiscus Beach Hotel	37	$120–$190	(800) 442-0121	A, D, MC, V
★★★	Hotel on the Cay	55	$95–$160	(800) 524-2035	A, DC, MC, V
★★★	Tamarind Reef Hotel	46	$145–$180	(800) 619-0014	A, MC, V
★★	Anchor Inn	30	$85–$145	(800) 524-2030	A, MC, V
★★	Cane Bay Reef Club	9	$90–$230	(800) 253-8534	A, MC, V
★★	Chenay Bay Beach Resort	50	$150–$235	(800) 548-4457	A, MC, V

ST. CROIX

ST. CROIX

ST. CROIX HOTELS		RMS	RATES	PHONE	CR CARDS
★★	Colony Cove	60	$140–$195	(800) 524-2025	A, D, MC, V
★★	Frederiksted Hotel	40	$75–$105	(800) 524-2025	A, MC, V
★★	Gentle Winds Resort	66	$150–$325	(800) 537-6242	
★★	Hilty House Inn	6	$70–$110	(340) 773-2594	
★★	Hotel Caravelle	43	$82–$142	(800) 524-0410	A, D, MC, V
★★	King's Alley Hotel	35	$79–$158	(800) 843-3574	A, D, DC, MC, V
★★	On the Beach Resort	20	$65–$250	(800) 524-2018	D, MC, V
★★	Pink Fancy Hotel	13	$65–$120	(800) 524-2045	A, MC, V
★★	Schooner Bay Resort	40	$110–$150	(800) 524-2025	A, D, MC, V
★★	Waves at Cane Bay	12	$85–$195	(800) 545-0603	A, D, MC, V
★	Club Comanche	42	$36–$86	(800) 524-2066	A, MC, V
★	Cottages by the Sea	20	$70–$115	(800) 323-7252	A, D, MC, V
★	Danish Manor Hotel	34	$49–$125	(800) 524-2069	A, D, DC, MC, V

ST. CROIX RESTAURANTS		PHONE	ENTRÉE	CR CARDS
Continental Cuisine				
★★★★	Kendrick's at Quin House	(340) 773-9199	$18–$26	A, MC, V
★★★	Top Hat	(340) 773-2346	$20–$30	A, D, DC, MC, V
French Cuisine				
★★★	Le St. Tropez	(340) 772-3000	$8–$25	A, MC, V
International Cuisine				
★★★★	Greathouse, The	(340) 773-8141	$18–$26	A, D, DC, MC, V
★★	Antoine's	(340) 773-0263	$7–$32	A, MC, V
★★	Tivoli Gardens	(340) 773-6782	$6–$30	A, MC, V
Regional Cuisine				
★★★★	Indies	(340) 692-9440	$17–$23	A, MC, V
★★★	Blue Moon	(340) 772-2222	$5–$20	A, MC, V
★★★	Cafe du Soleil	(340) 772-5400	$16–$23	A, MC, V
★★★	Waves at Cane Bay, The	(340) 778-1805	$15–$22	A, MC, V
★★	Harvey's	(340) 773-3433	$8–$10	
★★	Wahoo Willie's	(340) 773-6585	$7–$19	A, D, DC, MC, V

SINT EUSTATIUS

Oranje Bay, considered the best beach on Sint Eustatius stretches for a mile along the coast from January–July. Other times it narrows and almost disappears.

An eccentric little Caribbean backwater whose quaint appeal is known to relatively few, Sint Eustatius tucks quite a bit of history and character into its slight 12 square miles. More commonly known as Statia, the island has a closer link to the United States and a bigger storyline than might be guessed by armchair historians. It was once the Caribbean's richest port, a major trading center that helped funnel gunpowder and other goods to the nascent American colonies during the war of independence. But that was then. Today, as one of the three Dutch Windwards (nearby St. Maarten and Saba are the others), Statia is a Caribbean anomaly with a small handful of curious tourists checking out life off the beaten track. With almost nothing in the way of nightlife, shopping, resorts or beautiful beaches, what do they discover?

The island has an attractive landscape dominated by The Quill, a gently sloped and extinct volcanic cone that can be explored on foot in a few hours on a cool morning. There is a rich underwater scene that includes both unusual marine life and historical artifacts—all relatively pristine and healthy by Caribbean standards. And there is life among the islanders, including a small clutch of American and other ex-pats who sometimes resemble an extended family. The quirky island is sometimes unfairly compared to its sibling Saba, a lusher and steeper dot of green, but the two are dissimilar even in the type of hiking and diving they offer. What a visit to Statia is really about is peeking into one of the last undiscovered nooks of the Caribbean, and one can explore much of it in a leisurely two or three days. When combined with a trip to Sint Maarten and Saba, the three islands offer much of the best of the Caribbean: history and charm, beaches and diving, exploring and shopping.

BEST BETS FOR...

Bird's-Eye View

Measuring five miles long by two miles wide, Sint Eustatius has a distinctive profile. The south end of the elongated island is governed by the unmistakable swoop of a volcanic mountain, The Quill, which rises to 1968 feet—its last eruption is estimated to have taken place 4000 years ago. The northern end of Statia is a series of smaller hills, and nestled almost out-of-sight in one northwest valley is Statia Terminals, the oil transshipment facility that is the island's biggest employer. In between is an almost barren saddle rising just above sea level, where most of the 2100-strong population lives, along with a surfeit of free-ranging goats and cows that graze on anything, to the frustration of many. The island's tiny capital, Oranjestad, has vintage Dutch colonial structures and a fort dating back to 1636; it is divided in two sections referred to as Upper Town and Lower Town, separated by a small bluff that drops to Oranjestad Baai, where the carcasses of 18th-century ships lie disintegrating. Although much of Statia's original forests are long gone (the island once had 70 plantations), a small rainforest is tucked inside the Quill's crater and a few endemic species can be found; in 1994, an unusual morning glory written off as extinct decades ago was found on the Statia Terminals

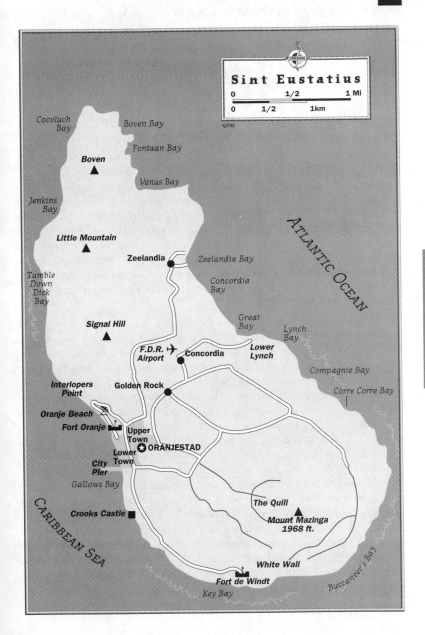

Sint Eustatius

0   1/2   1 Mi
0   1/2   1km
©FWI

Cocoluch Bay

Boven Bay

Fontaan Bay

Boven ▲

Venus Bay

Jenkins Bay

Little Mountain ▲

Zeelandia ●

Zeelandia Bay

ATLANTIC OCEAN

Concordia Bay

Tumble Down Dick Bay

Great Bay

Signal Hill ▲

Lynch Bay

F.D.R. Airport ✈ ●   Concordia

Lower Lynch

Compagnie Bay

Interlopers Point

Golden Rock ●

Corre Corre Bay

Oranje Beach

Fort Oranje

Upper Town

Lower Town ✪ ORANJESTAD

City Pier

Gallows Bay

The Quill ▲

Crooks Castle ■

Mount Mazinga 1968 ft.

CARIBBEAN SEA

White Wall

Fort de Windt ■

Buccaneer's Bay

Key Bay

property. Sint Eustatius lies 39 miles south of Sint Maarten and 17 miles southeast of Saba.

History

Initially inhabited by Carib Indians, Columbus may have happened across the island on his second voyage, though a Spanish settlement never materialized. The earliest historical record comes from Sir Francis Drake in 1595, who mentions "Estazia" in his journals. The Dutch founded the first settlement in 1636 and changed the name to St. Eustatius (after an obscure Second-century martyr), but the island changed hands 22 times over the next century-and-a-half before the Dutch could finalize their claim. During the 18th century, Statia emerged as the most prosperous island in the region, earning the nickname "Golden Rock," as trade became the most profitable way to make a living. At its peak in the late 1700s, more than 8000 people lived here, and as many as 3500 ships visited the free port each year, trading everything from African slaves to silk from the Far East—it was the island's wealthiest hour.

Statia has a unique connection to the United States. At the time of the American Revolution, Statia was a major port from which arms were shipped to General Washington's troops from the Netherlands and Belgium. On November 16, 1776, the island fired a salute to the *Doria*, a war brig flying the stars and stripes—Statia became the first foreign port to pay tribute to the just-declared nation. Legend has it that the gesture provoked retaliation by the British under the command of Admiral Rodney, who destroyed the town and its port, leading to the island's economic collapse. History books tell a somewhat different tale, for the British Crown under Rodney's command did not take the port until 1781, when he emptied the warehouses of goods, plundered the town and put the island's Dutch commander on trial. Changing trade routes, hurricanes and a gradual dismantling of the bricks that supported the town's warehouses were the real cause of the island's eclipse. The Emancipation Act of 1863 was a final death knell for any plantation industry and the few islanders who remained subsisted on farming until relatively recently. In 1982, an oil trans-shipment facility, Statia Terminals, opened in Tumble Down Dick Bay. Today 50 or more oil tankers per month dock to unload or load oil on its way from South America or the Middle East on its way to the United States and elsewhere.

People

The population is about 2100, made up mainly of descendants of African slaves, forced into labor on the more than 70 plantations that once dominated Sint Eustatius. More than 20 nationalities are represented on the small island. Instruction is in Dutch—the official language— though English and Spanish are also taught and widely spoken. A variety of religions are practiced on the island, including Roman Catholic, Methodist, Baptist, Anglican, Methodist, Seventh Day Adventist, Jehovah Witness, Baha'i Faith, and the World of Faith Ministry. The people are extraordinarily friendly and crime is rare. Those not working in tourism make their living by farming, trading and at the oil transshipment facility.

Beaches

The best beach for swimming is **Oranjestad Baai**, the black sand cove that stretches for a mile on either side of Oranjestad; excellent snorkeling can be found on the remains of the former city wall, 130 feet out from the shore. The sand comes and goes seasonally, however, which is why beach-lovers should not come to Statia with high hopes. The island's prettiest beach is **Zeelandia Baai**, a two-mile-long sweep of golden sand that is great for beach-combing, walking and wading—swimming in the rough surf is not advised. There are a few other places for swimming on the east coast, but check around locally for conditions—**Corre Corre Baai** has no sand, but the cove is protected by a reef which makes for good swimming.

Underwater

Still emerging from the shadow cast by her better-known little sister Saba, Sint Eustatius is possibly the best-kept dive secret in the Eastern Caribbean, and it's easy to understand why. If you're looking for an island with beaches, nightlife and resorts to complement a vivid underwater scene, you are kindly requested to skip Statia. This is a minimally developed destination visited by only a few hundred divers each year. But do head for Statia if you desire an

SINT EUSTATIUS

EXPLORING SINT EUSTATIUS

Locally known as Statia, this island is a 12-mile-square backwater and a shadow of its former self. Once sought after by many nations, the island has changed hands 22 times. Today, the Dutch-protected island is a perfect place to hike and dive, or learn more about Caribbean history.

Boven

Fort Oranje

Clinging to a cliff, this fort, constructed in 1636, protected the island for centuries. Restored in 1976, the fort has cannons on its ramparts and a 1939 plaque in the courtyard commemorating the fact that in 1776 St. Eustatius was the first country to recognize the United States of America.

Little Mountain

Signal Hill

Oranjestad

Situated on the west coast, facing the Caribbean, the capital city has an Upper and Lower Town. Filled with stone buildings and gaily painted gingerbread houses, Oranjestad is a great place to watch artisans at work making boats. Take a break with a loaf of bread purchased from the bakery that uses old-fashioned ovens.

Gallows Bay

Oranjestad

The Supermarket

This famous dive site has a depth of 60 feet and is reached by boat access from Lower Town. Two shipwrecks shelter gorgeous patches of coral and are populated with schools of soldier fish and squirrel fish, along with spotted moray eels and stingrays. Here is one of the few places you might see a flying gurnard, a fish with black and white spots and satiny blue pectoral fins.

Crooks Castle

Kay Bay

Boven Bay

Statia Diving

The warm waters surrounding Eustatius are filled with reefs and canyons, pinnacles and underwater mountains, all covered with coral and dotted with more than 200 shipwrecks. Most diving is in the 20–80 foot range, with visibility extending up to 100 feet. Snorkelers will find plenty to see as well. Choose from 16 charter sites, including the Crooks Reef site, which has huge elkhorn corals and sea fans.

Gilboa Hill

Historical Foundation Museum

Housed in an 18th century, red-roofed building, the museum occupies the space that once served as the headquarters for British Admiral Rodney in 1781. Today, you can tour the completely restored landmark which displays pre-Columbian artifacts.

elandia

F.D.R. Airport

Fair Play

Behind the Mountain

The Quill

This dramatic, dormant volcano is 1968 feet high, making it an island landmark. The crater encloses a rainforest filled with giant tree ferns and broad-leaf tropicals. You can spend a day bird watching or photographing flowers. The most direct trail is a moderate hike up a steep track that in 45 minutes takes you to the crater rim. Other trails wind around the crater above, huge, thick-trunked trees draped with vines.

The Quill Crater

Bucaneers Bay

Fort de Windt

Situated on the south side of the island, this fort was built between 1753 and 1775.

off-the-wall vacation to an island your friends have never heard of (and all your dive buddies know of Saba by now). The payoff, for those willing to "rough it" without a disco, is pristine diving through deep volcanic canyons and fissures, over shallow reefs and plunging walls, and around a bevy of quietly disintegrating 17th- and 18th-century trading ships. And those are just the documented sites; there are a number of unexplored areas offering true virgin dive possibilities.

Statia's wrecks provided a delightful bounty to early diver visitors. So much so that, although their wooden hulls were long gone, the government eventually ruled that nonresidents may dive only when accompanied by a local dive operator; today, the occasional bottle or pewter utensil unearthed is to be donated to the Oranjestad museum. Fortunately, there are still plenty of antiquities to see, but the reefs are the real star of Statia's underwater show, and you won't have to elbow your way in to do it. The spectacular and rare flying gurnard is regularly spotted on Statia, and larger pelagics frequent a number of the sites. Humpback whales cruise the area December through February. Perhaps the best snorkeling site is found 130 feet from shore at **City Wall**, a barricade that once represented the old sea wall for Lower Town and is now inhabited by reef fish and invertebrate life; watch for sea urchins.

Sint Eustatius is a diver's dream with coral reefs, marine life and many shipwrecks to explore.

Dive Shops

Dive Statia

Oranjestad; ☎ *(5993) 82435.*

The island's oldest shop is a small, low-key operation, with all sites within 15 minutes of the dock. Two-tank dive, $72, including equipment. Resort course $80; night dives and underwater photography courses available. PADI instructors provided on all dives. Two mountain bikes are also available for rent at $10 per day.

Golden Rock Dive Center

Oranjestad ☎ *(5993) 82964 or (800) 311-6658.*

The newer outfit on the island, which takes qualified divers out in search of new sites. Has the only covered dive boat on the island, and also does day trips to Saba and St. Kitts. Two-tank dive $90; one-hour snorkeling trips $25.

For hikers, Statia is a small treasure. With only 12 square miles to cover, the island realistically can be seen entirely on foot, albeit by dedicated walkers. But more sedate visitors will still want to climb **The Quill**, the classically shaped volcanic cone that dominates the island from every vantage point (although the best view is actually obtained from nearby St. Kitts). It represents one of the Caribbean's easier "high points" and rewards its guests with a lush crater rainforest (the only one on an otherwise arid island), where islanders hunt land crabs after dark. A three-hour guided tour of **Oranjestad** is easily arranged with local historians through the island museum or tourist office; they will also provide a walking map featuring a few trails and donkey tracks not listed here.

Although a few picayune hamlets dot the landscape, Oranjestad is Statia's only real town, as well as its capital, split in two by a 130-foot-high bluff. **Lower Town**, along Oranjestad Baai, was once the island's hub of activity—a freewheeling port that contained 280 warehouses, shops and dwellings as well as a slave house in 1784. During the 1800s, as trading declined, so did the town; many of the buildings were disassembled so their bricks could be recycled. A different bounty—precious glass **blue beads**—can be discovered by the lucky and patient. Originating in Holland and ranging in color from dark green to azure to opaline, the five-sided beads were used for trading with Africa (probably for slaves), though they are not found on any other Caribbean islands. The beads are usually spotted along the Oranjestad shore or in the water, but are increasingly rare (storms usually unearth a few)— local shops sell them for $50 and up.

Connecting Lower Town with Upper Town is the **Slave Walk**, a path built in 1803 to allow easier access over the bluff that divides the capital. **Upper**

Town still has a number of 18th century buildings intact, including the restored **Doncker House**, which Admiral Rodney inhabited in 1781 and now houses the worthwhile **Museum of the Historical Foundation**. There are several fine churches, including a synagogue named **Holen Dalim**, the second-oldest in the Western Hemisphere. Statia's Jews suffered at the hands of Admiral Rodney, who forced them to leave the island in 1781. Though the community is gone, the ruins of the synagogue and its nearby, weed-embraced burial grounds dating back to 1742 are maintained by the Historical Foundation. At the center of town is the restored **Fort Oranje**, which made history in 1776 as the first foreign land to recognize American sovereignty.

Historical Sites

Fort Oranje   ★★

Upper Town, Oranjestad.

Built by the Dutch in 1636 (over the ruins of a former French fort), Fort Oranje looks well-positioned atop the bluff overlooking Lower Town to ward off intruders, but history tells a different story. Statia was the first foreign entity to support the United States in the Revolutionary War, and a plaque here, presented by Franklin D. Roosevelt, gives thanks. The British retaliated by sacking the then-rich town and its harbor, the beginning of the end for Statia's importance as a major trading center. The fort was restored in honor of the U.S. Bicentennial is 1976. The tourist office across the street is a good place to pick up brochures and maps.

Museums and Exhibits

St. Eustatius Historical Museum   ★★★

Wilhelmina Way, Oranjestad.
Hours open: 9 a.m.–5 p.m.

This museum is housed in a beautifully restored 18th-century building once lived in by British Admiral Rodney in 1781. The museum's eclectic exhibits focus on Statia's sugar production, slave trading, 18th-century antiques, and pre-Columbian artifacts including a complete Arawak Indian skeleton. General admission: $2.

Sports

With the exception of diving and hiking (both of which are excellent), sporting activities are few and far between on Statia. Most are found at the Community Center, at the south end of Upper Town, which offers a lone tennis court with a changing room, as well as facilities for volleyball, basketball and softball.

Watersports

Dive Statia ☎ *(5993) 82435* is the island's most complete watersports center. They offer deep-sea fishing trips, snorkeling equipment, scuba instruction and excursions.

Where to Stay

Fielding's Best Value Hotels in Sint Eustatius	
★★ **La Maison Sur la Plage**	$65–$100
★★ **King's Well**	$55–$100
★★ **Talk of the Town**	$69–$98

Don't head to Statia for glitzy resorts. The **Old Gin House**, formerly the island's best hotel, closed in 1995 and no one has stepped in to fill its shoes. For now, the few accommodations are small, usually family-run inns with affordable rates and low-key amenities.

Inns

Golden Era   **$60–$88**   ★

Lower Town, ☎ *(800) 223-9815, (5993) 82345, FAX (5993) 82445.*
Single: $60–$70. Double: $75–$88.
This small hotel sits right at the water's edge below the fort. Guest rooms are quite basic, with air conditioning, phones and tiny private balconies. A restaurant serves Caribbean cuisine. The saltwater pool is the only other facility; the island's main beach is a few minutes walk. The rates aren't high, but the property is definitely worn at the edges. 20 rooms. Credit cards: A, D, MC, V.

King's Well   **$55–$100**   ★★

Oranjestad, ☎ *(5993) 82538.*
Single: $55–$70. Double: $65–$100.
Nice spot overlooking Lower Town and Statia's main beach, King's Well grew out of a popular restaurant, and both owe much of their success to a pleasant husband-and-wife management team. Rooms are simply decorated but spacious, and a few have kitchenettes; a balcony is shared by upper units. No air conditioning, but ceiling fans in all rooms—rates include full breakfast. Popular with divers. The beach is a five-minute walk; town is a little further. 8 rooms. Credit cards: D, MC, V.

La Maison Sur la Plage   **$65–$100**   ★★

Zeelandia, ☎ *(800) 692-4106, (5993) 82256, FAX (5993) 82831.*
Closed Date: September.
Single: $65–$85. Double: $80–$100.
Located at the north tip of Zeelandia Beach on the east coast, this small property offers accommodations in cottages with basic furnishings, private terraces and artwork; rooms are a little dark. Two units have air conditioning (for $5 additional per night). Facilities include a gourmet French restaurant, a bar, a TV lounge (you won't find one in your room), a small library and a pool. Quiet and secluded, and wonderful views of the beach which stretches for two miles toward The Quill, but

the sea is too rough for most swimmers. Rates include continental breakfast. 10 rooms. Credit cards: MC, V.

Talk of the Town　　　　　　　　$69–$98　　　　　　　　★★

Oranjestad, ☎ (800) 223-9815, (5993) 82236, FAX (5993) 82640.
Website: www.antyrus.com/tot/talk.html.
Single: $69–$81. Double: $86–$98.

This hotel is set near the airport, a mile-and-a-half from the beach, but does have a small pool. Rooms are simple but nice, with air conditioning, locally made furnishings, telephones, and cable TV. There are also three efficiencies with kitchenettes. The restaurant is fine. Though frills are few and the location is not ideal, this is still one of Statia's better choices. Rates include breakfast. 20 rooms. Credit cards: A, D, MC, V.

Where to Eat

Fielding's Highest Rated Restaurants in Sint Eustatius	
★★★　La Maison Sur La Plage	$16–$21
★★　Talk of the Town	$5–$20
★★　Blue Bead	$7–$18

Restaurants on Statia are as informal as their surroundings, though you'll find decent French food at **La Maison Sur la Plage**. Chinese food is popular, served at no less than four establishments.

Blue Bead　　　　　　　　$　　　　　　　　★★

Lower Town, ☎ (5993) 82873.
Lunch: 11:30 a.m.–2:30 p.m., entrées $3–$9.
Dinner: 6–9 p.m., entrées $7–$18.

Everyone winds up at Blue Bead sooner or later—this hangout draws locals, the yachtie crowd and other visitors, as well as government officials. The outdoor terrace setting is lovely, a blue- and yellow-trimmed house overlooking the remnants of Lower Town. An unexciting menu offers fried shrimp, T-bone steaks and chicken in Creole sauce, but check out the daily specials on the blackboard (posted on the kapok tree along the road). Sunday brunch is $10.50 and includes eggs benedict or steak and eggs, along with mimosas and bloody marys.

Cool Corner　　　　　　　　$　　　　　　　　★★

Oranjestaad ☎ (5993) 82523.
Lunch: 10 a.m.–4 p.m., entrées $8–$10.
Dinner: 4 p.m.–midnight, entrées $8–$10.

This hot spot (for Statia) beckons with a prime location near the local tourist office. A good place to meet the friendly townspeople, Cool Corner stays open late to serve the needs of the few night owls who may be prowling. Fare is Caribbean-Chinese, with curry plates and Cantonese specialties available. Credit cards: not accepted.

Kim Cheng's Chinese   **$**   ★★
> *Oranjestad,* ☎ *(5993) 82389.*
> *Lunch: entrées $5–$10.*
> *Dinner: entrées $5–$10. Closed: Sun.*

Also known as the Chinese Restaurant, this tiny eatery manages to produce plates heaped with hearty food in rather cramped surroundings. The fare is actually a pot-pourri of dishes encompassing West Indian, creole and Chinese.

L'Etoile   **$$**   ★★
> *Oranjestad,* ☎ *(5993) 82299.*
> *Lunch: Noon-4 p.m., entrées $7–$20.*
> *Dinner: 4–10 p.m., entrées $7–$20.*

What appears to be a roadhouse is really a welcoming room proffering tasty local food prepared by amiable Caren Henriquez. Its location on a hillside is a little out of the way, but a crowd of regulars keeps the place full. Though there are hamburgers, spareribs and hotdogs, try goat stew or stuffed crab for a true taste of Statia.

La Maison Sur la Plage   **$$$**   ★★★
> *Zeelandia,* ☎ *(5993) 82256.* Associated hotel: *La Maison Sur La Plage.*
> *Dinner: 6:30–9 p.m., entrées $16–$21.*

La Maison is somewhat out-of-the-way by Statia standards (two miles from town), but it's the island's best restaurant, and reasonable prices are the rule despite the French menu. Meals are served on a breezy, trellised terrace overlooking the windswept sands of Zeelandia and the Quill. Expect Gallic specialties like duck breast, beef fillets with green peppercorn sauce, lobster fricassee, and crepes for dessert. Reservations recommended. Credit cards: MC, V.

Talk of the Town   **$$**   ★★
> *Oranjestad,* ☎ *(5993) 82236.* Associated hotel: *Talk of the Town.*
> *Lunch: 11:30 a.m.–2 p.m., entrées $5–$20.*
> *Dinner: 7–10 p.m., entrées $5–$20.*

A Dutch family owns and operates this plant-filled, indoor-outdoor restaurant near the airport. It has a reputation for the best Creole in town, but the cuisine jumps often from one exotic clime to the next. Specialties include lobster stew, which can be ordered in advance. A good deal is the Dutch-style breakfast buffet with some American standards thrown in—all for under $10. Credit cards: A, MC, V.

Statia is no St. Thomas. You'll find a few items imported from Holland, including cosmetics, perfumes, liquors, cigarettes and jewelry at the **Mazinga Gift Shop** in Upper Town (Fort Oranje). One good native buy is **Mazinga Mist** (schnapps made from soursop) which you can pick up at **Dive Statia's bou-**

tique near the Old Gin House. The museum at Fort Oranje has a small selection of books and postcards, handcrafts, paintings and souvenirs.

Sint Eustatius Directory

Arrival and Departure

There are no direct flights from North America to the tiny airstrip on Sint Eustatius. The principal gateway is Sint Maarten's Juliana Airport which is served by **American Airlines** nonstop from New York's JFK, Miami and San Juan, Puerto Rico; by **USAir** out of Charlotte and Philadelphia; by **Continental** from Newark; and by several charter operators out of major cities (for additional service see "Arrival and Departure" in "Sint Maarten"). **Winair** ☎ *(5993) 82381* or *(800) 634-4907* makes the 20-minute hop to Statia several times a day from Sint Maarten, with additional daily flights from Saba (about $88 round-trip).

The departure tax is $5 for domestic flights, or $10 if you are leaving the Netherlands Antilles from Statia.

Business Hours

Shops open weekdays 8 a.m.–noon and 1–5 p.m. Banks are open Monday–Thursday 8:30 a.m.–1 p.m. and Friday 8:30 a.m.–1 p.m. and 4–5 p.m.

Climate

Daytime temperatures hover in the mid-80s during the day and drop to the 70s during the evening, year-round. Only 45 inches of rain fall a year.

Documents

U.S. and Canadian citizens need to show only proof of citizenship (current passport or one that expired less than five years ago, or voter's registration card or birth certificate with raised seal and a photo ID), plus an ongoing or return ticket.

Electricity

Current runs 110 volts, 60 cycles, same as in the U.S. No converter or transformer necessary.

Getting Around

In town, most destinations are within a mile or so, and walking is an agreeable way to experience the island. A three-hour island tour by taxi runs about $40. Cars can be rented at the airport for about $40 per day, or check with Elvin Schmidt regarding bike rentals ☎ *(5993) 82827.*

Language

The official language is Dutch (most of the signs are written so), but everyone speaks English. If you meet someone on the street, use the national greeting; "Awright, ok-a-a-y."

Medical Emergencies

Most emergencies are flown to Sint Maarten (though serious problems warrant a charter flight to San Juan, Puerto Rico), but there is a small hospital on the outskirts of Oranjestad.

Money

The official currency is the Netherlands Antilles florin (abbreviated NAf), also called the guilder. American dollars are generally accepted everywhere, but Canadians should change their money into florins (Barclays Bank in Wilhelminaweg) or in St. Maarten before coming. Only hotels and a few restaurants will accept credit cards. Imagine you are in the middle of nowhere.

Telephone

The country code is *(5993)*. To call St. Eustatius from the U.S., dial *1 +* *(5993)*, plus the five-digit local number.

Time

Atlantic Standard Time, one hour ahead of New York, except during Daylight Saving Time, when it is the same.

Tipping and Taxes

Restaurants, hotels and bars all add a 15 percent service charge. You don't need to tip anyone on top of this.

Tourist Information

There are three tiny tourist offices on the island: at the airport, in Lower Town opposite Ro-Ro Pier, and in the village center. For more information, call ☎ *(5993) 82433*, or in the U.S., you may request brochures through the **Saba and Sint Eustatius Tourist Office** ☎ *(800) 722-2394.*

Web Site

www.turq.com/statia

When to Go

Coronation Day and the **Queen's Birthday** are held on April 30, with ceremonies commemorating the coronation of Queen Beatrix of the Netherlands, and featuring special sports activities and picnics. Statia's **Carnival** is celebrated in July with local foods, steel bands, shows, games and competitions. November 16 is **Statia/America Day**, commemorating the first salute to the American flag by a foreign government in 1776; festivities include a re-enactment ceremony. December 26 is **Boxing Day**, when residents parade through the streets and local actors depict the social, cultural and political melee of the year gone by and stops are made at homes with rewards of food and drink.

SINT EUSTATIUS HOTELS	RMS	RATES	PHONE	CR. CARDS
★★ **King's Well**	8	$55–$100	(5993) 82538	D, MC, V
★★ **La Maison Sur la Plage**	10	$65–$100	(800) 692-4106	MC, V
★★ **Talk of the Town**	20	$69–$98	(800) 223-9815	A, D, MC, V

SINT EUSTATIUS HOTELS	RMS	RATES	PHONE	CR. CARDS
★ Golden Era	20	$60–$88	(800) 223-9815	A, D, MC, V

SINT EUSTATIUS RESTAURANTS	PHONE	ENTRÉE	CR. CARDS
Chinese Cuisine			
★★ Cool Corner	(5993) 82523	$8–$10	None
★★ Kim Cheng's Chinese	(5993) 82389	$5–$10	
French Cuisine			
★★★ La Maison Sur la Plage	(5993) 82256	$16–$21	MC, V
Regional Cuisine			
★★ Blue Bead	(5993) 82873	$3–$18	
★★ L'Etoile	(5993) 82299	$7–$20	
★★ Talk of the Town	(5993) 82236	$5–$20	A, MC, V

SINT EUSTATIUS

ST. JOHN

Maho Bay, St. John

St. John serves a captivating mix of both frontier outpost and trendy up-scale qualities that makes it one of the most polished and appealing of Caribbean islands. There's no airport, so St. John works its magic soon after you pull up to the ferry dock in the small harbor community of Cruz Bay. Board a safari bus heading away from town and one is quickly plunged into a lush, primeval jungle—it's a little like landing at *Jurassic Park*'s Isla Nublar. St. John has more than its fair share of aquamarine bays, snow-white beaches and lushly carpeted mountains to begin with, but it is the island's protection of these assets and minimal development of the land that makes it so special. Almost two-thirds of St. John (and much of its underwater territory) is part of the Virgin Islands National Park. As such, there are terrific adventures to be had both above and under water. All it takes is a good pair of boots and the park service map to mash one's way through densely packed forest or hike over well-marked trails that lead past 200-year-old plantation houses. Underwater, the views are just as spectacular, with rock formations, grottoes and wrecks that rate among the best in the Virgins.

Part of St. John's appeal is that you won't leave creature comforts far behind. A group of adventurous restaurants have developed, lively bars cluster around bantam Cruz Bay, and upscale shops sell an array of local arts, crafts, and clothing. And for such a small destination, the variety of accommodations on St. John is striking. On one end, there is the fine (and expensive) Caneel Bay, an island classic surrounded by seven fabled beaches, while on the other is Maho Bay Camp, an early foray into eco-tourism, and still a trendsetter. In between are bed-and-breakfasts, small guest houses, and dozens of villas for rent. The absence of sales tax here might drive some visitors into a frenzy, but once the shopper's dust settles, even these folks find a way to appreciate the natural environment that beckons at every turn. Thanks largely to the National Park and the minimal infrastructure, the island is unusually pristine—there is little trash littering the roads and trails, the beaches are immaculate, the residents care about their special surroundings. St. John took a beating from Hurricane Marilyn in 1995, leaving it even quieter than usual during 1996. But two years after the storm, the island is in terrific shape—greener and friendlier than ever.

BEST BETS FOR...

Bird's-Eye View

ST. JOHN

The smallest of the three settled U.S. Virgins, St. John lies a mere two miles east of St. Thomas. The island is bordered on the north and east by the British Virgin Islands just a few miles away and the southern shore faces the Caribbean Sea. There are a number of uninhabited islets and outcrops surrounding the island, or so Christopher Columbus fantasized when he named the group after St. Ursula and her 11,000 virgins. St. John is nine miles end to end, but much farther if you drive it. The lumpy topography rises to a mere 1277 feet at Bordeaux Mountain, though the winding, up-and-down nature of the roads suggests something far more dramatic. Two main roads traverse the western portion of the island: the Northshore Road which sticks

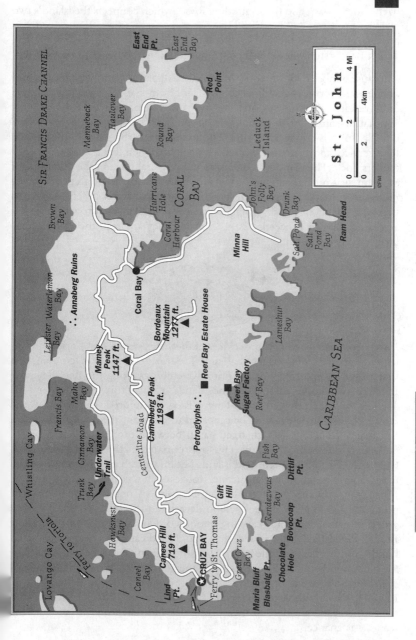

St. John

SIR FRANCIS DRAKE CHANNEL

East End Pt.

East End Bay

Red Point

Mennebeck Bay

Haulover

Round Bay

Leduck Island

Brown Bay

John's Folly Bay

Drunk Bay

CORAL BAY

Hurricane Hole

Coral Harbour

Salt Pond Bay

Ram Head

Annaberg Ruins

Minna Hill

Leinster Bay

Watermelon Bay

Coral Bay

Bordeaux Mountain 1277 ft.

Reef Bay Estate House

Mamey Peak 1147 ft.

Camelberg Peak 1193 ft.

Lameshur Bay

Centerline Road

Petroglyphs

Reef Bay Sugar Factory

Reef Bay

Francis Bay

Maho Bay

Cinnamon Bay

Trunk Bay

Underwater Trail

Whistling Cay

CARIBBEAN SEA

Hawksnest Bay

Gift Hill

Fish Bay

Dittlif Pt.

Caneel Bay

Caneel Hill 719 ft.

CRUZ BAY

Rendezvous Bay

Bovocoap Pt.

Lovango Cay

Ferry to Tortola

Lind Pt.

Ferry to St. Thomas

Great Cruz Bay

Maria Bluff

Blasbalg Pt.

Chocolate Hole

ST. JOHN

to the north coast, and the Centerline Road, which connects the island's two main towns, Cruz Bay and Coral Bay, via a mountain ridge. Scenic overlooks provide glimpses of the white sand lining impossibly beautiful coves; one, Trunk Bay, is surely among the most photographed beaches in the world.

Because almost two-thirds of the island has been a National Park for four decades, the territory is still virgin, by Caribbean standards anyway. A mere 3500 residents live on St. John, most of them in or near Cruz Bay, a tiny, ramshackle (flirting with fashionable) community surrounding a quaint harbor. St. John is connected to St. Thomas (and nearby Tortola) by regular ferry service, and the town buzzes with activity when ferries and cruise ship tenders dock. The island's second settlement, Coral Bay, on the other side of St. John, was once the biggest town and main harbor. Though the community still claims a few bars and restaurants, since the debut of ferry service to Cruz Bay a few years back, Coral Bay is now a bit of a ghost town. In general, the further one proceeds east, the further they are from the island's minimalist touristic pursuits.

History

Archaeologists have yet to decide whether the Arawaks or Caribs (the island's first pre-Columbian inhabitants), African slaves or a combination thereof were responsible for the primitive etchings along the Reef Bay trail. In 1493, Columbus discovered the islands of St. Croix, St. John and St. Thomas, and then shoved off to Puerto Rico. A hundred years later saw the arrival of Sir Francis Drake as he prepared to confront the Spanish troops in San Juan. While St. Croix changed hands between the French and Spanish, St. John (along with St. Thomas) was appropriated by the Danish West India Company. The two Dutch-held islands became a hub of business (St. Thomas), and a magnet for sugarcane, tobacco and cotton plantations (St. John). In 1717, the Danes established St. John's Coral Bay as a permanent port. In 1733, a great slave rebellion devastated the country, when a large group of slaves, ostensibly carrying bundles of wood, were admitted to Fort Berg in Coral Bay. Once inside, they brandished cane knives and massacred hundreds of settlers and the entire Danish garrison. The rebels held the fort for nine months until the Danes, with the support of two French warships and an army from Martinique, recaptured the island and rebuilt the factories. In 1848, slavery was abolished, and when planters eventually left the island, the former slaves divided up their properties and relied on the land and the sea for sustenance.

In 1917, with a view to protect its interest in the Panama Canal, the U.S. bought the Virgin Islands package—St. John, St. Thomas and St. Croix—from the Danes for a bargain $25 million. In 1952, before electricity served St. John, Laurance Rockefeller took a shine to the island, bought 5000 acres, and built his Caneel Bay Resort, which gave well-heeled visitors a chance to enjoy the pleasures of an undeveloped backwater. He later donated the land to the government, which added to it, and created the country's 29th National Park. With the advent later of the Cinnamon Bay and Maho Bay camps, more ecologically oriented travelers arrived on St. John's shores, ready to scale and sail the lush resources. A second resort, the Virgin Grand (now the Westin) opened in 1987, with a slew of high-class condos in its wake.

People

Little of St. John's culture is indigenous. In 1773 there was a slave population of more than 2000; legend has it that when Rockefeller arrived in the early '50s, there were barely 400 islanders. The population today is only about 3500, and although residents are protective of St. John's ecology, they are virtually 100 percent dependent on tourism for revenue. Reggae is a passion on the island, and the Rastafarian influence lies behind a few local superstitions: old timers still believe jumbies (spirits) caused the closing of the Reef Bay Sugar Factory in 1916. But most of St. John's residents today are American ex-pats who, keen to the laid-back lifestyle, spend their days casually selling wares in Cruz Bay. If you can abandon your cellular phone and datebook at home, it will take only a day or two to settle into the Virgin vibe known as "limin"—a kind of wrinkle-in-time sensation that renders you unable to do anything but lounge with a tropical drink and daydream.

Beaches

Trunk Bay is the picture-perfect beach of your dreams. Unfortunately, after perhaps a few too many magazine covers, it is almost always swamped with visitors throughout the day, many drawn to the 225-yard snorkeling trail. Not to worry, there are a couple dozen other beaches on St. John that may be a notch below Trunk Bay, but are resplendent nonetheless.

Winding east along the north coast road from Cruz Bay, the first beach you *won't* see is secluded **Salomon Bay**. Not coincidentally, it's also the nudist's choice—access is via the Lind Point Trail (which starts at the Visitor Center in Cruz Bay). Nearby, beautiful **Honeymoon Beach** is on the Caneel Bay property, but there are no guest rooms here so you'll probably be left alone to your Rockefeller-primed fantasies. The Caneel Bay peninsula is wrapped by a pearly necklace of well-kept coves (theoretically off-limits to non-guests) that ends with **Hawksnest Beach**, yet another splendid strand, though it too receives its share of day-trippers; Hawksnest has changing rooms and picnic tables. Two of Caneel's beaches are among the island's best: **Scott Beach** and **Turtle Bay**. The next two beaches are very popular, **Cinnamon Bay** (backed by the campground) and **Trunk Bay**. Cozy **Maho Bay** lies just below the tent cabin settlement of the same name, while **Francis Beach** is a memorable, less visited cove with bird-watching and nature trails nearby. On the south shore, **Great Cruz Bay**, backed by the Westin Resort, is also pleasant. Other beaches take a little more effort to reach, but the payoff might be a deserted cove to call your own. Among the best are three on the remote southern coast: **Reef Bay** (see "On Foot"), **Lameshur Bay** and **Saltpond Bay**.

Although there's plenty of beautiful underwater life to mirror the island's lush above-ground geography, diving on St. John tends to be shallow and mild, which makes it a great place to learn, or to visit if you've just been certified. There are relatively few surface conditions to complicate matters, although the northern coast is subject to swells in the winter (which usually renders these sites inaccessible). Several USVI operators visit the wonderful wreck of the *RMS Rhone* off the British Virgin Islands (you'll need a passport or birth certificate; see "Underwater" in "British Virgin Islands"). Dives off eastern St. Thomas are easily accessible from Cruz and Cinnamon bays. **Trunk Bay** has a heavily visited, 225-yard self-guiding underwater trail that will thrill first-time snorkelers, but better snorkeling lies off **Cinnamon Bay**, **Hawksnest Beach** or in **Leinster Bay** (at nearby Waterlemon Cay). The rangers at the Park Service headquarters in Cruz Bay will help you find other locations—remember, much of the National Park lies off-shore.

Dive Shops

Coral Divers

Coral Bay; ☎ *(340) 776-6850.*

Situated on the quieter east end of St. John, Coral Divers is a four-year-old NAUI training facility. Offers two-tank and night dives for $65. Resort course, $65.

Cruz Bay Watersports

Cruz Bay; ☎ *(800) 835-7730 or (340) 776-6234.*

The biggest operator on the island. Two-tank dive $78, or book it through St. John Watersports, ☎ *(340) 776-6256,* for $73. Snorkel trips, $25.

Low Key Watersports

Cruz Bay; ☎ *(800) 835-7718.*

PADI Five Star and I.D.C. facility with classrooms. Offers three-day "Executive" course with videos and manuals shipped to home address ($350); open water certification after dives on the island. Three vessels, group size under 12; weekly trips to the *Rhone* on Fridays ($130 including lunch, customs fees and all equipment). Two-tank dive $75, including equipment.

Paradise Watersports

Caneel Bay; ☎ *(340) 776-6111 or 693-8690.*

Smaller PADI and NAUI operation limits groups to eight with sites chosen by consensus. Resort courses and pool sessions; close to many of the eastern St. Thomas sites and occasional trips to the *Rhone*. Two-tank dive, $75.

After falling in love with its pristine, untouched beauty, in 1954 Laurance Rockefeller donated 5000 acres of prime St. John real estate to the U.S. government, which turned around and created the unique Virgin Islands National Park, eventually comprising just under two-thirds of the island's above-water territory, and a decent chunk of its underwater coral reefs and offshore islands. As such, there is virtually no comparison between St. John and the other U.S. Virgins when it comes to hiking; it's where the Virgins, well... practically live up to their name. With the possible exception of Martinique and Guadeloupe, St. John has the best-developed trail system in the Caribbean, offering a variety of short jaunts. Although the two longest trails come in under two-and-a-half miles, it's possible to make a few itinerary adjustments to create memorable all-day excursions, particularly in the vicinity of Lameshur. Pick up a copy of the free trail guide available at the park's Cruz Bay Visitor Center, which outlines 22 hiking possibilities; better yet, purchase a waterproof *Trails Unlimited* topo map (available in Cruz Bay) for a more detailed look at the island's geography. If you're visiting from St. Thomas for the day, two trails leave from the vicinity of Cruz Bay leading to Caneel Hill and Lind Point, and can be combined (using the Caneel Hill spur trail) for a shorter hike. Another enticing offering is the Park Service's guided outing which buses guests to the start of the Reef Bay Trail, near the top of Mamey Peak, for a mostly downhill and casual stroll past petroglyphs

ST. JOHN

Fielding ST. JOHN

EXPLORING THE VIRGIN ISLANDS NATIONAL PARK

Tiny St. John is remarkable in that much of its land is preserved as a U.S. National Park. Encompassing 11,560 acres on land and sea, the park contains a treasure-trove of sights. Hike through rain forests to see ruins of an old sugar plantation and ancient Carib petroglyphs. Settle down by a lagoon to bird-watch. Dive the varied reefs. When you're tired out, you can join the cruise-ship tourists in Cruz Bay for shopping or dining.

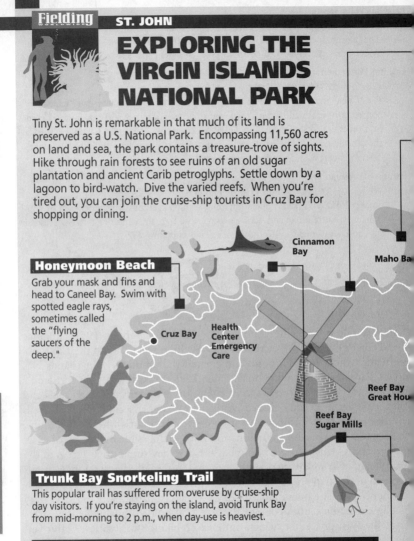

Cinnamon Bay

Maho Ba

Honeymoon Beach

Grab your mask and fins and head to Caneel Bay. Swim with spotted eagle rays, sometimes called the "flying saucers of the deep."

Cruz Bay

Health Center Emergency Care

Reef Bay Great Hou

Reef Bay Sugar Mills

Trunk Bay Snorkeling Trail

This popular trail has suffered from overuse by cruise-ship day visitors. If you're staying on the island, avoid Trunk Bay from mid-morning to 2 p.m., when day-use is heaviest.

Reef Bay Hike

Labeled on Park Service brochures as Trail 14, this two-hour hike follows a shady path downhill through both wet and dry forests filled with bird life. Dominant trees and plants are labeled, plus hikers pass by abandoned sugar plantations. Catch a Park Service boat back to Cruz Bay to bypass the uphill return walk. A five-hour guided hike is also available.

Cinnamon Bay Campground

Campers stay in screened canvas tents or rustic cottages at this concessionaire-operated site on the North Shore. A few bare tent sites are also available, and guests can stay up to 14 days. The self-guided, one-hour Cinnamon Bay Loop Trail begins near the entrance.

Francis Bay Trail

This trail begins at the north end of the Maho Bay Camp and winds by a pond that attracts various species of birds. Teals, white-cheeked pintails and wigeons are often sighted, as are pelicans and frigatebirds. In the bay, you might catch a glimpse of a green turtle.

Point

Annaberg Plantation

This short trail leads to the ruins of the island's best known sugar plantation. View the windmill and other ruins, then join the rangers at the interpretive center for talks about how the colonists and islanders once lived.

Coral
Bay

Coral Bay

Round Bay

East End

ameshur
ay

Red Point

Leduck Island

Salt Pond
Bay

Rams
Head

and sugar factory ruins to Reef Bay. Here hikers can swim and snorkel before being ferried back to Cruz Bay late in the afternoon. Other guided hikes are available and will provide an informative glimpse into the Caribbean ecosystem and the history of the Virgin Islands.

What Else to See

Although shopping and dining have gradually evolved to become a worthwhile pursuit in Cruz Bay, they still take a back seat to St. John's breathtaking natural environment. To orient yourself, begin with a stop at the **National Park Visitor Center**, a few hundred feet from the ferry dock, where park rangers will assist you in assembling an itinerary suitable for a few hours or a week. The Park Service also schedules nature walks and snorkeling trips. Take the scenic drive along **Centerline Road**—the ruins of the **Catherineberg Sugar Mill** are worth a visit, and feature a crumbling windmill yielding stupendous views. Another great roadside pullout is at the turnoff for **Bordeaux Mountain Road**, where a restaurant, **Le Chateaux de Bordeaux**, has a deck overlooking Coral Bay and the British Virgin Islands in the distance. Two peaceful spots missed by many day-trippers are **Saltpond Bay**, near the location of the environmentally sensitive **Concordia Eco-Tents** development (ask for a tour of the site), and **East End**, which has a delightful roadside restaurant serving local food. History is served up at the **Annaberg Sugar Mill Ruins**, a sugarmill and estate built in the 1720s overlooking Leinster Bay, and the park service regularly schedules living history demonstrations of how islanders survived in the post-slavery era. Back in **Cruz Bay**, two small museums are worth a stop. The **Elaine Ione Sprauve Museum and Library** honors a local activist with a collection old maps, drawings and displays showing the history of the island, while the **Museum of Cultural Arts** occupies an old 18th-century plantation house that contains photos and artifacts illustrating the survival of island arts. At present, Wednesday is the big cruise-ship day on St. John—a day when Cruz Bay and the most popular beaches are best avoided.

Museums and Exhibits

Elaine Ione Sprauve Museum   ★★★

>   *Enghied Street; Cruz Bay,* ☎ *(340) 776-6359.*
>   *Hours open: 9 a.m.–5 p.m.*
>   This small museum has exhibits on St. John's Danish West Indian history, as well as displays of locally created artwork.

Parks and Gardens

Virgin Islands National Park   ★★★★★

>   ☎ *(340) 776-6201*

ST. JOHN

No visit to St. John—or any of the U.S. Virgins—would be complete without at least a day spent at the breathtaking national park. It encompasses 11,560 acres and has 20 miles of trails to explore (see "On Foot" for additional hiking information). Stop by the Visitors Center next to the ferry dock in Cruz Bay (open daily from 8 a.m. to 4:30 p.m.) to peruse the exhibits, pick up a map, and get details of special ranger-led events. Highlights in the park include the Annaberg Ruins, a sugar plantation and mill from the 1720s; the Reef Bay Trail, which passes plantation ruins and petroglyphs; and Trunk Bay, a picture-postcard beach and the start of a marked underwater trail for snorkelers.

Tours

Guided Tours

The **St. John Taxi Association** will show you around the island in less-than-ideal safari buses for $30 for one or two people, $13 per person for three or more. The **St. John Island Tour** ☎ *(340) 774-4550* lasts two hours and costs $12 per person. Ranger-led tours are popular at **Virgin Islands National Park**; call ☎ *(340) 776-6201* for details. Finally, local personality **Miss Lucy** ☎ *(340) 776-6804* tailors private tours to individual interests, while **John Abraham** ☎ *(340) 776-6177* and **Wesley Easley** ☎ *(340) 693-8177* offer a friendly, insider's look at their island.

Watersports are an integral part of the St. John lifestyle. The island even has its own unique watersport: **SNUBA**—a hybrid of snorkeling and diving available at Trunk Bay (no lengthy training course or certification is necessary). In addition to the Trunk Bay underwater trail, another good **snorkeling** site is Flanagan's Cay off the southeast coast of St. John, and reached by the snorkel tour operators. The campgrounds offer extensive sports packages, including nature hikes and snorkeling trips. The Virgins are famous for spectacular **deep-sea fishing** for blue marlin with many world records to prove it—the best is found in the St. Croix Channel to the south and the Sir Francis Drake Channel in the east. Deep sea fishing is not allowed within the National Park boundary, but you can **rod-and-reel fish** from beaches.

Excellent sea conditions with balmy weather and numerous coves and sheltered anchorages create a superlative **sailing** environment. Every type of vessel, from sailfish to oceangoing yachts can be hired (though many do so on nearby St. Thomas or the British Virgin Islands, where the selection is even greater). **Boats** may be chartered with a full crew, but you'll need to know what you're doing if you're going to leave the crew behind. Many half- and full-day sailing excursions are available; check first with your hotel, which probably has a full and up-to-date list and can recommend what will best suit your needs. Operators on St. John are based in both Cruz Bay and Coral Bay. Because of the constant trade winds, **windsurfing** also finds a number of fans. The winds, whipping down the Sir Francis Drake Channel north of St. John, are funneled by two hills through the Narrows to the Windward Passage. Expert windsurfers can also cross the Pillsbury Sound to St. Thomas.

Constant trade winds off St. John thrill windsurfers.

Sea kayaking is quickly finding a niche in the U.S. and British Virgin Islands. The classic tour leaves from Virgin Gorda or Peter Island in the BVIs and heads toward St. John, the wind on your back for most of the way. En route on this ambitious trip, stops at Beef, Cooper, and Jost Van Dyke reward with hidden beaches and pristine snorkeling. You can stay at hotels and guest houses in a real bed nightly—which minimizes your load factor to a change of clothes, fresh water, swimsuit, a towel, mask and snorkel, sunscreen (essential) and hat—or, play "no-see-um" on beaches by pulling onto shore late, camping and leaving early before anyone catches you. If planning such a trip, you can take a kayak on the ferry to the British Virgins, but don't forget to bring your passport or birth certificate.

Tennis courts are provided at the Caneel Bay and Westin resorts; both have pro shops and instructors. A local outfit, **Connections**, acts as a booking service for day-sails, snorkeling and fishing trips; they're located in Cruz Bay near the ferry dock ☎ *(340) 776-6922.* Additional information on activities can be obtained by calling the **St. John Visitors' Bureau** ☎ *(340) 776-6450.*

Bicycling

Other islands are bigger or have higher peaks, but few concentrate as many fierce grades into a compact area as St. John. And note that although you may ride on the island's numerous dirt roads, bikes are strictly forbidden on the hiking trails. **Coral Bay Watersports**, which has a second location at Cinnamon Bay, has a small selection of mountain bikes, and they'll provide a drop-off at no charge (don't be a martyr—ask them to haul you up to the top of Bordeaux Mountain). Full day rentals are $25–$35, depending on the condition of the bike ☎ *(340) 776-6850.*

Guided hike

The **Virgin Islands National Park Service** provides a guided hike of the popular Reef Bay Trail several days a week. Participants are driven by van to the trailhead, and then descend the 2.2-mile path through tropical forest to visit petroglyphs and the ruins of former sugar estates before arriving at an isolated beach. The trip leaves from the Visitor Center at 9:45 a.m. and returns via boat from the beach at 3 p.m. $14.50 per person; reservations necessary ☎ *(340) 776-6330.*

Horseback Riding

Pony Express Riding Stables on Bordeaux Mountain provides trail rides ☎ *(340) 776-6494.* **Carolina Stables** in Coral Bay provides horse and donkey rides. Two-hour guided trips are $45, or a half-day trip to the Annaberg ruins is $75, including lunch ☎ *(340) 776-6922.*

Kayaking

Several outfits provide kayak rentals. One, **Arawak Expeditions**, specializes in fully supported camping odysseys from Peter Island (in the BVIs) that paddle their way back to St. John. $850 for the five day trip, $1095 for seven days, with a discount during summer. Half- and full-day guided tours around St. John are $40–$75, or rent one and paddle about on your own for $40 per day ☎ *(800) 238-8687* or ☎ *(340) 693-8312.* Other companies that provide rentals only include **Coral Bay Watersports** ☎ *(340) 776-6850* and **Low Key Watersports** ☎ *(340) 835-7718.* Single-seat kayaks start at about $20 for a half day, or $40 for the full day.

Watersports

St. John's two resorts, the Westin and Caneel Bay, have their own watersports facilities. Otherwise, there is a variety of providers that cover snorkeling, windsurfing and other activities. For general equipment rentals, try: **Coral Bay Watersports** ☎ *(340) 776-6850,* **Paradise Watersports** ☎ *(340) 693-8690,* **Low Key Watersports** ☎ *(340) 693-8999,* **Cinnamon Bay Watersports Center** ☎ *(340) 776-6330,* and **Cruz Bay Watersports** ☎ *(340) 776-6234.* For deep-sea fishing, call **Gone Ketchin** ☎ *(340) 693-8657,* **World Class Anglers** ☎ *(340) 779-4281,* and **Low Key Watersports** ☎ *(340) 693-8999.* For daysails and snorkeling trips, try **Jolly Mon Day Sailing** ☎ *(340) 776-6239* or **Proper Yachts** ☎ *(340) 776-6256.*

ST. JOHN

Where to Stay

Fielding's Highest Rated Hotels in St. John

★★★★★	**Caneel Bay Resort**	$250–$700
★★★	**Estate Concordia Studios**	$95–$190
★★★	**Gallows Point Suite Resort**	$145–$355
★★★	**Harmony Resort**	$95–$185
★★	**Serendip Condominiums**	$85–$155

Fielding's Best Back-to-Nature Eco-Tourism Experiences in St. John

★★	**Concordia Eco-Tents**	$60–$100
★★	**Maho Bay Campground**	$60–$98
★★	**Cinnamon Bay Campground**	$48–$105
★★★	**Estate Concordia Studios**	$95–$190
★★★	**Harmony Resort**	$95–$185

Fielding's Best Value Hotels in St. John

★★★	**Estate Concordia Studios**	$95–$190
★★	**Cinnamon Bay Campground**	$48–$105
★★	**Concordia Eco-Tents**	$60–$100
★★	**Maho Bay Campground**	$60–$98
★★	**Serendip Condominiums**	$85–$155

ST. JOHN

Although the quantity of bunks on St. John is relatively small, there is an eclectic variety of accommodations. The island's two resorts, **Caneel Bay** and **Westin Resort St. John**, take care of big spenders, while several guest houses, small inns and upscale campgrounds accommodate budget travelers. In between are a plethora of self-catering villas, apartments and condos, some of which are quite plush.

Over the past two decades, and through the dedication of a number of ecologically minded islanders, St. John has become known as a world leader in the creation of sustainable tourism. Laurance Rockefeller and Caneel Bay essentially invented tourism on St. John, but it was the elegant "camping" provided by his rustic beachfront cottages at **Cinnamon Bay** that really set the tone for developments. In 1976, entrepreneur Stanley Selengut, a civil engineer and carpenter, opened the **Maho Bay** (before the term "eco-tourism" existed, he notes), starting with 18 tent cottages on a pristine hillside at the edge of the National Park, connected by a series of elevated wooden walkways. It was his goal to provide "creature comforts for all the creatures." Maho was a success that eventually grew to 114 units and spawned an increasingly eco-conscious empire: **Harmony**, a condo-style site above Maho Bay; **Estate Concordia**, another development above remote Saltpond Bay; and the nearby **Concordia Eco-Tents**, which represents the current apex of Selengut's efforts to use recycled building materials, minimize waste, and integrate the tourist experience closely with the land. Maho Bay and its siblings have captured the eye of the press and public, and are popular throughout the year. As further testimony to their rapport with Mother Nature, the four creations suffered little at the hands of Hurricane Marilyn in 1995; the durable structures at Maho Bay were receiving guests just four days after the storm.

Hotels and Resorts

The Hyatt Regency St. John closed following the devastation of Hurricane Marilyn in 1995, but legal tangles (rather than hurricane damage) kept the resort shuttered for more than two years. At press time, the property will become the **Westin Resort St. John**, with a re-opening scheduled for November, 1997; reservations *(800) 937-8461* or *(340) 693-8000*. We will have a report on the hotel in next year's edition of *Fielding's Caribbean*. Until then, **Caneel Bay** is St. John's classic resort, a unique mix of rustic with luxury. Vacations integrating a stay at both Caneel and its sister property **Little Dix Bay** (in the British Virgins) can be arranged easily.

Caneel Bay Resort $250–$850   ★★★★★

Caneel Bay Peninsula, ☎ *(800) 928-8889, (340) 776-6111, FAX (340) 693-8280.*
Website: www.rosewood-hotels.com.
Single: $250–$700. Double: $250–$700. Cottage Rates Per Day: $475–$850.

Set on a 170-acre peninsular estate, this unique resort continues to do much right, as it has since Laurance Rockefeller bought it in 1952, when the operation was a seven-room plantation inn. The accommodations he built are now managed by Rosewood Hotels, but they didn't dare mess with the essentials—there's still no TV or phone by your bed, and air conditioning is limited solely to breezes through the jalousied windows. The rock-walled cottages and two-story wings are infused with a pleasing melange of colors and textures; each has a patio or balcony, minibar and coffeemaker. Rooms overlooking the tennis courts and garden areas offer the most seclusion (and are cheaper), while those on the beaches are beloved—just try to snare a cottage on Scott Beach for Christmas! Or, rent some or all of Cottage 7, once the Rockefeller home. Caneel's grounds offer 11 tennis courts, a small pool and an exercise room; there are seven lovely beaches from which to choose, with non-motorized watersports included in the rates. The resort's back-to-nature ambiance isn't for everyone—prim, sheltered types might resent a bug or two. There's very little nightlife, and the rates keep out most young folks (though summer brims with honeymooners). Caneel's size means long walks are common, so shuttle buses ply the grounds (anathema for the impatient), and those who are not surefooted will find strolling about in the black of night foolhardy. However, for those looking for a slow-paced retreat in a resort setting, Caneel remains one of the Caribbean's great escapes. 171 rooms. Credit cards: A, MC, V.

Apartments and Condominiums

Rental properties have become extremely popular on St. John—there are almost as many of these as there are hotel rooms—and they are a particularly good buy for families or other groups. Many of the sites are first-class private homes and villas, and deluxe condos are also available, most offering fully equipped kitchens, VCRs, stereos, patio grills; the bigger units have their own pools. There are more than 400 rental villas sprinkled throughout St. John, almost all of them within a mile or so of Cruz Bay. Most are represented by a dozen local rental firms, allowing you to shop around for exactly the arrangements and price you want. Among the bigger outfits are **Caribbean Villas** ☎ *(800) 338-0987 or (340) 776-6152;* **Villa Portfolio** ☎ *(800) 858-7989 or (809) 693-9100;* **Catered To** ☎ *(800) 424-6641 or (340) 776-6641;* **Windspree Vacation Homes** ☎ *(809) 693-5423;* **Vacation Vistas** ☎ *(340) 776-6462;* and **Destination St. John** ☎ *(800) 562-1901 or (340) 779-4647.* Prices vary considerably—in the summer it's possible to find small villas that rent for under $100 per night. Dozens of homes are represented by smaller firms (not listed above) plus many homeowners represent themselves; contact the **USVI Department of Tourism** for more information ☎ *(800) 372-USVI.* Remember that groceries are expensive on St. John and you'll want to procure most of your provisions on St. Thomas before ferrying over. Still, if you arrive on the island without fresh herbs, dried morels and fine wine, a quick stop at the lavishly-stocked **StarFish Market** in Boulon Center should help you fill your pantry with gourmet goodies.

Estate Concordia Studios   **$95–$190**   ★★★

Saltpond Bay, ☎ *(800) 392-9004, (340) 693-5855, FAX (340) 693-5960.*
Website: www.maho.org. E-mail: concordia@maho.org.
Single: $95–$190. Double: $95–$190.

Owned by the same folks who developed eco-sensitive Maho Bay Campground and Harmony, this property offers deluxe accommodations in an off-the-beaten-track setting on St. John's southeastern coast. The 51-acre estate looks out on Salt Pond Bay with lovely views of the beach below (a 20-minute walk). The nicest unit is the loft duplex, which has 20-foot cathedral ceilings, a wrap-around deck, two bathrooms, a full kitchen, two twin beds, ceiling fans, and a queen-size sofabed. There are also vaulted studios and efficiency suites, both with kitchens. The grounds include a luscious 20- by 40-foot swimming pool, laundry room, and store. The location is quite remote and a car is necessary—the nearest restaurant or shopping is several miles away in Coral Bay. 9 rooms. Credit cards: MC, V.

Gallows Point Suite Resort **$145–$355** ★★★

Cruz Bay, ☎ (800) 323-7229, (340) 776-6434, FAX (340) 776-6520.
Website: www.gallowspointresort.com. E-mail: gallows@islands.vi.
Single: $145–$355. Double: $145–$355.

This oceanfront resort showcases suites, ideally positioned on a point at the entrance to Cruz Bay's port—close enough to walk to town, but just beyond the (admittedly minimal) traffic. Each of the 15 buildings has four units—two down and two up, most without air conditioning, and most are privately owned and reflect the decorating taste of their owners. Garden units have sunken living rooms, while the larger upper suites have loft bedrooms and two baths. All are spacious and sleep four comfortably, with fully equipped kitchens, living and dining rooms, and ceiling fans; some units were showing wear on a recent visit. There's a restaurant and two bars on the premises. The tiny beach is too rocky for sunbathing (fine for snorkeling, though) but the free-form pool is large and inviting. A solid choice for families, but no kids under 5 allowed. 60 rooms. Credit cards: A, DC, MC, V.

Harmony Resort **$95–$185** ★★★

Maho Bay, ☎ (800) 392-9004, (340) 776-6240, FAX (340) 776-6504.
E-mail: mahony@maho.org.
Single: $95–$185. Double: $95–$185.

This noteworthy collection of cottages was built as much in harmony with nature as possible. Set high on a hill over the Maho Bay Campground (and run by the same folks), each unit is powered by the sun and wind and was built using recycled materials—even the nails came from recycled steel. You can even keep track of your energy use on computers installed in each unit. The spacious, one-room cottages are nicely done, with tile floors, wicker furniture, kitchenettes, living and dining areas, interesting artwork, ceiling fans, high wood-beamed ceilings, and decks. The shower-only baths are small but functional. There's no phones or TV, and for some reason, all the beds are twins (easily pushed together). It's a five- to seven-minute walk to the beach down a steep road. 12 rooms. Credit cards: MC, V.

Lavender Hill Estates **$140–$235** ★★

Cruz Bay, ☎ (800) 562-1901, (340) 776-6969, FAX (340) 776-6969.
Single: $140–$235. Double: $140–$235.

Set on a hillside within walking distance of Cruz Bay shops and restaurants, this complex offers condominium living. Each of the 12 units has full kitchens, nice views off the balconies, spacious living rooms, and one or two bedrooms. All are quite nice and have TVs and phones, but two-bedrooms rely on ceiling fans instead of air conditioners. There's a good-sized pool on the premises. 12 rooms. Credit cards: DC, D, MC, V.

Serendip Condominiums **$85–$155** ★★

Above Cruz Bay, ☎ (340) 776-6646, FAX (340) 776-6646.
Single: $85–$155. Double: $85–$155.

This secluded apartment-style complex is situated high in a valley above Cruz Bay and consists of eight one-bedroom units and two studios, each with kitchens, limited maid service, and dining areas. Furnishings are simple but adequate; the expansive balconies overlooking the Pillsbury Sound are wonderful. There are no facilities

on-site or within walking distance—you'll want a car. Excellent value. 10 rooms.
Credit cards: MC, V.

Low Cost Lodging

There are a few decent budget properties around Cruz Bay. Another nice spot, priced $100–130 per night, is **Frank Bay Bed and Breakfast**, which opened three pleasant rooms in 1995 ☎ *(800) 561-7290 or (809) 693-8617.*

Inn at Tamarind Court　　　　　　$38–$138　　★

Cruz Bay, ☎ *(800) 221-1637, (340) 776-6378, FAX (340) 776-6722.*
Single: $38–$118. Double: $68–$118. Suites Per Day: $118–$138.
This bustling spot is one of the USVI's least-expensive with particularly good rates for singles. Standard guest rooms specialize in garage sale decor, but all are clean, have air conditioning and private bath and are a good value. There are also a few suites, and a one-bedroom apartment ($98-118). For penny pinchers, there are six tiny economy rooms that share a pair of bathrooms, but sleep only one. Despite its slightly rundown exterior, Tamarind Court does a brisk business younger travelers, and the atmosphere is friendly and fun. A bar and restaurant are on the premises and rates include a continental breakfast. 20 rooms. Credit cards: A, D, MC, V.

Raintree Inn　　　　　　　　$65–$123　　★

Cruz Bay, ☎ *(800) 666-7449, (340) 693-8590, FAX (340) 693-8590.*
E-mail: raintree@islands.com.
Single: $65–$123. Double: $65–$123.
Located in the heart of Cruz Bay, rooms at this straightforward guest house are as simple as the rates suggest, but comfortable and with private baths. Each has air conditioning and a ceiling fan; there are also loft bedrooms and kitchens in three units—these sleep up to six. A pleasant wooden deck surrounds the inn, leading to the reliable restaurant. Smoking is forbidden. 11 rooms. Credit cards: A, D, MC, V.

Campgrounds

On St. John, a niche market has developed that locates a unique common ground between camping and a rustic cottage stay. The first foray into this field was Laurance Rockefeller's **Cinnamon Bay Campground**, which used prime land along a vivid beach to create a series of bungalows, later supplemented by tent and bare sites. In 1976, conservationist Stanley Selengut created the "site-sensitive" **Maho Bay**, which eventually gave birth to the ultimate in luxury camping, the **Concordia Eco-Tents**. In all three cases, it's not necessary to bring your sleeping bag or camping equipment. These accommodations may be simple, but you could arrive with a swimsuit, change of clothes and toothbrush and feel right at home (both Maho and Cinnamon have dining facilities on-site). You won't be pampered, but "roughing it" was never so easy for eco-sensitive travelers. All three are exceedingly popular and winter months book up early. Another option that may be worth investigating is **Hansen Bay Campground**, a beachfront facility at East End that provides a tent with sleeping mattress, gas lamp and stove, ice chest and sun-warmed showers for $35 a night; bare sites are $20 per night ☎ *(340) 693-5033.*

Cinnamon Bay Campground　　　$48–$105　　★★

Cinnamon Bay, ☎ *(800) 539-9998, (340) 776-6330, FAX (340) 776-6458.*
Single: $48–$105. Double: $48–$105.

Set in the woods just off Cinnamon Bay in the Virgin Islands National Park, this Rosewood Hotels-run campground offers everything from bare sites on which to pitch a tent ($17 per night) to rather ugly, Flintstone-style open-air cottages with electricity, simple cooking facilities, and two trundle beds with linens. In between, there are also small tents with wooden floors that lack electricity but do have gas lanterns and stoves—a great budget choice for true campers. Four bath houses provide toilets and showers, and meals can be had in the cafeteria. There's no pool, but the nearby beach is grand—cottage 10 sits right on the sand (and is priced a few dollars extra for the privilege). Many watersports are available. This spot doesn't require a hike to get to the beach (as at Maho Bay), but the set-up is more rustic. 113 rooms. Credit cards: A, MC, V.

Concordia Eco-Tents $60–$100   ★★★

Saltpond Bay, ☎ (800) 392-9004, (340) 693-5855, FAX (340) 693-5960.
Website: www.maho.org. E-mail: concordia@maho.org.
Single: $60–$100. Double: $60–$100.
Pushing the sustainable development envelope yet one step further, in 1994 Stanley Selengut unveiled his fourth project on St. John, a small group of wood and canvas eco-tents designed to maximize the ecological interaction guests experience on the island while minimizing their impact. The high-tech yet unpretentious tent cottages utilize solar and wind power, composting toilets, and have private baths with running water. Each of the units can sleep five or six on sofa beds. Guests may use Estate Concordia's pool, or hike to a beach at Saltpond Bay, 20 minutes away. This is the ultimate in combining simple creature comforts with a back-to-nature escape, and popular enough that more units are planned for 1998. 5 rooms. Credit cards: MC, V.

Maho Bay Campground $60–$98   ★★

Maho Bay, ☎ (800) 392-9004, (340) 776-6226, FAX (340) 776-6504.
E-mail: mahony@maho.org.
Single: $60–$98. Double: $60–$98.
Set on 14 forested acres in the Virgin Islands National Park, this gorgeous spot is for nature lovers who like to camp without sacrificing too many creature comforts. Accommodations are in cozy three-room tent-style cottages, with kitchenettes, a screened dining area, sofabeds, twin beds, living areas, private decks and electricity. Five communal bath houses have toilets and showers. The grounds include a sandy beach, simple restaurant and watersports. Each site is limited to two adults and two kids. The only drawback is the steep walk to the beach. Otherwise, for "roughing it," this is quite comfortable and nice, and very popular—book early for choice winter dates. No radios allowed. 114 rooms. Credit cards: MC, V.

Where to Eat

Fielding's Highest Rated Restaurants in St. John

★★★★	Chateau de Bordeaux, Le	$20–$30
★★★★	Equator	$28–$35
★★★★	Paradiso	$13–$23
★★★	Ellington's	$13–$28
★★★	Fish Trap, The	$8–$23
★★★	Mongoose Restaurant and Deli	$10–$20
★★★	Morgan's Mango	$7–$22

Fielding's Most Romantic Restaurants in St. John

♡♡♡♡♡	Chateau de Bordeaux, Le	$20–$30
♡♡♡♡	Ellington's	$13–$28
♡♡♡♡	Equator	$28–$35
♡♡♡	Paradiso	$13–$23

Fielding's Best Value Restaurants in St. John

★★★★	Paradiso	$13–$23
★★★	Morgan's Mango	$7–$22
★★★	Mongoose Restaurant and Deli	$10–$20
★★★	Fish Trap, The	$8–$23

ST. JOHN

No doubt spurred on by the culinary delights produced on the other side of the Pillsbury Sound, the restaurant scene on St. John has blossomed in recent years into a group of first-class operations that roll out an impressive array of international taste sensations. There's even room for a mini-empire of fine restaurants, operated by Chris Rosbrook and Winston Bennett. In addition to the fine **Le Chateau de Bordeaux** and their newly acquired Italian establishment, **Paradiso**, the pair owns the warped **Bad Art Bar** (drinks only) and recently reopened their long-celebrated (and hurricane-damaged) **Asolare**, where seafood is prepared with a dynamic Asian flare. The Bad Art Bar hangs its velvet Elvis and other tacky contributions from the artist wannabe world in Cruz Bay, kitty-corner from Chase Manhattan. The best ice cream parlor is **Luscious Licks**, scooping Ben and Jerry's alongside a few vegetarian items. "Local" food—saltfish and *funghi*, conch fritters, johnnycakes, calaloo, goat water—is harder to find on St. John than elsewhere in the Caribbean, but don't miss a trip out to **Vie's Snack Shack** on the east end.

Cafe Roma $ ★★

Cruz Bay, ☎ *(340) 776-6524.*
Dinner: 5–10 p.m., entrées $11–$16.
A touch of Italy in the tropics, this pretty trattoria overlooks the sights and sounds of Cruz Bay from a second-floor perch. No slouch on gustatory or olfactory senses either, the place is noted for dynamite pizza—there's a choice of a white or traditional tomato sauce as a base for several tasty toppings. Seafood is also a standout, especially shrimp with garlic cream sauce. An excellent choice for a varied selection of tropical drinks. Credit cards: MC, V.

Chateau de Bordeaux, Le $$$ ★★★★

Centerline Road; Bordeaux Mountain, ☎ *(340) 776-6611.*
Dinner: 5:30–8:45 p.m., entrées $20–$30. Closed: Mon.
This petite dazzler clings to the sides of Bordeaux Mountain in the center of the island, and its terrace commands an unparalleled view of the rising moon (if you're on St. John during a full moon, dinner here is a must!). Despite its unprepossessing exterior, within is a cozy room with hand-crocheted tablecloths, flickering oil lanterns and eclectic chandeliers. It's no surprise many honeymooners end up here, as this place just oozes romance. The cuisine is as good as the atmosphere—don't miss the roasted rack of lamb with a rosemary, honey and nut crust and a port wine and shallot reduction. A wild game special is featured each evening. This is one of the Caribbean's few non-smoking restaurants, though there's a deck where smokers can slip off to get their fix. The deck area is open through the day for burgers, fish and chicken sandwiches and drinks. Reservations recommended. Credit cards: A, MC, V.

Crash Landing Bar and Grill $ ★★

Cruz Bay, ☎ *(340) 693-7771.*
Dinner: 3–9 p.m., entrées $5–$16.
Crash Landing takes the cake for a colorful setting. A rooftop, nine-hole miniature golf course is free to guests; there's also darts, pool tables and occasional live entertainment. Most come for burgers, but check out the coconut shrimp with tequila lime sauce and the nightly pasta specials. Credit cards: D, MC, V.

Ellington's $$$ ★★★

Gallows Point; Cruz Bay, ☎ *(340) 693-8490.* Associated hotel: *Gallows Point.*
Dinner: 6–10 p.m., entrées $13–$28.
Some of the best seafood on the island is prepared here at this viewful spot positioned not far from the ferry dock. On a clear day, you can see St. Thomas from a

front-row seat on the terrace. After a tasty drink, dine on hearty seafood chowder followed by the daily special, which could be blackened something, or chicken Martinique in an exotic fruit sauce. Reservations recommended. Credit cards: A, MC, V.

Equator $$$ ★★★★

Caneel Bay, ☎ *(340) 776-6111.* Associated hotel: *Caneel Bay.*
Dinner: 7–9:30 p.m., entrées $28–$35.

Formerly the Sugar Mill, Caneel Bay's open-air dining terrace is the lovely setting for this restaurant, and the fusion of flavors from earth's girder is a novel concept. So, there's Tom Yam (a robust coconut and lemon grass soup from Thailand), a Moroccan crispy salad with feta on pita bread and a ginger barbecued pork tamale in banana leaf with mango chutney, just for starters. Entrees run the gamut from Teriyaki tuna and pickled lobster roll with tempura vegetables to a "classic" Indian curry with beef and cashews. With such global ambitions, you might expect some over-reaching—we found several dishes more salty than spicy, for instance—but the ambiance and service are tops, and make Equator a worthy addition to the St. John restaurant scene. Credit cards: A, MC, V.

Fish Trap $$ ★★★

Cruz Bay, ☎ *(340) 693-9994.* Associated hotel: *Raintree Inn.*
Lunch: 11 a.m.–3 p.m., entrées $6–$11.
Dinner: 4:30–9:30 p.m., entrées $8–$23. Closed: Mon.

Owned by a long-time St. John couple whose son Aaron runs the kitchen, the Fish Trap puts its effort into the food rather than on fancy trappings, which makes it a favorite with locals who enjoy well-prepared shellfish and surf and turf offerings. The blackened jumbo shrimp are popular, and the fries are dependable. Credit cards: MC, V.

Lime Inn $$ ★★

Lemon Tree Mall; Cruz Bay, ☎ *(340) 776-6425.*
Lunch: 11:30 a.m.–3 p.m., entrées $5–$9.
Dinner: 5:30–10 p.m., entrées $13–$19. Closed: Sun.

The local practice of limin' is strictly adhered to here and the congenial group of limers include veteran travelers as well as residents. Settle for a terrace seat to while away the hours with a steak or fresh fish entree cooked on their outdoor grill; the lunch salads are ambitious and varied. Hungry bargain hunters crowd the place Wednesday nights for the well-regarded, all-you-can-eat shrimp extravaganza ($18.95), but no reservations are taken, so line up early. Credit cards: A, MC, V.

Mongoose Restaurant and Deli $$ ★★★

Mongoose Junction; Cruz Bay, ☎ *(340) 693-8677.*
Lunch: 11:30 a.m.–5 p.m., entrées $6–$10.
Dinner: 5–10 p.m., entrées $10–$20.

A pleasant refueling spot for tired shoppers souvenir hunting at upscale Mongoose Junction, this eatery and bar offers a bevy of cooling fruity alcoholic drinks and plates of fresh seafood—the sesame-crusted tuna is a favorite. Patrons poise on a tree-shaded, tiled deck or at the bar, which serves light meals until 10 p.m. Live music on Friday and Saturday keeps the joint jumpin'. The deli is open from 7 a.m. to 9 p.m.—a perfect place to stock up for a beach picnic. Credit cards: A, MC, V.

Morgan's Mango $$ ★★★

Cruz Bay, ☎ *(340) 693-8141.*

Dinner: 6–10 p.m., entrées $7–$22.

There's often a crowd at this very popular dining spot in a gingerbread-trimmed house painted in pastels. One reason is an excellent bar and unusual Argentinean specialties interspersed with local seafood and chicken. Another is the woodsy patio where guests sit surrounded by trees and greenery. A plate-crowding hunk of prime beef comes accompanied by the piquant Pampas-style chimmichurri sauce—a spicy melding of oregano, peppers, garlic and olive oil. The bar is a happening spot with a vast array of tropical libations; live music on Thursdays. Credit cards: A, MC, V.

Paradiso $$$ ★★★★

Mongoose Junction; Cruz Bay, ☎ *(340) 693-8899.*

Dinner: 6–9:30 p.m., entrées $13–$23. Closed: Sun.

The words "suave" and "chic" appropriately describe this Italian restaurant all dolled up in burnished woods and marble which underwent an ownership change in 1996. Dine in air-conditioned comfort on daily seafood and pasta specials and designer pizzas prepared with signature flare; the osso d'agnello Milanese is a highlight. Paradiso also has an impressive wine list and well-mixed drinks. Reservations recommended. Credit cards: MC, V.

Vie's Snack Shack $ ★★

East End, ☎ *(340) 693-5033.*

Lunch: 10 a.m.–5 p.m., entrées $3–$6. Closed: Mon., Sun.

This is probably the best local cooking on St. John—but it's only open for lunch. But if you're out at East End when Vie's at the stove, don't miss it for conch fritters both sweet and savory, island-style beef or fish patties, garlic-fried chicken with johnny cakes, and seasonal fruit drinks. The homemade coconut and pineapple tarts are a must. Located four miles east of Coral Bay beneath Blackrock Hill.

Where to Shop

Though it can hardly hold a candle to the panoply of wares offered in Charlotte Amalie across the channel, the shopping is still duty free. There is no sales tax and a $1200 per person exemption from duty applies when returning to the U.S. A small, attractive mall, **Mongoose Junction**, is the hub of most shopping activities, featuring island clothing and T-shirts, jewelry, a bookstore and a well-stocked deli. Stop by **Bamboula** for folk art, artifacts and West Indian furniture. Liquor is also a bargain and anyone over 21 can return to the states with five bottles duty free (or six, if one is produced in the U.S. Virgin Islands).

St. John Directory

Arrival and Departure

Getting to St. John requires an extra hop as the island does not have an airport. **American**, **American Eagle**, **Delta** and **USAir** all have daily service into St. Thomas, the most convenient connection point. For information on these and other carriers, see "Arrival and Departure" in "St. Thomas."

Once on St. Thomas, visitors board one of the scheduled **ferries** that ply the link to St. John. Two routes are available: for those flying into St. Thomas, the one from downtown Charlotte Amalie is closest to the airport, while another dock is located at the eastern tip of St. Thomas at Red Hook. The ferry from Charlotte Amalie leaves almost hourly ($7 each way; about 45 minutes), while the ferry from Red Hook leaves hourly throughout the day ($3 each way; about 20 minutes). For additional information and departure times, call **Transportation Services** ☎ *(340) 776-6282* or **Varlack Ventures** ☎ *(340) 776-6412*. A car ferry is also provided by **Blue Lines** that leaves from Red Hook about every 90 minutes ($50 for car and passengers round-trip; about 25 minutes); call ahead to reserve a slot ☎ *(340) 777-6111*. The **Caneel Bay** and **Westin** resorts have their own ferry service to transport guests from St. Thomas to St. John. Ferries also work the route between St. John and Tortola daily, with more limited service available to Jost Van Dyke and Virgin Gorda (you'll need to bring a passport or birth certificate and photo identification to enter the British Virgin Islands).

The departure tax when leaving the U.S. Virgin Islands is $3.

Business Hours

Shops generally open weekdays 9 a.m.–5 p.m. Banks generally open Monday–Thursday 9 a.m.–2:30 p.m. and Friday 9 a.m.–2 p.m. and 3:30–5 p.m.

Climate

Temperatures during the summer, cooled by eastern trade winds, keep the temperature around 82 degrees Fahrenheit. Brief showers also keep things cool. Winter temperatures rise to 77 degrees Fahrenheit. Rainiest months are September-January, and about 40 inches of rainfall per year. April–August are the calmest sea conditions with the best visibility.

Documents

U.S. citizens do not need a passport to enter the U.S. Virgin Islands. However, a passport or birth certificate and photo identification is necessary to visit the British Virgins. If you wish to dive the *RMS Rhone*, or snorkel amid The Baths of Virgin Gorda they are but a short ferry ride away, but you'll first need to clear British Virgin Islands customs.

Electricity

Current runs at 110 volts at 60 cycles.

Getting Around

Several car rental companies in Cruz Bay compete for the tourist trade including **Avis** and **Hertz**, but rental rates are high—expect to spend about $50–$60 per day. Driving is on the left. Taxis meet all ferry landings, and two-hour island tours can be easily arranged through **Wesley Easley** ☎ *(340) 693-8177*. Other recommended guides are **Miss Lucy**, **George Simmonds**, **Jimmy Powell**, or **Calvin George**. Tours run $30 for two passengers, or $12 each for a group of three or more. There is no public transportation system on St. John, though hitching is common.

Language

The official language is English. Some locals speak a musical patois called Creole—a blend of English, African and Spanish. Some also speak Spanish.

Medical Emergencies

There is a small clinic in Cruz Bay, but serious emergencies are handled in Charlotte Amalie on St. Thomas.

Money

The official currency is the U.S. dollar.

Telephone

The new area code is *340*. To call St. John from the U.S., dial *1 + (340)* and the seven-digit local number. Since U.S. Virgin Islands are an incorporated territory, toll-free numbers that operate in the U.S. work here, and normal postage rates apply. You can also direct dial to the mainland.

Time

Atlantic Standard Time, one hour later than New York City; during Daylight Saving Time, it is the same as New York.

Tipping and Taxes

All hotels charge an 8 percent room tax. Most accommodations do not add the service charge common on other Caribbean islands, however Caneel Bay tacks on a 10 percent service charge to your final bill. If in doubt, ask at the time of your reservation; if a service charge is will not be added to your bill, a tip in the room is appreciated. Tips in restaurants are handled as in the U.S.; 15 percent is standard.

Tourist Information

The `St. John Tourist Office` is located around the corner from the Cruz Bay ferry dock and is open daily ☎ *(340) 776-6450*. They will help arrange an island tour. Additional travel information can be obtained through ☎ *(800) 372-USVI*.

Web Site

www.usvi.net or www.stjohnusvi.com

When to Go

St. John's **Carnival** events take place from June 18–July 4, including a food fair, boat races and the recreation of a carnival village. The St. John Carnival Parade takes place on July 4.

ST. JOHN HOTELS		RMS	RATES	PHONE	CR CARDS
★★★★★	Caneel Bay Resort	171	$250–$700	(800) 928-8889	A, MC, V
★★★	Estate Concordia Studios	9	$95–$190	(800) 392-9004	MC, V
★★★	Gallows Point Suite Resort	60	$145–$355	(800) 323-7229	A, DC, MC, V
★★★	Harmony Resort	12	$95–$185	(800) 392-9004	MC, V
★★	Cinnamon Bay Campground	113	$48–$105	(800) 539-9998	A, MC, V
★★	Concordia Eco-Tents	5	$60–$100	(800) 392-9004	MC, V
★★	Lavender Hill Estates	12	$140–$235	(800) 562-1901	D, DC, MC, V
★★	Maho Bay Campground	114	$60–$98	(800) 392-9004	MC, V
★★	Serendip Condominiums	10	$85–$155	(340) 776-6646	MC, V
★	Inn at Tamarind Court	20	$38–$118	(800) 221-1637	A, D, MC, V
★	Raintree Inn	11	$65–$123	(800) 666-7449	A, D, MC, V

ST. JOHN RESTAURANTS		PHONE	ENTRÉE	CR CARDS
Continental Cuisine				
★★★	Ellington's	(340) 693-8490	$13–$28	A, MC, V
French Cuisine				
★★★★	Chateau de Bordeaux, Le	(340) 776-6611	$20–$30	A, MC, V
Italian Cuisine				
★★★★	Paradiso	(340) 693-8899	$13–$23	MC, V
★★	Cafe Roma	(340) 776-6524	$11–$16	MC, V
Regional Cuisine				
★★★★	Equator	(340) 776-6111	$28–$35	A, MC, V
★★★	Mongoose Restaurant and Deli	(340) 693-8677	$6–$20	A, MC, V
★★★	Morgan's Mango	(340) 693-8141	$7–$22	A, MC, V
★★	Crash Landing Bar and Grill	(340) 693-7771	$5–$16	D, MC, V
★★	Lime Inn	(340) 776-6425	$5–$19	A, MC, V
★★	Vie's Snack Shack	(340) 693-5033	$3–$6	
Seafood Cuisine				
★★★	Fish Trap	(340) 693-9994	$6–$23	MC, V

ST. JOHN

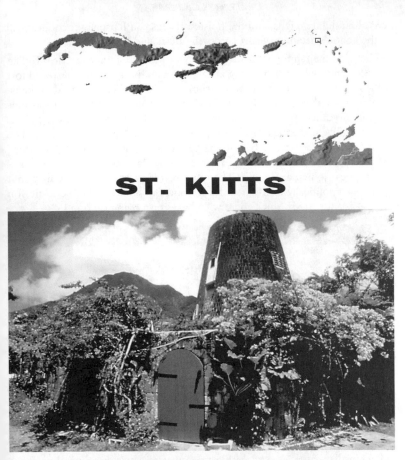

ST. KITTS

Quaint flower-bedecked cottages add to the charm of St. Kitts.

Boasting dark, humid rainforests presided over by colonies of vervet monkeys as well as secluded bays containing hidden beaches, St. Kitts is one of the Caribbean's treasures, with a little something to please everybody. Properly (though rarely) referred to as St. Christopher, the island was part of the British Empire just over a decade ago but, along with its sister Nevis, decided to go its own way in 1983. With a mere 44,000 inhabitants (9000 of them on Nevis), the nation is today one of the Western Hemisphere's smallest—though a referendum on secession being debated over on Nevis might make each smaller still. Sugarcane is the dominant crop on St. Kitts, but with a decline in sugar prices worldwide, tourism has been looked to as the economic force of the future. Fortunately, outside Basseterre and Frigate Bay, unhampered tranquillity reigns, and the noisiest things you'll usually encounter will be the gentle skittering of surf across the black and blonde sands.

Hikes into the rainforest or up the slopes of Mt. Liamuiga (a Carib Indian word for "fertile land") are a big attraction, as is the splendidly restored fort at Brimstone Hill. Your accommodations may be further immersed in the island's history if you overnight in one of the centuries-old plantation inns dotting the cane-covered slopes. Only about half the size of St. Kitts, Nevis hefts its bulk equally majestically out of the sea just across from its sister. The two islands are separated by a two-mile-wide channel of water, the Narrows—a proximity so close that from some vantage points the two sometimes appear joined at the hip. The quiet revolt on the Nevis side may split them apart politically in the near future but, rest assured, the blood ties on the two islands run so thick there will always be a common bond.

BEST BETS FOR...

Bird's-Eye View

Sixty-eight square-mile St. Kitts is part of the Caribbean's Leeward Islands, and is positioned with its sibling Nevis between Monserrat and Sint Eustatius at the northern end of a still-active volcanic chain. Shaped like an oversized tennis racket, St. Kitts has at least three distinct mountainous areas along its 19-mile length. The "handle" of the racket, the narrow southeastern peninsula that reaches to within two miles of Nevis, has several hills that rise sharply from the sea to just over a thousand feet. A number of scenic bays and a salt pond are carved into these hills, creating the island's few strands of white sand and producing luxuriant vistas. The six-mile-long peninsula is mostly undeveloped, but plans to build resorts on it have been bubbling for years, as a couple of now-abandoned structures testify to today. This "last frontier" was all but inaccessible only a few years ago—its beaches fabled, but seen by few—until a paved road was built in 1990 over steep Sir Timothy Hill connecting St. Kitts to its remote end.

The "neck" of the racket is a low-lying isthmus, Frigate Bay, where more than half of the island's hotel rooms are positioned. A spit of sand and scrub less than a mile wide, Frigate Bay has grown to include a golf course, a casino, restaurants and condominiums, but is bordered on either side by prime

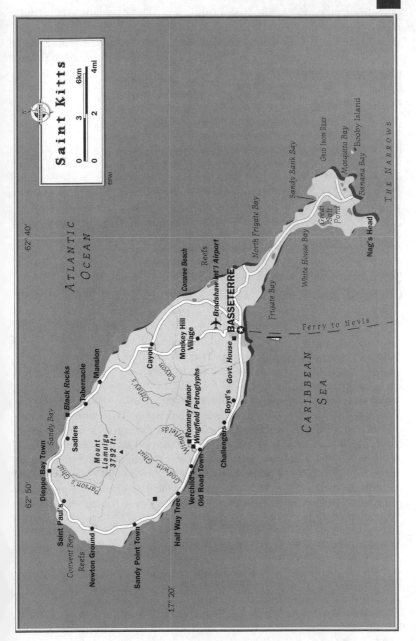

beachfront property. At the base of the racket lies Basseterre, the island's capital (population 20,000) which booms with an irrepressible West Indian vigor. Traffic police are crisply dressed and reggae blasts from music stores and cafes. Recently completed is a $16-million deep-water cruiseship facility.

Untrammeled by tourism, St. Kitts is a stunning combination of volcanic mountains, rainforest and golden beaches.

The island's second rise begins just northwest of Basseterre and leads up to an unnamed volcanic crest topping out above 2800 feet. Continuing northwest, a deep, jungle-choked ravine leads to Verchild's Mountain, and just beyond, the steep summit of 3792-foot Mt. Liamuiga, which has a gaping crater over a half-mile wide and 1500 feet deep. Usually swathed in mist, St. Kitts' volcanic range is infrequently seen from below. What most visitors remember about the larger end of the island is its extensive cloaking in green sugarcane. Though the sugar economy has fallen on hard times everywhere, the crop remains a chief export for St. Kitts. A delightfully rustic narrow-gauge railway cuts through the field like an oversized child's playtoy to haul the harvested cane from 44 plantations around the island to a processing plant before being loaded onto ships at the docks near Basseterre.

History

Columbus first sighted the island of St. Kitts, dubbing it—with a touch of immodesty—St. Christopher. The title was later shortened to St. Kitts by British tobacco planters, who ignored Spanish claims and moved in with their African slaves. For years the island remained lost in obscurity, inhabited by Carib Indians who found nourishment from the island in the form of turtles, iguanas and *mauby* liquor. In 1623, a daring group of settlers led by Sir Thomas Warner plopped themselves on the island, but were soon forced to share the beach uneasily with some French colonists. In 1690, during a French occupation, the Englishman Sir Timothy Thornhill led a party of soldiers in the dead of night through Friars Bay and over a steep hill full of thorn bushes and spiky acacia trees to surprise the French sentries, who thought the British could only attack from the sea. After taking Basseterre, the island's main city, the English troops spiked the fortress cannons so that other English troops could land in safety. The hill was later named Sir Timothy in honor of Thornhill. The 1783 Treaty of Versailles finally awarded sovereignty to the Brits. Independent from Britain since 1983, St. Kitts is dealing peacefully with the challenges of economy, but still maintains affectionate ties with the mother country. Queen Elizabeth II visited St. Kitts in 1985 and her portrait continues to grace island bank notes.

People

Comparing the two halves of this twin-island nation, fun-loving Kittians are more gregarious than their conservative neighbors on Nevis. The most festive event on genteel Nevis is horseback racing, while a raucous music festival was introduced on St. Kitts in 1996 to great acclaim. A little fishing, some gardening, long pauses to chat—that's the pattern of a day's dally on St. Kitts, where the remains of British *haut monde* mix colorfully with the Caribbean way of life. The political tie to England may be severed, but the countries remain close, and Kittians were delighted with Queen Elizabeth's comments about the island's unspoiled beauty, an opinion shared by Christopher Columbus. Yes, the British are aground, running many of the inns and hotels on the island. There are a few local artists, including sculptor Valentine Brown who lives in Dieppe Bay and is known for his finely crafted sculptures of faces and figures out of cedar. Style in St. Kitts is casual, though visitors are advised not to wear skimpy shorts, bikinis or bare chests away from the beach.

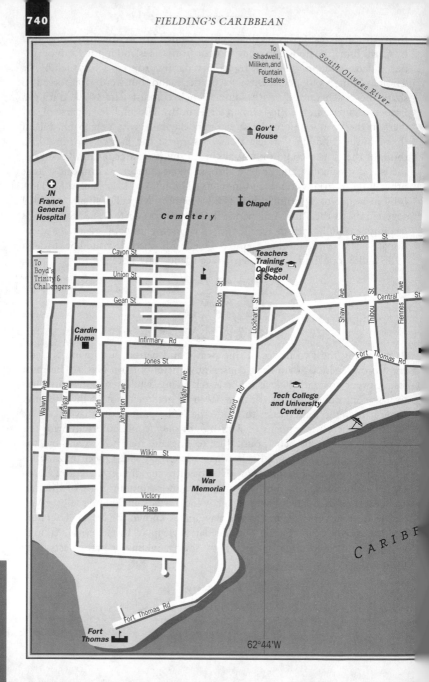

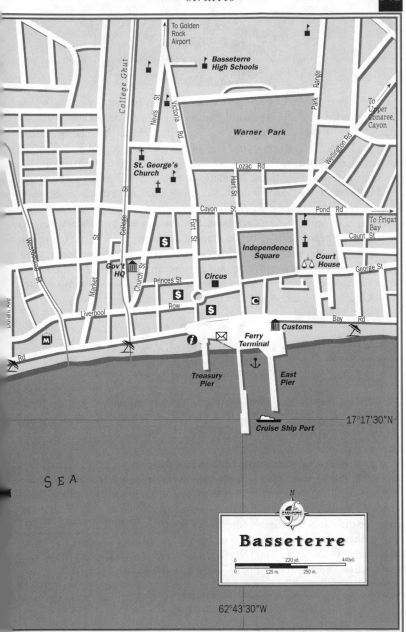

To Golden
Rock
Airport

**Basseterre
High Schools**

College Ghut

Nevis St

Victoria Rd

Warner Park

Park Range

To
Upper
Monaree,
Cayon

**St. George's
Church**

Lozac Rd

Hart St

To Frigate
Bay

Cayon St

Pond Rd

Wellington Rd

Westbourne St

Fort St

College St

Church St

**Gov't
HQ**

Market St

Princes St

Circus

**Independence
Square**

Caunt St

**Court
House**

George St

Row

Liverpool

Bay Rd

Customs

Dublin Ave

Rd

i

**Ferry
Terminal**

**Treasury
Pier**

**East
Pier**

17°17'30"N

Cruise Ship Port

S E A

N

FIELDING
WORLDWIDE

Basseterre

0	220 yd.	440yd.
0	125 m.	250 m.

62°43'30"W

ST. KITTS

Beaches

St. Kitts' best beaches lie in coves around the southeast peninsula, where white or golden sand faces the calm Caribbean on one side, and the choppier Atlantic on the other. **Frigate Bay** is one such divided personality, with a North and South strand on either side of the golf course and Jack Tar Village—they are probably the most popular on the island and possess a wide variety of watersports options. A mile southeast of Sir Timothy's Hill, **North** and **South Friar's Bay**, on either side of the peninsula, are a pair of good beaches. Near the end of the peninsula are several fine strands, each within a mile or two of one another: **Cockleshell Bay**, **Banana Bay** and **Major's Bay** are lovely, and **Turtle Beach** has a bar, restaurant and watersports. Snorkeling can be found throughout this area. Closer to Basseterre is **Conaree Beach**, used by many islanders, but as you continue around the larger wing of the island, the beaches become smaller, less reliable and are composed of gray or black sand. Ask at the plantation inns for their sun-sea-sand suggestions.

Underwater

Hundreds of wrecks are thought to rest off the sloping reefs of St. Kitts. Few of them have been discovered, and most are presumed to be long disintegrated, yet the island continues to inspire the dedicated wreck-diver. For the rest of us, the west coast offers inviting reefs, particularly at distant Sandy Point near the island's northern end, and in the channel between St. Kitts and Nevis, **The Narrows**. Probably the best overall area is **Grid Iron**, a six-mile undersea shelf rising to within 15 feet of the surface, located on a map by drawing a line between the coastline east of the St. Kitts airport, and the coast just off the Nevis airport (tiny **Booby Island** lies almost in its path). Although there are a number of dives on this formation, the star is **Monkey Shoals** (see "Underwater" in "Nevis"). Just a few dozen divers a week visit St. Kitts, and three shops compete for their favor.

Dive Shops

Kenneth's Dive Centre

Basseterre; ☎ *(869) 465-2670.*

Four decades of operation makes Kenneth, an ex-fisherman who used to free-dive for lobster 120 feet down, one of the most experienced in the region. PADI affiliated, with training through Instructor. Two-tank dive, $60, including all gear.

Pro Divers

Turtle Beach; ☎ *(869) 465-3223.*
Located at the remote southeast tip of St. Kitts, with easy access to the Narrows and Nevis sites. A PADI outfit with training through Assistant Instructor. Shore dives available. Two-tank dive $60, including all gear ($50 if you bring your own).

St. Kitts Scuba Ltd.

Basseterre; ☎ *(869) 465-1189.*
A PADI and NAUI certified outfit based at Bird Rock Hotel, St. Kitts Scuba began operation in 1995. Two tank dive $70, including equipment.

Northern St. Kitts is dominated by Mount Liamuiga and a rugged shoreline, including Black Rocks (above).

Defined trails to notable sites on St. Kitts are difficult to locate, a situation the government seems in no hurry to change (perhaps eco-tourism has not yet been identified as a potential money-maker?). You'll be reliant on one of the several hiking outfits that have sprung up on the island. St. Kitts' big **volcano hike** is easier than those on some islands, but is sufficiently spectacular to amply reward intrepid vacationers. One attractive trek not listed here, the **Mansion Source Trail**, ascends **Verchild's Mountain**, a 3100-foot summit one

Fielding WORLDWIDE   **ST. KITTS**

BEST OF ST. KITTS

Refined with a British air, yet offering lush rain forests and sandy beaches, St. Kitts attracts a wide variety of travelers. Immerse yourself in history with a visit to Arawak petroglyph sites and Brimstone Hill Fort, or enjoy watersports such as windsurfing and sailing.

Black Rocks

Fronting the Atlantic ocean at Sandy Bay, these volcanic rocks were formed when lava erupted from Mount Liamuiga. Centuries of surf action have given the rocks unusual shapes.

Dieppe Bay

St. Paul's

Newton Ground

Mt. Liamuiga

Brimstone Hill Fortress

Called the "Gibraltar of the West Indies," this large, imposing hill-top fort was built by the French and has cannons, ramparts, and cobbled courtyards. The museum displays weapons, uniforms and documents.

Romney

Half Way Tree

Mount Liamuiga Hike

The trail to the crater rim of this dormant volcano starts above the town of St. Paul's. A guide is recommended for this challenging, half-day adventure, but views aren't reliable from the summit due to the frequent clouds.

Romney Manor

Home to the Caribelle Batik Factory, this historic manor is surrounded by six acres of gardens, including a 350-year-old saman tree (sometimes called a rain tree). You can watch the batik artisans at work and purchase batik items.

Arawak Petroglyphs

Carved by ancient Indians, these petroglyphs remain mysteriously compelling today.

Ottley's Plantation

Now an elegant hotel, this manor house epitomizes the grandeur of a 1700s sugar plantation. Linger on the long veranda or stroll the verdant grounds.

Independence Square

Once a slave market, this landscaped square in Basseterre is surrounded by Georgian-style buildings. Other houses in the town are ornamented with intricate gingerbread details and long verandas.

Great Salt Pond

This large pond ranges from pink to red, depending on the time of year. Bird life is abundant in the scrub and along the nearby beaches—more than 25 species have been sighted.

Bradshaw International Airport

Basseterre

ey's

onkey
Hill

Southeast Peninsula

Take the Dr. Kennedy Simmonds Highway, a sleek, new road that winds past Frigate Bay through grassy hills until you reach Turtle Bay Beach, where you'll enjoy views of neighboring Nevis island.

Nag's Head

Turtle Bay

The Circus—Berkeley Memorial

Reflecting the island's British heritage, this square forms the town center in Basseterre. The monument to George Berkeley, former president of the General Legislative Counsil, is a well-known landmark.

ST. KITTS

mile southeast of **Mount Liamuiga** that features a pond surrounded by dense tropical vegetation. A variation, sometimes referred to as **Nine Turn Ghaut**, also ascends the area below Verchild's, but continues through a valley to Molineux on the other side of the island; trail conditions vary and may require a guide. 1:25,000 and 1:50,000 topographic maps are available; most of the island's trails are not detailed as the government has not yet assembled hiking information or identified and maintained major trails.

Trekking Tours

Greg's Tours

Basseterre; ☎ *(869) 465-4121.*

Explore the interior of the island with a naturalist bent. The all-day hike up Mount Liamuiga is $55 per person (minimum group of four), the shorter trip through the rain forest is $35 each (minimum of three).

Kriss Tours

Shadwell Estate; (869) 465-4042.

Kriss Berry invites you to explore the rain forest he has spent two decades exploring. The all-day hike to Mount Liamuiga is $45; a half-day rainforest adventure is $35; an overnight trip to a jungle campsite is $90 per person.

Basseterre is St. Kitts' center of business and commerce. Decimated by fire in 1867 and rebuilt in the Franco-British colonial style, Basseterre is now a bustling seaboard community of 20,000. The town boasts such Caribbean nuances as high-pitched, awningless roofs (to reduce their vulnerability in storms), shutters (to lessen sun glare but retain the essential flow of air through the interior spaces), and occasional outbursts of carpenter Gothic trim. Many of the renovations are due to the efforts of the "Basseterre Beautiful" organization, which has worked hard to restore sections of the old town, opening up new stores and courtyard cafes, and keeping the frilly, high-roofed architecture. The town hub is **The Circus**, built in tribute to London's Piccadilly Circus, with a memorial to Thomas Berkeley at its center. The **St. Christopher Heritage Society** is located on Bank Street and contains a photo collection and information on the island's history and culture, while the **Tourist Board** is found in **Pelican Mall**, just opposite the Circus. Nearby **Independence Square**, where slave auctions were held for 200 years, leads to **St. George's Church**, originally called Notre Dame when it was first completed by the French in 1670. Several fires burned the structure over the years. A subsequent earthquake in 1843 means the church has been rebuilt four times—the current building was completed in 1869.

The lovely southeast peninsula of St. Kitts, also known as **Salt Pond Estate**, extends toward the hulk of Nevis and has been the location of several unsuccessful development schemes. A seven-mile road extends from Frigate Bay down to the tip, where a bar and restaurant, **Turtle Beach**, hosts lively Sunday brunches and rents watersports equipment—watch for playful vervet monkeys in the surrounding hills. The St. Kitts-Nevis government promises that any development of this peninsula will be limited to a few select hotels that will have to comply with strict ecological and preservation laws. More than one abandoned structure tells a different story, but the peninsula and its treasured bays remain an idyllic retreat.

The 30-mile circuit of the island's mountainous northwest wing is a great day-trip. Driving up the west coast of the island from Basseterre, stop by **Romney Manor**, a 17th-century great house and plantation that suffered a major fire in 1995. The manor houses **Caribelle Batik**, which sells locally produced batiks and currently operates out of makeshift structures while plans for rebuilding Romney are debated. Next door is **Wingfield Estate**, once the home of Carib Chief Tegreman in 1623—remnants of St. Kitts' indian population, including petroglyphs, are nearby. Just down the hill from these historic sites is **Old Road Town**, the first permanent English settlement and original capital of the island. Continuing north on the main road, you'll soon encounter 800-foot-high **Brimstone Hill Fortress**, the most photographed tourist attraction on the island, and one of the most magnificent fortresses in the Caribbean. Rounding the northern wing of the island, you'll pass two of the island's historic inns: **Rawlings Plantation** is nestled in the fields of sugarcane above St. Paul's, while the **Golden Lemon** lies a few miles further on the shore next to a fishing village, **Dieppe Bay Town**—both are fine stops for breakfast, lunch or dinner. Scenically positioned off the coast to the northwest is **Sint Eustatius** and, on a clear day, **Saba**. A bit further along on the road as it heads back to Basseterre are the **Black Rocks**, coastal cliffs with a not-too-distant relationship to the summit of volcanic Mount Liamuiga above—the turnoff from the main road is not marked for northbound traffic.

Historical Sites

Brimstone Hill Fortress   ★ ★ ★ ★ ★

On the western slope of Mt. Liamuiga, ☎ *(869) 465-2609.*
Hours open: 9:30 a.m.–5:30 p.m.

This national park houses one of the Caribbean's largest and best-preserved fortresses, called the "Gibraltar of the West Indies" due to its sheer size. Set on top of an 800-foot basalt outcrop, the 38-acre fort dates back to 1690, and Brimstone saw several skirmishes between the French and the British, who alternated in their control of the fort. Although it was abandoned in 1850, today it is quite nicely restored, and you can see the officer's quarters, barracks, hospital and kitchen. A museum is devoted to military history. The park also includes nature trails through dense vegetation and features stunning views of neighboring islands—St. Eustatius and Nevis

ST. KITTS

are reliable sights, and on a clear day you can also see Montserrat, Saba, St. Maarten and St. Barthelemy. General admission: $5.

Watersports activities on St. Kitts are focused around Frigate Bay, where you can find options from **sailing** to **scuba**. **Windsurfing** is best at the end of the southeast peninsula, where breezy bays provide both shelter and challenge under the watchful eye of Nevis Peak; try Turtle Beach for board rentals. Facilities for many sports can be found at the Jack Tar Village, including **golf** at the 18-hole Frigate Bay Golf Club, though serious duffers won't want to miss the spectacular course at the Four Seasons Resort on Nevis. **Tennis** is available at many of the island hotels, and **horseback riding** can take the form of half-day outings into the rain forest or along rugged beaches from Trinity Stables in Conaree (it's worth checking into whether the sport has been resumed on the beautiful southeast peninsula). Greg's Safaris is the best-known and established guide for **nature walks** (see "On Foot"), but other outfits are riding the coattails of Greg's success.

Golf

The **Royal St. Kitts Golf Club** is the island's main links, an 18-hole championship course on the flats behind Jack Tar. It was designed by Peter Thomson in 1974— bring a few extra balls for the tricky water hazards. Green fees are $25–$35, cart rental (mandatory) is $30–$40, and club rental runs $10–$15 ☎ *(869) 465-8339*. There is also a nine-hole course near the airport that some of the locals use, **Golden Rock**, as well as the superlative **Four Seasons** course on Nevis.

Horseback Riding

Several outfits offer trail rides along the beach or through the rainforest: **Royal Stables** ☎ *(869) 465-2222* and **Trinity Stables** ☎ *(869) 465-2922*.

Watersports

Various locations,.

General watersports equipment and instruction can be found at **R.G. Watersports** ☎ *(869) 465-8050* and **Pro-Divers** ☎ *(869) 465-3223*. **Tropical Tours** ☎ *(869) 465-4167* and **Pelican Cove Marina** ☎ *(869) 465-2754* offer deep-sea fishing excursions. For boating and cruising, call **Kantours** ☎ *(869) 465-2098*, **Leeward Island Charters** ☎ *(869) 465-7474*, and **Tropical Tours** ☎ *(869) 465-4039*. **Leeward Island Charters** also provides day sails to Nevis aboard the 70-foot catamaran, the *Spirit of St. Kitts*. **Turtle Tours** offers guided kayak and snorkeling trips along the southeast peninsula ☎ *(869) 469-9094*.

Where to Stay

ⓕ	**Fielding's Highest Rated Hotels in St. Kitts**	
★★★★	**Golden Lemon Inn & Villas**	$160–$500
★★★★	**Ottley's Plantation Inn**	$190–$255
★★★★	**Rawlins Plantation**	$195–$395
★★★	**Frigate Bay Resort**	$77–$175
★★★	**Ocean Terrace Inn**	$61–$180

♡	**Fielding's Most Romantic Hotels in St. Kitts**	
★★★★	**Golden Lemon Inn & Villas**	$160–$500
★★★★	**Ottley's Plantation Inn**	$190–$255
★★★★	**Rawlins Plantation**	$195–$395

📖	**Fielding's Best Value Hotels in St. Kitts**	
★★★	**Ocean Terrace Inn**	$61–$180
★★★	**Frigate Bay Resort**	$77–$175
★★	**Timothy Beach Resort**	$65–$115
★★★★	**Ottley's Plantation Inn**	$190–$255

Accommodations on St. Kitts fall into two general categories—historic plantation inns, all north of Basseterre and set amid scenic volcanic slopes, and more contemporary condo-like structures, around and just southeast of Basseterre. The two groupings offer vastly different experiences, and a sub-category—the all-inclusive vacation—is proffered by the **Jack Tar Village Beach Resort**. Choose your accommodations carefully on this island, as most cater to very specific needs. If good beaches and a variety of nearby activities are important, you'll want to be in Frigate Bay; if solitude amid antiques and history is your cup of tea, choose one of the upscale inns, but you'll need a car for serious exploration. Several of the toll-free numbers listed below con-

ST. KITTS

nect directly to the island, allowing you to speak directly with the manager or perhaps even the owner. A pair of abandoned developments lie on the southeastern tip of the island facing Nevis. One day they may be a reality; for now they're unfinished eyesores.

Hotels and Resorts

With 242 rooms and a bustling casino, **Jack Tar Village** is by far the largest and busiest property on St. Kitts, though it has seen better days; it was purchased by the Allegro group in 1997 and renovations are planned. It caters to those who want the price of their vacation—room, food, activities and, perhaps, airfare—packaged and written in stone before they step foot on the island. A number of other, smaller properties have sprung up around Jack Tar, leading to a fair amount of development in Frigate Bay. Most of these newer hostelries are listed under Apartments and Condominiums.

Allegro's Jack Tar Village   **$175–$320**   ★★

Frigate Bay, ☎ *(800) 999-9182, (869) 465-8651, FAX (869) 465-1031.*
Single: $175–$210. Double: $250–$320.
Set on 20 acres on the isthmus between the Caribbean and Atlantic, this mass-market all-inclusive property was showing increasing wear in recent years—new owner Allegro Resorts promises a renovation. Guest rooms are scattered about the grounds in two-story buildings and are simple but comfortable and have modern conveniences; the beach is a five-minute walk. Most everything is included in the rates, from scuba lessons to tennis on four courts to nightly entertainment; even the greens fees at a nearby golf course are covered (though the mandatory golf cart is not—go figure). Rates include all meals and drinks, but the food takes a drubbing from most guests. Children under 12 stay and eat free at the resort (one per adult). 242 rooms. Credit cards: A, MC, V.

Bird Rock Beach Hotel   **$80–$175**   ★★

Bird Rock, ☎ *(800) 621-1270, (869) 465-8914, FAX (869) 465-1675.*
E-mail: birdrock@caribbeans.com.
Single: $80–$175. Double: $80–$175.
This small hotel is located on a bluff overlooking the sea, one mile from Basseterre. Accommodations are in standard rooms with air conditioning, balconies and cable TV, or in apartments with kitchens. Two- and three-bedroom units are also available. A restaurant serves continental and local cuisine, there are also two bars, a pool and tennis court on the premises. The speck of beach is more for snorkeling than sunning, but the management plans to expand it for 1998; the on-site dive shop supplies watersport equipment. 38 rooms. Credit cards: A, D, MC, V.

Fort Thomas Hotel   **$100–$160**   ★★

Fortlands, ☎ *(800) 851-7818, (869) 465-2695, FAX (869) 465-7518.*
Single: $100–$140. Double: $115–$160.
Built on the site of an old fort, this former Holiday Inn reopened in 1993 after extensive renovations. It caters mainly to business travelers who don't mind the fact that the beach is four miles away (they'll shuttle you over for free). Guest rooms are spacious but nothing special, though you can count on modern amenities and good housekeeping; otherwise rates are a bit high for what you get. The dining room

serves West Indian and international dishes. There are also a few bars and a pool. 52 rooms. Credit cards: A, MC, V.

Ocean Terrace Inn $61–$180 ★★★

Fortlands, ☎ (800) 524-0512, (869) 465-2754, FAX (869) 465-1057.
Single: $61–$132. Double: $81–$180.
Known throughout St. Kitts as "OTI," this informal inn, set on lushly landscaped hilltop grounds, overlooks the bay and Basseterre. Great views from all the air-conditioned rooms, which are modern and tasteful. There are also several one- and two-bedroom apartments and six suites. Two restaurants and three bars keep guests sated. Facilities include two pools, a business center and free transportation to the beach at Turtle Bay, a 20-minute ride. Popular especially with business travelers, but fine for vacationers. 57 rooms. Credit cards: A, DC, D, MC, V.

Apartments and Condominiums

A trend on St. Kitts in the '80s was a move toward condo-style properties, most of them located in (now) overbuilt Frigate Bay. What the area does have is a golf course, casino, restaurants, some nightlife and a good beach, and even better beaches along the beautiful southeast peninsula are close by. Additionally, there are good values to be found along here, none better than the **Timothy Beach Resort**, which overlooks Frigate Bay Beach. The swankest villas on the island are offered by the **Golden Lemon** (see "Inns").

Frigate Bay Resort $77–$267 ★★★

Frigate Bay, ☎ (800) 266-2185, (869) 465-8935, FAX (869) 465-7050.
E-mail: frigbay@caribsurf.com.
Single: $77–$175. Double: $77–$175. Suites Per Day: $175–$267.
Set just up from the beach, this hotel consists of four three-story buildings that face either the pool or the hills. Accommodations are air-conditioned and nicely done; many, but not all, have kitchens. There's a swim-up bar in the Olympic-size pool and a bar and restaurant on the premises. Watersports and an 18-hole golf course (free to guests) are within easy walk; the beach is five minutes away on foot. 64 rooms. Credit cards: A, MC, V.

Island Paradise Beach Village $135–$165 ★★

Frigate Bay, ☎ (800) 828-2956, (869) 465-8035, FAX (869) 465-8236.
Single: $135–$165. Double: $135–$165.
This complex of privately owned condominiums is located on the beach and consists of one- two- and three-bedroom units, all with fully equipped kitchens, living/dining areas, and balconies or patios. Some have TV and air conditioning, but not all, so be sure to make reservations accordingly; some include golf in the rates. There's a pool and Italian restaurant on the premises, while tennis and a casino are within walking distance. Good discounts for stays of a week of more. 62 rooms.

Sun 'n Sand Beach Resort $95–$270 ★★

Frigate Bay, ☎ (800) 223-6510, (869) 465-8037, FAX (869) 465-6745.
Single: $95–$270. Double: $95–$270.
Located near Jack Tar, this complex consists of apartment-style one-bedroom studios and charming cottages that house two-bedroom, two-bath units. All have phones, cable TV, kitchens and patios. There are two pools on-site (one for kids),

two tennis courts, and a beach bar and restaurant. The golf course is just across the street, and restaurants and shops are within walking distance. A good combination of self-catering and resort amenities. A 1997 renovation and expansion should leave this property polished for the 1998 season. 84 rooms. Credit cards: A, DC, D, MC, V.

Timothy Beach Resort $65–$165 ★★

Frigate Beach, ☎ *(800) 777-1700, (869) 465-8597, FAX (869) 465-7723.*
Single: $65–$115. Double: $65–$115. Suites Per Day: $95–$165.

This basic condominium complex is just off the beach, on the opposite side of the isthmus from Jack Tar. Accommodations range from standard guest rooms to one- and two-bedroom suites, some with full kitchens. All have air conditioning, phones, private balconies, and coffeemakers. There's a good cafe and bar on-site, as well as an inviting pool and tennis court; watersports await at the beach. Considering the location, one of St. Kitts' best values. 60 rooms. Credit cards: A, MC, V.

Inns

Like its sibling, Nevis, St. Kitts has a rich history visible in the form of plantation inns set on the slopes of a verdant volcano. Each has its own personality—stately **Ottley's** greets guests with well-tended lawns and rows of impressive royal palms, while the seaside **Golden Lemon** exudes eccentricity and color. With each of the following choices, you're 20 to 40 minutes from either the airport or Basseterre, and none have beaches nearby to speak of—a car is a must if solitude keeps you awake at night. Note that **Fairview** has a superb location and much history, too, but has slid several notches from its former glory when it was the first of the plantation homes to welcome tourists. The future of a fifth inn, **White House**, is uncertain; call ☎ *(869) 465-8162* to get an update.

Fairview Inn $80–$150 ★

Fairview, ☎ *(800) 223-9815, (869) 465-2472, FAX (869) 465-1056.*
Single: $80–$150. Double: $80–$150.

Located some ten minutes from Basseterre, this complex consists of cottages set around an 18th-century great house. Guest rooms, housed in the cottages, are small and motel-like, but decent enough if you want that "inn experience" on a budget. Only some are air-conditioned, and not all have ceiling fans, so be sure to make your requests accordingly. The site includes a pool, West Indian restaurant and a bar. You'll need a car to get around. 27 rooms. Credit cards: A, D, MC, V.

Golden Lemon Inn & Villas $160–$500 ★★★★

Dieppe Bay, ☎ *(800) 633-7411, (869) 465-7260, FAX (869) 465-4019.*
Single: $160–$333. Double: $245–$500.

Since 1961 one of the Caribbean's more unique inns, the Golden Lemon is located on a black-sand beach at St. Kitts' northern tip. Seven of the guest rooms are in the 17th-century great house, beautifully restored with lots of fine antiques. The rooms are individually furnished with smashing results—Oriental rugs, West Indian art, raised four-poster beds, ceiling fans (no air), verandas—no two are alike. The site also includes 15 villas with very private plunge pools. There's a main pool and tennis court, and a quaint fishing village out the front gate, otherwise the location encourages solitude and escape—the beach is just fair but snorkeling is good. Full breakfast is included in the rates; no kids under 18 allowed at this tony operation. Not for everyone, but those who love it keep coming back. 22 rooms. Credit cards: A, MC, V.

Ottley's Plantation Inn   **$190–$410**   ★ ★ ★ ★

Ottley's, ☎ (800) 772-3039, (869) 465-7234, FAX (869) 465-4760.
Website: www.interknowledge.com/stkitts-nevis/knkhot01.htm.
E-mail: ottleys@mail.caribsurf.com.
Single: $190–$230. Double: $215–$255. Suites Per Day: $275–$410.

This grand plantation inn sits on a 35-acre estate amid sugarcane fields that unroll magnificently down to the sea. Accommodations are in the 18th-century great house or in a charming cottage, all air-conditioned and sporting antique and wicker furniture, ceiling fans, phones and verandas. New for 1998 is a set of cottages with private plunge pools. The spectacular, spring-fed main pool is built into the ruins of a sugar mill, and there are nature trails for exploring the adjacent rainforest. There's little within walking distance, but they'll shuttle you to the beach. Room rates include breakfast; children under 10 discouraged most of the year. 17 rooms. Credit cards: A, MC, V.

Rawlins Plantation   **$195–$395**   ★ ★ ★ ★

St. Paul's, ☎ (800) 346-5358, (869) 465-6221, FAX (869) 465-4954.
Single: $195–$280. Double: $285–$395.

Located on 12 acres on the northern slopes of Mt. Liamuiga, the scenic views from this charming inn encompass fields of sugarcane, miles of ocean and St. Eustatius in the distance. It was built around the ruins of a 17th-century sugar mill at the north end of St. Kitts on well-landscaped grounds. Guest rooms are in cottages decorated with good local artwork, nice fabrics, four-poster beds, and antiques. No air conditioning, but breezes generally do the job. Guests can relax at the small spring-fed pool, play tennis on a grass court, or enjoy croquet. Breakfast and dinner are included in the MAP-only rates, and afternoon tea is a nice touch. You'll want a rental car to get around—Rawlins is quite isolated—though it's so peaceful and relaxing here you'll have to be motivated to move on. 10 rooms. Credit cards: A, MC, V.

Low Cost Lodging

Good deals can be found at some of the condo/apartment complexes in Frigate Bay listed above, particularly for families. Otherwise, among several options, head for the **Conaree Beach Cottages**, which makes up for a lack of luxury by being positioned right on the beach, just northeast of Basseterre ☎ *(869) 465-8475.* Another possibility is the **Morgan Heights Resort**, 10 minutes drive from Basseterre and a short stroll to the beach ☎ *(869) 465-8633.* **Trinity Inn Apartments** is a family-run operation located on Palmetto Point a few miles west of Basseterre ☎ *(869) 465-3226.* You can also ask around for rooms in private homes, but this option is best explored in person.

Where to Eat

Fielding's Highest Rated Restaurants in St. Kitts

★★★★★	**Royal Palm, The**	$50–$50
★★★★	**Golden Lemon**	$30–$50
★★★★	**Rawlins Plantation**	$35–$35
★★★	**Ballahoo**	$10–$21
★★★	**Chef's Place**	$5–$20
★★★	**Fisherman's Wharf**	$4–$26
★★★	**Georgian House, The**	$21–$27
★★★	**Patio, The**	$26–$30
★★★	**Turtle Beach Bar & Grill**	$16–$24

Fielding's Most Romantic Restaurants in St. Kitts

♡♡♡♡	**Rawlins Plantation**	$35–$35
♡♡♡♡	**Royal Palm, The**	$50–$50
♡♡♡	**Georgian House, The**	$21–$27
♡♡♡	**Golden Lemon**	$30–$50
♡♡♡	**Patio, The**	$26–$30

Fielding's Best Value Restaurants in St. Kitts

★★★	**Chef's Place**	$5–$20
★★★	**Fisherman's Wharf**	$4–$26
★★★	**Ballahoo**	$10–$21
★★	**PJ's Pizza**	$10–$20
★★★	**Georgian House, The**	$21–$27

For such a small island, St. Kitts has a wide spectrum of dining choices, from gourmet delights in historical settings to the homey kitchens of casual local hangouts. Typical St. Kittian delicacies include goat water (an ill-named stew), fried plantain, Creole bean soup, boiled saltfish, conch chowder, and poached parrotfish. The plantation inns have outdoor patios for candlelit dinners, while in Basseterre, dinner at the 400-year-old **Georgian House** is a leisurely, elegant evening in a high-ceilinged salon, with aperitifs enjoyed in the walled garden beneath the big mango tree. At the **Ocean Terrace Inn**, try the Two-Flavor Soup (pumpkin and broccoli) and carrot cake with local sugarcane sauce. Good West Indian food can be enjoyed with street theater at **Ballahoo**, a prime location overlooking the town center. Don't miss a swig of the island brew—Royal Extra Stout—or a glass of mauby, made from tree bark, or the local grapefruit soft drink, Ting.

Ballahoo   **$$**   ★★★
Fort Street; Basseterre, ☎ *(869) 465-4197.*
Lunch: 8 a.m.–6 p.m., entrées $2–$21.
Dinner: 6:30–10 p.m., entrées $10–$21. Closed: Sun.
This upper-level eatery overlooks the bustling downtown district that is Basseterre's version of Piccadilly Circus. The restaurant's customer base is a hodgepodge of cruise ship passengers, businesspeople and shoppers who find a wide variety of items to munch on, including fresh parrotfish fillets, *rotis*, burgers and yummy desserts. The place prides itself in presenting reasonably priced French wines. It's also a great location for West Indian or American-style breakfasts—be adventurous and have saltfish with your eggs instead of bacon. Credit cards: A, MC, V.

Chef's Place   **$**   ★★★
Church Street; Basseterre, ☎ *(869) 465-6176.*
Lunch: 8 a.m.–6 p.m., entrées $5–$10.
Dinner: 6–11 p.m., entrées $5–$20. Closed: Sun.
Get friendly owner Oliver Peetes to describe the West Indian specialties on the daily blackboard—he'll probably oblige. Then settle down on picnic tables outdoors with a streetside view and await generous helpings of *souse* (pigs feet stew with a special sauce) or lamb stew. Main dishes will be rounded out with rice, a tasty salad and island vegetables. Beverages are also homemade and may include *mauby*, a bittersweet and spicy brew made from tree bark, or fresh ginger beer for the less adventurous. Credit cards: not accepted.

Coconut Cafe   **$$**   ★★
Frigate Bay Beach, ☎ *(869) 465-3020.* Associated hotel: *Timothy Beach Resort.*
Lunch: 7 a.m.–4 p.m., entrées $3–$19.
Dinner: 4–11 p.m., entrées $13–$21.
Open to the sea breezes and steps away from the sand on the island's most popular swimming beach, this cafe dispenses three meals a day, but it's most popular for sunset cocktails and fresh seafood suppers to follow. There's steel band entertainment in season on Sunday and Wednesday evenings, and the bar stays open until the wee hours. Credit cards: A, D, MC, V.

Fisherman's Wharf　　　　　　$$　　　　　　★★★

Basseterre, ☎ *(869) 465-2754.* Associated hotel: *Ocean Terrace Inn.*
Dinner: 7–11 p.m., entrées $4–$26.

Eating here is like a beach cookout, with diners choosing meat, fish, or chicken to be grilled to order, and serving themselves from a salad and condiments buffet. Orders are taken to long wooden tables facing the oceanfront. Everything is reliably good, but the fresh lobster and shrimp are standouts. A steel band entertains on Friday. An institution. Credit cards: A, MC, V.

Georgian House, The　　　　　$$$　　　　　　★★★

Independence Square; Basseterre, ☎ *(869) 465-4049.*
Dinner: 6–10 p.m., entrées $21–$27.

This beautifully restored home, decorated with Georgian-era reproductions, is a showcase for a continental menu of seafood, chicken, and steaks, prepared with West Indian flourishes. Peas and rice accompany some of the main courses. Dinner is served nightly on a patio behind the house. Now operated by the owners of the White House. Reservations recommended. Credit cards: A, MC, V.

Golden Lemon　　　　　　　$$$　　　　　★★★★

Dieppe Bay Town, ☎ *(869) 465-7260.* Associated hotel: *Golden Lemon.*
Lunch: 11:30 a.m.–3 p.m., entrées $6–$12.
Dinner: 7-10 p.m., entrées $30–$50.

Some returning visitors would never dream of leaving St. Kitts without at least one visit to this fine restaurant. The three-course dinners are rotated frequently; owner Arthur Leaman creates the internationally themed menus himself. Gleaming antiques and crystal chandeliers accentuate the dining room and a breezy patio is a gathering spot for Sunday brunch and cocktails (11:30 a.m.–3 p.m.; $20). While touring by car, stop by for lunch, which features more informal offerings, including sandwiches, salads and fish dishes. Reservations recommended. Credit cards: A, DC, MC, V.

Patio, The　　　　　　　　$$$　　　　　　★★★

Frigate Bay Beach, ☎ *(869) 465-8666.*
Dinner: 7–8:30 p.m., entrées $26–$30. Closed: Sun.

Although talented chef Helen Mallalieu has gone to university, she trained a replacement and her father stills runs this restaurant positioned on the patio of their Frigate Bay Beach home. Diners face one of the prettiest private gardens on the island while feasting on specialties like pepper pot stew, broiled fresh seafood, and tropical desserts. Wines and liqueurs are complimentary with dinner. Reservations advised in high season. Credit cards: MC, V.

Rawlins Plantation　　　　　$$$　　　　　★★★★

St. Paul's, ☎ *(869) 465-6221.* Associated hotel: *Rawlins Plantation.*
Lunch: 12:30–2 p.m., prix fixe $23.
Dinner: 8 p.m. Seating, prix fixe $35.

Cap off a tour of the island with lunch or dinner at this splendidly restored estate on the northwest coast. A varied buffet of Creole specialties is served to diners on the terrace of the estate's great house, and offerings include curries, fritters, salads, vegetables and several international specialties. Call before noon to make a reservation for a fixed-price dinner of four courses with soup, salad, entree and a tantalizing dessert—possibly chocolate terrine with passion fruit sauce. Credit cards: A, MC, V.

Royal Palm, The $$$ ★★★★★

Ottley's Estate, ☎ *(869) 465-7234.* Associated hotel: *Ottley's Plantation.*
Lunch: Noon–3 p.m., entrées $8–$18.
Dinner: 8 p.m. Seating, prix fixe $50.

Possibly the most creative food on the island is served at this restaurant located in ruins of a sugar mill at Ottley's Plantation. The ever-changing menu has included delights like lobster quesadillas and sweet treats like mango mousse with raspberry sauce. Lunches, dinners and Sunday brunch with champagne are served in a location that couldn't be lovelier—the poolside dining room skirts a nearby rainforest. Fixed-price brunch is $25, and served from 11 a.m. to 2 p.m. Reservations recommended. Credit cards: A, MC, V.

Turtle Beach Bar & Grill $$$ ★★★

S.E. Peninsula Road, ☎ *(869) 469-9086.*
Lunch: 8 a.m.–6 p.m., entrées $16–$24.

Combine an afternoon of snorkeling (the preferred activity), scuba diving, or loafing on the beach with a notable barbecue of chicken, fish, meat, or lobster prepared at this off-the-beaten-track eatery on the southeast coast. Operated by the Ocean Terrace Inn, the Grill is also a cool place Sundays for a well-regarded West Indian buffet replete with live entertainment. Dinner is served only on Saturdays, from 7:30–10 p.m. Watersports equipment can be rented here as well. Credit cards: A, V.

Where to Shop

Shopping in Basseterre is concentrated in the area around **The Circus** and **Pelican Mall**—not coincidentally, also the docking place for cruise ships. T-shirts and duty-free items are found in mass quantities, but among the more unusual spots is the **Spencer Cameron Gallery** at North Independence Square which sells artwork from St. Kitts and around the world. Just below the Ballahoo Restaurant, **Island Hopper** provides a collection of art, pottery, textiles and fabrics. Duty-free items are available at **A Slice of the Lemon** on Fort Street where you can browse through pottery, teas, spices and condiments priced lower than those in St. Maarten or the U.S. Virgin Islands. The **St. Kitts Philatelic Bureau** in Pelican Mall sells a wide variety of the island's famous and collectable stamps.

Outside Basseterre, check into the **Plantation Picture House**, a gallery at Rawlings Plantation featuring the work of Kate Spencer, known for her portraits, landscapes and still lifes, some of them found on stone-washed silk scarves; a smaller store is also located on Fort Street in Basseterre. Located inside the Golden Lemon and with another shop in Basseterre is **Lemonaid**, which sells jewelry, antiques, imported crafts and Island to Island resort wear. Surrounded by lush gardens, **Caribelle Batik** creates and sells their colorful batiks at Romney Manner, above Old Road Town.

St. Kitts Directory

Arrival and Departure

At this time, no airline service connects St. Kitts' airport directly with North America, although winter charter flights are sometimes possible. Among the charter companies to check with are **Travel Charter** in Detroit ☎ *(810) 641-9677* and **T.N.T.** in Boston ☎ *(800) 262-0123*. Otherwise, most visitors travel to the island via San Juan, from where **American Eagle** provides three to five flights daily into St. Kitts. **LIAT** has daily service into St. Kitts from Anguilla, Antigua, Nevis, St. Maarten, St. Thomas and Tortola, with connecting service from a number of other islands through Antigua. The 10-minute hop between Nevis and St. Kitts is served by two local operations: **Air St. Kitts-Nevis** ☎ *(869) 465-8571* and **Nevis Express** ☎ *(869) 469-3346*. Public ferry service from Nevis, aboard the *Caribe Queen* or the *Spirit of Mount Nevis*, makes the 45-minute crossing between Charlestown and Basseterre one to three times daily for $4 one way ☎ *(869) 469-9373*.

The departure tax is $10.

Business Hours

Shops open Monday–Saturday 8 a.m.–noon and 1–4 p.m. Most close earlier on Thursday. Banks open Monday–Thursday 8 a.m.–3 p.m. and Friday 8 a.m.–5 p.m.

Climate

The climate is pleasant and moderate, with an average temperature of 75–85 degrees Fahrenheit. Humidity is low and constant northeast trade winds keep the islands cool. Annual rainfall averages 55 inches; the rainy season extends from June through November.

Documents

U.S. citizens need to present proof of citizenship (passport, voters registration or birth certificate), along with a return or ongoing ticket.

Electricity

The current runs 230 volts, 60 cycles AC. While the electricity supply at some hotels is 110 volts, AC transformers and adapters are generally needed.

Getting Around

Local transportation is available via **minibuses** and **taxis**. Numerous taxi rates are set, among them: from the airport into Basseterre, $5; to Frigate Bay, $10; to Dieppe Bay, $19. From Basseterre to Frigate Bay, $7; to Ottley's, $10.50; to Rawlings, $20. There is a 25 percent surcharge between 11 p.m. and 6 a.m. Prices for island tours by taxi are based on where you begin your trip: from Basseterre, an island tour is about $45; a two-hour tour of the southeast peninsula from Basseterre is $31. **Dave Charles** is a good choice for island taxi-tours ☎ *(869) 465-4253*. **Rental car** rates start at about $35 per day; you'll need to obtain a St. Kitts-Nevis drivers license for $12 at the police station on Canyon Street in Basseterre—drive on the left. Among the firms, all located in Basseterre, are **Avis** ☎ *(869) 465-6507* and **Budget** ☎ *(869) 466-5555*. and **TDC Rentals** ☎ *(869) 465-2991*. Day trips to Nevis are possible via air or fer-ry; see "Arrival and Departure" above.

Language

The official language of both St. Kitts and Nevis is English.

Medical Emergencies

There is a 24-hour emergency room at **Joseph N. France General Hospital** in Buckley ☎ *(869) 465-2551*. Also ask your hotel about physicians on call. Se-rious medical emergencies should be handled in San Juan, Puerto Rico.

Money

The official currency is the Eastern Caribbean dollar. The exchange rate is tied to the American dollar, and trades at about $2.70 for one U.S. dollar. Make sure you know which dollar is being used when your restaurant or hotel bill is calculated since both are widely accepted. You will get a better exchange rate by changing money at a local bank or paying with a credit card.

Telephone

The St. Kitts-Nevis area code *869*. To call St. Kitts from the U.S., dial *1 + (869)* and the local seven-digit number. International calls, telexes and tele-grams can be made from **Skantel** on Canyon Street in Basseterre ☎ *(869) 465-2219*.

Time

Atlantic Standard Time. That is to say, it's one hour ahead of New York time, except during Daylight Saving Time, when it is the same.

Tipping and Tax

Expect a 10 percent service charge added to most hotel and restaurant bills. The room tax is 7 percent.

Tourist Information

Good brochures and information can be found at the **St. Kitts Tourist Board**, *Pelican Mall, P.O Box 132, Basseterre*; ☎ *(869) 465-2620/4040*, FAX *(869) 465-8794*. In the U.S. ☎ *(212) 535-1234*.

Web Site

www.interknowledge.com/stkitts-nevis

When to Go

Carnival celebrations take place in a week-long spectacle the last week of De-cember, featuring calypso competitions, queen shows, street dancing and fes-tivals. The **St. Kitts Music Festival** draws international and regional artists in late June.

ST. KITTS HOTELS		RMS	RATES	PHONE	CR. CARDS
★★★★	Golden Lemon Inn & Villas	22	$160–$500	(800) 633-7411	A, MC, V
★★★★	Ottley's Plantation Inn	17	$190–$255	(800) 772-3039	A, MC, V
★★★★	Rawlins Plantation	10	$195–$395	(800) 346-5358	A, MC, V
★★★	Frigate Bay Resort	64	$77–$175	(800) 266-2185	A, MC, V
★★★	Ocean Terrace Inn	57	$61–$180	(800) 524-0512	A, D, DC, MC, V
★★	Allegro's Jack Tar Village	242	$175–$320	(800) 999-9182	A, MC, V
★★	Bird Rock Beach Hotel	38	$80–$175	(800) 621-1270	A, D, MC, V
★★	Fort Thomas Hotel	52	$100–$160	(800) 851-7818	A, MC, V
★★	Island Paradise Beach Village	62	$135–$165	(800) 828-2956	
★★	Sun 'n Sand Beach Resort	84	$95–$270	(800) 223-6510	A, D, DC, MC, V
★★	Timothy Beach Resort	60	$65–$115	(800) 777-1700	A, MC, V
★	Fairview Inn	27	$80–$150	(800) 223-9815	A, D, MC, V

ST. KITTS RESTAURANTS		PHONE	ENTRÉE	CR. CARDS
International Cuisine				
★★★★★	Royal Palm, The	(869) 465-7234	$8–$50	A, MC, V
★★★★	Golden Lemon	(869) 465-7260	$6–$50	A, DC, MC, V
★★★★	Rawlins Plantation	(869) 465-6221	$23–$35	A, MC, V
★★★	Georgian House, The	(869) 465-4049	$21–$27	A, MC, V
Regional Cuisine				
★★★	Ballahoo	(869) 465-4197	$2–$21	A, MC, V
★★★	Chef's Place	(869) 465-6176	$5–$20	None
★★★	Patio, The	(869) 465-8666	$26–$30	MC, V
★★★	Turtle Beach Bar & Grill	(869) 469-9086	$16–$24	A, V
★★	Coconut Cafe	(869) 465-3020	$3–$21	A, D, MC, V
Seafood Cuisine				
★★★	Fisherman's Wharf	(869) 465-2754	$4–$26	A, MC, V

ST. KITTS

ST. LUCIA

St. Lucia's dramatic countryside includes emerald hills, waterfalls, rainforest, volcanic mineral baths and pristine beaches.

Though it offers golden beaches seductively wrapped by steep mountains and lush highlands that are home to exotic and rare species of bird, plant and wild life—a panoply of the visual truisms the Caribbean is best known for—more than anything else, St. Lucia delivers spectacle. A vibrant, Eden-like vision, this is an island of lavish scenery—prodigious in the vicinity of its landmarks, the Pitons, and lush and colorful elsewhere, with an underwater scene that mirrors the grandeur of the above-water topography. Islanders are gradually catching the eco-tourism bug as they figure out that St. Lucia's chief draw is these wondrous natural resources. Every visitor should drive the sheer roads that wind through the emerald peaks and valleys along the southwestern coast, where jungle flowers scent the air and giggling children soap themselves under roadside water faucets. And to obtain the full Lucian experience, you must get out and tread toe to heel over the dramatic countryside, breathe in the rain forest, and even bathe in the volcano's hot mineral baths.

But the spirit of St. Lucia lies not only in the land but in the people as well—spirited, musical, and forever ready to party. Festivals carve the rhythm of life here, ranging from not one but two quaint, elaborate flower festivals—La Rose and La Marguerite—to a jazz festival in May that draws international musicians and a growing bevy of admirers. St. Lucia is the most developed of the British Windwards, with a bustling population of 143,000 that flirt with relative prosperity. Many are employed by the agricultural industry, but a growing number work directly or indirectly for the tourism sector, which is luring an increasing faction of Americans to its shores.

St. Lucia is well-connected by air to North America, and a surprisingly diverse range of accommodations—from simple inns and local hotels to all-inclusives and luxury resorts—have sprouted to make the island one of the region's most accessible to all kinds of budgets and agendas.

BEST BETS FOR...

Bird's-Eye View

At 238 square miles, pear-shaped St. Lucia is the second largest of the British Windwards, though its vertical heft makes it seem much larger. At 27 miles long, and 14 across at its widest, the island is positioned between Martinique and St. Vincent in the Eastern Caribbean. Like most of its sister Windwards Islands, St. Lucia has a mountainous interior crafted by volcanic activity over the centuries. This is most apparent in the southern half, where the highest mountains (topping out with Mount Gimie at 3118 feet), are overshadowed by a pair of spectacular volcanic plugs a mile and a half apart, Petit Piton and Gros Piton, that rise straight up out of the ocean to 2461 and 2619 feet respectively. Most of the southern half of the island is densely forested in tropical vegetation, with an abundance of flowers such as hibiscus, frangipani, orchids, jasmine and poinciana. A 19,000-acre national forest protects much of this primal area. The bright green jacquot, St. Lucia's own rare and indigenous parrot, is found here—the subject of a successful breeding and education program initiated by Paul Butler that has halted the parrot's slide toward extinction and more than doubled the population to

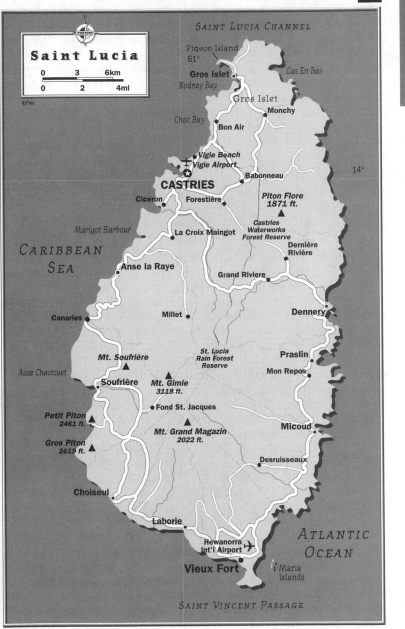

Saint Lucia

0   3   6km
0   2   4mi

©FWI

SAINT LUCIA CHANNEL

Pigeon Island 61°
Gros Islet
Cas En Bas
Rodney Bay
Gros Islet
Monchy
Choc Bay
Bon Air
Vigie Beach
Vigie Airport
CASTRIES
Babonneau
14°
Ciceron
Forestière
Piton Flore 1871 ft.
Marigot Harbour
La Croix Maingot
Castries Waterworks Forest Reserve
Dernière Rivière
CARIBBEAN SEA
Anse la Raye
Grand Riviere
Canaries
Millet
Dennery
St. Lucia Rain Forest Reserve
Praslin
Mt. Soufrière
Mon Repos
Ause Chastcuet
Soufrière
Mt. Gimie 3118 ft.
Petit Piton 2461 ft.
Fond St. Jacques
Mt. Grand Magazin 2022 ft.
Micoud
Gros Piton 2619 ft.
Desruisseaux
Choiseul
Laborie
ATLANTIC OCEAN
Hewanorra Int'l Airport
Vieux Fort
Maria Islands
SAINT VINCENT PASSAGE

almost 500. The northwest coast seems positively cosmopolitan by Caribbean standards, though Castries, the island's capital and victim of one too many fires (the last in 1948), is in need of a beautification project. About half of the 160,000-strong population lives on or near the busy coast between Castries and Gros Islet. Tourism has been growing steadily, with marinas and resorts filling up the coastline north and south of Castries. St. Lucia is trying to learn from the over-development mistakes that have occurred on other islands before it's too late. For now, agriculture remains the larger industry—bananas and coconuts mostly—though marijuana is a major unofficial crop. With the future of Caribbean banana exports increasingly cloudy, it is expected that tourism will become St. Lucia's biggest industry in the near future.

History

The first inhabitants of St. Lucia were probably Arawak Indians, and later Caribs, who did not appreciate the British invasion of their island in the early 17th century; for some time they managed to successfully fend off colonization. In 1650, the French overcame the resistance and settled a colony, completing a treaty with the Caribs in 1660. Over the next 164 years, the island exchanged hands 14 times between the French and British in an almost comical seesaw play of power. It was not until the issue of the 1814 Treaty of Paris that the British finally secured all rights. During this time, the Carib Indians were played as a pawn between the two powers until the British finally—and unceremoniously—exiled them to a still-existing reservation on Dominica. Although the island gained control of its own government on Feb. 22, 1979, its official head of state still remains the British throne, represented by a governor general, who appoints the 11 members of St. Lucia's Senate. The House of Assembly is elected by popular vote.

People

As in most neighboring states, about 87 percent of the inhabitants of St. Lucia are African, descendants of the slaves who were imported as plantation laborers in the 17th and 18th centuries. Almost 10 percent are mixed race; a few islanders are descended from indentured servants brought in from India and still others are of European origin. The rich mixture has produced a highly musical local patois, a combination of French, English and Spanish

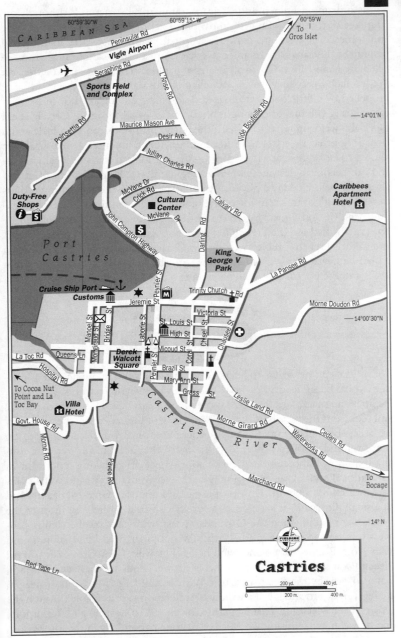

Castries

words utilizing a French and African grammatical structure. Although the language of tourism is English, most private conversations, jokes, street jibe and some court cases are conducted in patois. In most cases friendly and helpful, St. Lucians have retained a love of African and Caribbean rhythms—celebrated annually at Carnival, a calypso explosion held two days before Ash Wednesday. Every small town and village holds dances throughout the year, propelled by a little beer, rum, weed, and music pumped out of speakers at ear-splitting volume. Friday night block parties in the village of Gros Islet are especially welcoming to tourists; other neighborhoods can be a little more closed. Spurred by a less-than-ideal employment situation, some locals are known to be aggressive with visitors—offering guided tours or local wares—and can become aggravated when you refuse them. Be polite, but firm, and always ask before taking a photo. About 80 percent of the population profess to be Roman Catholics. Many of the older women continue to wear the madras head-tie and a modern version of the panniered skirt. Occupation by both the British and the French has left a population celebrating both cricket and savory French Creole cooking. St. Lucia has also given birth to two Nobel Laureates: Sir W. Arthur Lewis won the Nobel Prize in economics in 1979 and the poet Derek Walcott won the 1992 prize in literature.

Beaches

St. Lucia's prime goal is to keep its beaches open to the public, but as pristine as possible. Therefore, you will find only a few with restrooms, changing facilities and snack bars. The best way to locate *your* beach is to hire a sailboat and scope out the possibilities from sea, many of them deserted because they are accessible only by boat. Though there are some real lovelies located on the as yet undeveloped eastern Atlantic coast, they are difficult to reach, usually requiring some combination of four-wheel drive, hiking, and a bit of navigational savvy. One exception is a relatively quiet, gray-sand bay, **Cas En Bas**, located on the northern tip of the island opposite Gros Islet at the end of a small dirt road—it's a nice spot for windsurfing. Otherwise most of the beaches are found along the Caribbean coast, with the sand becoming progressively darker as you head south. Two popular gold-hued strands lead away from Rodney Bay—one wide beach juts west from Gros Islet toward **Pigeon Point** and is popular with locals on weekends, while **Reduit Beach** is watched over by the Rex properties. With several large hotels on or near it, Reduit can be crowded, but a variety of watersports are available through the resorts. **Choc Beach** and **Vigie Beach** are the closest to Castries and the airport, and they can be surprisingly devoid of visitors, particularly in the low season.

Continuing south, the beaches become progressively more exotic; charming **Anse La Raye** is a small beach at the fishing village of the same name—limited facilities, but plenty of shady palms. **Anse Cochon** is a remote cove of black volcanic sand, calm waters for swimming and a romantic setting accessible only by boat. At the end of a rutted road, **Anse Chastanet** offers spectacular snorkeling and diving—the steep drop-off leads quickly to tropical fish, a plethora of sponges and well-preserved coral life. **Anse des Pitons** is tucked between the Pitons, a dramatic setting reached by boat or via the road through Jalousie Resort. At the southern tip of the island, just southeast of Hewanorra Airport, is **Anse de Sables**, or Vieux Fort Beach—a comely, undeveloped expanse facing the Atlantic with miles of coconut palms.

Over the past several years, St. Lucia has emerged as one of the premier dive destinations in the Eastern Caribbean. The island has pristine reefs and vertigo-inducing walls, the latter best exemplified by a quick glance at St. Lucia's shoreside signature peaks, the Pitons, which plunge precipitously into the sea below. The resulting publicity in the dive community has created a popular product, similar to St. Lucia's neighboring attractions, Dominica and St. Vincent. Fortunately, diving was commercialized relatively recently on the island and the government has maintained a firm hand on the number of dive businesses it will license. The area surrounding the Pitons boasts many of the best dive sites, and is where the marine park is centered, but impressive dives are located along the entire length of the Caribbean side. A faint current runs along the coast, sometimes providing drift opportunities off Soufriére Bay, and visibility generally exceeds 75 feet. The coral is unusually clean on St. Lucia, with currents washing over shallower sites to give them an added sheen. Shore diving, is available on the reef at Anse Chastanet, immediately below the similarly named hotel (a great place for beginning divers to start their St. Lucia adventure). A diverse collection of unusual marine life can be found here: frogfish, sea horses, octopus, electric rays and much more. It's also an excellent night dive.

Dive Shops

Scuba St. Lucia

Soufriére; ☎ *(758) 459-7000.*

The region's only SSI facility (an instructor-trainer facility for Divers Alert Network); also a PADI Five Star facility. Ideally located at Anse Chastanet, this is St. Lucia's biggest and oldest operation, with a staff of 22. Two-tank dive, $66. Also features a two-day, four-dive introductory course for those wanting more than a resort course, but less than certification (starts at $200).

Dolphin Divers

Marigot Bay; ☎ *(758) 451-4974.*

A PADI Five Star facility and an Instructor Development Center with courses through Assistant Instructor. Opened in 1992 and works with smaller groups off a 32-foot catamaran dive boat. Two-tank dive, $70, including equipment ($60 if you bring your own).

On Foot

St. Lucia's volcanic spikes, The Pitons, are surrounded by dense jungle.

St. Lucia still contains extensive and marginally explored rainforest within the range of mountains which form a spine leading down the western side of the island. Mount Gimie (3118 feet) is St. Lucia's highest peak, but you'll need a guide to locate the difficult trail to its summit. Peak-baggers can tack le three other points: the two Pitons, the spectacular spires rising above the town of Soufriére, and Piton Flore, a peak within easy reach of the north coast resorts. The excellent *Ordnance Survey* 1:50,000 topographical map of St. Lucia can be found at a few bookstores in Castries. Be forewarned, however, that the considerable network of enticing tracks displayed on the map frequently are found to be overgrown and/or impossible to follow. Paths are often muddy, particularly following rain, of which the island's interior receives an ample share. A guide is strongly advised for the difficult ascent of the Pitons and any other extensive explorations; the helpful staff of the Forest and Lands Department can provide trail and guide information ☎ *(758) 450-2231* or *(758) 450-2078*. Also, beware of the rare *fer de lance*, the poisonous snake that lurks in St. Lucia's back yard; bites are infrequent, but can be deadly. Finally, for those seeking a gentler stroll, the Union Nature Trail offers a 45-minute gravel-paved loop through dry woodland forest; it is located in the hills beneath the community of Babonneau, east of Castries.

What Else to See

A driving tour is the best way to see St. Lucia, but be forewarned—road conditions vary from adequate to miserable, and driving is on the left. One bit of good news: the road between **Castries** (where many of the hotels are) and **Soufriére** (where most of the scenic attractions are located) has finally been improved after a three-and-a-half year construction period. Otherwise, begin your tour in **Castries**, the island's densely populated capital, where the harbor is nestled within a long-extinct volcanic crater. The town was a classic West Indian port a few decades ago, but a series of fires, as well as contemporary commerce and population expansion has conspired to replace most of the old Victorian wooden architecture with buildings of glass, steel and concrete. The best opportunity to experience the old hustle-bustle is on Saturday mornings, when **market** takes over at the corner of Jeremie and Peynier streets, and local farmers and island artisans lay out their wares for serious barter. Stop by **Derek Walcott Square**, where a 400-year-old *samaan* tree shades the Cathedral of the Immaculate Conception, built in 1897; the late-Victorian-era **Government House** stands nearby. Above and south of the town is **Morne Fortune** and **Fort Charlotte**, where good views can be had encompassing Castries, the Pitons, and Martinique on a clear day; see if you can note the difference at the fort between the French architecture and British walls built at different stages of occupation. The area north of Castries is heavily developed, and the village of **Gros Islet** comes wildly alive on Friday nights with a raging weekly street festival—the "jump-up" is noisy with *soca*, reggae and other beats of the Caribbean. The prominent peninsula just beyond Gros Ilet is **Pigeon Island**, connected by causeway to the coast and home to an 18th-century British naval garrison, a museum, and beaches for picnicking.

If you're not overnighting in the Soufriere area, a full day should be allotted to explore the west coast south of Castries. Picturesque **Marigot Bay** is a lush and slender harbor that was where Rex Harrison talked to the animals in the 1967 film *Doctor Doolittle*, now inhabited by yachties and others who enjoy the secluded location. The tiny fishing villages of **Anse la Raye** and **Canaries** are also charming, though afternoons are the best time to visit when the colorful boats come in with their daily catch. The island's oldest settlement, **Soufriére**, lies at the foot of sheer **Petit Piton**, one of the most dramatic settings a village could wish for. The new marketplace in Soufriére is decorated with colorful murals and gingerbread trim; otherwise the shabby town, at one time the capital of the island until it was destroyed by a hurricane in 1780, retains a Third World aura. Stop by the **Morne Coubaril Estate** above Soufriére, a working plantation that offers a 60-minute guided tour. The road that winds up and behind the Pitons affords more great views, though you may want to pull in at the dormant **drive-in volcano** and sulfur springs. It presents a face akin to a B-horror movie, complete with open pits of fuming sulfur and bubbling mud—guides are omnipresent and a good one will add to your exploration of the strange site. Also nearby is the **Diamond Mineral Baths**, constructed by order of Louis XVI when his doctors recommended the waters for French soldiers stationed in the area. At the southern tip of St. Lucia off Vieux Fort is the **Maria Islands Nature Reserve**, where a species of lizard and bird exist that are found nowhere else in the world.

Historical Sites

Fort Charlotte   ★★★

Morne Fortune.

Set atop a hill 853 feet above sea level and overlooking Port Castries, this fortress was started by the French in 1764 and finished 20 years later by the British. Today it holds government and education offices, but it's worth a trip for the great views if nothing else. The grounds include a military cemetery that dates back to 1782 where French and British soldiers are buried as well as six former governors.

Museums and Exhibits

Morne Coubaril Estate   ★★★★

Soufriere, ☎ (758) 459-7340
Hours open: 9 a.m.–5 p.m.

A working plantation estate that is also open to the public, Morne Coubaril was originally established in the 1700s. It has seen coconut, cocoa, manioc, sugarcane and more produced on its grounds; the 60-minute guided tour will explain how slaves lived and worked the plantation, how its bounty was processed (long before the days of electricity), and more. A fascinating overview of Caribbean plantation life and agriculture. General admission: $6.

Parks and Gardens

Maria Islands Nature Reserve ★★★

Off Vieux Fort, ☎ *(758) 454-5014.*

Hours open: 10 a.m.–4 p.m.

This reserve consists of two small islands in the Atlantic—one 25 acres, the other just four. It is home to a thriving population of birds and rare snakes and lizards. Great snorkeling off the larger island, Maria Major. The price to visit the island is $30 per person, arranged in advance through the reserve office in Vieux Fort. Note that the island is closed during breeding season, May through September.

Pigeon Island National Park ★★★★

Pigeon Point, ☎ *(758) 452-5005.*

Hours open: 9 a.m.–4 p.m.

This 40-acre one-time island is now connected to the mainland by a causeway. It has a long history and was used for all manner of operations before becoming a national park—pirates hid out here in the 1600s, the French and British militaries used it as a fort, and long before any of them, the Arawak Indians lived here. Ruins from some of these days still exist, but this is also a place to picnic and hang out on its picturesque beaches; there are great views from the breezy summit, 359 feet above Rodney Bay. There's also a spiffy interpretive center. General admission: $4.

Tours

Diamond Falls and Mineral Bath ★★

Soufriere Estate, Soufriere.

Hours open: 10 a.m.–5 p.m.

The water in these sulfuric mineral baths averages a toasty 106 degrees Fahrenheit. Louis XVI ordered them built in 1784 so French soldiers stationed in the area could soak the supposedly curative waters. Bring your suit so you, too, can "take the waters." General admission: $3.

Sulfur Springs ★★★

Soufriere

Hours open: 9 a.m.–5 p.m.

Called the world's only drive-in volcano, Qualibou Caldera encompasses a seven-acre crater complete with pool of boiling mud and sulfurous waters. The most recent major activity was a steam eruption around 1766, but otherwise, it's a good spot to see what a Caribbean volcano looks like. Drive to the entrance, where a guide will hop in your car for the tour around the site.

Sports

Watersports are available at most hotels, with **windsurfing**, **waterskiing**, **sailing** and other activities usually available. Strong windsurfers head for two spots: Anse de Sables, the bay on the southeastern tip of the island between the Hewanorra Airport and Maria Islands; or Cas en Bas, a cove on the northern tip of the island, also facing the Atlantic. Conditions for windsurfing are fine along the western coast, and particularly suitable for beginners, but more advanced windsurfers like the rougher, choppier waters of the Atlantic coast. **Tennis courts** are available at many of the island's larger resorts, and **golfers** can enjoy two moderate nine-hole courses. Half- and full-day **fishing** charters are available and can be arranged through hotels or resorts, or at the marinas at Rodney Bay and Castries. The main fishing season runs from January to June, reeling in tuna, kingfish and dolphin; the rest of the year the catch is closer to shore. St. Lucians depend on fishing for their livelihood, and you can join fishermen to use lines and pots to catch snapper, lobster and reef fish. Yachtsmen and day-trippers from Castries tend to congregate in Soufriére, beneath the Pitons. The region's major charter operator is **The Moorings**, operating out of Marigot Harbour and offering day cruises for four to six passengers with lunch and drinks—bareboat or with crew. Other day cruise operators can be found at Rodney Bay, with Stevens Yachts one of the most foremost names in the region. **Horseback riding** through the countryside or along beaches is also available.

Golf

The choices for duffers are limited to two nine-hole courses. **St. Lucia Golf and Country Club** ☎ *(758) 450-8523* in Cap Estate is open to the public and includes a 320-yard driving range. A better-maintained private course at **Sandals St. Lucia** ☎ *(758) 452-3081* is only available when not fully booked by guests at the island's two Sandals resorts.

Horseback Riding

At least two stables await the horseman (and woman): **International Riding Stables** ☎ *(758) 452-8139* and **Trim's** at Cas en Bas ☎ *(758) 452-8273*. Rides can be arranged through the countryside, along the beach, or to some of northern St. Lucia's sights, like Pigeon Island.

Watersports

If your hotel doesn't offer the watersports you're seeking try one of these. Deep-sea fishing: **Mako Watersports** ☎ *(758) 452-0412* and **Captain Mike's** ☎ *(758) 452-7044*. **Mistral Windsurfing** ☎ *(758) 452-8351* specializes in board rentals and instruction, as does **Island Windsurfing**, located on Anse de Sable Beach ☎ *(758) 454-7400*. For cruises and snorkel expeditions, call **Captain Mike's** ☎ *(758) 452-0216*, **Surf Queen** ☎ *(758) 452-8351*, **Brig Unicorn** ☎ *(758) 452-6811*, and **Cat Inc.** ☎ *(758) 450-7044*. Finally, **St. Lucian Watersports** ☎ *(758) 452-8351* offers waterskiing and parasailing in addition to general equipment rentals.

Where to Stay

Fielding's Highest Rated Hotels in St. Lucia

★★★★	Anse Chastanet	$120–$530
★★★★	LeSport	$290–$620
★★★★	Royal St. Lucian	$310–$600
★★★★	Windjammer Landing	$150–$450
★★★	East Winds Inn	$300–$700
★★★	Ladera Resort	$195–$690
★★★	Rendezvous	$325–$400
★★★	Rex St. Lucian Hotel	$140–$195
★★★	Sandals St. Lucia	$520–$1029
★★★	Wyndham Morgan Bay Resort	$265–$520

Fielding's Best Rooms With a View in St. Lucia

★★★	Ladera Resort	$195–$690
★★★★	Anse Chastanet	$120–$530
★★	Hummingbird Beach Resort	$30–$130
★★★★	Windjammer Landing	$150–$450
★★★	Marigot Beach Club	$83–$180

Fielding's Best Value Hotels in St. Lucia

★★	Hummingbird Beach Resort	$30–$130
★★	Orange Grove Hotel	$45–$83
★★	Islander Hotel	$55–$95
★★★	Marigot Beach Club	$83–$180
★★	Bay Gardens	$80–$125

St. Lucia offers an impressive range of lodging possibilities, from all-inclusive resorts to luxury hotels, intimate inns to budget digs—the best are surrounded by lush greenery and overlook gold- or black-sand beaches. Almost all accommodations are found in the relatively small coastal section between Castries and Gros Islet, yet the island's signature view—the Pitons—is located to the south, in the town of Soufriere, where a handful of hotels serve a growing clientele. Some families do best at all-inclusive resorts since everything is usually right out your door and you'll spend less time running around searching for activities to please everybody (though neither **Rendezvous** nor **Sandals** allows kids). Otherwise, for a memorable vacation, consider one of the island's more individualistic accommodations, where you'll get to know the staff on a first-name basis.

Note that although most hotels are located in or north of Castries, the larger planes that many visitors arrive on can only fly into Hewanorra Airport, on the island's southern tip (only smaller aircraft can land at Vigie Airport, just outside Castries). If flying into Hewanorra, allow a full 90 minutes for the drive to Castries.

Hotels and Resorts

St. Lucia has a variety of traditional resort accommodations, but the island also boasts some pretty unique hotels that aim to provide a full-blown tropical experience in the most memorable fashion. If you stay at **Ladera**, where rooms view Petit Piton from a stone's-throw distance, you won't want to go anywhere else, so fabulous is the setting—but **Anse Chastenet** has its own special view of the Pitons, with breathtaking snorkeling and diving on the beach below as well. A Mediterranean village is the setting for **Windjammer Landing**, a resort that continues to be popular for almost any type of vacation, while the **Royal St. Lucian** showcases an all-suite, all-deluxe haven for beach aficionados. Closed for almost two years, **Jalousie Plantation** was formally acquired by Hilton with plans for a late 1997 opening—we'll have a report on the resort for next year's edition.

Anse Chastenet   **$120–$630**   ★★★★

Anse Chastenet, ☎ (800) 223-1108, (758) 459-7000, FAX (758) 459-7700.
Single: $120–$375. Double: $166–$530. Suites Per Day: $380–$630.

Located two miles outside Soufriere at the end of a miserable road and nestled amid a 500-acre beachfront plantation, Anse Chastenet is a world apart. The resort sits astride a steep, forested ridge that descends to a silvery black-sand beach. Accommodations are found on the hillside or at beach level (sans view), but not one of the 49 beautifully designed rooms are alike. The least expensive units are captivating octagonal gazebos with ceiling murals that replicate a nighttime sky; there are also bungalows that hang out from the crest of the ridge into the forest to provide a treehouse setting (a towering pine vaults out of the shower and through the roof in one). Or spring for a premium unit at the top of the property—immense suites lit by rows of bobbing lanterns where one wall may be discretely omitted, providing you and your mate a private CinemaScope panorama of the Pitons. All rooms are individually decorated with fine contemporary international artwork and locally crafted furniture. The grounds include an excellent dive center (lots of scuba enthusiasts), two solid restaurants, two bars, and tennis courts. Service is swift, belying its

ST. LUCIA

outpost quality, by women in coyly knotted madras headwear. No pool or air conditioning, and lots of stairs, but no one's complaining. Mandatory MAP in winter. 49 rooms. Credit cards: A, DC, MC, V.

Bay Gardens $80–$125 ★★

Rodney Bay, ☎ *(758) 452-8060, FAX (758) 452-8059.*
E-mail: destangd@candw.lc.
Single: $80–$125. Double: $80–$125.
This new addition to St. Lucia's popular Rodney Bay area caters to business travelers, who are accommodated with professional service, a *New York Times* fax daily, and conference rooms, but it's a pleasant spot for vacationers, too. Standard rooms are a bit small, or you can spring for a junior suite; decor is attractive and fresh in all. Next to the marina, but not much view to speak of. Two pools, a very good restaurant and ice cream shop, and colorful island atmosphere, but make sure a large group won't be checking in during your visit. Reduit Beach is a ten-minute walk. 53 rooms. Credit cards: MC, V.

Ladera Resort $195–$690 ★★★

Soufriere, ☎ *(800) 738-4752, (758) 459-7323, FAX (758) 459-5156.*
Single: $195–$690. Double: $195–$690.
Set on a steep, vine-clad hillside 1000 feet above sea level, this romantic hideaway offers a stupendous view of the Pitons and beyond. Accommodations are in a hodge-podge of woodsy villas lining an airy ridge, each furnished with wicker, four-poster beds and 19th century French antiques. But the real selling point for these suites and villas is the completely open wall in each that affords a breathtaking view, yet still provides complete privacy. All units were revamped in 1996–97 to incorporate personal plunge pools (some larger than others) and a few also have a Jacuzzi—the property seems to finally be locating its niche. The food in the restaurant is fine; a bar and smallish communal pool round out the limited facilities. The location is pretty isolated, and the nearest beach is attained by (free) transport only. Expensive? Quite, but this one-of-a-kind spot is very special, and popular with lovers in search of real peace and seclusion. 19 rooms. Credit cards: A, MC, V.

Rex St. Lucian Hotel $140–$195 ★★★

Reduit Beach, ☎ *(800) 255-5859, (758) 452-8351, FAX (758) 452-8331.*
Single: $140–$195. Double: $140–$195.
Sitting on one of the island's best beaches, this sprawling Rex resort houses guests in nondescript rooms that are air-conditioned and comfortable enough. A much-needed renovation in 1996 spruced things up nicely, particularly the lobby and restaurant area. The grounds include two bars, a pool, two tennis courts, and watersports, including a certified windsurfing school; the beach is excellent, if sometimes crowded. Not the most luxurious resort on St. Lucia by any means, but the rates are fair, and the active set is kept happy. Formerly a 260-room property, 140 rooms were split off to form the Rex Papillion all-inclusive next door. 120 rooms. Credit cards: A, CB, DC, MC, V.

Royal St. Lucian $310–$600 ★★★★

Reduit Beach, ☎ *(800) 255-5859, (758) 452-9999, FAX (758) 452-9639.*
Single: $310–$600. Double: $310–$600.

Located on lovely Reduit Beach, this all-suite Rex resort delivers St. Lucia's most upscale vacation experience. Long on modern conveniences, short on lived-in personality, the three-story Royal added a pampering spa in 1997. Standard rooms are quite spacious and luxurious, with air-conditioning, mini-bar, bathrobes, and expansive, marble-tiled bathrooms—beachfront suites have huge sundecks overlooking the sea. The hotel's centerpiece is a tropical pool, complete with swim-up bar. Two restaurants, 24-hour room service, and tennis and watersports await next door at the Rex St. Lucian, the hotel's sister property. Elegant, and a heady rate card to prove it. 96 rooms. Credit cards: A, DC, MC, V.

All-Inclusives

Three couples-only properties make the biggest splash on the all-inclusive scene. Sandals, the Caribbean's chain of all-inclusive resorts, has two locations on the island: the original, **Sandals St. Lucia**, has the most expensive rate card of the ten Sandals properties, while **Sandals Halcyon** opened in 1994 on the site of the former Halcyon Beach Club at Choc Bay. **Rendezvous** offers a more low-key interpretation of the couples concept, and throws in a free, no-frills weddings, too. At all three of these properties, however, note that "couples only" is a strictly Southern Baptist interpretation—same-sex couples are not permitted past the guards at the entrance.

Extensive spa facilities characterize **LeSport**, where the beach, tennis courts, golf course and accommodations are only steps from each other. Not to be left out of the all-inclusive game, the Rex Resorts chain split the Rex St. Lucian into two hotels and created a new, 140-unit facility, **Rex Papillion**, to snare the all-inclusive crowd. Finally, if the convenience of an all-inclusive option appeals to you, but you don't want the hustle of a big resort, **East Winds Inn** (see "Inns") is an intimate, 26-room resort (though with a more limited roster of activities and amenities).

| Club St. Lucia | $106–$316 | ★★ |

Smuggler's Cove, ☎ (800) 777-1250, (758) 450-0551, FAX (758) 450-0281.
Single: $106–$161. Double: $206–$316.

This huge, moderately priced all-inclusive located just north of Pigeon Island appeals to both families and singles. Guestrooms are good-sized, if plain, spread around the 50-acre sloping property; note that the least expensive rooms rely on ceiling fans—you'll pay an extra $25–$30 per night (double) for an identical air-conditioned unit. Ocean view rooms are somewhat bigger with a Jacuzzi in the bathroom. There are three pools, a fitness center, two restaurants, a disco, nightly entertainment, and supervised children's programs. Rates include access to a private tennis club with nine courts and pro lessons. Sunfish sailing, waterskiing and other watersports await on two fair beaches. While it doesn't lay on all the frills available at some of the bigger all-inclusives, Club St. Lucia is a very good deal for the price, particularly for solo travelers. 312 rooms. Credit cards: A, D, MC, V.

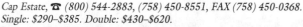

| LeSport | $290–$620 | ★★★★ |

Cap Estate, ☎ (800) 544-2883, (758) 450-8551, FAX (758) 450-0368.
Single: $290–$385. Double: $430–$620.

Prepare to be pampered at this all-inclusive situated at St. Lucia's secluded northern tip and encompassing some 18 acres. The resort's health spa, the Oasis, is a lavish

Moorish-themed facility with exercise classes, yoga and t'ai chi programs, and wonderful treatments like massages, facials and body wraps—two a day included in the rates. Guest rooms benefited from a recent renovation, with canopy beds and balconies that overlook a lovely beach, though a few common areas are in need of attention. Meals place an emphasis on healthful preparations, but there's just one dining room for breakfast, lunch and dinner. Tennis, golf, archery, watersports, nightly entertainment and bicycles are part of the package; you can even obtain full PADI certification as part of your stay. LeSport offers a less-boisterous all-inclusive experience, though for all its new-agey trappings, the resort is a bit soulless and the operation could be warmer. Minimum age is 10 years January-March. 102 rooms. Credit cards: A, DC, D, MC, V.

Rendezvous $325–$450 ★★★

Vigie Beach, ☎ (800) 544-2883, (758) 452-4211, FAX (758) 452-7419.
Double: $325–$400. Suites Per Day: $395–$450.
Now managed by SunSwept (which operates LeSport), this all-inclusive follows Sandals' twosomes-only formula, though at a more relaxed pace. Encompassing seven acres with two miles of beachfront at the end of Castries' Vigie runway, it houses guests in garden or oceanfront rooms in one- to three-story buildings. All rooms feature air conditioning, modern amenities, and balconies or patios. The Luxury Ocean Front Suites are best, with hammocks strung across attractive octagonal decks; standard rooms are fairly simple. The rates include all meals, drinks, and activities, and there's plenty to do: two pools, two tennis courts, watersports, exercise classes in the gym. There's daily entertainment in the Terrace Bar, and night owls appreciate the Piano Bar, which stays open until the last guest leaves. Tipping is not allowed. 100 rooms. Credit cards: A, MC, V.

Rex Papillion $272–$374 ★★

Reduit Beach, ☎ (800) 255-5859, (758) 727-4556, FAX (758) 452-8331.
Single: $272–$340. Double: $306–$374.
An annexed part of the Rex St. Lucian, Papillion is yet another of St. Lucia's long line of all-inclusives, but there's not much beyond the beach to make this one stand out. The least expensive rooms are spare and lack air conditioning, bathtub or TV, while pricier units add in these features and an extra few square feet; some boast an ocean view. The pool is a tad small for a resort of this size (usually brimming with kids) and the beach here is backed by a wall to keep out those not wearing a Papillion wristband. Rates include non-motorized watersports and a well-equipped fitness room, along with the usual meals and drinks. 140 rooms. Credit cards: A, MC, V.

Sandals Halcyon $474–$637 ★★★

Choc Bay, ☎ (800) 726-3257, (758) 452-5331, FAX (758) 452-5434.
Double: $474–$637.
This 22-acre resort joined the Sandals family in 1994 after a previous incarnation as the Halcyon Beach Club Hotel. Set on a nice beach four miles north of Castries, Halcyon has a more relaxed pace than Sandals St. Lucia. The rates cover everything from soup to nuts, with three restaurants and seven bars from which to choose—nightly theme parties are a big part of the scene. The main restaurant, The Pier, is

lovely, with great views from over the water. Recreational facilities include two tennis courts, three pools with swim-up bars, fitness center, watersports, plenty of organized tours, and nine holes of golf at Sandals St. Lucia (Halcyon guests may use all the facilities at the sister property). 170 rooms. Credit cards: A, MC, V.

Sandals St. Lucia $520–$1029 ★★★

Castries, ☎ (800) 726-3257, (758) 452-3081, FAX (758) 452-1012.
Double: $520–$686. Suites Per Day: $700–$1029.

Sandals' most expensive and deluxe venue, this 155-acre resort is set in a cove just outside Castries. Couples are housed in standard rooms that are nicely done with four-poster beds and modern amenities; there are also several different categories of suites with living rooms, VCRs, refrigerators, and terraces—some even have private plunge pools. Common-area features include three pools (one is the largest in the Eastern Caribbean), five restaurants, karaoke bar, a disco and theme nights. The rates include virtually everything, including tennis on five courts, nine holes of golf (club rental is extra), watersports (including diving), fitness classes, and lots of activities. Everything proceeds at a feverish pitch: the pool is always busy, the bars are always humming and Sandals' "playmakers" will do everything in their power to make sure you have a good time, whether you like it or not. 273 rooms. Credit cards: A, MC, V.

Wyndham Morgan Bay Resort $265–$520 ★★★

Choc Bay, ☎ (800) 996-3426, (758) 450-2511, FAX (758) 450-1050.
Single: $265–$345. Double: $360–$520.

This very American resort is located a mile north of Castries on a small beach. Guest rooms are modern and personality-neutered (you could be in Des Moines), but with all the creature comforts Wyndham strives for. The rates include all meals, drinks and activities, and there's plenty to keep guests busy: four tennis courts, a fitness center, watersports (scuba and fishing cost extra), and nightly entertainment. Children are kept occupied in organized programs. This 22-acre property offers a polished package, but little Lucian ambience. 238 rooms. Credit cards: A, D, MC, V.

Apartments and Condominiums

In addition to the options below, you can rent luxurious villas, or more basic digs that come with a kitchen. Decide on whether you want to be close to the tourist hub or away from it all; an apartment in rustic Soufriere will be more secluded than a number of other options. Fruits and vegetables can be picked up at the local market, and fish can be bought right off the boats. **Tropical Villas** ☎ *(758) 450-8240* and **Island Link Villa Service** ☎ *(758) 453-6341* are the primary sales agents.

Harmony Marina Suites $75–$135 ★★

Rodney Bay, ☎ (800) 446-2747, (758) 452-0336, FAX (758) 452-8677.
E-mail: harmony@candw.lc.
Single: $75–$115. Double: $75–$135.

This family-owned, apartment-style hotel is set on Rodney Bay, some 200 yards from Reduit Beach. Standard rooms are air-conditioned suites with coffeemakers and minifridge; some also have kitchenettes. Deluxe units have four-poster beds, Jacuzzi and a private sundeck. All are serviced by maids. The grounds include a pool, mini-market, good restaurant and a body therapy studio with massage and body wraps. A decent value and popular with families. 30 rooms. Credit cards: A, D, MC, V.

Tuxedo Villas $95–$135 ★★

Rodney Bay, ☎ *(758) 452-8553, FAX (758) 452-8577.*
Single: $95–$135. Double: $95–$135.
A recent addition to the Rodney Bay area, this block of apartments aims for "home away from home" atmosphere, and largely succeeds. Each of the bright, nicely decorated one- and two-bedroom units are self-contained, with cable TV, phone and full kitchen (a supermarket is a five-minute walk). The pool is small, but Reduit Beach is just across the street behind the Royal St. Lucian. An attractive, relaxed spot for independent types and families. 10 rooms. Credit cards: MC, V.

Windjammer Landing $150–$450 ★★★★

Labrelotte Bay, ☎ *(800) 958-7376, (758) 452-0913, FAX (758) 452-9454.*
Website: www.WLV-Resort.com.
Single: $150–$450. Double: $150–$450.
Set on 55 attractively landscaped acres on a hillside overlooking a man-made beach, Windjammer Landing is a village-style enclave of bright white Mediterranean suites and villas. All are spacious and beautifully done, with living and dining rooms, kitchenettes, air conditioners, and modern conveniences. Most of the villas, from one to four bedrooms each, have a private plunge pool; guests staying in the suites can use one of two shared swimming pools. Windjammer combines the best of self-sufficient housing (including a well-stocked on-site mini-mart), with the pampering of a resort, including nightly turndown, four bars and restaurants, two tennis courts, a fitness center and watersports. Parents can stash their kids in supervised programs, available year-round. The number of villas at the bustling property has been increasing over the years; it remains to be seen if the space will become over-developed. Until then, Windjammer is a very appealing resort concept that, while not cheap, provides solid value for the money. 133 rooms. Credit cards: A, DC, MC, V.

Inns

Staying at a smaller property affords a chance for interaction with islanders in more congenial surroundings, sometimes well off the beaten track. **Inns of St. Lucia** is an umbrella organization that covers more than two dozen smaller properties on the island. The common denominator doesn't seem to be that they're strictly intimate lodgings so much as smaller guys who grew tired of being elbowed out of the picture by the marketing efforts of the big resorts. Nonetheless, the portfolio for the organization—which includes properties ranging from three rooms to 62—is handy, and available through the **St. Lucia Tourist Board** ☎ *(800) 456-3984* or *(758) 452-4599.*

East Winds Inn $300–$700 ★★★

Labrelotte Bay, ☎ *(800) 223-9832, (758) 452-8212, FAX (758) 452-9941.*
Single: $300–$525. Double: $450–$700.
This small, garden-embroidered inn has carved out a pretty unique niche, to the point of near-invisibility among Americans vacationers. It's an all-inclusive, but offers none of the feverish pace or rah-rah attitude of a Sandals. But it's more than

a beach resort with a mandatory meal plan. The bar is stocked with top brands, like Roderer champagne, and meals include afternoon tea and a four-course dinner (including lobster on Fridays)—all part of the rates. Each of its bungalows has a king size bed and living area with a stocked mini-fridge and coffeemaker on the patio. Rooms rely on ceiling fans to keep things cool; deluxe units have attractive sunken rock-wall showers. There is a library and a pool with a swim-up bar, kayaking and snorkeling off the small beach and live entertainment several nights a week. UK customers, who love the private club feel, make up most of the clientele. 26 rooms. Credit cards: MC, V.

Hummingbird Beach Resort $30–$145   ★★

Soufriere, ☎ *(758) 459-7232, FAX (758) 459-7033.*
Single: $30–$95. Double: $40–$130. Suites Per Day: $95–$145.
Psst—interested in one of the Caribbean's great views for under $100 a night? This small inn is located at the north end of Soufriere, facing Petit Piton. The two least-expensive units are fine for low cost digs, though they share a bathroom and one lacks a view. Other guest rooms have the panorama, along with ceiling fans (no air), mosquito netting over four-poster beds, and cozy balconies—nicely atmospheric. There's also a suite with air conditioning, and a cute two-bedroom cottage that rents for $150–$250, perfect for two, or a family. The grounds are tropical and end at a fair black-sand beach; the pool is small but lovely. Good restaurant, and don't miss the giftshop, which sells the owner's batiks. 10 rooms. Credit cards: A, D, MC, V.

Marigot Beach Club $83–$180   ★★★

Marigot Bay, ☎ *(758) 451-4974, FAX (758) 451-4973.*
Single: $83–$180. Double: $83–$180.
This charming inn, formerly Doolittle's (but not to be confused with Marigot Bay Hotel a few hundred yards away), is perched at the base of a tropical hillside and accessible only by a one-minute ride on a gingerbread-trimmed ferry. Pleasant rooms with cathedral ceilings, small kitchenettes and large, screened porches are in the main building, while 10 one- two- and three-bedroom villas with screened, open-air living areas and kitchens lie up the hill. Trade winds into the idyllic bay ensure you won't mind the lack of air conditioners. The hotel caters to divers, with an on-site PADI shop as well as a variety of watersports (not included in rates), a boutique, gym ($8 per person, per day), a pool, bar and restaurant. The oasis-like beach looked scrawny during a 1997 visit, but owners were planning to replenish the sand. Note that you are miles from the island's other resorts and activities, but the setting is paradise. 22 rooms. Credit cards: A, MC, V.

Low Cost Lodging

There are quite a few budget-to-moderate options available on St. Lucia, some of which are covered in the portfolio created by the Inns of St. Lucia (see "Inns" above), but don't always trust a description sight unseen. Expect little in the way of location, air conditioning or decor at budget guest houses.

Candyo Inn $60–$90   ★

Rodney Bay, ☎ *(758) 452-0712, FAX (758) 452-0774.*
Single: $60–$75. Double: $60–$75. Suites Per Day: $75–$90.

You can walk to the beach in five minutes from this small hotel. The four guest rooms are standard and well-kept, with modern amenities like phones, TV, clock radios, and nice touches like bougainvillea on your pillow. The eight apartments have kitchens and more room to spread out; all accommodations are air-conditioned. Facilities are limited to a snack bar and pool. There are many restaurants within walking distance, and this well-run, well-located budget operation is a good deal. 12 rooms. Credit cards: A, MC.

Islander Hotel $55–$95   ★★
Rodney Bay, ☎ *(800) 278-5824, (758) 452-8757, FAX (758) 452-0958.*
Single: $55–$90. Double: $65–$95.
Guests at this laid-back hotel can choose from standard rooms (tall ceilings, skylight, minimalist decor) and ones with a kitchenette on the porch. All are air-conditioned and benefit from maid service. The grounds include a restaurant, terrace bar and nice pool. The beach is a five-minute walk away, and there are lots of nearby eateries. Not much character, but quite a bargain. 60 rooms. Credit cards: A, D, MC, V.

Orange Grove Hotel $45–$83   ★★
Bois D'Orange, ☎ *(800) 777-1250, (758) 452-9040, FAX (758) 452-8094.*
Single: $45–$70. Double: $55–$83.
A recently renovated hotel between Rodney Bay and Choc Bay, the Orange Grove is one of the island's better values, housing guests in an orange-trimmed 19th century French Colonial-style plantation. Room furnishings are simple but fresh—rattan furniture, tile floors and king size beds in all units. What keeps the price down is an isolated hilltop location, but there are nice views and the hotel provides a free daily shuttle to Choc Bay. 62 rooms. Credit cards: MC, V.

Still Beach Resort, The $65–$80   ★
Soufriere, ☎ *(758) 459-5179, FAX (758) 459-7301.*
Single: $65–$80. Double: $65–$80.
Named after the antique distillery on the terrace overlooking Soufriere Bay and the Pitons, this small apartment-style complex showcases a great view at a modest price, but little else. Accommodations are in spacious one-bedroom units or standard-size studios; each has a full kitchen, and shares a pleasant balcony with the other rooms. An OK black-sand beach is immediately below and town is a five-minute walk. In all, a fair deal for the scenery, but hope for neighbors you like at this intimate property. This same family's 300-acre working plantation one mile inland, also called The Still, has some comparably-priced rooms (and a huge pool) but the isolated location works against it. 5 rooms. Credit cards: A, D, MC, V.

Where to Eat

Fielding's Highest Rated Restaurants in St. Lucia

★★★★	Bang (between the Pitons)	$12–$19
★★★★	Green Parrot	$34–$41
★★★★	Piton	$45
★★★	Bistro, The	$11–$23
★★★	Capone's	$16–$32
★★★	Charthouse	$15–$34
★★★	Dasheene	$19–$27
★★★	Hummingbird	$15–$36
★★★	Jimmie's	$15–$25
★★★	San Antoine	$15–$28

Fielding's Most Romantic Restaurants in St. Lucia

♡♡♡♡♡	Dasheene	$19–$27
♡♡♡♡♡	Piton	$45
♡♡♡♡	Hummingbird	$15–$36
♡♡♡♡	San Antoine	$15–$28
♡♡♡	Green Parrot	$34–$41

Fielding's Best Value Restaurants in St. Lucia

★★	Kimlan's	$5–$6
★★★	Key Largo	$6–$17
★★★	La Creole	$1–$26
★★★	Bistro, The	$11–$23
★★★	Capone's	$16–$32

Although international cuisine has made its way into St. Lucia, efforts at upscale dining are stymied by the number of all-inclusive resorts (since guests have paid for meals up front, there's no incentive to splurge on a gourmet meal outside the hotel). Still, St. Lucia's fertile volcanic soil supports a cornucopia of exotic fruits and vegetables; the six types of local bananas are particularly delicious. Island chefs make inventive use of papayas, soursops, mangos, passionfruit and coconuts. Some restaurants take advantage of the unparalleled natural beauty, with stellar views available at some spots. Spectacular **Dasheen**—perfect for lunch or an afternoon cocktail—is barely kissing distance from Petit Piton, while **Hummingbird** is a more humble spot with Piton views across the bay. One of the most atmospheric eateries is **San Antoine**, perched in the hills overlooking Castries, which incorporates the walls of a 19th-century greathouse, with antique tableware to match. **Naked Virgin** in Castries is a good bet for traditional West Indian and Creole specialties such as callaloo, curry and pepperpot stew. Excellent jerk chicken, and green fig and saltfish (a local specialty), can be tried at **Jimmie's**.

Bang (between the Pitons) $ ★★★★
Soufriere, ☎ *(758) 459-7864.* Associated hotel: *Jalousie.*
Dinner: 4–11 p.m., entrées $12–$19.
Colin Tennant, aka Lord Glenconner, has a reputation that precedes him. He had the inspiration to purchase and develop a little island named Mustique a few decades back, and later bought a chunk of Lucian land between a couple of rocks named the Pitons. Jalousie was developed, but Mr. Tennant turned his focus to this restaurant, a collection of charming gingerbread houses that surround an outdoor dining area and informal stage, just off the beach. The food is solid and local, if unspectacular—stewed goat, callaloo soup, grilled chicken and fish—but the entertainment is sizzling: identical acrobatic twins who juggle sharp and fiery objects to music, roping much of the gasping crowd into the action. Check to make sure the show is scheduled for the night you visit (reservations are a good idea), and you might meet Lord Glenconner to boot. Credit cards: MC, V.

Bistro, The $$ ★★★
Rodney Bay, ☎ *(758) 452-9494.*
Dinner: 5–10:30 p.m., entrées $11–$23.
The British owners of this marina-side pub offer shrimp and calamari etouffee, wiener schnitzel, a varied, extensive seafood menu (dorado a specialty), West Indian pepperpot and pasta. Dining is on a wide elevated deck and nautical types and others like the 20 percent discount on food items before 6:30 p.m., sort of a Caribbean early bird special. Closed Thursdays in summer. Credit cards: A, MC, V.

Camilla's $$ ★★
7 Bridge Street, Soufriere, ☎ *(758) 459-5379.*
Lunch: 11:30 a.m.–2 p.m., entrées $4–$9.
Dinner: 6:30–9 p.m., entrées $8–$28.
A cute new establishment in rustic Soufriere, Camilla offers the best "local food" in the area. The lunch menu is uninspired, but look for a specials board that has more

interesting offerings, while dinner includes a fresh catch (pan fried, curry or Creole), beef (au poivre, stroganoff or Creole) and a large selection of shellfish. A pair of tables on the tiny, second-floor balcony are prime spots for viewing the Soufriere street scene. Credit cards: MC, V.

Capone's $$$ ★★★

Rodney Bay, ☎ *(758) 452-0284.*
Dinner: 4:30–10:30 p.m., entrées $16–$32. Closed: Mon.

Patrons are served by staff dressed as 1930s mobsters and a Jazz Age atmosphere predominates. But for all the fun, the Italian food is skillfully prepared if pricey. Dishes include fresh pastas, grilled fish, juicy steaks and veal. If the atmosphere is too heavy in the main dining room, there's a pizza parlor adjacent serving decent pies, burgers and sandwiches for lunch and dinner. Reservations recommended. Credit cards: A, MC, V.

Charthouse $$$ ★★★

Rodney Bay, ☎ *(758) 452-8115.*
Dinner: 6–10:30 p.m., entrées $15–$34. Closed: Sun.

St. Lucia's franchise of this popular, all-American steakhouse chain overlooks the Rodney Bay yacht harbor—a pretty setting. Guests like the service from a loyal staff (though regulars seem to get preferential treatment) and the food, which is steak, lobster (in season), tangy baby back ribs, and some Caribbean specialties—all familiar and well-prepared. The restaurant is a fern-filled wood-frame house that exudes warmth, but reserve early to get one of the few tables that actually overlooks the water. Reservations recommended. Credit cards: A, MC, V.

Dasheene $$$ ★★★

Soufriere, ☎ *(758) 459-7850.* Associated hotel: *Ladera Resort.*
Lunch: 11 a.m.–2:30 p.m., entrées $12–$17.
Dinner: 6:30–9:30 p.m., entrées $19–$27.

The lusty view from this hilltop aerie is unbeatable, nestled next to Petit Piton, just above Soufriere. Located in the rustic/chic villa resort, Ladera, Dasheene is named after an exotic leaf used in cooking, and the menu, which changes often, incorporates locally grown produce, prime meats and seafood—all under the auspices of new chef Robert Skeete. Fish and shellfish are delivered to the restaurant daily, and the desserts are renowned. A must for lunch for those making the daytrip from the Castries area to Soufriere. Bring a swim suit for a before-meal dip in the sublime pool. Reservations recommended. Credit cards: A, D, MC, V.

Ginger Lily $$ ★★

Rodney Bay, ☎ *(758) 452-8303.*
Lunch: 11:30 a.m.–2:30 p.m., entrées $6–$30.
Dinner: 6–11:30 p.m., entrées $6–$30.

Cantonese specialties are on hand at this popular restaurant near the resorts of Reduit Beach. There's a long list of familiar favorites, which pleases locals who flock here often when the urge hits. Combination dinners run up to $13 per person, and lunch specials are also available, with several courses for under $8 (lunch is served Tuesday-Saturday only). Credit cards: MC, V.

Green Parrot $$$ ★★★★

Red Tape Lane, Castries, ☎ *(758) 452-3399.* Associated hotel: *Green Parrot.*
Lunch: Noon–3 p.m., entrées $6–$30.
Dinner: 7 p.m.–midnight, prix fixe $34–$41.
Chef Harry brought his years of culinary expertise learned at Claridge's in London home to St. Lucia, and now cooks and entertains nightly at this lively spot on a hilltop in Morne Fortune, overlooking Castries. His spiced pumpkin creation, "soup oh la la" will make you say just that when you taste it—dinner offerings include curries, fish, and an avocado brimming with saltfish called "stuffed pussy." Portions are huge and no one goes away unsatisfied. Green Parrot is a wild scene on Wednesday and Saturday nights when belly or limbo dancers (including Harry) reign. On Monday's, women with a flower in their hair dine free when accompanied by gents in jacket and tie. Reservations recommended. Credit cards: A, D, MC, V.

Hummingbird $$$ ★★★

Soufriere, ☎ *(758) 459-7232.* Associated hotel: *Hummingbird Resort.*
Lunch: 10 a.m.–4 p.m., entrées $7–$21.
Dinner: 7–10 p.m., entrées $15–$36.
Combine lunch with a plunge in the pool at this restaurant located in a rustic inn on the Soufriere waterfront with lush views of Petit Piton. Visitors flock here when the house specialty, freshwater mountain crayfish, is in season. At other times, enjoy other tasty seafood dishes including offbeat choices like whelks and octopus, along with steaks, sandwiches and rich desserts—great selection of tropical drinks, too. One drawback: service can be slow and disjointed. The stone-walled, open-air dining room is decorated with batiks by the owner. Credit cards: A, D, MC, V.

Jimmie's $$$ ★★★

Vigie Marina, Castries, ☎ *(758) 452-5142.*
Lunch: 11 a.m.–4 p.m., entrées $5–$7.
Dinner: 4–11 p.m., entrées $15–$25. Closed: Sun.
Jimmie's garden-fringed bar has long been known as the place to meet and greet, but the cuisine, authentic West Indian specialties prepared by a chef who trained in fine restaurants in England, is also worth noting. Jimmie James offers delicious crepes stuffed with vegetables and seafood, saltfish and green fig (bananas)—a respected tradition—and the Friday and Saturday night special of *bouyon* (a robust pork, chicken and bean stew). And if you're feeling extravagant, order "the most expensive cocktail in the Caribbean"—a Vanessa Smile—for $75. At least it serves eight. The setting overlooks Vigie Marina, just outside Castries, where the ambience might be a bilge pump sputtering gently in the night. Somehow, it works. Credit cards: A, MC, V.

Key Largo $ ★★★

The Marina, Castries, ☎ *(758) 452-0282.*
Lunch: 11:30 a.m.–4 p.m., entrées $6–$17.
Dinner: 4–10 p.m., entrées $6–$17. Closed: Mon.
Sophisticated California-style pizzas on a patio are served at this small restaurant with its own outdoor brick oven. Try the house specialty, a pizza made with arti-

chokes and shrimp, or make do with one of several tasty salads. All manner of Italian coffee drinks are dispensed here as well. Credit cards: MC, V.

Kimlan's $ ★★

Micoud Street, Castries, ☎ *(758) 452-1136.*
Lunch: 7 a.m.–4 p.m., entrées $5–$6.
Dinner: 4–11 p.m., entrées $5–$6. Closed: Sun.
A local family runs this upper-level West Indian restaurant with a terrace positioned directly across from Columbus Square. Steaming bowls of curry, fish stews or chicken roti are served with rice, salad and provisions. A good spot for people watching, and for lighter snacks and ice cream.

La Creole $$ ★★★

Rodney Bay, ☎ *(758) 450-0022.*
Lunch: Noon–3 p.m., entrées $10–$26.
Dinner: 7–10 p.m., entrées $10–$26.
Don't judge a book—or in this case, a restaurant—by its cover. La Creole is housed on the second floor of a non-descript building just off the main road heading north, before Gros Islet; you'll have to hunt for a sign. But the French Creole delights that pour out of the kitchen are much like the real ones found in the French West Indies. Revel in the taste of accras (fritters), crab backs, lambi (conch) creole, crayfish broth, chicken colombo (curry), grilled shark with capers and more, just as found in the better Martinique establishments. Desserts are fabulous. Credit cards: MC, V.

Lime, The $$$ ★★

Rodney Bay, ☎ *(758) 452-0761.*
Lunch: 11 a.m.–3 p.m., entrées $4–$16.
Dinner: 6:30–10 p.m., entrées $11–$28. Closed: Tue.
Lots of locals hang out at the Lime, particularly on Monday nights, when live music draws a big crowd to the pleasant outdoor patio. Food is strictly by-the-book, but try the Lucian fish Creole or conch in one of several sauces for a taste of local. Steaks, burgers, *roti*, sauteed shrimp and lobster round out the menu. Credit cards: MC, V.

Piton $$$ ★★★★

Soufriere, ☎ *(758) 459-7000.* Associated hotel: *Anse Chastenet.*
Dinner: 7–9:30 p.m., prix fixe $45.
Great sunset views of the Pitons mingle with fine creole and continental food at this lovely, greenery-enhanced dining spot. The five-course fixed price menu changes daily, but might include a roast pork loin, grilled mahi mahi or vegetarian *gateaux*; desserts range from light to hefty. A beachside bar at this same resort, Trou au Diable, is a great place to dine between ocean dips, with *rotis*, pepperpot, chicken and beef *satays* or sandwiches to entice you away from snorkeling. The staff is quite welcoming at both places. Credit cards: A, DC, D, MC, V.

Rain $ ★★

Derek Walcott Square, Castries, ☎ *(758) 457-7246.*
Lunch: 9 a.m.–5 p.m., entrées $4–$19.
Dinner: 5–11 p.m., entrées $7–$21.
Rain embodies the romance, charm and Somerset Maugham aura of a steamy tropical novel. Located in an elegant and gingerbread-fringed, tin-roofed house over-

looking Derek Walcott Square, the restaurant remains a popular lunchtime choice with local businesses, despite a recently chaotic management history. The drinks are still heady and rum-based, but the dinner menu is not quite up to its sophisticated former self as the new owners look to find a niche. The new chef turns out good roti and grilled fish, and shish kabobs and steaks are decent. Credit cards: A, MC, V.

San Antoine   **$$$**   ★★★

Old Morne Rd., Castries, ☎ *(758) 452-4660.*
Lunch: Noon–2 p.m., entrées $15–$28.
Dinner: 6:30–midnight, entrées $15–$28. Closed: Sun.
The surroundings are old fashioned and gracious, with meals served in the main house of the old San Antoine Hotel. The elegant dining room, lit by candles at night, is run by an English couple who keep things purring along smoothly. Those looking for a special night out often choose this salon, which overlooks the twinkling lights of the harbor. The menu includes French and continental specialties, including seafood in parchment, pepper steak, or filet mignon with crayfish stuffing. A five-course fixed-price dinner is available for $34. Reservations recommended. Credit cards: A, MC, V.

Where to Shop

St. Lucia is not a big shopping destination, though the ardent browser will find a few treasures. In Castries, a new harborfront shopping complex, **Pointe Seraphine**, features a large variety of duty-free imports such as designer perfumes, crystal and china. You'll also find native crafts and resortwear, but avoid the complex when a cruise ship has docked. You'll find more variety of bananas than you ever knew existed on Saturday, market day, at the 100-year-old **Castries market**, which provides a chance to rub shoulders with hundreds of farmers' wives displaying luscious tropical fruits and vegetables, spices and local crafts; don't be shy about asking to sample a bite of tamarind, but keep a watch on your handbag and wallet. The **government handicraft store** at the waterfront provides a nice selection—woven fruit baskets are good buys for your kitchen back home. Other shops sell wood carvings, pottery and locally made baskets. Hand-screened clothing and colorful batik apparel are featured buys, particularly at the **Caribelle Batik** store. St. Lucia's artists tend to specialize in designs and portraits of the island's flora and fauna. More local crafts are available outside Castries—two spots that merit a visit are **Bagshaws**, a store selling silk-screened work by local artist Sydney Bagshaw, including shirts, skirts and a variety of other apparel (located across from the Sandals Halcyon); and the **Arts and Crafts Centre** near Choiseul on the southwest coast, where craftspeople are usually at work and baskets, dishes, tapestries and woodcarvings are a good buy.

ST. LUCIA

St. Lucia Directory

Arrival and Departure

St. Lucia has two airports—a smaller one, **Vigie**, on the edge of Castries and a larger airstrip suitable for jets, **Hewanorra**, at the southern tip at Vieux Fort. Since most of the hotels are located close to Castries, Vigie is far more convenient for most visitors, but you'll be flying in on a smaller plane. The hotels located near Soufriere are more convenient to Hewanorra.

American Airlines has flights into both airports daily out of their hub in San Juan, Puerto Rico (Vigie is served by **American Eagle**), allowing connections from a majority of U.S. cities they serve. **Air Jamaica** now serves Hewanorra several times a week out of both New York's JFK and their hub in Montego Bay, Jamaica, with connecting service out of major U.S. cities. **BWIA** offers direct flights into Hewanorra several times a week out of JFK and Miami; BWIA also has limited service from other islands in the region. Within the Caribbean, **LIAT** provides direct or nonstop service to Vigie out of Antigua, Barbados, Caracas, Carriacou, Dominica, Grenada, Guadeloupe, Martinique, St. Kitts, St. Vincent and Trinidad, as well as connecting service from most other islands. LIAT also has a daily flight between Hewanorra and St. Vincent, and a daily flight between Hewanorra and Vigie. The island's own **Helen Air** ☎ *(758) 452-7196* serves the short hops between St. Lucia and its neighbors. **Charter service** is increasingly available to St. Lucia out of major U.S. markets, though primarily in winter months.

L'Express des Iles provides scheduled hydrofoil service between Martinique and St. Lucia; daytrips are about $70 round-trip ☎ *(758) 452-2211*.

The airport departure tax is $11.

Business Hours

Shops open weekdays 8 a.m.–12:30 p.m. and 1:30–4 p.m. and Saturdays 8 a.m.–noon. Banks open Monday–Thursday 8 a.m.–3 p.m., Friday 8 a.m.–5 p.m. Some banks in Rodney Bay also open Saturday from 9 a.m.–noon.

Climate

Temperatures year-round average between 70 and 90 degrees Fahrenheit. Trade winds keep the air cool and humidity from becoming oppressive.

Documents

U.S. and Canadian citizens need to show a full and valid passport. British citizens need no passport if their stay does not exceed six months. An ongoing or return ticket must also be shown.

Electricity

Current runs 220 volts, 50 cycles, with a square three-pin plug. A few hotels use 110 volts, 50 cycles. Bring an adapter and converter plug.

ST. LUCIA

Getting Around

Travel between Castries and other towns, including Soufriere, can be accomplished in local minibuses, usually crowded with passengers, baggage and produce—you might share your seat with a carton of tomatoes. Buses leaving Castries for Soufriere and Vieux Fort can be picked up in front of the department store on Bridge Street; to get to Rodney Bay or Cap Estate, take the bus near the market on Jeremy Street. The price of your trip is based on distance.

Taxis will take you almost anywhere on the island. Drivers have excellent experience with the roads outside the capital and many have been trained as guides for tourists; **Christopher Moise** is one good choice ☎ *(758) 451-7521.* Cars are unmetered, but official rates have been set by the government that will cover almost any set of destinations. Before setting off, verify the price in advance, and in what currency—when someone says dollar, you must check whether they are referring to American or Eastern Caribbean currency. A taxi from Castries to Soufriere will cost $60, one-way.

Rental cars are easy to obtain, but note that St. Lucia's 281 miles of paved roads are steep, winding and potholed, and frequent rain showers means sections can be washed out—driving is on the left. You'll need to procure a local drivers license ($12, available through rental agencies or at the Immigrations Office on arrival). Most of the island's numerous rental firms are linked with major U.S. rental companies, which makes reservations easier and, if anything goes wrong, you can contact the head office back home. **Avis** ☎ *(800) 331-1212* or *(758) 452-2700,* **Budget** ☎ *(800) 527-0700* or *(758) 452-0233,* and **Hertz** ☎ *(800) 654-3131* or *(758) 452-0679* each have multiple locations around the island. Expect to pay about $50 a day for a stick-shift economy model without air conditioning (multi-day rentals are sometimes less); there may also be a per-kilometer charge.

Language

The official language is English, and spoken by everyone—though a good deal of French works its way into the local patois.

Medical Emergencies

A 24-hour emergency room is available at **St. Jude's Hospital**, Vieux Fort ☎ *(758) 454-6041* and **Victoria Hospital**, Hospital Road, Castries ☎ *(758) 452-2421.*

Money

The official currency is the Eastern Caribbean dollar, commonly referred to as E.C. It is pegged to the American dollar and trades at $2.70 to one U.S. dollar. American currency is accepted almost everywhere, but verify which currency is being used when you are quoted prices, particularly in smaller hotels and restaurants.

Telephone

The area code for St. Lucia is *(758).* All local numbers have seven digits—to call the island from the U.S., dial *1 + (758),* then the seven-digit number. International phone calls can be made at the offices of the **Cable and Wireless** in the George Gordon Building on Bridge Street in Castries ☎ *(758) 452-3301.* Phone cards from Cable and Wireless may save you money on overseas calls.

Time

Atlantic Standard Time, all year round, one hour later than New York time. During Daylight Saving Time, however, it is the same hour.

Tipping and Taxes

The government imposes an 8 percent occupancy tax on hotel rooms. Hotels and restaurants add a 10 percent service charge, but check your bill carefully. In restaurants it is customary to tip waiters or waitresses 10–15 percent if it has not already been added to the bill. Airport porters usually receive about 75 cents a bag.

Tourist Information

The main office of the **St. Lucia Tourist Board** is located at Point Seraphine, at the cruise ship port ☎ *(758) 452-2479.* They also have offices at Vigie Field, Vieux Fort and in Soufriere. There is also a U.S. office that can help with questions and brochures ☎ *(800) 456-3984* or *(212) 867-2950.*

Web Site

www.interknowledge.com/st-lucia

When to Go

January 1 and 2, the local **New Year's** celebration, culminates in a two-day street fair offering local foods, island music, and dancing and games for children. **Carnival** is celebrated the two days prior to Ash Wednesday in mid-February, with elaborate costumes, dancing until dawn and national calypso contests. The annual **St. Lucia Jazz Festival** takes place in the middle of May, with outdoor concerts at Pigeon Island and late-night performances at hotels around the Castries area. June 29 is the **Feast of St. Peter**, or Fisherman's Day, where priests bless the fishermen's brightly decorated boats. August 30 is the **Feast of St. Rose de Limt**, a spectacular flower festival dating back to the 18th century where members of La Rose Flower Society dress in costume to sing Creole songs and dance quadrilles in the streets. An annual culinary competition in October, **Annou T'juit Sent Lisi**, lures judges from throughout the region to sample fare from island restaurants and hotels. The annual **Billfish Tournament** is also held in October, as well as the island's second flower festival, the **Feast of St. Margaret Mary Alacoque**, which is based on African traditions shaped by political affiliations with France and England. November 22 is **St. Cecilia's Day**, celebrated by musicians who serenade through the streets of Castries. Early December brings the **Atlantic Rally for Cruisers**, the world's largest trans-Atlantic yacht race, when more than 100 yachts set sail for St. Lucia from the Canary Islands.

ST. LUCIA HOTELS	RMS	RATES	PHONE	CR. CARDS
★★★★ Anse Chastanet	49	$120–$530	(800) 223-1108	A, DC, MC, V
★★★★ LeSport	102	$290–$620	(800) 544-2883	A, D, DC, MC, V
★★★★ Royal St. Lucian	96	$310–$600	(800) 255-5859	A, DC, MC, V
★★★★ Windjammer Landing	133	$150–$450	(800) 958-7376	A, DC, MC, V
★★★ East Winds Inn	26	$300–$700	(800) 223-9832	MC, V
★★★ Ladera Resort	19	$195–$690	(800) 738-4752	A, MC, V
★★★ Marigot Beach Club	22	$83–$180	(758) 451-4974	A, MC, V
★★★ Rendezvous	100	$325–$400	(800) 544-2883	A, MC, V
★★★ Rex St. Lucian Hotel	120	$140–$195	(800) 255-5859	A, CB, DC, MC, V
★★★ Sandals Halcyon	170	$474–$637	(800) 726-3257	A, MC, V
★★★ Sandals St. Lucia	273	$520–$686	(800) 726-3257	A, MC, V
★★★ Wyndham Morgan Bay Resort	238	$265–$520	(800) 996-3426	A, D, MC, V
★★ Bay Gardens	53	$80–$125	(758) 452-8060	MC, V
★★ Club St. Lucia	312	$106–$316	(800) 777-1250	A, D, MC, V
★★ Harmony Marina Suites	30	$75–$135	(800) 446-2747	A, D, MC, V
★★ Hummingbird Beach Resort	10	$30–$130	(758) 459-7232	A, D, MC, V
★★ Islander Hotel	60	$55–$95	(800) 278-5824	A, D, MC, V
★★ Orange Grove Hotel	62	$45–$83	(800) 777-1250	MC, V
★★ Rex Papillion	140	$272–$374	(800) 255-5859	A, MC, V
★★ Tuxedo Villas	10	$95–$135	(758) 452-8553	MC, V
★ Candyo Inn	12	$60–$75	(758) 452-0712	A, MC
★ Still Beach Resort, The	5	$65–$80	(758) 459-5179	A, D, MC, V

ST. LUCIA RESTAURANTS	PHONE	ENTRÉE	CR. CARDS
Chinese Cuisine			
★★ Ginger Lily	(758) 452-8303	$6–$30	MC, V
Creole Cuisine			
★★★ La Creole	(758) 450-0022	$10–$26	MC, V
International Cuisine			
★★★★ Green Parrot	(758) 452-3399	$6–$41	A, D, MC, V

ST. LUCIA RESTAURANTS	PHONE	ENTRÉE	CR. CARDS
Italian Cuisine			
★★★ Capones	(758) 452-0284	$16–$32	A, MC, V
★★★ Key Largo	(758) 452-0282	$6–$17	MC, V
Regional Cuisine			
★★★★ Bang (between the Pitons)	(758) 459-7864	$12–$19	MC, V
★★★★ Piton	(758) 459-7000	$45	A, D, DC, MC, V
★★★ Charthouse	(758) 452-8115	$15–$34	A, MC, V
★★★ Dasheene	(758) 459-7850	$12–$27	A, D, MC, V
★★★ Hummingbird	(758) 459-7232	$7–$36	A, D, MC, V
★★★ Jimmie's	(758) 452-5142	$5–$25	A, MC, V
★★★ San Antoine	(758) 452-4660	$15–$28	A, MC, V
★★ Camilla's	(758) 459-5379	$4–$28	MC, V
★★ Kimlan's	(758) 452-1136	$5–$6	
★★ Lime, The	(758) 452-0761	$4–$28	MC, V
★★ Rain	(758) 457-7246	$4–$21	A, MC, V
Seafood Cuisine			
★★★ Bistro, The	(758) 452-9494	$11–$23	A, MC, V

SINT MAARTEN
SAINT MARTIN

Port la Royale Marina in Marigot, St. Martin, offers boat rentals, boutiques and excellent restaurants.

Half-Dutch, half-French, the island of Sint Maarten/Saint Martin provides a unique, bi-polar vacation for the price of one. Sint Maarten, the Dutch side, is part of the trio of islands that make up the Dutch Windwards (which includes nearby Sint Eustatius and Saba), while Saint Martin belongs to the French West Indies, a sub-prefecture of the French department of Guadeloupe, 140 miles to the southeast. A mere welcoming sign acts as the only border between the two sides—nary a customs officer in sight—and English is frequently a common denominator. The split personality doesn't end with linguistics, however, for each side of the island goes out of the way to define its own identity. Marigot, the capital of the more refined French side, is the place to go if you're looking for unique French shopping or fine Creole and Gallic cooking. The Dutch capital, Philipsburg, has a port catering to cruise ships, an array of some of the region's best duty-free shopping, and an upscale nightlife that includes more than a dozen casinos. Throw in a healthy dose of Caribbean cultures imported by the many nationalities that work on the island and you have a vibrant medley of not two, but at least three cohabiting influences.

Beyond a fine parcel of beaches, one thing consistent all the way around the island is massive development. It started in earnest on Sint Maarten during the 1960s, but two decades later the French side was embarking on an equally enthusiastic game of catch-up. The upshot is that, by the 1990s, well over 7000 hotel rooms had been built on the two sides of the small island and more than one million tourists annually had become essentially the sole economy. That providence was delivered a devastating wallop from Hurricane Luis in September 1995. The storm shuttered huge hotels, siphoned sand away from postcard-perfect beaches, and left thousands under- or unemployed as businesses tried to re-group. The storm ripped the roof off other problems—pollution, overcrowding, crime—that were already solidly in place, and the respective governments have been forced to acknowledge both how dependent they are on the tourism sector, and how fragile that market is. Two years later, more than 1000 rooms are still closed as hotel owners tussle with insurance companies and time-share owners, delaying their reopening indefinitely.

But as a whole, the island is physically back in shape and will soon re-emerge as a vacation hot spot. Despite the unusual twin-nation status, the island's long-standing popularity stems not from its uniqueness, but rather from the reliability and convenience of its vacation product—time-share properties are seemingly endless and many American visitors come once or twice a year. Slip into News Cafe, the island's popular bar and disco, and the one thing that stands out is how very *American* the atmosphere is. No, Sint Maarten/Saint Martin is not terribly Caribbean, but vacationers looking for a heady dose of duty-free shopping, a smattering of photogenic beaches, and some of the best, most varied dining in the region, will probably not leave disappointed.

The island must be doing something right. It did, after all, survive *Speed 2*.

BEST BETS FOR...

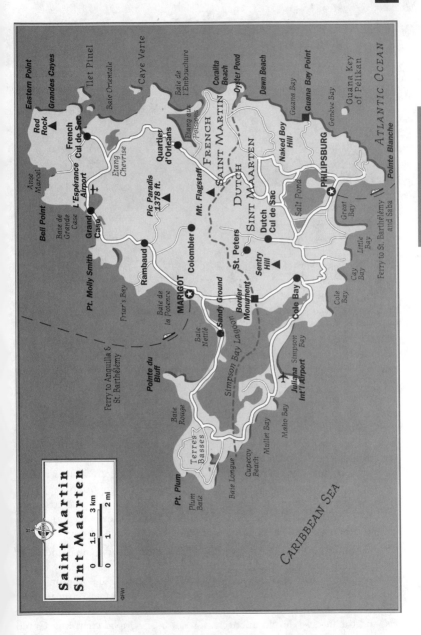

Saint Martin / Sint Maarten

ATLANTIC OCEAN

Eastern Point
Grandes Cayes
Îlet Pinel
Caye Verte
Red Rock
French Cul de Sac
L'Espérance Airport
Baie Orientale
Baie de l'Embouchure
Cocalita Beach
Oyster Pond
Dawn Beach
Guana Bay
Guana Bay Point
Guana Key of Pelikan
Geneve Bay
Grand Case
Baie de Grande Case
Bell Point
Pt. Molly Smith
Anse Marcel
Étang Chevrise
Quartier d'Orléans
Étang aux Poissons
FRENCH SAINT MARTIN
DUTCH SINT MAARTEN
PHILIPSBURG
Pointe Blanche
Pic Paradis 1378 ft.
Mt. Flagstaff
Naked Boy Hill
Rambaud
Colombier
St. Peters
Dutch Cul de Sac
Salt Pond
Great Bay
Friar's Bay
Baie de la Potence
MARIGOT
Sandy Ground
Sentry Hill
Ferry to St. Barthélemy and Saba
Little Bay
Cay Bay
Border Monument
Cole Bay
Cole Bay
Baie Nettlé
Ferry to Anguilla & St. Barthélemy
Pointe du Bluff
Baie Rouge
Simpson Bay Lagoon
Juliana Simpson Int'l Airport
Simpson Bay
Maho Bay
Terres Basses
Baie Longue
Mullet Bay
Cupecoy Beach
Pt. Plum
Plum Baie
CARIBBEAN SEA

Saint Martin
Sint Maarten

N

0   1.5   3 km
0   1   2 mi

©FWT

Simpson Bay Lagoon, with Saba in the background, is spectacular at sunset.

One of the smaller islands in the Eastern Caribbean, Sint Maarten/Saint Martin's 37-square-mile territory is almost three-fifths French-owned, while a little more than two-fifths of the land is Dutch. The western side of the island is low-lying and primarily comprised of Simpson Bay Lagoon, an excellent harbor for smaller craft shared by both the French and Dutch. The rest of the island is more hilly, almost conical, rising to 1378 feet at Paradise Peak. Coves scallop the coastline, some of which are backed by salt ponds (salt production was once a principal economy). Though the island is relatively scrubby and dry, one area of the French side, a sheltered valley named Colombier, is comparatively verdant. Though it once supported sugarcane and other crops, little of the island is used for produce today, preferring instead to import the fruits and vegetables it consumes, even including the guavaberries used for the island's famed guavaberry liqueur.

With about 60,000 residents (as of a pre-hurricane census), the island is the most populous per square mile of any in the Caribbean, particularly on the crowded Dutch side, where residents are tucked into dense communities in valleys that clamber up from Philipsburg, the Dutch capital. Marigot is the capitol of the French side—it is no longer the sleepy fishing village it once was, and the intense development has also now enveloped charming Grand

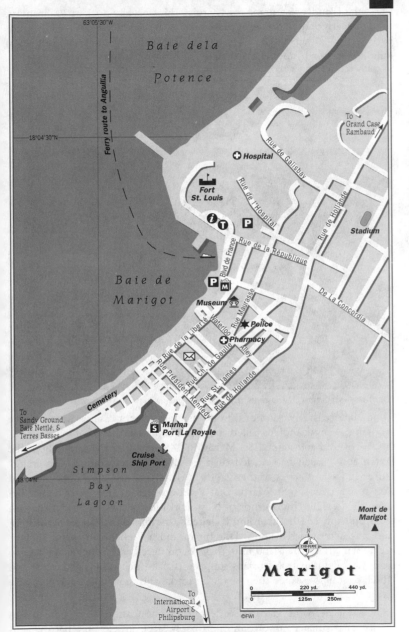

SINT MAARTEN
SAINT MARTIN

Baie de la Potence

Ferry route to Anguilla

63°05'30"W

18°04'30"N

To Grand Case Rambaud

Rue de Galisbay

Hospital

Rue de l'Hospital

Fort St. Louis

Rue de Hollande

Stadium

P

Rue de la République

Blvd de France

Baie de Marigot

De La Concordia

P

Museum

Rue Maurasse

Police

Rue de la Liberté

Rue Waterloo

Pharmacy

Alley

Rue Ch. de Gaulle

Rue Président Kennedy

Rue St. James

Rue de Hollande

Cemetery

To Sandy Ground, Baie Nettlé, & Terres Basses

Marina Port La Royale

Cruise Ship Port

Simpson Bay Lagoon

18°04'N

Mont de Marigot

N

Marigot

0   220 yd.   440 yd.
0   125m   250m

©FWI

To International Airport & Philipsburg

Case, the island's restaurant row. Cruise ships usually dock at Philipsburg, though Marigot now brings in passengers by tender. The island is surrounded by several other nearby Leeward Islands, including Anguilla, just seven miles to the north, and St. Barthelemy, 19 miles southeast.

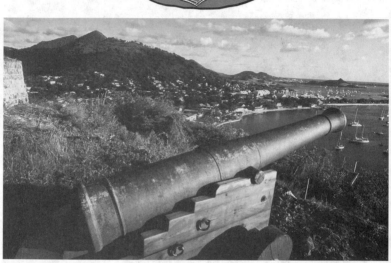

A cannon on Saint Martin recalls the days when pirates roamed the shores.

Long before the invasion of Europeans that brought casinos and duty-free shopping, Arawak Indians called the island *Sualouiga*—land of salt. Columbus discovered and named St. Martin in 1493, and by the 1630s both the Dutch and French had settled on the island. Pirates combed the craggy shores and secret coves of the island, burying treasure and booty they had won at sea. It was in St. Martin that Peter Stuyvesant (who would later become the last Dutch governor of New York) lost his leg in a struggle with the Spanish in 1640. According to legend, the binational division of the island was determined when a Dutchman and a Frenchman stood back to back, then circled the island until they encountered each other again, face to face. More legitimate historians suppose that a small group of French and Dutch prisoners escaped their Spanish captors and drew up an agreement to divide the island between them.

Sint Maarten/Saint Martin was destined for tourism in some part due to the fact that Juliana Airport, an improbably large airfield on a narrow isthmus along Simpson Lagoon, was created in 1943 for military rather than touristic reasons. After the war, the airport was ideal for bringing in larger planes filled with vacationers, and tourist arrivals began to pick up in the 1960s. Today, the number of overnight and cruise ship arrivals exceeds one million visitors annually.

In 1998, the island will celebrate 350 years of peaceful French-Dutch co-existence that began on March 23, 1648.

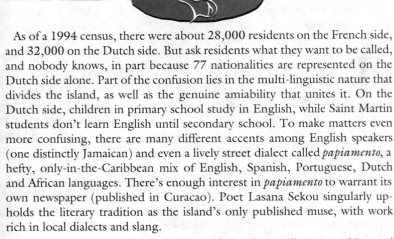

People

As of a 1994 census, there were about 28,000 residents on the French side, and 32,000 on the Dutch side. But ask residents what they want to be called, and nobody knows, in part because 77 nationalities are represented on the Dutch side alone. Part of the confusion lies in the multi-linguistic nature that divides the island, as well as the genuine amiability that unites it. On the Dutch side, children in primary school study in English, while Saint Martin students don't learn English until secondary school. To make matters even more confusing, there are many different accents among English speakers (one distinctly Jamaican) and even a lively street dialect called *papiamento*, a hefty, only-in-the-Caribbean mix of English, Spanish, Portuguese, Dutch and African languages. There's enough interest in *papiamento* to warrant its own newspaper (published in Curacao). Poet Lasana Sekou singularly upholds the literary tradition as the island's only published muse, with work rich in local dialects and slang.

Despite all the French sophistication and Dutch geniality, superstition and backwoods lore are still strong and thriving among long-time residents, kindled further by the many workers representing other West Indian cultures, particularly the Dominican Republic. The fervent love of calypso is also pure Caribbean, though the local lyrics lack the political bite known among more dissident communities. Calypso contests and parties are held regularly throughout the year. The island's colonial roots bore the first real signs of backlash in 1996 when a sign promoting the Sint Maarten/Saint Martin Carnival had depictions of a Dutch windmill and Eiffel Tower crossed out with spray paint—the protesters stated they didn't want symbols of Europe used to represent Caribbean culture.

Beaches

One of Sint Maarten/Saint Martin's chief draws has always been its beaches. Most of them have come back nicely following the ravages of Hurricane Luis, and the island's official count of 37 beaches may once again be accurate. Beginning on Dutch Sint Maarten's east side, **Dawn Beach** is a good place to begin the day, with spectacular sunrises followed by snorkeling to the colorful depths. **Guana Bay** is one of the island's few isolated strands, but a rugged current makes it more suitable for surfing than swimming. Though narrower than it once was, **Great Bay** is a mile-long beach set against the backdrop of busy Philipsburg (the best swimming is at the west end near the Great Bay Beach Hotel), while just around the corner is **Little Bay**, a sheltered cove with good snorkeling. **Simpson Bay Beach** is excellent and usually uncrowded for swimming and sunning, though it lies against the Juliana airstrip (the big jets land and take off mid-day), while **Maho Bay** is immediately under the flight path. A little further is **Mullet Bay**, long a favorite, and less crowded while the 600-room Mullet Bay Resort behind it is closed. A scenic beauty is **Cupecoy**, whose evanescent string of sand (widest in winter) is backed by eroding limestone cliffs dappled by cotton trees that provide caves and smaller coves—it's the site of a number of photos promoting Sint Maarten as a beach destination. Cupecoy is Sint Maarten's unofficial nude beach and gay hangout, and a spectacularly-perched bar, the Cliffside, serves sandwiches and drinks through the day.

The sand on the French side is equally prime, starting with **Baie Longue**, a velvety strip watched over by La Samanna. **Baie Rouge** is a little off the beaten path, but spectacular—a picturesque stretch of sand big enough to spread out away from the crowd. **Baie Nettle** was actually expanded in some places by the hurricane; it has also sprouted several resorts in the last few years. **Friar's Bay** is small and tricky to reach, but that works to its advantage, while **Grand Case** is a long expanse of narrow sand fringed by *lolos*, the roadside snack stands favored by the French. The calm, shallow waters of **Anse Marcel** are perfect for families, while nearby **Petites Cayes** is accessible only by boat or on foot. The most famous beach on the French side is lively **Baie Orientale**, an immensely popular clothing-optional spot with a naturist resort, Club Orient. Live music, casual restaurants, beachside vendors and watersports at Orientale do more to set the tone than concern over tan lines—the beach came through Luis fine and recently looked better, and busier, than ever.

Diving on Sint Maarten/Saint Martin is often lost within the shadows of the island's glittering nightlife and rippling canvas sails. The sport seems virtually an afterthought, most obviously displayed by the fact that day trips to Saba, St. Barthélémy and Anguilla are promoted eagerly by local dive shops. Sites close to shore have been over-fished and the coral degraded, and winds frequently whip up the seas, making access a bit bumpy. As locals will quietly explain, the island simply is not a major dive destination. And yet, there are at least two good wrecks—one ancient, the other very new—and the shallow reef structure is extensive, stretching for more than two miles off the island's coast. An excellent site, **One Step Beyond**, is not listed below; rough waters rarely make the location (seven miles southeast of Philipsburg) available to divers, but it yields large pelagics, coral arches and tunnels. The best of the rest are concentrated on the south coast around Philipsburg and visibility averages 60 to 80 feet (better in winter). Dive prices are a little steeper here than in most parts of the Eastern Caribbean. There are a few small operators on the French side, but using them requires familiarity with the French system of diving. In sum, most anyone serious about exploring the depths will visit a couple sites on this island, then beeline to nearby Saba, where the real excitement lies, but beginners and less worldly divers will be kept sufficiently happy. Snorkelers will find the island's coves and inlets ideal; try **Mullet Bay** or the waters off **Green Cay**, **Tintamarre** or **Ilet Pinel**.

Dive Shops

Lou Scuba Club

Baie Nettle, ☎ *(590) 87-16-61.*
The largest of several operators on the French side, Lou Couture is a PADI and CMAS instructor who charges about $65 a dive.

Ocean Explorers Dive Center

Simpson Bay, ☎ *(5995) 45252.*
A smaller, independent operation, the oldest on the island (35 years); PADI and NAUI affiliation, with courses to Assistant Instructor. Two-tank dive, $80 including equipment; maximum group size, 10 divers.

Trade Winds Dive Center

Philipsburg, ☎ *(5995) 75176.*
Conveniently located five minutes from major dive sites. Twelve-year-old operation; PADI and SSI-affiliated, with courses to Assistant Instructor. Two-tank dive, $85 including equipment ($5 per dive discount if you bring your own gear).

Fielding WORLDWIDE

ST. MARTIN

MEANDERING ON SAINT MARTIN / SINT MAARTEN

Slender fingers of land, green-clad hills rising above the bay, and world-famous soft-sand beaches are among the sights on this heavily developed isle. Ensconce yourself in a resort–the casinos are located on the Dutch side—or opt for the intimacy at a guest house, then grab your towel and walking shoes and start exploring.

Cupecoy Bay

Cupecoy Bay is located near the western end of landlocked Simpson Bay Lagoon. The beach is flanked with sandstone cliffs where Arawak Indian artifacts have been discovered in some of the small caves. Follow the footpath from Cupecoy Beach Resort to reach a more secluded stretch of beach.

Pt. du Bluff

Pt. du Plum

Pt. des Pierres a Chaux

Simpson Bay Lagoon

Marigot

Sometimes known as the "St. Tropez of the tropics," this capital of the French side of the island is a Francophile's heaven. Window shop at trendy boutiques or savor a croissant at one of the cafés, then stop in at the Match supermarket for French-style picnic fare. Take the pier road to the ferry dock to catch a ferry to Anguilla.

Simpson Bay

Juliana International Airport

Ocean Explorers Sea Walk

At Simpson Bay, no swimming or diving experience is required to join this underwater expedition. Don your swimsuit and a specially designed helmet and join your guide in a tour of the colorful reef life found in the bay.

Fort Amsterdam

Located at Little Bay on a hilly spit of land, this fort dates back to the late 17th century, when the Dutch constructed fortifications on top of an older Spanish fort.

Flat Island Marine Reserve

At Tintamerre Island, day-trippers enjoy hiking the flats, while divers explore the tugboat wreck dive site. Elkhorn coral is located in shallow water great for snorkeling. North of the island, underwater caves and arches attract dolphins.

Prickly Pear Caps

Charter a ketch tour to this set of atolls near Anguilla to the north. Snorkel or scuba dive the reefs that shelter massive stands of elkhorn coral.

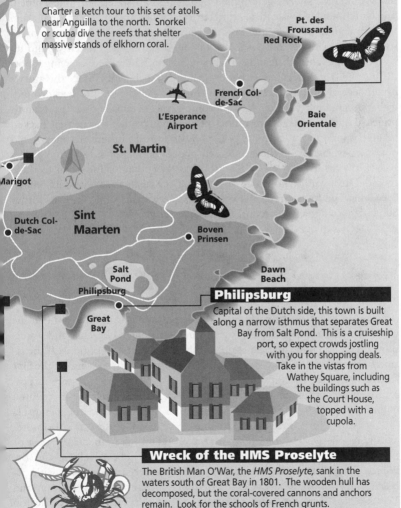

Pt. des Froussards
Red Rock

French Col-de-Sac

Baie Orientale

L'Esperance Airport

St. Martin

Sint Maarten

Marigot

Dutch Col-de-Sac

Boven Prinsen

Salt Pond

Philipsburg

Great Bay

Dawn Beach

Philipsburg

Capital of the Dutch side, this town is built along a narrow isthmus that separates Great Bay from Salt Pond. This is a cruiseship port, so expect crowds jostling with you for shopping deals. Take in the vistas from Wathey Square, including the buildings such as the Court House, topped with a cupola.

Wreck of the HMS Proselyte

The British Man O'War, the *HMS Proselyte,* sank in the waters south of Great Bay in 1801. The wooden hull has decomposed, but the coral-covered cannons and anchors remain. Look for the schools of French grunts.

On Foot

One of the better local legends has it that Sint Maarten/Saint Martin's national boundaries were determined by having two statesmen, one French, one Dutch, walk the island's perimeter to establish an equal territorial claim for each nation. Whether the Frenchman was a faster walker, slimmer or, as some say, the Dutchman was slowed by inebriation, the French wound up with the larger chunk of land (others suggest both men were carrying a bottle, but the Dutch beer was stronger than the French wine). Since this story's origin several hundred years ago, hiking has faded into the background, while shimmering beaches have become firmly established as the island's principal outdoor attraction. It doesn't help matters that this densely packed island has little room left for explorations on foot. But there are unexpected options, particularly on the less densely populated French side and on Terres Basses, the peninsula west of Simpson Bay. Keep your mind open to these sporadic strolls and you will be rewarded. The **Sint Maarten National Heritage Foundation** conducts interesting guided hikes of varying difficulty every other Sunday morning; a donation of $5 is requested ☎ *(5995) 24917.*

What Else to See

Unless you have a fort fetish, Sint Maarten/Saint Martin offers little in the way of cultural exploration and sightseeing—sticking to beaches and watersports, or shopping in **Marigot** and **Philipsburg** are your best options. If the island's forts do call to you, begin your explorations with a swing by the **Sint Maarten Museum** in Philipsburg which will help put the rich history in perspective. **Fort Amsterdam** is the most important, representing the first Dutch military outpost in the Caribbean—its ruins are found on the peninsula southwest of Philipsburg (just past the Divi Little Bay Resort). Also noteworthy on the Dutch side is **Fort Willem**, atop **Fort Hill** immediately west of Philipsburg, reached by a treacherous road that is best walked. On the French side is **Fort de Marigot**, built in 1767 and recently restored, with excellent views above Marigot and extending to Simpson Bay Lagoon and Terres Basses. You can drive part way up, but the steep climb to the top yields the best views.

Try to visit Marigot on Wednesday or Saturday morning, when the town comes alive with its traditional French West Indian **market**, now housed in an elaborate new enclosure. Above the town of Rambaud is **Colombier**, a village in a lush valley beneath Paradise Peak—it represents St. Martin at its most quiet and rural. Further up the coast is **Grand Case**, a seaside community dotted with charming Creole houses sporting gingerbread trim and whose restaurant row has earned the town the title "Gastronomique Center of Saint Martin." The hustle of nudist **Baie Orientale** is worth a visit—the sand is always lively with music and food. Don't miss the pastoral hamlet of **Orleans**— also known as the French Quarter, and the oldest French settlement on the island. Here you'll find small homes set among gardens alive with tropical blossoms. **Roland Richardson**, perhaps the island's best-known artist/conservationist/historian, captures these scenes on canvas and welcomes visitors into his Orleans studio on Thursdays ☎ *(590) 87-32-24.*

Most visitors take at least one day-trip to a neighboring island. Anguilla is easiest to reach, a 20-minute ferry ride from Marigot (see "Getting Around").

Sint Maarten's shops at Maho Bay offer French fashions, jewelry, perfumes and quality gift items.

Historical Sites

Saint Martin

Fort de Marigot   ★ ★ ★

Just off Rue de la Republique, Marigot.

Also known as Fort St. Louis, this ruin dates back to 1767 and is well preserved with some original cannons still intact. It's worth the steep climb (bring water) for the splendid views of Marigot and Simpson Bay Lagoon alone.

Museums and Exhibits
Sint Maarten

Courthouse of Sint Maarten ★★

Frontstreet, Philipsburg.

Located at the Philipsburg town square on bustling Frontstreet and overlooking the pier, this 1793 building was recently restored with glorious results. The second floor still functions as a courthouse, while the first floor is a post office. You'll definitely want to snap a picture of this colorful edifice.

Sint Maarten Museum ★★★

7 Front Street, Philipsburg.
Hours open: 10 a.m.–4 p.m.

This small museum is run by a headstrong Sint Maartener, Elsje Wilson-Bosch, a teacher dedicated to preserving the past of this rapidly developing island. The museum features a collection of military artifacts, ancient bottles and pottery, antiques, old photographs and maps. The Sint Maarten National Heritage Foundation (which Elsje is president of) also rescues the island's architecture and hopes to soon open the Belvedere Plantation Cultural Park around the ruins of a plantation great house and sugar factory. The museum is located on the second floor; open Sunday until noon only. General admission: $1.

Saint Martin

Museum of Marigot ★★★★

Sandy Ground Road, Marigot.
Hours open: 9 a.m.–6:30 p.m.

This new museum hosts an interesting exhibit, "On the Trail of the Arawaks." The collection focuses on pre-Columbian artifacts, including remains of indigenous inhabitants dating back to 1800 B.C. and ceramics from 550 B.C. There's also a reproduction of a 1,500-year-old Indian burial site (just discovered in 1994), early 20th-century photographs of the island, and displays on the plantation and slavery periods. Open Monday-Saturday from 9 a.m.–1 p.m. and from 3–6 p.m. Located next to the Royal Marina on the lagoon side. General admission: $5.

Parks and Gardens
Sint Maarten

Sint Maarten Zoo ★★

Madame Estate, Philipsburg.
Hours open: 9 a.m.–5 p.m.

This small zoo is especially suited to children (who get in for $2), with its playground and petting zoo. The facility was expanded following the hurricane and now features walk-through aviaries, a bat cave, and animals from the Caribbean and South America. General admission: $3.

Saint Martin

Butterfly Farm ★★★★

Le Galion Beach Road, Quartier d'Orleans.
Hours open: 9 a.m.–4:30 p.m.

If you're never given lepidopterans a second thought (or look) before, you certainly will after visiting this tranquil spot just south of Orient Beach, at Baie L'Embrouchure. Hundreds of rare and exotic butterflies fly free in a large screened-in garden replete with fish ponds, fountains and tropical foliage. Interesting exhibits showcase their egg laying, caterpillar and pupa stages, and you'll get to see butterflies emerge from their cocoons and fly off into the great beyond (or at least around their 900-square-meter home). Butterflies are free... but the fascinating tour costs $10.

Tours
Sint Maarten

Sint Maarten 12 Metre Challenge   ★★★★★
Bobby's Marina, Philipsburg.
If you've ever dreamed of racing in the America's Cup, this unique attraction allows you a taste of the action, with a front-row seat. Guests participate as crew on one of the actual America's Cup racing boats, including two incarnations of Stars and Stripes (the '86 and '87 winners), and several other multi-million dollar contenders. You and up to 17 others crew alongside three experts, racing against one or more of the other boats and a streamlined version of an actual America's Cup course. Everyone is assigned a duty, be it trimming the sails or grinding a winch, but previous sailing experience is not necessary. The two-hour adventure is not cheap ($60 per person), but for many it is the highlight of a visit to Sint Maarten. Races are held up to seven days a week in high season, but call the day before to book a seat.

Saint Martin

Pinel Island   ★★★★
Cul de Sac Bay
Just five bucks will get you a roundtrip boat ride from Orient Beach to this tiny island just off the coast. There you can snorkel (they rent equipment), sunbathe or dine in the casual restaurant. Chairs, umbrellas and restrooms are available at no charge.

Seaworld Explorer   ★★★
Grand Case Pier, Grande Case.
This semi-submarine has an open-air deck and underwater observatory hull that lets you view sealife in air-conditioned comfort—and without getting your hair wet. Trips depart from Grand Case Pier and explore the waters surrounding Creole Rock. A diver feeds the fishies to make sure tourists have lots to see. Tours cost $30 for adults, $20 for kids 2–12. Add $10 each ($7 for kids) for roundtrip transportation from your hotel.

Sports

Sailing is an island passion, and neophytes will receive a brisk immersion into the sport by partaking in the Sint Maarten 12-Metre Challenge, which uses actual America's Cup boats for races just off Great Bay. Visiting boaters have a variety of bays and marinas for mooring. On French Saint Martin, Baie Rouge provides good anchorage, Port la Royale and Marigot Bay are good sites for shopping, while Grand Case features excellent dining at all price levels. A top-class marina can be found at Port de Lonvilliers (Anse Marcel), with docking space for up to 60 boats (up to 73 feet), and boutiques, grocery, cafe and La Capitanerie, a ship's chandlery. At Oyster Pond, Captain Oliver's Marina serves the French side, while Oyster Pond Yacht Club is on the Dutch side of the placid bay. On Dutch Sint Maarten, Bobby's Marina and Great Bay Marina are the primary access into Philipsburg, while two marinas are also positioned in Cole Bay. Large enough to accommodate virtually any yacht, passage into Simpson Bay Lagoon is available from both the windward (French) and leeward (Dutch) sides of the island.

Sailing excursions from Saint Martin to other islands are easily arranged.

Day sails to other nearby islands are popular—Anguilla and St. Barthélémy are nearby favorites. Two types of vessels are commonly used: large catamarans holding 25 or more, or smaller sailboats that hold six to 10 for excursions to secluded beaches. Boats depart from Bobby's Marina and Great Bay Marina in Philipsburg, Simpson Bay Marina, Captain Oliver's in Oyster Pond, Port la Royale in Marigot Bay and the new marina at Anse Marcel, Port de Lonvilliers. Rates for a day sail with snorkeling, open bar and picnics run between $65–75 per person. **Sport fishing** is also prominent. Half- and full-day charters with tackle, bait and snacks are readily available at Bobby's Marina, Great Bay Marina, Simpson Bay Marina and Port la Royale Marina. December to April is the season for kingfish, dolphin and barracuda; tuna is available year-round. **Windsurfing** is increasingly popular, and many resorts offer rentals and lessons.

The focus sticks primarily to the ocean, but a few other sports are popular. Although the Mullet Bay Resort is still closed from the hurricane, **golf** at the 18-hole Joe Lee-designed course is now possible, though serious duffers won't be enthralled with its sometimes scruffy conditions. A new miniature golf course in Marigot will keep the kids happy. Several stables on both sides of the island provide **horseback riding**, while **tennis courts** can be located at most of the island's resorts.

Bicycling

A growing craze with islanders, bicycles are a terrific way to see Sint Maarten/St. Martin, as long as you're comfortable with the amount of traffic that circuits the roads with you. On Sunday, the numbers of local bikers taking to the hills and roads exceeds well over a hundred. For rentals, visit **Tri-Sport** in Simpson Bay, which rents Treks for $15 per day; they also provide tours for groups of three or more by appointment ☎ *(5995) 54384*. On the French side, **Frog's Legs Cyclery** in the Howell Center in Marigot also has bikes for $15 per day, and is run by one of the island's mountain bike experts—join him on his Sunday excursions ☎ *(590) 87-05-11*.

Golf

Mullet Bay Resort, Philipsburg.
The island's only links are an 18-hole course designed by Joe Lee, and located next to Mullet Bay Resort. It is not always green and can sometimes be a bit scruffy, but it's not usually crowded. Greens fees are about $105, including cart rental.

Horseback Riding

On the Dutch side, horses can be rented at **Crazy Acres** ☎ *(5995) 42793*. On the French side, try **Caid and Isa** at Anse Marcel ☎ *(590) 87-32-79* and the **O.K. Corral** at Oyster Pond ☎ *(590) 87-40-72*. The going rate is about $40 for a two-hour trail ride.

Watersports

If your hotel doesn't offer the watersports you're seeking, a slew of companies are happy to help. Dutch Side: for boating and cruises, try **Swaliga** ☎ *(5995) 22167*, **White Octopus** ☎ *(5995) 24096*, **Caribbean Watersports** ☎ *(5995) 42801*, **Bobby's Marina** ☎ *(5995) 22366*, and **Bluebeard** ☎ *(5995) 52898*. For deep-sea fishing, try **Wampum** ☎ *(5995) 22366*, **Sea Brat** ☎ *(5995) 24096*, and **Bobby's Marina** ☎ *(5995) 22366*. Scuba divers can call **Leeward Island Divers** ☎ *(5995) 42866*, **Tradewinds** ☎ *(5995) 75176*, **St. Maarten Divers** ☎ *(5995) 22446*, and **Ocean Explorers** ☎ *(5995) 45252*, which also runs a unique underwater "helmet" walk in which non-swimmers can stroll with the help of special apparatus that supply oxygen. French side: For boating and cruises, call **Marina de Captain Oliver** ☎ *(590) 87-33-47*, **Marina Port la Royale** ☎ *(590) 87-20-43*, or **Port de Lonvilliers** ☎ *(590) 87-31-94*. General watersports, **Nettle Bay Beach Club** ☎ *(590) 87-20-59* or **Kontiki Watersports** ☎ *(590) 87-46-89*. For scuba diving call **Lou Scuba** ☎ *(590) 87-16-61*, or **Meridien Dive Center** ☎ *(590) 87-67-90*.

Where to Stay

Fielding's Highest Rated Hotels in Sint Maarten/Saint Martin

★★★★★	La Samanna	$325–$700
★★★★	Esmeralda Resort	$180–$450
★★★★	Green Cay Village	$258–$343
★★★★	Le Meridien L'Habitation and Le Domaine	$190–$380
★★★★	Privilege Resort & Spa	$255–$575
★★★	Beachside Villas	$165–$325
★★★	Divi Little Bay Beach Resort	$135–$220
★★★	Maho Beach Hotel & Casino	$155–$390

Fielding's Small Places Worth Discovering on Sint Maarten/Saint Martin

★★★	L'Esplanade Caraibe Hotel	$100–$320
★★★	Pavillion Beach Hotel	$90–$260
★★★	Mary's Boon	$75–$195
★★	Pasanggrahan Royal Inn	$78–$148
★★	La Residence	$74–$98

Fielding's Best Value Hotels in Sint Maarten/Saint Martin

★★	Royale Louisiana	$60–$88
★★★	Mary's Boon	$75–$195
★★	La Residence	$74–$98
★★	Hevea	$40–$132
★★★	Horny Toad Guesthouse	$98–$180

Sint Maarten/Saint Martin has an amazing thicket of hotels encircling it 37 square miles. A couple decades ago, most were concentrated on th

Dutch side, but the French began pouring concrete in ernest in the 1980s. The result is a hodge-podge of choices, though in reality, many vacationers are locked into the island's array of time shares. If shopping or gambling opportunities are a priority, being positioned on the Dutch side may suit your needs. If fine food or more luxurious surroundings whet your appetite, consider basing yourself on the French side (most of the French hotels are newer). The style is more conspicuously European on the French side, while the Dutch cater to the cruise ship masses and others with equal abandon.

When comparing the options, note that the tax and service charge appearing on your final bill varies substantially from one hotel to the next. *In general*, a 5 percent hotel tax is standard on the French side, and a service charge is unusual. On the Dutch side, a 5 percent government tax is typical, while the service charge ranges from 10 to 15 percent, though a few smaller properties skip it altogether. Also be on the lookout for a Dutch "energy surcharge" of up to 5 percent a day. Whichever side of the island you select, always verify the tax and service charge that will be added to minimize any check-out surprises.

Where to Stay—Sint Maarten

Almost 4000 hotel rooms are scattered across Dutch Sint Maarten, providing a dense bevy of options, though little room is furnished for travelers on a budget. Lodging ranges from small historic inns where you can make friends with the proprietors, to time-share condos where you'll never meet the owners. The hotels positioned around Great Bay and Philipsburg tend to be older properties, while the Lowlands immediately northwest of the Juliana Airport was developed more recently, with the huge **Maho Beach Hotel and Casino** dominating the landscape. Both of these areas are quite busy; Philipsburg is riddled with cruise ship traffic on most days, while the hotels near Simpson Bay suffer from jet noise mid-day (especially weekends).

Although most properties are operational at press time, several of Sint Maarten's major resorts—**Mullet Bay**, **Port de Plaisance** and **Dawn Beach Hotel**—are suspended in limbo and closed until further notice; **Divi Little Bay Beach Resort** has some of its rooms ready now, with the rest of the room inventory scheduled to be phased in by 1998. Among other developments, the owners of **Oyster Bay Beach** plan to turn the hotel into a 200-room time share. Caravanserai, closed prior to Luis, will re-open in late 1997 as the **Millennium Beach Resort**; we'll have a report on it next year ☎ *(5995) 54000.*

Hotels and Resorts

The best of the luxury resorts have been opened on the French side, though **Oyster Bay Beach Hotel** provides frills on one of the last-to-be-developed pieces of land on Sint Maarten, and **Maho Beach Hotel and Casino** satisfies those looking for an all-encompassing, neon-trimmed high-rise vacation.

Divi Little Bay Beach Resort $135–$220   ★★★

Little Bay, ☎ *(800) 367-3484, (599) 5-22333, FAX (5995) 23911.*
Single: $135–$220. Double: $135–$220.

Located a mile out of Philipsburg and overlooking an attractive beach, this resort dates back to 1955, but it's only just coming up to speed again after a year-and-a-half of post-hurricane rebuilding. Accommodations run the gamut from standard guestrooms in casitas to suites with one to three bedrooms; most are part of Divi's time-share operation. All are comfortable, air-conditioned, and feature balconies or patios with nice ocean views. There's a restaurant and two bars, and other facilities include a pool, two tennis courts, shops and watersports on the pretty, quiet beach. It's about a 20-minute walk into town. 118 rooms. Credit cards: A, DC, MC, V.

Great Bay Beach Hotel $95–$290   ★★

Philipsburg, ☎ *(800) 223-0757, (5995) 22446, FAX (5995) 23859.*
Single: $95–$280. Double: $105–$290.

This large, older property sits at the end of Philipsburg and the town beach. Guest rooms are adequate, but nothing to write home about—they received a spruce-up in 1996. The 10 junior suites have very large bathrooms with whirlpool tubs, but are not necessarily worth the bump in price. There are two restaurants and three bars, one with entertainment and shows nightly. The grounds also include two pools, a casino, a tennis court, gym, and all the usual watersports at the pleasant beach. Rates provided are European Plan, but an all-inclusive set-up is also available. The size of this property guarantees you'll be sharing it with large groups. 285 rooms. Credit cards: A, DC, MC, V.

Holland House Beach Hotel $84–$200   ★★

Philipsburg, ☎ *(800) 223-9815, (5995) 22572, FAX (5995) 24673.*
Single: $84–$185. Double: $99–$200.

This five-story hotel is right in the center of Philipsburg on the town's narrow beach. Air-conditioned guest rooms have sitting areas, twin beds, TVs, and private balconies, though not all have views; most have small kitchenettes. Be sure to book a room on the bay side, or you'll suffer from the noisy street. There's a pleasant waterfront restaurant and bar, but no other facilities—much within walking distance, however, including a decent beach 10 minutes away. This is a well-run operation, serving both business and leisure travelers. 54 rooms. Credit cards: A, D, MC, V.

Maho Beach Hotel & Casino $155–$455   ★★★

Maho Bay, ☎ *(800) 223-0757, (5995) 52115, FAX (5995) 53604.*
Single: $155–$370. Double: $165–$390. Suites Per Day: $340–$455.

Set on a bluff above a small beach, this bustling, nine-story resort (the island's largest) is near the airport and can suffer from the roar of jets in the afternoon. Accommodations are straightforward and feature private balconies and large baths, all with bidets and some with whirlpool tubs. There are also 57 efficiency units with small kitchenettes. Facilities include a number of restaurants, two cafes, a nightclub and several bars, a large casino, two pools, four tennis courts, a health club, and all the usual watersports. With an atmosphere more Vegas than Caribbean, this spot appeals to conventioneers and those who like busy resorts with all the accompanying activity. 600 rooms. Credit cards: A, DC, MC, V.

Oyster Bay Beach Resort   **$120–$310**   ★★★

Oyster Pond, ☎ *(800) 231-8331, (5995) 22206, FAX (5995) 25695.*
Single: $120–$275. Double: $120–$275. Suites Per Day: $190–$310.
Located on a small peninsula at a quieter spot and surrounded on three sides by water, this property is part time-share, part hotel, but fairly appealing throughout. Accommodations are decorated in white wicker and pastel fabrics; each room has ceiling fans, air conditioners, and seaview patios. The 20 suites are luxurious, particularly the nice Tower Suites, but standard rooms are the best value. The restaurant is romantic, and there's also a comfortable lounge for quiet respites. Mile-long Dawn Beach is a 10-minute walk and quite lovely but not reliable for swimming; most guests prefer the saltwater pool. 40 rooms. Credit cards: A, DC, D, MC, V.

Summit Resort Hotel   **$95–$195**   ★★

Lowlands, ☎ *(800) 351-5656, (5995) 52150, FAX (5995) 52615.*
Single: $95–$180. Double: $105–$195.
Perched on a bluff in a residential neighborhood and overlooking Simpson Bay, this complex consists of apartment-style buildings clustered closely together. Accommodations are either studios or duplexes, all air-conditioned and boasting sitting areas and verandas. The more expensive rooms have kitchens. There's tennis, a restaurant and bar on the premises, and the large pool is nice. They'll shuttle you to Philipsburg or the beach (a 15-minute walk), but you'll probably want a car so you can travel on your own schedule. Has seen better days. 50 rooms. Credit cards: A, MC, V.

Apartments and Condominiums

Apartments, condos and time shares are big business on Sint Maarten. Among the nicest is the **Cupecoy Beach Club,** located above one of the island's most beautiful beaches.

Beachside Villas   **$165–$325**   ★★★

Simpson Bay Beach, ☎ *(5995) 54294, FAX (5995) 53349.*
Single: $165–$325. Double: $165–$325.
These Mediterranean-style villas are set on a fine, uncrowded beach and are quite elegant. All are individually owned but identically decorated, with two bedrooms, fully equipped kitchens, combination baths, living and dining areas, VCRs, and decks—an atrium is perfect for lazy breakfasts. Maids tidy up daily. Facilities are limited to a small pool with a deck built over the sand, but there are many restaurants and shops within a short distance. The only downside is the proximity to the airport, which means a loud roar when jets take off and land. No service charge added to the rates. 14 rooms. Credit cards: A, MC. V.

Belair Beach Hotel   **$205–$335**   ★★

Little Bay Beach, ☎ *(5995) 23366, FAX (5995) 25295.*
Single: $205–$335. Double: $205–$335.
This all-suite time-share is situated on Little Bay Beach, next to the Divi Little Bay. The condos at this four-story hotel are individually owned and rented out when the owners are elsewhere. Each unit has one-and-a-half bedrooms, two baths, small but full kitchens, living and dining rooms, VCRs, and private patios or balconies, and can sleep up to six. Facilities include a bar and restaurant and a tennis court—but the beach is right there, where watersports equipment can be rented. Request a unit

on an upper floor for more privacy. Good for families, but not one of the island's better values. 72 rooms. Credit cards: A, MC, V.

Cupecoy Beach Club $100–$350 ★★★

Cupecoy Beach, ☎ *(800) 955-9008, (215) 885-9008, FAX (215) 572-7731.*
Single: $100–$350. Double: $100–$350.

Situated on white sandstone cliffs above Cupecoy Beach (which comes and goes, depending on the season), this attractive Mediterranean-style condo complex offers standard rooms or one-bedroom suites, all privately owned. Each has air conditioning and spacious terraces; suites have a full kitchen (there are also two- and three-bedroom units). The pool has a swim-up bar, and they'll help arrange activities. A restaurant and casino are across the street. Little in the way of service or amenities, but one of the more spectacular locations available on the island. They have no local phone; the number shown is the management in Pennsylvania. 126 rooms.

Pelican Resort & Casino $95–$270 ★★

Simpson Bay, ☎ *(800) 550-7088, (5995) 42503, FAX (5995) 42133.*
Single: $95–$270. Double: $95–$270.

This full-service resort combines both condo living with full hotel amenities. The air-conditioned accommodations range from studios to two-bedroom suites, all colorfully done in tropical decor with fully equipped kitchens with dishwashers and microwaves; decor in some units dated. Facilities include two restaurants, a large casino, deli, health spa, five pools—two with swim-up bars—four tennis courts, and a marina. Extensive watersports include cruises aboard Pelican's catamaran. There's even a 24-hour doctor's office. With all that going on, this resort isn't for everyone—it's not exactly an idyllic escape, more like a teeming mini-city, and to get to the beach you'll have to brave steep hillsides. Especially suited to families with its two kiddie pools, playground and daycare center. 342 rooms. Credit cards: A, DC, D, MC, V.

Town House Villas $125–$250 ★★

Philipsburg, ☎ *(5995) 22898, FAX (5995) 22418.*
Single: $125–$250. Double: $125–$250.

Located on the edge of Philipsburg and right on the whisper of a beach, this complex consists of 11 duplex villas. Each has two bedrooms, 1.5 baths, living and dining rooms, and full kitchens. Patios are set along a nice courtyard. Maids keep things tidy. No facilities on the premises, but lots of shops and restaurants are a short stroll away. 12 rooms. Credit cards: A, MC, V.

White Sands Beach Club $79–$139 ★

Simpson Bay, ☎ *(5995) 54370, FAX (5995) 54370.*
Single: $79–$139. Double: $79–$139.

This beachcomber's hideaway is a little rundown, but offers good value on a nice beach. A motel-like wing houses eight of the simple units, each with kitchenettes. There are also four beach chalets without cooking facilities—the least expensive units, three of them right on the sand. Two two-bedroom villas are also available ($149–$215 per night). Within earshot of the airport. 14 rooms. Credit cards: A, MC, V.

Inns

Inns are not Sint Maarten's specialty, but a couple of charmers with lots of colorful history welcome guests. The **Pasanggrahan Royal Guest House** is the island's oldest hotel, originally built for Queen Wilhelmina, and has the creaking hardwood floors and fluttering ceiling fans to prove it. **Mary's Boon** was built by a notorious, gun-toting Caribbean legend, Mary Pomeroy, who disappeared in her private plane some time in the late '70s. "All the stories you've heard about Mary are true," say those who knew her. The food at Mary's Boon, the responsibility of one chef for more than two decades, is well respected.

Horny Toad Guesthouse $98–$180 ★★★

Simpson Bay Beach, ☎ (800) 417-9361 ext. 3013, (5995) 54323, FAX (5995) 53316.
Single: $98–$180. Double: $98–$180.
This former governor's residence combines guesthouse ambience with apartment living. It is located on a lovely beach that sometimes suffers from jet noise at the nearby airport. Each one-bedroom apartment is individually decorated and quite charming, with fully equipped kitchens, fresh flowers, and maid service. The friendly owners, Earle and Betty Vaughan, treat renters like personal guests, providing a gracious touch lacking in the fancier resorts. There are no facilities on-site, but there's plenty to do within walking distance. No kids under 7. No service charge added to the rates. 8 rooms.

Mary's Boon $75–$195 ★★★

Simpson Bay Beach, ☎ (5995) 54235, FAX (5995) 53403.
Website: www.marysboon.com. E-mail: marysboon@megatropic.com.
Single: $75–$175. Double: $90–$195.
Located next to the Juliana airport, 15 minutes from Philipsburg, this is an authentic West Indian beachcomber inn—not someone's idea of one. The long beach is quite nice, but can disappear during high tide. Accommodations are in large, recently remodeled studios with kitchenettes, patios and ceiling fans; most now have air conditioning. Public spaces are nicely accented with island art, tropical prints, and antiques—the owner's dogs are frequently seen. There's a terrific restaurant and honor bar, and a pool is planned for 1998. As with all the properties in this area, occasional airport noise—particularly the big jets midday—is intrusive. A favorite with "boonies," who return year after year. 15 rooms. Credit cards: MC, V.

Pasanggrahan Royal Inn $78–$148 ★★

Philipsburg, ☎ (800) 351-5656, (5995) 23588, FAX (5995) 22885.
Closed Date: September.
Single: $78–$148. Double: $78–$148.
A classic West Indian inn, the Pasanggrahan (it means "guest house" in Indonesian) occupies a 19th-century governor's house and was once the accommodations for Queen Wilhelmina on her periodic swings through the Dutch Windwards. Guest rooms are decorated in wicker and have balconies or patios; not all are air-conditioned and some are fairly run down. The studios are a better bet with their superior furnishings and kitchenettes. No pool (it sits on a narrow sliver of Great Bay Beach), and guests forego modern amenities like phones and TV, but are rewarded with a rich dose of historical charm, a noteworthy perk on this modern and developed island. The bar and restaurant are popular with locals, and afternoon tea is a treat.

Nestled at the quieter end of Philipsburg—lots within walking distance. 30 rooms.
Credit cards: A, MC.

Low Cost Lodging

Although a number of hotels drop their rates below the hundred-dollar mark in summer, there's precious little for budget travelers on Sint Maarten during the winter. One option is to hook up with another couple and share a condo or apartment. The new **Hotel L'Esperance** located in Cay Hill has attractive apartment-style rooms ☎ *(5995) 25355*. Another is the **Sea Breeze Hotel**, a pleasant and inexpensive hostelry ☎ *(5995) 26054*. Both are in a residential neighborhood a mile west of Philipsburg (you'll need a car).

Where to Stay—Saint Martin

About 3500 hotel rooms have been built on Saint Martin, many in the last decade during a building boom which has seemingly left no cove cement-free. The development has not reached the rampant level seen on the Dutch side, and a building moratorium has recently been debated. Although many Americans visit the island, accommodations on the French side are decidedly more European than is typically found in the Caribbean. English is spoken by most who work in the hotels.

An important note: most of the hotels have two rate cards—one in American dollars and one in French francs. However, the exchange rate between the two currencies changes daily. At press time, the franc was trading at its lowest rate in years and, as a result, a number of hotels did not raise their *dollar* rate card for the 1998 season. The situation may have changed by the time you read this, and if the franc has further declined, you'll want to negotiate your room rate carefully to make sure you are obtaining the best price. For hotels that did not provide prices in dollars, we have used an exchange rate of 5.5 francs for one U.S. dollar.

Hotels and Resorts

La Samanna, a swank oasis amid St. Martin's hubbub, is one of the Caribbean's great hotels, a bastion of tasteful retreat overlooking a priceless beach, and containing some of the most seductive rooms to be found anywhere in the region. Yes, it's true: the resort's caviar sampler (Beluga, Sevruga, et al) runs $500, though a bottle of glacial vodka comes with it. The flip side of La Samanna is probably **Le Meridien l'Habitation**, a mammoth development on the most "remote" corner of St. Martin—though rooms are appropriately deluxe, and the on-site spa delivers the goods, it's geared for French conventions and groups as well as typical vacationers (it was the site of a Bush-Mitterrand meeting in 1989). Another spa experience in more intimate surroundings is delivered just up the hill from l'Habitation at **Privilege Resort**.

Anse Margot   **$125–$274**   ★★★

Baie Nettle, ☎ (800) 742-4276, (590) 87-92-01, FAX (590) 87-92-13.
Single: $125–$167. Double: $150–$189. Suites Per Day: $211–$274.
Located a mile out of Marigot and opening onto Simpson Bay Lagoon, this Anchorage-owned hotel is a popular spot. Nine three-story buildings with pretty

gingerbread trim house the guestrooms and suites, all quite pleasant with air conditioners, refrigerators, and private balconies. The restaurant is a nice place for a romantic meal, and there's also a bar, two pools, and watersports on the beach. The clientele is predominantly European. 96 rooms. Credit cards: A, DC, D, MC, V.

Captain Oliver's Hotel   **$105–$205**   ★★★

Oyster Pond, ☎ *(800) 535-7289, (590) 87-40-26, FAX (590) 87-40-84.*
Single: $105–$140. Double: $160–$205.

Located on the French/Dutch border and fronting the pleasant Oyster Pond lagoon, this charming complex gets high marks for its peaceful grounds and attractive rooms. Guests are housed in attached pink bungalows that hold junior suites with kitchenettes, rattan furnishings, air conditioners, and private balconies. The well-landscaped grounds feature two restaurants, a bar, a 100-slip marina, a dive center, and a pool. Dawn Beach can be reached via water taxi, five minutes away. Appeals to yachties and others seeking a nautical ambience. The rates are a particularly good value for singles. 30 rooms. Credit cards: A, MC, V.

L'Esplanade Caraibe Hotel   **$100–$320**   ★★★

Grand Case, ☎ *(800) 633-7411, (590) 87-06-55, FAX (590) 87-29-15.*
Single: $100–$250. Double: $150–$320.

This newer hotel is set on a breezy hill overlooking Grande Case and the sea; both are an easy, five-minute walk. Accommodations are in suites with fully equipped kitchens, color TV, direct-dial phones, central air conditioning and ceiling fans, and furnished balconies. One-bedroom and loft suites have a king bed and a sleeper sofa in the living room; lofts have an additional half-bathroom downstairs. Facilities are limited to a small pool and a bar that's open for lunch only in high season, but St. Martin's Restaurant Row is just down the hill. Friendly, attentive service and a sophisticated ambience make this property a winner. 24 rooms. Credit cards: A, MC, V.

La Samanna   **$325–$1500**   ★★★★★

Baie Longue, ☎ *(800) 854-2252, (590) 87-64-00, FAX (590) 87-87-86.*
Website: www.orient-expresshotels.com/.
Closed Date: September.
Single: $325–$700. Double: $325–$700. Suites Per Day: $500–$1500.

Now operated by Orient-Express Hotels, this stellar spot is splendidly perched on 55 beachfront acres, and designed to resemble a Moorish Mediterranean village. Accommodations are in the main building and in villas scattered about the luscious beach. The corner Terrace Suite remains a Caribbean classic, while most of the rest are on the small side but still very elegant, with luxurious, Spanish-tiled bathrooms. Large patios, minibars, refrigerators, and air conditioning are standard throughout. The resort's well-heeled guests can play tennis on three courts, splash about in the idyllic pool, or frolic on the beach (windsurfing and waterskiing are included). The food is grand, the extensive wine cellar is one of the best in the region. La Samanna gets high marks for seclusion and sophistication on this otherwise cluttered isle. Attentive service and extra touches like fresh flowers every other day make this one of the Caribbean's premiere resorts—and one blessedly free of riffraff. The new owners promise to live up to La Samanna's polished reputation, though plans for a

100-person banquet room may not sit well with long-time customers. Full breakfast included in the rates. 82 rooms. Credit cards: A, MC, V.

Le Meridien L'Habitation and Le Domaine $190–$600   ★★★★

Anse Marcel, ☎ *(800) 543-4300, (590) 87-67-00, FAX (590) 87-30-38.*
Closed Date: September.
Single: $190–$380. Double: $190–$380. Suites Per Day: $290–$600.
Situated on 170 acres, this sprawling resort consists of the 251-room L'Habitation and the newer 145-room Le Domaine. All the guest rooms are beautifully decorated and comfortable, though those in Le Domaine are larger and more luxurious (and more expensive); some rooms have kitchenettes. The extensive grounds cater to resort lovers, with four restaurants, three bars, two lovely pools, six tennis courts, racquetball and squash courts, a marina and a gorgeous, quarter-mile beach. Other activities (not featured in the rates) include watersports, and guests can hike up to Privilege Fitness Center and Spa up the hill, a luxurious spot to work up a sweat or get a massage. Quite nice for those looking for that full-on resort setting, but a bit isolated, and big groups are not infrequent. 396 rooms. Credit cards: A, DC, MC, V.

Mont Vernon $120–$385   ★★★

Baie Orientale, ☎ *(800) 223-0888, (590) 87-62-00, FAX (590) 87-37-27.*
Website: www.interknowledge.com/st-martin/mont-vernon.
E-mail: tmcauban@ix.netcom.com.
Single: $120–$255. Double: $140–$275. Suites Per Day: $265–$385.
Situated at the non-nude end of mile-long Orient Beach, all accommodations at this colorful, plantation-style resort are in junior suites or larger, all rather spacious, comfortable and pleasant. The free-form pool is the island's biggest, and there are also two tennis courts and a fitness room for energetic types; the rates include a buffet breakfast. The beach has all variety of watersports and many topless bathers. Supervised programs keep little tykes busy during holidays and high season. Lots of conventioneers at this big and busy resort. 394 rooms. Credit cards: A, MC, V.

Pavillion Beach Hotel $90–$260   ★★★

Grand Case, ☎ *(800) 322-2223, (590) 87-96-46, FAX (590) 87-71-04.*
Single: $90–$240. Double: $130–$260.
This small hotel is set right on lovely Grand Case, with a sea view from each of its 17 rooms. Accommodations are either studios or suites, all large and inviting and boasting kitchenettes and air conditioning—there's also a great honeymoon suite. Request an upper floor for more privacy. There are no on-site facilities, but the central location puts much within walking distance. 17 rooms. Credit cards: A, D, MC, V.

Privilege Resort & Spa $255–$575   ★★★★

Anse Marcel, ☎ *(590) 87-38-38, FAX (590) 87-44-12.*
Single: $255–$575. Double: $255–$575. Suites Per Day: $350–$950.
Located high above Anse Marcel, Privilege is a relatively new choice for spa lovers, and is situated amid gorgeous, boulder-strewn gardens. The rooms and suites are quite elegant, with central air, mini-bars, TVs, VCRs and tropical furnishings. The spiffy spa offers hydrotherapy baths and every possible pampering service (not included in room rates). Other facilities include extensive tennis, squash, and racquetball facilities, swimming pools, aerobics classes, a high-tech exercise room, two

restaurants, two bars and a disco. Management quirks may be a drawback. 27 rooms. Credit cards: A, DC, MC, V.

Royale Louisiana $60–$88 ★ ★

Marigot, ☎ (590) 87-86-51, FAX (590) 87-96-49.
Single: $60–$66. Double: $82–$88.
Located in downtown Marigot above several shops, this hotel is a great bargain—if you don't mind that the only beach within walking distance is marginal at best. Air-conditioned guest rooms are small and simple but comfortable, with telephones and VCRs. Facilities are limited to a restaurant and bar, but there's much within walking distance. Since the beach is not terribly convenient, it's unfortunate that there's no pool, but it keeps the rates low. 58 rooms. Credit cards: MC, V.

Sol Hotel $90–$135 ★ ★

Oyster Pond, ☎ (800) 476-5849, (590) 87-38-10, FAX (590) 87-32-23.
Single: $90–$115. Double: $100–$135.
Fashioned in Georgian-style architecture and draped in bougainvillea, this little charmer overlooks Oyster Pond Marina and surrounds a pleasant pool area. Rooms are simple, but feature kitchenettes, air conditioning and a terrace for enjoying the view. Several rooms offer a Murphy bed to sleep a third adult. Dawn Beach is a 15-minute hike, and a bevy of watersports is available at the nearby marina. Rates include continental breakfast. 8 rooms. Credit cards: A, MC, V.

Apartments and Condominiums

You can actually spend as much money on a fabulous villa as you would at a chic resort on St. Martin. Two cases in point: the luxurious **Esmeralda Resort** and **Green Cay Village**, where the classification as villa complexes masks that they both provide many of the amenities of a full-service hotel. Only here you can have your own private pool. But more modest digs are also available, and may save you money, either via cooking at home, or by hooking up with another couple to split the accòmmodation costs. Among the villa rental companies are **Carimo** ☎ *(590) 87-57-58*, **Immobilier St. Martin Caraibes** ☎ *(590) 87-55-21*, and **West Indies Immobilier** ☎ *(590) 87-56-48*. In the U.S., call **WIMCO** toll-free ☎ *(800) 932-3222*.

Club Orient Resort $115–$340 ★ ★

Baie Orientale, ☎ (800) 476-5849, (590) 87-33-85, FAX (590) 87-33-76.
E-mail: clubo@virtualaccess.net.
Single: $115–$288. Double: $135–$340.
This pleasant hotel is known for its unique (in the Caribbean) "clothes-optional" policy which allows closet nudists to take it all off in a tame and relaxed environment. Located on a flat, scruffy peninsula on the Atlantic side of the island, guests are housed in wooden chalets that have living rooms, full kitchens and large porches, or in newer units in pine duplex cottages. The rooms are rustic by design (not run-down), and have some charm; all have air conditioners and ceiling fans, and facilities include a beachside restaurant, a bar and two tennis courts. No pool, but you're right on Orient Beach. 108 rooms. Credit cards: A, DC, D, MC, V.

Esmeralda Resort $180–$900 ★ ★ ★ ★

Baie Orientale, ☎ (800) 622-7836, (590) 87-36-36, FAX (590) 87-35-18.

Single: $180–$450. Double: $180–$450. Suites Per Day: $300–$900.
Situated on secluded grounds overlooking Orient Bay, this property consists of 18 posh villas that can be rented in their entirety or partially as standard guest rooms. Each villa has three to five rooms, are tastefully decorated and have all the modern conveniences; all units have at least a kitchenette. Each villa has its own pool, but you may be sharing it, depending on how much of the villa you rent. There are two restaurants, a bar, a large communal pool and three tennis courts. Watersports await on the mile-long beach. 65 rooms. Credit cards: A, MC, V.

Green Cay Village $258–$343 ★★★★

Baie Orientale, ☎ *(800) 476-5849, (590) 87-38-63, FAX (590) 87-39-27.*
Single: $258–$343. Double: $258–$343.
Perched atop Orient Bay, each villa at this Creole-inspired complex has its own small swimming pool. The villas are quite spacious and include a large living room with an entertainment center (VCR, cable TV, CD player), a full and modern kitchen, food for your first evening and a barbecue grill. Facilities include concierge services by the professional hotel staff and a tennis court. All of the villas are three-bedroom, but you can rent one or two of the bedrooms without sharing the unit (rates shown are for a one-bedroom arrangement); a seven-night minimum usually applies. Wonderfully managed and popular with savvy Americans. Rates include airport transfers and daily maid service. 16 rooms. Credit cards: A, DC, D, MC, V.

Grand Case Beach Club $105–$335 ★★★

Grand Case, ☎ *(800) 447-7462, (590) 87-51-87, FAX (590) 87-59-93.*
Single: $105–$335. Double: $105–$335.
Located at the end of Grand Case, this apartment complex consists of six white stucco buildings that offer nice ocean views. Accommodations include studios and one- and two-bedroom suites, all air conditioned and with rattan furnishings, fully equipped kitchens, satellite TV, wet bars, and nice balconies. Facilities include a restaurant, bar, tennis court and complete watersports. Small pool, but the beach is fine for swimming. This ideal spot is a great value in summer and very popular with Americans in winter. 71 rooms. Credit cards: A, DC, MC, V.

Nettle Bay Beach Club $125–$275 ★★★

Baie Nettle, ☎ *(800) 999-3543, (590) 87-68-68, FAX (590) 87-21-51.*
Single: $125–$275. Double: $125–$275.
Despite its size and location, Nettle Bay almost imparts a charming French country feel at check-in—outside the lobby are sea grapes, palms and a lot of sand. Accommodations range from standard guest rooms to villas to garden suites, all with full kitchens. The villas are large and bright, furnished in Philippine rattan, and come in one- and two-bedroom configurations. The garden suites are one-bedroom units with smaller kitchen areas. All are air-conditioned and have private terraces or patios. The grounds include three tennis courts, five pools, and a restaurant. A fair number of Americans. 230 rooms. Credit cards: A, DC, MC, V.

Inns

As on the Dutch side, there are not many true inns on St. Martin, but **La Residence** offers plenty of character.

La Residence   **$74–$98**   ★★
Marigot, ☎ *(800) 365-8484, (590) 87-70-37, FAX (590) 87-90-44.*
Single: $74–$80. Double: $92–$98.
This small hotel is in the heart of Marigot, one mile from the beach. Rooms are air-conditioned, modern, and comfortable, some have very high ceilings and a few offer kitchens. The French restaurant is quite good, and there's also a bar for unwinding. Popular with business travelers, as there is much within an easy walk, and the year-round rate structure makes prices quite reasonable in winter. 21 rooms. Credit cards: A, D, MC, V.

Low Cost Lodging

A few budget spots are found in Marigot, where the town's location away from a beach keeps rates low, particularly during the more expensive winter season. **Hevea** and **La Residence** (see "Inns," above) are reasonably priced year-round. A couple of other possibilities are **Chez Martine** in Grand Case, ☎ *(590) 87-51-59* and **Golfe** in Belleview, just outside Marigot, ☎ *(590) 87-92-05.*

Fantastic Guest House   **$45–$65**   ★
Marigot, ☎ *(590) 87-71-09, FAX (590) 87-73-51.*
Single: $45. Double: $65.
OK, so it's located above a car parts store, at least a mile from a decent beach. But this little guest house with the big name offers just about the least expensive room you'll find on the French side. That they're clean and have air conditioning is a nice bonus, and there's a splash pool on the roof top deck that overlooks Simpson Bay. The location on the outskirts of Marigot isn't exactly fantastic, but gourmands will find plenty within walking distance. And you never know when your car will break down. 19 rooms. Credit cards: A, MC, V.

Hevea   **$40–$132**   ★★
Grand Case, ☎ *(590) 87-56-85, FAX (590) 87-83-88.*
Associated Restaurant: *Hevea.*
Single: $40–$110. Double: $55–$132.
Located just across the street from the beach, this inn is housed in a restored Creole mansion surrounding a terra cotta courtyard. It has two guestrooms, three studios and three suites. Five are air conditioned; the other three make do with ceiling fans. Each of the rooms is a little different, but two are very special, with mahogany beds, mosquito nets and interesting trinkets. 8 rooms. Credit cards: MC, V.

Where to Eat

Fielding's Highest Rated Restaurants in Sint Maarten/Saint Martin

★★★★★	Fish Pot	$17–$31
★★★★★	Rainbow	$21–$30
★★★★	Antoine's	$15–$36
★★★★	Bye Bar Brazil	$10–$19
★★★★	L'Auberge Gourmande	$17–$28
★★★★	La Maison sur le Port	$17–$34
★★★★	Le Perroquet	$18–$26
★★★★	Le Pressoir	$18–$39
★★★	L'Escargot	$18–$31
★★★	La Rhumerie	$25–$45

Fielding's Most Romantic Restaurants in Sint Maarten/Saint Martin

♡♡♡♡♡	Le Pressoir	$18–$39
♡♡♡♡♡	Rainbow	$21–$30
♡♡♡♡	Antoine's	$15–$36
♡♡♡♡	L'Auberge Gourmande	$17–$28
♡♡♡♡	La Maison sur le Port	$17–$34

Fielding's Best Value Restaurants in Sint Maarten/Saint Martin

★★★	Mark's Place	$3–$13
★★★	Sambuca Ristorante	$8–$13
★★★★	Bye Bar Brazil	$10–$19
★★★	Chesterfield's	$7–$20
★★★★★	Fish Pot	$17–$31

With its strong French influence, Sint Maarten/Saint Martin has almost a legal obligation to serve world-class cuisine, and the island doesn't disappoint, with more than 300 restaurants to choose from on the two sides. Many have top gourmet kitchens to deliver full-on Gallic sensations, and a handful of restaurants serving traditional Creole cuisine can also be found (try **Le Palmier** or **Le Rhumerie**). But many other nationalities are well represented—in fact, the variety of international tastes delivered here is probably more expansive than on any other Caribbean island. Where else could you find a restaurant specializing in *Reunion Island* dishes? Seafood is omnipresent, and French wines are in abundance, but it all comes with a price. Before splurging on a hundred-dollar meal, ask around to see what spot is new or in fashion—fresh faces are always springing up. Among the newer establishments drawing raves are **L'Alabama** and **Le Tastevin**, both in Grand Case and **Michel Royer** (the chef formerly ensconced at Astrolabe) at Orient Beach. Grand Case continues to operate as the island's spectacular Restaurant Row, a half-mile long strip of dozens of beachfront eateries to satisfy almost any budget (a good rule-of-thumb: the restaurants on the waterfront side of the street are more expensive—you're paying, at least in part, for the view). Grand Case is such a hotbed of activity that it really requires a reconnaissance mission of sorts to scope out dinner for more than one night.

Cost-conscious eating can be a challenge, but it's not impossible. For gourmands, check out the *prix fixe* menu available at many restaurants, particularly on the French side. While this set, typically three-course menu won't usually include the house specialties, it's a good way to sample some of the island's better restaurants for less than $35 per person (not including wine or tip). **Back Street** in Philipsburg has a number of Chinese and Indian restaurants where a good meal can be had for $10–15. A colorful new eatery, **Kangaroo Court Caffe**, has taken over one of Philipsburg's oldest buildings, a former salt warehouse; it's a pleasant spot for early-morning coffee and baked goods, with sandwiches for lunch. Though Burger King and Taco Bell are now ubiquitous, tasty and inexpensive fast food, French Caribbean-style, is proffered by the **lolos**, family-run "chicken shacks" along the Boulevard de Grand Case and in Marigot. Here, a rack of ribs or grilled chicken with a side of rice and peas and johnny cake is about $6 (though lobster still tops $20); **Talk of the Town** is one Grand Case favorite. And, don't forget that the strong Euro influence means supermarkets like **Match** (near Marigot) stock fine cheese, pate, bread and wine, provisions for a fabulous picnic.

Sint Maarten

Antoine's	**$$$**	★★★★

103 Frontstreet; Philipsburg, ☎ (5995) 22964.
Lunch: 11 a.m.–5 p.m., entrées $6–$32.
Dinner: 5–10 p.m., entrées $15–$36.

A lovely new post-hurricane setting on a breezy patio adorned with colorful local art makes this restaurant a good choice for a celebratory or romantic dinner. Cuisine is classic French with Italian touches. Some of the specialties offered bring back memories of a rich past; to wit, duck with brandy and cherries, lobster thermidor, frog legs in garlic butter and a ravishing chocolate souffle. When in season, fresh local crayfish makes a welcome appearance. The fixed-price menu is a good bet at $29. Reservations recommended. Credit cards: A, MC, V.

Cheri's Cafe $$ ★★

Maho Bay, ☎ *(5995) 53361.*
Lunch: 11 a.m.–4:30 p.m., entrées $6–$12.
Dinner: 4:30–1:30 a.m., entrées $12–$17.
Cheri Batson, owner of the legendary cafe and bar that bears her name, must share the honors for the success of her hugely popular eating establishment with her steak purveyor—customers are always raving about the quality and quantity of the grilled beef. But most go for the scene—the place is just plain fun, and nobody sits down for long when the house band, Ramon, starts to play. Still, burgers good enough to make you homesick are also on the menu, along with the inevitable grilled seafood.

Chesterfield's $ ★★★

Great Bay Marina, Philipsburg, ☎ *(5595) 23484.*
Lunch: 11:30 a.m.–2:30 p.m., entrées $7–$12.
Dinner: 5:30–10 p.m., entrées $7–$20.
Rub epaulets with the boating crowd at this pierside restaurant with a casual, congenial ambience. The food is well-prepared, with a host of seafood, duckling and beef dishes served with flair at lunch and dinner. A companionable group gathers for happy hour on a daily basis. Credit cards: not accepted.

Da Livio Ristorante $$$ ★★★

159 Frontstreet; Philipsburg, ☎ *(5995) 22690.*
Dinner: 6–10 p.m., entrées $16–$32. Closed: Sun.
Classic Italian is the focus at this charming and friendly Philipsburg restaurant offering alfresco dining on a seaside terrace. Antipasto, lobster cocktail and beef carpaccio are nice starters, while house pasta specialties include a classic manicotti with spinach and ricotta cheese, and a homemade lasagne. Lobster fra diavolo and several veal items round out the menu. Credit cards: A, DC, MC, V.

Greenhouse, The $$ ★★

Bobby's Marina, Philipsburg, ☎ *(5995) 22941.*
Lunch: 11 a.m.–5 p.m., entrées $6–$10.
Dinner: 5–10 p.m., entrées $11–$25.
An all-purpose eatery that serves American favorites and exotic Indonesian specialties, the Greenhouse has a harbor location and a dining room lush with plant life. Guests can play pool, throw darts and dance as well as dine. It jumps daily at happy hour, which actually lasts a little longer; good for twofers and gratis hors d'oeuvres. Credit cards: A, MC, V.

Grill & Ribs Co., The $ ★★

Old Street Shopping Center, Philipsburg, ☎ *(5995) 27723.*
Lunch: 11 a.m.–4 p.m., entrées $5–$6.

Dinner: 4–10 p.m., entrées $5–$14.

This informal place is the island's best-known and best-loved ribarama. For a reasonable price of $12.95, diners can chow down on an unlimited amount of baby back pork or beef ribs. The Grill & Ribs Co. has two locations to choose from: a second-story alfresco terrace eatery at the Old Street Shopping Center, or the rib place behind Pizza Hut on Simpson Bay Beach. Other offerings include chicken fajitas, burgers, chicken and sandwiches heaped with a side of fries. Credit cards: not accepted.

L'Escargot $$$ ★★★

84 Frontstreet; Philipsburg, ☎ (5995) 22483.
Lunch: 11 a.m.–3 p.m., entrées $8–$23.
Dinner: 6:30–11 p.m., entrées $18–$31.

Snail fanciers and others will enjoy a meal at this venerable grande dame of a restaurant, which has been in the same spot for over 25 years. The delectable delicacy is a specialty, and it shows up stuffed in mushrooms and in various other ways. The rest of the menu is largely French, encompassing duck, seafood, and meat dishes. Reservations recommended. Credit cards: A, MC, V.

Le Bec Fin $$$ ★★★

119 Front Street; Philipsburg, ☎ (5995) 22976.
Lunch: 11 a.m.–3:30 p.m., entrées $6–$14.
Dinner: 6–10 p.m., entrées $16–$31.

Ascend a flight of stairs to this second-floor dining salon in a pleasant courtyard. At night, the ambience is candlelit and intimate, during the day try to snag a table overlooking the sea; there are only a few of them available. The kitchen really shines with its seafood preparations, especially lobster, served grilled or flamed in brandy. Lunch is served downstairs in the cafe. Reservations recommended. Credit cards: A, MC, V.

Le Perroquet $$$ ★★★★

72 Airport Road, Philipsburg, ☎ (5995) 54339.
Dinner: 6–10:30 p.m., entrées $18–$26. Closed: Mon.

This restaurant, situated on the lagoon in a typical West Indian house near the airport, serves atypical meals. Servers wheel a cart to your table with a choice of nightly specials—which often include filets of ostrich or boar steaks. For less adventurous palates, fresh red snapper or beef dishes are usually available. The view of Simpson Bay Lagoon from the plant-filled porch is lovely. Closed June and September. Reservations recommended. Credit cards: A, MC, V.

Lynette's Grill and Seafood Restaurant $$$ ★★★

Airport Road, Simpson Bay, ☎ (5995) 52865.
Lunch: Noon–4 p.m., entrées $7–$17.
Dinner: 6–10:30 p.m., entrées $12–$29.

Lynette's is the spot for authentic West Indian dishes prepared with casual flair in upscale surroundings near the foot of the Juliana airstrip. Grilled fish, shrimp and lobster are usually excellent, while barbecued chicken or ribs, chateaubriand and rack of lamb are a tip of the hat to heartier appetites. Or you can stick to the local specialties, like conch Creole, stewed goat or fish and *funghi*. The service is always friendly, and local recording artist King Beau Beau gyrates and sings merrily on Tuesday and Friday evenings. Credit cards: A, MC, V.

Mark's Place $ ★★★

Food Center shopping mall, Philipsburg.
Lunch: 12:30–2:30 p.m., entrées $3–$13.
Dinner: 6:30–9:30 p.m., entrées $3–$13.

A longtime favorite that moved during the post-Luis turmoil from French Cul de Sac to Philipsburg's Food Center shopping mall, the West Indian food served here is hearty, plentiful, and varied. On a given night you could have lobster bisque with a curry of conch or goat, or a crab back appetizer and swordfish, but some note that the quality dropped when Mark switched national allegiance (or maybe that's just a French thing?). Either way, it's hard to quibble with the reasonable prices. And the crowds keep coming—Mark's Place is usually jammed. Credit cards: A, MC, V.

Sambuca Ristorante $ ★★★

46 Airport Road, Simpson Bay, ☎ (5995) 52633.
Lunch: 11:30 a.m.–4:30 p.m., entrées $5–$8.
Dinner: 6–11 p.m., entrées $8–$13.

An attractive new Italian ristorante near the Juliana airport, Sambuca serves up tasty and inexpensive pizzas and pastas (the fusilli with chicken and broccoli is delicious), while specialties include eggplant parmigiana, a ribeye topped with peperoncini, carmelized onions and mushrooms, and chicken marsala. Desserts include a pretty decent tiramisu. A casino is being built upstairs as we go to press. Credit cards: MC, V.

Seafood Galley, The $ ★★

Bobby's Marina, Philipsburg, ☎ (5995) 23253.
Lunch: 11 a.m.–3 p.m., entrées $7–$18.
Dinner: 6–10 p.m., entrées $7–$18. Closed: Sun.

Although this pier-side establishment has a clubby restaurant offering hot plates of fresh fish and seafood, some people bypass it and head straight for the adjoining raw bar. There they can graze all night from a generous menu of oyster shooters, clams on the half shell, or crab claws. Lunchtime is popular for the view and the hearty sandwiches and egg dishes. Credit cards: A, MC, V.

Shivsager $$ ★★★

#3 Frontstreet; Philipsburg, ☎ (5995) 22299.
Dinner: 6:30–10 p.m., entrées $11–$22.

The island's best Indian food is served up at this simply decorated Philipsburg restaurant across from the Barclay's Bank. There's a tandoori oven for kebabs and chicken *tikka*, while the chicken marsala and the mutton *rogan josh* are other recommended items. Samosas, fish and shrimp curry, chicken *mankhanwalia* and a variety of *naans* help to round out an authentic dining experience. Credit cards: A, MC, V.

Trattoria Italiana $ ★★

Maho Bay.
Lunch: Noon–, entrées $9–$15.
Dinner: –midnight, entrées $9–$15.

A nice plate of pasta or steaming pizza for about $10—could it be? Tucked in the alley behind Cheri's, opposite the Maho Beach Hotel, this down-home trattoria serves decent Italian for reasonable prices (look for the line streaming out the door on most nights). The list of pastas encompasses hearty spaghetti, macaroni and ravioli dishes, while the pizzas include a pretty decent quattro stagioni (ham, mushrooms, artichokes and sweet bell pepper).

Wajang Doll, The $$$ ★★★
137 Frontstreet, Philipsburg, ☎ *(5995) 22687.*
Dinner: 7–10 p.m., entrées $19–$25. Closed: Sun.
It helps to come here with a big group and a healthy appetite for this restaurant's 14- to 19-item Javanese feasts. This cuisine, known as *rijstaffel* (rice table), originated in the former Dutch colony of Indonesia. Seemingly endless plates of savory and spicy seafood, meats and chicken are devoured over a mountain of fragrant rice. They can be embellished with "try them if you dare" hot pepper *sambals*. Couples and singles won't feel left out, as smaller and cheaper versions are available as well as a la carte dishes. Reservations recommended. Credit cards: A, MC, V.

Saint Martin

Bye Bar Brazil $$ ★★★★
47 Boulevard de Grand Case, Grand Case, ☎ *(590) 87-76-49.*
Dinner: 7 p.m.–1 a.m., entrées $10–$19. Closed: Tue.
Locals love to hang out here and talk literature and politics into the wee hours with Michel, the opinionated (but gracious) owner of this unpretentious spot in the heart of Grand Case. Though most come for the socializing, the food is fine—try the *feijoada completa*, a black bean stew with a variety of meats that is Brazil's national dish, or simple country French dishes, like *porc a chavallon*, hearty marinated pork with onions and potatoes. Michel is more famous for his *caipirinha*—a wonderful concoction of rum, sugar and lime—as well as his selection of whiskeys, including 35 or so single malts from Scotland. The entire wine list is available by the glass, with many tasty choices under $5. Credit cards: MC, V.

Captain Oliver's Restaurant $$ ★★
Oyster Pond, ☎ *(590) 87-30-00.* Associated hotel: *Captain Oliver's.*
Lunch: Noon–5 p.m., entrées $7–$21.
Dinner: 6:30-11 p.m., entrées $13–$21.
A popular outdoor restaurant/snackbar/store on a deck facing the sea, Captain Oliver's sits below its namesake resort. A thoroughly democratic place, the good captain has provided a choice of flavors to fit every budget. There's a snack shack dispensing brochettes, Indonesian lamb chops and other inexpensive meals (open noon to midnight daily). The centerpiece, though, is the oceanfront restaurant, where basic international cuisine, with an emphasis on seafood, is served for lunch and dinner. Service is spotty, and expect a 15 percent surcharge after 6 p.m. Credit cards: A, DC, MC, V.

Claude Mini Club $$$ ★★
Front de Mer, Marigot, ☎ *(590) 87-50-69.*
Lunch: Noon–3 p.m., entrées $12–$25.
Dinner: 7:30–10 p.m., entrées $18–$35.
Locals who like to stuff themselves silly with food as good as mother makes are grateful for the continuing success of the gargantuan French-Creole buffet served

here on Wednesdays and Saturday nights. The feast includes all the wine you can drink, so bring a friend who can help you down the stairs. On other days sample lobster soufflé and other French specialties. The setting is lots of fun: a jungly, tropical terrace above the street, facing the harbor. The buffet is $40 per person, or the fixed priced dinner is $25. Closed for lunch Sunday. Credit cards: A, MC, V.

Coco Beach Bar   **$$$**   ★★★

Orient Beach, ☎ *(590) 87-34-62.* Associated hotel: *Esmeralda Resort.*
Dinner: 6–10 p.m., entrées $12–$36.

By day Coco Beach bar is just one of a number of plain open-air eateries competing for the tourist dollar on clothing-optional Orient Beach. But at night, it becomes a quaint little candlelit restaurant, with tastefully set tables and a diverse menu, which includes caesar salad, stuffed crab, filet mignon, and grilled lobster with pasta. Soft lapping ocean waves provide atmospheric background music. Despite an often-full house, service is among the best on the island. Credit cards: A, MC, V.

Fish Pot   **$$$**   ★★★★★

82 Boulevard de Grand Case, Grand Case, ☎ *(590) 87-50-88.*
Dinner: 6–10:30 p.m., entrées $17–$31.

One of the many dining terraces sitting above the shimmering beach at Grand Case, and one of the best. A cold, creamy cauliflower soup with chips of bacon is sublime; fish and meat entrées are given their due. For dessert, try the croustillant de banane. The service is a bit formal—waiters in natty, color-coordinated red bows and vests— and a few nag that it's overrated, but the view of Anguilla and soft rustle of the sea under the prime front-row tables is hard to beat. Small selection of kosher and vegetarian items. Reservations recommended. Credit cards: A, MC, V.

Hevea   **$$$**   ★★★

Boulevard de Grand Case, Grand Case, ☎ *(590) 87-56-85.* Associated hotel: *Hevea.*
Dinner: 6:30–10 p.m., entrées $17–$28.

Set in a restored Creole mansion that is also an intimate inn, this 10-table French eatery is charming and romantic. The size of the dining room ensures consistent quality of the French cuisine served here. The proprietors, who hail from Nice, use top ingredients and believe that simplicity is key—sauces made with fresh herbs, wine reductions, or wild mushrooms are often used to subtly accentuate, never overpower, lamb, duck breast, or a signature red snapper en papillote or lobster thermidor. The three-course Creole menu for $29 is a good deal. Closed Mondays in the low season. Reservations recommended. Credit cards: MC, V.

Kontiki   **$$**   ★★★

Orient Beach, ☎ *(590) 87-43-27.*
Lunch: 11 a.m.–, entrées $11–$25.
Dinner: 9:30 p.m., entrées $11–$25.

A Thor Heyerdahl fantasy gone gloriously haywire, Kontiki is perched between the palms and seagrapes of Orient Beach, in a clutch of thatched-roof huts on the sand. The hip, inspired setting is a front for an eclectic menu suitable for a beached lunch—artichoke and leek salad, grilled fish and barbecued chicken and other meats; there's also a sushi bar. Live music takes over by late afternoon (usually jazz or blues), jet skis buzz madly in the water, and beautiful people abound (no, we're not referring to the naturists just down the sand). Credit cards: MC, V.

L'Auberge Gourmande $$$ ★★★★

89 Boulevard de Grand Case, Grand Case, ☎ *(590) 87-73-37.*
Dinner: 6:30–10 p.m., entrées $17–$28. Closed: Wed.
The setting is a quaint, converted residence sporting jalousied windows. Guests dine in a comfortable room, although increased noise on the streets of Grand Case may affect a romantic tete-a-tete. Soups are a specialty and are interestingly prepared, including a lovely fish soup. Grilled fish is reliable, or go all out and order the sweetbreads and shrimp in puff pastry or roast lamb with herbs. Two seatings nightly, 7 and 9 p.m. Reservations recommended. Credit cards: A, MC, V.

La Maison sur le Port $$$ ★★★★

Rue de la Republique, Marigot, ☎ *(590) 87-56-38.*
Lunch: Noon–2:30 p.m., entrées $11–$14.
Dinner: 6–10:30 p.m., entrées $17–$34. Closed: Sun.
Positioned in a lovely colonial-style house overlooking the harbor, chef Christian Verdeau presents impeccably prepared but rather small portions of duck (a specialty), lobster and other prime meats and seafood. The veranda is especially popular for sunset views. A good value for the excellent quality of the ingredients, and a warm welcome is reserved for all comers. Closed June and September. Reservations recommended. Credit cards: A, CB, MC, V.

La Rhumerie $$$ ★★★

Route de Colombier ☎ *(590) 87-56-98.*
Dinner: 7–10 p.m., entrées $25–$45. Closed: Thurs.
A lovely countryside setting far from the citified pace of Saint Martin is the spot for this French and Creole restaurant. Avocado *farcee*, stuffed crab backs, herbed conch and a widely praised smoked chicken are menu highlights. Desserts are heavenly and include bananas flambee and *profiteroles*, or simply papayas drizzled with lime. As a topper, try one of the flavored rums that sit elegantly in jars on the bar counter—passion fruit, prune, coconut and others. La Rhumerie would be the perfect escape for lunch, but it's open for dinner only. Closed the months of September–October. Reservations recommended. Credit cards: MC, V.

Le Palmier $$ ★★

Lady Fish Road, Sandy Ground, ☎ *(590) 87-50-71.*
Lunch: Noon–3 p.m., entrées $10–$30.
Dinner: 6:30–10:30 p.m., entrées $10–$30.
Madras tablecloths and a colorful selection of fruit-saturated rum in bottles are virtually the only decor at this little spot next to the bridge into Sandy Ground. A low-key outfit serving traditional French Creole food, Le Palmier specializes in snapper in Creole sauce, curried goat, octopus stew and, of course, delightful accras morue. The staff is sweet, though English is not spoken by all. Credit cards: MC, V.

Le Pressoir $$$ ★★★★

Boulevard de Grand Case, Grand Case, ☎ *(590) 87-76-62.*
Dinner: 6:30–10:30 p.m., entrées $18–$39.

A newer Grand Case favorite, named after the rusting salt grinding machine in front, Le Pressoir occupies an old Creole house and trades sea views for homey decor accented by local art. Soups are refined delights—cold cream of asparagus and chives or lobster bisque. Entrees include a half-lobster with stuffed mussels and crayfish, and rabbit tournedos in a banana and lime sauce. A wonderful evening is assured. Credit cards: D, MC, V.

Rainbow $$$ ★★★★★

176 boulevard de Grand Case, Grand Case, ☎ *(590) 87-55-80.*
Lunch: Noon–2 p.m., entrées $11–$17.
Dinner: 6–10:30 p.m., entrées $21–$30. Closed: Sun.

Going on its 18th year, David and Fleur's romantic seaside eatery is not inexpensive, but the simple blue and white wooden cottage belies the gastronomique delights that pour forth from the kitchen of Frederick Lecullier, the restaurant's new chef. The always-evolving menu leans to French contemporary, with a succulent spicy shrimp salad and a number of grilled meat and fish dishes prepared with flair. Always-fashionable, Rainbow remains a true "in" spot with locals. Closed annually from mid-September through October. Credit cards: A, MC, V.

Surf Club South $$ ★★

French Cul de Sac, ☎ *(590) 29-50-40.*
Dinner: 3–10 p.m., entrées $14–$19.

New Jersey natives will do a double take as they come upon the Garden State Parkway, Turnpike and other highway signs prominently displayed along the road out of Orient Beach (en route to Grand Case). Andy and Cheryl, Jersey expatriates, run this funky spot, which boasts of a "New Jersey menu" (lots of burgers and cheese steaks). It's a happening spot, especially on Sunday for the New Jersey Shore Party, when they give out free mimosas and bloody marys from noon 'til 2 p.m. and live music kicks in at 6 p.m. Bring your bathing suit for the pool.

FIELDING'S CHOICE:

Little known to the outside world is the special purple and bittersweet guavaberry liqueur produced on the island ever since Dutch colonists settled in the 18th century. During the Christmas holidays, it's customary to go from home to home serenading for samples. Every family makes a different brew, which is usually fully consumed by the end of the Christmas season. The Sint Maarten Guavaberry Company now makes the liqueur locally, and offers shade, seating and a few samples at the Guavaberry Shop on 10 Front St. in Philipsburg. Try a guavaberry colada (blended with cream of coconut and pineapple juice), or a guavaberry screwdriver (mixed with orange juice). A bottle sells for less than $15 and is duty-free because it is an island craft.

Where to Shop

Philipsburg, capital of Dutch Sint Maarten, is full of shops and markets.

Shopping is a major industry here, and Sint Maarten/Saint Martin's duty-free shops carry all the typical products one would expect to find at 25–50 percent discounts: china, jewelry, crystal, perfumes and fashions. Prices are usually quoted in U.S. dollars and virtually all sales clerks speak English. Bargaining is not part of the culture on either side of the island, though discounts are sometimes offered to those paying by traveler's checks. Before beginning your shopping splurge, it pays to know what the prices are at home.

Marigot is the main shopping area of French Saint Martin—be prepared to pay in French francs if you want a good exchange. The **Gold Mine** reputedly carries the largest diamond inventory in the Caribbean. High fashion designs can be found in the **Galerie Perigourdine** shopping complex, across from the post office, and the **Marina Royale** has another good collection of shops. **Ma Doudou** makes traditional West Indian fruit-imbued rums of coconut, orange and other flavors—the bottles make inexpensive and attractive gifts for about $12. Local art shown in galleries and studios can sometimes be reasonable and several local artists are known outside the region; besides Roland Richardson in Orleans (see "What Else to See"), seek out the work of Genevieve Curt at the **Tropical Gallery**. Other fine names are the painter Alexandre Minguet, and the Lynn family (husband, wife and two sons) who have a

Grand Case gallery open "by chance." There is a twice-weekly **market** in **Marigot** (Wednesday and Saturday mornings), where locals sell their spices, fruits, vegetables and handicrafts. Marigot's **Port la Royale** is a beehive of activity after dawn; hang out here if you want to meet yachties and even local schooner captains cruising in from other islands with new goods. Shopping in Grand Case is limited to the narrow main street.

Philipsburg and the Dutch side is less fashion-oriented than Saint Martin, and you'll need to wander past the maze of T-shirt and trinket shops, but you can find memorable leather products (**Domina**), clothes (**Maurella Senesi**) and jewelry (**Caribbean Gems**). The **Shipwreck Shop** on Frontstreet has an eclectic array of island goods, maps, and Lord & Hunter spices. Gucci, H. Stern Jewelers, Little Switzerland, Benetton and other name brands are represented in Philipsburg. **Sualouiga Festival** is an open market held on Fridays in Philipsburg, with local food, handicrafts, exhibits and music. Another area to hunt for bargains is the **Maho** complex.

On the French side, shops are generally open Monday through Friday from 9 a.m.–noon, and from 2–6 p.m. Shops on Sint Marten are typically open 8 a.m.–noon, and 2–6 p.m. Monday through Friday; most Dutch shops are also open Saturday mornings and Philipsburg stores will usually open on Sundays if a cruise ship has landed.

Sint Maarten/St. Martin Directory

Arrival and Departure

Sint Maarten's Juliana Airport is one of the best-connected in the Caribbean (a small airstrip on the French side, L'Esperance, connects Saint Martin with the nearby French islands only). **American Airlines** has daily nonstop flights from New York's JFK and Miami, as well as several flights daily from its hub in San Juan, Puerto Rico. **Continental** serves Sint Maarten several times weekly out of Newark, and **USAirways** flies to the island on weekends from Charlotte and Philadelphia. **Northwest** provides seasonal service out of Minneapolis. **Charter service** is available from a number of North American cities, especially in winter; contact your travel agent or the island's information line: ☎ *(800) STMAARTEN* or *(212) 953-2084*. Of the regional carriers, **LIAT** offers direct or nonstop service from Anguilla, Antigua, St. Croix, St. Kitts, St. Thomas and Tortola. **BWIA** offers limited service to Juliana from Jamaica and Barbados. **Winair** connects Sint Maarten with Saba and Sint Eustatius, as well as other nearby islands. **ALM Antillean** flies in from Aruba, Bonaire and Curacao. **Air Martinique**, **Air Guadeloupe** and **Air St. Barts** serve the French islands out of both Juliana and L'Esperance.

There is a departure tax from Juliana Airport of $12, or $5 if you are headed for other islands in the Netherlands Antilles. The departure tax from L'Esperance is $3, usually written into the price of the ticket.

Business Hours

On the Dutch side, shops open Monday–Saturday 8 a.m.–noon and 2–6 p.m. Banks open Monday–Thursday 8 a.m.–1 p.m. and Friday from 8:30 a.m.–1 p.m. and 4–5 p.m. On the French side, shops open Monday–Saturday 9 a.m.–12:30 p.m. and 3–7 p.m. Some shops take a longer or shorter siesta, so call ahead. Banks open weekdays 8:30 a.m.–1:30 p.m.

Climate

Sunshine prevails on the island and it is warm year-round. Temperatures during the winter average 80 degrees Fahrenheit; in the summer, it gets a little warmer. Constant trade winds keep the climate pleasant.

Documents

U.S. citizens entering either the Dutch or French side of the island must have a valid passport (or one that has expired no more than five years prior), or a notarized or original birth certificate and a government-issued photo identification. Those entering the island via the French side for a stay of more than three weeks must have a valid passport. As a duty-free port, there is no customs facility on the island.

Electricity

The Dutch side is wired for 110 volts, 60 cycles. The French side is set up for 220 AC, 50 cycles—American and Canadian appliances require French plug converters and transformers.

Getting Around

Taxis are prevalent at Juliana Airport, and expensive. Sample rates from the airport to Philipsburg are $12, to Maho $6, to Marigot $12, and $20 to Grand Case. Between 10 p.m. and midnight, rates rise 25 percent; after midnight, 50 percent. The taxi stand in Marigot is located near the tourist office ☎ *(590) 87-56-54*; in Grand Case ☎ *(590) 87-75-79*. **Car rentals** are easy and abundant on the island; rates start at about $35 per day. In addition to numerous local firms, several of the name American outfits provide rentals on the French and/or Dutch side, including **Avis**, **Budget**, **Dollar**, **Hertz** and **National**. Among the local firms, **Paradise Island Car Rental** is a reliable outfit based near the Maho complex ☎ *(5995) 52361*.

Local transportation is via **minibus**, which are a convenient way to get to major population centers, but less so if you're headed to out-of-the-way beaches like Baie Longue or Baie Orientale. Most routes start or end in Philipsburg or Marigot, and transport between these two points is particularly easy, for $1. However, some itineraries may involve a change of bus. For instance, a trek from the Maho Bay area to Marigot will usually involve two buses; one from Maho to Cole Bay, and another to Marigot. Tell your driver where you are going when you board the bus and ask him to point out where to wait for your connection.

Daytrips to neighboring islands are simple and popular. Closest and easiest to reach is **Anguilla**, which is a five-minute flight from Juliana, or a 20-minute ferry ride that leaves from the Marigot marina every 30 minutes ($10 each way). **St. Barthélémy** can be reached by plane from either Juliana or L'Esperance airport (about $95), or via ferry. *White Octopus*, a 75-foot catamaran, makes the 90-minute crossing from Bobby's Marina in Philipsburg on Tuesday and Thursday; $25 one way (plus $5 tax), open bar included ☎ *(5995) 23170.* Gustavia Express serves St. Barts from both Philipsburg ($36 one way) and Marigot ($40), several times a week ☎ *(590) 27-77-24.* The Edge makes a 40-minute trip to St. Barts three times a week from the Pelican Resort Marina ($50 round trip) ☎ *(5995) 42640.* **Saba** is reached 20-minute by Winair flight from Juliana several times daily, or via boat. *Voyager*, a ferry that makes the round trip several times a week ($40 one way or $60 round trip) ☎ *(5995) 24096.* The Edge also makes three trips a week to Saba from the Pelican Marina (45 minutes, $60 round trip) ☎ *(5995) 42640.* Lunch and island tour packages are available once on Saba for an additional $30. Scheduled service to **Sint Eustatius** is via air only, with several Winair flights daily out of Juliana. For additional information on transportation to these four islands, see "Arrival and Departure" in their respective chapters. You will be hit with a $12 departure tax for day trips to Anguilla, St. Barts, or other non-Dutch islands; $5 for trips to other islands in the Netherlands Antilles. A word to the wise: inter-island ferry service can be a highly unsettling experience for those with sensitive stomachs. If in doubt, fly—it is not uncommon for a substantial portion of the passengers to become seasick during the crossings to Saba or St. Barts (Anguilla is both a shorter and usually less roiled trip).

Language

French is the official language of Saint Martin and Dutch is the official language of Sint Maarten. English is spoken everywhere on the Dutch side, and in most establishments catering to tourists on the French side.

Medical Emergencies

There is a hospital in Marigot ☎ *(590) 29-57-57*, and another in Philipsburg ☎ *(5995) 22111*. Hotels can contact English-speaking physicians for you. There are about 18 doctors practicing general medicine and specialists in many fields. There are several pharmacies in Saint Martin, and a clinic and pharmacy at Maho Bay. Serious emergencies may warrant a trip to San Juan.

Money

The official currency on the French side is the French franc, and the guilder on the Dutch side, but U.S. dollars are accepted everywhere. Prices are usually quoted in U.S. dollars, particularly in Sint Maarten, but pay attention to the exchange rate used to calculate menu prices, especially on the French side. The rates of exchange fluctuates, but at press time the French franc was trading at about 5.5 to the dollar, while Dutch guilders were about 1.80 to the dollar.

Telephone

The international dialing code for the Dutch side is *(5995)*; to call Sint Maarten from the U.S., dial *011 + (5995)* and the five-digit local number.

The international dialing code for the French side is *(590)*; to call Saint Martin from the U.S., dial *011 + (590)* and the six-digit local number.

It's a toll call when phoning from one side of the island to the other. To call Saint Martin from the Dutch side, dial 06, followed by the six-digit local number. To call Sint Maarten from the French side, dial *19 + (5995)*, followed by the five-digit local number.

The cheapest way to call the U.S. from Sint Maarten/Saint Martin is to use a phone card at a public phone. These are found at the pier in Philipsburg and at the square in Marigot.

Time

Saint Martin/Sint Maarten is one hour ahead of Eastern Standard Time in New York. French St. Martin uses the 24-hour system of telling time; hence, 1 p.m. in the afternoon is 13 hours.

Tipping and Taxes

Most Sint Maarten hotels include a 5 percent tax and 10–15 percent service charge in their quoted room rates—some add an energy surcharge. On the French side, a 5 percent hotel tax is usual, the service charge is not, but you'll need to check to make sure. There is no tax on meals; if a service charge (usually 10–15 percent) is not added to your restaurant bill, a tip is appropriate.

Tourist Information

The **Dutch Sint Maarten Tourist Office** is located at Wathey Square in Philipsburg ☎ *(5995) 223-37*. The **French Saint Martin Tourist Office** is located at the waterfront in Marigot ☎ *(590) 87-57-21*. In the United States, information on Dutch Sint Maarten is obtained through ☎ *(800) STMAARTEN* or ☎ *(212) 953-2084*; for French Saint Martin ☎ *(212) 529-8484*. The French side also maintains an information center at ☎ *(900) 990-0040*, but be forewarned you'll be charged.95 per minute on your phone bill.

Web Site

www.st-maarten.com AND www.interknowledge.com/st-martin

When to Go

La Fete des Rois, or **Epiphany**, is celebrated on the French side on January 5 with feasting, dancing and a cake known as *galette des rois*. The French side Carnival is in February, during the five days leading up to Ash Wednesday; the Dutch respond with their Carnival a few weeks later at Easter. During both events, beauty contests, food competitions, concerts, jump-ups and parades fill the streets. The three-day **Heineken Regatta** has emerged as one of the region's major sailing events, held in March around the island. April 30 is the **Queen's Birthday**, honoring the queen of Holland, but celebrated on both sides; festivities for the French national holiday, **Bastille Day**, are similarly island-wide, on July 14. **Schoelcher Day** is a French holiday on July 21 in honor of Victor Schoelcher, the French parliamentarian who led the campaign against slavery; festivities include boat racing in Grand Case (using colorful Anguillan sailing vessels), a mini-marathon, and bike race. On November 11,

Concordia Day (or Sint Maarten/Saint Martin Day) is celebrated—the date commemorates the long-standing peaceful co-existence of the two countries. Festivities include a ceremony at the border monument at Simpson Bay and a 20-mile "Around the Island" relay race, which is based on the folk tale of how the island's borders were established.

SINT MAARTEN/ SAINT MARTIN HOTELS		RMS	RATES	PHONE	CR. CARDS
Sint Maarten					
★★★	Beachside Villas	14	$165–$325	(5995) 54294	A, MC
★★★	Cupecoy Beach Club	126	$100–$350	(800) 955-9008	
★★★	Divi Little Bay Beach Resort	118	$135–$220	(800) 367-3484	A, DC, MC, V
★★★	Horny Toad Guesthouse	8	$98–$180	(800) 417-9361, x3013	
★★★	Maho Beach Hotel & Casino	600	$155–$390	(800) 223-0757	A, DC, MC, V
★★★	Mary's Boon	15	$75–$195	(5995) 54235	MC, V
★★★	Oyster Bay Beach Resort	40	$120–$275	(800) 231-8331	A, D, DC, MC, V
★★	Belair Beach Hotel	72	$205–$335	(5995) 23366	A, MC, V
★★	Great Bay Beach Hotel	285	$95–$290	(800) 223-0757	A, DC, MC, V
★★	Holland House Beach Hotel	54	$84–$200	(800) 223-9815	A, D, MC, V
★★	Pasanggrahan Royal Inn	30	$78–$148	(800) 351-5656	A, MC
★★	Pelican Resort & Casino	342	$95–$270	(800) 550-7088	A, D, DC, MC, V
★★	Summit Resort Hotel	50	$95–$195	(800) 351-5656	A, MC, V
★★	Town House Villas	12	$125–$250	(5995) 22898	A, MC, V
★	White Sands Beach Club	14	$79–$139	(5995) 54370	A, MC, V
Saint Martin					
★★★★★	La Samanna	82	$325–$700	(800) 854-2252	A, MC, V
★★★★	Esmeralda Resort	65	$180–$450	(800) 622-7836	A, MC, V
★★★★	Green Cay Village	16	$258–$343	(800) 476-5849	A, D, DC, MC, V
★★★★	Le Meridien L'Habitation and Le Domaine	396	$190–$380	(800) 543-4300	A, DC, MC, V
★★★★	Privilege Resort & Spa	27	$255–$575	(590) 87-38-38	A, DC, MC, V
★★★	Anse Margot	96	$125–$189	(800) 742-4276	A, D, DC, MC, V
★★★	Captain Oliver's Hotel	30	$105–$205	(800) 535-7289	A, MC, V
★★★	Grand Case Beach Club	71	$105–$335	(800) 447-7462	A, DC, MC, V

SINT MAARTEN/ SAINT MARTIN HOTELS	RMS	RATES	PHONE	CR. CARDS
★★★ L'Esplanade Caraibe Hotel	24	$100–$320	(800) 633-7411	A, MC, V
★★★ Mont Vernon	394	$120–$275	(800) 223-0888	A, MC, V
★★★ Nettle Bay Beach Club	230	$125–$275	(800) 999-3543	A, DC, MC, V
★★★ Pavillion Beach Hotel	17	$90–$260	(800) 322-2223	A, D, MC, V
★★ Club Orient Resort	108	$115–$340	(800) 476-5849	A, CB, D, DC, MC, V
★★ Hevea	8	$40–$132	(590) 87-56-85	MC, V
★★ La Residence	21	$74–$98	(800) 365-8484	A, D, MC, V
★★ Royale Louisiana	58	$60–$88	(590) 87-86-51	MC, V
★★ Sol Hotel	8	$90–$135	(800) 476-5849	A, MC, V
★ Fantastic Guest House	19	$45–$65	(590) 87-71-09	A, MC, V

SINT MAARTEN/SAINT MARTIN RESTAURANTS	PHONE	ENTRÉE	CR. CARDS
Sint Maarten			
American Cuisine			
★★★ Chesterfield's	(5595) 23484	$7–$20	None
★★ Cheri's Cafe	(5995) 53361	$6–$17	
★★ Greenhouse	(5995) 22941	$6–$25	A, MC, V
★★ Grill & Ribs Co., The	(5995) 27723	$5–$14	None
French Cuisine			
★★★★ Antoine's	(5995) 22964	$6–$36	A, MC, V
★★★★ Le Perroquet	(5995) 54339	$18–$26	A, MC, V
★★★ L'Escargot	(5995) 22483	$8–$31	A, MC, V
★★★ Le Bec Fin	(5995) 22976	$6–$31	A, MC, V
Indian Cuisine			
★★★ Shivsager	(5995) 22299	$11–$22	A, MC, V
Indonesian Cuisine			
★★★ Wajang Doll, The	(5995) 22687	$19–$25	A, MC, V
Italian Cuisine			
★★★ Da Livio Ristorante	(5995) 22690	$16–$32	A, DC, MC, V
★★★ Sambuca Ristorante	(5995) 52633	$5–$13	MC, V

SINT MAARTEN SAINT MARTIN

SINT MAARTEN/SAINT MARTIN RESTAURANTS	PHONE	ENTRÉE	CR. CARDS
★★ **Trattoria Italiana**		$9–$15	
Regional Cuisine			
★★★ **Lynette's Grill and Seafood Re**	(5995) 52865	$7–$29	A, MC, V
★★★ **Mark's Place**		$3–$13	A, MC, V
Seafood Cuisine			
★★ **Seafood Galley, The**	(5995) 23253	$7–$18	A, MC, V

Saint Martin

	PHONE	ENTRÉE	CR. CARDS
American Cuisine			
★★ **Surf Club South**	(590) 29-50-40	$14–$19	
Creole Cuisine			
★★★ **La Rhumerie**	(590) 87-56-98	$25–$45	CB, MC, V
★★ **Le Palmier**	(590) 87-50-71	$10–$30	MC, V
French Cuisine			
★★★★★ **Fish Pot**	(590) 87-50-88	$17–$31	A, MC, V
★★★★★ **Rainbow**	(590) 87-55-80	$11–$30	A, MC, V
★★★★ **L'Auberge Gourmande**	(590) 87-73-37	$17–$28	A, MC, V
★★★★ **La Maison sur le Port**	(590) 87-56-38	$11–$34	A, CB, MC, V
★★★★ **Le Pressoir**	(590) 87-76-62	$18–$39	D, MC, V
★★★ **Hevea**	(590) 87-56-85	$17–$28	MC, V
★★ **Claude Mini Club**	(590) 87-50-69	$12–$35	A, MC, V
Latin American Cuisine			
★★★★ **Bye Bar Brazil**	(590) 87-76-49	$10–$19	MC, V
Regional Cuisine			
★★★ **Coco Beach Bar**	(590) 87-34-62	$12–$36	A, MC, V
★★★ **Kontiki**	(590) 87-43-27	$11–$25	MC, V
★★ **Captain Oliver's Restaurant**	(590) 87-30-00	$7–$21	A, DC, MC, V

ST. THOMAS

St. Thomas has 34 dive sites and offers excellent snorkeling.

Few metropolitan sights are as breathtaking as the one of St. Thomas's glittering Charlotte Amalie harbor, particularly when seen high above from Paradise Point at dusk. Enormous cruise ships ply the water, the downtown area bustles with shoppers, homes trickle up the verdant slopes, and comely swathes of sand can be seen in the distance. It's a seductive vision, and for many it defines the quintessential Caribbean paradise. In fact, St. Thomas is the most cosmopolitan of the U.S. Virgin Islands, and perhaps the most unabashedly commercial destination in the entire Caribbean, as well. With the capacity for up to ten cruise ships docking in a single day, and an extensive infrastructure in hot pursuit of the tourist dollar, the island will be a serious turnoff to anyone in search of genuine retreat and tranquillity. If, on the other hand, your vacation is geared toward shopping, fine dining and Americanized nightlife, St. Thomas may be exactly what you're looking for. One notable who vacationed here in January 1997 was President Clinton and family, who stayed in a three-bedroom villa, took day sails and dined on conch fritters and soursop juice at a local restaurant.

St. Thomas needed the attention. The island suffered an *annus horribilis* or two after Hurricane Marilyn delivered its body blow in September 1995. The "storm of the century" churned a path of destruction that left St. Thomas reeling. And compounding the damage by Marilyn, several violent incidents made their way into the American press in 1996, as if to provide potential visitors one more reason to choose another island for their hard-earned vacation. While the resorts are back open, the hills are verdant again, and the beaches have crept back to their former size, the crime is unsettling. Realistically, however, one need only take the kind of precautions here that one would use visiting any American city—keep belongings close at hand, avoid flashing jewelry in public, and be cautious about where you walk after dark. Long-time residents are understandably troubled by the increasing development and congestion, but at the same time cherish the easy (by Caribbean standards) access to life's finer things, be it a good cup of coffee and bagel with cream cheese, or the high fashions trundled out by Charlotte Amalie clothiers. And, in the end, this is probably what many of St. Thomas' visitors are looking for: an urbane and accessible sojourn, albeit one ringed by glistening white sand and swaying palms.

St. Thomas is about 40 miles north of St. Croix and just two miles west of St. John, the sister islands that make up the bulk of the 68 or so U.S. Virgin Islands. The island lies about 75 miles east of Puerto Rico. With an official population of 48,166 residents for its 32 square miles, St. Thomas vies with Saint Martin/Sint Maarten as the most populous island in the Caribbean per square mile, and homes crawl along ridges and down valleys in every direction—only the western tip of the island remains relatively undeveloped. Sometimes referred to as "Rock City" for the way it is draped onto steep slopes, Charlotte Amalie is the hub of most non-beach activities. Although a

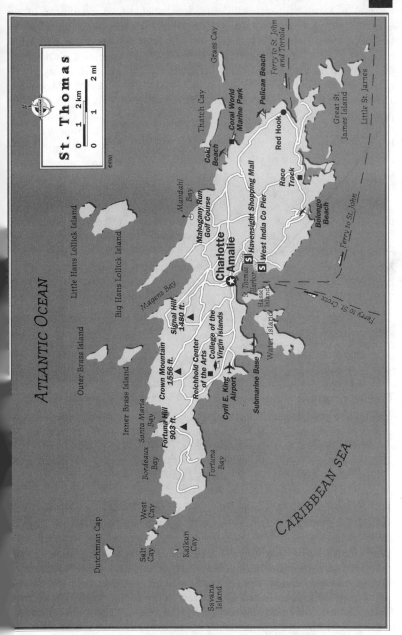

St. Thomas

N

0   1   2 km
0   1   2 mi

ewi

ATLANTIC OCEAN

Dutchman Cap

Savana Island

Salt Cay
West Cay

Kalkun Cay

Outer Brass Island

Inner Brass Island

Little Hans Lollick Island

Big Hans Lollick Island

Grass Cay

Thatch Cay

Ferry to St. John and Tortola

Great St. James Island

Little St. James

Fortuna Hill 903 ft.

Fortuna Bay

Bordeaux Santa Maria Bay

Crown Mountain 1556 ft.

Reichhold Center for the Arts

College of the Virgin Islands

Cyril E. King Airport

Submarine Base

Water Island

Hassel Island

St. Thomas Harbor

Signal Hill 1480 ft.

Magens Bay

Mandahl Bay

Mahogany Run Golf Course

Charlotte Amalie

Havensight Shopping Mall

West India Co Pier

Race Track

Coki Beach

Coral World Marine Park

Pelican Beach

Red Hook

Bolongo Beach

Ferry to St. John

Ferry to St. Croix

CARIBBEAN SEA

few inns are nestled into the hills immediately behind the town, most of the island's 2000-plus rooms lie along the coastline, where a succession of pretty beaches invite sunning and relaxing. Viewed from a distance, Magens Bay is a world treasure, though by late morning the sand is covered with day-trippers fresh off the cruise ships, each one in search of the pristine beauty promised in glossy brochures. The island rolls to its apex at Crown Mountain, 1556 feet high, and a slender spine of ridges taper off east and west of this point. St. Thomas is easy to navigate by auto, but also time-consuming—there is a daily traffic jam that clogs downtown Charlotte Amalie at rush hour, particularly late afternoon when a contingent of cruise ships are loading package-laden passengers for the trip to the next port.

The tram to Paradise Point offers a bird's eye view of the St. Thomas harbor.

History

As with St. Croix and St. John, Columbus discovered these islands on his third voyage in 1493. A plan for colonizing St. Thomas was signed by Frederick III of Denmark, but the first settlement failed. Charlotte Amalie, St. Thomas's first permanent European settlement, dates back to 1671. Set on a grand circular harbor, the town was laid out by planners in Denmark who had never seen the mountainous 32-square mile island. Danish control of the Virgin Islands ended when the U.S. bought St. Croix, St. Thomas and St. John for $25 million in order to protect its interests in the Panama Canal. Today, the self-governing unincorporated territory has a nonvoting delegate to the U.S. House of Representatives.

People

For many years, the U.S. Virgin Islands have been sold to vacationers as an American paradise, and St. Thomas is where the flag flies most brightly. The population, though predominantly black African, is diverse and includes a long-standing Hebrew community of about a hundred families. One noteworthy St. Thomian was Impressionist Camille Pissarro, who was not French but a Dutch West Indian, and who spent his formative years drawing and painting here. St. Thomas's lengthy history as part of Denmark is seen today primarily in the form of architecture and street names. Many islanders can be curt to the point of rudeness, particularly taxi drivers (who, some locals pointedly note, "run the island" with their considerable clout). The icy veneer melts somewhat in Charlotte Amalie's shops when you roll out your wallet for purchases. The surliness can be excused to some degree by the fact that this island is invaded literally by thousands of cruise ship passengers every day—although given that tourism is virtually the only business on St. Thomas, it might be prudent to receive outsiders with a little more warmth. St. Thomas also has a colorful Carnival celebration in April which is quite festive with parades, costumed Mocko Jumbies on stilts, and steel bands.

Beaches

One of St. Thomas's biggest appeals remains its collection of shimmering beaches, lead by spectacular **Magens Bay**, on the north coast of the island (opposite Charlotte Amalie). Magens is one of the few island beaches that doesn't have a chain of hotels along its perimeter, and a self-guiding nature trail adds to the attraction. Despite an admission price and parking fee ($1 per person and $1 per car), it is also the most crowded, with a steady stream of cruise-ship passengers landing on its sand throughout the day. Magens is perhaps best appreciated from the dazzling viewpoint at Mountain Top, where a bar and shopping mall are a diversion for island tours.

But there are plenty of other beaches to choose from. Among the best are **Coki Beach**, where snorkeling is excellent and a *pate* stand provides local snacks; **Limetree Beach**, just east of the Morningstar Resort and popular not just for swimming but iguana sightings; **Brewer's Bay**, near the university and airport runway, and **Hull Bay**, just east of Magens Bay, where calm waters greet bathers and provide anchorage for local fishermen, but winter brings swells off a long reef ideal for surfing. Of the beaches with major hotels along their length, the choice spots are **St. John's Bay** (also known as Sapphire Beach, after the resort), **Morningstar Beach**, and **Lindbergh Beach**. Although the latter suffers from the noise of jets, particularly midday, Lindbergh is the local pick. A couple off-the-beaten-track beauties where swimming conditions are less reliable are **Stumpy Bay Beach** on the island's western end, and **Bluebeard's Beach**, on the eastern tip just past the Ritz-Carlton.

St. Thomas probably does more dive business than any other destination in the Eastern Caribbean, resulting in a profusion of operators. Most of the diving is easily accessible and not difficult, and certification and resort courses are very popular. Make sure the dive shop you select is not one of the cattle-drive operators geared toward massive groups of cruise-ship passengers. Locals will reluctantly point out that St. Thomas (like St. John) doesn't offer a lot of big fish and there are no real walls, but decent reef dives are available off the cays clustered around the island, particularly on its eastern half (see "Underwater" in "St. John" for some of the shared destinations in the Pillsbury Sound). Shore diving is nice from Coki Bay. Several good wrecks ornament the St. Thomas depths, and local dive shops offer weekly excursions to the wreck of the *RMS Rhone* in the British Virgins; prices vary, but be sure to bring your passport or birth certificate if you want to make the trip. Visibility normally averages 80 to 100 feet. A recompression chamber is available at the St. Thomas Naval Hospital.

Dive Shops

Chris Sawyer Dive

Redhook; ☎ *(800) 882-2965 or (340) 775-7320.*
NAUI and PADI affiliated (a Five Star facility), with four separate shops spread around the island. Groups limited to 12 divers, perfect safety record over 15-year operation. Two-tank dive, $70. Handicapped instruction. Weekly trips on Friday.

Coki Beach Dive Club

Coki Beach; ☎ *(800) 474-2654 or (340) 775-4220.*
Resort courses and easy access to shore dives off Coki (one tanks, $20). PADI and SSI affiliated with courses through Divemaster.

Dive In

Sapphire Beach Resort and Marina; ☎ *(800) 524-2090 or (340) 775-6100.*
PADI and NAUI operation with certification courses through Divemaster and resort courses. Two-tank dives $70; night dives $55, including all equipment.

St. Thomas Diving Club
Bolongo Bay; ☎ *(800) 538-7348 or (340) 776-2381.*
A PADI Five Star facility with training through Instructor. Popular with locals, offers private charters. Two-tank dive, $80, night dives $65.

Bustling St. Thomas is undeniably beautiful, but it's also heavily developed and densely populated. Its relatively compact, 14-by-three-mile size, coupled with a population approaching 50,000, means that truly virgin territory is long gone. Paved roads lead to the island's highest point, Crown Mountain (1556 feet), and snake to the crests of other scenic vistas. So, where does a walker go? In addition to the paths listed below, your best opportunity for escape lie on the two islands just south of Charlotte Amalie. **Hassel Island** (recently adopted as part of the National Park) features nice beaches and a long-abandoned ruin, **Fort Cowell**, but is currently reachable only by private boat. Nearby **Water Island**, the fourth largest of the U.S. Virgins, was an Army base during World War II and later, its (now-closed) hotel may have served as inspiration for Herman Wouk's *Don't Stop the Carnival.* The island has a small population and a manufactured, quarter-mile strip of sand; impromptu ferry service is provided to Water Island by its residents. A St. Thomas walking itinerary also should include a tour of charming **Charlotte Amalie**, which buzzes with activity when cruise ships are docked, and even when they aren't. For better appreciation of the capital's history, pick up a **Historic District Guide** from the tourist office.

Of course, serious hikers need only step onto the ferry in Charlotte Amalie or Red Hook to visit **St. John**, where the national park provides 22 hiking possibilities (see "On Foot" in "St. John" for more information).

Scenic and busy **Charlotte Amalie** is worth a half day of exploration and shopping. Schedule it for a rainy day if the clouds are so inclined. The **Government House** is a bit of a bore, while the Virgin Islands Museum, housed in **Fort Christian**, might harbor a few ghosts—it was the center of social and political activity on the island for several hundred years. It's a striking Danish building of red brick and the oldest structure still in use on the island. Also

ST. THOMAS

ST. THOMAS HIGHLIGHTS

Popular with the cruise-ship set, St. Thomas is the most developed of the U.S. Virgin Islands. Shopping and resort activities can consume an entire vacation and leave your wallet considerably lighter. Although crowds sometimes make the island seem more like an urban jungle, its many historic buildings and mountaintop views are legendary.

Magens Bay

You won't be alone here, but never mind—the soft, sandy beach at Magens Bay is considered a St. Thomas "must." Located on the north coast, this superb beach has picture-postcard views.

Mountain Top

Take a taxi ride to this lookout on the top of St. Peter, and enjoy a banana daiquiri in the bar that claims to have invented the concoction.

Magens Bay

Charlotte Amalie

Charlotte Amalie

Capital of the U.S. Virgin islands and a shopper's paradise, this pretty, colonial town was once a notorious gathering place for Caribbean pirates. Today, the Danish-style town is generally overrun with tourists.

Blackbeard's Castle

Rumored to be the stronghold of the notorious pirate Edward Teach, this interesting structure has been converted into a privately owned inn. Enjoy a tasty lunch and a swim (you don't have to be a registered guest during the daytime). Come in the evening for live jazz.

Shopping St. Thomas

Charlotte Amalie offers shopping on Waterfront, Main Street and Back Street, as well as the Vendors Plaza near Emancipation Gardens and Havensight Mall close to the cruise-ship dock.

Drake's Seat

Best viewed at dusk, when it is the prettiest and the crowds have thinned, this mountain lookout is the legendary place where Sir Francis Drake once kept watch over his fleet. You can see the British Virgin Islands, Drake's Passage, and other St. Thomas landmarks such as Mountain Top and Hull Bay.

Coral World Marine Park

This small complex near Coki Beach is a great way to introduce kids to the wonders of coral reefs. The 80,000-gallon reef tank is the main attraction, but also visit the predator tanks, the "touch" tank and the walk-in observatory.

Red Hook

This town on the eastern end of the island is the jumping-off place for ferry service to St. John and the Virgin Islands National Park. The docks are great for strolling, and if you want to shop, you'll find merchants in the waterfront arcade.

St. John

ackbeard's Castle

Atlantis Submarines

Tour the underwater world of St. Thomas in a 1.5-mile tour of the Buck Island Reef in the hugely popular Atlantis submarine. Book ahead for a tour that departs from Havensight Mall.

Fort Christian

The island's oldest standing structure, this imposing brick-red fort dates back to the 17th century, when Danish colonists began constructing a redoubt to guard the harbor. The Fort has been used as a jail, a courthouse, a police station, and a church. Now it houses the Virgin Island Museum.

ST. THOMAS

worth visiting are some of the historic churches, particularly the **St. Thomas Synagogue**, which celebrated its bicentennial in 1996. The steep **99 Steps** that rise to the top of Government Hill were the product of over-zealous 18th-century Danish engineers who wanted the city laid out in a grid (and actually, there are 103 steps). Near the top of the steps is **Blackbeard's Castle**, a recently designated National Historic Landmark, and reputedly once the haunt of pirate Edward Teach—it's now a hotel and restaurant. Just outside Charlotte Amalie, above the cruise ship dock, is **Paradise Point**, a terrific scenic overlook reached by aerial tram or via a winding road that begins just past the tram station. The view of the town and harbor at sunset is unbeatable.

Another day can be devoted to exploring the rest of the island. **Tillett Gardens** in the Tutu area is the site of funky and delightful arts and crafts studios, a "peaceful sanctuary of creativity and wonderment," in the words of English silkscreen artist Jim Tillett—classical and other concerts are often hosted here. **Mountain Top** is commercialized, but no one can deny the spectacular view down to Magens Bay (it's the spot where banana daiquiris were invented), while nearby **Drake's Seat** is, according to legend, the spot where Sir Francis Drake observed ships passing through the dozens of British Virgins and (what is now called) Drake's Passage. The **Estate St. Peter Greathouse and Botanical Gardens** sprawls over 11 lush acres on the northern slopes of the island, with an observation deck providing views of nearby islands. The meticulously landscaped gardens offer self-guided nature trails through such exotic flora as the umbrella plant from Madagascar, the cane orchid of China, and bird of paradise from South Africa. The University of the Virgin Islands (just north of the airport) is home to the **Reichhold Center for the Arts**, a 1200-seat amphitheater in a spectacular setting on Brewer's Bay that is host to a wide variety of performances, from classical to jazz, ballet to South African dance troupes, and more. Event and ticket information can be obtained through your hotel concierge or ☎ *(340) 693-1559.*

Wednesday is typically the biggest day for **cruise ship dockings** on St. Thomas. It's a bad time for shopping, exploration of Charlotte Amalie, or visiting Magens Bay, when you'll have to compete for elbow room. Bury yourself in a book next to your hotel's pool, or to head over to the **British Virgin Islands** for a daytrip away from the masses (see "Getting Around")—a cruise ship also lands on **St. John** on Wednesdays. By contrast, few if any cruise ships dock on Fridays—a good day for exploring the island's tourist attractions. A few important sights were shuttered following Hurricane Luis: **Coral World**, an underwater observatory at Coki Point, was heavily damaged and awaiting repairs as we went to press, while the **Arboretum** at Magens Bay was turned upside down by Luis just after a 1995 refurbishing.

Historical Sites

Fort Christian   ★★★★

At the harbor, ☎ *(340) 776-4566.*
Hours open: 8:30 a.m.–4:30 p.m.

This striking brick fortress is the oldest building still in daily use in the Virgin
Islands, and a U.S. national landmark dating back to 1672. It has housed everything
from the entire St. Thomas colony to a jail to a church over the years, and is now
home to an art gallery, book store and, in former dungeons, the Virgin Islands
Museum, which traces island history. The museum recently completed a $900,000
renovation. It also boasts (per the governor's wife) the cleanest bathroom in town.

Historic Churches   ★★★

Various locations.

Charlotte Amalie is home to several historic churches well worth a look. The Frederick Lutheran Church (Norre Gade) is the Western Hemisphere's second-oldest
Lutheran church. All Saints Anglican Church on Garden Street was built in 1848 to
celebrate the end of slavery. The Dutch Reformed Church on Nye Gade was built
in 1844, but actually dates back to 1744 (the original was destroyed by a fire in
1804). Finally, the Cathedral of St. Peter and St. Paul in Kronprindsens Alley was
built in 1848 and is enhanced by murals done in 1899 by Belgian artists.

St. Thomas Synagogue   ★★★★

Synagogue Hill, ☎ *(340) 774-4312.*
Hours open: 9 a.m.–4 p.m.

Founded in 1796, this is the oldest synagogue in continuous use under the American flag, and the second-oldest in the Western Hemisphere. The current structure
was built in 1833 by Sephardic Jews, and functions today for some 120 Jewish families on the island. Many of the relics are unique—including an 850-year-old meno-
rah and torah scrolls from Sint Eustatius. The floor is sand, symbolic of the desert
through which Moses and the Israelis wandered for 40 years. A well-received bicentennial celebration, commemorating 200 years of Jewish life on St. Thomas, took
place in 1996. The full name, incidentally, is *Synagogue of Berecha V'Shalom
V'Gemilath Chasidim,* or "Blessings and Peace and Acts of Piety."

Museums and Exhibits

Seven Arches Museum   ★★★

Government Hill, ☎ *(340) 774-9259.*
Hours open: 10 a.m.–3 p.m.

This Danish house was built in 1800 and is now a private home, but they'll let you
in to see its historic furnishings and antiques. The grounds include a separate
kitchen and a walled garden, the perfect spot to quaff the drink included in the
admission fee. General admission: $8.

Parks and Gardens

Estate St. Peter Greathouse Gardens   ★★★★

Route 40 and Barrett Hill Road, Above Hull Bay, ☎ *(340) 774-4999.*
Hours open: 9 a.m.–4 p.m.

As you stroll the grounds of these new gardens, it's hard to believe this verdant spot was completely leveled by Hurricane Hugo in 1989, and again by Marilyn in 1995. Owners Sylvie and Howard DeWolfe did an amazing job restoring everything to its former glory. The gardens are perched 1000 feet above Hull Bay and Magens Bay Beach on the island's north side. Self-guided trails lead through more than 200 varieties of Caribbean plants and trees, as well as imported treasures like the tropical day lily from Asia and South African bird of paradise. There's also ponds, waterfalls and a rainforest—not to mention sweeping views from the observation deck, a thousand feet above sea level, where you can spot more than 20 other Virgin Islands. The recreated great house is filled with contemporary Caribbean furnishings and locally done artwork. General admission: $8.

Tours

Atlantis Submarine   ★ ★ ★

Havensight Mall, Charlotte Amalie, ☎ *(340) 776-5650.*

A treat for all but the claustrophobic, this modern voyage seats 46 people in air-conditioned comfort on a 65-foot sub built specifically as a tourist attraction. The 50-minute ride provides non-divers a taste of the underwater sights 90 feet down off Little Buck Island (a different one than the Buck Island near St. Croix). Regular stars of the show include a green moray eel, blue chromis and yellow-tail snapper scooting through the sea whips, brain and pillar coral. The trip is a pricy $72 for adults, $36 for teens and $27 for children (kids under 3 feet tall are not permitted).

Coral World   ★ ★ ★

Coki Point.

Hours open: 9 a.m.–6 p.m.

Non-swimmers can see what all the fuss is about at this five-acre marine park, home to 21 aquariums, a touch tank, an 80,000-gallon tank showcasing the world's largest living man-made reef. The highlight is the underwater observatory, an air-conditioned room 20 feet below sea level through which you can observe all sorts of sea life, an especially exciting sight at feeding time. The grounds also include duty-free shops, a bar and restaurant, and a pretty beach where they rent snorkel and scuba equipment (showers and changing rooms are available). Heavily damaged by Hurricane Marilyn, Coral World is scheduled to re-open in 1998.

Guided Tours

St. Thomas is easily explored on your own, but if you'd like to spare the expense of renting a car, take a guided tour. **Destination Virgin Islands** ☎ *(340) 776-2424* offers walking tours, beach and shopping trips, and excursions to St. John and St. Croix; prices vary. The **St. Thomas Islands Tour** ☎ *(340) 774-7668* explores the island in two hours for $14 per person; another excursion takes in the many splendid views and costs $20. **Tropic Tours** ☎ *(340) 774-1855* offers various shopping and scenic tours; call for prices. Also try **Smitty Island Tour** ☎ *(340) 775-2787*, a 3.5-hour tour in air-conditioned vans which goes to Drake's Seat, Mountain Top and Magen's Bay ($35); and **Timmy Island Tour** ☎ *(340) 775-9529*, whose 2.5-hour tour includes Red Hook, Sapphire Beach overlook, Magen's Bay, Mountain Top, and Charlotte Amalie ($25).

Paradise Point Tramway ★★★

Havensight, ☎ (340) 774-9809.
Hours open: 8:30 a.m.–6:30 p.m.

This tramway offers a 3.5-minute ride up to 697-foot high Paradise Point where a splendid view of Charlotte Amalie and the cruise ship harbor awaits. You can wander among the shops, have a quiet drink or just soak in the scenery. When going up, try to snag the last car; coming down, hop in the first car for unobstructed views. $5 for kids under 13; kids under 6 are free. Note that a rugged road snakes up the slope for those who want the view without buying the ride. General admission: $10.

Seaborne Seaplane Adventure ★★★★

Charlotte Amalie Harbor, ☎ (340) 777-4491.

Amazing views abound on this 45-minute flight aboard the twin-engine seaplane Vistaliner. Bring lots of film, because you'll be snapping away like mad as you fly over some 100 islands of the U.S. and British Virgin Islands. The entire tour takes 1.5 hours (it's exciting to take off and land from the ocean) and is greatly enhanced by extra-large windows, lively narration via headphones (which can also be plugged right into your video camera) and an interesting booklet that gives details on the islands spotted. Great fun! General admission: $79.

Virgin Islands Ecotours ★★★★★

#2 Estate Nadir, ☎ (340) 779-2155.

A new addition to St. Thomas is this kayaking outfit providing 2.5-hour tours through the St. Thomas Marine Sanctuary and mangrove lagoon, where the juvenile reef fish grow up. The two-person ocean kayaks are stable and easy to paddle, and snorkel and safety gear is also provided. A bit expensive, but an excellent and enjoyable introduction to Caribbean marine ecology. Two tours daily: 9:30 a.m. and 1 p.m. Price is $50 per person.

All manner of watersports activities are enjoyed on St. Thomas. **Sportfishing** is devoted primarily to the blue marlin—from March to June, marlin are found to the south in the Caribbean, while the fish navigate the waters of the Atlantic to the north of the island July through September. Other fish common to the area include kingfish, wahoo, dolphin, white marlin and Allison tuna, and some 21 world records have been set here in recent years. On this side of the Virgins is a 100-fathom drop-off bordering the Puerto Rico Trench, the deepest hole in the Atlantic. Because the Virgin Islands lie in the Trade Winds Belt, fishing can always be done on the leeward side. Red Hook is the main center of operations for boat charters. Many operators offer half- and full-day boat excursions on a variety of craft; full-day fishing expeditions usually come equipped with equipment, picnic, beer and ice.

Surfing attracts a few fans during the winter when the waves roll in at Hull Bay, just west of Magens Bay. **Windsurfing** is best on the eastern end of the island—winds peak around noon, with Morningstar Beach offering some of the gentlest conditions. **Kayaking** is possible along the scenic coast, and can be arranged at some of the bigger resorts including Sapphire Beach. **Snorkeling** and **diving** equipment is sold by Mask and Fin (across from Fort Christian in Charlotte Amalie), and can provide good information about the best snorkeling locations.

Horse racing is a party event on St. Thomas, involving thoroughbred horses, panmutuel and daily double betting. Events are held approximately monthly, usually on a local holiday or Sunday. English-style **riding lessons** are offered at Rosenthal Riding Ring, which also provides trail rides. **Tennis** is available at a number of resorts, and two public courts are found at the Sub Base. St. Thomas also has a spectacular 18-hole championship **golf** course, Mahogany Run, designed by George and Tom Fazio. There's also a free, nine-hole course at the University of the Virgin Islands.

Golf

St. Thomas's **Mahogany Run** is an especially scenic and challenging one, a par-70 known designed by George and Tom Fazio and known for its dramatic 13th and 14th holes, which hug cliffs overlooking the Atlantic. If you play the Devil's Triangle—holes 13, 14 and 15—without a penalty shot, they'll award you a poster. A 270,000-gallon desalination plant opened in 1997. Greens fees are $85 (check for off-season discounts); the mandatory cart fee is $15. Nine holes can be played before 8 a.m. and after 3 p.m.; a twilight rate kicks in after 2 p.m. Several resorts, including Ritz-Carlton, Renaissance Grand, Wyndham Sugar Bay and Sapphire Beach offer golf packages ☎ *(340) 777-6006* or *(800) 253-7103*.

Watersports

If your hotel doesn't offer the equipment you need, these companies are happy to help out. For boat charters, try: **Regency Yacht Vacations** ☎ *(340) 776-5950* or *(800) 524-7676*, **Island Yachts** ☎ *(340) 775-6666* or *(800) 524-2019*, **Avery's Marine** ☎ *(340) 776-0113*, **Coconut Charters** ☎ *(340) 775-5959*, **Nightwind** ☎ *(340) 775-4110*, and **New Horizons** ☎ *(340) 775-1171*. For scuba and snorkel instruction and excursions, try: **Seahorse Dive** ☎ *(340) 774-2001*, **Adventure Center** ☎ *(340) 774-2990*, **Dean Johnston's Diving** ☎ *(340) 775-7610* and **Hi-Tec Water Sports** ☎ *(340) 774-4650*. Deep-sea fishers can call **Fish Hawk** ☎ *(340) 775-9058* and **St. Thomas Sportfishing Center** ☎ *(340) 775-7990*.

ST. THOMAS

Where to Stay

Fielding's Highest Rated Hotels in St. Thomas

★★★★★	Ritz-Carlton, St. Thomas, The	$200–$525
★★★★	Elysian Beach Resort	$175–$375
★★★★	Renaissance Grand Beach Resort	$225–$445
★★★★	Sapphire Beach Resort and Marina	$225–$440
★★★★	Secret Harbour Beach Resort	$169–$495
★★★	Colony Point Pleasant Resort	$170–$360
★★★	Island Beachcomber	$95–$145
★★★	Magens Point Hotel	$150–$300
★★★	Wyndham Sugar Bay Resort	$180–$580

Fielding's Inns With Character on St. Thomas

★★★	Hotel 1829	$65–$185
★★	L'Hotel Boynes	$85–$175
★★	Galleon House	$49–$119
★★	Blackbeard's Castle	$60–$175
★★★	Island Beachcomber	$95–$145

Fielding's Best Value Hotels in St. Thomas

★★	Best Western Carib Beach Resort	$89–$149
★★	Mafolie Hotel	$65–$135
★★★	Island Beachcomber	$95–$145
★★	Galleon House	$49–$119
★★★	Hotel 1829	$65–$185

Most of the accommodations on St. Thomas are concentrated into two areas. The first surrounds Charlotte Amalie and the island's scenic main harbor, and extends to near the airport on the west and to Bolongo Bay on the east. This hotel group is where you'll find the most variety, from the all-inclusive **Bolongo Beach Club** to the classic island inn **Hotel 1829**; from family-owned guest houses like **Villa Santana** to the 516-room **Marriott** complex at the harbor entrance. The second area lies along the island's eastern tip facing St. John, where a group of large hotels and apartment/condo complexes dot the coastline between Coki Point and Nazareth Bay. The big resorts, like **Sapphire Beach** and the **Renaissance Grand Beach** tend to be expensive, while **Secret Harbour Beach Resort** and other apartment/condo facilities can be easier on the wallet, particularly for families. This portion of the island tends to be quieter than around Charlotte Amalie, but your commute into town will be up to a half-hour each way, despite the relatively short distance.

Hurricane Marilyn did a real number on St. Thomas, and many accommodations suffered extensive damage. In addition to the physical toll, the fallout paved the way for a number of properties to change hands, led by the swank Grand Palazzo, which re-opened under the **Ritz-Carlton** banner in 1996. Fortunately, most hotels underwent a full makeover when the insurance monies came through, which means many of St. Thomas's properties look better than ever. The two-sided Marriott resort, **Frenchman's Reef** and **Morning Star Beach**, was not scheduled to complete its $45 million renovation until late 1997—we'll have a report on the newly polished property (the largest on the island) in the next edition of *Fielding's Caribbean*.

Hotels and Resorts

There is no shortage of hotels and resorts to choose from on St. Thomas, in all styles, shapes, colors and sizes. Start by organizing your priorities. Do you want to be near shopping, or on a secluded beach? Do you want a smaller, more intimate property or would you prefer a full-service resort with an array of on-site activities? Remember that the view or beach access your room offers will almost always affect the price of accommodations. In some cases, you'll save big bucks by opting for a room that is only a minute or two further from the sand. If you want a no-holds-barred luxury escape, look no further than the island's new **Ritz-Carlton**, which is setting new standards for service and pampering.

Best Western Carib Beach Resort   **$89–$149**   ★★

Lindbergh Bay, ☎ (800) 792-2742, (340) 774-2525, FAX (340) 777-4131.
Website: www.st-thomas.com/caribbeach.
Single: $89–$149. Double: $89–$149.
This Best Western hotel is located on a very small, man-made beach (you can tan but there's no ocean access—a better stretch of sand is nearby). Each basic room is air-conditioned and has a private balcony, cable TV, telephones, refrigerator and coffee maker. Facilities include a restaurant and a small pool. Located just a stone's throw from the airport, so expect some noise from jets. Though this place is rather

bare-bones compared to St. Thomas' many glittering resorts, there's something agreeable about it. 69 rooms. Credit cards: A, DC, D, MC, V.

Best Western Emerald Beach Resort   **$129–$239**   ★★★

Lindbergh Bay, ☎ *(800) 233-4936, (340) 777-8800, FAX (340) 776-3426. Website: www.st-thomas.com/emeraldbeach. Single: $129–$239. Double: $129–$239.*

Located near the foot of the airport runway, this smaller hotel has decent guest-rooms that won't win any prizes for originality, but are modern and comfortable nonetheless, with newly added refrigerators and coffee makers. Facilities include a bar and restaurant, pool and tennis court. There's watersports for hire at the nice public beach, just steps away. Note that jet noise from the nearby airport can be intrusive. 90 rooms. Credit cards: A, DC, D, MC, V.

Blackbeard's Castle   **$60–$175**   ★★

Charlotte Amalie, ☎ *(800) 344-5771, (340) 776-1234, FAX (340) 776-4321. E-mail: Blackbeards.stt@worldnet.att.net. Single: $60–$150. Double: $60–$150. Suites Per Day: $125–$175.*

This inn is built around a National Historic Landmark, a stone tower once reportedly used by pirates and now boasting a gay following today. Standard guest rooms are quite small, with simple furnishings, air conditioners—some have tiny balconies. There are also apartment-style suites with more amenities and appealing decor. The grounds include two pools and a well regarded restaurant; wonderful views abound and downtown Charlotte Amalie is within walking distance. After extensive hurricane damage, the hotel re-opened in 1997. 22 rooms. Credit cards: A, D, MC, V.

Bluebeard's Castle Hotel   **$140–$395**   ★★★

Charlotte Amalie, ☎ *(800) 524-6599, (340) 774-1600, FAX (340) 774-5134. Single: $140–$235. Double: $140–$235. Suites Per Day: $255–$395.*

Set high up on a hill with splendid views of the harbor and beyond, this venerable hotel is built around a 17th-century tower. Lodgings are found in villas and range from studios to one-bedroom suites, all air-conditioned, blandly decorated, and boasting balconies or terraces. There's nightly entertainment in the lounge, three restaurants, a large pool, two tennis courts, and a fitness center. The location is nice—it's a 15-minute walk down to Charlotte Amalie, or they'll shuttle you over to the beach for free. Group businesses and local weddings dominate here, so individual travelers can feel lost in the shuffle; a haphazard staff doesn't help. 184 rooms. Credit cards: A, DC, D, MC, V.

Bolongo Beach Club and Villas   **$135–$225**   ★★★

Bolongo Bay, ☎ *(800) 524-4746, (340) 775-1800, FAX (340) 775-3208. Single: $135–$215. Double: $145–$225.*

This busy, family-owned property offers full resort amenities and a lovely palm-studded beach. Guestrooms have white tile floors, two double or king beds, shower-only baths and a small refrigerator. The west wing is quietest, while those in the center have the nicest views, but all are quite close to the beach. Definitely request a second-floor unit for more privacy, but ground-level rooms open onto the beach. The grounds include lighted tennis and volleyball courts, a new health club, a pretty pool complete with swim-up bar, two restaurants, and all the watersports one could want, including daily boat trips and a dive shop. Guests may choose from an all-inclusive or semi-inclusive plan—the latter (prices above) includes continental breakfast, a variety of non-motorized watersports and introductory scuba diving. 116 rooms. Credit cards: A, DC, D, MC, V.

Colony Point Pleasant Resort $170–$360   ★ ★ ★

Coki Point, ☎ *(800) 524-2300, (340) 775-7200, FAX (340) 776-5694.*
Single: $170–$360. Double: $170–$360.

This 15-acre all-suite property lies on a steep hillside overlooking Smith Bay, Coki Point and the British Virgins—and although it's between two of the island's biggest hotels (Sugar Bay and the Renaissance) it's surprisingly peaceful here. Guests are put up in junior suites or spacious one- and two-bedroom units, all with full kitchens and living and dining areas; views from most rooms are superb. If you choose not to do your own cooking, two restaurants will do the job. Facilities include three oleander-covered pools, a tennis court and complimentary non-motorized watersports on the nearby beach; a series of short nature trails wind around the property. Guests also get free use of a car for four hours each day (a $12.50-per-day insurance/gas fee is mandatory). 134 rooms. Credit cards: A, DC, D, MC, V.

Island Beachcomber $95–$145   ★ ★ ★

Lingbergh Bay, ☎ *(800) 982-9898, (340) 774-5250, FAX (340) 774-5615.*
Single: $95–$140. Double: $100–$145.

Set right on a fine beach, this hotel has a faithful clientele—they say some 80 percent of the guests are repeaters who don't mind the occasional jet noise from the nearby airport. Guests are put up in comfortable, air-conditioned rooms facing the lush garden or beach; all have cable TV, phones, refrigerators, and patios or porches. The restaurant is open-air and reasonably priced, and there's also a beach bar. No pool, but the sea is calm and good for swimming. Snorkeling equipment and water rafts are complimentary (other watersports cost extra), and they'll shuttle you into town for free. A pleasantly informal spot with the kind of friendly staff we'd like to see at more Caribbean resorts. 48 rooms. Credit cards: A, DC, D, MC, V.

Renaissance Grand Beach Resort $225–$925   ★ ★ ★ ★

Coki Point, ☎ *(800) 468-3571, (340) 775-1510, FAX (340) 775-3757.*
Single: $225–$445. Double: $225–$445. Suites Per Day: $450–$925.

One of St. Thomas' mega-resorts catering to both leisure travelers and meeting trade, the Renaissance doesn't offer a lot of true island flavor, but no one seems to mind—the grounds are lush with flowers, and iguanas lope about. Guestrooms, redone in 1996, are quite plush with marble floors and attractive furnishings; rates are based on proximity to water. A few hundred dollars more buys a two-story townhouse suite or a one-bedroom unit with an indoor whirlpool. Recreational options include six tennis courts, two pools, an excellent health club, and lots of watersports. There's also two restaurants and bars, and organized programs for the kids. Like many of St. Thomas's beaches, the one here is rather narrow but that doesn't crimp the selection of watersports. If you want a big resort setting, you'll find just about all you could want, but be warned that conventions and incentive groups make up almost half the clientele; a major function can take out the pool area or beach for an afternoon and/or evening. 290 rooms. Credit cards: A, DC, D, MC, V.

Ritz-Carlton, St. Thomas, The $200–$925 ★★★★★

Great Bay, ☎ (800) 241-3333, (340) 775-3333, FAX (340) 775-4444.
Single: $200–$525. Double: $200–$525. Suites Per Day: $475–$925.

Luxury mavens should be happily impressed with this swank, bougainvillea-draped production located at St. Thomas's eastern tip. Teeming with Italian Renaissance accents and formerly known as the Grand Palazzo, the 15-acre property was acquired by the Ritz-Carlton Hotel chain in 1996. A fresh coat of peach warms the formerly all-white color scheme, while the resort's spouting lion fountains, acres of pink Italian marble, and swooping free-form pool are gleaming once again. The lobby area is quite elegant, though its austere formality may be a turn-off for some—this is not a place for paddling about in a wet swimsuit. Accommodations are in plush junior suites with marble baths, tasteful wicker and *faux* antique furnishings. Wonderful views of St. John and the BVIs from most balconies, but note that all rooms are identical and prices are dictated by how high your floor is (and $125 extra per night—in season—is quite a pop for the unencumbered view; if you're springing for the top floor, at least make sure you get one of the attractive pergola-topped units). A few one-bedroom suites are also available. Facilities include a good beach, three tennis courts, a full health club with modern exercise equipment, a 56-foot catamaran for ocean cruises, two elegant restaurants, several bars; watersports, including a dive shop, are not part of the rates. The resort surrounds a blip of a "nature preserve" where birds chirp, cluck and coo through the day. The entire site is wheelchair accessible. 152 rooms. Credit cards: A, D, MC, V.

Sapphire Beach Resort and Marina $225–$440 ★★★★

Sapphire Beach, ☎ (800) 524-2090, (340) 775-6100, FAX (340) 775-4024.
Website: www.usvi.net/hotel/sapphire.
Single: $225–$440. Double: $225–$440.

Located on one of St. Thomas' best beaches, this well-liked resort encompasses 35 picturesque acres. It's a bit out of the way, so you'll want to rent a car to get around. The oversized accommodations are attractive, with large balconies, fresh flowers, and fully equipped kitchens; most are right on the beach. The two-story villa units have two baths, two balconies, and two queen-size sofa beds in addition to the bedroom (great for families). Maids tidy up daily, and room service is available. Watersports and supervised children's programs are free. There's also a restaurant, a posh pool with nice views of neighboring islands, three bars, and a 67-slip marina. Kids under 12 stay and eat for free. 171 rooms. Credit cards: A, D, MC, V.

Windward Passage $99–$200 ★★

Charlotte Amalie, ☎ (800) 524-7389, (340) 774-5200, FAX (340) 774-1231.
Single: $99–$145. Double: $109–$170. Suites Per Day: $170–$200.

The rates are fairly reasonable at this busy commercial hotel, located downtown in the heart of the shopping district and overlooking the harbor. Guestrooms are basic but fine, and the 11 more expensive suites offer sitting areas, hair dryers and refrigerators. There is a restaurant, bar and pool, but no other facilities on the property.

ST. THOMAS

Most of the guests are business travelers, as the beach is beyond walking distance. 151 rooms. Credit cards: A, DC, D, MC, V.

Wyndham Sugar Bay Resort $180–$580   ★★★

Coki Point, ☎ *(800) 996-3426, (340) 777-7100, FAX (340) 777 7200.*
Single: $180–$290. Double: $360–$580.

Located just east of Coki Point, this monolithic resort opened in 1992 and has switched hands several times in the ensuing few years—the new management by Wyndham showcases an all-inclusive policy. The large hillside complex consists of nine buildings that wrap around a bluff above a small beach. The property has fairly standard room interiors, but they vaunt spectacular views from their rocky perch—all balconies face out to the ocean. Down below are all the usual resort diversions including a spiffy pool complete with grotto, bar and waterfalls, plus seven tennis courts, a fitness room, two restaurants, four bars, and watersports at the beach (cramped when the resort is full). Rates include unlimited meals and drinks (during bar hours) and a daily activities program. 300 rooms. Credit cards: A, DC, D, MC, V.

Apartments and Condominiums

For some St. Thomas visitors, the villa life is the way to go. One family that went this way is President and Mrs. Clinton, who checked in with Chelsea to the three-bedroom **Sand Dollar** overlooking Magens Bay in 1997. You can rent this one-time St. Thomas White House too, for $3150–$4950 per week ☎ *(340) 777-6090.* But if money's no object, look no further than **Little St. James**, a 72-acre islet off St. Thomas' east end available through McLaughlin Anderson Villas. This four-bedroom villa is impeccably furnished in Haitian and European antiques and comes with a small private beach. Rates at Little St. James, including meals, wine and spirits, start at $3000 *per day,* for two.

Actually, for a family or a pair of couples that might otherwise rent two rooms at a resort, the villa life can be surprisingly affordable, usually providing a private pool and more seclusion for much less than the price of two rooms at the Ritz-Carlton. St. Thomas agencies that handle villas and private homes include **McLaughlin Anderson Villas** ☎ *(800) 537-6246* or *(340) 776-0635,* **Pineapple Village Villas** ☎ *(800) 874-1786* or *(340) 775-5516,* and **Calypso Realty** ☎ *(800) 747-4858* or *(340) 774-1620* (Calypso also specializes in villas for physically challenged visitors).

For those of us who are happier with simpler comforts, apartments and condos are numerous and may fill the bill nicely. U.S.-style supermarkets make self-catering a breeze, but be prepared for high food prices. You can always bring staples from home, soft packages of soup, etc., that will fit easily into the unused corners of a suitcase. The largest condo agency on the island is **Ocean Property Management**, which oversees 60 units in four separate condominium developments: **Secret Harbourview Villas**, **Sapphire Village**, **Sapphire Bay West** (aka Crystal Cove), and the **Anchorage**. Rates for a studio start at $115 per night during the summer season ☎ *(800) 874-7897* or *(340) 775-2600.*

Elysian Beach Resort $175–$375   ★★★★

Cowpet Bay, ☎ *(800) 753-2554, (340) 775-1000, FAX (340) 776-0910.*
Single: $175–$375. Double: $175–$375.

This resort, set on a hill above a peaceful cove, houses guests in a variety of nicely done guestrooms or loft units with full kitchens and one to three bedrooms. Sporting facilities include a large and elaborate pool, a tennis court, an excellent and well-equipped health club and complimentary watersports on the nice beach including sailboats, kayaks and windsurfers. Dining choices range from the elegant Palm Court to the casual Oasis outdoor grill. It's peaceful, and there's less going on here than at some island properties—a plus or minus, depending upon your preference. Rates include continental breakfast. 180 rooms. Credit cards: A, DC, D, MC, V.

Magens Point Hotel $150–$300 ★ ★ ★

Magens Bay Road, ☎ *(800) 524-2031, (340) 777-6000, FAX (340) 777-6055.*
Single: $150–$300. Double: $150–$300.
Set on a hillside next to the Mahogany Run Golf Course and overlooking the beach, this informal operation consists of studio and one- and two-bedroom suites with cooking facilities. There's a convenience store, bar, pool, and two tennis courts on-site, and they'll shuttle you to the beach or golf course (about a half mile away) at no charge. All here is quite casual, and the property underwent a post-hurricane makeover. Good on-site restaurant with a rotating menu of continental and West Indian cuisine. 54 rooms. Credit cards: A, DC, D, MC, V.

Pavilions & Pools $180–$260 ★ ★ ★

Near Red Hook, ☎ *(800) 524-2001, (340) 775-6110, FAX (340) 775-6110.*
Single: $180–$260. Double: $180–$260.
This villa resort is located seven miles from Charlotte Amalie, near Sapphire Beach. Each of the 25 air-conditioned villas has one bedroom, living/dining areas, complete kitchens, and private, decent-sized pools. Maids tidy up daily, and the rates are quite reasonable for self-sufficient types—the beach is a five-minute walk. There's a restaurant and open-air bar that occasionally hosts live entertainment. Guests can play tennis on the courts at the nearby Sapphire Bay Beach Resort for a fee; watersports equipment can be rented there as well. 25 rooms. Credit cards: A, MC, V.

Secret Harbour Beach Resort $169–$495 ★ ★ ★ ★

Nazareth Bay, ☎ *(800) 524-2250, (340) 775-6550, FAX (340) 775-1501.*
E-mail: shb.vi@worldnet.att.net.
Single: $169–$495. Double: $169–$495.
All accommodations are in suites at this secluded (for St. Thomas) resort set on a fine beach. Lodging is in spacious studios and one- and two-bedroom condos with full kitchens, quality tropical furnishings, air conditioning and ceiling fans, and enormous balconies. Facilities include an extensive watersports center, a pool and two tennis courts; the resort's restaurant, Blue Moon Cafe, is well-liked by locals and guests. The narrow, coconut tree-dotted beach is lovely, and the sea here is so calm it sports one of the island's few swim floats. This operation combines the best of self-sufficient and resort living. 60 rooms. Credit cards: A, MC, V.

Villa Santana $85–$195 ★ ★

Charlotte Amalie, ☎ *(340) 776-1311, FAX (340) 776-1311.*
Website: www.st-thomas.com/villasantana. E-mail: santana@islands.vi.
Single: $85–$195. Double: $85–$195.
Located high on Denmark Hill in a residential area of Charlotte Amalie, Villa Santana was built in 1857 by Mexico's exiled General Santa Anna and today is a nicely atmospheric guest house. Stone-walled rooms are tastefully appointed with wooden

shutters, rattan furniture, kitchenettes and ceiling fans (no air conditioning but good ventilation), and are spread over three cozy, two-story buildings with sparkling views. A small pool and lawn keeps things inviting. An adjacent three-bedroom villa is available for weekly rentals. A tad pricey, but perfect for someone who wants easy access to town without the overload of a big hotel. 5 rooms. Credit cards: A.

Inns

The number of inns available on St. Thomas is limited—the focus here has long been on larger and newer hotels. But **Hotel 1829** oozes with character, providing a romantic excursion into an earlier era.

Admiral's Inn $79–$149   ★★

Charlotte Amalie, ☎ *(800) 544-0493, (340) 774-1376, FAX (340) 774-8010.*
Website: www.admirals.com. E-mail: admirals@admirals.com.
Single: $79–$149. Double: $79–$149.
This brightly painted inn is not in one of St. Thomas' better neighborhoods, but on the other hand, the area is home to a number of good restaurants. Guestrooms, located on the hillside, are air-conditioned and have private baths and satellite TV, and new furnishings following 1995's hurricanes. The inn's four acres include a Chart House restaurant and a pool. A continental breakfast is included in the rates. 13 rooms. Credit cards: A, D, MC, V.

Hotel 1829 $65–$235   ★★★

Charlotte Amalie, ☎ *(800) 524-2002, (340) 776-1829, FAX (340) 776-4313.*
Single: $65–$175. Double: $75–$185. Suites Per Day: $170–$235.
This atmospheric inn was built in 1829 by a French sea captain for his bride. It's located in the heart of Charlotte Amalie, with lots of dining and shopping within walking distance. Now a National Historic Site, the hotel accommodates guests in brick-walled rooms enhanced with antiques, air conditioners, minibars and VCRs. The price you pay depends on the size of your room, which varies widely—definitely request one in the original building (the rest were added in the late 1920s and are too dark). The continental restaurant is well-regarded, and there's also a wonderful bar and a tiny pool. Not especially suited to small children or the physically challenged, as there are many steep stairs to negotiate. 15 rooms. Credit cards: A, MC, V.

L'Hotel Boynes $85–$175   ★★

Charlotte Amalie, ☎ *(800) 377-2905, (340) 774-5511, FAX (340) 774-8509.*
E-mail: sboynes@islands.vi.
Single: $85–$175. Double: $85–$175.
This intimate, bed-and-breakfast style inn provides excellent views of the cruise ship harbor from its perch on Blackbeard's Hill. Every room has its own personality and color scheme—the best are the Red Room with its teak parquet floor and private sun terrace, and the Marble Room, from which you can almost leap out of a king-size four-poster mahogany bed into the small pool. All rooms have private bathrooms and air conditioning—high ceilings, antiques and whimsical elements abound (one unique room has its bed positioned in the chimney and a bathtub in the corner). A charming and welcome addition to the St. Thomas hotel scene. Rates include continental breakfast and airport transfers. 8 rooms. Credit cards: A, MC, V.

ST. THOMAS

Low Cost Lodging

Lodging is not inexpensive on St. Thomas overall, but there are a few family-run budget choices available, particularly if you don't mind a bathroom down the hall. One option, the **Bunker Hill Hotel**, has rooms from $59 to $90, though it's a somewhat colorless property in a so-so Charlotte Amalie neighborhood ☎ *(340) 774-8056;* **Ramsey's Guest House** ☎ *(340) 774-6521,* **Miller Manor** ☎ *(340) 774-1535* and **Sea Horse Cottages** ☎ *(340) 775-9231* are other possibilities. Additional options can be provided by the **Virgin Island Tourist Office** ☎ *(800) 372-USVI.*

Danish Chalet Inn $60–$95   ★

Charlotte Amalie, ☎ *(800) 635-1531, (340) 774-5764, FAX (340) 777-4886.*
Single: $60–$95. Double: $60–$95.
This pleasant if simple bed and breakfast is on a hill within walking distance of Charlotte Amalie. Most rooms have air conditioning, but can be a little tight; a few share a bathroom and are priced less. The $1 honor bar in front is welcoming, and the Jacuzzi in back provides a little splash. Homey and unpretentious. 11 rooms. Credit cards: MC, V.

Galleon House $49–$119   ★★

Charlotte Amalie, ☎ *(800) 524-2052, (340) 774-6952, FAX (340) 774-6952.*
Single: $49–$109. Double: $59–$119.
Delightful family-run inn with character and homey touches. Six economy rooms (two with shared bath) are in the main building, a rustic house with a player piano out on the veranda. Newer lodgings are in two apartment-style buildings up on the hillside—air conditioning, ceiling fans, coffee maker and fridge are standard, as is a nice view of Charlotte Amalie. There's a small pool and sundeck and the garden is nicely kept, with iguanas crawling through the kenip tree and orchids that bloom in September. Lots of restaurants and shopping within a short stroll. Rates include a full breakfast from a rotating menu. 14 rooms. Credit cards: A, D, MC, V.

Island View Guest House $45–$100   ★

Charlotte Amalie, ☎ *(800) 524-2023, (340) 774-4270, FAX (340) 774-6167.*
Website: www.st-thomas.com/islandviewguesthouse.
E-mail: islandview@worldnet.att.net.
Single: $45–$90. Double: $50–$95. Suites Per Day: $84–$100.
This informal guest house is five minutes out of Charlotte Amalie and perched high on a hill with great harbor views. Guestrooms are quite simple, but comfortable enough. Most, but not all, have private baths, and those who want air conditioners or a kitchenette will pay an extra fee. There's an honor bar and small pool on the premises, and continental breakfast is complimentary. 15 rooms. Credit cards: A, MC, V.

Mafolie Hotel $65–$135   ★★

Mafolie Hill, ☎ *(800) 225-7035, (340) 774-2790, FAX (340) 774-4091.*
Website: www.st-thomas.com/mafolie/.
Single: $65–$135. Double: $75–$135.
Set high on a hill overlooking Charlotte Amalie, this Mediterranean-style villa hotel is a great deal for those who can handle steep climbs. Guestrooms are simple and basic; all have air conditioners and phones. There's a pool and the views are stunning. A shuttle to Magens Bay is gratis, but town is too far to walk, so a car is still handy. Continental breakfast is included in the rates. 23 rooms. Credit cards: A, MC, V.

Where to Eat

Fielding's Highest Rated Restaurants in St. Thomas

★★★★	Craig and Sally's	$14–$28
★★★★	Herve Restaurant and Wine Bar	$16–$26
★★★★	Ritz-Carlton Dining Room, The	$22–$32
★★★★	Virgilio's	$16–$39
★★★	Agave Terrace	$18–$38
★★★	Chart House	$16–$37
★★★	Epernay Champagne Bar	$13–$22
★★★	Hotel 1829	$29–$29
★★★	L'Escargot	$15–$27
★★★	La Scala	$13–$25

Fielding's Most Romantic Restaurants in St. Thomas

♡♡♡♡	Agave Terrace	$18–$38
♡♡♡♡	Herve Restaurant and Wine Bar	$16–$26
♡♡♡♡	Hotel 1829	$29–$29
♡♡♡	Cafe Wahoo	$17–$24
♡♡♡	L'Escargot	$15–$27

Fielding's Best Value Restaurants in St. Thomas

★★★	Zorba's	$10–$20
★★★★	Craig and Sally's	$14–$28
★★★	Victor's New Hide Out	$11–$20
★★★	Epernay Champagne Bar	$13–$22
★★★	La Scala	$13–$25

Locals dine out almost as frequently as visitors on St. Thomas, which accounts for the extraordinary range of dining options with cuisines hailing from nearly every corner of the world. Splurging on Sunday brunch at the big resorts is a national pastime, but otherwise restaurants are pleasantly informal and frequently open-air—casual dress, even shorts, generally pass muster. Prices can edge to the expensive, but primarily this is because of the high cost of importing food rather than due to some local conspiracy. Visitors on a budget will be able to locate good food at a reasonable price.

Seafood, lobster and conch top the list at many island restaurants, but local specialties include *fungi*, a dumpling made from corn meal, and *maubi*, a foamy beverage made from bark and herbs. *Souse* is a stew made from a pig's head, tail and feet, drenched in lime juice, and traditionally served at special events. Johnny cakes (fried bread), and *pate* (turnovers plump with goat, beef or saltfish) can be found at a few roadside stands, particularly at Magens Bay. But it's always worth keeping an eye out for local food. One renowned spot, **Eunice's Terrace**, occasioned a late evening visit from the Clintons during their 1997 vacation here (they dined on conch fritters and triggerfish, and provided the restaurant a hefty boost in notoriety). Near Eunice's Coki Point location is **Elizabeth's Kitchen**, a little shack where a plate of scrumptious hogfish, sweet potato and salad will set you back only a few dollars. By most accounts, **Victor's New Hideout** serves the best local food and draws repeaters throughout the day and night—that is, those who can locate the spot near the submarine base.

Several noteworthy eateries were lost to Hurricane Marilyn, or through post-storm fallout. The healthy appetite for fine food is such that new restaurants are springing up as St. Thomas tourism resumes its pace. One such contender is **La Scala**, spawned by the team responsible for Chateau de Bordeaux on St. John; another is **Herve**, the creation of the former manager of Hotel 1829. The Blue Marlin changed hands in 1997 and is now **Cafe Wahoo**, while the beloved **Old Stone Farmhouse** was scheduled to re-open as we went to press.

Agave Terrace $$$ ★★★

6400 Estate Smith Bay, ☎ *(340) 775-4142.* Associated hotel: *Point Pleasant Resort.*
Dinner: 6–10 p.m., entrées $18–$38.

It may be a little hard to find, with a hilltop resort location on the northeastern end of the island. But even non-guests should try to make it here for a leisurely dinner on the patio while the light is still good for an unparalleled view of the Caribbean sea in the distance. The cuisine is mostly seafood, with Mediterranean as well as Caribbean accents, and the chef is delighted to create any dish (within reason) that a customer requests. A live steel band performs Tuesday and Thursday. Reservations recommended. Credit cards: A, MC, V.

Cafe Wahoo $$$ ★★

6300 Smith Bay Road; Red Hook, ☎ *(340) 775-6350.*
Lunch: 11:30 a.m.–2:30 p.m., entrées $7–$11.
Dinner: 6–10 p.m., entrées $17–$24. Closed: Wed.
Upscale seafood in a casual atmosphere is the focus at this new Red Hook spot. Salads and sandwiches are served for lunch, with pasta and seafood taking over at night—highlights include a seared tuna with sesame seed crust and wasabi mustard dipping sauce, and flambeed jumbo shrimp served over pasta with a gin-cream sauce. The food is good, but the real reason to come is the pleasant setting overlooking the Red Hook marina; it's also a good spot to camp out if you miss one of the midday ferries. Credit cards: A, MC, V.

Chart House $$$ ★★★

Villa Olga; Frenchtown, ☎ *(340) 774-4262.* Associated hotel: *Admiral's Inn.*
Dinner: 5:30–10 p.m., entrées $16–$37.
Salad bar lovers flock here for a huge spread of many items, including passable caviar. Dinner specialties include sizzling steaks, juicy prime rib, chicken, lobster and pasta (the grilled salmon over orzo is a treat); the salad bar is included. All this bounty is consumed on a terrace overlooking the sea, situated in a 19th century building which was once home to Russian diplomats. Don't overlook the famous "mud pie" if you still have room. Credit cards: A, DC, MC, V.

Craig and Sally's $$$ ★★★★

22 Estate Honduras; Frenchtown, ☎ *(340) 777-9949.*
Lunch: 11:30 a.m.–3 p.m., entrées $9–$13.
Dinner: 5:30–10 p.m., entrées $14–$28. Closed: Mon., Tue.
A talented husband and wife team combine his knowledge of fine wines and her culinary expertise in the operation of this muraled restaurant in Frenchtown, creating "passionate cuisine." Although there are several dining areas, it's often crowded; the word is out on the creative Mediterranean, Asian and other specialties prepared here. The menu changes daily, but sun-kissed tomatoes, broiled peppers or salsas made with market picked fruits are used liberally on plump scallops, chicken or swordfish. Sally's desserts recall a childhood learning to bake at mother's elbow—there's key lime pie and killer chocolate cakes. The wine list has received an award of excellence citation from *Wine Spectator* for three years running. Lunch is served Wednesday–Friday only. Reservations recommended. Credit cards: A, MC, V.

Cuzzin's $ ★★

Back Street; Charlotte Amalie, ☎ *(340) 777-4711.*
Lunch: 11 a.m.–4 p.m., entrées $6–$16.
Dinner: 5–9:30 p.m., entrées $10–$18. Closed: Sun.
Authentic island cuisine awaits in this local's hangout, a cute yellow brick building with wooden shutters. Specialties include stewed conch, curried chicken and other local dishes and drinks like sea moss (milk, sugar, seaweed and nutmeg). Each entree comes with a choice of three side dishes such as potato stuffing, rice and beans, yams and macaroni and cheese. The daring will like the homemade hot sauce that accompanies some meals. Credit cards: A, D, MC, V.

Epernay Champagne Bar   **$$**   ★★★

24 B Honduras Street; Frenchtown, ☎ *(340) 774-5343.*
Dinner: 4:30 p.m.–1 a.m., entrées $13–$22. Closed: Sun.
Before or after a night on the prowl, nestle here for champagne by the glass; sample
up to six different varieties. A grazing menu of sophisticated snacks covers the
globe. There's sushi, caviar and goat cheese. A small selection of entrées are also
available. Food is served from 5 p.m. to 12 a.m.; it's open later on weekends. Wine
and desserts are also available. Credit cards: A, MC, V.

Eunice's Terrace   **$$**   ★★

66-67 Smith Bay, Route 38, ☎ *(340) 775-3975.*
Lunch: 11 a.m.–5 p.m., entrées $6–$11.
Dinner: 6–10 p.m., entrées $10–$28.
Don't let the junk yard out back put you off. An island success story, Eunice's estab-
lishment grew quickly from a simple food stand to a two-story building with a pop-
ular bar on Smith Bay (just west of the Renaissance). The West Indian cuisine that
built her reputation is among the best on the island. There's a daily menu, but lip-
smacking conch fritters, broiled fish, fungi, and peas and rice are usually available.
Don't miss Eunice's incomparable tropical rum cake (available in a gift box for $4).
Closed for lunch on Sunday. Credit cards: A, MC, V.

Gladys' Cafe   **$**   ★★

17 Main Street; Charlotte Amalie, ☎ *(340) 774-6604.*
Lunch: 10:30 a.m.–4 p.m., entrées $6–$13.
This spot, set in an alleyway in Charlotte Amalie, is where locals congregate for
breakfast (served from 7 a.m.) and Caribbean-style lunches. Besides the standard
burgers and sandwiches, the menu offers up conch in lemon butter sauce, sauteed
shrimp and other West Indian favorites. On Fridays, Gladys serves dinner with live
jazz music until 1 a.m.; entrées $16-18. The brick walls, covered in murals, feature
pigs flying; and a blackboard with Gladys' thought of the day, such as "the effect of
hope is astounding." Credit cards: A, MC, V.

Hard Rock Cafe   **$**   ★

International Plaza, Charlotte Amalie, ☎ *(340) 777-5555.*
Lunch: 10 a.m.–4 p.m., entrées $8–$17.
Dinner: 4 p.m.–midnight, entrées $8–$17.
This memorabilia-laden, retro-rock burger palace draws a cruise ship crowd
throughout the day. As with all Hard Rocks, Bob Marley mementoes intermingle
with the gold Beatles records behind glass frames—the music can be loud, but the
burgers, barbecue ribs, nachos and fajitas are reliable. No dinner served Sundays.
Credit cards: A, MC, V.

Herve Restaurant and Wine Bar   **$$$**   ★★★★

Government Hill; Charlotte Amalie, ☎ *(340) 777-9703.*
Lunch: 11:30 a.m.–2:30 p.m., entrées $6–$18.
Dinner: 6–10 p.m., entrées $16–$26. Closed: Sun.
Pronounced "air-VAY," this new eatery is located in the historic district, next door
to Hotel 1829, with generous views extending into the Charlotte Amalie harbor.
The menu combines classic French and a dash of Caribbean with contemporary

ST. THOMAS

American—specialties include lobster and coquille St. Jacques, pan-seared Norwegian salmon with tomatoes and capers, and a black sesame-crusted tuna in a ginger-raspberry sauce. Lunches are lighter, with salad Nicoise, shrimp crepes, quiche and sandwiches. Classic turn-of-the-century black-and-white prints of St. Thomas decorate the walls of the restaurant, while a separate wine bar provides hot and cold appetizers. Reservations recommended. Credit cards: A, MC, V.

Hook, Line and Sinker $ ★★

#2 The Waterfront; Frenchtown, ☎ *(340) 776-9708.*
Lunch: 11:30 a.m.–4 p.m., entrées $5–$10.
Dinner: 6–10 p.m., entrées $6–$20.
Yachties tie up to this seaside eatery that's a reliable meet and greet. There's a nice outdoor deck, and offerings are reasonably priced—dinner highlights include steak au poivre and almond-crusted yellowtail. The Sunday brunch (10 a.m to 2:30 p.m.) is popular with locals, but breakfast is available every day. Credit cards: A, MC, V.

Hotel 1829 $$$ ★★★

Government Hill; Charlotte Amalie, ☎ *(340) 776-1829.* Associated hotel: *Hotel 1829.*
Dinner: 6–10 p.m., prix fixe $29. Closed: Sun.
The restaurant in this restored Government Hill hotel has much-sought tables on a terrace, while the dark brick-walled interior room is air conditioned and offers another form of romance—wherever you sit, the cuisine is good, if expensive. Continental cuisine is the focus, including grilled lobster tail and rack of lamb. Other specialties include a wilted spinach salad and dessert souffles—the raspberry chocolate is especially toothsome. The new menu is a three-course prix-fixe. Reservations recommended. Credit cards: A, MC, V.

L'Escargot $$$ ★★★

#12 Submarine Base, ☎ *(340) 774-6565.*
Lunch: 11:45 a.m.–2:45 p.m., entrées $7–$15.
Dinner: 6–10 p.m., entrées $15–$27. Closed: Sun.
A long-established dining room, this classic French restaurant is one of a few eateries located at a submarine base, near the airport. Two dining areas are available: an al fresco terrace, or a wine cellar for more formal meals. Specialties are continental favorites like rack of lamb or lobster thermidor—all simply and impeccably prepared, but with an Italian flair that allows room for an angel hair pasta topped with scampi and pesto. Reservations recommended. Credit cards: A, MC, V.

La Scala $$$ ★★★

Palm Passage; Charlotte Amalie, ☎ *(340) 774-2206.*
Lunch: 11 a.m.–3 p.m., entrées $10–$17.
Dinner: 5:30–9 p.m., entrées $13–$25. Closed: Sun.
Another fine creation from the creative team responsible for Chateau de Bordeaux and Asolare on St. John, La Scala is a great addition to the St. Thomas restaurant scene. Pizzas, pastas and sandwiches fill out the lunch menu, while dinner brings a huge osso bucco of lamb, pan-seared red snapper, and other items prepared with Italian sizzle. The food is fresh and tasty, and the pleasant alfresco courtyard dining is next to a large bar made from coral. A live jazz happy hour is planned for Thursdays. Credit cards: A, MC, V.

Polly's $ ★

Tillet Gardens, Smith Bay Road, ☎ *(340) 775-4550.*
Lunch: 11:30 a.m.–3:30 p.m., entrées $5–$12.
Dinner: 4:30–9:30 p.m., entrées $5–$15. Closed: Sun.
Enjoy burgers, sandwiches and salads at lunch, plus an array of fresh Mexican items including fajitas, chimichangas and margaritas at this casual open-air cafe in Tillet Gardens. If you're lucky, you'll get to watch the daily iguana feedings. The restaurant is a true oasis in a peaceful garden setting, though the real reason to come here is to check out the fascinating artisans' shops that surround it—you can even invest in a pre-prandial massage! Credit cards: A, MC, V.

Raffles $$ ★★★

The Marina; Compass Point, ☎ *(340) 775-6004.*
Dinner: 6:30–10:30 p.m., entrées $10–$25. Closed: Mon.
Always a local favorite, a post-hurricane makeover has brought an elegant new look to Raffles—pink chiffon, West Indian masks and high-backed peacock chairs for an English boudoir feel—the salon is still cooled by gentle ceiling fans and ocean breezes. The menu also survived, including steaks flambeed at tableside. Other specialties include fresh fish, conch sauteed in wine and garlic, and marinated duck. Chocoholics will die for Peter's Paradise, a chocolate basket filled with white chocolate mousse, almonds and drizzled with raspberry puree. Credit cards: A, MC, V.

Ritz-Carlton Dining Room, The $$$ ★★★★

Red Hook, ☎ *(340) 775-3333.* Associated hotel: *Ritz-Carlton St. Thomas.*
Dinner: 6:30–10 p.m., entrées $22–$32.
A chef with a background in cooking for luxury health spas in California and Florida holds court at this, the Ritz-Carlton resort's crown jewel. Weight watchers can delight in the fact that many of the delectable meals are prepared in natural juices and infusions, instead of heavy cream sauces. Alas, the calories await in the desserts, one of which is caramel ice cream encased in chocolate. Apparently, this ensures a return to the fat farm. The surroundings here are some of the most luxurious on the island—everything exudes a rosy glow and all is pretty in pink. A pianist helps further the romantic mood. Divine! Reservations recommended. Credit cards: A, MC, V.

Victor's New Hide Out $$ ★★★

103 Submarine Base, ☎ *(340) 776-9379.*
Lunch: 11:30 a.m.–3 p.m., entrées $9–$11.
Dinner: 5–10 p.m., entrées $11–$20.
Chef Victor left quiet Montserrat 30 years ago for more action (little did he know what he was leaving behind), and he cooks his West Indian specialties for an appreciative crowd of locals, tourists, and the occasional celebrity. The ubiquitous conch and curried chicken dishes are available, as well as his signature dish, Lobster Montserrat, cooked with fruit and cream sauce. Newcomers should probably arrive by taxi, as the hilltop hideaway is a little hard to find. Credit cards: A, MC, V.

Virgilio's $$$ ★★★★

18 Dronningens Gade; Charlotte Amalie, ☎ *(340) 776-4920.*
Lunch: 11:30 a.m.–4 p.m., entrées $13–$22.
Dinner: 4–10:30 p.m., entrées $16–$39. Closed: Sun.

ST. THOMAS

It looks dumpy from the outside, but a true haven awaits inside this wonderful restaurant. The walls are covered with eclectic artwork, the ceilings twinkle with tiny lights and display cases proudly spotlight a huge wine cellar—1000 bottles, plus an extensive collection of cordials. The food is as good as the atmosphere. The huge menu offers up 40 kinds of homemade pastas, fish, chicken and vegetarian specialties. Save room for a luscious dessert such as bananas Foster or crepes suzette prepared tableside. You'll find few tourists among the upscale locals who dine here regularly, and the continued success has grown a wine bar and bistro across the street. Reservations recommended. Credit cards: A, MC, V.

Zorba's $$ ★★★

Government Hill; Charlotte Amalie, ☎ *(340) 776-0444.*
Lunch: 10:30 a.m.–3:30 p.m., entrées $7–$13.
Dinner: 6–10 p.m., entrées $10–$20.

The bright whites of Greece animate this festive deli and restaurant located on Government Hill, and featuring scintillating fresh bread baked on the premises. A few shrimp and fish entrées, but most dishes embrace chicken and lamb with generous appetizers of baba ganush, tabouli and a chilled octopus in white wine, garlic and lemon. Macrobiotic and vegetarian platters available and a small outdoor patio is quite pleasant. Closed Sunday for lunch, but live entertainment is served on Sunday nights. Credit cards: A, MC, V.

Where to Shop

St. Thomas moves to a mercantile beat. Charlotte Amalie was declared a free port in 1755, a move that opened the island for trade with both the European powers and the growing American colonies. Today there are literally hundreds of duty-free shops to tempt shoppers in and around Charlotte Amalie. Jewelry, electronics, china, linen and perfume shops crowd Main Street (also known as Dronnigens Gade) and the alleys and passageways that bisect it, with a number of stores having a second outlet at the Havensight Mall just outside town near the cruise ship dock. Reputable establishments generally avoid the sidewalk barker come-ons that grow more shrill as one moves west on Main Street.

Most visitors leave toting at least one bottle of local rum, Cruzan, which is priced about $3 a fifth. But U.S. residents may bring home $1200 in goods free of duty, with the next $1000 subject to a 5 percent duty. Members of a household may make a joint declaration, entitling a family of four to a $4800 duty-free allowance. There is no sales or luxury tax, and products manufactured in the USVI (clothing, and handicrafts like jams or local jewelry) do not count toward your duty-free exemption. Unset precious gems, original paintings and binoculars are also exempt. The best buys traditionally include jewelry, fine china, crystal and perfume, while bargains can also be found in gems, watches and electronic products (verify the service warranty). However, it pays to do a little research before you arrive on island. By familiarizing yourself with prices on items you are interested in at home, you can separate the good deals from those that offer little or no savings. Finesse in bargaining also goes a long way.

Beyond the name brand stores, there are a number of specialty shops worth investigating. Artisans from Jamaica, Haiti, the Dominican Republic and Martinique are represented and **The Gallery** has a two-room studio featuring fine Caribbean folk art including work from some of the island's top primitivists. Another favorite is **Down Island Traders**, next to Post Office Alley on the waterfront, where you choose everything from edible delicacies such as marmalades and jellies to sweet Caribbean rum balls, fiery mustards, fruit chutneys and exotic spices. Down Island also has an extensive collection of Haitian and Jamaican wall hangings, handmade cloth and wooden dolls, including the famous Caribbean worry doll. At **Mango Tango** in the Al Cohen building (across the street from Havensight), you can stock up on wooden masks from Jamaica, wooden carvings from Trinidad and original and print work from the Virgin Islands. **Tillet Gardens Craft Complex**, located in Tutu across from the Four Winds Plaza, features the work of Jim Tillet, who creates screen-painted maps of the Caribbean, cruising maps of the Virgin Islands, and abstract paintings; other local artists are also represented. **Color of Joy** is a boutique that features watercolors and prints by St. Thomas painter Corinne Van Rensselaer, as well as varied gifts from the islands. A small annex, the **Caribbean Enamel Guild** features hand-painted jewelry, boxes and various accessories. The best time to visit Tillet Gardens is during the popular **Arts Alive** arts and craft fairs, held on-site three times a year. For more information ☎ *(340) 775-1929.*

If shopping is a big part of your St. Thomas itinerary, pick up a free copy of *St. Thomas This Week*, a bright yellow magazine that provides shopping information and a detailed map of Charlotte Amalie's shopping district; it can be found at the St. Thomas airport, as well as in San Juan's airport. Charlotte Amalie stores are generally open 9 a.m. to 5 p.m. Monday through Saturday, though they will sometimes open on Sunday if cruise ship business warrants.

St. Thomas Directory

Arrival and Departure

The most comprehensive service to St. Thomas is via **American Airlines**, which provides daily nonstop flights from Miami and New York's Kennedy Airport. **American Eagle** provides more than a dozen flights daily out of San Juan, Puerto Rico, allowing easy connections on American Airlines from throughout North America. **Delta** provides daily nonstop service out of Atlanta. **USAirways** flies to St. Thomas nonstop daily from Philadelphia. **Carnival**, **Continental**, **Pan Am**, **TWA** and **United** fly into San Juan where you may connect to American Eagle, **Air St. Thomas** or **Carib Air**. At press time, the St. Thomas/St. John Hotel Association was negotiating to bring in charter service to St. Thomas out of the New York area for 1998; call for more information ☎ *(340) 774-6835.*

Inter-island service is provided by **LIAT**, which offers nonstop or direct service to St. Thomas from Anguilla, Antigua, St. Kitts, St. Maarten and Tortola, with connecting service from a number of other islands available through Antigua. Among the other regional carriers connecting St. Thomas to Caribbean destinations are **Air Anguilla** (Anguilla, St. Croix, St. Maarten), **Air St. Thomas** (San Juan, St. Barts, Virgin Gorda), **Bohlke International Airways** (St. Croix), and **American Eagle** (St. Croix). Scheduled seaplane service is available from the Ramada Yacht Haven marina in Charlotte Amalie to Christiansted in St. Croix every 30 minutes in the morning and afternoon on **Seaborne Seaplane** ☎ *(340) 777-4491*; $45 one way for USVI residents, or $50 for visitors (reservations necessary). For information on ferry service to and from the other Virgin Islands, see "Getting Around," below.

The departure tax when leaving the U.S. Virgin Islands is $3.

Business Hours

Shops generally open weekdays 9 a.m.–5 p.m. Banks generally open Monday–Thursday 9 a.m.–2:30 p.m. and Friday 9 a.m.–2 and 3:30–5 p.m.

Climate

Summer temperatures, cooled by eastern trade winds, hover around 82 degrees Fahrenheit. Winter temperatures range from 77 degrees, dipping to 69 degrees at night and rising as high as 84 degrees. The rainy season runs September–January, though the sun shines nearly every day. The average rainfall is about 40 inches per year, and showers are usually brief.

Documents

U.S. citizens do not need a passport, though proof of identity is necessary for departure. But if you plan to visit the British Virgin Islands, you must show proof of citizenship (passport, or birth certificate with photo ID).

Electricity

Current runs at 110 volts, 60 cycles.

Getting Around

Cabs are not metered but each driver must carry the current fare structure. Rates are per person, but drop if two or more are going to the same destination. Sample rates from Charlotte Amalie are: to Red Hook $9 for one, or $5 each for two or more; to the airport, $4.50 and $4; to Magens Bay, $6.50 and $4. If you are traveling between two points that aren't on the official list, negotiate firmly ahead of time. Note that when you board at a popular departure point (for instance, at Red Hook when a ferry comes in), you'll need patience while drivers try to fill the cab with other passengers headed in your general direction. There are open-air taxi buses between Charlotte Amalie and Red Hook for $3. The buses leave the Market Place every hour from 8:15 a.m. to 5:15 p.m.; buses leave Red Hook every hour from 7:15 a.m. to 4:15 p.m. A two-hour island tour for one or two passengers runs $30, with additional passengers paying $12 each.

Rental cars are easily obtained, typically from one of the name American agencies like Budget, for about $50 per day. Comparing prices and reserving your car ahead of your trip will usually net the best deals. No special license or permit is required, but driving is on the left.

Ferries are the primary transportation between St. Thomas and the other Virgins and daytrips are easy and popular. **Virgin Hydrofoil** ☎ *(340) 776-7417* provides daily service to St. Croix at 7:15 a.m. and 3:15 p.m. (return trips are 9:15 a.m. and 5 p.m.); $37 one-way or $70 round-trip (75 minutes). Ferries to Cruz Bay, St. John, originate hourly from Red Hook ($3 each way; about 20 minutes) or almost hourly from Charlotte Amalie ($7, about 45 minutes)—for exact schedules, call **Transportation Services** ☎ *(340) 776-6282* or **Varlack Ventures** ☎ *(340) 776-6412*. **Blue Lines** has a car ferry that plies the route between Red Hook and Cruz Bay every 90 minutes ($50 round-trip for car and passengers, about 25 minutes); call to reserve slot ☎ *(340) 777-6111*. For information on ferry service to West End, Road Town and Virgin Gorda, see "Arrival and Departure" in "British Virgin Islands;" you'll need a passport or a birth certificate and photo identification for entry into the BVIs. **Per Dohm's Water Taxi** provides speedy charter service between Red Hook and St. John or the BVIs ☎ *(340) 775-6501*. A ferry also connects downtown Charlotte Amalie with the Frenchman's Reef Hotel and Morningstar Beach hourly ($4, about 15 minutes).

Language

English is the official language. Locals also speak a native patois, a mixture of English, African and Spanish. Some people are bilingual in Spanish.

Medical Emergencies

A 160-bed hospital with a decompression chamber is available on St. Thomas and can handle most emergencies.

Money

The official currency is the American dollar. There is no sales tax.

Telephone

The new area code for the U.S. Virgin Islands is *(340)* and standard intrastate toll charges apply. Since the USVI is an incorporated territory, toll-free *(800)* numbers on the island can be accessed from the mainland. Regular U.S. postage rates also apply.

Time

Atlantic Standard Time, which means an hour later than New York City, except during Daylight Saving Time, when it is the same.

ST. THOMAS

Tipping and Taxes

The USVI hotel occupancy tax is 8 percent. Some hotels also add a service charge to your final bill, but between the big resorts, small hotels and guest houses, there's no consistent schedule and a few even throw in an energy surcharge. *Most* hotels do *not* add a service charge, but verify the individual policy directly with your hotel at the time of booking. If a service charge is not added to your bill, a tip in the room is appropriate. Restaurant tips are handled as in the U.S.; 15 percent is standard, but verify that it hasn't already been added to your bill.

Tourist Information

The U.S. Virgin Islands **Department of Tourism** has information booths at the airport, at Emancipation Garden in Charlotte Amalie, and in Havensight Mall near the cruise ship dock ☎ *(340) 774-8784* or *(800) 372-USVI*. You can also pick up brochures, rest your feet, and even check shopping bags at an island-sponsored hospitality lounge in the Old Customs House next to Little Switzerland. You may write to the **St. Thomas Visitors Bureau** at *P.O. Box 6400, St. Thomas, VI 00804*. Local offices for the USVI Department of Tourism are found in Atlanta, Chicago, Los Angeles, Miami, New York and Washington D.C.

Web Site

www.usvi.net OR www.st-thomas.com

When to Go

The island's biggest annual event is the **Virgin Islands Carnival**, a month-long festival held in April and featuring mocko jumbies, a greased pig contest, steel pan bands, a mile-long parade, fireworks, a food fair and *J'ouvert*—daybreak dancing that begins at 4 a.m. Easter weekend brings the **Rolex Cup Regatta**, an international sailing event held in the waters off St. Thomas. Other sea-faring events include the American **Yacht Harbor Billfish Tournament**, held in July, and the **V.I. Atlantic Open Blue Marlin Tournament**, held in August.

ST. THOMAS HOTELS		RMS	RATES	PHONE	CR. CARDS
★★★★★	Ritz-Carlton, St. Thomas, The	152	$200–$525	(800) 241-3333	A, D, MC, V
★★★★	Elysian Beach Resort	180	$175–$375	(800) 753-2554	A, D, DC, MC, V
★★★★	Renaissance Grand Beach Resort	290	$225–$445	(800) 468-3571	A, D, DC, MC, V
★★★★	Sapphire Beach Resort and Marina	171	$225–$440	(800) 524-2090	A, D, MC, V
★★★★	Secret Harbour Beach Resort	60	$169–$495	(800) 524-2250	A, MC, V
★★★	Best Western Emerald Beach Resort	90	$129–$239	(800) 233-4936	A, D, DC, MC, V
★★★	Bluebeard's Castle Hotel	184	$140–$235	(800) 524-6599	A, D, DC, MC, V

ST. THOMAS

ST. THOMAS HOTELS		RMS	RATES	PHONE	CR. CARDS
★★★	Bolongo Beach Club and Villas	116	$135–$225	(800) 524-4746	A, D, DC, MC, V
★★★	Colony Point Pleasant Resort	134	$170–$360	(800) 524-2300	A, D, DC, MC, V
★★★	Hotel 1829	15	$65–$185	(800) 524-2002	A, MC, V
★★★	Island Beachcomber	48	$95–$145	(800) 982-9898	A, D, DC, MC, V
★★★	Magens Point Hotel	54	$150–$300	(800) 524-2031	A, D, DC, MC, V
★★★	Pavilions & Pools	25	$180–$260	(800) 524-2001	A, MC, V
★★★	Wyndham Sugar Bay Resort	300	$180–$580	(800) 996-3426	A, D, DC, MC, V
★★	Admiral's Inn	13	$79–$149	(800) 544-0493	A, D, MC, V
★★	Best Western Carib Beach Resort	69	$89–$149	(800) 792-2742	A, D, DC, MC, V
★★	Blackbeard's Castle	22	$60–$150	(800) 344-5771	A, D, MC, V
★★	Galleon House	14	$49–$119	(800) 524-2052	A, D, MC, V
★★	L'Hotel Boynes	8	$85–$175	(800) 377-2905	A, MC, V
★★	Mafolie Hotel	23	$65–$135	(800) 225-7035	A, MC, V
★★	Villa Santana	5	$85–$195	(340) 776-1311	A
★★	Windward Passage	151	$99–$170	(800) 524-7389	A, D, DC, MC, V
★	Danish Chalet Inn	11	$60–$95	(800) 635-1531	MC, V
★	Island View Guest House	15	$45–$95	(800) 524-2023	A, MC, V

ST. THOMAS RESTAURANTS		PHONE	ENTRÉE	CR. CARDS
American Cuisine				
★★★	Chart House	(340) 774-4262	$16–$37	A, DC, MC, V
★	Hard Rock Cafe	(340) 777-5555	$8–$17	A, MC, V
Continental Cuisine				
★★★	Hotel 1829	(340) 776-1829	$29–$29	A, MC, V
★★★	L'Escargot	(340) 774-6565	$7–$27	A, MC, V
★★★	Raffles	(340) 775-6004	$10–$25	A, MC, V
Greek Cuisine				
★★★	Zorba's	(340) 776-0444	$7–$20	A, MC, V
International Cuisine				
★★★★	Craig and Sally's	(340) 777-9949	$9–$28	A, MC, V

ST. THOMAS

ST. THOMAS RESTAURANTS	PHONE	ENTRÉE	CR. CARDS
★★★★ Herve Restaurant and Wine Bar	(340) 777-9703	$6–$26	A, MC, V
★★★★ Ritz-Carlton Dining Room, The	(340) 775-3333	$22–$32	A, MC, V
★★★ Epernay Champagne Bar	(340) 774-5343	$13–$22	A, MC, V
★★ Hook, Line and Sinker	(340) 776-9708	$5–$20	A, MC, V
Italian Cuisine			
★★★★ Virgilio's	(340) 776-4920	$13–$39	A, MC, V
★★★ La Scala	(340) 774-2206	$10–$25	A, MC, V
Mexican Cuisine			
★ Polly's	(340) 775-4550	$5–$15	A, MC, V
Regional Cuisine			
★★★ Victor's New Hide Out	(340) 776-9379	$9–$20	A, MC, V
★★ Cuzzin's	(340) 777-4711	$6–$18	A, D, MC, V
★★ Eunice's Terrace	(340) 775-3975	$6–$28	A, MC, V
★★ Gladys' Cafe	(340) 774-6604	$6–$13	A, MC, V
Seafood Cuisine			
★★★ Agave Terrace	(340) 775-4142	$18–$38	A, MC, V
★★ Cafe Wahoo	(340) 775-6350	$7–$24	A, MC, V

ST. THOMAS

ST. VINCENT AND THE GRENADINES

Picturesque St. Vincent's terrain ranges from rugged cliffs to lush valleys and beaches with golden and black sand.

Perhaps nothing symbolizes the delightfully offbeat and vibrant aura of St. Vincent better than its national emblem—the St. Vincent parrot. The bird's head is ivory-colored with a splash of bright yellow above the eyes. Around the neck is a band of lavender accented by soft hues of turquoise, while the bird's body and wings are a rich and luminous golden-brown. For flourish, the tail feathers are bolts of deep indigo, sunflower orange and emerald green. There is no mistaking this lavish bird for any other and St. Vincent is pretty special, too.

Boat excursions and hiking trails lead to cascading waterfalls and mineral springs on St. Vincent.

As most islanders will conscientiously point out, the nation is actually St. Vincent *and* the Grenadines, encompassing the larger island as well as a spread of smaller outposts that pepper the junction of the Caribbean and Atlantic en route to Grenada. The Grenadines have drawn yachties for decades. Today, many visitors barely step foot on St. Vincent, if at all, choosing instead to dash straight for the picturesque smaller islands, where they find postcard-perfect beaches and barefoot escapes worthy of a Wall Street banker's best getaway fantasies. Bequia, the largest, is a quirky tourism frontier that still clings to a tradition of whaling under oar and sail. Electricity came in 1969, a small airport opened in 1992, yet fortunately, the feared floodgates of visitors are but a trickle. Several Grenadines—Mustique and Petit St. Vincent in particular—have been developed for a posh crowd that wouldn't be caught dead in a traditional West Indian guest house.

But St. Vincent has an irrepressible backwater charm all its own that is missed by many Caribbean connoisseurs. From the bustling streets of its port and capital, Kingstown, one of the last Caribbean towns to step into the 20th century, to the heights of La Soufriere, the island's quietly simmering volcano, to vine-embroidered valleys swirled by mist, St. Vincent is a study in contrasts when paired with the Grenadines. Kingstown has some well-preserved Georgian architecture, along with a fabulous Romanesque-style church. The a majority of the population lives the more simple existence afforded by the island's agrarian economy. Though a 1997 scandal cast an unfavorable light on St. Vincent's judicial system, all eyes are now focused on

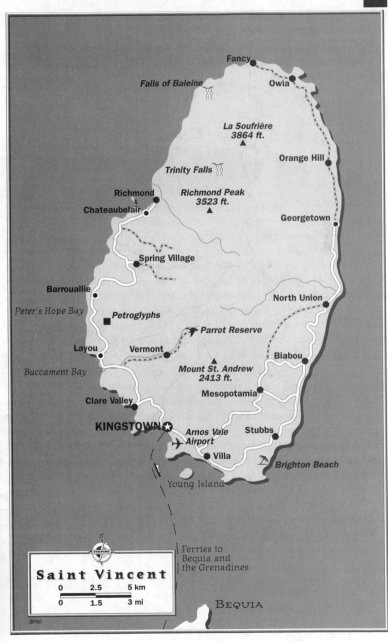

Fancy

Falls of Baleine

Owia

La Soufrière
3864 ft.
▲

Orange Hill

Trinity Falls

Richmond

Richmond Peak
3523 ft.
▲

Chateaubelair

Georgetown

Spring Village

Barrouallie

North Union

Peter's Hope Bay

■ Petroglyphs

Parrot Reserve

Layou

Vermont

Biabou

Buccament Bay

▲
Mount St. Andrew
2413 ft.

Mesopotamia

Clare Valley

KINGSTOWN ✪

Arnos Vale
Airport

Stubbs

Villa

Brighton Beach

Young Island

N

Ferries to
Bequia and
the Grenadines

Saint Vincent

0   2.5   5 km

0   1.5   3 mi

BEQUIA

©FWI

the construction of a cruise ship pier in Kingstown that may substantially change the pace of life on the island.

BEST BETS FOR...

Bird's-Eye View

Lush and lovely, with large expanses of undeveloped territory in its northern reaches, 130-square-mile St. Vincent is one of the region's volcanic creations. Steep ridges of black rock reach into the clouds, culminating at the summit of La Soufriere, a 3864-foot peak. Its gaping, mile-wide crater was the site of serious activity in 1979, but the volcano slumbers peacefully for the moment. On the slopes of La Soufriere and other peaks are verdant valleys splintered by rushing streams and waterfalls, while the lower hillsides are punctuated by fields of banana, breadfruit and coconut palms. The island's 111,000-strong population is concentrated along the coasts, predominantly around Kingstown, the capitol of St. Vincent and the Grenadines.

The Grenadines taper off from St. Vincent to the south like the tail of a kite, and although they each have their own personality, the uniting theme is a drier landscape and velvety white-sand beaches, some of them fairly magnificent. There are dozens of islands, not including Carriacou and Petit Martinique, the Grenadines that are politically linked to Grenada. Bequia is the largest and most developed, with a population of 5055, and connected to St. Vincent via one-hour ferry ride or 10-minute plane hop. Two others, Union Island and Canouan, have a population that skitters into four digits—the latter has been the focus of a major development project involving resorts, villas and an 18-hole championship golf course. But the bulk of the attention tends to focus on Mustique, an island that was developed for the jet set in the 1960s, and on a pair of privately-owned outposts, Palm Island and Petit St. Vincent, each with a small upscale resort that lures vacationers in search of unqualified retreat from civilization.

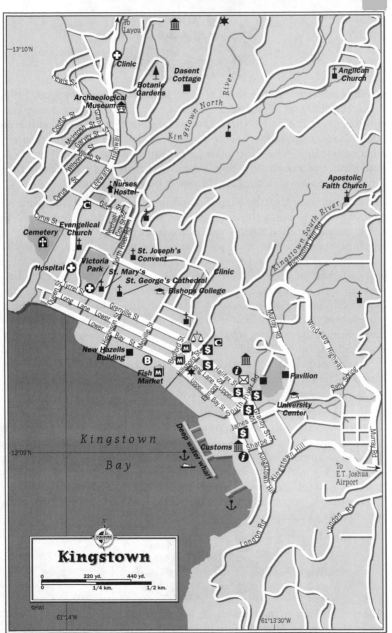

Kingstown

0   220 yd.   440 yd.
0   1/4 km.   1/2 km.

©FWI

History

Columbus marked the presence of St. Vincent on his third voyage in 1498, but luckily didn't go ashore since the resident Carib Indians might have cannibalized him. The native tribes here were more tenacious than those on other islands, keeping the European conquistadors at bay longer than any other island. In 1763 a treaty allowed the British to take control of the island. Sixteen years later, they found themselves battling the French, but the Treaty of Versailles in 1783 gave the power back to England.

Some years later, Captain Bligh took off for Tahiti from England with his crew of the *Bounty*, only to be mutinied by them and pushed out to sea. In 1793 he finally reached St. Vincent on his own, equipped with a canoeful of breadfruit seedlings, which became the progenitors of a crop that would eventually make the island famous. In 1795, the native population sided with the French and burned down British plantations during a ferocious battle; a year later the Brits triumphantly quelled the rebellion. At that time, the Brits decided to deport the rest of the native Indians to British Honduras (now known as Belize), where their ancestors live today. Until 1979 the island was under British rule, at which time it received independent statehood, along with the other Grenadines, within the Commonwealth. It is governed by a governor-general appointed by the Crown on the advice of the prime minister. The Parliament's House of Assembly is elected every five years.

The country landed in hot water in 1997 when an American yachting pair was detained on circumstantial evidence for the murder of a well-liked water taxi operator from Bequia. The couple's family stirred the U.S. media with stories of corrupt Vincentians looking for bribes, while on Bequia the pair's lifestyle was questioned and local politics seasoned the stew. After nine months in jail where they faced death by hanging, and with the island's prime minister suffering under the glare of "Nightline" and other news outlets, the couple was quickly tried and released for lack of evidence (at press time, no other suspects have emerged).

People

Vincentians are a friendly and open lot, and visitors are made to feel welcome. Most are of African, East Indian and Portuguese descent, and the total population is nearly 120,000—almost all live on St. Vincent, many of them in or near Kingstown, the nation's capitol. The majority of Vincentians are Protestant, with Roman Catholics a healthy minority. Agriculture is still a major island employer. Bananas are the dominant crop, but the future of exports beyond the next few years is in doubt; other produce includes arrowroot (a thickening agent for cooking, but also used to coat computer paper), coconuts and sweet potato. St. Vincent and the Grenadines are a constitutional monarchy within the Commonwealth of Great Britain.

Beaches

St. Vincent has its share of beaches, but most are of black sand, which is sometimes coarse and hot to the touch. The hub of most sun-sea-sand activities on St. Vincent is **Villa**, which encompasses **Indian Bay** and **Blue Lagoon**, facing Young Island. The beaches here are narrow and gray, but pleasant in spots. On the west coast of the island are better beaches, including **Wallilabou**, where the sea is calm and the sand uncrowded. Also worth checking out is **Cumberland Bay** and, just past Chateaubelair, remote **Richmond Beach**. Otherwise, beach-lovers will want to head south to where the white sand coves of the Grenadines unfurl splendidly.

Underwater

Diving in St. Vincent and the Grenadines still appeals to the adventurous spirit. The reefs remain pristine and new sites continue to be discovered. As on Dominica and St. Lucia, visibility is usually excellent despite significant rain runoff, because the main island's soil is mostly volcanic (and heavier), allowing it to sink quickly to the depths rather than mucking up the waters. However, unlike the aforementioned destinations, St. Vincent is not known for its walls. This is a place for reefs, which flourish on the tongues of ancient lava flows snaking into the sea, and for its extensive fish activity. There is an abundance of smaller life, including the unusual and rare frog fish, and frequent sightings of seahorses. Additionally, black coral, which usually grows deeper than recreational diving allows, is found much nearer sea level here, in some spots as close as 27 feet below the surface. Somehow, these beautiful underwater forests, whose branches come in six different colors, have not been leveled.

A few dive shops are also sprinkled among the Grenadines. Bequia features several excellent dive locations, all within a few minutes of the main boat dock—the island's west coast is all part of a marine park. **Devil's Table** is a flat reef sitting in Bequia's main harbor, with channels of sand amid the coral structure; terrific detail, including occasional frog fish and sea horses. **The Wall** is a sheer, dramatic plunge from a ledge at 30 feet to a sandy floor 120 feet down, while **The Boulders** is a delightful drift dive among coral encrusted monoliths.

Although Union Island offers decent snorkeling and diving, better sites are just a couple miles away, off the Tobago Cays and Mayreau. One area, **Mayreau Gardens**, allows three different drift dives of intermediate difficulty; the strong current discourages fishermen from visiting the reef. There is an excellent wreck, the *HMS Purina*, a 140-foot English gunship that went down in 1918 just off Mayreau. Much of its superstructure is still intact, and with a maximum depth of just 40 feet, the site is terrific for beginners. For experienced divers, ten miles east of Union Island is **Sail Rock**, a dynamic and isolated location which requires very calm seas to visit; the rock outcrop draws barracudas by the dozens and a plethora of nurse sharks. **Horseshoe Reef**, which wraps around the Tobago Cays, offers superb snorkeling.

Four dive shops (**Dive St. Vincent**, **Dive Bequia**, **Dive Canouan** and **Grenadine Dive** on Union Island) have worked out a mix-and-match package which will appeal to island-hoppers: 10 dives spread among the four shops for $400, including all equipment. Other packages (which lock you into one location) are also available.

Dive Shops

Dive St. Vincent

Villa, St. Vincent; ☎ *(784) 457-4714.*

Oldest operator on the island (since 1977), featuring resort courses and entry level certifications, and handling referrals. PADI and NAUI affiliated. Two tank dive $90, including equipment. Owner Bill Tewes made it onto the local .45-cent postcard stamp.

Grenadines Dive

Clifton, Union Island; ☎ *(784) 458-8138.*

Owner Glenroy Adams, a NAUI instructor, has been on Union Island since 1988. His staff is all PADI, with courses to Divemaster. Two-tank dive, $90, including equipment. Dives Mayreau and the Tobago Cays.

Dive Bequia

Port Elizabeth, Bequia; ☎ *(784) 458-3504.*

Bob Sachs conducted much of the original dive exploration in and around Bequia, opening his shop in 1983. PADI and NAUI affiliated, with courses to Divemaster. Two tank dive, $75 with your own equipment (or $85 without).

Dive Canouan

Canouan; ☎ *(784) 458-8044.*

A newer outfit that works out of the Tamarin Beach Hotel. Two tank dive $80, including all equipment. Offers a yacht rendezvous service within the surrounding islands.

On Foot

Somehow, St. Vincent feels like a forgotten outpost. Many tourists use the island simply as a jumping-off point for the Grenadines, but there is a smoldering volcano, **La Soufrière** (up until recently the most actively-monitored in the Caribbean), treks into rain forests which are home to the few remaining St. Vincent parrots, and splendid waterfalls. The Forestry Department has guides to some of the island's trails, and the 1:50,000 *Ordnance Survey* map is helpful for exploration. Hikers should carry insect repellent (mosquitoes are prevalent), and be prepared for rainy weather and muddy trails.

In Bequia, hikes from Admiralty Bay lead over unpaved roads and footpaths, but are relatively easy, and arrive at such places as **Mt. Pleasant**, where there is a spectacular view. The northern part of the island is covered with gentle hills good for hiking. There are no roads or cars on Mayreau, but from the bay you can take a track to the tiny hilltop village in the center of the island; here you can see a great view of **Tobago Cays**. One of the most idyllic paradises in the Caribbean, Tobago Cays consists of four uninhabited islets ringed by pure white beaches and clear blue waters. From a beach anywhere here, you can walk/paddle to see clusters of tropical fish swimming through the coral gardens. **Petit Rameau**, the northernmost cay, has a short trail through heavy mangroves along a sandy beach.

What Else to See

The capital city of Kingstown holds much of interest for the visitor. The waterfront is a good place to start; you'll see everything plying the waters from luxury yachts to commercial fishing boats. On Back Street, **St. Mary's Catholic Church**, which dates to 1893, is an exotic blend of Romanesque, Moorish and Georgian architecture. Just across the street is another house of worship, **St. George's Cathedral**, a Georgian structure with a vintage graveyard. Also worth checking out is the **National Museum**, ☎ *(784) 456-1787,* open just Wednesdays from 9 a.m. to noon and Saturdays from 3–6 p.m., a tiny enclave of Indian pottery that's the project of curator Dr. Earle Kirby, a local archaeologist. If you're on the island during a Saturday, be sure to head for the **market** at Bay Street, where exotic fruits, fresh-from-the-sea fish and all sorts of vegetables are snapped up by islanders and visitors alike.

St. Mary's Catholic Church, St. Vincent

Historical Sites

Fort Charlotte ★★★

Kingstown, ☎ *(784) 456-1830*
Hours open: 6 a.m.–6 p.m.
Construction on this fort was started around 1791 and was completed in 1812. Much of the impressive structure is in ruins today, but well worth a visit for the stunning views from its perch some 650 feet above sea level of Kingstown and the Grenadines. Check out the murals inside that tell the history of black Caribbeans.

Parks and Gardens

Botanical Gardens   ★★★

Kingstown, ☎ *(784) 457-1003*
Hours open: 7 a.m.–4 p.m.

Located on a hillside north of town, this 20-acre garden is the oldest in the Western Hemisphere, dating back to 1765. Among the teak, mahogany and cannonball trees and exotic plants and flowers are breadfruit trees descended from seedlings brought over by Captain Bligh in 1793. The lush grounds also include a pagoda, lily pond, and the Archeological Museum, located in a West Indian house and displaying artifacts from pre-Columbian days. There is also a small aviary with about three dozen St. Vincent parrots kept for the island's successful breeding program. Admission to the gardens is free, but once there, it's worth a couple of dollars to hire a guide for an hour-long tour.

Tours

Half- and full-day tours to the Vermont Nature Trail, La Soufriere, Trinity Falls, Mesopotamia Valley and other sights on St. Vincent can be arranged through two land-based tour operators: Clint and Mildred Hazell's **Hazeco Tours** ☎ *(784) 457-8634* and **SVG Tours** ☎ *(784) 458-4534*. Excursions by chartered speed boat from St. Vincent to the Falls of Baleine, Mustique and the southern Grenadines are handled by **Fantasea Tours** ☎ *(784) 457-4477.*

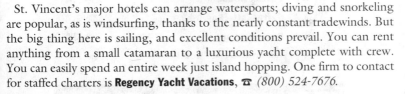

St. Vincent's major hotels can arrange watersports; diving and snorkeling are popular, as is windsurfing, thanks to the nearly constant tradewinds. But the big thing here is sailing, and excellent conditions prevail. You can rent anything from a small catamaran to a luxurious yacht complete with crew. You can easily spend an entire week just island hopping. One firm to contact for staffed charters is **Regency Yacht Vacations**, ☎ *(800) 524-7676.*

Bicycling

Cycling is a nascent activity in St. Vincent, but rewarding for anyone with the thighs to tackle the island's roller coaster roads. **Sailor's Cycle Center** ☎ *(784) 457-1712* is the sole rental agency for now, offering a variety of both mountain and road bikes for $10 per day. Owner Trevor Bailey is head of the local cycling association and leads impromptu trips for visitors.

Watersports

Various locations, Kingstown.

Most watersports can be found at your hotel, and those staying on the Grenadines can be outfitted at the resorts. For boating and cruising, call **Barefoot Yacht Charters** ☎ *(784) 456-9526* or **Lagoon Marina** ☎ *(784) 458-4308*, both on St. Vincent. On Bequia, call **Frangipani Yacht Services** ☎ *(784) 458-3255.*

Where to Stay

	Fielding's Highest Rated Hotels in St. Vincent and its Grenadines	
★★★★	Cotton House	$190–$890
★★★★	Petit St. Vincent Resort	$385–$770
★★★★	Young Island Resort	$210–$640
★★★	Camelot Inn	$225–$275
★★★	Firefly	$200–$250
★★★	Grand View Beach Hotel	$104–$270
★★★	Palm Island Beach Club	$174–$415
★★★	Plantation House	$126–$369
★★★	Saltwhistle Bay Club	$200–$450
★★★	Tamarind Beach Hotel	$160–$300

	Fielding's Best Barefoot Escapes in St. Vincent and The Grenadines	
★★★★	Cotton House	$190–$890
★★★	Saltwhistle Bay Club	$200–$450
★★	Petit Byahaut	$160–$310
★★★	Tamarind Beach Hotel	$160–$300

	Fielding's Best Value Hotels in St. Vincent and the Grenadines	
★★	Cobblestone Inn	$65–$76
★★	Spring on Bequia	$50–$205
★★	Frangipani Hotel	$30–$150
★★★	Plantation House	$126–$369
★★	Lagoon Marina and Hotel	$65–$95

Where to Stay—St. Vincent

Most accommodations on St. Vincent are located either in Kingstown or around Villa; the former include true West Indian guest houses in a bustling town, while the latter sit on or near the fair beach at Villa. Beach buffs will find more to their liking in the Grenadines, but good black sand options lie on the west coast, north of Kingstown. Note that most properties do not have air conditioning, but trade winds and ceiling fans usually do the trick.

Hotels and Resorts

Thankfully, St. Vincent has yet to go the way of the high-rise resort. With a couple of exceptions, lodging tends to be pretty basic, and inexpensive. At the other end of the spectrum is Young Island, a romantic private island paradise located a few hundred feet off the shores of St. Vincent, at Villa. Inquire about Young's "sailaway" options which allow you to spend some of your nights aboard one of their yachts in the Grenadines.

Beachcombers Hotel   **$60–$80**   ★

Villa, ☎ *(784) 458-4283, FAX (784) 458-4385.*
Single: $60. Double: $80.
This basic property accommodates guests in five different buildings—most rooms are air-conditioned and three have kitchenettes, all are on the small side. TVs available on request. Facilities are limited to a decent bar and restaurant, with watersports available on the pleasant beach that faces Young Island. Fine for those in search of beachcomber ambiance. 13 rooms. Credit cards: A, D, MC, V.

Camelot Inn   **$225–$325**   ★★★

Kingstown, ☎ *(800) 223-6510, (784) 456-2100, FAX (784) 456-2233.*
Single: $225–$275. Double: $225–$275. Suites Per Day: $300–$325.
Occupying an 18th-century plantation house that has been transformed into a high-amenity hotel, Camelot is set in a garden overlooking Kingstown. The guest rooms are bright and tastefully appointed in Spanish rattan—most have balcony views of town or the surrounding mountains. Extras include air conditioning, bathrobes, hair dryer and nightly turndown, all thanks to Camelot's Director, Mrs. Ballantyne, formerly of the St. James Club in Antigua. There's a pool, well-equipped gym and tennis court, and a restaurant delivers fine dining. The formal ambiance is a bit of a mismatch for lived-in St. Vincent, but for those wanting an upscale option close to town, Camelot fills the bill. The rates are MAP and include breakfast, dinner and afternoon tea, plus a city tour and a massage. 22 rooms. Credit cards: A, MC, V.

Grand View Beach Hotel   **$104–$270**   ★★★

Villa Point, ☎ *(800) 223-6510, (784) 458-4811, FAX (784) 457-4174.*
E-mail: granview@caribsurf.com.
Single: $104–$180. Double: $130–$270.
A former plantation house is the focal point of this well-run property, located on a striking promontory overlooking a small beach and Young Island. As the name suggests, the views here are indeed grand. Rooms are fairly polished and comfortable, with air conditioning, safes and balconies. The hotel's eight acres include tennis and squash courts, a small pool, a health club, a reading room, and a restaurant serving

West Indian fare. Don't come looking for a resort, but do come for the tranquil surroundings and friendly, family-run service. 19 rooms. Credit cards: A, DC, MC, V.

Lagoon Marina and Hotel   **$65–$95**   ★★

Villa, ☎ *(800) 742-4276, (784) 458-4308, FAX (784) 458-4308.*
Website: www.cpscaribnet.com/ads/lagoon/lagoon.html. E-mail: lagoon@cpsnet.com.
Single: $65–$95. Double: $65–$95.
This simple hotel overlooks Blue Lagoon and its marina, and is often filled with sea folk. Rooms are on the second floor—they're basic, but all have nice, large patios (the five with air conditioning are $10 extra). The bar and restaurant do a brisk business with marina customers, and there's also a pool and small watersports center on the fair black-sand beach. It's a little set off from the Villa scene, but quieter. 19 rooms. Credit cards: A, MC, V.

Sunset Shores Beach Hotel   **$90–$140**   ★★

Villa, ☎ *(800) 223-6510, (784) 458-4411, FAX (784) 457-4800.*
Website: www.cpscaribnet.com/ads/sunset/sunset.html. E-mail: sunset@cpsnet.com.
Single: $90–$120. Double: $115–$140.
This motel-like property is one of St. Vincent's few commercial hotels and sits on a fair beach. Guestrooms are air-conditioned and comfortable enough; they form a horseshoe around an attractive courtyard that faces Young Island. Facilities include a small pool, a bar and restaurant, and watersports on the beach. Kingstown is some 10 minutes away by car. 32 rooms. Credit cards: A, D, MC, V.

Villa Lodge Hotel   **$95–$120**   ★★

Villa, ☎ *(784) 458-4641, FAX (784) 457-4468.*
Single: $95–$110. Double: $105–$120.
Set on a hillside and overlooking the sea, this converted home is popular, friendly, and family run. Guestrooms are air-conditioned and simply furnished; most have balconies or patios, all are blanketed with tired carpets. The restaurant serves West Indian fare, and the large pool is a nice alternative to the small beach, which is within walking distance. The management also runs the Breezeville Apartments next door, eight bright and airy one- and two-bedroom apartments for about the same price. 10 rooms. Credit cards: A, D, MC, V.

Young Island Resort   **$210–$640**   ★★★★

Young Island, ☎ *(800) 223-1108, (784) 458-4826, FAX (784) 457-4567.*
E-mail: Y-Island@caribsurf.com.
Single: $210–$550. Double: $300–$640.
A Caribbean classic, Young is one of the region's original private island resorts, a choice 35-acre rock outcrop embraced by sand on one edge. To reach it, you board a bumpkin launch that putt-putts the 200 yards across from Villa. Accommodations are lovely and varied, in cottages scattered about the hillside or set on the beach—each are comfortable, cooled by ceiling fans, tropically decorated, with patios; a few with private plunge pools and many have open-air rock showers with vines that crawl up the black lava cliffs. There is a lagoon-style pool, tennis court, a small beach with a "floating" swim-up bar, and nonmotorized watersports. The grounds are a lush tangle of greenery and flowers, with St. Vincent parrots squawking from cages, and hammocks swaying beneath thatch huts—it feels more Tahitian than Carib-

bean, but it all works. The Friday night manager's cocktail party is a don't-miss affair held in an alcove at the base of another islet next door, a sheer rock tower lit by dozens of torches. Despite the steep rates, the atmosphere is casual and informal—this is not a luxury haven so much as a romantic escape. The resort is undergoing a remodeling that should brighten up decor that was leaning to frumpy. Rates are MAP and include breakfast and dinner daily. 30 rooms. Credit cards: A, D, MC, V.

Inns

Most accommodations in St. Vincent come with an "inn" feeling about them. That's the nature of the St. Vincent life. Some can be found in Kingstown, others in the highlands away from the hustle of city life.

Cobblestone Inn   **$65–$76**   ★★
Kingstown, ☎ *(784) 456-1937, FAX (784) 456-1938.*
Single: $65. Double: $76.
This harborside inn dates back to 1814 and was originally intended as a sugar and arrowroot warehouse. Guestrooms are small but comfortable and air-conditioned, and all have private baths. Request one in the back to avoid street noise, but be warned that all are rather dark. The bar and restaurant are popular with locals, and the in-town location attracts mostly business travelers. There's no pool; the beach is a 10-minute drive away. 19 rooms. Credit cards: A, MC, V.

Low Cost Lodging

It is possible to find cheap lodgings in simple hotels in the Kingstown area. The style is usually West Indian, with very basic furnishings. Cleanliness is usually not a problem.

Heron Hotel   **$45–$59**   ★
Kingstown, ☎ *(784) 457-1631, FAX (784) 457-1189.*
Single: $45. Double: $59.
Located on the waterfront within walking distance of the town center, this is a classic West Indian guest house, with lots of charm between the warped floorboards to prove it. The rooms are very basic and old-fashioned, and lack modern amenities like TV but have air conditioners, phone and private baths; most have lovely cathedral ceilings. The restaurant is similarly no-frills, but the reasonably priced meals are tasty enough. 15 rooms. Credit cards: D, MC, V.

Umbrella Beach Hotel   **$42–$62**   ★
Villa, ☎ *(784) 458-4651, FAX (784) 457-4930.*
Single: $42–$52. Double: $52–$62.
If you're on a tight budget and want the convenience (and economy) of having a kitchenette, this may be just the spot. The rooms are very basic and a bit run down, but they are clean and colorfully painted with sweetly dilapidated charm. The location is handy, right near the fair beach and several restaurants. 9 rooms. Credit cards: A, DC, MC, V.

Campgrounds
Petit Byahaut   **$160–$310**   ★★
Petit Byahaut Bay, ☎ *(784) 457-7008, FAX (784) 457-7008.*
Website: www.outahere.com/petitbyahaut. E-mail: trio@mcw.gov.vc.
Closed Date: July–October.

Single: $160–$190. Double: $250–$310.

Nature-lovers used to roughing it at U.S. campgrounds will feel pampered at this solar-powered haven, located three miles north of Kingstown in a secluded and unspoiled 50-acre valley that descends to a black sand beach. The remote spot has no phone or electricity, and is reached only by boat or trail. Accommodations are in large tents that sit on roofed wooden decks spread around the valley. Each has a queen-size bed and hammock, but little else; the al fresco toilet, sink and sun-warmed shower in back are sheltered by bush (the less-expensive sites share a toilet and shower). Rates include all meals and some watersports; diving is extra, as are drinks—dinner is served by candlelight overlooking the bay. Snorkeling, diving and kayaking off the beach are excellent. Petit Byahaut is impressively expensive—you're buying the isolation, not the amenities—but it may be just the ticket for well-heeled adventurous types seeking an offbeat alternative. Credit cards: not accepted.

Where to Eat

	Fielding's Highest Rated Restaurants in St. Vincent and The Grenadines	
★★★★	**Basil's Bar and Raft**	$15–$32
★★★	**French Restaurant**	$17–$25
★★★	**Gingerbread Cafe**	$13–$18
★★★	**Mac's Pizzeria**	$7–$30
★★★	**Pepperpot**	$10–$15

	Fielding's Most Romantic Restaurants in St. Vincent and the Grenadines	
♥♥♥♥	**Basil's Bar and Raft**	$15–$32
♥♥♥♥	**French Restaurant**	$17–$25
♥♥♥	**Gingerbread Cafe**	$13–$18
♥♥♥	**Mac's Pizzeria**	$7–$30

	Fielding's Best Value Restaurants in St. Vincent and the Grenadines	
★★	**Heron Restaurant**	$5–$10
★★	**Basil's Bar and Restaurant**	$3–$17
★★★	**Gingerbread Cafe**	$13–$18
★★★	**Mac's Pizzeria**	$7–$30
★★★★	**Basil's Bar and Raft**	$15–$32

Where to Eat—St. Vincent

Don't come to St. Vincent for international dining. Though everyone talks about **The French** (as in the French Restaurant), you'll be better off investing in West Indian cuisine, which is reliable and much less expensive.

Specialties include goat stew, fresh seafood, breadfruit dishes and callaloo soup. For a special evening out, try **Young Island**, where a rotating five-course menu is a good deal at $35 per person ($40 for the Wednesday and Saturday night buffet). The food at the new **Camelot Inn** is drawing praise, but dressing up is the order of the day.

Basil's Bar and Restaurant $ ★★

Bay Street, Kingstown, ☎ *(784) 457-2713.* Associated hotel: *Cobblestone Inn.*
Lunch: 10 a.m.–4 p.m., prix fixe $11.
Dinner: 4 p.m.–midnight, entrées $3–$17. Closed: Sun.
Those who can't get to Basil Charles' overwater fantasy in Mustique make the scene at his second hangout. Lunchtime buzzes with hungry diners going back and forth from a tasty buffet. The spread includes salads and desserts, and a la carte burgers, sandwiches, egg dishes, and seafood are also available. Nighttime is more romantic, with candlelit tables and simple grills on the menu, plus French wines at decent prices. There's a Chinese buffet on Friday evenings. Credit cards: A, MC, V.

French Restaurant $$$ ★★★

Villa Beach, Kingstown, ☎ *(784) 458-4972.* Associated hotel: *Umbrella Beach Hotel.*
Lunch: Noon–2 p.m., entrées $8–$10.
Dinner: 7–9:30 p.m., entrées $17–$25. Closed: Sun.
Behind a homey white picket fence lies an informal French restaurant that is pleasing in its simplicity. Guests sit on plain folding chairs, feet planted on rough wooden floors in a windowless structure open to salty breezes. Succulent lobster couldn't get much fresher, retrieved as they are live from an on-site pool—the Parisian chef serves the juicy crustaceans flambeed in brandy, sliced in crepes, or broiled. Other items pale in comparison, but include a variety of fish offerings in traditional French sauces, all prepared with island-grown herbs and spices. The dining room overlooks Villa Beach and Young Island. Reservations recommended. Credit cards: A, MC, V.

Heron Restaurant $ ★★

Upper Bay Street, Kingstown, ☎ *(784) 457-1631.* Associated hotel: *Heron Hotel.*
Lunch: Noon–1:30 p.m., entrées $5–$10.
Dinner: 7–10 p.m., prix fixe $5–$10. Closed: Sat., Sun.
A friendly local couple run this budget restaurant that's popular for American bacon and eggs breakfasts. Lunch features soups, salads, and sandwiches, and a soup-to-nuts supper is served daily for a set price (reservations required). Market fresh vegetables are a standout.

Pepperpot $ ★★★

Villa, ☎ *(784) 457-4337.*
Lunch: Noon–4 p.m., entrées $10–$15.
Dinner: 4–11 p.m., entrées $10–$15. Closed: Wed.
An inspired menu of regional favorites is offered here, keyed by the flags of various Caribbean nations. The smorgasbord of tastes includes black bean soup from Cuba, jerk chicken from Jamaica, and pepperpot from Guyana, plus less typical choices like Uncle Gringo's chicken salad from Montserrat, and grilled fish in passionfruit sauce from Dominica. St. Vincent's national dish—Bul Jol—is also featured. Less adventurous types can stick with pizza, but all will enjoy the view of bobbing yachts and Young Island. Live music on Monday and Friday nights in season. Credit cards: MC, V.

The Grenadines

Bequia offers many dive challenges.

Bequia

Other Grenadines may offer prettier beaches, tonier resorts or a more escapist air, but none have the bucolic sweetness of Bequia (pronounced beckwee), located nine miles south of St. Vincent. The largest and most populated of St. Vincent's Grenadines, six-square-mile Bequia has a spindly shape indented by several bays, the most scenic being Admiralty Bay, overlooked by the main village, Port Elizabeth. Because it is low (about 800 feet at its highest) and small, there is no rainforest environment, but an array of crops are grown here, including pigeon peas, cassava, citrus fruits, mango and Bequia plums.

The ferry dock in Port Elizabeth buzzes throughout the day, yachts anchor and the town hums with simple commerce, much of which is tourist oriented, particularly since 1992, when the island's airstrip opened for business (though from St. Vincent, most still arrive by ferry). Visitors will quickly note that Bequia, like the other Grenadines, is anything but action-packed.

There are a few music bars in Port Elizabeth (check out the jump-up at the **Reef and Harpoon Saloon**), but otherwise days are filled with watersports (available at the main hotels), casual exploration and even a little shopping. **Sergeants Model Boat Shop** sells handcrafted wooden boats by wood carver

Lawson Sergeant; **Noah's Arcade** sells locally crafted pottery, batiks and woven goods; the **Bequia Bookshop** has a small but fine collection of maps, books and photographic supplies. All three of these (and most other) shops are located in Port Elizabeth. Just south of the dock is the **Frangipani Hotel**, birthplace of current Prime Minister Sir James Mitchell; the Frangi (as everyone calls it) and the **Gingerbread Restaurant** next door are an essential island hub that everyone passes through at least once during their visit.

A second town, **Paget Farm** (also known as Derrick), was once the center of Bequia's whaling interests. Athneal Ollivierre, a local folk hero known as the Last Harpooner, lives here and has a small museum devoted to the dying practice of whaling under oar and sail (the last harpooning was more than a decade ago, by Ollivierre)—the whaling station on Petit Nevis is visible a mile off the southern coast of Bequia. Another site worth visiting is **Moonhole**, a 100-foot natural arch on the westernmost tip of Bequia. More notable than the arch is the twenty home development built into the rock by Tom Johnston in the 1960s—he utilized the natural contours of the cliff to create his handsome and unique dwellings.

There are five main beaches on the island, the best of which is **Lower Bay**, Bequia's longest runway of sand and located at the south end of Admiralty Bay—several beach bars, including **De Reef**, keep things upbeat, but the atmosphere is usually as tranquil as the sea is calm here. Next door, **Princess Margaret Beach** (aka Tony Gibbons Beach) is tucked behind a bluff closer to town—there is no development here, and it's no more than a ten-minute walk using the short trail from the Plantation House. On the east side of Bequia are **Friendship Bay**, **Hope Bay** and **Industry Bay**, which offer decent swimming and sunning. Snorkeling is good around Moonhole and at reef-protected Park Bay, where a light current will carry you next door to Industry Bay; for diving information, see "Underwater" earlier in this chapter.

Where to Stay

Lodging in Bequia is geared for total relaxation. Each property is unique and exudes a certain personal ambiance.

Hotels and Resorts

Plantation House	$126–$369	★★★

Admiralty Bay, ☎ *(784) 458-3425, FAX (784) 458-3612.*
Single: $126–$277. Double: $171–$369.
Located on a 10-acre spread at the edge of Port Elizabeth, this French-managed resort centers around a pretty, colonial-style house wrapped by a wide veranda on three sides—a nice place for people-watching and harbor-gazing. Rooms are in the modern main house or in sweet cottages set back from the short, narrow beach. All are attractively decorated, air-conditioned and comfortable, if somewhat spare. There's a pool, tennis court and beach bar on the premises, and a dive shop and watersports center (rates include non-motorized watersports and mountain bikes).

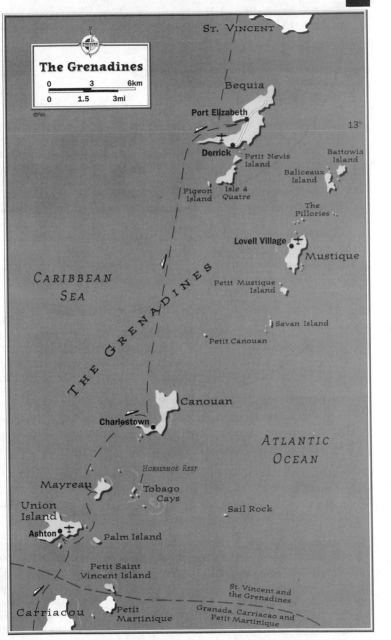

N

The Grenadines

| 0 | 3 | 6km |
| 0 | 1.5 | 3mi |

©FWA

ST. VINCENT

Bequia

Port Elizabeth

13°

Derrick

Petit Nevis Island

Battowia Island

Baliceaux Island

Pigeon Island

Isle à Quatre

The Pillories

Lovell Village

Mustique

CARIBBEAN SEA

Petit Mustique Island

THE GRENADINES

Savan Island

Petit Canouan

Canouan

Charlestown

ATLANTIC OCEAN

HORSESHOE REEF

Mayreau

Tobago Cays

Sail Rock

Union Island

Ashton

Palm Island

Petit Saint Vincent Island

St. Vincent and the Grenadines

Carriacou

Petit Martinique

Granada, Carriacao and Petit Martinique

Pleasant and nicely designed, Plantation House is Bequia's most upscale property and caters to a Euro clientele, yet uneven management has been an issue for some guests. Still, a good if pricey spot for families. 27 rooms. Credit cards: A, MC, V.

Inns

Frangipani Hotel $30–$150   ★★

Port Elizabeth, ☎ *(784) 458-3255, FAX (784) 458-3824.*
E-mail: Frangi@caribsurf.com.
Single: $30–$130. Double: $40–$150.

This West Indian inn dates back to 1920 when it was the family home of the island's current prime minister. The least-expensive rooms are guesthouse style, in the main house, one of which was Sir Mitchell's as a young boy (he is still a part owner and stops by frequently). These charmers share a pair of bathrooms and a deck that overlooks Admiralty Bay. Newer units are up on the hill, with lovely Guyanese teak or Italian tile floors, stone walls and four-poster beds draped with mosquito netting; ceiling fans keep things cool. There's no pool, but the beach is a 10-minute walk. A good restaurant and bar (a local hangout), tennis court and watersports center are available. No overstated luxury here, but casual types will love the ambiance. 15 rooms. Credit cards: A, D, MC, V.

Old Fort Country Inn $90–$160   ★★

Mount Pleasant, ☎ *(784) 458-3440, FAX (784) 457-3340.*
Single: $90–$120. Double: $130–$160.

This unique, hilltop inn occupies a fortified plantation house built by the French in 1765 or earlier, making it possibly the oldest structure on the island. Otmar Schaedle, a German history and music professor, bought the estate as a holiday house for his family, but fell in love with Bequia and decided to turn it into a guest house. The atmosphere is not for everyone: children and animals scamper about, rooms are rustic, and the beach is a long walk down the hill. But for travelers content to share time and space with a happy family, Old Fort is a welcome home away from home. The pleasant rooms are filled with local and tasteful European art—the unit on the top floor is the best—and views soar for miles (you can see Grenada on a clear day). The dining room is one of the island's best with Billie Holiday and classical music playing throughout the day, there's a modest pool, and the Schaedles will assist with excursions. A happy find for anyone who's ever enjoyed a European country inn. 6 rooms. Credit cards: MC, V.

Spring on Bequia $50–$205   ★★

Spring Estate, ☎ *(784) 458-3414, FAX (784) 457-3305.*
Closed Date: Mid-June through October.
Single: $50–$175. Double: $70–$205.

A mile outside Port Elizabeth is pastoral, 28-acre Spring Estate, a former coconut plantation that is now home to a languid and romantic 10-room inn. The distinctive architecture is more Frank Lloyd Wright than West Indian—the floors, walls and showers are made of hand-cut bluebitch stone with wood furnishings in a Scandinavian style. A hammock yawns across the stone terrace of each unit—views look down onto Spring Bay a few hundred yards away. There's a tennis court and an elegant pool (largest on the island), and the Sunday curry buffet is a popular hit. Din ner is by candlelight; a full English breakfast is also available. Otherwise, this tranquil spot is a refuge for lovers who enjoy longing gazes, board games and the comfy retreat of a good book. The booking office in Minneapolis is at ☎ *(612) 823-1202.* 10 rooms. Credit cards: A, DC, D, MC, V.

Where to Eat

No great claims to chefdom here, but do get ready for home-style island cooking with lots of fresh seafood. Most of the eating places are along the waterfront within walking distance of each other.

Gingerbread Cafe   **$$**   ★★★
Gingerbread Complex, ☎ *(784) 458-3800.*
Lunch: Noon–2 p.m., entrées $4–$10.
Dinner: 7:30–6:30 p.m., entrées $13–$18.
This cute Hansel and Gretelish stone cottage is the place to go for Italian coffees, fresh limeade and fruit juices, and the appropriate cakes and breads to go with them. Sit here at leisure all day at an outdoor table with a book and gaze out at the activity in the harbor. Next door, the Gingerbread Restaurant serves tasty meals highlighted by curry, the house specialty, prepared with chicken, beef, fish or shrimp, and with appropriate sides of mango chutney, banana raita, etc. Credit cards: A, MC, V.

Mac's Pizzeria   **$$**   ★★★
Box 23, Belmont Beach, ☎ *(784) 458-3474.*
Lunch: 11 a.m.–4 p.m., entrées $7–$30.
Dinner: 4–10 p.m., entrées $7–$30. Closed: Mon.
Bequia veterans daydream about the 15-inch lobster pizzas that this terraced restaurant is famous for. Besides the pies, quiches, salads and sandwiches, Mac's home-bakes all its scrumptious breads and bakery goods, and the banana bread, plump with raisins and flavored with rum, is especially delicious. The menu also features East Indian samosas (fried pastries stuffed with curried vegetables or meats), crunchy conch nuggets, and chunky pita bread sandwiches. Though Mac passed away, this place remains a winner. Credit cards: MC, V.

Mustique

Ultra-posh Mustique is more famous than actually visited, and the owners of the 70 or so smashing villas here—Mick Jagger, Raquel Welch, Princess Margaret, et al—are no doubt happy to keep it that way. Though fabulously expensive, it is nonetheless quite accessible, to those who can afford it.

The genesis of Mustique's present-day jet setter community date back to 1958, when Scotsman Colin Tennant, who was entranced by the two-square-mile island's rolling hills and glimmering beaches, bought it for entertaining royalty and friends. The purchase price: reportedly about $100,000. At the time, about 100 people lived on Mustique in a dilapidated hamlet called Cheltenham (near the location of today's Cotton House), and had a meager existence based on farming and fishing. Tennant had a master-stroke when he gave England's Princess Margaret a 10-acre plot as a wedding gift in 1960—the whimsical present would later become a catalyst for the island's fame. Within a few years, Tennant had built a new village for the inhabitants, a sea island cotton plantation was started, and Mustique flirted with self-sufficiency. In 1968, however, Tennant created the Mustique Company, which entered into an agreement with the St. Vincent government to develop the island for tourism and private homes, to be limited to 140 estates. An airstrip was built, the first villas were constructed, and famed British theatrical designer Oliver Messel helped to create Cotton House, still the only hotel on the island (there is also a four-room guest house). Some of Mustique has been left wild, while other parts are manicured—the villas (some also designed by Messel) are spread throughout the island

Today, exclusivity and a kind of managed serenity reign on Mustique. There is no scheduled plane or ferry service for travelers, effectively keeping the daytripping riff raff at bay (though a private ferry owned by the Mustique Company, the **Robert Junior**, transports employees to and from Kingstown daily). There is a fine restaurant at **Cotton House**, and another at **Firefly**, but **Basil's** is the place to be seen. Beach lovers will find a handful of sandy treasures—**Macaroni Bay** is the loveliest. Exploring on foot will occupy a leisurely day or two, but otherwise, organized activities are few and far between.

At present, 52 of the villas are available for weekly rentals; all come with cook and maid, and most have a private pool and *Architectural Digest* pedigree. Options range from two- and three-bedroom villas that start at $2500 per week in summer, and $4000 in winter, to Princess Margaret's six-bedroom **Les Jolies Eaux**, which starts at $7000 per week in summer (all rates subject to five percent government tax and an eight percent administrative fee; credit cards are accepted). For reservations, call **Resorts Management** ☎ *(800) 225-4255* or *(212) 696-4566.*

Where to Stay

Cotton House   **$190–$1500**   ★★★★

Mustique, ☎ *(800) 223-1108, (784) 456-4777, FAX (784) 456-5887.*
Single: $190–$790. Double: $290–$890. Suites Per Day: $490–$1500.
Built on the remains of an old sugar plantation, this hotel underwent an overhaul in 1997 that has taken it from its former restrained polish to a tony little operation worthy of the most primped Mustique customers—with the prices to prove it. Guests are accommodated in tasteful cottages on a gentle rise set back from a beach; standard guestrooms, junior suites, or full suites are available, all poshly decorated and sporting balconies or patios. The roster of in-room amenities includes a CD player, minibar and fridge. The grounds are beautifully manicured, with hammocks dangling everywhere and oversized cushions dappling the lawn—perfect for an afternoon tea. There is a pool surrounded by Romanesque columns, two tennis courts and a fine beach. Cotton House is also home to a highly regarded and

revamped restaurant and bar that draws the locals. Now operated by the Mustique Company, a recent management shake-up is behind them and the well-heeled should once again be coddled with finesse. The rates are all-inclusive and cover select watersports, laundry service on arrival, all meals and drinks; a room-only rate also is available in low season. 20 rooms. Credit cards: A, DC, MC, V.

Firefly   **$200–$250**   ★ ★ ★
Mustique, ☎ *(784) 456-3414, FAX (784) 456-4565.*
Single: $200–$250. Double: $200–$250.
Part guest house, part social hub, part secret hideaway, Firefly is the black sheep of Mustique, and all the better for it. The establishment is a three-story stone house built against a hill—the restaurant and bar occupies the top floor (where guests enter), with rooms down below. Each of the four units are a little different (two are a bit tight), but are open on one side to the view—one even has a stone shower platform that is suspended above the pool; the nearest beach is a ten-minute walk. Each room has a balcony or patio and three contain four-poster beds; all are fan-cooled. Firefly's new owners, Stan and Elizabeth Clayton, have remodeled the rooms and restaurant beautifully, but kept the special mix of informality and exclusivity that has always been a Firefly trademark. Rates include a full breakfast. 4 rooms. Credit cards: A, MC, V.

Where to Eat

Basil's Bar and Raft   **$$$**   ★ ★ ★ ★
Britannia Bay, ☎ *(784) 458-4621.*
Lunch: entrées $11–$28.
Dinner: entrées $15–$32.
A watering hole with one of the loveliest settings anywhere, Basil's is not just a bar—it's a way of life. This unique establishment is a thatch-roofed structure built over the pale turquoise waters of Britannia Bay. Owner Basil Charles has a great thing going—it's the only nightlife spot on Mustique and everyone ends up here sooner or later, including titled lords and ladies, *People* magazine cover girls and rock-and-roll boys. There's good seafood served daily along with lamb chops, chicken satay, or come for the ever-popular "Wenz-d-night" barbecue ($28, or $32 with lobster); jazz sometimes on Sunday afternoons. It's open from 8 a.m. until the last guest goes home. Credit cards: A, MC, V.

Canouan

Located some 25 miles south of St. Vincent and slinking tentatively into a tourism economy for the last two decades, Canouan boasts pearlescent white sand beaches fringed by coral reefs. The dry and scrubby island is dominated by cacti and acacia—the highest point is Mount Royal (877 feet). The main settlement, Charlestown, sits next to a sliver of airstrip. A Swiss firm has leased almost two-thirds of the three-square-mile island for an ambitious hotel, condo and golf course development that is slowly wending its way toward completion. With a population of just 768, the island's character is in the throws of evolution.

Where to Stay

Tamarind Beach Hotel   **$160–$300**   ★★★

Canouan, ☎ (800) 223-1108, (784) 458-8044, FAX (784) 458-8851.
E-mail: cantbh@caribsurf.com.
Single: $160–$240. Double: $220–$300.

Canouan's main resort is this modern and attractive European venture that opened in 1995 and is just now finding its footing in the outback of the Grenadines. Guest rooms are in three two-story buildings that open onto the beach—each has wood paneling, rattan furnishings and breezy balconies, with extras like in-room safes and hair dryers. The restaurant is in one of two palapa-roofed buildings and serves reliable Italian cuisine from a Milanese chef. Sunfish and windsurfing equipment is included; the management will help put together diving and day sails. Rates are MAP and include breakfast and dinner. Credit cards: A, MC, V.

Union Island

Of the Grenadines, four-square-mile Union Island was awarded the lion's share of topographical personality—its profile of ridges and peaks is unmistakable from a distance, rising dramatically to 999-foot Mt. Toboi. The 1514 islanders live primarily in Ashton, though nearby Clifton is the hub of activity, particularly for the yachties who frequent this outpost—a small airport opened here in 1993. Though Union has beaches, the two best, **Chatham Bay** and **Bloody Bay**, are accessible only by boat or on foot. The island is not the most appealing of Grenadines (it is considered a transshipment point for northbound drugs, one reason the U.S. has built a Coast Guard facility on nearby Petit Martinique), but Union serves as a good base for daytrips to the Tobago Cays, Mayreau and Palm Island, all of which can be arranged through the several hotels.

Where to Stay

Anchorage Yacht Club   **$100–$165**   ★★

Union Island, ☎ (784) 458-8221, FAX (784) 458-8365.
Single: $100–$165. Double: $100–$165.

Most who come to this motel-like property are en route to the Grenadines, though this French-owned spot is a pleasant place to spend your vacation. Guestrooms are spacious and air conditioned and have nice harbor views off the balconies. The twice-weekly jump-ups are well attended; the fine restaurant and bar keep guests occupied with local gossip the rest of the time. The hotel sits right on a nice beach, where a dive shop handles watersports rentals. There's also a shark pool on the premises, as well as a busy marina. 10 rooms. Credit cards: D, MC, V.

Grenadine Resort Islands

Barefoot fantasies are brought to life on three small islands in the southern Grenadines: **Palm Island**, **Petit St. Vincent** and **Mayreau**. Their common calling card—gently rustling palms and inviting white-sand beaches—draw yachtsmen and the occasional smaller cruise ship. The first two spots were built in the 1960s by inspired entrepreneurs who still run them today—they remain popular places to escape from the pressures of life, though they appeal to a different clientele (Palm is more rustic and laid-back while PSV, as everyone calls it, is decidedly upscale).

Mayreau (pronounced My-ro), the largest island of the three, has a population of 189 that shares their island with its sole resort, the **Saltwhistle Bay Club**. There are two restaurants here, **Dennis' Hideaway** ☎ *(784) 458-8594*, a down-home establishment where the owner plays guitar several nights a week, and **Island Paradise** ☎ *(784) 458-8068*, which is located on a hill and offers wonderful sunset views. Excellent diving is found off Mayreau, and the beautiful Tobago Cays are nearby.

Each of these islands is connected to the world through Union Island, and although scheduled air service is available to Union from St. Vincent and Grenada, you may find passage via Barbados is the easiest route (have your travel agent check all the options carefully to avoid spending more time in transit than on the beach). For information on Young Island, see "Hotels and Resorts" in the St. Vincent section.

Where to Stay

Palm Island Beach Club   **$174–$415**   ★★★

Palm Island, ☎ (800) 999-7256, (784) 458-8824, FAX (784) 458-8804.
Website: www.palmislandresorts.com. E-mail: palm@caribsurf.com.
Closed Date: September.
Single: $174–$295. Double: $270–$415.
This private, 130-acre paradise is still called Prune Island on a few maps, but that name is left over from before John Caldwell came ashore and planted a few thousand palms. After requesting an official name change, he and his family built a low-key resort that remains popular for its lovely grounds and fine hospitality. Accommodations are in rustic stone and wood duplex cottages, each very comfortable and cooled by ceiling fans. Palm Island boasts a bevy of beaches, including Casuarina—one of the Grenadines' best—but note that the spot is visited by smaller cruise ships and yachts. Complimentary watersports include windsurfing, Sunfish and snorkel gear; diving can be arranged. There's a tennis court, and a nature trail (named "Highway 90") winds around the island, but otherwise, activities are of the do-it-yourself type. Rates include three meals daily; Palm Island is reached by 10-minute water taxi from Union Island. 24 rooms. Credit cards: A, D, MC, V.

Petit St. Vincent Resort $385–$770   ★★★★

Petit St. Vincent, ☎ (800) 854-9326, (784) 458-8801, FAX (513) 242-6951.
Closed Date: September–October.
Single: $385–$600. Double: $490–$770.

Known to aficionados simply as PSV, this private island resort is surrounded by ravishing white beaches and a gin clear sea. Accommodations are in 22 large one-bedroom wood and bluebitch stone cottages sprinkled around one end of the 113-acre island. Regulars have their favorites, but note that units 6–13 step right onto the main beach, while 16–19 are clustered above a "private" dollop of sand; 20–22 trade instant beach access for lovely views. The cottages vaunt sun terraces, cool terra-cotta tile floors and luxurious bathrooms with handsome stone showers. Each comes equipped with a PSV trademark flagpole—if you want room service, hoist the yellow flag, if you prefer to be left alone, raise the red one. The steep rates include Hobie Cats and Sunfish, windsurfing and snorkeling equipment; diving, waterskiing and deep sea fishing are extra but can be arranged. There's also a tennis court and fitness trail; the restaurant serves solid, sometimes adventurous cuisine (meals are included in the rates, but drinks are extra). Once a week dinner is a beach barbecue with a local band from a neighboring island. The resort celebrates its 30th year in 1998 and continues to lure an upscale, sophisticated crowd in search of those rare commodities: privacy and seclusion. The island is reached via 20-minute boat ride from Union Island. 22 rooms. Credit cards: A, MC, V.

Saltwhistle Bay Club $200–$450   ★★★

Mayreau, ☎ (800) 999-7256, (784) 458-8444, FAX (784) 458-8944.
Single: $200–$300. Double: $300–$450.

This casual hideaway is Mayreau's only lodging choice, tucked into a 22-acre estate of palm and sea grape trees. Guests are housed in spacious, yet rustic one-bedroom stone bungalows that rely on ceiling fans to keep things cool. The setting is idyllic—lovely tropical grounds unroll to an amazing beach and a crystal-clear sea that is well-appreciated by divers. Facilities include a bar, restaurant, and a few watersports are free of charge (scuba and catamaran excursions to neighboring islands are extra). Though you can walk to Station Hill (the island's sole hamlet—population, about 200), there's virtually nothing in the way of nightlife; Saltwhistle Bay has an early-to-bed, early-to-rise barefoot charm. Rates are MAP, and include breakfast and dinner daily. 10 rooms. Credit cards: A, MC, V.

Where to Shop

St. Vincent is not a duty-free port, so don't come expecting great bargains on imported merchandise. Some things to look out for are colorful batiks and tie-died fabrics at **Batik Caribe** *(Wallilabou Bay, ☎ (784) 458-7270)*, and woven items, wood carvings, books and other locally made crafts at **St. Vincent Craftsmen** *(James Street, Kingstown, ☎ (784) 457-1288)*. **Noah's Arcade**

(Bay Street, Kingstown, ☎ *(784) 457-1513)* has a good selection of local arts and handiworks; they also have a shop on Bequia at Port Elizabeth ☎ *(784) 458-3424).* If you're a stamp collector, you'll love **St. Vincent Philatelic Services** *(Lower Bay Street, Kingstown,* ☎ *(784) 457-1911),* the Caribbean's largest bureau. Note that stores usually close from noon to 1:00 for lunch.

St. Vincent and the Grenadines Directory

Arrival and Departure

St. Vincent and the Grenadines became a link closer to North America with the introduction of daily **American Eagle** service to the small airport outside Kingstown in 1996. These flights originate in San Juan, Puerto Rico, allowing easy connections from a number of cities via **American Airlines** and other carriers. However, other routes are still worth investigating, including via Barbados and Grenada (both of which have direct air service to the U.S.), particularly if you are going on to the Grenadines—Bequia, Mustique, Union Island and Canouan all have small air strips with scheduled and/or charter service available. **LIAT** provides nonstop or direct service to St. Vincent from Antigua, Barbados, Dominica, Grenada, St. Lucia, Tobago and Trinidad, with flights to Union Island from St. Vincent and Grenada. Airlines that serve the Grenadines from St. Vincent, Barbados and Grenada include **Airlines of Carriacou** ☎ *(473) 444-1475*, **St. Vincent Grenadines Air** ☎ *(784) 456-5610* and **Mustique Airways** ☎ *(784) 458-4380.* For information about ferry travel to the Grenadines from St. Vincent, see "Getting Around," below.

The departure tax is $8.

Business Hours

Most shops open weekdays 8 a.m.–noon and 1–4 p.m., Saturday 8 a.m.–noon. Banks open Monday–Thursday 8 a.m.–1 or 3 p.m. and Friday 8 a.m.–5 p.m. Some banks take a two-hour break from 1–3 p.m. on Friday.

Climate

Temperatures all year round average 78–80 degrees Fahrenheit, cooled by gentle northeast trade window. Rain is heavier in the mountains of St. Vincent than in the Grenadines, which are generally flatter.

Documents

U.S. and Canadian citizens must have a passport; all visitors must hold return or ongoing tickets. Visas are not required.

Electricity

Current runs 220/40 v. 50 cycles.

Getting Around

Island roads are like roller coasters, with potholes providing additional navigational excitement—driving is on the left. Unless you have an international drivers license, a local license is necessary, about $15; **car rentals** start at about $50 per day. No American firms are represented on St. Vincent; try **David's** in

Kingstown ☎ *(784) 456-4026* or **UNICO Auto Rentals** at the airport ☎ *(784) 456-5744*. If driving conditions sound daunting, you may be better off hiring a taxi or obtaining a guided tour.

Sample **taxi** fares are $8 from the St. Vincent airport to Villa or Kingstown. It's also possible to hop on a **local bus**—most routes start or end in Kingstown and fares within the Kingstown-Villa area are less than a dollar; fares as far as Georgetown or Richmond are less than $3.

Trips to **Bequia**, **Canouan**, **Mayreau** and **Union Island** from St. Vincent are easy, either by air (see "Arrival and Departure," above) or sea. The latter choice is an inexpensive way to see the Grenadines, but it's not a good option for anyone prone to seasickness. The four main vessels that head south from Kingstown include the *MV Barracuda*, *MV Admiral I* and *II*, and *Coasta de Gale*, each of which has a weekly schedule, available from the Department of Tourism. Between the four ships, the one-hour crossing to Bequia is served several times daily ($4 each way, $5 on weekends). Scheduled service to the southern islands is less frequent, but each is reached several times a week. It pays to study a ferry schedule carefully to plan an island-hopping itinerary; the longest trip, St. Vincent to Union Island, takes four hours on a nonstop ferry, or ten hours on one that calls at several islands en-route.

Of the private islands, **Young Island** is reached by a tiny shuttle from Villa Beach that makes the two-minute crossing continuously throughout the day and evening. **Mustique** is reached by air only (and frowns on daytrippers); **Petit St. Vincent** and **Palm Island** welcome day visitors at the discretion of the management. The easiest way to reach some of the smaller islands is via chartered boat: **Fantasea Tours** is based at Villa Beach and does private or group tours of the Grenadines by speedboat ☎ *(784) 457-4477*.

Language

English is spoken everywhere, often with a Vincentian patois or dialect.

Medical Emergencies

The government **General Hospital** ☎ *(764) 456-1185*, is located at the west end of Kingstown. There is also **Bequia Casualty Hospital** at Port Elizabeth. Serious emergencies require airlift to Barbados or San Juan, Puerto Rico.

Money

The official currency is the Eastern Caribbean dollar, called the "EC" locally. The exchange rate is tied to U.S. currency at $2.70 for one American dollar. Most hotels, restaurants and shops accept U.S. dollars, but you'll get your best rate of exchange at a bank, or by using a credit card.

Telephone

The new area code for St. Vincent and the Grenadines, scheduled to replace the old *(809)* code soon after we go to press, is *(784)*. To call St. Vincent from the U.S., dial *1 + (784)*, plus the seven-digit local number.

Time

Atlantic Standard Time, one hour ahead of New York time, except during Daylight Saving Time, when it is the same.

Tipping and Taxes

The hotel tax is 10 percent. A 10 percent service charge is added to the bill at most hotels and restaurants.

Tourist Information

The **St. Vincent and the Grenadines Department of Tourism** will send brochures and assist with trip planning. In the U.S., they can be reached at ☎ *(212) 687-4981* or *(800) 729-1726*. The main office in St. Vincent is located in Kingstown ☎ *(784) 457-1502*. There is also an office in Bequia ☎ *(784) 458-3286* and in Clifton Harbour on Union Island.

Web Site

www.vincy.com

When to Go

Easterval is a Union Island Easter weekend festivity, with boat races, cultural shows and a calypso competition. The same weekend also features the **Bequia Easter Regatta**, which draws competitors from throughout the region with yacht races, sports and games. The first Monday in May is **Fisherman's Day**, a Kingstown event dedicated to local fisherman, with various competitions. **Carnival**, or **Vincy Mas**, is celebrated in Kingstown the last week of June and first week of July, with street dancing, a costumed masquerade, steel band and calypso competitions and a beauty pageant. The **Canouan Annual Yacht Race** is a week-long sailing event held on Canouan in early August; highlights include fishing competitions, greasy pig and donkey races, cricket matches and calypso competitions. **Nine Mornings** is held during the nine days preceding **Christmas Day**, with parades, bicycle races, caroling and stringbands.

ST. VINCENT AND THE GRENADINES HOTELS	RMS	RATES	PHONE	CR. CARDS
St. Vincent				
★★★★ **Young Island Resort**	30	$210–$640	(800) 223-1108	A, D, MC, V
★★★ **Camelot Inn**	22	$225–$275	(800) 223-6510	A, MC, V
★★★ **Grand View Beach Hotel**	19	$104–$270	(800) 223-6510	A, DC, MC, V
★★ **Lagoon Marina and Hotel**	19	$65–$95	(800) 742-4276	A, MC, V
★★ **Petit Byahaut**	7	$160–$310	(784) 457-7008	None
★★ **Sunset Shores Beach Hotel**	32	$90–$140	(800) 223-6510	A, D, MC, V
★★ **Villa Lodge Hotel**	10	$95–$120	(784) 458-4641	A, D, MC, V
★ **Beachcombers Hotel**	13	$60–$80	(784) 458-4283	A, D, MC, V
★ **Heron Hotel**	15	$45–$59	(784) 457-1631	D, MC, V
★ **Umbrella Beach Hotel**	9	$42–$62	(784) 458-4651	A, DC, MC, V

ST. VINCENT AND THE GRENADINES

ST. VINCENT AND THE GRENADINES HOTELS	RMS	RATES	PHONE	CR. CARDS
Bequia				
★★★ Plantation House	27	$126–$369	(784) 458-3425	A, MC, V
★★ Frangipani Hotel	15	$30–$150	(784) 458-3255	A, D, MC, V
★★ Old Fort Country Inn	6	$90–$160	(784) 458-3440	MC, V
★★ Spring on Bequia	10	$50–$205	(784) 458-3414	A, D, DC, MC, V
Mustique				
★★★★ Cotton House	20	$190–$890	(800) 223-1108	A, DC, MC, V
★★★ Firefly	4	$200–$250	(784) 456-3414	A, MC, V
Canouan				
★★★ Tamarind Beach Hotel		$160–$300	(800) 223-1108	A, MC, V
Union Island				
★★ Anchorage Yacht Club	10	$100–$165	(784) 458-8221	D, MC, V
Grenadine Resort Islands				
★★★★ Petit St. Vincent Resort	22	$385–$770	(800) 854-9326	A, MC, V
★★★ Palm Island Beach Club	24	$174–$415	(800) 999-7256	A, D, MC, V
★★★ Saltwhistle Bay Club	10	$200–$450	(800) 999-7256	A, MC, V

ST. VINCENT AND THE GRENADINES RESTAURANTS	PHONE	ENTRÉE	CR. CARDS
St. Vincent			
French Cuisine			
★★★ French Restaurant, The	(784) 458-4972	$8–$25	A, MC, V
Regional Cuisine			
★★ Basil's Bar and Restaurant	(784) 457-2713	$11–$17	A, MC, V
★★★ Pepperpot	(784) 457-4337	$10–$15	MC, V
★★ Cobblestone Roof Top	(784) 456-1937	$5–$6	A, MC, V
★★ Heron Restaurant	(784) 457-1631	$5–$10	
Bequia			
★★★ Gingerbread Cafe	(784) 458-3800	$4–$18	A, MC, V
★★★ Mac's Pizzeria	(784) 458-3474	$7–$30	MC, V
Mustique			
★★★★ Basil's Bar and Raft	(784) 458-4621	$11–$32	A, MC, V

TOBAGO

The quiet turquoise waters of Tobago are great for snorkeling.

The sister island of nearby Trinidad, Tobago is a verdant, languid jewel in the Caribbean. Of the two, Tobago is where tourism is more developed, though it remains quiet and laid-back, even by Caribbean standards. People visit these two islands for different reasons. On Trinidad, the rhythms and harmonies of steel pan bands set the pace, artists and playwrights are nurtured, and the spice of East Indian curry wafts through its restaurants. On quiet Tobago, ecological resources—gentle green hills navigated by squawking parrots, placid bays populated with manta rays—take the front seat, with cultural assets registering as an also-ran. Tobago is the destination where Trinidadians go when they want to get away from it all (particularly following Carnival). And though the smaller island's economic status continues to play catch-up with Trinidad's relatively prosperous and cosmopolitan life-style, the gap is slowly closing.

A larger percentage of Tobago's visitors are from Europe and South America than most other Caribbean destinations—relatively few Americans (beyond the diving community) are familiar with the island. Yet three expensive, new resorts were built and opened on Tobago in 1995. None of this activity seems to have severely or negatively impacted the quiet, relaxed atmosphere that dominates away from the developed southwestern tip of the island. Forays into the bucolic hills and bays beyond Scarborough and Plymouth, the island's two main population areas, remain an essential and rewarding part of any vacation to Tobago.

BEST BETS FOR...

Bird's-Eye View

Located in the extreme southeastern corner of the Caribbean, just 70 miles off the Venezuelan coast of South America, Tobago is 21 miles from its larger sibling, Trinidad. The island covers 116 square miles—less than a fifteenth the size of Trinidad—and is 27 miles in length, nine miles wide at the center. Although Tobago's high point is only about 1900 feet, the eastern three-quarters of the island is consistently hilly and has very few roads or trails to access the highlands. The northeastern tip of Tobago is where the mountains are steepest and several points are dramatically scooped to provide beautiful coves of sand within the larger Tyrrel's and Man O' War bays on either side of this end of the island. The steep, jungle-like slopes between the two bays are populated by a wide variety of parrots and other birds, while below the surface of the water lie most of the island's best dive sites. The coastline on this end of the island is dotted with fishing villages that drowse in the sun—their brightly painted *pirogues* hauled up on the shore beneath coconut palms and sea grapes. Just inland are farms and plantations of brilliant green—the northern coast between Plymouth and L'Anse Fourmi is a succession of improbably located towns high on the scenic ridges.

The other end of the island has an entirely different appearance. From a geographical standpoint, as one proceeds west from the island's capital, Scarborough, the hills roll along modestly for a few miles, then peter out as on

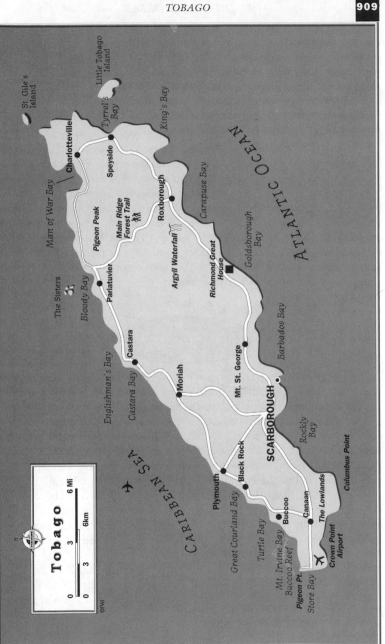

approaches the Lowlands. Additionally, the weather tends to be drier, creating scrublands and coconut groves, rather than the dense jungle found on the other end. The southwestern corner is hemmed by Crown Point and Pigeon Point, and an airport bisects the peninsula. More than half of Tobago's accommodations are located here, and it's the sheer mass of population and increasing development from Scarborough and Plymouth to the west that most defines the bustling character of this end of the island. Elsewhere, Tobago moves along at an unhurried pace.

Several areas have been designated as protected reserves or sanctuaries. The Tobago Forest Reserve is the oldest forest reserve in the western hemisphere, dating back to 1764. Another important sanctuary is Little Tobago Island, which lies just offshore from the fishing village of Speyside. Here can be found important nesting grounds for an enormous number of species, including Audubon's shearwater, the red-footed booby, the sooty fern, the red-billed tropic-bird and at least 600 species of butterflies—a lepidopterist's dream. The Buccoo Reef off Pigeon Point is now protected, but a fair amount of damage has been done to the coral; enforcement of environmental laws on Tobago is somewhat haphazard.

History

Most historians believe Tobago was discovered in 1498 by Columbus, who supposedly dubbed it "Bella Forma" (beautiful form). Its present name was derived from the word tobacco, which the native Caribs cultivated. In 1641, a Baltic duke received permission to settle a number of Courlanders on the north side of the island, but the Dutch took over in 1658, remaining in control until 1662. For the next few centuries, the island changed hands at least a dozen times among world powers who considered Tobago a treasure. Not only the Dutch, but the French and English fought each other for control, not to mention pirate invasions and settlers from Latvia. The conflicts formed the stuff of legends. Bloody Bay, on the island's west coast, earned its name after a 17th-century clash between combined French and Dutch forces against a British fleet (the latter was the victor). History records that the battle was so "sanguinary" that the water became red with blood. In another ferocious struggle, more than 1700 lives were lost in the battle of Roodklyn Bay, fought between the Dutch and the French. Eventually Tobago was declared neutral territory and promptly became a haven for pirates and treasure hunters. (In fact, rumors of treasure still buried on Pirate's Bay abound today.) During the early 19th century, Tobago was a leading contender in the British and French sugarcane industry, producing more sugar per square acre than any other island. When the sugar industry went bust, Tobago also went bankrupt, and in 1888 the island was tacked to nearby Trinidad by a British colonial government that didn't know what to do with it. In 1962, both islands gained independence from Britain and became a republic within the Commonwealth in 1976. Although only about 4 percent of Trinidad and Tobago's 1.3 million population lives on the smaller island, today Tobago has its own 12-seat House of Assembly, which runs many local services. (For more information, see "History" in "Trinidad.")

People

Tobago's population has been on the upswing over the last decade or so, as new resorts have been built and Trinidadians have come over to work them; the current population figure is about 51,000. Unlike Trinidad, where almost half the population is of East Indian background, about 90 percent of Tobagonians are of African descent. Their food, folklore, music and religion are all African-based. Although the official language on both islands is English, it's spoken with a more lilting, softer accent on Tobago. In general, islanders are extremely friendly and helpful, and perhaps because the island's economy depends on tourism, visitors seem to receive special attention. There's less crime here than on Trinidad, as everyone will tell you, but the problems on the larger island (usually tied to drugs) are frequently exaggerated, while those on Tobago are often shrugged off. Take simple precautions with valuables and you are unlikely to encounter any problems.

Trinidad has its Carnival, and Tobago has its Heritage Festival. Held the last two weeks of July, the nostalgic event taps into the history of the island, and features old-time weddings, traditional local music played with fiddles and tambourines, and showcases the complex courting rituals and dances of days gone by. Each village presents one aspect of the island's heritage, showing off its own versatility in music, dance, drama, arts and cooking.

Beaches

The beach most point to as Tobago's best is **Pigeon Point**, one mile north of the Crown Point Airport. It's also where cruise ship passengers are carted to by the hundreds when they dock—hardly an attribute that contributes to making Pigeon Point the Caribbean beach of your dreams. Still, its placid turquoise waters are nice for swimming, the snorkeling on nearby **Buccoo Reef** can be quite good, and sunsets along the coast are often terrific—there's also a quaint, photogenic pier. The peninsula is privately owned, and a fee ($2 per person) is charged for day use; there's a beach bar, picnic tables and huts and full changing facilities available. A half-mile south is **Store Bay**, next to the Coco Reef Resort, a small public beach that can be quite festive, particularly on weekends. This is Tobago's most happening beach, where young Rastas sell local arts and crafts—expect the vibe to be lively.

Coco Reef Resort, Tobago

Continuing the opposite direction along the north coast, two good beaches are watched over by resorts: **Turtle Bay** and **Great Courland Bay**. Both offer good swimming amid calm waters and are clean and well-kept, but can be relatively busy in season. As you continue east along this coast, however, the coves of sand meet fishing villages—frequently idyllic settings. Check out usually-deserted **King Peter's Bay** (accessed by a difficult road), **Englishman's Bay** and **Bloody Bay**. Around the northeastern tip are several prizes, the best being **Pirate's Bay**, reached via a half-mile trail out of Charlotteville. There are similar coves and bays along the southern coast, but the water tends to be rougher as it faces the Atlantic.

Underwater

Unlike the murky reefs of Trinidad, Tobago is an excellent dive location which is only on the cusp of being discovered by Americans. Big pelagics are frequently spotted here, closer to the surface than in most of the Eastern Caribbean, including manta rays, dolphins, and even the occasional hammerhead or whale shark. As on Trinidad, Venezuela's Orinoco River filters freshwater nutrients onto Tobago's reefs, courtesy of the Guyana Current, but usually without the heavy dose of silt found off the larger island. The Orinoco can still limit visibility in the "bad water" rainy season (July through November), but the good news is that the multitude of currents that swirl around Tobago make drift-diving a dependable specialty. On the Atlantic side, currents of up to three knots are a regular occurrence, although the patterns and directions shift constantly, requiring the insight of a local dive operator. The island is not an ideal beginner's destination—not because the diving is difficult, but because some of Tobago's dive shops are staffed by cowboys who can be less than attentive to the needs of neophytes.

The island's best diving is found around **Little Tobago Island** just off Speyside, and along Tobago's **north coast**, although an area referred to as **The Shallows**, in the channel between Trinidad and Tobago, features several excellent advanced dives. **Kelliston Deep** is famous as the location for the world's biggest known brain coral, some 16 feet high. Year-round visibility at Little Tobago averages 80 to 100 feet; on the southern half of the island, expect 50 to 60 feet in the dry season, and 40 or 50 during the rainy season. Sections of famed **Buccoo Reef** have been overused and abused, in part by glass-bottom boat operators who allow visitors to walk on the reef. The result: some of Buccoo is now a heap of dead coral attracting few fish. If you take a snorkel trip to Buccoo, make sure you're visiting its living sections or, better, head for some of the other bays that curl along the island's Caribbean coast. Pirate Bay, just north of Man O' War Bay, is particularly lovely, and **Tyrrel's Bay** (off Speyside) also features spots accessible from the shore.

Dive Shops

Aqua Marine Dive Ltd.
Scarborough; ☎ *(868) 660-4341.*
PADI International Resort, training facility and Five Star operation, based at Blue Waters. Courses available to instructor level. Two-tank dive, $70. Two scheduled dives daily; groups limited to 15.

Dive Tobago, Ltd.
Pigeon Point; ☎ *(868) 639-0202.*
Oldest shop on Tobago (since 1977), catering primarily to Europeans. Three dives daily in small groups of six to eight. Two-tank dive $80 with equipment, or $70 if you bring your own. PADI- and NAUI-affiliated, with certification to Divemaster.

Man Friday Diving
Charlotteville; ☎ *(868) 660-4676.*
Five-year-old, PADI-affiliated shop with courses to Divemaster. Groups limited to six, prefers to work with experienced divers. Two-tank dive, $70.

Tobago Dive Experience
Black Rock and Speyside; ☎ *(868) 639-0191.*
Two-tank dive, $70. PADI- and NAUI-affiliated, with courses to Divemaster. Two locations; the Speyside shop is part of Manta Lodge.

WANDERING ROBINSON CRUSOE'S ISLAND

"I was in an Island environ'd every Way with the Sea, no Land to be seen," wrote Daniel Defoe's hero in the classic tale. Legend has it that Tobago inspired Defoe's writings. Feel like Crusoe yourself as you explore this laid-back neighbor to more sophisticated Trinidad.

Bucco Reef Restricted Area

Situated on the leeward side of Tobago's west end, this proposed marine park is a transitional zone that includes non-Caribbean influences, such as outflow from the Orinoco River. The major reef crests a lagoon, and diving is popular along the outer reef, where depths reach 60 feet.

Arnos Vale

This rustic resort north of Grafton was once a plantation. Set on a hillside, it's a superb place to bird-watch. Look for jacamars, motmots and doves. The reefs beyond the shore are perfect for snorkelers and novice divers.

Pigeon Point

This famous beach is a Caribbean classic—azure water, white sand and a line of royal palms. Swimming is excellent, as is bird-watching in the mangrove lagoon. A fee is charged for entrance; avoid the spot on cruise ship days.

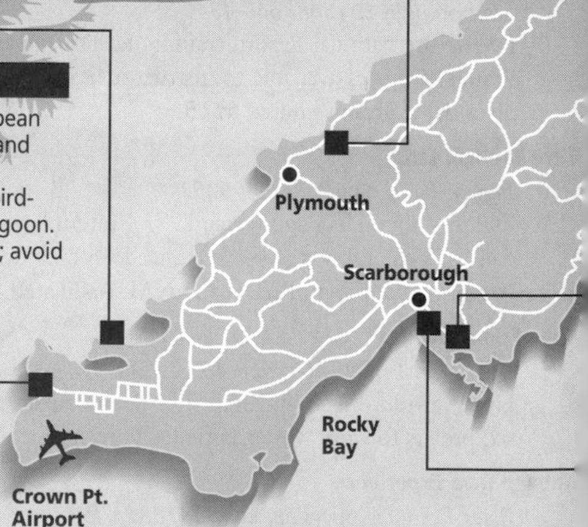

Castara

N

Plymouth

Scarborough

Rocky Bay

Crown Pt. Airport

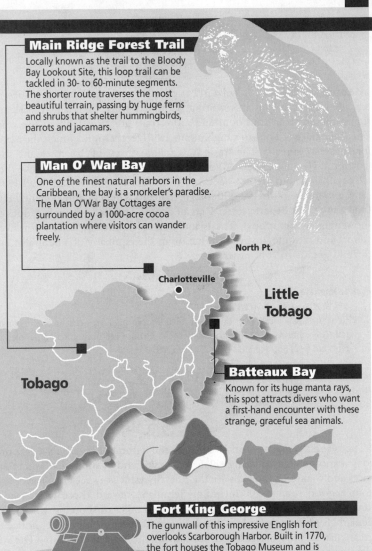

Main Ridge Forest Trail

Locally known as the trail to the Bloody Bay Lookout Site, this loop trail can be tackled in 30- to 60-minute segments. The shorter route traverses the most beautiful terrain, passing by huge ferns and shrubs that shelter hummingbirds, parrots and jacamars.

Man O' War Bay

One of the finest natural harbors in the Caribbean, the bay is a snorkeler's paradise. The Man O'War Bay Cottages are surrounded by a 1000-acre cocoa plantation where visitors can wander freely.

North Pt.

Charlotteville

Little Tobago

Tobago

Batteaux Bay

Known for its huge manta rays, this spot attracts divers who want a first-hand encounter with these strange, graceful sea animals.

Fort King George

The gunwall of this impressive English fort overlooks Scarborough Harbor. Built in 1770, the fort houses the Tobago Museum and is surrounded by immaculate gardens.

Scarborough

No hustle, no bustle, no glitz, no glamour—this island capital exudes the feel of the old-time Caribbean. Soak up the sun and enjoy the charm of this quaint, quiet city.

On Foot

Relaxed and unspoiled, Tobago has plenty of exploration possibilities, but few identified trails at this writing. Coupled with Trinidad, the island is riding the eco-tourism boom and more trails are reportedly in the works. The **Main Ridge** is Tobago's high point, 1890 feet, around which the island's forest reserve spreads. The **Argyle Waterfall**, just west of Roxborough, is well worth the 10-minute walk/wade off the main road (guides will make themselves obvious, but are not necessary). There is a book of trails available locally, and the helpful 1:50,000 map of Tobago is dependably obtained at the **Land and Survey Department** in Port of Spain, Trinidad (though it does not show trails or elevations). The island's complex interior, filled with diverse animal and bird life, invites exploration in the company of a naturalist, who can add greatly to your experience.

Trekking Tours

Pioneer Journeys

☎ *(868) 660-4327 or (868) 660-5175.*

Renson Jack, a local forest ranger, and Pat Turpin organize acclaimed all-day naturalist expeditions into Tobago's wilderness. Groups are limited to 12 people, and rates are $42–55, depending on hike selected.

What Else to See

The island's star attractions are mostly the natural ones. Don't miss a drive to Tobago's east-end fishing villages, **Speyside** and **Charlotteville**, where zinc roofs and wandering animals are the rule. Speyside is a speck of a town, but a couple good restaurants, including Jemma's, reward those who stop for lunch. A boat trip to **Little Tobago Island**, two miles offshore, is worthy, particularly for hikers or birdwatchers. As you head out of Speyside, notice the great rusting waterwheel at the turnoff for the Blue Waters Inn. The road climbs steeply to a ridge, but before heading down into Charlotteville, watch for the dirt road that leads off to the right. After one mile, the road takes you to **Flagstaff Hill**, the site of an American military lookout during World War II. The view from the manicured lawns is superb, and at sunset pairs of parrots swoop and screech madly through the jungle below. **Charlotteville** is a picture-perfect West Indian village. Swimming is okay in town, or head along an obvious 20-minute path to secluded **Pirate's Bay**. Legend has it that treasure is buried here, but not a single piece of gold has ever turned up.

From Charlotteville, those with a four-wheel-drive can continue along the north coast toward **Bloody Bay** on a difficult road. Or retrace your tracks back to Roxborough and take the well-paved **Parlatuvier Road** through the lush **Tobago Forest Reserve** where trails quickly deposit you into the thick of the jungle. Rejoin the **Northside Road** at Bloody Bay and continue west past beautiful coves and more fishing villages, until the road heads into the hills where quaint villages are perched along the main ridge. In **Golden Lane**, seek out the grave of **Gang Gang Sara**, an African woman rumored to be a witch who once flew to Tobago and took up residence. When she tried to leave, we're told, she lost her power to fly because she had eaten salt while on the island. Just prior to reaching the Arnos Vale Hotel is another photo-worthy waterwheel and rusting processing plant which has been turned into a restaurant and nature preserve.

Scarborough, the eccentric capital of Tobago, is also worth a tour, but try to visit on Saturday when the market is running at full speed. The weekly market is an explosion of shouts, colors and aromas as the turbaned vendors lay out piles of fresh vegetables and fruits. Bargaining is a necessity, but don't try so hard for a good deal that you miss biting down on a delicious papaya or a ripe golden tomato. From here, you may walk or drive up to **Fort King George**, 450 feet above the sea and the island's most significant historical monument, though the museum is open only on weekdays. Just below is the **National Fine Arts Centre**, which houses a collection of paintings and crafts.

Argyle Waterfalls   ★★★
Roxborough.
This three-tiered waterfall is just outside the town of Roxborough, and plunges into a green lagoon perfect for swimming. It's only a 10-minute walk from the road and easy to find, but guides will make their presence known and can be aggressive. If the scene here (or at Rainbow Falls just inland from Goodwood) is too much, head for King's Bay a little further up the coast, where the falls are next to the road and guides don't bother offering to show you the way.

Historical Sites

Fort King George   ★★
Scarborough, ☎ *(868) 639-3970*
Hours open: 9 a.m.–5:30 p.m.
Tobago's best-preserved historical building is this fort perched on a hill above Scarborough. English troops built it in 1779 and over the years it traded hands between the English and French. You can inspect its ruins and cannons, and on a clear day you can see forever—or at least to Trinidad. The Barrack Guard House is the site of the Tobago Museum, whose exhibits center on Amerindian pottery and relics, military artifacts, and documents from the slave era. General admission: $1.

Tours

Adventure Farm and Nature Reserve   ★★

Arnos Vale Road, Plymouth.

This 12-acre plantation grows mangoes, citrus, bananas and papaya, and rears sheep and goats in its pasture. You can come and pick your own fruit (they charge market prices) or enjoy the birdwatching. Open to the public daily except Saturday from 7 a.m. to 9 a.m. and 5 to 6 p.m.; a caretaker acts as guide for an extra $1. Nearby, just past the Arnos Vale Hotel, is a rusting waterwheel and machinery in the woods, which was converted to a restaurant and museum. General admission: $3.

Buccoo Reef   ★★★★

Off Pigeon Point, ☎ *(868) 639-8519.*

Although much of this large, accessible reef has suffered from visitors walking on the coral, the better guides will take you to the less-damaged portions. The 10,000-year-old reef is spectacular and a stop at the Nylon Pool (a surreal, natural shallow pool in the lagoon) is mandatory. Two-and-a-half hour tours via glass-bottomed boats available daily for $10; departure times vary by season.

A highlight for many on Tobago is the Mount Irvine Golf Course, one of the better greens in the Caribbean. The leading beachfront hotels boast their own watersports programs. Other tour operators can be found in the vicinity of Pigeon Point; in rural areas, arrangements can frequently be made with local fishermen. Horseback riding is offered at the Palm Tree Village Resort, which has its own stables, ☎ *(868) 639-4347.* There are several professional sports associations on the island that will provide information on their respective activities.

Golf

Mount Irvine Hotel, ☎ *(868) 639-8871.*
Hours open: 6:30 a.m.–3 p.m.

The 18-hole, par-72 **Mount Irvine Golf Course** is among the Caribbean's most scenic, covering 125 acres of rolling hills and overlooking the sea. Great views from the clubhouse, too. Greens fees are $46, a cart is $35, and club rental is $17, with a discount to guests of the hotel.

Watersports

Various locations.

If your hotel can't supply the necessary aqua activity, try one of these. Sailing: **Viking Sail/Yacht Chartering Limited** ☎ *(868) 639-9209.* Deep-sea fishing: **Gerald deSilva** ☎ *(868) 639-7108.* Windsurfing: **Windsurfing Association of Trinidad and Tobago** ☎ *(868) 659-2457.* General watersports: **Blue Waters Inn** ☎ *(868) 660-4341,* and **Mt. Irvine Watersports** ☎ *(868) 639-9379.*

Where to Stay

	Fielding's Highest Rated Hotels in Tobago	
★★★★	Coco Reef Resort	$154–$350
★★★★	Le Grand Courlan	$200–$275
★★★	Arnos Vale Hotel	$120–$285
★★★	Grafton Beach Resort	$162–$225
★★★	Kariwak Village Hotel	$75–$120
★★★	Manta Lodge	$75–$170
★★★	Mount Irvine Bay Hotel	$165–$350
★★★	Palm Tree Village	$75–$130
★★★	Rex Turtle Beach Hotel	$110–$200

	Fielding's Most Romantic Hotels in Tobago	
★★★★	Coco Reef Resort	$154–$350
★★★★	Le Grand Courlan	$200–$275
★★★	Arnos Vale Hotel	$120–$285

	Fielding's Best Value Hotels in Tobago	
★★★	Kariwak Village Hotel	$75–$120
★★	Hampden Inn	$40–$60
★★	Sandy Point Beach Club	$35–$80
★★★	Palm Tree Village	$75–$130
★★	Speyside Inn	$55–$95

Most of Tobago's tourist accommodations are concentrated in and around the airport, squeezed between Crown Point and Pigeon Point. All manner of rooms can be found here—resorts, condos and guest houses—though the area can sometimes become congested with activity. Most of the other mod-

TOBAGO

erate-to-expensive properties will be found northeast of here, near Plymouth, on or near some of the better beaches. Little is found in Scarborough or through the middle portion of the island, until you reach the northeast tip, where two fine dive properties, the **Manta Lodge** and **Blue Waters Inn**, are located.

On the hotel front, Tobago is currently suffering an embarrassment of riches. Three resorts opened in 1995. Limited air service to Tobago means rooms go empty, even in high season, but their loss is your gain. If you want a resort vacation, compare the rates and amenities of the various big hotels. If you're on a budget, you will find a surfeit of low-cost rooms under $75 in high season—and under $50 in low season.

Hotels and Resorts

Coco Reef is the creation of Bermudan hotelier John Jefferis, who made the resort a five-year labor of love—it replaces the old Crown Radisson that previously occupied this coral coast between Crown Point and Pigeon Point. Meanwhile, the Grafton Beach Resort empire spawned **Le Grand Courlan** with the hope of luring vacationers for serious pampering and spa treatments; rooms are luxurious, but the operation leaves something to be desired. Those who want easy access to the island's golf course will want to stay at **Mount Irvine Bay**, where country-club charm mingles with old-fashioned Caribbean style. Two popular spots that always stay busy are the **Rex Turtle Beach** and **Grafton Beach**—well-worn properties with good beaches, solid amenities and moderate prices that make up for what they lack in glitzy style.

Despite the current oversupply of resort rooms, at press time, construction was about to begin on a 200-room **Tobago Hilton** in the Lowlands area with an adjoining nine-hole golf course and condo development.

Arnos Vale Hotel   **$120–$285**   ★★★

> *Plymouth,* ☎ *(868) 639-2881, FAX (868) 639-4629.*
> *Single: $120–$285. Double: $120–$285.*
> Located in a coastal valley 15 minutes north of Scarborough, this self-contained resort has undergone a refurbishing to help match the lush surroundings. The sloping grounds include acres of fruit orchards—the bounty of which often enhance the meals served at the hotel's restaurant. Accommodations are located on the hillside or in apartment-style dwellings near the nice beach; all are air-conditioned. Facilities include two bars, a pool and a few watersports. There are lots of stairs between the beach and lobby/restaurant area. 30 rooms. Credit cards: A, DC, MC, V.

Blue Waters Inn   **$75–$130**   ★★

> *Batteaux Bay,* ☎ *(800) 742-4276, (868) 660-4341, FAX (868) 660-5195.*
> *Website: www.trinidad.net/bwi-tobago. E-mail: bwitobago@trinidad.net.*
> *Single: $75–$115. Double: $85–$130.*
> Set in a beautiful protected cove with a good beach, this dive inn is almost 90 minutes from the airport, but provides a requisite escape to make the drive worthwhile. Guestrooms are basic and some rely on sea breezes to keep cool. One- and two-bedroom self-catering efficiencies (the nearest store is miles), and luxury bungalows are

also available for $175 per night and up. The surrounding rainforest keeps nature lovers happy, but those who want to see the island will want to rent a car—the location is isolated. There's a tennis court, kayaks, windsurfing, a restaurant and bar on the grounds, but no pool. Birdwatching excursions are offered, but diving is the main draw and excellent sites are less than ten minutes from your door, which goes a ways to make up for the long drive to get here. 38 rooms. Credit cards: A, MC, V.

Coco Reef Resort $154–$350 ★★★★
Crown Point, ☎ *(800) 221-1294, (868) 639-8571, FAX (868) 639-8574.*
Single: $154–$350. Double: $154–$350.
Guests are greeted to the sparkling new Coco Reef Resort via a subdued hallway that leads into a grand, arching two-story lobby with 30-foot palms, statues and a vibrant papaya-and-white color scheme. Guest rooms feature Saltillo tile floors and wicker furnishings, with most of the units opening onto nice views of the Caribbean and Pigeon Point. The coup de grace is a "lover's cottage" nestled on a rocky promontory next to the resort and featuring a private porch perfect for sunset ($1100–$1650 per night). An artificial sand beach and lagoon seems a little manicured, but the mosaic-tiled pool is appealing and other fine beaches are close by. A cozy and cool champagne bar, Bobster's, features undulating walls and murals of Caribbean entertainers, and an open-air gourmet restaurant provides fine food. Probably Tobago's best-run resort. 135 rooms. Credit cards: A, DC, MC, V.

Grafton Beach Resort $162–$400 ★★★
Black Rock, ☎ *(800) 223-6510, (868) 639-0191, FAX (868) 639-0030.*
Website: www.grandehotels.com. E-mail: grafton@trinidad.net.
Single: $162–$225. Double: $162–$225. Suites Per Day: $300–$400.
This busy resort, 15 minutes out of Scarborough and practically joined at the hip with the new Grand Courlan next door, attracts a mostly European clientele. Guestrooms are nicely appointed with balconies, teak furnishings, minibars and modern comforts. The four suites also have Jacuzzis. There's lots to do: a large pool with a swim-up bar, shuffleboard, two air-conditioned squash courts, a well-equipped gym, two restaurants and three bars. A dive shop, Diamond Divers, takes care of sporting needs on the nice beach, and there is frequent evening entertainment. 112 rooms. Credit cards: A, DC, MC, V.

Kariwak Village Hotel $75–$120 ★★★
Crown Point, ☎ *(800) 544-7631, (868) 639-8545, FAX (868) 639-8441.*
E-mail: Kariwak@tstt.net.tt.
Single: $75–$120. Double: $75–$120.
This sweet island getaway is nicely designed and quite popular with both visitors and locals. Accommodations are in nine octagonal stucco cottages tightly configured around a swimming pool with a pleasant ambience. Rooms are basic, but most guests will spend their time out at the pool, or at Store Bay Beach, a 10-minute walk. Couch potatoes can camp out in the TV lounge to get their fix. The restaurant is a local favorite, and on the weekends, a popular spot to hear live music. They'll help arrange tours and watersports. 18 rooms. Credit cards: A, DC, MC, V.

Manta Lodge $75–$170 ★★★
Speyside, ☎ *(800) 544-7631, (868) 660-5268, FAX (868) 660-5030.*

Website: www.trinidad.net/tobagodive. E-mail: dive-manta@trinidad.net.
Single: $75–$135. Double: $95–$170.

The newer of Tobago's two scuba-oriented resorts, Manta delivers a simple elegance that belies its dive lodge concept. Delightful touches include handpainted manta ray dining tables, and a ceramic moray eel that writhes over the length of the restaurant's bar—most of these accents are by the owner's wife and mother, both artists with a nice feel for whimsy. Rooms are spare but tasteful in design—the standard units (priced less without air conditioning) are a good buy; the deluxe loft rooms are nice but lack a sea view and are a bit overpriced. Manta is geared to divers: there's not much of a beach and you'll need a car to go just about anywhere of note. But below the water offshore are the huge manta rays of Speyside that glide through the blue with inspiring grace. 22 rooms. Credit cards: A, DC, MC, V.

Le Grand Courlan $200–$425   ★★★★

Black Rock, ☎ *(800) 223-6510, (868) 639-0191, FAX (868) 639-0030.*
Website: www.grandhotels.com. E-mail: legrand@trinidad.net.
Single: $200–$275. Double: $200–$275. Suites Per Day: $375–$425.

A sibling to the long-popular Grafton, Le Grand Courlan shares the former's hillside and beach bar below, but works hard to create an elegant luxury resort with a full spa and the largest gym on the island. Standard rooms are impressively furnished with king beds, Asian rugs and nice amenities like personalized stationery, seaweed loofa soap in the bathroom and a fruit tray on arrival. Some rooms also feature a semi-private Jacuzzi (not all of them functioning) and there are elegant suites. The airy restaurant downstairs from the lobby features local and Guyanese teak, and the large pool has an attractive swim-up bar; the beach is a five-minute walk. The operation is still a bit shaky after a rocky 1995 opening—it has potential, but the resort is overpriced until it attains it. 78 rooms. Credit cards: A, MC, V.

Mount Irvine Bay Hotel $165–$1000   ★★★

Mount Irvine Bay, ☎ *(800) 221-1294, (868) 639-8871, FAX (868) 639-8800.*
Single: $165–$350. Double: $165–$350. Suites Per Day: $510–$1000.

Highlighted by a solid, well-maintained 18-hole golf course, Mt. Irvine has been Tobago's leading resort choice for many years, but now shares the spotlight with several polished newer properties. The amenities and grounds still shine, but Mt. Irvine's seems more in touch with 1960s country club life than with the focus of many of today's Caribbean vacationers. There's plenty to keep travelers occupied off the greens, though, with two tennis courts, the island's largest pool, and watersports on the nearby beach. There's also two restaurants and two bars, with frequent entertainment once the sun goes down. Lodging is in well-appointed guestrooms and in 46 fairly plush cottages. There are six one- and two-bedroom suites decorated with beautiful mahogany antiques. 105 rooms. Credit cards: A, DC, MC, V.

Rex Turtle Beach Hotel $110–$200   ★★★

Courland Bay, ☎ *(800) 255-5859, (868) 639-2851, FAX (868) 639-1495.*
Single: $110–$200. Double: $110–$200.

If you're visiting this hotel between May and October, you might get a chance to see leatherback turtles laying their eggs on the beach at Courland Bay—hence the name. It's decent any time of the year here, though, with a fine mile-long beach, full dive shop, two tennis courts, and small pool to keep guests happy. Accommodations are comfortable, though central air would be a great improvement. Additional facilities include two restaurants and two bars at this pleasant spot, popular with British families. 125 rooms. Credit cards: A, DC, MC, V.

Apartments and Condominiums

A fair amount of variety can be found in the self-catering department; you can splurge on luxury homes and apartments (with a live-in chef and maid) or you can hole up in a cottage and do your own cooking. Most of your supplies will be best procured at the Scarborough market on Saturday, when fruits, vegetables, meats and more are put up for sale. Bring any unusual staples you think you'll need because supplies at grocery stores are limited and those you do find will be expensive. For more information and rates, contact the **Tobago Villas Agency**, ☎ *(868) 639-8737*. **Plantation Beach Villas** offers a selection of six two-story, three-bedroom villas, ☎ *(868) 639-9377*.

Crown Point Beach Hotel $55–$105   ★

Store Bay Beach, ☎ *(868) 639-8781, FAX (868) 639-8731.*
Single: $55–$105. Double: $55–$105.
Set on seven acres, this time share condominium resort is eight miles from Scarborough, but a two-minute walk from Store Bay Beach, one of the island's nicer coves. Accommodations are in studios and one-bedroom units with air conditioning and kitchenettes; maids tidy up daily. There's a restaurant, bar, two tennis courts, and a supermarket on the premises. Accommodations are very simple, but cheap. 100 rooms. Credit cards: A, DC, MC, V.

Man O' War Bay Cottages $55–$70   ★

Charlotteville, ☎ *(868) 660-4327, FAX (868) 660-4328.*
Single: $55–$70. Double: $60–$70.
Set on a 1000-acre cocoa plantation, these rustic cottages boast an idyllic location right on the beach, just outside Charlotteville, but little else. Configurations vary from one to four bedrooms, all with kitchens, fans and verandas. Maid and cook service is available for an extra charge; upkeep is skimpy. Otherwise, this spot is popular with birdwatchers and those really looking to get away from it all. You'll want a car for mobility. 6 rooms. Credit cards: MC, V.

Palm Tree Village $75–$130   ★ ★ ★

Little Rockley Bay, ☎ *(800) 223-6510, (868) 639-4347, FAX (868) 639-4180.*
Single: $75–$120. Double: $85–$130.
This self-styled village is located a five-minute drive from Scarborough and is across the street from a public beach. Guests can stay in the hotel wing with its 20 standard air-conditioned rooms; there are also 18 villas with two to four bedrooms, large living areas, kitchens and patios ($145 and up). Maid service is available, as are cooks. Facilities include a restaurant, bar, small pool, gym and tennis court—horseback riding on the beach can be arranged. 20 rooms. Credit cards: A, DC, MC, V.

Sandy Point Beach Club $35–$80   ★ ★

Crown Point, ☎ *(800) 223-6510, (868) 639-8533, FAX (868) 639-8495.*
Single: $35–$80. Double: $35–$80.

Accommodations at this airport-close resort are in studios and one-bedroom suites, all with air conditioners, kitchenettes, and pleasing decor. The beach is not great for swimming, so guests splash about in the pool (fine for laps) or take the free shuttle to the beach at Pigeon Point. The casual restaurant serves varied fare for those not into cooking. This friendly spot is a great bargain. 50 rooms. Credit cards: DC, MC, V.

Inns

The bright new **Manta Lodge** in Speyside is geared to divers and lacks a real beach, but those content with a remote retreat will be happy if they have a set of wheels at their beck and call. The **Richmond Guest House** offers a beautiful country location and courteous family management, but is well off the beaten track and perhaps too quiet.

Richmond Great House   **$70–$170**   ★★

Belle Garden, ☎ (800) 544-7631, (868) 660-4467, FAX (868) 660-4467.
Single: $70–$120. Double: $85–$120. Suites Per Day: $120–$170.
Located on the coast halfway between Scarborough and Speyside on a verdant hillside, this unique former plantation house brims with interesting African art, local antiques and character. The 200-year-old house offers a handful of nicely decorated and colorful rooms, each individually done, with spacious newer (but viewless) rooms in the basement. The beach is a 10-minute drive; there's a restaurant here, which is good since other choices are fair distance. 12 rooms. Credit cards: A, MC, V.

Speyside Inn   **$55–$95**   ★★

Speyside, ☎ (868) 660-4852, FAX (868) 660-4852.
Single: $55–$80. Double: $70–$95.
Located just outside the fishing village of Speyside, this laid-back charmer is a seaside family-run inn with simple, but nicely decorated rooms. No air conditioning, but ceiling fans and pleasant balconies do the trick for most. No pool, but you can swim in Tyrrel's Bay across the street from the rocky shoreline. A restaurant and bar is on the premises, and a couple more are within walking distance; rates include breakfast. 7 rooms. Credit cards: A, MC, V.

Low Cost Lodging

Lots of possibilities exist on Tobago, and because room prices on the island are generally low, some of the options are surprisingly good. Guest houses are listed by the Tobago branch of TIDCO but you may want to see them and gauge their location before committing, ☎ (868) 639-2125. The new German-owned **Hampden Inn** is a good buy though its location is less than ideal and you'll want to lay out some cash for a car or bike rental while staying. Also worth considering for slightly more money is the **Conrado Beach Resort** which sits in a prime location next to Pigeon Point ☎ (868) 639-0145.

Arthur's by the Sea   **$50–$70**   ★

Crown Point, ☎ (800) 223-9815, (868) 639-0196, FAX (868) 639-4122.
Single: $50–$70. Double: $50–$70.
This small hotel is situated on a busy street a few minutes' walk from Store Bay Beach. The air-conditioned guestrooms are simple and basic, but in good shape and with private patios. All but two rooms now have TVs. There's a restaurant (lunch and dinner by request), bar and small pool on the premises; 10-minute walk to the beach. 15 rooms. Credit cards: A, DC, MC, V.

Hampden Inn

$40–$60 ★★

Lowlands, ☎ *(868) 639-7522, FAX (868) 639-7522.*
Single: $40–$48. Double: $50–$60.

This homey guest house features a series of one-story buildings facing a thatched-roof bar and restaurant that serves good local food. Rooms are spare, and on-site activities limited, but the friendly management goes out of the way to showcase the best of Tobago to its mostly European clientele. You'll need a car to go anywhere beyond the beach (10-minute walk), but bicycle rentals are available. An excellent budget choice. 10 rooms. Credit cards: MC, V.

Where to Eat

Fielding's Highest Rated Restaurants in Tobago

★★★★	Eleven Degrees North	$15–$26
★★★★	La Tartaruga	$11–$17
★★★	Dillon's Seafood	$12–$27
★★★	Jemma's Sea View Kitchen	$10–$27
★★★	Old Donkey Cart House	$20–$25
★★★	Papillon	$15–$25
★★★	Rouselle's	$13–$26

Fielding's Most Romantic Restaurants in Tobago

♥♥♥♥	La Tartaruga	$11–$17
♥♥♥	Eleven Degrees North	$15–$26
♥♥♥	Jemma's Sea View Kitchen	$10–$27
♥♥♥	Rouselle's	$13–$26

Fielding's Best Value Restaurants in Tobago

★★★★	La Tartaruga	$11–$17
★★★★	Eleven Degrees North	$15–$26
★★★	Jemma's Sea View Kitchen	$10–$27
★★★	Rouselle's	$13–$26
★★★	Papillon	$15–$25

Since Tobago aspires to be a resort destination, the food tends to be a tad more refined than what is found on Trinidad. Continental cuisine is served in most of the resorts and at a few local restaurants—led by the Italian at the excellent **La Tartaruga**. Otherwise, local cuisine centers on seafood, curries and traditional Caribbean fare. Prices are reasonable by Caribbean standards

Favorites include curried crab and dumplings, and *rotis*, chicken or beef and potatoes in a curry sauce wrapped in a thin, unleavened bread. During Heritage and other island festivals, *pacro* can be found—it's reputed to hold aphrodisiacal powers. Near the Crown Point Airport, along Milford Road, there are a number of stands that prepare authentic local food. Here you'll be able to sample *roti* and conch, crab and kingfish, or *doubles*, a burrito-like package containing chickpeas, chutney and hot pepper. Among the numerous small eateries that bridge the difference between roadside stand and restaurant, the better choices include **Sharon and Phoebe's** in Charlotteville, and the **Riverside Restaurant** in Parlatuvier.

Black Rock Cafe $$$ ★ ★

Black Rock, ☎ *(868) 639-7625.*
Lunch: Noon–4 p.m., entrées $3–$8.
Dinner: 6:30–10 p.m., entrées $13–$32.

A tin-roofed roadside house has been opened to the breeze for this pleasant low-key eatery specializing in seafood and curried dishes. Surf and turf runs $32, but crayfish, shrimp and lobster items are a better deal. Credit cards: A, MC, V.

Blue Crab $ ★ ★

Robinson Street; Scarborough, ☎ *(868) 639-2737.*
Lunch: 11 a.m.–3 p.m., entrées $4–$6. Closed: Sat., Sun.

The hardworking family that runs this popular spot whips up good meals that combine the cuisines of East India, Portugal and Creole. Fresh vegetables and fruits from their own gardens are used in the preparation of such delights as pumpkin soup and homemade ice cream and fruit wines. Lunches are served on the wide terrace of the traditional West Indian building and are very popular with the local business community. The fresh catch might include bonito, red snapper, kingfish or shark. Dinner is available by advance reservation only from Wednesday through Friday. Reservations recommended. Credit cards: A, MC, V.

Dillon's Seafood $$$ ★ ★ ★

Airport Road, ☎ *(868) 639-8765.*
Dinner: 6–10 p.m., entrées $12–$27. Closed: Mon.

A charter captain and fisherman runs this modern restaurant—which assures that all fish and seafood is so fresh it snaps back at you. There's lobster thermidor, or island kingfish in a tomato sauce, and fish soup. Some of the food though, could use a braver hand with the salt shaker or the spice rack. Reservations required. Credit cards: A, MC, V.

Eleven Degrees North $$$ ★ ★ ★ ★

Store Bay Road; Crown Point, ☎ *(868) 639-0996.*
Dinner: 6:30–11:30 p.m., entrées $15–$26.

"New world cuisine" is celebrated at this Crown Point establishment, with a spicy selection originating from Mexico, Cajun country and, of course, the Caribbean— the seafood enchilada is popular. Grilled meats and a catch of the day round out the fine menu. The one-of-a-kind, lacquered tables created by the owners are lovely and local artists are showcased on the walls of the restaurant. Stop by on a night live entertainment is scheduled. Credit cards: MC, V.

Jemma's Sea View Kitchen $$ ★★★

Windward Road. Speyside, ☎ *(868) 660-4066.*
Lunch: 9 a.m.–4 p.m., entrées $10–$20.
Dinner: 4–9 p.m., entrées $10–$27. Closed: Sat.

The kids, big and small, will enjoy eating in a real treehouse overlooking Tyrell's Bay. You may have to fight for space though, as there are only 10 tables. The emphasis is on local dishes, served in generous portions by an amiable staff. Specialties include callaloo soup, grilled seafood, and crab and dumplings. It's a great place to stop on a circle-island tour or a day at the beach.

La Tartaruga $$ ★★★★

Buccoo Bay, Plymouth, ☎ *(868) 639-0940.*
Dinner: 7–11 p.m., entrées $11–$17. Closed: Mon., Sun.

Fresh is the key word at this intimate, friendly spot. The delightful Italian owner and chef prepares delicious pasta that's homemade daily. Sauces are embellished with garden-grown herbs and fish is delivered to his door from a reliable source. The service, by a well-trained staff, is as quick as it gets on the island. Recommended dishes include spaghetti with dorado in a sauce of olive oil and pepper, served with tomatoes. Stop by for a drink, an espresso, homemade ice cream or dessert such as ricotta cakes and amaretto cheesecake. Reservations recommended. Credit cards: A, MC, V.

Old Donkey Cart House $$$ ★★★

Bacolet Street, Bacolet, ☎ *(868) 639-3551.*
Lunch: Noon–3 p.m., entrées $3–$10.
Dinner: 6:30 p.m.–midnight, entrées $20–$25.

The Viennese owner of this charming restaurant in a white colonial house is the island's only authority on German wines, which are a specialty of the place. These fine vintages accompany well-prepared local fish, steaks and pastas. Start your meal with some excellent cheese. At lunch, sandwiches are served on homebaked bread (lunch weekdays only). Reservations recommended. Credit cards: A, MC, V.

Papillon $$$ ★★★

Buccoo Bay Road, ☎ *(868) 639-0275.*
Lunch: entrées $15–$25.
Dinner: entrées $15–$25.

Chef Jakob Straessle's cuisine may not be on the cutting edge of chic, but the Swiss restaurateur always delivers reliably tasty old favorites like lobster thermidor, served with a choice of soup, rice and salad. Also featured are conch in season, cooked in coconut milk. Dine in air-conditioned comfort in a rustic, out-of-the-way lodge. Credit cards: A, DC, MC, V.

Rouselle's $$$ ★★★

Old Windward Road; Bacolet, ☎ *(868) 639-4738.*
Dinner: 3–11 p.m., entrées $13–$26. Closed: Sun.

Charlene and Bobbie, the delightful couple was run this friendly seaview establishment, place a high priority on good vibes in a pleasant setting. Neither were cook a few years ago when they started out, but have developed a reputation for the car they put into their menu, evidenced by a fine and cool cucumber soup and a delectable grouper (when available)—a generous usage of local herbs and spices accents most of the dishes. Reservations are a good idea for this small spot. Credit cards: MC, V.

Compared to the cascade of goods available on Trinidad, Tobago's share represents a mere trickle. The Saturday **market** in Scarborough usually finds a few vendors selling leather sandals and belts, carved gourds and hand-wrought jewelry. A small area for vendors has been developed behind Store Bay; although what will be sold there isn't yet known. Two **malls** cater to the obvious and uninspiring: **Scarborough Mall** in the center of town and, slightly more fashionable, **Breeze Mall** on Milford Road. You'll find more original items in designer boutiques such as the **Cotton House** on Bacolet Street in Scarborough; it creates and sells brilliantly colored batik and tie-dye fabrics. Tobago's own fashion mavens head for **Nairobi,** above the Starting Gate Pub off Shirvan Road. A local jeweler, Jose Andres, is especially revered for his unique jewelry made from indigenous woods, bone, coral and seedpods. Finally, the large resorts have their own small gift shops, but expect the prices to be heavily inflated.

Tobago Directory

Arrival and Departure

American Eagle began nonstop daily service to Tobago from its hub in San Juan, Puerto Rico, in 1996, allowing easier connections from North America. The only hitch is that the flight currently arrives very late at night—a real consideration if you're staying at any of the hotels around Speyside, 90 minutes away. It's also possible to fly to Port of Spain, Trinidad, and connect to one of **Air Caribbean's** five to eight daily flights to Tobago's Crown Point Airport; the trip takes about 25 minutes. Port of Spain is served by **American Airlines** out of Miami and by **BWIA** out of Miami and JFK in New York (allow at least an hour for your connection as airport customs and immigrations in Port of Spain can be time-consuming when a big flight lands). Alternatively, you may fly to Grenada or Barbados (see "Arrival and Departure" in "Grenada" and "Barbados"), and connect to the daily **LIAT** flight to Tobago. A final option is too lengthy to warrant serious consideration except by those on a tight budget: an almost-daily passenger **ferry** plies the route between Port of Spain and Scarborough, but the crossing takes about five hours and the return trip from Tobago usually leaves at 11 p.m. A round-trip tourist-class ticket is $10, or a cabin runs $28; the departure schedule changes frequently, but there is usually no crossing on Saturday. The Port Authority in Port of Spain can be reached at ☎ *(868) 625-3055*, in Tobago ☎ *(868) 639-2416.*

There is a $15 departure tax collected when you leave the country.

Business Hours

Shops open Monday–Thursday 8 a.m.–4 p.m., Friday 8 a.m.–6 p.m. and Saturday 8 a.m.–noon. Banks open Monday–Thursday 9 a.m.–2 p.m. and Friday 9 a.m.–noon and 3–5 p.m.

Climate

Weather conditions are very comfortable, with temperatures averaging 83 degrees Fahrenheit. The wet season runs June to December, with rainfall in mostly short sharp bursts. Tobago is slightly cooler and less humid than Trinidad. Because Tobago is a scant 11 degrees above the equator, the climate is decidedly tropical.

Documents

A passport is required for entry, as is a return or ongoing ticket. An American drivers license will suffice for car rental.

Electricity

Current runs either 115 or 220 volts at 60 cycles. While many hotels have 115 volt current, it is advisable to travel with a small transformer just in case.

Getting Around

Although Tobago is small, you'll need a car if you want to travel outside the Crown Point area. Get one at the Crown Point Airport from **Baird's Rental**, ☎ *(868) 639-7054* or **Thrifty**, ☎ *(800) 367-2277* or *(868) 639-0357.* On the northeast tip of the island, one outfit, **Paradise Rentals**, operates out of the Blue Waters Inn, ☎ *(868) 660-4341.* Ask for a map, and remember to drive on the left. Note that the north coast road between L'Anse Fourmi and Charlotteville is rutted and suitable for four-wheel-drive vehicles only.

Taxis charge fixed fares to the major hotels from the airport. Fares from the airport to any of the nearby Crown Point hotels run about $4, while a taxi to Plymouth is $20 and to Speyside is about $40 (or $50 after 9 p.m.).

There are several good tour operators on the island. **Pioneer Journeys** works out of the Man O' War Bay Cottages in Charlotteville and does a variety of trips into the Forest Reserve ☎ *(868) 660-4327.* Fredericka at **Good Time Tours** is reported to be a pleasant guide ☎ *(868) 639-6816.*

Language

English is the official language and is spoken with a rich, melodious accent. The old French-based patois has almost died out.

Medical Emergencies

There is a fair hospital in Scarborough, but more serious emergencies require an air lift to Port of Spain or, in an extreme, to San Juan, Puerto Rico. There is an extensive network of health centers and clinics, both public and private. Both government and private doctors practice. The nearest decompression chamber for divers is in Trinidad.

Money

The official currency is the Trinidad and Tobago dollar (written as TT$), which floats against other currencies. At press time, the exchange rate hovered around 6.2 TT to 1 American dollar. Most prices in smaller restaurants are listed in the local currency, though all will accept U.S. dollars and all but the smallest restaurants now take credit cards. There are several banks in Scarborough that will exchange your dollars for smaller purchases.

Telephone

The new area code for Trinidad and Tobago is *(868)*. To call form the U.S., dial *1 + (868)*, plus the seven-digit local number.

Time

Atlantic Standard Time, one hour ahead of New York City, except during Daylight Saving Time, when it is the same.

Tipping

Most hotels and restaurants add a 10 percent service charge to your bill at check-out and all but the smaller spots add a 15 percent VAT tax on top. If the service charge is not included in your hotel or restaurant bill, be sure to leave something equivalent.

Tourist Information

Tourist information is doled out by the **Trinidad and Tobago Tourism and Industrial Development Company**, known everywhere on the islands as TIDCO. Local TIDCO offices are at the Crown Point Airport, ☎ *(868) 639-0509* and in Scarborough, ☎ *(868) 639-2125*. The TIDCO office in Port of Spain can be reached by toll-free number, ☎ *(888) 595-4TNT* or *(868) 623-6022*.

When to Go

Carnival explodes on Trinidad in February with steel bands, parades and lots of local food and drink (see "What Else to See" in "Trinidad"). The day after Carnival finishes on Ash Wednesday, Tobago is flooded by partiers who come to the smaller island to crash and unwind. The **Round the Gulf Sailing Competition** takes place in March. The **Tobago Arts Festival** occurs March–April. Goat and crab races take place in April. The **Indo-Caribbean Festival of the Arts** takes place in May. The **Tobago Heritage Festival** is held the last two weeks of July. The **Tobago Music Festival** takes place in November and December. The **Tobago Christmas Pageant**, with local music and dance, is in December.

TOBAGO HOTELS		RMS	RATES	PHONE	CR. CARDS
★★★★	Coco Reef Resort	135	$154–$350	(800) 221-1294	A, DC, MC, V
★★★★	Grand Courlan, Le	78	$200–$275	(800) 223-6510	A, MC, V
★★★	Arnos Vale Hotel	30	$120–$285	(868) 639-2881	A, DC, MC, V
★★★	Grafton Beach Resort	112	$162–$225	(800) 223-6510	A, DC, MC, V
★★★	Kariwak Village Hotel	18	$75–$120	(800) 544-7631	A, DC, MC, V

TOBAGO

TOBAGO HOTELS	RMS	RATES	PHONE	CR CARDS
★★★ Manta Lodge	22	$75–$170	(800) 544-7631	A, DC, MC, V
★★★ Mount Irvine Bay Hotel	105	$165–$350	(800) 221-1294	A, DC, MC, V
★★★ Palm Tree Village	20	$75–$130	(800) 223-6510	A, DC, MC, V
★★★ Rex Turtle Beach Hotel	125	$110–$200	(800) 255-5859	A, DC, MC, V
★★ Blue Waters Inn	38	$75–$130	(800) 742-4276	A, MC, V
★★ Hampden Inn	10	$40–$60	(868) 639-7522	MC, V
★★ Richmond Great House	12	$70–$120	(800) 544-7631	A, MC, V
★★ Sandy Point Beach Club	50	$35–$80	(800) 223-6510	DC, MC, V
★★ Speyside Inn	7	$55–$95	(868) 660-4852	A, MC, V
★ Arthur's by the Sea	15	$50–$70	(800) 223-9815	A, DC, MC, V
★ Crown Point Beach Hotel	100	$55–$105	(868) 639-8781	A, DC, MC, V
★ Man O' War Bay Cottages	6	$55–$70	(868) 660-4327	MC, V

TOBAGO RESTAURANTS	PHONE	ENTRÉE	CR CARDS
International Cuisine			
★★★ Old Donkey Cart House	(868) 639-3551	$3–$25	A, MC, V
Italian Cuisine			
★★★★ La Tartaruga	(868) 639-0940	$11–$17	A, MC, V
Regional Cuisine			
★★★★ Eleven Degrees North	(868) 639-0996	$15–$26	MC, V
★★★ Dillon's Seafood	(868) 639-8765	$12–$27	A, MC, V
★★★ Jemma's Sea View Kitchen	(868) 660-4066	$10–$27	
★★★ Rouselle's	(868) 639-4738	$13–$26	MC, V
★★ Black Rock Cafe	(868) 639-7625	$3–$32	A, MC, V
★★ Blue Crab	(868) 639-2737	$4–$6	A, MC, V
Seafood Cuisine			
★★★ Papillon	(868) 639-0275	$15–$25	A, DC, MC, V

TRINIDAD

One of the Magnificent Seven mansions, Trinidad

The largest and most-populated of the Lesser Antilles, yet one of the least-touristed as well, Trinidad offers a rich smorgasbord of cultural and natural attractions set against the backdrop of the Eastern Caribbean's center of commerce and trade—Port of Spain. During the 1970s, oil revenue made the two-island nation (which includes sister island Tobago) the region's wealthiest and most cosmopolitan, allowing it to eschew tourism as an un-needed intrusion. But as finances plummeted in the 1980s, the country began courting tourists on Tobago—long the spot where Trinidadians vaca-tioned—and recently has begun developing tourism on the larger island as well. Eco-tourism, in particular, is considered the best avenue for expanding the infrastructure for visitors. Still, increasing tourist arrivals will be a long haul on Trinidad, where accommodations are primarily in hotels geared to

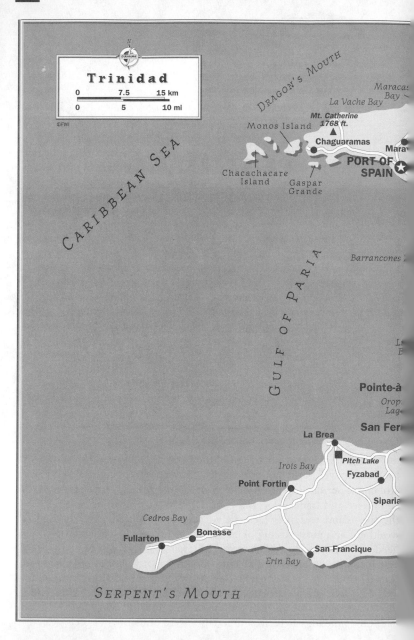

Trinidad

0   7.5   15 km
0   5   10 mi

©FWI

DRAGON'S MOUTH

Maracas Bay

La Vache Bay

Mt. Catherine 1768 ft.

Monos Island

CARIBBEAN SEA

Chaguaramas

Mara

PORT OF SPAIN

Chacachacare Island

Gaspar Grande

GULF OF PARIA

Barrancones

L B

Pointe-à

Orop Lag

San Fer

La Brea

Pitch Lake

Irois Bay

Fyzabad

Point Fortin

Siparia

Cedros Bay

Bonasse

Fullarton

San Francique

Erin Bay

SERPENT'S MOUTH

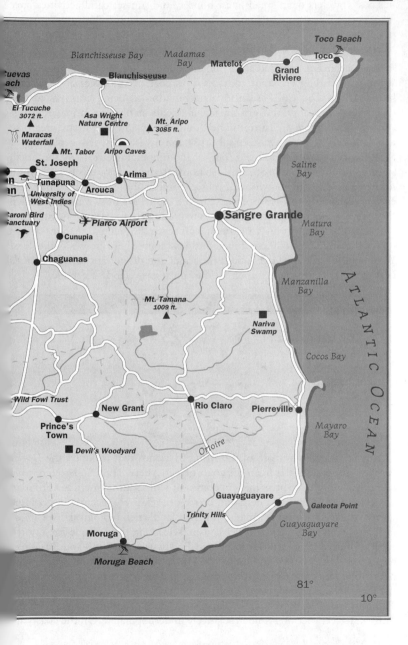

business travelers or in small guest houses, and sun-sea-sand activities have yet to be polished for the masses. But this large island holds numerous appeals and deserves more than a cursory glance from adventurous travelers interested in touring the Caribbean off the beaten track.

About a third of Trinidad's 1.2 million residents live in Port of Spain, a vibrant and bustling city that contains a number of embassies and business headquarters. The city has an unfair reputation as being crime-filled and dangerous—in reality, most of the few incidents involving tourists are drug-related. With simple precautions one would take in any large metro area (like avoiding Port of Spain's eastern suburbs), the city is well worth exploring for a day or two before heading to one of the mountain retreats or the north coast's small inns. Port of Spain is also home to the Caribbean's best Carnival festivities, a dizzying blowout of music, parades and exotic costumes held every February. For the rest of the year, the capital is a busy waterfront town filled with colorful gingerbread houses that compete for attention with ramshackle stalls and short high-rises as at least seven distinct nationalities stream down the streets intent on doing business somewhere between the First World and Third. Also dynamic is the food, and dinner at one of the city's best restaurants is usually unpretentious, inexpensive and delectable.

BEST BETS FOR...

Bird's-Eye View

Trinidad is at the bottom of the string of islands that make up the Lesser Antilles, just eight miles from the coast of Venezuela. The 1864-square-mile island has more than proximity in common with South America—Trinidad was once part of the continent and broke off, relatively recently in geologic terms, which is the primary reason for the island's rich biological diversity. A lush mountain range flexes its verdant muscle along the 50-mile-long north coast, climaxed by Cerro del Aripo and El Tucuche, at 3083 and 3075 feet respectively, the island's highest peaks. Much of the eastern end of this range has neither trails nor roads, only a single, winding route through the center: the Blanchisseuse Road, provides access between Arima and the north coast. The southern two-thirds of the island are a series of rolling plains, with the southeastern corner of Trinidad relatively underpopulated. On the coasts are

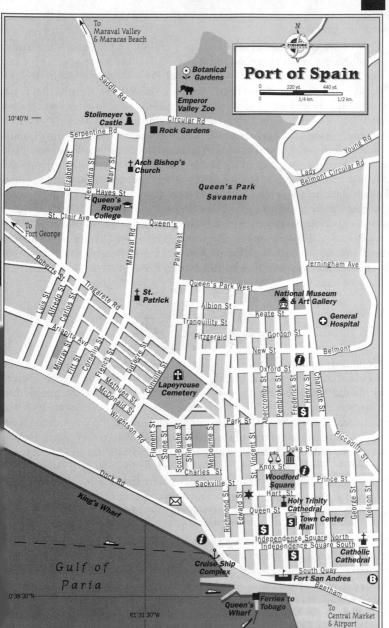

To Maraval Valley & Maracas Beach

N

FIELDING

Port of Spain

| 0 | 220 yd. | 440 yd. |
| 0 | 1/4 km. | 1/2 km. |

Saddle Rd

10°40'N

Botanical Gardens

Emperor Valley Zoo

Stolimeyer Castle

Serpentine Rd

Circular Rd

Rock Gardens

Young Rd

Elizabeth St

Alexandra St

Mary St

Arch Bishop's Church

Lady

Belmont Circular Rd

Hayes St

Queen's Royal College

Queen's Park Savannah

St. Clair Ave

Queen's

To Fort George

Park West

Maraval Rd

Jerningham Ave

Roberts St

Tragarete Rd

St. Patrick

Queen's Park West

National Museum & Art Gallery

Luis St

Alfredo St

Carlos St

Ariapita Ave

Murray St

Fitt St

Cornelio St

French St

Galafore St

Conville St

Albion St

Keate St

General Hospital

Tranquility St

Fitzgerald L.

Gordon St

New St

Belmont

Oxford St

Abercromby St

Pembroke St

Frederick St

Henry St

Charlotte St

Methuen St

McDonald St

Wrightson Rd

Lapeyrouse Cemetery

Piccadilly St

Flament St

Stone St

Scott-Bushe St

Shine St

Melbourne St

Park St

St. Vincent St

Duke St

Dock Rd

Charles St

Richmond St

Edward St

Knox St

Woodford Square

Prince St

George St

Nelson St

King's Wharf

Sackville St

Hart St

Holy Trinity Cathedral

Queen St

Town Center Mall

Gulf of Paria

Independence Square North

Independence Square South

Catholic Cathedral

Cruise Ship Complex

South Quay

Fort San Andres

B

0°38'30"N

Beetham

Queen's Wharf

Ferries to Tobago

To Central Market & Airport

61°31'30"W

important swamps—the Caroni is just south of Port of Spain, and the Nariva faces the Atlantic.

Port of Spain is Trinidad and Tobago's capital, and it sits at the western end of the mountain range, on the Gulf of Paria, which separates the island from Venezuela. The official population of Port of Spain is about 46,000, but a series of suburbs—Diego Martin, Maraval, St. Ann's, Barataria, Tunapuna—extend into the surrounding hillsides and lowlands to create a much larger community of about 350,000. Port of Spain's unofficial hub is not its downtown, but an expansive park, the Queen's Park Savannah, and a commanding hotel, the Trinidad Hilton, looks down on the greens. The west edge of the park is faced by The Magnificent Seven, a row of impressive colonial mansions built in 1904–1910 in architectural styles embracing a French château, a Scottish castle, and more, although most are vacant now as the community attempts to find new uses for the manors. Along the park's northern perimeter is the President's House, which is surrounded by the 70-acre Botanical Gardens and the Emperor Valley Zoo. The 2.5-mile one-way drive around the park is called the world's largest roundabout; you'll encounter it often on your trips in and around the city.

History

Columbus stumbled upon Trinidad and Tobago in 1498. Since then, the two islands have been a battlefield of contention among the French, Dutch, British and Spanish. Trinidad was long viewed as a source for Amerindian slaves, so the island was fiercely guarded, in contrast to Tobago which was nearly deserted by the Spanish. In 1592, an inland capital was erected at St. Joseph, stimulating interest in the cultivation of tobacco and cocoa. During the middle of the 18th century, plagues swept through the area, decimating the settlement and forcing the Spanish governor to move to a more coastal location, less vulnerable to jungle diseases and Indian raids. Port of Spain took its time to develop, first attracting a slow stream of settlers, followed by Christian missionaries intent on civilizing the Indians. Both tobacco and cocoa production soon fell off, the former a victim of competition among the northern islands, the latter a victim of blight. In 1776, the Spanish government offered land grants and tax incentives to Roman Catholic settlers; in response, numerous French planters from French Caribbean countries poured in to establish farms. By the end of the century, prosperous Frenchmen had gained control of the government, spreading the lilt of their patois and their tasty cuisine islandwide. During the Napoleonic Wars in 1797, the British sent a fleet to Trinidad, which swiftly overcame the resident Spaniard who had been too distracted fighting off Indians. In 1815, Tobago came under British control and was made a ward of Trinidad in 1897.

In the 1970s, offshore petroleum discoveries propelled Trinidad to the enviable status of the wealthiest nation in the Caribbean. Literacy rose to 90 percent, roads were paved, electricity installed. Signs of abject poverty, common among West Indian nations, nearly disappeared. In 1962, Sir Eric Williams, the father of Trinidad and Tobago's new independence from British rule, vowed to avoid what he called the mistakes of his Caribbean neighbors, which in his mind, was servile catering to tourists. As such, tourism was ignored for several decades. However, during the mid-1980s, resources plummeted, and the challenge of the Trinidadian government is to reestablish economic stability and ensure conservation of the island's natural resources.

People

Racially dynamic—40 percent East Indian and 40 percent African for starters—Trinidad is home to about 1.2 million people who live in relative prosperity by Caribbean standards, despite the nation's oil bust. Children are kept healthy by plentiful fish and fruit, as well as by free medical care, and are taught in schools that have a higher literacy rate than those in the United States. In addition to the predominant Indian and African, the population has intermingled with Chinese, Arab, British and remnant Carib Amerindian peoples. The cultural jetsam takes its biggest influence from the conquerors who stayed the longest—Spain, France and Holland. But also important is the legacy left by the Africans who arrived as slaves, and the indentured servants from India brought in to replace the slaves after abolition. Then add in the Chinese who proved unfit to harvest sugar but adept at everything else, Syrians bearing textiles, and former British estate owners whose descendants wouldn't leave for anything. Consequently, skin color is less an issue in this country, where intercultural cooperation has received lots of elbow grease.

As many Trinidadians will passionately explain, music is the true life blood of the island, and every Trini is an expert about what's hot at any particular moment. Lyrics—sometimes bawdy, sometimes political—hold the soul of the people, and calypso has morphed into *soca* (which is faster), *kaiso* (calypso/soca), *rapso* (told in rap), and the latest is *chutney*, a blending of calypso with authentic Indian folk music. The importance of music on the island is also a historical footnote. A century ago, the British outlawed African drums in Trinidad for allegedly inciting passions leading to violence. People switched to beating on bamboo, biscuit tins, hubcaps and, as local petroleum exploitation surged on, musicians began using oil drums. Someone soon figured out that the pitch changed after much pounding, particularly when dented, and the steel pan was born. The music was further legitimized when Harry Belafonte exported the calypso sound to the rest of the world (he is still considered a hero by many locals in the music industry). In the months leading up to Carnival, pan music can be heard everywhere on the island, from Sunday mass to jazz ensembles to 120-piece orchestras during Carnival's Panorama. Although Carnival is only a two-day event, the planning stage for parade floats and costumes begin months in advance, and by January, a few weeks before the festivities, Port of Spain has worked itself into a feverish pitch in delirious preparation. At the point of the actual event, the city grinds to a halt, and then collapses from exhaustion at its conclusion—usually decamping to Maracas Bay on the north coast, or to Tobago.

Because the country pursued tourism on Tobago before ever contemplating there was an audience who might enjoy Trinidad, the smaller island's beaches are better known. The reality is that Trinidad has many fine beaches, though most are remote and still unpublicized. The best lie on the north coast, with **Maracas Bay** leading the pack due to its proximity to Port of Spain—it's a 35-minute drive, the closest good beach to the city. Maracas received facility upgrades in 1996 that lead to an expanded parking lot and a series of structures for food service and restrooms; the beach is the place to unwind after Carnival, but it's popular year-round, particularly on weekends (watch valuables and don't leave them in your car). Continuing east along the north coast, **Las Cuevas Bay** has partially submerged caves and is just as nice as Maracas, but the extra five miles of road keeps the crowds down—the hulking mass of El Tucuche rises majestically behind the palms. The town of Blanchisseuse has a series of small coves tucked between the rock cliffs, and at the end of the road, a long stretch of golden sand—nearby **Damier Beach** is popular with surfers.

Elsewhere, there are other beauties, though swimming conditions can be tricky—inquire locally before diving in. On the other end of the north coast are several fine coves—**Grande Riviere**, **Toco Bay** and **Salybia Bay**. **Shark River** (near Grande Riviere) is a popular local freshwater swimming spot. Although the waters are calm, Trinidad's west coast (south of Port of Spain) offers little for bathers, but on the eastern Atlantic coast, **Manzanilla Bay** or Queen's Beach is a long stretch of sand fronted by stands of coconut. Further south **Mayaro Bay** is also lovely. Note that several of Trinidad's beaches, particularly around the northeast tip of the island at Grande Riviere and Matura, are nesting areas for leatherback turtles from March to August. Heed all signs during this period to avoid disturbing nests.

If you ask about diving on Trinidad, you'll be steered straight to Tobago in the blink of an eye. If you pry further, you'll probably be told—in no uncertain terms—"There's no diving on Trinidad." Well, that's right, but only to a degree. Tobago's stunning reefs and giant mantas are stiff competition for any neighboring island, but most particularly for Trinidad, which has a few complicating factors visiting divers need to consider. The first is the Orinoco, Venezuela's massive river, which flows straight to Trinidad. While this has the positive effect of steering rich nutrients into Trinidad's reef system, it also brings silt, reducing visibility to just 20–50 feet during the January–May dry season, and a ghastly 10 or 20 feet during the June–December rainy season. Suffice to say that "blue water" feeling one attains on most Caribbean islands simply isn't found here. To make matters worse, the Orinoco's colder waters settle into the depths below the surface and create a thermocline, which means that diving down past 35 or 40 feet is like entering a refrigerator, by Caribbean standards, anyway.

In sum, Trinidad remains an offbeat dive destination nurtured by locals, and visited by few outsiders, but suitable as a jumping-off point for the more dynamic sites on Tobago. Decent snorkeling is possible at Toco Beach (beware again of rough water) or around St. Peter's Bay, just west of Port of Spain.

Dive Shops

Ron's Watersports

Port-of-Spain; ☎ *(868) 673-0549.*

PADI certified, with courses through Assistant Instructor. Two tank dive, $60 including equipment. Ron also organizes reasonably priced day-trips to Tobago.

Trinidad is the biggest island in the Eastern Caribbean, and not just in geographic terms. The island was once part of the South American continent—some say as recently as 6000 years ago—and, as such, it has more in common

TRINIDAD

with nearby Venezuela than it does with other Caribbean islands. This is most magnificently displayed by the island's diverse wildlife. A few of the highlights are the unique golden tree frog, ocelot, armadillo, peccary, porcupine, deer and red howler monkeys. In addition to the almost-extinct bush turkey and the brilliant scarlet ibis, the avian population includes more than 400 species of birds, 617 types of butterflies and some 60-odd species of bat. Further, on the ground are 2300 different flowering shrubs and plants, including 700 kinds of orchids and a number of carnivorous species that grow in swampy areas. To its credit, Trinidad, richly endowed with oil deposits, began protecting its natural resources well before eco-tourism became a marketing concept. At this writing, there are 13 official wildlife sanctuaries that shelter much of the island's swamps and mountain forests.

The downside for adventurous hikers is that much of the country's wildlife is not easily visited without a guide. Consequently, there are few tour operators who accommodate the growing demand for wilderness exploration. At the top of the list is Asa Wright Nature Center, a lodge and bird sanctuary set in the rainforest of the Northern Range, at an elevation of 1200 feet.

What Else to See

Trinidad's Carnival is the Caribbean's most celebrated annual spectacle with islanders working all year on floats and costumes.

Several scenic drives invite you to explore Trinidad. A common daytrip is to head out of Port of Spain via the Eastern Main Road to Arima and then into the mountains laced with *christophene* vines via the Blanchisseuse Road. A stop at **Asa Wright** is mandatory (see "On Foot"), as is a break for an afternoon dip in **Blanchisseuse** or **Maracas** before returning through Maraval. An even longer trip heads out to the northeastern point of the island, to **Toco**, **Grande Riviere** and **Matelot**—beautiful villages struggling to keep pace with the economics of modern Trinidad (allow three hours each way, plus stops for the beaches and scenery).

The island's two major **coastal swamps** can only be explored with a guide, but they are rewarding excursions. The **Nariva Swamp** is the largest and most varied wetland on the island, containing many species of reptiles and amphibians, including caimans, anaconda and several varieties of poisonous snakes. The critically endangered manatee is found here, and a dazzling variety of parrots, macaws and toucans wing through regularly. The Nariva's **Bush Wildlife Sanctuary** is strictly off-limits, except by permit issued by the Forestry Department, ☎ *(868) 662-5114.* The **Caroni Swamp** is also protected, but access is easier through one of the individuals who conducts tours. Endangered leatherback turtles, the largest species of marine turtle, conduct their nocturnal egg-laying from March to July each year on several beaches around Trinidad's northeastern tip. The females deposit between 80 and 125 eggs in their laboriously dug nests—a moving event that the Forestry Department regulates onlookers for the protection of the species.

Two curious geologic phenomena are found in southwest Trinidad. **Pitch Lake** is an immense reservoir of tar that supplies the island with all its resurfacing needs (excavate a truck-load and the hole fills up overnight). Disappointed visitors sometimes note the lake looks a bit like a vast parking lot. Tour guides are aggressive, but will assist in making the site interesting—try Amena Hosein, recommended by TIDCO, ☎ *(868) 648-7697.* A holy site to some Hindus, the **Devil's Woodyard** is the major of several Trinidad spots known for sputtering mud volcanoes. In 1997, the first major eruption in almost four decades spewed hot mud and gas up to 200 feet in the air for six minutes, submerging everything within a one-mile radius under a layer of clay. It's located outside Prince's Town, just east of San Fernando.

Many visitors are surprised that **pan** and **calypso** is hard to find on Trinidad outside the winter prelude to Carnival. One reliable spot is the Hilton's Tuesday night Poolside Fiesta or Sunday Brunch where live music and colorful costumes spill into the outdoor dining area ☎ *(868) 624-3211.*

Festivals

Carnival ★★★★★

Port of Spain, ☎ *(868) 627-1354*

Trinidad's famous Carnival officially lasts just two days, from sunrise on Monday to midnight on Tuesday before Ash Wednesday—1998 dates are February 23 and 24. However, the unofficial season starts right after Christmas when creation of the colorful floats and outrageous costumes begins. Started by the French plantocracy 200 years ago, the festival was adopted by the island's blacks as a celebration of the end of slavery. Today, the joyous festival is eagerly anticipated by Trinidadians all year long. Most everyone dons elaborate costumes they've spent months making, then parades through the streets to the beat of steel bands. Tourists are welcome to join a troupe from a few hundred to thousands of costumed revelers. Note that Port of Spain hotel prices, particularly budget accommodations, double or triple during carnival; book rooms by Christmas.

Museums and Exhibits

National Museum ★★★

117 Frederick Street, Port of Spain, ☎ *(868) 623-5941.*
Hours open: 10 a.m.–6 p.m.

The museum's exhibits center on Trinidad's geography and history, with artifacts from pre-Columbian times. The highlight is a large art gallery with changing displays and a permanent exhibit on the works of famed 19th-century painter Michel Jean Cazabon.

Parks and Gardens

Royal Botanical Gardens ★★★

Queen's Park Savannah, Port of Spain, ☎ *(868) 622-3530.*
Hours open: 9:30 a.m.–5:30 p.m.

Located in the two-mile Queen's Park Savannah, these lush gardens cover 70 colorful acres on land that was once a sugar plantation. The grounds include the President's House, an 1875 Victorian mansion home to the president of Trinidad and Tobago, and the **Emperor Valley Zoo** ☎ *(868) 625-2264*, named after the huge Emperor butterflies common in the area. The gardens, laid out in 1820, showcase specimens from around the world.

Tours

Asa Wright Nature Center ★★★★★

Spring Hill Estate; Arima, ☎ *(868) 667-4655.*
Hours open: 9 a.m.–5 p.m.

This 730-acre estate turned wildlife sanctuary and mountain lodge is a must for bird watchers, with more than 130 species recorded on the grounds. Thirteen varieties of hummingbirds alone regularly call on the feeders that dangle off the inn's veranda, and brilliant purple and green honeycreepers add another palette of color to the cool mountain air. Three miles of trails cover the densely forested slopes. One leads to the lek of the white-bearded manakin—their exotic courtship dance is fascinating, another goes to caves that are home to the world's most accessible colony of oilbirds (this one is limited to guests staying three nights or more at the lodge; see "Accommodations"). Guided tours are offered daily at 10:30 a.m. and 1:30 p.m.; reservations are suggested. Allow at least 90 minutes by car from Port of Spain. General admission: $6.

Caroni Bird Sanctuary   ★★★★
Butler Highway, Port of Spain.
Hours open: 4 p.m.–6:30 p.m.
This sanctuary comprises 40 square miles of mangrove swampland bisected by waterways, located just a few miles southeast of Port of Spain. Come at sunset to see the national bird, the scarlet ibis, come home to roost—an amazing, colorful sight that takes place daily just before sundown. Boat tours are conducted by **Winston Nanon** ☎ *(868) 645-1305* for $10, or check with **Humming Bird Tours** in Port of Spain ☎ *(868) 623-3300.*

Sailing is one of the lures the government hopes will bring new travelers to the island, and the center of the activity is Chaguaramas, where **weekly races** are held. The local **yachting association** is a good source of information on daytrips or longer charters ☎ *(868) 634-4376.* **Deep-sea fishing** is found in the Dragon's Mouth, the channel that surrounds the islands off Trinidad's northwest tip—mackerel, kingfish, wahoo, yellowtail tuna, barracuda, red snapper and groupers are the most common catch. **Surfing** has become a local passion of late and the Surfing Association of Trinidad and Tobago welcomes visitors. Conditions are generally favorable year-round, and the biggest swells happen off Toco Point. **Windsurfing** is best at Chaguaramas.

Golf
Trinidad has four courses for duffers; the best are also the closest to Port of Spain. The island's only 18-hole course is at **St. Andrew's Golf Club** in Maravel ☎ *(868) 629-2314.* The **Chaguaramas Golf Course** has nine holes ☎ *(868) 634-4349.*

Watersports
A variety of companies are happy to assist with watersports. Deep-sea fishing: **Bayshore Charters** ☎ *(868) 637-8711* and **Trinidad and Tobago Game Fishing Association** ☎ *(868) 624-5304.* Boating and sailing: **Island Yacht Charters** ☎ *(868) 637-7389.* Windsurfing: **Windsurfing Association of Trinidad and Tobago** ☎ *(868) 659-2457.* General watersports equipment and instruction: **Ron's Watersports** ☎ *(868) 622-0459* and the **Surfing Association of Trinidad and Tobago** ☎ *(868) 637-4355.*

Where to Stay

Fielding's Highest Rated Hotels in Trinidad

★★★★	Trinidad Hilton	$150–$225
★★★	Asa Wright Nature Center	$106–$210
★★★	Holiday Inn Trinidad	$99–$185
★★★	Kapok Hotel	$76–$92

Fielding's Best Escape from Port-of-Spain Hotels in Trinidad

★★	Mt. Plaisir Estate	$48–$81
★★★	Asa Wright Nature Center	$106–$210
★★	Laguna Mar Resort	$45–$75
★★	Pax Guest House - Mt. St. Benedict	$45–$85

Fielding's Best Value Hotels in Trinidad

★★	Monique's Guest House	$45–$55
★★★	Kapok Hotel	$76–$92
★★	Laguna Mar Resort	$45–$75
★★	Pax Guest House - Mt. St. Benedict	$45–$85
★★	Mt. Plaisir Estate	$48–$81

Because Trinidad took a long time to recognize its tourism potential, accommodations tend to fall into two categories: business hotels (usually high-rises) or quaint guest houses. All of the former establishments are in Port of Spain, while the latter, family-run outfits seem to be springing up everywhere. In both cases, accommodations are inexpensive by Caribbean standards, though the 10 percent service charge, 15 percent VAT (the heftiest hotel tax in the region) and a sometimes overlooked $1.25-per-day energy surcharge can add up to a shock when you get your final bill. The biggest plus is that high season lasts only a couple weeks on this island—during Carnival in February, when Port of Spain room rates more than double and five-night minimums become the rule. Book Carnival dates by Christmas to secure the lodgings you want. Otherwise, Trinidad boasts what are easily the lowest winter room rates in the Eastern Caribbean. None of the Port of Spain or mountain hostelries are anywhere near a beach and, for the moment, Trinidad law prevents any hotel developments on the beautiful north coast beaches, though there are a few small properties nearby. In fact, Trinidad is the one major Caribbean island with no real resorts.

Trinidad's airport is a 30-minute drive from downtown Port of Spain and further still from the north coast—a few visitors opt for one of two airport hotels for their first or last night on the island. The better of these two crash pads is the 17-room **Airport View Guesthouse** in a three-story building above a convenience store located a mile from the terminal, but rooms are strictly spartan ☎ *(868) 664-3186*. A much better choice if you need airport-close accommodations is **Pax Guest House**, about a 15-minute drive from the terminal in the foothills above Tunapuna.

Hotels and Resorts

The premier hotel is the **Trinidad Hilton**, an island institution since 1962 when it opened. The Hilton serves as an important meeting and social hub for many of Trinidad's business and political leaders, as well as visiting dignitaries (U.S. Secretary of State Warren Christopher in 1996, et al). Although other properties are a notch below the Hilton, what the **Kapok**, **Normadie** and others lack in amenities and service, they make up for in laid-back charm. Other island possibilities include the **Valley Vue Hotel**, in a curious location well away from any other Port of Spain facilities, next to a hillside water park with slides, ☎ *(868) 623-3511*, and much further south, the **Farrel House Hotel**, just outside San Fernando where much of the island's oil business is conducted ☎ *(868) 659-2230*.

Holiday Inn Trinidad   **$99–$185**   ★★★
Port of Spain, ☎ *(800) 465-4329, (868) 625-3366, FAX (868) 625-4166.*
Single: $99–$175. Double: $109–$185.
This 13-story downtown hotel overlooks the harbor and attracts mainly business travelers and conventioneers, but very few vacationers. Accommodations are standard tried-and-true Holiday Inn: modern, air-conditioned, cable TV, and balcony with nice city views. Those staying on the executive floor pay extra for upgraded rooms and a private lounge. There's a revolving rooftop restaurant, a pool with a swim-up bar and a small fitness center. 221 rooms. Credit cards: A, DC, MC, V.

Kapok Hotel   **$76–$143**   ★★★
Port of Spain, ☎ *(868) 922-6441, FAX (868) 622-9677.*
Website: www.trinidad.net/kapok. E-mail: kapok@trinidad.net.
Single: $76–$79. Double: $89–$92. Suites Per Day: $130–$143.
Located five minutes from downtown, near Queen's Park Savannah, the ten-story Kapok is a business-oriented hotel, but doesn't have an overly corporate feel and goes out of its way to accommodate vacationers. Most of the rattan-furnished guest-

TRINIDAD

rooms have a fridge, and the six suites have full kitchens; there are also some cozy studios with a kitchenette. The Tiki Village Restaurant offers Polynesian fare, and there's also a cocktail lounge, koi ponds and a nice tile-lined pool. Quite decent for the rates, but beware the south-facing lower floors which can suffer from traffic noise. 71 rooms. Credit cards: A, DC, MC, V.

Laguna Mar Resort $45–$75 ★★

Blanchisseuse, ☎ *(868) 628-3731, FAX (868) 628-3737.*
E-mail: owl@opus-networx.com.
Single: $45–$55. Double: $65–$75.

This simple lodge lies on a 28-acre property at the end of the road outside Blanchisseuse and is a five-minute walk from a regal sweep of sand. Rooms are simple but clean and the beds are draped in mosquito netting. A small, affiliated restaurant, the Cocos Hut, serves good food. Laguna Mar aspires to be a resort (another six rooms are planned), but its low-key charm is a chief sales point—the lovely beach is another. 6 rooms. Credit cards: MC, V.

Normandie Hotel $60–$95 ★★

Port of Spain, ☎ *(868) 624-1181, FAX (868) 624-1184.*
Single: $60–$85. Double: $70–$95.

This two-story hotel is located in St. Ann's Valley, near the botanical gardens. The mixed-use complex includes a restaurant, disco, pool, art gallery and shopping arcade with local wares. Guestrooms are air-conditioned and comfortable, but on the dark side. The loft-style rooms are a little more money, but perfect for families. A nice inexpensive alternative to Port of Spain's business hotels, and in a good neighborhood near the President's House. 53 rooms. Credit cards: A, DC, MC, V.

Trinidad Hilton $150–$225 ★★★★

Port of Spain, ☎ *(800) 445-8667, (868) 624-3211, FAX (868) 624-4485.*
Single: $150–$205. Double: $170–$225.

This commercial hotel receives few vacationers, but remains the best-run property on the island—a prerequisite for some Port of Spain visitors. The 12-floor hotel sits on a hillside overlooking Queen's Park Savannah, and is entered via the top floor—it's known locally as the "upside-down hotel." The main lobby area is always buzzing with activity, and the Tuesday Night Poolside Fiesta and Sunday Brunch are the island's most dependable year-round spots for steel band entertainment. The air-conditioned guest rooms and suites have all the modern conveniences, and some include fax and computer hook-ups. Facilities include two restaurants, three bars, a pool, and two tennis courts. Guests are mainly American, and more than 90 percent of the rooms are occupied by business travelers who appreciate the nice trappings. What the Hilton lacks in local color it makes up through attentive service. 394 rooms. Credit cards: A, DC, MC, V.

Inns

Trinidad's mountain inns are special retreats, each with its own unique flavor. Both are well away from Port of Spain and other conveniences, but deliver hiking, birdwatching and eco-tourism at their unrefined best. Complete meal service is available at both.

Asa Wright Nature Center   **$106–$210**   ★★★

Arima Valley, ☎ *(800) 426-7781, (868) 667-4655, FAX (868) 623-8560.*
Single: $106–$139. Double: $160–$210.

This much-lauded retreat is devoted to preserving Trinidad's rich wildlife, and draws bird-lovers from around the globe. Located two hours out of Port of Spain and some 1200 feet up, it is a former coffee, cocoa and citrus plantation converted into a 730-acre wildlife sanctuary in 1967. Two tall-ceilinged guestrooms are in the turn-of-the-century main house, and are romantic and furnished with antiques but can suffer a bit from din of footsteps during the day. The rest are located in cottages; all are basic but quite peaceful. The lush grounds and neighboring rainforest attract winged friends throughout the day, including 13 varieties of hummingbirds. The rates include three meals, afternoon tea and rum punch—a good thing, since this spot is way off on its own. 25 rooms.

Mt. Plaisir Estate   **$48–$81**   ★★

Grande Riviere, ☎ *(868) 670-8381, FAX (868) 680-4553.*
Single: $48–$81. Double: $48–$81.

Looking for a real sojourn with nature, far from the trappings of civilization? This beachside inn is nestled in a small rural town on the little visited northeast coast, three hours from Port of Spain. The spacious rooms are basic, but filled with colorful local crafts and furniture that provide a bucolic ambiance. But the beach is the main draw, "home" to as many as 3000 nesting sea turtles who have been returning every two years to this one spot for endless decades to lay their eggs. During the peak nesting period, mid-March through mid-July, as many as several dozen leatherback turtles each night deposit up to a hundred eggs apiece in the sand; hatchlings appear two months later. Swimming is fine, hiking opportunities are nearby, but note that you are miles from any other facilities (Mt. Plaisir's restaurant is fine). The rustic inn attracts many Trinidadians and does a steady business during turtle season—the owners will set you up with a local family if their rooms are full. We thought long and hard about including this blissful place because the last thing it needs is a fleet of shutterbugging Americans to "discover" it. But the beach has been declared a protected area and the community is now proudly involved in guarding the wildlife—an ideal interpretation of eco-tourism at its best. 9 rooms.

Pax Guest House - Mt. St. Benedict   **$45–$85**   ★★

Tunapuna, ☎ *(868) 662-4084, FAX (868) 662-4084.*
Single: $45–$55. Double: $75–$85.

Located on a 600-acre monastery complex amid forested slopes, Pax Guest House was bought by Gerard and Oda Ramsawak in 1993 and they worked hard to upgrade and polish the weathered guest facilities—the property was "the most luxurious on the island" when it opened in 1932, though the building dates to 1916. The result is simple, somewhat rustic accommodations, peacefully situated amid the Caribbean's largest Benedictine settlement (monastery tours are available). Most rooms share bathroom facilities, but six have private bath. Daytime activities focus on birdwatching and hiking, and the afternoon tea is an island institution taken by Cuban President Fidel Castro, the Dalai Lama and other visiting dignitaries. Rates include full breakfast and three-course dinner, a must if you're overnighting without a car (Port of Spain is 40 minutes away). Pax is also an excellent place to begin or end a trip to Trinidad—the airport is a short drive. 18 rooms.

Low Cost Lodging

As the government has worked to develop a tourism infrastructure for Trinidad during the past decade, it has encouraged bed-and-breakfasts and guest houses, particularly during Carnival when rooms at hotels become scarce. The choices are endless, even within Port of Spain, and the **Trinidad and Tobago Bed and Breakfast Society** maintains a list of properties it has inspected and approved for public consumption, ☎ *(868) 627-BEDS.* Among the small hostelries that we like are **Zollna House** in Maraval Valley ☎ *(868) 628-3731,* **Carnetta's House** also in Maraval Valley, ☎ *(868) 628-2732,* **Alcazar Guest House** near Queen's Park Savannah, ☎ *(868) 628-8612,* and **Second Spring**, on the rocky coast at Blanchisseuse, ☎ *(868) 664-3909.* All of these locations have common areas shared by guests and owners.

Alicia's House   **$30–$58**   ★

Port of Spain, ☎ *(868) 623-2802, FAX (868) 623-8560.*
Single: $30–$40. Double: $50–$58.
One of Port of Spain's small budget inns, Alica's is a five-minute walk from the Presidents House and the Hilton in a pleasant residential area, St. Ann's. Four different room types, each named after flowers, but the best is the Admiral Rodney which features mahogany antique furnishings, an oval bathtub and ample space. All units have air conditioning and refrigerators. A small dining room serves breakfast, and a pool is available. 17 rooms. Credit cards: A, MC, V.

Monique's Guest House   **$45–$55**   ★ ★

Port of Spain, ☎ *(868) 628-3334, FAX (868) 622-3232.*
Single: $45–$55. Double: $45–$55.
This small hotel is run by the friendly Mike and Monique Charbonne, who opened it in 1973 as the first guest house on the island. It's located in Maravel Valley, an affluent suburb amid lush hills a couple miles from downtown Port of Spain. Rooms are nicely furnished, air-conditioned and spotless, and the small restaurant serves bargain fare; guests can splash about in a nearby pool. But the best reason for staying here is the attentive hospitality; they love their island and do all they can to expose visitors to its highlights. An excellent value. 11 rooms. Credit cards: A, MC, V.

Par-May-La's   **$30–$50**   ★

Port of Spain, ☎ *(868) 628-2008, FAX (868) 628-4707.*
Single: $30. Double: $50.
Simple accommodations in a good neighborhood near the French, German and American embassies. The apartment-style building was built in 1993 and most of the spare but clean rooms are on the second floor and feature air conditioning and lock boxes. Popular with Europeans and backpackers; rates include breakfast. 14 rooms. Credit cards: MC, V.

Where to Eat

	Fielding's Highest Rated Restaurants in Trinidad	
★★★★	Chateau de Poisson, Le	$9–$26
★★★★	Veni Mange	$8–$10
★★★	Hong Kong City	$8–$20
★★★	Monsoon	$4–$5
★★★	Rafters	$6–$21
★★★	Singho	$7–$12
★★★	Surf Country Inn	$9–$17
★★★	Tiki Village	$6–$13
★★★	Woodford Cafe	$3–$6

	Fielding's Most Romantic Restaurants in Trinidad	
♥♥♥♥	Chateau de Poisson, Le	$9–$26
♥♥♥♥	Surf Country Inn	$9–$17
♥♥	Tiki Village	$6–$13
♥♥	Veni Mange	$8–$10

	Fielding's Best Value Restaurants in Trinidad	
★★★	Woodford Cafe	$3–$6
★★★	Monsoon	$4–$5
★★★	Tiki Village	$6–$13
★★★	Singho	$7–$12
★★★★	Chateau de Poisson, Le	$9–$26

Though far from gourmet, food is a highlight of a trip to Trinidad. Seven distinct cultures have influenced the cuisine of Trinidad. Spanish settlers cooked up *pastelles*, tamales concocted by placing meats, raisins, capers and fresh herbs atop grated corn or cornmeal and folded in bright green leaves instead of the usual corn husks. The French introduced herbs such as broad-leaved thyme and basil. Tamarind was brought in by the British from the East Indies for sauces still used today in red snapper. Otherwise, in many restaurants, the influence of both India and South America is more prominent than on most other Caribbean islands. But some of the best specialties are found at street vendors, from doubles, the local equivalent of a burrito, to shark-and-bake, the ubiquitous Maracas Bay specialty of fried shark wrapped in bread. The **Breakfast Shed** is a colorful scene for tasty bowls of hot fish soup, all prepared fresh on the premises at one of a dozen or so counters. On the other end of the spectrum, **Chateau de Poisson** deserves the fast acclaim it has built for its careful preparations of memorable seafood dishes. One hold-over from the British is afternoon tea; in town, try **La Maison Rustique**, where Maureen Chin Asiong serves freshly baked pastries and cakes with tea Monday–Friday from 2–6 p.m., ☎ *(868) 622-1512*. The tea at **Pax Guest House** is one of the oldest traditions on the island, served daily from 3–6 p.m. and taken by a number of visiting diplomats as well as the guests of the hotel ☎ *(868) 662-4084*.

Breakfast Shed $ ★★

Waterfront; Port of Spain, ☎ *(868) 627-2337.*
Lunch: 5 a.m.–3 p.m., entrées $2–$3. Closed: Sun.
Join the wharf rats at this colorful Trini institution near the cruise ship dock, across the street from the Holiday Inn. Fellow diners are working people and early risers who like the breakfasts served from 5 a.m. The two primary offerings from the shed's female cooks (who each have their own counter) are hot and pungent fish soup—about $2 for a large bowl, and fish-and-bake, a few cents less and served with pepper sauce, crushed fresh on the premises. Lunch (the only other meal served) is accompanied by plantains, rice and peas and other plate stretchers. So down home, the hall-like room is called "Holiday Out" by regulars. A must-see on any budget.

Chaconia Inn $$ ★★

106 Saddle Road, Port of Spain, ☎ *(868) 628-8603.* Associated hotel: *Chaconia Inn.*
Lunch: 11 a.m.–2 p.m., entrées $12–$19.
Dinner: 7–11 p.m., entrées $12–$19.
The dining rooms of this motel-like spot in a Port of Spain suburb serve a double purpose: at lunch in the Lounge, business folk gather for a no-frills lunch of fish, pasta, pork and some vegetarian offerings. Sandwiches are tasty and moderately priced. And once a week, a West Indian barbecue is the attraction at the modern, plant-filled alfresco roof garden atop the hotel. A bar serves drinks until 2 p.m. Credit cards: A, DC, MC, V.

Chateau de Poisson, Le $$ ★★★★

Corner of Ariapita and Cornelio; Port of Spain, ☎ *(868) 622-6087.*
Lunch: 11:30 a.m.–2:30 p.m., entrées $6–$22.
Dinner: 7–10 p.m., entrées $9–$26. Closed: Sun.

An excellent seafood restaurant located in a quaint gingerbread cottage in the Woodbrook neighborhood. Though lobster selections are priced as high as $26, the extensive menu features many other succulent fish preparations. Try *Moqueca*, a Brazilian curry that makes a vibrant sauce for several dishes, or the Spanish crawfish, a local favorite. Seafood lovers should aim for the Thursday night buffet ($16); a lunch buffet is also served on Wednesday and Friday for $7. Credit cards: A, MC, V.

Hong Kong City $$ ★★★

86 Tragarete Road, Port of Spain, ☎ *(868) 622-3949.*
Lunch: entrées $8–$20.
Dinner: entrées $8–$20.
Spicy, creative Tri-Chi food is served amidst gaudy red and gold trappings. Bright Oriental lanterns hang from an intricately decorated ceiling. Chinese food-loving Trinidadians favor pepper shrimp, pork with dasheen and other delights. Karaoke nights sometimes, for those who enjoy that sort of thing. For more Chinese food around town, try: **New Shay-Shay Ten**, *81 Cipriani Blvd.,* ☎ *(868) 627-8089,* and in San Fernando area **Soong's Great Wall**, *97 Circular Road,* ☎ *(868) 652-2583.* Credit cards: A, DC, MC, V.

Monsoon $ ★★★

72 Tragarete Road; Port of Spain, ☎ *(868) 628-7684.*
Lunch: 11 a.m.–4 p.m., entrées $4–$5.
Dinner: 4–10 p.m., entrées $4–$5. Closed: Sun.
This brisk, but stylish East/West Indian restaurant is probably the most popular in town for curries and flatbread *(paratha)*. Lunch is a fast-paced affair, and very busy; many people take advantage of the take-out service. Complete meals built around shrimp, chicken, and fish include several vegetables, lentils and rice. There are great *rotis*, or dough wrapped around spiced conch or chicken, and fresh-squeezed, exotic drinks. The Wednesday night buffets are a good bet for a well-rounded feast—the seven-course meal is about $11. Credit cards: A, DC, MC, V.

Rafters $$ ★★★

6A Warner Street, Port of Spain, ☎ *(868) 628-9258.*
Lunch: 11:30 a.m.–4 p.m., entrées $6–$21.
Dinner: 4–11 p.m., entrées $6–$21. Closed: Sun.
Meat and potatoes people and seafood lovers all get their culinary kicks here: On Wednesday, a buffet of fresh local sea creatures is featured; on Thursdays, Fridays and Saturdays chefs carve hunks of roast beef and other meats nonstop until it's all gone. In an adjacent lounge, snacks and sandwiches are available for folks with more prudent appetites and pocketbooks. The restaurant resides in a lovely old restored dry goods store. Credit cards: A, DC, MC, V.

Singho $ ★★★

Long Circular Mall, Port of Spain, ☎ *(868) 628-2077.*
Lunch: 11:30 a.m.–7 p.m., entrées $5–$7.
Dinner: 7:30–11 p.m., entrées $7–$12.
Solid Cantonese food is the star at this tony eatery in the gargantuan Long Circular Mall. Decor features an aquarium, and meals run on the lines of cashew chicken,

TRINIDAD

spareribs in black bean sauce, and curries. Regulars and tourists like to stop in Wednesday nights for the Chinese buffet. Credit cards: A, MC, V.

Surf Country Inn $$ ★★★

Lower Village; Blanchisseuse, ☎ *(868) 669-2475.*
Lunch: 10 a.m.–6 p.m., entrées $9–$17.

Perched on a series of decks that overlooks the undulating north coast, this father and son operation is very popular for Sunday brunch, when Port of Spain families make the 90-minute drive to Blanchisseuse for a meal at this scenic spot. The food is good too—snapper en papillote is the signature dish, but the king fish poached in spicy garlic sauce is also tasty. Reservations essential for Sunday. Credit cards: A, MC, V.

Tiki Village $ ★★★

16-18 Cotton Hill, Port of Spain, ☎ *(868) 622-6441.* Associated hotel: *Kapok Hotel.*
Lunch: 11:30 a.m.–7 p.m., entrées $6–$13.
Dinner: 7:30–9 p.m., entrées $6–$13.

The island's version of Trader Vic's sits atop the plush Kapok Hotel, with a night vista of the glittering city lights; at lunch, Queens Park Savannah is spread out in all its glory. Food is average to good, with a dim sum lunch served from 11 a.m. to 3 p.m. on weekends and holidays. Management thoughtfully provides cards for diners to mark their choices on. The regular menu features Polynesian-style fish, steaks and chicken. Credit cards: A, DC, MC, V.

Veni Mange $ ★★★★

67 Ariapita Avenue; Port of Spain, Port of Spain, ☎ *(868) 624-7533.*
Lunch: 11:30 a.m.–2:30 p.m., entrées $8–$10. Closed: Sat., Sun.

Come and eat, say local media star Allyson Hennesey and co-owner and sister Rosemary Hezekiah, in the local lingo. A cross between Julia Child and Oprah Winfrey, Allyson manages to run the best West Indian lunch spot in town and host her own TV talk show. Specialties include tasty crab backs, hollowed out crab shells filled with peppered meat and a spicy mix of peppers and tomatoes. Hearty soups, including pumpkin and callaloo, are also recommended. Credit cards: not accepted.

Woodford Cafe $ ★★★

62 Tragarete Road; Port of Spain, ☎ *(868) 622-2233.*
Lunch: 11 a.m.–4 p.m., entrées $3–$6.
Dinner: 4–10 p.m., entrées from $3.

Opened by the proprietors of Monsoon at the other end of the block, this Port of Spain diner is hit with the local business community at lunch, but dinners are equally good. The stewed and Creole dishes are served with sides of callaloo, steamed pumpkin, dasheen and other West Indian specialties. The Guyanese pepper pot served on Fridays is highly recommended ($5). Credit cards: A, MC, V.

Where to Shop

Relative prosperity has kept the number of local crafts to a minimum; on the other hand it has allowed for artisans to develop their trade and flourish without the assistance of tourists. The latest in island-inspired jewelry, hand-painted T-shirts and batiks can be found at the extensive shopping area connected to the Normandie Hotel, on **Nook Avenue** in St. Ann's (behind the Presidents House). The pleasant mall shelters art galleries, crafts stores, a newsstand and more. Art Creators is just around the corner on **St. Ann's Road** and features the best local artists. The **Drag Mall** located on Charlotte Street just east of downtown is a good spot for inexpensive local handicrafts and leather goods (visit the spot with someone who knows the area).

For residents, Port of Spain's primary shopping area is eight-block-long **Frederick Street**, a humming scene any day of the week when the avenue bustles with activity. Calypso and soca music is always a great buy—ask for a disc highlighting the best of the most recent Carnival. **Rhyner's Record Shop** on Prince Street sells the new along with the old; **Metronome**, on the Western Main Road, is another good music source.

Trinidad Directory

Arrival and Departure

Piarco Airport is 30 miles east of Port of Spain and serves as the island's main point of entry. **American Airlines** provides daily nonstop jet service out of Miami. **BWIA** offers daily nonstop flights to Piarco Airport from Miami, New York's Kennedy Airport and Toronto. **Air Canada** also provides service to the island. **LIAT** and **BWIA** offer nonstop inter-island flights to Barbados, Grenada and St. Lucia. **Air Caribbean** connects Trinidad with Tobago and there is also a **ferry** between the two islands (see "Arrival and Departure" in "Tobago"). Customs and immigration at Piarco is lengthy when a large jet lands.

Taxis are plentiful at the airport when you land and run about $20 into Port of Spain. **Buses** (or Maxi Taxis) run on the hour from the airport to the city's South Quay Bus Terminal; the price is about $1, but you'll then need a taxi to get to any Port of Spain hotels.

The airport departure tax is about $14.

Business Hours

Shops open Monday–Thursday 8 a.m.–4 p.m., Friday 8 a.m.–6 p.m. and Saturday 8 a.m.–noon. Banks open Monday–Thursday 9 a.m.–2 p.m. and Friday 9 a.m.–noon and 3–5 p.m.

Climate

Trinidad has a tropical climate, with a dry season that runs from January–June, and a wet season the for rest of the year. Temperatures are fairly uniform year-round. In Port of Spain, average temperature in January is 78 degrees Fahrenheit, in July 79 degrees Fahrenheit. Annual rainfall is around 60 inches.

Documents

U.S. and Canadian citizens, as well as those of the United Kingdom, may enter the country with a valid passport if they only plan to stay less than two months. An ongoing or return ticket is also required. An immigration card is handed to you upon arrival (or on the plane) which must be filled out and handed in as you depart. Do not lose it. A visa is required for longer stays. Long delays in clearing customs have often been reported. To facilitate customs, pack as lightly and unostentatiously as possible.

Electricity

Current runs 110 or 220 volts, AC 60 cycles. Ask your hotel when making reservations what kind of transformer or adapter you will need.

Getting Around

On an island this big and diverse, you'll want to explore, and gas is inexpensive by Caribbean standards, though rental cars are not. One American firm is represented at the airport—**Thrifty's**, ☎ *(800) 367-2277* or *(868) 669-0602*—or you can use a local firm which is usually cheaper. Try **Kalloo's Auto Rentals**, ☎ *(868) 669-5673* or **Singh's Auto Rentals**, ☎ *(868) 664-5417*; both have locations at the airport and in Port of Spain. In any case, you will obtain a well-used set of wheels for your journeys—inspect your car's condition carefully on pick-up; the numerous dings and dents will be laboriously tallied when you return. Port of Spain is full of crazy drivers who taunt each other into dangerous maneuvers. Do your best to avoid driving yourself around in the city, or at least downtown. Conditions are usually less unsettling in the country, though potholes are not uncommon in less-visited areas and driving after dark requires a lot of nerve on the dark and winding roads.

Private taxis do not pick up any other passengers and take you straight to your destination. Take one for longer trips or destinations not on the public route. Rates are not usually observed during Carnival, when anything goes since demand is so high. Adjust and go with the flow or you will drive yourself crazy arguing. You can explore the north coast by taxi, but always negotiate a fixed price in advance. Public transportation around the island is good, if initially a little bewildering to outsiders. **Route (shared) taxis** and **maxi taxis** (color-coded minibuses) provide inexpensive rapid transit. Those with yellow stripes operate within Port of Spain, those with red stripes are for eastern Trinidad. Destinations within Port of Spain are under $1; Port of Spain to Maracas Bay is $3, to Toco, $5. The maxi taxi terminus in Port of Spain is on South Quay.

Language

The official language is English, spiced with a rich slew of local idioms. There is also some facility in Chinese, Hindi, Spanish and French, due to the large amount of immigrants.

Medical Emergencies

There are several adequate hospitals in Port of Spain, including the **St. Clair Medical Center** and **Mount Hope**, a large teaching facility. There is also an extensive network of health centers and clinics, both public and private; both government and private doctors practice. Trinidad has several decompression chambers for divers. Other serious emergencies, however, may require an airlift to San Juan, Puerto Rico. Ask your hotel to suggest the nearest pharmacy, though carrying your own prescription medicine is advised.

Money

The Trinidad and Tobago dollar (written as TT$) has been devalued twice in the past few years. At press time, the exchange rate was about 6.2 "TT" to one American dollar. You can exchange money in most major hotels, though banks usually offer a slightly better rate. Most shops, restaurants and hotels will accept American dollars if you run out of "TT", but generally all prices are listed in the local currency. Traveler's checks are accepted in major businesses, as are all major credit cards.

Telephone

The new area code for Trinidad and Tobago is *(868)*. To call the islands from the U.S. dial *1 + (868)* plus the seven-digit local number. Telegraphs, telefax, teletype, and telex can be sent through the Textel office at *1 Edward Street, Port-of-Spain;* ☎ *(868) 625-4431*.

Time

Atlantic Standard Time.

Tipping and Taxes

Restaurants and hotels usually add a 15 percent Value Added Tax (called VAT). Most also add an additional 10 percent service charge. If they have not (check your bill carefully), add your own comparable tip if you find the service satisfactory.

Tourist Information

Trinidad and Tobago's **Tourism and Industrial Development Company** (TIDCO) is the political unit responsible for luring visitors to island shores, and a toll-free number is provided to Americans looking for vacation brochures or other resources, ☎ *(888) 595-4TNT* or *(868) 623-6022*. TIDCO is located in Port of Spain at 10-14 Phillips Street. They are well-staffed, eager to promote tourism in Trinidad, and can provide maps, brochures and assistance in finding bed-and-breakfast situations. They are particularly helpful in securing accommodations during Carnival, when beds become scarce.

When to Go

The **Kaiso House** calypso tent opens in January. **Carnival** and many associated events take place in February (see "What Else to See"). **Leatherback turtle nesting** season is from March until July. The four-day Muslim **Hosay** festival takes place in June. **Steelband Week** takes place in August. The **Pan Jazz Festival** takes place in November. The **Hindu Divali Festival** is celebrated in November.

TRINIDAD HOTELS		RMS	RATES	PHONE	CR. CARDS
★★★★	Trinidad Hilton	394	$150–$225	(800) 445-8667	A, DC, MC, V
★★★	Asa Wright Nature Center	25	$106–$210	(800) 426-7781	
★★★	Holiday Inn Trinidad	221	$99–$185	(800) 465-4329	A, DC, MC, V
★★★	Kapok Hotel	71	$76–$92	(868) 922-6441	A, DC, MC, V
★★	Laguna Mar Resort	6	$45–$75	(868) 628-3731	MC, V
★★	Monique's Guest House	11	$45–$55	(868) 628-3334	A, MC, V
★★	Mt. Plaisir Estate	9	$48–$81	(868) 670-8381	
★★	Normandie Hotel	53	$60–$95	(868) 624-1181	A, CB, DC, MC, V
★★	Pax Guest House - Mt. St. Benedict	18	$45–$85	(868) 662-4084	
★	Alicia's House	17	$30–$58	(868) 623-2802	A, MC, V
★	Par-May-La's	14	$30–$50	(868) 628-2008	MC, V

TRINIDAD RESTAURANTS		PHONE	ENTRÉE	CR. CARDS
Chinese Cuisine				
★★★	Hong Kong City	(868) 622-3949	$8–$20	A, DC, MC, V
★★★	Singho	(868) 628-2077	$5–$12	A, MC, V
★★★	Tiki Village	(868) 622-6441	$6–$13	A, DC, MC, V
Regional Cuisine				
★★★★	Chateau de Poisson, Le	(868) 622-6087	$6–$26	A, MC, V
★★★★	Veni Mange	(868) 624-7533	$8–$10	None
★★★	Monsoon	(868) 628-7684	$4–$5	A, DC, MC, V
★★★	Rafters	(868) 628-9258	$6–$21	A, DC, MC, V
★★★	Surf Country Inn	(868) 669-2475	$9–$17	A, MC, V
★★★	Woodford Cafe	(868) 622-2233	$3–$6	A, MC, V
★★	Breakfast Shed	(868) 627-2337	$2–$3	
★★	Chaconia Inn	(868) 628-8603	$12–$19	A, DC, MC, V

TURKS & CAICOS ISLANDS

Situated on a 12 mile sandy beach, Grace Bay Club in Providenciales, is one of the highest rated resorts in the Turks and Caicos.

With some islands in the Caribbean already overdeveloped or well on their way to becoming so, Turks and Caicos (KAY-Kos) remain a breath of fresh air. The region is an archipelago of eight inhabited islands and nearly three dozen smaller cays at the southwestern tip of the Bahamas, some 90 miles north of Havana. Though tourism has slowly emerged over the last two decades as the principal source of revenue (financial services ranks a distant second), the islands have yet to—and hopefully never will—succumb to the overdevelopment that has plagued destinations such as St. Maarten and parts of Jamaica. Indeed, these quirky islands are only now being discovered by the masses who find it a quick hop from the East Coast (under ninety minutes by jet from Miami). Don't let the boast of three "international" airports—one on Providenciales, one on Grand Turk and one on South Caicos—fool you. In 1996, the nation had just 87,794 visitors, albeit up 11 percent over the previous year. The singular major resort area to speak of lies on a breathtaking, 12-mile stretch of powder-soft, white sand beach on Providenciales, nicknamed Provo, the archipelago's most populous island with 6000 residents. Three resorts—Club Med, Beaches and Turquoise Reef—and one condominium, Ocean Club, account for about 900 rooms here, but the island's dozen or so other hotels typically have less than 30 rooms each. The sprinkling of accommodations on the remaining islands are even tinier and largely attract the sort of traveler looking for a kickback casual escape. Even on Providenciales—where the limestone island's stunning beaches, pristine reefs and aquamarine waters are proving a strong lure for divers, snorkelers and sport fishermen—the attitude among the natives toward the influx of visitors ranges from embracing to ambivalent to borderline hostile. Largely, it's ambivalent, which sometimes peaks through in the service—or lack thereof.

Turks and Caicos—two island groups separated by the Christopher Columbus passage 22-miles wide and more than 7000 feet deep—together total 260 square miles; Provo claims 44 of those while the next most popular island with visitors, Grand Turk, totals just seven square miles.

Cockburn Town on Grand Turk, the seat of government and the capital has about 4300 residents. North Caicos, called the "garden island" due to its relatively high rainfall, a plethora of accommodations, and favorite of birders, has some interesting caves and a pond frequented by pink flamingos. Middle Caicos is the largest of the chain but the least developed with only 275 residents, while South Caicos is a fishing center for spiny lobster, bonefish and queen conch. Salt Cay, once the world's largest producer of salt, today has fewer than 100 residents. Pine Cay is privately owned, while East and West Caicos are uninhabited.

That is for now. At presstime, Chief Minister Derek Taylor was pushing to transform this sleepy British dependent territory into "the Monte Carlo of the Caribbean" via a $350 million development of East Caicos. A Canadian based real estate investment and development company has an option agreement to establish a resort town and cruise port facility big enough to allow berthing for up to eight cruise ships simultaneously. It would be the first port in the Caribbean built specifically for cruise ships rather than cargo vessels. The plan calls for six major resort hotels, an 18-hole golf course and all the usual bells-and-whistles that accompany this sort of development. A new airport would also be built on South Caicos to service the proposed Caicos cruise port and resort. If the project comes to fruition, it would radically alter

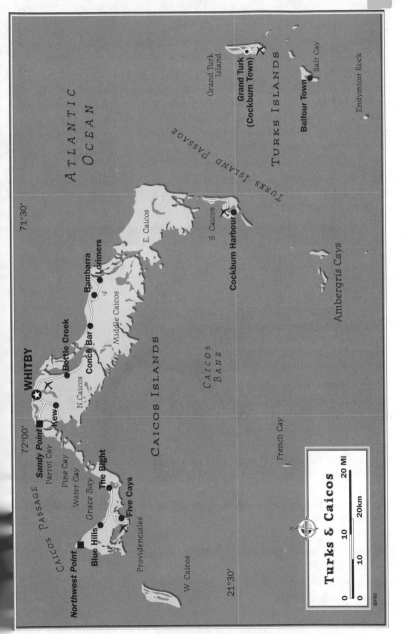

a nation—almost doubling its population—that previously hasn't even flirted with the idea of hyper-development. Opposition was swiftly voiced on the political front as well as from environmental groups, particularly Reefkeepers International, dedicated to preserving reefs globally.

Throughout the islands, much emphasis is put on the preservation of its natural beauty and rich sea life (the diving ranks among the Caribbean's best). In 1992, the government set up an extensive series of national parks, nature reserves and sanctuaries to protect the reefs and coastlines of these unique islands. The islands even have an unofficial mascot, JoJo, a wild Atlantic bottlenose dolphin who has made these waters home since 1980 and often swims with snorkelers and divers off Provo. Declared a "national treasure" by the Ministry of Natural Resources in 1989, JoJo is so beloved he even has his own warden who looks after him and tends his wounds when he gets too close to boats.

BEST BETS FOR...

Bird's-Eye View

Turks—which refers to the indigenous Turk's head cactus—and Caicos—the Spanish word for small islands—are part of the same geological structures that make up the Bahamas. In fact, they were actually the same country until 1874, when Great Britain divided the territories to make governing easier. Located 575 miles southeast of Miami, these low-lying, coraline islands are arrayed around the edges of two large limestone platforms. Caicos the westernmost bank, is the base of six primary islands—West Caicos, Provo, North Caicos, Middle Caicos, East Caicos and South Caicos—as well a 30 smaller cays. The Caicos are encircled by a barrier reef lying one to two miles offshore.

The Turk islands get about 21 inches of rain each year, while the somewhat lusher Caicos receive some 40 inches. Temperatures average 85 degree Fahrenheit in the summer and 77 degrees in the winter. The scrubby land scape is comprised of tidal flats, mangrove swamps and small hills sometime peppered with palmettos, frangipanis, acacia trees and a smattering of imported palms. The isolated cays and uninhabited larger islands are home to nesting seabirds, nesting green and hawksbill sea turtles, curly-tailed lizard and the Turks & Caicos rock iguana, but the latter's number is rapidly dwindling due to encroaching development. Wild donkeys wander Grand Turk, where gardens are walled to protect foliage from random munching by the small beasts. On Provo, the locals claim that last century the salt miners cut down the native trees, altering the island's face to present day. No matter. Even the lush tropics—which none of these islands are—would have difficulty competing with the main attraction here: dazzling clear water, dappled with the full spectrum of blue from aquamarine to cobalt. The islands are known for their white powder beaches—230 miles in all—and excellent wall diving, with abundant marine life and visibility up to 200 feet.

History

Some historians speculate that Grand Turk was the first landfall made by Columbus in 1492, but since the islands had no obvious riches, the fleet quickly moved on. A few years later, he was followed by Ponce de León, searching for the fountain of youth. For 900 years prior, the Taino and Lucayan Amerindians had occupied these islands, having originated in the Orinocco region in South America—peace-loving tribes who had survived by fishing, farming and trading dried conch meat and conch pearls in Hispaniola to the south. Only 40 years after their first European contact, the native tribes were totally wiped out by enslavement, disease and abuse. With the exception of an odd shipwrecked sailor, the islands remained uninhabited for more than 200 years.

In 1668, Bermudian salt rakers arrived. They divided the tidal lakes on Salt Cay, Grand Turk and South Caicos into salt pans (called *salinas*), controlled the flooding and evaporating of the sea water and raked out the salt, creating an industry that was the mainstay of the economy until 1967. Indeed, in 1777 salt sold for a stunning $40 a bushel in the U.S. During much of that time frame, buccaneers hiding out in the Caicos preyed on treasure vessels passing through the Caicos Passage. Colorful legends still abound about Calico Jack Rackman and the two women pirates Anne Bonney and Mary Reed. By 1789 planters loyal to the crown arrived from the newly formed United States and set up cotton plantations, which failed. By the mid-1800s, the British Loyalists abandoned their plantations, leaving behind their slaves. The most extensive plantation ruins may be seen at Yankeetown on West Caicos and Wade's Green on North Caicos.

With the exception of Provo, time appears to have stopped on these islands. On Salt Cay, abandoned windmills stand as ghostly sentinels over the

Fielding   **TURK AND CAICOS ISLANDS**

BEAUTIFUL BY NATURE

"Beautiful by nature" is the official motto of this cluster of islands and cays, where it is said that Columbus made his first landfall. Ignored (for now) by the resort-set, favored (in growing numbers) by international bankers, and beloved (with good reason) by divers, this chain of islands offers 230 miles of powder-white beaches, innumerable dive spots and landscapes that range from tropical forest to salt ponds.

West Caicos

North Caicos

Caicos Islands

Governor's Beach

Located on the west coast of the island, this long stretch of white sand beckons sun-worshippers and beach-combers.

The Black Forest

On the island's leeward side, just a seven-minute boat ride from shore, this underwater "forest" of black coral is located at a depth of 35 feet. Novice-to-intermediate divers will sight fairy basslets and brilliantly colored corals.

Grand Turk Wall

At this famous dive site, divers of all levels can get up close and personal with the Wall, which drops 7000 ft. into the ocean. Along its upper reaches divers can see gorgonians and other corals.

Grand Turk

This island serves as the administrative headquarters for the colony, but life is far from urban-hectic. Dotted with caves that invite exploration, the island was once a major salt producer, and the remnants of the industry can still be seen today.

Turks and Caicos National Museum

Sixteenth-century cannons line the entrance to this superb museum, which includes extensive displays of the Molasses Reef wreck of 1513, one of the oldest authenticated European shipwrecks in the Caribbean.

East
Caicos

Cockburn Town

The capital is a small town of narrow streets lined with low stone walls. Houses reflect typical Bermudian-style architecture, with red roofs and long verandas.

South
Caicos

Turks Islands

Salt Cay

Encompassing only 2.5 square miles, this tiny island was once the world's largest salt producer. The diving is excellent. Stroll the beaches, or explore the abandoned windmills, salt sheds and ponds.

abandoned salinas. Middle Caicos only recently got its first paved road. Grand Turk appears to have taken the role of keeper of the flame with its main tourist attractions, The Turks & Caicos National Museum and a 140-plus-year-old lighthouse. The capital is locked into another century with its Bahamian architecture and small one-way streets. Ironic, then, that another new world explorer, astronaut John Glenn, splashed down here when he returned to the Earth's atmosphere and was debriefed at the U.S. Air Force base—since closed—on Grand Turk.

People

"Belongers," as the 15,000 residents of Turks and Caicos are called, are a welcoming and friendly lot. Most are descendants of African slaves or Bermudian salt rakers. About 4000 expatriates—Americans, Brits, Canadians, French and Swedes—round out that number. The population of Provo was steadily declining until tourism began to blossom in the late 1980s. Young people were frequently leaving their home island to pursue hospitality careers or other dreams on more prosperous islands. That trend has reversed with Provo's population almost doubling in the past five years. The islands are a British Dependent Territory and English is the official language. Besides tourism, the principal source of employment, locals work in the fishing and financial services industries. Crime remains almost nonexistent, but use common sense on Provo, where more development inevitably leads to petty crimes. The pace is slow here, and social life revolves around the church. whose choirs are magnificent. Visitors are more than welcome to drop into a Sunday service—if for no other reason than to enjoy the music.

Beaches

The crowning glory of the Turks and Caicos are the wide stretches of pris tine beaches—often miles long and all public from the low tide line to th dune line—that have the consistency of talcum powder. The calm, iridescen waters of **Grace Bay** on Provo enchanted the captains of industry in the earl '60s, and it remains relatively unspoiled despite the buildup launched b Club Med in 1984. On its far reaches it's still not heavily used, and it's heav enly for an early morning stroll. The best snorkeling is found at Smith's Ree off **Erebus Beach** at the mouth of the Turtle Cove Pond, and off **White Hous** beach in the shallows. An isolated beach where you can find treasures from as far away as South America is **Long Bay**, three miles long on the southeastern shore. Tiki huts provide shade at **Malcolm Roads**, a two-mile beach accessible only via four-wheel drive. Grand Turk's entire leeward shore is edged by one long beach. **Governor's Beach** is the most popular picnic and party spot.

Although its walls are comparable in many ways to those of the world re-nowned Cayman Islands, diving amid the Turks and Caicos Islands still feels a little like an insider's secret. But the reality is that one dive shop has been established for over a quarter-century now, and the number of divers visiting the islands has skyrocketed over the past decade. You may not be touring vir-gin reefs and walls, but the undersea display is still pristine, with magnificent visibility (almost always exceeding 100 feet, and approaching 200 feet dur-ing the summer months), and you won't have to deal with the crowds who pack the Caymans year-round.

The archipelago is actually two separate geological structures divided by the Columbus Passage, a narrow 22-mile-long undersea trench, 7000 feet deep, which connects the Caribbean Sea with the Atlantic Ocean. Each of the island groups, the Caicos to the west and the smaller Turks to the east, are essentially great mesas rising from either side of the passage, with a water depth rarely exceeding 20 feet and temperatures hover around 80°F. Most of the barrier reef surrounding the islands is undistinguished. But two great wall formations, both running roughly southwest to northeast, provide the impressive diving: one drops into the Turks Passage immediately west of Grand Turk and Salt Cay (discussed in the Turks section below), the other wall abuts the Caicos Passage, just west of Provo and West Caicos.

Providenciales

The Provo dive shops typically visit four different areas. **Grace Bay**, the long sweep of water immediately north of The Bight, features a tapered spur-and-groove barrier reef from 30 feet down to 60, where a mini-wall starts and drops to about 100 feet below the surface; these sites are close to most of the Provo operators. To the north, **Pine Cay** also features a spur-and-groove reef system of rolling undersea mountains that drop from 50 feet down to 150; two easier sites are usually frequented here, **Football Field** and **Meridian Club Reef**. **Northwest Point**, about a 45-minute boat ride from Grace Bay, over-looks the wall, which lies about a third-mile off the Provo west coast. The wall starts 45 to 50 feet below the surface, descends another hundred feet to a ledge or platform only a few feet wide in some places, and then drops for thousands of feet into the abyss. The fourth area lies off uninhabited **West Caicos**, where the wall parallels the island as close as 500 feet from the shore; these sites are over an hour away from the dive shops on Provo, but yield some of the best diving in the island chain. In winter months, when winds blow from the northeast, the wall sites offer the best visibility, while the barrier reefs are best during the summer as winds come in from the southeast.

Feather Duster worm, Providenciales, Turks/Caicos

There are some sites along **South Caicos**, 40 miles east of Provo, as well as idyllic diving off remote, uninhabited **French Cay**, but these are generally visited only by the several live-aboard boats which troll the waters, and only sporadically at that. Otherwise, neither the Provo operations nor the Turk dive shops visit their counterparts' sites; the distances by sea are much too far for day trips. A recompression chamber is available at Menzies Medical Practice on Provo.

Dive Shops

Art Pickering's Provo Turtle Divers

Turtle Cove Marina, ☎ *(800) 887-0477 or (649) 946-4232.*
Turks and Caicos oldest dive shop opened in 1970. Three boats, one with a 20 diver capacity. A PADI outfit, but can do NAUI and SSI referrals. Two tank-dive $70.

Caicos Adventures

Turtle Cove Marina, ☎ *(800) 513-5822 or (649) 941-3346.*

Two tank dive $70. Uses two boats, one carries 14, the other 20. Specialty is West Caicos, diving uncharted sites. Buffet lunch on deserted beach, uninhabited island, reef and nurse sharks, eagle rays, wall starts at 35–45 feet and drops to 6000 feet.

Dive Provo

Grace Bay; ☎ *(649) 946-5029 or (800) 234-7768.*
Two tank dive, $60. Night dive Wednesday and Friday, $50. Based at Turquoise Reef Resort. Only PADI five-star facility in Turks and Caicos, courses to divemaster. Complete underwater photo/video center.

Flamingo Divers

Turtle Cove Marina; ☎ *(800) 204-9282 or (649) 946-4193.*
Open since 1988, PADI and SSI affiliated, with courses to assistant instructor. Two-tank dive price $60. Uses two smaller boats for groups of 14 or less. Trips to French Cay, weather permitting. Complete line of rentals for diving and photo gear.

Sea Dancer/Peter Hughes Diving

☎ *(800) 932-6237 or (305) 669-9391.*
One of two live-aboard boats plying the Turks and Caicos waters, the *Sea Dancer* visits West Caicos, Great and Little Inagua and Hogsty Reef (the latter islands are in the Bahamas). All-inclusive prices for the seven-day trip, $999–1399 (based on type of berth selected). The *Sea Dancer* sleeps 18 and departs every Saturday out of Provo (summer trips focus exclusively on the Bahamas). Beginners with referrals may obtain their open water certification on the *Sea Dancer* ($180).

Turks and Caicos Aggressor

☎ *(800) 348-2628 or* ☎ */FAX (649) 946-4494.*
Seven-day, all-inclusive live-aboard trips, $1495. Includes five-and-a-half days of diving and all food; trips depart every Saturday from Provo. Instructor available on all dives, and certification courses are $300 (open water certification $150). Sixteen-passenger boat visits West Caicos, French Cay, Provo and South Caicos. Incorporates whale watching itinerary in January and February (additional $400).

Grand Turk

If Provo is an escape from well-known destinations, Grand Turk, which has been dived for only the past decade, is quieter still. The Turks Island Passage serves as a conduit between the Caribbean and Atlantic, providing much of the rich marine life into the region. Summer months draw mantas to the passage, and January through March brings humpback whales that swim quite close to Grand Turk and actually hover off Salt Cay on their annual trek to and from their winter breeding grounds off the Dominican Republic. The massive wall plunges from a point only a quarter-mile off Grand Turk's shoreline, and the crest of the wall sits at an average of just 30 to 40 feet below the surface. There are virtually no currents, and the minimal rain run-off allows visibility to average 120 feet year-round, but it can extend much further in the calm summer months. Weather permitting, the Grand Turk dive shops sometimes make the long trip to **Salt Cay**, which features lovely sites, but only Porpoise Divers makes the occasional haul even further south to the **H.M.S. Endymion**. Salt Cay is, for now, the last frontier of Turks and Caicos destinations, averaging under 500 dive visitors a year; spectacular snorkeling amid giant coral formations in 15 feet of water is available at **Point Pleasant**.

Dive Shops

Blue Water Divers

Front Street, Cockburn Town; ☎ *(649) 946-2432.*

Two-tank dive, $55; single-tank dive, $30; night dives, $35. Resort courses, $85; PADI training to Divemaster. Largest group size, eight.

Oasis Divers

Front Street, Cockburn Town, ☎ *(800) 892-3995 or* ☎*/FAX (649) 946-1128.*

PADI instruction up to divemaster. Two tank morning dive $50. $30 1 tank afternoon dive, $35 1 tank night dive. 2–10 person boats. Amazing Abyss on south side of island, eagle rays, big grouper, beautiful reef. Snorkel trips to Gibbs Cay $40 with lunch.

Sea Eye Diving

Duke Street, Cockburn Town; ☎ *(649) 946-1407.*

PADI and NAUI instruction to assistant instructor. Largest group size, 12. Two-tank dive, $55. Snorkeling trips to Gibbs Cay twice weekly, $35 with lunch.

South Cay Divers

Salt Cay; ☎ *(649) 946-6906 or FAX (649) 946-6927. E-mail s.c.divers☆caribsurf.com.*

Brian Sheedy started the diving on Salt Cay, opening his shop in 1988; the island now features nine moored sites. PADI affiliated, courses available to Divemaster. Single-tank dives, $30, packages also available. Grand Turk trips; visits the 1790 British warship wreck, *Endymion*, and Great Sand Cay weather permitting. Horseback riding is available

Although hiking doesn't figure prominently in the sporting landscape these islands, the long strands of beaches offer great trails along the coast lines. On Grand Turk, hike to the **Lighthouse**, made from cast iron and shipped from England in 1852, located atop the cliffs at Northeast Point. The small, uninhabited cays dotting these waters also offer a myriad of day trip opportunities for exploring by foot. The government has been taking steps to make them handier for hikers while protecting nature at the same time. For example, on Little Water Cay, off the leeward tip of Provo, the government has opened the **Rock Iguana Nature Trail**, a boardwalk designed to be nonintrusive. Scores of boats are available for rent to take you to vi the 33 protected areas of the Turks & Caicos. Just pack plenty of drinks, food and sunscreen.

What Else to See

Turks and Caicos National Museum—island expert Brian Riggs is the caring curator—gives you a glimpse into the early days of the islands, reaching back to the tribal population. A special exhibit on the **Molasses Reef** wreck, found on the southern reaches of the Caicos Bank, is fascinating.

Museums and Exhibits
Providenciales

Caicos Conch Farm ★★

☎ *(649) 946-5330*
Hours open: 9 a.m.–5 p.m.

This unusual, high-tech farm allows visitors to learn about these tasty critters from the breeding stage to eggs to maturation at age 4. You can watch a video on their production, and a touch tank allows for up-close inspections. Over 2.5 million conch are being farmed for their colorful pink shells, pearls and nutty-flavored meat. Admission is $6.00 for adults and $3.00 for children. General admission: $6.

Grand Turk

Turks & Caicos National Museum ★★

Guinep House, Cockburn Town, ☎ *(649) 946-2160.*
Hours open: 9 a.m.–4 p.m.

Housed in a more than 150-year-old, Bermuda-style building with white-washed stone walls, this small museum, opened in 1991, centers on the island's people and natural history starting with its earliest inhabitants, the Lucayan Tainos. The highlights of the collection are artifacts gathered from the wreck of a caravel—possibly a slaver—that sank on Molasses Reef in 1513, one of the earliest shipwrecks found in the Americas. General admission: $5.

Sports

Grand Turk

Watersports

Known for its game and bottom fishing just outside its protective reef, Grand Turk boasts some of the area's most knowledgeable boat captains. **Captain Ossie Virgil** (☎ *(649) 946-2018*) often finishes well in the local tournaments.

Providenciales

Biking

Cycling remains a sport in search of an audience, but Provo provides the best roads and easy flat terrain. From the Grace Bay area, North West Point is about 15 miles and travels through small villages on its way to this remote territory. The Lower Bight Road, running along the north coast to the Leeward Marina, makes a pleasant five-mile ride. **Scooter Bob's** (☎ *(649) 946-4684*) at the Turtle Cove Marina rents single speed bikes ($12.50 a day) and Yamaha single- or double-seater scooters ($25/$35 a day). **Provo Fun Cycles** (☎ *(649) 946-5868; e-mail: naseem@carib-surf.com*) specializes in Honda motorcycles, scooters and bikes.

Provo Golf Club

Providenciales, ☎ *(649) 946-5991.*
Hours open: 7 a.m.–7 p.m.

This challenging course, designed by Karl Litten and opened in 1991, is ranked as one of the Top 10 Caribbean courses. Owned by the local water company, the 6560-yard course has 18 holes and a par of 72. The air-conditioned West Indian-style club house overlooks the 18th hole and—with its vaulted ceilings, cushy leather couches and chairs scattered about—makes a good meeting place. Fairways Bar and Grill, a driving range and pro shop are also on premises. Greens fees are $95, cart included. Internet: *www.provogolfclub.com; e-mail: provgolf@carib-surf.com;* or toll-free ☎ *(888) 296-1121.*

Watersports

These islands are especially known for their excellent beaches and typically calm waters, as well as for their salt flats that yield remarkable bone-fishing. An island pro Arthur Dean, offers guided bone fishing, shark and bottom fishing tours through **Silver Deep** (☎ *(649) 946-5612*). Bone fishing takes extreme skill as you stalk the skittish fish, which feed on the mud flats. For cruising to the small, uninhabited islands in the archipelago, Dean at the Turtle Cove Marina or **Sand Dollar Cruisin** (☎ *(649) 946-5407*), also on Provo, has several choices ranging in price from $25–$85. **J & B Tours** (☎ *(649) 946-5047; e-mail: jbtours@caribsurf.com or interne http://www.nobis.com/jbtours*) can arrange power boat rentals, private charters beach cruises, fishing excursions (bone and bottom fishing), waterskiing in Grac Bay and a sunset cruise to see the luminescent green glow worm in the shallows o Caicos Banks. **Minx** (☎ *(649) 946-5122*) takes up to six on a 41 ft. trimaran. Fc windsurfing, kayaking or sea cycles, try **Windsurfing Provo** (☎ *(649) 946-5040*).

FIELDING'S CHOICE:

Both Grand Turk and Salt Cay, down to the Mouchoir and Silver Banks off Hispaniola, are the southern terminus of the migrational route of the Atlantic herd of some 2500 humpback whales. Sightings happen daily in February and March, and divers frequently have a chance encounter both in water and from the boat.

Where to Stay

![f]	**Fielding's Highest Rated Hotels in Turks and Caicos Islands**	
★★★★★	Grace Bay Club	$355–$755
★★★★★	Meridian Club, The	$400–$675
★★★★	Beaches	$357–$610
★★★★	Club Med Turkoise	$133–$360
★★★	Erebus Inn	$105–$225
★★★	Ocean Club	$165–$650
★★★	Turquoise Reef Resort & Casino	$125–$260
★★★	White House, The	$100–$300
★★★	Windmills Plantation, The	$475–$595
★★	Prospect of Whitby Hotel	$140–$270

![camera]	**Fielding's Best Places to Escape the Paparrazzi in Turks & Caicos Islands**	
★★★★★	Meridian Club, The	$400–$675
★★★	Windmills Plantation, The	$475–$595
★★	Prospect of Whitby Hotel	$140–$270

![coins]	**Fielding's Best Value Hotels in Turks and Caicos Islands**	
★★	Turks Head Inn	$55–$85
★★	Sunworshippers Pelican Beach Club	$70–$120
★★	Turtle Cove Inn & Marina	$85–$130
★★★	Erebus Inn	$105–$225
★★	Guanahani Beach Resort	$95–$150

Most tourists head for Provo, which has the largest number of accommodations, including a smashing Club Med and the new Beaches, another all-inclusive. At the extravagant-but-worth-it end of the spectrum is the Mediterranean-style **Grace Bay Club**. The **Meridian Club**, on tiny Pine Cay, shines as an exclusive-but-barefoot friendly hideaway. On Salt Cay, **Windmills Plantation** is ideal for relaxing getaways; you don't even have to bring your own reading material: Its library has more than 1000 books. Until now, the choices on Grand Turk were extremely limited, but the new owners of Turks Head Inn are striving to make it a showplace worthy of its intriguing history.

Hotels and Resorts
Grand Turk

Arawak Inn and Beach Club   **$120–$140**   ★ ★

☎ *(649) 946-2277, FAX (649) 946-2279.*
Website: www.4arawak.com. E-mail: arawak@caribsurf.com.
Single: $120–$140. Double: $120–$140.

This small, two-story hotel, three miles out of town on the southernmost end of the island and on the beach, caters to divers and families looking to escape the hustle and bustle. The island's three dive shops cater to the Arawak's guests, picking them up on the beach for dives. Arawak is also the only hotel on the island if you want shore diving: The 7000 ft. wall is only 200 yards out. Each room has a living room and full kitchen equipped with toaster and coffeemaker. The living room couch pulls out into a queen-size bed. Before their transformation in 1995, the original rooms served as officers' housing—explaining the spaciousness— for the now-abandoned U.S. Air Force Base that used to be on the island. Units downstairs are tiled; upstairs are carpeted. All have lockers that divers can use for storage. On-site is a pool—one of the few on Grand Turk that works well—and a restaurant. Management is eager to accommodate requests. Send an e-mail before you arrive, for instance, and you'll find your refrigerator stocked to your specifications. Plans are to add 54 more rooms, which will be smaller, in the next two years. 16 rooms. Credit cards: A, MC, V.

Guanahani Beach Resort   **$95–$150**   ★ ★

Pillory Beach, ☎ *(800) 577-3872, (649) 946-1459, FAX (649) 946-1460.*
E-mail: GTHotels@caribsurf.com.
Associated Restaurant: Shipwreck Restaurant & Lounge.
Single: $95–$130. Double: $100–$150.

This small hotel, on the edge of Pillory Beach where Columbus supposedly landed, is a 20-minute walk from Cockburn Town. Guestrooms—all with oceanviews and balconies—are simple and have AC and ceiling fans to keep cool. This property attracts mainly divers and has an excellent dive shop across the street and resident instructor. Snorkeling is available right off the beach. Facilities include a restaurant, bar and oceanside pool at this low-key spot. Often offers good packages for divers. 16 rooms. Credit cards: A, MC, V.

Sitting Pretty Hotel, The   **$63–$220**   ★ ★

Cockburn Town, ☎ *(800) 577-3872, (649) 946-2666, FAX (649) 946-2668.*
Single: $63–$215. Double: $95–$220.

Located on the narrow main road in town and fronting the white sand beach, the small guestrooms of this quiet hotel are generally pleasant with ceiling fans, and balconies with French doors; most are air conditioned. The newer beachfront suites also have kitchenettes. The grounds include two bars and a small pool where barbecues are held on Friday nights. Meals are served buffet-style at the poolside terrace. Scooter rentals and Sea Eye Diving (PADI and NAUI instruction) are across the street. 23 rooms. Credit cards: A, MC, V.

Sunworshippers Pelican Beach Club   **$70–$120**   ★★

Sapodilla Bay, ☎ *(809) 946-4488, FAX (809) 946-4488.*
Single: $70–$95. Double: $70–$120.
Located at this island's south end and overlooking a pretty bay, this small hotel is unique for its wonderful pastry shop, where pastries are baked fresh each day by the owner himself. Guestrooms are simple and airy with ceiling fans and ocean views. There's a dive shop on the pleasant beach, a bar and restaurant, and a small pool. 25 rooms. Credit cards: A, MC, V.

Pine Cay

Meridian Club, The   **$400–$675**   ★★★★★

Pine Cay, ☎ *(800) 331-9154, FAX (649) 946-5128.*
Single: $400–$600. Double: $475–$675.
This casual hideaway, a six-minute plane ride from Provo, is tucked onto its own 800-acre island, privately owned by American and Canadian families. Aging, well-heeled baby boomers who long to doff their shoes and hectic schedules—and who can afford to vanish from the office—come here as well as a sprinkling of honeymooners and the rich and famous. The modest accommodations line a two-mile, untrammeled beach. One of the few changes since the club opened in 1973 is that the airy rooms—with tiled screened-in porches and outdoor showers—have recently been updated with bold Caribbean prints and Haitian paintings. A single phone that accepts outgoing credit card calls only is tucked into a bush by the tennis court. The idea at this unspoiled and well-managed retreat is pure escape—no phones (cellular or otherwise), faxes, TV, newspapers, or radios to remind you of the outside world. Overhead paddle fans and trade winds make up for the lack of air conditioners. The bar is on the verandah where guests gather in the evenings. Visiting chefs, as well as the club's own, constantly change menus at the restaurant, which serves three meals a day, including candlelit dinners spanning several courses. Active types make use of the pool, tennis court, watersports and nature trails meandering through the scrubby terrain dotted with seven freshwater ponds. A handful of privately-owned cottages are sometimes available for $3000 a week rent. Children under 12 are not allowed. 12 rooms.

Providenciales

Grace Bay Club   **$355–$1255**   ★★★★★

Grace Bay, ☎ *(800) 946-5757, (649) 946-5757, FAX (649) 946-5758.*
Associated Restaurant: *Grace Bay Club. Closed Date: September.*
Single: $355–$495. Double: $355–$755. Suites Per Day: $355–$1255.
Devastatingly gorgeous, this Mediterranean red-tiled roof enclave stands out as an oasis of luxury on Grace Bay, a crescent-moon, powdered sugar beach. Quiet court-

yards and splashing fountains add to the peaceful air of this island's standout, which affords plenty of privacy for those who value it. (No children under age 12 either, which helps keep noise to a minimum.) Masterfully crafted details—hardwood shutters, Guatemalan and Turkish rugs, quarried tile floors—give a feeling of built-to-last that is sometimes lacking in the islands. Your choice is luxe, deluxe and more luxurious with suites only, each with a living room and terrace overlooking the turquoise clear waters of the bay. Maids clean your room twice daily. All suites are air conditioned, with two bathrooms in each as well as designer kitchens. Although the pampering comes with a hefty price tag, Grace Bay lives up to its promises. On-premise facilities include a gourmet open-air restaurant, bar, pool, Jacuzzi, two lighted tennis courts and most watersports. Boat excursions for snorkeling (some of the finest in the Caribbean), shuttle to the nearby golf course, and use of Sunfish and Hobie-Cat boats are all complimentary. You can catch up on the world with your daily fax of *The New York Times* over afternoon tea or....not. Here you may find you don't care so much. 22 rooms. Credit cards: A, MC, V.

Le Deck Hotel $110–$325   ★★

Grace Bay, ☎ *(649) 946-5547, FAX (649) 946-5770.*
Single: $110–$185. Double: $135–$245. Suites Per Day: $210–$325.
This older, two-story hotel is located on Grace Bay's lovely sandy beach within easy walking distance of magnificent coral reefs for snorkeling. Nothing fancy, but the air-conditioned guestrooms are clean and simple. Upper floor rooms are slightly more expensive. It also has a one-bedroom condo available. Facilities include a pool, watersports, a popular bar and Le Jardin, a restaurant. Couples ages 25-35 are the primary clientele at this informal spot. 25 rooms. Credit cards: A, MC, V.

Turquoise Reef Resort & Casino $125–$400   ★★★

Grace Bay, ☎ *(800) 992-2015, (649) 946-5555, FAX (649) 946-5629.*
Associated Restaurant: *Portofino.*
Single: $125–$260. Double: $155–$260. Suites Per Day: $300–$400.
This rambling, low-rise resort—formerly a Ramada—is adjacent to 12 miles of white sandy beach that is part of the Princess Alexandra National Marine Park. The plain vanilla accommodations—island-anywhere-decor—are outfitted with balcony or patio, cable TV, air conditioning and tile floors. Service is sometimes lacking. Facilities include **Dive Provo**, a PADI dive shop and watersports center, a fitness club, two lit tennis courts, and three restaurants (**Portofino**, the gourmet offering, dishes out some of the island's only Italian fare.) The **Provo Golf Course** is across the street. Nightly entertainment, weekly theme parties and the island's only casino—no great shakes—appeal to those who want a small dose of Club Med. A recent addition is the Kids on Vacation Club ($48 a day), which is open Monday-Friday 9 a.m.–5 p.m. for any child (age 2 1/2 to 12 years) who is vacationing on the island. Overall, this hotel tries hard but misses the mark unless you've only come to dive and golf. Inquire about packages. 228 rooms. Credit cards: A, MC, V.

Turtle Cove Inn & Marina $85–$150   ★★

Turtle Cove Marina, ☎ *(800) 633-7411, (649) 946-4203, FAX (649) 946-4141.*
Associated Restaurant: *The Terrace.*
Single: $85–$130. Double: $85–$130. Suites Per Day: $115–$150.

This laid-back hotel with its own marina, houses guests in air-conditioned rooms with TV, small refrigerators and phones. Two restaurants on-site, including The Terrace, a surprise and delight for discerning diners. Sporting facilities include a pool, bike rentals, and watersports, including diving. Snorkelers can take advantage of free bus service to a reef and beach. Within easy walking distance of restaurants, bars and scooter rentals. 32 rooms. Credit cards: A, MC, V.

North Caicos

| **Prospect of Whitby Hotel** | **$140–$270** | ★★ |

☎ *(649) 946-7119, FAX (649) 946-7114.*
Single: $140–$225. Double: $170–$270. Suites Per Day: $225–$380.
Situated on seven miles of beach, this isolated hotel bills itself as perfect for escaping the outside world. Rooms are spacious and air conditioned, with basic but comfortable furnishings. There's a pool, tennis court, bar and restaurant on the premises, and management handles watersports requests. 28 rooms. Credit cards: A, MC, V.

All Inclusives
Providenciales

| **Beaches** | **$357–$949** | ★★★★ |

Grace Bay, ☎ *(800) 726-3257, (649) 946-8000, FAX (649) 946-8001.*
Website: www.SANDALS.com.
Single: $357–$405. Double: $514–$610. Suites Per Day: $643–$949.
This resort is a new concept from the Sandals chain, which operates successful couples-only all-inclusives in Jamaica and other Caribbean islands. Although still all-inclusive, Beaches is open to everyone, including teens and kids, for whom extensive facilities and activities are provided. Remember that prices include many extras including all meals, sport activities, airport transfers and more. It has a minimum two-night stay. This frenetic site gives nearby Club Med a run for its money with a free-form pool with a swim-up bar, two restaurants, grill, a cocktail lounge, and a pastry shop. Guestrooms come equipped with satellite TV, minibar, coffeemaker and hairdryer, A/C and ceiling fans. Recreational facilities include a dive shop, top-of-the-line fitness center and lighted tennis courts. Big spenders may opt for the handful of suites or villas available. The two-bedroom Presidential villa rents for $12,850 for seven nights. 225 rooms. Credit cards: A, MC, V.

| **Club Med Turkoise** | **$133–$360** | ★★★★ |

Grace Bay, ☎ *(800) 258-2633, (649) 946-5500, FAX (649) 946-5497.*
Single: $133–$360. Double: $133–$360.
This large Club Med is one of the best in the chain. Set on 70 acres with a mile-long beachfront on the startlingly clear turquoise waters of Grace Bay, it attracts mainly couples and singles devoted to scuba diving and other watersports. Lodging—a cut above some of the older Club Med properties, but still small— is found in low-rise buildings lining the beach, all with two double beds and ceiling fans. The extensive facilities include three restaurants, a theater complex, a pool, eight tennis courts, a fitness center, a dive center and a nightclub. The rates include all activities, meals, circus workshops and watersports, though you'll pay extra for bonefishing, diving and golf. Children from age 12 and teens are welcome, though unlike the family-

oriented Club Meds, there are no special facilities for them. Rates range from $931 to $1811 per person per week, plus a one-time $30 membership fee and a $50 annual fee. 298 rooms. Credit cards: A, DC, MC, V.

Salt Cay

Windmills Plantation   **$475–$695**   ★★★

North Beach, ☎ (800) 822-7715, (649) 946-6962, FAX (649) 946-6930.
E-mail: windmills-six@webtv.net.
Closed Date: June-September.
Single: $475. Double: $595. Suites Per Day: $650–$695.
Arriving at this tiny, all-inclusive resort you have the feeling of being on an island that time forgot. Owner/manager Guy Lovelace has created a carnival of color and an eccentric mix of architectural styles on a pristine, 2.5 mile stretch of beach. Each of the four suites has a private verandah or patio and is uniquely decorated with a four-poster bed and antiques. Dinner is served by candlelight in the fine restaurant. Airport transfers, all meal and beverages (including house wines) as well as the pool, snorkeling and diving are included in the rates. 4 rooms. Credit cards: A, MC, V.

Apartments and Condominiums
Providenciales

Ocean Club   **$165–$860**   ★★★

Grace Bay, ☎ (800) 457-8787, (649) 946-5880, FAX (649) 946-5845.
Website: www.ocean-club.com. E-mail: oceanclu@caribsurf.com.
Associated Restaurant: *Gecko Grille.*
Single: $165–$235. Double: $175–$650. Suites Per Day: $495–$860.

This deluxe condominium complex sits on lushly landscaped grounds fronting Grace Bay Beach. Accommodations are found in five, pale turquoise buildings, painted to match the waters in front of the complex. The housing ranges from studio suites to three-bedroom, 1900-sq.-ft. oceanfront suites that accommodate up to eight people. All suites have modern amenities—including a phone system with voice mail—screened balconies and full kitchens. The condo has a bar—which doles out complimentary coffee in the mornings and chips and salsa during happy hour—and an excellent restaurant on-site, as well as a pool and lighted tennis court. Two children under age 12 can stay free when sharing a suite with an adult paying full price. The Ocean Club is across the street from the island's golf course. 86 rooms. Credit cards: A, D, MC, V.

White House, The   **$100–$450**   ★★★

☎ (649) 941-3713, FAX (649) 941-3713.
Single: $100–$150. Double: $200–$300. Suites Per Day: $250–$450.
This sleek, ultra-modern villa—lots of glass and angles—looks like something straight off the old TV show *Miami Vice.* Located on the middle of the lengthy beach for which Provo's north shore is noted, The White House sits in front of the prime snorkeling spot on the island. Each unit has cablevision, barbecue and outside shower. Or the villa can be rented as a whole to accommodate up to 20 people. The lap pool, adjacent to the beach, invites lingering. The owner *(cell ☎ (649) 941-0370)* is in the midst of building 12 condominiums next door. 6 rooms. Credit cards: A, MC, V.

Inns
Grand Turk

Turks Head Inn   **$55–$85**   ★★

Cockburn Town, ☎ *(649) 946-2466, FAX (649) 946-2825.*
Website: www. Grand-Turk.com. E-mail: turkshead@caribsurf.com.
Associated Restaurant: *Treetops Terrace.*
Single: $55. Double: $85.
Located on Duke Street, this antique-filled, Bermudan-style inn, surrounded by walled gardens, dates back to 1840 and was the governor's guest house and American Consulate in prior years. It had fallen into a state of disrepair, but was purchased by investors with extensive hotel experience in England in May 1997. The four upstairs guestrooms have been completely restored with period antiques to the former glory of the original Caribbean mansion. Two rooms have balconies overlooking the garden. Each also has modern amenities and a private bath suite. Five additional rooms were under renovation at presstime. The popular pub has been expanded, and Treetops Terrace, a new restaurant in the gardens, overlooking the beach opened in August 1997. The menu features lamb shanks, lobster and rib-eye steaks. A new garden bar was being added, too, with plans for live music evenings.
4 rooms. Credit cards: A, MC, V.

Providenciales

Erebus Inn   **$105–$420**   ★★★

Turtle Cove, ☎ *(800) 323-5655, (649) 946-4240, FAX (649) 946-4704.*
Associated Restaurant: *Sunset Bar & Grill.*
Single: $105–$225. Double: $105–$225. Suites Per Day: $315–$420.
Set on a hillside above Turtle Cove on Provo's north coast, this cheerful spot accommodates guests in comfortable rooms, four cottages or a villa. All have telephones with computer dataport, TV, and air-conditioning. There's a restaurant, publike bar with darts, two pools and two lighted clay tennis courts. A surprise is this small property's large, well-equipped health club, which offers aerobics Monday through Friday. A free shuttle takes you over to a nearby beach. Two small conference rooms for meetings of 30 or fewer were added in 1997. 21 rooms. Credit cards: A, D, MC, V.

Where to Eat

Fielding's Highest Rated Restaurants in Turks and Caicos Islands

★★★★★	Anacaona	$27–$32
★★★★	Terrace Restaurant, The	$18–$24
★★★	Gecko Grille	$16–$30

Fielding's Most Romantic Restaurants in Turks and Caicos Islands

♡♡♡♡	Anacaona	$27–$32
♡♡♡♡	Gecko Grille	$16–$30
♡♡♡	Terrace Restaurant, The	$18–$24
♡♡	Banana Boat Caribbean Grill	$12–$22
♡♡	Water's Edge Bistro, The	$9–$23

Fielding's Best Value Restaurants in Turks and Caicos Islands

★★★★	Terrace Restaurant, The	$18–$24
★★	Pub on the Bay	$6–$16
★★	Hey, Jose's Caribbean Cantina	$10–$14
★★★★★	Anacaona	$27–$32
★★★	Gecko Grille	$16–$30

Restaurants are as casual as everything else on the islands, but since virtually all foodstuffs are imported, prices can be high. Seafood figures heavily on all menus, where you're apt to frequently see grouper, tuna, reef-dwelling hogfish (a local favorite), conch and spiny lobster. Goat roti (an East Indian curried dish) and turtle are also widely available. Foods are often heavily seasoned with tangy or biting spices, and Cajun blackening and Jamaican jerking are popular ways of preparing white-meat fish, shellfish and chicken. Interestingly enough, the resort area in Provo has developed a reputation for attracting talented and inventive young chefs who are causing a stir among gourmands. For nightlife, head to the islands' sole casino, the Port Royale at the Turquoise Reef Resort and Casino on Provo. Though life here is quite informal, you'll notice that locals like to dress up for an evening out.

Grand Turk

Water's Edge Bistro, The   **$$**   ★★

Cockburn Town, ☎ *(649) 946-1680.*
Lunch: 11 a.m.–4 p.m., entrées $4–$9.
Dinner: 4–10 p.m., entrées $9–$23. Closed: Mon.

This open-air, wood-framed restaurant is set on a small point along the main road in Grand Turk. If you like a hearty breakfast, start your day here. Likewise, if you like a stout drink, you'll find the locals at this bar. It can satisfy your taste for a Bloody Mary with Sunday Brunch, too. The simple menus offer grilled, salmon-colored grouper, fish (grouper,too) and chips and an appetizer of grouper bites. It also boasts of the best burger on the island. Indeed, it certainly beats most stateside as well. Big spenders spring for the lobster, caught off the coast. No pretense, just plain fun.

Providenciales

Anacaona   **$$$**   ★★★★★

Grace Bay, ☎ *(649) 946-5050.* Associated hotel: *Grace Bay Club.*
Dinner: 6–10 p.m., entrées $27–$32.

If you only have one night to splurge, make it here. Three 35 ft. thatched roofed pavilions front the sea. The discreetly spaced tables display gleaming glassware and a single candle encased in a hurricane lamp. Each, of course, has a view of the sea. Ceiling fans lazily stir the air and torches enhance the glow of the star-filled night sky. Chef Joseph Warde, formerly the chef of an English country house hotel, has mastered island-style cooking and brings his own nouvelle continental flair to the ever-changing menu. Starters include blackened lobster salad with pineapple and red pepper salsa or salmon smoked on the premises and served with wheat bread and lemon. The red snapper with aubergine feuillantine, onion confit and star anise sauce melts in your mouth. Another winner is the rack of lamb with herb crust served with ratatouille. Terrific wine list, homemade desserts and Italian coffee drinks. Reservations are a must. Credit cards: A, MC, V.

Banana Boat Caribbean Grill   **$$**   ★★

Turtle Cove Marina, ☎ *(649) 941-5706.*
Lunch: 11 a.m.–4 p.m., entrées $4–$9.
Dinner: 4–10 p.m., entrées $12–$22.

Dockside at the Turtle Cove Marina, this casual eatery serves up what most come to the Caribbean expecting: good tropical drinks, conch fritters, raw oysters and jerk chicken, with a healthy dollop of Jimmy Buffett-laid back cool. Noted for its Colorado black angus steaks—a good choice for divers starved after a long-day underwater—the menu is nonetheless weighted toward Caribbean standards like grilled grouper salad and curry chicken. Main dishes include salad, potato and vegetable. Good pick for a casual lunch for burgers or sandwiches. In-season, splurge on the Caicos lobster sandwich. Credit cards: A, MC, V.

Gecko Grille　　　　　　　$$$　　　　　★★★

☎ *(649) 946-5885.* Associated hotel: *Ocean Club.*
Dinner: 6–9:30 p.m., entrées $16–$30. Closed: Mon., Tue.

The extensive wine list and a bar with most choices of rum on the island are just two of the distinctions that make Gecko Grille a good choice for a special night on Provo. Local artist Pamela Leach painted the interiors with a vivid banana leaf mural while wood craftsman Doug Carlson constructed the elegant bar in the center of the air-conditioned restaurant. Outside the dining patio is lined with torches, and palms are bedecked with twinkling lights. Chef John Brubaker, who grows his own herbs in a kitchen garden out back, likes to make dining an adventure at his restaurant, borrowing from whatever international cuisines strike his fancy and mesh with the ingredients he can procure. The Italian breads—the white cheese pizza is a favorite take-out item—that come from the half-ton brick oven have become noted on the island. Salads are stylish compositions of vegetables sprinkled with cheese and balsamic vinaigrette. He delights in adding twists to old favorites, like adding a coating of almonds to cracked conch. Dessert is a specialty here with creme brulee taking centerstage. Credit cards: MC, V.

Hey, Jose's Caribbean Cantina　　　$　　　　★★

Central Square, Leeward Highway, ☎ *(649) 946-4812.*
Lunch: Noon–3 p.m., entrées $6–$9.
Dinner: 6–11 p.m., entrées $10–$14. Closed: Sun.

This unlikely find is a Tex-Mex restaurant that has developed a well-earned reputation for the frothy margaritas, as well as platters of sizzling fajitas that match most you can get stateside. Housed in a shopping center, it's short on intimacy, but long on good food. Pizza, burgers and chicken are also available. Reservations recommended. Credit cards: A, MC, V.

Pub on the Bay　　　　　　$　　　　★★

☎ *(649) 941-3090.*
Lunch: 11 a.m.–5 p.m., entrées $4–$10.
Dinner: 5–10 p.m., entrées $6–$16. Closed: Sun.

If you tire of resort row in Grace Bay, take a 15-minute walk to Blue Hills. You'll pass a Seventh Day Adventist church on the way to this cinder-block building. Tuesday nights owners Charles and Zenith Palmer throw a seafood buffet from 6:30 p.m. to 10 p.m. with live music. On the menu that night are conch fritters, cracked conch, fish fingers, chicken wings, ribs, macaroni and potato salads. Across the way by the beach is a thatched-roof gazebo with a sand-covered floor. Park yourself at one of the wooden tables and watch the local fishing boats while you munch on conch fritters or turtle steak in the evening.

Terrace Restaurant, The　　　$$$　　　★★★★

☎ *(649) 946-4763.* Associated hotel: *Turtle Cove Inn.*
Lunch: 11:30 a.m.–5 p.m., entrées $12–$18.
Dinner: 5–10 p.m., entrées $18–$24. Closed: Sun.

If you crave the conch for which the Caicos islands have become noted, head to the palm-tree lined deck at the Turtle Cove Inn. Chef/Owners Clive Whent and Stuart Grey prove that they know how to fashion these tasty critters into all sorts of delectable dishes from conch roulade encasing a snapper mousse to a creamy conch chowder flavored with bacon and potato. The duo marry their classical European training with Caribbean-style cooking. The results explain the difficult time you'll have getting a table unless you make reservations when you first arrive on Provo. The eclectic menu stars fish caught from local waters with an occasional nod to meat-eaters. A good bet: roast chicken stuffed with tiger shrimp, leeks and parmesan cheese served with a tomato and coriander sauce. All main courses come with vegetables and au gratin potatoes or a salad, and the wait staff keeps you well-supplied with steamy homemade bread. Save room for dessert—especially homemade ice cream in flavors like mango and pumpkin. The softly lit, tropical foliage surrounding the patio makes for a romantic evening. Inside, local artists contributed to casually elegant decor. Credit cards: MC, V.

Top o' the Cove   **$**   ★
☎ *(649) 946-4694.*
Lunch: 6:30 a.m.–3:30 pm, entrées $4–$12.
Homesick New Yorkers and other bagel lovers will likely find their way to this small delicatessen next to an auto parts store. The white interior highlighted with blue makes for cheery surroundings if you want to eat your bagel or muffin on the spot. Also a good spot to get items for a picnic.

Where to Shop

There's not much in the way of shopping here, though Provo has a few outlets worth mentioning. Baskets woven from fresh grass and rag rugs are craft specialties. For Caribbean artworks, try **Bamboo Gallery**, ☎ *(649) 946-4748)* or **Caribbean Art Company** in Ports of Call across the street from Turquoise Reef. You'll find other shops at Market Place, Plantation Hills and Central Square along Provo's Leeward Highway. The post office is a good place to pick up colorful stamps that make good, inexpensive souvenirs.

Turks and Caicos Directory

Arrival and Departure

Travel to and from the Turks and Caicos is made easy by **American Airlines** ☎ *(800) 433-7300*, the country's primary carrier, which flies into Provo from Miami twice daily. **Northwest Airlines** ☎ *(800) 447-4747* arrives each Sunday from Detroit. **Air Jamaica** ☎ *(800) 523-5585* has regular service now via its hub in Montego Bay. Transfers to Grand Turk are handled by **Turks and Caicos Airways**, with small, six-passenger planes. TCA also flies a 19-passenger jet, offering alternative service from Nassau and Miami as well as other destinations. **Bahama Air** has flights three times a week. Air travel to all other inhabited islands is also offered by TCA as well as several small carriers such as **InterIsland** ☎ *(649) 941-5481*.

A departure tax of $15 for anyone over age 12 is collected at the airport.

Business Hours

Shops generally open weekdays 8 a.m.–4 p.m. Banks open Monday–Thursday 8:30 a.m.–2:30 p.m. and Friday 8:30 a.m.–12:30 p.m. and 2:30–4:30 p.m.

Climate

Temperatures range from 75–85 degrees F. from November -May, spiraling up to the 90s in June through October. Constant trade winds keep the heat bearable. There is no marked rainy season. Hurricane season runs June-October.

Documents

Visitors are required to write a valid passport (or proof of citizenship in the form of a birth certificate, voter's registration card plus a photo ID and return ticket).

Electricity

Current runs 110 volts, 60 cycles, the same as in the United States.

Getting Around

Those who've come to the Turks and Caicos for watersports and trekking will find that a cab to and from the airport is probably the only transportation they will need. Major hotels are within walking distance of a beach; those that aren't offer a shuttle service. However, restaurants and most attractions to Provo are located about a $10 taxi trip from most hotels, making a scooter or rental car necessary.

Taxis are unmetered, and rates, posted in the taxis, are regulated by the government. A trip between Provo's airport and most major hotels runs $15. On Grand Turk, a trip from the airport to town is about $4.; from the airport to the hotels outside town $5–$10.

Rental cars are available on the island. On Provo, **Budget** ☎ *(649) 946-4079* or *(800) 527-0700* offers the lowest rates, which average $40–$50 per day.

A bus runs into town from most hotels on Providenciales, running about $2–$4 one-way.

Language

The official language of the Turks and Caicos is English.

Medical Emergencies

Emergency medical care is provided at the **Provo Health Medical Centre** downtown ☎ *(809) 946-4201*, including eye and dentalwork. The government **Blue Hills Clinic** has a doctor and midwife on call ☎ *(809) 946-4228*. Grand Turk has a hospital on the north side of town. Other islands organize emergency air service to the closest hospital available.

Money

The official currency of the Turks and Caicos is the U.S. dollar.

Telephone

The area code is *649*. To dial direct from the U.S., dial *011* (international access) + *809* (country code) + local number. To make international calls from the Turks and Caicos, it's best to go to the Cable & Wireless office in Provo ☎ *(649) 946-4499* and Grand Turk ☎ *(649) 946-2200*. These offices are open Monday–Thursday 8 a.m.–4:30 p.m., Friday 8 a.m.–4 p.m. You can make calls from local phones with the use of a credit card purchased in increments of $5, $10 and $20.

Time

Atlantic Standard Time, meaning one hour earlier than New York. During daylight saving time, it is the same time as New York.

Tipping and Taxes

Hotels charge a seven percent government tax and add a 10–15 percent service charge to your bill. In a restaurant, it's appropriate to leave a 10–15 percent tip if it is not added already; check so you don't duplicate efforts. Taxi drivers expect a small tip.

Tourist Information

The **Turks and Caicos Islands Tourist Board** has a toll-free number on the islands ☎ *(800) 241-0824.* or *(649) 946-2321; FAX (649) 946-2733.*

Water

Outside of Providenciales, where desalinators have transformed much of the island into a riot of flowers, water remains a precious commodity. Drink only from the decanter of fresh water provided by the hotel, but tap water is safe for brushing your teeth and other hygienic purposes.

Web Site

www.ttg.co.uk/t&c/index.htm

When to Go

Late April to the end of November is off-season, when you can save 15–50 percent on hotel rates.

TURKS & CAICOS ISLANDS

TURKS AND CAICOS ISLANDS HOTELS	RMS	RATES	PHONE	CR. CARDS
Grand Turk				
★★ Arawak Inn and Beach Club	16	$120–$140	(649) 946-2277	A, MC, V
★★ Guanahani Beach Resort	16	$95–$150	(800) 577-3872	A, MC, V
★★ Sitting Pretty Hotel, The	23	$63–$220	(800) 577-3872	A, MC, V
★★ Sunworshippers Pelican Beach Club	25	$70–$120	(809) 946-4488	A, MC, V
★★ Turks Head Inn	4	$55–$85	(649) 946-2466	A, MC, V
North Caicos				
★★ Prospect of Whitby Hotel	28	$140–$270	(649) 946-7119	A, MC, V

TURKS AND CAICOS ISLANDS HOTELS

		RMS	RATES	PHONE	CR. CARDS
★★★★★	**Meridian Club, The**	12	$400–$675	(800) 331-9154	

Pine Cay

Providenciales

		RMS	RATES	PHONE	CR. CARDS
★★★★★	**Grace Bay Club**	22	$355–$755	(800) 946-5757	A, MC, V
★★★★	**Beaches**	225	$357–$610	(800) 726-3257	A, MC, V
★★★★	**Club Med Turkoise**	298	$133–$360	(800) 258-2633	A, DC, MC, V
★★★	**Erebus Inn**	21	$105–$225	(800) 323-5655	A, D, MC, V
★★★	**Ocean Club**	86	$165–$650	(800) 457-8787	A, D, MC, V
★★★	**Turquoise Reef Resort & Casino**	228	$125–$260	(800) 992-2015	A, MC, V
★★★	**White House, The**	6	$100–$300	(649) 941-3713	A, MC, V
★★	**Le Deck Hotel**	25	$110–$245	(649) 946-5547	A, MC, V
★★	**Turtle Cove Inn & Marina**	32	$85–$130	(800) 633-7411	A, MC, V

Salt Cay

		RMS	RATES	PHONE	CR. CARDS
★★★	**Windmills Plantation, The**	4	$475–$595	(800) 822-7715	A, MC, V

TURKS AND CAICOS ISLANDS RESTAURANTS

		PHONE	ENTREE	CR.C ARDS

Grand Turk

American Cuisine

		PHONE	ENTREE	CR.C ARDS
★★	**Water's Edge Bistro, The**	(649) 946-1680	$4–$23	

Providenciales

		PHONE	ENTREE	CR.C ARDS
★	**Top o' the Cove**	(649) 946-4694	$4–$12	

Mexican Cuisine

		PHONE	ENTREE	CR.C ARDS
★★	**Hey, Jose's Caribbean Cantina**	(649) 946-4812	$6–$14	A, MC, V

Regional Cuisine

		PHONE	ENTREE	CR.C ARDS
★★★★	**Terrace Restaurant, The**	(649) 946-4763	$12–$24	MC, V
★★	**Banana Boat Caribbean Grill**	(649) 941-5706	$4–$22	A, MC, V
★★	**Pub on the Bay**	(649) 941-3090	$4–$16	

Seafood Cuisine

		PHONE	ENTREE	CR.C ARDS
★★★★★	**Anacaona**	(649) 946-5050	$27–$32	A, MC, V
★★★	**Gecko Grille**	(649) 946-5885	$16–$30	MC, V

INDEX